PAGES PACKED WITH ESSENTIAL INFORMATION

"Value-packed, unbeatable, accurate, and comprehensive."

—The Los Angeles Times

"The guides are aimed not only at young budget travelers but at the independent traveler; a sort of streetwise cookbook for traveling alone."

—The New York Times

"Unbeatable; good sight-seeing advice; up-to-date info on restaurants, hotels, and inns; a commitment to money-saving travel; and a wry style that brightens nearly every page."

—The Washington Post

THE BEST TRAVEL BARGAINS IN YOUR BUDGET

"All the dirt, dirt cheap."

—People

"Let's Go follows the creed that you don't have to toss your life's savings to the wind to travel—unless you want to."

—The Salt Lake Tribune

REAL ADVICE FOR REAL EXPERIENCES

"The writers seem to have experienced every rooster-packed bus and lunar-surfaced mattress about which they write."

—The New York Times

"[Let's Go's] devoted updaters really walk the walk (and thumb the ride, and trek the trail). Learn how to fish, haggle, find work—anywhere."

—Food & Wine

"A world-wise traveling companion—always ready with friendly advice and helpful hints, all sprinkled with a bit of wit."

—The Philadelphia Inquirer

A GUIDE WITH A SPIRIT AND A SOCIAL CONSCIENCE

"Lighthearted and sophisticated, informative and fun to read. [Let's Go] helps the novice traveler navigate like a knowledgeable old hand."

—Atlanta Journal-Constitution

"The serious mission at the book's core reveals itself in exhortations to respect the culture and the environment—and, if possible, to visit as a volunteer, a student, or a teacher rather than a tourist."

—San Francisco Chronicle

LET'S GO PUBLICATIONS

TRAVEL GUIDES

Australia
Austria & Switzerland
Brazil
Britain
California
Central America
Chile
China
Costa Rica
Costa Rica, Nicaragua & Panama
Eastern Europe
Ecuador
Egypt
Europe
France
Germany
Greece
Guatemala & Belize
Hawaii
India & Nepal
Ireland
Israel
Italy
Japan
Mexico
New Zealand
Peru
Puerto Rico
Southeast Asia
Spain & Portugal with Morocco
Thailand
USA
Vietnam
Western Europe
Yucatán Peninsula

ROADTRIP GUIDE

Roadtripping USA

ADVENTURE GUIDES

Alaska
Pacific Northwest
Southwest USA

CITY GUIDES

Amsterdam
Barcelona
Berlin, Prague & Budapest
Boston
Buenos Aires
Florence
London
London, Oxford, Cambridge & Edinburgh
New York City
Paris
Rome
San Francisco
Washington, DC

POCKET CITY GUIDES

Amsterdam
Berlin
Boston
Chicago
London
New York City
Paris
San Francisco
Venice
Washington, DC

LET'S GO

WESTERN EUROPE

Jason Meyer Book Editor

Associate Editors

Ronan Devlin **Jun Li**
Krysten Keches **Lingbo Li**
Nickclette Izuegbu

Researcher-Writers

Rachel Banay **Andrew Moore**
Amanda Mangaser **Emily Naphtal**
Megha Majumdar **Alyssa Stachowski**
Ashley messina **Catherine Zielinski**

R. Derek Wetzel Map Editor
Vanessa J. Dube Managing Editor

Editors

Courtney A. Fiske **Russell Ford Rennie**
Charlie E. Riggs **Sara Plana**
Olga I. Zhulina

CONTENTS

HOW TO USE THIS BOOK

Conquering the great continent that is **Europe** is no easy task. Yes, dear reader, there are many mysteries in this Old World. That is why you have come to us. We will be your Virgil, teaching you the art of budget travel. We will guide you through Genoa's labyrinthine *vicoli* and Granada's *Alhambra.* From Santa's Workshop in northern Finland to strangely perched rocks in Salisbury, Western Europe—like a coffee shop in Amsterdam—has it. And our gritty, dutiful researchers have fanned out to Irish shoals and Kreuzberg wine bars, between Greece's pirate party ships and Austria's posh ski towns, to bring you the freshest, most comprehensive travel guide ever produced. Here's how to use it:

COVERING THE BASICS. The first chapter is **Discover** (p. 1). Read it before you go. Its purpose is to help you find the best this Earth has to offer. If you prefer people telling you what to do (or just want some ideas), check out this chapter's **suggested itineraries.** The **Essentials** (p. 7) section gets down to the nitty-gritty, detailing the info you'll need to get around and stay safe on your journey. The **Transportation** (p. 33) section will help you get to and around Europe, while the **Beyond Tourism** (p. 45) chapter suggests ways to work and volunteer your way across the Continent. Then we get to the meat of the book: 13 **country chapters,** organized alphabetically. The **Appendix** (p. 595) has a weather chart for major cities and a handy dandy phrasebook with nine languages to help you say "I'm lost" or "another round, please," land a bed, or find your way to a bathroom no matter where you are.

TRANSPORTATION INFO. Because you've told *Let's Go* you're traveling on budget airlines, we've created a new transportation format to help you navigate getting to where you really want to go from that random town an hour away: **Regional Hubs,** listed in the Intercity Transportation section of major cities. We've also collected info on bus, ferry, and train routes; these range from solid Spanish AVE schedules to, well, any transportation in Romania.

RANKINGS AND FEATURES. Our researchers list establishments in order of value from best to worst, with absolute favorites denoted by the *Let's Go* thumbpick. Since the lowest price does not always mean the best value, we've incorporated a system of price ranges (❶-❺) for food and accommodations. Tipboxes come in a variety of flavors: warnings, helpful hints and resources, insider deals, cheap finds, and then a smattering of stuff you should know.

AWESOMENESS. From ☎ codes to avoiding scams, from the best borscht to the boldest brews, we'll guide you through the souvenir-cluttered jungle of the old-school Europa to the most authentic food, craziest nightlife, and most mind-bendingly beautiful landscapes around. Start in Brussels, in Stockholm, in Bucharest. Open this bad boy up, and select your own adventure.

A NOTE TO OUR READERS. The information for this book was gathered by Let's Go researchers from May of 2008 through August of 2009. Each listing is based on one researcher's opinion, formed during his or her visit at a particular time. Those traveling at other times may have different experiences since prices, dates, hours, and conditions are always subject to change. You are urged to check the facts presented in this book beforehand to avoid inconvenience and surprises.

RESEARCHERS

Rachel Banay *Britain and Ireland*

After graduating from Harvard and hopping around Northern Ireland for *Let's Go Britain*, Rachel joined the Europe team for a whirlwind tour of the Republic of Ireland. She impressed us with her ability to explore big cities within a single day and still have the time and energy to hit the pubs with new friends Guinness and Jameson.

Danny Bilotti *Venice, Milan, Munich, Vienna, Amsterdam, Brussels*

Fame seemed to follow this California-born Economics major wherever he went, bumping into both John Malkovich and Furious Pete (a record-holding competitive eater). We were a little concerned about sending him off to represent Let's Go, given that he said he was most looking forward to embarrassing America abroad—but we're pretty sure he failed in that regard, and succeeded in most others, including charming us with great coverage of Munich.

Paul Katz *Lisbon, Madrid, Seville, Nice, Paris*

Paul kept us laughing in the office all summer with his enthusiastically cheesy video blogs. Having traveled extensively in Latin America, this was his first extended trip to Europe, and he braved the language barrier and the hostile Parisian nightclub bouncers with admirable courage. Always going out of his way to improve our coverage and organization, we hope he'll remember us someday when he has his own travel show and turns those cheesy video blogs into hour-long films.

Amanda Mangaser *Croatia, Greece, and Turkey*

While traveling the world, perhaps only in a swimsuit, Amanda's excitement about international exploration and vivid writing style left us anxiously waiting for more. Personal adversity, ferry schedules, cardboard box surprises, weeks in Athens... nothing affected her wit or charm. Top prize for tales from the road on our most awesome route.

Megha Majumdar *Sweden*

A native of India, Megha joined *Let's Go* eager to begin researching her route. She covered a whopping five countries in just seven weeks, smiling through it all. Despite computer troubles and a rigorous itinerary, she added new coverage, savored blood sausage, climbed medieval towers, and even outwitted a swarm of vicious insects.

RESEARCHERS

Ashley Messina *Czech Republic, Hungary, Poland, Slovakia*

Ashley fearlessly and flawlessly traversed four countries, expertly sampling local cuisines and always finding the top-shelf tea. Whether it was partying in Prague or finding the best *pierogi* in Poland, her excellent writing and timely, flawless copy kept the office running smoothly.

Andrew Moore *Finland, Iceland, Norway*

This accomplished skier was legendary for his crazy tales of roughin' it in Scandinavia—often choosing to forgo lodging expenses and sleep by the river and in a hotel lobby. Subsisting on mostly yogurt, he epitomized the B in budget. He'll soon be using his thrifty, hard-working charms as a US State Department employee.

Emily Naphtal *Austria, Switzerland*

Packing in four countries in two months, Emily proved to be quite the fighter. She biked through Slovenian castles and caves, experienced the EuroCup Fancamp in Salzburg, and even went skydiving after a computer meltdown in the Swiss Alps. Add a steaming cup of cappuccino and it was all in day's work for this determined researcher.

Alyssa Stachowski *Belgium, Denmark, Netherlands*

Ridiculous, memorable moments filled the daily travels of Alyssa. Her tales never failed to amaze with their unique twists and turns, grooves and bumps. Ask about Copenhagen, Møn, and of course, Amsterdam—she may just leave you flabbergasted and hilariously entertained.

REGIONAL RESEARCHERS AND RESEARCH MANAGERS

LET'S GO BARCELONA

Jesse Barron *Research Manager*

Sèph Kramer, Justine Lescroart *Researchers*

LET'S GO BERLIN, PRAGUE, & BUDAPEST

David Andersson *Research Manager*

Justin Keenan, Rachel Nolan *Researchers*

LET'S GO FLORENCE

Beatrice Franklin *Research Manager*

Marykate Jasper, Beryl Lipton *Researchers*

LET'S GO GREECE

Andrew Fine *Research Manager*

Charlotte Alter, Jillian Goodman,
Sarah Mortazavi, Ansley Rubinstein, Phoebe Stone *Researcher-Writers*

LET'S GO LONDON, OXFORD, CAMBRIDGE, & EDINBURGH

Jesse Barron *Research Manager*

Jack Holkeboer, Sara O'Rourke *Researchers*

LET'S GO ROME

Beatrice Franklin *Research Manager*

Emily Chertoff, Justin Monticello *Researchers*

LET'S GO WESTERN EUROPE

Claire Shepro *Research Manager*

Danny Bilotti, Paul Katz *Researchers*

ACKNOWLEDGMENTS

TEAM EUROPE THANKS: Vanessa J. Dube for the edits, advice, and treats. Mr. Wetzel for providing clear direction and guidance. The digital saviours, InDesign tamers, and all-around playas PROD. Sam and Inés, leading the way with smiles and veteran wisdom. Laura Gordon for random fun and slosh ball. Pod-tastic award goes to Ricaloha, true audiophiles and brethren Mississippi-haters. Crunchalicious teams BRI/ITA/S&P/GER/FRA. The newly rebranded EUR Presents: Nick Traverse. Rachel, Amanda, Megha, Ashley, Andrew, Emily, Alyssa, and Catherine; thanks for blazing glorious trails of epic proportion through The Continent. Your coverage truly made this book possible, and your stories from the road kept us entertained all summer long.

THE EDITORS THANK: First and foremost our lord (Jay-C) and savior (Starbucks, Terry's Chocolate Orange). We also owe gratitude to Barack Obama (peace be upon Him), the Oxford comma, the water cooler, bagel/payday Fridays, the HSA "SummerFun" team for being so inclusive, Rotio (wherefore art thou Rotio?), the real Robinson Crusoe, the Cambridge weather and defective umbrellas, BoltBus, Henry Louis Gates, Jr. (sorry 'bout the phone call), the office blog, gratuitous nudity, the 20-20-20 rule and bananas (no more eye twitches), the Portuguese flag, trips to the beach (ha!), sunbathing recently married Mormon final club alums, non-existent free food in the square, dog-star puns, and last but not least, America. The local time in Tehran is 1:21am.

But seriously, the MEs and RMs, our researchers (and all their wisdom on tablecloths and hipsters), LGHQ, HSA, our significant others (future, Canadian, and otherwise), and families (thanks Mom).

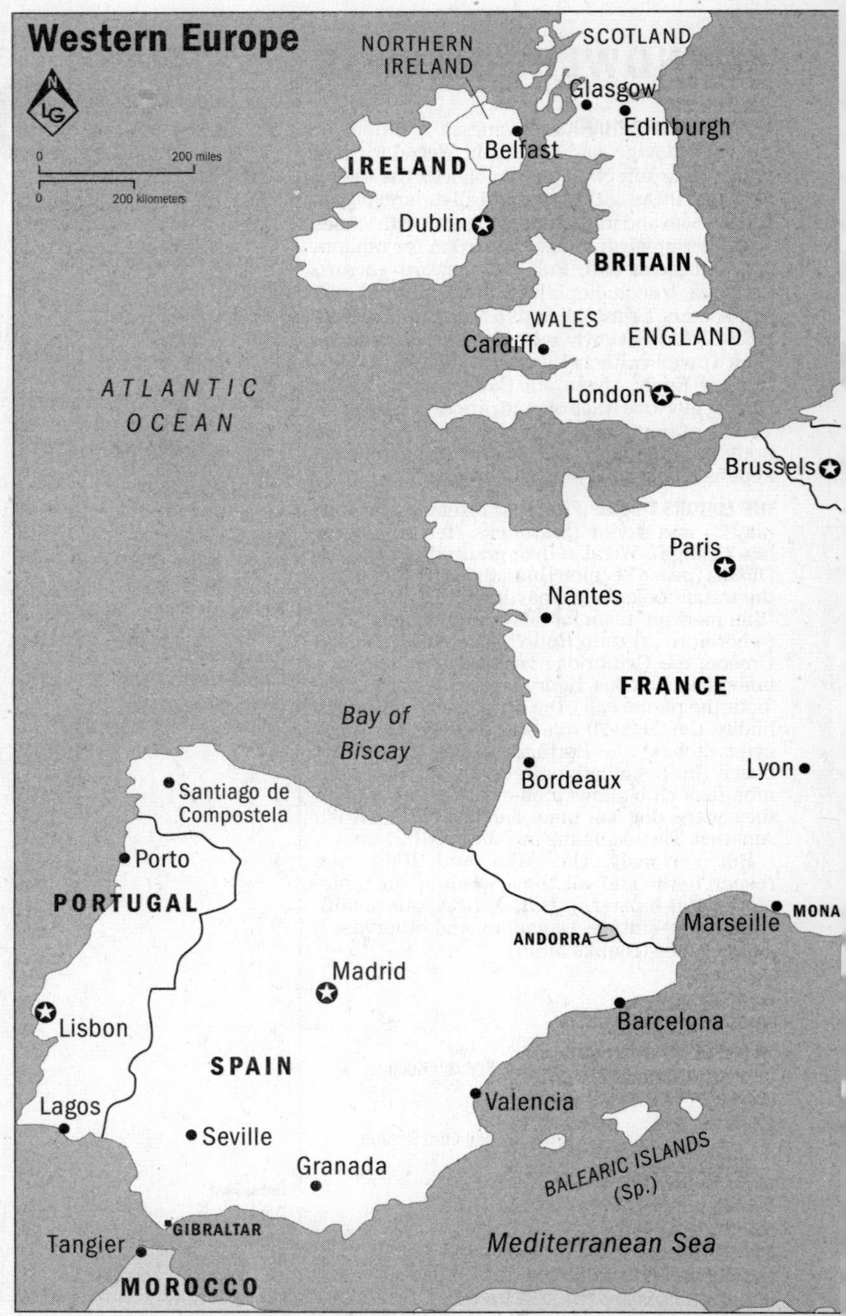
Western Europe
0
200 miles
0
200 kilometers
NORTHERN IRELAND
SCOTLAND
Glasgow
Edinburgh
Belfast
IRELAND
Dublin
BRITAIN
WALES
ENGLAND
Cardiff
London
ATLANTIC OCEAN
Brussels
Paris
Nantes
FRANCE
Bay of Biscay
Bordeaux
Lyon
Santiago de Compostela
Porto
PORTUGAL
ANDORRA
Marseille
MONA
Madrid
Barcelona
Lisbon
SPAIN
Valencia
Lagos
Seville
Granada
BALEARIC ISLANDS (Sp.)
GIBRALTAR
Tangier
Mediterranean Sea
MOROCCO

NORWAY
RUSSIA
North Sea
SWEDEN
Riga
LATVIA
DENMARK
Baltic Sea
LITHUANIA
Copenhagen
Vilnius
RUSSIA
Gdansk
Hamburg
BELARUS
NETHERLANDS
Amsterdam
Berlin
Warsaw
GERMANY
POLAND
BELGIUM
Bonn
Frankfurt
Lux. City
Prague
Kraków
LUXEMBOURG
CZECH REPUBLIC
UKRAINE
SLOVAKIA
Munich
Salzburg
Bratislava
Zürich
Vienna
Geneva
Bern
LIECHTENSTEIN
AUSTRIA
Budapest
SWITZERLAND
HUNGARY
SLOVENIA
Ljubljana
Milan
Venice
ROMANIA
CROATIA
Zagreb
Florence
BOSNIA AND HERZEGOVINA
Belgrade
Nice
Sarajevo
SERBIA
SAN MARINO
Adriatic Sea
BULGARIA
Corsica (Fr.)
MONTENEGRO
Podgorica
Skopje
Rome
ITALY
Tirana
F.Y.R. MACEDONIA
Sardinia (It.)
Naples
ALBANIA
Tyrrhenian Sea
GREECE
Aegean Sea
Ionian Sea
Athens
Sicily
TO MALTA

PRICE RANGES ❶ ❷ ❸ ❹ ❺ WESTERN EUROPE

Our researchers list establishments in order of value from best to worst, honoring our favorites with the Let's Go thumbs-up (☒). Because the best *value* is not always the cheapest *price*, we have incorporated a system of price ranges based on a rough expectation of what you will spend. For **accommodations,** we base our range on the cheapest price for which a single traveler can stay for one night. For **restaurants** and other dining establishments, we estimate the average amount one traveler will spend in one sitting. The table below tells you what you'll *typically* find in Western Europe at the corresponding price range, but keep in mind that no system can allow for the quirks of individual establishments. For country-specific information, a table at the beginning of each country chapter lists the price ranges for each bracket.

ACCOMMODATIONS	WHAT YOU'RE *LIKELY* TO FIND
❶	Campgrounds and dorm rooms, both in hostels and actual universities. Expect bunk beds and a communal bath. You may have to provide or rent towels and sheets. Be ready for things to go bump in the night.
❷	Upper-end hostels or lower-end hotels and pensions. You may have a private bathroom, or there may be a sink in your room and communal shower in the hall.
❸	A small room with a private bath or pension. Should have decent amenities, such as phone and TV. Breakfast may be included in the price of the room.
❹	Should have bigger rooms than a ❸, with more amenities or in a more convenient location. Breakfast probably included.
❺	Large hotels or upscale chains. Rooms should elicit an involuntary "wow." If it's a ❺ and it doesn't have the perks you want, you've paid too much.

FOOD	WHAT YOU'RE *LIKELY* TO FIND
❶	Probably street food, a *gelateria*, corner *crêperie*, or a fast-food joint, but also university cafeterias and bakeries (yum). Soups, gyros, kebab, and other simple dishes in minimalist surroundings. Usually takeout, but you may have the option of sitting down.
❷	Sandwiches, *bocadillos*, appetizers at a bar, or low-priced entrees and *tapas*. Most *trattorie* or ethnic eateries are a ❷. Either takeout or a sit-down meal (sometimes with servers!), but only slightly more fashionable decor.
❸	Mid-priced entrees, pub fare, seafood, and exotic pasta dishes. More upscale ethnic eateries. Since you'll have a waiter, tip will set you back a little extra.
❹	A *brasserie* or somewhat fancy restaurant. Entrees tend to be heartier or more elaborate, but you're really paying for decor and ambience. Few restaurants in this range have a dress code, but some may look down on T-shirts and sandals.
❺	Your meal might cost more than your room, but there's a reason—it's something fabulous, famous, or both. Slacks and dress shirts may be expected. Offers foreign-sounding food and a decent wine list.

DISCOVER WESTERN EUROPE

Some things never change. Aspiring writers still spin romances in Parisian garrets; a cool glass of sangria in the Plaza Mayor tastes sweeter than ever; and iconic treasures, from the inside-out architecture of the Pompidou Center to the hulking slabs of Stonehenge, continue to inspire wonder in new generations of wayfarers. And yet, sights that used to lie on the fringes of Western Europe have come into prominence: the ice-covered fjords of Norway, the bright Blue Lagoon of Iceland, and the quaint fishing villages of the Basque country. With this new focus, the old and the very old unfold before enterprising travelers as they fan out across the Continent, reshaping the Old World's venerable culture to fit an increasingly international world.

As the European Union expanded from a small clique of Atlantic nations trading coal and steel to a 27-member commonwealth with a parliament and a central bank, Amsterdam and Madrid have suddenly found themselves competing with Budapest and Kraków for global attention. Still, "Old Europe's" niche as a destination has been aided by the proliferation of small airlines, clearing the way for a new era of budget globetrotting. Whether it's Dublin's pubs, Lyon's upscale bistros, or Croatia's dazzling beaches that call to you, *Let's Go Western Europe 2010* will help keep you informed and on-budget.

TACKLING WESTERN EUROPE

Anyone who tells you that there is any one "best way" to see Europe should be politely ignored. This book is designed to facilitate all varieties of travel, from a few days in Paris to a breathless, continent-wide summer sprint to a leisurely year (or two) abroad. This chapter is made up of tools to help you create your own itinerary: **themed categories** let you know where to find your museums, mountains, and madhouses, while the **suggested itinerary** outlines a path across Western Europe. Look to chapter introductions for country-specific itineraries and for more detailed information.

WHEN TO GO

While summer sees the most tourist traffic in Western Europe, the best mix of value and accessibility comes in late spring and early fall. To the delight of skiing and ice-climbing enthusiasts, traveling during the low season (mid-Sept. to June) brings cheaper airfares and accommodations, in addition to freedom from hordes of fannypack-toting tourists. On the flip side, many attractions, hostels, and tourist offices close in the winter, and in some rural areas local transportation dwindles or shuts down altogether. Most of the best **festivals** (p. 6) also take place in summer. For more on when to visit, see the **Weather Chart** on p. 595 and the **Essentials** section at the beginning of each chapter.

WHAT TO DO

MUSEUMS

Western Europe has kept millennia worth of artistic masterpieces close to home in strongholds like the Louvre, the Prado, and the Vatican Museums. European museums do not merely house art, however. They also have exhibits on erotica, clocks, corpses, sea otters, leprosy, marijuana, chocolate, puppets and secret police—in short, whatever can be captioned. A trip across Europe qualifies as little more than a stopover without an afternoon among some of its paintings, sculptures, and artifacts—whether they include the pinnacles of Western culture, or more risqué fare. Whether your museum tastes lie in the classy or the sassy, Europe has a collection for you.

THE SUBLIME
AUSTRIA: ÖSTERREICHISCHE GALERIE (p. 70). Venetian paintings, an Egyptian burial chamber, and medieval arms in the world's 4th-largest art collection impress the history nerd in all of us.
BRITAIN: THE BRITISH MUSEUM (p. 124). Holding world artifacts like Egypt's Rosetta Stone or Iran's Oxus Treasure, the British Museum contains almost nothing British at all.
BRITAIN: TATE MODERN (p. 123). Organized thematically, this former power station turned modern art powerhouse is as much a masterpiece as any of the works in its galleries.
FRANCE: THE LOUVRE (p. 203). Six million visitors come each year to see 35,000 works of art, including Da Vinci's surprisingly small painting of art's most famous face, the *Mona Lisa*.
GERMANY: GEMÄLDEGALERIE (p. 272). With over 1000 works from 1200 to 1800 by the likes of Bruegel and Raphael, it's no wonder this is one of the most visited museums in Germany.
GREECE: NATIONAL ARCHAEOLOGICAL MUSEUM (p. 326). Athens itself may be museum enough for some, but this building collects what's too small to be seen with a placard on the street.
ITALY: GALLERIA BORGHESE (p. 397). Vivid paintings and graceful sculpture by Bernini, Caravaggio, Rubens, and Titian are a sight for sore eyes after staring at miles of Renaissance canvases.
ITALY: VATICAN MUSEUMS (p. 397). Look for the School of Athens here; the painting tops off a mind-blowing amount of Renaissance and other art, including the incredible Raphael Rooms.
THE NETHERLANDS: RIJKSMUSEUM (p. 462). Renovations shouldn't deter visitors who come to see the pinnacles of the Dutch Golden Age, including Rembrandts and Vermeers, that line the walls.
SPAIN: MUSEO DEL PRADO (524). It's an art-lover's heaven to see hell, as painted by Hieronymus Bosch. Velázquez's famous 10 by 9 ft. painting *Las Meninas* is as luminous as it is tall.

THE RIDICULOUS
BELGIUM: MUSEUM OF COCOA AND CHOCOLATE (p. 90). Chocolate lovers will delight in the sight, smell, and taste of this unique museum in Brussels, which displays the history of the cacao fruit.
GERMANY: SCHOKOLADENMUSEUM (p. 293). This chocolate museum, detailing the chocolate-making process, has gold fountains that spurt out samples that make this a magical experience.
THE NETHERLANDS: CANNABIS COLLEGE (p. 460). Cannabis College is just like college, except there are no libraries, no lectures, no studying, no liquor, no dorms, and no full-time students.

ARCHITECTURE

European architecture is a huge part of the continent's appeal. Royal lines from the early Welsh dynasties and Greek ruling families to the Bourbons, Hapsburgs, and Romanovs have all been outlasted by the emblems of their magnificence. Monarchs were careless of expense, and jealous of each other; Louis XIV's palace at Versailles (p. 208), a byword for opulence, whetted the ambition of rival monarchs and spurred the construction of competing palaces. No expense was spared for God, either, as the many cathedrals, monasteries, synagogues, and mosques rising skyward from their cityscapes attest.

ROYAL REALTY	SACRED SITES
AUSTRIA: SCHLOß SCHÖNBRUNN (p. 69). If the palace isn't impressive enough, check out the classical gardens that extend behind for four times the length of the structure.	**BRITAIN: WESTMINSTER ABBEY** (p. 115). Royal weddings and coronations take place in the sanctuary; nearby, poets and politicians from the earliest kings to Winston Churchill rest in peace.
BRITAIN: BUCKINGHAM PALACE (p. 116). Britain's royal family has lived in Buckingham Palace since 1832, guarded by everybody's favorite stoic, puffy-hatted guards.	**ITALY: SISTINE CHAPEL** (p. 395). Each fresco on its famous ceiling depicts a scene from Genesis. Michelangelo painted himself as a flayed human skin hanging between heaven in hell.
FRANCE: VERSAILLES (p. 208). Once home to the entire French court, the lavish palace, manicured gardens, and Hall of Mirrors epitomize Pre-Revolutionary France's regal extravagance.	**GERMANY: KÖLNER DOM** (p. 293). With a 44m ceiling and 1350 sq. m of stained glass illuminating the interior with particolored sunlight, Cologne's cathedral is Germany's greatest.
GERMANY: NEUSCHWANSTEIN (p. 310). A waterfall, an artificial grotto, a Byzantine throne room, and a Wagnerian opera hall deck out the inspiration for Disney's Cinderella Castle.	**GREECE: THE PARTHENON** (p. 325). Keeping vigil over Athens from the Acropolis, the Parthenon, civilization's capital since the 5th century BC, is a necessary pilgrimage for any humanist.
SPAIN: THE ALHAMBRA (p. 544). The Spanish say, *"Si mueres sin ver la Alhambra, no has vivido."* ("If you die without seeing the Alhambra, you have not lived.") We agree.	**SPAIN: SAGRADA FAMILIA** (p. 557). Though it looks like it's already melting, Antoni Gaudí's cathedral isn't even finished. The world's most visited construction site, it should be done in 2026.

OUTDOORS

As Europe is the seat of modern Western civilization, its museums and ruins tend to draw more people than its mountains and rivers. But for any traveler, budget or otherwise, solo or companioned, expert or neophyte, an excursion outdoors can round off (or even salvage, as the case may be) any journey. Mountains crowned with trees or icy glaciers continue to challenge mankind and dwarf the manmade, just as they did when civilization began.

HARDCORE THRILL-SEEKIN'
ITALY: MT. VESUVIUS (p. 436). The only active volcano on the Continent is overdue for another eruption. Scientists say the explosion will be more violent than the one that buried Pompeii in AD 79.
SPAIN: PAMPLONA (p. 565). While not outdoorsy in the traditional sense, the Running of the Bulls in Pamplona attracts runners and adrenaline junkies from all over the world.
SWITZERLAND: INTERLAKEN (p. 579). Thanks to its mild climate and pristine landscape, Interlaken is Europe's adventure sports capital, with every adrenaline-inducing opportunity imaginable.

THE GRAND TOUR (2 months)

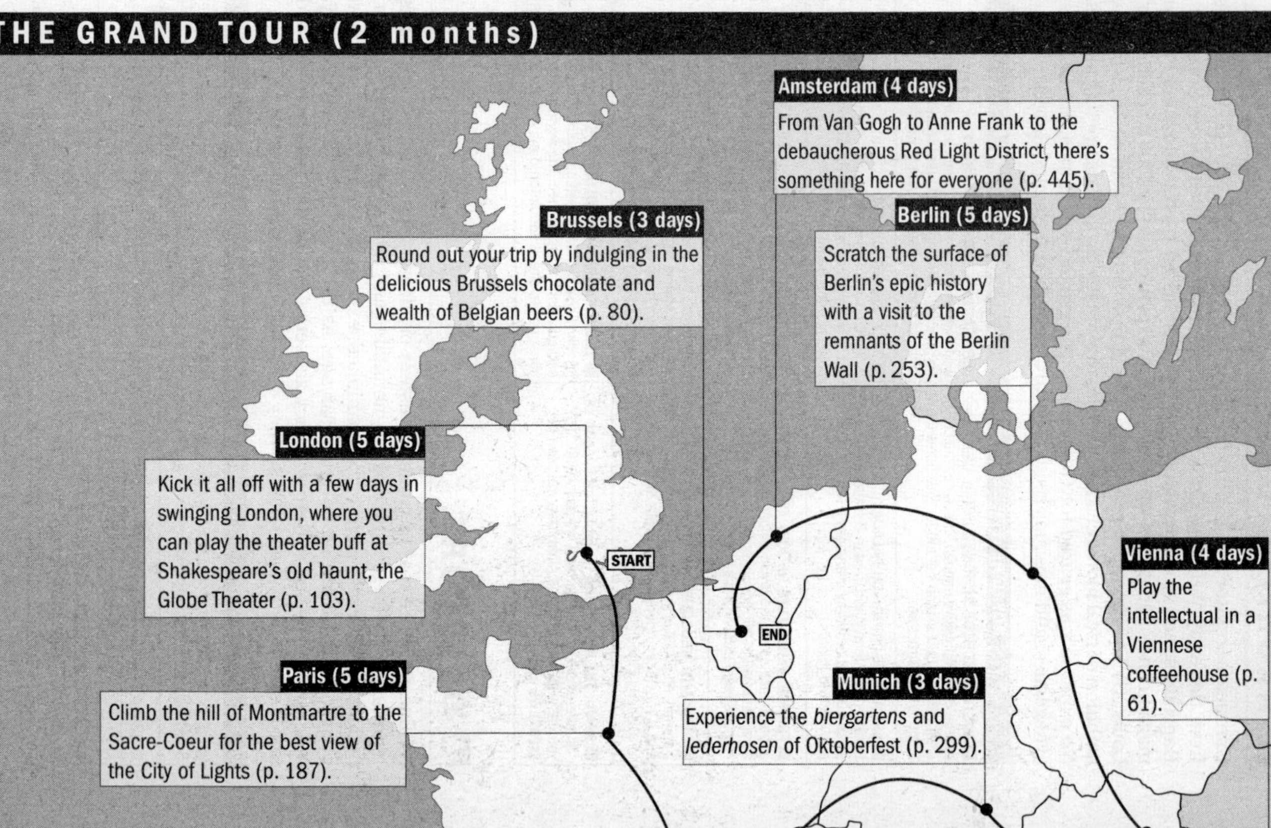

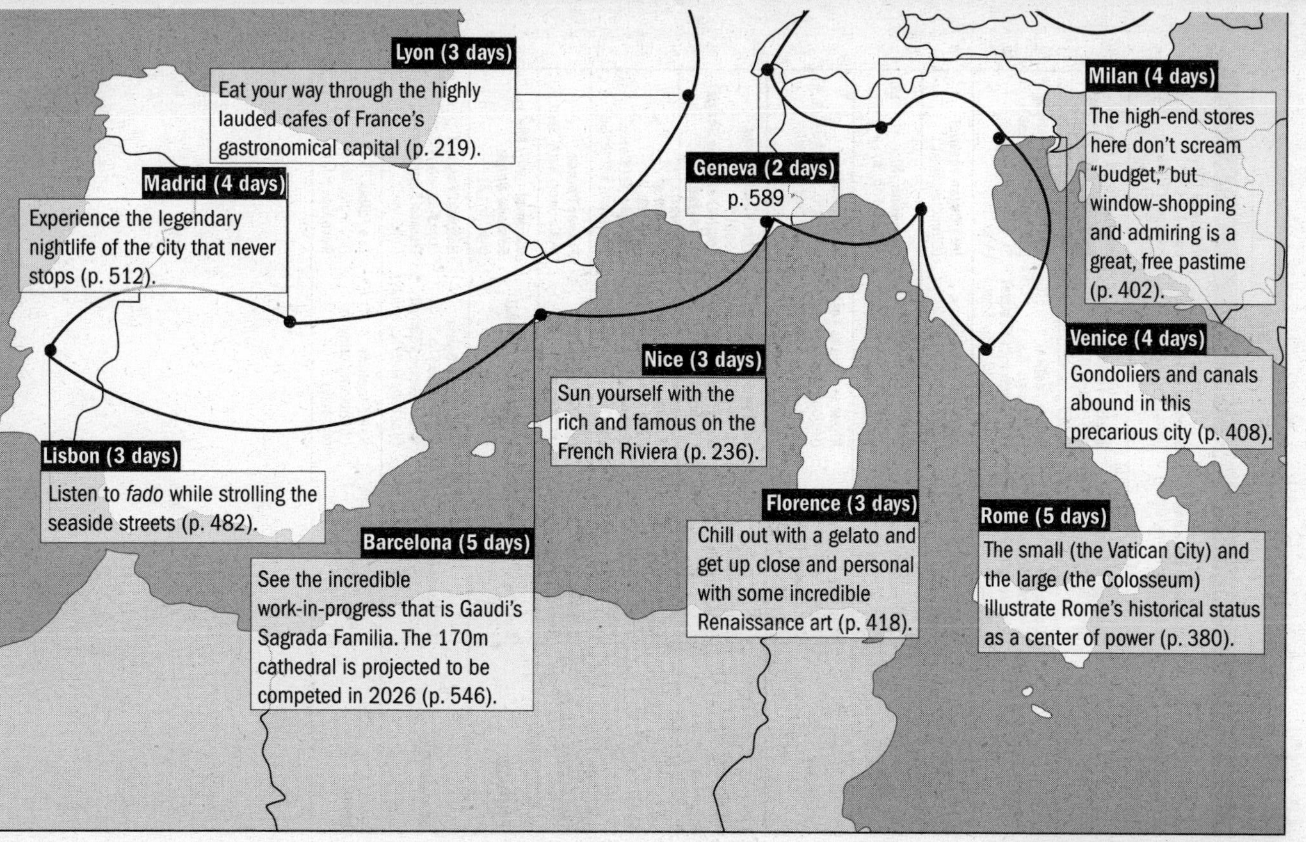
Lyon (3 days)
Eat your way through the highly lauded cafes of France's gastronomical capital (p. 219).
Madrid (4 days)
Experience the legendary nightlife of the city that never stops (p. 512).
Geneva (2 days)
p. 589
Milan (4 days)
The high-end stores here don't scream "budget," but window-shopping and admiring is a great, free pastime (p. 402).
Venice (4 days)
Gondoliers and canals abound in this precarious city (p. 408).
Nice (3 days)
Sun yourself with the rich and famous on the French Riviera (p. 236).
Lisbon (3 days)
Listen to *fado* while strolling the seaside streets (p. 482).
Florence (3 days)
Chill out with a gelato and get up close and personal with some incredible Renaissance art (p. 418).
Rome (5 days)
The small (the Vatican City) and the large (the Colosseum) illustrate Rome's historical status as a center of power (p. 380).
Barcelona (5 days)
See the incredible work-in-progress that is Gaudi's Sagrada Familia. The 170m cathedral is projected to be competed in 2026 (p. 546).

FESTIVALS

COUNTRIES	APR. - JUNE	JULY - AUG.	SEPT. - MAR.
AUSTRIA AND SWITZERLAND	**Vienna Festwochen** (early May to mid-June)	**Salzburger Festspiele** (late July-Aug.)	**Escalade** (Geneva; Dec. 11-13) **Fasnacht** (Basel; Mar. 2-4)
BELGIUM	**Festival of Fairground Arts** (Wallonie; late May)	**Gentse Feesten** (Ghent; mid- to late July)	**International French Language Film Festival** (Namur; late Sept.)
BRITAIN AND IRELAND	**Bloomsday** (Dublin; May 2) **Wimbledon** (London; late June-early July)	**Fringe Festival** (Edinburgh; Aug.) **Edinburgh Int'l Festival** (mid-Aug. to early Sept.)	**Matchmaking Festival** (Lisdoonvarna; Sept.) **St. Patrick's Day** (Mar. 17)
CZECH REPUBLIC	**Prague Spring Festival** (May-June)	**Int'l Film Festival** (Karlovy Vary; July)	**Int'l Organ Festival** (Olomouc; Sept.)
FRANCE	**Cannes Film Festival** (May 13-24)	**Festival d'Avignon** (July-Aug.) **Bastille Day** (July 14)	**Carnevale** (Nice, Nantes; Jan 25-Feb. 5)
GERMANY	**May Day** (Berlin; May 1) **Christopher St. Day** (late June)	**Rhine in Flames Festival** (various locations in the Rhine Valley; throughout summer)	**Oktoberfest** (Munich; Sept. 19-Oct. 4) **Fasching** (Munich; Feb. 1-5)
HUNGARY	**Danube Festival** (Budapest; June)	**Golden Shell Folklore** (Siófok; June) **Sziget Rock Festival** (Budapest; Aug.)	**Éger Vintage Days** (Sept.) **Festival of Wine Songs** (Pécs; Sept.)
ITALY	**Maggio Musicale** (Florence; May to mid-June)	**Il Palio** (Siena; July 2, Aug. 16) **Umbria Jazz Festival** (July)	**Carnevale** (late Feb.) **Scoppio del Carro** (Florence; Easter Su)
THE NETHERLANDS	**Queen's Day** (Apr. 30) **Holland Festival** (June)	**Gay Pride Parade** (early Aug.)	**Flower Parade** (Aalsmeer; early Sept.)
PORTUGAL	**Burning of the Ribbons** (Coimbra; early May)	**Lisbon Beer Festival** (July)	**Carnaval** (early Mar.) **Semana Santa** (Apr. 5-12)
SCANDINAVIA	**Midsummer** (June 19-25)	**Savonlinna Opera Festival** (July) **Quart Music Festival** (Kristiansand; early July)	**Helsinki Festival** (late Aug.-early Sept.) **Tromsø Film Festival** (mid-Jan.)
SPAIN	**Feria de Abril** (Sevilla; mid-Apr.)	**San Fermines** (Pamplona; early to mid-July)	**Las Fallas** (Valencia; Mar.) **Carnaval** (Mar.)

ESSENTIALS

PLANNING YOUR TRIP

AT A GLANCE

Passport (p. 7). Required for all non-EU citizens traveling in Europe.

Visa (p. 8). Not required for citizens of Australia, Canada, Ireland, New Zealand, the UK, and the US for stays shorter than 90 days in a 6-month period in most European countries.

Work Permit (p. 9). Required for all non-EU citizens planning to work in any European country.

Vaccinations (p. 17). Visitors to Europe should be up to date on vaccines, especially for diphtheria, hepatitis A, hepatitis B, and mumps.

EMBASSIES AND CONSULATES

CONSULAR SERVICES

Information about European consular services abroad and foreign consular services in Europe is located in individual country chapters; it can also be found at **www.embassiesabroad.com** and **www.embassyworld.com.**

TOURIST OFFICES

Information about national tourist boards in Europe is located in individual country chapters; it can also be found at **www.towd.com.**

DOCUMENTS AND FORMALITIES

PASSPORTS

REQUIREMENTS. Citizens of Australia, Canada, Ireland, New Zealand, the UK, and the US need valid passports to enter European countries and to re-enter their home countries. Most countries do not allow entrance if the holder's passport expires within six months. Returning home with an expired passport is illegal and may result in a fine and/or delays upon re-entry.

NEW PASSPORTS. Citizens of Australia, Canada, Ireland, New Zealand, the UK, and the US can apply for a passport at their local passport office and at most post offices and courts of law. Applications must be filed at least two months before the departure date, though most passport offices offer rush services for a very steep fee. Be warned that even "rushed" passports can take up to two weeks to arrive. Citizens living abroad who need a passport or renewal should contact the nearest passport office or consulate of their home country.

ONE EUROPE. European unity has come a long way since 1958, when the European Economic Community (EEC) was created to promote European solidarity and cooperation. Since then, the EEC has become the European Union (EU), a mighty political, legal, and economic institution. On May 1, 2004, 10 South, Central, and Eastern European countries—Cyprus, the Czech Republic, Estonia, Hungary, Latvia, Lithuania, Malta, Poland, Slovakia, and Slovenia—were admitted into the EU, joining 15 other member states: Austria, Belgium, Denmark, Finland, France, Germany, Greece, Ireland, Italy, Luxembourg, the Netherlands, Portugal, Spain, Sweden, and the UK. On January 1, 2007, two others, Bulgaria and Romania, came into the fold, bringing the tally of member states to 27.

What does this have to do with the average non-EU tourist? The EU's policy of **freedom of movement** means that most border controls have been abolished and visa policies harmonized. Under this treaty, formally known as the **Schengen Agreement,** you're still required to carry a passport (or government-issued ID card for EU citizens) when crossing an internal border, but, once you've been admitted into one country, you're free to travel to the other participating states. Most EU states are already members of Schengen (except for Bulgaria, Cyprus, Ireland, Romania, and the UK), as are Iceland and Norway. In 2009, Cyprus, Liechtenstein, and Switzerland will bring the total number of countries in the Schengen Agreement to 27. Britain and Ireland have also formed a **common travel area,** abolishing passport controls between the UK and the Republic of Ireland.

For more important consequences of the EU for travelers, see **The Euro** (p. 11) and **Customs in the EU** (p. 9).

PASSPORT MAINTENANCE. Photocopy the page of your passport with your photo, as well as your visas, traveler's check serial numbers, and any other important documents. Carry one set of copies in a safe place, apart from the originals, and leave another set at home. Consulates also recommend that you carry an expired passport or an official copy of your birth certificate in a part of your baggage separate from other documents.

If you lose your passport, immediately notify the local police and the nearest embassy or consulate of your home government. To expedite its replacement, you must show ID and proof of citizenship. It also helps to know all information previously recorded in the passport. In some cases, a replacement may take weeks to process, and it may be valid only for a limited time. Any visas stamped in your old passport will be lost. In an emergency, ask for temporary traveling papers that will permit you to re-enter your home country.

VISAS, INVITATIONS, AND WORK PERMITS

VISAS. As of August 2008, citizens of Australia, Canada, Ireland, New Zealand, the UK, or the US did not need a visa to visit the following countries for fewer than 90 days: Andorra, Austria, Belgium, Britain, Denmark, France, Germany, Greece, Ireland, Italy, Liechtenstein, Luxembourg, the Netherlands, Portugal, Spain, and Switzerland. For travelers planning to spend more than 90 days in any European country, visas cost US$35-200 and typically allow you six months in that country. Visas can usually be purchased at a consulate or at www.itseasypassport.com/services/visas/visas.htm.

Double-check entrance requirements at the nearest embassy or consulate of your destination for up-to-date information before departure. US citizens can also consult http://travel.state.gov/travel.

WORK PERMITS. Admission as a visitor does not include the right to work, which is authorized only by a work permit. Entering a country in Europe to study typically requires a special study visa, though many study-abroad programs are able to subsidize it. For more info, see **Beyond Tourism,** p. 45.

IDENTIFICATION

When you travel, always carry at least two forms of identification on your person, including a photo ID; a passport and a driver's license or birth certificate is usually adequate. Never carry all of your IDs together; split them up in case of theft or loss, and keep photocopies in your luggage and at home.

STUDENT, TEACHER, AND YOUTH IDENTIFICATION. The **International Student Identity Card** (ISIC), the most widely accepted form of student ID, provides discounts on some sights, accommodations, food, and transportation; access to a 24hr. emergency helpline; and insurance benefits for US cardholders (see **Insurance,** p. 16). Applicants must be full-time secondary or post-secondary school students. Because of the proliferation of fake ISICs, some services (particularly airlines) require additional proof of student identity.

The **International Teacher Identity Card** (ITIC) offers teachers the same insurance coverage as the ISIC and similar but limited discounts. For travelers who are under 26 years old but are not students, the **International Youth Travel Card** (IYTC) also offers many of the same benefits as the ISIC.

Each of these identity cards costs US$22. ISICs and ITICs are valid until the new year unless purchased between September and December, in which case they are valid until the beginning of the following new year. IYTCs are valid for one year from the date of issue. To learn more about ISICs, ITICs, and IYTCs, see www.myisic.com. Many travel agencies issue the cards; for more info, see the **International Student Travel Confederation** (ISTC) website (www.istc.org).

The **International Student Exchange Card** (ISE Card) is a similar identification card available to students, faculty, and youths aged 12 to 26. The card provides discounts, medical benefits, access to a 24hr. emergency helpline, and the ability to purchase student airfares. An ISE Card costs US$25; for more info, call in the US ☎800-255-8000, or visit www.isecard.com.

CUSTOMS

CUSTOMS IN THE EU. As well as freedom of movement of people (p. 8), travelers in the European Union can also take advantage of the freedom of movement of goods. This means that there are no customs controls at internal EU borders (i.e., you can take the blue customs channel at the airport), and travelers are free to transport whatever legal substances they like as long as it is for their own personal (non-commercial) use—up to 800 cigarettes, 10L of spirits, 90L of wine (including up to 60L of sparkling wine), and 110L of beer. Duty-free allowances were abolished on June 30, 1999, for travel between the original 15 EU member states; this now also applies to Cyprus and Malta. However, travelers between the EU and the rest of the world still get a duty-free allowance when passing through customs.

When you enter a European country, you must declare certain items from abroad and pay a duty on those articles if they exceed a set allowance. Note that goods purchased at **duty-free** shops are not exempt from duty or sales tax; "duty-free" merely means that you do not need to pay a tax in the country of purchase. Duty-free allowances were abolished for travel between EU member states but still exist for those arriving from outside the EU. Upon returning home, you must likewise declare all articles acquired abroad and pay a duty on the value of articles in excess of your home country's allowance. In order to expedite your return, make a list of any valuables brought from home and register them with customs before traveling abroad, and be sure to keep receipts for all goods acquired in foreign countries.

MONEY

CURRENCY AND EXCHANGE

The currency chart on the next page is based on August 2008 exchange rates between euro and Australian dollars (AUS$), Canadian dollars (CDN$), New Zealand dollars (NZ$), British pounds (UK£), and US dollars (US$). Check the currency converter on websites like www.xe.com or www.bloomberg.com, or a large newspaper, for the latest exchange rates.

As a general rule, it's cheaper to convert money in Europe than in the United States. While currency exchange will probably be available in your arrival airport, it's wise to bring enough currency to last for the first 24-72hr. of your trip, since airport rates are generally less competitive.

EURO (€)		
	AUS$1 = €0.58	1€ = AUS$1.72
	CDN$1 = €0.65	1€ = CDN$1.55
	NZ$1 = €0.47	1€ = NZ$2.14
	UK£1 = €1.18	1€ = UK£0.85
	US$1 = €0.70	1€ = US$1.44

When exchanging money abroad, try to go only to banks or official exchange establishments that have at most a 5% margin between their buy and sell prices. Because you lose money with every transaction, convert large sums (unless the currency is depreciating rapidly), but no more than you'll need.

If you use traveler's checks or bills, carry some in small denominations (the equivalent of US$50 or less) for times when you are forced to exchange money at disadvantageous rates, but bring a range of denominations, as charges may be levied per check cashed. Store your money in a variety of forms; ideally, at any given time you will be carrying some cash, some traveler's checks, and an ATM and/or credit card. All travelers should also consider carrying some US dollars (about US$50 worth), which are often preferred by local tellers.

CREDIT, ATM, AND DEBIT CARDS

Where they are accepted, credit cards often offer superior exchange rates—up to 5% better than the retail rate used by banks and other currency exchange establishments. Credit cards may also offer services such as insurance or emergency help and are sometimes required to reserve hotel rooms or rental cars. **MasterCard** (a.k.a. **EuroCard** in Europe) and Visa (e.g., **Carte Bleue**) are the most frequently accepted cards; **American Express** cards work at some ATMs and at American Express offices and major airports.

The use of ATM cards is widespread in Europe. Depending on the system that your home bank uses, you can most likely access your personal bank account from abroad. ATMs get the same wholesale exchange rate as credit cards, but there is often a limit on the amount of money you can withdraw per day. There is also typically a surcharge of US$1-5 per withdrawal.

Debit cards are as convenient as credit cards but withdraw money directly from the holder's checking account. A debit card can be used wherever its associated credit card company (usually MasterCard or Visa) is accepted. Debit cards often also function as ATM cards and can be used to withdraw cash from associated banks and ATMs throughout Europe.

The two major international money networks are **MasterCard/Maestro/Cirrus** (for ATM locations ☎+1-800-424-7787 or www.mastercard.com) and **Visa/PLUS** (for ATM locations ☎+1-800-847-2911 or www.visa.com). Most ATMs charge a transaction fee that is paid to the bank that owns the ATM.

PINS AND ATMS. To use a cash or credit card to withdraw money from a cash machine (ATM) in Europe, you must have a four-digit Personal Identification Number (PIN). If your PIN is longer than four digits, ask your bank whether you can just use the first four or whether you'll need a new one. Credit cards don't usually come with PINs, so, if you intend to hit up ATMs in Europe with a credit card to get cash advances, call your credit-card company before leaving to request one.

Travelers with alphabetic, rather than numerical, PINs may also be thrown off by the lack of letters on European cash machines. The following are the corresponding numbers to use: 1 = QZ; 2 = ABC; 3 = DEF; 4 = GHI; 5 = JKL; 6 = MNO; 7 = PRS; 8 = TUV; and 9 = WXY. Note that if you mistakenly punch the wrong code into the machine three times, it will swallow your card.

TRAVELER'S CHECKS

Traveler's checks are one of the safest means of carrying funds. American Express and Visa are the most recognized brands. Many banks and agencies sell them for a small commission. Check issuers provide refunds if the checks are lost or stolen, and many provide additional services, such as toll-free refund hotlines abroad, emergency message services, and assistance with lost and stolen credit cards or passports. Traveler's checks are readily accepted in most of Western Europe. Ask about toll-free refund hotlines and the location of refund centers when purchasing checks, and always carry emergency cash.

THE EURO. As of January 1, 2009, the official currency of 16 members of the European Union—Austria, Belgium, Cyprus, Finland, France, Germany, Greece, Ireland, Italy, Luxembourg, Malta, the Netherlands, Portugal, Slovenia, and Spain—will be the euro.

The currency has some important—and positive—consequences for travelers hitting more than one euro-zone country. For one thing, money-changers across the euro-zone are obliged to exchange money at the official, fixed rate (below) and at no commission (though they may still charge a small service fee). Second, euro-denominated traveler's checks allow you to pay for goods and services across the euro-zone, again at the official rate and commission-free. At the time of printing, €1 = US$1.54 = CDN$1.62 = NZ$2.15. For more info, check an online currency converter or www.europa.eu.int.

American Express: Checks available with commission at select banks, at all AmEx offices, and online (www.americanexpress.com; available for US residents only). Cardholders can also purchase checks by phone (☎800-528-4800). Cheques for Two can be signed by either of 2 people traveling together.

Travelex: Thomas Cook MasterCard and Interpayment Visa traveler's checks available. For information about Thomas Cook MasterCard in Canada and the US call ☎800-223-7373, UK ☎0800 622 101; elsewhere, call UK ☎+44 1733 318 950. For Interpayment Visa in Canada and the US ☎800-223-7373, in the UK ☎0800 515 884; elsewhere, call UK ☎+44 1733 318 949. For more info, visit www.travelex.com.

Visa: Checks available (generally with commission) at banks worldwide. For office locations, call the Visa Travelers Cheque Global Refund and Assistance Center: in Australia ☎800-882-426, New Zealand ☎800-447-002, UK ☎0800 895 078, US ☎800-227-6811; elsewhere, call UK collect ☎+44 2079 378 091. Visa also offers TravelMoney, a pre-paid debit card that can be reloaded online or by phone. For more info on Visa travel services, see http://usa.visa.com/personal/using_visa/travel_with_visa.html.

GETTING MONEY FROM HOME

The easiest and cheapest solution for running out of money while traveling is to have someone back home make a deposit to the bank account linked to your credit card or ATM card. Failing that, consider one of the options below.

WIRING MONEY

It is possible to arrange a **bank money transfer**, which means asking a bank back home to wire money to a bank in Europe. This is the cheapest way to transfer cash, but it's also the slowest, usually taking several days or more. Note that some banks may only release your funds in local currency, potentially sticking you with a poor exchange rate; inquire about this in advance. Money transfer services like **Western Union** are faster and more convenient than bank transfers, but also much pricier. Western Union has many locations worldwide. To find one, visit www.westernunion.com, or call: Australia ☎800 173 833, Canada and US ☎800-325-6000, UK ☎0800 833 833. To wire money using a credit card (Discover, MasterCard, or Visa), call in Canada and the US ☎800-225-5227, UK ☎0800 833 833. Money transfer services are also available to **American Express** cardholders and at selected **Thomas Cook** offices.

US STATE DEPARTMENT (US CITIZENS ONLY)

In serious emergencies only, the US State Department will forward money within hours to the nearest consular office, which will then disburse it according to instructions for a US$30 fee. If you wish to use this service, you must contact the Overseas Citizens Service division of the US State Department (from overseas ☎202-501-4444, toll-free 888-407-4747).

COSTS

The cost of your trip will vary depending on where you go, how you travel, and where you stay. The most significant expenses will probably be your round-trip (return) airfare to Europe (see **Getting to Europe: By Plane**, p. 33) and a rail pass or bus pass (see **Getting around Europe**, p. 36).

STAYING ON A BUDGET

Your daily budget will vary greatly from country to country. A bare-bones day in Europe would include camping or sleeping in hostels and buying inexpensive food in supermarkets. A slightly more comfortable day would include sleeping in hostels or guesthouses and the occasional budget hotel, eating one meal per day at a restaurant, and going out at night. For a luxurious day, the sky's the limit. In any case, be sure to factor in emergency reserve funds (at least US$200) when planning how much money you'll need for your trip.

TIPS FOR SAVING MONEY

Some simple ways to save include searching out free entertainment, splitting accommodation and food costs with trustworthy fellow travelers, and buying food in grocery stores. Full- or multi-day local transportation passes can also save you valuable pocket change. Bring a **sleepsack** to save at hostels that charge for linens, and do your **laundry** in the sink (unless you're explicitly prohibited from doing so). Museums often have certain days when admission is free—check websites in advance for deals. If you are eligible, consider getting an ISIC or an IYTC; many sights and museums offer reduced admission to students and youths. Drinking at bars and clubs quickly becomes expensive. It's cheaper to buy alcohol at a supermarket and imbibe before going out. That said, don't go overboard. Though staying within your budget is important, don't do so at the expense of your health or a great travel experience.

TIPPING AND BARGAINING

In most European countries, a 5-10% gratuity is included in the food service bill. Additional tipping is not expected, but an extra 5-10% for good service is not unusual. Where gratuity is not included, 10-15% tips are standard and rounding up to the next unit of currency is common. Many countries have their own unique tipping practices with which you should familiarize yourself before visiting. In general, tipping in bars and pubs is unnecessary and money left on the bar may not make it into the bartender's hands. For other services such as taxis or hairdressers, a 10-15% tip is usually recommended. Watch other customers to gauge what is appropriate. Bargaining is useful in Greece, and in outdoor markets across Europe.

TAXES

The EU imposes a value added tax (VAT) on goods and services, usually included in the sticker price. Non-EU citizens visiting Europe may obtain a refund for taxes paid on retail goods, but not for taxes paid on services. As the VAT is 15-25%, it might be worthwhile to file for a refund. To do so, you must obtain Tax-Free Shopping Cheques, available from shops sporting the Europe Tax-Free Shopping logo, and save your receipts. Upon leaving the EU, present your goods, invoices, and passport to customs and have your checks stamped. Then, go to an ETS cash refund office on site or file for a refund once back home. Keep in mind that goods must be taken out of the country within three months of purchase, and that most countries require minimum purchase amounts per store to become eligible for a refund. See www.globalrefund.com for more info and downloads of relevant forms.

PACKING

Pack lightly. Lay out only what you absolutely need, then take half the clothes and twice the money. The **Travelite FAQ** (www.travelite.org) is a good resource for tips on traveling light. The online **Universal Packing List** (http://upl.codeq.info) will generate a customized list of suggested items based on your trip length, the expected climate, your planned activities, and other factors. If you plan to do a lot of hiking, also consult **The Great Outdoors**, p. 26.

Adapters and Converters: In Europe, electricity is 230V AC, enough to fry any 120V North American appliance. Americans and Canadians should buy an adapter (changes the shape of the plug; US$10-30) and a converter (changes the voltage; US$10-30); don't use an adapter without a converter unless appliance instructions explicitly state otherwise. Australians and New Zealanders, who use 230V at home, won't need a converter, but will need a set of adapters. For more on all things adaptable, check out http://kropla.com/electric.htm.

SAFETY AND HEALTH

GENERAL ADVICE

In any type of crisis situation, the most important thing to do is **stay calm.** Your country's embassy abroad is usually your best resource in an emergency; registering with that embassy upon arrival in the country is often a good idea. *Let's Go* lists consulates in the **Practical Information** section of large cities.

DRUGS AND ALCOHOL. Drug and alcohol laws vary widely throughout Europe. "Soft" drugs are legal in the Netherlands, while in much of Eastern Europe drug possession may lead to a heavy prison sentence. If you carry **prescription drugs,** include both a copy of the prescriptions themselves and a note from a doctor, especially at border crossings. **Public drunkenness** is culturally unacceptable and against the law in many countries; it can also jeopardize your safety.

TERRORISM AND CIVIL UNREST. In the wake of September 11 and the war in Iraq, be vigilant near embassies and be wary of big crowds and demonstrations. Pay attention to travel warnings and comply with security measures.

Overall, risks of civil unrest tend to be localized and rarely directed toward tourists. Tensions remain in Northern Ireland, especially around July "marching season," which reaches its height July 4-12. Notoriously violent separatist movements include the ETA, a Basque group that operates in southern France and Spain, and FLNC, a Corsican separatist group in France. The November 17 group in Greece is known for anti-Western acts, though they have not targeted tourists, to date. The box below lists offices to contact and webpages to visit to get the most updated list about travel advisories.

TRAVEL ADVISORIES. The following government offices provide travel information and advisories by telephone, by fax, or via the web:

Australian Department of Foreign Affairs and Trade: ☎+61 26 261 1111; www.dfat.gov.au.

Canadian Department of Foreign Affairs and International Trade (DFAIT): ☎+1-800-267-8376; www.dfait-maeci.gc.ca. Visit the website for the booklet *Bon Voyage...But*.

Ireland Department of Foreign Affairs: ☎353 1 478 0822; www.foreignaffairs.gov.ie.

New Zealand Ministry of Foreign Affairs and Trade: ☎+64 4 439 8000; www.mfat.govt.nz.

United Kingdom Foreign and Commonwealth Office: ☎+44 20 7008 1500; www.fco.gov.uk.

US Department of State: ☎+1-888-407-4747; http://travel.state.gov. Visit the website for the booklet *A Safe Trip Abroad*.

PERSONAL SAFETY

EXPLORING AND TRAVELING

To avoid unwanted attention, try to blend in. Respecting local customs (in many cases, dressing more conservatively than you would at home) may ward off would-be hecklers. Familiarize yourself with your surroundings before setting out, and carry yourself with confidence. Avoid checking maps on the street. If you are traveling alone, be sure someone at home knows your itinerary, and never tell anyone you meet that you're by yourself. When walking at night, stick to busy, well-lit streets and avoid dark alleyways. If you ever feel uncomfortable, leave the area as quickly and directly as you can.

There is no sure-fire way to avoid all the threatening situations you might encounter while traveling, but a good **self defense course** will give you concrete ways to react to unwanted advances. **Impact, Prepare,** and **Model Mugging** can refer you to local self defense courses in Australia, Canada, Switzerland and the US. Visit the website at www.modelmugging.org for more info.

If you are using a **car,** learn local driving signals and wear a seatbelt. Children under 40 lbs. should ride only in specially designed carseats, available for a small fee from most car rental agencies. Study route maps before you hit the road and, if you plan on spending a lot of time driving, consider bringing spare parts. For long drives in desolate areas, invest in a mobile phone (p. 21) and a roadside assistance program (p. 41). Park your vehicle in a garage or well-traveled area and use a steering wheel locking device in larger cities. **Sleeping in your car** is very dangerous, and it's also illegal in many countries. For information on the perils of **hitchhiking,** see p. 44.

POSSESSIONS AND VALUABLES

Never leave your belongings unattended; crime occurs in even the most safe-looking hostels and hotels. Bring your own padlock for hostel lockers, and don't ever store valuables in a locker. Be particularly careful on **buses** and **trains;** horror stories abound about determined thieves who wait for travelers to fall asleep. Carry your bag or purse in front of you where you can see it. When traveling with others, sleep in alternate shifts. When alone, use good judgment in selecting a train compartment: never stay in an empty one, and use a lock to secure your pack to the luggage rack. Use extra caution if traveling at night or on overnight trains. Try to sleep on top bunks with your luggage stored above you (if not in bed with you), and keep important documents like your passport and other valuables on you at all times.

There are a few steps you can take to minimize the financial risk associated with traveling. First, **bring as little with you as possible.** Second, buy a few combination **padlocks** to secure your belongings either in your pack or in a hostel or train station locker. Third, **carry as little cash as possible.** Keep your traveler's checks and ATM/credit cards in a **money belt**—not a "fanny pack"—along with your passport and ID cards. Fourth, **keep a small cash reserve separate from your primary stash.** This should be about US$50 (US$ or euro are best) sewn into or stored in the depths of your pack, along with your traveler's check numbers and photocopies of your passport and other important documents.

In large cities **con artists** often work in groups and may involve children. Beware of certain classics: sob stories that require money, rolls of bills "found" on the street, mustard spilled (or saliva spit) onto your shoulder to distract you while they snatch your bag. **Never let your passport and your bags out of your sight.** Hostel workers will sometimes stand at bus and train station arrival points to try to recruit tired and disoriented travelers to their hostel; never believe strangers who tell you that theirs is the only hostel open. Beware of **pickpockets** in city crowds, especially on public transportation. Also, be alert in public telephone booths: if you must say your calling card number, do so very quietly; if you punch it in, make sure no one can look over your shoulder.

If you will be traveling with electronic devices, check whether your homeowner's insurance covers loss, theft, or damage when you travel. If not, you might consider purchasing a low-cost separate insurance policy. **Safeware** (☎+1-800-800-1492; www.safeware.com) specializes in covering computers. State rates vary, but average US$200 for global coverage up to $4000.

PRE-DEPARTURE HEALTH

In your **passport,** write the names of any people you wish to be contacted in case of a medical emergency, and list any allergies or medical conditions. Matching a prescription to a foreign equivalent is not always easy, safe, or possible, so if you take prescription drugs, consider carrying up-to-date prescriptions or a statement from your doctor stating the medication's trade name, manufacturer, chemical name, and dosage. While traveling, be sure to keep all medication with you in your carry-on luggage. Before you leave, make sure you have the proper vaccinations necessary for your destination. For more country-specific info, go to www.cdc.gov/vaccines.

INSURANCE

Travel insurance covers four basic areas: medical/health problems, property loss, trip cancellation/interruption, and emergency evacuation. Though regular insurance policies may well extend to travel-related accidents, you may consider purchasing separate travel insurance if the cost of potential trip cancellation, interruption, or emergency medical evacuation is greater than you can absorb. Prices for independent travel insurance generally run about US$50 per week for full coverage, while trip cancellation/interruption may be purchased separately at a rate of US$3-5 per day, depending on length of stay.

Medical insurance (especially university policies) often covers costs incurred abroad; check with your provider. **Australians** traveling in Finland, Ireland, Italy, the Netherlands, Sweden, or the UK are entitled to many of the services that they would receive at home as part of the Reciprocal Health Care Agreement. **Homeowners' insurance** often covers theft during travel and loss of travel documents (passport, plane ticket, rail pass, etc.) up to US$500.

ISIC and **ITIC** (p. 9) provide basic insurance benefits to US cardholders, including US$100 per day of in-hospital sickness for up to 100 days and US$10,000 of accident-related medical reimbursement (see www.myisic.com for details). Cardholders have access to a toll-free 24hr. helpline for emergencies. **American Express** (☎+1-800-528-4800) grants most cardholders automatic collision and theft insurance on car rentals made with the card.

USEFUL ORGANIZATIONS AND PUBLICATIONS

The American **Centers for Disease Control and Prevention** (**CDC;** ☎+1-800-311-3435; www.cdc.gov/travel) maintains an international travelers' hotline and an informative website. Consult the appropriate government agency of your home country for consular information sheets on health, entry requirements, and other issues for various countries (see the listings in the box on **Travel Advisories,** p. 14). For quick information on health and other travel warnings, call the **Overseas Citizens Services** (M-F 8am-8pm from US ☎+1-888-407-4747, from overseas ☎+1-202-501-4444), or contact a passport agency, embassy, or consulate abroad. For information on medical evacuation services and travel insurance firms, see the US government's website http://travel.state.gov/travel/abroad_health.html or the **British Foreign and Commonwealth Office** (www.fco.gov.uk). For general health information, contact the **American Red Cross** (☎+1-202-303-4498; www.redcross.org).

STAYING HEALTHY

Common sense is the simplest prescription for good health while you travel. Drink lots of fluids to prevent dehydration and constipation, and wear sturdy, broken-in shoes and clean socks.

COMES IN HANDY. A small bottle of liquid hand cleanser, a stash of moist towelettes, or even a package of baby wipes can keep your hands and face germ-free and refreshed on the road. The hand cleanser should have an alcohol content of at least 70% to be effective.

ONCE IN WESTERN EUROPE

ENVIRONMENTAL HAZARDS

Heat exhaustion and dehydration: Heat exhaustion leads to nausea, excessive thirst, headaches, and dizziness. Avoid it by drinking plenty of fluids, eating salty foods (e.g., crackers), abstaining from dehydrating beverages (e.g., alcohol and caffeinated beverages), and wearing sunscreen. Continuous heat stress can eventually lead to heatstroke, characterized by a rising temperature, severe headache, delirium, and cessation of sweating. Victims should be cooled off with wet towels and taken to a doctor.

Sunburn: Always wear sunscreen (SPF 30 or higher) when spending time outdoors. If you get sunburned, drink more fluids than usual and apply an aloe-based lotion. Severe sunburns can lead to sun poisoning, a condition that can cause fever, chills, nausea, and vomiting. Sun poisoning should always be treated by a doctor.

Hypothermia and frostbite: A rapid drop in body temperature is the clearest sign of overexposure to cold. Victims may also shiver, feel exhausted, have poor coordination or slurred speech, hallucinate, or suffer amnesia. Do not let hypothermia victims fall asleep. To avoid hypothermia, keep dry, wear layers, and stay out of the wind. When the temperature is below freezing, watch out for frostbite. If skin turns white or blue, waxy, and cold, do not rub the area. Drink warm beverages, stay dry, and slowly warm the area with dry fabric or steady body contact until a doctor can be found.

High Altitude: Allow your body a couple of days to adjust to less oxygen before exerting yourself. Note that alcohol is more potent and UV rays are stronger at high elevations.

INSECT-BORNE DISEASES

Many diseases are transmitted by insects—mainly mosquitoes, fleas, ticks, and lice. Be aware of insects in wet or forested areas, especially while hiking and camping. Wear long pants and long sleeves, tuck your pants into your socks, and use a mosquito net while sleeping. Apply insect repellents such as DEET and soak or spray your gear with permethrin (licensed in the US only for use on clothing). **Ticks**—which can carry Lyme and other diseases—can be particularly dangerous in rural and forested regions.

Tick-borne encephalitis: A viral infection of the central nervous system transmitted during the summer by tick bites (primarily in wooded areas) or by consumption of unpasteurized dairy products. The risk of contracting the disease is relatively low, especially if precautions are taken against tick bites.

Lyme disease: A bacterial infection carried by ticks and marked by a circular bull's-eye rash of 2 in. or more. Later symptoms include fever, headache, fatigue, and aches and pains. Antibiotics are effective if administered early. Left untreated, Lyme disease can cause problems in joints, the heart, and the nervous system. If you find a tick attached to your skin, grasp the head with tweezers as close to your skin as possible and apply slow, steady traction. Removing a tick within 24hr. greatly reduces the risk of infection. Do not try to remove ticks with petroleum jelly, nail polish remover, or a hot match. Ticks usually inhabit moist, shaded environments and heavily wooded areas. If you are going to be hiking in these areas, wear long clothes and DEET.

Other insect-borne diseases: Lymphatic filariasis is a roundworm infestation transmitted by mosquitoes. Infection causes enlargement of extremities and has no vaccine. **Leishmaniasis,** a parasite transmitted by sand flies, can occur in rural areas of Western Europe. Common symptoms are fever, weakness, and swelling of the spleen, as well as skin sores. There is a treatment, but no vaccine.

FOOD- AND WATER-BORNE DISEASES

Prevention is the best cure: be sure that your food is properly cooked and the water you drink is clean. Watch out for food from markets or street vendors that may have been cooked in unhygienic conditions. Other culprits are raw shellfish, unpasteurized milk, and sauces containing raw eggs. If the region's tap water is known to be unsanitary, peel fruits and vegetables before eating them and avoid tap water (including ice cubes and anything washed in tap water). Buy bottled water, or purify your own water by bringing it to a rolling boil or treating it with **iodine tablets;** note that some parasites have exteriors that resist iodine treatment, so boiling is more reliable. Always wash your hands.

Giardiasis: Transmitted through parasites and acquired by drinking untreated water from streams or lakes. Symptoms include diarrhea, cramps, bloating, fatigue, weight loss, and nausea. If untreated, it can lead to severe dehydration. Giardiasis occurs worldwide.

Hepatitis A: A viral infection of the liver acquired through contaminated water or shellfish from contaminated water. Symptoms include fatigue, fever, loss of appetite, nausea, dark urine, jaundice, vomiting, aches and pains, and light stools. The risk is highest in rural areas and the countryside, but it is also present in urban areas. Ask your doctor about the Hepatitis A vaccine or an injection of immune globulin.

Traveler's diarrhea: Results from drinking fecally contaminated water or eating uncooked and contaminated foods. Symptoms include nausea, bloating, and urgency. Try quick-energy, non-sugary foods with protein and carbohydrates to keep your strength up. Over-the-counter anti-diarrheals (e.g., Imodium) may counteract the problem. The most dangerous side effect is dehydration; drink 8 oz. of water with tsp. of sugar or honey and a pinch of salt, try uncaffeinated soft drinks, or eat salted crackers. If you develop a fever or your symptoms don't go away after 4-5 days, consult a doctor. Consult a doctor immediately for treatment of diarrhea in children.

Sexually transmitted infections (STIs): Gonorrhea, chlamydia, genital warts, syphilis, herpes, HPV, and other STIs are easier to catch than HIV and can be just as serious. Though condoms may protect you from some STIs, oral or even tactile contact can lead to transmission. If you think you may have contracted an STI, see a doctor immediately.

OTHER HEALTH CONCERNS

MEDICAL CARE ON THE ROAD

While healthcare systems in Western Europe tend to be quite accessible and of high quality, medical care varies greatly across Eastern and Southern Europe. Major cities such as Prague have English-speaking medical centers or hospitals for foreigners. In general, medical service in these regions is not up to Western standards; though basic supplies are usually there, specialized treatment is not. Tourist offices may have names of local doctors who speak English. In the event of a medical emergency, contact your embassy for aid and recommendations. All EU citizens can receive free or reduced-cost first aid and emergency services by presenting a **European Health Insurance Card.**

If you are concerned about obtaining medical assistance while traveling, you may wish to employ special support services. The **MedPass** from **GlobalCare, Inc.,** 6875 Shiloh Rd. East, Alpharetta, GA 30005, USA (☎800-860-1111; www.globalcare.net), provides 24hr. international medical assistance, support, and medical evacuation resources. The **International Association for Medical Assistance to Travelers (IAMAT;** US ☎+1-716-754-4883, Canada 519-836-0102; www.iamat.org) has free membership, lists English-speaking doctors worldwide, and offers detailed info on immunization requirements and sanitation. If your regular insurance policy does not cover travel abroad, you may wish to purchase additional coverage. For more information, see p. 16.

Those with medical conditions may want to obtain a **MedicAlert** membership (US$40 per year), which includes among other things a stainless steel ID tag and a 24hr. collect-call number. Contact the MedicAlert Foundation International, 2323 Colorado Ave., Turlock, CA 95382, USA (☎+1-888-633-4298, outside US ☎+1-209-668-3333; www.medicalert.org).

WOMEN'S HEALTH

Women traveling in unsanitary conditions are vulnerable to urinary tract **infections.** Over-the-counter medicines can sometimes alleviate symptoms, but if they persist, see a doctor. Vaginal yeast infections may flare up in hot and humid climates. Wearing loose-fitting trousers or a skirt and cotton underwear will help, as will over-the-counter remedies. Bring supplies if you are prone to infection, as it may be difficult to find the brands you prefer on the road. **Tampons, pads,** and **contraceptive devices** are widely available in most of Western Europe, but can be hard to find in areas of Eastern Europe. **Abortion** laws also vary from country to country. In much of Western Europe, abortion is legal during at least the first 10-12 weeks of pregnancy, but remains illegal in Ireland, Monaco, and Spain, except in extreme circumstances.

KEEPING IN TOUCH

BY EMAIL AND INTERNET

Email is popular and easily accessible in most of Europe. Although in some places it's possible to forge a remote link with your home server, in most cases this is a much slower (and thus more expensive) option than taking advantage of free **web-based email accounts** (e.g., **www.gmail.com** and www.hotmail.com). **Internet cafes** and the occasional free Internet terminal at a public library or university are listed in the **Practical Information** sections of major cities. For lists of additional cybercafes in Europe, check out www.cybercaptive.com, www.netcafeguide.com, and www.cybercafe.com.

WARY WI-FI. Wireless hot spots make Internet access possible in public and remote places. Unfortunately, they also pose **security risks.** Hot spots are public, open networks that use unencrypted, unsecured connections. They are susceptible to hacks and "packet sniffing"—ways of stealing passwords and other private information. To prevent problems, disable ad hoc mode, turn off file sharing and network discovery, encrypt your email, turn on your firewall, beware of phony networks, and watch for over-the-shoulder creeps.

Increasingly, travelers find that taking their **laptop computers** on the road with them can be a convenient option for staying connected. Laptop users can call an Internet service provider via a modem using long-distance phone cards specifically intended for such calls. Another option is **Voice over Internet Protocol (VoIP).** A particularly popular VoIP provider, **Skype,** allows users to contact other users for free, and to call landlines and mobile phones for an additional fee. Some Internet cafes allow travelers to connect their laptops to the Internet. Lucky travelers with wireless-enabled computers may be able to take advantage of an increasing number of Internet "hot spots," where they can get online for free or for a small fee. Newer computers can detect these hot spots automatically; otherwise, websites like www.jiwire.com, www.wififreespot.com, and www.wi-fihotspotlist.com can help you find them. For information on insuring your laptop and other electronics while traveling, see p. 16.

BY TELEPHONE

CALLING HOME FROM EUROPE

Prepaid phone cards are a common and relatively inexpensive means of calling abroad. Each one comes with a Personal Identification Number (PIN) and a toll-free access number. Call the access number and then follow the directions for dialing your PIN. To purchase prepaid phone cards, check online for the best rates; www.callingcards.com is a good place to start. Online providers generally send your access number and PIN via email, with no actual "card" involved. You can also call home with prepaid phone cards purchased in Europe (see **Calling Within Europe,** p. 21).

PLACING INTERNATIONAL CALLS. All international dialing prefixes and country codes for Europe are shown in a chart on the **Inside Back Cover** of this book. To place international calls, dial:

1. The **international dialing prefix.** To call from **Australia,** dial 0011; **Canada** or the **US,** 011; **Ireland, New Zealand,** or the **UK,** 00.
2. The **country code** of the country you want to call. To call **Australia,** dial 61; **Canada** or the **US,** 1; **Ireland,** 353; **New Zealand,** 64; the **UK,** 44.
3. The **city/area code.** *Let's Go* lists the city/area codes for cities and towns in Europe opposite the city or town name, next to a ☎, as well as in every phone number. If the first digit is a zero (e.g., 020 for London), omit the zero when calling from abroad (e.g., dial 20 from **Canada** to reach **London**).
4. The **local number.**

Another option is to purchase a **calling card,** linked to a major national telecommunications service in your home country. Calls are billed collect or to your account. To obtain a calling card, contact the appropriate company listed below. Where available, there are often advantages to purchasing calling cards online, including better rates and immediate access to your account. Companies that offer calling cards include: **AT&T Direct** (US ☎800-364-9292; www.att.com); **Canada Direct** (☎800-561-8868; www.infocanadadirect.com); **MCI** (☎800-777-5000; www.minutepass.com); **Telecom New Zealand Direct** (www.telecom.co.nz); **Telstra Australia** (☎1800 676 638; www.telstra.com). To call home with a calling card, contact the operator for your service provider by dialing the appropriate toll-free access number. Placing a **collect call** through an international operator can be expensive but may be necessary in case of an emergency. You can frequently call collect without even possessing a company's calling card just by calling its access number and following the instructions. *Let's Go* lists access numbers in the **Essentials** sections of each chapter.

CALLING WITHIN EUROPE

The simplest way to call within a country is to use a public pay phone. However, much of Europe has switched to a **prepaid phone card** system, and in some countries you may have a hard time finding coin-operated phones. Prepaid phone cards (available at newspaper kiosks and tobacco stores), which carry a certain amount of phone time depending on the card's denomination, usually save time and money in the long run. Another kind of prepaid phone card comes with a PIN and a toll-free access number. Instead of inserting the card into the phone, you call the access number and follow the directions on the card. These cards can be used to make international as well as domestic calls..

MOBILE PHONES

Mobile phones are an increasingly popular option for travelers calling within Europe. In addition to greater convenience and safety, mobile phones often provide an economical alternative to expensive landline calls. Virtually all of Western Europe has excellent coverage. The international standard for mobile phones is **Global System for Mobile Communication** (GSM). To make and receive calls in Europe, you need a **GSM-compatible phone** and a **subscriber identity module (SIM) card,** a country-specific, thumbnail-sized chip that gives you a local phone number and plugs you into the local network. Many SIM cards are prepaid, and incoming calls are free. When you use up the prepaid time, you can buy additional cards or vouchers (usually available at convenience stores) to "top up" your phone. For more info on GSM phones, check out www.telestial.com, www.orange.co.uk, www.roadpost.com, or www.planetomni.com. Companies like **Cellular Abroad** (www.cellularabroad.com) rent mobile phones that work in a variety of destinations around the world.

GSM PHONES. Just having a GSM phone doesn't mean you're necessarily good to go when you travel abroad. The majority of GSM phones sold in the United States operate on a different **frequency** (1900) than international phones (900/1800) and will not work abroad. Tri-band phones work on all three frequencies (900/1800/1900) and will operate through most of the world. Additionally, some GSM phones are **SIM-locked** and will only accept SIM cards from a single carrier. You'll need a **SIM-unlocked** phone to use a SIM card from a local carrier when you travel.

TIME DIFFERENCES

All of Europe falls within 3hr. of **Greenwich Mean Time (GMT).** For more info, consult the time zone chart on the **Inside Back Cover.** GMT is 5hr. ahead of New York time, 8hr. ahead of Vancouver time, 10hr. behind Sydney time, and 12hr. behind Auckland time. Iceland is the only country in Europe to ignore Daylight Saving Time; fall and spring switchover times vary in countries that do observe Daylight Saving. For more info, visit www.worldtimeserver.com.

BY MAIL

SENDING MAIL HOME FROM EUROPE

Airmail is the best way to send mail home from Europe. From Western Europe to North America, delivery time averages about seven days. **Aerogrammes,** printed sheets that fold into envelopes and travel via airmail, are available at post offices. Write "airmail" or "*par avion*" (or *por avión*, *mit Luftpost*, *via aerea*, etc.) on the front. Most post offices will charge exorbitant fees or simply refuse to send aerogrammes with enclosures. **Surface mail** is by far the cheapest and slowest way to send mail. It takes one to two months to cross the Atlantic and one to three to cross the Pacific—good for heavy items you won't need for a while, such as souvenirs that you've acquired along the way. Check the **Essentials** section of each chapter for country-specific postal info.

SENDING MAIL TO EUROPE

To ensure timely delivery, mark envelopes "airmail" in both English and the local language. In addition to standard postage systems, **Federal Express** (Australia ☎+61 13 26 10, Canada and the US +1-800-463-3339, Ireland +353 800 535 800, New Zealand +64 800 733 339, the UK +44 8456 070 809; www.fedex.com) handles express mail services from most countries to Europe.

There are several ways to arrange pick-up of letters sent to you while you are abroad. Mail can be sent via **Poste Restante** (General Delivery, *Lista de Correos*, *Fermo Posta*, *Postlagernde Briefe*, etc.) to almost any city or town in Europe with a post office, though it can be unreliable in Eastern Europe. See individual country chapters for more info on addressing Poste Restante letters. The mail will go to a special desk in a town's central post office, unless you specify a post office by street address or postal code. It's best to use the largest post office, since mail may be sent there regardless. It's usually safer and quicker, though more expensive, to send mail express or registered. Bring your passport for pick-up; there may be a small fee. If the clerks insist that there is nothing for you, ask them to check under your first name as well. *Let's Go* lists post offices in the **Practical Information** section for each city and most towns.

American Express's travel offices throughout the world offer a free **Client Letter Service** (mail held up to 30 days and forwarded upon request) for cardholders who contact them in advance. Some offices provide these services to non-cardholders (especially AmEx Travelers Cheque holders), but call ahead to make sure. *Let's Go* lists AmEx locations for most large cities in **Practical Information** sections; for a complete list, visit www.americanexpress.com/travel.

ACCOMMODATIONS

HOSTELS

Many hostels are laid out dorm-style, often with large single-sex rooms and bunk beds, although private rooms sleeping two to four are becoming more common. They sometimes have kitchens, bike or moped rentals, storage areas, airport transportation, breakfast and other meals, laundry facilities, and Internet. There can be drawbacks: some hostels close during certain daytime "lockout" hours, have a curfew, don't accept reservations, impose a maximum stay, or—less frequently—require that you do chores. In Western Europe, a hostel dorm bed will average around US$15-30 and a private room around US$30-50.

A HOSTELER'S BILL OF RIGHTS. There are certain standard features that we do not include in our hostel listings. Unless we state otherwise, you can expect that every hostel has free hot showers, no lockout, no curfew, some system of secure luggage storage, and no key deposit.

ESSENTIALS

HOSTELLING INTERNATIONAL

Joining the youth hostel association in your own country (listed below) automatically grants you membership privileges in **Hostelling International (HI),** a federation of national hosteling associations. Non-HI members may be allowed to stay in some hostels but will have to pay extra. HI hostels are scattered throughout Western Europe and are typically less expensive than private hostels. HI's umbrella organization's website (www.hihostel.com), which lists the web addresses and phone numbers of all national associations, can be a great place to begin researching hosteling in a specific region. Other comprehensive hosteling websites include www.hostels.com and www.hostelplanet.com.

Most HI hostels also honor **guest memberships**—you'll get a blank card with space for six validation stamps. Each night you'll pay a nonmember supplement and earn one guest stamp; get six stamps and you're a member. In some countries you may need to remind the hostel reception. A new membership benefit is the **FreeNites program,** which allows hostelers to gain points toward free rooms. Most student travel agencies sell HI cards, as do all of the national hosteling organizations listed below. All prices listed below are valid for **one-year memberships** unless otherwise noted.

Australian Youth Hostels Association (YHA), 422 Kent St., Sydney, NSW 200 (☎02 9261 1111; www.yha.com.au). AUS$42, under 26 AUS$32.

Hostelling International-Canada (HI-C), 205 Catherine St. Ste. 400, Ottawa, ON K2P 1C3 (☎613-237-7884; www.hihostels.ca). CDN$35, under 18 free.

An Óige (Irish Youth Hostel Association), 61 Mountjoy St., Dublin 7 (☎01 830 4555; www.irelandyha.org). EUR€20, under 18 EUR€10.

Hostelling International Northern Ireland (HINI), 22-32 Donegall Rd., Belfast BT12 5JN (☎028 9032 4733; www.hini.org.uk). UK£15, under 25 UK£10.

Scottish Youth Hostels Association (SYHA), 7 Glebe Cres., Stirling FK8 2JA (☎01786 89 14 00; www.syha.org.uk). UK£8, under 16 free.

Youth Hostels Association (England and Wales), Trevelyan House, Dimple Rd., Matlock, Derbyshire DE4 3YH (☎01629 592 600; www.yha.org.uk). UK£16, under 26 UK£10.

Hostelling International-USA, 8401 Colesville Rd., Ste. 600, Silver Spring, MD 20910 (☎301-495-1240; www.hiayh.org). US$28, under 18 free.

BOOKING HOSTELS ONLINE. One of the easiest ways to ensure you've got a bed for the night is by reserving online. Click to the Hostelworld booking engine through www.letsgo.com, and you'll have access to bargain accommodations from Argentina to Zimbabwe with no added commission.

OTHER TYPES OF ACCOMMODATIONS

YMCAS AND YWCAS

Young Men's Christian Association (YMCA) and **Young Women's Christian Association (YWCA)** lodgings are usually cheaper than a hotel but more expensive than a hostel. Not all locations offer lodging; those that do are often located in urban downtowns. Many YMCAs accept women and families; some will not lodge those under 18 without parental permission. **World Alliance of YMCAs,** 12 Clos Belmont, 1208 Geneva, SWI (☎41 22 849 5100; www.ymca.int), has more info and a register of Western European YMCAs with housing options.

European Alliance of YMCAs (YMCA Europe), Na Porici 12, CZ-110 00 Prague 1, Czech Republic (☎420 224 872 020; www.ymcaeurope.com). Maintains listings of European YMCAs with opportunities to volunteer abroad.

HOTELS, GUESTHOUSES, AND PENSIONS

In Western Europe, **hotel singles** cost about US$30 (€20) per night, **doubles** US$40 (€26). You'll typically share a hall bathroom; a private bathroom and hot showers may cost extra. Some hotels offer "full pension" (all meals) and "half pension" (no lunch). Smaller **guesthouses** and **pensions** are often cheaper than hotels. If you make reservations in writing, note your night of arrival and the number of nights you plan to stay. After sending you a confirmation, the hotel may request payment for the first night. Often it's easiest to reserve over the phone.

BED & BREAKFASTS (B&BS)

For a cozy alternative to hotel rooms, **B&Bs** (private homes with rooms available to travelers) range from acceptable to sublime. Rooms generally cost about €35 for a single and €70 for a double in Western Europe. Any number of websites provide listings for B&Bs. Check out **InnFinder** (www.inncrawler.com), **InnSite** (www.innsite.com), or **BedandBreakfast.com** (www.bedandbreakfast.com).

UNIVERSITY DORMS

Many **colleges** and **universities** open their residence halls to travelers when school is not in session; some do so even during term-time. Getting a room may take a couple of phone calls and require advanced planning, but rates tend to be low and many offer free local calls and Internet. Where available, university dorms are listed in the **Accommodations** section of each city.

HOME EXCHANGES AND HOSPITALITY CLUBS

Home exchange offers the traveler various types of homes (houses, apartments, condominiums, villas, even castles), plus the opportunity to live like a native and to cut down on accommodation fees. For more info, contact **HomeExchange.com Inc.**, P.O. Box 787, Hermosa Beach, CA 90254, USA (☎310-798-3864 or toll free 800-877-8723; www.homeexchange.com), or **Intervac International Home Exchange** (www.intervac.com; see site for phone listings by country).

Hospitality clubs link their members with individuals or families abroad who are willing to host travelers for free or for a small fee to promote cultural exchange and general good karma. In exchange, members usually must be willing to host travelers in their own homes; a small membership fee may also be required. **The Hospitality Club** (www.hospitalityclub.org) is a good place to start. **Servas** (www.servas.org) is an established, more formal, peace-based organization, and requires a fee and an interview to join. As always, use common sense when planning to stay with or host someone you do not know.

LONG-TERM ACCOMMODATIONS

Travelers planning to stay in Western Europe for extended periods of time may find it most cost-effective to rent an **apartment.** Rent varies widely by region, season, and quality. Besides the rent itself, prospective tenants usually are also required to front a security deposit and the last month's rent. Generally, for stays shorter than three months, it is more feasible to **sublet** than lease your own apartment. Sublets are also more likely to be furnished. Out of session, it may be possible to arrange to sublet rooms from university students on summer break. It is far easier to find an apartment once you have arrived at your destination than to attempt to use the Internet or phone from home. By staying in a hostel for your first week or so, you can make local contacts and, more importantly, check out your new digs before you commit.

CAMPING

With Europe's vast terrain encompassing beaches, mountains, and plains, **camping** always has some new adventure to offer. Furthermore, you can explore nature for prices refreshingly easy on the wallet. Most towns have several campgrounds within walking distance, occasionally offering a cheap shuttle service to reach them. Even the most rudimentary *campings* (campgrounds) provide showers and laundry facilities, though almost all forbid campfires. In addition to tent camping, other patrons opt to drive RVs across Europe. Campgrounds usually charge a flat fee per person (usually around €4-6) plus a few euro extra for electricity, tents, cars, or running water. Most larger campgrounds also operate on-site general stores or cafes perfect for a quick, cheap bite. In some countries, it is illegal to pitch your tent or park your RV overnight along the road; look for designated camping areas within national parks, recognized campgrounds, or ask landowners permission before setting up residency on private property. In Sweden, Finland, and Norway, the **right of public access** permits travelers to tent one night in Scandinavia's forests and wilderness for free.

If planning on using campgrounds as your go-to accommodation, consider buying an **International Camping Carnet** (ICC, US$45). Available through the association of **Family Campers and RVers** (☎800-245-9755; www.fcrv.org), the card entitles holders to discounts at some campgrounds and may save travelers from having to leave their passport as a deposit. National tourist offices offer more info on country-specific camping. Additionally, check out **Interhike** (www.interhike.com) which lists campgrounds by region. First-time campers may also want to peruse **KarmaBum Cafe** (www.karmabum.com) for suggested itineraries, packing lists, blogs, and camping recipes. For more info on outdoor activities in Western Europe, see **The Great Outdoors,** p. 26.

THE GREAT OUTDOORS

LEAVE NO TRACE. *Let's Go* encourages travelers to embrace the "Leave No Trace" ethic, minimizing their impact on natural environments. Trekkers should set up camp on durable surfaces, use cookstoves instead of campfires, bury human waste away from water supplies, bag trash and carry it out with them, and respect wildlife and natural objects. For more detailed information, contact the **Leave No Trace Center for Outdoor Ethics,** P.O. Box 997, Boulder, CO 80306 (☎800-332-4100 or 303-442-8222; www.lnt.org).

Camping can be a great way to see Europe on the cheap. There are organized **campgrounds** outside most cities. Showers, bathrooms, and a small restaurant or store are common; some sites have more elaborate facilities. Prices are low, usually US$5-15 per person plus additional charges for tents and cars. While camping is a cheaper option than hosteling, the cost of transportation to and from campgrounds can add up. Some public grounds allow **free camping,** but check local laws. Many areas have additional park-specific rules. **The Great Outdoor Recreation Pages** (www.gorp.com) provides excellent general info.

USEFUL RESOURCES

There are a variety of publishing companies that offer hiking guidebooks to meet the educational needs of the novice or the expert. For information about biking, camping, and hiking, write or call the publishers listed below to receive a free catalog. Campers heading to Europe should consider buying an **International Camping Carnet.** Similar to a hostel membership card, it's required at a few campgrounds in addition to providing discounts at others. It is available in North America from the **Family Campers and RVers Association** (www.fcrv.org) and in the UK from **The Caravan Club** (see below).

Automobile Association, Contact Centre, Carr Ellison House, William Armstrong Dr., Newcastle-upon-Tyne NE4 7YA, UK (☎08706 000 371; www.theaa.com). Publishes *Caravan and Camping Europe* and *Britain & Ireland* (UK£10) as well as road atlases for Europe as a whole and for Britain, France, Germany, Ireland, Italy, and Spain.

The Caravan Club, East Grinstead House, East Grinstead, West Sussex RH19 1UA, UK (☎01342 326 944; www.caravanclub.co.uk). For UK£36, members get access to campgrounds, insurance services, equipment discounts, maps, and a magazine.

Sierra Club Books, 85 2nd St., 2nd fl., San Francisco, CA 94105, USA (☎415-977-5500; www.sierraclub.org). Publishes general resource books on hiking and camping.

The Mountaineers Books, 1001 SW Klickitat Way, Ste. 201, Seattle, WA 98134, USA (☎206-223-6303; www.mountaineersbooks.org). Over 600 titles on hiking, biking, mountaineering, natural history, and conservation.

WILDERNESS SAFETY

Staying **warm, dry,** and **well hydrated** are the keys to a happy and safe wilderness experience. Before any hike, prepare yourself for an emergency by packing a first-aid kit, a reflector, a whistle, high-energy food, extra water, raingear, a hat, gloves, and several **extra pairs of socks.** For warmth, wear wool or insulating synthetic materials designed for the outdoors. Cotton is a bad choice as it takes a ridiculously long time to dry and loses its insulating effect when wet.

Check **weather forecasts** often and pay attention to the skies when hiking, as weather patterns can change suddenly, especially in mountainous areas. Always let someone—a friend, your hostel staff, a park ranger, or a local hiking organization—know when and where you are going. Know your physical limits and do not attempt a hike beyond your ability.

CAMPING AND HIKING EQUIPMENT

WHAT TO BUY

Good camping equipment is both sturdy and light. North American suppliers tend to offer the most competitive prices.

Sleeping Bags: Most sleeping bags are rated by season; "summer" means 30-40°F (around 0°C) at night; "four-season" or "winter" often means below 0°F (-17°C). Bags are made of down (warm and light, but expensive, and miserable when wet) or of synthetic material (heavy, durable, and warm when wet). Prices range from US$50-250 for a summer synthetic and from US$200-300 for a good down winter bag. Sleeping bag pads include foam pads (US$10-30), air mattresses (US$15-50), and self-inflating mats (US$30-120). Bring a stuff sack to store your bag and keep it dry.

Tents: The best tents are free-standing (with their own frames and suspension systems), set up quickly, and only require staking in high winds. Low-profile dome tents are the best all around. 2-person tents start at US$100, 4-person tents at US$160. Make sure your tent has a rain fly and seal its seams with waterproofer. Other useful accessories include a battery-operated lantern, a plastic groundcloth, and a nylon tarp.

Backpacks: Internal-frame packs mold to your back, keep a lower center of gravity, and flex to allow you to hike difficult trails, while external-frame packs are more comfortable for long hikes over even terrain, as they carry weight higher and distribute it more evenly. Make sure your pack has a hip-belt to transfer weight to your legs. Any serious backpacking requires a pack of at least 4000 cu. in., plus 500 cu. in. for sleeping bags in internal-frame packs. Sturdy backpacks cost anywhere from US$125 to US$420—your pack is an area where it doesn't pay to economize. On your hunt for the perfect pack, fill up each prospective model with something heavy, strap it on, and walk around the store to get a sense of how the model distributes weight. Either buy a rain cover (US$10-20) or store your belongings in plastic bags inside your pack.

Boots: Be sure to wear hiking boots with good ankle support. They should fit snugly and comfortably over 1-2 pairs of wool socks and a pair of thin liner socks. Break in boots over several weeks before you go to spare yourself from blisters.

Other Necessities: Synthetic layers, like those made of polypropylene or polyester, and a pile jacket will keep you warm even when wet. A space blanket (US$5-15) will help you to retain body heat and doubles as a groundcloth. Durable plastic water bottles are vital. Carry water-purification tablets for when you can't boil water. Virtually every organized campground in Europe forbids fires or the gathering of firewood, so you'll need a camp stove and a propane-filled fuel bottle to operate it. Keep in mind you may have to buy some equipment after you arrive because of airline restrictions. Also bring a first-aid kit, pocketknife, insect repellent, and waterproof matches or a lighter.

ORGANIZED ADVENTURE TRIPS

Organized adventure tours offer another way of exploring the wild. Activities include hiking, biking, skiing, skydiving, canoeing, kayaking, rafting, climbing, photo safaris, and archaeological digs. Organizations that specialize in camping and outdoor equipment like REI and EMS (see above) are also a good source for information. Some companies, like the ones below, list organized tour opportunities throughout Europe.

Specialty Travel Index, PO Box 458, San Anselmo, CA 94979, USA (US ☎888-624-4030, elsewhere 415-455-1643; www.specialtytravel.com).

Ecotravel (www.ecotravel.com). Online directory of various programs in Europe and throughout the world. Includes itineraries, guides, and articles.

NatureTrek, Cheriton Mill, Cheriton, Alresford, Hampshire, SO24 0NG (☎01962 733051; www.naturetrek.co.uk). Offers responsible travel opportunities all over the globe.

SPECIFIC CONCERNS

SUSTAINABLE TRAVEL

As the number of travelers on the road rises, the detrimental effect they can have on natural environments is an increasing concern. With this in mind, *Let's Go* promotes the philosophy of **sustainable travel.** Through sensitivity to issues of ecology and sustainability, today's travelers can be a powerful force in preserving as well as restoring the places they visit.

ECOTOURISM RESOURCES. For more info on environmentally responsible tourism, contact one of the organizations below:

Conservation International, 2011 Crystal Dr., Ste. 500, Arlington, VA 22202, USA (☎+1-800-406-2306 or 703-341-2400; www.conservation.org).

Green Globe, Green Globe vof, Verbenalaan 1, 2111 ZL Aerdenhout, The Netherlands (☎+31 23 544 0306; www.greenglobe.com).

International Ecotourism Society, 1333 H St. NW, Ste. 300E, Washington, D.C. 20005, USA (☎+1-202-347-9203; www.ecotourism.org).

United Nations Environment Program, 39-43 Quai André Citroën, 75739 Paris Cedex 15, France (☎+33 1 44 37 14 50; www.uneptie.org/pc/tourism).

Ecotourism, a rising trend in sustainable travel, focuses on the conservation of natural habitats—mainly, on how to use them without exploitation or overdevelopment. Travelers can make a difference by doing advance research, by supporting organizations and establishments that pay attention to their carbon "footprint," and by patronizing establishments that strive to be environmentally friendly. **International Friends of Nature** (www.nfi.at) has info about sustainable travel options in Europe. For more info, see **Beyond Tourism,** p. 45.

RESPONSIBLE TRAVEL

Your tourist dollars can make a big impact on the destinations you visit. The choices you make during your trip can have potent effects on local communities—for better or for worse. Travelers who care about the destinations they explore should become aware of the social, cultural, and political implications of their choices. Simple decisions such as buying local products, paying fair prices for products or services, and attempting to speak the local language can have a strong, positive effect on the community.

Community-based tourism aims to channel tourist money into the local economy by emphasizing tours and cultural programs run by members of the host community. This type of tourism also benefits the tourists themselves, as it often takes them beyond the traditional tours of the region. The *Ethical Travel Guide*, a project of **Tourism Concern** (☎+44 20 7133 3330; www.tourismconcern.org.uk), is an excellent resource for info on community-based travel, with a directory of 300 establishments in 60 countries.

TRAVELING ALONE

Traveling alone can be extremely beneficial, providing a sense of independence and a greater opportunity to connect with locals. On the other hand, solo travelers are more vulnerable targets of harassment and street theft. If you are traveling alone, look confident, try not to stand out as a tourist, and be especially careful in deserted or very crowded areas. Stay away from areas that are not well lit. If questioned, never admit that you are traveling alone. In Eastern Europe, be particularly careful about train travel; some travelers find it safer to ride in more crowded compartments and to avoid traveling at night. Maintain regular contact with someone who knows your itinerary, and always research your destination before traveling. For more tips, pick up *Traveling Solo* (6th ed.) by Eleanor Berman (Globe Pequot Press; 2008), visit www.travelaloneandloveit.com, or subscribe to **Connecting: Solo Travel Network,** 689 Park Rd., Unit 6, Gibsons, BC V0N 1V7, Canada (☎+1-604-886-9099; www.cstn.org; membership US$50).

WOMEN TRAVELERS

Women exploring on their own inevitably face some additional safety concerns. Single women can consider staying in hostels which offer single rooms that lock from the inside or in religious organizations with single-sex rooms. It is a good idea to stick to centrally located accommodations and to avoid solitary late-night journeys or metro rides.

Always carry extra money for a phone call, bus, or taxi. **Hitchhiking** is never safe for lone women, or even for two women traveling together. Look as if you know where you're going, and approach older women or couples for directions if you're lost or uncomfortable. Generally, the less you look like a tourist, the better off you'll be. Dress conservatively, especially in rural areas. Wearing a conspicuous **wedding band** sometimes helps prevent unwanted advances.

Your best answer to verbal harassment is no answer at all; feigning deafness, pretending you don't understand the language, or staring straight ahead will usually do the trick. Seek out a police officer or a passerby if you are being harassed. Memorize the emergency numbers in places you visit, and consider carrying a whistle. A self defense course will both prepare you for a potential attack and raise your level of awareness of your surroundings (see recommendations on self defense, p. 15). Also, it might be a good idea to talk with your doctor about the health concerns that women face when traveling (p. 19).

GLBT TRAVELERS

Attitudes toward gay, lesbian, bisexual, and transgendered (GLBT) travelers are particular to each region in Europe. On the whole, countries in Northern and Western Europe tend to be queer-friendly, while Eastern Europe harbors enclaves of tolerance in cities amid stretches of cultural conservatism. Countries like Romania that outlawed homosexuality as recently as 2002 are becoming more liberal today, and can be considered viable destinations for GLBT travelers. Listed below are contact organizations that offer materials addressing some specific concerns. **Out and About** (www.planetout.com) offers a weekly newsletter addressing travel concerns and a comprehensive site addressing gay travel concerns. The online newspaper **365gay.com** has a travel section, and the French-language site **netgai.com** (http://netgai.com/international/Europe) includes links to country-specific resources.

Gay's the Word, 66 Marchmont St., London WC1N 1AB, UK (☎+44 20 7278 7654; http://freespace.virgin.net/gays.theword). The largest gay and lesbian bookshop in the UK, with both fiction and non-fiction titles. Mail-order service available.

Giovanni's Room, 345 S. 12th St., Philadelphia, PA 19107, USA (☎+1-215-923-2960; www.queerbooks.com). An international lesbian and gay bookstore with mail-order service (carries many of the publications listed below).

International Lesbian and Gay Association (ILGA), 17 Rue de la Charité, 1210 Brussels, BEL (☎+32 2 502 2471; www.ilga.org). Provides political information, such as homosexuality laws of individual countries.

ADDITIONAL RESOURCES.

Spartacus International Gay Guide 2008 (US$22).

The Damron Men's Travel Guide 2006. Gina M. Gatta, Damron Co. (US$22).

The Gay Vacation Guide: The Best Trips and How to Plan Them. Mark Chesnut, Kensington Books (US$15).

TRAVELERS WITH DISABILITIES

European countries vary in accessibility to travelers with disabilities. Some tourist boards, particularly in Western and Northern Europe, provide directories on the accessibility of various accommodations and transportation services. If these services are not available, contact establishments directly. Those with disabilities should inform airlines and hotels of their disabilities when making reservations; some time may be needed to prepare special accommodations. Call ahead to restaurants, museums, and other facilities to find out if they are wheelchair-accessible. **Guide dog owners** should inquire as to the quarantine policies of each destination country.

Rail is the most convenient form of travel for disabled travelers in Europe. Many stations have ramps, and some trains have wheelchair lifts, special seating areas, and special toilets. All Eurostar, some InterCity (IC), and some EuroCity (EC) trains are wheelchair-accessible. CityNightLine trains, French TGV (high speed), and Conrail trains feature special compartments. In general, the countries with the most **wheelchair-accessible rail networks** are: Denmark (IC and Lyn trains), France (TGVs and other long-distance trains), Germany (ICE, EC, IC, and IR trains), Ireland (most major trains), Italy (EC and IC trains), the Netherlands (most trains), Sweden (X2000s, most IC and IR trains), and Switzerland (all IC, most EC, and some regional trains). Austria, Poland, and the UK offer accessibility on selected routes. Bulgaria, the Czech Republic, Greece, Hungary, Slovakia, and Spain's rail systems have limited wheelchair accessibility. For those who wish to rent cars, some major **car rental** agencies (e.g., Hertz) offer hand-controlled vehicles for those with disabilities.

USEFUL ORGANIZATIONS

Access Abroad, www.umabroad.umn.edu/access. Devoted to making study abroad available to students with disabilities. The site is maintained by Disability Services, University of Minnesota, 230 Heller Hall, 271 19th Ave. S., Minneapolis, MN 55455, USA (☎+1-612-626-7379).

Accessible Journeys, 35 W. Sellers Ave., Ridley Park, PA 19078, USA (☎+1-800-846-4537; www.disabilitytravel.com). Designs tours for wheelchair users and slow walkers. The site has tips and forums for all travelers.

Flying Wheels, 143 W. Bridge St., Owatonna, MN 55060, USA (☎+1-507-451-5005; www.flyingwheelstravel.com). Specializes in escorted trips to Europe for people with physical disabilities. Plans custom trips worldwide.

The Guided Tour, Inc., 7900 Old York Rd., Ste. 114B, Elkins Park, PA 19027, USA (☎+1-800-783-5841; www.guidedtour.com). Organizes travel programs for persons with developmental and physical challenges in Ireland, Italy, Spain, and the UK.

Society for Accessible Travel and Hospitality (SATH), 347 5th Ave., Ste. 605, New York, NY 10016, USA (☎+1-212-447-7284; www.sath.org). An advocacy group that publishes free online travel information and the travel magazine *Open World*. Annual membership US$49, students and seniors US$29.

MINORITY TRAVELERS

In general, minority travelers will find a high level of tolerance in large cities; small towns and the countryside are less predictable. The increasingly mainstream reality of anti-immigrant sentiments means that travelers of African or Arab descent (regardless of their citizenship) may be the object of unwarranted assumptions and even hostility. Anti-Semitism remains a very real problem in many countries, especially in France, Austria, and much of Eastern Europe. Discrimination is particularly forceful against Roma (gypsies) throughout much of Eastern Europe. Jews, Muslims, and other minority travelers should keep an eye out for skinheads, who have been linked to racist violence in Central and Eastern Europe and elsewhere. **The European Union Agency for Fundamental Rights (FRA),** Rahlgasse 3, 1060 Vienna, AUT (☎43 15 80 30; www.eumc.europa.eu), publishes a wealth of country-specific statistics and reports. Travelers can consult **United for Intercultural Action,** Postbus 413, NL-1000 AK, Amsterdam, NTH (☎31 20 683 4778; www.unitedagainstracism.org), for a list of over 500 country-specific organizations that work against racism and discrimination.

DIETARY CONCERNS

Vegetarians will find no shortage of meat-free dining options throughout most of Northern and Western Europe, although **vegans** may have a trickier time outside urban centers, where eggs and dairy can dominate traditional dishes. The cuisine of Eastern Europe still tends to be heavy on meat and gravy, although major cities often boast surprisingly inventive vegetarian and ethnic fare.

The travel section of **The Vegetarian Resource Group's** website, at www.vrg.org/travel, has a comprehensive list of organizations and websites that are geared toward helping vegetarians and vegans traveling abroad. The website for the **European Vegetarian Union (EVU),** at www.europeanvegetarian.org, includes links to dozens of veggie-friendly organizations. For more info, consult *The Vegetarian Traveler: Where to Stay if You're Vegetarian, Vegan, Environmentally Sensitive*, by Jed and Susan Civic (Larson Publications; 1997), *Vegetarian Europe*, by Alex Bourke (Vegetarian Guides; 2000), and the indispensable, multilingual

Vegan Passport (The Vegan Society; 2005), along with the websites www.vegdining.com, www.happycow.net, and www.vegetariansabroad.com.

Those looking to keep **kosher** will find abundant dining options across Europe; contact synagogues in larger cities for information, or consult www.kashrut.com/travel/Europe for country-specific resources. Your own synagogue or college Hillel should have access to lists of Jewish institutions across the nation. Hebrew College Online also offers a searchable database of kosher restaurants at www.shamash.org/kosher. Another good resource is the *Jewish Travel Guide*, edited by Michael Zaidner (Vallentine Mitchell; 2004). Travelers looking for **halal** groceries and restaurants will have the most success in France and Eastern European nations with substantial Muslim populations; consult www.zabihah.com for establishment reviews. Keep in mind that if you are strict in your observance, you may have to prepare your own food.

OTHER RESOURCES

TRAVEL PUBLISHERS AND BOOKSTORES

The Globe Corner Bookstore, 90 Mt. Auburn St., Cambridge, MA 02138 (☎617-497-6277; www.globecorner.com). Sponsors an Adventure Travel Lecture Series and carries a vast selection of guides and maps to every imaginable destination. Online catalog includes atlases and monthly staff picks of outstanding travel writing.

Hippocrene Books, 171 Madison Ave., New York, NY 10016 (☎718-454-2366; www.hippocrenebooks.com). Publishes foreign-language dictionaries and learning guides, along with ethnic cookbooks and a smattering of guidebooks.

WORLD WIDE WEB

Almost every aspect of budget travel is accessible via the web. In 10min. at the keyboard, you can make a hostel reservation, get advice on travel hot spots from other travelers, or find out how much a train ride costs. Listed here are some regional and travel-related sites to start off your surfing; other relevant websites are listed throughout the book. Because website turnover is high, use search engines (e.g., www.google.com) to strike out on your own.

LET'S GO ONLINE. Plan your next trip on our newly redesigned website, **www.letsgo.com.** It features the latest travel info on your favorite destinations, as well as tons of interactive features: make your own itinerary, read blogs from our trusty researcher-writers, browse our photo library, watch exclusive videos, check out our newsletter, find travel deals, and buy new guides. We're always updating and adding new features, so check back often!

TRANSPORTATION

GETTING TO WESTERN EUROPE

BY PLANE

When it comes to airfare, a little effort can save you a bundle. Tickets sold by consolidators, couriers, and standby seating are good deals, but last-minute specials, airfare wars, and charter flights often beat these fares. The key is to hunt around, be flexible, and ask about discounts. Students, seniors, and those under 26 should never pay full price for a ticket.

AIRFARES

Airfares to Europe peak between mid-June and early September; holidays are also expensive. The cheapest times to travel are November to mid-December and January to March. Midweek (M-Th morning) round-trip flights run US$60-$120 cheaper than weekend flights, but they are generally more crowded and less likely to permit frequent-flier upgrades. Not fixing a return date ("open return") or arriving in and departing from different cities ("open jaw") is usually significantly pricier than buying a round-trip. Flights between Europe's capitals or regional hubs (Amsterdam, London, Paris, Prague, Warsaw, Zürich) tend to be cheaper than those to more rural areas.

If your European destinations are part of a more extensive globe-hop, consider a round-the-world (RTW) ticket. Tickets usually include at least five stops and are valid for about a year; prices range from US$1600-$5000. Try **Northwest Airlines/KLM** (☎800-225-2525; www.nwa.com) or **Star Alliance** (www.staralliance.com), a consortium of 16 airlines including United.

BUDGET AND STUDENT TRAVEL AGENCIES

While agents specializing in flights to Europe can make your life easy, they may not find you the lowest possible fare—they get paid on commission. Travelers holding **ISICs** and **IYTCs** (p. 9) qualify for big discounts from student travel agencies. Most flights from budget agencies are on major airlines, but in peak season some may sell seats on less reliable chartered aircrafts.

STA Travel, 9/89 5900 Wilshire Blvd., Ste. 900, Los Angeles, CA 90036, USA (24hr. reservations and info ☎800-781-4040; www.statravel.com). A student and youth travel organization with over 150 offices worldwide, including US offices in many college towns. Ticket booking, travel insurance, rail passes, and more.

The Adventure Travel Company, 124 McDougal St., New York, NY 10021, USA (☎1800 467 4594; www.theadventuretravelcompany.com). Offices across Canada and the US including Champaign, New York, San Francisco, Seattle, and San Diego.

USIT, 19-21 Aston Quay, Dublin 2, Ireland (☎+353 1 602 1906; www.usit.ie). Ireland's leading student/budget travel agency has 20 offices throughout Northern Ireland and the Republic of Ireland. Offers programs to work, study, and volunteer worldwide.

COMMERCIAL AIRLINES

Commercial airlines' lowest regular offer is the **APEX** (Advance Purchase Excursion) fare, which provides confirmed reservations and allows "open-jaw" tickets. Generally, reservations must be made seven to 21 days ahead of departure, with seven- to 14-day minimum stay and 90-day maximum stay restrictions. These fares carry hefty cancellation and change penalties (fees rise in summer). Use **Expedia** or **Travelocity** to get an idea of the lowest published fares, then use the resources listed here to try to beat those fares. Low-season fares should be appreciably cheaper than the high-season ones listed here.

TRAVELING FROM NORTH AMERICA

Basic round-trip fares to **Europe** range from roughly US$400-1500: to **Frankfurt**, US$450-1250; **London**, US$250-550; **Paris**, US$600-1400. Standard commercial carriers like **American** (☎800-433-7300; www.aa.com), **United** (☎800-538-2929; www.united.com), and **Northwest** (☎800-225-2525; www.nwa.com) will probably offer the most convenient flights, but they may not be the cheapest. Check **Lufthansa** (☎800-399-5838; www.lufthansa.com), **British Airways** (☎800-247-9297; www.britishairways.com), **Air France** (☎800-237-2747; www.airfrance.us), and **Alitalia** (☎800-223-5730; www.alitaliausa.com) for cheap tickets from US destinations to all over Europe. You might find an even better deal on one of the following airlines if any of their limited departure points is convenient for you.

Icelandair: ☎800-223-5500; www.icelandair.com. Stopovers in Iceland for no extra cost on most flights. New York to Frankfurt Apr.-Aug. US$900-1000; Sept.-Oct. US$600-800; Dec.-Mar. US$500. For last-minute offers, subscribe to their "Lucky Fares" email list.

Finnair: ☎800-950-5000; www.finnair.com. Cheap round-trips from New York, San Francisco, and Toronto to Helsinki; connections throughout Europe. New York to Helsinki June-Sept. US$1250; Oct.-May US$830-1200.

FLIGHT PLANNING ON THE INTERNET. The Internet may be the budget traveler's dream when it comes to finding and booking bargain fares, but the array of options can be overwhelming. Many airline sites offer special last-minute deals online, though some require membership logins or email subscriptions. Try www.airfrance.com, www.britishairways.com, www.icelandair.com, and www.lufthansa.de. **STA** (www.sta.com) and **StudentUniverse** (www.studentuniverse.com) provide quotes on student tickets, while **Expedia** (www.expedia.com), **Orbitz** (www.orbitz.com), and **Travelocity** (www.travelocity.com) offer full travel services. **Priceline** (www.priceline.com) lets you specify a price, and obligates you to buy any ticket that meets or beats it; **Hotwire** (www.hotwire.com) offers bargain fares but won't reveal the airline or flight times until you buy. Other sites that compile deals include www.bestfares.com, www.flights.com, www.lowestfare.com, www.onetravel.com, and www.travelzoo.com. There are tools available to sift through multiple offers; **Booking Buddy** (www.bookingbuddy.com), **SideStep** (www.sidestep.com), and **Kayak** (www.kayak.com) let you enter your trip information once and search multiple sites. Spain-based **eDreams** (www.edreams.com) is convenient to book budget flights within Europe.

TRAVELING FROM THE UK AND IRELAND

Because of the many carriers flying from the British Isles to the continent, we only include discount airlines or those with cheap specials here. The **Air Travel Advisory Bureau** in London (www.atab.co.uk) provides referrals to travel agencies that offer discounted airfares. **Cheapflights** (www.cheapflights.co.uk) publishes bargains. For more info on budget airlines like Ryanair, see p. 35.

Aer Lingus: Ireland ☎08 18 36 50 00; www.aerlingus.com. Round-trip tickets from Cork, Dublin, and Shannon to destinations across Europe (€15-300).

bmibaby: UK ☎08 712 240 224; www.bmibaby.com. Departures from throughout the UK to destinations across Europe. Fares from UK£25.

TRAVELING FROM AUSTRALIA AND NEW ZEALAND

Air New Zealand: New Zealand ☎0800 73 70 00; www.airnz.co.nz. Flights from Auckland to London.

Qantas Air: Australia ☎13 13 13, New Zealand 0800 808 767; www.qantas.com.au. Flights from Australia to London for around AUS$2400.

Singapore Air: Australia ☎13 10 11, New Zealand 0800 808 909; www.singaporeair.com. Flights from Adelaide, Auckland, Brisbane, Christchurch, Melbourne, Perth, Sydney, and Wellington to Western Europe.

Thai Airways: Australia ☎13 00 65 19 60, New Zealand 09 377 3886; www.thaiair.com. Major cities in Australia and New Zealand to Frankfurt and London.

BEFORE YOU BOOK. The emergence of no-frills airlines has made hopscotching around Europe by air increasingly affordable. Many budget airlines save money by flying out of smaller, regional airports. A flight billed as Paris to Barcelona might in fact be from Beauvais (80km north of Paris) to Girona (104km northeast of Barcelona). For a more detailed list of these airlines by country, check out www.whichbudget.com.

easyJet: UK ☎0871 244 2366; www.easyjet.com. 104 destinations including links to Eastern Europe. Also serves Egypt, Morocco, and Turkey.

Ryanair: Ireland ☎0818 303 030, UK 0871 246 00 00; www.ryanair.com. Serves 132 destinations in Austria, Belgium, the Czech Republic, France, Germany, Ireland, Italy, Latvia, the Netherlands, Poland, Portugal, Scandinavia, Spain, the UK, and Morocco.

SkyEurope: UK ☎0905 7222 747; www.skyeurope.com. 40 destinations in 19 countries around Central and Eastern Europe, including the Czech Republic and Slovakia.

Sterling: Denmark ☎70 10 84 84, UK ☎870 787 8038. www.sterling.dk. The first Scandinavian-based budget airline. Connects Denmark, Norway, and Sweden to 40 cities across Europe.

Wizz Air: Hungary ☎06 90 181 181, Poland ☎ 03 00 50 30 10; www.wizzair.com. 50 destinations in Belgium, Bulgaria, Croatia, France, Germany, Greece, Hungary, Ireland, Italy, the Netherlands, Norway, Poland, Romania, Slovenia, Spain, Sweden, and the UK.

You'll have to buy shuttle tickets to reach the airports of many of these airlines, and add an hour or so to your travel time. After round-trip shuttle tickets and fees for checked luggage or other services that might come standard on other airlines, that €0.01 sale fare can suddenly jump to €20-100. Be particularly aware of baggage allowances, which are generally small and strictly policed. Prices for no-frills airlines vary dramatically; shop around, book months ahead, pack light, and stay flexible to nab the best fares.

AIR COURIER FLIGHTS

Those who travel light should consider courier flights. Couriers help transport cargo on international flights by using their checked luggage space for freight. Generally, couriers are limited to carry-ons and must deal with complex flight restrictions. Most flights are round-trip only, with short fixed-length stays (usually one week) and a limit of one ticket per issue. Most of these flights also operate only out of major gateway cities. Round-trip courier fares from the US to Europe run about US$200-500. Most flights leave from L.A., Miami, New York, or San Francisco in the US, and from Montreal, Toronto, or Vancouver in Canada. Generally, you must be over 18 (in some cases 21). In summer, the most popular destinations require an advance reservation. Super-discounted fares are common for "last-minute" flights (3-14 days ahead).

Air Courier Association, 1767A Denver West Blvd., Golden, CO 80401, USA (☎800-461-8556; www.aircourier.org). Departure cities throughout Canada and the US to Western Europe (US$150-650). 1-year membership US$39, plus some monthly fees.

International Association of Air Travel Couriers (IAATC; www.courier.org). Courier and consolidator fares from North America to Europe. 1-year membership US$45.

Courier Travel (www.couriertravel.org). Searchable online database. 6 departure points in the US to various European destinations. Membership US$40 per household.

STANDBY FLIGHTS

Traveling standby requires considerable flexibility. Companies dealing in standby flights sell vouchers, along with the promise to get you to your destination (or near it) within a certain window of time (typically 1-5 days). You call in before your specific window of time to hear your flight options and the probability that you will be able to board each flight. You can then decide which flights you want to try to make, show up at the right airport at the appropriate time, present your voucher, and board if space is available. Vouchers can usually be bought for both one-way and round-trip travel. You may receive a refund only if every available flight within your date range is full; if you opt not to take an available (but less convenient) flight, you can only get credit toward future travel. Read agreements carefully, as tricky fine print abounds. To check on a company's service record in the US, contact the **Better Business Bureau** (☎703-276-0100; www.bbb.org). It is difficult to receive refunds, and clients' vouchers will not be honored when an airline fails to receive payment in time.

GETTING AROUND WESTERN EUROPE

GOING MY WAY, SAILOR? In Europe, fares are listed as either **single** (one-way) or **return** (round-trip). "Period returns" require you to return within a specific number of days; "day return" means you must return on the same day. Round-trip fares on trains and buses in Europe are simply twice the one-way fare. Unless stated otherwise, *Let's Go* always lists single fares.

BY PLANE

A number of European airlines offer discount coupon packets. Most are only available as add-ons for transatlantic passengers, but some are stand-alone offers. **Europe by Air's** FlightPass allows non-EU residents to country-hop to over 150 European cities for US$99 or $129 per flight, plus tax. (☎888-321-4737; www.europebyair.com.) **Iberia's** Europass allows passengers flying from the US to Spain to add a minimum of two additional destinations in Europe for $139 per trip. (US ☎800-772-4642; www.iberia.com.)

BY TRAIN

Trains in Europe are generally comfortable, convenient, and reasonably fast, although quality varies by country. Second-class compartments, which seat two to six, are great places to meet fellow travelers. However, trains can be unsafe, especially in Eastern Europe. For safety tips, see p. 15. For long trips, make sure you are on the correct car, as trains sometimes split at crossroads. Towns listed in parentheses on European train schedules require a switch at the town listed immediately before the parentheses.

You can either buy a **rail pass**, which allows you unlimited travel within a region for a given period of time, or rely on individual point-to-point tickets as you go. Almost all countries give students or youths (usually defined as anyone under 26) direct discounts on regular domestic rail tickets, and many also sell a student or youth card that provides 20-50% off all fares for up to a year.

RESERVATIONS. While seat reservations are required only for selected trains (usually on major lines), you are not guaranteed a seat without one (usually US$5-30). You should strongly consider reserving in advance during peak holiday and tourist seasons (at the very latest, a few hours ahead). You will also have to purchase a **supplement** (US$10-50) or special fare for high-speed or high-quality trains such as Spain's AVE, Switzerland's Cisalpino, Finland's Pendolino, Italy's ETR500 and Pendolino, Germany's ICE, and certain French TGVs. InterRail holders must also purchase supplements (US$3-20) for trains like EuroCity, InterCity, and many TGVs; supplements are often unnecessary for Eurail Pass and Europass holders.

OVERNIGHT TRAINS. On night trains, you won't waste valuable daylight hours traveling and you can avoid the hassle and expense of staying at a hotel. However, the main drawbacks include discomfort, sleepless nights, and the lack of scenery. The risk of theft also increases dramatically at night, particularly in Eastern Europe. **Sleeping accommodations** on trains differ from country to country. **Couchettes** (berths) typically have four to six seats per compartment (supplement about US$10-50 per person); **sleepers** (beds) in private sleeping cars offer more privacy, but are more expensive (supplement US$40-150). If you are using a rail pass valid only for a restricted number of days, inspect train schedules to maximize the use of your pass: an overnight train or boat journey often uses up only one of your travel days if it departs after 7pm.

SHOULD YOU BUY A RAIL PASS?. Rail passes were designed to allow you to jump on any train in Europe, go wherever you want whenever you want, and change your plans at will. In practice, it's not so simple. You still must stand in line to validate your pass, pay for supplements, and fork over cash for seat and couchette reservations. More importantly, rail passes don't always pay off. Estimate the point-to-point cost of each leg of your journey; add them up and compare the total with the cost of a rail pass. If you are planning to spend a great deal time on trains, a rail pass will probably be worth it. But especially if you are under 26, point-to-point tickets may be cheaper.

A rail pass won't always pay for itself in the Balkans, Belgium, Eastern Europe, Greece, Iceland, Ireland, Italy, Luxembourg, the Netherlands, Portugal, or Spain, where train fares are reasonable, distances short, or buses preferable. If, however, the total cost of your trips nears the price of the pass, the convenience of avoiding ticket lines may be worth the difference.

MULTINATIONAL RAIL PASSES

EURAIL PASSES. Eurail is valid in most of Western Europe: Austria, Belgium, Denmark, Finland, France, Germany, Greece, Italy, Luxembourg, the Netherlands, Norway, Portugal, the Republic of Ireland, Spain, Sweden, and Switzerland. It is **not valid** in the UK. **Eurail Global Passes,** valid for a number of consecutive days, are best for those planning on spending extensive time on trains every few days. Other types of global passes are valid for any 10 or 15 (not necessarily consecutive) days within a two-month period, and are more cost-effective for those traveling longer distances less frequently. **Eurail Pass Saver** provides first-class travel for travelers in groups of two to five (prices are per person). **Eurail Pass Youth** provides parallel second-class perks for those under 26. Passholders receive a timetable for major routes and a map with details on bike rental, car rental, hotel, and museum discounts. Passholders also often receive reduced fares or free passage on many boat, bus, and private railroad lines. The **Eurail Select Pass** is a slimmed-down version of the Eurail Pass: it allows five to 10 days of unlimited travel in any two-month period within three, four, or five bordering European countries. **Eurail Select Passes** (for individuals) and **Eurail Select Pass Saver** (for people traveling in groups of two to five) range from US$505/429 per person (5 days) to US$765/645 (10 days). The **Eurail Select Pass Youth** (2nd class), for those ages 12-25, costs US$279-619. You are entitled to the same **freebies** afforded by the Eurail Pass, but only when they are within or between countries that you have purchased.

PICKY PASSES. In **Eastern Europe**, finding a pass is complicated. **Global passes** aren't accepted anywhere in Eastern Europe except Hungary and Romania; **Select passes** apply to Bulgaria, Croatia, and Slovenia, as well as Hungary and Romania; and **Regional passes** are available for all of those countries, with the exception of Bulgaria and the additions of the Czech Republic and Poland.

SHOPPING AROUND FOR A EURAIL. Eurail Passes can be bought only by non-Europeans from non-European distributors. These passes must be sold at uniform prices determined by the EU. However, some travel agents tack on a US$10 handling fee, and others offer certain bonuses with purchase, so shop around. Also, remember that pass prices rise annually, so if you're planning to travel early in the year, you can save cash by purchasing before January 1 (you have 3 months from the purchase date to validate your pass in Europe). It's best to buy a Eurail before leaving; only a few places in major cities sell them, and at a marked-up price. You can get a replacement for a lost pass only if you have purchased insurance on it under the **Pass Security Plan** (US$14). Eurail Passes are available through travel agents, student travel agencies like STA (p. 33), and **Rail Europe** (Canada ☎800-361-7245, US 888-382-7245; www.raileurope.com). It is also possible to buy directly from Eurail's website, www.eurail.com. Shipping is free to North America, Australia, and New Zealand.

OTHER MULTINATIONAL PASSES. If you have lived for at least six months in one of the European countries where **InterRail Passes** are valid, they are an economical option. The InterRail Pass allows travel within 30 European countries (excluding the passholder's country of residence). The **Global Pass** is valid for a given number of days (not necessarily consecutive) within a 10 day to one-month period. (5 days within 10 days, adult 1st class €329, adult 2nd class €249, youth €159; 10 days within 22 days €489/359/239; 1 month continuous €809/599/399.) The **One Country Pass** unsurprisingly limits travel to one country (€33 for 3 days). Passholders receive free admission to many museums, as well as **discounts** on accommodations, food, and many ferries to Ireland, Scandinavia, and the rest of Europe. Passes are available at www.interrailnet.com, as well as from travel agents, at major train stations throughout Europe, and through online vendors (www.railpassdirect.co.uk).

DOMESTIC RAIL PASSES

If you are planning to spend a significant amount of time within one country or region, a national pass—valid on all rail lines of a country's rail company—may be more cost-effective than a multinational pass. Many national passes are limited and don't provide the free or discounted travel on private railways and ferries that Eurail does. Some of these passes can be bought only in Europe, some only outside Europe; check with a rail agent or with national tourist offices.

NATIONAL RAIL PASSES. The domestic analogs of the Eurail pass, national rail passes are valid either for a given number of consecutive days or for a specific number of days within a given time period. Though they will usually save travelers some money, the passes may actually be a more expensive alternative to point-to-point tickets, especially on Easter. For more info, check out www.raileurope.com/us/rail/passes/single_country_index.htm.

RAIL-AND-DRIVE PASSES. Many countries (as well as Eurail) offer rail-and-drive passes, which combine car rental with rail travel—a good option for travelers who wish both to visit cities accessible by rail and to travel in the surrounding areas. Prices range US$300-2400. Children under 11 cost US$102-500, and adding more days costs US$72-105 per day (see **By Car,** p. 40).

FURTHER READING & RESOURCES ON TRAIN TRAVEL

Info on rail travel and rail passes: www.raileurope.com or www.eurail.com.

Point-to-point fares and schedules: www.raileurope.com/us/rail/fares_schedules/index.htm. Calculate the cost-effectiveness of buying a rail pass.

Railsaver: www.railpass.com/new. Uses your itinerary to calculate the best rail pass for your trip.

European Railway Server: www.railfaneurope.net. Links to rail servers throughout Europe.

Thomas Cook European Timetable, updated monthly, covers all major and most minor train routes in Europe. Buy directly from Thomas Cook (www.thomascooktimetables.com).

BY BUS

In some cases, buses prove a better option than train travel. In Britain and Hungary, the bus and train systems are on par; in the Baltics, Greece, Ireland, Spain, and Portugal, bus networks are more extensive, efficient, and often more comfortable; in Iceland and parts of northern Scandinavia, bus service is the only ground transportation available. In the rest of Europe, bus travel is more of a gamble. Scattered offerings from private companies are often cheap, but sometimes unreliable. Amsterdam, Athens, London, Munich, and Oslo are centers for lines that offer long-distance rides across Europe. **International bus passes** allow unlimited travel on a hop-on, hop-off basis between major European cities, often at cheaper prices than rail passes.

Eurolines, offices in 19 countries (UK ☎8717 81 81 81; www.eurolines.co.uk or www.eurolines.com). The largest operator of Europe-wide coach services. Unlimited

15-day (high season €329, under 26 €279; low season €199/169) or 30-day (high season €439/359; low season €299/229) travel passes offer unlimited transit among 40 major European cities. Discount passes €29 or €39.

Busabout, 258 Vauxhall Bridge Rd., London, SW1V 1BS, UK (☎020 7950 1661; www.busabout.com). Offers 3 interconnecting bus circuits. 1 loop US$639; 2 loops US$1069; 3 loops US$1319. Flexipass with 6 stops $549; additional stops $59. Also sells discounted international SIM cards (US$9; from US$0.29 per min.).

BY CAR

Cars offer speed, freedom, access to the countryside, and an escape from the town-to-town mentality of trains. Although a single traveler won't save by renting a car, four usually will. If you can't decide between train and car travel, you may benefit from a combination of the two; RailEurope and other rail pass vendors offer rail-and-drive packages. Fly-and-drive packages are also often available from travel agents or airline/rental agency partnerships. Before setting off, know the laws of the countries in which you'll be driving (e.g., both seat belts and headlights must be on at all times in **Scandinavia**, and remember to drive on the left in **Ireland and the UK**). For an informal primer on European road signs and conventions, check out www.travlang.com/signs. The **Association for Safe International Road Travel** (ASIRT) can provide more specific information about road conditions (☎301-983-5252; www.asirt.org). ASIRT considers road travel (by car or bus) to be relatively safe in Denmark, Ireland, the Netherlands, Norway, Sweden, Switzerland, and the UK, and relatively **unsafe** in Turkey and many parts of Eastern Europe. Western Europeans use **unleaded gas** almost exclusively, but it's not available in many gas stations in Eastern Europe.

RENTING A CAR

Cars can be rented from a US-based firm **(Alamo, Avis, Budget, or Hertz)** with European offices, from a European-based company with local representatives (Europcar), or from a tour operator (Auto Europe, Europe By Car, or Kemwel Holiday Autos) that will arrange a rental for you from a European company. Multinationals offer greater flexibility, but tour operators often strike better deals. Ask airlines about special fly-and-drive packages; you may get up to a week of free or discounted rental. See **Costs and Insurance**, p. 40, for more info. Minimum age requirements vary but tend to fall in the range of 21-25, with some as low as 18. There may be an additional insurance fee for drivers under 25. At most agencies, to rent a car, you'll need a driver's license from home with proof that you've had it for a year or an **International Driving Permit** (p. 41). Car rental in Europe is available through the following agencies:

Auto Europe (Canada and the US ☎888-223-5555; www.autoeurope.com).

Budget (Australia ☎1300 36 28 48, Canada ☎800-268-8900, New Zealand ☎0800 283 438, UK 87 01 56 56 56, US 800-527-0700; www.budget.com).

Europcar International (UK ☎18 70 607 5000; www.europcar.com).

Hertz (Canada and the US 800-654-3001; www.hertz.com).

COSTS AND INSURANCE

Expect to pay US$200-600 per week, plus tax (5-25%), for a tiny car with a manual transmission; automatics and larger vehicles can double or triple the price. Reserve and pay in advance if at all possible. It is less expensive to reserve a car from the US than from Europe. Rates are lowest in Belgium, Germany, the

Netherlands, and the UK, higher in Ireland and Italy, and highest in Scandinavia and Eastern Europe. National chains often allow one-way rentals, with pick-up in one city and drop-off in another. There is usually a minimum hire period and sometimes an extra drop-off charge of several hundred dollars.

Many rental packages offer unlimited kilometers, while others offer a fixed distance per day with a per-kilometer surcharge after that. Be sure to ask whether the price includes **insurance** against theft and collision. Remember that if you are driving a conventional vehicle on an **unpaved road** in a rental car, you are almost never covered by insurance. Always check if prices quoted include tax and collision insurance; some credit cards provide insurance, allowing their customers to decline the collision damage waiver. Ask about discounts and check the terms of insurance, particularly the size of the deductible. Beware that cars rented on an **American Express or Visa/MasterCard Gold** or **Platinum** credit cards in Europe might not carry the automatic insurance that they would in some other countries. Check with your credit card company. Insurance plans almost always come with an **excess** (or deductible) for conventional vehicles; excess is usually higher for younger drivers and for 4WD. This provision means you pay for all damages up to the specified sum, unless they are the fault of another vehicle. The excess you will be quoted applies to collisions with other vehicles; other collisions ("single-vehicle collisions") will cost you even more. The excess can often be reduced or waived for an additional charge. Remember to return the car with a **full tank** of gas to avoid high fuel charges. Gas prices are generally highest in Scandinavia. Throughout Europe, fuel tends to be cheaper in cities than in outlying areas.

LEASING A CAR

Leasing can be cheaper than renting, especially for more than 17 days. It is often the only option for those aged 18 to 21. The cheapest leases are agreements to buy the car and then sell it back to the manufacturer. Leases generally include insurance coverage and are not taxed. The most affordable ones usually originate in Belgium, France, or Germany. Expect to pay US$1000-2000 for 60 days. **Renault Eurodrive** leases new cars in a tax-free package to qualifying non-EU citizens (Australia ☎9299 33 44, Canada ☎450-461-1149, New Zealand ☎0800 807 778, US ☎212-730-0676; www.renault-eurodrive.com).

ON THE ROAD

Road conditions and **regional hazards** are variable throughout Europe. Steep, curvy mountain roads may be closed in winter. Western European roads are generally excellent, but each area has its own dangers. In Scandinavia, for example, drivers should be on the lookout for moose and elk; on the Autobahn, the threat may come from cars speeding by at 150kph. In this book, region-specific hazards are listed in country introductions. Carry emergency equipment with you (see **Driving Precautions**, below) and know what to do in case of a breakdown. Car rental companies will often have phone numbers for emergency services.

DRIVING PERMITS AND CAR INSURANCE

INTERNATIONAL DRIVING PERMIT (IDP). To drive a car in **Europe**, you must **be over 18** and have an **International Driving Permit (IDP)**, though certain countries (such as the UK) allow travelers to drive with a valid American or Canadian license for a limited number of months. It may be a good idea to get an IDP anyway, in case you're in a situation (e.g., you get in an accident or become stranded in a small town) **where the police do not know English; information on the**

IDP is printed in 11 languages, including French, German, Italian, Portuguese, Russian, Spanish, and Swedish. Your IDP must be issued in your home country before you depart. An application for an IDP usually requires a photo, a current license, an additional form of identification, and a fee of around US$20. To apply, contact your country's automobile association (i.e., the AAA in the US or the CAA in Canada). Be wary of buying IDPs from unauthorized online vendors.

CAR INSURANCE. If you rent, lease, or borrow a car, you will need an International Insurance Certificate, or Green Card, to certify that you have liability insurance and that it applies abroad. Green Cards can be obtained at car rental agencies, car dealerships (for those leasing cars), some travel agents, and some border crossings. Rental agencies may require you to purchase theft insurance in countries they consider to have a high risk of auto theft.

DRIVING PRECAUTIONS. When traveling in summer, bring substantial amounts of **water** (5L per person per day) for drinking and for the radiator. For long drives to unpopulated areas, register with police before beginning the trip, and again upon arrival at the destination. Check with the local automobile club for details. Make sure tires are in good repair and have enough air, and get good maps. A **compass** and a **car manual** can also be very useful. Always carry a **spare tire** and **jack, jumper cables**, extra **oil, flares,** a **flashlight** (torch), and **heavy blankets** (in case your car breaks down at night or in winter). A **mobile phone** may help in an emergency. If you don't know how to change a tire, learn, especially if you're traveling in deserted areas. Blowouts on dirt roads are very common. If the car breaks down, stay with your car to wait for help.

BY CHUNNEL FROM THE UK

Traversing 27 mi. under the sea, the Chunnel is undoubtedly the fastest, most convenient, and least scenic route from England to France.

BY TRAIN. Eurostar, Eurostar House, Waterloo Station, London SE1 8SE (UK ☎08 705 186 186; www.eurostar.com) runs frequent trains between London and the continent. Ten to 28 trains per day run to 100 destinations including Paris (4hr., US$75-400, 2nd class), Disneyland Paris, Brussels, Lille, and Calais. Book online, at major rail stations in the UK, or at the office above.

BY BUS. Eurolines provides bus-ferry combinations (see p. 39).

BY CAR. Eurotunnel, Customer relations, P.O. Box 2000, Folkestone, Kent CT18 8XY (UK ☎08 705 353 535; www.eurotunnel.co.uk) shuttles cars and passengers between Kent and Nord-Pas-de-Calais. Return fares for vehicle and all passengers range from UK£223-253 with car. One-way starts at UK£49, two- to five-day return for a car UK£165-298. Book online or via phone. Travelers with cars can also look into sea crossings by ferry (see below).

BY BOAT

Most long-distance ferries are quite comfortable; the cheapest ticket typically includes a reclining chair or couchette. Fares jump sharply in July and August. ISIC holders can often get student fares, and Eurail Pass holders get reductions and sometimes free trips. You'll occasionally have to pay a port tax (around US$10). The fares below are **one-way** for **adult foot passengers** unless otherwise noted. Though standard round-trip fares are usually twice the one-way fare, **fixed-period returns** (usually within 5 days) may be cheaper. Ferries run **year-round** unless otherwise noted. Bringing a **bike** costs up to US$15 in high season.

FERRIES FROM BRITAIN AND IRELAND

Ferries are frequent and dependable. The main route across the English Channel from Britain to France is Dover-Calais. The main ferry port on England's southern coast is Portsmouth, with connections to France and Spain. Ferries also cross the Irish Sea, connecting Northern Ireland with Scotland and England, and the Republic of Ireland with Wales. For more information, see the directory at www.seaview.co.uk/ferries.html.

Brittany Ferries: UK ☎0871 2440 744, France ☎825 828 828, Spain ☎942 360 611; www.brittany-ferries.com. **Cork** to **Roscoff, FRA** (14hr.); **Plymouth** to **Roscoff, FRA** (6hr.) and **Santander, SPA** (18hr.); **Poole** to **Cherbourg, FRA** (4hr.); **Portsmouth** to **St-Malo, FRA** (10hr.) and **Caen, FRA** (5hr.).

DFDS Seaways: UK ☎0871 522 9955; www.dfdsseaways.co.uk. **Harwich** to **Cuxhaven** (19hr.) and **Esbjerg, DEN** (18hr.); **Newcastle** to **Amsterdam, NTH** (16hr.), and **Haugesund, NOR** (18hr.); **Dover** to **Calais, FRA** (1-2hr.).

Irish Ferries: Northern Ireland ☎353 818 300 400; Republic of Ireland ☎08 18 30 04 00, Great Britain ☎87 05 17 17 17; www.irishferries.com. **Rosslare** to **Pembroke** (3hr.) and **Cherbourg** or **Roscoff, FRA** (18hr.). **Holyhead** to **Dublin, IRE** (2-3hr.).

P&O Ferries: UK ☎08 705 980 333; www.poferries.com. **Dover** to **Calais, FRA** (1hr., 25 per day, UK £14); **Hull** to **Rotterdam, NTH** (10hr.) and **Zeebrugge, BEL** (12hr.).

FERRIES IN SCANDINAVIA

Ferries run to many North Sea destinations. Booking ahead is not necessary for deck passage. Baltic Sea ferries sail between Poland and Scandinavia.

Color Line: Norway ☎0810 00 811; www.colorline.com. Ferries run from 6 cities and towns in Norway to **Frederikshavn** and **Hirtshal, DEN** (€24-80); **Strömsand, SWE** (€9-22); **Kiel, GER** (€98-108). Car packages from €137. Student discounts available.

Tallinksilja Line: Finland ☎09 180 41, Sweden ☎08 22 21 40; www.tallinksilja.com. Connects Helsinki and Turku to **Sweden** (€18-116) and **Stockholm, SWE** to **Tallinn, EST** (€20-33); **Rostock, GER** (€91-133); **Riga, LAT** (€22-32). Eurail passes accepted.

Viking Line: Finland ☎0600 415 77, Sweden ☎0452 40 00; www.vikingline.fi. Ferries run between **Helsinki** and **Turku, FIN** to destinations in **Estonia** and **Sweden**. M-Th and Su cruises min. age 18, F-Sa 21. One-way €33-59. Eurail discounts available.

MEDITERRANEAN AND AEGEAN FERRIES

Mediterranean ferries may be the most glamorous, but they can also be the most turbulent. Ferries run from Spain to Morocco, from Italy to Tunisia, and from France to both Morocco and Tunisia. Reservations are recommended, especially in July and August. Schedules are erratic, with varying prices for similar routes. Shop around, and beware of small companies that don't take reservations. Ferries traverse the Adriatic from Ancona, ITA to Split, CRO and from Bari, ITA to Dubrovnik, CRO. They also cross the Aegean, from Ancona, ITA to Patras, GCE and from Bari, ITA to Igoumenitsa and Patras, GCE. **Eurail** is valid on certain ferries between Brindisi, ITA and Corfu, Igoumenitsa, and Patras, GCE. Many ferry companies operate on these routes.

BY MOPED AND MOTORCYCLE

Motorized bikes and **mopeds** don't use much gas, can be put on trains and ferries, and are a good compromise between costly car travel and the limited range of bicycles. However, they're uncomfortable for long distances, dangerous in the rain, and unpredictable on rough roads. Always wear a helmet, and never ride with a backpack. If you've never ridden a moped before, a twisting Alpine road is not the place to start. Expect to pay about US$20-35 per day; try auto repair shops, and remember to bargain. **Motorcycles** are more expensive and normally require a license, but are better for long distances. Before renting, ask if the price includes tax and insurance. Avoid handing your passport over as a deposit; if you have an accident or mechanical failure you may not get it back until you cover all repairs. Pay ahead of time instead.

BY THUMB

WARNING. Let's Go strongly urges you to consider the risks before you choose to hitch. We do not recommend hitchhiking, and none of the information presented here is intended to do so.

No one should hitch without careful consideration of the risks involved. Hitching means entrusting your life to an unknown person and risking theft, assault, sexual harassment, and unsafe driving. However, some travelers report that hitchhiking in Europe allows them to meet locals and travel in areas where public transportation is sketchy. **Britain** and **Ireland** are probably the easiest places in Western Europe to get a lift. Hitching in **Scandinavia** is slow but steady. Long-distance hitching in the developed countries of northwestern Europe demands close attention to expressway junctions, rest stop locations, and destination signs. Hitching in southern Europe is generally mediocre. Hitchhiking at night can be particularly dangerous; experienced hitchers stand in well-lit places. For women traveling alone or even two women traveling together, hitching is simply too dangerous. A man and a woman are a safer combination, two men will have a harder time, and three will go nowhere. Experienced hitchers pick a spot outside of built-up areas, where drivers can stop, return to the road without causing an accident, and have time to look over potential passengers as they approach. Hitching (or even standing) on super-highways is usually illegal: one may only thumb at rest stops or at the entrance ramps to highways. Finally, success often depends on appearance.

Most Western European countries have ride services that pair drivers with riders; fees vary according to destination. **Eurostop** (www.taxistop.be/index_ils.htm), Taxistop's ride service, is one of the largest in Europe. Also try **Allostop** in France (French-language website www.allostop.net) and **Verband der Deutschen Mitfahrzentralen** in Germany (German-language website www.mitfahrzentrale.de). Not all organizations screen drivers and riders; ask ahead.

BEYOND TOURISM

A PHILOSOPHY FOR TRAVELERS

HIGHLIGHTS OF BEYOND TOURISM IN WESTERN EUROPE

EXCAVATE old skulls and castles in **France** (p. 186).

PROTECT hatchling sea turtles on the coasts of **Greece** (p. 319).

POLITICK as an intern at NATO in **Belgium** (p. 80).

TEACH English to European campers across **Italy** (p. 379).

As a tourist, you are always a foreigner. Sure, hostel-hopping and sightseeing can be great fun, but connecting with a foreign country through studying, volunteering, or working can extend your travels beyond tourist traps. Instead of feeling like a stranger in a strange land, you can understand Europe like a local. Instead of being that tourist asking for directions, you can be the one who gives them (and correctly!). All the while, you get the satisfaction of leaving Europe in better shape than you found it (after all, it's being nice enough to let you stay here). It's not wishful thinking—it's Beyond Tourism.

As a **volunteer** in Western Europe, you can unleash your inner superhero with projects from building homes in Ireland to digging up ancient treasures in Italy. This chapter is chock-full of ideas to get involved, whether you're looking to pitch in for a day or run away from home for a whole new life in activism.

The powers of **studying** abroad are beyond comprehension: it actually makes you feel sorry for those poor tourists who don't get to do any homework.

Working abroad immerses you in a new culture and can bring some of the most meaningful relationships and experiences of your life. Yes, we know you're on vacation, but these aren't your normal desk jobs. (Plus, it doesn't hurt that it helps pay for more globetrotting.) If you're an EU citizen, work will be far easier to come by, but there are still options for those not so blessed.

SHARE YOUR EXPERIENCE. Have you had a particularly enjoyable volunteer, study, or work experience that you'd like to share with other travelers? Post it to our website, www.letsgo.com!

VOLUNTEERING

Feel like saving the world this week? Volunteering can be a powerful and fulfilling experience, especially when combined with the thrill of traveling in a new place. Europe offers an endless varieties of opportunities to volunteer, with exciting choices from teaching English to ecological conservation.

Most people who volunteer in Europe do so on a short-term basis at organizations that make use of drop-in or once-a-week volunteers. The best way to find opportunities that match your interests and schedule may be to check with local or national volunteer centers. As always, read up before heading out.

Those looking for longer, more intensive volunteer opportunities usually choose to go through a parent organization that takes care of logistical details and often provides a group environment and support system—for a fee. There are two main types of organizations—religious and secular—although there are rarely restrictions on participation for either. Websites like **www.volunteerabroad.com**, **www.servenet.org**, and **www.idealist.org** allow you to search for volunteer openings both in your country and abroad.

I HAVE TO PAY TO VOLUNTEER? Many volunteers are surprised to learn that some organizations require large fees or "donations," but don't go calling them scams just yet. While such fees may seem ridiculous at first, they often keep the organization afloat, covering airfare, room, board, and administrative expenses for the volunteers. If you're concerned about how a program spends its fees, request an annual report or finance account. A reputable organization won't refuse to inform you of how volunteer money is spent. Pay-to-volunteer programs might be a good idea for young travelers who are looking for more support and structure (such as pre-arranged transportation and housing) or anyone who would rather not deal with the uncertainty of creating a volunteer experience from scratch.

ONLINE DIRECTORIES: VOLUNTEERING

www.alliance-network.org. Various international service organizations.
www.idealist.org. Provides extensive listings of service opportunities.
www.worldvolunteerweb.org. Lists organizations and events around the world.

COMMUNITY DEVELOPMENT

If working closely with locals and helping in a hands-on fashion appeals to you, check out community development options. Many returning travelers report that working among locals was one of their most rewarding experiences.

Global Volunteers, 375 E. Little Canada Rd., St. Paul, MN 55109, USA (☎800-487-1074; www.globalvolunteers.org). A variety of 1- to 3-week volunteer programs throughout Europe. Fees range US$2000-3000, including room and board but not airfare.

Habitat for Humanity, 121 Habitat St., Americus, GA 31709, USA (☎800-422-4828; www.habitat.org). A Christian non-profit organization coordinating 9- to 14-day service trips in Britain, Germany, Greece, Hungary, Ireland, the Netherlands, Poland, Portugal, and Switzerland. Participants aid in building homes. Program around US$1000-2200.

Service Civil International Voluntary Service (SCI-IVS), 5505 Walnut Level Rd., Crozet, VA 22932, USA (☎206-350-6585; www.sci-ivs.org). Arranges placement in 2- to 3-week outdoor service camps (workcamps), or 3-month teaching opportunities throughout Europe. 18+. Registration fee US$235, including room and board.

Volunteer Abroad, 7800 Point Meadows Dr., Ste. 218 Jacksonville, FL 32256, USA (☎720-570-1702; www.volunteerabroad.com/search.cfm). Volunteer work in Europe.

CONSERVATION

As more people realize that long-cherished habitats and structures are in danger, diverse programs have stepped in to aid the concerned in lending a hand.

Club du Vieux Manoir, Ancienne Abbaye du Moncel, 60700 Pontpoint, FRA (☎33 03 44 72 33 98; http://cvmclubduvieuxmanoir.free.fr). Offers year-long and summer programs restoring castles and churches throughout France. €15 annual membership and insurance fee. Costs €14 per day, including food and tent.

Earthwatch Institute, 3 Clock Tower Pl., Ste. 100, P.O. Box 75, Maynard, MA, 01754, USA (☎978-461-0081; www.earthwatch.org). Arranges 2-day to 3-week programs promoting the conservation of natural resources. Fees vary based on program location and duration. Costs range US$400-4000, including room and board but not airfare.

The National Trust, P.O. Box 39, Warrington, WA5 7WD, UK (☎ 44 017 938 176 32; www.nationaltrust.org.uk/volunteers). Arranges numerous volunteer opportunities, including Working Holidays. From £60 per week, including room and board.

World-Wide Opportunities on Organic Farms (WWOOF), PO Box 2154, Winslow Buckingham, MK18 3WS England, UK (www.wwoof.org). Arranges volunteer work with organic and eco-conscious farms around the world. You become a member of WWOOF in the country in which you plan to work; prices vary by country.

HUMANITARIAN AND SOCIAL SERVICES

Western Europe's complex, war-torn history offers up opportunities to help rebuild. Numerous peace programs can prove to be fulfilling for volunteers.

Brethren Volunteer Service (BVS), 1451 Dundee Ave., Elgin, IL 60120, USA (☎800-323-8039; www.brethrenvolunteerservice.org). Peace and social justice based programs. Minimum commitment of 2 yr., must be 21 to serve overseas. US$75 fee for background check; US$500 fee for international volunteers.

Simon Wiesenthal Center, 1399 South Roxbury Dr., Los Angeles, CA 90035, USA (☎800-900-9036; www.wiesenthal.org). Fights anti-Semitism and Holocaust denial throughout Europe. Small, discretionary donation required for membership.

Volunteers for Peace, 1034 Tiffany Rd., Belmont, VT 05730, USA (☎802-259-2759; www.vfp.org). Arranges placement in camps throughout Europe. US$30 membership required for registration. Programs average US$250-500 for 2-3 weeks.

STUDYING

It's hard to dread the first day of school when London is your campus and exotic restaurants are your meal plan. A growing number of students report that studying abroad is the highlight of their learning careers. If you've never studied abroad, you don't know what you're missing—and, if you have studied abroad, you do know what you're missing.

Study-abroad programs range from basic language and culture courses to university-level classes, often for college credit. In order to choose a program that best fits your needs, research as much as you can before making your decision—determine costs and duration as well as what kinds of students participate in the program and what sorts of accommodations are provided. (Since when was back-to-school shopping this fun?)

In programs that have large groups of students who speak the same language, there is a trade-off. You may feel more comfortable in the community, but you will not have the same opportunity to practice a foreign language or to befriend other international students. For accommodations, dorm life provides a better opportunity to mingle with fellow students, but there is less of a chance to experience the local scene. If you live with a family, you could potentially build lifelong friendships with natives and experience day-to-day life in more depth, but you might also get stuck sharing a room with their pet iguana. Conditions can vary greatly from family to family.

UNIVERSITIES

Most university-level study-abroad programs are conducted in the local language, although many programs offer classes in English as well as lower-level language courses. Savvy linguists may find it cheaper to enroll directly in a university abroad, although getting college credit may be more difficult. You can search **www.studyabroad.com** for various programs that meet your criteria, including your desired location and focus of study. If you're a college student, your friendly neighborhood study-abroad office is often the best place to start.

ONLINE DIRECTORIES: STUDY ABROAD

These websites are good resources for finding programs that cater to your particular interests. Each has links to various study-abroad programs broken down by a variety of criteria, including desired location and focus of study.

www.petersons.com/stdyabrd/sasector.html. Lists study-abroad programs at accredited institutions that usually offer cross credits.

www.studyabroad.com. A great starting point for finding college- or high-school-level programs in foreign languages or specific academic subjects. Also includes information for teaching and volunteering opportunities.

www.westudyabroad.com. Lists language courses and college-level programs.

AMERICAN PROGRAMS

The following is a list of organizations that can either help place students in university programs abroad or that have their own branch in Western Europe.

American Institute for Foreign Study, College Division, River Plaza, 9 W. Broad St., Stamford, CT 06902, USA (☎800-727-2437; www.aifsabroad.com). Organizes programs for high school and college study at universities in Austria, Britain, the Czech Republic, France, Hungary, Ireland, Italy, Russia, and Spain. Summer programs US$4900-6500; Semester-long programs US$11,000-16,000. Scholarships available.

Council on International Educational Exchange (CIEE), 7 Custom House St., 3rd fl., Portland, ME, 04101, USA (☎800-407-8839; www.ciee.org/study). Sponsors work, volunteer, academic, and internship programs in Belgium, Britain, the Czech Republic, France, Hungary, Ireland, Italy, the Netherlands, Spain, and Turkey for around US$14,000 per semester. Also offers volunteer opportunities. US$30 application fee.

International Association for the Exchange of Students for Technical Experience (IAESTE), 10400 Little Patuxent Pkwy. Ste. 250, Columbia, MD 21044, USA (☎410-997-3068; www.iaeste.org). Offers 8- to 12-week internships in Europe for college students who have completed 2 years study in a particular trade.

School for International Training, College Semester Abroad, Kipling Rd., P.O. Box 676, Brattleboro, VT 05302, USA (☎888-272-7881 or 802-258-7751; www.sit.edu/studyabroad). Programs in Europe cost around US$10,000-16,000. Also runs The Experiment in International Living (☎800-345-2929; fax 802-258-3428; www.usexperiment.org), 3- to 5-week summer programs that offer high school students homestays, community service, ecological adventure, and language training in Europe for US$5900-7000.

AUSTRALIAN PROGRAMS

The following organizations place Australian students in programs in Europe.

World Exchange Program Australia, (☎1 300 884 733; www.wep.org.au). Places Australian high school students for 3 months to 1 year in high schools abroad. Group study tours also available. Costs for one semester in Europe are AUS$8950-6290.

Innovative Universities European Union Centre (IUEU), (☎298 507 915 ; www.iueu.edu.au). Offers undergraduates from Flinders, La Trobe and Macquarie universities a chance to study abroad for one semester in their Global Citizenship program.

LANGUAGE SCHOOLS

Enrolling at a language school has two major perks: a slightly less rigorous courseload and the ability to teach you exactly what slang those kids in Mainz are using to insult you under their breath. There can be great variety in language schools—independently run, affiliated with a larger university, local, international—but one thing is constant: they rarely offer college credit. Their programs are also well-suited for younger high-school students who might not feel comfortable with older students in a university program. Some worthwhile organizations to explore include:

Association of Commonwealth Universities (ACU), Woburn House, 20-24 Tavistock Sq., London WC1H 9HF, UK (☎020 7380 6700; www.acu.ac.uk). Publishes information about Commonwealth Universities, including those in Cyprus and the UK.

Eurocentres, Seestr. 247, CH-8038 Zürich, SWI (☎41 1 485 50 40; www.eurocentres.com). Language programs for beginning to advanced students with homestays in Britain, France, Germany, Ireland, Italy, Spain, and Switzerland.

Language Immersion Institute, SCB 106, State University of New York at New Paltz, 1 Hawk Dr., New Paltz, NY 12561, USA (☎845-257-3500; www.newpaltz.edu/lii). 2-week summer language courses and some overseas courses in French, German, Greek, Hungarian, Italian, Polish, Portuguese, Spanish, and Swedish. Around US$1000 for a 2-week course, not including accommodations.

Sprachcaffe Languages Plus, 413 Ontario St., Toronto, ON M5A 2V9, CAN (☎888-526-4758; www.sprachcaffe.com). Language classes in France, Germany, Italy, the Netherlands, and Spain for US$200-500 per week. Homestays available. Also offers French and Spanish language and travel programs for teenagers.

BEYOND TOURISM

WORKING

Nowhere does money grow on trees (though *Let's Go*'s researchers aren't done looking), but there are still some pretty good opportunities to earn a living and travel at the same time. As with volunteering, work opportunities tend to fall into two categories. Some travelers want long-term jobs that allow them to integrate into a community, while others seek out short-term jobs to finance the next leg of their travels. In Europe, people who want to work long-term should look for jobs like teaching English, taking care of local children, and other opportunities that can be found through a bit of research and luck. People looking for short term work have options like picking fruit and working for summer programs abroad. **Transitions Abroad** (www.transitionsabroad.com) also offers updated online listings for work over any time span.

Employment opportunities for those who want short-term work may be more limited and are generally contingent upon the city or region's economic needs. In addition to local papers, international English-language newspapers, such as the International Herald Tribune (www.iht.com), often list job opportunities in their classified sections. If applicable, travelers should also consult federally run employment offices. Note that working abroad often requires a special work visa; see the box below for info about obtaining one.

VISA INFORMATION. **EU Citizens:** The EU's 2004 and 2007 enlargements led the 15 previous member states (EU-15) to fear that waves of Eastern European immigrants would flood their labor markets. This fear caused some members of the union to institute a transition period of up to seven years during which citizens of the new EU countries may still need a visa or permit to work. EU-15 citizens generally have the right to work in the pre-enlargement countries for up to three months without a visa; longer-term employment usually requires a work permit. By law, all EU-15 citizens are given equal consideration for jobs not directly related to national security. **Everyone else:** Getting a work visa in Europe is difficult for non-EU citizens. Different countries have varying policies for granting work permits to those from non-EU countries. It is possible for students to work part-time without a work permit in some countries. In 2007, the EU introduced the "blue card" program, aimed at long term, skilled workers, which requires an employment contract in place before immigration.

LONG-TERM WORK

If you're planning to spend more than three months working in Western Europe, search for a job well in advance. International placement agencies are often the easiest way to find employment abroad, especially for those interested in teaching English. Although often only available to college students, **internships** are a good way to segue into working abroad; although they are often un- or underpaid, many say the experience is valuable. Be wary of advertisements for companies claiming to be able get you a job abroad for a fee—often the same listings are available online or in newspapers. Some organizations include:

Escapeartist.com (jobs.escapeartist.com). International employers post directly to this website; various jobs in Western European countries advertised.

International Cooperative Education, 15 Spiros Way, Menlo Park, CA, 94025, USA (☎650-323-4944; www.icemenlo.com). Finds summer jobs in Belgium, Britain, Germany, and Switzerland. $250 application fee and $700 placement fee.

StepStone (www.stepstone.com, branches across Europe listed at www.stepstone.com/EN/Company/Locations). Database covering international employment in Austria, Belgium, Britain, Denmark, France, Germany, Italy, the Netherlands, Norway, Portugal, and Sweden. Several search options and a list of openings.

TEACHING ENGLISH

While some elite private American schools offer competitive salaries, let's just say that teaching jobs abroad pay more in personal satisfaction and emotional fulfillment than in actual cash. Perhaps this is why volunteering as a teacher instead of getting paid is a popular option. Even then, teachers often receive some sort of a daily stipend to help with living expenses. For countries that have a low cost of living, even though salaries at private schools may be low compared to those in the US, the low cost of living makes it much more profitable. In almost all cases, you must have at least a bachelor's degree to be a full-fledged teacher, although college undergraduates can often get summer positions teaching or tutoring. Many schools require teachers to have a **Teaching English as a Foreign Language (TEFL)** certificate. You may still be able to find a teaching job without one, but certified teachers often find higher-paying jobs.

Those who can't speak the local language don't have to give up their dream of teaching, either. Private schools usually hire native English speakers for English-immersion classrooms where no local language is spoken. (Teachers in public schools will more likely work in both English and the local language.) Placement agencies or university fellowship programs are the best resources for finding teaching jobs. The alternative is to contact schools directly or to try your luck once you arrive in Europe. In the latter case, the best time to look is several weeks before the start of the school year. The following organizations are extremely helpful in placing teachers in Europe.

International Schools Services (ISS), 15 Roszel Rd., P.O. Box 5910, Princeton, NJ 08543, USA (☎609-452-0990; www.iss.edu). Hires teachers for more than 200 international and American schools around the world; candidates should have 2 years teaching experience and/or teacher certification. 2-year commitment expected.

Teaching English as a Foreign Language (TEFL), TEFL Professional Network Ltd., 72 Pentyla Baglan Rd., Port Talbot, SA12 8AD, UK (www.tefl.com). Maintains an extensive database of openings throughout Europe. Offers job training and certification.

AU PAIR WORK

Au pairs are typically women aged 18-27 who work as live-in nannies, caring for children and doing light housework in foreign countries in exchange for room, board, and a small spending allowance or stipend. One perk of the job is that it allows you to get to know Western Europe without the high expenses of traveling. Drawbacks, however, can include mediocre pay and long hours. Average weekly pay will vary depending on location. Much of the au pair experience depends on the family with which you are placed. The agencies below are a good starting point for looking for employment.

Childcare International, Ltd., Trafalgar House, Grenville Pl., London NW7 3SA (☎44 020 8906 3116; www.childint.co.uk). Offers au pair and nanny placement.

InterExchange, 161 6th Ave., New York, NY, 10013, USA (☎212-924-0446; www.interexchange.org). Au pair, internship, and short-term work placement in France, Germany, the Netherlands, and Spain. US$495-595 placement fee and US$75 application fee.

Sunny AuPairs (☎44 020 8144 1635, in US 503-616-3026; www.sunnyaupairs.com). Online, worldwide database connecting au pairs with families. No placement fee.

SHORT-TERM WORK

Believe it or not, traveling for long periods of time can be hard on the wallet. Many travelers try their hand at odd jobs for a few weeks at a time to help pay for another month or two of touring around. Work options vary across the continent, but work possibilities might include picking fruit or serving. A popular option is to work several hours a day at a hostel in exchange for free or discounted room and/or board. Most often, these short-term jobs are found by word of mouth or by expressing interest to the owner of a hostel or restaurant. Due to high turnover in the tourism industry, many places are eager for help. *Let's Go* lists temporary jobs of this nature whenever possible; look in the Practical Information sections of larger cities or see below.

FURTHER READING ON BEYOND TOURISM.

Alternatives to the Peace Corps: A Guide of Global Volunteer Opportunities, by Paul Backhurst. Food First Books, 2005.

The Back Door Guide to Short-Term Job Adventures: Internships, Summer Jobs, Seasonal Work, Volunteer Vacations, and Transitions Abroad, by Michael Landes. Ten Speed Press, 2005.

Green Volunteers: The World Guide to Voluntary Work in Nature Conservation, ed. Fabio Ausenda. Universe, 2007.

How to Get a Job in Europe, by Cheryl Matherly and Robert Sanborn. Planning Communications, 2003.

How to Live Your Dream of Volunteering Overseas, by Joseph Collins, Stefano DeZerega, and Zahara Heckscher. Penguin Books, 2002.

International Job Finder: Where the Jobs Are Worldwide, by Daniel Lauber and Kraig Rice. Planning Communications, 2002.

Live and Work Abroad: A Guide for Modern Nomads, by Huw Francis and Michelyne Callan. Vacation-Work Publications, 2001.

Overseas Summer Jobs 2002. Peterson's Guides and Vacation Work, 2002.

Volunteer Vacations:

Short-Term Adventures That Will Benefit You and Others, by Doug Cutchins, Anne Geissinger, and Bill McMillon. Chicago Review Press, 2006.

Work Abroad: The Complete Guide to Finding a Job Overseas, by Clayton Hubbs. Transitions Abroad Publishing, 2002.

Work Your Way Around the World, by Susan Griffith. Vacation-Work Publications, 2007.

AUSTRIA (ÖSTERREICH)

With Vienna's high culture and the Alps's high mountains, Austria offers different extremes of beauty. Many of the world's most famous composers and thinkers, including Mozart and Freud, called Austria home. Today, its small villages brim with locally brewed beer, jagged peaks draw hikers and skiers, and magnificent palaces, museums, and concerts are omnipresent. Stroll along the blue Danube River or relax in a Viennese coffeehouse and listen to a waltz.

LIFE AND TIMES

HISTORY

HOLY ROMANS AND HAPSBURGS (800-1740). Austria has been both a barrier between and a meeting point for Eastern and Western Europe ever since the Holy Roman Emperor **Charlemagne** conquered the Bavarians in AD 788. The German **King Otto I** took control of the Holy Roman Empire after Charlemagne's death and named **Leopold of Babenberg** ruler of much of present-day Austria.

The last Babenberg died childless in the 13th century, and **Rudolf of Hapsburg** established his dynasty in the resulting power vacuum. Six centuries of Hapsburg kings proved that the wedding vow is just as politically powerful as the sword. **Maximilian I,** who became ruler of the Netherlands through his wife in 1477, is credited with the adaptation of Ovid's couplet, "Let other nations go to war; you, happy Austria, marry." His son **Philip the Handsome** married into Spanish royalty, endowing his grandson, **Charles V,** with an empire that covered wide swaths of Europe and parts of the Americas. The vast fortunes of the **Hapsburgs** left behind many monuments and castles in Austria; the **Hofburg** (p. 69) palace still dazzles with Hapsburgian grandeur.

Despite Austria's vast territory, Martin Luther's **Protestant Reformation** shook the reins of the Hapsburgs in the 16th and 17th centuries. Peasants left the Catholic Church en masse, and Protestant nobles doggedly fought the Catholic Hapsburgs in the **Thirty Years' War** (1618-48). Soon after, the Ottoman Turks besieged Vienna until **Prince Eugene of Savoy** drove them out. The plucky Eugene would triumph again, this time over the French in the **War of Spanish Succession** (1701-14). His palace, **Schloß Belvedere,** now houses a superb art collection.

CASTLES CRUMBLE (1740-1914). When **Maria Theresa,** daughter of Charles VI, ascended the throne in 1740, her neighbors were eager to infringe on the Hapsburg domain. Aware of this, she forged an alliance with France by marrying her daughter **Marie Antoinette** to the future **King Louis XVI.** The decapitation of Marie Antoinette during the French Revolution made relations between the two nations less than friendly; after the Revolution, **Napoleon Bonaparte** mercilessly conquered many Austrian territories. French troops invaded Vienna, where Napoleon took up residence in Maria Theresa's favorite palace, **Schönbrunnn,** and married her granddaughter.

Ironically, Napoleon's temporary success led to the establishment of a consolidated Austrian empire that could defend itself against the imperial aggressions of France. In 1804, Franz II renounced his claim to the defunct Holy Roman crown and proclaimed himself **Franz I,** Emperor of Austria. During the **Congress of Vienna** (1814-15), which redrew the map of Europe, Chancellor **Klemens von Metternich** renewed Austria's power base. Calm prevailed until the spring of 1848, when the philosophy from the French **bourgeois revolution** reached Austria. Students and workers revolted, seizing the palace and demanding a constitution with freedom of the press. The movement was divided and the rebellions were quashed. Nevertheless, the emperor was eventually pressured to abdicate in favor of his nephew, **Franz Josef I,** whose 68-year reign remains the second-longest in the recorded history of Europe.

Austria's political status continued to shift throughout Franz Josef's reign. Prussia, Austria's powerful northern neighbor, dominated European politics under **Otto von Bismarck** and defeated Austria in 1866. A year later, Franz Josef was outmaneuvered by Hungarian nobles and agreed to end the Austrian Empire to form the dual **Austro-Hungarian Empire.** Non-German speakers were marginalized within the new empire until 1907, when the government ceded basic civil rights to its peoples and instituted universal male suffrage. Unfortunately, these concessions to the empire's Slavic minority came too late. Burgeoning nationalist sentiments, especially among the South Slavs in the Balkans, led to severe divisions within the empire.

MODERNITY APPROACHES (1914-2000). The divisions within the Austro-Hungarian Empire gave way to open conflict at the turn of the 20th century. The assassination of Austrian archduke and heir to the throne **Franz Ferdinand** by a Serbian nationalist in Sarajevo in June 1914 sparked **World War I:** Austria's declaration of war against Serbia set off a chain reaction that spread throughout Europe. Franz Josef died in 1916, leaving the throne to his reluctant grandnephew **Karl I,** who struggled in vain to preserve the empire. On November 11, 1918, Karl finally surrendered, and the 640-year-old Hapsburg dynasty was replaced by the **First Republic of Austria.**

Between 1918 and 1938, Austria experienced its first taste of parliamentary democracy. Immediately after the war, the Republic suffered massive inflation, unemployment, and near economic collapse, which did not stabilize until the 1920s. In 1933, the weak coalition government gave way when **Engelbert Dollfuss,** the Austrian chancellor, declared martial law and abolished freedom of the press. Two years later, Dollfuss was assassinated by Austrian **Nazis**, who hoped for an alliance between Germany and Austria that Dollfuss opposed. In 1938, Austrian Nazis got their wish when Germany annexed Austria in the **Anschluß.** While **World War II** continued, tens of thousands of Austrian Jews, political dissidents, disabled people, Roma (gypsies), and homosexuals were sent to endure the horrible conditions of Nazi concentration camps.

After Soviet troops "liberated" Vienna in 1945, Allied troops divided Austria into four zones of occupation. During the occupation, the Soviets tried to make Austria a Communist state, but instead settled on an agreement that the nation would be permanently neutral. As in much of Western Europe, the American Marshall Plan helped jump-start the economy, laying the foundation for Austria's present prosperity. The **Federal Constitution** (1945) and the **Austrian State Treaty** (1955) established Austrian sovereignty and formed the basis for the current Austrian nation, often referred to as the **Second Republic.** Today, Austria is led by a president, elected for six-year terms, and a chancellor, usually the majority party's leader. A bicameral parliamentary legislature and strong provincial governments perform the main work of governance. Historically, the government has been dominated by a coalition of two parties: the socialist **Social Democratic Party** (SPÖ) and the Christian-conservative **People's Party** (ÖVP). Together, the two parties have built one of the world's most successful economies, with low unemployment and low inflation rates.

During the 1990s, the country moved toward stronger unification with Europe, joining the **European Union** in 1995. Austria faced European criticism, however, when its far-right **Freedom Party** (FPÖ) claimed 27% of the vote in the 1999 national elections. Led by the infamous **Jörg Haider,** the FPÖ maintained a strong anti-immigrant stance; Haider has made remarks that some have interpreted as neo-Nazi sentiments. Several hundred thousand protestors turned out on the day that members of the FPÖ were to be sworn in to parliament, and several EU countries ceased cooperation with the government until 2000.

TODAY

EUROSKEPTIC. Beginning in 2002, the popularity of the Freedom Party began to fall precipitously; a splinter group of the Freedom Party, the **Alliance for the Future of Austria** (BZÖ), enjoyed popularity for a few subsequent years. **Heinz Fischer,** a member of the SPÖ, is Austria's Federal president, although the role is largely ceremonial, with political parties and their leaders holding most of the power. The Chancellor of Austria is **Alfred Gusenbauer,** also the leader of the SPÖ. Austria has become known as one of the most "euroskeptic" members of the EU, consistently opposing measures to promote free movement of labor from Eastern Europe and the entry of Turkey into the Union. Pundits argue that such skepticism stems from lingering resentment in Austria over its political ostracization by other EU nations in the 90s. In 2006, the Social Democrats and the People's Party agreed on a coalition.

PEOPLE AND CULTURE

DEMOGRAPHICS. Although almost 90% of Austria's eight million people identify as German, nearly all have ties to other ethnic groups that belonged to the former empire. The 10% of the population that does not identify as German is made up mostly of recent immigrants. An emphasis on education is responsible for sky-high literacy rates (100%). Unemployment is around 4%.

LANGUAGE. While German is the nation's official language, Austrians often add a diminutive "*-erl*" (instead of the High German "*-chen*" or "*-lein*") to words. Also, Austrians don't greet each other with the standard *Guten Tag*, but instead opt for *Servus* (ZER-vus) or *Grüß Gott* (grOOs got).

LITERATURE. One of the earliest and most impressive works of Austrian literature is the German-language heroic epic *Song of the Nibelungs* (c. 1200), whose author is unknown. **Johann Nestroy** (1801-62) wrote biting comedies and satires like *The Talisman* (1840), lampooning social follies. His contemporary, **Adalbert Stifter** (1805-68), wrote short stories and novels, such as *The Condor* (1840) and *Indian Summer* (1857), which represent the height of Austria's classical style. Beginning around 1890, a growing recognition within Austria of the nation's *fin-de-siècle* social turmoil transformed Austrian literature. **Karl Kraus** (1874-1936) unmasked the crisis, **Arthur Schnitzler** (1862-1931) dramatized it, **Georg Trakl** (1887-1914) commented on it in symbolic verse, and **Hugo von Hofmannsthal** (1874-1929) penned its eulogy. Many of Austria's literary titans, such as **Franz Kafka** (1883-1924) and **Marie von Ebner-Eschenbach** (1830-1916), lived in the Hapsburg protectorate of Bohemia, and conversed with other writers in coffeehouses. Kafka's surrealist style is most famously elucidated in *The Metamorphosis* (1915), in which the narrator comes to terms with his unexpected transformation into a cockroach. Ebner-Eschenbach is considered the greatest female Austrian writer for her vivid individual portraits and her defense of women's rights.

When the Austro-Hungarian monarchy suddenly gave way to democracy, novelists **Robert Musil** (1880-1942) and **Joseph Roth** (1894-1939) charted the transformation. In post-war Austrian society, **Ingeborg Bachmann's** (1926-73) novels told stories of personal transformation through a feminist perspective, while **Thomas Bernhard** (1931-89) critiqued Austrian society and the inherent brutality of human nature. **Peter Handke** (1942-present) has written many experimental novels and co-wrote the screenplay for **Wim Wenders's** *Wings of Desire* (1987). The wildly popular crime novels of **Wolf Haas** (1960-present) have been adapted into films, including *Komm, süßer Tod* ("Come, Sweet Death"; 1998, film 2000) and *Silentium!* (1999, film 2004).

SCIENCE AND PHILOSOPHY. **Gregor Mendel** (1822-84) studied trait inheritance in pea pods and later became the father of modern genetics. The world's most famous psychoanalyst, **Sigmund Freud** (1856-1939), developed theories of sexual repression and the subconscious. His former home in Vienna is now a museum (p. 71).The **Austrian School of Economics** began developing libertarian economic theories in 1871. One of its most influential members, **Friedrich Hayek** (1899-1992), received the 1974 Nobel Prize in Economics. The **Vienna Circle** championed logical positivism in the early 20th century, and **Ludwig Wittgenstein** (1889-1951) published *Tractatus Logico-Philosophicus* (1921), which he believed solved all of philosophy's problems.

MUSIC. **Josef Haydn** (1732-1809) defined the classical period and created a variety of new musical forms that led to the sonata and the symphony. **Wolfgang Amadeus Mozart** (1756-91), a prodigy and brilliant composer, produced such pieces as *The Marriage of Figaro*, *Eine Kleine Nachtmusik* (A Little Night Music), and the unfinished *Requiem*. **Ludwig van Beethoven** (1770-1827) lived in Vienna for much of his life and composed some of his most famous works there. The expressive lines of **Franz Schubert** (1797-1828) incorporated the classical style as well as the Romantic Movement, music characterized by swelling melodies and harmonies. Mainly self-taught, Schubert began his *Unfinished Symphony* in 1822. Later in the 19th century, **Johannes Brahms** (1833-97) reintroduced Classical forms into Romanticism. The exhilarating waltzes of **Johann Strauss the Elder** (1804-49) and his son, creatively named **Johann Strauss the Younger** (1825-99), kept Vienna dancing for much of the century. **Arnold Schönberg** (1874-1951) rejected tonal keys at the turn of the 20th century, producing a highly abstracted sound.

VISUAL ARTS. Aided by the Hapsburg Empire's extensive patronage, Austria has maintained a rich artistic tradition. The flowering of Austrian architecture is represented in the cherub-covered facades of the **Baroque** style, exhibited exquisitely in the **Schönbrunn** and **Hofburg** (p. 69) palaces. The **Ringstraße**. a broad boulevard encircling Vienna, is an example of Austria's 19th-century **Modernism**. Modern Austrian art began in the 20th century with the works of **Gustav Klimt** (1862-1916), who founded the **Secession** movement. **Oskar Kokoschka** (1886-1980) and **Egon Schiele** (1890-1918) worked at the same time as Klimt and were tangentially involved with the Secessionists. Also around 1900, Modernist architects deviated from the Viennese Academy's conservatism. This gave rise to the **Jugendstil** movement (Art Nouveau), which formulated an ethic of functional buildings with artistic touches in the smallest details, an idea embraced by **Otto Wagner** (1841-1918). Travelers can still see Jugendstil apartments near Stephanspl. in Vienna (p. 61). In the 1920s and early 1930s, the Social Democratic administration built thousands of apartments in large **municipal projects** in a style reflecting the assertiveness of workers' movements and the ideals of **urban socialism.**

HOLIDAYS AND FESTIVALS

Holidays: Almost everything closes on public holidays. New Year's Day (Jan. 1); Epiphany (Jan. 6); Easter (Apr. 13); Labor Day (May 1); Ascension (May 21); Corpus Christi (June 11); Assumption (Aug. 15); Austrian National Day (Oct. 26); All Saints' Day (Nov. 1); Immaculate Conception (Dec. 8); Christmas (Dec. 25); Boxing Day (Dec. 26).

Festivals: Vienna celebrates *Fasching* (Carnival) from New Year's until the start of Lent. Austria's best summer music festivals are the *Wiener Festwochen* (early May to mid-June; www.festwochen.at) and the *Salzburger Festspiele* (late July-late August; www.salzburgerfestspiele.at).

ESSENTIALS

FACTS AND FIGURES

OFFICIAL NAME: Republic of Austria.

CAPITAL: Vienna.

MAJOR CITIES: Graz, Innsbruck, Salzburg.

POPULATION: 8,205,000.

LAND AREA: 82,400 sq. km.

LANGUAGE: German.

RELIGIONS: Roman Catholic 74%, Protestant 5%, Muslim 4%, Other/None 17%.

PERCENTAGE OF AUSTRIA'S LAND AREA COVERED BY THE ALPS: 62.

WHEN TO GO

Between November and March, prices in western Austria double and travelers need reservations months in advance. The situation reverses in the summer, when the eastern half of the country fills with tourists. Accommodations are cheaper and less crowded in the shoulder seasons (May-June and Sept.-Oct.). Cultural opportunities also vary with the seasons: the Vienna State Opera has no shows in July or August, and the Vienna Boys' Choir only performs May-June and Sept.-Oct.

DOCUMENTS AND FORMALITIES

EMBASSIES. Foreign embassies in Austria are in Vienna (p. 62). Austrian embassies abroad include: **Australia,** 12 Talbot St., Forrest, Canberra, ACT, 2603 (☎02 6295 1533; www.austriaemb.org.au); **Canada,** 445 Wilbrod St., Ottawa, ON, K1N 6M7 (☎613-789-1444; www.austro.org); **Ireland,** 15 Ailesbury Ct., 93 Ailesbury Rd., Dublin, 4 (☎01 269 45 77); **New Zealand,** Level 2, Willbank House, 57 Willis St., Wellington, 6001 (☎04 499 63 93); **UK,** 18 Belgrave Mews West, London, SW1X 8HU (☎020 7344 3250; www.bmaa.gv.at/london); **US,** 3524 International Ct., NW, Washington, D.C., 20008 (☎202-895-6700; www.austria.org).

VISA AND ENTRY INFORMATION. EU citizens do not need a visa. Citizens of Australia, Canada, New Zealand, and the US do not need a visa for stays of up to 90 days, beginning upon entry into any of the countries in the EU's freedom-of-movement zone. For more info, see p. 8. For stays of longer than 90 days, all non-EU citizens need visas, available at Austrian embassies. For American citizens, visas are $80 or free of charge for students studying abroad.

TOURIST SERVICES AND MONEY

TOURIST OFFICES. For general info, contact the **Austrian National Tourist Office,** Margaretenstr. 1, A-1040 Vienna (☎588 66 287; www.austria.info). All tourist offices are marked with a green "i"; most brochures are available in English.

MONEY. The **euro (€)** has replaced the **schilling** as the unit of currency in Austria. As a general rule, it's cheaper to exchange money in Austria than at home. Railroad stations, airports, hotels, and most travel agencies offer exchange services, as do banks. If you stay in hostels and prepare most of your own food, expect to spend €30-60 per day. Accommodations start at about €12 and a basic sit-down meal usually costs around €8. Menus will say whether service is included (*Preise inklusive* or *Bedienung inklusiv*); if it is, a tip is not expected. If not, 10% will do. Austrian restaurants expect you to seat yourself, and servers will not bring the bill until you ask them to do so. Say "*Zahlen bitte*" (TSAHL-en BIT-uh) to settle your accounts, and give tips directly to the server. Don't expect to bargain, except at street markets.

EMERGENCY	Ambulance: ☎144. Police: ☎133. Fire: ☎122.

TRANSPORTATION

BY PLANE. The only major international airport is Vienna's **Schwechat-Flughafen (VIE).** Other airports are in Innsbruck, Graz, Linz, and Salzburg. From London-Stansted, **Ryanair** (☎3531 249 7791; www.ryanair.com) flies to the latter three. For more info on flying to Austria, see p. 33.

BY TRAIN. The **Österreichische Bundesbahn** (ÖBB; www.oebb.at), Austria's state railroad, operates an efficient system with fast and comfortable **trains.** Eurail and InterRail passes are valid in Austria, but they do not guarantee a seat without a reservation. The **Austria Rail** pass allows three to eight days of travel within any 15-day period on all rail lines. It also entitles holders to 40% off **bike rentals** at train stations (2nd-class US$148 for three days).

BY BUS. The Austrian **bus system** consists mainly of PostBuses, which cover areas inaccessible by train. Buy tickets at the station or from the driver. Call ☎43 17 11 01 from abroad or ☎0810 222 333 within Austria from 7am-8pm.

BY CAR. Driving is a convenient way to see the more isolated parts of Austria, but gas is costly, an international license is required, and some small towns prohibit cars. The roads are well maintained and well marked, and Austrian drivers are quite careful. **Mitfahrzentralen** (ride-share services) in larger cities pair drivers with riders for a small fee. Riders then negotiate fares with the drivers. Be aware that not all organizations screen their participants; ask ahead.

BY BIKE. Bicycles are a great way to get around Austria, as roads in the country are generally smooth and safe. Many train stations rent **bikes** and allow you to return them to any participating station.

KEEPING IN TOUCH

TELEPHONES. Wherever possible, use a **calling card** for international phone calls, as long-distance rates for national phone services are often exorbitant. Prepaid phone cards and major credit cards can be used for direct international calls but are still less cost-efficient. For info on **mobile phones,** see p. 21. The most popular companies are A1, One, and T-mobile. Direct-dial access numbers for calling out of Austria include: **AT&T Direct** (☎0800 200 288); **British Telecom** (☎0800 890 043); **Canada Direct** (☎0800 200 217); **MCI WorldPhone** (☎0800 999 762); **Sprint** (☎0800 200 236); **Telecom New Zealand** (☎0800 200 222).

PHONE CODES	**Country code:** 43. **International dialing prefix:** 00 (for Vienna, dial 00 431). For more info on how to place international calls, see **Inside Back Cover.**

MAIL. Letters take one or two days within Austria. Airmail (€1.40) to North America takes four to seven days, and up to nine days to Australia and New Zealand. Mark all **letters** and packages *"mit Flugpost"* (airmail). Aerogrammes are the cheapest option. To receive mail in Austria, have mail delivered **Poste Restante.** Mail will go to the main post office unless you specify a subsidiary by street address. Address mail to be held according to the following example: LAST NAME, First name, Postlagernde Briefe, Postal code City, AUSTRIA.

ACCOMMODATIONS AND CAMPING

AUSTRIA	❶	❷	❸	❹	❺
ACCOMMODATIONS	under €16	€16-26	€27-34	€35-55	over €55

Always ask if your lodging provides a **guest card** *(Gästekarte)*, which grants discounts on activities, museums, and public transportation. The **Österreichischer Jugendherbergsverband-Hauptverband (ÖJH)** runs the over 80 **HI hostels** in Austria. Because of the rigorous standards of the national organization, these are usually very clean and orderly. Most charge €18-25 per night for dorms, with a €3-5 HI discount. **Independent hostels** vary in quality, but often have more personality and foster a lively backpacking culture. Slightly more expensive **Pensionen** are similar to American and British B&Bs. In small to mid-sized towns, singles will cost about €20-30, but expect to pay twice as much in big cities. **Hotels** are expensive (singles over €35; doubles over €48). Cheaper options have "Gasthof," "Gästehaus," or "Pension-Garni" in the name. Renting a **Privatzimmer** (room in a family home) is an inexpensive option. Contact the tourist office about rooms (€16-30). **Camping** in Austria is less about getting out into nature than having a cheap place to sleep; most sites are large plots glutted with RVs and are open in summer only. Prices run €10-15 per tent site and €5-8 per extra person. In the high Alps, hikers and mountaineers can retire to the well-maintained system of **Hütten** (mountain huts) where traditional Austrian fare and a good night's rest await them. Reserve ahead.

HIKING AND SKIING. Almost every town has hiking trails in its vicinity; consult the local tourist office. Trails are marked with either a red-white-red marker (only sturdy boots and hiking poles necessary) or a blue-white-blue marker (mountaineering equipment needed). Most mountain hiking trails and mountain huts are open only from late June to early September. Western Austria is one of the world's best skiing regions; the areas around Innsbruck and Kitzbühel are full of runs. High season runs from November to March.

FOOD AND DRINK

AUSTRIA	❶	❷	❸	❹	❺
FOOD AND DRINK	under €5	€5-10	€11-16	€17-25	over €25

Loaded with fat, salt, and cholesterol, traditional Austrian cuisine is bad for your skin, your heart, and your figure. *Wienerschnitzel* is a breaded meat cutlet (usually veal or pork) fried in butter. Natives nurse their sweet teeth with *Sacher Torte* (a rich chocolate cake layered with marmalade) and *Linzer Torte* (a light yellow cake with currant jam). Austrian beers are outstanding—try Stiegl, a Salzburg brew; Zipfer, from Upper Austria; and Styrian Gösser.

EAT YOUR VEGGIES. Vegetarians should look on the menu for *Spätzle* (noodles), *Eierschwammerl* (mushrooms), or anything with *"Vegi"* in it.

AUSTRIA

BEYOND TOURISM

Austria caters more to tourism than volunteerism; there are only limited opportunities to give back, so your best bet is to find them through a placement service. Short-term work abounds at hotels, ski resorts, and farms. For more info on opportunities across Europe, see **Beyond Tourism,** p. 45.

Actilingua Academy, Glorietteg. 8, A-1130 Vienna (☎431 877 6701; www.actilingua.com). Study German in Vienna (from €419) for 2 to 4 weeks, with accommodation in dorms, apartments, or with a host family.

Bergwald Projekt/Mountain Forest Project, Hauptstr. 24, 7014 Trin (☎081 630 4145; www.bergwaldprojekt.ch). Organizes week-long conservation projects in the forests of Austria, Germany, and Switzerland.

Concordia, 19 North Street, Portslade, Brighton, BN41 1DH, UK (☎012 7342 2218; www.concordia-iye.org.uk). British volunteer organization that directs community projects in Austria, which have in the past included renovating historic buildings and parks and directing a youth drama project.

VIENNA (WIEN) ☎01

War, marriage, and Hapsburg maneuvering transformed Vienna (pop. 1,700,000) from a Roman camp along the Danube into Europe's political linchpin, engendering a culture of luxury and intrigue that lingers today. Beethoven and Mozart made Vienna an everlasting arbiter of high culture, and the tradition continues with the city's prestigious orchestras and world-class museums. Freud, Klimt, and Kafka gave voice to the unique energy that drives the city's art and culture forward. Its dozens of coffeehouses radiate artistic and intellectual energy—on any given afternoon, cafes turn the sidewalks into a sea of umbrellas while bars and clubs pulse with techno and indie rock until dawn.

INTERCITY TRANSPORTATION

Flights: Wien-Schwechat Flughafen (VIE; ☎01 700 70; www.viennaairport.com), 18km from the city center, is home to **Austrian Airlines** (☎01 517 89; www.aua.com). The **S-Bahn** (☎65 17 17) stops at Wien Mitte (30min., 2-3 per hr., €3). The **Vienna Airport Lines bus** (☎930 00 23 00) goes to Südbahnhof (20min.) and Westbahnhof (40min.; 2 per hr.; €6, round-trip €11). The **City Airport Train (CAT;** ☎01 25 250; www.cityairporttrain.com) takes only 16min. to reach Wien Mitte (2 per hr. 6:05am-11:35pm; online €8, round-trip €15; from a ticket machine €9, round-trip €16; on board €10, children up to 14 free; Eurail not valid).

Budget Airlines: M.R. Štefánik International Airport (BTS; ☎421 2 3303 3353; www.letiskobratislava.sk) in Bratislava, Slovakia serves as a gateway to Western Europe. In addition to domestic flights from Slovakia, budget airlines **SkyEurope** (☎48 50 11 11; www.skyeurope.com) and **Ryanair** (www.ryanair.com; see **Transportation,** p. 33) run shuttle buses to and from Vienna (1-1½hr., 7-8 per day, 363Sk). Vienna-bound **trains** (☎20 29 11 11; www.zsr.sk) depart from **Bratislava Hlavná Stanica** every hr. (1hr., round-trip 283Sk). **Buses** make a similar journey, leaving from **Mlynské nivy 31** (1hr., every hr., 400Sk). Another option is to sail to Vienna (1hr., 2 per day, 150Sk) with **Lodná osobná doprava,** Fajnorovo nábr. 2 (☎52 93 22 26; open daily 8:30am-5:30pm).

Trains: Vienna has 2 train stations with international connections. Call ☎05 17 17 or check www.oebb.at for detailed train info. Credit cards accepted.

Westbahnhof, XV, Mariahilferstr. 132. Info counter open daily 7:30am-9pm. Trains go to: **Innsbruck** (4-5hr., 7 per day, €54); **Salzburg** (2-3hr., every hr., €43); **Amsterdam, NTH** (12hr., 4 per day, €135); **Berlin, DEU** (9-11hr., every 2hr., €100-130); **Budapest, HUN** (3hr., 17 per day, €36); **Hamburg, DEU** (9-12hr., 6 per day, €80); **Munich, DEU** (5hr., 10 per day, €72); **Paris, FRA** (14-24hr., 2 per day, €70-160); **Zürich, CHE** (9hr., 3 per day, €88).

Südbahnhof, X, Wiener Gürtel 1a. Info counter open daily 7am-8pm. Trains go south and east to: **Graz** (2hr., every hr., €30); **Kraków, POL** (7hr., 4 per day, €46); **Prague, CZR** (4-5hr., 8 per day, €44); **Rome, ITA** (13-18hr., 6 per day, €75-100); **Venice, ITA** (7-11hr., 6 per day, €50-70).

Buses: Buses in Austria are rarely cheaper than trains; compare prices before buying a ticket. **Postbus** (☎0810 222 333; www.postbus.at) provides regional bus service and **Eurolines** (☎798 29 00; www.eurolines.at) connects to international destinations. Buses leave from the city stations at **Erdberg, Floridsdorf, Heiligenstadt, Hütteldorf, Kagran, Reumannplatz,** and **Wien Mitte/Landstraße.**

ORIENTATION

Vienna is divided into 23 **Bezirke** (districts). District numbering begins in the city center, **Innenstadt.** The borders of the center, the **Ringstraße** (ring road) on three sides and the Danube Canal on the fourth, were originally the location of a wall that protected the city from invaders. At the center of the Innenstadt lies **Stephansplatz** and the pedestrian district. The best way to reach Innenstadt is to take the U-bahn to Stephanspl. (U1, U3) or **Karlsplatz** (U1, U2, U4); **Schwedenplatz** (U1, U4) is close to the city's nightlife. Tram lines 1 and 2 circle the Innenstadt on the Ringstr., with line 2 heading clockwise and 1 counterclockwise.

The **Ringstraße** consists of different segments, such as Opernring and Kärntner Ring. Many of Vienna's attractions lie within District I, right in the center and immediately around the Ringstr. Districts II-IX spread out from the city center following the clockwise traffic of the Ring. The remaining districts expand from yet another ring road, the **Gürtel** (Belt). Similar to the Ring, this major thoroughfare has numerous segments, including Margaretengürtel, Neubaugürtel, and Währinger Gürtel. Like Vienna's street signs, *Let's Go* indicates the district number in Roman/Arabic numerals before the street and number.

LOCAL TRANSPORTATION

Public Transportation: Wiener Linien (☎790 91 00; www.wienerlinien.at). The **U-Bahn** (subway), **Straßenbahn** (tram), **S-Bahn** (elevated tram), and **bus lines** operate on a 1-ticket system, so you can transfer between modes of transportation without having to buy a new ticket. Purchase tickets at a counter, machine, on board, or at a tobacco shop *(trafik)*. A **single fare** (€1.70 in advance, €2.20 on board) lets you travel to any destination in the city and switch from bus to U-Bahn to tram to S-Bahn in any order, provided your travel is uninterrupted. Other ticket options include a **1-day pass** (€5.70), **3-day rover ticket** (€14), **7-day pass** (valid M 9am to the next M 9am; €14), and an **8-day pass**(valid any 8 days, not necessarily consecutive; can be split between several people, but must be validated for each person; €27). The **Vorteilscard** (Vienna Card; €19) allows for 72hr. of travel and discounts at museums and sights, and can be purchased at the ticket office and hotels. To avoid a €60 fine from plainclothes inspectors, **validate your ticket** by punching it in the machine. Tickets need only be stamped once. Regular trams and subway cars do not run midnight-5am. **Night buses** run 2 per hr., 12:30-4:30am, along most routes; "N" signs designate night bus stops. A night bus schedule and **discount passes** are available from Wiener Linien info offices (open M-F 6:30am-6:30pm, Sa-Su 8:30am-4pm) in the Karlspl., Stephahnspl., Westbahnhof, and some other U-Bahn stations, and at the **tourist office** (see below).

Taxis: ☎313 00, ☎401 00, ☎601 60, or ☎814 00. Stands at Südbahnhof, Karlspl. in the city center, Westbahnhof, and by the Bermuda Dreieck. Rates outside the city are not regulated, and should be negotiated. **Accredited taxis** have yellow-and-black signs on the roof. Base rate M-Sa €2.50 plus €0.20 per 0.2km; base rate Su 11pm-6am €3; holidays slightly more expensive. €2.50 surcharge for calling a taxi.

Bike Rental: Pedal Power, II, Ausstellungsstr. 3 (☎01 729 72 34; www.pedalpower.at). €17 per 4hr., €28 per day, students €14/€21. Delivery available. 2½hr. guided tours in English and German. €23, students €17. Open daily May-Sept. 8am-7pm; Mar.-Apr. and Oct. 8am-6pm.

AUSTRIA

PRACTICAL INFORMATION

Tourist Office: I, Albertinapl. (☎01 245 55; www.vienna.info), on the corner of Maysederg. Follow Operng. up 1 block from the Opera House and look for the massive sign above the corner. Books rooms with €2.90 fee. Open daily 9am-7pm.

Embassies and Consulates: Australia, IV, Mattiellistr. 2-4 (☎01 50 67 40). Open M-F 8:30am-4:30pm. **Canada,** I, Laurenzerberg 2 (☎01 531 38 30 00). Open M-F 8:30am-12:30pm and 1:30-3:30pm. **Ireland,** I, Rotenturmstr. 16-18, 5th fl. (☎01 715 42 46). Open M-F

9:30-11am and 1:30-4pm. **New Zealand,** III, Salesianerg. 15 (☎01 318 85 05). **UK,** III, Jaurèesg. 10 (☎01 716 13 53 33, after hours for UK nationals in emergencies only ☎0676 569 40 12). Open M-F 9:15am-12:30pm and 2-3:30pm. **US,** X, Boltzmanng. 16 (☎01 31 33 90). Open M-F 8-11:30am. 24hr. emergency services.

Currency Exchange and Banks: ATMs are your best bet. Nearly all accept Cirrus/MC/V. **Banks** generally give the best available exchange rate. Most open M-W and F 8am-3pm, Th 8am-5:30pm. **Train station** exchanges have long hours (daily 7am-10pm at the Westbahnhof), but charge 1% with a €6 minimum fee. Stay away from the 24hr. bill-exchange machines in Innenstadt, as they generally charge outrageous fees.

Luggage Storage: Lockers available at all train stations. €2-3.50 per 24hr.

Emergency: ☎141.

24hr. Pharmacy: ☎15 50. Consulates have lists of English-speaking doctors.

Hospital: Allgemeines Krankenhaus, IX, Währinger Gürtel 18-20 (☎01 40 40 00).

Internet Access: C@llCenter West, XV, Mariahilferstr. 149. €1.40 per 30min., €2.50 per hr. Open daily 9am-midnight. **ARI-X,** VII (☎01 9911 151 612), corner of Kaiserstr. and Lerchenfelderstr. €1 per hr. Open M-Sa 9am-11pm, Su noon-11pm.

Post Office: Hauptpostamt, I, Fleischmarkt 19 (☎01 0577 677 10 10). Open daily 6am-10pm. Branches throughout the city and at the train stations; look for yellow signs with trumpet logos. **Postal Codes:** A-1010 (1st district) through A-1230 (23rd district).

ACCOMMODATIONS AND CAMPING

Hunting for cheap rooms in Vienna during high season (June-Sept.) can be unpleasant; call for reservations at least five days ahead. For info on camping near Vienna, visit www.campingwien.at.

Hostel Ruthensteiner, XV, Robert-Hamerlingg. 24 (☎01 893 42 02; www.hostelruthensteiner.com). Knowledgeable staff, spotless rooms, kitchen, and a courtyard with a massive chess set. Guitars and piano available for guest use. Breakfast €2.50. Linens €2. Internet €2 per 40min. Key deposit €10. 5-night max. stay. Reception 24hr. 8-bed dorms €18; singles €32; doubles €50, with bath €54; quads €72/80. AmEx/MC/V. ❷

Wombats City Hostel, (☎01 897 23 36; www.wombats-hostels.com) has 2 separate locations. **"The Lounge"** (XV, Mariahilferstr. 137). Exit Westbahnhof and turn right on Mariahilferstr. The bright walls and leather couches add a modern touch to the college dorm atmosphere. Loud, popular bar in the basement vault, 24hr. reception, and no curfew make this a more social hostel. **"The Base"** (XV, Grang. 6). Continue on Mariahilferstr., turn right on Rosinag., and left on Grang. On a quiet street farther from the train station, this wildly colorful hostel compensates with an in-house pub, guided tours, and nightly English-language movies. Breakfast €3.50 daily 7:30-10am. Laundry €4.50. Internet €2 per hr. Free Wi-Fi in the lobby. Dorms €21; doubles €50. MC/V. ❷

Westend City Hostel, VI, Fügerg. 3 (☎01 597 67 29; www.westendhostel.at), near Westbahnhof. A rose-filled courtyard and plain dorms provide travelers a peaceful place to spend the night. Breakfast included. Internet €4 per hr. Free Wi-Fi. Reception 24hr. Check-out 10:30am. Lockout 10:30am-2pm. Open from mid-Mar. to Nov. Dorms €20-23; singles €52-65; doubles €62-80. Cash only. ❷

Pension Kraml, VI, Brauerg. 5 (☎01 587 85 88; www.pensionkraml.at). U3: Zieglerg. Exit on Otto-Bauer-G., take the 1st left onto Königsegg., then 1st right. Large plush rooms in rich red. Lounge has cable TV. Breakfast included. Reception 24hr. Singles €35; doubles €56, with shower €66, with full bath €76; triples €78/€87. 3- to 5-person apartment with bath €99-135. Cash only. ❸

Camping Neue Donau, XXII, Am Kleehäufel 119 (☎01 202 40 10; www.campingwien.at/nd). U1: Kaisermühlen. Take the Schüttaustr. exit, cross the street, then take bus #91a to

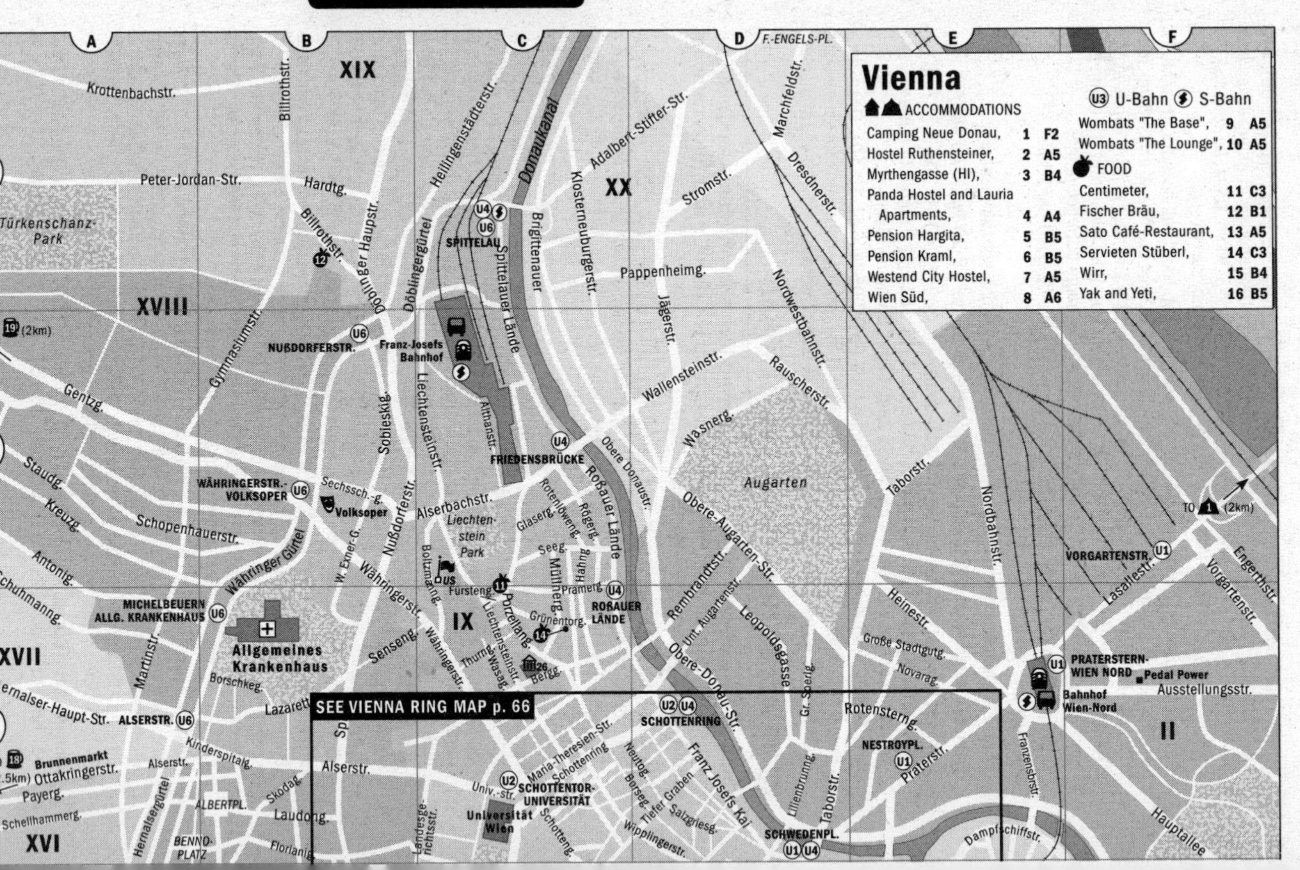
Vienna
ACCOMMODATIONS
Camping Neue Donau, 1 F2
Hostel Ruthensteiner, 2 A5
Myrthengasse (HI), 3 B4
Panda Hostel and Lauria Apartments, 4 A4
Pension Hargita, 5 B5
Pension Kraml, 6 B5
Westend City Hostel, 7 A5
Wien Süd, 8 A6
U3 U-Bahn S-Bahn
Wombats "The Base", 9 A5
Wombats "The Lounge", 10 A5
FOOD
Centimeter, 11 C3
Fischer Bräu, 12 B1
Sato Café-Restaurant, 13 A5
Servieten Stüberl, 14 C3
Wirr, 15 B4
Yak and Yeti, 16 B5
SEE VIENNA RING MAP p. 66
Donaukanal
Augarten
Türkenschanz-Park
Liechtenstein Park
Allgemeines Krankenhaus
Universität Wien
Franz-Josefs Bahnhof
Bahnhof Wien-Nord
Pedal Power
Volksoper
SPITTELAU
NUßDORFERSTR.
FRIEDENSBRÜCKE
WÄHRINGERSTR.-VOLKSOPER
MICHELBEUERN ALLG. KRANKENHAUS
ALSERSTR.
ROßAUER LÄNDE
SCHOTTENRING
SCHOTTENTOR-UNIVERSITÄT
SCHWEDENPL.
NESTROYPL.
VORGARTENSTR.
PRATERSTERN-WIEN NORD
XIX
XX
XVIII
XVII
XVI
IX
II
TO (2km)
TO (2.5km)
Brunnenmarkt

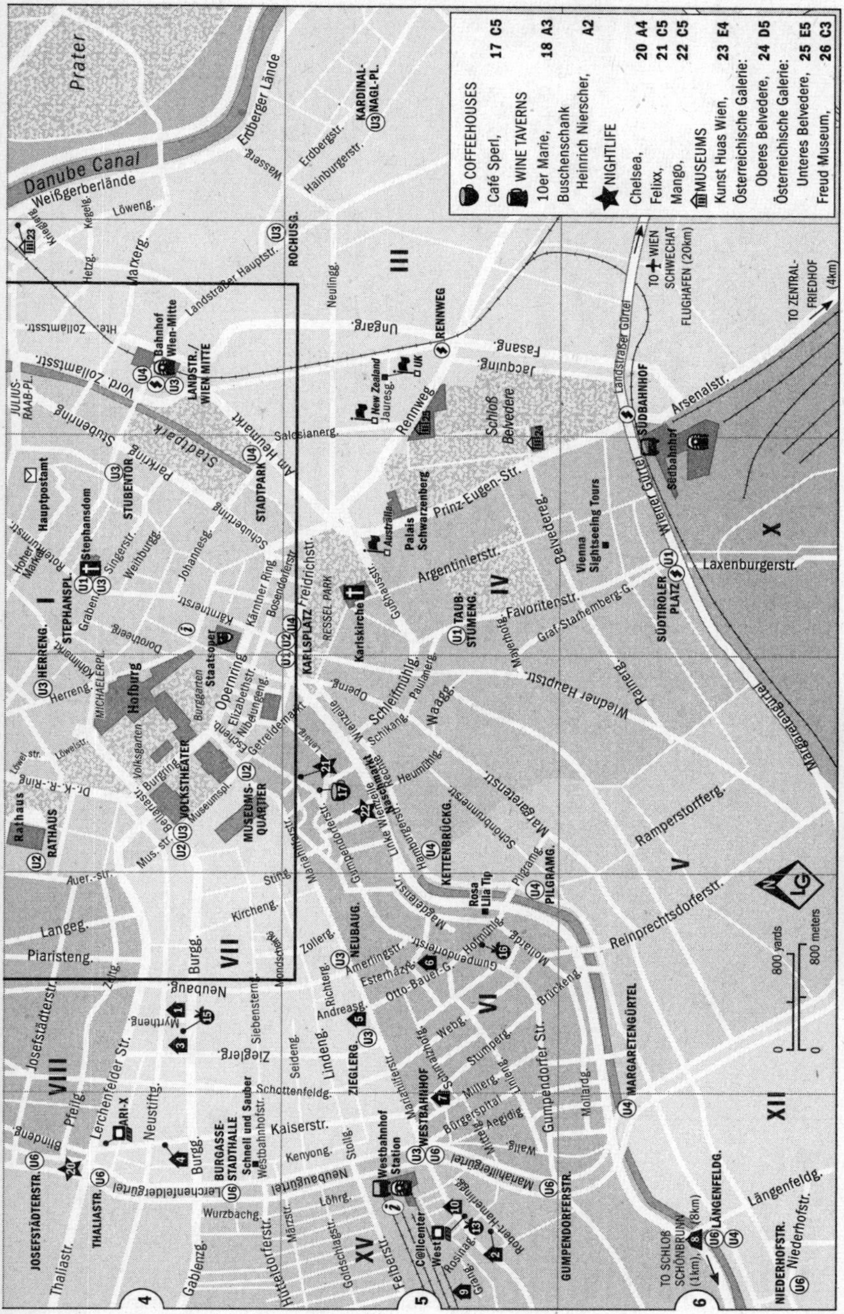

COFFEEHOUSES
Café Sperl, 17 C5
WINE TAVERNS
10er Marie, 18 A3
Buschenschank Heinrich Nierscher, A2
NIGHTLIFE
Chelsea, 20 A4
Felixx, 21 C5
Mango, 22 C5
MUSEUMS
Kunst Huas Wien, 23 E4
Österreichische Galerie: Oberes Belvedere, 24 D5
Österreichische Galerie: Unteres Belvedere, 25 E5
Freud Museum, 26 C3
Prater
Danube Canal
Stadtpark
Hofburg
Stephansdom
Staatsoper
Karlskirche
Schloß Belvedere
Palais Schwarzenberg
Südbahnhof
Westbahnhof Station
Rathaus
TO WIEN SCHWECHAT FLUGHAFEN (20km)
TO ZENTRALFRIEDHOF (4km)
TO SCHLOß SCHÖNBRUNN (1km), (8km)
800 yards
800 meters

AUSTRIA

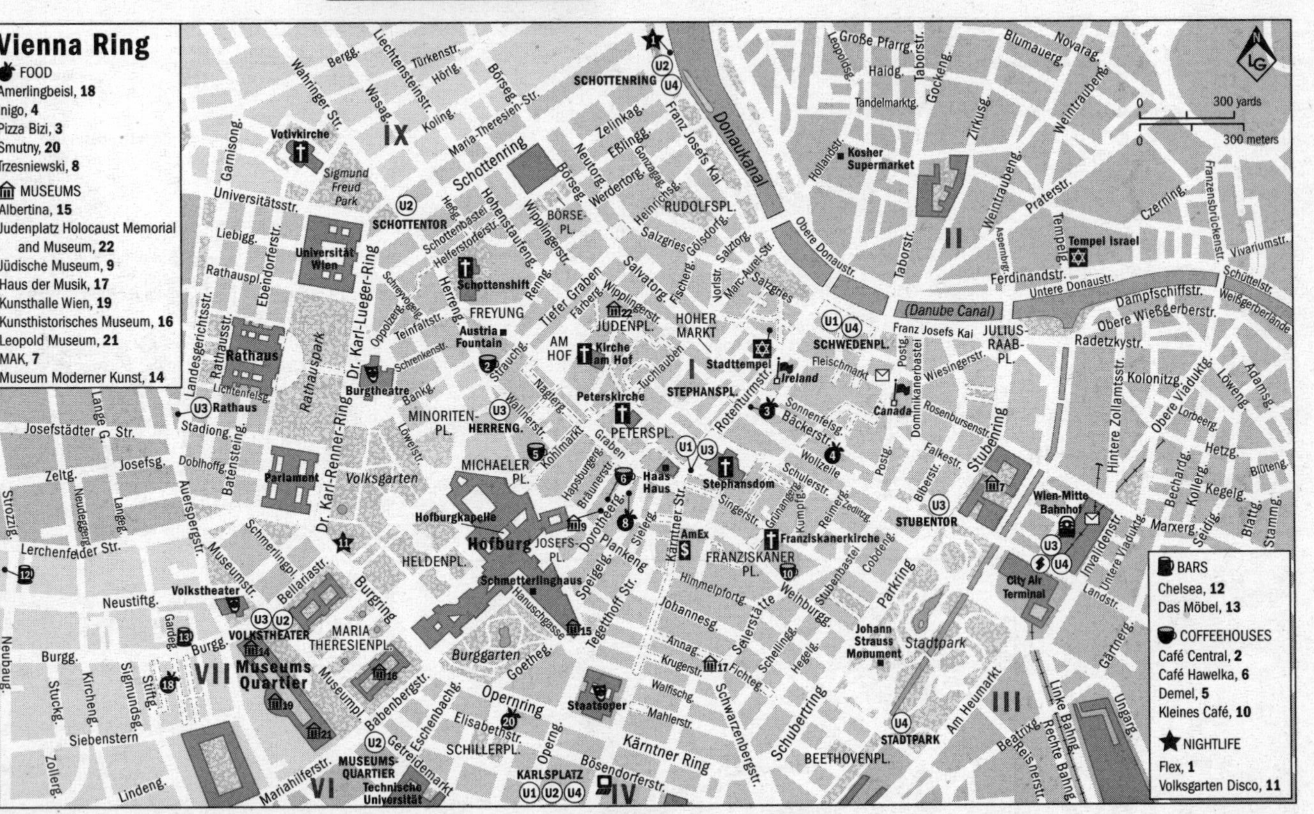

Vienna Ring
FOOD
Amerlingbeisl, 18
Inigo, 4
Pizza Bizi, 3
Smutny, 20
Trzesniewski, 8
MUSEUMS
Albertina, 15
Judenplatz Holocaust Memorial and Museum, 22
Jüdische Museum, 9
Haus der Musik, 17
Kunsthalle Wien, 19
Kunsthistorisches Museum, 16
Leopold Museum, 21
MAK, 7
Museum Moderner Kunst, 14
BARS
Chelsea, 12
Das Möbel, 13
COFFEEHOUSES
Café Central, 2
Café Hawelka, 6
Demel, 5
Kleines Café, 10
NIGHTLIFE
Flex, 1
Volksgarten Disco, 11
0 300 yards
0 300 meters

Kleehäufel. 4km from the city center and adjacent to Neue Donau beaches, though not directly on the water. Kitchen, showers, and supermarket. Boat and bike rental available. Laundry €4.50. Reception 8am-12:30pm and 3-6:15pm. Open Easter-Sept. €6-7 per person; €10-12 per tent. AmEx/MC/V. ❶

FOOD

Viennese food is all about meat: *Tafelspitz* (boiled beef), *Gulasch* (goulash), and *Wiener Schnitzel* (deep-fried, breaded veal or pork cutlet) are all traditional. But vegetarians need not fear—there's plenty of tasty non-meat fare in this bustling metropolis. The city boasts elaborate sweets, including *Mohr in Hemd* (chocolate and hazelnut soufflé draped in hot chocolate sauce) and the renowned *Sacher Torte*. Restaurants that call themselves *Stüberln* ("little sitting rooms") or advertise *Schmankerl* serve traditional Viennese fare.

Innenstadt restaurants are expensive. The neighborhood north of the university, where Universitätsstr. and Währingerstr. meet (U2: Schottentor), is more budget-friendly. Affordable restaurants line **Burggasse** in District VII and the area around Rechte and Linke Wienzeile near Naschmarkt (U4: Kettenbrückeng). The **Naschmarkt** hosts Vienna's biggest produce market. (Open M-F 6am-6:30pm and Sa 6am-2pm.) The **Brunnenmarkt** (XVI, U6: Josefstädterstr.) has Turkish flair. There's a **kosher** supermarket at II, Hollandstr. 10. (☎01 216 96 75. Open M-Th 8:30am-6:30pm and F 8am-2pm.)

B.Y.O.B. When shopping at Austrian supermarkets, bring your own bag; most supermarkets charge €0.05-0.20 per bag. Come early, too—many supermarkets close M-Sa at around 6:30-7pm and often close Su.

INSIDE THE RING

Trzesniewski, I, Dorotheerg. 1 (☎01 512 32 91). From Stephansdom, follow the signs 3 blocks down on the left side of the Graben. Once Kafka's favorite, this stand-up establishment has been serving delicious open-faced mini-sandwiches (€1) for over 100 years. They're mainly egg- and cucumber-based, but can also include salmon, onion, paprika, and herring—presumably no angsty vermin. Open M-F 8:30am-7:30pm and Sa 9am-5pm. Cash only. ❶

Smutny, I, Elisabethstr. 8 (☎01 587 13 56; www.smutny.com), U6: Karlspl. A traditional Viennese restaurant serving *Wiener schnitzel* (€15) and *Fiakergulash* (goulash with beef, egg, potato, and sausage; €12). Open daily 10am-midnight. AmEx/MC/V. ❸

Inigo, I, Bäckerstr. 18 (☎01 512 74 51; www.inigo.at). Founded by a Jesuit priest, Inigo aids the chronically unemployed by hiring them as cooks. Hearty entrees served with a complimentary salad in a cheery interior or the church square. Vegetarian entrees €8-10. Soups €4. Salads €2-7. Open M-Th and Sa 9:30am-midnight. AmEx/MC/V. ❷

OUTSIDE THE RING

Yak and Yeti, VI, Hofmühlg. 21 (☎01 595 54 52; www.yakundyeti.at). U3: Zieglerg. This Himalayan restaurant serves *momos* (Nepalese dumplings; €8-11) and other ethnic specialties. Eat meditatively under the prayer flags in their lush garden. Lunch buffet €6.50. All you can eat specials T and Th evening €10. Entrees €7-13. Try a mango mousse (€4.50) for dessert. Open M-F 11:30am-2:30pm and 6-10:30pm, Sa 11:30am-10:30pm. MC/V. ❸

Fresco Grill IX, Liechtensteinstr. 10 (☎660 467 89 83; www.frescofrill.at). U2: Schottentor. Head north along Liechtensteinstr. Vienna's best burritos in a hip, relaxed atmosphere. Hang out and enjoy a 1½L pitcher of beer (€3) with free chips and salsa. Free Wi-Fi. Burritos €4.50-5.50. Open daily in summer M-F noon-9pm, in winter 11am-11pm. 5% student discount. Check website for freebies. MC/V. ❷

COFFEEHOUSES

For years these venerable establishments have been havens for artists, writers, and thinkers: Vienna's cafes saw Franz Kafka brood about solitude, Theodor Herzl plan the creation of Israel, and Sigmund Freud ponder the perversity of the human mind. The only dictat of coffeehouse etiquette is that you linger; the waiter *(Herr Ober)* will serve you when you sit down and then leave you to sip your *Mélange* (coffee and steamed milk), read, and contemplate life's great questions. When you're ready to leave, ask to pay with a *"Zahlen, bitte."*

Café Central, I, Herreng. 14 (☎01 533 37 63; www.palaisevents.at), at the corner of Strauchg. With green-gold arches and live music, this luxurious coffeehouse transports patrons to a world of bygone manners and opulence. The house specialty is coffee with apricot liqueur (€5.90). Open M-Th and Sa 7:30am-10pm, F and Su 10am-10pm. AmEx/MC/V.

Kleines Café, I, Franziskanerpl. 3. Escape from the busy pedestrian streets with a *Mélange* (€3.30) and chat with locals on a leather couch in the sotthing interior or by the fountain in the square. Sandwiches €3-5. Croissants, apple *(apfel)* strudel, and curd strudel €2.10. Eggs €7. Open daily 10am-2am. Cash only.

Café Sperl, VI, Gumpendorferstr. 11 (☎01 586 41 58; www.cafesperl.at). U2: Museumsquartier. Marble tables and crystal chandeliers adorn one of Vienna's oldest, most elegant cafes. Sept.-June Su live piano 3:30-5:30pm. Open Sept.-June M-Sa 7am-11pm, Su 11am-8pm; July-Aug. M-Sa 7am-11pm. AmEx/MC/V.

WINE TAVERNS (HEURIGEN)

Those tired of high culture can find Dionysian release on the outskirts of the city in a number of wine taverns, hidden from the disapproving eyes and powdered wigs of opera ticket salesmen. Marked by a hanging branch, *Heurigen* serve *Heuriger* (wine) and Austrian delicacies, often in a relaxed outdoors setting akin to German beer gardens. The wine is from the most recent harvest; good *Heuriger* is white, fruity, and full-bodied. Open in summer, *Heurigen* cluster in the Viennese suburbs where the grapes grow. Tourist buses head to the most famous region, **Grinzing,** in District XIX; you'll find better atmosphere in the hills of **Sievering, Neustift am Walde** (both in District XIX), and **Neuwaldegg** (in XVII). True Heuriger devotees make the trip to **Gumpoldskirchen.**

Buschenschank Heinrich Nierscher, XIX, Strehlg. 21 (☎01 440 21 46). U6: Währingerstr. Tram #41 to Plötzleinsdorf (the last stop); then take bus #41A to Plötzleinsfriedhof (the 2nd stop) or walk up Pötzleinsdorfer Str., which becomes Khevenhüller Str.; go right on Strehlg. Enjoy a glass of *Heuriger* (€2.50) in the oversized country kitchen or the backyard overlooking the vineyards. Select a tray of meat, cheese, and bread for a light supper (€4-6). Open M and Th-Su 3pm-midnight. Cash only.

10er Marie, XVI, Ottakringerstr. 222-224 (☎01 489 46 47). U3: Ottakring. Turn left on Thaliastr., then right onto Johannes-Krawarik. Locals frequent the large garden behind the yellow house. Though it lacks its own vines, this wine garden is most accessible from the interior, perfect for tipsy patrons who need to take the subway home. ¼L of wine €2. Open M-Sa 3pm-midnight. MC/V.

SIGHTS

Vienna's contrasting streets are by turns stately, residential, and decaying. Unlike nearby cities in Germany, Vienna was largely unaffected by the destruction of WWII, which means that visitors can enjoy the same buildings that Freud and Kafka wandered by. To wander on your own, grab a copy of *Vienna from A to Z* (€3.60) from the tourist office. The office also leads themed English-language walking tours (€12). Contact **Pedal Power,** II, Ausstellungsstr. 3 (☎01 729 72 34; www.pedalpower.at) for **cycling tours** (€23). **Bus tours** (€35) are given by **Vienna Sightseeing Tours,** IV, Goldegg. 29 (☎01 712 46 83; www.viennasightseeing.at).

STEPHANSDOM AND GRABEN. In the heart of the city, the massive **Stephansdom** is one of Vienna's most treasured landmarks. For a view of the old city and the church's mosaic roof, take the elevator up the North Tower. Or, to work off that strudel, climb the 343 steps of the slightly higher South Tower. *(☎01 515 52 35 26. North Tower open daily Apr.-June and Sept.-Oct. 8:30am-5:30pm; Nov.-Mar. 8:30am-5pm; July-Aug. 9am-5pm. €4.50. South Tower open daily 9am-5:30pm. €3.50.)* Downstairs, skeletons of plague victims fill the **catacombs.** The **Gruft** (vault) stores urns containing the Hapsburgs' innards. *(Tours in English. M-Sa 2 per hr. 10-11:30am and 1:30-4:30pm, Su and holidays 1:30-4:30pm. Cathedral tour daily 3:45pm. €4.50, children €1. MC/V.)* From Stephanspl., follow Graben to see Jugendstil architecture, including Otto Wagner's red marble **Grabenhof** and the underground public toilet complex designed by the fortuitously-named **Adolf Loos.**

HOFBURG PALACE. Previously a medieval castle, this imperial palace was the Hapsburgs' home until 1918. Wing by wing, it was expanded continuously over 800 years. Now home to the President's office and a few small museums, its grandest assets are in the **royal treasury.** The palace is best admired from its **Michaelplatz** and **Heldenplatz** entrances. *(☎01 533 75 70; www.hofburg-wien.at and www.kmh.at. U3: Herreng. Open daily Sept.-June 9am-5:30pm, July-Aug. 9am-8pm. €10, students €7.50.)*

HOHER MARKT AND STADTTEMPEL. Once both a market and an execution site, **Hoher Markt** was home to the Roman encampment **Vindobona.** Roman ruins lie beneath the shopping arcade across from the fountain. *(Open Tu-Su 9am-6pm. €4, students €3. MC/V.)* The biggest draw is the 1914 Jugendstil **Ankeruhr** (clock), whose figures—from Marcus Aurelius to Maria Theresa—rotate past the Viennese coat of arms accompanied by the tunes of their times. To find it, look across the square from the Roman Museum; it's in the corner, connecting two buildings on the second floor. *(1 figure appears every hr. All figures appear at noon.)* Hidden on Ruprechtspl. is the **Stadttempel,** the only synagogue in Vienna to escape destruction during Kristallnacht. *(Seitenstetteng. 4. Mandatory guided tours M and Th at 11:30am and 2pm. €2, students €1.)*

AM HOF AND FREYUNG. Once a medieval jousting square, Am Hof now houses the **Kirche am Hof** (Church of the Nine Choirs of Angels) and **Collalto Palace,** where Mozart gave his first public performance. Just west of Am Hof is **Freyung,** the square with the **Austriabrunnen** (Austria Fountain) in the center. Medieval fugitives took asylum in the **Schottenstift** (Monastery of the Scots), giving rise to the name *Freyung* or "sanctuary." Today, the annual **Christkindl market** fills the plaza with baked goods and holiday cheer (Dec. 1-24).

SCHLOSS SCHÖNBRUNN. Schönbrunn began as a humble hunting lodge, but because of Maria Theresa's efforts became a splendid palace. The **Imperial Tour** passes through the dazzling **Hall of Mirrors,** where six-year-old Mozart played. The longer **Grand Tour** also visits Maria Theresa's exquisite 18th-century rooms, including the ornate **Millions Room.** *(Schönbrunnerstr. 47. U4: Schönbrunn. ☎01 811 132 39; www.schoenbrunn.at. Open daily July-Aug. 8:30am-6pm; Apr.-June and Sept.-Oct. 8:30am-5pm; Nov.-Mar. 8:30am-4:30pm. Imperial Tour 22 rooms; 35min.; €9.50, students €8.50. Grand Tour 40 rooms; 50min.; €13/12. English-language audio tour and/or booklet included.)* The

COFFEE CULTURE

Vienna is the world's coffee capital, but for those used to *mocha lattes* or half-caff lite soys, understanding the jumble of German words on the *Kaffeehaus* menu can be daunting. Here's a cheat-sheet for deciphering the menu:

A **Mokka** or a **Schwarzer** is strong, pure black espresso and nothing more. The **Kleiner Brauner** ("small brown") lightens the espresso with milk or cream, while the **Verlängerter** lowers the stakes yet again with weaker coffee. The quintessential Viennese cafe drink, a **Mélange** melds black espresso with steamed milk, sometimes capping it with a dollop of whipped cream. The **Kapuziner** ("the monk") also consists of espresso with gently foamed milk but is more commonly known by its Italian name, "cappuccino." The **Einspanner** is a strong black coffee heaped with whipped cream and sometimes a dash of chocolate shavings. **Eiskaffee,** or hot coffee with vanilla ice cream, is refreshing on hot summer days.

Vienna's specialty coffee drinks combine espresso with a variety of liqueurs for caffeine with a punch. Some cafes serve the **Maria-Theresia,** with orange liqueur, or the **Pharisär,** with rum and sugar. Other liqueurs include **Marillen** (apricot) and **Kirsche** (cherry). Or, for a protein boost, try the milk-less mocha **Kaisermelange,** stirred with brandy and an egg yolk. Be prepared to shell out €6-7 for an indulgent delight.

gardens behind the palace contain a **labyrinth** and a profusion of manicured greenery, flowers, and statuary. *(Park open daily 6am-dusk. Labyrinth open daily July-Aug. 9am-7pm; Apr.-June and Sept. 9am-6pm; Oct. 9am-5pm; Nov. closed. Park free. Labyrinth €2.90, students €2.40.)*

KARLSKIRCHE. Situated in Karlspl., **Karlskirche** (the Church of St. Borromeo) is an eclectic masterpiece. Under restoration as of 2007, it combines a Neoclassical portico with a Baroque dome. An elevator takes visitors up to a somewhat precarious platform with a dazzling new view over the church. Climb the stairs to view the city from the highest point, although the view is somewhat obscured by grates. *(IV, Kreuzherreng. 1. U1, 2, or 4 to Karlspl. ☎01 504 61 87. Open M-Sa 9am-12:30pm and 1-7pm, Su 1-7pm. €6, students €4.)*

ZENTRALFRIEDHOF. The Viennese describe the Central Cemetery as half the size of Geneva but twice as lively. **Tor II** (Gate 2) contains the tombs of Beethoven, Brahms, Schubert, Strauss, and an honorary monument to Mozart, whose true resting place is an unmarked pauper's grave in the **Cemetery of Saint Marx,** III, Leberstr. 6-8. **Tor I** (Gate 1) holds the old **Jewish Cemetery,** where many headstones are cracked and neglected. *(XI, Simmeringer Hauptstr. 234. Tram #71 from Schwarzenbergpl. or Simmering. ☎01 76 04 10; www.friedhoefewien.at. Open daily May-Aug. 7am-7pm; Mar.-Apr. and Sept.-Oct. 7am-6pm; Nov.-Feb. 8am-5pm. Free.)*

MUSEUMS

With a museum around every corner, Vienna can exhaust even the most zealous of travelers. The **Vienna Card** (€19), available at the tourist office, large U-bahn stops, and most hostels, tries to make the task a little easierl it entitles holders to museum and transit discounts for 72hr.

ÖSTERREICHISCHE GALERIE (AUSTRIAN GALLERY). The grounds of **Schloß Belvedere** house the Österreichische Galerie's two museums, along with a classic Austrian garden and a carriage museum. Home to Klimt's **The Kiss** and one of David's portraits of Napoleon on horseback, the **Oberes (Upper) Belvedere** supplements its magnificent collection of 19th- and 20th-century art with the Austrian Museum of Baroque Art and the Austrian Museum of Medieval Art. *(III, Prinz-Eugen-Str. 27. Walk from the Südbahnhof or take tram D from Schwarzenbergpl. to Schloß Belvedere, or take U1 to Suditorolerplatz. €9.50, students €6. MC/V.)* The **Unteres (Lower) Belvedere** hosts temporary exhibits of contemporary art. *(Unteres Belvedere, III, Rennweg 6. Tram #71 from Schwarzenbergpl. to Unteres Belvedere. €9.50, students*

€6. Both Belvederes ☎01 79 55 70; www.belvedere.at. Open daily 10am-6pm. Lower Belvedere open W 10am-9pm. Combo ticket €13.50, students €9.50.)

KUNST HAUS WIEN. Artist-environmentalist **Friedenreich Hundertwasser** built this museum without straight lines—even the floor bends. Arboreal "tree tenants" grow from the windowsills and the top floor. Check out his designs for a model city and a new flag for New Zealand. *(III, Untere Weißgerberstr. 13. U1 or 4 to Schwedenpl., then tram 1 to Radetzkypl. ☎01 712 04 91; www.kunsthauswien.at. Open daily 10am-7pm. Each exhibit €9, both €12; students €7/9. MC/V.)*

ÖSTERREICHISCHES MUSEUM FÜR ANGEWANDTE KUNST (MAK). This intimate, eclectic museum is dedicated to design. It examines the smooth curves of Thonet bentwood chairs, the intricacies of Venetian glass, and the steel heights of modern architecture. *(I, Stubenring 5. U3: Stubentor. ☎01 71 13 60; www.mak.at. Open Tu 10am-midnight, W-Su 10am-6pm. €7.90, students €5.50. Sa and holidays free. MC/V.)*

KUNSTHISTORISCHES MUSEUM (MUSEUM OF FINE ARTS). One of the world's largest art collections boasts Italian paintings, Classical art, and an Egyptian burial chamber. The main building contains works by Venetian and Flemish masters. Across the street in the Neue Burg wing of the Hofburg Palace, the **Ephesos Museum** exhibits findings from excavations in Turkey. The **Sammlung alter Musikinstrumente** includes Beethoven's harpsichord and Mozart's piano. *(U2: Museumsquartier. Across from the Burgring and Heldenpl., to the right of Maria Theresienpl. ☎01 525 24 41; www.khm.at. Main building open Tu-Th 10am-9pm, F-Su 10am-6pm; Ephesos and Sammlung open M and W-Su 10am-6pm. €10, students €7.50. Audio tour €3. AmEx/MC/V.)*

MUSEUMSQUARTIER. Central Europe's largest collection of modern art, the **Museum Moderner Kunst (MUMOK)** highlights Classical Modernism, Fluxus, Photo Realism, Pop Art, and Viennese Actionism in a building made from basalt lava. *(Open M-W and F-Su 10am-6pm, Th 10am-9pm. €9, students €6.50. AmEx/MC/V.)* The **Leopold Museum** has the world's largest Schiele collection. *(Open M, W-Su 10am-7pm, Th 10am-9pm. €10, students €6.50. AmEx/MC/V.)* Themed exhibits of contemporary artists fill **Kunsthalle Wien.** *(U2: Museumsquartier. ☎01 52 57 00; www.mqw.at. Open M-W and F-Su 10am-7pm, Th 10am-10pm. Exhibition Hall 1 €8.50; students M €7, W-Su €6. Exhibition Hall 2 €6/3.50/4.50. Both €11/7/9. "Art" combination ticket admits visitors to all 2 museums; €22. "Duo" ticket admits to Leopold and MUMOK; €17, students €11.)*

FREUD MUSEUM. See the home of the founder of psychoanalysis, Sigmund Freud. It contains bric-a-brac, like his report cards and certificate of circumcision—potential clues to all his hang-ups? Don't bring your mother along... *(IX, Bergg. 19. U2: Schottentor. ☎01 319 15 96; www.freud-museum.at. Open daily July-Sept. 9am-6pm; Oct.-June 9am-5pm. €7, students €4.50. MC/V.)*

ENTERTAINMENT

Many of classical music's greats lived, composed, and performed in Vienna. Beethoven, Haydn, and Mozart wrote their best-known masterpieces here. A century later, Berg, Schönberg, and Webern revolutionized the music world. Today, Vienna hosts many budget performances, though prices rise in the summer. The **Bundestheaterkasse,** I, Hanuschg. 3, sells tickets for the Staatsoper, the Volksoper, and the Burgtheater. (☎01 514 44 78 80. Open from June to mid-Aug. M-F 10am-2pm; from mid-Aug. to June M-F 8am-6pm, Sa-Su 9am-noon.)

Staatsoper, I, Opernring 2 (☎01 514 44 22 50; www.wiener-staatsoper.at). Vienna's premier opera performs nearly every night Sept.-June. No shorts. Seats €3.50-254. 500 standing-room tickets go on sale 80min. before every show (1 per person; €2-3.50);

arrive 2hr. before curtain. Box office in the foyer open M-F 9am until 1hr. before curtain, Sa 9am-noon; 1st Sa of each month and during Advent 9am-5pm. MC/V.

Wiener Philharmoniker Orchestra (☎01 505 65 25; www.wienerphilharmoniker.at). The Philharmonic plays in the Musikverein, Austria's premier concert hall. To purchase tickets, visit the box office, Bösendorferstr. 12, well in advance of performances. Tickets also available at Lothinringerstrasse 20. MC/V.

NIGHTLIFE

With one of the highest bar-to-cobblestone ratios in the world, Vienna is a great place to party if you know where to look. Take U1 or 4 to Schwedenpl., which will drop you within blocks of the **Bermuda Dreieck** (Bermuda Triangle), a hot clubbing area. If you make it out alive, head down **Rotenturmstraße** toward Stephansdom or walk around the area between the synagogue and **Ruprechtskirche.** Slightly outside the Ring, the streets off **Burggasse** and **Stiftgasse** in District VII and the **university quarter** in Districts XIII and IX have outdoor courtyards and hip bars. For listings, pick up the indispensable *Falter* (€2.60).

Chelsea, VIII, Lerchenfeldergürtel 29-31. U6: Thaliastr. or Josefstädterstr. (☎01 407 93 09; www.chelsea.co.at), under the U-Bahn between the 2 stops. Austrian and international bands pack this underground club to the brim twice a week, while weekend DJs spin techno-pop. Concerts start at 10pm. ½L beer €3.50. Cover €6-13 for performances, bar free. Happy hour 4-5pm. Open M-Sa 6pm-4am, Su 4pm-3am. Cash only.

Siebensternbraeu, VII, Siebensterngasse 19 (☎01 523 86 97; www.7stern.at), between Stiftgasse and Kirchengasse. This brewhouse has a Bavarian feel and beer garden to match. Traditional Austrian fare along with beer brewed in the massive kettles at the center of the establishment. 7 varieties of home-brewed beer €3.50 per ½L. Food €7-16. Open T-Su 11am-midnight. Garden and kitchen open until 11pm. AmEx/MC/V.

Krah Krah, I, Rabensteig. 8 (☎01 533 81 93; www.krah-krah.at). A Bermuda Dreieck bar, Krah Krah has 49 beer varieties, including many lesser-known Austrian brews. Be careful with the Kulmbach Kulminator 28, the "world's strongest beer" (0.3L, €4.90) which has been known to destroy happy-go-lucky backpackers. Happy hour M-F 3:30-5:30pm. Open M-Sa 11am-2am, Su 11am-1:30am. MC/V.

Das Möbel, VII, Burgg. 10 (☎01 524 94 97; www.das-moebel.at). U2 or 3: Volkstheater. An artsy crowd chats on metal couches and Swiss-army tables, all created by designers and for sale. Don't leave without seeing (and sullying) the post-modern bathroom. Internet free for 15min., €0.90 per 15min. thereafter. Open daily 11am-1am. Cash only.

Flex, I, Donaulände (☎01 533 75 25; www.flex.at), near the Schottenring U-Bahn station (U2 or U4) down by the Danube. Grab a beer or bring your own and sit by the river with other partiers. DJs start spinning techno, reggae, house, ska, or electronic at 11pm in the most famous dance club in the city. Beer €3.50. Cover €4-10, free after 3:30am. Open daily 8pm-4am. Cash only.

Volksgarten Disco, I, Burgring 1 (☎01 532 42 41; www.volksgarten.at). U2: Volkstheater. Pool, dance floor, and bangin' young crowd make this one of Vienna's most exclusive clubs. Cover €5-15. Open June-Aug. M 8pm-2am, Th 8pm-4am, F 11pm-6am, Sa 9pm-6am; Sept.-May M 8pm-2am, Th 8pm-4am, F and Sa 11pm-6am. AmEx/MC/V.

passage, I, the corner of Burgring. and Babenbergerstr. (☎01 961 88 00; www.sunshine.at). What used to be an underground walkway is now a collection of small but fashionable nightclubs. Getting in can be difficult—dress to impress. Club Cosmopolitan plays soul music, Club Fusion spins house, and disco blares from the Bachelor Club. Hours vary by season; check the website. Cash only.

Mango, VI, Laimgrubeng. 3 (☎01 920 47 14; www.mangobar.at). U2: Museumsquartier. Mango advertises itself as "the place where young gays meet," and it's easy to see why people are drawn to its casual atmosphere, golden walls, and pop music. Open daily 9pm-4am. Cash only.

Why Not, I, Tiefer Graben 22 (☎01 920 47 14; www.why-not.at). Gay and lesbian clientele dances late into the night amid 4 discoballs in Vienna's only GLBT disco. Drinks from €3. Cover after midnight €9 includes 2 drinks. Open F-Sa 10pm-4am. Cash only.

FESTIVALS

Vienna hosts several important festivals, mostly musical. The **Wiener Festwochen** (May-June) has a diverse program of concerts, exhibitions, and plays. (☎01 58 92 20; www.festwochen.or.at.) In May, over 4000 people attend **Lifeball,** Europe's largest AIDS charity event and Vienna's biggest gay celebration. With the Lifeball Style Police threatening to dispose of under-dressed guests (make-up and hair-styling are musts), come looking like you deserve to mix and mingle with Bill Clinton, Elton John, and other celebrities. (☎01 595 56 77; www.lifeball.org. Tickets €75-150.) Democrats host **The Danube Island Festival** in late June, which celebrates with fireworks and concerts, hosting up to to a million partiers in years past. (☎01 535 35 35; www.donauinselfest.at. Free.) The *Staatsoper* and *Volkstheater* host **Jazzfest Wien** (☎01 503 56 47; www.viennajazz.org) during the first weeks of July.

BELGIUM
(BELGIQUE, BELGIË)

Surrounded by France, Germany, and The Netherlands, Belgium is a convergence of different cultures. Appropriately, the small country attracts an array of travelers: chocoholics, Europhilés, and art-lovers all come together in Belgium. Sweet-toothed foreigners flock to Brussels, the home of filled chocolate, to nibble confections from one of 2000 cocoa-oriented specialty shops and to brush shoulders with diplomats en route to European Union and NATO headquarters. In Flanders, Gothic towers surround cobblestone squares, while visitors below admire Old Masters' canvases and guzzle monk-brewed ale. Wallonie has less tourist infrastructure, but the caves of the Lesse Valley and the forested hills of the Ardennes compensate with their stunning natural beauty.

DISCOVER BELGIUM: SUGGESTED ITINERARY

ONE WEEK. Plan for at least two days in **Brussels** (p. 80). Head north to the elegant boulevards of **Antwerp,** then go west to the winding streets and canals of romantic **Bruges** (p. 86).

LIFE AND TIMES

HISTORY

Charlemagne ruled Belgium as part of his **Holy Roman Empire** around AD 800, but squabbles among grandsons following his death divided the country into separate regions: **Flanders** (p. 86), the Flemish-speaking province in the north, and **Wallonie,** the French-speaking province in the south. From the 15th century on, conquering powers—including Austria, Denmark, and France—attempted to unite and rule Belgium, but none could quell the area's aversion to foreign occupation. In the early 1800s, the people of the north and south provinces cooperated to launch a rebellion against the Dutch king who controlled the country. They cited religious differences between Protestant rulers and the Catholic population as well as competing economic ideologies regarding trade to support their coup. In 1831, the Belgians emerged victorious as rulers of a new, independent country committed to tariff-protected trade, albeit certainly one with intact regional divisions.

The new **constitutional monarchy,** under the reign of Belgian **Leopold I,** spent its first year fending off Dutch invaders craving a rematch. However, France stepped in, forcing the Dutch to back off. By 1839, all major European powers recognized Belgium as sovereign and neutral, the latter becoming crucial to its history. Under the rule of Leopold I and **Leopold II,** who rose to power in

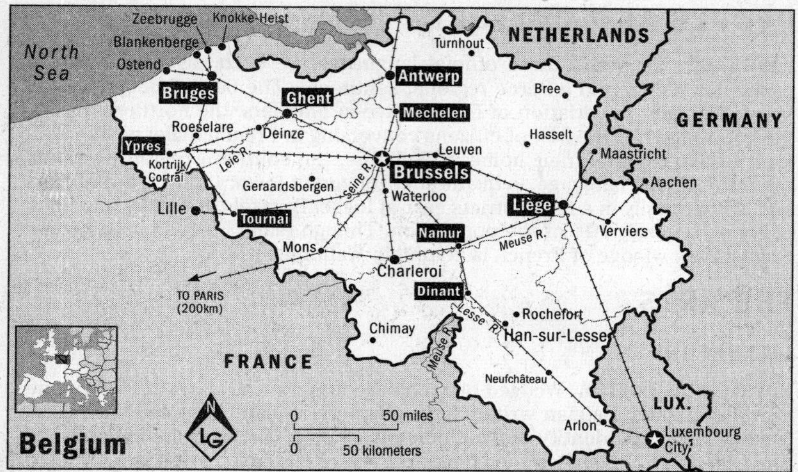

1865, Belgium became a major industrial power as well as an imperial international player. In 1885, Belgium acquired the **Congo Free State,** which Leopold II governed as personal property. He proved a grossly negligent ruler, brutally oppressing and slaughtering the native Congolese. Conversely, in Europe, Leopold instituted progressive reforms by introducing universal male suffrage.

German armies invaded Belgium during both **World Wars,** upsetting the country's neutrality. During WWI, **King Albert I** and his army spent four years in the trenches trying to repel the invaders. When the Nazis invaded in 1940, **King Leopold III** surrendered almost immediately. Post-war criticism of this move made Leopold unpopular, forcing him to hand power to his son **Baudouin** in 1951. Following WWII, Belgium shed much of its former neutrality by joining **NATO,** which is headquartered in Brussels, and the **Benelux** economic union with the Netherlands and Luxembourg. Baudouin, who ruled until 1993, continued this trend with Belgium's entrance into the European Coal and Steel Community, the predecessor to the **European Union.**

TODAY

Under the Belgian Constitution of 1831, the Belgian king, currently **Albert II,** is the official head of state, accountable to the democratically elected parliament. The prime minister, currently **Yves Leterme,** conducts day-to-day affairs. He is appointed by the monarch but must come from the majority party, which currently is the **Christian Democratic and Flemish** party. Leterme attempted to resign on July 14, 2008, but his resignation was rejected by Albert II. Internal divisions fall along language lines: constitutional amendments in 1994 made Belgium a federal state with local governments centered in Flemish-speaking Flanders, French-speaking Wallonie, and bilingual **Brussels** (p. 80). Even the powerful political parties, the **Socialists** on the left, the **Christian Democrats** in the center, and the **Liberals** on the right, organize through separate Flemish- and French-speaking branches. Since the late 1970s, Belgium's far-right parties have won votes on nationalist and anti-immigrant platforms.

PEOPLE AND CULTURE

LANGUAGE. Belgium's three official languages are each associated with a particular region and a fierce regional sentiment. The 60% of Belgians who speak Flemish—a variation of Dutch—live in Flanders, the northern part of the country, while the 31% of citizens conversing in French dialects, like Walloon Brabant, make their home in Wallonie, the southern region. German, the third official language, is the mother tongue of fewer than 1% of Belgians and is heard only in a few districts east of Liège. Brussels, officially bilingual, is home to nearly 10% of the population. Though many Flemish speak some English, knowledge of French is helpful in Wallonie.

THE ARTS

LITERATURE

NOVELS AND POETRY. Wedged between the literary traditions of France and the Netherlands, Belgian writers have characteristically grappled with questions of language, identity, and nationhood. In 1867, **Charles de Coster** published *The Legend of Ulenspiegel*, an allegorical tale of a Flemish prankster trying to free himself from the control of a Spanish king. The book became a rallying cry for Flemish regionalism, although no one missed the irony that the tale was written in French. In 1937, the **Monday Group** of Surrealist authors proclaimed that Belgian literature did not exist, and that Francophone Belgian writers should embrace the French canon. Francophonie—French literature outside France—has become a theme of Belgian literature, and many Belgian writers are expatriates. Surrealist poet **Henri Michaux** traveled in Africa, even becoming a French citizen at the end of his life. Fictionalized versions of her own forays into Asia pervade young novelist **Amélie Nothomb's** satirical stories.

COMIC STRIPS AND MYSTERIES. In the 20th century, Belgian talent made its presence known in comic strips and detective novels. Perhaps it was British writer Agatha Christie's tribute to this tradition that her famous moustached detective, **Hercule Poirot,** was Belgian. In Brussels, museums are dedicated to the history of cartooning, specifically to the work of **Georges Remi,** better known as Hergé, creator of **Tintin,** and to **Peyo,** papa of the **Smurfs.** The enigmatic **Georges Simenon** wrote a 76-novel mystery series on cunning **Commissaire Maigret.**

VISUAL ARTS

ARCHITECTURE. The 14th-century cathedrals of Bruges and Ghent exemplify Gothic architecture. Belgium's own contribution came much later, when **Victor Horta,** a native of Ghent, reacted against Classicism's heavy formality to champion a lighter Art Nouveau style in the late 19th century. Enthusiasm for Horta's trademark curvy, asymmetrical lines waned, however, by World War I, and many of his buildings were demolished. Exhibits at the **Musée Horta** in Brussels reflect Horta's particular style.

ON THE CANVAS. As a member of the Flemish Primitive school of painting, **Jan van Eyck** excelled beyond his peers and transformed the art of oil painting, lavishing minute detail on his canvases without sacrificing the tenderness of his presentation. His best-known painting, the 1432 *Adoration of the Mystic Lamb*, adorns the altarpiece of St-Baafskathedraal in Ghent. **Pieter Bruegel the Elder** is known as "peasant Bruegel" for his non-sacred works, as depicted in pieces like the 1567 *Peasant Wedding Feast.* **Peter Paul Rubens** remains Antwerp's artistic hero. In the early 17th century, he represented the female body in his Italian Renaissance-style canvases, establishing a specific and enduring ideal of beauty. In the 20th century, **René Magritte** gained fame with his Surrealist paintings that portrayed jarring juxtapositions of everyday objects. His most famous painting, *The Betrayal of Images* (1929), pairs the image of a pipe with the caption, *ceci n'est pas une pipe* ("this is not a pipe").

HOLIDAYS AND FESTIVALS

Holidays: New Year's Day (Jan. 1); Epiphany (Jan. 6); Good Friday (Apr. 11, Apr. 2); Easter (Apr. 12-13, Apr. 4-5); Ascension (May 1); Labor Day (May 1); Pentecost (May 11-12, May 23-24); Corpus Christi (May 22); Flemish Community Day (July 11); National Day (July 21); Assumption (Aug. 15); French Community Day (Sept. 27); All Saints' Day (Nov. 1); Armistice Day (Nov. 11); Christmas (Dec. 25-26).

Festivals: Ghent hosts **Gentse Feesten** (mid to late July; www.gentsefeesten.be), which brings *al fresco* theater, puppet performances, the 10 Days Off (www.10daysoff.be) dance festival, and free music and food to the city's streets. Antwerp runs films, circuses, plays, and concerts in its **Zomer van Antwerpen** festival (mid-July to mid-August; www.zva.be). Bruges's **Cactus Festival** (mid-July; www.cactusfestival.be) draws alt-pop and hip-hop acts for a weekend, with nearby camping available. Eastern Belgium's **Pukkelpop** (mid-Aug.; www.pukkelpop.be) is a festival for the alternative music set.

ESSENTIALS

FACTS AND FIGURES

OFFICIAL NAME: Kingdom of Belgium.

CAPITAL: Brussels.

MAJOR CITIES: Antwerp, Ghent, Liège.

POPULATION: 10,584,534.

LAND AREA: 30,500 sq. km.t

TIME ZONE: GMT +1.

LANGUAGES: Dutch (60%), French (40%).

RELIGIONS: Roman Catholic (75%), Protestant (25%).

FRENCH FRIES: Invented in Belgium during the 18th century, despite what the name suggests. Served with mayonnaise.

VARIETIES OF BEER: Over 500.

WHEN TO GO

May, June, and September are the best months to visit Belgium, with temperatures around 18-22°C (64-72°F) in Brussels and Antwerp, and approximately 6°C (10°F) higher in Liège and Ghent. July and August tend to be rainy and hot. Winters are cool, typically 2-7°C (36-45°F), and somewhat colder in the Ardennes.

DOCUMENTS AND FORMALITIES

EMBASSIES AND CONSULATES. Foreign embassies in Belgium are in Brussels. Belgian embassies abroad include: **Australia** and **New Zealand,** 19 Arkana St., Yarralumla, ACT 2600 (☎02 62 73 25 02; www.diplomatie.be/canberra); **Canada,** 360 Albert St., Ste. 820, Ottawa, ON, K1R 7X7 (☎613-236-7267; www.diplomatie.be/ottawa); **Ireland,** 2 Shrewsbury Rd., Ballsbridge, Dublin 4 (☎01 205 71 00; www.diplomatie.be/dublin); **UK,** 17 Grosvenor Crescent, London, SW1X 7EE (☎020 7470 3700; www.diplomatie.be/london); **US,** 3330 Garfield St., NW, Washington, D.C., 20008 (☎202-333-6900; www.diplobel.us).

VISA AND ENTRY INFORMATION. EU citizens do not need a visa. Citizens of Australia, Canada, New Zealand, and the US do not need a visa for stays of up to 90 days, beginning upon entry into any of the countries in the EU's freedom-of-movement zone. For stays longer than 90 days, all non-EU citizens need visas (around US$85), available at Belgian consulates. Visit www.diplobel.us. For US citizens, visas are issued a few weeks after application submission.

TOURIST SERVICES AND MONEY

EMERGENCY	**Ambulance:** ☎100. **Fire:** ☎100. **Police:** ☎101.

TOURIST OFFICES. **Bureaux de Tourisme,** marked by green-and-white or blue signs labeled "i," are supplemented by **Info Jeunes/Info-Jeugd,** info centers that help people find work and secure accommodations in Wallonie and Flanders, respectively. The **Belgian Tourist Information Center (BBB),** Grasmarkt 63, Brussels (☎025 04 03 90), has national tourist info. The weekly English-language *Bulletin* (www.thebulletin.be; €2.80 at newsstands) has cultural events and news.

MONEY. The **euro (€)** has replaced the Belgian **franc** as the unit of currency in Belgium. **ATMs** generally offer the best exchange rates. **Credit cards** are used widely throughout Belgium, most notably in the country's major cities. A bare-bones day in Belgium might cost €35, while a more comfortable day runs about €50-65. Tipping is not common, though rounding up is. Restaurant bills usually include a service charge, although outstanding service warrants an extra 5-10% tip. Give bathroom attendants €0.25 and movie and theater attendants €0.50.

BUSINESS HOURS. **Banks** are generally open Monday through Friday 9am-4pm but often close for lunch midday. **Stores** are open Monday through Saturday 10am-5pm or 6pm; stores sometimes close on Mondays, but may be open Sundays in summer. Most **sights** are open Sundays but closed Mondays; in Bruges and Tournai, museums close Tuesdays or Wednesdays.

TRANSPORTATION

BY PLANE. Most international flights land at **Brussels International Airport** (**BRU;** ☎27 53 87 98; www.brusselsairport.be), located roughly 20min. away from Brussels. Budget airlines, like **Ryanair** and **easyJet,** fly out of **Brussels South Charleroi Airport** (**CRL;** ☎71 25 12 11; www.charleroi-airport.com), about 1hr. south of Brussels, and Brussels International Airport. The Belgian national airline, **Brussels Airlines** (☎070 35 11 11, US ☎516-740-5200, UK ☎087 0735 2345; www.brusselsairlines.com), flies to Brussels from most major European cities.

BY TRAIN AND BUS. The extensive and reliable **Belgian Rail** (www.b-rail.be) network traverses the country. **Eurail** is valid in Belgium. A **Benelux Tourrail Pass** (US$210, under 26 US$160) allows five days of unlimited train travel in a one-month period in Belgium, the Netherlands, and Luxembourg. Travelers with time to explore Belgium's nooks and crannies might consider the **Rail Pass** (€70) or Go Pass (under 26 only; €45), both of which allow 10 single trips within the country over a one-year period and can be transferred among travelers. Because trains are widely available, buses are used primarily for local transport. Single tickets are €1.50, and are cheaper when bought in packs.

BY FERRY. **P&O Ferries** (☎070 70 77 71, UK ☎087 0598 03 33; www.poferries.com) from Hull, BRI to Zeebrugge, north of Bruges (12hr., 7pm, from €150).

BY CAR, BIKE, AND THUMB. Belgium honors drivers' licenses from Australia, Canada, the EU, and the US. New Zealanders must contact the New Zealand Automobile Association (☎0800 822 422; www.aa.co.nz) for an International Driving Permit. **Speed limits** are 120kph on motorways, 90kph on main roads, and 50kph elsewhere. **Biking** is popular, and many roads in Flanders have bike lanes. Wallonie has started to convert old railroad beds into bike paths. **Hitchhiking** is illegal in Belgium. *Let's Go* does not recommend hitchhiking.

KEEPING IN TOUCH

PHONE CODES	**Country code:** 32. **International dialing prefix:** 00. For more info on how to place international calls, see **Inside Back Cover.**

TELEPHONE. Most pay phones require a **phone card** (from €5), available at post offices, supermarkets, and newsstands. Whenever possible, use a calling card for international phone calls, as long-distance rates for national phone services are often very high. Calls are cheapest 6:30pm-8am and weekends. **Mobile phones** are an increasingly popular and economical option. Major mobile carriers include Vodafone, Base, and Mobistar. When dialing within a city, the city code must still be dialed. For operator assistance within Belgium, dial ☎12 07; for international, dial ☎12 04 (€0.25). Direct-dial access numbers for calling out of Belgium include: **AT&T** (☎0800 100 10); **British Telecom** (☎0800 100 24); **Canada Direct** (☎0800 100 19); **Telecom New Zealand** (☎0800 100 64).

MAIL. Post offices are open Monday to Friday 9am-5pm, with a midday break. Sent within Belgium, a letter (up to 50g) costs €0.46 for non-priority and €0.52 for priority. Within the EU, costs are €0.80, and for the rest of the world €0.90. Additional info is available at www.post.be. Poste Restante available.

ACCOMMODATIONS AND CAMPING

BELGIUM	❶	❷	❸	❹	❺
ACCOMMODATIONS	under €10	€10-20	€21-30	€31-40	over €40

Hotels in Belgium are fairly expensive, with rock-bottom singles from €30 and doubles from €40-45. Belgium's 31 **HI youth hostels** are run by the **Flemish Youth Hostel Federation** (www.vjh.be) in Flanders and **Les Auberges de Jeunesses** (www.laj.be) in Wallonie. Expect to pay around €18 per night, including linens, for modern, basic hostels. Private hostels cost about the same but are usually nicer, although some charge separately for linen. **Hotels** are noticeably more expensive than the nicest hostel; make reservations in advance to secure accommodations. Most receptionists speak some English. Reservations are a good idea, particularly in summer and on weekends. **Campgrounds** charge about €4 per night and are common in Wallonie but not in Flanders. An International Camping Card is unnecessary in Belgium.

FOOD AND DRINK

BELGIUM	❶	❷	❸	❹	❺
FOOD	under €5	€5-9	€10-13	€14-18	over €18

Belgian cuisine, acclaimed but expensive, fuses French and German styles. An evening meal may cost as much as a night's accommodations. Fresh seafood appears in *moules* or *mosselen* (steamed mussels) and *moules frites* (steamed mussels with french fries), the national dishes, which are often tasty and reasonably affordable (€14-20). *Frites* (french fries) are ubiquitous and budget-friendly; Belgians eat them dipped in mayonnaise. Look for *friekots* ("french fry shacks") in Belgian towns. Belgian **beer** is a source of national pride, its consumption a national pastime. More varieties—over 500, ranging from ordinary pilsners (€1) to Trappist ales (€3) brewed by monks—are produced here than in any other country. Beer is even an ingredient in the national dish, *carbonnades flamandes*, a beef stew. Leave room for chocolate **pralines** from Leonidas or Neuhaus and Belgian **waffles** *(gaufres)*, sold on the street and in cafes.

BEYOND TOURISM

Volunteer *(benévolat)* and work opportunities in Belgium focus on its strong international offerings, especially in Brussels, which is home to both NATO and the EU. Private-sector short- and long-term employment is listed at www.jobsabroad.com/Belgium.cfm. A selection of public-sector job and volunteer opportunities is listed below. For more info on opportunities across Europe, see the **Beyond Tourism** chapter, p. 45.

Amnesty International, r. Berckmans 9, 1060 Brussels (☎02 538 8177; www.amnesty-international.be). One of the world's foremost human rights organizations has offices in Brussels. Paid positions and volunteer work available.

The International School of Brussels, Kattenberg-Botisfort 19, Brussels (☎02 661 42 11; www.isb.be). The ISB hires teachers for positions lasting more than one full year Must have permission to work within Belgium.

North Atlantic Treaty Organization (NATO), bd. Leopold III, 1110 Brussels (www.nato.int). Current students and recent graduates (within 1yr.) who are nationals of a NATO member state and fluent in 1 official NATO language (English or French), with a working knowledge of the other, can apply for 6-month internships. Requirements and application details available at www.nato.int/structur/interns/index.html. Application deadlines are far ahead of the program's start dates.

BRUSSELS (BRUXELLES, BRUSSEL) ☎02

The headquarters of NATO and the capital of the European Union, Brussels (pop. 1,200,000) is a dish best served piping hot in your finest china at a banquet full of diplomats and functionaries. Despite their numbers, these civil servants aren't the only ones with claims to Belgium's capital; beneath the drone of parliamentary procedure bustles the spirited clamor of locals and their profound appreciation of *frites*, beer, and whimsy. In a city that juxtaposes old and new, skyscrapers and historic buildings are plastered with three-story comics by local artists. Brussels defiantly remains a colorful city of character and history, much like its symbol, the ever-streaming *Manneken Pis*.

TRANSPORTATION

Flights: Brussels Airport (BRU; ☎090 07 00 00, €0.45 per min.; www.brusselsairport.be) is 14km from the city and accessible by train. **South Charleroi Airport (CRL;** ☎02 71 25 12 11; www.charleroi-airport.com) is 46km outside the city, between

Brussels and Charleroi, and serves a number of European airlines, including **Ryanair.** From the airport, **Bus A** runs to the Charleroi-ZUID train station, where you can catch a train to Brussels. There is also a bus service which goes from the airport to Brussels's Gare du Midi (1hr., buy tickets on board). Timetables can be found on the website.

Trains: (☎02 555 2555; www.sncb.be). All international trains stop at **Gare du Midi;** most also stop at **Gare Centrale** or **Gare du Nord.** Trains run to: **Antwerp** (45min., €6.10); **Bruges** (45min., €12); **Liège** (1hr., €17); **Amsterdam, NTH** (3hr.; €43, under 26 €34); **Cologne, DEU** (2hr.; €26, under 26 €22); **Luxembourg City, LUX** (1hr., €28.80); **Paris, FRA** (1hr., €55-86). **Eurostar** goes to **London, ENG** (2hr., €79-224, with Eurail or Benelux pass from €75, under 26 from €60).

Public Transportation: The **Société des Transports Intercommunaux Bruxellois** (**STIB;**☎090 01 03 10, €0.45 per min.; www.stib.be) runs the **Métro (M), buses,** and **trams** daily from 5:30am-12:30am. 1hr. ticket €1.70, 1-day pass €4.50, 3-day pass €9, 5 trips €7, 10 trips €11.50. Check the website for more info.

HOLD THAT STUB. Always hold on to your receipt or ticket stub to avoid steep fines on public transportation. Although enforcement may appear lax, authorities do conduct spot checks and could charge a fine.

ORIENTATION AND PRACTICAL INFORMATION

Most major attractions are clustered around **Grand-Place,** between the **Bourse** (Stock Market) to the west and the **Parc de Bruxelles** to the east. One **Métro** line circles the city and another bisects it, while efficient **3/4 trams** run north-south. Signs list street names in both French and Flemish; *Let's Go* lists all addresses in French. The concrete hills of Brussels make biking inconvenient, so don't plan on maneuvering through the bustle of the city by bike. Since cars rule the streets, the best way to get around is either by foot or tram.

Tourist Office: Brussels International Tourism and Congress (**BITC;** ☎02 548 0452; www.brures.com). M: Bourse. On Grand-Place in the Town Hall. The official tourist office books accommodations in the city for no charge and sells the **Brussels Card,** which provides free public transport, a city map, and access to 25 museums for 1, 2, or 3 days (€20/28/33). Open daily Easter-Dec. 9am-6pm; Jan.-Easter M-Sa 9am-6pm.

Embassies and Consulates: Australia, 6-8 r. Guimard (☎02 286 0500; www.austemb.be). **Canada,** 2 av. Tervuren (☎02 741 0611; www.international.gc.ca/brussels). **Ireland,** 50 r. Wiertz (☎02 235 6676). **New Zealand,** 1 sq. de Meeus (☎02 512 1040). **UK,** 85 r. d'Arlon (☎02 287 6211; www.british-embassy.be). **US,** 27 bd. du Régent (☎02 508 2111; www.brussels.usembassy.gov).

Currency Exchange: Travelex, Nord Station (☎02 513 2845). Open M-F 10am-5pm, Sa 10am-7pm, Su 10am-4pm.

English-Language Bookstore: Sterling Books, 38 r. du Fossé aux Loups (☎02 223 6223; www.sterlingbooks.be). M: De Brouckère. Largest independent English-language bookstore in Belgium. Open M-Sa 10am-7pm, Su noon-6:30pm. MC/V.

GLBT Resources: The tourist office offers the *Rainbow Map,* which has information on nightlife, hotels, and events.

Laundromat: Wash Club, 68 r. du Marché au Charbon. M: Bourse. Wash €3.50 per 8kg, €7 per 18kg. Open daily 7am-10pm.

Pharmacy: Neos-Bourse Pharmacie, 61 bd. Anspach at r. du Marché aux Poulets (☎02 218 0640). M: Bourse. Open M-Sa 8:30am-6:30pm.

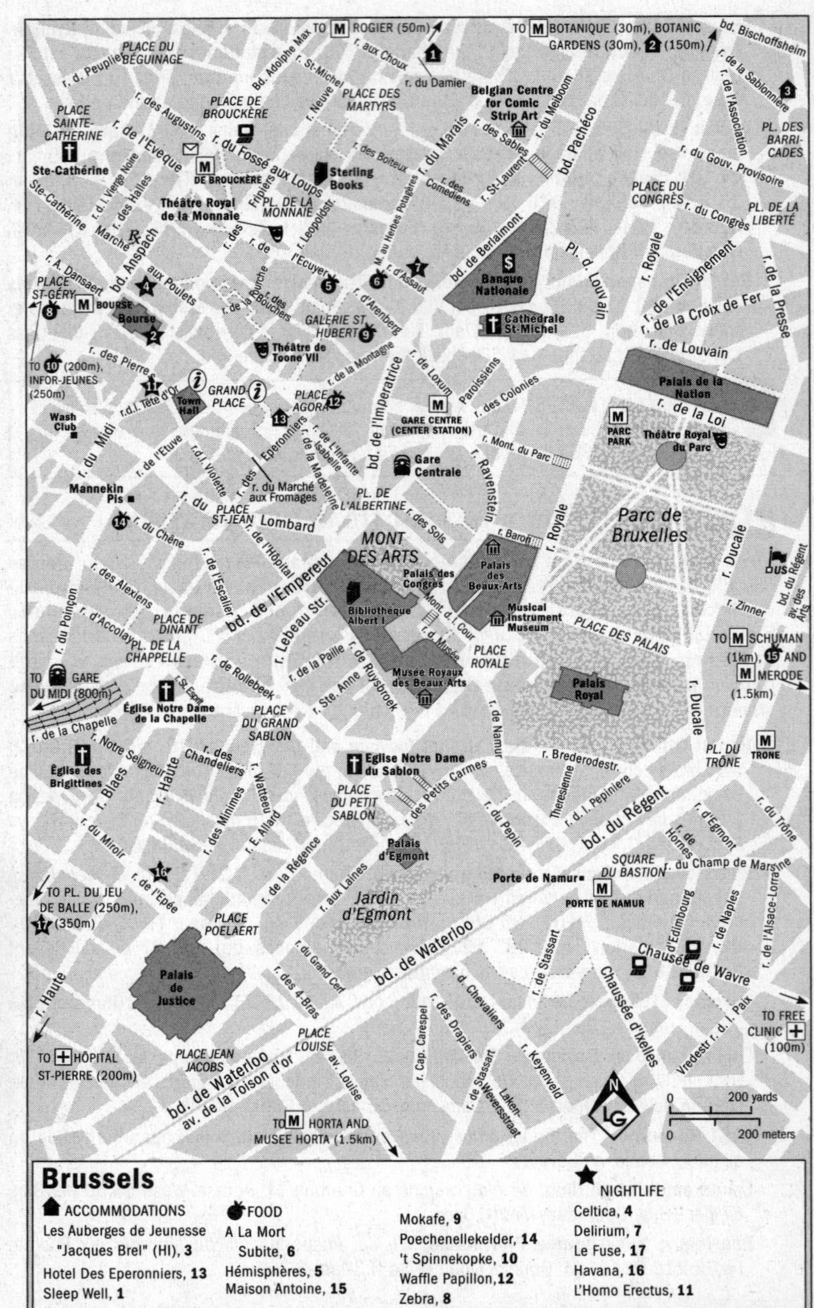

Brussels
ACCOMMODATIONS
Les Auberges de Jeunesse "Jacques Brel" (HI), 3
Hotel Des Eperonniers, 13
Sleep Well, 1
FOOD
A La Mort Subite, 6
Hémisphères, 5
Maison Antoine, 15
Mokafe, 9
Poechenellekelder, 14
't Spinnekopke, 10
Waffle Papillon, 12
Zebra, 8
NIGHTLIFE
Celtica, 4
Delirium, 7
Le Fuse, 17
Havana, 16
L'Homo Erectus, 11
TO M ROGIER (50m)
TO M BOTANIQUE (30m), BOTANIC GARDENS (30m), 2 (150m)
PLACE DU BÉGUINAGE
PLACE SAINTE-CATHERINE
Ste-Cathérine
PLACE DE BROUCKÈRE
DE BROUCKÈRE
PLACE DES MARTYRS
Belgian Centre for Comic Strip Art
Sterling Books
Théâtre Royal de la Monnaie
PL. DE LA MONNAIE
PLACE ST-GÉRY
BOURSE
Bourse
GALERIE ST HUBERT
Théâtre de Toone VII
Banque Nationale
Cathédrale St-Michel
PLACE DU CONGRÈS
PL. DE LA LIBERTÉ
PL. DES BARRICADES
Palais de la Nation
TO 10 (200m), INFOR-JEUNES (250m)
Wash Club
Town Hall
GRAND-PLACE
PLACE AGORA
GARE CENTRE (CENTER STATION)
Gare Centrale
PARC PARK
Théâtre Royal du Parc
Parc de Bruxelles
Mannekin Pis
PLACE ST-JEAN
PL. DE L'ALBERTINE
MONT DES ARTS
Palais des Congrès
Bibliothèque Albert I
Palais des Beaux-Arts
Musical Instrument Museum
PLACE DES PALAIS
PLACE ROYALE
Musée Royaux des Beaux-Arts
Palais Royal
TO M SCHUMAN (1km), 15 AND M MERODE (1.5km)
PLACE DE DINANT
PL. DE LA CHAPPELLE
TO GARE DU MIDI (800m)
Église Notre Dame de la Chapelle
PLACE DU GRAND SABLON
Église des Brigittines
Église Notre Dame du Sablon
PLACE DU PETIT SABLON
PL. DU TRÔNE
TRONE
Palais d'Egmont
Jardin d'Egmont
SQUARE DU BASTION
Porte de Namur
PORTE DE NAMUR
TO PL. DU JEU DE BALLE (250m), 17 (350m)
PLACE POELAERT
Palais de Justice
PLACE LOUISE
PLACE JEAN JACOBS
TO HÔPITAL ST-PIERRE (200m)
TO FREE CLINIC (100m)
TO M HORTA AND MUSEE HORTA (1.5km)
bd. de Waterloo
av. de la Toison d'or
av. Louise
Chaussée de Wavre
Chaussée d'Ixelles
bd. du Régent
bd. de l'Empereur
bd. Anspach
bd. Pachéco
bd. de Berlaimont
bd. de l'Imperatrice
r. Royale
r. Ducale
r. de la Loi
r. de Louvain
r. Ravenstein
r. du Midi
r. Haute
r. Blaes
0 200 yards
0 200 meters

Medical Services: St. Luc's, 10 av. Hippocrate (☎02 764 1111), near Grand-Place. **Clinique St Etienne Kliniek,** 100 r. du Meridien (☎02 225 9111).

Internet: Internet cafes with phone booths can be found on ch. de Wavre. M: Porte de Namur. Most charge €1-2 per hr.

Post Office: (☎02 226 9700; www.laposte.be). At the corner of bd. Anspach and r. des Augustins. M: De Brouckère. Open M-F 8am-7pm, Sa 10:30am-6:30pm. **Poste Restante.**

NO LADIES' CHOICE. Women navigating Brussels on their own are often the target of unwanted advances from male admirers. While sexual harassment is illegal in Belgium, isolated incidents are rarely prosecuted. Consider venturing out with a companion.

ACCOMMODATIONS

Lodging is much cheaper in Brussels than in other European capitals, but can be difficult to find, especially on weekends in summer. Overall, accommodations are well-kept and centrally located. The **BITC** (see **Practical Information,** p. 81) books rooms for no fee, and sometimes offers discounts.

Sleep Well, 23 r. du Damier (☎02 218 5050; www.sleepwell.be). M: Rogier. "Star" service is similar to staying in a hotel (visitors get rooms with private bath and TV), while "non-Star" service is like being in a hostel. Whichever you choose, the bar, pool table, lounge, and colorful common spaces make it a fun place to be. Breakfast and linens included. Free storage. Laundry €2.50. Lockout for non-Star 11am-3pm. Check-in 3pm. Check-out 11am. Non-star dorms €18-23; singles €30; doubles €54; triples €72. Star singles €42; doubles €60, triples €85. Discounts after 1st night for all non-Star rooms except singles. MC/V. ❷

Les Auberges de Jeunesse "Jacques Brel" (HI), 30 r. de la Sablonnière (☎02 218 0187). M: Botanique. Spacious rooms surround a courtyard with a picturesque fountain. Breakfast and linens included. Bring lock and towel. Free laundry. Free internet 7pm-midnight. Reception 8am-1am. Lockout noon-3pm. Dorms €19-21; singles €34; doubles €52; triples and quads €63-84. €3 HI discount. MC/V. ❷

FOOD

Brussels has earned its reputation as one of the culinary capitals of Europe, although the city's restaurants are often more suited to the five-star set than to the student traveler. Inexpensive eateries cluster outside **Grand-Place.** Vendors along **Rue du Marché aux Fromages** to the south hawk cheap Greek and Middle Eastern food until late at night, while the smell of lobster and seafood permeates the air on **Rue des Bouchers.** *Frites* vendors are scattered throughout the city and offer mountains of golden fries in white paper cones for around €3. An **AD Delhaize** supermarket is on the corner of bd. Anspach and r. du Marché aux Poulets. (M: Bourse. Open M-Th and Sa 9am-8pm, F 9am-9pm, Su 9am-6pm.) **Grocery stores** such as **Carrefour** can be found throughout the city and are a great way to save while still getting quality Belgian treats like their famous chocolates and **waffles** (you can get about 10 for the price of one from vendors).

Poechenellekelder, 5 r. du Chêne (☎02 511 9262; www.poechenellekelder.com). If the ongoing trickle of water from *Manneken Pis* makes you parched, head across the street for a drink amid hanging marionettes in this 3-story bar. Opt for outdoor seating to watch the tourists giggle at the miniscule statue while you bask in the sunlight enjoying

WAFFLING THE ISSUE

At the base of the budget tourist's food pyramid in Belgium lies an auspicious dietary group: the waffle (*gaufre* in French, *wafel* in Dutch). There are two types of Belgian waffles, both made on such particular waffle irons that they can not be made well elsewhere.

Brussels waffles are flat and more or less rectangular. They're light and airy, and bear some resemblance to ones eaten in the US (the kind served at diner brunches, not the ones that emerge from the freezer, pop out of the toaster, and beg to be drowned in high fructose corn syrup). Belgian recipes tend to use beaten egg whites and yeast as leavening agents, which give them their light, crisp texture. **De Lièges** waffles, ubiquitous on Belgian streets, are generally smaller, sweeter, and denser than their counterparts, and have a crunchy caramelized-sugar crust.

Pause at a cafe for a Brussels waffle, and savor it with a knife and fork. Approach a street vendor for a hand-held Liège waffle and continue to wander (in search of your next waffle?). Both can be topped with chocolate, fruit, or ice cream, or dusted with powdered sugar. Waffles generally cost about €1.50, though prices mount with the toppings. Since you can't visit Belgium without sampling its waffles, you might as well indulge!

a drink. Coffee (€2-6) is supplemented by a menu of *tartines* (open-faced sandwiches; €4-7) and *pâté* (€8). Beer €2-8. Open Tu-Su 11am-2am. Cash only. ❸

A La Mort Subite, 7 r. Montagne-aux-Herbes-Potagères (☎02 513 1318; www.alamortsubite.com). M: Gare Centrale or De Brouckère. Across from Galeries Royals St. Hubert. Feel classy—but not out of place—while ordering an omelette (€4.30-8.70) or Gueuze Mort Subite (Belgian beer; €4) brewed specifically for the restaurant. Open M-Sa 11am-1am, Su 12-11pm. MC/V. ❷

In 't Spinnekopke, 1 pl. du Jardin aux Fleurs (☎02 511 8695). M: Bourse. Tucked away near a small square with a fountain. Locals "inside the spider's head" savor the authentically Belgian menu. Entrees €15-25. Open M-F noon-3pm, 6pm-midnight, Sa 6pm-midnight. Kitchen closes at 11pm. AmEx/MC/V. ❺

Hémisphères, 29 r. Leopold (☎02 513 9370; www.hemispheres-resto.be). This restaurant, art gallery, and "intercultural space" serves Middle Eastern, Indian, and Asian fare. Couscous with veggies or meat €11-15. Entrees €7-15. Concerts 1 Sa per month. Open M-F noon-3pm and 6-10:30pm, Sa 6:30pm-late. MC/V. ❹

Da-Kao II, 19 r. Van Artevelde (☎02 512 6716). Large, budget-friendly portions of Vietnamese and Thai food. Entrees €5-12. Open M-Sa 12pm-3pm and 6pm-midnight. Cash only. ❶

Zebra, 31 pl. St-Géry. (☎02 513 5116). M: Bourse. Hipsters abound in this centrally located cafe and bar. Known for its mixed drinks. Also serves juices, milkshakes, and light but filling sandwiches (€5), salads (€6.50), and soups (€3.50). Open M-Th and Su 11am-1am, F-Sa 11am-2am. Kitchen open 11am-9pm. AmEx/MC/V over €12. ❶

Mokafe, in Galeries Royals St. Hubert (☎02 511 7870). Pause at this old time coffee shop for a shopping break. Pastries €1-3. Crepes €4-6. Waffles €5. Mixed drinks €6. Open daily 7am-midnight. AmEx/MC/V. ❷

Maison Antoine, 1 pl. Jourdan. M: Schuman. The Maison, a famed fast-food kiosk in the center of a parking lot, has served the best *frites* (€2-2.20) in town for 58 years. Nearby is a romantic park with sculptures where you and your *frites* can have some one-on-one time. Make sure to get a side of flavored mayo (€0.50). Open M-Th and Su 11:30am-1am, F-Sa 11:30am-2am. ❶

Gaufre de Bruxelles, Pl. Agora. (☎02 514 0171; www.belgiumwaffle.com). An outdoor seating area and hordes of hungry Belgians separate this waffle pavilion from the competition. Delicious waffles (€2.60-5.50) come topped with homemade ice cream. Add chocolate, whipped cream, strawberries, or bananas (€1.50-4.20) if you're feeling indulgent. Open daily 7am-midnight. AmEx/MC/V. ❶

SIGHTS

GRAND-PLACE AND ENVIRONS. Three blocks behind corner of r. de l'Étuve and r. du Chêne, is Brussels's m **Mannekin Pis,** a tiny fountain of a boy peeing cont it commemorates a young Belgian who defused a Grand-Place. In reality, the fountain was installed hood with water during the reign of Albert and Isabelle. To gap, a statue of a squatting girl *(Jeanneken)* now pees down an alley Bouchers. Victor Hugo once called the statued and gilded Grand-Place "the most beautiful square in the world."

During the day, be sure to visit **La Maison du Roi** (King's House), now the city museum, whose most riveting exhibit is the collection of clothes worn by *Mannekin Pis*. It's also home to the town hall, where 40min. guided tours reveal over-the-top decorations and an impressive collection of paintings. *(La Maison du Roi ☎02 279 4350. Open Tu-Su 10am-5pm. €3. Town Hall ☎02 548 0445. English-language tours Tu-W 3:15pm, Su 10:45am and 12:15pm; arrive early. €3, students €2.50.)* You'll find an extremely brief introduction to the brewing process and a quiet spot to enjoy Belgium's famed beers at the **Belgian Brewer's Museum.** *(10 Grand-Place. 2 buildings left of the town hall. ☎02 511 4987; www.beerparadise.be. Open daily 10am-5pm. €6, includes 1 beer.)* Nearby, the **Museum of Cocoa and Chocolate** tells of Belgium's other renowned edible export. Cacao fruits grow on display, and the smell of chocolate permeates the air as an expert demonstrates the art of working with chocolate. *(11 r. de la Tête d'Or. ☎02 514 2048; www.mucc.be. Open July-Aug. and holidays daily 10am-5pm; Sept.-June Tu-Su 10am-4:30pm. €5.50, students €4.50.)* The top floor of **Parking 58** provides an unobstructed view of the entire city from the Palace of Justice to Atomium. Take the elevator to the 10th floor and enjoy a sunset fit for a bureaucrat. *(1 r. de l'Eveque near St. Kateljine. Free.)* In the skylit **Galeries Royals Saint-Hubert arcade,** one block behind Grand-Place, a long covered walkway is lined with shops whose wares range from *haute couture* to marzipan frogs. North of Gare Centrale, the **Cathédrale Saint-Michel et Sainte-Gudule** hosts royal affairs under its soaring ribbed vaults. At times, music from a pipe organ or carillon serenades visitors. *(Pl. Ste-Gudule. Open M-F 7am-6pm, Sa-Su 8:30am-3pm. Free.)*

MONT DES ARTS. The **Musées Royaux des Beaux-Arts** encompass the **Musée d'Art Ancien,** the **Musée d'Art Moderne,** and several contemporary exhibits. The museums steward a huge collection of Belgian art, including Bruegel's famous *Landscape with the Fall of Icarus*, and pieces by Rubens. Other masterpieces on display include David's *Death of Marat* and paintings by Delacroix, Gauguin, Seurat, and van Gogh. Connected by a tunnel and requiring a separate ticket, the **Musée Magritte** houses the works of the famed Surrealist and Brussels native René Magritte. The great hall is itself a work of architectural beauty and the panoramic view of Brussels from the fourth floor of the Magritte alone justifies the price of admission. *(3 r. de la Régence. M: Parc. ☎02 508 3211; www.fine-arts-museum.be. Open Tu-Su 10am-5pm. Some wings close noon-2pm. Each museum costs €8, under 26 €2, under 18 free; combination tickets costs €13, under 26 €3, under 18 free. 1st W of each month 1-5pm free. Audio tour €2.50.)* The **Musical Instrument Museum (MIM)** houses over 1500 instruments; stand in front of one and your headphones automatically play a sample of its music. *(2 r. Montagne de la Cour. ☎02 545 0130; www.mim.fgov.be. Open Tu-F 9:30am-4:45pm, Sa-Su 10am-5pm. €5, students €4. 1st W of each month 1-5pm free.)*

BELGIAN CENTER FOR COMIC STRIP ART. Comic strips *(les BD)* are a serious business in Belgium. Today, a restored warehouse designed by famous architect Victor Horta pays tribute to what Belgians call the Ninth Art. Tintin

Smurfs make several appearances, and amusing displays document strip history, while the library has thousands of books available to, n, scholarly researchers. *(☎02 191 980; www. comicscenter.net. R. des Sables. M: gier. Open Tu-Su 10am-6pm. Students with ISIC €6.)*

ENTERTAINMENT AND NIGHTLIFE

The weekly *What's On*, part of the *Bulletin* newspaper and available free at the tourist office, contains info on cultural events. The **Théâtre Royal de la Monnaie,** on pl. de la Monnaie, is renowned for its opera and ballet. (M: De Brouckère. ☎02 229 1200, box office ☎02 70 39 39; www.lamonnaie.be. Tickets from €8, half-price tickets go on sale 20min. prior to the event.) The **Théâtre Royal de Toone VII,** 66 r. du Marché-aux-herbes, stages marionette performances, a distinctly Belgian art form, and houses an intimate bar with marionettes hanging from the ceiling. (☎02 513 5486; www.toone.be for show times and prices. Shows generally in French; English available for groups upon request. F 8:30pm, Sa 4pm and 8:30pm; occasionally Tu-Th. €10, students €7.) **Nova,** 3 r. d'Arenberg, screens foreign and independent films, both contemporary and historic. Live performances take place downstairs. The website lists future festivals. The theater holds a free "Open Screen" on the last Thursday of every month at 8:30pm, in which any filmmaker can screen a 15min. piece. (☎02 511 2477; www.nova-cinema.com. €5, students €3.50.)

On summer nights, live concerts on Grand-Place and the Bourse bring the streets to life. The *All the Fun* pamphlet, available at the tourist office, lists the newest clubs and bars. On **Place St-Géry,** patios are jammed with a laid-back crowd of students and backpackers. **Zebra** (p. 84) and a host of other bars are lively until late. **O'Reilly's Irish Pub,** pl. de la Bourse, nearby, is packed with travelers and TVs—a comforting spot for the homesick. It has large breakfast, lunch, and dinner menus, plus lots of beer. (☎25 521 0481. Open M-Th and Su 11am-1am, F-Sa 11am-4am. Free Wi-Fi. AmEx/MC/V.) Choose from over 2000 beers at carefree **Delirium,** 4A impasse de la Fidélité. (☎02 251 4434; www.deliriumcafe.be. Jam session Th and Su 11pm. Open daily 10am-4am.) **Celtica,** 55 r. aux Poulets, might have the world's longest happy hour: throbbing techno accompanies €2 drafts 1pm-midnight. The bar downstairs is more relaxed, and a DJ spins upstairs. (☎02 514 3253; www.celticpubs.com. Bar open daily 1pm-late. Disco open Th-Sa 10pm.) More techno blares amid the crowd of beautiful people at **Le Fuse,** 208 r. Blaes. (☎02 511 9789; www.fuse.be. Cover €5 before midnight, €8 after. Open Sa 10pm-late.) **Havana,** 4 r. de l'Epee, plays everything from salsa to techno. (☎02 502 1224; www.havana-brussels.com. Open W-Su 7pm-late. Live music on W, F, and Sa. AmEx/MC/V.) **GBLT nightlife** in Brussels primarily centers on r. des Pierres and r. du Marché au Charbon, next to Grand-Place. **L'Homo Erectus,** 57 r. des Pierres, is extremely popular. (☎02 514 7493; www.lhomoerectus.com. Open daily 3pm-3am.)

FLANDERS (VLAANDEREN)

BRUGES (BRUGGE) ☎050

Bruges (pop. 117,000) is arguably Belgium's most romantic city. Canals carve their way through rows of pointed brick houses and cobblestone streets en route to the breathtaking Gothic Markt. The city's buildings remain some of the best-preserved examples of Northern Renaissance architecture. Though a bit crowded, Bruges is a relaxing getaway to catch your breath.

TRANSPORTATION

Trains leave from the **Stationsplein,** a 10min. walk south of the city. (Open daily 4:30am-11pm. Info desk open daily 8am-7pm.) Trains head to: Antwerp (1hr., 2 per hr., €13); Brussels (1hr., 1-3 per hr., €12); Ghent (20min., 3 per hr., €5.60); Knokke (30min., 2 per hr., €3); Ostend (15min., 3 per hr., €3.30).

ORIENTATION AND PRACTICAL INFORMATION

Bruges is enclosed by a circular canal, with the train station, Stationsplein, just beyond its southern extreme. The historic district is entirely accessible by foot, while bikes are popular for countryside visits. The dizzying **Belfort** looms high over the center of town, presiding over the handsome **Markt.** On the easternmost edge of the city, the beautiful, windmill-lined **Kruisvestraat** and serene **Minnewater Park** have stretches of gorgeous green land, ideal for picnicking.

Tourist Office: In and Uit, 't Zand 34 (☎050 44 46 46; www.brugge.be). From the train station, head left to 't Zand and walk for 10min.; the tourist office is located inside the red concert hall. Books accommodations for a €2.50 fee and €20 deposit, and sells helpful **maps** (€0.50) and **information guides** (€1). Open M-W and F-Su 10am-6pm, Th 10am-8pm. A smaller **branch** is located inside the train station (Stationsplein). Open M-F 10am-5pm and Sa-Su 10am-2pm.

Tours: 5 companies offer 30min. **boat tours** of Bruges's extensive canals. (Mar.-Nov., 2-4 per hr., €6); inquire at tourist office for a list. **QuasiMundo Tours** has 3 different bike tours of Bruges and the countryside (3-4hr.). Tours depart daily at 10am and 7pm from Bruges, 1pm from the countryside. (☎050 33 07 75; www.quasimundo.com. Tours Mar.-Oct. €20, under 26 €18; includes free drink.)

Currency Exchange: Goffin, Steenstraat 2, is near the Markt and charges no commission on cash exchange (☎050 34 04 71. Open M-Sa 9am-5:30pm.

Luggage Storage: At the train station. €2.60-3.60.

Laundromat: Belfort, Ezelstr. 51. Wash €3-6, dry €1. Open daily 7am-10pm.

Bike Rental: At the train station (☎050 30 23 28). Passport required. €6.50 per day. Koffieboontje, Hallestr. 4 (☎050 33 80 27; www.adventure-bike-renting.be), to the right of the Belfort. €7 per 4hr.; €10 per day, students €7 per day. Open daily 9am-10pm.

Police: Hauwerstr. 7 (☎050 44 89 30).

Hospitals: A. Z. St-Jan (☎050 45 21 11; not Oud St-Janshospitaal, a museum). **St-Lucas** (☎050 36 91 11). **St-Franciscus Xaveriuskliniek** (☎050 47 04 70).

Internet: Teleboutique Brugge, Predikherenstr. 48, is one of the cheapest options. €2 per hour. Open daily 10am-10pm. Cash only.

Post Office: Markt 5. Open M and W-F 9am-6pm, Sa 9:30am-12:30pm.

WATCH THAT BIKE! In Bruges, bike lanes are marked in red stone. To forestall cyclists' ire—and their tires—pedestrians should avoid these areas.

BELGIUM

ACCOMMODATIONS

Snuffel Backpacker Hostel, Ezelstr. 47-49 (☎050 33 31 33; www.snuffel.be). Take bus #3 or 13 (€1.30) from the station to the stop after Markt, then take the 1st left. Colorful rooms decorated by local artists. Helpful staff leads free walking tours every other day. The on-site bar's Happy hour is so cheap that even locals frequent it (9-10pm, beer €1).

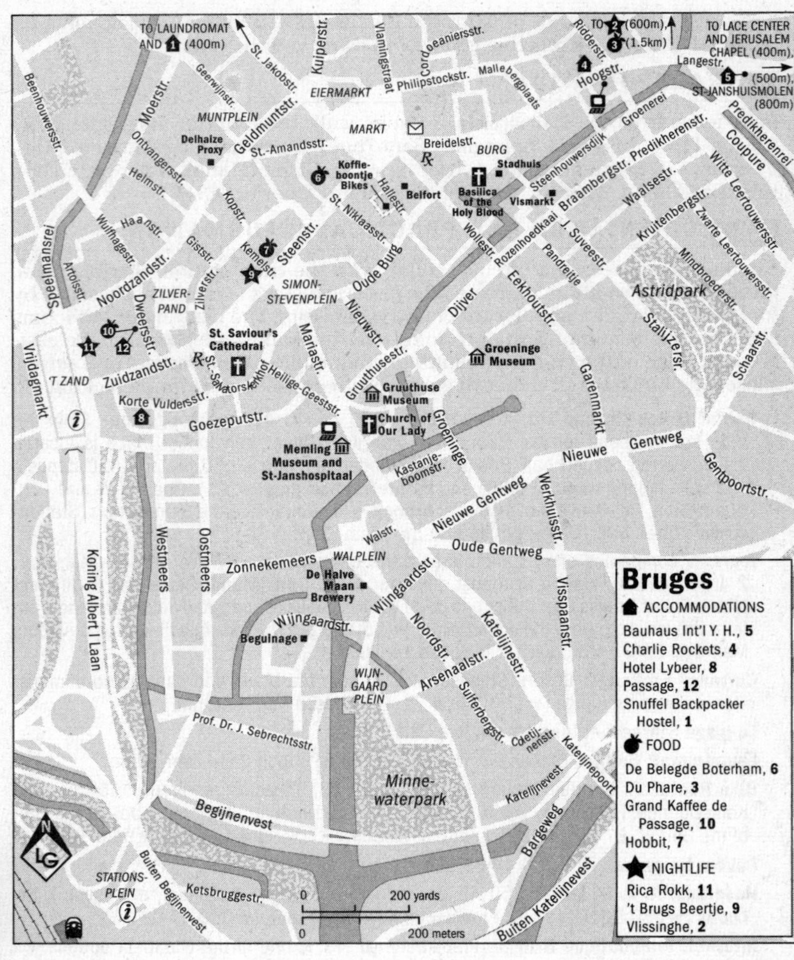

Guests also get a free Bruges card, which gives access to museums and offers many discounts. Kitchen. Bike rental €6 per day. Breakfast €3. Lockers available; bring lock or rent one. Linens included. Internet €2 per hr.; free Wi-Fi. Key deposit €5. Reception 7:30am-midnight. Dorms €14; doubles €36; quads €60-64. AmEx/MC/V. ❷

Passage, Dweersstr. 26 (☎050 34 02 32; www.passagebruges.com). Old-world, refined hostel-hotel-cafe in an ideal location. Safes available. Breakfast €5; included in private rooms. Free beer at bar with purchase of dinner. Internet €4 per hr. Reception 9am-11pm; need code to get in after close. Open mid-Feb. to mid-Jan. Dorms €14; singles €25-45; doubles €45-60; triples and quads €75-90. AmEx/MC/V. ❷

Hotel Lybeer, Korte Vuldersstr. 31 (☎050 33 43 55; www.hostellybeer.com). Charming and convenient. Breakfast and linens included. Free Internet. Reception 7:30am-11pm. Dorms €14-24; singles €23-38; doubles €43-65; triples €70-80. AmEx/MC/V. ❸

Bauhaus International Youth Hostel and Hotel, Langestr. 133-137 (☎500 34 10 93; www.bauhaus.be). Take bus #6 or 16 from the station; ask to stop at the hostel. A giant candelabra and popular bar lead the way to airy rooms. Bike rental €9 per day. Breakfast and linens included. Lockers €1.50. Internet €3 per hr. Reception 8am-midnight. Dorms €14-15; singles from €26; doubles from €40; triples from €57. AmEx/MC/V. ❷

Charlie Rockets, Hoogstr. 19 (☎050 33 06 60; www.charlierockets.com). Americans might feel at home at this wannabe Charlie Rockets in a converted movie theatre, equipped with pool tables, darts, and, of course, 50s decor. The in-house bar is popular with locals and travelers not spending the night. Breakfast €3. Lockers €3. Linens included. Internet €2 per 20min. Dorms €16. MC/V. ❷

FOOD

Inexpensive restaurants can be hard to find in Bruges. Seafood lovers should splurge at least once on the city's famous *mosselen* (mussels; €15-22) found at the **Vismarkt,** near the Burg. (Open Tu-Sa 8am-1pm.) Restaurants close early in Bruges (around 10pm), so plan in advance for nighttime cravings; grab groceries at **Delhaize Proxy,** Noordzandstr. 4, near the Markt. (Open M-Sa 9am-7pm.)

Grand Kaffee de Passage, Dweersstr. 26-28 (☎050 34 02 32). Next to the Passage hostel. Traditional Belgian cuisine in a candlelit setting. Try the excellent Flemish stew (€11). Desserts are inexpensive and delectable (€2-5). Entrees €8-15. Open daily 5-11pm. Closed from mid-Jan. to mid-Feb. AmEx/MC/V. ❸

Du Phare, Sasplein 2 (☎050 34 35 90; www.duphare.be). From the Burg, walk down Hoogstr. and turn left at the canal onto Verversdijk, crossing to the right side at the second bridge. Follow the canal for 20min. to Sasplein. Bus #4 stops right outside. This jazz and blues bistro serves international fare (€11-20). Open M and W 11:30am-2:30pm and 7pm-midnight, Tu and F-Sa 11:30am-2:30pm and 6:30pm-midnight, Su 11:30am-midnight. Reservations recommended F-Sa. AmEx/MC/V. ❸

Hobbit, Kemelstr. 8-10 (☎050 33 55 20; www.hobbitgrill.be). Try filling meats and pastas off funny newsprint menus. Entrees €7-11. Open daily 6pm-1am. AmEx/MC/V. ❷

De Belegde Boterham, Kleine St-Amandsstr. 5 (☎050 34 91 31). Health-conscious spot serves sandwiches (€7-8) and innovative salads (€11) in its chic interior or on mismatched tables outside. Open M-Sa noon-4pm. Cash only. ❷

SIGHTS

Filled with Gothic and neo-Gothic buildings and crisscrossed by canals, picturesque Bruges is best experienced on foot. Avoid visiting Bruges on Mondays, when museums are closed. If you plan to visit many museums, consider a cost-saving combination ticket (€15, includes admission to 5 museums).

MARKT AND BURG. The medieval **Belfort** (belfry) looms over the Markt; climb its 366 steep steps for a city view. *(Belfort open Tu-Su 9:30am-5pm. Last entry 4:15pm. €5. Bell concerts mid-June to Sept. M, W, and Sa 9pm, Su 2:15pm; Oct. to mid-June W and Sa-Su 2:15pm.)* Behind the Markt, the Burg is dominated by the finely detailed facade of the **Stadhuis** (Town Hall). Inside, wander through the gilded **Gothic Hall,** where residents of Bruges still get married. *(☎050 44 81 10. Open Tu-Su 9:30am-4:30pm. €2.50, under 26 €1.50. Audio tour included.)* This ticket will also get you into **Liberty of Bruges Museum,** which contains an ornate fireplace. *(Open M-Sa 9:30am-12:30pm and 1:30-5pm).* Tucked in a corner of the Burg next to the Stadhuis, the **Basilica of the Holy Blood** supposedly holds the blood of Christ in a spectacularly ornate sanctuary upstairs. *(Basilica open daily Apr.-Sept. 9:30am-noon and 2-6pm; Oct.-Mar. 10am-noon and 2-4pm; closed W afternoon. Holy Relic can be viewed at 11am and 2-4pm. Museum €1.50.)*

MUSEUMS. From the Burg, follow Wollestr. left and then head right on Dijver and walk through the garden to reach the **Groeninge Museum,** small for its price but full of beautiful portraits and works by Jan van Eyck and Hans Memling. *(Dijver 12. ☎050 50 44 87. Open Tu-Su 9:30am-5pm. €8, under 26 €6. Audio tour included.)* Formerly a palace, the nearby **Gruuthuse Museum** houses a large collection of 16th- and 17th-century tapestries. *(Dijver 17. ☎050 44 87 62. Open Tu-Su 9:30am-5pm. €6, students €4. Audio tour included.)* Continue on Dijver as it becomes Gruuthusestr. and walk under the stone archway to enter the **Memling Museum,** in Oud St-Janshospitaal, a brick building that was a hospital in medieval times. The museum reconstructs everyday life in the hospital and has several paintings by its namesake, Hans Memling. *(Mariastr. 38. ☎050 44 87 71. Open Tu-Su 9:30am-5pm, ticket office closes 4:30pm. €8, under 26 €5. Audio tour included.)*

OTHER SIGHTS. The 14th-century **Church of Our Lady,** at Mariastr. and Gruuthusestr., contains Michelangelo's famous work, *Madonna and Child.* *(Open Tu-F 9:30am-5pm, Sa 9:30am-4:45pm, Su 12:30-5pm; last entry 4:30pm. Church free. Tomb viewing €2.50, students €1.50. Ticket for the tomb included in Gruuthuse Museum ticket.)* Sophisticated beer aficionados will enjoy the accompanying samples at 150-year-old **De Halve Maan,** a beer museum and brewery. *(Welplein 26. ☎50 33 26 97; www.halvemaan.be. 45min. tours Apr.-Sept. 1 per hr. M-F 11am-4pm, Sa-Su 11am-5pm; Oct.-Mar. tours M-F 11am and 3pm, Sa-Su 1 per hr. 11am-4pm. €5, includes beer.)* For God-sanctioned fun, wander the grounds of the **Beguinage,** home to nuns who share their flower-covered yard with passersby. The Beguine's house displays furnishings typical of medieval Flemish households. *(From Simon Stevinplein, follow Mariastr., and turn right on Wijngaardstr.; at the canal, turn right and cross the footbridge. ☎050 33 00 11. Open Mar.-Nov. daily 10am-noon and 1:45-5pm; gate open 6:30am-6:30pm. Church and garden free; house €2, under 26 €1.)* Walk along the river to see the windmills; to enter, go down to 235-year-old windmill **St-Janshuismolen,** which still gives occasional flour-grinding demonstrations in summer when the wind is right. *(☎050 33 00 44. Open May-Sept. daily 9:30am-12:30pm and 1:30-5pm. €2, under 26 €1.)*

FESTIVALS AND NIGHTLIFE

Bruges plays host to the **Cactusfestival** (☎050 33 20 14; www.cactusfestival.be. €25 per day, €63 for 3 days), a series of alt-pop and hip-hop concerts the first full weekend in July. The city also sponsors **Klinkers,** an open-air music and film series that's free to the public during the months of July and August (☎50 33 20 14; www.klinkers-brugge.be).

Although Bruges is not known for its wild party destination, the town definitely knows how to enjoy beer. The packed pubs offer a wide selection of Belgium's finest brews. At **'t Brugs Beertje,** Kemelstr. 5, off Steenstr., you can sample some of the 250 varieties of beer. (☎050 33 96 16. Open M, Th and Su 4pm-12:30am, F-Sa 4pm-2am.) Stop by Bruges's oldest pub, **Vlissinghe,** Blekersstr. 2, established in 1515. From the Burg, take Hoogstr. and turn left onto Verversdijk immediately before the canal. Cross the second bridge onto Blekersstr. (☎050 34 37 37. Open W-Sa 11am-midnight, Su 11am-7pm.) Steer clear of the pricey tourist-trap clubs behind the Markt. Belgian students tend to prefer the dance floor of **Rica Rokk,** 't Zand 6, where shots are €3 and a liter of beer starts at €19. (☎050 33 24 34; www.maricarokk.com. Open daily 9:30am-5am.) The tourist office has a limited list of **GLBT establishments.** For tips on Bruges nightlife, pick up a free "Use-It" map at your hostel.

BRITAIN

After colonizing two-fifths of the globe, spearheading the Industrial Revolution, and winning every foreign war in its history but two, Britain seems intent on making the world forget its tiny size. It's hard to believe that the rolling farms of the south and the rugged cliffs of the north are only a day's train ride apart, or that people as diverse as clubbers, miners, and monks all occupy a land area roughly the size of Oregon. Beyond the fairytale cottages and sheep farms of "Merry Olde England," today's Britain is a high-energy destination driven by international influence. Though the sun may have set on the British Empire, a colonial legacy survives in multicultural urban centers and a dynamic arts and theater scene. Brits now eat kebabs and curry as often as they do scones, and dance clubs in post-industrial settings draw as much attention as elegant country inns.

DISCOVER BRITAIN: SUGGESTED ITINERARIES

THREE DAYS. Spend it all in **London** (p. 103), the city of tea, royalty, and James Bond. After a stroll through **Hyde Park,** head to **Buckingham Palace** for the changing of the guard. Check out the renowned collections of the **British Museum** and the **Tate Modern.** Stop at famed **Westminster Abbey** and catch a play at Shakespeare's **Globe Theatre** before grabbing a drink in the **East End.**

ONE OR TWO WEEKS. Start in **London** (4 days), to explore the museums, theaters, and clubs. Tour the college greens in **Cambridge** (2 days; p. 143) and **Oxford** (2 days). Don't miss Shakespeare's hometown, **Stratford-upon-Avon** (1 day; p. 139). Energetic **Edinburgh** (4 days) will keep you busy, especially during festival season.

LIFE AND TIMES

HISTORY

THE ANCIENT ISLE (3200 BC TO AD 450). Britain's prehistoric residents left little but stones and mysteries in their wake. These relics of the past gave way to Roman occupation of "Britannia" (England and Wales) by the end of the 1st century AD. You can still see remnants of their rule in the resort spa they built at **Bath** (p. 132) and in the coast-to-coast fortification of **Hadrian's Wall,** built during the early 1st century to ward off invaders from ancient Scotland. The 5th century AD saw the decline of the Roman Empire, leaving Britannia vulnerable to raids. The Angles and Saxons flooded in from Denmark and Germany to establish their own kingdoms in the south.

CHRISTIANITY AND THE NORMANS (450-1066). Christianity came to Britain in AD 597 when **Augustine** converted King Æthelbert and founded England's first Catholic church at **Canterbury** (p. 132). The religion continued to flourish during the reign of Edward the Confessor, the last Anglo-Saxon king, and the reign of his successor, a bastard Norman named **William I.** Better known as "The Conqueror," he invaded from northern France in 1066 and defeated the Anglo-Saxons at the pivotal **Battle of Hastings,** seizing the crown. William made French the language of the educated elite and introduced feudalism, doling out vast tracts of land to the royals and subjugating English tenants to French lords.

BLOOD AND DEMOCRACY (1066-1509). The Middle Ages were a time of conquest and infighting until 1215, when noblemen forced King John to sign the **Magna Carta,** the document that inspired modern English democracy. The first "modern" parliament convened 50 years later. While English kings expanded the nation's boundaries, the **Black Death** ravaged its population, killing up to one-third of all Britons between 1349 and 1361. Many more fell in the **Hundred Years' War** (1337-1453), a squabble over the French throne in which England lost most of its holdings in France. Following this defeat, England turned its attention back home for the **War of the Roses** (1455-85), a lengthy crisis of royal succession between the Houses of Lancaster and York.

REFORMATION, RENAISSANCE, AND REVOLUTION (1509-1685). In a desperate effort to produce a male heir, England's most infamous king, **Henry VIII,** married six women. The marriages ended in disaster, with two of his wives facing execution. Stymied by the Pope's refusal to allow him to divorce, Henry rejected Catholicism and established the **Church of England** in 1534. His daughter, **Elizabeth I,** later inherited the throne and cemented the success of the Protestant Reformation. The first union of England, Wales, and Scotland took place in 1604, when James VI of Scotland ascended the throne as **James I** of England.

In a move to eliminate royal power, the monarchy was abolished during the **English Civil War** (1639-1651), and the first **British Commonwealth** was founded with **Oliver Cromwell** as its hopelessly despotic Lord Protector. To the relief of the masses, the Republic collapsed under the lackluster leadership of Cromwell's son Richard, but the subsequent **Restoration** of **Charles II** to the throne in 1660 did not cure England's troubles. Debates over whether to bar Charles' Catholic brother **James II** from the throne established the first political parties: the **Whigs,** who supported reform, and the Tories, who backed hereditary succession.

PARLIAMENT AND THE CROWN (1685-1783). **James II** took the throne in 1685, but lost it just three years later to his son-in-law, Dutch Protestant **William of Orange,** in the bloodless **"Glorious Revolution."** Supporters of James II (called **Jacobites)** remained a threat until 1745, when James II's grandson Charles, commonly known as **Bonnie Prince Charlie,** failed in his attempt to recapture the throne. William and his wife Mary issued a **Bill of Rights,** ushering in a more liberal age. By the end of Britain's victory over France in the **Seven Years' War** (1756-1763), the nation had risen to great economic and political prominence, with extensive colonial holdings across the Atlantic. Meanwhile, Parliament prospered thanks to the ineffectual leadership of **Georges I, II,** and **III.** The office of Prime Minister soon eclipsed the monarchy as the true seat of power.

EMPIRE AND INDUSTRY (1783-1832). During the 18th and 19th centuries, Britain came to rule more than one-quarter of the world's population and two-fifths of its land, despite the loss of the American colonies in 1783, becoming an empire on which "the sun never set." The **Napoleonic Wars** (ca. 1800-1815) revived the rivalry with France and added to Britain's colonial holdings. The **Industrial Revolution** also fueled Britain as a world power and saw many cities, such as Manchester, flourish as farmers shifted to urban factories. The **gold standard,** adopted by Britain in 1821, stimulated international trade and solidified the value of the pound.

THE VICTORIAN ERA (1832-1914). During the long, stable rule of **Queen Victoria** (1837-1901), a series of **Factory** and **Reform Acts** dealt with social difficulties, many of them stemming from rapid industrialization. The legislation limited child labor, capped the average work day, and increased male voting rights.

Trade unions, also a product of progressive reform, found a political voice in the **Labour Party** by 1906. Yet pressures to alter the position of other marginalized groups proved ineffectual as the rich embraced fin-de-siècle decadence.

THE WORLD WARS (1914-1945). The **Great War** (1914-1918), as World War I was known until 1939, scarred the national spirit with the loss of a generation of young men, and dashed Victorian dreams of a peaceful, progressive society. The 1930s brought depression, as well as mass unemployment. Tensions in Europe escalated once again with Germany's reoccupation of the Rhineland and subsequent invasion of Poland. Britain declared war on Germany on September 3, 1939. However, even the Great War had failed to prepare the British Isles for the utter devastation of **World War II**. German air raids began with the **Battle of Britain** in the summer of 1940 as the Luftwaffe devastated many English cities. The fall of France in 1940 precipitated the creation of a war cabinet, led by the eloquent **Winston Churchill.** In 1944, Britain and the Allied Forces launched the **D-Day Invasion** of Normandy, shifting the tide of the war and leading to the defeat of Germany and its allies in May 1945.

THE POST-WAR YEARS (1945-1990). Post-war Britain faced economic hardship with enormous war debt and non-existent infrastructure. Increasing immigration from former colonies and a growing rift between rich and poor worsened social tensions. Britain joined the **European Economic Community (EEC)** in 1971, a move that received a lukewarm approbation from many Britons; the relationship between Britain and the Continent remains a contentious issue today. When unemployment and economic unrest culminated in a series of public service strikes in 1979, the nation grasped for change, electing "Iron Lady" **Margaret Thatcher** as prime minister. Thatcher dismantled vast segments of the welfare state, bringing dramatic prosperity to many but sharpening the class divide. Aggravated by her resistance to the EEC, the Conservative Party conducted a vote of no confidence that led to Thatcher's 1990 resignation and the appointment of **John Major.**

THE NEW MILLENNIUM (1990-2005). After the British pound fell out of the EEC's monetary regulation system in 1993, Major and the Conservative Party became less popular. Under the leadership of the youthful **Tony Blair,** the Labour Party refashioned itself into the alternative for discontented middle-class voters and garnered two landslide electoral victories in 1997 and 2001. Blair nurtured relations with the European Union and maintained inclusive, moderate economic and social positions. The British government's support of American foreign policy on the Kosovo crisis (and again in the wake of the September 11 attacks) earned Blair the moniker of "little Clinton." His government also initiated domestic devolution in Scotland and Wales, a move toward local governance that delegated some power to the Scottish Parliament and the Welsh National Assembly—both inaugurated in 1999. The **Good Friday Agreemen**t (1998) was a first step toward Northern Irish autonomy. In July 2005 the **Irish Republican Army** (IRA) announced a permanent ceasefire. In April 2007, the **Ulster Volunteer Force** (UVF) announced a disarmament, officially ending the conflict.

TODAY

RULE BRITANNIA. Since the 1700s, the monarch (currently **Queen Elizabeth II**) has served a symbolic role, leaving real power to **Parliament,** which consists of the **House of Commons,** with its elected **Members of Parliament** (MPs), and the **House of Lords,** most of whom are government-appointed Life Peers. All members of the executive branch, which includes the **prime minister** and the **cabinet,** are also MPs. This fusion of legislative and executive functions—called the "efficient secret" of the British government—ensures the swift passage of the majority party's programs into bills. The prime minister is never directly elected to the post. Rather, the MPs of the ruling party choose a leader who then becomes the prime minister. The two main parties are the **Labours** and the **Conservatives** (Tory), roughly representing the left and right.

CURRENT EVENTS. In the May 2005 general election, Labour maintained control of Parliament, giving Blair a third term, although its majority in the House of Commons dropped. Blair's continued support of US foreign policy and his political alliance with President George W. Bush caused discontent in Britain, particularly since the war in Iraq. In February 2003, nearly one million people gathered in London to protest military intervention in Iraq. Blair's political positions remained controversial after a series of **terrorist attacks** in July 2005. Four suicide bombs detonated on public transport in London on the morning of July 7, killing 52, less than a day after the city earned the right to host the 2012 Summer Olympics; a failed second attack occurred two weeks later. The July 7 bombings marked the deadliest attack in London since WWII. Blair's critics also pointed to his stance on the euro—that Britain will convert to the currency when the economy is ready—as an equivocation and a political maneuver. The fate of the pound and Britain's participation in the EU remain heated issues, and British opinion remains, as ever, distrustful of integration with the rest of Europe. In late 2006, Blair announced that he would not seek a fourth term. He stepped down from his post as Prime Minister on June 27, 2007, passing power on to fellow Labour Party colleague **Gordon Brown.** Brown's tenure, after a promising start, was soured by his clumsy handling of an early election issue. The reinvigorated Conservative (Tory) Party opposition is led by **David Cameron.** The Tories' impressive performance in the local elections of May 2008 has even caused some Labour MPs to call for Brown's replacement.

A ROYAL MESS. The world mourned the death of the "People's Princess," **Diana,** in a Paris car crash in 1997. **Queen Elizabeth II**—a matronly, practical character—earned praise when she began paying income tax in 1993 and threw a year-long **Golden Jubilee** for the 50th year of her reign in 2002. **Prince Charles** and his paramour **Camilla Parker-Bowles** married in April 2005 after a 35-year romance; the Queen did not attend the service. A quick visit to a drug rehab clinic in 2002 heralded the onset of adult celebrity—and tabloid notoriety—for **Prince Harry,** the younger of Charles and Diana's sons. Before his entry into the British military as an officer, Harry offended the British public by dressing as a Nazi soldier for a costume party. In 2007, Harry was featured in news stories again when British military officers prevented him from serving in Iraq, against the Prince's wishes. Harry's increasing fame, however, still does not detract from the rapt attention devoted to second-in-line **Prince William.** Having earned a degree in geography from the University of St. Andrews, William is seen by some as a reluctant future successor to his father; he has also joined the military and received his Royal Air Force wings in April 2008.

PEOPLE AND CULTURE

CUSTOMS AND ETIQUETTE. The United Kingdom is home to 60 million Britons, a dynamic and varied population made up of local subcultures. Stiff upper-lipped public schoolboys and post-punk Hoxton rockers sit next to Burberry-clad football hooligans ("chavs") on the eerily quiet Tube. There is little that a traveler can do that will inadvertently cause offense. That said, the English do place weight on proper decorum, including politeness ("thanks" comes in many varieties, including "cheers"), queueing (that is, lining up—never disrupt the queue), and keeping a certain respectful distance. You'll find, however, that the British sense of humor—fantastically wry, explicit, even raunchy—is somewhat at odds with any notion of their coldness or reserve.

FOOD AND DRINK. Historically, England has been derided for its horrific cuisine. But do not fear the gravy-laden, boiled, fried, and bland traditional nosh! Britain's cuisine is in the midst of a gourmet revolution, and even travelers on a backpacker's budget can taste the benefits. In the spring of 2005, a panel of more than 600 chefs, food critics, and restaurateurs voted 14 British restaurants into the world's top 50; the Fat Duck in Berkshire was named the world's best. Popular television chef Jamie Oliver led a well-publicized

RULES OF THE PUB

British pubs are governed by a set of complex and often unwritten rules. Here's a primer to help you avoid some common mistakes:

1. If you expect someone to come around to your seat, you'll be waiting for some time. At most British pubs, you order at the bar.
2. So you've gotten up to go to the bar. But, before you go, check your table number so that the server knows where to bring your food.
3. Get your wallet out right away: most pubs require payment when you place your order.
4. In groups, it's common to buy drinks in rounds. One person goes to the bar and buys drinks for the whole table, someone else buys the next round, and so on.
5. Put away that pack of cigarettes—as of 2007, it's illegal to smoke in enclosed public spaces.
6. Don't jump the invisible queue. Even if patrons aren't physically lining up to buy drinks, the bartender usually serves them in the order they come to the bar.
7. Don't tip as you leave. If you're impressed by the service, offer to buy the bartender a drink.
8. Pubs don't open before 11am, before which time you probably shouldn't be drinking anyway.
9. You may have seen a pub called the "Red Lion" or the "White Horse" in several towns, but they're not related to one another.
10. Keep your eyes on the clock. Licencing laws require most pubs to close by 11pm, so be sure to heed the call for "last orders" (sometimes indicated by a bell).

and successful campaign to increase the British government's spending on school lunches. Still, the best way to eat in Britain is to avoid British food. Thanks to its colonial legacy, ethnic food is ubiquitous, and Britain offers some of the best tandoori and curry outside India.

THE ARTS

LITERATURE

Geoffrey Chaucer tapped into the spirited side of Middle English. His *Canterbury Tales* (1387) is among the best comedic works of all time. Under Elizabeth I, English drama flourished with the appearance of the first professional playwrights, among them **William Shakespeare,** the son of a glove-maker from Stratford-upon-Avon (p. 139). The British Puritans of the late 16th and early 17th centuries produced a huge body of obsessive and brilliant literature, including **John Milton's** epic *Paradise Lost* (1667). In 1719, **Daniel Defoe** started the era of the English novel with his popular, island-bound *Robinson Crusoe.* By the end of the century, **Jane Austen** satirized the modes and manners of her time in novels like *Pride and Prejudice* (1813). Victorian poverty and social change spawned the sentimental novels of **Charles Dickens.** The **Romantic** movement of the early 1800s found its greatest expression in poetry. The watershed *Lyrical Ballads* (1798) by **William Wordsworth** and **Samuel Taylor Coleridge** included classics like *The Rime of the Ancient Mariner*. In the early 20th century, **Virginia Woolf** spoke up on behalf of female writers. She and the Irish expatriate **James Joyce** were among the ground-breaking practitioners of **Modernism** (ca. 1910-1990). One of the movement's poetic champions was **T.S. Eliot;** his influential poem *The Waste Land* (1922) portrays London as a fragmented desert awaiting redemption. **D.H. Lawrence** explored tensions in the British working-class family while **E.M. Forster's** half-Modernist, half-Romantic novels like *A Passage to India* (1924) reveal a disillusionment with imperialism. The end of the empire and the growing gap between the classes splintered British literature in several directions. Postcolonial voices like **Salman Rushdie's** and **Zadie Smith's** have become an important literary force.

Britain has also produced some enduring volumes of children's literature, like **Lewis Carroll's** *Alice's Adventures in Wonderland* (1865), **C.S. Lewis's** *Chronicles of Narnia* (1950-1956), and **Roald Dahl's** *Charlie and the Chocolate Factory* (1964). In **J.R.R. Tolkien's** grandiose epics *The Hobbit* (1937) and *The Lord of the Rings* (1954-56), elves, wizards, men, and little folk go to battle over the fate of Middle Earth. Recently, **J.K. Rowling** has won over readers around the world with her tales of juvenile wizardry in the *Harry Potter* series.

MUSIC

During the Renaissance, English ears were tuned to cathedral anthems, psalms, madrigals, and the occasional lute performance. **Henry Purcell** rang in the Baroque era with England's first great opera, *Dido and Aeneas* (1689). Today's audiences are familiar with the operettas of **W.S. Gilbert** and **Arthur Sullivan.** The pair were rumored to hate each other, but nonetheless managed to produce gems like *The Pirates of Penzance* (1879). A renaissance of more serious music began under **Edward Elgar,** whose *Pomp and Circumstance* (1901) is most often heard at graduation ceremonies. The devastation of World War I and II provoked **Benjamin Britten's** heartbreaking *War Requiem* (1962). Later 20th-century trends, including the wildly popular musicals of **Sir Andrew Lloyd Webber,** were toward commercial music.

The **British Invasion** groups of the 1960s infiltrated the world with daring, controversial sound. **The Beatles,** fresh out of Liverpool, were the ultimate trendsetters, still influential nearly four decades after their break-up. The edgier lyrics and grittier sound of the Rolling Stones shifted teens' thoughts from "I Want To Hold Your Hand" to "Let's Spend the Night Together." Over the next 20 years, England imported the urban "mod" sound of **The Who** and guitar gurus Eric Clapton of **Cream** and Jimmy Page of **Led Zeppelin.** In the mid-1970s, British rock split, as the theatrical excesses of glam rock performers like **Queen, Elton John,** and **David Bowie** contrasted with the conceptual, album-oriented art rock popularized by **Pink Floyd.** Punk rock bands, including **The Sex Pistols** and **The Clash,** emerged from Britain's industrial centers in the 1970s.

British bands continue to achieve popular success on both sides of the Atlantic thanks to the 1980s advent of America's MTV. **Dire Straits, Duran Duran, the Eurythmics, Boy George, Tears for Fears,** and the **Police** have all enjoyed many top-10 hits. England's influence on dance music comes from the **Chemical Brothers** and **Fatboy Slim,** among others. **Oasis** embodied a dramatically indulgent breed of rock 'n' roll stardom, while the tremendous popularity of American grunge rock inspired then-wannabes **Radiohead,** who have since been hailed as one of the most creative and influential British rock bands since The Beatles. The UK also produced some brilliantly awful pop, including **Robbie Williams** (survivor of the bubblegummy **Take That**), who continues to be a stadium-filling force. Sadly, the **Spice Girls** have not enjoyed the same longevity.

These days, **Coldplay** is still one of the UK's best-selling rock exports. Modern post-punk and New Wave bands like **Bloc Party** and **Franz Ferdinand** enjoy indie credit and impressive fan bases. A product of instant Internet success, **Lily Allen** has established herself as a major player in the world of commercial pop, winning audiences with an upbeat sound and sassy attitude. Similarly, **Amy Winehouse's** deep and soulful jazz vocals made her the first British artist to win five Grammys. The British have also created a new genre: bands like **The Streets** and **Dizzee Rascal** play **UK Garage,** a blend of skittering beats, heavy bass, and urban rapping, which is now the official sound of every UK club.

VISUAL ARTS

ARCHITECTURE. Houses of worship began as stone churches, but gave way to massive cathedrals like the one at Winchester. The Normans introduced the round arches and thick walls of **Romanesque** architecture, erecting squat castles such as the Tower of London (p. 118). The **Gothic** period ushered in the more intricate buildings like **King's College Chapel** in Cambridge (p. 144). Christopher Wren's dome on **St. Paul's Cathedral** (p. 118) and Tudor homes like Henry VIII's **Hampton Court** attest to the capabilities of Renaissance architecture. During the Victorian period, British nostalgia gave us the neo-Gothic **Houses of Parliament** (p. 116) and the Neoclassical **British Museum** (p. 124). Today, **Richard Rogers** and **Norman Foster** vie for bragging rights as England's most influential designers, dotting London with a host of Millennium constructions. A team of architects created the **London Eye,** the largest observation wheel in the world and one of the city's most popular attractions.

FILM. British film has a checkered past marked by cycles of relative independence from Hollywood, followed by increasing drains of talent to America. The **Royal Shakespeare Company** has produced such heavyweights as **Dame Judi Dench** and **Sir Ian McKellen,** who both then made the transition to film. Earlier Shakespeare impresario **Laurence Olivier** worked both sides of the camera in *Henry V* (the 1944 brainchild of government-sponsored WWII propaganda), and his *Hamlet* (1948) is still the hallmark Dane. Master of suspense **Alfred Hitchcock** snared audiences with films produced in both Britain and the US, and Scotsman **Sean Connery** downed the first of many martinis as **James Bond** in *Dr. No* (1962). During the early 1980s, two British films, *Chariots of Fire* (1981) and *Gandhi* (1983) earned high accolades during a period dominated by major American productions (some of which, interestingly, were partially filmed in British studios, including 1980's *Star Wars: The Empire Strikes Back*). **Kenneth Branagh** has focused his talents on adapting Shakespeare for the screen, with glossy, acclaimed works like *Hamlet* (1996). Around the turn of the century, British films including *The Full Monty* (1997), *Billy Elliot* (2000), *Bend It Like Beckham* (2002), and *Love Actually* (2003) achieved massive success across the pond. The *Harry Potter* film franchise, which kicked off in 2001, continues to break box-office records. Films such as *The History Boys* (2006) and *The Queen* (2006) are recent landmarks in British cinema.

ON THE CANVAS. Britain's early religious art shifted to secular patronage and court painters. Portrait artist **Thomas Gainsborough** (1727-88) propagated an interest in landscape painting, which peaked in the 19th century with the Romanticism of **J. M. W. Turner** and **John Constable.** The Victorian era saw movements like **Dante Gabriel Rossetti's** (1828-82) Italian-inspired pre-Raphaelite school. Modernist trends like Cubism and Expressionism were picked up by painter **Wyndham Lewis** (1882-1957) and sculptor **Henry Moore** (1898-1986). WWII inspired experimental works by painters **Francis Bacon** (not to be confused with the Renaissance thinker) and **Lucian Freud.** The precocious **Young British Artists** of the 1990s include sculptor **Rachel Whitbread** and multimedia artist **Damien Hirst.** From the late 1990s into the early 2000s, the creations of acclaimed anonymous graffiti artist and stencilist **Banksy** have appeared in cities around the world.

HOLIDAYS AND FESTIVALS

Holidays: New Year's Day (Jan. 1, 2010); Epiphany (Jan. 6, 2010); Good Friday (Apr. 10, 2010); Easter Sunday and Monday (Apr. 4-5, 2010); Ascension (May 13, 2010); Pentecost (May 23, 2010); Corpus Christi (June 3, 2010); Bank Holidays (May 3, May 31, and Aug. 30, 2010); Assumption (Aug. 15, 2010); All Saints' Day (Nov. 1, 2010); Christmas (Dec. 25, 2010); Boxing Day (Dec. 26, 2010).

Festivals: Scotland's New Year's Eve celebration, *Hogmanay,* takes over the streets in Edinburgh and Glasgow. The *National Eisteddfod of Wales* (August 2010) has brought Welsh writers, musicians, and artists together since 1176. One of the largest music and theater festivals in the world is the *Edinburgh International Festival* (mid-Aug. to early Sept. 2010); also highly recommended is the *Edinburgh Fringe Festival* (Aug.

2010). Manchester's Gay Village hosts *Manchester Pride* (www.manchesterpride.com) in August, and London throws a huge street party at the *Notting Hill Carnival* (August 2010). Bonfires and fireworks abound on England's *Guy Fawkes Day* (Nov. 5, 2010) in celebration of a conspirator's failed attempt to destroy the Houses of Parliament in 1605.

ESSENTIALS

FACTS AND FIGURES

OFFICIAL NAME: United Kingdom of Great Britain and Northern Ireland.

CAPITAL: London.

MAJOR CITIES: Cardiff, Edinburgh, Glasgow, Liverpool, Manchester.

POPULATION: 60,776,000.

LAND AREA: 244,800 sq. km.

TIME ZONE: GMT.

LANGUAGE: English; also Welsh and Scottish Gaelic.

RELIGIONS: Christian: Protestant and Catholic (72%), Muslim (3%).

TOTAL NUMBER OF HARRY POTTER BOOKS SOLD: 400,000,000.

WHEN TO GO

It's wise to plan around the high season (June-Aug.). Spring and fall are better times to visit; the weather is reasonable and flights are cheaper, though there may be less transportation to rural areas. If you plan to visit the cities, the low season (Nov.-Mar.) is most economical. Keep in mind, however, that sights and accommodations often close or have reduced hours. In Scotland, summer light lasts almost until midnight, but in winter, the sun may set as early as 3:45pm. Regardless of when you go, it will rain—always.

IT'S ALL BRITISH TO ME. The United Kingdom is a political union of England, Northern Ireland, Scotland, and Wales. This is also referred to as Britain, not to be confused with the island of Great Britain, which only includes England, Scotland, and Wales. *Let's Go* uses United Kingdom and Britain interchangeably. This chapter covers Great Britain. For further information about Northern Ireland, see p. 360.

DOCUMENTS AND FORMALITIES

EMBASSIES AND CONSULATES. Foreign embassies in Britain are located in London (p. 103). British embassies abroad include: **Australia,** Commonwealth Ave., Yarralumla, ACT 2600 (☎02 6270 6666; http://bhc.britaus.net); **Canada,** 80 Elgin St., Ottawa, ON, K1P 5K7 (☎613-237-1530; www.britainincanada.org); **Ireland,** 29 Merrion Rd., Ballsbridge, Dublin, 4 (☎01 205 3700; www.britishembassy.ie); **New Zealand,** 44 Hill St., Thorndon, Wellington, 6011 (☎04 924 2888; www.britain.org.nz); **US,** 3100 Mass. Ave. NW, Washington, D.C., 20008 (☎202-588-7800; www.britainusa.com).

VISA AND ENTRY INFORMATION. EU citizens do not need a visa. Citizens of Australia, Canada, New Zealand, and the US do not need a visa for stays of up to 6 months. Students planning to study in the UK for six months or more must obtain a student visa (around US$90). For a full list of countries whose citizens require visas, call your British embassy or visit www.ukvisas.gov.uk.

TOURIST SERVICES AND MONEY

EMERGENCY Ambulance, Fire, and Police: ☎999.

TOURIST OFFICES. Formerly the British Tourist Authority, **Visit Britain** (☎020 8846 9000; www.visitbritain.com) is an umbrella organization for regional tourist boards. Tourist offices in Britain are listed for each city and town. They stock maps and provide info on sights and accommodations.

IT'S JUST A TIC. Tourist offices in Britain are known as Tourist Information Centres, or TICs. Britain's National Parks also have National Park Information Centres, or NPICs. This chapter refers to all offices as TICs and NPICs.

MONEY. The British unit of currency is the **pound sterling** (£), plural pounds sterling. One pound is equal to 100 **pence,** with standard denominations of 1p, 2p, 5p, 10p, 20p, 50p, £1, and £2 in coins, and £5, £10, £20, and £50 in notes. **Quid** is slang for pounds. Scotland has its own bank notes, which can be used interchangeably with English currency, though you may have difficulty using Scottish £1 notes outside Scotland. As a rule, it's cheaper to exchange money in Britain than at home. ATMs offer the best exchange rates. Many British department stores, such as Marks & Spencer, also offer excellent exchange services. Tips in restaurants are often included in the bill, sometimes as a "service charge." If gratuity is not included, tip your server about 12.5%. A 10% tip is common for taxi drivers, and £1-3 is usual for bellhops and chambermaids. To the relief of budget travelers from the US, tipping is not expected at pubs and bars in Britain. Aside from open-air markets, don't expect to bargain. For more info on money in Europe, see p. 10.

BRITISH POUND(£)		
	AUS$1 = £0.47	£1 = AUS$2.14
	CDN$1 = £0.51	£1 = CDN$1.97
	EUR€1 = £0.79	£1 = EUR€1.27
	NZ$1 = £0.38	£1 = NZ$2.62
	US$1 = £0.54	£1 = US$1.86

TRANSPORTATION

BY PLANE. Most international flights land at **London's Heathrow** (**LHR;** ☎0870 000 0123; www.heathrowairport.com) or **Gatwick** (**WSX;** ☎0870 000 2468; www.gatwickairport.com) airports; **Manchester (MAN)** and **Edinburgh (EDI)** also have international airports. **Budget airlines,** like Ryanair and easyJet, fly out of many locales, including **Stansted Airport** (p. 104) and **Luton Airport,** (p. 104). The national airline, **British Airways** (☎0870 850 9850, US ☎800-247-9297; www.britishairways.com), offers discounted youth fares for those under 24. For more info on traveling by plane around Europe, see p. 33.

BY TRAIN. Britain's main carrier is **National Rail Enquiries** (☎08457 484 950). The country's train network is extensive, criss-crossing the length and breadth of the island. Prices and schedules often change; find up-to-date information from their website (www.nationalrail.co.uk/planmyjourney) or **Network Rail** (www.networkrail.co.uk; schedules only). **Eurostar** trains run to Britain from the Continent through the Chunnel. The **BritRail Pass,** sold only outside Britain, allows unlimited travel in England, Scotland, and Wales (www.britrail.net). In Canada and the US, contact **Rail Europe** (Canada ☎800-361-7245, US ☎888-382-7245; www.raileurope.com). Eurail passes are not valid in Britain. Rail discount cards (£20), available at rail stations and through travel agents, grant 33% off most point-to-point fares and are available to those ages 16-25 or over 60, full-time students, and families. In general, traveling by train costs more than by bus. For more info on train travel in Europe, see p. 37.

BY BUS. The British distinguish between **buses,** which cover short routes, and **coaches,** which cover long distances; *Let's Go* refers to both as buses. **National Express** (☎08705 808 080; www.nationalexpress.com) is the main operator of long-distance bus service in Britain, while **Scottish Citylink** (☎08705 505 050; www.citylink.co.uk) has the most extensive coverage in Scotland. The **Brit Xplorer Pass** offers unlimited travel on National Express buses (7-day £79, 14-day £139, 28-day £219). **NX2 cards** (£10), available online for ages 16-26, reduce fares by up to 30%. Plan ahead for the cheapest rides, National Express's **Fun Fares,** which are only sold online (limited number of tickets out of London from £1).

BY CAR. To drive, you must be 17 and have a valid license from your home country; to rent, you must be over 21. Britain is covered by a high-speed system of **motorways** (M-roads) that connect London to other major cities. Visitors should be able to handle **driving on the left side** of the road and driving **manual transmission** ("stick shift" is far more common than automatic). Roads are generally well maintained, but gasoline (petrol) prices are high. In London, driving is restricted during weekday working hours, with charges imposed in certain congestion zones; parking can be similarly nightmarish.

BY FERRY. Several ferry lines provide service between Britain and the Continent. Ask for discounts; ISIC holders can sometimes get student fares, and Eurail pass-holders are eligible for reductions and free trips. **Seaview Ferries** (www.seaview.co.uk/ferries.html) has a directory of UK ferries. Book ahead in summer. For more info on boats to Ireland and the Continent, see p. 42.

BY BIKE AND BY FOOT. Much of the British countryside is well suited to biking. Many cities and villages have rental shops and route maps. Large-scale *Ordnance Survey* maps, often available at TICs, detail the extensive system of long-distance hiking paths. TICs and NPICs can provide extra information.

BY THUMB. Hitchhiking or standing on M-roads is illegal; one may only thumb at rest stops or at the entrance ramps to highways. Despite this, hitchhiking is fairly common in rural parts of Scotland and Wales (England is tougher) where public transportation is spotty. *Let's Go* does not recommend hitchhiking.

KEEPING IN TOUCH

PHONE CODES	**Country code:** 44. **International dialing prefix:** 00. Within Britain, dial city code + local number, even when dialing inside the city. For more info on how to place international calls, see **Inside Back Cover.**

EMAIL AND THE INTERNET. Internet access is ubiquitous in big cities, common in towns, and sparse in rural areas. Internet cafes or public terminals can be found almost everywhere; they usually cost £2-6 per hour, but you often pay only for the time used. For more info, see www.cybercafes.com. Public libraries usually have free or inexpensive Internet access, but you might have to wait or make an advance reservation. Many coffee shops, particularly chains such as Caffe Nero and Starbucks, offer Wi-Fi for a fee.

TELEPHONE. Most public **pay phones** in Britain are run by British Telecom (BT). Public phones charge at least 30p and don't accept 1, 2, or 5p coins. A BT Chargecard bills calls to your credit card, but most pay phones now have readers where you can swipe credit cards directly (generally AmEx/MC/V). The number for the operator in Britain is ☎100, the international operator ☎155. Whenever possible, use a **calling card** for international phone calls, as long-distance rates for national phone services are often very high. **Mobile phones** are an increasingly popular and economical option. Major mobile carriers include T-Mobile, Vodafone, and O2. Direct-dial access numbers for calling out of Britain include: **AT&T Direct** (☎0800 890 011); **Canada Direct** (☎0800 096 0634 or 0800 559 3141); **Telecom New Zealand Direct** (☎0800 890 064); **Telstra Australia** (☎0800 890 061). For more info on calling home from Europe, see p. 20.

MAIL. **Royal Mail** has tried to standardize their rates around the world. Check shipment costs with the Postal Calculator at www.royalmail.com. **Airmail** is the best way to send mail home from Britain. Just write "Par Avion—Airmail" on the top left corner of your envelope or stop by any post office to get a free airmail label. Letters sent via Airmail should be delivered within three working days to European destinations and five working days to Australia, Canada, and the US. To receive mail in the UK, have mail delivered **Poste Restante.** Mail will go to the main post office unless you specify a subsidiary by street address. Address mail to be held according to the following example: First Name, Last Name, Poste Restante, post office address, Postal Code, UK. Bring a passport to pick up your mail; there may be a small fee.

ACCOMMODATIONS AND CAMPING

GREAT BRITAIN	❶	❷	❸	❹	❺
ACCOMMODATIONS	under £15	£15-20	£21-30	£31-40	over £40

Hostelling International (HI) hostels are prevalent throughout Britain. They are run by the **Youth Hostels Association of England and Wales** (**YHA;** ☎08707 708 868; www.yha.org.uk), the **Scottish Youth Hostels Association** (**SYHA;** ☎01786 891 400; www.syha.org.uk), and **Hostelling International Northern Ireland** (**HINI;** ☎028 9032 4733; www.hini.org.uk). Dorms cost around £12-15 in rural areas, £15-20 in larger cities, and £20-35 in London. Make reservations at least a week in advance, especially in more touristed areas on weekends and during the summer. You can book **B&Bs** by calling directly, or by asking the local TIC to help you. TICs usually charge a flat fee of £1-5 plus 10% deposit, deductible from the amount you pay the B&B proprietor. **Campgrounds** tend to be privately owned and cost £3-10 per person per night. It is illegal to camp in national parks.

FOOD AND DRINK

GREAT BRITAIN	❶	❷	❸	❹	❺
FOOD	under £6	£6-10	£11-15	£16-20	over £20

A pillar of traditional British fare, the cholesterol-filled, meat-anchored **full English breakfast** is still served in most B&Bs across the country. Beans on toast or toast smothered in Marmite (the most acquired of tastes—a salty, brown spread made from yeast) are breakfast staples. The best native dishes for lunch or dinner are roasts—beef, lamb, and Wiltshire hams—and **Yorkshire pudding,** a type of popover drizzled with meat juices. Despite their intriguing names, **bangers and mash** and **bubble and squeak** are just sausages and potatoes and cabbage and potatoes, respectively. Pubs serve savory meat pies like **Cornish pasties** (PASS-tees) or **ploughman's lunches** consisting of bread, cheese, and pickles. **Fish and chips** (french fries) are traditionally drowned in malt vinegar and salt. **Crisps,** or potato chips, come in an astonishing variety, with flavors like prawn cocktail. Britons make their desserts (often called "puddings" or "afters") exceedingly sweet and gloopy. **Sponges, trifles, tarts,** and the ill-named **spotted dick** (spongy currant cake) will satiate the sweetest tooth. To escape English food, try Chinese, Greek, or Indian cuisine. British **"tea"** refers to both a drink, served strong and milky, and to a social ritual. A high tea might include cooked meats, salad, sandwiches, and pastries, while the oft-stereotyped afternoon tea comes with finger sandwiches, scones with jam and **clotted cream** (a sinful cross between whipped cream and butter), and small cakes. **Cream tea,** a specialty of Cornwall and Devon, includes scones or crumpets, jam, and clotted cream.

BEYOND TOURISM

There are many opportunities for volunteering, studying, and working in Britain. As a volunteer, you can participate in projects ranging from archaeological digs to lobbying for social change. Explore your academic passions at the country's prestigious institutions or pursue an independent research project. For more info on opportunities across Europe, see **Beyond Tourism,** p. 45.

The National Trust, Volunteering and Community Involvement Office, P.O. Box 39, Warrington WA5 7WD (☎0870 458 4000; www.nationaltrust.org.uk/volunteering). Arranges numerous volunteer opportunities, including volunteer work on holidays.

The Teacher Recruitment Company, Pennineway Offices (1), 87-89 Saffron Hill, London EC1N 8QU (☎0845 833 1934; www.teachers.eu.com). International recruitment agency that lists positions across the country and provides info on jobs in the UK.

University of Oxford, College Admissions Office, Wellington Sq., Oxford OX1 2JD (☎01865 288 000; www.ox.ac.uk). Large range of summer programs (£880-3780) and year-long courses (£8880-11,840).

ENGLAND

A land where the stately once prevailed, England is now a youthful, hip, and forward-looking nation on the cutting edge of art, music, and film. But traditionalists can rest easy; for all the moving and shaking in large cities, scores of ancient towns, opulent castles, and comforting cups of tea still abound.

LONDON ☎020

London offers visitors a bewildering array of choices: Leonardo at the National Gallery or Hirst at the Tate Modern; Rossini at the Royal Opera or Les Misérables at the Queen's; Bond Street couture or Camden cutting-edge—you could spend your entire stay just deciding what to do. London is not often described as a unified city but rather as a conglomeration of villages, whose heritage and traditions are still evolving. Thanks to the feisty independence and diversity of each area, the London "buzz" is continually on the move.

INTERCITY TRANSPORTATION

Flights: Heathrow (**LON;** ☎08700 000 123) is London's main airport. The **Piccadilly Line** heads from the airport to central London (1hr., 20 per hr., £4-10). **Heathrow Connect** runs to **Paddington** (20min., 2 per hr., £10), as does the more expensive **Heathrow Express** (15min.; 4 per hr.; £15.50, round-trip £29). From **Gatwick Airport** (**LGW;** ☎08700 002 468), the **Gatwick Express** heads to **Victoria** (30min.; 4 per hr., round-trip £28.90).

Regional Hubs: London Luton Airport (**LTN;** ☎1582 405 100; www.london-luton.co.uk) serves as a hub for **easyJet, Ryanair,** and **Wizz Air.** First Capital Connect (☎0845 026 4700; www.firstcapitalconnect.co.uk) and Midland Mainline (☎0870 010 1296; www.midlandmainline.com) run **trains** between London King's Cross and Luton (30min.-1hr., 3-4 per hr., £10-20). Easybus (www.easybus.co.uk) and National Express (☎08705 808 080; www.nationalexpress.com) operate **buses** between London Victoria and Luton (1hr., 2-3 per hr., from £2). **London Stansted Airport (STN;** ☎0870 000 0303; www.stanstedairport.com) is the main hub for **Ryanair,** and also serves **easyJet** and **Wizz Air.** The Stansted Express (☎0845 600 7245; www.stanstedexpress.com) train shuttles between London Liverpool and Stansted (45min., 4 per hr., £15-24). Easybus runs **buses** between London Baker St. and Stansted and National Express runs **buses** from London Victoria (1hr., 3-6 per hr., from £2).

Trains: London has 8 major train stations: **Charing Cross** (southern England); **Euston** (the northwest); **King's Cross** (the northeast); **Liverpool Street** (East Anglia); **Paddington** (the west and south Wales); **St. Pancras** (the Midlands and the northwest); **Victoria** (the south); **Waterloo** (the south, the southwest, and the Continent). All stations are linked by the subway, referred to as the **Underground** or **Tube** (⊖). Itineraries involving a change of stations in London usually include a crosstown transfer by Tube. Get information at the station ticket office or from the **National Rail Enquiries Line** (☎08457 484 950; www.britrail.com).

Buses: Long-distance buses (coaches) arrive in London at **Victoria Coach Station,** 164 Buckingham Palace Rd. ⊖Victoria. **National Express** (☎08705 808 080; www.nationalexpress.com) is the largest operator of intercity services.

ORIENTATION

The **West End,** stretching east from Park Lane to Kingsway and south from Oxford St. to the River Thames, is the heart of London. In this area you'll find aristocratic **Mayfair,** the shopping near **Oxford Circus,** the clubs of **Soho,** and the boutiques of **Covent Garden.** Heading east of the West End, you'll pass legalistic **Holborn** before hitting the ancient **City of London** ("the City"), the site of the original Roman settlement and home to the Tower of London. The City's eastern border encompasses the ethnically diverse, working-class **East End.**

Westminster encompasses the grandeur of **Trafalgar Square** and extends south along the Thames; this is the location of both royal and political London, with the Houses of Parliament, Buckingham Palace, and Westminster Abbey. Farther west lies rich, snooty **Chelsea.** Across the river, the **South Bank** has an incredible variety of entertainment and museums. To the south, **Brixton** is one of the hottest nightlife spots in town, besides touristy Leicester Square and Piccadilly Circus. The huge expanse of **Hyde Park** lies west of the West End; along its southern border are chic **Knightsbridge** and posh **Kensington.** North of Hyde Park is the media-infested **Notting Hill** and the B&B- and hostel-filled **Bayswater.** Bayswater, Mayfair, and **Marylebone** meet at Marble Arch, on Hyde Park's northeast corner; from there, Marylebone stretches west to meet academic **Bloomsbury,** north of Soho and Holborn. **Camden Town, Islington, Hampstead,** and **Highgate** lie to the north of Bloomsbury and the City. A good street atlas is essential. **London A to Z** (£10) is available at newsstands and bookstores.

LOCAL TRANSPORTATION

Public Transportation: Run by **Transport for London (TfL;** 24hr. info ☎020 7222 1234; www.thetube.com). The **Underground** or **Tube** (⊖) is divided into 6 concentric zones; fares depend on the number of zones crossed. Buy your ticket before you board and pass it through automatic gates at both ends of your journey. Runs approximately 5am-11:30pm. See Tube map in the front of this guide. **Buses** are divided into 4 zones. Zones 1-3 are identical to the Tube zones. Buses run 5:30am-midnight, after which a network of **Night Buses,** prefixed by "N," take over. Fares £2. **Travelcard** valid on all TfL services. 1-day Travelcard from £5.30 (Zones 1-2).

Licensed Taxicabs: An illuminated "taxi" sign on the roof of a black cab signals availability. Tip 10%. For pickup (min. £2 charge), call **Taxi One-Number** (☎08718 718 710).

Minicabs: Private cars. Cheaper but less reliable–stick to a reputable company. **London Radio Cars** (☎020 8905 0000; www.londonradiocars.com) offers 24hr. pickup.

PRACTICAL INFORMATION

Tourist Information Centre: Britain Visitor Centre, 1 Regent St. (www.visitbritain.com). ⊖Piccadilly Circus. Open M 9:30am-6:30pm, Tu-F 9am-6:30pm, Sa-Su 10am-4pm. **London Information Centre,** 1 Leicester Pl. (☎020 7930 6769; www.londoninformationcentre.com). ⊖Leicester Sq. Open M-F 8am-midnight, Sa-Su 9am-6pm.

Tours: The Big Bus Company, 35-37 Grosvenor Gardens (☎020 7233 7797; www.bigbus.co.uk). ⊖Victoria. Multiple routes and buses every 5-15min. 1hr. walking tours and Thames cruise. Buses start at central office and at hubs throughout the city. £20. £2 discount for online purchase. AmEx/MC/V. **Original London Walks** (☎020 7624 3978, recorded info ☎020 7624 9255; www.walks.com) offers themed walks, from "Haunted London" to "Slice of India." Most 2hr. £6, students £5, under 16 free.

Embassies: Australia, Australia House, Strand (☎020 7379 4334). ⊖Temple. Open M-F 9am-5pm. **Canada,** MacDonald House, 1 Grosvenor Sq. (☎020 7258 6600). ⊖Bond St. Open M-F 9am-5pm. **Ireland,** 17 Grosvenor Pl. (☎020 7235 2171). ⊖Hyde Park Corner. Open M-F 9:30am-1pm and 2:15-5pm. **New Zealand,** New Zealand House, 80 Haymarket (☎020 7930 8422). ⊖Piccadilly Circus. Open M-F 9am-5pm. **US,** 24 Grosvenor Sq. (☎020 7499 9000). ⊖Bond St. Open M-F 8:30am-5:30pm.

Currency Exchange: Banks, such as **Barclays, HSBC, Lloyd's,** and **National Westminster** (NatWest) have the best rates. Branches open M-F 9:30am-4:30pm. Call ☎0895 456 6524 for the nearest **American Express** location.

GLBT Resources: London Lesbian and Gay Switchboard (☎020 7837 7324; www.queery.org.uk). 24hr. helpline and information service.

Police: London is covered by 2 police forces: the **City of London Police** (☎020 7601 2222) for the City and the **Metropolitan Police** (☎020 7230 1212) for the outskirts. At least 1 station is open 24hr. Call ☎020 7230 1212 for the nearest station.

Pharmacies: Most pharmacies open M-Sa 9:30am-5:30pm; a "duty" chemist in each district opens Su; hours limited. **Zafash Pharmacy,** 233-235 Old Brompton Rd. (☎020 7373 2798), ⊖Earl's Ct., is 24hr. **Bliss Chemist,** 5-6 Marble Arch (☎020 7723 6116), ⊖Marble Arch, is open daily 9am-midnight.

Hospitals: Charing Cross, Fulham Palace Rd. (☎020 8846 1234), entrance on St. Dunstan's Rd., ⊖Hammersmith. **Royal Free,** Pond St. (☎020 7794 0500), ⊖Belsize Park.

Central London

● SIGHTS

Sight	Grid
Apsley House, **1**	C4
Barbican Hall, **2**	E3
British Library, **4**	D2
British Museum, **5**	D3
Buckingham Palace, **6**	C4
Cabinet War Rooms, **7**	D4
Chinatown, **9**	D4
Courtauld Institute, **10**	D4
The Houses of Parliament, **14**	D4
Kensington Palace, **17**	B4
London Eye, **18**	D4
Marble Arch, **20**	C3
Millennium Bridge, **21**	E4
Monument, **22**	F4
Museum of London, **23**	E3
National Gallery, **24**	D4
National Portrait Gallery, **25**	D4
Natural History Museum, **26**	B5
Royal Courts of Justice, **29**	E3
The Royal Mews, **31**	C4
St. Martin-in-the-Fields, **38**	D4
St. Mary-le-Bow, **39**	E3
St. Pancras Chambers, **40**	D2
St. Paul's Cathedral, **41**	E3
Science Museum, **43**	B5
Shakespeare's Globe Theatre, **44**	E4

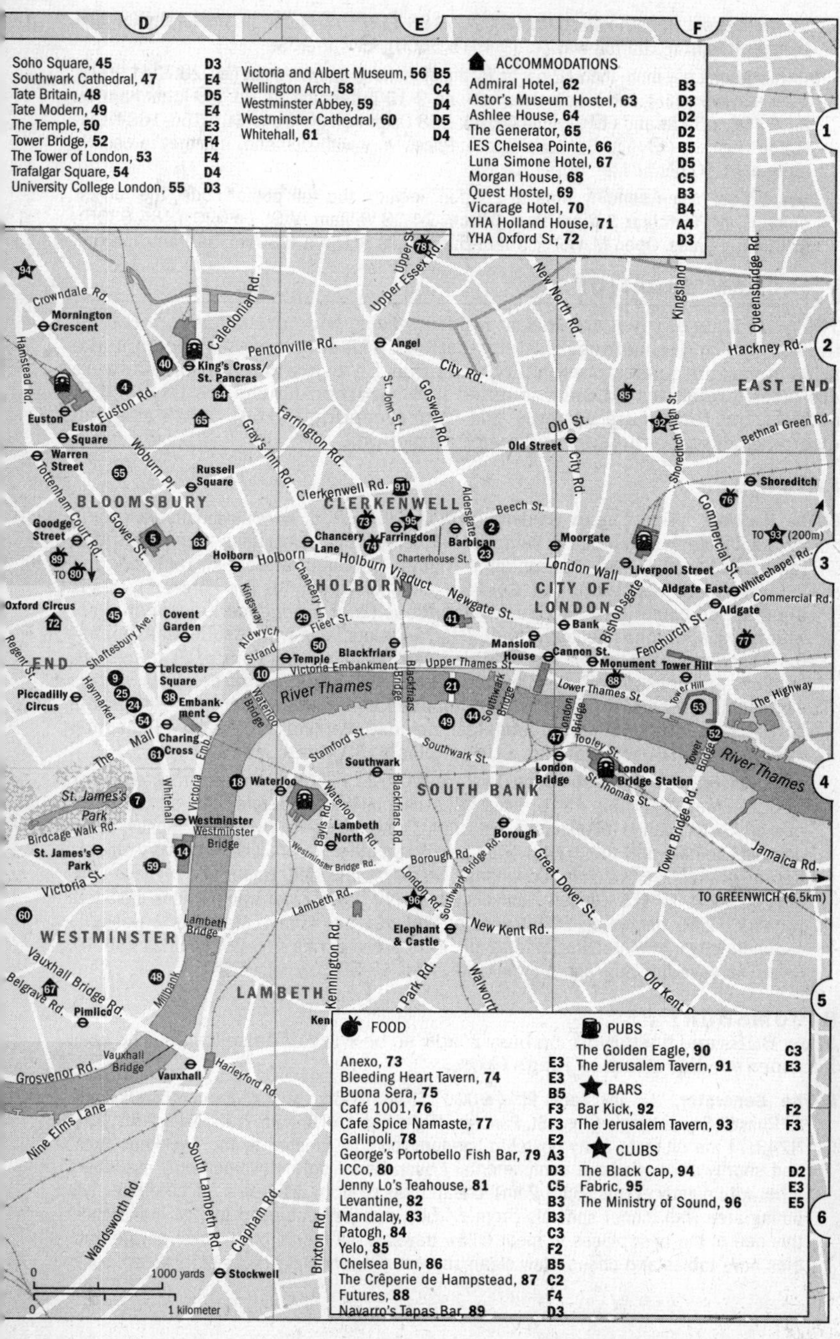
D
E
F
Soho Square, 45 D3
Southwark Cathedral, 47 E4
Tate Britain, 48 D5
Tate Modern, 49 E4
The Temple, 50 E3
Tower Bridge, 52 F4
The Tower of London, 53 F4
Trafalgar Square, 54 D4
University College London, 55 D3
Victoria and Albert Museum, 56 B5
Wellington Arch, 58 C4
Westminster Abbey, 59 D4
Westminster Cathedral, 60 D5
Whitehall, 61 D4
ACCOMMODATIONS
Admiral Hotel, 62 B3
Astor's Museum Hostel, 63 D3
Ashlee House, 64 D2
The Generator, 65 D2
IES Chelsea Pointe, 66 B5
Luna Simone Hotel, 67 D5
Morgan House, 68 C5
Quest Hostel, 69 B3
Vicarage Hotel, 70 B4
YHA Holland House, 71 A4
YHA Oxford St, 72 D3
FOOD
Anexo, 73 E3
Bleeding Heart Tavern, 74 E3
Buona Sera, 75 B5
Café 1001, 76 F3
Cafe Spice Namaste, 77 F3
Gallipoli, 78 E2
George's Portobello Fish Bar, 79 A3
ICCo, 80 D3
Jenny Lo's Teahouse, 81 C5
Levantine, 82 B3
Mandalay, 83 B3
Patogh, 84 C3
Yelo, 85 F2
Chelsea Bun, 86 B5
The Crêperie de Hampstead, 87 C2
Futures, 88 F4
Navarro's Tapas Bar, 89 D3
PUBS
The Golden Eagle, 90 C3
The Jerusalem Tavern, 91 E3
BARS
Bar Kick, 92 F2
The Jerusalem Tavern, 93 F3
CLUBS
The Black Cap, 94 D2
Fabric, 95 E3
The Ministry of Sound, 96 E5
1
2
3
4
5
6
Crowndale Rd.
Mornington Crescent
Hamstead Rd.
Caledonian Rd.
Pentonville Rd.
King's Cross/ St. Pancras
Angel
Upper Essex Rd.
Upper St.
New North Rd.
Kingsland Rd.
Queensbridge Rd.
Hackney Rd.
EAST END
City Rd.
St. John St.
Goswell Rd.
Euston Rd.
Euston
Euston Square
Farringdon Rd.
Gray's Inn Rd.
Old St.
Old Street
Shoreditch High St.
Bethnal Green Rd.
Warren Street
Woburn Pl.
Russell Square
Tottenham Court Rd.
BLOOMSBURY
Clerkenwell Rd.
CLERKENWELL
Aldersgate
Beech St.
City Rd.
Shoreditch
Commercial St.
Goodge Street
Gower St.
Chancery Lane
Farringdon
Barbican
Moorgate
TO 93 (200m)
TO 80
Holborn
Holborn
Holburn Viaduct
Charterhouse St.
London Wall
Liverpool Street
Whitechapel Rd.
Kingsway
Chancery Ln.
HOLBORN
Newgate St.
CITY OF LONDON
Aldgate East
Commercial Rd.
Oxford Circus
Covent Garden
Fleet St.
Bank
Bishopsgate
Aldgate
Aldwych
Shaftesbury Ave.
Regent St.
Strand
Blackfriars
Mansion House
Fenchurch St.
END
Temple
Victoria Embankment
Upper Thames St.
Cannon St.
Monument
Tower Hill
Leicester Square
Waterloo Bridge
Blackfriars Bridge
Southwark Bridge
Lower Thames St.
Tower Hill
The Highway
Piccadilly Circus
Haymarket
River Thames
Embankment
London Bridge
Charing Cross
The Mall
Victoria Emb.
Stamford St.
Southwark St.
Tooley St.
Southwark
London Bridge
London Bridge Station
Tower Bridge
River Thames
Whitehall
Waterloo
Waterloo Rd.
SOUTH BANK
St. Thomas St.
St. James's Park
Victoria
Westminster
Westminster Bridge
Baylis Rd.
Lambeth North
Blackfriars Rd.
Borough
Tower Bridge Rd.
Birdcage Walk Rd.
St. James's Park
Westminster Bridge Rd.
Borough Rd.
Southwark Bridge Rd.
Great Dover St.
Jamaica Rd.
Victoria St.
London Rd.
TO GREENWICH (6.5km)
Lambeth Rd.
Lambeth Bridge
Elephant & Castle
New Kent Rd.
WESTMINSTER
Kennington Rd.
Park Rd.
Walworth
Old Kent R
Vauxhall Bridge Rd.
Belgrave Rd.
Millbank
LAMBETH
Pimlico
Vauxhall Bridge
Grosvenor Rd.
Vauxhall
Harleyford Rd.
Nine Elms Lane
South Lambeth Rd.
Wandsworth Rd.
Clapham Rd.
Brixton Rd.
0
1000 yards
0
1 kilometer
Stockwell

St. Thomas's, Lambeth Palace Rd. (☎020 7188 7188), ⊖Waterloo. **University College London Hospital,** Grafton Way (☎08 4515 5500), ⊖Warren St.

Internet: Don't pay more than £2 per hr. Try the ubiquitous **easyInternet** (☎020 7241 9000; www.easyeverything.com). Locations include 9-16 Tottenham Ct. Rd. (⊖Tottenham Ct. Rd.); 456/459 Strand (⊖Charing Cross); 358 Oxford St. (⊖Bond St.); 160-166 Kensington High St. (⊖High St. Kensington). Prices vary with demand, but they're usually around £1.60 per hr. Min. 50p-£1.

Post Office: When sending mail to London, include the full postal code. The largest office is the **Trafalgar Square Post Office,** 24-28 William IV St. (☎020 7484 9305), ⊖Charing Cross. Open M, W-F 8:30am-6:30pm, Tu 9:15am-6:30pm, Sa 9am-5:30pm.

ACCOMMODATIONS

The best deals in town are **student residence halls,** which rent out rooms over the summer and sometimes Easter vacations. **B&B** encompasses accommodations of varying quality, personality, and price. Be aware that in-room showers are often prefabricated units jammed into a corner. Linens are included at all **YHAs,** but towels are not; buy one from reception (£3.50). YHAs also sell discount tickets to theaters and major attractions.

BAYSWATER

The Pavilion, 34-36 Sussex Gardens (☎020 7262 0905; www.pavilionhoteluk.com). ⊖Paddington or Edgeware Rd. With over 30 themed rooms, including "Honky Tonk Afro" (dedicated to the 70s), "Casablanca Nights" (recalling a Moorish fantasy), and 2 James Bond inspired pads ("Gold Finger" and "Diamonds Are Forever"), this is the place to come for a hilariously sumptuous hotel experience. Decadent decor with funky additions like zebra print, Grecian busts, or Warhol-esque Marilyn photos accompany flatscreen TVs. Priding itself on its connection to all things art, fashion, and rock & roll, the Pavilion has hosted a number of celebrity visitors and fashion shoots: a naked Naomi Campbell and an impatient Kate Beckinsale both posed here. Continental breakfast included. Parking £10 per day. Reception 24hr. Singles £60-85; doubles £100; triples £130. AmEx/MC/V. ❺

Quest Hostel, 45 Queensborough Terr. (☎020 7229 7782; www.astorhostels.com). ⊖Queensway. Night Bus #N15, 94, 148. A chummy staff operates this simple backpacker hostel with a blackboard welcoming new check-ins by name. Mostly co-ed dorms (1 female-only room). Nearly all have bath; otherwise, facilities on every other fl. Recently refurbished kitchen. Continental breakfast included. Under-bed luggage storage; padlocks £2 (£5 deposit). Lockers £1.50 per day; £7 per week. Linens included. Laundry £2.50 per wash, £0.50 per dry. Wi-Fi £1 per 40min. Max stay 2 weeks in summer; longer in winter. Reception 24hr. 4- to 9-bed dorms £16-25; doubles £35-40. Rates increase July-Aug. and on weekends. Ages 18-35 only. MC/V. ❶

BLOOMSBURY

Many B&Bs and hostels are on busy roads, so be wary of noise levels. The area becomes seedier closer to King's Cross.

The Generator, 37 Tavistock Pl. (☎020 7388 7666; www.generatorhostels.com). ⊖Russell Sq. or King's Cross St. Pancras. Night Bus #N19, N35, N38, N41, N55, N91, N243. At the ultimate party hostel in London, you'll be greeted by the "Welcome Host" and shortly after offered a complimentary beer. Co-ed dorms (women-only available), a bar with nightly events (6pm-2am), cheap pints (6-9pm, £1.50), a full cafeteria-style dining area with dinner specials (from £4.50), and well-equipped lounge areas make this one of the best places to meet fellow travelers. All rooms have sinks; private doubles have tables and chairs. New clean showers. Continental breakfast included. Lockers (padlocks £4), free towels and linens, laundry (wash £2; dry £0.50 per 10min.), cash machine, charge station (for any phone or iPod) and an in-house travel shop that sells Tube, train, and theater tickets. Small safes £1 per day, £5 per week.; larger safes £3/10. Internet £1 per 30min. Wi-Fi £1.50 per hr.; £4 per 3hr. Reception 24hr. Reserve 1 week in advance for Sa-Su. Online booking. Credit card required with reservation. 4- to 12-bed dorms £15-25; singles £50-65; doubles with 2 twin beds £50-65; triples £60-75; quads £80-100; 6-bed private rooms £120-150. Discounts for long stays. 18+. MC/V. ❶

YHA St. Pancras International, 79-81 Euston Rd. (☎020 7388 9998; www.yha.org.uk). ⊖King's Cross St. Pancras. Night Bus #N10, N73, N91, 390. Opposite the British Library and St. Pancras Tube. After a £1.6 million refurbishment, this hostel has come out sparkling, with a sunken bar-cafe (beers from £2.20; pub style mains £5.50) and clean, spacious rooms with plush wall-to-wall carpets and wooden bunks. Family bunk rooms, single-sex dorms, basic doubles, and premium doubles (with bath and TV) are sparkling. Kitchen and elevators available. Breakfast £3.50-5. Linens included. Laundry (wash and dry £4.50). Wi-Fi £1.50 per 15min.; £3 per 30min. 1 week max. stay. Reserve dorms 1 week in advance for Sa-Su or summer, 2 weeks for doubles. 4- to 6-bed dorms £23-32, under 18 £18-25; doubles £63, with bath £68. £3 discount with HI, ISIC, or NUS card. MC/V. ❷

George Hotel, 58-60 Cartwright Gardens (☎020 7387 8777; www.georgehotel.com). ⊖Russell Sq. Night Bus #N10, N73, N91, 390. Spacious rooms with flatscreen satellite TV, radio, tea/coffee facilities, phone, and alarm clock, plus hair dryer and iron on request. The front rooms on the 1st fl. have high ceilings and tall windows; others have bay windows. Full English breakfast included. Free internet and Wi-Fi. Reserve 3 weeks in advance for summer; 48hr. cancellation policy. Singles £50, with shower

£75; doubles £69/75, with bath £89; triples £79/89/99; basic quads £89. Discounts for stays over 4 days. MC/V. ❸

KENSINGTON AND EARL'S COURT

Astor Hyde Park, 191 Queensgate (☎020 7581 0103; www.astorhostels.co.uk). ⊖South Kensington or Gloucester Rd. Set in a recently renovated Victorian walk-up, this social backpacker's hostel offers clean, spacious rooms outfitted with full ensuite baths and decorated with modern art. Sleek lounge with flatscreen TV and dining hall with pool table. Regular F night parties. Breakfast included; occasional hostel dinners £3-4. Lockers under beds; padlock £2. Safes £1.50 per day, £7 per week. Free luggage storage before check-in and after check-out. Wash £2.50; dry 50p per 20min. Internet 50p per 15min. Free Wi-Fi. Reception 24hr. Dorms in summer £15-25, in winter £13-20; doubles £35-40/25-30. Ages 18-35 only. AmEx/MC/V. ❶

Vicarage Hotel, 10 Vicarage Gate (☎020 7229 4030; www.londonvicaragehotel.com). ⊖High St. Kensington. Night Bus #27, N28, N31, N52. Walking on Kensington Church St. from Kensington High St., you'll see 2 streets marked Vicarage Gate; take the 2nd on your right. Immaculately maintained Victorian house with ornate hallways, TV lounge, and elegant bedrooms; all have shiny wood furnishings, tea and coffee sundries, and hair dryers. Rooms with private baths have TV. Full English breakfast included. Free Wi-Fi. Best to reserve 2 months in advance with 1 night's deposit; personal checks accepted for deposit with at least 6 weeks notice. Singles £55, with private bathroom £93; doubles £93/122; triples £117/156; quads £128/172. AmEx/MC/V. ❸

OTHER NEIGHBORHOODS

YHA Oxford Street (HI), 14 Noel St. (☎020 7734 1618; www.yha.org.uk). ⊖Oxford Circus. Night Bus: more than 10 Night Buses run along Oxford St., including #N7, N8, and N207. Small, clean, bright rooms with limited facilities but an unbeatable location for nightlife. Some doubles have bunk beds, sink, mirror, and wardrobe; others have single beds and wardrobes. Clean communal toilets and showers. Spacious, comfy TV lounge. Huge, well-equipped kitchen. Laundry available. Towels £3.50. Wi-Fi £3 per hr. Travelcards sold at reception; discount tickets to popular attractions. Reserve at least 2 weeks in advance. 3- to 4-bed dorms £22-27, under 18 £17-21; 2-bed dorms £27-34. MC/V. ❷

Morgan House, 120 Ebury St. (☎020 7730 2384; www.morganhouse.co.uk). ⊖Victoria. A touch of pizzazz makes this B&B a neighborhood standout. A boistrous couple rents mid-sized rooms with floral decor and country-style furnishings. Many have fireplaces and all have TV, kettle, and phone for incoming calls (pay phone downstairs). English breakfast included. Wi-Fi available. Reserve 2-3 months in advance. 48hr. cancellation policy. Singles with sink £52; doubles with sink £72, with bath £92; triples £92/112; quads with bath £132. MC/V. ❸

IES Chelsea Pointe, (☎020 7808 9200; www.iesreshall.com), corner of Manresa Rd. and King's Rd., entrance on Manresa Rd. ⊖Sloane Sq., then Bus #11, 19, 22, 319; ⊖South Kensington, then Bus #49. Night Bus #N11, N19, N22. Brand new university residence offers clean, basic dorms. Amenities include phones, a modern kitchen, laundry service, and 5 TV/DVD lounges. Linens provided but guests must wash them. Free Wi-Fi. 1 week min. stay. Reservations recommended. 72hr. cancellation policy. Wheelchair-accessible. More availability during summer and winter school breaks. Singles £300-360 per week; doubles £394 per week. In the heart of trendy Chelsea, these prices are unheard of. AmEx/MC/V. ❸

FOOD

Any restaurant charging under £10 for a main course is relatively inexpensive. For the best and cheapest ethnic restaurants, head to the source: Whitechapel for Bangladeshi baltis, Chinatown for dim sum, South Kensington for French pastries, Edgware Road for shawarma. The best places to get your own ingredients are street markets (see **Shopping, p. 128**). To buy groceries, try supermarket chains **Tesco, Safeway, Sainsbury's,** or **Marks & Spencer.**

BAYSWATER

Aphrodite Taverna, 15 Hereford Rd. (☎020 7229 2206). ⊖Bayswater or Notting Hill Gate. Zealously decorated walls feature an abundance of Aphrodite sculptures. Fabulous menu includes traditional favorites like *dolmedes* (stuffed grape leaves; £8.50), *keftedes* (Greek meatballs; £8.50), hummus, *tzaziki,* and *tambouli.* £1 cover is amply rewarded with baskets of freshly baked pita and other appetizers. Cafe Aphrodite next door offers some of Taverna's specialties at cheaper prices as well as a full sandwich menu (from £3). Takeaway available. Restaurant open M-Sa noon-midnight. Cafe open daily 8am-5pm. AmEx/MC/V. Restaurant ❷. Cafe ❶

Durbar Tandoori, 24 Hereford St. (☎020 7727 1947; www.durbartandoori.co.uk). ⊖Bayswater. Enjoy the refined dining room and revel in the inexpensive goodness of London's oldest family-owned Indian restaurant, which celebrated 50 years in 2006. Generous portions of dishes from regions throughout India. Vegetarian and meat entrees from £6. Bargain take-away lunch box £6. Chef's special dinner for 2 £25. Open M-Th and Sa-Su noon-2:30pm and 5:30-11:30pm, F 5:30-11:30 pm. AmEx/MC/V. ❷

Khan's Restaurant, 13-15 Westbourne Grove (☎020 7727 5420; www.khansrestaurant.com). ⊖Bayswater. This family-run restaurant celebrated its 30th birthday in 2009. Hearty portions of Indian favorites served among faux palm tree pillars. The extensive menu features tandoori specialties (chicken tikka; £5.80) as well as other meat, chicken, and seafood dishes (fish curry; £6.40). Thalis £9.50-£11. Takeaway available. Open M-Th noon-2:45pm and 6-11:45pm; F-Su 6pm-midnight. AmEx/MC/V. ❷

BLOOMSBURY

Navarro's Tapas Bar, 67 Charlotte St. (☎020 7637 7713; www.navarros.co.uk). ⊖Goodge St. Colorful, bustling tapas restaurant with blue tiled walls, brightly painted furniture, and flamenco music straight from Seville. The authenticity carries over to the excellent food—try the spicy fried potatoes (*patatas bravas;* £4.90), spinach with chickpeas (*espinacas con garbanzos;* £5) or one of the many brochettes of lamb, chicken, or prawns (£12-15). Tapas £4-15; 2-3 per person is plenty. £10 min. purchase. Reservations recommended for dinner. Open M-F noon-3pm and 6-10pm, Sa 6-10pm. AmEx/MC/V. ❸

Newman Arms, 23 Rathbone St., (☎020 7636 1127). ⊖Tottenham Court Rd. or Goodge St. A pub with a famous upstairs pie room and restaurant. Connoisseurs at 10 sought-after tables dig into homemade pies (with potatoes and vegetables; £10). Most are filled with seasonal game, but there's always a vegetarian option. Just-as-comforting desserts like spotted dick, puddings, and crumbles. Pints from £3. Book in advance. Pub open M-F noon-12:30am. Restaurant open M-Th noon-3pm and 6-9pm, F noon-3pm. MC/V. ❷

CHELSEA

Buona Sera, at the Jam, 289A King's Rd. (☎020 7352 8827). ⊖Sloane Sq., then Bus #19 or 319 (or a 10-15min. walk along King's). With patented "bunk" tables stacked high into the air and plants for effect, the treetop-esque dining experience alone justifies a visit; the mouth-watering Italian fare makes it practically mandatory. Waiters climb small wooden ladders to deliver generous plates of pasta (£8.20-11) along with fish and steak dishes (£12-15). Enjoy, but don't drop your fork. Open M 6pm-midnight, Tu-F noon-3pm and 6pm-midnight, Sa-Su noon-midnight. Reservations recommended F-Sa; for a higher bunk always reserve. AmEx/MC/V. ❸

Chelsea Bun, 9A Limerston St. (☎020 7352 3635). ⊖Sloane Sq., then Bus #11 or 22. Chelsea-ites spill into this spirited and casual Anglo-American diner, which serves heaping portions of everything from the "Ultimate Breakfast" (3 eggs, 3 pancakes, sausages, hash browns, bacon, burger, french toast, kitchen sink; £11) to Tijuana Benedict (eggs with chorizo sausage and tomato; £0). Also serves a plethora of sandwiches, salads, pasta, and burgers £2.80-9.20. Extensive vegetarian and vegan options. Early-bird specials available M-F 7am-noon (£2.20-3.20) and breakfast (from £4) served until 6pm. £3.50 min. per person lunch, £5.50 dinner. Open M-Sa 7am-midnight, Su 8am-7pm. MC/V. ❷

THE CITY OF LONDON

CafeSpice Namaste, 16 Prescot St. (☎020 7488 9242; www.cafespice.co.uk). ⊖Tower Hill or DLR: Tower Gateway. Somewhat out of the way, but well worth the trek. Bright, festive decorations bring a zany feel to this old Victorian warehouse with courtyard seating. Extensive menu of Goan and Parsi specialties. Meat mains are on the pricey side (from £14.30), but vegetarian dishes (from £5.50) are tasty and affordable. Varied wine list and excellent, if expensive, desserts. Open M-F noon-3pm and 6:15-10:30pm, Sa 6:30-10:30pm. Reservations recommended. AmEx/MC/V. ❸

CLERKENWELL AND HOLBORN

The Clerkenwell Kitchen, 31 Clerkenwell Close (☎020 7101 9959; www.theclerkenwellkitchen.co.uk). ⊖Farringdon. Hidden in a former warehouse among the twists and turns of the Close, this hip cafe specializes in sustainable food production. Every day the staff prepares 6 dishes, 2 puddings, and a selection of takeaway sanwiches, pastries, and tarts, almost all of which are made with organic and local ingredients. Dishes like spinach, onion, and feta tart and crab and fennel linguini £4.50-11. Open M-W and F 8am-5pm, Th 8am-11pm; breakfast 8-11am, lunch noon-3pm, snacks 3-5pm. MC/V. ❷

Bleeding Heart Tavern (☎020 7404 0333), on the corner of Greville St. and Bleeding Heart Yard. ⊖Farringdon. This jovial pub has guarded the entrance to Bleeding Heart Yard since 1746, and maintains the same motto: "drunk for a penny and dead drunk for two." Roast suckling pig with sage, apple, and onion stuffing (£14). Classic beer-battered haddock with marrow fat peas (£11). Open M-F 7-10:30am, noon-2:30pm, 6-10:30pm. Upstairs pub open M-F 11:30am-11pm. AmEx/MC/V. ❷

EAST LONDON

Café 1001, 91 Brick Lane, Dray Walk (☎7247 9679; www.cafe1001.co.uk), in an alley just off Brick Ln. ⊖Aldgate East. This massive warehouse-turned-artists' den feels more like a never-ending block party than a cafe. Young students, artists and assorted hipster types lounge in couches in the spacious upstairs or at the numerous picnic tables that dominate the alleyway, while staff dole out fresh homemade food to eat in or take away. Choose from a variety of premade salads (3 for £3.50) and healthy main dishes (£5.95 including 3 side salads) at the buffet, or grab a massive sandwich (from £3.50) and pastry (from £.80) at the cafe side. Selections of wine and beer (£2-4). Outdoor barbecue weather permitting (burgers £4, with fries £4.50). Nightly DJs or live bands 8pm-close, W live jazz. Open M-Th and Su 6am-midnight, F-Sa 6am-12:30am. ❶

Chaat, 36 Redchurch St. (☎020 7739 9595; www.chaatlondon.co.uk). ⊖Liverpool St. A sleek but cozy restaurant, tea room, and bar, Chaat is the perfect place to do just that--over delicious Bangladeshi food, served in five courses. Start with a "Chit Chaat" like samosas or tomato, ginger, and coriander soup; follow it with a veggie or meat dish; add a "Mopper" (rice or bread) and an accompaniment like dhal or pan-fried okra; and finish with a homemade dip. Doubles as an art gallery. All 5 "parts" £13.95. Reservations recommended. Open M-Sa 6:30-11pm. AmEx/MC/V. ❷

MARYLEBONE AND REGENT'S PARK

Le Relais de Venise "L'Entrecote," 120 Marylebone Ln. (☎020 7486 0878; www.relaisdevenice.com). ⊖Bond St. 2nd location at 5 Throgmorton St., The City (☎020 7638 6325). This wildly popular French restaurant ventures across the channel; the queue is usually down the street. There's only one dish on the menu: steak, fries, and salad (£19). Pace yourself: as soon as you're done, they'll bring you more. Delicious desserts £5. Open M-Th noon-2:30pm and 6-10:45pm, F noon-2:45pm and 6-10:45pm, Sa 12:30-3:30pm and 6:30-10:45pm, Su 12:30-3:30pm and 6:30-10:30pm. AmEx/MC/V. ❹

Patogh, 8 Crawford Pl. (☎020 7262 4015). ⊖Edgware Rd. With just 10 tables and a cave-like interior, this charming Persian restaurant gives new meaning to "hole in the wall." Generous portions of sesame-seed flatbread (£2) and freshly prepared starters (£2-4) will whet your appetite; flame-grilled kebabs like kebab *koobideh* (minced lamb kebab) with bread, rice, or salad (£5-12) could feed you for days. Takeaway available. Open daily noon-midnight. Cash only. ❷

NORTH LONDON

Gallipoli Cafe Bistro, 102 Upper St. (☎020 7359 0630), **Gallipoli Again,** 120 Upper St. (☎0207 359 1578), and **Gallipoli Bazaar,** 107 Upper St. (☎020 7226 5333). ⊖Angel. Three's usually a crowd, but not with this group of tasty Upper St. eateries. In fact, they only bring the crowds. Dark walls, patterned tiles, and hanging lamp and lanterns provide the background to spectacular Lebanese, Turkish, and Mediterranean delights like hummus, falafel, *kisir* (simliar to tabouleh), kebab, and *moussaka.* Try one of the set meals for 2, which come with a selection of hot and cold appetizers (£11-15 per person). Gallipoli Cafe was the original; Gallipoli Again opened in response to its immense popularity (with the added bonus of an outdoor patio); and Gallipoli Bazaar, which sits between the other two, serves up *sheesha* and food in tea-room surroundings. Again and Bazaar wheelchair-accessible. Open M-Th 10:30am-11pm, F-Sa 10:30am-midnight, Su 10:30am-11pm. Reservations recommended F-Sa. MC/V. ❷

Le Crêperie de Hampstead, 77 Hampstead High St. (www.hampsteadcreperie.com). ⊖Hampstead. Proof that good things come in small packages, this metal stand, topped with a traditional Parisian street sign, serves phenomenal crepes that are worth the wait. Most savory crepes are made with some combination of spinach, mushroom, ratatouille, asparagus, cream, egg, cheese and ham (£3.40-4.50). The most popular sweet crepe is the Banana Maple Cream Dream, with banana, walnuts, maple syrup, and cream (£4.30). Open M-Th 11:45am-11pm, F-Su 11:45am-11:30pm. Cash only. ❶

THE WEST END

Busaba Eathai, 8-13 Bird St. (☎020 7518 8080; www.busaba.com). ⊖Oxford St. Also at 106-110 Wardour St., Soho (☎7255 8686). Incense, floating candles, and slick wood paneling make you feel like you're dining in a Buddhist temple. Large, tightly-packed communal tables ensure a lively wait for the affordable, filling dishes. Students and locals line up for stir fry, curry, pad thai, and other wok creations (£6.20-11). Tons of vegetarian dishes. Open M-Th noon-11pm, F-Sa noon-11:30pm, Su noon-10pm. AmEx/MC/V. ❷

The Breakfast Club, 33 D'Arblay St. (☎020 726 5454; www.thebreakfastclubsoho.com). A favorite spot for the irreverent brunch-goer, serving creative twists on classics like eggs benedict, pancakes, burritos and burgers. Large family-style tables with red-

checkered table cloths. Specials like The Full Monty (bacon, sausage, beans, tomatoes, mushrooms; £6.20) or The Number wrap (goat cheese, roasted red peppers and eggplant, pesto, tomato chutney; £6). Full Metal Jacket Potatoes with a variety of toppings £4.50-5.50. Super smoothies £3.50. Open M-F 8am-6pm, Sa 9:30am-5pm, Su 10am-4pm. Cash only. ❶

Golden Dragon, 28-29 Gerrard St. (☎020 1705 2503). ⊖Leicester Sq. The ritziest and best-known dim sum joint in Chinatown. Golden Dragon's 2 large red-and-gold rooms (yes, there are dragons) are packed on the weekends with families and couples taking in the cheery atmosphere and shoveling in the dumplings—from veggie staples to minced prawn and sugar cane treats (each dish £2.40-3.20). Regular dinner items £6.20-22. Dim sum £15-25. Open M-Th noon-11:30pm, F-Sa noon-midnight, Su 11am-11pm. Dim sum served M-Sa noon-5pm, Su 11am-5pm. AmEx/MC/V. ❹

OTHER NEIGHBORHOODS

George's Portobello Fish Bar, 329 Portobello Rd. (☎020 8969 7895). ⊖Ladbroke Grove. A London institution, George's garners praise from all who enter: Naked Chef Jamie Oliver, for one, raves about the place. George opened up here in 1961, and with his daughter now at the helm, the fish and chips are still as good as ever. Cod, rockfish, plaice, and skate come with a huge serving of chunky chips (from £7) and the popular barbecue ribs (£7) are made according to a secret recipe. With only a couple outdoor tables, seating is so scarce that on Sa, a seat costs £3 per person. Open M-F 11am-11:45pm, Sa 11am-9pm, Su noon-9:30pm. Cash only. ❷

Rock and Sole Place, 47 Endell St. (☎020 7836 3785). ⊖Covent Garden. There's a reason Rock and Sole's been around since 1871: messy and delicious fried fish in an equally no-frills environment. A self-proclaimed "master fryer" (qualifications unclear) turns out tasty haddock, cod, halibut, and sole filets (all with chips; £9 takeaway, £11 sit down), while customers gather around the crowded diner tables inside, or the large wooden picnic tables under the giant tree outside. Extras like mushy peas, baked beans, coleslaw, or curry or gravy sauce £0.50-1.50. Open M-Sa 11:30am-11:45pm, Su noon-10:30pm. MC/V. ❷

Jenny Lo's Teahouse, 14 Eccleston St. (☎020 7259 0399). ⊖Victoria. The daughter of the late Ken Lo, at one point one of the most famous Cantonese chefs in the UK, Jenny Lo serves some of the best noodles in town. A healthy variety of Vietnamese, Thai, and Wok noodles (everything from *ho fun* to *wun tun*) brings a crowd every time the clock strikes noon. Of course, to top off the meal, Jenny offers a selection of Chinese, mint, and "therapeutic" teas (£1.90). Vegetarian options abound. Takeaway and delivery available over £5 per person. Noodles £7-8.50. Open M-F noon-3pm and 6-10pm. Cash only. ❷

SIGHTS

WESTMINSTER

The City of Westminster, now a borough of London, has been the seat of British power for over 1000 years. William the Conqueror was crowned in Westminster Abbey on Christmas Day, AD 1066, and his successors built the Palace of Westminster, which today houses Parliament.

WESTMINSTER ABBEY. Founded as a Benedictine monastery, Westminster Abbey has evolved into a house of kings and queens both living and dead. Almost nothing remains of **St. Edward's Abbey:** Henry III's 13th-century Gothic reworking created most of the current grand structure. Britons buried or commemorated inside the Abbey include: **Henry VII; Mary, Queen of Scots; Elizabeth I;** and the scholars and artists honored in the **"Poet's Corner"** (Jane Austen, the

Brontë sisters, Chaucer, Shakespeare, and Dylan Thomas). A door off the east cloister leads to the **Chapter House,** the original meeting place of the House of Commons. Next door to the Abbey (through the cloisters), the lackluster **Abbey Museum** is in the Norman undercroft. Just north of the Abbey, **St. Margaret's Church** enjoys a strange status: as a part of the Royal Peculiar, it is neither under the jurisdiction of the diocese of England nor the archbishop of Canterbury. Since 1614, it's been the official worshipping place of the House of Commons. *(Parliament Sq. ⊖Westminster. Abbey ☎7654 4900, Chapter House 7222 5152; www.westminster-abbey.org. No photography. Abbey open M-Tu and Th-F 9:30am-3:45pm, W 9:30am-7pm, Sa 9:30am-1:45pm, Su open for services only. Museum open daily 10:30am-4pm. Partially wheelchair-accessible. Abbey and Museum £15, students and children 11-17 £12, families of 4 £36. Services free. 1hr. tours £3 Apr.-Oct. M-F 10, 10:30, 11am, 2, 2:30pm, Sa 10, 10:30, 11am; Oct.-Mar. M-F 10:30, 11am, 2, 2:30pm, Sa 10:30, 11am. Audio tours available; free. M-F 9:30am-3:30pm, Sa 9:30am-1pm. AmEx/MC/V.)*

BUCKINGHAM PALACE. The Palace has been the official residence of the British monarchs since 1837, when a youthful Queen Victoria decamped from nearby Kensington Palace to set up housekeeping in this English Taj Mahal. With 755 rooms and a suite of state chambers decorated with Rembrandt and Vermeer, **Buckingham Palace** celebrates the splendor and power of 19th-century English monarchy. The Palace is open to visitors from late July to late September every year, but don't expect to meet the Queen—the State Rooms are the only rooms on view, and they are used only for formal occasions. "God Save the Queen" is the rallying cry at the Queens Gallery, dedicated to exhibits of absurdly valuable items from the Royal Collection. Detached from the palace and tour, the **Royal Mews** acts as a museum, stable, riding school, and working carriage house. The main attraction is the Queen's collection of coaches, including the Cinderella-like "Glass Coach" used to carry royal brides, including Princess Diana, to their weddings, and the State Coaches of Australia, Ireland, and Scotland. Another highlight is the 4 ton **Gold State Coach,** which can occasionally be seen wheeling around the streets in the early morning on practice runs for major events. To witness the Palace for free, attend a session of the **Changing of the Guard.** Show up well before 11:30am and stand in front of the Palace in view of the morning guards, or use the steps of the Victoria Memorial as a vantage point. *(⊖St. James's Park, Victoria, Green Park, or Hyde Park Corner. ☎020 7766 7324; www.the-royal-collection.com. Palace open late July to late Sept. daily 9:30am-6:30pm, last admission 4:15pm. £15, students £14, children 6-17 £8.50, under 5 free, families of 5 £67. Advance booking is recommended and required for disabled visitors. Queens Gallery open daily 10am-5:30pm, last admission 4:30pm. Wheelchair-accessible. £8, students £7, families £22. Royal Mews open late July to late Sept. daily 10am-5pm, last admission 4:15pm; Mar.-July and late Sept. to late Oct. M-Th and Sa-Su 11am—4pm, last admission 3:15pm. Wheelchair-accessible. £7, seniors £6, children under 17 £4.50, families £19. Changing of the Guard Apr. -late July daily, Aug.-Mar. every other day, excepting the Queen's absence, inclement weather, or pressing state functions. Free.)*

THE HOUSES OF PARLIAMENT. Soaring like a spike against the London skyline, the **Palace of Westminster** is one of the most recognizable buildings in the city. It has been home to both the House of Lords and the House of Commons (together known as Parliament) since the 11th century, when Edward the Confessor established his court here. Standing guard on the northern side of the building is the Clock Tower, nicknamed **Big Ben,** after the robustly proportioned Benjamin Hall, a former Commissioner of Works. **Victoria Tower,** at the south end of the palace building, contains copies of every Act of Parliament since 1497. A flag flying from the top signals that Parliament is in session. When the Queen is in the building, a special royal banner is flown instead. Visitors with enough patience or luck to make it inside the chambers can hear the occasional debates between members of both the Lords and the Commons. *(Parliament Sq., in Westminster. Queue for both Houses forms at St. Stephen's entrance, between Old and New Palace Yards. ⊖Westminster. ☎08709 063 773; www.parliament.uk/visiting/visiting.cfm. "Line of Route" Tour: includes both Houses. UK residents can contact their MPs for tours year-round, generally M-W mornings and F. Foreign visitors may tour Aug.-Sept. Book online, by phone, or in person at Abingdon Green ticket office (open mid-July) across from Palace of Westminster. Open Aug. M-Tu and F-Sa 9:15am-4:30pm, W-Th 1:15-4:30pm; Sept. M and F-Sa 9:15am-4:30pm, Tu-Th 1:15-4:30pm. 1¼hr. tours depart every few min. £12, students £8. MC/V.)*

PARLIAMENTARY PROCEDURE. Arrive early in the afternoon to minimize waiting, which often exceeds 2hr. Keep in mind that the wait for Lords is generally shorter than the wait for Commons. To sit in on Parliament's "question time" (40min.; M-W 2:30pm, Th-F 11am) apply for tickets several weeks in advance through your embassy in London.

ST. JAMES'S PARK AND GREEN PARK. The streets leading up to Buckingham Palace are flanked by two expanses of greenery: **St. James's Park** and **Green Park.** In the middle of St. James's Park is the placid St. James's Park Lake and the pelicans who call it home—the lake and the grassy area surrounding it are an official waterfowl preserve. In the back corner, closest to the palace, is a children's playground in memory of Princess Diana. Across the Mall, the lush **Green Park** is the creation of Charles II; it connects Westminster and St. James's. "Constitution Hill" refers not to the King's interest in political theory but to his daily exercises. If you sit on one of the lawn chairs scattered enticingly around both parks, an attendant will magically materialize and demand money. Alternatively, bring a blanket to picnic for free. *(The Mall. ⊖St. James's Park or Green Park. Open daily 5am-midnight. Lawn chairs available, weather permitting, Mar.-Oct. 10am-6pm, June-Aug. 10am-10pm. £3 for 2hr., student deal £30 for the season. Last rental 2hr. before closing. Summer walks in the park some M 1-2pm, including tour of Guard's Palace and Victoria Tower Gardens. Book in advance by calling ☎7930 1793.)*

WESTMINSTER CATHEDRAL. Following Henry VIII's divorce from the Catholic Church, London's Catholic community remained without a cathedral until 1884, when the Church purchased a derelict prison on what used to be a monastery site. The Neo-Byzantine church looks somewhat like a fortress and is now one of London's great religious landmarks. An elevator, well worth the minimal fee, carries visitors up the striped 273 ft. bell tower for an all-encompassing view of Westminster, the river, and Kensington. *(Cathedral Piazza, off Victoria St. ⊖Victoria. ☎7798 9055; www.westminstercathedral.org.uk. Open M-F 7am-7pm, Sa-Su 8am-7pm. Free, suggested donation £2. Bell tower open M-F 9:30am-5:15pm and Sa-Su 10am-4:45pm. Tower £5, students £2.50, families £11. Organ recitals in the winter Su 4:45pm.)*

WHITEHALL. Synonymous with the British civil service, **Whitehall** refers to the stretch of road connecting Trafalgar Sq. with Parliament Sq. From 1532 until a devastating fire in 1698, it was the home of the monarchy and one of the grandest palaces in Europe, although today little remains. Toward the north end of Whitehall, **Great Scotland Yard** marks the former headquarters of the Metropolitan Police. Nearer Parliament Sq., heavily guarded steel gates mark the entrance to Downing Street. In 1735, No. 10 was made the official residence of the First Lord of the Treasury, a position now permanently identified with the Prime Minister. His neighbors, the Chancellor of the Exchequer, and the Parliamentary Chief Whip, live at No. 11 and No. 12, respectively. When Tony Blair's family was too big for No. 10, he switched houses with Gordon Brown, a move that proved convenient when Brown was appointed Prime Minister in

2007. The street is closed to visitors, but if you wait long enough, you might see the PM. South of Downing St., in the middle of Whitehall, Edward Lutyen's *Cenotaph* (1919) stands, a proud tribute to WWI dead. Many of the islands in the middle of the road hold statues honoring monarchs and military heroes, a testament to the avenue's identity as the center of civil service. *(Between Trafalgar Sq. and Parliament Sq. ⊖Westminster, Embankment, or Charing Cross.)*

CHELSEA

CHELSEA PHYSIC GARDEN. Founded in 1673 to provide medicinal herbs to locals, the Physic Garden remains a carefully ordered living repository of useful, rare, and just plain interesting plants. *(66 Royal Hospital Rd.; entrance on Swan Walk. ⊖Sloane Sq., then Bus #137. ☎020 7352 5646; www.chelseaphysicgarden.co.uk. Open from early Apr. to June and Sept.-Oct. W-F noon-5pm, Su noon-6pm; July-Aug. M-Tu and Th-F noon-5pm, W noon-10pm; Feb. Su 10am-4pm; during Chelsea Flower Show (late May) and Chelsea Festival (mid-June) M-F noon-5pm. Tea served M-Sa from 12:30pm, Su from noon. Call ahead for wheelchair access. £8, students and children under 16 £5.)*

THE CITY OF LONDON

ST. PAUL'S CATHEDRAL. Originally built in 604 AD, the majestic St. Paul's is a cornerstone of London's architectural and historical legacy. Architect Christopher Wren's masterpiece is the fifth cathedral to occupy the site. Two years after the Great Fire of 1666, construction of the present cathedral began. Inside, the nave leads to the second-tallest freestanding dome in Europe (after St. Peter's in the Vatican), its height accentuated by the tricky perspective of the paintings on the inner surface. Climbing the 259 narrow steps is exhausting, but the views from the top of the dome are extraordinary and worth the trip: a panoramic cityscape. Circling the base of the inner dome, the **Whispering Gallery** is a perfect resounding chamber: whisper into the wall, and your friend on the other side will hear you—or, theoretically, he or she could if everyone else weren't trying the same thing. Far, far below the lofty dome, the crypt is packed wall-to-wall with plaques and tombs of great Britons and, of course, the ubiquitous gift shop. Lord Nelson commands a prime location, with radiating galleries of gravestones and tributes honoring other military heroes, from Epstein's bust of T.E. Lawrence (of Arabia) to a plaque commemorating the casualties of the Gulf War. The magnificently carved stone of the exterior is warmed and softened by the cathedral gardens which curve round the sides in a ramble of roses and clipped grass. *(St. Paul's Churchyard. ⊖St. Paul's. ☎020 7246 8350; www.stpauls.co.uk. Open M-Sa 8:30am-4pm; last entry 3:45pm. Dome and galleries open M-Sa 8:30am-4pm. Open for worship daily 7:15am-6pm. Partially wheelchair-accessible. Admission £11, students £8.50, children 7-16 £3.50, worshippers free. Group of 10 or more £0.50 discount per ticket. 1½-2hr. "Supertour" M-F 10:45, 11:30am, 1:30, 2pm; £3, students £2.50, children 7-16 £1; English only. Audio tours in English, Chinese, French, German, Italian, Japanese, Russian, and Spanish; 9am-3:30pm; £4, students £3.50.)*

ST. PAUL'S FOR POCKET CHANGE. To gain access to the Cathedral's nave for free, attend an Evensong service (M-Sa 5pm, 45min). Arrive at 4:50pm to be admitted to seats in the choir.

BRITAIN

THE TOWER OF LONDON. The turrets of this multi-functional block—serving as palace, prison, royal mint, and museum over the past 900 years—are impressive not only for their appearance but also for their integral role in England's history. A popular way to get a feel for the Tower is to join one of the theatrical

Yeoman Warders' Tours. Queen Anne Boleyn passed through Traitor's Gate just before her death, but entering the Tower is no longer as perilous as it used to be. **St. Thomas's Tower** begins the self-guided tour of the Medieval Palace. At the end of the **Wall Walk**—a series of eight towers—is **Martin Tower,** which houses an exhibit that traces the history of the British Crown and is now home to a fascinating collection of retired crowns (without the gemstones; those have been recycled into the current models); informative plaques are much better here than in the **Jewel House,** where the crown jewels are held. With the exception of the Coronation Spoon, everything dates from after 1660, since Cromwell melted down the original booty. The centerpiece of the fortress is White Tower, which begins with the first-floor **Chapel of St. John the Evangelist.** Outside, Tower Green is a lovely grassy area—not so lovely, though, for those once executed there. *(Tower Hill, next to Tower Bridge, within easy reach of the South Bank and the East End. ⊖Tower Hill or DLR: Tower Gateway. ☎0870 751 5175, ticket sales 0870 756 6060; www.hrp.org.uk. Open Mar.-Oct. M and Su 10am-6pm, Tu-Sa 9am-6pm; buildings close at 5:30pm, last entry 5pm. Nov.-Feb. M and Su 10am-5pm, Tu-Sa 9am-5pm; buildings close at 4:30pm, last entry 4pm. Tower Green open only by Yeoman tours, after 4:30pm, or for daily services. £17, concessions £15, children 5-15 £9.50, children under 5 free, families of 5 £47. Tickets also sold at Tube stations; buy them in advance to avoid long queues at the door. "Yeoman Warders' Tours" meet near entrance; 45min.-1hr., every 30min. M and Su 10am-3:30pm, Tu-Sa 9:30am-3:30pm. Audio tours in 9 languages including English. £4, concessions £3.)*

TOWER BRIDGE. Not to be mistaken for its plainer sibling, London Bridge, Tower Bridge is featured in most movies set in London. A relatively new construction—built in 1894—its bright blue suspension cables connect the banks of the Thames, raising it above the cluster of other bridges in the area. The Victorian steam-powered lifting mechanism remained in use until 1973, when electric motors took over. Although clippers no longer sail into London very often, there's still enough large river traffic for the bridge to be lifted around 1000 times per year and five or six times per day in the summer. Call for the schedule or check the signs posted at each entrance. Historians and technophiles will appreciate the **Tower Bridge Exhibition,** which combines scenic 140 ft. glass-enclosed walkways with videos presenting a history of the bridge. *(Entrance to the Tower Bridge Exhibition is through the west side (upriver) of the North Tower. ⊖Tower Hill or London Bridge. ☎020 7403 3761, for lifting schedule 7940 3984; www.towerbridge.org.uk. Open daily Apr.-Sept. 10am-5:30pm; Oct.-Mar. 9:30am-5pm. Wheelchair-accessible. £7, students £5, children 5-16 £3.)*

THE SOUTH BANK

SHAKESPEARE'S GLOBE THEATRE. This incarnation of the Globe is faithful to the original, thatch roof and all. The original burned down in 1613 after a 14-year run as the Bard's preferred playhouse. Today's reconstruction had its first full season in 1997 and now stands as the cornerstone of the International Shakespeare Globe Centre. The informative exhibit inside covers the theater's history and includes displays on costumes and customs of the theater, as well as information on other prominent playwrights of Shakespeare's era. There's also an interactive display where you can trade lines with recorded Globe actors. Try to arrive in time for a tour of the theater itself. Tours that run during a matinee skip the Globe but are the only way to gain admission to the neighboring **Rose Theatre,** where both Shakespeare and Christopher Marlowe performed. For info on performances, see p. 127. *(Bankside, close to Bankside pier. ⊖Southwark or London Bridge. ☎020 7902 1400; www.shakespeares-globe.org. Open Mar. daily 9am-5pm (exhibit and tours); Apr.-Sept. M-Sa 9am-12:30pm (exhibit and Globe tour) and 12:30-5pm (exhibit and Rose Tour), Su 9-11:30am (exhibit and Globe)* *and noon-5pm (exhibit and Rose); Oct.-Apr. daily 10am-5pm (exhibit). Wheelchair-accessible. £11, concessions £8.50, children 5-15 £6.50, families of 5 £28.)*

SOUTHWARK CATHEDRAL. A site of worship since AD 606, the cathedral has undergone numerous transformations in the last 1400 years: it was a convent in 606, a priory in 1106, a parish church in 1540, and finally, a cathedral since 1905. Shakespeare's brother Edmund is buried here. During the reign of Queen Mary, many high-profile Protestant martyrs were tried in the retrochoir. Near the center, the archaeological gallery is actually a small excavation by the cathedral wall, revealing a first-century Roman road. Free organ recitals on Mondays from 1:10 to 1:50pm. *(Montague Close. ⊖London Bridge. ☎020 7367 6700; www.southwark.anglican.org/cathedral. Open M-F 8am-6pm, Sa-Su 9am-6pm. Wheelchair-accessible. Free, suggested donation £4. Groups are asked to book in advance; group rates available. Camera permit £2; video permit £5.)*

LONDON EYE. At 135m (430 ft.), the British Airways London Eye, also known as the Millennium Wheel, is the biggest observational wheel in the world. The ellipsoidal glass "pods" give uninterrupted views from the top during each 30min. revolution. *(Jubilee Gardens, between County Hall and the Festival Hall. ⊖Waterloo. ☎087 990 8883; www.londoneye.com. Open daily May-June 10am-9pm; July-Aug. 10am-9:30pm; Sept. 10am-9pm; Oct.-Apr. 10am-8pm. Wheelchair-accessible. Buy tickets from the box office at the corner of County Hall before joining the queue at the Eye. Advance booking recommended, but check the weather. £17, concessions £14, children under 16 £8.50.)*

GET HIGH FOR FREE. If paying £20 for the London Eye seems a bit steep for a bird's-eye view of the city, climb the tower at the nearby Tate Modern (p. 123), which gives a similar view for free.

BLOOMSBURY AND MARYLEBONE. During the early 20th century, Gordon Sq. resounded with the philosophizing and womanizing of the Bloomsbury Group, a set of intellectuals including John Maynard Keynes, Bertrand Russell, Lytton Strachey, and Virginia Woolf. Marylebone's most famous resident (and address) never existed: 221b Baker St. was the fictional home of Sherlock Holmes, but 221 Baker St. is actually the headquarters of the Abbey National Bank.

REGENT'S PARK. When Crown Architect John Nash designed Regent's Park, he envisioned a residential development for the "wealthy and good." Fortunately for us commonfolk, Parliament opened the space to all in 1811, creating London's handsomest and most popular recreation area. Most of the park's top attractions and activities lie near the **Inner Circle,** a road that separates the meticulously maintained **Queen Mary's Gardens** from the rest of the grounds. While the few villas in the park—The Holme and St. John's Lodge—are private residences for the unimaginably rich and are not available for public viewing, the formal **Gardens of St. John's Lodge** ("The Secret Garden"), on the northern edge of the Inner Circle, give a peek into the backyard of one such mansion. The climb up Primrose Hill, just north of Regent's Park proper, offers a splendid view of central London. *(⊖Baker St., Regent's Park, Great Portland St., or Camden Town. ☎020 7486 7905, police ☎020 7706 7272; www.royalparks.org. Open daily 5am-dusk. Free.)* The famous **Open Air Theatre,** which began in 1932, is now Britain's premier outdoor Shakespeare theater and stages performances from May to Sept. *(☎020 826 4242; www.opentheatre.org. £10-30.)*

BRITISH LIBRARY. The British Library is a paradox: the sleekest, most modern of buildings (finished in 1998) contains in its vast and comprehensive holdings some of the oldest and most precious English literary and historical documents. Most of the library is underground, with 12 million books on 200 miles of shelving; the above-ground brick building is home to cavernous reading rooms and a museum. Displayed in a glass cube toward the rear of the building, the 65,000 volumes of the King's Library, collected by George III, were bequeathed to the nation in 1823 by his less bookish son, George IV. Treasures of the British Library Room include Beethoven's tuning fork, Tudor documents, and original manuscripts of *Beowulf, Jane Eyre, and Tess of the D'Urbervilles. (96 Euston Rd. ⊖King's Cross St. Pancras. ☎020 7412 7332; www.bl.uk. Grab a free map at the main info desk. Open M and W-F 9:30am-6pm, Tu 9:30am-8pm, Sa 9:30am-5pm, Su 11am-5pm. Wheelchair-accessible. Free.)*

OTHER BLOOMSBURY SIGHTS. A co-founder and key advisor of **University College London,** social philosopher Jeremy Bentham still watches over his old haunts; his body has sat on display in the **South Cloister** since 1850, wax head and all, as requested in his will. *(Main entrance on Gower St. South Cloister entrance through the courtyard, in the back right corner. ⊖Euston. ☎020 7679 2000; www.ucl.ac.uk. Quadrangle gates close at midnight; access to Jeremy Bentham ends at 6pm. Wheelchair-accessible. Free.)*

CLERKENWELL AND HOLBORN

Clerkenwell buildings are beautiful from the outside but inaccessible to tourists; walk the **Clerkenwell Historic Trail** to see the exteriors. *(Free maps at the 3 Things Coffee Room, 53 Clerkenwell Close. ☎020 7125 37438. ⊖Farringdon. Open daily 8am-8pm.)*

THE TEMPLE. Named after the crusading Order of the Knights Templar, this complex of buildings houses legal and parliamentary offices, but it hasn't lost its clerical flavor: silent, suited barristers hurry by at all hours, clutching briefcases. The charming network of gardens and the medieval church remain open to the enterprising visitor. Make sure to see the **Inner Temple Gateway,** between 16 and 17 Fleet St., the 1681 fountain of **Fountain Court** (featured in Dickens's *Martin Chuzzlewit*), and Elm Court, tucked behind the church, a tiny yet exquisite garden ringed by massive stone structures. *(Between Essex St. and Temple Ave.; church courtyard off Middle Temple Ln. ⊖Temple or Blackfriars. Free.)*

KENSINGTON AND EARL'S COURT

Nobody took much notice of Kensington before 1689, when the newly crowned William III and Mary II moved into Kensington Palace. In 1851, the Great Exhibition brought in enough money to finance museums and colleges. Now that the neighborhood is home to expensive stores like Harrods and Harvey Nichols, it's hard to imagine the days when the area was known for taverns and highwaymen (robbers galloping on horseback).

HYDE PARK AND KENSINGTON GARDENS. Enclosed by London's wealthiest neighborhoods, **Hyde Park** has served as the model for city parks around the world, including Central Park in New York and Paris's Bois de Boulogne. **Kensington Gardens,** contiguous with Hyde Park and originally part of it, was created in the late 17th century when William and Mary set up house in Kensington Palace. *(Framed by Kensington Rd., Knightsbridge, Park Ln., and Bayswater Rd. ⊖Queensway, Lancaster Gate, Marble Arch, Hyde Park Corner, or High St. Kensington. ☎020 7298 2100; www.royalparks.org.uk. Park open daily 6am-dusk. Free. "Liberty Drive" rides available Tu-F 10am-5pm for seniors and the disabled; ☎077 6749 8096. A full program of music, performance, and children's activities takes place during the summer; see park notice boards for details.)* In the middle of the park is the **Serpentine,** officially known as the "Long Water West of the Serpentine Bridge." Doggy-paddling tourists and boaters have made it London's busiest swimming hole. Nowhere near the water, the **Serpentine Gallery** holds contemporary art and is free and open to the public daily from 10am to 6pm. *(⊖Hyde Park Corner. Boating: ☎020 7262 1330. Open Apr.-Sept. daily 10am-5pm or later in* *fine weather. £5 per 30min., £7 per hr.; children £2/3. Deposit may be required for large groups. Swimming at the Lido, south shore: ☎ 020 7706 3422. Open from June to early Sept. daily 10am-5:30pm. Lockers and sun lounges available. £4, after 4pm £3; students £3/2; children 1p/80p; families £9. Gallery open daily 10am-5pm. Free.)* At the northeast corner of the park, near Marble Arch, you can see free speech in action as proselytizers, politicos, and flat-out crazies dispense wisdom to bemused tourists at **Speaker's Corner** on Sundays, the only place in London where demonstrators can assemble without a permit.

KENSINGTON PALACE. In 1689 William and Mary commissioned Christopher Wren to remodel Nottingham House into a palace. Kensington remained the principal royal residence until George III decamped to Kew in 1760, but it is still in use—Princess Diana lived here. It was here that the young Victoria was awakened from her canopied bed in 1837 and told the crown was hers. Royalty fanatics can tour the rather underwhelming **Hanoverian State Apartments,** with *trompe l'œil* paintings by William Kent, or the **Royal Ceremonial Dress Collection,** a magnificent spread of tailored and embroidered garments. *(On the western edge of Kensington Gardens; enter through the park. ⊖High St. Kensington, Notting Hill Gate, or Queensway. ☎ 020 7937 9561; www.hrp.org.uk/kensingtonpalace. Open daily 10am-6pm; last entry 1hr. before closing. Wheelchair-accessible. £13, students £11, children 5-15 £6.30, families of 5 £34. Combo passes with Tower of London or Hampton Court available; discounts for online purchases. MC/V.)*

KNIGHTSBRIDGE AND BELGRAVIA

APSLEY HOUSE. Named for Baron Apsley, the house later known as "No. 1, London" was bought in 1817 by the Duke of Wellington, whose heirs still occupy a modest suite on the top floor. Most visitors come for Wellington's fine art collection, much of which was given to him by the crowned heads of Europe following the Battle of Waterloo. The old masters hang in the Waterloo Gallery, where the duke held his annual Waterloo banquet around the stupendous silver centerpiece, now displayed in the dining room. *(Hyde Park Corner. ⊖Hyde Park Corner. ☎ 020 7499 5676; www.english-heritage.org.uk/london. Open Apr.-Oct. W-Su 11am-5pm; Nov.-Mar. W-Su 11am-4pm. Wheelchair-accessible. £5.70, students £4.80, children 5-18 £2.90. Joint ticket with Wellington Arch £7/6/3.50. Audio tours free. MC/V.)*

WELLINGTON ARCH. Standing at the center of London's most infamous intersection, the Wellington Arch was ignored by tourists and Londoners alike until April 2001, when the completion of a restoration project revealed the interior to the public. Exhibits on the building's history and the changing nature of war memorials play second fiddle to the two observation platforms which provide nice views of Buckingham Palace gardens, Green Park, and Hyde Park. *(Hyde Park Corner. ⊖Hyde Park Corner. ☎ 020 7930 2726; www.english-heritage.org.uk/london. Open W-Su Apr.-Oct. 10am-5pm, Nov.-Mar. 10am-4pm. Wheelchair-accessible. £3.50, students £3, children 5-16 £1.80. Joint tickets with Apsley House available. MC/V.)*

THE WEST END

TRAFALGAR SQUARE. John Nash first suggested laying out this square in 1820, but it took almost 50 years for London's largest traffic roundabout to take on its current appearance. The square is named in commemoration of the defeat of Napoleon's navy at Trafalgar—England's greatest naval victory. It has traditionally been a site for public rallies and protest movements, but it is packed with tourists, pigeons, and the ever-ubiquitous black taxis on a daily basis. Towering over the square is the 170 ft. granite **Nelson's Column,** which until recently was one of the world's tallest displays of decades-old pigeon droppings. Now, thanks to a deep clean sponsored by the Mayor, this monument to naval hero Lord Nelson sparkles once again. *(⊖Charing Cross.)*

ST. MARTIN-IN-THE-FIELDS. The fourth church to stand here, James Gibbs's 1726 creation is instantly recognizable: the rectangular portico building supporting a soaring steeple has made it the model for countless Georgian churches in Ireland and America. Handel and Mozart both performed here, and today the church hosts frequent concerts with some of Europe's premier symphonies and conductors. In order to support the church's maintenance, a delicious cafe, book shop, and art gallery dwell in the Crypt. *(St. Martin's Ln., northeast corner of Trafalgar Sq.; crypt entrance on Duncannon St. ⊖Leicester Sq. or Charing Cross. ☎020 7766 1100; www.smitf.org. Call or visit website for hours and further information.)*

SOHO. A glitteringly eclectic conglomeration of squares and tourist capitalists, Soho is one of the most diverse areas in central London. **Old Compton Street** is the center of London's GLBT culture. In the 1950s, immigrants from Hong Kong started moving en masse to the few blocks just north of Leicester Sq., around Gerrard St. and grittier Lisle St., which now form Chinatown. Gaudy, brash, and world-famous, **Piccadilly Circus** is made up of four of the West End's major arteries (Piccadilly, Regent St., Shaftesbury Ave., and the Haymarket). In the middle of all the glitz and neon stands Gilbert's famous **Statue of Eros.** *(⊖Piccadilly Circus.)* Lined with tour buses, overpriced clubs, and generic cafes, Leicester Sq. is one destination that Londoners go out of their way to avoid due to throngs of tourists. *(⊖Piccadilly Circus or Leicester Sq.)* A calm in the midst of the storm, Soho Square is a rather scruffy patch of green space popular with picnickers. Its removed location makes the square more hospitable and less trafficked than Leicester. *(⊖Tottenham Ct. Rd. Park open daily 10am-dusk.)*

MUSEUMS AND GALLERIES

Centuries spent as the capital of an empire, together with a decidedly English penchant for collecting, have given London a spectacular set of museums. Art lovers, history buffs, and amateur ethnologists won't know which way to turn. Even better news for museum lovers: since 2002, admission to all major collections is free in celebration of the Queen's Golden Jubilee.

MAJOR COLLECTIONS

TATE MODERN. Sir Giles Gilbert Scott's mammoth building, formerly the Bankside power station, houses the second half of the national collection (the other set is held in the National Gallery). The Tate Modern is probably the most popular museum in London, as well as one of the most famous modern art museums in the world. The public galleries on the third and fifth floors are divided into four themes. The collection is enormous, but gallery space is limited—works rotate frequently. If you are dying to see a particular piece, head to the museum's computer station on the fifth floor to browse the entire collection. The seventh floor has unblemished views of the Thames and north and south of London. *(Main entrance on Bankside, on the South Bank; 2nd entrance on Queen's Walk. ⊖Southwark or Blackfriars. From the Southwark Tube, turn left up Union, then left on Great Suffolk, then left on Holland. ☎020 7887 8000; www.tate.org.uk. Open M-Th and Su 10am-6pm, F-Sa 10am-10pm. Free; special exhibits can be up to £10. Free tours meet on the gallery concourses: Level 3 at 11am and noon, Level 5 at 2 and 3pm. 5 types of audio tours include highlights, collection tour, architecture tour, children's tour, and tours for the visually impaired; £4, concessions £3.50. Free talks M-F 1pm; meet at the concourse on the appropriate level. Wheelchair-accessible on Holland St.)*

NATIONAL GALLERY. The National Gallery is an enormous gallery stuffed with masterpieces. Unless you have a few years, you will have to power past the magnificent collections of Titians, Botticellis, DaVincis, and medieval art. Don't miss the fabulously detailed *Arnolfini Wedding Portrait* by Van Eyck or Van Gogh's iconic *Sunflowers*. Founded by an Act of Parliament in 1824, the Gallery has grown to hold an enormous collection of Western European paintings, ranging from the 1200s to the 1900s. Numerous additions have been made, the most recent (and controversial) being the massive modern Sainsbury Wing, which holds almost all of the museum's large exhibitions as well as restaurants and lecture halls. If pressed for time, head to **Art Start** in the Sainsbury Wing, where you can design and print out a personalized tour of the paintings you want to see. Themed audio tours and family routes also available from the information desk. *(Main entrance (Portico Entrance) on north side of Trafalgar Sq. ⊖Charing Cross or Leicester Sq. ☎020 7747 2885; www.nationalgallery.org.uk. Wheelchair-accessible at Sainsbury Wing on Pall Mall East, Orange St., and Getty Entrance. Open M-Th and Sa-Su 10am-6pm, F 10am-9pm. Special exhibitions in the Sainsbury Wing occasionally open until 10pm. Offers themed workshops (£30-40), lectures (£3-18), and courses (£30-45) to accompany exhibitions. Free, suggested donation £5; some temporary exhibitions £5-10, seniors £4-8, students and ages 12-18 £2-5. 1hr. tours start at Sainsbury Wing information desk. Tours daily 11:30am and 2:30pm. Audio guides £3.50, students £3. AmEx/MC/V for ticketed events.)*

NATIONAL PORTRAIT GALLERY. Take a vast and magnificent tour of the *Who's Who* in Great Britain, beginning with priceless portraits of the Tudors and ending with today's celebrities. Try to trace family resemblances through the royal families (the Stuarts' noses) or admire the centuries of changing costume: velvet, taffeta, fabulously-patterned brocade. The famous picture of Shakespeare with an earring hangs near the Queen Elizabeth portraits in the Tudor wing. New facilities include an IT Gallery, with computers to search for pictures and print out a personalized tour, and a third-floor restaurant offering an aerial view of London, although the inflated prices will limit most visitors to coffee. To see the paintings in chronological order, take the escalator in the Ondaatje Wing to the top floor. *(St. Martin's Pl., at the start of Charing Cross Rd., Trafalgar Sq. ⊖Leicester Sq. or Charing Cross. ☎020 7312 2463; www.npg.org.uk. Open M-W and Sa-Su 10am-6pm, Th-F 10am-9pm. Wheelchair-accessible on Orange St. Free lectures Tu 3pm. Free gallery talks Sa-Su afternoons. Free live music F 6:30pm. General admission free; some special exhibitions free, others up to £6. Popular events require tickets, available from the information desk. Audio tours £2.)*

BRITISH MUSEUM. With 50,000 items from all corners of the globe, the magnificent collection is expansive and, although a bit difficult to navigate, definitely worth seeing. Most people don't even make it past the main floor, but they should—the galleries upstairs and downstairs are some of the best. Must-sees include the Rosetta stone, which was the key in deciphering ancient Egyptian hieroglyphs and the ancient mummies. *(Great Russell St. ⊖Tottenham Court Rd., Russell Square, or Holborn. ☎020 7323 8000; www.britishmuseum.org. Great Court open M-W and Su 9am-6pm, Th-Sa 9am-11pm (9pm in winter); galleries open daily 10am-5:30pm, selected galleries open Th-F 10am-8:30pm; library open M-W and Sa 10am-5:30pm, Th 10am-8:30pm, F noon-8:30pm. Free 30-40min. tours daily starting at 11am from the Enlightenment Desk. "Highlights Tour" daily 10:30am, 1, 3pm; advanced booking recommended. Wheelchair-accessible. Free; £3 suggested donation. Temporary exhibitions around £5, concessions £3.50. "Highlights Tour" £8, concessions £5. Audio tours £3.50, family audio tours for 2 adults and up to 3 children £10. MC/V.)*

VICTORIA AND ALBERT MUSEUM. As the largest museum of decorative (and not-so-decorative) art and design in the world, the V&A has over 9 mi. of corridors open to the public and is twice the size of the British Museum. It displays "the fine and applied arts of all countries, all styles, all periods." Unlike the

British Museum, the V&A's documentation is consistently excellent and thorough. Highlights include the Glass Gallery, the Japanese and Korean areas with suits of armor and kimonos, and the Indian Gallery. Themed itineraries (£5) available at the desk can help streamline your visit, and **Family Trail** cards suggest kid-friendly routes. *(Main entrance on Cromwell Rd., wheelchair-accessible entrance on Exhibition Rd. ⊖South Kensington. ☎020 7942 2000; www.vam.ac.uk. Open M-Th and Sa-Su 10am-5:45pm, F 10am-10pm. Wheelchair-accessible. Free tours meet at rear of main entrance: introductory tours daily 10:30, 11:30am, 1:30, 3:30pm, plus W 4:30pm; British gallery tours daily 12:30 and 2:30pm. Talks and events meet at rear of main entrance. Free lunchtime talks W 1:15pm; free gallery talks Th 1pm (45-60min); F talks 7-8pm with big names in art, design and fashion industries, £8, concessions £6. Admission free.)*

TATE BRITAIN. Tate Britain is the foremost collection on British art from 1500 to the present, including pieces from foreign artists working in Britain and Brits working abroad. There are four Tate Galleries in England; this is the original Tate, opened in 1897 to house Sir Henry Tate's collection of "modern" British art and later expanded to include a gift from famed British painter J.M.W. Turner. Turner's modest donation of 282 oils and 19,000 watercolors can make the museum feel like one big tribute to the man. The annual and always controversial **Turner Prize** for contemporary visual art is still given here. Four contemporary British artists are nominated for the £40,000 prize; their short-listed works go on show from late October through late January. In 2008, the exhibition moves temporarily to the Liverpool branch of the Tate. The Modern British Art Gallery, featuring works by Vanessa Bell and Francis Bacon, is also worth a look. *(Millbank, near Vauxhall Bridge, in Westminster. ⊖Pimlico. Information ☎7887 8008, M-F exhibition booking 7887 8888; www.tate.org.uk. Open daily 10am-5:50pm, last entry 5pm. Wheelchair-accessible via Clore Wing. Free; special exhibitions £7-11. Audio tours free. See website for free tours and lectures.)*

OTHER MUSEUMS AND GALLERIES

Courtald Institute, Somerset House, Strand, just east of Waterloo Bridge (☎020 7420 9400; www.courtauld.ac.uk). ⊖Charing Cross or Temple. Small, outstanding collection ranges from 14th-century Italian icons to 20th-century abstractions. Manet's *A Bar at the Follies Bergères,* Van Gogh's *Self-Portrait with Bandaged Ear,* and a room devoted to Degas bronzes. Open daily 10am-6pm, last admission at 5:30pm. Wheelchair-accessible. £5, concessions £4, under 18 free.

Cabinet War Rooms, Clive Steps, far end of King Charles St. (☎020 7930 6961; www.iwm.org.uk). ⊖Westminster. Churchill and his strategists lived and worked underground here from 1939 to 1945. Highlights include the room with the top-secret transatlantic hotline—the official story was that it was Churchill's personal toilet. Open daily 9:30am-6pm; last admission 5pm. £12, students £9.50, under 16 free. MC/V.

British Library Galleries, 96 Euston Rd. (☎020 7412 7332; www.bl.uk). ⊖King's Cross St. Pancras. Stunning display of books, manuscripts, and related artifacts from around the world and throughout the ages. Highlights include the 2nd-century *Unknown Gospel,* The Beatles' hand-scrawled lyrics, a Gutenberg Bible, and pages from Leonardo da Vinci's notebooks. Open M and W-F 9:30am-6pm, Tu 9:30am-8pm, Sa 9:30am-5pm, Su 11am-5pm. Wheelchair-accessible. Free. Audio tours £3.50, concessions £2.50.

ENTERTAINMENT

Although West End ticket prices are sky high and the quality of some shows questionable, the city that brought the world Shakespeare, the Sex Pistols, and Andrew Lloyd Webber still retains its unique theatrical edge. London is a city of immense talent, full of up-and-comers, experimenters, and undergrounders.

COMEDY

On any given night, you'll find at least 10 comedy clubs in operation: check listings in *Time Out* or in a newspaper. London comedians flee in August, when most head to Edinburgh to take part in the annual festivals (p. 160); consequently, plenty of comedians try out material in July. The UK's top comedy club, **Comedy Store,** founded in a strip club, sowed the seeds that gave rise to *Absolutely Fabulous* and *Whose Line is it Anyway?* All 400 seats have decent views of stage. Grab a £6 burger at the bar before the show. (1a Oxendon St, in Soho. ⊖Piccadilly Circus. Club inquiries ☎020 7839 6642, tickets ☎08700 602 340; www.thecomedystore.co.uk. Tu contemporary news-based satire; W and Su London's well-reviewed **Comedy Store Players** improv; Th-Sa standup. Shows Tu-Th and Su 8pm; F-Sa 8pm and midnight, sometimes only at midnight. Book in advance. 18+. Tu-W and F midnight shows and all Su shows £16; concessions £13; Th-F early show and all Sa shows £15. Happy hour 6:30-7:30pm. Box office open M-Th and Su 6:30-9:30pm, F-Sa 6:30pm-1:15am. AmEx/MC/V.) One of the few comedy venues to specialize in sketch comedy, the **Canal Cafe Theatre,** sits above the Bridge House pub; in North London. Cozy red velvet chairs and a raised rear balcony means that everyone gets a good view. Get dinner below and enjoy your drinks around the small tables. (Delamere Terr. ⊖Warwick Ave. ☎020 7289 6056; www.canalcafetheatre.com. Box office opens 30min. before performance. Weekly changing shows W-Sa 7:30 and 9:30pm; £5, concessions £4. "Newsrevue," Th-Sa 9:30pm and Su 9pm, is London's longest-running comedy sketch show, a satire of weekly current events; £9, concessions £7. £1.50 membership included in ticket price. MC/V.)

CLASSICAL MUSIC

Barbican Hall, Silk St. (☎020 7638 4141; www.barbican.org.uk), in the City of London. ⊖Barbican or Moorgate. Recently refurbished, Barbican Hall is one of Europe's leading concert halls, with excellent acoustics and a nightly performance program. The resident **London Symphony Orchestra** plays here frequently. Many summer events sell out; it's worth checking what's going on early. Call in advance for tickets, especially for popular events. Otherwise, the online and phone box offices sometimes have good last-minute options. £6-35. Also includes the 2 venues below:

English National Opera, London Coliseum, St. Martin's Ln. (☎7632 8300; www.eno.org), in Covent Garden. ⊖Charing Cross or Leicester Sq. 500 balcony seats (£16-21) for sale every performance. Innovative, updated productions of classics as well as contemporary work. Wheelchair-accessible. Purchase best-available, standby student tickets (£15), and balcony tickets (£10) at box office 3hr. before show. Call to verify availability. Half-price tickets for those under 17. Box office open M-Sa 10am-8pm. AmEx/MC/V.

Holland Park Theatre, Holland Park (box office ☎0845 223 097; www.rbkc.gov.uk/hollandpark), in Kensington and Earl's Court. ⊖High St. Kensington or Holland Park. Open-air performance space in the atmospheric grounds of a Jacobean mansion. Performances from June to early Aug. Tu-Sa 7:30pm, occasional matinees Sa 2:30pm. Box office in the Old Stable Block just to the west of the opera open M-F 1-6pm, performance days until 8pm. Tickets £10-54; occasional concessions £3 off mid-price tickets. Special allocation of tickets for wheelchair users. AmEx/MC/V.

JAZZ

Jazz Café, 5 Parkway (☎020 7534 6955; www.jazzcafe.co.uk), in North London. ⊖Camden Town. Famous and popular. Crowded front bar and balcony restaurant overlook the dance floor and stage. Shows can be pricey at this nightspot, but the top roster of jazz, hip-hop, funk, and Latin performers (£10-30) explains Jazz Café's popularity.

F-Sa jazzy DJs spin following the show. Box office open M-Sa 10:30am-5:30pm. Cover £5-10. Open M-Th and Su 7pm-2am, F-Sa 7pm-3:30am. 18+. MC/V.

Ronnie Scott's, 47 Frith St. (☎020 7439 0747; www.ronniescotts.co.uk), in Soho. ⊖Tottenham Court Rd. or Leicester Sq. London's oldest and most famous jazz club, having hosted everyone from Dizzy Gillespie to Jimi Hendrix. Supporting and main acts alternate throughout the night. Table reservations essential for big-name acts. There's limited unreserved standing room at the bar; if it's sold out, try coming back at the end of the headliner's first set, around midnight. Traditional English dishes £12-24, mixed drinks £5-11. Box office open M-F 9:30am-5:30pm. Club open M-Sa 6pm-3am, Su 6pm-midnight. Tickets £26, restricted viewing £20. AmEx/MC/V.

POP AND ROCK

The Monto Water Rats, 328 Grays Inn Rd. (☎020 7813 1079; www.themonto.com), in Bloomsbury. ⊖King's Cross St. Pancras. Where young indie rock bands come in search of a record deal. Bob Dylan had his UK debut here in 1962 and Oasis was signed here after their 1st London gig. Generous gastropub lunches (fish and chips £5-6) M-F noon-3pm. Tickets £6. Open for coffee M-F 8:30am-midnight. Music M-Sa 8pm-late (headliner 9:45pm). MC/V.

02 Academy, Brixton, 211 Stockwell Rd. (☎020 7771 3000; www.brixton-academy.co.uk), in South London. ⊖Brixton. A former Art Deco cinema. The sloping floor ensures that even those at the back have a chance to see the band. Recent performers include Lenny Kravitz, Pink, the Offspring, and Franz Ferdinand. Box office open only on performance evenings; order online or by telephone. Tickets £20-40.

THEATER

London's West End is dominated by musicals and plays that run for years, if not decades. For a list of shows and discount tickets, head to the **tkts** booth in Leicester Sq. (⊖Leicester Sq. www.tkts.co.uk. Most shows £20-30; up to £2.50 booking fee per ticket. Open M-Sa 10am-7pm, Su noon-3pm. MC/V.)

REPERTORY

Shakespeare's Globe Theatre, 21 New Globe Walk (☎020 7087 7398; www.shakespeares-globe.org), in the South Bank. ⊖Southwark or London Bridge. Innovative, top-notch performances at this faithful reproduction of Shakespeare's original 16th-century playhouse. Choose among 3 covered tiers of hard, backless wooden benches (cushions £1 extra) or stand through a performance as a "groundling"; come 30min. before the show to get as close as you can. Should it rain, the show must go on, and umbrellas are prohibited. For tours of the Globe, see p. 119. Wheelchair-accessible. Performances from mid-May to late Sept. Tu-Sa 7:30pm, Su 6:30pm; June-Sept. Tu-Sa 2 and 7:30pm, Su 1 and 6:30pm. Box office open M-Sa 10am-6pm, 8pm on performance days; Su 10am-5pm, 7pm on performance days. New plays from £20, others from £15, yard (standing) £5.

National Theatre, South Bank (info ☎020 7452 3400, box office 7452 3000; www.nationaltheatre.org.uk), in the South Bank. ⊖Waterloo or Embankment. Founded by Laurence Olivier, the National Theatre opened in 1976 and has been at the forefront of British theater ever since. Tickets typically start at £10. Complicated pricing scheme, which is liable to change from show to show; contact box office for details. Wheelchair-accessible. Box office open M-Sa 9:30am-8pm. AmEx/MC/V.

"OFF-WEST END"

The Almeida, Almeida St. (☎020 7359 4404; www.almeida.co.uk), in North London. ⊖Angel. The top fringe theater in London. Shows M-Sa 7:30pm, Sa matinees 3pm;

occasional W matinees 3pm, other weekday matinees 2:30pm. Tickets usually £8-32, occasionally as high as £46. Wheelchair-accessible. MC/V.

The King's Head, 115 Upper St. (☎020 7226 1916; www.kingsheadtheatre.org), in North London. ⊖Angel or Highbury and Islington. Above an attached pub, this theater focuses on new writing and rediscovered works. Alums include Hugh Grant, Gary Oldman, and Anthony Minghella. Shows Tu-Sa 8pm, Sa 3:30pm. £10-20, concessions £2.50 off; matinees £5 off. Occasional lunchtime shows and M night short-run shows; call for schedule. MC/V.

SHOPPING

London has long been considered one of the fashion capitals of the world. Unfortunately, the city features many underwhelming chain stores in addition to its one-of-a-kind boutiques. The truly budget-conscious should stick to window-shopping in Knightsbridge and on Regent Street. Vintage shopping in Notting Hill is also a viable alternative; steer clear of Oxford Street, where so-called vintage clothing was probably made in 2002 and marked up 200%.

DEPARTMENT STORES

Selfridges, 400 Oxford St. (☎020 0870 837 7377; www.selfridges.com). ⊖Bond St. Tourists may flock to Harrods, but Londoners head to Selfridges. You'll find all the biggies here—Gucci, Chanel, Dior—but there are also more affordable brands. Styles run the gamut from traditional tweeds to space-age clubwear. Departments specialize in every product imaginable, from antiques and scented candles, not to mention key cutting and theater tickets. With 18 cafes and restaurants, a hair salon, an exchange bureau, and even a hotel, shopaholics need never leave. Massive Jan. and July sales. Wheelchair-accessible. Open M-Sa 9:30am-9pm, Su noon-6pm. AmEx/MC/V.

Harrods, 87-135 Brompton Rd. (☎020 7730 1234; www.harrods.com). ⊖Knightsbridge. In the Victorian era, this was *the* place for the wealthy to shop; over a century later, it is less of a provider of goods than a tourist extravaganza. Given the sky-high prices, it's no wonder that only souvenir-seekers and oil sheiks actually shop here. Open M-Sa 10am-8pm; Su 11:30am-6pm, browsing only 11:30am-noon. Wheelchair-accessible. AmEx/MC/V/gold/diamonds.

Harvey Nichols, 109-125 Knightsbridge (☎020 7235 5000; www.harveynichols.com). ⊖Knightsbridge. Imagine Bond St., Rue St. Honoré, and 5th Ave. all rolled up into one store: in contrast to the pomp and circumstance of the other H down the street, Harvey is about serious shopping. 5 of its 7 fl. are devoted to the sleekest, sharpest fashions from the biggest names to the hippest unknowns. Sales from late June to late July and from late Dec. to late Jan. Open M-Sa 10am-9pm, Su 11:30-6pm, browsing only 11:30am-noon. Wheelchair-accessible. AmEx/MC/V.

STREET MARKETS

Better for people-watching than hardcore shopping, street markets may not bring you the big goods but they are a much better alternative to a day on Oxford Street. **Portobello Road Markets** (www.portobelloroad.co.uk) includes foods, antiques, secondhand clothing, and jewelry. In order to see it all, come Friday or Saturday when everything is sure to be open. (⊖Notting Hill Gate; also Westbourne Park and Ladroke Grove. Stalls set their own times.) **Camden Passage Market** (www.camdenpassageislington.co.uk) is more for looking than for buying—London's premier antique shops line these charming alleyways. (Islington High St., in North London. ⊖Angel. Turn right from the Tube; it's the alleyway that starts behind "The Mall" antiques gallery on Upper St. Stalls open W 7:30am-6pm and Sa 9am-6pm; some stores open daily, but W is the best day to go.) Its overrun sibling **Camden Markets** (☎020 7969 1500) mostly includes cheap clubbing gear and tourist trinkets; avoid the canal areas. The best bet is to stick with the **Stables Market,** farthest north from the Tube station. (Make a sharp right out of the Tube station to reach Camden High St., where most of the markets start. All stores are accessible from ⊖Camden Town. Many stores open daily 9:30am-6pm; Stables open F-Su.) **Brixton Market** has London's best selection of Afro-Caribbean fruits, vegetables, spices, and fish. It is unforgettably colorful, noisy, and fun. (Along Electric Ave., Pope's Rd., and Brixton Station Rd., and inside markets in Granville Arcade and Market Row; in South London. ⊖Brixton. Open M-Sa 10am-sunset.) Formerly a wholesale vegetable market, **Spitalfields** has become the best of the East End markets. On Sundays, food shares space with rows of clothing by 25-30 independent local designers. (Commercial St., in East London. ⊖Shoreditch (during rush hour), Liverpool St., or Aldgate East. Crafts market open M-F 10am-4pm, Su 9am-5pm. Antiques market open Th 9am-5pm.) **Petticoat Lane Market** is Spitalfield's little sister market, on Petticoat Ln., off of Commercial Street. It sells everything from clothes to crafts, and is open M-F 10am-2:30pm and Su 9am-2pm. Crowds at this market can be overwhelming at times; head to the **Sunday (Up) Market** for similar items in a calmer environment. (☎020 7770 6100; www.bricklanemarket.com. Housed in a portion of the old Truman Brewery just off Hanbury St., in East London. ⊖Shoreditch or Aldgate East. Open Su 10am-5pm.)

NIGHTLIFE

From pubs to taverns to bars to clubs, London has all the nightlife that a person could want. First-time visitors may initially head to the **West End,** drawn by the flashy lights and pumping music of Leicester Sq. For a more authentic experience, head to the **East End** or **Brixton.** Soho's **Old Compton Street** is still the center of GLBT nightlife. Before heading out for the evening, make sure to plan out **Night Bus** travel. Listings open past 11pm include local Night Bus routes. Night Buses in the West End are ubiquitous—head to Trafalgar Sq., Oxford St., or Piccadilly Circus to catch buses to all destinations.

PUBS

The Court London, 108A Tottenham Court Rd. (☎087 2148 1508). ⊖Goodge St. A lighthearted pub that's all about students, with pool tables, televised sporting events, regular DJ nights, and deals on drinks and food. Pleasant outdoor picnic-style seating area. Jukebox. Burger and beer £3.75. "Screaming" burger (with bacon, cheese, onion rings, and BBQ sauce) and beer £5.75. Wine from £1; beer from £2. Mixed drinks M £2.50. Open M-Th 11am-midnight, F-Sa 11am-1am, Su noon-6pm. AmEx/MC/V.

The Jerusalem Tavern, 55 Britton St. (☎020 7490 4281; www.stpetersbrewery.co.uk). ⊖Farringdon. Tiny and wonderfully ancient, this showcase pub for the beers of the St. Peter's Brewery has many nooks and crannies, which fill with locals at lunchtime and at night. The availability of brews changes with the seasons and is advertised on a chalkboard outside. Specialty ales (£3.40) like grapefruit or cinnamon, several organic ales, Golden Ale, Honey Porter, Summer Ale, and Suffolk Gold are available in season. Pub grub £6.50-8.50. Sourdough sandwiches £6.80. Open M-F 11am-11pm. Lunch served daily noon-3pm, dinner served Tu-Th 5-9:30pm. MC/V.

The Golden Eagle, 59 Marylebone Ln. (☎020 7935 3228). ⊖Bond St. The quintessence of "olde worlde"—both in terms of clientele and charm—this is one of the friendliest pubs around. Sidle up and join locals for the authentic pub sing-alongs (Tu and Th-F 8:30-11pm) around the piano in the corner. Beer and cider £2.40-3.50. Open M-Sa 11am-11pm, Su noon-7pm. MC/V.

BARS

Lab, 12 Old Compton St. (☎020 7437 7820; www.lab-townhouse.com). ⊖Leicester Sq. or Tottenham Court Rd. With restroom signs for "bitches" and "bastards," the only thing this bar takes seriously is its stellar drink selection. Drink sections like "high and mighty," "short and sexy," and "streets ahead" fill the book-length menu. Licensed mixologists serve up the award-winning concoctions (£6.80-7.50), while hip 20-somethings lounge in the colorful retro atmosphere. DJs spin house and funk nightly from 8pm. Open M-Sa 4pm-midnight, Su 4pm-10:30pm. Cash only.

The Old School Yard, 111 Long Ln. (☎020 7357 6281; www.theoldschoolyard.com). ⊖Borough. Just like Cat Stevens imagined it. Blue skies and fluffy clouds adorn the ceiling, sports trophies and Teenage Mutant Ninja Turtles paraphernalia cover the walls, and old-time tunes fill the air. The drink menu comes on notebook paper, organized by subject: don't know much about history? Go for geography and try a Manhattan. Beers from £3.30. Mixed drinks from £4.90. Happy Hour Tu-Sa 5:30-8pm, Su all day; mixed drinks £4.50, beers £2.50. Occasional events like Show-ke-oke (karaoke to Westerns) and Flair bartending competition. Open Tu-Th 5:30-11:30pm, F-Sa 5:30pm-12:30am, Su 5:30-10:30pm. AmEx/MC/V.

Vibe Bar, 91-95 Brick Ln. (☎020 7426 0491; www.vibe-bar.co.uk). ⊖Aldgate East or Liverpool St. Night Bus. Once the home of the Truman Brewery, this funky bar is heavy on style and light on pretension. Vibe prides itself on promoting new artists and combining music and visual displays. Dim lighting, brick interior, and mural-covered walls give the place an artsy, casual feel. In the summer, pour into the outdoor courtyard for drinking, BBQ, and general revelry. Free internet. DJs spin hip hop, garage, techno, and more M-Th and Su 11am-11:30pm. Cover F-Sa after 8pm £4. Open M-Th and Su 11am-11:30pm, F-Sa 11am-1am. AmEx/MC/V over £10.

CLUBS

Ministry of Sound, 103 Gaunt St. (☎020 7378 6528; www.ministryofsound.com). ⊖Elephant and Castle; take the exit for South Bank University. Night Bus #N35, N133, N343. A mecca for serious clubbers worldwide—arrive before it opens or stand in line all night. Emphasis on dancing rather than decor, with a massive main room, smaller 2nd dance floor, and perpetually packed overhead balcony bar. Multiple artists often take over different venues on the same night. Dress to impress. Cover varies; usually £10-20. Hours depend on event; generally F 10pm-6am, Sa 11pm-7am, Su 10:30pm-3:30am. AmEx/MC/V.

Club Surya, 156 Pentonville Rd. (☎020 8888 2333; www.club4climate.com/surya). ⊖King's Cross. The first ecological club in London, this nightclub seeks to enlighten (the name means Sun God). The bar area is made out of melted cell phones, the tables consist of old magazines, and downstairs, the music runs on the energy created by those on the electrifying dance floor. Also uses wind turbines and solar panels, hires local artists for the decor, and dedicates a portion of the profits to charity. Free entry for those who can prove they've traveled there by foot, bike, or public transport. Mixed drinks £7. Cover F-Sa £10-15. Open M-Th and Su 9am-11pm, F-Sa 9am-midnight. AmEx/MC/V.

GLBT NIGHTLIFE

Many venues have Gay and Lesbian nights on a rotating basis. Check *TimeOut* and look for flyers/magazines floating around Soho: *The Pink Paper* (free from newsagents) and *Boyz* (www.boyz.co.uk; free at gay bars and clubs).

The Edge, 11 Soho Sq. (☎020 7439 1313; www.edge.uk.com). ⊖Oxford Circus or Tottenham Court Rd. A friendly "polysexual" drinking spot just off Soho Sq. offers several types of venues, complete with Häagen Dazs ice cream and £14 bottles of wine. 4 floors of stylish brick, silver, or hot pink. Relaxed bar on the ground fl., sleek black lounge bar on the 1st fl., piano bar decked out in white on the 2nd, and a newly refurbished disco dance bar, with lit up dance floor, on the top fl. Piano bar Tu-Sa. Live jazz last W of the month. DJs and dancing F-Sa. Cover Th-Sa after 10pm £2. Open M-Sa noon-1am, Su noon-11pm. MC/V.

The Black Cap, 171 Camden High St. (☎020 7428 2721; www.theblackcap.com). ⊖Camden Town. North London's most popular gay bar and cabaret is always buzzing and draws an eclectic male and female crowd. The rooftop patio is the highlight of the place, with plenty of tables for outside revelry. Live shows and club scene downstairs F-Su nights and some weeknights (times vary; call for details). Cover for downstairs M-Th and Su before 11pm £2, 11pm-close £3; F-Sa before 11pm £3, 11pm-close £4. Open M-Th noon-2am, F-Sa noon-3am, Su noon-1am. Kitchen open noon-10pm.

G-A-Y Late, 5 Goslett Yard (☎020 7434 9592; www.g-a-y.co.uk), off Charing Cross Rd. ⊖Tottenham Court Rd. Frequently besieged by teenage girls on weekends. Madonna previewed 6 songs from her newest album here. G-A-Y (you spell it out when you say it) has become a Soho institution. Mixed drinks £5. Dancers on Tu, W "Slag Tags" (get a # at the door and when you see someone you like, text to the screen), Th "Porn Idol" ("Gay Girlz" in the pop room with a female stripper), F "Camp Attack" with 4 decades of music. Wheelchair-accessible. Cover varies from £1-15; check website for details. Open M, W-Th, and Su noon-2am; F-Sa noon-5am. Cash only.

SOUTHERN ENGLAND

History and myth shroud Southern England. Cornwall, the alleged birthplace of King Arthur, was the last stronghold of the Celts in England, but traces of older Neolithic communities linger in the stone circles their builders left behind. In WWII, German bombings uncovered long-buried evidence of an invasion by Caesar, whose Romans dotted the countryside with settlements. William the Conqueror left his mark in the form of awe-inspiring castles and cathedrals. Apart from this pomp and circumstance lies a less palpable presence: the voices of British literati such as Jane Austen, Geoffrey Chaucer, Charles Dickens, and E.M. Forster echo above the sprawling pastures and seaside cliffs.

SALISBURY ☎01722

Let's be honest– you're only here as a stopover on the way to **Stonehenge.** **Trains** run from South Western Rd., west of town across the River Avon, to London Waterloo (1hr., 2 per hr., £29.50). National Express **buses** (☎08705 808 080) go from 8 Endless St. to London (3hr., 3 per day, £14). Wilts and Dorset buses (☎01722 336 855) run to Bath (X4; every hr., £4.50) and Winchester (#68; 1hr., 8 per day, £4.65). An **Explorer** ticket is good for one day of travel on Wilts and Dorset buses (£7.50, child £4.50). The **TIC** is on Fish Row, in back of the Guildhall in Market Sq. (☎01722 334 956; www.visitsalisbury.com. Open June-Sept. M-Sa 9:30am-6pm, Su 10:30am-4:30pm; Oct.-May M-Sa 9:30am-5pm.)

DAYTRIP FROM SALISBURY: STONEHENGE AND AVEBURY. A ring of colossal stones amid swaying grass and indifferent sheep, Stonehenge has been battered for millennia by winds whipping at 80km per hour and visited by legions of people for over 5000 years. The monument, which has retained its present shape since about 1500 BC, was once a complete circle of 6.5m tall stones weighing up to 45 tons each. Sensationalized religious and scientific explanations for Stonehenge's purpose add to its intrigue. Some believe the stones are oriented as a calendar, with the position of the sun on the stones indicating the time of year. Admission to Stonehenge includes a 30min. audio tour. Ropes confine the throngs to a path around the outside of the monument. From the roadside or from Amesbury Hill, 2km up the A303, you can get a free view of the stones. There are also many walks and trails that pass by; ask at the Salisbury TIC. *(☎01980 624 715. Open daily June-Aug. 9am-7pm; mid-Mar. to May and Sept. to mid-Oct. 9:30am-6pm; mid-Oct. to mid-Mar. 9:30am-4pm. £6.50, students £5.20.)*

A question for the world: why is **Avebury's** stone circle, larger and older than its favored cousin Stonehenge, often so lonely during the day? Avebury gives an up-close and largely untouristed view of its 98 stones, dated to 2500 BC and standing in a circle with a 300m diameter. For the direct route, take the Stonehenge Tourbus, which leaves from the Salisbury train station. (Every hour, starting at 9:30am. £11 for tour, £17 with Stonehenge admission, students £14.) Wilts and Dorset **buses** (☎336 855) run daily service from the Salisbury train station and bus station (#3, 5, and 6; 30min.-2hr.; round-trip £4-8). The first bus leaves Salisbury at 9:45am, and the last leaves Stonehenge at 4:05pm. Check a schedule before you leave; intervals between drop-offs and pickups are at least 1hr. Wilts and Dorset also runs a tour bus from Salisbury (3 per day, £7.50-15). The closest lodgings are in **Salisbury** (see above).

BATH ☎01225

Perhaps the world's first tourist town, Bath (pop. 90,000) has been a must-see for travelers since AD 43, when the Romans built an elaborate complex of baths to house the town's curative waters. In 1701, Queen Anne's trip to the springs re-established the city as a prominent meeting place for artists, politicians, and intellectuals; it became an English social capital second only to London. No longer an upper-crust resort, today Bath plays host to crowds of tourists eager to appreciate its historic sites and well-preserved elegance.

TRANSPORTATION AND PRACTICAL INFORMATION. **Trains** leave from Dorchester St. for: Birmingham (2hr., 2 per hr., £36); Bristol (15min., every 10-15min., £6); London Paddington (1.5hr., 2 per hr., £47-66.50); London Waterloo (2hr., every hr., £28.20). National Express **buses** (☎08717 818 181) run from Bath Bus Station to London (3hr., every hr., £17.50) and Oxford (2hr., 1 per day, £9.50). The train and bus stations are near the south end of Manvers St. Walk toward the town center and turn left on York St. to reach the **TIC,** in Abbey Chambers, which books rooms for £3 and a 10% deposit. (☎9067 112 000; www.visitbath.co.uk. Open June-Sept. M-Sa 9:30am-6pm, Su 10am-4pm; Oct.-May M-Sa 9:30am-5pm, Su 10am-4pm.) **Postal Code:** BA1 1AJ.

ACCOMMODATIONS AND FOOD. B&Bs line Pulteney Rd. and Pulteney Gardens. Conveniently located **Bath Backpackers ❶**, 13 Pierrepont St., is a relaxed backpackers' lair with music-themed dorms, TV lounge, and "dungeon" bar. (☎01225 446 787; www.hostels.co.uk. Kitchen available. Internet £2 per hr. Luggage storage £2 per bag. Reception 8am-11pm. Check-out 10:30am. Reserve ahead in summer. 4-bed dorms £16-18, 8-bed £14-16, 10-bed £13-15. MC/V.) **St. Christopher's Inn ❷**, 16 Green St., has clean rooms and a downstairs pub. (☎01225 481 444; www.st-christophers.co.uk. Dorms £16-23.50. Discount for online booking. MC/V.) **Riverside Cafe ❶**, below Pulteney Bridge, serves light dishes and delicious coffee. Patrons have a gorgeous view of the River Avon. (☎01225 480 532; www.riversidecafebar.co.uk. Sandwiches and soups £5-6. Open M-Sa 9am-9pm, Su 9am-5pm. MC/V.) Try the exotic vegetarian dishes, or the superb chocolate fudge cake (£5.25) at **Demuths Restaurant ❸**, 2 N. Parade Passage. (☎01225 446 059; www.demuths.co.uk. Entrees from £12. Open M-F and Su 10am-5pm and 6-10pm, Sa 9am-5pm and 6-10pm. Reserve ahead in summer. MC/V.) For groceries, head to the **Sainsbury's** supermarket on Green Park Rd. (☎01225 444 737. Open M-F 8am-10pm, Sa 7:30-10pm, Su 11am-5pm.)

SIGHTS. In 1880, sewer diggers uncovered the first glimpse of an extravagant feat of Roman engineering. For 400 years, the Romans harnessed Bath's bubbling springs, where nearly 1,000,000L of 47°C (115°F) water flow every day. The **Roman Baths Museum,** Abbey Church Yard, shows the complexity of Roman architecture and engineering, which included central heating and internal plumbing. (☎01225 447 785; www.romanbaths.co.uk. Open daily July-Aug. 9am-10pm; Sept.-Oct. and Mar.-June 9am-6pm; Nov.-Feb. 9am-5:30pm. £10.50, concessions £9, children £6.80, families £30. Joint ticket with Museum of Costume £14/12/8.30/38. Audio tour included.) Next to the baths, the towering **Bath Abbey** meets masons George and William Vertue's oath to build "the goodliest vault in all England and France." The Abbey's underground **Heritage Vaults,** built over medieval monk burial grounds, display the history of the abbey. (☎01225 422 462; www.bathabbey.org. Open M-Sa 9am-6pm, Su 1-2:30pm and 4:30-5:30pm. Vaults open daily 10am-4pm. Requested donation £2.50.) Walk up Gay St. to **The Circus,** a classic Georgian block where painter Thomas Gainsborough and 18th-century prime minister William Pitt lived. Near The Circus, the **Museum of Costume,** on Bennett St., has a dazzling parade of 400 years of fashions, from 17th-century silver tissue garments to J. Lo's racy Versace ensemble. (☎01225 477 785; www.fashionmuseum.co.uk. Open daily Mar.-Oct. 10:30am-6pm; Nov.-Feb. 10:30am-5pm. £7, concessions £6, children £5, family £20.)

EAST ANGLIA AND THE MIDLANDS

The rich farmland and watery flats of East Anglia stretch northeast from London, cloaking the counties of Cambridgeshire, Norfolk, Suffolk, and parts of Essex. Mention of The Midlands inevitably evokes grim urban images, but there is a unique heritage and quiet grandeur to this smokestacked landscape. Even Birmingham, the region's much-maligned center, has its saving graces, among them a lively nightlife scene and the Cadbury chocolate empire.

OXFORD ☎01865

For nearly a millennium, the University of Oxford has been churning out talent, including 47 Nobel Prize winners, 25 British prime ministers, 86 Archbishops of Canterbury, 12 saints, six kings, and Hugh Grant. Its 38 colleges are home to impossibly intricate church ceilings, serene quads, and paintings that are older than many countries. But don't forget to come down from the ivory tower and explore the city of Oxford—a surprisingly modern metropolis of 150,000, where scaffolding creeps up ancient spires and even 11th-century buildings have been retrofitted with Wi-Fi.

TRANSPORTATION

Trains: Station on Botley Rd., down Park End. Ticket office open M-F 5:45am-8pm, Sa 7:30am-8pm, Su 7:15am-8pm. Trains (☎08457 000 125) to: **Birmingham** (1hr., 2 per hr., £23); **Glasgow** (5-7hr., every hr., £93); **London Paddington** (1hr., 2-4 per hr., £19-24); **Manchester** (3hr., 2 per hr., £57).

Buses: Station on Gloucester Green. Stagecoach (☎01865 772 250; www.stagecoachbus.com; ticket office open M-F 9am-5pm, Sa 9:30am-1pm). National Express (☎08717 818 181; www.nationalexpress.com; ticket office open M-Th 8:30am-5:45pm, F-Sa 8:30am-6pm, Su 9am-4:30pm). The Oxford Bus Company (☎01865 785 400; www.oxfordbus.co.uk; ticket office in Debenhams Department store, at the corner of George St. and Magdalen St., open M-W 9:30am-6pm, Th 9am-8pm, F-Sa 9am-7pm).

Public Transportation: The Oxford Bus Company Cityline (☎01865 785 400) and Stagecoach Oxford (☎01865 772 250) offer frequent service to: **Abingdon Road** (Stagecoach #32, 33, Oxford Bus X3); **Banbury Road** (Stagecoach #2, 2A, 2B, 2D); **Cowley Road** (Stagecoach #1, 5A, 5B, 10, Oxford Bus #5); **Iffley Road** (Stagecoach #3, Oxford Bus #4, 4A, 4B, 4C). Fares are low (£0.60-£1.40).

Taxis: Radio Taxis (☎01865 242 424). **ABC** (☎01865 770 077). Both 24hr.

Boat Rental: Magdalen Bridge Boat House, Magdalen Bridge (☎01865 202 643; www.oxfordpunting.co.uk). Rents punts and rowboats (£14 per hr.) or chauffered punts (£20 per 30min.). Open daily 9:30am-9pm or dusk (whichever comes first).

ORIENTATION

Oxford's colleges stand around **Saint Mary's Church,** which is the spiritual heart of both the university and the greater city. The city's center is bounded by **George Street** and connecting **Broad Street** to the north and **Cornmarket** and **High Street** in the center. Directly south of the city center, the wide open spaces of **Christ Church Meadow** are surrounded by a horseshoe-shaped bend in the Thames. To the northwest, the district of **Jericho** is less touristed and is the unofficial hub of student life. Across Magdalen bridge, the corridor surrounding **Cowley Road** is a vibrant and diverse residential area that feels like its own city. **Banbury** to the north and **Abingdon** to the south are quieter, quainter towns surrounded by gorgeous countryside.

PRACTICAL INFORMATION

Tourist Information Centre: 15-16 Broad St. (☎01865 252 200; www.visitoxford.org). The busy staff books rooms for £4 plus a 10% deposit. Distributes free black-and-white maps (nicer colored maps £1.30), restaurant lists, accommodation lists, and monthly *In Oxford* guides. Open M-Sa 9:30am-5pm.

.**Banks:** Lining Cornmarket St. The **TIC** (p. 134) has a commission-free **bureau de change,** as does **Marks & Spencer,** 13-18 Queen St. (☎01865 248 075). Open M-W and F-Sa 8am-7pm, Th 8am-8pm, Su 10:30am-5pm.

Police: St. Aldates and Speedwell St. (☎01865 505 505).

Pharmacy: Boots, Cornmarket St. (☎01865 247 461). Open M-W and F-Sa 8:30am6pm, Th 8:30am-7pm, Su 11am-5pm.

Hospital: John Radcliffe Hospital, Headley Way (☎01865 741 166). Take bus #13.

Internet Access: Free at the **Oxford Central Library** (above). **Links Communications,** 33 High St. (☎01865 204 207). £1 per 45min. Open M-Sa 10am-8:30pm, Su 11am-8:30pm.

Post Office: 102-104 St. Aldates (☎08457 223 344). **Bureau de change.** Open M and W-Sa 9am-5:30pm, Tu 9:30am-5:30pm. **Postcode:** OX1 1ZZ.

ACCOMMODATIONS

Book at least a week ahead from June to September, especially for singles. B&Bs (from £30) line the main roads out of town. Try www.stayoxford.com for affordable options.

Central Backpackers, 13 Park End St. (☎01865 242 288; www.centralbackpackers.co.uk), a short walk from the train station. Spacious rooms and clean bathrooms. Have a few drinks on the rooftop terrace—where guests frequently barbecue in the summer time. Light sleepers beware: booming bass from nearby clubs may keep you awake on weekends (but shouldn't you be out partying anyway?). Kitchen available. Female-only dorms available. Continental breakfast included. Free luggage storage and lockers. Laundry £3.50. Free internet and Wi-Fi. 12-bed dorms £16; 8-bed £17; 6-bed £18; 4-bed £19. MC/V. ❶

Oxford Backpackers Hostel, 9A Hythe Bridge St. (☎01865 721 761; www.hostels.co.uk), halfway between the bus and train stations. A self-proclaimed "funky hostel" with murals and music playing in the hallway. The bathrooms may be a little dirty, and the chairs in the common area may be losing their stuffing, but after a few drinks from the inexpensive bar, who's going to notice? Self-catering kitchen. Female-only dorm available. Continental breakfast included. Luggage storage £2. Laundry £2.50. Internet £1 per 30min. 8-bed dorms £15-16; 4-bed £17-19. MC/V. ❶

FOOD

Gloucester Green Market, behind the bus station, is full of tasty treats, fresh fruit, and assorted junk (Open W 9am-5pm). The **Covered Market** has produce and deli goods. Enter on High St. between Cornmarket St. and Turl St. (open M-Sa 8:30am-5:30pm, Su 10am-4pm). Across Magdalen Bridge, you'll find cheap restaurants on **Cowley Road** that serve international food in addition to fish and chips. For a meal on the go, try a sandwich from a **kebab van,** usually found on Broad St., High St., Queen St., or St. Aldates.

Chiang Mai Kitchen, Kemp Hall Passage (☎01865 202 233), hidden in an alley to the right of the Starbucks at 127 High St. Tasty Thai cuisine at unbeatable prices. Enjoy the fresh herbs and spices (flown in weekly from Bangkok) while soaking up the peaceful decor. Play it safe with pad thai (£9) or get exotic with jungle curry with wild venison (£9.50). Special vegetarian menu. Open M-Sa noon-2:30pm and 6-10:30pm, Su noon-2:30pm and 6-10pm. AmEx/MC/V. ❷

COLLEGES

The **Tourist Information Centre** sells a map (£1.25) and gives out the *Welcome to Oxford* guide, which lists the visiting hours for all of the colleges. Hours can also be accessed online at www.ox.ac.uk/visitors/colls.html. Note that those hours change without explanation or notice, so confirm in advance.

CHRIST CHURCH

COLLEGE. "The House" has Oxford's grandest quad and its most distinguished students, counting 13 past prime ministers among its alumni. Charles I made Christ Church his headquarters for three and a half years during the Civil Wars and escaped dressed as a servant when the city was besieged. Lewis Carroll first met Alice, the dean's daughter, here. The dining hall and Tom Quad serve as shooting locations for Harry Potter films. Look for rowing standings chalked on the walls and for the beautiful exterior of Christ Church's **library.** Spreading east and south from the main entrance, **Christ Church Meadow** compensates for Oxford's lack of "backs" (the riverside gardens in Cambridge). *(Down*

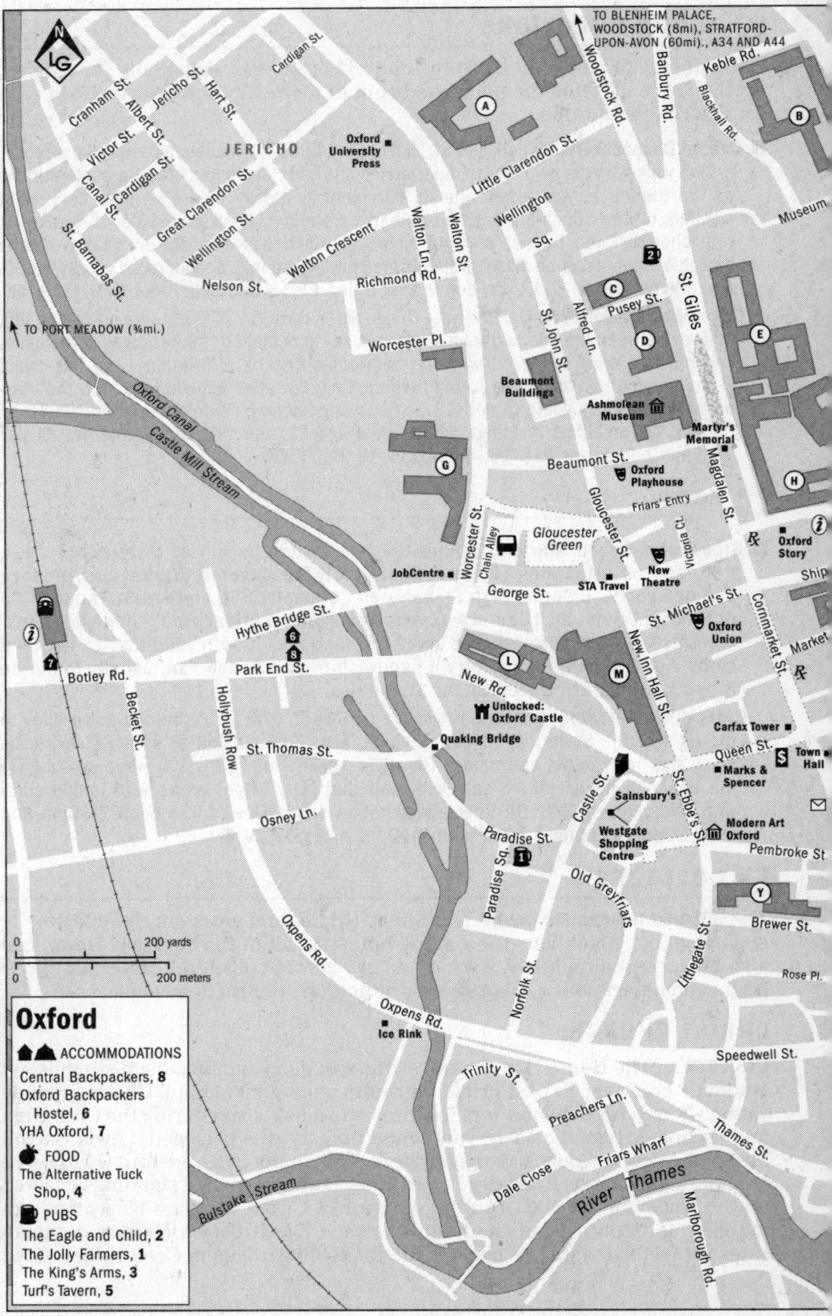

Oxford
ACCOMMODATIONS
Central Backpackers, 8
Oxford Backpackers Hostel, 6
YHA Oxford, 7
FOOD
The Alternative Tuck Shop, 4
PUBS
The Eagle and Child, 2
The Jolly Farmers, 1
The King's Arms, 3
Turf's Tavern, 5
TO BLENHEIM PALACE, WOODSTOCK (8mi), STRATFORD-UPON-AVON (60mi)., A34 AND A44
TO PORT MEADOW (¾mi.)
JERICHO
Oxford University Press
Cranham St.
Jericho St.
Hart St.
Albert St.
Victor St.
Cardigan St.
Canal St.
Great Clarendon St.
Wellington St.
St. Barnabas St.
Nelson St.
Walton Crescent
Richmond Rd.
Walton Ln.
Walton St.
Little Clarendon St.
Wellington Sq.
Woodstock Rd.
Banbury Rd.
Keble Rd.
Blackhall Rd.
Museum
St. Giles
Pusey St.
Alfred Ln.
St. John St.
Worcester Pl.
Beaumont Buildings
Ashmolean Museum
Martyr's Memorial
Magdalen St.
Beaumont St.
Oxford Playhouse
Friars' Entry
Gloucester St.
Victoria Ct.
Oxford Story
Oxford Canal
Castle Mill Stream
Worcester St.
Chain Alley
Gloucester Green
JobCentre
STA Travel
New Theatre
George St.
Ship
St. Michael's St.
Oxford Union
Cornmarket St.
Market
Hythe Bridge St.
Park End St.
Botley Rd.
Becket St.
Hollybush Row
New Rd.
Unlocked: Oxford Castle
New Inn Hall St.
Carfax Tower
Quaking Bridge
St. Thomas St.
Queen St.
Town Hall
Marks & Spencer
Castle St.
St. Ebbe's St.
Sainsbury's
Westgate Shopping Centre
Modern Art Oxford
Pembroke St.
Osney Ln.
Paradise St.
Paradise Sq.
Old Greyfriars
Brewer St.
Littlegate St.
Rose Pl.
Oxpens Rd.
Norfolk St.
Ice Rink
Speedwell St.
Trinity St.
Preachers Ln.
Thames St.
Friars Wharf
Dale Close
River Thames
Bulstake Stream
Marlborough Rd.
0
200 yards
200 meters

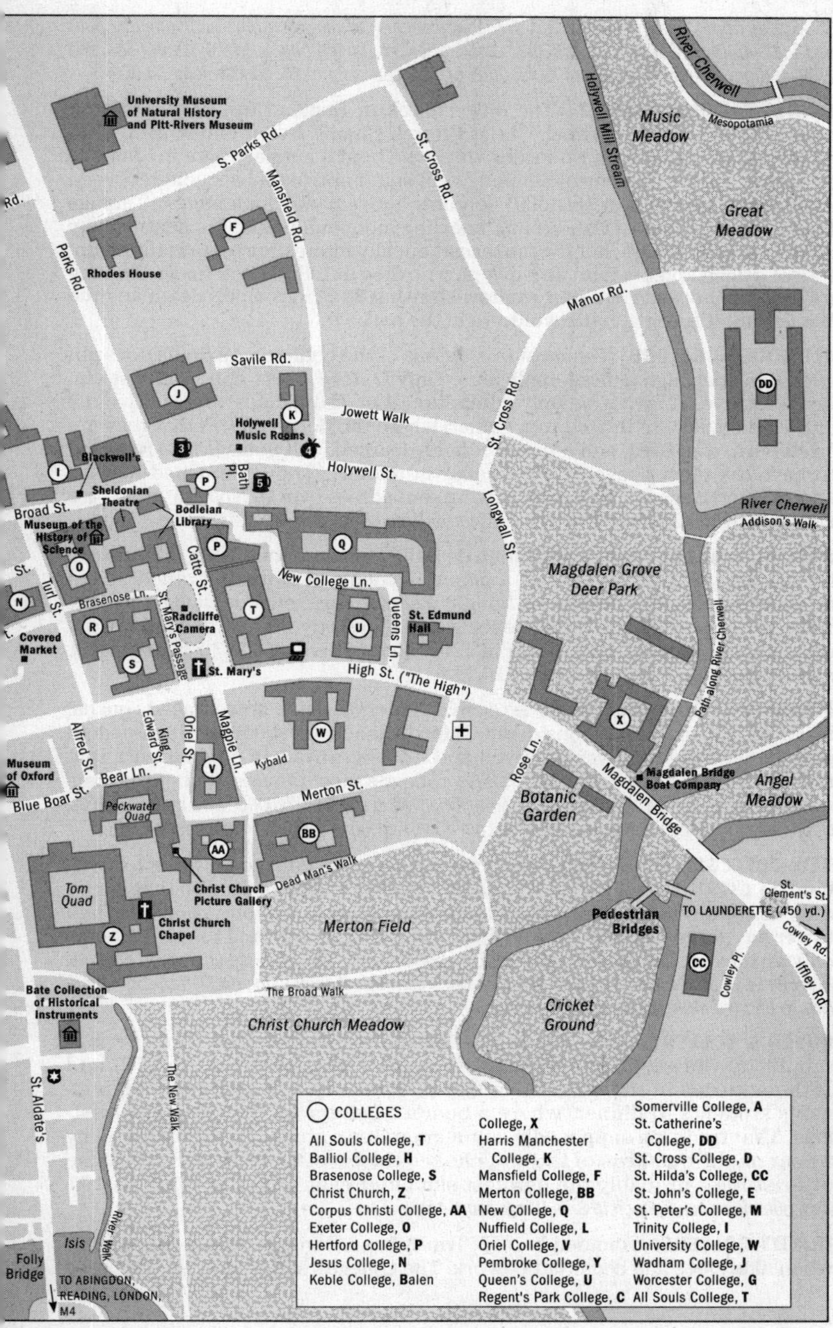
University Museum of Natural History and Pitt-Rivers Museum
S. Parks Rd.
St. Cross Rd.
Mansfield Rd.
Parks Rd.
Rhodes House
River Cherwell
Holywell Mill Stream
Music Meadow
Mesopotamia
Great Meadow
Manor Rd.
Savile Rd.
Jowett Walk
Holywell Music Rooms
Blackwell's
Holywell St.
Bath Pl.
Sheldonian Theatre
Bodleian Library
Broad St.
Museum of the History of Science
Catte St.
Longwall St.
Addison's Walk
New College Ln.
Magdalen Grove Deer Park
Turl St.
Brasenose Ln.
St. Mary's Passage
Radcliffe Camera
Queens Ln.
St. Edmund Hall
Covered Market
St. Mary's
High St. ("The High")
Path along River Cherwell
Alfred St.
King Edward St.
Oriel St.
Magpie Ln.
Kybald
Rose Ln.
Museum of Oxford
Bear Ln.
Blue Boar St.
Merton St.
Botanic Garden
Magdalen Bridge
Magdalen Bridge Boat Company
Angel Meadow
Peckwater Quad
Tom Quad
Christ Church Picture Gallery
Dead Man's Walk
Christ Church Chapel
Merton Field
Pedestrian Bridges
St. Clement's St.
TO LAUNDERETTE (450 yd.)
Cowley Rd.
Cowley Pl.
Iffley Rd.
Bate Collection of Historical Instruments
The Broad Walk
Christ Church Meadow
Cricket Ground
St. Aldate's
The New Walk
River Walk
Isis
Folly Bridge
TO ABINGDON, READING, LONDON, M4
COLLEGES
All Souls College, T
Balliol College, H
Brasenose College, S
Christ Church, Z
Corpus Christi College, AA
Exeter College, O
Hertford College, P
Jesus College, N
Keble College, Balen
College, X
Harris Manchester College, K
Mansfield College, F
Merton College, BB
New College, Q
Nuffield College, L
Oriel College, V
Pembroke College, Y
Queen's College, U
Regent's Park College, C
Somerville College, A
St. Catherine's College, DD
St. Cross College, D
St. Hilda's College, CC
St. John's College, E
St. Peter's College, M
Trinity College, I
University College, W
Wadham College, J
Worcester College, G
All Souls College, T

BRITAIN

St. Aldates from Carfax. ☎01865 286 573; www.chch.ox.ac.uk. Open M-F 10:15am-11:45am and 2:15-4:30pm, Sa-Su 2:15-4:30pm. Last entry 4pm. Dining hall open 10:30am-noon and 2:30-4:30pm. Chapel services M-F 6pm; Su 8, 10, 11:15am, 6pm. £6, concessions £4.50.)

CHRIST CHURCH CHAPEL. The only church in England to serve as both a cathedral and college chapel, Christ Church Chapel was founded in AD 730 by Oxford's patron saint, St. Frideswide, who built a nunnery here in honor of two miracles: the blinding of her persistent suitor and his subsequent recovery. A stained-glass window (c. 1320) contains a rare panel depicting St. Thomas Becket, archbishop of Canterbury, kneeling moments before his death. Many clergy are buried here, but the most aesthetically interesting tomb is the sculpture of a dead knight (John de Nowers, who died in 1386). Look for the floating toilet in the bottom right of a window showing St. Frideswide's death and the White Rabbit fretting in the windows in the hall.

ALL SOULS COLLEGE. The most prestigious of the colleges, All Souls does not even consider high school applicants. Only Oxford's best and brightest students receive an invitation-only admission offer. Candidates who survive the entrance exams are invited to a dinner, where the dons confirm that they are "well-born, well-bred, and only moderately learned." All Souls is also reported to have the most heavenly wine cellar in the city. The Great Quad may be Oxford's most serene, as hardly a living soul passes over it. *(Corner of High St. and Catte St. ☎01865 279 379; www.all-souls.ox.ac.uk. Open Sept.-July M-F 2-4pm. Free.)*

BALLIOL COLLEGE. When Lord John de Balliol insulted the Bishop of Durham, he was assigned two penances: a public whipping at Durham Cathedral and an act of charity. For charity, he bought a small house outside the Oxford city walls and gave scholars a few pence a week to study there. This community officially became Balliol College in 1266. *(Broad St. ☎01865 277 777; www.balliol.ox.ac.uk. Open daily 2-5pm. £1, students £0.50.)*

MAGDALEN COLLEGE. With extensive grounds and flower-laced quads, Magdalen (MAUD-lin) is considered Oxford's handsomest college. It has a deer park flanked by the River Cherwell and Addison's Walk, a circular path that touches the river's opposite bank. The college's most famous alumnus is playwright Oscar Wilde. *(On High St., near the Cherwell. ☎01865 276 000; www.magd.ox.ac.uk. Open daily July-Sept. noon-6pm; Oct.-Mar. 1pm-dusk; Apr.-June 1-6pm. £4, concessions £3.)*

NEW COLLEGE. This is the self-proclaimed first real college of Oxford. It was here, in 1379, that William of Wykeham dreamed up an institution that would offer a comprehensive undergraduate education under one roof. The bell tower has gargoyles of the seven deadly sins on one side and the seven heavenly virtues on the other—all equally grotesque. *(New College Ln. gate in summer, Holywell St. Gate in winter. ☎01865 279 555. Open daily from Easter to mid-Oct. 11am-5pm; from Nov. to Easter 2-4pm. £2, concessions £1.)*

QUEEN'S COLLEGE. Although the college dates back to 1341, Queen's was rebuilt by Christopher Wren and Nicholas Hawksmoor in the 17th and 18th centuries in the distinctive Queen Anne style. A trumpet call summons students to dinner, where a boar's head graces the table at Christmas. That tradition supposedly commemorates a student who, attacked by a boar on the outskirts of Oxford, choked the beast to death with a volume of Aristotle—probably the nerdiest slaughter ever. *(High St. ☎01865 279 120; www.queens.ox.ac.uk. Open to Blue-Badge tours only.)*

TRINITY COLLEGE. Founded in 1555, Trinity has a Baroque chapel with a limewood altarpiece and cedar latticework. The college's series of eccentric presidents includes Ralph Kettell, who would come to dinner with a pair of scissors to chop anyone's hair that he deemed too long. *(Broad St. ☎01865 279 900; www.trinity.ox.ac.uk. Open daily 10am-noon and 2-4pm. £1.50, concessions £0.80.)*

UNIVERSITY COLLEGE. Built in 1249, this soot-blackened college vies with Merton for the title of oldest, claiming Alfred the Great as its founder. *(High St. ☎01865 276 602; www.univ.ox.ac.uk. Entry at the discretion of the lodge porter.)*

MUSEUMS

ASHMOLEAN MUSEUM. The grand Ashmolean—Britain's finest collection of arts and antiquities outside London and the country's oldest public museum—opened in 1683. The museum is undergoing extensive renovations until November 2009. *(Beaumont St. ☎01865 278 000. Open Tu-Sa 10am-5pm, Su noon-5pm. Free. Tours £2.)*

NIGHTLIFE

- **The Turf Tavern,** 4 Bath Pl. (☎01865 243 235; www.theturftavern.co.uk), hidden off Holywell St. Arguably the most popular student bar in Oxford, this 13th-century pub is tucked in an alley off an alley, but that doesn't stop just about everybody in Oxford from partaking of its 11 different ales. Bob Hawke, future prime minister of Australia, downed a yard of ale (over 2 pints) in a record 11 seconds here while at the university. The Turf is also allegedly the spot where Bill Clinton "didn't inhale" as a Rhodes Scholar. Quiz night Tu 8:30pm. Open M-Sa 11am-11pm, Su noon-10:30pm. Kitchen open noon-7pm.
- **Lava/Ignite,** Park End St. (☎01865 250 181; www.parkend.co.uk), across the street from Thirst. The epicenter of Oxford's student nightlife; be prepared to wait in line to get in. DJs on 3 different dance floors spin the latest techno, pop, and R&B. Look for promoters down the street handing out discount stickers. No sneakers. Cover £3-7.
- **Thirst,** 7-8 Park End St. (☎01865 242 044; www.thirstbar.com). Lounge bar with a DJ and backdoor garden, where you can smoke hookah (£10) with your drinks. Arguably the most popular student hangout in Oxford. Student discount on mixed drinks (from £2.80) M-Th and Su with student ID. Open M-W and Su 7:30pm-2am, Th-Sa 7:30-3am. MC/V over £10.
- **The King's Arms,** 40 Holywell St. (☎01865 242 369; www.kingsarmsoxford.co.uk). Oxford's unofficial student union. Until 1973, the bar was the last male-only pub in the UK. Now, the "KA" has plenty of large tables for all patrons even when it's busy. Features a rotating selection of tasty Young's cask ale. Open daily 10:30am-midnight. Kitchen open 11:30am-9pm. MC/V.

STRATFORD-UPON-AVON ☎01789

Shakespeare was born here, and this fluke of fate has made Stratford-upon-Avon a major stop on the tourist superhighway. Proprietors tout the dozen-odd properties linked, however remotely, to the Bard and his extended family; shops and restaurants devotedly stencil his prose and poetry on their windows and walls. But, behind the sound and fury of rumbling tour buses and chaotic swarms of daytrippers, there lies a town worth seeing for the beauty of the Avon and for the riveting performances in the Royal Shakespeare Theatre.

THENCE, AWAY! Trains (☎08457 484 950) arrive at Station Rd., off Alcester Rd., and run to: Birmingham (50min., 2 per hr., £5.90); London Marylbone (2hr., 2 per hr., £45); and Warwick (25min., 9 per day, £4.50). National Express **buses** (☎08717 818 181) go to: London (3-4hr., 4 per day, £15.80) and Oxford (1hr., 1 per day, £8). Local Stratford Blue bus #X20 stops at Wood and Bridge St.,

SHAKESPEAREAN DISSES

In Stratford-upon-Avon, you can see where Shakespeare is buried, walk through his childhood abode, and sit on a bench where he kissed babes. But what no tour guide will tell you is how Will slung out insults. the following might come in handy, in Stratford and beyond:

1. **Wipe thy ugly face, thou loggerheaded toad-spotted barnacle!** I'm sorry, you're just not attractive enough for me.
2. **Bathe thyself, thou rank reeling-ripe boar-pig!** One way to tell that guy in your hostel that he could use a shower.
3. **Thou puny milk-livered measel!** You're a coward!
4. **Thou dost intrude, thou infectious fat-kidneyed woldwarp!** Sometimes, you just need some personal space.
5. **Thou vain idle-headed strumpet!** You spend too much time in front of that mirror.
6. **Clean thine ears, thou lumpish boil-brained lout!** What? You didn't hear me the first time?
7. **Thy breath stinks with eating toasted cheese.** Your breath is offensive. Brush your teeth.
8. **Remove thine ass hence, thou beslubbering beetle-headed clotpole!** For that drunkard in the club who just won't leave you alone.
9. **Thou droning boil-brained harpy!** To let your tour guide know that you're not that interested.
10. **I'll see thee hang'd, thou villainous ill-breeding ratsbane!** Only to be used when you're truly furious.

and goes to Birmingham (1hr., every hr., £4). The TIC, **Bridgefoot,** is across Warwick Rd. (☎0870 160 7930; www.shakespeare-country.co.uk. Open Apr.-Oct. M-Sa 9am-5:30pm, Su 10am-4pm; Nov.-Mar. M-Sa 9am-5pm, Su 10am-3:30pm.) Surf the **Internet** at Cyber Junction, 28 Greenhill St. (☎263 400. £4 per hr. Open M-F 10am-6pm, Sa 10:30am-5:30pm.) **Postal Code:** CV37 6PU.

TO SLEEP, PERCHANCE TO DREAM. B&Bs line Evesham Place, Evesham Road, Grove Road, and Shipston Road, but reservations are a must. **Carlton Guest House ❸,** 22 Evesham Pl., has spacious rooms and spectacular service. (☎293 548. Singles £24-30; doubles £52; triples £60-78. Cash only.) To reach **YHA Stratford (HI) ❷,** Wellsbourne Rd., follow B4086 from the town center (35min.), or take bus #X18 or 15 from Bridge St. (10min., every hr., £2.) This isolated hostel caters mostly to school groups and families and is a solid, inexpensive option for longer stays. (☎01789 297 093; www.stratfordyha.org.uk. Breakfast included. Internet £1 per 15min. Dorms £19.95-24.50. £3 HI discount. MC/V.)

Classy yet cozy, **The Oppo ❸,** 13 Sheep St., receives rave reviews from locals. (☎01789 269 980. Entrees from £9. M-Th noon-2pm and 5-9:30pm, F-Sa noon-2pm and 5-11pm, Su 6-9:30pm. MC/V.) **Hussain's ❷,** 6a Chapel St., a favorite of Ben Kingsley, offers Stratford's best Indian menu, featuring tandoori with handcrushed spices. (☎01789 276 506; www.hussainsindiancuisine.co.uk. Entrees from £6. Open daily 12:30-2:30pm and 5pm-midnight. AmEx/MC/V.) A **Somerfield** supermarket is in Town Sq. (☎292 604. Open M-Sa 8am-7pm, Su 10am-4pm.)

THE PLAY'S THE THING. Stratford's Will-centered sights are best seen before 11am, when daytrippers arrive, or after 4pm, when crowds disperse. Fans can buy an **All Five Houses ticket** for admission to all official Shakespeare properties: Anne Hathaway's Cottage, Mary Arden's House, Hall's Croft, New Place and Nash's House, and Shakespeare's Birthplace. (Tickets available at all houses. £14.50, concessions £12.50.) The **Three In-Town Houses** pass covers the latter three sights. (£10.60, concessions £9.30.) **Shakespeare's Birthplace,** on Henley St., is part period re-creation and part exhibit of Shakespeare's life and works. (☎01789 201 806. Open in summer M-Sa 9am-5pm, Su 9:30am-5pm; mid-season daily 10am-5pm; winter M-Sa 10am-4pm, Su 10:30am-4pm. £8, students £7.) **New Place,** on Chapel St., was Stratford's finest home when Shakespeare bought it in 1597; now only the foundation remains, the house itself destroyed by a disgruntled 19th-century owner to spite Bard tourists. (Summer M-Sa 9:30am-5pm, Su 10am-5pm; mid-season daily 11am-5pm; winter M-Sa 11am-4pm. £4, concessions £3.50.) New Place can be viewed from **Nash's House,** on Chapel St., which belonged to the first husband of Shakespeare's granddaughter. **Hall's Croft** and **Mary Arden's House** also capitalize on connections to Shakespeare's extended family and provide exhibits on Elizabethan daily life. (Open daily 9:30am-5pm in summer, 10am-5pm in mid-season, and 10am-4pm in winter. £7, concessions £6.) Pay homage to the Bard's grave in the **Holy Trinity Church,** Trinity St. (☎01789 266 316. Open daily 8:30am-6pm. Last admission 20min. before close. Requested donation £1.50.)

The **Royal Shakespeare Company** sells well over one million tickets each year. The Royal Shakespeare Theatre and the Swan Theatre, the RSC's more intimate neighbor, are currently undergoing a £100 million renovation and will re-open in 2010. The company will continue to perform shows down the road at **The Courtyard Theatre.** Visitors can get backstage tours and a glimpse at the high-tech stage to be installed at the Royal Shakespeare Theatre. Tickets are sold through the box office in the foyer of the Courtyard Theatre. (☎01789 0844 800 1110; www.rsc.org.uk. Open M and W-Sa 9:30am-8pm, Tu 10am-8pm. Tickets £10-48. Tickets £5 for ages 16-25. Standing room £5. Standby tickets in summer £15; winter £12. Disabled travelers should call ahead to advise the box office of their needs; some performances feature sign language interpretation or audio description.) The Shakespeare Birthplace Trust hosts a **Poetry Festival** every Sunday evening in July and August. Past participants include Seamus Heaney, Ted Hughes, and Derek Walcott. (☎01789 292 176. Tickets £7-15.) Theater crowds abound at the **Dirty Duck Pub,** 66 Waterside, where RSC actors make appearances almost nightly. (☎01789 297 312; www.dirtyduck.co.uk. Open daily 10am-midnight. AmEx/MC/V.)

DAYTRIP FROM STRATFORD: WARWICK CASTLE. From the towers of 14th-century **Warwick Castle,** the countryside unfolds like a medieval kingdom. This spectacular castle, one of England's finest, has dungeons with life-sized wax soldiers preparing for battle, while wax "knights" and "craftsmen" discuss their trades in the festival village. Visit the eagles and peacocks and climb to the top of Guy's tower for a panoramic view of the entire countryside. Events include summer jousting tournaments, storytelling, and live concerts. Ask at the TIC in Stratford-upon-Avon about discounted tickets. (☎0870 442 2000; www.warwick-castle.com. Open daily Apr.-Sept. 10am-6pm; Oct.-Mar. 10am-5pm. £17.95, concessions £12.95, children £10.95, families £52. Audio tours £3.) **Trains** arrive at the station off Coventry Rd. and run to Birmingham (40min., 2 per hr., £5.20), London Marylebone (2hr., 3 per hr., £15-41), and Stratford (25min., every hour., £4.50). Local **buses** #16 and 18 also stop at Market Pl. from Stratford (20min., 3-4 per hr.).

BIRMINGHAM ☎0121

Birmingham (pop. 1,000,000), second in Britain only to London in population, is the hub of Midlands nightlife and offers a thriving arts scene. It is steadfastly defended by fun-loving "Brummies" as one of the UK's most lively cities.

TRANSPORTATION. Trains run from **New St. Station** (☎08457 484 950) to: Liverpool Lime Street (2hr., every hr., £23.60); London Euston (2hr, every 30min., £61.50); Manchester Piccadilly (2hr., 2 per hr., £25.50); Oxford (1hr., at least 1 per hr., £23). Book in advance for lower prices.

Luggage storage £6 per day. National Express **buses** (☎08717 818 181; www.nationalexpress.com.) leave from **Digbeth Station** (temporarily on Oxford St.) for: Cardiff (1hr., 4 per day, £21.50), Liverpool (1hr., 5 per day, £10.80), London Heathrow (2hr., every hr., £28), Manchester (2hr., every 2 hr., £12), Oxford (2hr., 5 per day., £11).

ORIENTATION AND PRACTICAL INFORMATION. Birmingham is at the center of train and bus lines between London, central Wales, southwest England, and all northern destinations. The TIC, **The Rotunda,** 150 New St., books rooms for free and offers listings and flyers for budget accommodations. (☎0844 888 3883; www.visitbirmingham.com. Branch at the junction of New and Corporation St. Open M, W-Sa 9:30am-5:30pm, Tu 10am-5:30pm, Su 10:30am-4:30pm.) **Postal Code:** B2 4TU.

ACCOMMODATIONS AND FOOD. Hagley Road has several budget B&Bs—the farther away from downtown, the lower the prices. Take bus #9, 109, 126, or 139 from Colomore Row to Hagley Rd. Near the bus stop, **Birmingham Central Backpackers ❷,** 58 Coventry St., has tidy ensuite rooms and a large comfortable common area with colorful pastel walls and a TV projection screen. The full bar also stocks plenty of snacks and simple items for dinner. (☎0121 643 0033; www.birminghambackpackers.com. Breakfast included. Internet 50p for 30min. Laundry £3.50. Beds from £16. MC/V.) **Canalside Cafe ❶,** 35 Worcester Bar, serves baguettes, chili, and vegetarian dishes. (☎0121 441 9862. Most sandwiches £4-5. Open M-F and Su noon-11pm, Sa noon-10pm. Cash only.) Get groceries from **Sainsbury's,** Martineau Pl., 17 Union St. (☎0121 236 6496. Open M-F 7am-9pm, Sa 7am-8pm, Su 11am-5pm.)

SIGHTS AND ENTERTAINMENT. Birmingham has a long-standing reputation as a grim, industrial metropolis. To counter this bleak stereotype, the city has revitalized its central district with a visitor magnet: shopping—and lots of it. The epic **Bullring,** Europe's largest retail establishment, is the foundation of Birmingham's material-world makeover. Recognizable by the wavy, scaled **Selfridges** department store, the center has more than 140 shops and cafes. (☎0121 632 1500; www.bullring.co.uk. Open M-F 9:30am-8pm, Sa 9am-8pm, Su 11am-5pm.) Twelve minutes south of town by rail or bus lies **Cadbury World,** a cavity-inducing celebration of the famed chocolate empire. Take a train from New St. to Bournville, or bus #84 from the city center. (☎0121 451 4159. Open Mar.-Oct. daily 10am-3pm; Nov.-Feb. Tu-Th and Sa-Su 10am-3pm. Reserve ahead. £13, students £10.) The **Birmingham International Jazz Festival** brings over 200 performers to town during the first two weeks of July. (☎0121 454 7020; www.birminghamjazzfestival.com.)

Broad Street, with trendy cafe-bars and clubs, gets rowdy on weekends; as always, exercise caution at night. Pick up the bi-monthly *What's On* to discover Birmingham's latest hot spots. **The Yardbird,** Paradise Pl., is an excellent alternative to the club scene. No dress code, no cover, no pretense—just good music, big couches, and drinks with friends. DJs spin beats on Friday, with live music on Saturdays. (☎0121 212 2524; www.myspace.com/theyardbirdbirmingham. M-W and Su noon-midnight, Th-Sa noon-2am. Cash only.) A popular bar at the heart of city nightlife, **Rococo Lounge,** 260 Broad St., has a large outdoor patio and red retro-modern furnishings. Half price on Friday. (☎0121 633 4260; www.rococolounge.com. M-Th noon-2am, Sa-Su noon-3am.) A gay-friendly scene centers around Lower Essex Street.

CAMBRIDGE ☎01223

Unlike museum-oriented, metropolitan Oxford, Cambridge is a town for students before tourists. It was here that Newton's theory of gravity, Watson and Crick's model of DNA, Byron's and Milton's poetry, and Winnie the Pooh were born. No longer the exclusive academy of upper-class sons, the university feeds the minds of female, international, and state-school pupils alike. At exams' end, Cambridge explodes in Pimm's-soaked glee, and May Week is a swirl of celebration on the River Cam.

TRANSPORTATION

Trains: (☎08456 007 245). Station on Station Rd. (How original.) Ticket office open daily 5am-11pm. Trains to **London King's Cross** (45min., 3 per hr., £14) and **Ely** (20min., 3 per hr., round-trip £3.70).

Buses: Station on Drummer St. Ticket booth open M-Sa 9am-5pm; tickets often available onboard. **National Express** (☎08705 808 080) buses and airport shuttles pick up at stands on Parkside St. along Parker's Piece park. Buses to: **London Victoria** (2hr., every hr., £12); **Gatwick** (4hr., every hr., £31); **Heathrow** (2½hr., 2 per hr., £28); **Stansted** (1hr., every hr., £12). **Stagecoach Express** (☎01604 676 060) runs to **Oxford** (3hr., every 30min., from £11).

Public Transportation: Stagecoach (☎01223 423 578) runs **CitiBus** from the train station to the city center and around town (£5 for all-day ticket).

Taxis: Cabco (☎01223 312 444) and **Camtax** (☎01223 313 131). Both available 24hr.

Bike Rental: Station Cycles, Corn Exchange St. (☎01223 307 125). £9 per day; £50 deposit. Lock included. Open M-Sa 8am-7pm and Su 10am-6pm. AmEx/MC/V.

ORIENTATION

Cambridge has two central avenues; the main shopping street starts at **Magdalene Bridge** and becomes **Bridge Street, Sidney Street, Saint Andrew's Street, Regent Street,** and **Hills Road.** The other main thoroughfare starts as **Saint John's Street,** becoming **Trinity Street, King's Parade,** and **Trumpington Street.** From the Drummer St. bus station, **Emmanuel Street** leads to the shopping district near the TIC. To get to the TIC from the train station, turn right onto Hills Rd. and follow it ¾ mi.

PRACTICAL INFORMATION

Tourist Information Centre: Wheeler St. (☎09065 268 006; www.visitcambridge.org), 1 block south of Market Sq. Books rooms for £5 and a 10% deposit. Local Secrets Card gives city-wide discounts. Sells National Express tickets. Open Easter-Oct. M-F 10am-5:30pm, Sa 10am-5pm, Su 11am-3pm; Nov.-Easter M-F 10am-5:30pm, Sa 10am-5pm.

Police: Parkside (☎01223 358 966).

Hospital: Addenbrookes Hospital, Long Rd. (☎01223 245 151). Take Cambus C1 or C2 from Emmanuel St. (£1) and get off where Hills Rd. intersects Long Rd.

Internet Access: Available at: **Jaffa Net Cafe,** 22 Mill Rd. (☎01223 308 380). From £1 per hr. 10% student discount. Open daily 10am-10pm. **Budget Internet Cafe,** 30 Hills Rd. (☎01223 362 214). 75p per 30min. Open daily 9am-11pm. AmEx/MC/V. **Web and Eat,** 32 Hills Rd. (☎01223 314 168). 70p per 30min. Open daily 8am-11pm.

Post Office: 9-11 St. Andrew's St. (☎08457 223 344). **Bureau de change.** Open M and W-Sa 9am-5:30pm, Tu 9:30am-5:30pm. **Postcode:** CB2 3AA.

ACCOMMODATIONS

John Maynard Keynes, who studied and taught at Cambridge, tells us that low supply and high demand usually mean one thing: high prices.

Tenison Towers Guest House, 148 Tenison Rd. (☎01223 363 924; www.cambridgecitytenisontowers.com). Sunny rooms and freshly baked muffins in a Victorian house. Free Wi-Fi. Singles £40; doubles £60-66; triples £84. Cash only. ❹

Warkworth Guest House, Warkworth Terr. (☎01223 363 682). Spacious ensuite rooms near the bus station in a Victorian mansion. Breakfast included. Free Wi-Fi in lounge. Singles £55; twins and doubles £75; ensuite triples £90; families £95. MC/V. ❺

FOOD

Clown's, 54 King St. (☎01223 355 711). The staff at this cozy Italian eatery will remember your name if you come more than once. Children's artwork plasters the orange walls. Huge portions of pasta and dessert (£2.50-7). Set menu includes a drink, salad, small pasta, and cake (£7.50). Open daily 8am-11pm. Cash only; accepts Euro. ❷

The Regal, 38-39 St. Andrews St. (☎01223 366 459). The largest pub in the UK. 3 floors, 2 bars, and lots of slot machines. Check out the value menu (£3-4) for classic fare. Cheap pints (£1.50-2.50) to accompany your meal. Free Wi-Fi. Open M-Th and Su 9am-midnight, F-Sa 9am-2am. AmEx/MC/V over £5. ❶

SIGHTS

KING'S COLLEGE. King's College was founded by Henry VI in 1441 as a partner school to Eton: it was not until 1873 that students from other prep schools were admitted. Today, however, King's is the most socially liberal of the Cambridge colleges, drawing more of its students from state schools than any other. Its most stunning attraction is the Gothic **King's College Chapel.** From the southwest corner of the courtyard, you can see where Henry's master mason left off and the Tudors began work—the earlier stone is off-white. John Maynard Keynes, EM Forster, and Salman Rushdie all lived in King's College. *(King's Parade. ☎01223 331 100. Chapel and grounds open M-Sa 9:30am-5pm, Su 10am-5pm. Last entry 4:30pm. Contact TIC for tours. Listing of services and musical events available at porter's lodge. Choral services 10:30am, often 5:30pm. £5, students £3.50. Audio tour £2.50.)*

TRINITY COLLEGE. Henry VIII intended the College of the Holy and Undivided Trinity (founded in 1546) to be the largest and richest in Cambridge. The alma mater of Sir Isaac Newton, who lived in E staircase for 30 years, the college has many other equally illustrious alumni: literati Dryden, Byron, Tennyson, and Nabokov; atom-splitter Ernest Rutherford; philosopher Ludwig Wittgenstein; and Indian statesman Jawaharlal Nehru. The **Wren Library** houses alumnus AA Milne's handwritten copies of *Winnie the Pooh* and Newton's personal copy of his *Principia.* Pass through the drab **New Court** (Prince Charles's former residence) to get to the **Backs,** where you can enjoy the view from **Trinity Bridge.** *(Trinity St. ☎01223 338 400. Chapel and courtyard open daily 10am-5pm. Easter-Oct. £2.50, concessions £1.30, children £1, families £4.40; Nov.-Easter free for all.)*

SAINT JOHN'S COLLEGE. Established in 1511 by Lady Margaret Beaufort, mother of Henry VIII, St. John's centers on a paved plaza rather than a grassy courtyard. The **Fellows' Room** in Second Court spans 93 ft. and was the site of

D-Day planning. *(St. John's St. ☎01223 338 600. Open M-F 10am-5pm, Sa-Su 9:30am-5:30pm. Evensong Tu-Su 6:30pm. £3, concessions £2.)*

QUEENS' COLLEGE. Queens' College has the only unaltered Tudor courtyard in Cambridge, but the main attraction is the **Mathematical Bridge.** *(Silver St. ☎01223 335 511. Open Mar.-Oct. daily 10am-5pm. £2.)*

FITZWILLIAM MUSEUM. The museum fills an immense Neoclassical edifice, built in 1875 to house Viscount Fitzwilliam's collections. Egyptian, Chinese, Japanese, Middle Eastern, and Greek antiquities downstairs are joined by 16th-century German armor. Upstairs, galleries feature works by Rubens, Monet, Van Gogh, and Picasso. *(Trumpington St. ☎01223 332 900. Open Tu-Sa 10am-5pm, Su noon-5pm. Call about lunchtime and evening concerts. Free; suggested donation £3.)*

ENTERTAINMENT

PUNTING. Punting on the Cam is as traditional and obligatory as afternoon tea. Touristy and overrated? Maybe, but it's still a blast. Punters take two routes—from Magdalene Bridge to Silver St. or from Silver St. to Grantchester. The shorter, busier, and more interesting first route passes the colleges and the Backs. To propel your boat, thrust the pole behind the boat into the river-bed and rotate the pole in your hands as you push forward. Punt-bombing—jumping from bridges into the river alongside a punt to tip it—is an art form. Some more ambitious punters climb out midstream, scale a bridge while their boat passes underneath, and jump back down from the other side. Be wary of bridge-top pole-stealers. You can rent at **Scudamore's,** Silver St. Bridge. (☎01223 359 750; www.scudamores.com. M-F £16 per hr., Sa-Su £18 per hr. £80 deposit. MC/V.) Student-punted tours (£14, students £12) are another option.

NIGHTLIFE

The Eagle, 8 Benet St. (☎01223 505 020). Cambridge's oldest pub (in business since 1525) is in the heart of town and packed with boisterous tourists. When Watson and Crick rushed in to announce the discovery of DNA, the barmaid insisted they settle their 4-shilling tab. Check out the RAF room, where WWII pilots stood on each other's shoulders to burn their initials into the ceiling. Open M-Sa 11am-11pm, Su noon-10:30pm. AmEx/MC/V over £5.

The Anchor, Silver St. (☎01223 353 554). This jolly-looking pub, overflowing with beer and good cheer, is anchored right on the Cam. Scoff at amateur punters colliding under Silver St. Bridge or savor a pint at the same spot from which Pink Floyd's Syd Barrett drew his inspiration. Open M-Th and Su 11am-11pm, F-Sa 11am-midnight. Kitchen open M-Sa noon-10pm, Su noon-9pm. AmEx/MC/V.

FESTIVALS

May Week, actually in June—you would expect a better understanding of simple chronology from those bright Cambridge students. A celebration of the end of the term, the week is crammed with concerts, plays, and balls followed by recuperative riverside breakfasts and 5am punting. The boat clubs compete in races known as the **bumps.** Crews attempt to ram the boat in front before being bumped from behind. The celebration includes **Footlights Revue,** a series of skits by current undergrads. Past performers have included future *Monty Python* stars John Cleese and Eric Idle. £250 per person.

SCOTLAND

Half the size of England with only a tenth the population, Scotland possesses open spaces and wild natural splendor unrivaled by its neighbor to the south. The craggy Highlands, beaches of the western coast, and mists of the Hebrides are awe-inspiring, while the farmland to the south and tiny fishing villages to the east convey a more subtle beauty. The Scots revel in a distinct culture ranging from the fevered nightlife of Glasgow and the festival atmosphere of Edinburgh to the tight-knit communities of the Orkney and Shetland Islands. The Scots defended their independence for hundreds of years before reluctantly joining England to create Great Britain in 1707, and they only regained a separate parliament in 1999. The mock kilts and bagpipes of the big cities can grow tiresome; discover Scotland's true colors by venturing off the beaten path to find Gaelic-speaking B&B owners, peat-cutting crofters, and fishermen setting out in skiffs at the crack of dawn.

GETTING TO SCOTLAND

Buses from London (8-12hr.) are generally the cheapest option. National Express (☎08457 225 333; www.nationalexpress.com) **buses** connect England and Scotland via Edinburgh and Glasgow. Trains are faster (4-6hr.) but more expensive. National Express also runs **trains** (☎08457 225 333; www.nationalexpress.com) from London to Edinburgh and Glasgow. Fares vary depending on when you buy (£27-£100). A pricier option is the **Caledonian Sleeper,** run by First Scotrail (☎08456 015 929; www.firstgroup.com/scotrail), which leaves London Euston near midnight and gets to Edinburgh at 7am (£20-140). The cheapest airfares between England and Scotland are available from no-frills airlines. **easyJet** (☎0871 244 2366; www.easyjet.com) flies to Edinburgh and Glasgow from London Gatwick, Luton, and Stansted. The fares are web-only; book in advance and fly for as little as £5. **Ryanair** (☎08712 460 000; www.ryanair.com) flies to Edinburgh and to Glasgow Prestwick (1hr. from the city) from Dublin and London. **British Airways** (☎0844 493 0787; www.britishairways.com) sells round-trip tickets between England and Scotland from £85.

TRANSPORTATION

In the Lowlands (south of Stirling and north of the Borders), **trains** and buses run many routes frequently. In the Highlands, Scotrail and National Express trains run a few routes. Many stations are unstaffed—buy tickets on board. A great money-saver is the **Freedom of Scotland Travelpass,** which allows unlimited train travel and transportation on most Caledonian MacBrayne ("CalMac") ferries. Purchase the pass before traveling to Britain at any BritRail distributor. **Buses** tend to be the best and cheapest way to travel. **Traveline Scotland** has the best information on all routes and services (☎0871 200 2233; www.travelinescotland.com). **Scottish Citylink** (☎08705 505 050; www.citylink.co.uk) runs most intercity routes; **Postbuses** (Royal Mail customer service ☎08457 740 740) pick up passengers and mail once or twice a day in the most remote parts of the country, typically charging £2-5 (and sometimes nothing). Many travelers find that they can be a reliable way to get around the Highlands. **HAGGiS** (☎0131 557 9393; www.haggisadventures.com) and **MacBackpackers** (☎01315 589 900;

www.macbackpackers.com) cater to the young and adventurous, with a number of tours departing from Edinburgh. Both run hop-on, hop-off excursions that let you travel Scotland at your own pace (usually under three months).

EDINBURGH ☎0131

A city of elegant stone set between rolling hills and ancient volcanoes, Edinburgh (ED-in-bur-ra; pop. 500,000) is the pride of Scotland. Since King David I granted it "burgh" (town) status in 1130, Edinburgh has been a haven for forward-thinking intellectuals and innovative artists. Today, world-class universities craft the next generation of Edinburgh's thinkers. Businessmen, students, and lots of backpackers mix amid the city's medieval architecture and mingle in lively pubs and cutting-edge clubs. In August, Edinburgh becomes a mecca for the arts, drawing talent and crowds from around the globe to its International and Fringe Festivals.

INTERCITY TRANSPORTATION

Edinburgh lies 45 mi. east of Glasgow and 405 mi. northwest of London on Scotland's east coast, on the southern bank of the Firth of Forth.

Flights: Edinburgh International Airport (☎0870 040 0007), 7 mi. west of the city. Lothian Airlink (☎0131 555 6363) shuttles between the airport and Waverley Bridge (25min.; every 10-15min.; £3.50, children £2, round-trip £6/3). Flights to major international cities, including **New York City** (9hr.), as well as UK destinations such as **Birmingham, London Gatwick, London Heathrow,** and **Manchester.**

Trains: Waverley Station, between Princes St., Market St., and Waverley Bridge. Free bike storage beside platforms 1 and 11. Ticket office open M-Sa 4:45am-12:30am, Su 7am-12:30am. Trains (☎08457 484 950) to: **Aberdeen** (2½hr.; M-Sa every hr., Su 8 per day; £34); **Glasgow** (1hr., 4 per hr., £9.70); **Inverness** (3½hr., every 2hr., £32); **London King's Cross** (4¾hr., 2 per hr., £108); **Stirling** (50min., 2 per hr., £6.10).

Buses: The modern **Edinburgh Bus Station** is on the eastern side of St. Andrew Sq. Open daily 6am-midnight. Ticket office open daily 8am-8pm. National Express (☎08705 808 080) to **London** (10hr., 4 per day, £30). Scottish Citylink (☎08705 505 050; www.citylink.co.uk) to **Aberdeen** (2½hr., every hr., £23), **Glasgow** (1hr.; M-Sa 4 per hr., Su 2 per hr.; £6), and **Inverness** (4½hr., 8-10 per day, £25). A bus-ferry route via Stranraer goes to **Belfast** (2 per day, £28) and **Dublin, IRE** (2 per day, £32). Megabus also serves Edinburgh; for cheapest fares, book ahead online at www.megabus.com or call ☎0900 160 0900 (7am-10pm).

LOCAL TRANSPORTATION

Public Transportation: Although walking is usually the fastest and easiest way around the city center, Edinburgh has a comprehensive bus system. Lothian (☎0131 555 6363; www.lothianbuses.com) operates most buses. Exact change required (£1.10, children 70p). Buy a 1-day **Daysaver** ticket (£3, children £2.40) from any driver or in the Lothian Travelshops (☎0131 555 6363) on Waverley Bridge, Hanover St., and Shandwick Pl. Open M-Sa 8:15am-6pm. **Night buses** cover selected routes after midnight (£3). First Edinburgh (☎0870 872 7271) also operates local buses. Traveline (☎0870 608 2608; www.traveline.co.uk) has more information.

Taxis: Stands located at all train and bus stations. **City Cabs** (☎0131 228 1211). **Central Radio Taxis** (☎0131 229 2468). **Central Taxis Edinburgh** (☎0131 229 2468; www.taxis-edinburgh.co.uk).

Car Rental: The TIC has a list of rental agencies, most from £25 per day. **Thrifty,** 42 Haymarket Terr. (☎0131 337 1319). **Avis,** 100 Dalry Rd. (☎0131 337 6363).

Bike Rental: Biketrax, 11-13 Lochrin Pl. (☎0131 228 6633; www.biketrax.co.uk). Mountain bikes £12 per ½-day, £16 per day. Open M-F 9:30am-6pm, Sa 9:30am-6pm, Su noon-5pm. **Edinburgh Cycle Hire,** 29 Blackfriars St. (☎01680 300 301), off High St., organizes cycle tours. Mountain bikes £10-15 per day, £50-70 per week. Open daily 10am-6pm.

ORIENTATION

Edinburgh's city center is divided into two halves, on either side of the train tracks, **Old Town** and **New Town.** The two are connected by three bridges: **North Bridge, Waverley Bridge,** and **The Mound.** The bridges cross over **Waverley Station,** which lies directly between Old Town and New Town. The **Royal Mile** and **Edinburgh Castle** are in Old Town and are the center of most tourist activities, while New Town plays host to upscale shopping. When reading maps, remember that Edinburgh is a multidimensional city—many streets that appear to intersect are actually on different levels. The terrain is hilly, and valleys are often spanned by bridges with streets running under them. Elevations are connected by many narrow stairway alleys known as "closes." Two miles northeast of New Town, **Leith** is the city's seaport on the Firth of Forth.

PRACTICAL INFORMATION

TOURIST AND FINANCIAL SERVICES

Tourist Information Centre: Waverley Market, 3 Princes St. (☎0845 22 55 121), north of Waverley Station. Helpful and often mobbed, the mother of all Scottish TICs books rooms for £4 plus a 10% deposit; sells bus, museum, tour, and theater tickets; and has free maps and pamphlets. **Bureau de change.** Open July-Aug. M-Sa 9am-7pm, Su 10am-7pm; Sept.-June M-Sa 9am-5pm, Su 10am-5pm.

Budget Travel: STA Travel, 27 Forrest Rd. and 72 Nicholson St. (both ☎0131 230 8569). Open M-Sa 10am-6pm, Su 11am-5pm.

Beyond Tourism: In the summer, young travelers are employed by festival organizers to help manage offices, set up, etc. Hostel notice boards often help employment agencies seeking temporary workers. **Temp Agency** (☎0131 478 5151). **Wesser and Partner** (☎01438 356 222, www.wesser.co.uk). **Kelly Services** (☎0131 220 2626).

LOCAL SERVICES

Luggage Storage: At the Waverley train station or the bus station. £5 per item per day.

Camping Gear:Millets the Outdoor Store, 12 Frederick St. (☎0131 220 1551). All the essentials, but no rentals. Open M-W and F-Sa 9am-6pm, Th 9am-8pm, Su 10:30am-5:30pm.

Library: Central Library (☎0131 242 8000), on George IV Bridge. Free Internet. Open M-Th 10am-8pm, F 10am-5pm, Sa 9am-1pm.

GLBT Resources:Edinburgh Lesbian, Gay, and Bisexual Centre, 58A-60 Broughton St. (☎0131 478 7069). **Gay Edinburgh**(www.visitscotland.com).

Disabled Services: Contact the TIC prior to traveling for a free *Accessible Scotland* guide or check www.edinburgh.org and www.capability-scotland.org.uk for info on access to restaurants and sights. **Shopmobility,** The Mound (☎0131 225 9559), by the National Gallery, lends motorized wheelchairs for free. Open Tu-Sa 10am-4pm.

Public Toilets and Showers: In the "Superloo" at the train station. Shower, toilet, and towel £3. Toilet 20p. Open daily 4am-12:45am.

EMERGENCY AND COMMUNICATIONS

Police: Headquarters at Fettes Ave. (☎0131 311 3131; www.lbp.police.uk). Other stations at 14 St. Leonard's St. (☎0131 662 5000) and 188 High St. (☎0131 226 6966). Blue **police information boxes** are scattered throughout the city center, with tourist information and an emergency assistance button.

Pharmacy: Boots, 48 Shandwick Pl. (☎0131 225 6757) and 101-103 Princes St. (☎0131 225 8331). Open M-W and F-Sa 8am-6:30pm, Th 8am-8pm, Su 10am-6pm.

Hospitals: Royal Infirmary of Edinburgh, 51 Little France Cres. (☎0131 536 1000, emergencies 536 6000). **Royal Hospital for Sick Children,** 9 Sciennes Rd. (☎0131 536 0000).

Internet Access: Signs to internet cafes are on every other corner along the Royal Mile. **E-Corner,** 54 Blackfriars St. (☎0131 558 7858). £1 per 30min. with terminals and Wi-Fi. Open M-F 10am-9pm, Sa 10am-8pm, Su noon-8pm. Free at the **Central Library** (p. 149). Many cafes throughout Old Town also offer internet access.

Post Office: St. James Centre (☎0131 556 9546). **Bureau de change.** Open M-Sa 9am-5:30pm. Branch at 46 St. Mary's St. (☎0131 556 6351). Open M-Tu and Th-F 9am-12:30pm and 1:30-5:30pm, Sa 9am-noon. **Postcode:** EH1 3SR.

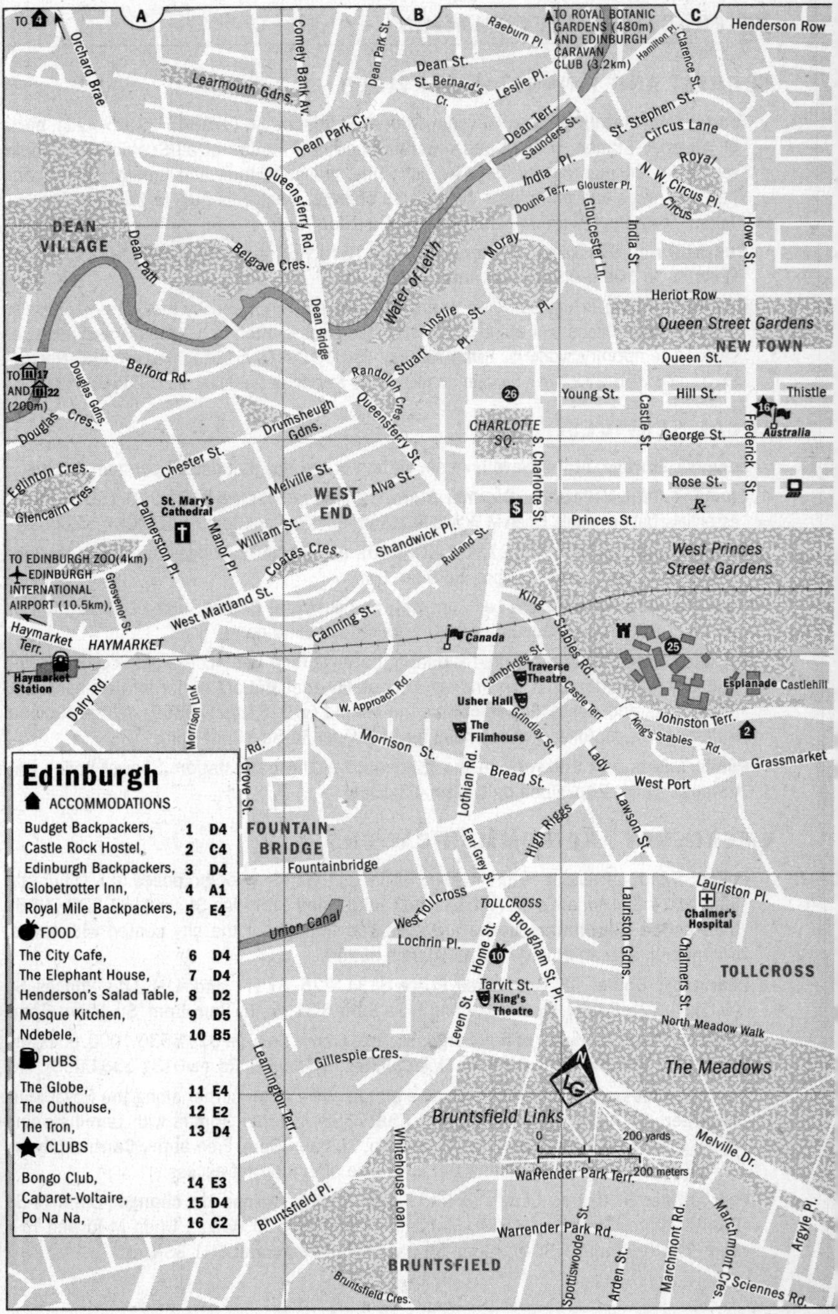

Edinburgh
ACCOMMODATIONS
Budget Backpackers, 1 D4
Castle Rock Hostel, 2 C4
Edinburgh Backpackers, 3 D4
Globetrotter Inn, 4 A1
Royal Mile Backpackers, 5 E4
FOOD
The City Cafe, 6 D4
The Elephant House, 7 D4
Henderson's Salad Table, 8 D2
Mosque Kitchen, 9 D5
Ndebele, 10 B5
PUBS
The Globe, 11 E4
The Outhouse, 12 E2
The Tron, 13 D4
CLUBS
Bongo Club, 14 E3
Cabaret-Voltaire, 15 D4
Po Na Na, 16 C2
A
B
C
TO 4
TO ROYAL BOTANIC GARDENS (480m) AND EDINBURGH CARAVAN CLUB (3.2km)
TO 17 AND 22 (200m)
TO EDINBURGH ZOO(4km)
EDINBURGH INTERNATIONAL AIRPORT (10.5km),
Orchard Brae
Learmouth Gdns.
Comely Bank Av.
Dean Park St.
Raeburn Pl.
Henderson Row
Dean St.
St. Bernard's Cr.
Leslie Pl.
Hamilton Pl.
Clarence St.
Dean Park Cr.
Dean Terr.
Saunders St.
St. Stephen St.
Circus Lane
Royal Circus
N. W. Circus Pl.
India Pl.
Doune Terr.
Glouster Pl.
Queensferry Rd.
DEAN VILLAGE
Dean Path
Belgrave Cres.
Water of Leith
Moray Pl.
Gloucester Ln.
India St.
Howe St.
Heriot Row
Queen Street Gardens
NEW TOWN
Dean Bridge
Ainslie Pl.
Stuart St.
Queen St.
Belford Rd.
Douglas Gdns.
Douglas Cres.
Randolph Cres.
Young St.
Hill St.
Thistle
Castle St.
Drumsheugh Gdns.
Queensferry St.
CHARLOTTE SQ.
S. Charlotte St.
George St.
Australia
Frederick St.
Eglinton Cres.
Glencairn Cres.
Chester St.
Melville St.
WEST END
Alva St.
Rose St.
St. Mary's Cathedral
Palmerston Pl.
Manor Pl.
William St.
Princes St.
Coates Cres.
Shandwick Pl.
Rutland St.
West Princes Street Gardens
Grosvenor St.
West Maitland St.
King Stables Rd.
Haymarket Terr.
HAYMARKET
Canning St.
Canada
Haymarket Station
Dalry Rd.
Cambridge St.
Traverse Theatre
Esplanade
Castlehill
W. Approach Rd.
Usher Hall
Castle Terr.
Johnston Terr.
Morrison Link
The Filmhouse
Grindlay St.
King's Stables Rd.
Morrison St.
Grove St.
Lothian Rd.
Bread St.
Lady Lawson St.
Grassmarket
West Port
FOUNTAIN-BRIDGE
High Riggs
Earl Grey St.
Fountainbridge
Lauriston Pl.
West Tollcross
TOLLCROSS
Lauriston Gdns.
Chalmer's Hospital
Union Canal
Brougham St.
Lochrin Pl.
Home St.
Tarvit St.
King's Theatre
Chalmers St.
TOLLCROSS
Leven St.
North Meadow Walk
Gillespie Cres.
Leamington Terr.
The Meadows
Bruntsfield Links
0
200 yards
200 meters
Melville Dr.
Whitehouse Loan
Warrender Park Terr.
Bruntsfield Pl.
Warrender Park Rd.
Spottiswoode St.
Arden St.
Marchmont Rd.
Marchmont Cres.
Argyle Pl.
BRUNTSFIELD
Bruntsfield Cres.
Sciennes Rd.

BRITAIN

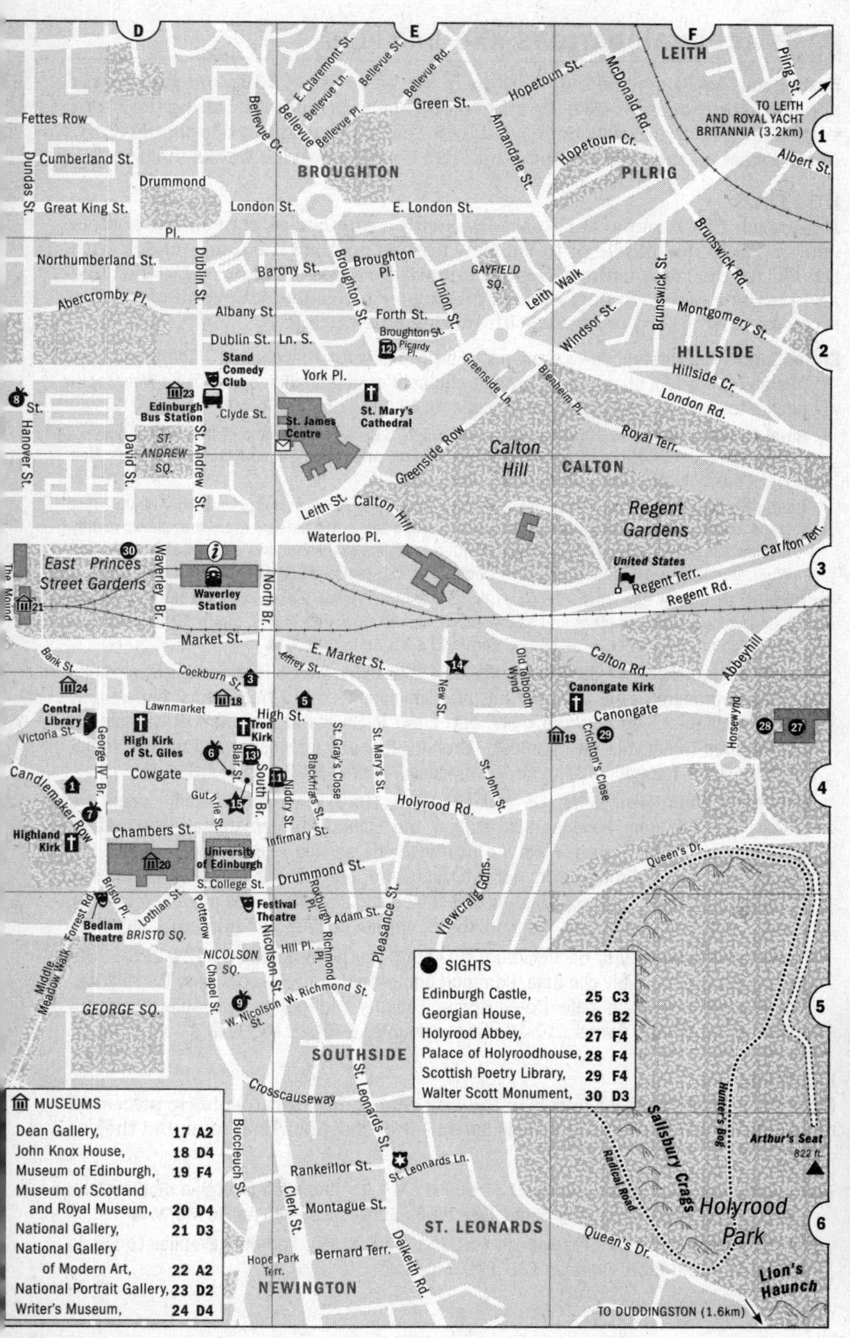
LEITH
TO LEITH AND ROYAL YACHT BRITANNIA (3.2km)
BROUGHTON
PILRIG
HILLSIDE
CALTON
Calton Hill
Regent Gardens
East Princes Street Gardens
Waverley Station
Edinburgh Bus Station
Stand Comedy Club
St. James Centre
St. Mary's Cathedral
United States
Canongate Kirk
Central Library
High Kirk of St. Giles
Tron Kirk
Highland Kirk
University of Edinburgh
Festival Theatre
Bedlam Theatre
SOUTHSIDE
ST. LEONARDS
NEWINGTON
Salisbury Crags
Holyrood Park
Arthur's Seat 822 ft.
Lion's Haunch
TO DUDDINGSTON (1.6km)
SIGHTS
Edinburgh Castle, 25 C3
Georgian House, 26 B2
Holyrood Abbey, 27 F4
Palace of Holyroodhouse, 28 F4
Scottish Poetry Library, 29 F4
Walter Scott Monument, 30 D3
MUSEUMS
Dean Gallery, 17 A2
John Knox House, 18 D4
Museum of Edinburgh, 19 F4
Museum of Scotland and Royal Museum, 20 D4
National Gallery, 21 D3
National Gallery of Modern Art, 22 A2
National Portrait Gallery, 23 D2
Writer's Museum, 24 D4

BRITAIN

ACCOMMODATIONS AND CAMPING

Hostels and **hotels** are the only options in the city center; **B&Bs** and **guesthouses** appear on the edges of town. Be sure to ook ahead in summer. During the Festival (from late July to early Sept.) and New Year's, prices often rise significantly. Many locals let their apartments; the TIC's booking service works magic.

HOSTELS

Edinburgh is a backpacker's paradise, with a number of convenient hostels smack-dab in the middle of town. New hostels open all the time—check with the TIC for the latest listings. Hostels range from the small and cozy to the huge and party-oriented. Expect cliques of long-term residents. Several also offer more expensive private rooms with varying amenities.

Scotland's Top Hostels (www.scotlands-top-hostels.com). This chain's 3 Edinburgh hostels all have a fun, relaxed environment and comfortable facilities. Also runs MacBackpacker tours in the city and around Scotland. All three run free Th pub crawls.

Royal Mile Backpackers, 105 High St. (☎0131 557 6120). The smallest of the chain's hostels. Well-kept and cozy, with a community feel (and free tea and coffee). Shared laundry facilities. Free Wi-Fi. 8-bed dorms £13-15. AmEx/MC/V. ❶

Castle Rock Hostel, 15 Johnston Terr. (☎0131 225 9666, www.castlerockedinburgh.com). Just steps from the castle, with a party atmosphere and a top-notch cinema room that shows nightly movies. Ask about their haircut offer: £10 with a complimentary shot of vodka. Breakfast £2. Free Wi-Fi. Dorms £13-15; doubles £30-34; triples £45-51. AmEx/MC/V. ❶

High St. Hostel, 8 Blackfriars St. (☎0131 557 3984). Ideally located just off the Royal Mile. Laid-back party environment and 16th-century architecture. Pub crawls, movie nights, and pool competitions. Free Wi-Fi. 4- to 18-bed dorms £13-15. AmEx/MC/V. ❶

Budget Backpackers, 37-39 Cowgate (☎0131 226 2351; www.budgetbackpackers.co.uk). The most modern of the Old Town hostels. Spacious 2- to 12-bed rooms; female-only dorms available. Free city tour daily; pub crawl M-Sa starting at 9pm. Breakfast £2. Lockers free (bring your own padlock). Laundry £1 each for washer and dryer. Internet £1 per 30min. Reception 24hr. Key-card access. Rooms £9-24. 18+. MC/V. ❷

Globetrotter Inn, 46 Marine Dr. (☎0131 336 1030; www.globetrotterinns.com), a 15min. bus ride from Waverley train station and Edinburgh International Airport. Large grounds next to the Firth of Forth. An hourly shuttle service runs to and from the city, although a shop, TV room, gym, hot tub, and 24hr. bar make it tempting to stay put. Curtained bunks offer privacy. Light breakfast included. Free Wi-Fi and internet terminals. Lockers free. Key-card access. Dorms £15-19; ensuite doubles and twins £46. MC/V. ❶

Edinburgh Backpackers, 65 Cockburn (CO-burn, you pervert) St. (☎0131 220 2200; www.hoppo.com). Lively clientele. Common areas, pool table, jukebox, and TV. 15% discount at the downstairs cafe. Co-ed dorms. Laundry and internet available. Check-out 10am. 8- to 16-bed dorms £10-19; private doubles £45-52. MC/V. ❶

HOTELS

Most of the independent hotels in the city center have stratospheric prices. At the affordable end are budget **chain hotels**—they may lack character, but they're comfortable.

Greenside Hotel, 9 Royal Terr. (☎0131 557 0121). A refurbished Georgian building with views of the Firth from its top floors. Free Wi-Fi. Singles £25-60. AmEx/MC/V. ❺

Grassmarket Hotel, 94 Grassmarket (☎0131 220 2299). Formerly Premier Lodge. In the heart of Old Town. Doubles £80-120. MC/V. ❺

B&BS AND GUESTHOUSES

B&Bs cluster in three colonies, all of which you can walk to or reach by bus from the city center. Try Gilmore Pl., Viewforth Terr., or Huntington Gardens in the **Bruntsfield** district, south from the west end of Princes St. (bus #11, 16, or 17 west/southbound); Dalkeith Rd. and Minto St. in **Newington,** south from the east end of Princes St. (bus #7, 31, or 37, among others); or **Pilrig,** northeast from the east end of Princes St. (bus #11 east/northbound). See www.visitscotland.com/listings/edinburgh-guest-houses.html for a complete list or call the TIC.

Ardenlee Guest House, 9 Eyre Pl. (☎0131 556 2838; www.ardenlee.co.uk), near the beautiful Royal Botanic Gardens. Take bus #23 or 27 from Hanover St. northbound to the corner of Dundas St. and Eyre Pl. In a Victorian building with a welcoming red carpet running up the stairs. Comfortable beds complete with teddy bears. £25-45 per person; prices rise during July and August. Free Wi-Fi. MC/V. ❹

Relax Guest House, 11 Eyre Place (☎0131 556 1433; www.relaxguesthouse.co.uk), in New Town. Ensuite rooms and a calm vibe. An impressive whisky selection in the fully licensed bar helps guests relax. Low-season £25-60 per person, high-season £45-60. AmEx/MC/V. ❹

Robertson Guest House, 5 Hartington Gardens (☎0131 229 2652; www.robertson-guesthouse.com). Bus #11, 16, or 17 from George St. Quiet and welcoming, with ensuite rooms and a relaxing garden patio. An original tile mosaic in front of the door has survived for 135 years. £29-75 per person. MC/V. ❹

CAMPING

Edinburgh Caravan Club Site, Marine Dr. (☎0131 312 6874), by the Firth. Take bus #27 from The Mound, get off at Silvernose, and walk 15min. down Marine Dr. Clean and family-friendly. Electricity, shop, hot water, showers, and laundry. £4.60-6 per person; £4.80-7.60 per pitch for members. £7 per pitch for non-members. MC/V. ❶

FOOD

Edinburgh's restaurants offer a range of cuisines. If it's traditional fare you're after, find everything from pub haggis to creative "modern Scottish" at the city's top restaurants. For food on the cheap, many **pubs** offer student and hosteler discounts in the early evening, while fast-food joints are scattered across New Town. Takeaway shops on **South Clerk, Leith Street** and **Lothian Road** have affordable Chinese and Indian fare. For groceries, try **Sainsbury's,** 9-10 St. Andrew Sq. (☎0131 225 8400; open M-Sa 7am-10pm, Su 9am-8pm) or the **Tesco** on Earl Grey St. (☎0131 221 0650; open daily 6am-11pm).

OLD TOWN

The Mosque Kitchen, 19A West Nicholson Street, tucked away in the courtyard of Edinburgh's modern central mosque. A jumble of long tables make up an outdoor cafeteria. Popular with students. Heaping plates of curry (£4) are hard to beat. Open M-Th and Sa-Su 11:30am-7pm, F noon-1pm and 1:45-7pm (closes briefly for F prayers). Cash only. ❶

The City Cafe, 19 Blair St. (☎0131 220 0125), right off the Royal Mile behind Tron Kirk. This perennially popular Edinburgh institution is a cafe by day and a flashy pre-club spot by night. Sip a milkshake and people-watch from the cafe's heated street-side seating. Happy hour daily 5-8pm. Open daily during the festival 11am-3am; otherwise 11am-1am. Kitchen open M-Th until 10pm, F-Su until 10pm. MC/V. ❷

Maxies Bistro and Wine Bar, 5B Johnston Terrace (☎0131 226 7770, www.maxies.co.uk). For 35 years, this local institution has poured some of the world's tastiest wines on their romantic second-story patio overlooking Old Town. Eclectic menu with everything from pasta to Mexican (entrees £7-13). Vegetarian dishes £7. Open daily 11am-midnight. AmEx/MC/V. ❷

The Elephant House, 21 George IV Bridge (☎0131 220 5355). Harry Potter and Albus Dumbledore were born here on scribbled napkins. A perfect place to chill, chat, and read a newspaper. Exotic teas and coffees and the best shortbread in the universe. Great views of the castle. Coffee and 1hr. of internet £2.50. Open daily 8am-11pm. MC/V. ❶

NEW TOWN

Valvonna & Crolla, 19 Elm Row (☎0131 556 6066; www.valvonacrolla.co.uk), off Leith Walk. Beloved of foodies across the UK, this deli has been selling Italian wine, gourmet meats, and other delicious groceries since 1934. In back, the cafe serves Scottish takes on Italian specialties, complete with wine pairings. Open M-Th 8:30am-5:30pm, F-Sa 8am-6pm, Su 10:30am-3:30pm. Reservations recommended on weekends. MC/V. ❷

The Basement, 10A-12A Broughton St. (☎0131 557 0097; www.thebasement.org.uk). Menu changes daily, with plenty of vegetarian options. Energetic vibe draws students, artists, performers, and other creative types. Entrees £6-9.50, set 2-course lunch £8. Mexican night Sa-Su. Kitchen open M-Sa noon-10:30pm, Su 12:30-10:30pm. Bar open until 1am. Reservations recommended on weekends. AmEx/MC/V. ❷

Henderson's Salad Table, 94 Hanover St. (☎0131 225 2131). The flagship of Edinburgh's vegetarian scene. The bar gets going at night, offering a range of organic wines, beers, and spirits. Free Wi-Fi. Seriously good salads £2.10-7.30. Open M-Sa 8am-11pm. Kitchen open 11:30am-10pm. AmEx/MC/V. ❶

Mussel Inn, 61-65 Rose St. (☎0131 225 5979; www.mussel-inn.com). Succulent local shellfish in a friendly, relaxed environment. Gourmet entrees £11-18. Open M-Th noon-3pm and 5:30-10pm, F-Sa noon-10pm, Su noon-10pm. MC/V. ❸

SIGHTS

TOURS

Edinburgh is best explored by foot, but Lothian buses run several hop-on, hop-off open-top bus tours around the major sights, beginning at Waverley Bridge. **City Sightseeing Edinburgh** is popular; others include the **Majestic Tour** to New Haven and the Royal Yacht Britannia, vintage **MacTours,** and **Edinburgh Tours.** (General tour bus information ☎0131 220 0770; www.edinburghtour.com. All tours run Apr.-Oct. every 20-30min. £10, concessions £9. Tickets can be used for reduced admission at many attractions.) A 24hr. Edinburgh **Grand Tour** ticket (£13, concessions £11) combines all four.

While a great array of tour companies in Edinburgh tout themselves as "the original" or "the scariest," the most worthwhile of the bunch is **McEwan's Edinburgh Literary Pub Tour.** Led by professional actors, this 2hr., booze-filled crash course in Scottish literature meets outside the Beehive Inn on Grassmarket. (☎0800 169 7410; www.edinburghliterarypubtour.co.uk. May-Sept. daily 7:30pm; Oct. and Mar.-Apr. Th-Su 7:30pm; Nov.-Feb. F 7:30pm. £8, concessions £7. £1 discount for online booking.) The popular **City of the Dead Tour,** convening nightly outside St. Giles's Cathedral, promises a one-on-one encounter with the MacKenzie poltergeist. (☎0131 225 9044; www.blackhart.uk.com. Daily Easter-Halloween 8:30, 9:15, 10pm; Halloween-Easter 7:30, 8:30pm. £8.50, concessions £6.50.) **Mercat Tours,** leaving from Mercat Cross, enters Edinburgh's spooky underground vaults, relying upon long ghost stories rather than staged frights. (☎0131 225 5445; www.mercattours.com. £7.50-8.50, families £20-23.)

OLD TOWN

Edinburgh's medieval center, the **Royal Mile,** is the heart of Old Town and home to many attractions—it's an energetic traveler's playground. The Mile gets its name from the royal edifices on either end: **Edinburgh Castle** on top of the hill and the **Palace of Holyrood** anchoring the bottom of the hill. The top of the Mile is known as **Castle Hill.** Continuing east downhill from the castle, the street becomes **Lawnmarket,** then **High Street,** then **Canongate,** and finally ends at **Holyrood.** Each segment is packed with attractions and souvenir shops.

CASTLE HILL AND LAWNMARKET

EDINBURGH CASTLE. Looming over the city center atop a dormant volcano, Edinburgh Castle dominates the skyline. Its oldest surviving building is tiny, 12th-century **Saint Margaret's Chapel,** built by King David I of Scotland in memory of his mother. The castle compound developed over the course of centuries; the most recent additions date to the 1920s. The central **Palace,** begun in the 1430s, was home to Stuart kings and queens and contains the room where Mary, Queen of Scots, gave birth to James VI. It also houses the **Scottish Crown Jewels,** which are older than those in London. The storied (although visually unspectacular) **Stone of Scone,** more commonly known as the Stone of Destiny, is also on permanent display. Other sections of the sprawling compound, like the Scottish National War Memorial, the National War Museum of Scotland, and the 15th-century monster cannon Mons Meg, definitely merit a visit, despite the uphill climb. The **One O'Clock Gun** fires from Monday to Saturday. Guess what time. Buy tickets online to skip the queues. *(☎0131 225 9846; www.edinburghcastle.gov.uk. Open daily Apr.-Oct. 9:30am-6pm; Nov.-Mar. 9:30am-5pm. Last entry 45min. before closing. Free guided tours of the castle depart regularly from the entrance. £13, concessions £10.50, children £6.50. Excellent audio tour £3.50, concessions £2.50, children £1.50.)*

CAMERA OBSCURA AND WORLD OF ILLUSIONS. Climb **Outlook Tower** to see the 150-year-old camera obscura, which captures moving color images of the street below. On the top floor, a guide uses the lever-operated camera to show you around the city from the comfort of a darkroom. The museum's dazzling exhibits use lights, mirrors, lenses, and other 19th-century technology to create illusions that still manage to amaze and confound visitors; displays with more modern technology are equally astonishing and amusing, including a photographic face-morphing booth and a hall of holograms. *(☎0131 226 3709. Open daily July 9:30am-7pm; Aug 9:30am-7:30pm; Sept.-Oct. and Apr.-June 9:30am-6pm; Nov.-Mar. 10am-5pm. Presentations every 20min., last presentation 1hr. before closing. £8.50, concessions £6.75, children £5.75.)*

THE SCOTCH WHISKY EXPERIENCE. Learn about the "history and mystery" of Scotland's most famous export at the Scotch Whisky Heritage Centre, located right next to the castle. The first portion is a Disney-style barrel ride with animatronic displays that explain the careful process of distillation. Then you learn the characters of different regions' whiskies and choose whichever suits your fancy. *(350 Castle Hill. ☎0131 220 0441; www.scotchwhiskyexperience.co.uk. Open daily June-Sept. 10am-5:30pm; Oct.-May 10am-5pm. Tours every 15min. £11, concessions £8.50.)*

HIGH STREET

High St. marks the middle of the Royal Mile with *kirks* (churches) and monuments. Watch for sandwich board signs advertising ghost or underground tours—many convene throughout the day and night along High St.

HIGH KIRK OF SAINT GILES. This *kirk* is Scotland's principal church, sometimes known as **Saint Giles's Cathedral.** From its pulpit, Protestant reformer

John Knox delivered the sermons that drove the Catholic Mary, Queen of Scots, into exile. Stained-glass windows illuminate the structure, whose crown spire is one of Edinburgh's hallmarks. The 20th-century **Thistle Chapel** honors the Most Ancient and Most Noble Order of the Thistle, Scotland's prestigious chivalric order. The church is flanked on the east by the stone **Mercat Cross,** marking the site of the medieval market ("mercat"), and on the west by the **Heart of Midlothian,** inlaid in the pavement. According to legend, spitting on the Heart protects you from being hanged in the square. It appears as though many visitors are under the impression that they get extra protection if they spit their gum on the Heart. The cathedral hosts free concerts throughout the year. *(Where Lawnmarket becomes High St. ☎0131 225 9442. Open M-F 9am-7pm, Sa 9am-5pm, Su 1-5pm. Suggested donation £1.)*

HOLYROOD

Holyrood, at the lower end of the Royal Mile, is mostly occupied by the huge palace, park, and parliament.

PALACE OF HOLYROODHOUSE. This Stuart palace at the base of the Royal Mile remains Queen Elizabeth II's official Scottish residence. As a result, only parts of the ornate interior are open to the public. Once home to Mary, Queen of Scots, whose bedchamber is on display, the palace is every inch a king-ly residence. Dozens of portraits inside the **Great Gallery** chronicle its proud history. On the palace grounds lie the ruins of **Holyrood Abbey,** built by King David I in 1128 and ransacked during the Reformation. Most of the ruins date from the 13th century, but only a single doorway remains from the original construction. Located in a recently renovated 17th-century schoolhouse near the palace entrance is the **Queen's Gallery,** which displays exhibits from the royal art collection. *(At the bottom of the Royal Mile. ☎0131 556 5100. Open daily Apr.-Sept. 9:30am-6pm; Nov.-Mar. 9:30am-4:30pm. Last entry 1hr. before closing. No entry while royals are in residence (often June-July). Palace £10, concessions £9, children £6, under 5 free, families £26.50. With admission to Queen's Gallery £14/12.50/8/free/38.50. Audio tour free.)*

HOLYROOD PARK. A true city oasis, Holyrood Park is filled with hills, moorland, and lochs. At 823 ft., **Arthur's Seat,** the park's highest point, affords the best views of the city and Highlands. Considered a holy place by the Picts, the name "Arthur's Seat" is derived from "*Ard-na-Saigheid,*" Gaelic for "the height of the flight of arrows." Traces of forts and Bronze Age terraces dot the surrounding hillside. From the Palace of Holyroodhouse, the walk to the summit takes about 45min. **Queen's Drive** circles the park and intersects with Holyrood Rd. by the palace.

HOLYROOD SCOTTISH PARLIAMENT BUILDING. After years of controversy and massive budget overdraws, the new Scottish Parliament Building is functional and open to visitors. A winner of numerous architectural awards, the building is highly geometric, with steel, glass, oak, and stone fanning out every which way. Architect Enric Miralles was influenced by the surrounding landscapes, the paintings of Charles Rennie Mackintosh, and boats on the seashore. *(☎0131 348 5200; www.scottish.parliament.uk. Open Apr.-Oct. M and F 10am-6pm, Tu-Th 9am-7pm, Sa-Su 10am-4pm; Nov.-Mar. M and F-Su 10am-4pm, Tu-Th 9am-7pm. Hours may vary; call ahead. Guided tours on non-business days £6, concessions and children £3.60, under 5 free. Free tickets to the parliamentary sessions; book in advance.)*

ELSEWHERE IN THE OLD TOWN

Believe it or not, there is more to Old Town than the Royal Mile.

GREYFRIARS TOLBOOTH AND HIGHLAND KIRK. Off George IV Bridge, the 17th-century *kirk* rests in a churchyard that, while lovely, is estimated to contain 250,000 bodies and has long been considered haunted. A few centuries ago, the infamous body snatchers Burke and Hare dug up corpses here before resorting to murder in order to keep the Edinburgh Medical School's anatomy laboratories well supplied. A more endearing claim to fame is the loyal pooch Greyfriars Bobby, whose much-photographed statue sits at the southwestern corner of George IV Bridge in front of the churchyard's gates. *(Beyond the gates, atop Candlemakers Row. ☎0131 225 1900. Open for touring Easter-Oct. M-F 10:30am-4:30pm and Sa 10:30am-2:30pm. Free.)*

THE NEW TOWN

Don't be fooled by the name—Edinburgh's New Town, a masterpiece of Georgian design, has very few buildings with 20th century birthdays. James Craig, an unknown 23-year-old architect, won the city-planning contest in 1767. His rectangular grid of three parallel streets (**Queen, George,** and **Princes**) linking two large squares (**Charlotte** and **Saint Andrew**) reflects the Scottish Enlightenment belief in order. Queen St. and Princes St., the outer streets, were built up on only one side to allow views of the Firth of Forth and Old Town. Princes St., Edinburgh's main shopping drag, is also home to the venerable **Jenners,** the Harrods of Scotland. *(☎0131 225 2442. Open M-W and F 9:30am-6pm, Th 9:30am-7pm, Sa 9am-6pm, Su 11:30am-5:30pm. AmEx/MC/V.)*

WALTER SCOTT MONUMENT. Statues of Sir Walter and his dog preside inside the spire of this Gothic "steeple without a church." Climb 287 narrow, winding steps past carved figures of Scott's most famous characters to reach the top. An eagle's-eye view of Princes St., the castle, and the surrounding city awaits. The journey to the top is not recommended for those who suffer from claustrophobia or vertigo. *(Princes St. between The Mound and Waverley Bridge. ☎0131 529 4098. Open daily Apr-Sept. 10am-7pm; Oct.-Mar. 10am-4pm. £3.)*

MUSEUMS

NATIONAL GALLERIES OF SCOTLAND

Edinburgh's four major galleries are an elite group, housing work by Scots and non-Scots alike. *(☎0131 624 6200; www.nationalgalleries.org. All open daily during the festivals 10am-6pm; otherwise 10am-5pm. All free.)*

NATIONAL GALLERY OF SCOTLAND. Housed in a grand 19th-century building designed by William Playfair, this gallery has a superb collection of works by Renaissance, Romantic, and Impressionist masters, including Raphael, Titian, El Greco, Turner, and Gauguin. Sprawling, wall-sized works illustrate important moments in Scottish history. Don't miss the octagonal room, which displays Poussin's entire *Seven Sacraments.* The basement houses a selection of Scottish art. The impressionist room upstairs shows several works by Monet. *(On The Mound between the halves of the Princes St. Gardens).* Next door is the **Royal Academy,** connected by an underground tunnel, which hosts exhibits from the National Gallery and runs a high-profile show each summer. *(At the corner of The Mound and Princes St. Special late night Th until 7pm. Exhibit prices vary, many are free; visit www.royalscottishacademy.org for information.)*

SCOTTISH NATIONAL GALLERY OF MODERN ART. In the west end of town, this permanent collection includes works by Braque, Matisse, and Picasso as well as a post-war collection with works by Andy Warhol and Damien Hirst. The landscaping in front of the museum, a bizarre spiral of grass set into a pond, represents the concept of chaos theory with dirt and greenery. *(75 Belford Rd. Ride bus #13 from Hanover St. or walk along the Water of Leith Walkway. Special exhibits £5-10.)*

OTHER MUSEUMS AND GALLERIES

MUSEUM OF SCOTLAND AND ROYAL MUSEUM. The superbly designed Museum of Scotland traces the whole of Scottish history through an impressive collection of treasured objects and decorative art. Highlights include the working **Corliss Steam Engine** and the **Maiden,** Edinburgh's guillotine, used on High St. around 1565. The rooftop terrace provides a 360° view. Gallery and audio tours in various languages are free. The Royal Museum has rotating exhibits on natural history, European art, and ancient Egypt, to name a few. The **Millennium Clock,** a towering, ghoulish display of figures representing human suffering in the 20th century, chimes three times per day. Free tours, from useful intros to 1hr. circuits of the highlights, leave from the Main Hall's totem pole in the Royal Museum and the Museum of Scotland's Hawthornden Court. *(Chambers St. ☎0131 247 4422; www.nms.ac.uk. Both open daily 10am-5pm. Free.)*

ENTERTAINMENT

For all the latest listings and local events in Edinburgh, check out *The List* (£2.25; www.list.co.uk), available at newsstands, or *The Skinny*, a monthly music magazine with concert listings (free, available in most hostels; www.theskinny.co.uk). Watch for ads in pubs and clubs. The Fringe festival publishes its own program of activities, available in hard copy from the Fringe office and online at www.edfringe.com.

COMEDY, FILM, AND THEATER

The Stand Comedy Club, 5 York Pl. (☎0131 558 7272; www.thestand.co.uk). Hilariously unhinged acts perform every night in front of a mural of a guy aiming a pistol at his own sombrero (that is, a mural of a guy watching bad standup comedy, likely at a lesser venue than The Stand). Free lunchtime improv Su 1:30pm. Special program with 17 shows per day for the Fringe Festival. Call ahead. Tickets £1-13. MC/V for tickets only.

Festival Theatre, 13-29 Nicholson St. (☎0131 529 6000; www.eft.co.uk). Stages predominantly ballet and opera, turning entirely to the Fringe in August. Box office open M-Sa 11am-8pm and before performances. Tickets £5-55. MC/V.

King's Theatre, 2 Leven St. (☎0131 529 6000; www.eft.co.uk). Promotes musicals, opera, and the occasional pantomime. Box office open 1hr. before show and between matinee and evening performances. Tickets also available through the Festival Theatre. MC/V.

Traverse Theatre, 10 Cambridge St. (☎0131 228 1404; www.traverse.co.uk). Presents almost exclusively new drama and experimental theater with lots of local Scottish work. Box office open daily 10am-6pm. Ticket prices vary, usually around £7-12, up to £18 during Festival. MC/V.

Royal Lyceum Theatre, 30 Grindlay St. (☎0131 248 4848; www.lyceum.org.uk). The finest in Scottish and English theater, with many international productions. Box office open M-Sa 10am-6pm, performance nights 10am-8pm. Tickets £4-26, students half-price. AmEx/MC/V.

Bedlam Theatre, 11B Bristo Pl. (☎0131 225 9893). A university theater with student productions, ranging from comedy and drama to F night improv, all in a converted church. A Fringe Festival hot spot. Box office open M-Sa 10am-6pm. Tickets £4-5.

LIVE MUSIC

The Jazz Bar, 1A Chambers St. (☎0131 220 4298). Not just a jazz venue: you can also see blues, hip-hop, funk, and more. Classy and relaxing vibe, with stone walls and red lighting. 3 shows most days: "Tea Time" (acoustic, T-Su 5-8:30pm, free entry, free Wi-Fi), "Early Gig" (mostly jazz, daily 8:30-11pm, cover £1-5), and "Late N' Live" (daily 11:30pm-3am, or 5am during Festival, cover £1-5). Always packed on weekends. Cash only for cover. MC/V at bar over £5.

Whistle Binkie's, 4-6 South Bridge (☎0131 557 5114). A subterranean pub with 2 live shows every night, open to bands of any genre. Mostly local rock cover bands, with some folk music thrown in. Gets busy later at night. Open daily until 3am. AmEx/MC/V over £5.

The Mitre, 131-133 High St. (☎0131 652 3902). Live music starts every night at 9:30pm in this traditional pub on the Royal Mile. Haunted by the ghost of 17th-century Bishop John Spottiswool, whose throne is buried under the bar in concrete that mysteriously repels the drills of workmen seeking to excavate. Beautiful Jacobean ceiling. Mostly acoustic folk and covers, with lots of Scottish ballad sing-alongs. Open M-Th and Su noon-midnight, F-Sa noon-1am. AmEx/MC/V.

SHOPPING

From ritzy department stores to funky vintage shops, Edinburgh has something for every shopper and every wallet. If you want to get in touch with your Scottish heritage, tourist shops along the **Royal Mile** sell Highland outfits, cashmere sweaters, tartan towels, and will even trace your family history for around £10. New Town generally caters to big spenders—major chains line **Princes Street,** and **Multrees Walk** off St. Andrew's Square houses upscale designer shops like Louis Vuitton. The pedestrian **Rose Street** has smaller boutiques and plenty of pubs to whet your whistle (while you can still afford a whistle). Big malls include **St. James Shopping Centre** (off Leith St.; open M-W and F 9am-6pm, Th 9am-8pm, Sa 9am-6:30pm, Su 10am-6pm) and **Princes Mall** (Princes St.; open M-W and F-Sa 9am-6pm, Th 9am-7pm, Su 11am-5pm). For (slightly) more affordable shopping, stick to **Old Town.** The **Grassmarket, Cockburn Street,** and **Lothian Road** are all full of diverse and interesting shops.

STREET MARKETS

Edinburgh Farmers Market, Castle Terrace. Under the shadow of Castle Rock, local farmers sell a variety of fresh, tasty produce. Open Sa 9am-2pm.

The Eating Place, Castle St. A big market with produce from all around Scotland. Last Th of the month noon-6pm.

NIGHTLIFE

Edinburgh is known internationally for its festivals, but its nightly festivities are a big draw as well. Some Festival-goers even skip the theatres altogether and spend their time doing two things—sleeping and partying. During the Fringe, the city turns into what some have described as a month-long Mardi Gras: packed streets, loud revelry, and nonstop performances. The sun rises around 4am in the summer, so partying until dawn is easy.

PUBS

Pubs on the **Royal Mile** tend to attract a mixed crowd of old and young, tourists and locals. Students and backpackers gather in force each night in the Old Town. Casual pub-goers groove to live music on **Grassmarket, Candlemaker Row,** and **Victoria Street.** The New Town also has its share of worthy watering holes, some historical and most strung along **Rose Street,** parallel to Princes St. Wherever you are, you'll usually hear last call sometime between 11pm and 1am, or 3am during the Festival.

TOURIST TO PURIST. Don't order your Scotch on the rocks if you want to avoid looking like a tourist. Scotch whisky should be drunk neat, with no ice. Locals may mix with a splash of water—real pros ask for mineral water from the region in which the whisky was distilled.

The Tron, 9 Hunter Sq. (☎0131 226 0931), behind Tron Kirk. Friendly student bar. Downstairs is a mix of alcoves and pool tables. Frequent live music. Burger and a pint £3.50 after 3pm, or get 2 meals for just £6.50. "Pound-a-pint" W. Open during the Festival daily 10am-3am; otherwise M-Sa noon-1am, Su 12:30pm-1am. Kitchen open until 9pm. AmEx/MC/V over £5.

Royal Mile Tavern, 127 High St. (☎0131 557 9681). This easygoing pub has managed to avoid the high prices and tourist gimmicks of its Royal Mile neighbors. Live music every night (don't miss the popular "Acoustic Dave" Sa). Flash your hostel card for a £2.50 pint or to see the cheap "Backpacker food" menu. Open daily 8am-1:30pm. MC/V.

The Outhouse, 12A Broughton St. (☎0131 557 6668). Hidden up an alleyway off Broughton St. and well worth the hunt. More stylish than your average pub but just as cheap, with one of the best beer gardens in the city. Free Wi-Fi. Happy hour daily 5-8pm. Open daily noon1am. Kitchen open M, W, Su 1-7pm; Tu, Th, F-Sa 1pm-late. MC/V over £5.

The Three Sisters, 139 Cowgate (☎0131 622 6801). Loads of space for dancing, drinking, and lounging. Attracts a young crowd to its 3 bars (Irish, Gothic, and American). Beer garden sees close to 1000 people pass through on Sa nights. Open daily 9am-1am. Kitchen open M-Th 9am-9pm, F-Su 9am-8pm. MC/V.

Blue Moon Cafe, 36 Broughton St. (☎0131 557 0911), entrance around the corner on Barony St. A popular GLBT pub serving food to a mixed gay and straight crowd in a chic setting. Open daily 10am-11pm. Kitchen open until 10pm. MC/V.

CLUBS

Edinburgh may be best known for its pubs, but the club scene is none too shabby. It is, however, in constant flux, with club nights switching between venues and drawing a very different clientele from one night to the next. Consult *The List* (£2.25), a comprehensive guide to events, available from any local newsstand, for the night's hot spot. Clubs cluster around the city's once-disreputable **Cowgate,** just downhill from and parallel to the Royal Mile; most close at 3am (5am during the Festival). Smart street wear is a must.

Cabaret-Voltaire, 36-38 Blair St. (☎0131 220 6176; www.thecabaretvoltaire.com). Most clubbers agree that "Cab-Volt" is the place to be in Edinburgh. Playing everything from jazz to breakbeat, this innovative club knows how to throw a party. Cavernous interior packs a loyal crowd. Cover free-£2 on weeknights, £5-10 on weekends. Open daily 7pm-3am.

Bongo Club, 37 Holyrood Rd. (☎0131 558 7604), off Canongate. Particularly noted for its hip hop and immensely popular "Messenger" (reggae; 1 Sa per month) and "Headspin" (funk and dance; 1 Sa per month) nights. Occasionally hosts live music. Cafe with free internet during the day. Cover £3-7. Open M-W and Su 10am-midnight, Th-F 10am-3am. MC/V.

CC Bloom's, 23-24 Greenside Pl. (☎0131 556 9331), on Leith St. No cover and a new up-and-coming DJ each night at this gay club. Karaoke Th and Su nights. Open daily 4pm-3am. MC/V.

FESTIVALS

Edinburgh has special events year-round, but the real show is in August. Prices rise, pubs and restaurants stay open later than late (some simply don't close), and street performers have the run of the place. What's commonly referred to as "the Festival" actually includes a number of independently organized events. For more information, check out www.edinburghfestivals.co.uk.

Edinburgh Festival Fringe (☎0131 226 0000; www.edfringe.com), generally in Aug. Longer and more informal than the International, the Fringe is the world's biggest arts festival, showcasing everything from Shakespeare to coconut-juggling dwarfs. It began in 1947, when 8 theater companies arrived in Edinburgh uninvited and had to book "fringe" venues to perform. Today, the Fringe draws more visitors to Edinburgh than any other event, and their box office sells well over a million tickets every year. Anyone who can afford the small registration fee can perform; this orgy of eccentricity attracts a multitude of good and not-so-good acts and guarantees a wild month. Theater is the main focus, but comedy is increasingly popular. Impromptu street performances take place constantly. Head to the **Half Price Hut** bright and early to grab tickets for that day's shows at 50% off. *The Fringe* program, published in late spring, has a full listing of festivities (available free in just about every doorway of the city). Tickets available online, by phone, in person, or by post at The Fringe Office, 180 High St., Edinburgh EH1 1QS. Tickets up to £25. Open M-F 10am-5pm, during Festival daily 10am-9pm.

Edinburgh International Festival (☎0131 473 2000; www.eif.co.uk), normally in late Aug. and early Sept., but check website for this year's dates. Founded in 1947 to reunite European countries through culture after WWII, the International Festival was the first of its kind. It still attracts the top performers from all over the globe, mainly in the realms of classical music, ballet, opera, and drama. **The Hub** (where Lawnmarket meets Castle Hill) is a former church that serves as the Festival's main box office. It also hosts lectures on art, philosophy, history, and more. The most popular single event is the festival's grand finale: a spectacular **Fireworks Concert** with pyrotechnics choreographed to orchestral music. Most tickets go on sale in early Apr., when the full program is published. Tickets to the biggest events sell out well in advance, but at least 50 tickets for major events are held and sold on the day of the performance at the venue. Throughout the festival, visitors can buy tickets at the door 1hr. prior to showtime. Selected shows are ½-price on the day of performance. Bookings can be made by post, phone, web, or in person at The Hub, Edinburgh's Festival Centre, Castlehill, Edinburgh EH1 2NE. Tickets £7-60, students and children ½-price on some shows. The Hub is open from early Apr. to late July M-Sa 10am-5pm; from late July to early Apr. daily 10am-5pm.

Hogmanay (☎0131 529 3914; www.edinburghshogmanay.org), New Year's Eve. The long, dark winter can't stop the party. Hogmanay is Scotland's traditional New Year's Eve celebration, a nationwide party with pagan roots, having long marked the turn of the calendar and the return of the sun,. Official events in Edinburgh include concerts, torchlight processions, and a street party that packs the Royal Mile and bursts into a rousing rendition of "Auld Lang Syne" at midnight. New Year's Day sees a number of options to shake that hangover, from a triathlon to a mid-winter dip in the Forth. Many events are free, though some require tickets to limit numbers. The Hub also provides ticket information. Tickets and program available starting in Oct.

DENMARK (DANMARK)

Straddling the border between Scandinavia and continental Europe, Denmark packs majestic castles, pristine beaches, and thriving nightlife onto the compact Jutland peninsula and its network of islands. Vibrant Copenhagen boasts the busy pedestrian thoroughfare of Strøget and the world's tallest carousel in Tivoli Gardens, while beyond the city, fairytale lovers can tour Hans Christian Andersen's home in rural Odense. In spite of the nation's historically homogenous population, its Viking past has given way to a dynamic multicultural society that draws in visitors as it turns out Legos and Skagen watches.

LIFE AND TIMES

HISTORY

The Danes evolved from nomadic hunters to farmers during the Stone Age before taking to the water as **Vikings,** sacking everything from the English coast to Constantinople and ruling the North Sea. Denmark—then called Jutland—was unified and Christianized in the 10th century by **King Harold Bluetooth.** Under the rule of Harold's descendants, the empire grew to include all of modern Norway, Iceland, and England. Various disputes plagued the Danish throne until 1282 when the **Danehof,** a council composed of high nobles and church leaders, established control over state affairs. In 1397, Denmark united with Norway and Sweden under the rule of **Queen Margrethe I,** until Sweden seceded from the union in the 1520s after a violent conflict. During the 16th century, the **Protestant Reformation** swept through Denmark, and **Lutheranism** was established as the national religion. Over several centuries, the **Thirty Years' War** (1618-1648), the **Napoleonic Wars** (1799-1815), the **War of 1864,** and a series of squabbles with Sweden resulted in severe financial and territorial losses. Denmark's policy of neutrality during **WWI** proved fiscally beneficial, allowing the country to profit from trade with the warring nations. During WWII, Nazi forces occupied Denmark, but the underground **Danish Resistance Movement** safely evacuated most of the nation's 8000 Jewish citizens to Sweden. After the war, Denmark took its place on the international stage, becoming a founding member of **NATO** in 1949 and joining the **European Union** in 1973.

TODAY

Prime Minister **Anders Fogh Rasmussen** leads Denmark's unicameral legislature, the Folketing, while **Queen Margrethe II** remains the nominal head of state. Support for the European Union has been underwhelming; the country rejected the EU's common defense policy as well as the increasingly popular euro. Periodic economic setbacks have increased support for conservative groups, and the far-right **Danish People's Party** has garnered an increasing share of the vote since 1996. In response to the party's lobbying, the government passed a controversial anti-immigration bill in 2002 that imposed stringent citizen-

ship requirements and limited spouses' rights of entry. The bill led many native Copenhageners to cross the Øresund Bridge—nicknamed the "Love Bridge"—into neighboring Sweden to remain with their foreign partners.

In recent years, several high-profile incidents in Denmark have highlighted tensions with Muslims, who make up approximately 2% of the population. In 2005, the Danish Supreme Court upheld the firing of a Muslim resident for her refusal to remove her headscarf at work. Later that year, Danish newspaper *Jyllands-Posten* published a series of controversial cartoons of the prophet Muhammad, some of which were reprinted in newspapers around the world. Clerics in Denmark and leaders of Islamic nations organized protests, and over 130 people were killed in violent demonstrations worldwide. In response to the conflict, **Naser Khader,** a Muslim member of the Danish Parliament, founded the **Democratic Muslims Network** and organized a job fair that resulted in Danish companies hiring hundreds of Muslims, a positive step toward peaceful relations.

PEOPLE AND CULTURE

DEMOGRAPHICS AND LANGUAGE. Denmark has traditionally been home to a homogenous population of Scandinavian descent. Immigration increased during the last decades of the 20th century, but the influx of foreigners has declined since the passage of new restrictions in 2002. Today immigrants make up about 8% of the population. Danish is the official language of Denmark, although natives of Greenland and the Faroe Islands speak local dialects. The Danish add æ (pronounced like the "e" in egg), ø (pronounced "euh"), and å (sometimes written aa; pronounced "oh" with tightly pursed lips) to the end of the alphabet; thus Århus would follow Skagen in an alphabetical listing of cities. *Let's Go* indexes these under "ae," "o," and "a." Nearly all Danes speak English, but for basic Danish words and phrases, see **Phrasebook: Danish,** p. 596.

THE ARTS

Denmark's wide cultural influence ranges from fairy tales to philosophy. **Hans Christian Andersen's** famous tales, including *"The Little Mermaid"* and *"The Ugly Duckling,"* have delighted children around the world since their initial publication in 1835. Nineteenth-century philosopher and theologian **Søren Kierkegaard** developed the term "leap of faith," the idea that religious belief is beyond the bounds of human reason. **Karen Blixen** gained fame under the pen name Isak Dinesen, detailing her experiences in Kenya in *Out of Africa* (1937). **Carl Nielsen** composed six symphonies with unique tonal progressions that won him international recognition by the early 20th century.

HOLIDAYS AND FESTIVALS

Holidays: New Year's Day (Jan. 1); Easter (Apr. 12); Queen's Birthday (Apr. 16); Worker's Day (May 1); Whit Sunday and Monday (May 11-12); Constitution Day (June 5); Midsummer's Eve (June 23); Christmas (Dec. 24-26).

Festivals: In early Spring before the start of Lent, Danish children assault candy-filled barrels with birch branches on **Fastelavn** (Shrovetide), while adults take to the streets for carnivals. Guitars ring out over Roskilde during the **Roskilde Festival** (July 3-6), just before Copenhagen and Århus kick off their annual **jazz festivals** in mid-to-late July.

ESSENTIALS

FACTS AND FIGURES

OFFICIAL NAME: Kingdom of Denmark.

CAPITAL: Copenhagen.

MAJOR CITIES: Aalborg, Århus, Odense.

POPULATION: 5,485,000.

LAND AREA: 42,400 sq. km.

LANGUAGES: Danish. Pockets of Faroese, Greenlandic, and German. English is nearly universal as a second language.

WHEN TO GO

Denmark is best between May and September, when days are usually sunny and temperatures average 10-16°C (50-61°F). Winter temperatures average 0°C (32°F). Although temperate for its northern location, Denmark can turn rainy or cool at a moment's notice; always pack a sweater and an umbrella.

DOCUMENTS AND FORMALITIES

EMBASSIES AND CONSULATES. All foreign embassies in Denmark are based in Copenhagen (p. 168). A number of Danish embassies are abroad. They include: **Australia,** Gold Fields House, Level 14, 1 Alfred St., Circular Quay, Sydney, NSW, 2000 (☎02 92 47 22 24; www.gksydney.um.dk/en); **Canada,** 47 Clarence St., Ste. 450, Ottawa, ON, K1N 9K1 (☎613-562-1811; www.ambottawa.um.dk/en); **Ireland,** Harcourt Road, 7th floor, Block E, Iveagh Court, Dublin 2 (☎01 475 6404; www.ambdublin.um.dk/en); **New Zealand,** Forsyth Barr House, Level 7, 45 Johnston Street, P.O. Box 10-874, Wellington, 6036 (☎04 471 0520; www.danish-consulatesnz.org.nz); **UK,** 55 Sloane St., London, SW1X 9SR (☎020 73 33 02 00; www.amblondon.um.dk/en); **US,** 3200 Whitehaven St., NW, Washington, D.C., 20008 (☎202-234-4300; www.denmarkemb.org).

VISA AND ENTRY INFORMATION. EU citizens don't need visas. Citizens of Australia, Canada, New Zealand, and the US do not need a visa for stays of up to 90 days, beginning upon entry into any of the countries in the EU's freedom-of-movement zone. For stays longer than 90 days, non-EU citizens need a residence or work permit. For more info visit www.um.dk/en.

TOURIST SERVICES AND MONEY

EMERGENCY	**Ambulance, Fire,** and **Police:** ☎112.

TOURIST OFFICES. The **Danish Tourist Board** has offices in most cities throughout the country, with its main office in Copenhagen at Islands Brygge 43 (☎3288 9900; www.visitdenmark.dt.dk). The website offers a wealth of info as well as an online booking tool for accommodations.

MONEY. The Danish unit of currency is the **krone (kr),** plural **kroner.** One krone is equal to 100 **øre.** The easiest way to get cash is from **ATMs;** cash cards are widely accepted, and many machines give advances on **credit cards.** Money and **traveler's checks** can be exchanged at most **banks** for a fee of 30kr. Denmark has a high cost of living, which it passes along to visitors; expect to pay 100-150kr for a hostel bed, 450-800kr for a hotel room, 80-130kr for a day's groceries, and 50-90kr for a cheap restaurant meal. A bare-bones day might cost 250-350kr, and a slightly more comfortable one 400-600kr. There are no hard and fast rules for **tipping.** In general, service at restaurants is included in the bill, but it's always polite to round up your bill to the nearest 10kr, and to leave an additional 10-20kr for exceptional service. Exchange rates:

DANISH KRONER (KR)		
	AUS$1 = 4.42KR	10KR = AUS$2.26
	CDN$1 = 4.63KR	10KR = CDN$2.16
	EUR€1 = 7.46KR	10KR = EUR€1.34
	NZ$1 = 3.49KR	10KR = NZ$2.86
	UK£1 = 9.42KR	10KR = UK£1.06
	US$1 = 4.82KR	10KR = US$2.08

BUSINESS HOURS. Shops are normally open Monday to Thursday from about 9 or 10am to 6pm and Friday until 7 or 8pm; they are always open Saturday mornings and in Copenhagen, they stay open all day Saturday. Regular banking hours are Monday to Wednesday and Friday 10am-4pm, Thursday 10am-6pm.

TRANSPORTATION

BY PLANE. International flights arrive at **Kastrup Airport** in Copenhagen (**CPH;** ☎3231 3231; www.cph.dk). Flights from Europe also arrive at **Billund Airport,** outside Århus (**BLL;** ☎7650 5050; www.billund-airport.dk). Smaller airports in Århus and Esbjerg serve as hubs for budget airline **Ryanair** (☎353 12 49 77 91; www.ryanair.com). **SAS** (Scandinavian Airlines; Denmark ☎70 10 20 00, UK 0870 60 72 77 27, US 800-221-2350; www.scandinavian.net), the national airline company, offers youth discounts to some destinations.

BY TRAIN AND BY BUS. The state-run rail line in Denmark is **DSB;** their helpful route planner is online at www.rejseplanen.dk. **Eurail** is valid on all state-run routes. The **ScanRail** pass is good for rail travel through Denmark, Finland, Norway, and Sweden, as well as many discounted ferry and bus rides. Remote towns are typically served by buses from the nearest train station. Buses are reliable and can be less expensive than trains.

RAIL SAVINGS. ScanRail passes purchased outside Scandinavia may be cheaper, depending on the exchange rate, and they are also more flexible. Travelers who purchase passes within Scandinavia can only use three travel days in the country of purchase. Check www.scanrail.com for more info.

BY FERRY. Several companies operate ferries to and from Denmark. **Scandlines** (☎33 15 15 15; www.scandlines.dk) arrives from Germany and Sweden and also operates domestic routes. **Color Line** (Norway ☎47 81 00 08 11; www.colorline.com) runs ferries between Denmark and Norway. **DFDS Seaways** (UK ☎08715 229 955; www.dfdsseaways.co.uk) sails from Harwich, BRI to Esbjerg and from Copenhagen to Oslo, NOR. For more info, check www.aferry.to/ferry-to-denmark-ferries.htm. Tourist offices help sort out the dozens of smaller ferries that serve Denmark's outlying islands.

BY BIKE AND BY THUMB. With its flat terrain and well-marked bike routes, Denmark is a cyclist's dream. You can rent bikes (50-80kr per day) from designated shops as well as from some tourist offices and train stations. The **Dansk Cyklist Forbund** (☎3332 3121; www.dcf.dk) provides info about cycling in Denmark and investing in long-term rentals. Pick up *Bikes and Trains* at any train station for info on bringing your bike on a train, which can cost up to 50kr. **Hitchhiking** on motorways is illegal. *Let's Go* does not recommend hitchhiking.

KEEPING IN TOUCH

PHONE CODES	**Country code:** 45. **International dialing prefix:** 00. For more info on international calls, see **Inside Back Cover.**

EMAIL AND THE INTERNET. In Copenhagen and other cities, you can generally find at least one Internet cafe; expect to pay 15-30kr per hr. DSB, the national railroad, maintains Internet cafes in some stations as well. In smaller towns, access at public libraries is free; reserve a slot in advance.

TELEPHONE. **Pay phones** accept both coins and phone cards, available at post offices or kiosks in 100kr denominations. **Mobile phones** (p. 21) are a popular and economical alternative. For domestic directory info, dial ☎118; for international info, dial ☎113. International direct dial numbers include: **AT&T Direct**

(☎8001 0010); **Canada Direct** (☎8001 0011); **MCI WorldPhone** (☎8001 0022); Sprint (☎8001 0877); **Telecom New Zealand** (☎8001 0064).

MAIL. Mailing a postcard or letter to Australia, Canada, New Zealand, or the US costs 8kr; to elsewhere in Europe it costs 7kr. Domestic mail costs 4.50kr.

ACCOMMODATIONS AND CAMPING

DENMARK	❶	❷	❸	❹	❺
ACCOMMODATIONS	under 100kr	100-160kr	161-220kr	221-350kr	over 350kr

Denmark's hotels are uniformly expensive, so **youth hostels** *(vandrehjem)* tend to be mobbed by budget travelers of all ages. HI-affiliated **Danhostels** are the most common, and are often the only option in smaller towns. Facilities are clean, spacious, and comfortable, often attracting families as well as backpackers. Eco-conscious tourists can choose from one of the six Danhostels that have earned a **Green Key** (www.green-key.org) for their environmentally friendly practices. Room rates vary according to season and location; dorms range from 100 to 200kr per night, with a 35kr HI discount. Linens cost 40-60kr; sleeping bags are not permitted. Reserve ahead, especially in summer and near beaches. Danhostel check-in times are usually a non-negotiable 3-4hr. window. For more info, contact the **Danish Youth Hostel Association** (☎3331 3612; www.danhostel.dk). Independent hostels, found mostly in cities and larger towns, draw a younger crowd and tend to be more sociable, although their facilities are rarely as nice as those in Danhostels. Most tourist offices can help you book a room in **private homes** (150-250kr).

Denmark's 496 **campgrounds** (about 60kr per person) range from one star (toilets and drinking water) to three stars (showers and laundry) to five stars (swimming, restaurants, and stoves). Info is available at **DK-Camp** (☎7571 2962; www.dk-camp.dk). You'll need a **Camping Card Scandinavia** (125kr for 1yr. membership; available at www.camping.se; allow at least 3 weeks for delivery), valid across Scandinavia and sold at campgrounds as well as through the Danish Youth Hostel Association. Campsites affiliated with hostels generally do not require a card. If you plan to camp for only a night, you can buy a 24hr. pass (20kr). The **Danish Camping Council** *(Campingrådet)*, Mosedalvej 15, 2500 Valby (☎39 27 88 44; www.campingraadet.dk), sells passes and the Camping Denmark handbook (95kr). When camping, utilize their many campgrounds; sleeping in train stations, in parks, or on public property is illegal in Denmark.

FOOD AND DRINK

DENMARK	❶	❷	❸	❹	❺
FOOD	under 40kr	40-70kr	71-100kr	101-150kr	over 150kr

A "danish" in Denmark is a *wienerbrød* (Viennese bread), found in bakeries alongside other flaky treats. Traditionally, Danes have favored open-faced sandwiches called *smørrebrød* for a more substantial meal. For cheap eats, look for lunch specials *(dagens ret)* and all-you-can-eat buffets. National beers include Carlsberg and Tuborg; bottled brews tend to be cheaper than drafts. A popular alcohol is *snaps* (or *aquavit)*, a clear liquor flavored with fiery spices, usually served chilled and unmixed. Many vegetarian *(vegetarret)* options are the result of Indian and Mediterranean influences, and salads and veggies *(grønsager)* can be found on most menus. Expect to pay around 120kr for a sit-down meal at a restaurant and 40-80kr in cafes and ethnic takeaways.

BEYOND TOURISM

For short-term employment in Denmark, check www.jobs-in-europe.net. For more info on opportunities across Europe, see Beyond Tourism, p. 45.

The American-Scandinavian Foundation (AMSCAN), 58 Park Ave., New York, NY, 10016, USA (☎212-879-9779; www.amscan.org/jobs/index.html). Has an extensive list of volunteer and job opportunities throughout Scandinavia.

Vi Hjælper Hinanden (VHH), Aasenv. 35, 9881 Bindslev, DEN, c/o Inga Nielsen (☎98 93 86 07; www.wwoof.dk). For 50kr, the Danish branch of World-Wide Opportunities on Organic Farms (WWOOF) provides a list of farmers currently accepting volunteers.

COPENHAGEN (KØBENHAVN)

The center of Europe's oldest monarchy and the largest city in Scandinavia, Copenhagen (pop. 1,800,000) embodies a laid-back spirit. Historically, a major Baltic port with many canals and lakes, the city's lush greenways encourage a sense of pride among its inhabitants. The Strøget, the city's famed pedestrian thoroughfare, now bustles with Middle Eastern restaurants and cybercafes, and neon signs glimmer next to angels in the architecture. The up-and-coming districts of Vesterbro and Nørrebro reverberate with some of Europe's wildest nightlife, while the hippie paradise of Christiania swings to a more downbeat vibe. Despite its size, Copenhagen manages to hold on to its small town appeal with its narrow streets dotted by gabled houses.

INTERCITY TRANSPORTATION

Flights: Kastrup Airport (CPH; ☎3231 3231; www.cph.dk). **Trains** connect the airport to København H (13min., 6 per hr., 20kr or 2 clips). Ryanair flies into nearby **Sturup Airport** in Malmö, SWE (**MMX;** ☎40 613 1000; www.sturup.com) at low rates.

Trains: København H (Hovedbanegården or Central Station; domestic travel ☎7013 1415, international 7013 1416; www.dsb.dk). Trains run to: **Berlin, GER** (8hr., 9 per day, 803kr); **Hamburg, GER** (5hr., 5 per day, 537kr); **Malmö, SWE** (25min., every 20min., 71kr); **Oslo, NOR** (8hr., 2 per day, 821kr); **Stockholm, SWE** (5hr., 1 per 1-2hr., 1040kr). For international trips, fares depend on seat availability and can drop to as low as 50% of the quotes listed above; **book at least 2 weeks in advance.**

ORIENTATION

Copenhagen lies on the east coast of the island of **Zealand** *(Sjælland)*, across the Øresund Sound from Malmö, Sweden. The 28km **Øresund Bridge,** which opened on July 1, 2000, established the first "fixed link" between the two countries. Copenhagen's main train station, København H, lies near the city center. Just north of the station, **Vesterbrogade** passes **Tivoli** and **Rådhuspladsen,** the main square, then cuts through the city center as **Strøget** (STROY-yet), the world's longest pedestrian thoroughfare. As it heads east, Strøget goes through a series of names: **Frederiksberggade, Nygade, Vimmelskaftet, Amagertorv,** and **Østergade.** The city center is bordered to the west by five **lakes,** outside of which are the less-

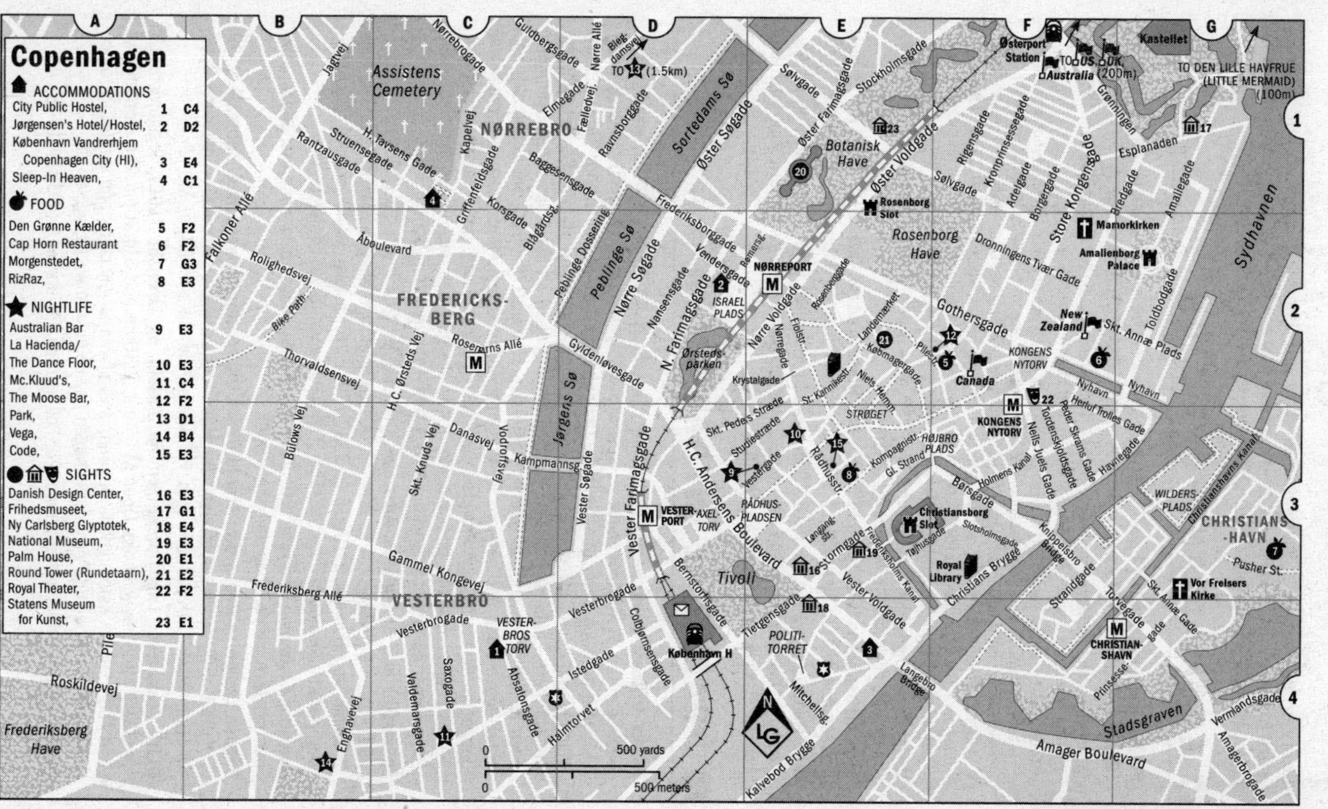

Copenhagen
ACCOMMODATIONS
City Public Hostel, 1 C4
Jørgensen's Hotel/Hostel, 2 D2
København Vandrerhjem Copenhagen City (HI), 3 E4
Sleep-In Heaven, 4 C1
FOOD
Den Grønne Kælder, 5 F2
Cap Horn Restaurant 6 F2
Morgenstedet, 7 G3
RizRaz, 8 E3
NIGHTLIFE
Australian Bar 9 E3
La Hacienda/ The Dance Floor, 10 E3
Mc.Kluud's, 11 C4
The Moose Bar, 12 F2
Park, 13 D1
Vega, 14 B4
Code, 15 E3
SIGHTS
Danish Design Center, 16 E3
Frihedsmuseet, 17 G1
Ny Carlsberg Glyptotek, 18 E4
National Museum, 19 E3
Palm House, 20 E1
Round Tower (Rundetaarn), 21 E2
Royal Theater, 22 F2
Statens Museum for Kunst, 23 E1
NØRREBRO
FREDERICKS-BERG
VESTERBRO
CHRISTIANS-HAVN
Assistens Cemetery
Botanisk Have
Rosenborg Have
Tivoli
Sortedams Sø
Peblinge Sø
Jørgens Sø
Sydhavnen
Stadsgraven
Kastellet
TO DEN LILLE HAVFRUE (LITTLE MERMAID) (100m)
TO 13 (1.5km)
500 yards
500 meters

touristy communities of **Vesterbro, Nørrebro,** and **Østerbro.** Vesterbro and Nørrebro are home to many of the region's immigrants, while some of Copenhagen's highest-income residents live on the wide streets of Østerbro.

LOCAL TRANSPORTATION

Public Transportation: Copenhagen has an extensive public transportation system. **Buses** (☎3313 1415; www.moviatrafik.dk) run daily 5:30am-12:30am.

S-togs (subways and suburban trains; ☎3314 1701) run M-Sa 5am-12:30am, Su 6am-12:30am. S-tog tickets are covered by Eurail, ScanRail, and InterRail passes.

Metro (☎015 1615; www.m.dk) is small but efficient. All 3 types of public transportation operate on a zone system. To travel any distance, a 2-zone **ticket** is required (19kr; additional zones 9.50kr), which covers most of Copenhagen. For extended stays, the best deal is the **rabatkort** (rebate card; 120kr), available from supermarkets, corner stores, and kiosks, which offers 10 2-zone tickets at a discount. The **24hr. pass** (115kr), grants unlimited bus and train transport in the Northern Zealand region, as does the **Copenhagen Card** (see Practical Information below).

Night buses, marked with an "N," run 12:30-5:30am on limited routes and charge double for bus fare; they do accept the 24hr. pass as payment.

Taxis: Københavns Taxa (☎3535 3535) and **Hovedstadens Taxi** (☎3877 7777) charge a base fare of 19kr and then 11-16kr/km. København to Kastrup Airport costs 200kr.

Bike Rental: City Bike (☎3616 4233; www.bycyklen.dk) lends bikes mid-Apr. to Nov. from 110 racks all over the city for a 20kr deposit. Anyone can return your bike and claim your deposit, so keep an eye on it.

PRACTICAL INFORMATION

Tourist Offices: Copenhagen Right Now, Vesterbrog. 4A (☎7022 2442; www.visitcopenhagen.dk). From København H, cross Vesterbrog. toward the Axelrod building. Open M-F 9am-4pm, Sa 9am-2pm. Sells the **Copenhagen Card** (1-day 199kr; 3-day 429kr), which grants free or discounted admission to most sights and unlimited travel throughout Northern Zealand; however, cardholders will need to keep up an almost manic pace to justify the cost. **Use It,** Rådhusstr. 13 (☎3373 0620; www.useit.dk), has indispensable info and services for budget travelers. Offers *Playtime,* a comprehensive budget guide to the city. Provides daytime luggage storage, has free **Internet** (max. 20min.), holds mail, and finds lodgings for no charge. Open mid-June to mid-Sept. daily 9am-7pm; mid-Sept. to mid-June M-W 11am-4pm, Th 11am-6pm, F 11am-2pm.

Embassies and Consulates: Australia, Dampfærgev. 26, 2nd fl. (☎7026 3676). **Canada,** Kristen Bernikowsg. 1 (☎3348 3200). **Ireland,** Østbaneg. 21 (☎3542 3233). **New Zealand,** Store Strandst. 21, 2nd fl. (☎3337 7702). **UK,** Kastelsv. 36-40 (☎3544 5200). **US,** Dag Hammarskjölds Allé 24 (☎3555 3144). www.um.dk for complete list.

Currency Exchange: Forex, in København H. 20kr commission for cash exchanges, 10kr per traveler's check. Open daily 8am-9pm.

English-Language Bookstore: Arnold Busck International Boghandel, Købmagerg. 49 (☎3373 3500; www.arnoldbusck.dk). Has a considerable selection of literature. Open M 10am-6pm, Tu-Th 9:30am-6pm, F 9:30am-7pm, Sa 10am-4pm. MC/V.

GLBT Resources: Landsforeningen for Bøsser og Lesbiske (LBL), Teglgårdstr. 13 (☎3313 1948; www.lbl.dk). Open M-F noon-2:30pm and 3-4:30pm. The monthly *Out and About,* which lists nightlife options, is available at gay clubs and the tourist office Other resources include www.copenhagen-gay-lfe.dk and www.gayguide.dk.

Police: Headquarters at Halmtorvet 20; Politigarden, Politiorvet 1 (☎3314 1448)

24hr. Pharmacy: Steno Apotek, Vesterbrog. 6C (☎3314 8266), across from the Banegårdspl. exit of København H. Ring the bell at night. Cash only.

Medical Services: Doctors on Call (☎7013 0041 M-F 8am-4pm; ☎7020 1546 evenings/weekends; 400-600kr fee). Emergency rooms at **Amager Hospital,** Italiensv. 1 (☎3234 3234), **Frederiksberg Hospital,** Nordre Fasanv. 57 (☎3834 7711), and **Bispebjerg Hospital,** Bispebjerg Bakke 23 (☎3531 3531).

Internet: Free at **Use It** and **Copenhagen Hovedbibliotek (Central Library),** Krystalg. 15 (☎3373 6060). Coffee shop on 1st fl. Open M-F 10am-7pm, Sa 10am-2pm. Boomtown, Axeltorv. 1-3 (☎3332 1032; www.boomtown.net), directly opposite the Tivoli main entrance. 30kr per hr. Open 24hr.

Post Office: In København H. Open M-F 8am-9pm, Sa-Su 10am-4pm. Address mail as follows: LAST NAME, First name, Post Denmark, Hovedbanegårdens Posthus, Hovedbanegården, 1570 Copenhagen V, DENMARK. **Use It** also holds mail for 2 months.

ACCOMMODATIONS

Comfortable and inexpensive accommodations can be hard to find near the city center, but pedestrian-friendly streets and the great public transportation system ensure that travelers are never far from the action. Reserve well ahead in the summer. Be sure to check out early, as 10am is the standard.

Sleep-In Heaven, Struenseeg. 7 (☎3535 4648; www.sleepinheaven.com), in Nørrebro. M: Forum. Take bus 5A from the airport or from København H. (dir.: Husum; every 10-20min.) to Stengade. Go down Stengade and take your first right on Korsgade. Slight right to continue on Korsgade, left on Kapelvej, quick right onto HansTavsensGade and left into the alley. Laid-back hostel with friendly vibe and warm and helpful staff. Smoke-free. Breakfast 40kr. Linens 40kr. Lockers (refundable deposit). Free Wi-Fi. Max. 5-night stay. Reception and security guard 24hr. Dorms 145-160kr; doubles 500kr; triples 600kr. Ages 16-35. AmEx/MC/V; 5% surcharge. ❷

City Public Hostel, Absalonsg. 8 (☎3331 2070). Go down Vesterbrogade and take a left on Absalonsg., just before the Copenhagen Museum. Cheap rates and great location attracts a diverse crowd of travelers to this hostel with a rocker-styled reception area. Breakfast 30kr-40kr. Locks for storage 30kr. Linens and pillow 40kr, towel 10kr. Internet available. Reception 24hr. Open May-Aug. Dorms 110-150kr. Cash only. ❷

Jørgensen's Hostel/Hotel Jørgensen, Rømersg. 11 (☎3313 8186; www.hoteljoergensen.dk). M: Nørreport. Small yet comfortable rooms in a convenient location. Breakfast and linens included. Max. 5-night stay. Dorm lockout 11am-3pm. 6- to 14-bed dorms 150kr. Singles 475-625kr and doubles 575-750kr; include TV and private ensuite bathrooms. Under age 35. Cash only for dorms; AmEx/MC/V for private rooms. ❷

Danhostel: København Vandrerhjem Copenhagen City (HI), H.C. Andersens Bvd. 50 (☎3311 8585; www.danhostel.dk/copenhagencity). A popular 15-story resting place, only 5min. from the city center, feels more like a hotel than a hostel. Great for large groups. Breakfast 50kr. Linens 60kr. Internet 14kr per 20min; 29kr per hr. Bike rental 100kr per day. Reception 24hr. Check-in 2-5pm. Reserve ahead. Single-sex-dorms 145-180kr; private rooms 580-720kr. 35kr HI discount. AmEx/MC/V. ❷

FOOD

Stylish cafes serving delectable dishes are plentiful throughout the streets of Copenhagen, but be prepared to spend some cash. For delicious, less expensive food, try local *Schawarma* and kebab shops that line **Strøget** (full meal 40-70kr). For less authentically Danish food, budget travelers stop by the many all-you-can-eat pizza, pasta, and ethnic buffets down **Vesterbrogade** (from 70kr). Traditional cuisine includes *smørebrød* (open-faced sandwiches) and can be found on any street in Copenhagen. Green grocers in **Vesterbro** along **Istedgade** provide fresh fruits and veggies (cash only.)

RizRaz, Kompagnistr. 20 (☎3315 0575; www.rizraz.dk). M: Kongens Nytorv. This relaxed restaurant has plenty of seating, an extensive Mediterranean and Middle Eastern influenced menu with a vegetarian lunch buffet (69kr), and beautiful paintings for sale. Dinner 79kr. Grill order (includes buffet) from 119kr. Open daily 11:30am-midnight. AmEx/MC/V. Also at Store Kannikestr. 19 (☎3332 3345). ❸

Den Grønne Kælder, Pilestr. 48 (☎3393 0140). M: Kongens Nytorv. Enjoy the vegetarian and vegan menu, rotated monthly and made from organic ingredients, in this cozy basement cafe. Try the local favorite "legendary hummus." Takeout 40-60kr. Lunch 50kr. Dinner starts at 105kr. Open M-Tu and Th-Sa 11am-10pm, W 1-10pm. Cash only. ❷

Morgenstedet, Langgaden, Bådsmandsstr. 43 (☎3295 7770; www.morgenstedet.dk), in Christiania. Walk down Pusher St. and take a left at the end, then take a right up the concrete ramp at the bike shop and a left before the bathrooms; it will be on your right. Sit in the enclosed outdoor dining area surrounded by lush bushes and flowerbeds and whet your appetite with the rotating menu of vegetarian cuisine. Soup with bread 45kr. Entrees 70kr. Desserts 25kr. Open Tu-Su noon-9pm. Cash only. ❷

Cap Horn. Nyhavn 21 (☎3312 8504; www.caphorn.dk) M: Kongens Nytorv. Enjoy an old-fashioned, nautical atmosphere inside or take in the charming view of the canal on the outdoor patio at this upscale restaurant, a local favorite. Open daily 9am-1am. Brunch 11am-2pm, 98kr. Kitchen closes at 11pm. MC/V. ❷

SIGHTS

Flat Copenhagen lends itself to exploration by bike. Walking tours are detailed in *Playtime* (available at **Use It, p. 170**). Window-shop down pedestrian **Strøget** until you reach Kongens Nytorv; opposite is the picturesque **Nyhavn,** where T**Hans Christian Andersen** penned his first fairy tale. On a clear day, take the 6.4km walk along the five **lakes** on the western border of the city center or grab a bike and ride. Relax in the city hall square and listen to the street music as you enjoy an ice cream treat or a hot dog from local vendors. Most museums are free and some have extended hours on Wednesdays.

CITY CENTER. **Tivoli Gardens,** the famed 19th century amusement park, features newly-built rides, an aquarium, concert hall, and theatre. Located across the street from Central Station. **Tivoli Illuminations,** an evocative light show, is staged on Tivoli Lake each night 30min. before closing. *(Vesterbrogade 3 ☎3315 1001; www.tivoligardens.com. Open mid-Sept. to mid-Apr. M-Th and Su 11am-10pm, F 11am-12:30am, Sa 11am-midnight; mid-Aug. to mid-Sept. M-Th and Su 11am-midnight, F-Sa 11am-12:30am. Admission 85kr. Rides 10-60kr. Admission with unlimited rides 285kr. AmEx/MC/V.)* From Tivoli, cross Tietgensgade to find **Ny Carlsberg Glyptotek,** home to ancient art from the 19th and 20th centuries. Also features a beautiful greenhouse garden. Tickets for free guided tours go quickly. *(Dantes Pl. 7. ☎3341 8141; www.glyptoteket.dk. Open Tu-Su 10am-4pm. 50kr, students and children free. Su free. Wheelchair-accessible. Tours mid-June to Aug. W 2pm. MC/V.)* Across H.C. Andersens Bvd., aquaint yourself with the latest trends from furniture to model cars at the **Danish Design Center,** which displays exhibitions of Danish and international design. The **Flow Market Exhibition** downstairs, encourages consumers to think with sustainable growth in mind, selling items such as "inner calmness" and "clean air." *(H.C. Andersens Bvd. 27. ☎3369 3369; www.ddc.dk. Open M-Tu and Th-F 10am-5pm, W 10am-9pm, Sa-Su 11am-4pm. 50kr, seniors, youth ages 12-18 and students 25kr. W after 5pm free. AmEx/*

MC/V.) The **National Museum's** vast collections include several large rune stones, ancient Viking art, and the ethnographic exhibit, "People of the Earth." To reach the National Museum from H.C. Andersens Bvd., turn onto Stormg., take a right on Vester Volf., and go left on Ny Vesterg. *(Ny Vesterg. 10. ☎3313 4411. www.natmus.dk. Open Tu-Su 10am-5pm. Free. 1 hr. guided tours at noon, 1, 2pm on Sa, Sun, and holidays.)*

The home of Parliament *(Folketing)* and the royal reception rooms, **Christiansborg Slot** displays vivid modernist tapestries that were designed by Bjørn Nørgård and presented to the Queen on her 50th birthday. Visitors can tour the subterranean ruins underneath the Slot. *(Longangstraede 21. ☎3392 6300; www.ses.dk/christrainsborg. Ruins open daily May-Sept. 10am-4pm; Oct.-Apr. Tu-Su 10am-4pm. Ruins 40kr, students 30kr. Guided Castle tour daily Tu-Su at 11:30am and 1:30pm. Adults 65kr, students 55kr.)* Overlook the greater Copenhagen area from atop the impressive **Round Tower** *(Rundetaarn)*. Today, anyone can view the night sky through the astronomical telescope during the winter months. *(Købmagerg. 52A. ☎3373 0373; www.rundetaarn.dk. Open daily May 20-Sept. 21. 10am-8pm, Sept. 21-May 20 10am-5pm. Observatory open mid-Oct.-mid-Mar. Tu, W 7-10pm. 25kr. AmEx/MC/V.)*

CHRISTIANSHAVN. In 1971, a few dozen flower children established the "free city" of **Christiania** in an abandoned Christianshavn fort. Today, the thousand-odd residents continue the tradition of artistic expression and an alternative lifestyle. Buildings surrounded by gorgeous bushes and flowerbeds are covered in ornate graffiti and murals. Vendors sell clothing and jewelry; nearby spots like **Woodstock Cafe** and **Cafe Nemoland** offer cheap beer and diverse crowds. Recent government crackdowns have driven Pusher Street's once open drug trade underground, and arrests for possession have become commonplace. It's a sensitive subject so don't ask; let local people do the talking. Careful: do not take pictures on Pusher Street. *(Main entrance on Prinsesseg. Take bus #66 or 2A (runs every 5min.) from København H.)* **Vor Frelsers Kirke** (Our Savior's Church), who has recently reopened its gold-accented interior to the public, is great for a quieter time. *(Sankt Annæg. 9. M: Christianshavn or bus #66. Turn left onto Prinsesseg. ☎3257 2798; www.vorfrelserskirke.dk. Spire ☎3254 1573. Church free. Spire 20kr. Cash only.)*

FREDERIKSTADEN. Northeast of the city center, Edvard Eriksen's tiny **Little Mermaid** *(Lille Havfrue)* statue honors Hans Christian Andersen's beloved tale. *(S-tog: Østerport. Turn left out of the station, go left on Folke Bernadottes Allé, bear right on the path bordering the canal, go left up the stairs, and then head right along the street.)* Head back along the canal and turn left across the moat to reach **Kastellet,** a rampart-enclosed 17th-century fortress that's now a park. *(Center of Churchill Park. ☎3311 2233. Open daily 6am-10pm.)* On the other side of Kastellet, the **Frihedsmuseet** (Museum of Danish Resistance) documents the German occupation from 1940-45, when the Danes helped over 7000 Jews escape to Sweden. *(At Churchillparken. ☎3313 7714. Open May-Sept. Tu-Su 10am-5pm; Oct.-Apr. Tu-Su 10am-3pm. English-language tours July-Sept. Tu and Th 11am. Free.)* Walk south down Amalieng. to reach **Amalienborg Palace,** a complex of four enormous mansions that serve as the winter residences of the royal family. Several apartments are open to the public, including the studies of 19th-century Danish kings. The changing of the guard takes place at noon on the vast plaza. *(☎3312 0808; www.rosenborgslot.dk. Open May-Oct. daily 10am-4pm; Nov.-Apr. Tu-Su 11am-4pm. 50kr, students 30kr. Combined ticket with Rosenborg Slot 80kr. MC/V.)*

The **State Museum of Fine Arts** displays an eclectic collection of Danish and international art between its two buildings, which are linked by an impressive glass-roof gallery. *(Sølvg. 48-50. S-tog: Nørreport. Walk up Øster Voldg or take bus 6A ☎3374 8494; www.smk.dk. Open Tu and Th-Su 10am-5pm, W 10am-8pm. English-language tours July-Aug. Sa-Su 2pm. Permanent collection free. Special exhibits 80kr, students 50kr. W free. AmEx/MC/V.)* Opposite the museum, the **Baroque Rosenborg Slot** built by King Christian IV in the 17th century as a summer residence, shows off the crown jewels

BIKING TOUR OF COPENHAGEN

TIME: 4hr. With visits to Rosenborg Slot and Christianborg Slot, 6hr.
DISTANCE: About 6km.
SEASON: Year-round, although Rosenborg Slot has reduced hours Nov.-Apr.

In Copenhagen, biking is the new black. From chic women in heels to businessmen in suits, biking is the European way to travel; not to mention a great way to burn off the delicious buffets you'll be devouring. Copenhagen's flat land makes the city an ideal spot for scenic cycling as you tour fine churches, museums, and of course, castles. Rentals from **City Bike** (p. 170) are a great way to explore Copenhagen, but be sure to stake one out early. Careful: the rules require that you only ride the bikes in the city center. The eastern banks of the five western lakes are fair game, but if you cross over to the other side of the lakes, you'll face a 1000kr fine. Don't ride at night with a City Bike—and make sure you keep an eye on your City Bike when exploring the castles and museums, as anyone can take your bike, not to mention your 20kr!

When biking through the city, you should bypass pedestrian thoroughfares like Strøget to avoid strolling couples and bedazzled tourists. If you want to ride out into the beautiful countryside, ask your hostel about rental bikes. They can be a great alternative and you may get a better quality bike. You can take your bike onto an S-tog for 10kr. In Denmark, you are legally required to use lights when riding at night, and police are not shy about handing out 400kr fines to enforce this law. Helmets are recommended, but not mandatory.

The tour starts and ends in **Rådhus-Pladsen.** Begin by carefully making your way down busy Hans Christian Andersens Boulevard.

1. BOTANISK HAVE. Take a right onto Nørre Voldg. and follow it until you see the gates leading into the University of Copenhagen's lush **Botanical Gardens** (p. 176). Wander along paths lined with more than 13,000 species of plants, or hone in on the **Palm House** to view its extravagant orchids, cycads, and other tropical rarities. Explore the grounds to the **Faculty of Science of the University of Copenhagen,** located just north of the Gardens atop a hill along Øster Voldg.

2. STATENS MUSEUM FOR KUNST AND ROSENBORG SLOT. Next, head back onto Øster Voldg. At the intersection with Sølvg., you'll see the gates of the **Statens Museum for Kunst** (State Museum of Fine Arts; p. 173) to the north and the spires of **Rosenborg Slot** to the south. The latter served as the 16th-century summer house of King Christian IV, and the royal family took refuge here in 1801 when the British navy was shelling Copenhagen. Lock up your bike and pop inside for a look at the Sculpture Street in the museum or Denmark's crown jewels in the Slot's treasury, and don't forget to wander the King's Gardens.

3. ROUND TOWER. Backtrack down Øster Voldg. and turn left onto Gothersg. Make a right onto Landemærket and then hop off again to scale the heights of the **Round Tower** (p. 173), a onetime royal observatory that still affords a sweeping view of the city.

4. AMALIENBORG PALACE. Head back up to Gothersg. and turn right. Pass by **Kongens Nytorv,** the 1670 "new square" that turns into a skating rink each winter, and take a left onto Bredg. Keep your eyes peeled for the gilded dome of the **Marmorkirken** (Marble Church) on your left, and then turn right to enter the octagonal plaza of **Amalienborg Palace** (p. 173), a set of four Rococo mansions that the queen and her family call home. Check out the Amalienborg Museum to admire the luxurious furnishings of 19th century King Frederik VII's room.

5. NYHAVN. Continue on through the plaza, turn right on Toldbodg., and then right before the bridge onto Nyhavn. Part of the city's old waterfront, Nyhavn was known for centuries as a seedy strip for sailors to find grog, women, and a tattoo artist sober enough to wield a firm needle. Over the past 30 years, Copenhagen has embarked on a clean-up campaign, and today you're more

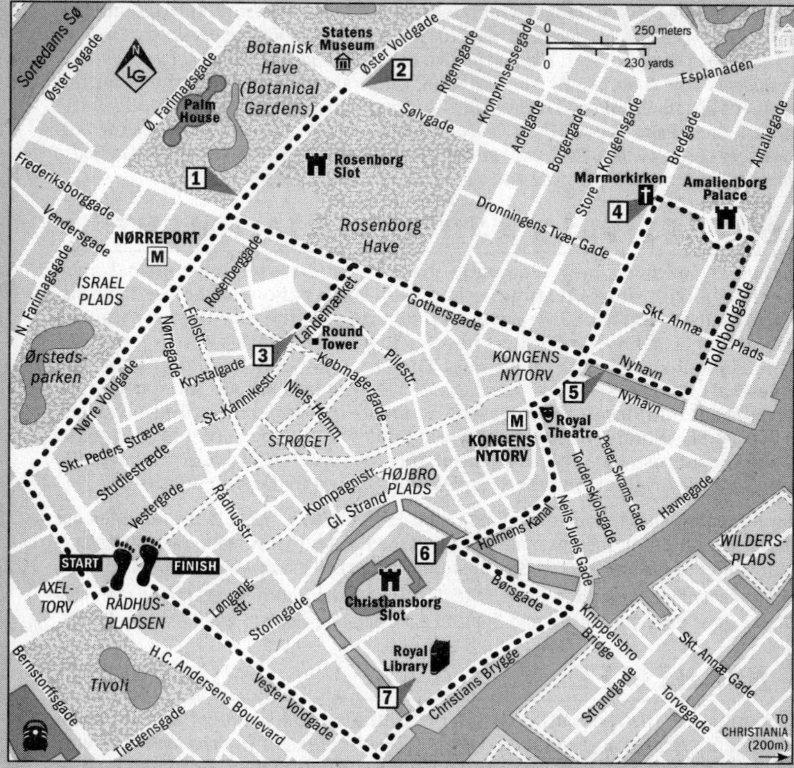

likely to find an upscale deli serving smørrebrod than a tumbledown soup kitchen. Whenever a scrap of sunshine can be found, the good people of Copenhagen are soaking it up along the wharf, joined by Swedes from Malmö in search of cheap Danish beer.

6. CHRISTIANBORG SLOT. Walk your bike through Kongens Nytorv, and then thread your way between the **Royal Theater** (p. 176) and the metro station down Neils Juels G. Turn right onto Holmens Kanal and cross the bridge to reach **Christiansborg Slot** (p. 173), seat of the Danish Parliament. Look for the 103m tower; it's difficult to miss. If you arrive before 3:30pm, try to catch a tour of the **Royal Reception Rooms,** or head down into the ruins of the four previous castles underneath the present-day building. The first castle was demolished to make way for a larger one, the next two burned down in fires, and the Hanseatic League dismantled the fourth castle stone by stone after they captured the city in 1369.

7. SLIDING INTO HOME. You're in the home stretch. Head east toward the **Knippelsbro Bridge** and **Christiania** (p. 173), taking in the industrial skyline before lugging your bike down the steps to Christians Brygge below. Turn right and bike along the canal. Keep watch for the Black Diamond annex of the **Royal Library,** built in 1996 from black marble imported from Zimbabwe. Make a quick stop to check your email at one of the two free terminals inside. Make a right onto Vester Voldg. and coast back up to the Rådhus. You've earned the right to call it a day. Now you can relax and watch the fireworks from Tivoli, while treating yourself to an ice cream cone.

and the opulent **Unicorn Throne,** which legend holds is constructed from unicorn horns. *(Øster Voldg. 4A. M: Nørreport. ☎3315 3286; www.rosenborgslot.dk. Open daily June-Aug. 11am-5pm; May and Sept. 10am-4pm; Oct. daily 11am-3pm; Nov.-Apr. Tu-Su 11am-2pm. 50kr, students 40kr. AmEx/MC/V.)* About 13,000 plant species thrive in the beautiful gardens of **Botanisk Have.** Tropical and subtropical plants mingle happily in the iron-and-glass **Palm House.** *(Øster Farimagsgade 2B. ☎3532 2221 botanik.snm.ku.dk/english. Gardens open daily May-Sept. 8:30am-6pm; Oct.-Apr. daily Tu-Su 8:30am-4pm. Palm House open daily May-Dec. 10am-3pm; Jan.-Apr. daily Tu-Su 10am-3pm. Free.)*

FESTIVALS AND ENTERTAINMENT

Whether showcasing new cinematic pictures or entertaining musical acts, Copenhagen isn't short on summer festivals. During the world-class **Copenhagen Jazz Festival** (☎3393 2013; www.festival.jazz.dk), the city teems with free outdoor concerts. Past performers have included Ray Charles, Oscar Peterson, Herbie Hancock, and Dizzy Gillespie. The city truly comes alive for the **Nat-Film Festival** (☎3312 0005; www.natfilm.dk) during late March and early April. International and domestic releases compete for Danish distribution deals. **Zulu Sommerbio** (Summer Cinema; www.zulu.dk) holds free screenings in parks and squares across the city throughout July and August. Movies are normally shown in their original languages and accompanied by Danish subtitles.

Royal Theater, August Bournoville Pass. 1, (☎3369 6969) is home to the world-famous Royal Danish Ballet. The box office is just off the Konges Nytorv metro and sells same-day half-price tickets. Open M-Sa 10am-6pm. Tickets online at www.billetnet.dk.

Tivoli ticket office, Vesterbrog. 3, (☎3315 1012). Sells half-price tickets for the city's theaters. Open daily mid-Apr. to mid-Sept. 11am-8pm; mid-Sept. to mid-Apr. 9am-5pm.

NIGHTLIFE

In Copenhagen, the real parties begin on Thursday night; many bars and clubs have cheaper drinks and reduced covers. The streets near the **city center,** as well as of **Nørrebro** and **Vesterbro,** are lined with hip, crowded bars. Look for fancier options along **Nyhavn,** where laid-back Danes bring their own beer and sit on the pier; open containers are legal within the city limits. Copenhagen has a thriving gay and lesbian scene; check out *Playtime* or *Out and About* for listings.

PARTNER UP. The areas behind København H, the central train station, can be unsafe, especially at night. Explore with caution and bring a friend.

Vega, Enghavev. 40 (☎3325 7011; www.vega.dk), in Vesterbro. Bus 10. "Party time! Always crowded! Always a good time!" is what locals exclaim about this locale. One of Copenhagen's largest and most popular nightclubs, it showcases 4 floors, 5 dance rooms, 2 concert venues, and a popular bar. Dress well. Bar 18+; club 20+. Club cover after 1am 60kr. Bar open F-Sa 9pm-5am. Club open F-Sa 11pm-5am. MC/V.

Code, Radhusstraede 1 (☎3326 3626; www.code.dk), in Central Copenhagen. By day, an open cafe with a wide range of sandwiches. By night, a gay bar & lounge with an exotic cocktail selection. Shows 8pm-midnight. DJs on weekends 10pm-5am. MC/V.

The Australian Bar, Vesterg. 10 (☎2024 1411). M: Nørreport. Tucked away in the basement of an enclave, this relaxed bar has cheap drinks, pool tables, an arcade, and a dance-club playlist where you pick the music (8 songs/25kr). Beer 10-20kr. Mixed drinks 30kr. Reduced prices Th. Open M-W and Su 4pm-2am, Th-Sa 4pm-5am. MC/V.

La Hacienda/The Dance Floor, Gammel Torv 8 (☎3311 7478; www.la-hacienda.dk). M: Nørreport. Choose between **La Hacienda,** a laid-back lounge playing soul and hip hop, and **The Dance Floor,** a 2-story trance-driven club. Cover for men 150kr, women 130kr, 75kr before midnight; includes 1 champagne and 1 beer. Dress: Stylish and modern. 18+. Open F 11pm-8am, Sa 11pm-10am. AmEx/MC/V.

The Moose Bar, Sværtev. 5 (☎3391 4291). M: Kongens Nytorv. Rowdy local spirit dominates in this popular bar, famous for its cheap beer and its jukebox playing classic rock hits. Beer 29kr, 2 for 32kr. 2 mixed drinks 30-35kr. Happy hour with reduced prices Tu, Th, and Sa 9pm-close. Open M and Su 1pm-3am, Tu-Sa 1pm-6am. AmEx/MC/V.

FRANCE

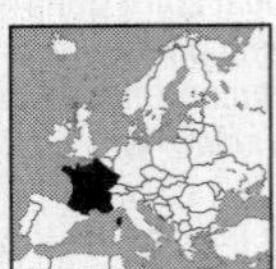

With its lavish châteaux, lavender fields, medieval streets, and sidewalk cafes, France conjures up any number of postcard-ready scenes. To the proud French, it is only natural that outsiders flock to their history-steeped homeland. Although France may no longer manipulate world events, the vineyards of Bordeaux, the museums of Paris, and the beaches of the Riviera draw more tourists than any other nation in the world. Centuries-old farms and churches share the landscape with inventive, modern architecture; street posters advertise jazz festivals as well as Baroque concerts. The country's rich culinary tradition rounds out a culture that cannot be sent home on a four-by-six.

DISCOVER FRANCE: SUGGESTED ITINERARIES

THREE DAYS. Don't even think of leaving **Paris,** the City of Light (p. 187). Explore the shops and cafes of the **Latin Quarter,** then cross the **Seine** to reach **Île de la Cité** to admire **Sainte-Chapelle** and the **Cathédrale de Notre Dame.** Visit the wacky **Centre National d'Art et de Culture Georges Pompidou** before swinging through **Marais** for food and fun. The next day, stroll down the **Champs-Élysées,** starting at the **Arc de Triomphe,** meander through the **Jardin des Tuileries,** and over to the **Musée d'Orsay.** See part of the **Louvre** the next morning, then spend the afternoon at **Versailles.**

ONE WEEK. After three days in **Paris,** explore the châteaux of the **Loire Valley** (1 day; p. 209). Head to **Rennes** for medieval sights and modern nightlife (1 day; p. 211), then to the dazzling island of **Mont-St-Michel** (1 day; p. 214).

BEST OF FRANCE, THREE WEEKS. Begin with three days in Paris, then daytrip to the royal residences at **Versailles.** Whirl through the **Loire Valley** (2 days) before traveling to the wine country of **Bordeaux** (1 day; p. 226). Check out the rose-colored architecture of **Toulouse** (1 day; p. 228) before sailing through **Aix-en-Provence** (p. 235) and sunny **Provence** (3 days). Let loose in **Marseille** (2 days; p. 230), and bask in the glitter of the Riviera in **Nice** (2 days; p. 236). Then show off your tan in the Alps as you travel **Lyon** (2 days; p. 219) to revel in their wild nightlife. Finish your trip with some German flavor in **Strasbourg** (1 day; p. 216), where trains will whisk you away to your next European adventure.

LIFE AND TIMES

HISTORY

FROM GAULS TO GOTHS (25,000 BC-AD 900). The first Frenchmen appeared in 25,000 BC, covering the caves of the **Dordogne Valley** with graffiti. By 4500 BC Neolithic people carved the famous stone **monoliths** (menhirs) at **Carnac,** which were admired by the Celtic Gauls, who arrived from the east around 600 BC to trade with Greek colonists in **Marseille** (p. 230). Fierce resistance from the Gauls and their leader **Vercingétorix** kept the Romans out of their territory until Julius Caesar's victory at Alesia in 52 BC. When Rome fell in AD 476, Gothic tribes plundered the area and moved on, leaving the Franks in control of **Gaul**

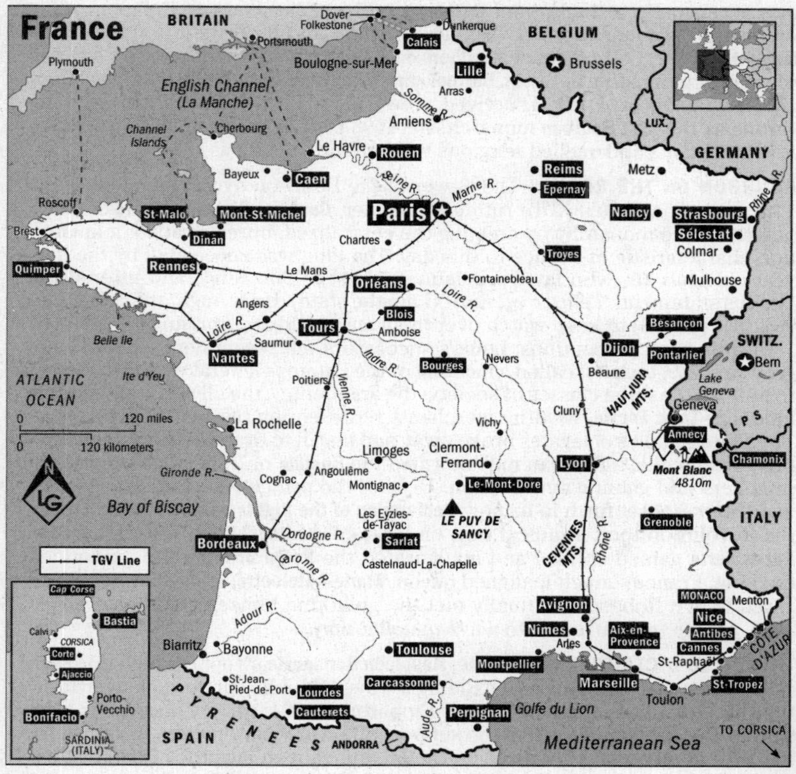

(now France). The Frankish king, **Clovis,** founded the Merovingian dynasty and was baptized in AD 507. Later, **Charlemagne,** who began the Carolingian dynasty, expanded his domain, the **Holy Roman Empire,** into Austria. The **Treaty of Verdun** in AD 843 resolved territorial squabbles after Charlemagne's death, dividing the empire between his three grandsons.

ENGLISH INTERFERENCE. After the death of the last Carolingian king, the noble-elected **Hugh Capet** consolidated power. When **Eleanor of Aquitaine,** the former queen of Capet's descendant Louis VII, married into the English Plantagenet dynasty in the 12th century, a swath of land stretching from the Channel to the Pyrénées became English territory. This opened the door for England's **Edward III** to claim the French throne, triggering the **Hundred Years' War** in 1337. French defeat seemed imminent when England crowned Henry VI king of France 90 years later, but salvation arrived in the form of a 17-year-old peasant, **Jeanne d'Arc** (Joan of Arc). Leading the French army disguised as a man, she won a string of victories and swept the English off the continent before she was burned at the stake for heresy in Rouen (p. 212) in 1431.

POPES AND PROTESTANTS. Hoping to wrest Jerusalem from the Saracens, **Pope Urban II** declared the First Crusade in 1295 from **Clermont,** convincing thousands to take up arms. In the 16th century, religious conflict between **Hugue-**

nots (French Protestants) and **Catholics** initiated the Wars of Religion. After orchestrating a marriage between her daughter and Protestant prince **Henri de Navarre** in 1572, Catholic queen **Catherine de Médici** inadvertently set off a series of events culminating in the **St. Bartholomew's Day Massacre.** While over 3000 Parisian Huguenots died, Henri survived, converted to Catholicism, and rose to the throne as the first **Bourbon** monarch. His 1598 **Edict of Nantes** granted tolerance for Protestants and quelled religious warfare for a century.

BOURBON ON THE ROCKS. The power of the Bourbon dynasty peaked in the 17th century as Louis XIII's ruthless minister, **Cardinal Richelieu,** consolidated power for the monarchy by creating the centralized, bureaucratic administration characteristic of France to this day. The king was succeeded by the five-year-old **Louis XIV,** who later proclaimed himself "Sun King" and uttered the famous statement: *"l'état, c'est moi"* (I am the state). He brought the nobility to **Versailles** (p. 208) to keep watch over them and avoid any uprisings.

Despite such precautions, Louis's successors felt resentment against them grow. In 1789, **Louis XVI** called a meeting of the Estates-General with representatives from the three classes of society: the aristocracy, the clergy, and the revolutionary **Third Estate,** wealthy merchants representing the rest of the people. The Third Estate's delegates broke away and began to draft their own constitution. Meanwhile, a Parisian mob stormed the **Bastille** on July 14, freeing seven prisoners and gaining ammunition. Despite the principles of *liberté, égalité,* and *fraternité* set forth in its new **Declaration of the Rights of Man and the Citizen,** the Revolution took a radical turn under the **First Republic** in 1792. **Maximilien Robespierre** gained control and inaugurated the **Reign of Terror.** He guillotined the king, France's much-maligned queen, **Marie-Antoinette,** and other perceived rivals. When Robespierre finally met the guillotine himself (without trail) in 1794, power was entrusted to a five-man **Directory.**

THE LITTLE DICTATOR. Meanwhile, **Napoleon Bonaparte** swept through northern Italy into Austria with his army. Riding a wave of public support, he overthrew the Directory, and crowned himself Emperor in 1804. After a disastrous invasion of Russia, Napoleon lost the support of a war-weary nation. In return for his 1814 abdication, he was given the Mediterranean island of **Elba.** Restless "ruling" just one small island, Napoleon left Elba and landed with an army at Cannes in March 1815. King **Louis XVIII** fled to England as Napoleon marched north. His ensuing **Hundred Days'** rule ended on the battlefield at **Waterloo,** where combined Prussian and British forces triumphed over him. Napoleon was banished again, this time to remote St. Helena, where he died in 1821.

WAR, PEACE, AND MORE WAR. Concerned about the changing balance of power in Europe after Germany's 1871 unification, France, Britain, and Russia forged the **Triple Entente** to counter Germany, Italy, and the Austro-Hungarian Empire's Triple Alliance. When **WWI** suddenly erupted in 1914, German armies swarmed into France but quickly became bogged down in intractable trench warfare. The war ended in 1918, but not before 1.3 million Frenchmen had died. The 1930s found France ill-equipped to deal with Hitler's mobilization across the Rhine. In May 1940, Germany swept through Belgium and invaded France from the north, seizing it by June. With the north under German occupation, WWI hero **Maréchal Pétain's** puppet state ruled the rest of the country from Vichy and answered to the Germans. Those who escaped joined the French government-in-exile under **General Charles de Gaulle.** At his insistence, French troops led the Liberation of Paris on August 25, 1944.

FOURTH REPUBLIC AND POST-COLONIAL FRANCE. While drafting the Fourth Republic's constitution, de Gaulle's provisional government established female suffrage and nationalized energy companies. De Gaulle's 1946 retirement left the Republic without a strong leader. Twenty-five different governments ruled France over the next 14 years until de Gaulle returned to power in 1958. Concurrently, the remnants of France's 19th-century **colonial empire** were crumbling. The 1950s witnessed the systematic and sometimes bloody dismantling of the remaining colonies. In 1958, with a new constitution in hand, the nation declared itself the **Fifth Republic.** In May 1968, student protest grew into a full-scale revolt, and 10 million state workers went on strike in support of social reform. The government responded by deploying tank and commando units, and another revolution seemed inevitable. Crisis was averted only with the return of the Gaullists. The aging de Gaulle had lost his magic touch, however, and he resigned following a referendum defeat in 1969.

THE 1980S AND BEYOND. In 1981, **François Mitterrand** became France's first Socialist president, helping his party gain a majority in the Assemblée Nationale. Far-reaching social programs implemented early in the administration gave way to compromise with the right, and Mitterrand was forced to appoint the Conservative **Jacques Chirac** as prime minister. In an unprecedented power-sharing relationship called *"cohabitation,"* Mitterrand controlled foreign affairs, leaving domestic power to Chirac. The French elected Chirac president in 1995. The 2002 presidential elections shocked the world when far-right nationalist **Jean-Marie Le Pen,** leader of the **Front National (FN),** beat left-wing candidate Lionel Jospin in the preliminary elections. He was defeated by Chirac, who was reelected in an 82% landslide amid protest against Le Pen's anti-immigration policies, reputed racism, and dismissive remarks about the Holocaust.

TODAY

Facing an increasingly global society, France continues to negotiate tradition and modernity. In February 2004, the National Assembly sparked controversy by backing a bill enforcing **laïcité,** the strict separation between church and state. The new law banned all religious symbols, most notably Muslim headscarves, in public schools. While some view the bill as discriminating against Muslims, then-Prime Minister Jean-Pierre Raffarin affirmed it would maintain the long-standing secular tradition of French public education. **Gay rights** have also been a point of controversy in recent years. In 1999, the **Civil Solidarity Pact (PACS)** made France the first Catholic country to legally recognize homosexual unions. In foreign policy, France's opposition to the US-led war in Iraq made headlines in 2003. Although Franco-German cooperation has played a central role in the European Union's economic policies, integration has met with resistance from the French, who worry about losing their autonomy and national character. In May 2005, the French voted against the adoption of the EU constitution, fearing unemployment and the disintegration of the welfare system. Chirac consequently named the more conservative **Dominique de Villepin** as prime minister in order to boost public confidence. In October 2005, riots erupted across France after two teenage immigrants were killed in an altercation with the police in a low-income suburb of Paris. Thousands of cars were torched in nearly 300 towns in protest of France's intolerance before the violence stopped. Only a few months later, more riots paralyzed the country when students protested a new labor law that they feared would erode job stability. In France's 2007 presidential elections, the Socialist party's **Ségolène Royal** faced off against **Nicolas Sarkozy,** who represented the Union for a Popular Movement (UMP). Sarkozy, promising immigration reform and more jobs for the unemployed, beat Royal by only five points.

HOLIDAYS AND FESTIVALS

Holidays: New Year's Day (Jan. 1, 2010); Epiphany (Jan. 6, 2010); Good Friday (Apr. 10, 2010); Easter Sunday and Monday (Apr. 4-5, 2010); Ascension (May 13, 2010); Pentecost (May 23, 2010); Corpus Christi (June 3, 2010); Bastille Day (July 14, 2010); Assumption (Aug. 15, 2010); All Saints' Day (Nov. 1, 2010); Christmas (Dec. 25, 2010).

Festivals: Many cities celebrate a pre-Lenten Carnaval—for the most over-the-top festivities, head to **Nice** (Jan. 25-Feb. 5). The internationally renowned **Cannes Film Festival** (May 13-24; www.festival-cannes.com) caters to the rich, famous, and creative. In 2010, the **Tour de France** will begin July 3. (www.letour.fr). The **Festival d'Avignon** (July-Aug.; www.festival-avignon.com) is famous for its theater productions.

ESSENTIALS

WHEN TO GO

In July, Paris starts to shrink; by August it is devoid of Parisians, animated only by tourists and the pickpockets who love them. The French Riviera fills with Anglophones from June to September. During these months, French natives flee to other parts of the country, especially the Atlantic coast. Early summer and fall are the best times to visit Paris—the city has warmed up but not completely emptied out. The north and west have cool winters and mild summers, while the less-crowded center and east have a more temperate climate. From December through April, the Alps provide some of the world's best skiing, while the Pyrénées offer a calmer, if less climatically dependable, alternative.

FACTS AND FIGURES

OFFICIAL NAME: French Republic.

CAPITAL: Paris.

MAJOR CITIES: Lyon, Marseille, Nice.

POPULATION: 60,880,000.

LAND AREA: 547,000 sq. km.

TIME ZONE: GMT+1.

LANGUAGE: French.

RELIGION: Roman Catholic (88%), Muslim (9%), Protestant (2%), Jewish (1%).

CHEESE VARIETIES: Over 500.

FRANCE

DOCUMENTS AND FORMALITIES

EMBASSIES AND CONSULATES. Foreign embassies in France are in **Paris** (p. 188). French embassies abroad include: **Australia,** Level 26, St-Martins Tower, 31 Market St., Sydney NSW 2000 (☎+61 02 92 68 24 00; www.ambafrance-au.org); **Canada,** 1501, McGill College, Bureau 1000, Montréal, QC H3A 3M8 (☎+1-878-4385; www.consulfrance-montreal.org); **Ireland,** 36 Ailesbury Rd., Ballsbridge, Dublin, 4 (☎+353 1 227 5000; www.ambafrance.ie); **New Zealand,** 34-42 Manners St., Wellington (☎+64 384 25 55; www.ambafrance-nz.org); **UK,** 21 Cromwell Rd., London SW7 2EN (☎+44 207 073 1000; www.consulfrance-londres.org); **US,** 4101 Reservoir Rd., NW, Washington, D.C., 20007 (☎+1-202-944-6195; www.consulfrance-washington.org).

VISA AND ENTRY INFORMATION. EU citizens do not need a visa. Citizens of Australia, Canada, New Zealand, and the US do not need a visa for stays of up to 90 days, beginning upon entry into any of the countries in the EU's freedom-of-movement zone. For more info, see p. 8. For stays longer than 90 days, all non-EU citizens need Schengen visas (around US$81), available at French consulates and online at www.consulfrance-washington.org.

TOURIST SERVICES AND MONEY

EMERGENCY	**Ambulance:** ☎15. **Fire:** ☎18. **Police:** ☎17. **General Emergency:** ☎112.

TOURIST OFFICES. The **French Government Tourist Office** (**FGTO;** www.franceguide.com), also known as Maison de la France, runs tourist offices (called *syndicats d'initiative* or *offices de tourisme*) and offers tourist services to travelers abroad. In smaller towns, the **mairie** (town hall) may also distribute maps and pamphlets, help travelers find accommodations, and suggest excursions.

MONEY. The **euro (€)** has replaced the franc as the unit of currency in France. For more info, see p. 11. As a general rule, it's cheaper to exchange money in France than at home. Be prepared to spend at least €40-60 per day and considerably more in Paris. Tips are generally included in meal prices at restaurants and cafes, as well as in drink prices at bars and clubs; ask or look for the phrase *service compris* on the menu. If service is not included, tip 15-20%. Even when service is included, it is polite to leave a *pourboire* of up to 5% at a cafe, bistro, restaurant, or bar. Workers such as concierges may expect at least a €1.50 tip for services beyond the call of duty; taxi drivers expect 10-15% of the metered fare. Tipping tour guides and bus drivers €1.50-3 is customary.

France has a 19.6% **value added tax** (**VAT;** TVA in French), a sales tax applied to a wide range of goods and services. The prices included in *Let's Go* include VAT. In the airport upon exiting the EU, non-EU citizens can claim a refund on the tax paid for goods purchased at participating stores. In order to qualify for a refund in a store, you must spend at least €175; make sure to ask for a refund form when you pay. For more info on qualifying for a VAT refund, see p. 13.

TRANSPORTATION

BY PLANE. Most transatlantic flights to Paris land at **Roissy-Charles de Gaulle** (**CDG;** ☎01 48 62 22 80). Many continental and charter flights use **Orly** (**ORY;** ☎01 49 75 15 15). Aéroports de Paris (www.aeroportsdeparis.fr) has info about both. **Paris Beauvais Tillé** (**BVA;** ☎38 92 68 20 66; www.aeroportbeauvais.com) caters to budget travelers, servicing airlines like Ryanair (UK ☎0905 566 0000; www.ryanair.com). For more info on flying to France, see p. 33. Once in France, most people prefer other travel modes unless heading to **Corsica.**

BY TRAIN. The French national railway company, **SNCF** (☎0892 35 35 35; www.sncf.fr), manages one of Europe's most efficient rail networks. Among the fastest in the world, **TGV** (www.tgv.com) trains (*train à grande vitesse;* high-speed) now link many major French cities, as well as some European destinations, including Brussels, Geneva, Lausanne, and Zürich. *Rapide* trains are slower. Local Express trains are actually the slowest option. French trains offer discounts of 25-50% on tickets for travelers under 26 with the **Carte 12-25** (€52; good for 1yr.). Locate the *guichets* (ticket counters), the *quais* (platforms), and the *voies* (tracks), and you will be ready to roll. Terminals can be divided into *banlieue* (suburb) and the bigger *grandes lignes* (intercity trains). While some select trains require reservations, you are not guaranteed a seat without one (usually US$5-30). Reserve ahead during holidays and high seasons.

If you are planning to spend a great deal of time on trains, a rail pass might be worthwhile, but in many cases—especially if you are under 26—point-to-point tickets may be cheaper. **Eurail** is valid in France. Standard **Eurail Passes,** valid for a given number of consecutive days, are best for those planning on traveling long distances. **Flexipasses,** valid for any 10 or 15 (not necessarily consecutive) days within a two-month period, are more cost-effective for those traveling longer distances less frequently. **Youth Passes** and **Youth Flexipasses** provide the same second-class perks for those under 26. It is best to purchase a pass before going to France. For prices and more info, contact student travel agencies, **Rail Europe** (Canada ☎800-361-7245, US 888-382-7245; www.raileurope.com), or **Flight Centre** (US ☎866-967-5351; www.flightcentre.com)

SELF-VALIDATE=GREAT. Validate *(composter)* your ticket! Orange validation boxes lie around every station, and you must have your ticket stamped with the date and time by the machine before boarding the train.

BY BUS. Within France, long-distance buses are a secondary transportation choice, as service is relatively infrequent. However, in some regions buses are indispensable for reaching out-of-the-way towns. Bus services operated by SNCF accept rail passes. *Gare routière* is French for "bus station."

BY FERRY. Ferries across the **English Channel** (La Manche) link France to England and Ireland. The shortest and most popular route is between Dover, BRI and Calais (1hr.) and is run by **P&O Stena Line** (☎08 25 12 01 56; www.posl.com) and **SeaFrance** (☎08 25 04 40 45; www.seafrance.com). **Norfolkline** (☎44 0870 870 1020; www.norfolkline-ferries.com) provides an alternative route from Dover, BRI to Dunkerque (1hr.). **Brittany Ferries** (France ☎0825 82 88 28, UK ☎0871 244 0744; www.brittany-ferries.com) travels from Portsmouth to Caen (5¾hr.), Cherbourg (4½hr.), and St-Malo (10¾hr.). For more info on English Channel ferries, see p. 42.

BY CAR. Drivers in France visiting for fewer than 90 days must be 18 years old and carry either an **International Driving Permit (IDP)** or a valid EU-issued or American driving license. You need to also have the vehicle's registration, national plate, and current insurance certificate on hand; French car rental agencies provide necessary documents. Agencies require renters to be 20, and most charge those aged 21-24 an additional insurance fee (€20-25 per day). If you don't know how to drive stick, you may have to pay a hefty premium for a car with automatic transmission. French law requires that both drivers and passengers wear seat belts. The almost 1,000,000km of French roads are usually in great condition, due in part to expensive tolls paid by travelers. Check www.francetourism.com/practicalinfo for more info on travel and car rentals.

BY BIKE AND BY THUMB. Of Europeans, the French alone may love **cycling** more than football. Renting a **bike** (€8-19 per day) beats bringing your own if you're only touring one or two regions. Hitchhiking is illegal on French highways, although some people describe the French's ready willingness to lend a ride. *Let's Go* does not recommend hitchhiking.

KEEPING IN TOUCH

PHONE CODES	**Country code:** 33. **International dialing prefix:** 00. When calling within a city, dial 0 + city code + local number. For more info on how to place international calls, see **Inside Back Cover.**

EMAIL AND THE INTERNET. Internet is readily available throughout France. Only the smallest villages lack Internet cafes, and in larger towns Internet cafes are well equipped and widespread, though often pricey. In addition to the locations suggested here, check out www.cybercaptive.com for more options.

TELEPHONE. Whenever possible, use a **calling card** for international phone calls, as long-distance rates for national phone services are often very high. Publicly owned **France Télécom** pay phones charge less than their privately owned counterparts. They accept *Télécartes* (phonecards), available in 50-unit (€7.50) and 120-unit (€15) denominations at newspaper kiosks and tabacs. **Mobile phones** are an increasingly popular and economical option. Major mobile carriers include Orange, Bouyges Telecom, and SFR. *Décrochez* means pick up; you'll then be asked to *patientez* (wait) to insert your card; at *numérotez* or *composez*, you can dial. The number for general info is ☎12; for an international operator, call ☎00 33 11. International direct dial numbers include: **AT&T Direct** ☎0 800 99 00 11; **Canada Direct** ☎0 800 99 00 16 or 99 02 16; **MCI WorldPhone** ☎0 800 99 00 19; **Telecom New Zealand** ☎0 800 99 00 64; **Telstra Australia** ☎0 800 99 00 61.

MAIL. Send mail from **La Poste** offices (www.laposte.net. Open M-F 9am-7pm, Sa 9am-noon). Airmail between France and North America takes five to 10 days; writing *"prioritaire"* on the envelope should ensure delivery in about five days at no extra charge. To send a 20g airmail letter or postcard within France or from France to another EU destination costs around €0.54, to a non-EU European country €0.75, and to Australia, Canada, New Zealand, or the US €0.90. To receive mail in France, have it delivered **Poste Restante.** Mail will go to the main post office unless you specify a subsidiary by street address. Address mail to be held as follows: Last name, First name, Poste Restante, postal code, city, France. Bring a passport to pick up your mail; there may be a small fee.

FRANCE

ACCOMMODATIONS AND CAMPING

FRANCE	❶	❷	❸	❹	❺
ACCOMMODATIONS	under €15	€15-27	€28-38	€39-55	over €55

The **French Hostelling International (HI)** affiliate, **Fédération Unie des Auberges de Jeunesse** (**FUAJ;** ☎01 44 89 87 27; www.fuaj.org), operates 150 hostels within France. A dorm bed in a hostel averages €10-15. Some hostels accept reservations through the **International Booking Network** (www.hostelbooking.com). Two or more people traveling together can save money by staying in cheap hotels rather than hostels. The French government employs a four-star hotel rating system. *Gîtes d'étapes* are rural accommodations for cyclists, hikers, and other amblers in less-populated areas. After 3000 years of settlement, true wilderness in France is hard to find, and it's illegal to **camp** in most public spaces, including national parks. Instead, look for organized *campings* (campgrounds), replete with vacationing families and programmed fun. Most have toilets, showers, and electrical outlets, though you may have to pay €2-5 extra for such luxuries; you'll often need to pay a fee for your car, too (€3-8).

FOOD AND DRINK

FRANCE	❶	❷	❸	❹	❺
FOOD	under €7	€7-12	€13-18	€19-33	over €33

French chefs cook for one of the world's most finicky clienteles. The largest meal of the day is *le déjeuner* (lunch), while a light croissant with or without *confiture* (jam) characterizes *le petit déjeuner* (breakfast). A complete French meal includes an *apéritif* (drink), an *entrée* (appetizer), a *plat* (main course), salad, cheese, dessert, fruit, coffee, and a *digestif* (after-dinner drink). The French drink **wine** with virtually every meal; *boisson comprise* entitles you to a free drink (usually wine) with your food. In France, the legal drinking age is 16. Most restaurants offer a *menu à prix fixe* (fixed-price meal) that costs less than ordering *à la carte*. The *formule* is a cheaper, two-course version for the hurried luncher. Odd-hour cravings between lunch and dinner can be satisfied at *brasseries* or creperies, the middle ground between cafes and restaurants. *Service compris* means the tip is included in *l'addition* (the check). It's easy to get a satisfying dinner for under €10 with staples such as cheese, pâté, wine, bread, and chocolate. For a budget-friendly **picnic,** get fresh produce at a *marché* (outdoor market) and then hop between specialty shops. Start with a *boulangerie* (bakery) for bread, proceed to a *charcuterie* (butcher) for meats, and then *pâtisseries* (pastry shops) and *confiseries* (candy shops) to satisfy a sweet tooth. When choosing a cafe, remember that major boulevards provide more expensive venues than smaller places on side streets. Prices are also cheaper at the *comptoir* (counter) than in the *salle* (seating area). For **supermarket** shopping, look for the chains **Carrefour, Casino,** and **Monoprix.**

BEYOND TOURISM

As the most visited nation in the world, France benefits economically from the tourism industry. Yet the country's popularity has adversely affected some French communities and their natural life. Throw off the *touriste* stigma and advocate for immigrant communities, restore a crumbling château, or educate others about the importance of environmental issues while exploring France. For more info on opportunities across Europe, see **Beyond Tourism,** p. 45.

Care France, CAP 19, 13 r. Georges Auric, 75019 Paris (☎01 53 19 89 89; www.carefrance.org). An international organization providing volunteer opportunities, ranging from combating AIDS to promoting education.

Club du Vieux Manoir, Ancienne Abbaye du Moncel, 60700 Pontpoint (☎03 44 72 33 98; cvmclubduvieuxmanoir.free.fr). Year-long and summer work restoring castles and churches. €14 membership and insurance fee; €12.50 per day, plus food and tent.

International Partnership for Service-Learning and Leadership, 815 2nd Ave., Ste. 315, New York, NY 10017, USA (☎212-986-0989; www.ipsl.org). An organization that matches volunteers with host families, provides intensive French classes, and requires 10-15hr. per week of service for a year, semester, or summer. Ages 18-30. Based in Montpellier. Costs range US$7200-US$23,600.

PARIS ☎01

Paris (pah-ree; pop. 2,153,600), a cultural and commercial center for over 2000 years, draws millions of visitors each year, from students who come to study to tourists who snap endless pictures of the Eiffel Tower. The City of Light, Paris is a source of inspiration unrivaled in beauty. Priceless art fills its world-class museums and history is found in its Roman ruins, medieval streets, Renaissance hotels, and 19th-century boulevards. A vibrant political center, Paris blends the spirit of revolution with a reverence for tradition, devoting as much energy to preserving conventions as it does to shattering them.

INTERCITY TRANSPORTATION

Flights: Some budget airlines fly into **Aéroport de Paris Beauvais Tillé (BVA),** 1hr. outside of Paris (p. 183). **Aéroport Roissy-Charles de Gaulle (CDG, Roissy;** ☎3950; www.adp.fr), 23km northeast of Paris, serves most transatlantic flights. 24hr. English-speaking info center. The **RER B** (a Parisian commuter rail line) runs to central Paris from Terminals 1 and 2. (35min.; every 15min. 5am-12:30am; €13). **Aéroport d'Orly (ORY;** ☎01 49 75 15 15), 18km south of Paris, is used by charters and continental flights.

Trains: Paris has 6 major train stations: **Gare d'Austerlitz** (to the Loire Valley, southwestern France, Portugal, and Spain); **Gare de l'Est** (to Austria, eastern France, Czech Republic, southern Germany, Hungary, Luxembourg, and Switzerland); **Gare de Lyon** (to southern and southeastern France, Greece, Italy, and Switzerland); **Gare du Nord** (to Belgium, Britain, Eastern Europe, northern France, northern Germany, the Netherlands, and Scandinavia); **Gare Montparnasse** (to Brittany and southwestern France on the TGV); **Gare St-Lazare** (to). All are accessible by Métro.

Buses: Gare Routière Internationale du Paris-Gallieni, 28 av. du Général de Gaulle, outside Paris. ⓂGallieni. Eurolines (☎08 92 89 90 91, €0.34 per min.; www.eurolines.fr) sells tickets to most destinations in France and bordering countries.

ORIENTATION

The **Seine River** (SEHN) flows from east to west through Paris with two islands, **Île de la Cité** and **Île St-Louis,** situated in the city's geographical center. The Seine splits Paris in half: the **Rive Gauche** (REEV go-sh; Left Bank) to the south and the **Rive Droite** (REEV dwaht; Right Bank) to the north. Modern Paris is divided into 20 *arrondissements* (districts) that spiral clockwise outward from the center of the city. Each *arrondissement* is referred to by its number (e.g. the Third, the Sixteenth). Sometimes it is helpful to orient yourself around central Paris's major monuments: on Rive Gauche, the sprawling **Jardin du Luxembourg** lies in the southeast; the **Eiffel Tower,** visible from many points in the city, stands in the southwest; moving clockwise and crossing the Seine to Rive Droite, the **Champs-Élysées** and **Arc de Triomphe** occupy the northwest, and the **Sacré-Coeur** stands high in the northeast. *Let's Go Western Europe* splits Paris into five sections according to geographical grouping of *arrondissements*: the **city center** (1*er*, 2*ème*, 3*ème*, and 4*ème*); **Left Bank East** (5*ème*, 6*ème*, and 13*ème*); **Left Bank West** (7*ème*, 14*ème*, and 15*ème*); **Right Bank East** (10*ème*, 11*ème*, 12*ème*, 18*ème*, 19*ème*, and 20*ème*); **Right Bank West** (8*ème*, 9*ème*, 16*ème*, and 17*ème*).

LOCAL TRANSPORTATION

Public Transportation: The **Métro** (Ⓜ) runs from 5:30am-1:20am. Lines are numbered and are referred to by their number and final destinations; connections are called *correspondances*. Single-fare tickets within the city cost €1.60; *carnet* of 10 €11.40. Buy extras for when ticket booths are closed (after 10pm) and hold onto your ticket until you exit. The **RER** (Réseau Express Régional), the commuter train to the suburbs, serves as an express subway within central Paris. Keep your ticket: changing to and getting off the RER requires sticking your validated ticket into a turnstile. Watch the signboards next to the RER tracks and check that your stop is lit up before riding. Buses use the same €1.40 tickets (validate in the machine by the driver). Buses run 7am-8:30pm, **Autobus de Nuit** until 1:30am, and **Noctambus** 1 per hr. 12:30am-5:30am at stops marked with a blue "N" inside a white circle, with a red star on the upper right-hand side. The **Mobilis pass** covers the Métro, RER, and buses (€5.80 for a 1-day pass in Zones 1 and 2). A **Carte Orange weekly pass** *(carte orange hebdomadaire)* costs €16.80 and expires on Su; photo required. Refer to the front of the book for maps of Paris's transit network.

CONSTANT VIGILANCE. The following stations can be dangerous at night: Anvers, Barbès-Rochechouart, Château d'Eau, Châtelet, Châtelet-Les-Halles, Gare de l'Est, Gare du Nord, and Pigalle. If concerned, take a taxi, or sit near the driver on a Noctilien bus.

Taxis: Alpha Taxis (☎01 53 60 63 50). **Taxi 75** (☎01 78 41 65 05). Taxis take 3 passengers (4th passenger €2-3 surcharge). **Tarif A,** daily 7am-7pm (€0.86 per km). **Tarif B,** M-Sa 7pm-7am, Su 24hr., and from the airports and immediate suburbs (€1.12 per km). **Tarif C,** from the airports 7pm-7am (€1.35 per km). In addition, there is a €2.20 base fee and min. €5.60 charge. It is customary to tip 15% and polite to add €1 extra.

Bike Rental: Vélib (www.en.velib.paris.fr). Self-service bike rental. Over 1450 terminals and 20,000 bikes in Paris. Buy a subscription (day €1, week €5, year €29) and rent bikes from any terminal in the city. Rentals under 30min. free. Available 24hr.

PRACTICAL INFORMATION

Tourist Offices: Bureau Gare d'Austerlitz, 13ème (☎01 45 84 91 70). ⓂGare d'Austerlitz. Open M-Sa 8am-6pm.**Bureau Gare de Lyon,** 12ème (☎01 43 43 33 24). ⓂGare de Lyon. Open M-Sa 8am-6pm. **Bureau Tour Eiffel,** Champs de Mars, 7ème (☎08 92 68 31 12). ⓂChamps de Mars. Open daily May-Sept. 11am-6:40pm. **Montmartre Tourist Office,** 21 pl. du Tertre, 18ème (☎01 42 62 21 21). ⓂAnvers. Open daily 10am-7pm.

Currency Exchange: American Express, 11 rue Scribe, 9ème (☎01 53 30 99 00; parisscribe.france@kanoofes.com). ⓂOpéra or RER Auber. Exchange counters open M-Sa 9am-6:30pm; member services open M-F 9am-5pm, Sa 9am-noon and 1-5pm. **Thomas Cook,** 26 av. de l'Opéra, 1er (☎01 53 29 40 00; fax 47 03 32 13). ⓂGeorges V. Open M-Sa 9am-10:55pm, Su 8am-6pm.

GLBT Resources: SOS Homophobie, 63 rue Beaubourg, 3ème (☎01 48 06 42 41). Open M-F 8-10pm.

Laundromats: Ask at your hostel or hotel for the closest laundry facilities. **Multiservices,** 75 rue de l'Ouest, 14ème (☎01 43 35 19 51). Wash €3.50, dry €2 per 20min. Open M-Sa 8:30am-8pm. **Laverie Net A Sec,** 3 pl. Monge, 5ème. Wash €4 per 6kg, dry €1 per 9min. Soap €1. Open daily 7:30am-10pm.

Crisis Lines: Poison: ☎01 40 05 48 48. In French, but some English assistance is available. **SOS Help!** (☎01 46 21 46 46). An anonymous, confidential hotline for English speakers in crisis. Open daily (including holidays) 3-11pm. **Rape: SOS Viol** (☎08 00 05 95 95). Open M-F 10am-7pm.

Pharmacies: British and American Pharmacy, 1 rue Auber, pl. de l'Opéra, 9ème (☎01 42 65 88 29). ⓂOpéra or RER Auber. Sells hard-to-find Anglophone brands in addition to French products. English-speaking staff. Open daily 8am-8:30pm. **Pharmacie Beaubourg,** 50 rue Rambuteau, 3ème (☎01 48 87 86 37). ⓂRambuteau. Open M-Sa 8am-8pm, Su 10am-8pm. **Pharmacie des Halles,** 10 bd. de Sébastopol, 1er (☎01 42 72 03 23). ⓂChâtelet-Les Halles. Open M-Sa 9am-midnight, Su 9am-10pm. **Pharmacie Gacha,** 361 rue des Pyrénées, 20ème (☎01 46 36 59 10). ⓂPyrénées or Jourdain. Open M-F 9am-8pm, Sa 9am-7pm.

Medical Services: American Hospital of Paris, 63 bd. Victor Hugo, Neuilly (☎01 46 41 25 25). ⓂPort Maillot, then bus #82 to the end of the line. **Centre Médicale Europe,** 44 rue d'Amsterdam, 9ème (☎01 42 81 93 33). ⓂSt-Lazare. Open M-F 8am-7pm, Sa 8am-6pm. **Hôpital Bichat,** 46 rue Henri Buchard, 18ème (☎01 40 25 80 80). ⓂPort St-Ouen. Emergencies. **SOS Dentaire,** 87 bd. Port-Royal, 13ème (☎01 40 21 82 88). RER Port-Royal. No walk-ins. Open daily 9am-6pm and 8:30-11:45pm. **SOS Médecins** (☎01 48 07 77 77). Makes house calls. **SOS Oeil** (☎01 40 92 93 94). Eye care. Open daily 6am-11pm.

Internet Access: Cyber Cube, 5 rue Mignon, 6ème (☎01 53 10 30 50). ⓂSt-Michel or Odéon. €0.15 per min., €30 per 5hr., €40 per 10hr. Open M-Sa 10am-10pm. **easyInternetcafé,** 6 rue de la Harpe, 5ème (☎01 55 42 55 42). ⓂSt-Michel. €3 per hr. Open M-Sa 7:30am-8pm, Su 9am-8pm.

Post Office: There are post offices in each arrondissement. Most open M-F 8am-7pm, Sa 8am-noon. **Federal Express** (☎08 20 12 38 00). Call for pickup or dropoff at 63 bd. Haussmann, 8ème. ⓂHavre-Caumartin. Open M-F 9am-7:30pm, Sa 9am-5:30pm.

ACCOMMODATIONS

Accommodations in Paris are expensive. You don't need *Let's Go* to tell you that. Expect to pay at least €20 for a hostel dorm-style bed and €28 for a hotel single. Hostels are a better option for single travelers, whereas staying in a hotel is more economical for groups. Paris's hostels skip many standard restrictions (e.g., curfews) and tend to have flexible maximum stays. Rooms fill quickly after morning check-out; arrive early or reserve ahead. Most hostels and *foyers* include the *taxe de séjour* (€0.10-2 per person per day) in listed prices.

CITY CENTER

Centre International de Paris (BVJ) Louvre, 20 rue Jean-Jacques Rousseau (☎01 53 00 90 90; www.auberges-de-jeunesse.com). ⓂLouvre or Palais-Royal. 3-building hostel with glass-enclosed courtyard. Bright, spacious, unadorned rooms with 4-9 beds are single-sex, except for groups. Breakfast and

WASTE NOT, WANT NOT

While contemporary French cuisine is renowned for its sophistication, the roots of French cooking can be found in some not-so-sophisticated parts of nature's most delicious creatures.

1. Pied de Porc (pig's feet): usually chopped, seasoned, and delicately fried.

2. Tête de Veau (calf's head): rolled up, sliced, and served to the applause of French diners everywhere. A national favorite.

3. L'Os à moelle (bone marrow): served on its own with salt, parsley, and eaten with a spoon.

4. Boudin (blood sausage): mentioned as far back as Homer's *Odyssey*. Now you too, sitting "beside a great fire," can "fill a sausage with fat and blood and turn it this way and that."

5. Foie Gras ("fatty" goose liver): some American cities have banned the sale of *foie gras* but the French hold fast to tradition.

6. Whole Fish: the best meat on any fish is behind the eye. So when the whole thing arrives on a plate, carpe diem!

7. Tripe (stomach): it's pretty meta–your intestines are digesting intestines.

8. Tail: can be eaten on its own, in a stew, or you name it.

9. Groin: in French, pigs say "groin," not "oink." So when you order this, you're also imitating it.

10. Filet (muscle): who knew?

linens included. Towels €3.50. Lockers €2. Internet €1 per 10min. Reception 24hr. Beds can be reserved in advance for a max. of 3 nights; extend your reservation once there. Rooms held for only 5-10min. after stated arrival time; call if you'll be late. Under 36 only. No alcohol. Dorms €29; doubles €62. Cash only. ❷

Hotel Picard, 26 rue de Picardie (☎01 48 87 53 82; hotel.picard@wanadoo.fr). ⓂRépublique. Welcoming, family-run hotel with superb location. Lovely rooms come in many permutations–blue, pink, with exterior window, with rooftop views–so ask ahead to see what's available. Rooms with showers also come with TV. Breakfast €5. Hall showers €3. Reserve 2 weeks ahead. Singles €44, with shower €65, with full bath €75; doubles €53/83/94; triples with full bath €114. 5% discount with *Let's Go*. MC/V. ❸

Grand Hôtel Jeanne d'Arc, 3 rue de Jarente (☎01 48 87 62 11; www.hoteljeannedarc.com). ⓂSt-Paul. More like an elegant homestyle inn than a budget hotel. Cozy, stylish carpeted rooms with cable TV, toilets, and baths or showers. Stylish common room, loaded with travel guides and other books to borrow. Breakfast €7. Free internet and Wi-Fi. Wheelchair-accessible room. Reserve 2-3 months in advance, earlier for Sept.-Oct. Singles €60-84; doubles €84-97; triples €116; quads €146. MC/V. ❺

Hôtel des Jeunes (**MIJE;** ☎01 42 74 23 45; www.mije.com). 3 distinct hostels (below) in beautiful old Marais *hôtels particuliers* (mansions). Reception at all 3 locations; main welcome desk at Le Fourcy. Especially popular with school groups. Arranges airport pickup and drop-off and reservations for sights, restaurants, and shows. Restaurant in a vaulted cellar in Le Fourcy. Public phones. Breakfast and in-room shower included. Lockers free with €1 deposit. Linens included. Internet €1 per 10 min. 1-week max. stay. Reception 7am-1am. Reservations only held until noon; if you're arriving later, call ahead to confirm. Lockout noon-3pm. Quiet hours after 10pm. Reserve months ahead online and 2-3 weeks ahead by phone. No alcohol. 4- to 9-bed dorms €30-32; singles €49; doubles €72; triples €90. MIJE membership required (€2.50). Cash only. ❷

Maubuisson, 12 rue des Barres. ⓂHôtel de Ville or Pont Marie. Half-timbered former convent on a silent street by a monastery. Accommodates more individual travelers than groups.

Le Fourcy, 6 rue de Fourcy. ⓂSt-Paul or Pont Marie. Large courtyard ideal for meeting travelers.

Le Fauconnier, 11 rue du Fauconnier. ⓂSt-Paul or Pont Marie. Ivy-covered, sun-drenched building steps away from the Seine and Île St-Louis.

LEFT BANK EAST

Port-Royal Hôtel, 8 blvd de Port-Royal (☎01 43 31 70 06; www.hotelportroyal.fr). ⓂLes Gobelins. Bright, spacious rooms, a beautiful garden courtyard, 2 comfortable sitting rooms, and a location just steps from the metro more than compensate for this elegant hotel's distance from the Latin Quarter's major sights. Hall showers €2.50. Breakfast €5.50. Wheelchair-accessible. Reserve well in advance. Singles with sink €41-53; doubles with sink €53, with full bath €79; triples with full bath €84-89. Cash only. ❹

Hôtel Marignan, 13 rue du Sommerard (☎01 43 54 63 81; www.hotel-marignan.com). ⓂMaubert-Mutualité. Hostel friendliness with hotel privacy. Clean, freshly decorated rooms with (nonfunctioning) fireplaces and classic wood moulding. Breakfast included. Kitchen for guest use, self-service laundry, and Wi-Fi. Singles €47-52, with toilet €55-60, with full bath €75; doubles €60-68/69-80/80-95; triples €80-90/90-105/105-115; quads with toilet €105-115, with full bath €120-153; quints with toilet €120-125, with full bath €145-155. AmEx/MC/V. ❹

Hôtel de Nesle, 7 rue du Nesle (☎01 43 54 62 41; www.hoteldenesleparis.com). ⓂOdéon. Every room in this wonderfully quirky hotel represents a particular figure (e.g., Molière) or locale (e.g., Africa). Some rooms with full bath; North African room with Turkish *hammam*. Adorable lobby with ceiling made of dried flowers (you'll understand when you see it). Garden with duck pond. Reserve by phone; confirm 2 days in advance with arrival time. Singles €55-85; doubles €75-100. Extra beds €15. MC/V. ❹

Centres Internationaux du Séjour de Paris: CISP "Kellermann", 17 bd. Kellermann (☎01 44 16 37 38; www.cisp.fr). ⓂPorte d'Italie. 363-bed hostel looks like a retro spaceship on stilts. Cafeteria (buffet €11), laundry service, and TV lounge. Breakfast included. Free Wi-Fi and parking. Reception 24hr. Check-in noon. Check-out 9:30am. Reserve 1 month ahead. 8-bed dorms €20; 2- to 4-bed €26. Singles with full bath €39; doubles with full bath €56. MC/V. ❶

LEFT BANK WEST

Hôtel de Blois, 5 rue des Plantes (☎01 45 40 99 48; www.hoteldeblois.com). ⓂMouton-Duvernet, Alésia, or Gaîté. Flowers adorn rooms with clean bathrooms, lush carpets, hair dryers, phones, and TVs. Welcoming owner keeps scrapbook of previous guests' thank-you notes. 5 floors; no elevator. Breakfast €6.50. Wi-Fi €5 per hr., €26 per day. Reception 7am-10:30pm. Check-in 3pm. Check-out 11am. Reserve ahead. Singles and doubles with shower and toilet €55-70, with bathtub €75-85. AmEx/MC/V. ❹

FIAP Jean-Monnet, 30 rue Cabanis (☎01 43 13 17 00, reservations 43 13 17 17; www.fiap.asso.fr). ⓂGlacière. Like a standard college dorm. 500-bed student center. Spotless rooms with bath and phones. 2 restaurants, outdoor terrace, and *discothèque* every W and F night. Breakfast included. Internet €5 per hr. Wheelchair-accessible. Reception 24hr. Check-out 9am. Curfew 2am. Reserve 2-4 weeks ahead; hostel often booked for summer before June. Be sure to specify if you want a dorm bed. 3- to 4-bed dorms €32; 5- to 6-bed €25. Singles €55; doubles €70. MC/V. ❷

Aloha Hostel, 1 rue Borromée (☎01 42 73 03 03; www.aloha.fr). ⓂVolontaires. Frequented by international crowd. Varnished doors and cheery checkered sheets. Free city tour daily 10am. Breakfast included. Linen €3, deposit €7. Towels €3/6. Internet €2 per 30min.; free Wi-Fi. Reception 24hr. Lockout 11am-5pm. Curfew 2am. Reserve 1 week ahead. Apr.-Oct. dorms €23; doubles €50. Nov.-Mar. €4 less. Cash only. ❷

Three Ducks Hostel, 6 pl. Étienne Pernet (☎01 48 42 04 05; www.3ducks.fr). ⓂFélix Faure. Courtyard palm trees, beach-style shower sheds, airy rooms, and bar. Small 4- to 12-bed dorm rooms and a modest kitchen. Breakfast included. Linen €3.50. Towels €1. Internet €2 per 3hr. Reception 24hr. Lockout noon-4pm. Reserve online 1 week ahead, earlier for doubles. In summer 4- to 12-bed dorms €19; 3-bed €21; doubles €46. In winter 4 to 12-bed dorms €23; 3-bed €25; doubles €52. MC/V. ❶

RIGHT BANK WEST

Perfect Hôtel, 39 rue Rodier (☎01 42 81 18 86 or 42 81 26 19; www.paris-hostel.biz). ⓂAnvers. Lives up to its name. Rooms with balcony by request. Caring staff. Well-stocked kitchen, free coffee, and a beer vending machine (€1.50). Be careful in neighborhood after dark. Breakfast included. Reception 24hr. Reserve 1 month ahead. Singles €44, with toilet €60; doubles €50/60. Extra bed €19. Cash only. ❸

Hôtel Champerret Héliopolis, 13 rue d'Héliopolis (☎01 47 64 92 56; www.champerret-heliopolis-paris-hotel.com). ⓂPorte de Champerret. Superb staff. 22 brilliant rooms, each with hair dryer, phone, shower, and TV; several with little balconies opening onto a terrace. Breakfast €9.50. Free Wi-Fi. Wheelchair-accessible. Reception 24hr. Reserve 2 weeks ahead via email, fax, or phone. Singles €77; doubles €90, with bath €96; triples with bath €108. Check website for discounts of up to 15%. AmEx/MC/V. ❺

Woodstock Hostel, 48 rue Rodier (☎01 48 78 87 76; www.woodstock.fr). ⓂAnvers. Beatles-decorated VW Bug adorns the lobby wall. Communal kitchen and hostel (but definitely not hostile) cat. Breakfast included. Linen €2.50; €2.50 deposit. Internet and Wi-Fi €2 per 30min. 2-week max. stay. Lockout 11am-3pm. Curfew 2am. Reserve ahead. High-season 4- or 6-bed dorms €22; doubles €50. Low-season 4- or 6-bed dorms €19; doubles €22. Cash only. ❷

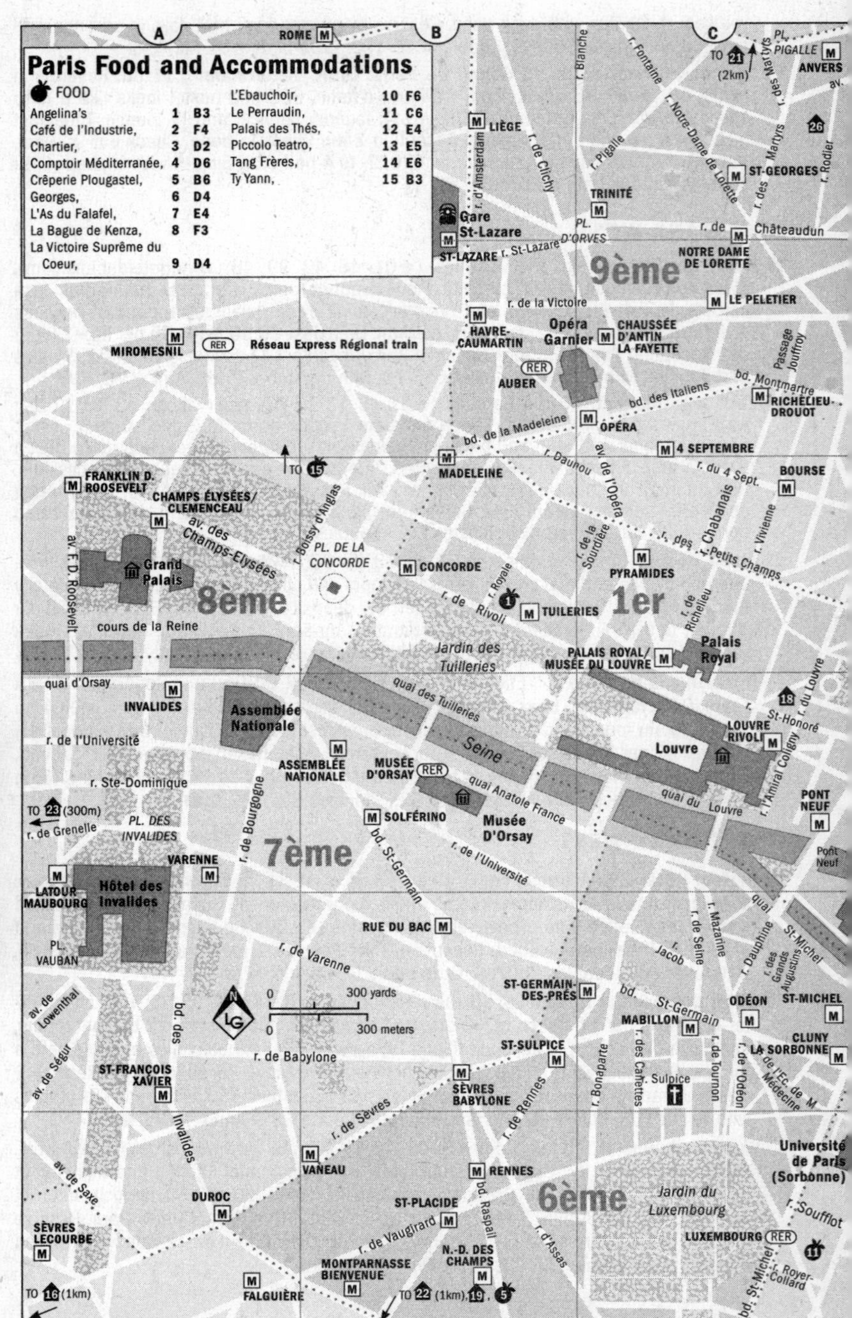
Paris Food and Accommodations
FOOD
Angelina's, 1 B3
Café de l'Industrie, 2 F4
Chartier, 3 D2
Comptoir Méditerranée, 4 D6
Crêperie Plougastel, 5 B6
Georges, 6 D4
L'As du Falafel, 7 E4
La Bague de Kenza, 8 F3
La Victoire Suprême du Coeur, 9 D4
L'Ebauchoir, 10 F6
Le Perraudin, 11 C6
Palais des Thés, 12 E4
Piccolo Teatro, 13 E5
Tang Frères, 14 E6
Ty Yann, 15 B3
RER Réseau Express Régional train
8ème
9ème
1er
7ème
6ème
Gare St-Lazare
Opéra Garnier
Grand Palais
PL. DE LA CONCORDE
Jardin des Tuilleries
Palais Royal
Louvre
Assemblée Nationale
Musée D'Orsay
Hôtel des Invalides
Seine
Jardin du Luxembourg
Université de Paris (Sorbonne)
St. Sulpice
ROME
LIÈGE
TRINITÉ
ST-GEORGES
ANVERS
PIGALLE
ST-LAZARE
NOTRE DAME DE LORETTE
LE PELETIER
HAVRE-CAUMARTIN
CHAUSSÉE D'ANTIN LA FAYETTE
AUBER
MIROMESNIL
RICHELIEU-DROUOT
OPÉRA
4 SEPTEMBRE
MADELEINE
BOURSE
FRANKLIN D. ROOSEVELT
CHAMPS ÉLYSÉES/ CLEMENCEAU
CONCORDE
PYRAMIDES
TUILERIES
PALAIS ROYAL/ MUSÉE DU LOUVRE
LOUVRE RIVOLI
INVALIDES
ASSEMBLÉE NATIONALE
MUSÉE D'ORSAY
SOLFÉRINO
PONT NEUF
VARENNE
LATOUR MAUBOURG
RUE DU BAC
ST-GERMAIN-DES-PRÉS
ODÉON
ST-MICHEL
MABILLON
CLUNY LA SORBONNE
ST-SULPICE
SÈVRES BABYLONE
ST-FRANÇOIS XAVIER
VANEAU
RENNES
DUROC
ST-PLACIDE
LUXEMBOURG
SÈVRES LECOURBE
N.-D. DES CHAMPS
MONTPARNASSE BIENVENUE
FALGUIÈRE
TO 21 (2km)
TO 15
TO 23 (300m)
TO 16 (1km)
TO 22 (1km), 19
r. Blanche
r. Fontaine
r. Notre-Dame de Lorette
r. des Martyrs
r. Rodier
r. d'Amsterdam
r. de Clichy
r. Pigalle
r. de Châteaudun
PL. D'ORVES
r. St-Lazare
r. de la Victoire
Passage Jouffroy
bd. Montmartre
bd. des Italiens
bd. de la Madeleine
r. Daunou
av. de l'Opéra
r. du 4 Sept.
r. Chabanais
r. Vivienne
r. des Petits Champs
r. de la Sourdière
r. Boissy d'Anglas
av. des Champs-Elysées
av. F. D. Roosevelt
cours de la Reine
r. Royale
r. de Rivoli
r. de Richelieu
r. St-Honoré
r. du Louvre
quai d'Orsay
quai des Tuilleries
quai Anatole France
quai du Louvre
r. de l'Amiral Colligny
r. de l'Université
r. Ste-Dominique
r. de Grenelle
PL. DES INVALIDES
r. de Bourgogne
bd. St-Germain
Pont Neuf
quai St-Michel
PL. VAUBAN
r. de Varenne
r. Mazarine
r. de Seine
r. Jacob
r. Dauphine
r. des Grands Augustins
av. de Lowenthal
bd. des Invalides
300 yards
300 meters
r. de Babylone
av. de Ségur
r. des Canettes
r. de Tournon
r. de l'Odéon
r. de l'Ec. de Médecine
r. Bonaparte
r. de Rennes
r. de Sèvres
av. de Saxe
bd. Raspail
r. de Vaugirard
r. d'Assas
r. Soufflot
r. Royer-Collard
bd. St-Michel

FRANCE

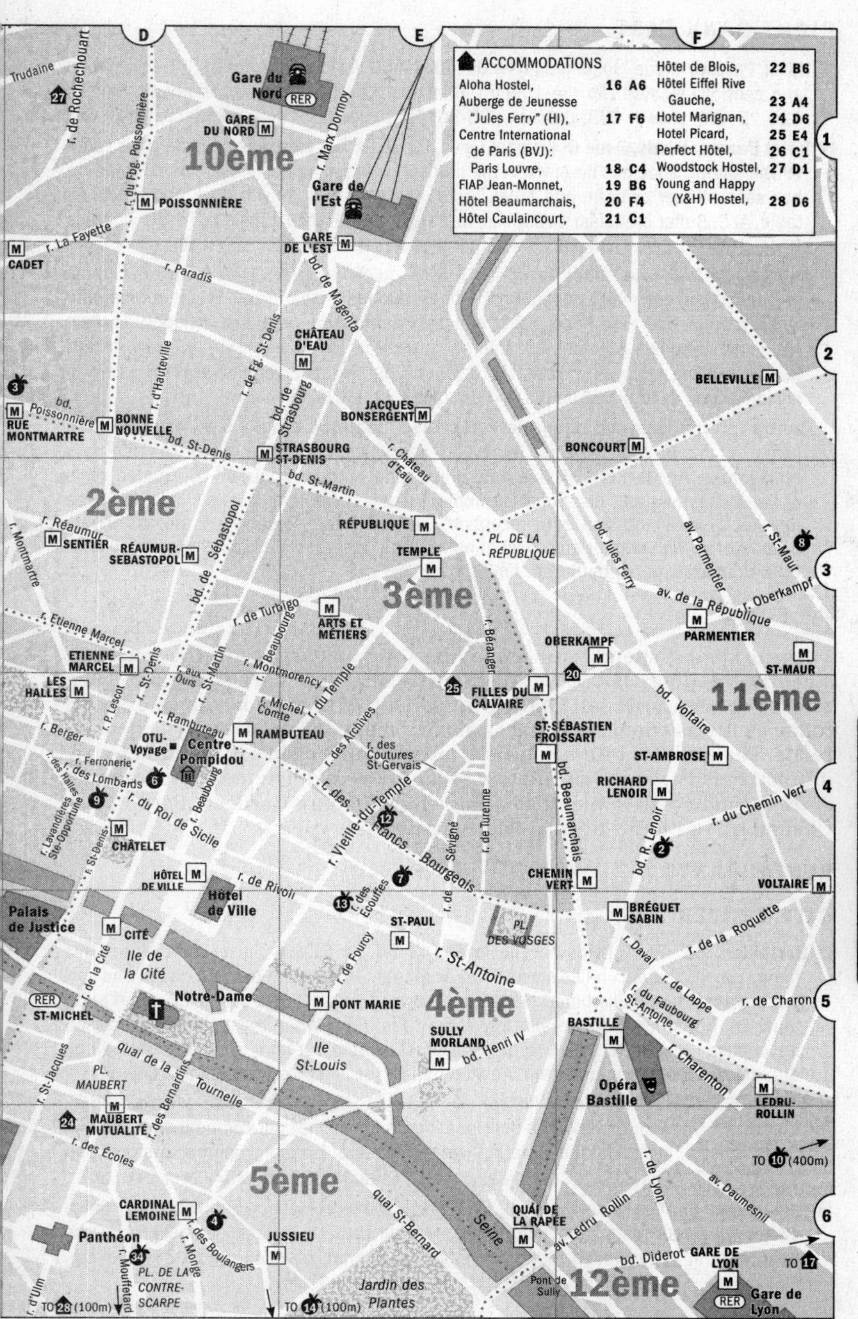
ACCOMMODATIONS
Aloha Hostel, 16 A6
Auberge de Jeunesse "Jules Ferry" (HI), 17 F6
Centre International de Paris (BVJ): Paris Louvre, 18 C4
FIAP Jean-Monnet, 19 B6
Hôtel Beaumarchais, 20 F4
Hôtel Caulaincourt, 21 C1
Hôtel de Blois, 22 B6
Hôtel Eiffel Rive Gauche, 23 A4
Hotel Marignan, 24 D6
Hotel Picard, 25 E4
Perfect Hôtel, 26 C1
Woodstock Hostel, 27 D1
Young and Happy (Y&H) Hostel, 28 D6
D
E
F
1
2
3
4
5
6
10ème
2ème
3ème
11ème
4ème
5ème
12ème
Gare du Nord
RER
GARE DU NORD
Gare de l'Est
GARE DE L'EST
Trudaine
r. de Rochechouart
r. du Fbg. Poissonnière
r. Marx Dormoy
POISSONNIÈRE
r. La Fayette
CADET
r. Paradis
bd. de Magenta
CHÂTEAU D'EAU
r. de Fg. St-Denis
r. d'Hauteville
bd. de Strasbourg
JACQUES BONSERGENT
BELLEVILLE
bd. Poissonnière
RUE MONTMARTRE
BONNE NOUVELLE
bd. St-Denis
STRASBOURG ST-DENIS
r. Château d'Eau
BONCOURT
bd. St-Martin
RÉPUBLIQUE
PL. DE LA RÉPUBLIQUE
r. Réaumur
SENTIER
RÉAUMUR-SEBASTOPOL
bd. de Sébastopol
TEMPLE
bd. Jules Ferry
av. Parmentier
r. St-Maur
r. Montmartre
av. de la République
r. Oberkampf
r. de Turbigo
ARTS ET MÉTIERS
r. Etienne Marcel
r. Beaubourg
r. Béranger
PARMENTIER
ETIENNE MARCEL
OBERKAMPF
ST-MAUR
r. Montmorency
r. St-Denis
r. aux Ours
r. St-Martin
r. du Temple
FILLES DU CALVAIRE
bd. Voltaire
LES HALLES
r. Michel Comte
r. Rambuteau
r. P. Lescot
RAMBUTEAU
r. des Archives
ST-SÉBASTIEN FROISSART
r. Berger
OTU-Voyage
Centre Pompidou
r. des Coutures St-Gervais
ST-AMBROSE
r. Ferronerie
r. des Lombards
r. des Halles
bd. Beaumarchais
RICHARD LENOIR
r. Vieille-du-Temple
r. du Roi de Sicile
r. des Francs Bourgeois
r. de Turenne
r. de Sévigné
r. du Chemin Vert
r. Lavandières Ste-Opportune
CHÂTELET
bd. R. Lenoir
HÔTEL DE VILLE
r. de Rivoli
CHEMIN VERT
VOLTAIRE
Hôtel de Ville
r. des Ecouffes
Palais de Justice
CITÉ
ST-PAUL
PL. DES VOSGES
BRÉGUET SABIN
r. de la Roquette
r. Daval
Ile de la Cité
r. de la Cité
r. de Fourcy
r. St-Antoine
r. de Lappe
r. de Charonne
RER
ST-MICHEL
Notre-Dame
PONT MARIE
r. du Faubourg St-Antoine
BASTILLE
SULLY MORLAND
bd. Henri IV
Ile St-Louis
r. Charenton
quai de la Tournelle
r. St-Jacques
PL. MAUBERT
Opéra Bastille
LEDRU-ROLLIN
MAUBERT MUTUALITÉ
r. des Bernardins
r. des Écoles
TO 10 (400m)
r. de Lyon
av. Daumesnil
quai St-Bernard
Seine
av. Ledru Rollin
CARDINAL LEMOINE
QUAI DE LA RAPÉE
Panthéon
r. des Boulangers
r. Monge
JUSSIEU
bd. Diderot
GARE DE LYON
PL. DE LA CONTRE-SCARPE
r. Mouffetard
r. d'Ulm
TO 28 (100m)
TO 14 (100m)
Jardin des Plantes
Pont de Sully
Gare de Lyon
TO 17

RIGHT BANK EAST

Hôtel Palace, 9 rue Bouchardon (☎01 40 40 09 45). ⓂStrasbourg-St-Denis. Clean and centrally located (for the 10ème). Breakfast €4. Reserve 2 weeks ahead. Singles €20-25, with shower €33; doubles €28-30/40; triples €55; quads €65-75. MC/V. ❶

Hôtel Beaumarchais, 3 rue Oberkampf (☎01 53 36 86 86; www.hotelbeaumarchais.com). ⓂOberkampf. Spacious hotel worth the money. Eye-popping decor. Each carpeted room has safe, shower or bath, and toilet. Suites include TV room with desk and breakfast table. A/C. Buffet breakfast €10. Reserve 2 weeks in advance. Singles €75-90; doubles €110-130; 2-person suites €150-170; triples €170-190. AmEx/MC/V. ❺

Auberge de Jeunesse "Jules Ferry" (HI), 8 bd. Jules Ferry (☎01 43 57 55 60; paris.julesferry@fuaj.org). ⓂRépublique. 99 beds. Modern, clean, and bright rooms with sinks, mirrors, and tiled floors. Party atmosphere. Kitchen. Breakfast included. Lockers €2. Linen included. Laundry €3. Internet access in lobby. 1-week max. stay. Reception and dining room 24hr. Lockout 10:30am-2pm. No reservations; arrive 8-11am to secure a bed. 4- to 6-bed dorms and doubles €22. MC/V. ❷

Centre International du Séjour de Paris: CISP "Maurice Ravel", 6 av. Maurice Ravel (☎01 43 58 96 00; www.cisp.fr). ⓂPorte de Vincennes. Large, clean rooms. Lively atmosphere. Art displays, sizable auditorium, and outdoor pool (€3-4). Guided tours of Paris. Cafeteria and restaurant available. Breakfast, linen, and towels included. Free Internet. 1-week max. stay. 24hr. reception. Curfew 1:30am. Reserve 1-2 months ahead. 8-bed dorms with shower and toilet in hall €20; 2- to 4-bed €26. Singles with full bath €39; doubles with full bath €56. AmEx/MC/V. ❶

FOOD

When in doubt, spend your money on food in Paris. Skip the museum, sleep in the dingy hotel, but **eat well.** Paris's culinary scene has been famous for centuries, and eating in the City of Light remains as exciting today as it was when Sun King Louis XIV made feasts an everyday occurrence. The city also offers delicious international dishes in addition to traditional cuisine. As an alternative to a pricey sit-down meal, stop into an *épicerie* and create a picnic lunch for Luxembourg Gardens, Parc Buttes Chaumont, or on the steps at Sacré-Coeur. *Bon appetit!*

RESTAURANTS

CITY CENTER

Berthillon, 31 rue St-Louis en l'Île (☎01 43 54 31 61). ⓂCité or Pont Marie. This family-run institution, on l'Île since 1954, is reputed to have the best ice cream and sorbet in Paris. Flavors like blood orange and honey nougat. Single scoop €2, double €3, triple €4. Open from Sept. to mid-July W-Su 10am-8pm. When the main store is closed in summer, get your Berthilion fix at the counter located out front of the touristy Taverne du Sergeant Recruteur just down the street at 41 rue St-Louis en l'Île. Cash only. ❶

Bistrot Victoires, 6 rue de la Vrilliére (☎01 42 61 43 78). ⓂBourse or Palais Royal. Classic Art Nouveau bistro offers delicious fare at prices that put competition to shame. Giant salads, including the amazing *salade océane* (salmon, shirmp, oysters, and squid), €8-9. *Plats* €10-11. Open daily noon-3pm and 7-11pm. MC/V over €10. ❷

404, 69 rue des Gravilliers (☎01 42 74 57 81). ⓂArts et Métiers. Sophisticated family-owned Maghrebi restaurant. Enjoy your meal on the airy terrace out back or in the beautifully lit stone-walled dining room. Mouthwatering couscous (€15-24) and *tag-*

ines (€15-19). Several vegetarian options. Open M-F noon-2:30pm and 8pm-midnight, Sa-Su noon-4pm and 8pm-midnight. AmEx/MC/V. ❹

Briezh Café, 109 rue Vielle du Temple (☎01 42 74 13 77; www.breizhcafe.com). Ⓜ Filles du Calvaire. Relaxed Breton *crêperie* uses high-quality ingredients (organic veggies, raw milk, *normand* sausage) to make simple, unpretentious, and tremendously delicious buckwheat *crêpes* and *galettes* (€3-11). Open W-Su noon-11pm. AmEx/MC/V. ❷

Chez Janou, 2 rue Roger Verlomme (☎01 42 72 28 41). Ⓜ Chemin-Vert. Classic Provençal bistro. Lively atmosphere. Try the *ratatouille* or the goat cheese and spinach salad (both €9). Chocolate mousse (€9) brought in an enormous self-serve bowl. Over 80 kinds of *pastis.* Packed every night. Open daily noon-midnight. Kitchen open M-F noon-3pm and 8pm-midnight, Sa-Su noon-4pm and 8pm-midnight. Reservations recommended. MC/V. ❷

Chez Hanna, 54 rue des Rosiers (☎01 42 74 74 99). Ⓜ St-Paul or Hôtel de Ville. Less mobbed that its more famous neighbor L'As (see below), local favorite Chez Hanna is proof that long lines do not the better falafel make. Falafel special (€5) served only at the window—eat inside and you'll have to spring for the more expensive falafel platters (€9-12). Open daily 11am-11pm. MC/V, min. €15. ❶

L'As du Falafel, 34 rue des Rosiers (☎01 48 87 63 60). Ⓜ St-Paul or Hôtel de Ville. A very close 2nd to Chez Hanna, this kosher stand serves what (renowned falafel expert?) Lenny Kravitz terms "the best falafel in the world." Come lunchtime, it's got the massive lines and tourist crowd to prove it. Falafel special €5. Lemonade €4. Open M-Th and Su noon-midnight, F noon-7pm. MC/V. ❶

La Victoire Suprême du Coeur, 29-31 rue du Bourg Tibourg (☎01 40 41 95 03; www.vscoeur.com). Ⓜ Hôtel de Ville. Run by the devotees of Indian spiritual leader and high-profile vegetarian Sri Chinmoy. Classics like seitan "steak" with mushroom sauce (€15). M-F vegan lunch buffet €13. 2-course dinner *menu* €19. Open Su-F noon-3pm and 6:30-10:30pm, Sa noon-3pm and 6:30-11pm. Cash only. ❸

LEFT BANK EAST

Comptoir Méditerranée, 42 rue du Cardinal Lemoine (☎01 43 25 29 08; www.savannahcafe.fr). Ⓜ Cardinal Lemoine. Savannah Café's little sister, run by the same welcoming owner. More Lebanese deli than restaurant, serving fresh, colorful dishes. Select from 18 hot or cold options to make your own plate (€6.80-12). Sandwiches €4.40. Tantalizing pastries €1.30. Homemade lemonade €2.50. Open M-Sa 11am-10pm. T

Tang Frères, 48 av. d'Ivry, 13*ème* (☎01 45 70 80 00). Ⓜ Porte d'Ivry. A sensory-overload, this huge shopping center in the heart of Chinatown contains a bakery, *charcuterie,* fish counter, flower shop, and grocery store. Exotic fruits (durian €7.80 per kg), cheap Asian beers (can of Kirin €0.85, 6-pack of Tsingtao €3.72), rice wines (€3.50 per 0.5-liter), and sake (€4.95-6.80). Noodles, rice, soups, spices, teas, and tofu in bulk. Also at 174 rue de Choisy. Ⓜ Place d'Italie. Open Tu-Sa 10am-8:30pm. MC/V. ❶

Le Comptoir du Relais, 5 carrefour de l'Odéon (☎01 44 27 07 97). Ⓜ Odéon. Local-heavy and hyper-crowded. Focuses on pork and other meats. *Pâté* on toast €10-12. Salads €10-22. *Plats* €14-22. Top it off with coffee-infused *crème brûlée* (€7). Open M-F noon-6pm, dinner seating 8:30pm, Sa-Su noon-11pm. Reserve ahead for weekday dinner; reservations not accepted for lunch or weekends. MC/V. ❸

Chez Gladines, 30 rue des 5 Diamants (☎01 45 80 70 10). Ⓜ Place d'Italie. Intimate seating. Southwestern French and Basque specialties (€7.30-12). Well-deserved acclaim draws crowds; to avoid them, come before 7:30pm or after 11pm. Large salads

€6.50-9. Beer €2. Espresso €1. Open M-Tu noon-3pm and 7pm-midnight, W-F noon-3pm and 7pm-1am, Sa-Su noon-4pm and 7pm-midnight. Cash only. ❷

Tang Frères, 48 av. d'Ivry (☎01 45 70 80 00). ⓂPorte d'Ivry. Also at 174 rue de Choisy. ⓂPlace d'Italie. A sensory overload, this huge shopping center in the heart of Chinatown contains a bakery, *charcuterie,* fish counter, flower shop, and grocery store. Exotic fruits (durian €7.80 per kg), cheap Asian beers (can of Kirin €0.85; 6-pack of Tsingtao €3.80), rice wines (€3.50 per 500mL), and sake (€5-6.80). Noodles, rice, soups, spices, teas, and tofu in bulk. Open Tu-Sa 10am-8:30pm. MC/V. ❶

LEFT BANK WEST

Les Cocottes, 135 rue St-Dominique (☎01 45 50 10 31). ⓂÉcole Militaire. A simpler, less expensive version of Christian Constant's popular haute cuisine establishments. Fresh, beautifully presented, and delicious comfort food. Try *cocottes* (cast-iron skillets filled with anything from pig's feet and pigeon to fresh vegetables; €12-16). Don't miss "La Fabuleuse" *tarte au chocolat* (€8). Open M-Th noon-2:30pm and 7-11pm, F-Sa noon-3pm and 7-10:30pm. AmEx/MC/V. ❸

Stéphane Secco, 20 rue Jean-Nicot (☎01 43 17 35 20). ⓂLa Tour-Maubourg. Another location at 25 bd. de Grenelle, 15ème (☎01 45 67 17 40). This delightful, pink-fronted *boulangerie-pâtisserie* is the perfect place to pick up supplies for a picnic on the nearby Seine. Creative quiches and *tartes* (€2-3 for a *petit*), rich desserts (macaroons €1-2), and bread with everything from herbs to apricots (€1-3). Open Tu-Sa 7:30am-8:30pm. Cash only. ❶

Crêperie Plougastel, 47 rue du Montparnasse (☎01 42 79 90 63). ⓂMontparnasse-Bienvenüe. Ambience and prompt staff set this cozy *crêperie* apart. Dessert *crêpes* feature homemade caramel. *Formule* (generous mixed salad and choice of 2 *galettes* and 5 dessert *crêpes*) €15. *Cidre* €2.90. Open daily noon-11:30pm. MC/V. ❸

RIGHT BANK WEST

Ty Yann, 10 rue de Constantinople (☎01 40 08 00 17). ⓂEurope. Breton chef and owner Yann cheerfully prepares outstanding *galettes* (€8-10) and *crêpes.* Decorated with Yann's mother's pastoral paintings. Chew on *La vaniteuse* (€8), with sausage sauteed in cognac, Emmental cheese, and onions. Create your own *crêpe* €6-7. Takeout 15% less. Open M-F noon-3:30pm and 7:30-10:30pm, Sa 7:30-10:30pm. MC/V. ❷

Chez Haynes, 3 rue Clauzel (☎01 48 78 40 63). ⓂSt-Georges. Paris's 1st African-American-owned restaurant opened in 1949. Louis Armstrong, James Baldwin, and Richard Wright enjoyed the delicious New Orleans soul food. Ma Sutton's fried honey chicken €14. Sister Lena's BBQ spare ribs €16. Soul food Tu-Sa, Brazilian Su. Live music F-Sa nights; cover €5. Open Tu-Su 7pm-midnight; hours vary. AmEx/MC/V. ❷

La Fournée d'Augustine, 31 rue des Batignolles (☎01 43 87 88 41). ⓂRome. Lines out the door at lunch. Closet-size *pâtisserie* bakes an absolutely fantastic baguette (€1). Fresh sandwiches (€3-4) range from light fare like goat cheese and cucumber to the more substantial grilled chicken and veggies. *Pain au chocolat* €1.10. Lunch *formule* €5.80-7. Open M-Sa 7:30am-8pm. AmEx/MC/V over €10. ❷

Ladurée, 16 rue Royale (☎01 42 60 21 79; www.laduree.com). ⓂConcorde or FDR. Also at 75 av. des Champs-Élysées, 8ème (☎01 40 75 08 75); 21 rue Bonaparte, 6ème (☎01 44 07 64 87); 62 bd. Haussmann, 9ème (☎01 42 82 40 10). Ever wanted to dine inside a Fabergé egg? Rococo decor attracts a jarring mix of well-groomed shoppers and tourists. Among the 1st Parisian *salons de thé.* Infamous mini macaroons in 16 varieties (€2). Boxes of Chocolats Incomparables from €18. Open M-Sa 8:30am-7pm, Su 10am-7pm. Lunch served until 3pm. AmEx/MC/V. ❸

RIGHT BANK EAST

Le Cambodge, 10 av. Richerand (☎01 44 84 37 70). ⓂRépublique. Inexpensive and delicious Cambodian restaurant. Good vegetarian options. *Plats* €7-10. M-Sa noon-2:30pm and 8-11:30pm. No reservations; wait up to 90min. MC/V. ❷

Marché St-Quentin, 85 bis bd. de Magenta. ⓂGare de l'Est or Gare du Nord. Outside: a huge construction of iron and glass, built in the 1880s, renovated in 1982, and covered by a glass ceiling. Inside: stalls of all varieties of produce, meat, cheese, seafood, and wine. Open Tu-Sa 8am-1pm and 3:30-7:30pm, Su 8am-1pm. ❶

Le Bar à Soupes, 33 rue Charonne (☎01 43 57 53 79; www.lebarasoupes.com). ⓂBastille. Small, bright cafe. Big bowls of delicious, freshly made soup (€5-6). 6 varieties change daily. €9.50 lunch *menu* is an astonishing deal; it comes with soup, a roll, wine or coffee, and cheese plate or dessert. Friendly staff will make your day. Gooey *gâteau chocolat* €4. Open M-Sa noon-3pm and 6:30-11pm. MC/V. ❷

Café de l'Industrie, 15-17 rue St-Sabin (☎01 47 00 13 53). ⓂBreguet-Sabin. Happening cafe. Diverse menu. *Vin chaud* €4.50. Salads €8.50-9. Popular brunch platter (served Sa-Su; changes weekly) €12-15. Open daily 10am-2am. MC/V.

L'Ébauchoir, 45 rue de Citeaux (☎01 43 42 49 31; www.lebauchoir.com). ⓂFaidherbe-Chaligny. Funky, lively French restaurant. Daily changing menu features delicious concoctions of seafood and meat. Vegetarian dishes upon request. Impressive wine list. *Entrées* €8-15. *Plats* €17-25. Desserts €7. Lunch *menu* €15. Open M 8-11pm, Tu-Sa noon-11pm. Kitchen open noon-2:30pm and 8-11pm. MC/V. ❸

Ay, Caramba!, 59 rue de Mouzaïa (☎01 42 41 23 80; http://restaurant-aycaramba.com). ⓂPré-St-Gervais. Bright yellow Tex-Mex restaurant in a drab, residential neighborhood transforms chic Parisian dining into a homegrown fiesta. Patrons salsa to live Latino singers F-Sa nights. Tacos €18. Margaritas €7. *Nachos rancheros* €7. Open Tu-Th 7:30pm-midnight, F-Su noon-3pm and 7:30pm-midnight. AmEx/MC/V. ❸

Refuge Café, 54 av. Daumesnil (☎01 43 47 25 59). ⓂGare de Lyon. Whimsical, ivy-covered cafe-restaurant seems to be out of a fairy tale. Art exhibits every month. Salads €11-15. *Plats* €15-23. *Formules* €14-22. Open M-Sa 8am-midnight. ❸

SAVE YOUR WALLET, HAVE A PICNIC. As a major tourist attraction, Montmartre has inevitably high prices. Save a couple euro by avoiding its touristy cafes, and picnic in Paris. Buy a *croque monsieur* or ham sandwich *à emporter* and eat on the church's steps.

SIGHTS

While it would take weeks to see all of Paris's monuments, museums, and gardens, the city's small size makes sightseeing easy and enjoyable. In a few hours, you can walk from the Bastille in the east to the Eiffel Tower in the west, passing most major monuments along the way. A solid day of wandering will show you how close the medieval Notre Dame is to the modern Centre Pompidou and the funky *Latin Quarter* to the royal Louvre—the diversity of Paris is all the more amazing for the compact area in which it unfolds.

CITY CENTER

In the 3rd century BC, Paris consisted only of the **Île de la Cité,** inhabited by the Parisii, a Gallic tribe of merchants and fishermen. Today, all distance-points in France are measured from *kilomètre zéro*, a sundial in front of Notre Dame. On the far west side of the island is the **Pont Neuf** (New Bridge), actually Paris's oldest bridge—and now the city's most popular make-out spot. *(Ⓜ️Pont Neuf.)* To the east of Île de la Cité is the tiny **Île St-Louis. Rue St-Louis-en-l'Île** rolls down the center, and is a welcome distraction from busy Parisian life. There's a wealth of ice cream parlors, upscale shops, and boutique hotels, but not much to see. *(Ⓜ️Pont Marie.)* On the right bank, the **Marais** is home to some of Paris's best falafel (p. 194), museums, and bars, as well as much of Paris's Orthodox Jewish community. At the end of **rue des Francs-Bourgeois** sits the **place des Vosges,** Paris's oldest public square. Molière, Racine, and Voltaire filled the grand parlors with their *bon mots,* while Mozart played a concert here. Victor Hugo lived at no. 6, which is now a museum devoted to his life. *(Ⓜ️Chemin Vert or St-Paul.)*

CATHÉDRALE DE NOTRE DAME DE PARIS. This 12th- to 14th-century cathedral, begun under Bishop Maurice de Sully, is one of the world's most famous and beautiful examples of medieval architecture. After the Revolution, the building fell into disrepair—it was even used to shelter livestock—until Victor Hugo's 1831 novel *Notre Dame de Paris* (a.k.a. The Hunchback of Notre Dame) inspired citizens to lobby for the cathedral's restoration. The apocalyptic facade and seemingly weightless walls—effects produced by Gothic engineering and optical illusions—are inspiring even for the most church-weary. The cathedral's biggest draws are its enormous stained-glass rose windows that dominate the transept's northern and southern ends. A staircase inside the towers leads to a perch from which gargoyles survey the city. The best time to view the Cathedral is late at night, when you can see the full facade without mobs blocking the view. *(Ⓜ️Cité. ☎01 42 34 56 10, crypt 55 42 50 10, towers 53 10 07 00; www.notredamedeparis.fr. Cathedral open daily M-F 8am-6pm, Sa-Su 8am-7:15pm. Treasury open M-F 9:30am-6pm, Sa 9:30am-6:30pm, Su 1:30-6:30pm. Last entry 15min. before close. Crypt open Tu-Su 10am-6pm. Last entry 5:30pm. Towers open June-Aug. M-F 10am-6:30pm, Sa-Su 10am-11pm; Sept. and Apr.-May daily 10am-6:30pm; Oct.-Mar. daily 10am-5:30pm. Last entry 45min. before closing. Mass M-Sa 8, 9am, noon, 5:45, 6:15pm; Su 8:30, 9:30, 10 (high mass with Gregorian chant), 11:30am (international mass), 12:45, and 6:30pm. Free. Treasury €3, ages 12-25 €2, ages 5-11 €1. Crypt €4, over 60 €3, under 26 €2, under 12 free. Towers €8, ages 18-25 €5, under 18 free. Audio tours €5 with ID deposit; includes visit of treasury. Tours begin at the booth to the right as you enter.)*

STE-CHAPELLE, CONCIERGERIE, AND PALAIS DE JUSTICE. The Palais de la Cité contains three vastly different buildings. **Ste-Chapelle** remains the foremost example of flamboyant Gothic architecture and a tribute to the craft of medieval stained glass. On sunny days, light pours through the **Upper Chapel's** windows, illuminating frescoes of saints and martyrs. Around the corner is the Conciergerie, one of Paris's most famous prisons; Marie-Antoinette and Robespierre were incarcerated here during the Revolution. *(6 bd. du Palais, within Palais de la Cité. Ⓜ️Cité. ☎01 53 40 60 97; www.monum.fr. Open daily Nov.-Feb. 9am-5pm and Mar.-Oct. 9:30am-6pm, last entry 30min. before closing. €8, seniors and ages 18-25 €5, under 18 free. Cash only.)* Built after the great fire of 1776, the **Palais de Justice** houses France's district courts. *(4 bd. du Palais, within the Palais de la Cité. Enter at 6 bd. du Palais. Ⓜ️Cité. ☎01 44 32 51 51. Courtrooms open M-F 9am-noon and 1:30pm-end of last trial. Free.)*

LEFT BANK EAST

The Latin Quarter, named for the prestigious universities that taught in Latin until 1798, lives for its ever-vibrant student population. Since the student riots in May 1968, many artists and intellectuals have migrated to the cheaper outer *arrondissements,* and the haute bourgeoisie have moved in. The 5*ème* still presents the most diverse array of bookstores, cinemas, and jazz clubs in the city. Shops and art galleries are found around **St-Germain-des-Prés** in the 6*ème*.

FRANCE

Farther east, the residential 13*ème* doesn't have much to attract the typical tourist, but its diverse neighborhoods offer an authentic view of Parisian life.

JARDIN DU LUXEMBOURG. Parisian sunbathers flock to these formal gardens. The site of a medieval monastery, and later home to 17th-century French royalty, the gardens were liberated during the Revolution. *(ⓂOdéon or RER: Luxembourg. Entrance at bd. St-Michel. Open daily sunrise-sunset. Guided tours in French depart from pl. André Honorat June every W; July-Oct. and Apr.-May 1st W of each month.)*

ODÉON. The **Cour du Commerce St-André** is one of the most picturesque walking areas in the 6*ème*, with cobblestone streets, centuries-old cafes (including Le Procope), and outdoor seating. Just south of bd. St-Germain, the Carrefour de l'Odéon, a favorite Parisian hangout, has more bistros and cafes. *(ⓂOdéon.)*

ÉGLISE ST-GERMAIN-DES-PRÉS. Paris's oldest standing church, **Église de St-Germain-des-Prés** was the centerpiece of the **Abbey of St-Germain-des-Prés,** the crux of Catholic intellectual life until it was disbanded during the Revolution. Worn away by fire and even a saltpetre explosion, the abbey's exterior looks appropriately world-weary. Its interior frescoes, redone in the 19th century, depict the life of Jesus in striking maroon, green, and gold.*(3 pl. St-Germain-des-Prés. ⓂSt-Germain-des-Prés. ☎01 55 42 81 33; www.eglise-sgp.org. Open daily 8am-7:45pm. Info office open July-Aug. M-F 10am-noon and 2-7pm; Sept.-June M 2:30-6:45pm, Tu-F 10:30am-noon and 2:30-6:45pm, Sa 3-6:45pm.)*

PLACE ST-MICHEL AND ENVIRONS. At the center of the Latin Quarter, bd. St-Michel, which divides the 5*ème* and 6*ème*, is filled with bookstores, boutiques, cafes, and restaurants. Tourists pack pl. St-Michel, where the 1871 Paris Commune and the 1968 student uprising began. You can find many traditional bistros on nearby r. Soufflot, the street connecting the Luxembourg Gardens to the Pantheon, and smaller restaurants on r. des Fossés St-Jacques. *(ⓂSt-Michel.)*

LA SORBONNE. The Sorbonne is one of Europe's oldest universities, founded in 1253 by Robert de Sorbon as a dormitory for 16 theology students. Nearby place de la Sorbonne, off bd. St-Michel, is flooded with cafes, bookstores, and during term-time, students. The **Chapelle de la Sorbonne,** which usually houses temporary exhibits on arts and letters, is undergoing renovations through 2009. *(45-47 r. des Écoles. ⓂCluny-La Sorbonne or RER: Luxembourg.)*

PANTHÉON. Though it looks like a religious monument, the Pantheon, occupying the Left Bank's highest point, celebrates France's great thinkers. The crypt houses the tombs of Marie and Pierre Curie, Victor Hugo, Jean Jaurès, Rousseau, Voltaire, and Émile Zola. On the main level, Foucault's Pendulum confirms the rotation of the earth. *(Pl. du Panthéon. ⓂCardinal Lemoine or RER: Luxembourg. ☎01 44 32 18 04. Open daily Apr.-Sept. 10am-6:30pm, Oct.-Mar. 10am-6pm. Last entry 45min. before closing. Crypt open daily 10am-6pm. €7.50, ages 18-25 €4.80, under 18 and 1st Su of the month Oct.-Mar. free. MC/V. Conservative dress required.)*

LEFT BANK WEST

EIFFEL TOWER. Gustave Eiffel wrote of his tower: "France is the only country in the world with a 300m flagpole." Designed in 1889 as the tallest structure in the world, the Eiffel Tower was conceived as a modern monument to engineering that would surpass the Egyptian pyramids in size and notoriety. Critics dubbed it a "metal asparagus" and a "Parisian tower of Babel." Writer Guy de Maupassant ate lunch every day at its ground-floor restaurant—the only place in Paris, he claimed, from which he couldn't see the offensive thing. Nevertheless, when it was inaugurated in March 1889 as the centerpiece of the World's Fair, the tower earned Parisians' love: nearly two million people ascended it during the fair. Some still criticize its glut of tourists, trinkets, and vagrants, but don't believe the anti-hype—the tower is worth seeing. *(ⓂBir-Hakeim or Trocadéro. ☎01 44 11 23 23; www.tour-eiffel.fr. Elevator open daily from mid-June to Aug. 9am-12:45am, last entry 11pm; from Sept. to mid-June 9:30am-11:45pm, last entry 11pm. Stairs open daily from mid-June to Aug. 9am-12:45am, last entry midnight; from Sept. to mid-June 9:30am-6:30pm, last entry 6pm. Elevator to 2nd fl. €8, under 25 €6.40, under 12 €4, under 3 free; elevator to summit €13/9.90/7.50/free. Stairs to 1st and 2nd fl. €4.50/3.50/3/free.)*

PARC ANDRÉ CITROËN. The futuristic Parc André Citroën was created by landscapers Alain Provost and Gilles Clément in the 1990s. Hot-air balloon rides offer spectacular aerial views of Paris. *(ⓂJavel or Balard. ☎01 44 26 20 00; www.ballondeparis.com. Open in summer M-F 8am-9:30pm, Sa-Su 9am-9:30pm; in winter M-F 8am-5:45pm, Sa-Su 9am-5:45pm. Guided tours leave from the Jardin Noir; €3-6.)*

INVALIDES. The gold-leaf dome of the **Hôtel des Invalides,** built by Napoleon as a hospital for crippled and ill soldiers, shines at the center of the *7ème*. The grassy **Esplanade des Invalides** runs from the hôtel to the Pont Alexandre III, a bridge with gilded lampposts from which you can catch a great view of the Invalides and the Seine. Both housed inside the Invalides complex, the **Musée de l'Armée** and **Musée de l'Ordre de la Libération,** documenting the Free France movement under General de Gaulle, are worth a look; the real star, however, is the **Musée des Plans-Reliefs,** which features dozens of enormous, detailed models of French fortresses and towns, all made around 1700. Napoleon's tomb is also here, resting in the Église St-Louis. *(127 r. de Grenelle. ⓂInvalides. Enter from either pl. des Invalides or pl. Vauban and av. de Tourville.)*

CATACOMBS. Originally excavated to provide stone for building Paris, the Catacombs were converted into a mass grave in 1785 when the stench of the city's public cemeteries became unbearable. Paris's "municipal ossuary" now has dozens of winding tunnels and hundreds of thousands of bones. *(1 av. du Colonel Henri Roi-Tanguy. ⓂDenfert-Rochereau; exit near ⓂMouton Duvernet. ☎01 43 22 47 63. Open Tu-Su 10am-4pm. €7, over 60 €5.50, ages 14-26 €3.50, under 14 free.)*

BOULEVARD DU MONTPARNASSE. In the early 20th century, avant-garde artists like Chagall, Duchamp, Léger, and Modigliani moved to Montparnasse. Soviet exiles Lenin and Trotsky talked strategy over cognac in cafes like Le Dôme, Le Sélect, and La Coupole. After WWI, Montparnasse attracted American expats like Calder, Hemingway, and Henry Miller. Chain restaurants and tourists crowd the now heavily commercialized street. Classic cafes like pricey La Coupole still hold their own, however, providing a wonderful place to sip coffee, read Apollinaire, and daydream away. *(ⓂMontparnasse-Bienvenüe or Vavin.)*

RIGHT BANK WEST

ARC DE TRIOMPHE. Napoleon commissioned the Arc, at the western end of the Champs-Élysées, in 1806 to honor his Grande Armée. In 1940, Parisians were brought to tears by the sight of Nazis goose-stepping through the Arc. At the end of the German occupation, a sympathetic Allied army made sure that a French general would be the first to drive under the arch. The terrace at the top has a fabulous view. The **Tomb of the Unknown Soldier** has been under the Arc since November 11, 1920, and an eternal flame has been burning since 1921. *(ⓂCharles de Gaulle-Étoile. Use the pedestrian underpass on the right side of the Champs-Élysées facing the arch. Buy your ticket in the pedestrian underpass before going up to the ground level. Open daily Apr.-Sept. 10am-11pm; Oct.-Mar. 10am-10:30pm. Last entry 30min. before close. Wheelchair-accessible. €9, ages 18-25 €5.50, under 17 free.)*

LA DÉFENSE. Outside the city limits, west of the 16*ème*, the skyscrapers and modern architecture of La Défense make up Paris's newest (unofficial) *arrondissement*, a playground for many of Paris's biggest corporations. Its centerpiece is hard to miss: the Grande Arche de la Défense stretches 35 stories into the air and is shaped like a hollow cube. The roof of this unconventional office covers one hectare—Notre Dame could fit in its concave core. *(Ⓜ/RER: La Défense or bus #73. If you take the RER, buy your ticket before going through the turnstile. ☎01 47 74 84 24. Open Apr.-Sept. daily 10am-6pm; Oct.-Mar. M-F 9:30am-5:30pm. Grande Arche open daily 10am-7pm. Last entry 6:30pm. €7.50, students, under 18, and seniors €6.)*

OPÉRA GARNIER. The exterior of the Opéra Garnier—with its newly restored multi-colored marble facade, sculpted golden goddesses, and ornate columns and friezes—is as impressive as it is kitschy. It's no wonder that Oscar Wilde once swore he saw an angel floating on the sidewalk. Inside, Chagall's whimsical ceiling design contrasts with the gold and red that dominate the theater. For shows, see **Entertainment**, p. 204. *(ⓂOpéra. ☎08 92 89 90 90; www.operadeparis.fr. Concert hall and museum open daily 10am-5pm. Last entry 30min. before close. Concert hall closed during rehearsals; call ahead. 90min. tours in English July-Aug. daily 11:30am, 2:30pm; Sept.-June W and Sa-Su 11:30am, 2:30pm. €8, students and under 25 €4, under 10 free. Tours €12, students €9, under 10 €6, seniors €10.)*

PLACE DE LA CONCORDE. Paris's most infamous public square, built between 1757 and 1777, is the eastern terminus of the Champs-Élysées at its intersection with the Jardin des Tuileries. During the Revolution and Reign of Terror, the area became known as the *place de la Révolution*, site of the guillotine that severed the heads of 1343 aristocrats, including Louis XVI, Marie Antoinette, and Robespierre. In 1830, the square was optimistically renamed *concorde* (peace) and the 3200-year-old Obélisque de Luxor, given to Charles X by the Viceroy of Egypt, replaced the guillotine. *(ⓂConcorde.)*

AVENUE DES CHAMPS-ÉLYSÉES. Extending from the Louvre, Paris's most famous thoroughfare was a piecemeal project begun under the reign of Louis XIV. The center of Parisian opulence in the early 20th century, with flashy mansions towering above exclusive cafes, the Champs has since undergone a bizarre kind of democratization. Shops along the avenue now range from designer fashion to cheap trinkets. While it may be an inelegant spectacle, the Champs offers some of the city's best people-watching—tourists, wealthy barhoppers, and even authentic Parisians crowd its broad sidewalks. *(ⓂCharles de Gaulle-Étoile. Runs from the pl. Charles de Gaulle-Étoile southeast to the pl. de la Concorde.)*

FRANCE

RIGHT BANK EAST

CIMITIÈRE PÈRE LACHAISE. This cemetery holds the remains of such famous Frenchmen as Balzac, Bernhardt, Colette, David, Delacroix, Piaf, La Fontaine, Haussmann, Molière, Proust, and Seurat within its peaceful paths and elaborate sarcophagi. Foreigners buried here include Chopin, Modigliani, Gertrude Stein, and Oscar Wilde, though the most frequently visited grave is that of Jim Morrison. French Leftists make a ceremonial pilgrimage to the **Mur des Fédérés** (Wall of the Federals), where 147 *communards* were executed in 1871. *(16 rue du Repo. ⓂPère Lachaise. ☎01 55 25 82 10. Open from mid-Mar. to early Nov. M-F 8am-6pm, Sa 8:30am-6pm, Su and holidays 9am-6pm; from Nov. to mid-Mar. M-F 8am-5:30pm, Sa 8:30am-5:30pm, Su and holidays 9am-5:30pm. Free.)*

BASILIQUE DU SACRÉ-COEUR. This ethereal basilica, with its signature shining white onion domes, was commissioned to atone for France's war crimes in the Franco-Prussian War. During WWII, 13 bombs were dropped on Paris, all near the structure, but miraculously no one was killed. *(35 rue du Chevalier-*

de-la-Barre. Ⓜ Anvers, Abbesses, or Château-Rouge. ☎ 01 53 41 89 00; www.sacre-coeur-montmartre.fr. Basilica open daily 6am-11pm. Crypt open daily 9am-5:30pm. Dome open daily 9am-6pm. Mass daily 10pm. Wheelchair-accessible. Free. Dome €5.)

PLACE DE LA BASTILLE. This intersection was once home to the famous **Bastille Prison,** stormed on July 14, 1789, sparking the French Revolution. Two days later, the National Assembly ordered the prison demolished, but the ground plan of the prison's turrets remains embedded in the road near r. St-Antoine. At the center of the square is a monument of the winged Mercury holding a torch of freedom, symbolizing the movement towards democracy. *(Ⓜ Bastille.)*

OPÉRA DE LA BASTILLE. One of Mitterrand's Grands Projets, the Opéra opened in 1989 to loud protests over its unattractive design. It has been described as a huge toilet because of its resemblance to the city's coin-operated *pissoirs.* The opera has not struck a completely sour note, though; it has helped renew local interest in the arts. The guided tour offers a behind-the-scenes view of the world's largest theater. *(130 rue de Lyon. Ⓜ Bastille. ☎ 01 40 01 19 70; www.operadeparis. 1hr. tour almost every day, usually at 1 or 5pm; call ahead for schedule. €11, over 60 and students €9, under 18 €6. Open M-Sa 10:30am-6:30pm.)*

BAL DU MOULIN ROUGE. Along bd. de Clichy and bd. de Rochechouart, you'll find many Belle Époque cabarets, including the Bal du Moulin Rouge, immortalized by Toulouse-Lautrec's paintings, Offenbach's music, and Baz Luhrmann's 2001 blockbuster. The crowd consists of tourists out for an evening of sequins, tassels, and skin. The revues are still risqué, but the real shock is the price of admission. *(82 bd. de Clichy. Ⓜ Blanche. ☎ 01 53 09 82 82; www.moulin-rouge.com.)*

MUSEUMS

No visitor should miss Paris's museums, which are universally considered to be among the world's best. Cost-effective for visiting more than three museums or sights daily, the **Carte Musées et Monuments** offers admission to 65 museums in greater Paris. It is available at major museums, tourist office kiosks, and many Métro stations. A pass for one day is €15, for three days €30, for five days €45. Students with art or art history ID can get into art museums free. Most museums, including the Musée d'Orsay, are closed on Mondays.

MUSÉE D'ORSAY. If only the *Académiciens* who turned the Impressionists away from the Louvre could see the Musée d'Orsay. Now considered masterpieces, these "rejects" are well worth the pilgrimage to this mecca of modernity. The collection, installed in a former railway station, includes painting, sculpture, decorative arts, and photography from 1848 until WWI. On the ground floor, Classical and Proto-Impressionist works are on display, including Manet's *Olympia*, a painting that caused scandal when it was unveiled in 1865. Other highlights include Monet's *Poppies*, Renoir's *Bal au moulin de la Galette*, Dégas's *La classe de danse*, and paintings by Cézanne, Gauguin, Seurat, and Van Gogh. The top floor offers one of the most comprehensive collections of Impressionist and Post-Impressionist art in the world. In addition, the exterior and interior balconies offer supreme views of the Seine and the jungle of sculptures below. Don't miss Rodin's imperious *Honoré de Balzac.* (62 *rue de Lille. Ⓜ Solférino or RER: Musée d'Orsay. Enter at entrance A off 1 rue de la Légion d'Honneur. ☎ 01 40 49 48 14; www.musee-orsay.fr. Open Tu-W and F-Su 9:30am-6pm, Th 9:30am-9:45pm. Last entry 1hr. before closing. 1hr. English-language tours usually Tu-Sa 11:30am and 2:30pm; call ahead to confirm. Wheelchair-accessible; call ☎ 01 40 49 47 14 for info. €8, ages 18-25 €5.50, under 18 free. €5.50 for everyone Tu-W and F-Su after 4:15pm, Th after 6pm. Tours €7.50, ages 18-25 €5.70, under 18 free. Audio guides €5.)*

CROWDLESS CULTURE. Orsay's undeniably amazing collection draws massive crowds, marring an otherwise enjoyable museum. A Sunday morning or Thursday evening visit will avoid the tourist throngs.

MUSÉE DU LOUVRE. No visitor has ever allotted enough time to thoughtfully ponder every display at the Louvre, namely because it would take weeks to read every caption of the over 30,000 items in the museum. Its masterpieces include Hammurabi's Code, Jacques-Louis David's *The Oath of the Horatii* and *The Coronation of Napoleon*, Delacroix's *Liberty Leading the People*, Vermeer's *Lacemaker*, Leonardo da Vinci's *Mona Lisa*, the classically sculpted *Winged Victory of Samothrace*, and the *Venus de Milo*. Enter through I. M. Pei's stunning glass Pyramid in the Cour Napoléon, or skip the line by entering directly from the Métro. The Louvre is organized into three different wings: Denon, Richelieu, and Sully. Each is divided according to the artwork's date, national origin, and medium. *(Ⓜ Palais Royal-Musée du Louvre. ☎ 01 40 20 53 17; www.louvre.fr. Open M, Th, and Sa 9am-6pm, W and F 9am-10pm. Last entry 45min. before closing; some galleries close up to 30min. before the museum itself closes. Free 1½hr. tours July-Aug. M-Sa in English 11am, 2, 3:45pm; in French 11:30am; sign up at the info desk. Admission €9; W and F after 6pm €6; under 18 free. Free W and F after 6pm for those under 26 and 1st Su of the month for everybody. Audio guide rental €6, under 18 €2; deposit of driver's license, passport, or credit card; available to reserve online.*

CENTRE POMPIDOU. This inside-out building has inspired debate since its 1977 opening. Whatever its aesthetic merits, the exterior's chaotic colored piping provides an appropriate shell for the Cubist, Conceptual, Fauvist, and Pop works inside. The **Musée National d'Art Moderne** is the Centre Pompidou's main attraction. *(Pl. Georges-Pompidou. Ⓜ Rambuteau, Hôtel de Ville, or RER Châtelet-Les Halles. ☎ 01 44 78 12 33; www.centrepompidou.fr. Centre open M and W-Su 11am-10pm; museum open M, W, and F-Su 11am-9pm; Th 11am-11pm; last ticket sales 1 hr. before closing. €12, under 26 €9, under 18 free; 1st Su of the month free.)*

MUSÉE RODIN. The 18th-century Hôtel Biron holds hundreds of sculptures by Auguste Rodin, including the *The Thinker*, *Bourgeois de Calais*, and *La Porte d'Enfer*. Bring a book and relax amid the gracious gestures of bending flowers and flexing sculptures. *(79 rue de Varenne. Ⓜ Varenne. ☎ 01 44 18 61 10; www.musee-rodin.fr. Open Tu-Su Apr.-Sept. 9:30am-5:45pm; Oct.-Mar. 10am-5:45pm. Last entry 30min. before closing. Gardens open Tu-Su Apr.-Sept. 9:30am-6:45pm; Oct.-Mar. 10am-6:45pm. €6, under 18 and 1st Su of the month free. Special exhibits €7. Permanent collections and special exhibits together €10. Garden €1. Audio tours €4.)*

FRANCE

MUSÉE JACQUEMART-ANDRÉ. The 19th-century mansion of Nélie Jacquemart and her husband contains a world-class collection of Renaissance art, including *Madonna and Child* by Botticelli and *St. George and the Dragon* by Ucello. *(158 bd. Haussmann. ☎ 01 45 62 11 59. Ⓜ Miromesnil. Open daily 10am-6pm. Last entry 30min. before close. €10, students and ages 7-17 €7.30, under 7 free. 1 free child ticket per 3 purchased tickets. English headsets included.)*

MUSÉE DE CLUNY. The Musée de Cluny, housed in a monastery built atop Roman baths, holds one of the world's finest collections of medieval art. Works include **La Dame et La Licorne** (The Lady and the Unicorn), a striking 15th-century tapestry series. *(6 pl. Paul-Painlevé. Ⓜ Cluny-La Sorbonne. Info ☎ 01 53 73 78 00, reception 53 73 78 16. Open M and W-Su 9:15am-5:45pm; last entry at 5:15pm. Closed Jan. 1, May 1, and Dec. 25. Temporarily free; prices TBD.)*

EXPLORA SCIENCE MUSEUM. Dedicated to bringing science to young people, the Explora Science Museum is the star attraction of La Villette, in the complex's Cité des Sciences et de l'Industrie. The building's futuristic architecture only hints at the close to 300 exhibits inside. *(30 av. Corentin-Cariou. Ⓜ Porte de la Villette. ☎ 01 40 05 80 00; www.cite-sciences.fr. Museum open Tu-Sa 10am-6pm, Su 10am-7pm. Last entry 30min. before close. Médiathèque open Tu-Su noon-6:45pm. 1½hr. Cité des Enfants programs Tu-Su 10:30am, 12:30, 2:30, 4:30pm. €8, under 25 €6, under 7 free. Planetarium supplement €3, under 7 free. Médiathèque free. Aquarium free. Cité des Enfants €6.)*

MUSÉE CARNAVALET. Housed in Mme. de Sévigné's 16th-century *hôtel particulier*, this museum presents room after room of historical objects and curiosities from Paris's origins through the present day. *(23 rue de Sévigné. ☎ 01 44 59 58 58; www.paris.fr/musees/musee_carnavalet. Ⓜ Chemin Vert. Open Tu-Su 10am-6pm; last entry 5pm. Free. Special exhibits €7, under 26 €4, seniors €6, under 14 free.)*

MAISON DE BALZAC. Honoré de Balzac hid from bill collectors in this three-story hillside mansion, his home from 1840-1847. Here in this tranquil retreat, he wrote a substantial part of *La Comédie Humaine;* today's visitors can see his original manuscripts, along with his beautifully embroidered chair and desk at which he purportedly wrote and edited for 17hr. a day. *(47 rue Raynouard. Ⓜ Passy. ☎ 01 55 74 41 80; www.paris.fr/musees/balzac. Open Tu-Su 10am-6pm. Last entry 30min. before closing. Permanent collection free. Guided tours and temporary exhibits €4, families and seniors €3, students under 26 €2, under 12 free.)*

MUSÉE PICASSO. When Picasso died in 1973, his family paid the French inheritance tax in artwork. The French government put this collection, which includes work from his Cubist, Surrealist, and Neoclassical years, on display in 1985 in the 17th-century Hôtel Salé. *(5 rue de Thorigny. Ⓜ Chemin Vert. ☎ 01 42 71 25 21; www.musee-picasso.fr. Open M and W-Su Apr.-Sept. 9:30am-6pm; Oct.-Mar. 9:30am-5:30pm. Last entry 45min. before close. €8.50, ages 18-25 €6.50, under 18 and 1st Su of the month free.)*

FRANCE

ENTERTAINMENT

Pick up one of the weekly bibles of Parisian entertainment, *Pariscope* (€0.40) and *Figaroscope* (€1), at any newsstand or *tabac*. *Pariscope* includes an English-language section. For concert listings, check the free magazine *Paris Selection*, available at tourist offices. Free concerts are often held in churches and parks, especially during summer festivals. They are extremely popular, so plan to arrive early. **FNAC** stores sell concert tickets.

OPERA AND THEATER

La Comédie Française, pl. Collette, 1er (☎ 08 25 10 16 80 or 44 58 14 00; www.comedie-francaise.fr). Ⓜ Palais-Royal. Founded by Molière; the granddaddy of all French theaters. Generally, you don't need to speak French to understand the jokes. Box office open daily 11am-6pm and 1hr. before shows. Tickets €11-35.

Opéra de la Bastille, pl. de la Bastille, 12ème (☎ 08 92 89 90 90; www.operadeparis.fr). Ⓜ Bastille. Opera and ballet with a modern spin. Subtitles in French. Rush tickets 15min. before show for students under 25 and seniors. €7-196. AmEx/MC/V.

Opéra Comique, 5 rue Favart, 2ème (☎ 01 42 44 45 46 or 08 25 01 01 23; www.opera-comique.com). Ⓜ Richelieu-Drouot. Operas on a lighter scale. €6-95. MC/V.

Opéra Garnier, pl. de l'Opéra, 9ème (☎ 08 92 89 90 90; www.operadeparis.fr). Ⓜ Opéra. Mostly ballet, chamber music, and symphonies. Tickets usually available 2 weeks ahead. Operas €7-160; ballets €6-80. Box office open M-Sa 10:30am-6:30pm. AmEx/MC/V.

JAZZ AND CABARET

Bal du Moulin Rouge, 82 bd. de Clichy, 9ème (☎01 53 09 82 82; www.moulin-rouge.com). Ⓜ Blanche. See **Sights,** p. 202. World-famous cabaret's reviews remain risqué. Be prepared to stand if it's a busy night. Elegant attire required; no shorts, sneakers, or sportswear permitted. Shows nightly 9pm (€99), 11pm (€89; includes champagne). 7pm dinner and 9pm show €145-175. Occasional lunch shows €95-125. MC/V.

SHOPPING

In a city where Hermès scarves serve as slings for broken arms and department store history stretches back to the mid-19th century, shopping is nothing less than an art form. Consumerism is as diverse as the citizens are, from the wild club wear sold near **rue Étienne-Marcel** to the off-the-beaten path boutiques in the **18ème** or the **Marais.** The great *soldes* (sales) of the year begin after New Year's and at the very end of June, with the best prices at the beginning of February and the end of July. If at any time of year you see the word *braderie* (clearance sale) in a store window, enter without hesitation.

A true gem, **Gabrielle Geppert,** 31-34 Galerie Montpensier, 1*er*, is a favorite of Sharon Stone. Find an assort of gold leather and snakeskin bags, rhine-studded sunglasses in all colors, fur purses, enormous necklaces and earrings—all by vintage designers: Chanel, Louis Vuitton, Prada, and Gucci. (☎01 42 61 53 52; www.gabriellegeppert.com. Ⓜ Palais-Royale. Open M-Sa 10am-7:30pm. MC/V.) **Abbey Bookshop,** 29 rue de la Parcheminerie, 5*ème*, is a laid-back shop overflows with new and used English-language titles, as well as Canadian pride courtesy of expat owner Brian. There's an impressive basement collection of anthropology, sociology, history, music, motherhood, and literary criticism titles. They're also happy to take special orders. (☎01 46 33 16 24; www.abbeybookshop.net. Ⓜ St-Michel or Cluny. Open M-Sa 10am-7pm, sometimes later.)

Paris's department stores are as much sights as they are shopping destination, especially in December, when the stores go all out to decorate their windows. **Galeries Lafayette,** 40 bd. Haussmann, 9*ème*, can be chaotic but carries it all. (☎01 42 82 34 56; www.galerieslafayette.com. Ⓜ Chaussée d'Antin-Lafayette or Havre-Caumartin. Open M-W and F-Sa 9:30am-7:30pm, Th 9:30am-9pm. AmEx/V.) **Au Bon Marché,** 24, rue de Sèvres, 7*ème*, is Paris's oldest, most exclusive, and most expensive, with items ranging from scarves to smoking accessories, *haute couture* to home furnishings. Across the street is **La Grande Épicerie de Paris** (38 rue de Sèvres), the celebrated gourmet food annex. (☎01 44 39 80 00. Ⓜ Sèvres-Babylone. Store open M-W and F 9:30am-7pm, Th 10am-9pm, Sa 9:30am-8pm. *Épicerie* open M-Sa 8:30am-9pm. AmEx/MC/V.)

NIGHTLIFE

In the 5*ème* and 6*ème*, bars draw students, while Paris's young and hip, queer and straight swarm the **Marais,** the center of Paris's GLBT life. Great neighborhood spots are springing up in the Left Bank's outlying areas, particularly in the 13*ème* and 14*ème*. A slightly older crowd congregates around **Les Halles,** while the outer *arrondissements* cater to locals. The **Bastille,** another central party area, is more suited to pounding shots than sipping Bordeaux.

Clubbing in Paris is less about hip DJs' beats than about dressing up and getting in. Drinks are expensive, and clubbers consume little beyond the first round. Many clubs accept reservations, so come early to assure entry on busy nights. Bouncers like tourists because they generally spend more money, so speaking English might actually give you an edge. Clubs heat up between 2 and 4am. Tune in to Radio FG (98.2 FM) or Radio Nova (101.5 FM) to find out about

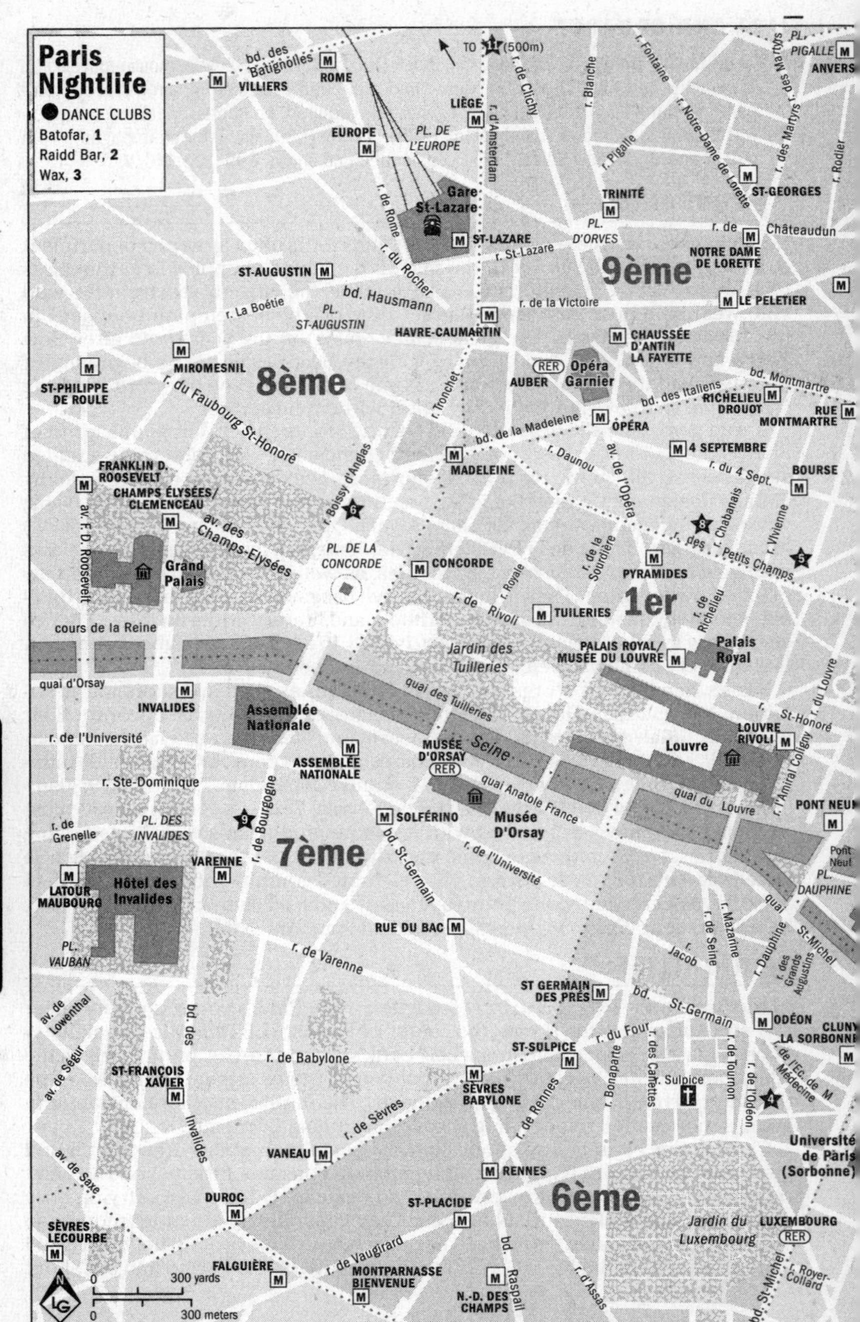
Paris Nightlife
DANCE CLUBS
Batofar, 1
Raidd Bar, 2
Wax, 3
TO 1 (500m)
bd. des Batignolles
VILLIERS
ROME
LIÈGE
EUROPE
PL. DE L'EUROPE
r. de Clichy
r. d'Amsterdam
r. Blanche
r. Fontaine
PL. PIGALLE
ANVERS
r. des Martyrs
r. Notre-Dame de Lorette
r. Pigalle
r. Rodier
ST-GEORGES
TRINITÉ
Gare St-Lazare
r. de Rome
ST-LAZARE
r. St-Lazare
PL. D'ORVES
r. de Châteaudun
NOTRE DAME DE LORETTE
9ème
r. du Rocher
ST-AUGUSTIN
bd. Hausmann
r. La Boétie
PL. ST-AUGUSTIN
r. de la Victoire
LE PELETIER
HAVRE-CAUMARTIN
CHAUSSÉE D'ANTIN LA FAYETTE
MIROMESNIL
ST-PHILIPPE DE ROULE
8ème
RER
Opéra Garnier
AUBER
bd. Montmartre
bd. des Italiens
RICHELIEU DROUOT
RUE MONTMARTRE
r. Tronchet
r. du Faubourg St-Honoré
bd. de la Madeleine
OPÉRA
4 SEPTEMBRE
MADELEINE
r. Daunou
av. de l'Opéra
r. du 4 Sept.
BOURSE
FRANKLIN D. ROOSEVELT
CHAMPS ÉLYSÉES/ CLEMENCEAU
r. Boissy d'Anglas
6
r. Chabanais
8
r. Vivienne
av. des Champs-Elysées
r. de la Sourdière
r. des Petits Champs
5
av. F. D. Roosevelt
PL. DE LA CONCORDE
CONCORDE
r. Royale
PYRAMIDES
Grand Palais
r. de Rivoli
TUILERIES
1er
r. de Richelieu
cours de la Reine
Jardin des Tuilleries
PALAIS ROYAL/ MUSÉE DU LOUVRE
Palais Royal
quai d'Orsay
quai des Tuilleries
r. du Louvre
r. St-Honoré
INVALIDES
Assemblée Nationale
Seine
LOUVRE RIVOLI
Louvre
r. de l'Université
ASSEMBLÉE NATIONALE
MUSÉE D'ORSAY
RER
r. de l'Amiral Coligny
r. Ste-Dominique
quai Anatole France
quai du Louvre
PONT NEUF
r. de Grenelle
PL. DES INVALIDES
9
r. de Bourgogne
SOLFÉRINO
Musée D'Orsay
bd. St-Germain
r. de l'Université
Pont Neuf
PL. DAUPHINE
VARENNE
7ème
LATOUR MAUBOURG
Hôtel des Invalides
quai St-Michel
r. Mazarine
r. de Seine
RUE DU BAC
PL. VAUBAN
r. de Varenne
r. Jacob
r. Dauphine
r. des Grands Augustins
ST GERMAIN DES PRÉS
bd. St-Germain
av. de Lowenthal
bd. des Invalides
ODÉON
CLUNY LA SORBONNE
r. du Four
ST-SULPICE
r. de Babylone
av. de Ségur
ST-FRANÇOIS XAVIER
SÈVRES BABYLONE
r. Bonaparte
r. des Canettes
r. de Tournon
r. de l'Odéon
r. de l'Ec. de Médecine
4
r. de Rennes
r. de Sèvres
Université de Paris (Sorbonne)
VANEAU
av. de Saxe
RENNES
DUROC
ST-PLACIDE
6ème
SÈVRES LECOURBE
Jardin du Luxembourg
LUXEMBOURG
RER
r. de Vaugirard
FALGUIÈRE
MONTPARNASSE BIENVENUE
bd. Raspail
r. d'Assas
bd. St-Michel
r. Royer-Collard
N.-D. DES CHAMPS
0
300 yards
0
300 meters

FRANCE

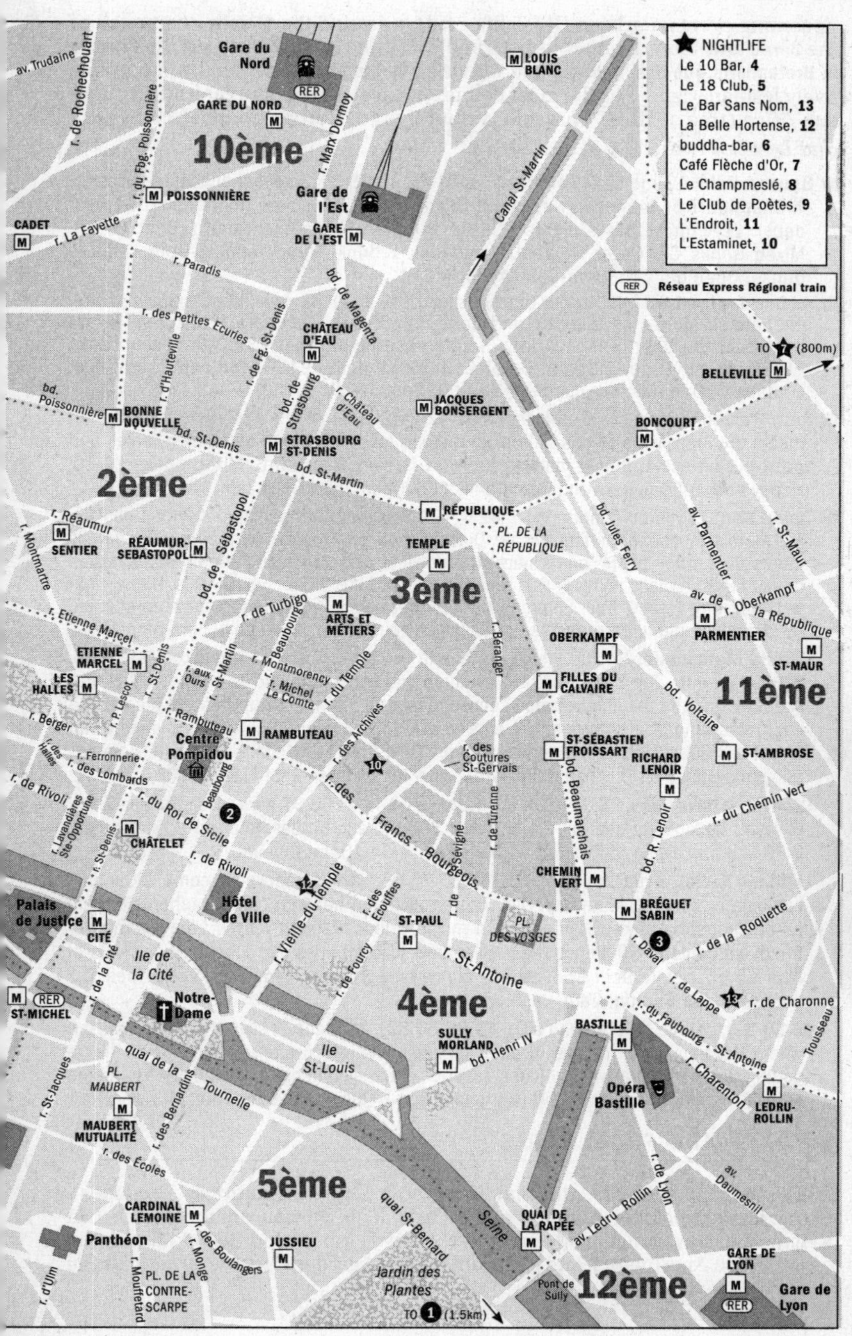
NIGHTLIFE
Le 10 Bar, 4
Le 18 Club, 5
Le Bar Sans Nom, 13
La Belle Hortense, 12
buddha-bar, 6
Café Flèche d'Or, 7
Le Champmeslé, 8
Le Club de Poètes, 9
L'Endroit, 11
L'Estaminet, 10
RER Réseau Express Régional train
10ème
2ème
3ème
4ème
5ème
11ème
12ème
Gare du Nord
GARE DU NORD
Gare de l'Est
GARE DE L'EST
LOUIS BLANC
POISSONNIÈRE
CADET
CHÂTEAU D'EAU
JACQUES BONSERGENT
BONNE NOUVELLE
STRASBOURG ST-DENIS
BELLEVILLE
TO 7 (800m)
BONCOURT
RÉPUBLIQUE
PL. DE LA RÉPUBLIQUE
TEMPLE
SENTIER
RÉAUMUR-SEBASTOPOL
ARTS ET MÉTIERS
OBERKAMPF
PARMENTIER
ST-MAUR
ETIENNE MARCEL
LES HALLES
FILLES DU CALVAIRE
RAMBUTEAU
Centre Pompidou
ST-SÉBASTIEN FROISSART
RICHARD LENOIR
ST-AMBROSE
CHÂTELET
CHEMIN VERT
BRÉGUET SABIN
Hôtel de Ville
Palais de Justice
CITÉ
ST-PAUL
PL. DES VOSGES
Ile de la Cité
ST-MICHEL
Notre-Dame
BASTILLE
SULLY MORLAND
Ile St-Louis
Opéra Bastille
LEDRU-ROLLIN
PL. MAUBERT
MAUBERT MUTUALITÉ
CARDINAL LEMOINE
Panthéon
JUSSIEU
QUAI DE LA RAPÉE
GARE DE LYON
Gare de Lyon
PL. DE LA CONTRE-SCARPE
Jardin des Plantes
Pont de Sully
TO 1 (1.5km)
Seine
Canal St-Martin
av. Trudaine
r. de Rochechouart
r. du Fbg. Poissonnière
r. Marx Dormoy
r. La Fayette
r. Paradis
bd. de Magenta
r. des Petites Ecuries
r. de Fg. St-Denis
r. d'Hauteville
bd. de Strasbourg
r. Château d'Eau
bd. Poissonnière
bd. St-Denis
bd. St-Martin
r. Réaumur
r. Montmartre
bd. de Sébastopol
bd. Jules Ferry
av. Parmentier
r. St-Maur
av. de la République
r. Oberkampf
r. de Turbigo
r. Etienne Marcel
r. Béranger
r. Beaubourg
r. Montmorency
r. Michel Le Comte
r. du Temple
r. St-Denis
r. aux Ours
r. St-Martin
r. P. Lescot
r. Berger
r. Rambuteau
r. des Archives
r. des Coutures St-Gervais
bd. Voltaire
r. Ferronnerie
r. des Halles
r. des Lombards
r. de Rivoli
r. du Roi de Sicile
r. des Francs Bourgeois
bd. Beaumarchais
r. Lavandières Ste-Opportune
r. de Turenne
bd. R. Lenoir
r. du Chemin Vert
r. de Sévigné
r. des Ecouffes
r. Vieille-du-Temple
r. de Fourcy
r. St-Antoine
r. Daval
r. de la Roquette
r. de Lappe
r. de Charonne
r. Trousseau
r. du Faubourg St-Antoine
r. Charenton
r. de la Cité
bd. Henri IV
quai de la Tournelle
r. St-Jacques
r. des Bernardins
r. des Écoles
quai St-Bernard
r. de Lyon
av. Daumesnil
av. Ledru Rollin
r. des Boulangers
r. Monge
r. Mouffetard
r. d'Ulm

FRANCE

upcoming events. Parisian GLBT life centers around the **Marais,** comprised of the *3ème* and *4ème*. Numerous bars and clubs line **rue du Temple, rue Ste-Croix de la Bretonnerie, rue des Archives,** and **rue Vieille du Temple,** while the *3ème* boasts a lively lesbian scene. For the most comprehensive listing of organizations, consult *Illico* (free at GLBT bars and restaurants) or Zurban's annual *Paris Gay and Lesbian Guide* (€5 at any kiosk).

Banana Café, 13 rue de la Ferronerie (☎01 42 33 35 31; www.bananacafeparis.com). ⓂChâtelet. *Très branché* (way cool). Scantily clad men pole dance amid tropical decor. Legendary theme nights. "Go-Go Boys" Th-Sa midnight-dawn. Beer €5.50. Mixed drinks €8. Cover F-Sa €10; includes 1 drink. Happy hour 6-9pm; 2 for 1 drinks. Open daily 5:30pm-6am. AmEx/MC/V.

Au Duc des Lombards, 42 rue des Lombards (☎01 42 33 22 88; www.ducdeslombards.com). ⓂChâtelet. Murals of Ellington and Coltrane cover the exterior of this premier jazz joint. Still the best in French jazz. 3 sets each night. Beer €3.50-5. Mixed drinks €8-10. Music 10pm-1:30am. Cover €19-25, students €12 if you call in advance, couples €30 in advance. Open M-Sa 5pm-2am. MC/V.

Andy Wahloo, 69 rue des Gravilliers (☎01 42 71 20 38). ⓂArts et Métiers. Andy Warhol meets the Arab world at this Moroccan-themed lounge bar with traffic-sign tables and paint-bucket seats. Smoke hookah as live DJs spin. Beer €5-6. Mixed drinks €9-10. Happy hour 5-8pm; beer and mixed drinks €5. Open Tu-Sa 5pm-2am. AmEx/MC/V.

Raidd Bar, 23 rue du Temple (☎01 42 77 04 88; www.raiddbar.com). ⓂHotel de Ville. The Marais's most happening gay bar. Disco globes, sexy topless bartenders, and a lively dance floor. After 11pm, performers strip down in glass-enclosed shower stalls. Mixed drinks €8-9. Tu disco night; W 80s and house; Th DJ VIP; F-Sa club; Su 90s. Happy hour 5-11pm; buy 1 get 1 free. Enforces a strict door policy; women must be accompanied (preferably outnumbered) by men (ideally gorgeous ones). Open daily 5pm-5am. V.

L'Étoile Manquante, 34 rue Vieille du Temple (☎01 42 72 48 34; www.cafeine.com). ⓂHôtel de Ville. The brown leather banquets and concentric circles on the ceiling may seem to straddle the line between conventional and funky, but pop into the technological fantasyland of a bathroom (be sure to avoid the model trains) and you'll know not to put this quirky cafe in the normal column. Beer from €2.50. Mixed drinks €9. Salads and sandwiches €4-9. Open daily 9am-2am. Kitchen open until 1:15am. MC/V.

L'Académie de la Bière, 88 bis bd. de Port Royal (☎01 43 54 66 65; www.academie-biere.com). ⓂVavin. 12 kinds of beer on tap and over 300 more in bottles. Beer €4-9. Happy hour 3:30-7:30pm. Open M-Th and Su 10am-2am, F-Sa 10am-3am. MC/V.

Le Piano Vache, 8 rue Laplace (☎01 46 33 75 03; www.lepianovache.com). ⓂCardinal Lemoine or Maubert-Mutualité. Dim, poster-plastered bar with cow paraphernalia from its butcher-shop days. Often shown in music videos. Patrons ranges from alternative-trendy students to 30-something intellectuals to celebrities like Johnny Depp. Pints of beer €5.50, before 9pm €5. Live Jazz concerts M. Theme nights 9pm-2am. Open M-F noon-2am, Sa-Su 9pm-2am. Cash only.

Le 10 Bar, 10 rue de l'Odéon (☎01 43 26 66 83). ⓂOdéon. A classic student hangout where Parisian youth indulge in deep philosophical discussion. Either that or they're getting drunk and making fart jokes. Jukebox plays everything from Édith Piaf to Aretha Franklin. Famous *sangria* €3.50 (€3 before 8pm). Open daily 6pm-2am. MC/V.

DAYTRIPS FROM PARIS

VERSAILLES. Louis XIV, the Sun King, built and held court at Versailles's extraordinary palace, 12km west of Paris. The **château** embodies the Old Regime's extravagance, especially in the newly renovated **Hall of Mirrors,** the ornate State Apartments, and the fountain-filled gardens. Arrive as soon as the château opens to avoid horrendous crowds. The line to buy tickets is to the left of the courtyard, while the line to get into the château is to the right; skip the former line by buying a day pass at the Versailles tourist office, 2bis av. de Paris, or skip the latter line by buying a combo guided tour and entrance ticket to the right of the château ticket office. *(☎01 30 83 78 89; www.chateauversailles.fr. Château open Tu-Su Apr.-Oct. 9am-6:30pm; Nov.-Mar. 9am-5:30pm. Last entry 30min. before closing. Admission to palace and self-guided tour through entrance A €8, after 3:30pm €6, under 18 free. Various other passes and guided tours also available. For group discounts and reservations call ☎08 10 81 16 14.)* A shuttle (round-trip €6, 11-18 €4.50) runs through the gardens to Louis XIV's pink marble hideaway, the **Grand Trianon,** and Marie-Antoinette's **Petit Trianon,** including her pseudo-peasant Hameau, or hamlet. *(www.train-versailles.com. Both Trianons open daily Apr.-Oct. noon-6:30pm; Nov.-Mar. noon-5:30pm. Last entry 30min. before closing. Apr.-Oct. €9, 2hr. before closing €5, under 18 free; Nov.-Mar. €5, under 18 free.)* Take the RER C5 train from Ⓜ Invalides to the Versailles Rive Gauche station (30-40min., 4 per hr., round-trip €5.60). Make sure you keep your RER (not Métro) ticket to exit at the Versailles station.

CHARTRES. Chartres's phenomenal cathedral is one of the most beautiful surviving creations of the Middle Ages. Arguably the finest example of early Gothic architecture in Europe, the cathedral retains nearly all of its original 12th- and 13th-century stained-glass windows, many featuring the stunning "Chartres blue." Climb the spiral staircase to the top of the 16th-century Flamboyant Gothic left tower (Tour Jehan-de-Beauce), built 300 years after the rest of the cathedral, for dizzying views. *(☎02 37 21 75 02; www.cathedrale-chartres.com. Open daily 8:30am-7:30pm. No casual visits during mass. Mass M-F 11:45am and 6:15pm, Tu and F 9am and 6:15pm; Sa 11:45am and 6pm; Su 9:15 (Latin), 11am, 6pm (in the crypt). Call the tourist office for info on concerts in the cathedral. €10, students and children €5.)* **Trains** run from Paris's Gare Montparnasse (1hr., 1 per hr., round-trip €26). The cathedral towers are visible to the left from outside the station.

LOIRE VALLEY (VAL DE LOIRE)

TRANSPORTATION

Faced with widespread grandeur, many travelers plan overly ambitious itineraries—two châteaux per day is a reasonable goal. The city of Tours is the region's best rail hub. However, train schedules are inconvenient, and many châteaux aren't accessible by train. **Biking** is the best way to explore the region. Many stations distribute the invaluable *Châteaux pour Train et Vélo* booklet.

ORLÉANS ☎02 38

A gateway from Paris into the Loire, Orléans (pop. 200,000) cherishes its historical connection to **Joan of Arc,** who marched triumphantly past the **rue de Bourgogne** in 1429 after liberating the city from a British siege. Most of Orléans's highlights are near place Ste-Croix. With stained-glass windows that depict Joan's story, the **Cathédrale Sainte-Croix,** pl. Ste-Croix, is Orléans's crown jewel. (Open daily July-Aug. 9:15am-7pm; Sept.-June reduced hours.)

One block from the train station, **Hôtel de L'Abeille ❹,** 64 r. Alsace-Lorraine, has been owned by the same family since 1919. Twenty-nine comfortable rooms with antique furniture and fireplaces (albeit non-functional) are worth the price. (☎02 38 53 54 87; www.hoteldelabeille.com. Continental breakfast €8.50, in bed €9.50. Wi-Fi in lobby. Singles with shower €47, with full bath €51; doubles €62-66/69-79; triples and quads €95-110. AmEx/MC/V.) Rue de

FRANCE

Bourgogne and rue Ste-Catherine have a variety of cheap buffets and a lively bar scene at night. At **Mijana ❸,** 175 r. de Bourgogne, a charming Lebanese couple prepares gourmet cuisine. (☎02 38 62 02 02; www.mijanaresto.com. Take-out sandwiches €4-6. Appetizers €7.20-8.50. *Plats* €14-17. Lunch specials, including *menu traditionel* €17.75. Open M-Sa noon-1:30pm, 7-10pm. Vegetarian options. Open M-Sa noon-1:30pm and 7-10pm. AmEx/MC/V over €15.) **Trains** leave from the Gare d'Orléans on pl. Albert I. to: Blois (40min.; at least 15 per day; €9.70 under 26 €7); Nantes (2hr.; M-F 3 per day, Sa-Su 2 per day; €35); Paris Austerlitz (1hr., every hr., €13); Tours (1hr., every 30min., €18). The **tourist office,** is located at 2 pl. de l'Étape. (☎02 38 24 05 05; www.tourisme-orleans.com. Open July-Aug. 9:30am-7pm; June 9:30am-1pm and 2-6:30pm; May and Sept. Tu-Sa 9:30am-1pm and 2-6pm; Oct.-Apr. reduced hours.) **Postal Code:** 45000.

BLOIS ☎02 54

Awash in a rich regal history, Blois (pop. 51,000) is one of the Loire's most charming, popular cities. Once home to monarchs Louis XII and François I, Blois's gold-trimmed **Château** was the Versailles of the late 15th and early 16th centuries. Housed within are well-preserved collections and historical museums with excellent temporary exhibits. While the royal apartments showcase extravagant and elegant pieces, the **Musée des Beaux-Arts** features a gallery of 16th- to 19th-century portraits, and the **Musée Lapidaire** exhibits sculptures from nearby châteaux. (☎02 54 90 33 33. Open daily Apr.-June. 9am-6:30pm; July and Aug. 9am-7pm; Sept 9am-6:30pm.; Oct.-Mar. 9am-noon and 2-5:30pm. Ticket booth closes 30min. before château. Admission including 2 museums €7.50, students under 25 €5, under 17 €3.) Bars and *boulangeries* on r. St-Lubin and r. des Trois Marchands tempt those en route to the 12th-century **Abbaye St-Laumer,** also called the **Église St-Nicolas.** (Open daily 9am-6:30pm. Su Mass 9:30am.) Five hundred years of expansions and additions to **Cathédrale St-Louis,** one of Blois's architectural jewels, have endowed it with an eclectic mix of styles. (Open daily 7:30am-6pm; crypt open June-Aug.) A spectacular view from the **Jardin de l'Evêché,** behind the cathedral, runs past the rooftops and winding alleys of the old quarter, stretching along the brilliant Loire.

Hôtel du Bellay ❷, 12 rue des Minimes, is a rustic old house, hidden away in a quiet, centrally located nook of the city, contains 12 clean but well-lived in rooms. (☎02 54 78 23 62; http://hoteldubellay.free.fr. Breakfast €5. Reception 24hr. Reservations recommended at least 3 weeks ahead. Singles and doubles with sink €25, with toilet €27, with shower €28, with bath €37; triples and quads €54-62. MC/V.) Fragrant *pâtisseries* entice visitors on **rue Denis Papin,** while **rue St-Lubin, place Poids du Roi,** and **place de la Résistance** offer more dining options. At night, the château's "Son et Lumière" light show brightens Blois.

Trains leave pl. de la Gare for Amboise (20min., 15 per day, €6.20); Angers via Tours (1hr., 9-11 per day, €24); Orléans (30-50min., 14 per day, €9.70); Paris via Orléans (1hr., 8 per day, €26); Tours (40min., 8-13 per day 8am-7pm, €9.20). **Transports Loir-et-Cher (TLC;** ☎02 54 58 55 44; www.TLCinfo.net) sends **buses** from the station to nearby Chambord and Cheverny (3 per day mid-May to early Sept.; €12; students €9; reduced entry to châteaux with bus ticket). Rent a **bike** from Bike in Blois, 8 rue Henri Drussy, near pl. de la Résistance. (☎02 54 56 07 73; www.locationdevelos.com. €14 standard bike or €38 tandem bike per day; price reduction for extra days. Open M-F 9:15am-1pm and 3-6:30pm, Su 10:30am-1pm and 3-6:15pm. Cash only.) The **tourist office** is on pl. du Château. (☎02 54 90 41 41; www.bloispaysdechambord.com. Open Apr.-Sept. M-Sa 9am-7pm, Su 10am-7pm; Oct.-Mar. reduced hours.) **Postal Code:** 41000.

BRITTANY (BRETAGNE)

RENNES

☎02 99

The cultural capital of Brittany, Rennes (pop 212,000) flourishes from September to June because of its large, rowdy student population. Ethnic eateries, colorful nightspots, and crowds of university students enliven the cobblestone streets and half-timbered houses of the *vieille ville.* Medieval architecture peppers Rennes's *vieille ville*, particularly **rue de la Psalette** and **rue St-Guillaume.** At the end of r. St-Guillaume, turn left onto r. de la Monnaie to visit the **Cathédrale St-Pierre,** a 19th-century masterpiece with a solid, Neoclassical facade and frescoed, gilded interior. (Open daily 9:30am-noon and 3-6pm.) The **Musée des Beaux-Arts,** 20 q. Émile Zola, houses an excellent collection including Baroque and Breton masterpieces but few famous works. (☎02 23 62 17 45; www.mbar.org. Open Tu 10am-6pm, W-Su 10am-noon and 2-6pm. €4.30, students €2.20, under 18 free; with special exhibits €5.40/2.70/free.) Across the river and up r. Gambetta is the lush **Jardin du Thabor,** one of the most beautiful gardens in France. (☎02 99 28 56 62. Open daily June-Aug. 7:30am-8:30pm; Sept.-June 7:30am-6:30pm.) Rennes is a **partygoer's dream,** especially during term time. Look for action in **place Ste-Anne, place St-Michel,** and **place de Lices.** In a former prison, **Delicatessen,** 7 impasse Rallier du Baty, has swapped jailhouse bars for heavy beats. (Drinks €6-10. Cover €5-15. Open Tu-Sa midnight-5am.)

The **Auberge de Jeunesse (HI)** ❶, 10-12 Canal St-Martin, has simple dorms. Take the metro (dir.: Kennedy) to Ste-Anne. Follow r. de St-Malo to the right of the church downhill onto r. St-Martin; the hostel will be on the right after the bridge. (☎02 99 33 22 33; rennes@fuaj.org. Breakfast and linens included. Reception 7am-11pm. Dorms €17. MC/V.) **Rue St-Malo** has many ethnic restaurants, while the *vieille ville* contains traditional brasseries. **Le St-Germain des Champs (Restaurant Végétarien-Biologique)** ❸, 12 r. du Vau St-Germain, serves vegetarian *plats* for €10. (☎02 99 79 25 52. Open M-Sa noon-2:30pm. MC/V.)

Trains leave pl. de la Gare for: Caen (3hr., 4 per day, €33); Paris (2hr., 1 per hr., €53-65); St-Malo (1hr., 15 per day, €14.90); Tours (3hr., 4 per day, €37) via Le Mans. Buses go from 16 pl. de la Gare to Angers (2hr., 2 per day, €14) and Mont-St-Michel (1hr., 4 per day, €10). Local **buses** run Monday through Saturday 5:15am-12:30am and Sunday 7:25am-midnight. The metro line uses the same ticket (€1.10, day pass €4, carnet of 10 €11). To get from the train station to the **tourist office** is at 11 r. St-Yves. (☎02 99 67 11 11; www.tourisme-rennes.com. Open July-Aug. M-Sa 9am-7pm, Su 11am-1pm and 2-6pm; Sept.-June M 1-6pm, Tu-Sa 10am-6pm, Su 11am-1pm and 2-6pm.) **Postal Code:** 35000.

ST-MALO

☎02 99

St-Malo (pop. 52,000) combines all the best of northern France: sandy beaches, imposing ramparts, and cultural festivals. East of the walled city is **Grande Plage de Sillon,** the town's largest and longest beach. The slightly more sheltered **Plage de Bon Secours** lies to the west and features the curious (and free) **Piscine de Bon Secours,** three cement walls that hold in a deep pool of salt water even when the tide recedes. The best view of St-Malo is from the château's **watchtower,** part of the **Musée d'Histoire,** which houses artifacts from St-Malo's naval past. (☎02 99 40 71 57. Open Apr.-Sept. daily 10am-12:30pm and 2-6pm; Oct.-Mar. reduced hours. €5.20, students €2.60.) The **"Centre Patrick Varangot" (HI)** ❶, 37 av. du Révérend Père Umbricht, has 242 beds near the beach. From the train station, take bus #5 (dir.: Croix Désilles) or #10 (dir.: Cancale). By foot (30min.) from the station, turn right and go straight at the roundabout onto av. de Moka. Turn right on av. Pasteur, which becomes av. du Révérend Père Umbricht. (☎02 99 40 29 80; www.centrevarangot.com. Breakfast included. Linens included. Laundry €4. Free Internet and Wi-Fi. Reception daily 8am-11pm. Dorms €16.50-19; singles €25-29. MC/V.) The best eateries lie farther from the walls of the *vieille ville*. For scoops of gelato, head to **Le Sanchez ❶**, 9 r. de la Vieille Boucherie at pl. du Pilori. (☎02 99 56 67 17. 1 scoop €2, 2 scoops €3. Super Sanchez 3-scoop sundae €4.80. Open mid-June to mid-Sept. daily 8:30am-midnight; Apr. to mid-June daily 8:30am-7:30pm; mid-Sept to Mar. M-Tu and Th-Su 8:30am-7:30pm. MC/V min. €15 charge.) **Trains** run to Dinan (1hr., 5 per day, €8.50), Paris (4hr., 14 per day, €59.40-73.20), and Rennes (1hr., 14 per day, €12.40). The **tourist office** is in esplanade St-Vincent. (☎08 25 13 52 00. Open July-Aug. M-Sa 9am-7:30pm, Su 10am-6pm; Sept.-June reduced hours.) **Postal Code:** 35400.

NORMANDY

ROUEN ☎02 35

Madame Bovary—literature's most famous desperate housewife—may have criticized Rouen (pop. 106,000), but Flaubert's hometown is no provincial hamlet. Historically important as the capital of Normandy and the city where **Joan of Arc** burned at the stake in 1431, Rouen today boasts splendid Gothic cathedrals and buzzing urban energy. The most famous of Rouen's "hundred spires" belong to the **Cathédrale de Notre-Dame,** pl. de la Cathédrale. The central spire, standing at 495 feet, is the tallest in France. Art lovers may also recognize the cathedral's facade from Monet's celebrated studies of light. (Open Apr.-Oct. M 2-7pm, Tu-Sa 7:30am-7pm, Su 8am-6pm; Nov.-Mar. M 2-7pm, Tu-Sa 7:30am-noon and 2-6pm, Su 8am-6pm.) The **Musée Flaubert et d'Histoire de la Médicine,** 51 r. de Lecat, down r. de Crosne from pl. de Vieux-Marché, houses a large collection of bizarre paraphernalia on both subjects. (☎02 35 15 59 95; www.chu-rouen.fr. Open Tu 10am-6pm, W-Sa 10am-noon and 2-6pm. €3, 18-25 €1.50, under 18 free.) **Hotel des Arcades ❸,** 52 r. de Carmes, is down the street from the cathedral. (☎02 35 70 10 30; www.hotel-des-arcades.fr. Breakfast €6.50. Singles €29-36, with shower €40-46; doubles €30-37/41-47; triples with shower €57. AmEx/MC/V.) Cheap eateries surround place du Vieux-Marché and the Gros Horloge area. **Chez Wam ❶,** 67 r. de la République, near l'Abbatiale St-Ouen, serves delicious *kebab-frites* (kebabs with fries; €4) ideal for picnics at the nearby **Jardins de l'Hôtel de Ville.** (☎02 35 15 97 51. Open daily 10am-2am. Cash only.) **Trains** leave r. Jeanne d'Arc, on pl. Bernard Tissot, for Lille (3hr., 3 per day, €30) and Paris (1hr., 1 per hr., €19.30). The **tourist office** is at 25 pl. de la Cathédrale. (☎02 32 08 32 40; www.rouentourisme.com. Open May-Sept. M-Sa 9am-7pm, Su 9:30am-12:30pm and 2-6pm; Oct.-Apr. M-Sa 9:30am-6:30pm.) **Postal Code:** 76000.

CAEN ☎02 31

Although Allied bombing leveled three-quarters of its buildings during WWII, Caen (pop. 114,000) has successfully rebuilt itself into an active university town. Caen's biggest (and priciest) draw is the **Mémorial de Caen,** which powerfully, tastefully, and creatively explores WWII, from the "failure of peace" to modern prospects for global harmony. (☎02 31 06 06 44; www.memorial-caen.fr. Open mid-Feb. to mid-Nov. daily 9am-7pm; mid-Nov. to mid-Feb. Tu-Su 9:30am-6pm. €17-18; students, seniors, and 10-18 €15-16, under 10 free. Prices vary by season.) The ruins of William the Conqueror's enormous **château** (ramparts free and open for visiting), sprawl above the center of town. The **Musée de Normandie,** within the château grounds on the left, traces the cultural evolution of people living on Norman soil from the beginning of civilization to the present. (☎02 31 30 47 60; www.musee-de-normandie.caen.fr. Open June-Sept. daily 9:30am-6pm; Oct.-May M and W-Su 9:30am-6pm. Free.) At night, Caen's already busy streets turn boisterous; well-attended bars and clubs pumping music populate the area around **rue de Bras, rue des Croisiers,** and **rue St-Pierre.**

The cheap and spacious four-bed dorms at **Auberge de Jeunesse (HI) ❶,** Résidence Robert Rème, 1 68 r. Eustache Restout, make its distance from town (3km) worth the trek. Take bus # 5, dir. Fleury Cimetière, to Lycée Fresnel (15min.); go back half a block in the direction the bus came from, then take a right on r. Restout, the hostel is on the left. (☎02 31 52 19 96; fax 02 31 84 29 49. Breakfast €2. Linens €2.50. Laundry wash €3, dry €1.50. Free Wi-Fi. Reception 5-9pm. Check-out 10am. Open daily June-Sept. Dorms €11. Cash only.) Eateries can be found near the château and around **Place Courtonne** and **Église St-Pierre.**

Trains run to: Paris (2hr., 11 per day, €29.80); Rennes (3hr., 2 per day, €31.10); Rouen (1hr., 9 per day, €22.30); Tours (3hr., 3 per day, €51). Bus Verts **buses** (☎08 10 21 42 14) cover the rest of Normandy. Twisto, operating **local buses** and **trams,** has schedules at its office on 15 r. de Gêole. (☎02 31 15 55 55; www.twisto.fr; €1.27, carnet of 10 €10.10.) The **tourist office** is in pl. St-Pierre. (☎02 31 27 14 14; www.caen.fr/tourisme. Open July-Aug. M-Sa 9am-7pm, Su 10am-1pm and 2-5pm; Mar.-June and Sept. M-Sa 9:30am-6:30pm, Su 10am-1pm; Oct.-Feb. M-Sa 9:30am-1pm and 2-6pm, Su 10am-1pm.) **Postal Code:** 14000.

BAYEUX ☎02 31

Escaping relatively unscathed from WWII, beautiful Bayeux (pop. 15,000) is an ideal base for exploring nearby D-Day beaches, especially in summer when more buses run. Visitors should not miss the 900-year-old **Tapisserie Bayeux,** 70m of embroidery depicting William the Conqueror's invasion of England. The tapestry is displayed in the **Centre Guillaume le Conquérant,** on r. de Nesmond. (Open daily May-Aug. 9am-7pm; mid-Mar. to Apr. and Sept.-mid-Nov. 9am-6:30pm; mid-Nov. to mid-Mar. 9:30am-12:30pm and 2-6pm. €7.70, students €3.80, under 10 free.) Close by, **Cathédrale Notre-Dame** was the tapestry's original home. (Open daily July-Sept. 8:30am-7pm; Oct.-Dec. 8:30am-6pm; Jan.-Mar. 9am-5pm; Apr.-June 8am-6pm. French-language tours of the Old Town, including access to the labyrinth and treasury; 5 tours per day July-Aug., €4.) The **Musée de la Bataille de Normandie,** bd. Fabian Ware, recounts the D-Day landing and subsequent 76-day struggle for northern France. (☎02 31 51 46 90. Open daily May-Sept. 9:30am-6:30pm; Oct.-Apr. 10am-12:30pm and 2-6pm. English-language film about every 2hr. €6.50, students €3.80.) **Le Maupassant ❸,** 19 r. St-Martin, in the center of town, has cheerful rooms. (☎02 31 92 28 53; h.lemaupassant@orange.fr. Breakfast €5.95. Singles €29; doubles with shower €40; quads with bath €69. Extra bed €10. MC/V.) **Trains** leave pl. de la Gare for Caen (20min., 23 per day, €5.50) and Paris (2hr., 12per day, €32). The **tourist office** is at r. St-Jean. (☎02 31 51 28 28; www.bayeux-bessin-tourism.com. Open July-Aug. M-Sa 9am-7pm, Su 9am-1pm and 2-6pm; Sept.-June reduced hours.) **Postal Code:** 14400.

FRANCE

DAYTRIP FROM BAYEUX: D-DAY BEACHES. On June 6, 1944, more than a hundred thousand Allied soldiers invaded Normandy's beaches, leading to France's liberation and the downfall of Nazi Europe. Army Rangers scaled 30m cliffs under heavy fire at the **Pointe du Hoc,** between Utah and Omaha Beaches, to capture a strongly fortified German naval battery. Having achieved their objective, the Army Rangers held the battery against counter attacks for two days past their anticipated relief. Of the 225 men in the division, only 90 survived. Often referred to as "Bloody Omaha," **Omaha Beach,** next to Colleville-sur-Mer and east of the Pointe du Hoc, is the most famous D-Day beach. On

June 6, Allied preparatory bombings missed the German positions due to fog, while the full-strength German bunkers inflicted an 85% casualty rate on the first waves of Americans; ultimately, over 800 soldiers died on the beach. The 9387 graves at the **American Cemetery** stretch throughout expansive grounds on the cliffs overlooking the beach. *(Open daily 9am-6pm.)* To Omaha's east and just west of Gold Beach is **Arromanches,** a small town where the ruins of the Allies' temporary **Port Winston** lie in a giant semi-circle off the coast. The Arromanches **360° Cinéma** combines images of modern Normandy and 1944 D-Day. *(Open daily June-Aug. 9:40am-6:40pm; Sept.-May reduced hours. €4.20, students €3.70.)*

Reaching the beaches can be difficult without a car. Some sites are accessible by **Bus Verts** from Caen on lines #1, 3, and 4 and from Bayeux on lines 70 and 74; more buses run in July-Aug., including a special D-Day line from Bayeux and Caen to Omaha Beach (€1.55-10.20). Normandy Sightseeing Tours, based in Bayeux, runs **guided tours** with English-speaking guides. *(☎02 31 51 70 52; www.normandywebguide.com. Reservations required. ½-day tour €40-45, students €35-40; full-day tour €75/65. Pick-up at train station, pl. du Québec, or your hotel. MC/V.)*

MONT-ST-MICHEL ☎02 33

Once regarded as a paradise, the fortified island of Mont-St-Michel is a medieval wonder. Stone and half-timbering enclose the town's narrow main street which leads steeply up to the abbey's twisting stairs. Adjacent to the abbey church is **La Merveille** (the Marvel), a 13th-century Gothic monastery, while four crypts support the church and keep it balanced on the hilltop. (Open daily May-Aug. 9am-7pm; Sept.-Apr. 9:30am-6pm. €8.50, 18-25 €5.) Hotels on Mont-St-Michel are expensive, starting at €50 per night. Cheap beds are only 1.8km away at the **Camping du Mont-St-Michel ❶,** rte. du Mont-St-Michel (☎02 33 60 22 10; www.le-mont-St-michel.com. Laundry €6.10. Wi-Fi at adjoining Hôtel Motel Vert. Reception 24hr. Check-out 2pm. Gates closed 11pm-6am. Open from Feb. to mid-Nov. €4-5 per adult, €2-3 per child, €5-9 per tent site; dorms €8.60. MC/V). Courriers Bretons (☎02 99 19 70 70), runs **buses** from Mont-St-Michel to Rennes (1hr., 2-3 per week, €2.50). The **tourist office** is to the left of the entrance. (☎02 33 60 14 30; www.ot-mont-saintmichel.com. Open July-Aug. daily 9am-7pm; Apr.-June M-Sa 9am-12:30pm and 2-6:30pm, Su 9am-noon and 2-6pm; Oct.-Dec. and Jan.-Mar. M-Sa 9am-noon and 2-6pm, Su 10am-noon and 2-5pm; Sept. M-Sa 9am-6pm, Su 10am-noon and 2-6pm.) **Postal Code:** 50170.

FLANDERS AND PAS DE CALAIS

LILLE ☎03 20

A long-time international hub with rich Flemish ancestry and the best nightlife in the north, Lille (pop. 220,000) has abandoned its industrial days to become a stylish metropolis. The impressive **Palais des Beaux-Arts,** on pl. de la République (M: République), has the second-largest art collection in France, with a comprehensive display of 15th- to 20th-century French and Flemish masterpieces. (Open M 2-6pm, W-Su 10am-6pm. €10, students €7.) The aptly named **La Piscine,** 23 r. de L'Espérance (M: Gare Jean Lebas), has creative exhibits and a collection that includes works from the 19th and early 20th centuries displayed—where else?—around an indoor pool. (Open Tu-Th 11am-6pm, F 11am-8pm, Sa-Su 1-6pm. €3.50, F students free.) Dating from the 15th century, the **Vieille Bourse** (Old Stock Exchange), pl. Général de Gaulle, is now home to regular book markets. (Open Tu-Su 9:30am-7:30pm.)

To reach the affable **Auberge de Jeunesse (HI) ❶**, 12 r. Malpart, circle left around the train station, then turn right on r. du Molinel, left on r. de Paris, and right on r. Malpart. (☎03 20 57 08 94; lille@fuaj.org. Breakfast and linens included. Reception 24hr. Lockout 11am-3pm. Open late Jan. to mid-Dec. 3- to 6-bed dorms €18. €3 HI discount. MC/V.) **La Pâte Brisée ❷**, 65 r. de la Monnaie, in *vieux* Lille, is garden-themed. (☎03 20 74 29 00. *Menus* €8.50-19.90. Open M-F noon-10:30pm, Sa-Su noon-11pm. MC/V.) At night, students swarm the pubs on **rue Solférino** and **rue Masséna,** while *vieux* Lille has a trendier bar scene.

Trains leave from Gare Lille Flandres, on pl. de la Gare (M: Gare Lille Flandres), for Paris (1hr., 20 per day, €37-50) and Brussels, BEL (1hr., 1-3 per day, €18-24). Gare Lille Europe, on r. Le Corbusier (M: Gare Lille Europe), sends Eurostar trains to Brussels, BEL (40min., 15 per day, €18-24) and London, BRI (1hr., 15 per day, €110-175), and TGVs to Paris (1hr., 6 per day, €37-50). Eurolines **buses** (☎03 20 78 18 88) also leave there for Amsterdam, NTH (5hr., 2 per day, round-trip €47); Brussels, BEL (3 per day, 1hr., round-trip €22); London, BRI (5hr., 2 per day, round-trip €61). The **tourist office,** pl. Rihour (M: Rihour), is inside the Palais Rihour. (☎03 20 21 94 21; www.lilletourism.com. Open M-Sa 9:30am-6:30pm, Su 10am-noon and 2-5pm.) **Postal Code:** 59000.

CALAIS ☎03 21

Calais (pop. 80,000) is a relaxing Channel port where people speak English as often as French. Rodin's famous sculpture **The Burghers of Calais** stands in front of the Hôtel de Ville, at bd. Jacquard and r. Royale, though most come for the **beaches.** Clean and pleasant **Centre Européen de Séjour/Auberge de Jeunesse (HI) ❶**, av. Maréchal Delattre de Tassigny, is less than a block from the beach and offers a bar and library. (☎03 21 34 70 20; www.auberge-jeunesse-calais.com. Wi-Fi €1 per 2 hr. Singles €26; doubles €21. €3 HI discount. AmEx/MC/V.) Open-air morning **markets** are on pl. Crèvecoeur (Th and Sa) and pl. d'Armes (W and Sa). For more info on **ferries** to Dover, BRI see p. 43. During the day, free **buses** connect the ferry terminal and Gare Calais-Ville on bd. Jacquard, where **trains** leave for Boulogne (30min., 11 per day, €8), Lille (1hr., 16 per day, €16), and Paris (3hr., 6 per day, €30-60). The **tourist office** is at 12 bd. Clemenceau. (☎03 21 96 62 40; www.ot-calais.fr. Open June-Aug. M-Sa 10am-1pm and Su 10am-1pm and 2-6:30pm; Sept.-May 10am-1pm.) **Postal Code:** 62100.

CHAMPAGNE AND BURGUNDY

REIMS ☎03 26

From the 26 monarchs crowned in its cathedral to the bubbling champagne of its famed *caves* (cellars), everything Reims (pop. 191,000) touches turns to gold. The **Cathédrale de Notre-Dame,** built with golden limestone taken from the medieval city walls, features sea-blue stained-glass windows by Marc Chagall, hanging chandeliers, and an impressive royal history. (☎03 26 47 55 34. Open daily 7:30am-7:30pm. Free. English-language audio tour €5.) The adjacent **Palais du Tau,** 2 pl. du Cardinal Luçon, houses original statues from the cathedral's facade alongside majestic 16th-century tapestries. (☎03 26 47 81 79. Open May-Aug. Tu-Su 9:30am-6:30pm; Sept.-Apr. 9:30am-12:30pm and 2-5:30pm. €6.50, 18-25 €4.50, under 18 free.) **Champagne Pommery,** 5 pl. du Général Gouraud, gives the best tours of Reims's champagne caves. Its 75,000L *tonneau* (vat) is one of the largest in the world; it, along with the *maison*'s modern art exhibits, can be viewed in the lobby free of charge. (☎03 26 61 62 56; www.pommery.com. Reservations recommended, €10-17.)

The **Centre International de Séjour/Auberge de Jeunesse (HI) ❶**, chaussée Bocquaine, has clean rooms. (☎03 26 40 52 60. Breakfast included. Free Wi-Fi. Wheelchair-accessible. Reception 24hr. Dorms €19, with toilet and shower €22; singles €28/41; doubles €21/28; triples with shower €22. €3 HI discount. MC/V.) Restaurants, and bars crowd **place Drouet d'Erlon,** Reims's nightspot. **Trains** leave bd. Joffre for Épernay (20min., 11 per day, €4.80) and Paris (1hr., 11 per day, €21). The **tourist office** is at 2 r. Guillaume de Machault. (☎03 26 77 45 00; www.reims-tourisme.com. Open mid-Apr. to mid-Oct. M-Sa 9am-7pm, Su 10am-6pm; mid-Oct. to mid-Apr. M-Sa 9am-6pm, Su 11am-6pm.) **Postal Code:** 51100.

ÉPERNAY ☎03 26

Champagne's showcase town, Épernay (pop. 26,000) is rightly lavish and seductive. Palatial mansions, lush gardens, and champagne companies distinguish the aptly named **avenue de Champagne.** Here you'll find Moët & Chandon, 20 av. de Champagne, producers of the king of all champagnes: **Dom Perignon.** (☎03 26 51 20 20; www.moet.com. Reservations required. Open daily 9:30-11:30am and 2-4:30pm. Tours with several tasting options for those 18+ €13-25, 10-18 €8, under 10 free.) Ten minutes away is **Mercier,** 70 av. de Champagne, producers of the self-proclaimed "most popular champagne in France." Tours are in roller-coaster-style cars that tell the story of its Willy-Wonka-like founder, Eugène Mercier. (☎03 26 51 22 22. Open mid-Mar. to mid-Nov. daily 9:30-11:30am and 2-4:30pm; mid-Nov. to mid-Dec. and mid-Feb. to mid-Mar. M and Th-Su 9:30-11:30am and 2-4:30pm. Wheelchair-accessible. 30min. tour €8-15.) Budget hotels are rare in Épernay, but **Hôtel St-Pierre ❷,** 1 r. Jeanne d'Arc, offers spacious rooms at unbeatable prices. (☎03 26 54 40 80; fax 57 88 68. www.villasaintpierre.fr. Breakfast €6. Reception 7am-10pm. Singles €21, with shower €30; doubles €24/36. MC/V.) Ethnic food, as well as pricier Champagne-soaked cuisine, line **rue Gambetta,** near the tourist office. Bakeries and delis sporadically dot the area around **place des Arcades** and **place Hugues Plomb.**

Trains leave Cours de la Gare for Paris (1hr., 18 per day, €19) and Strasbourg (3hr., 3 per day, €40). From the station, walk through pl. Mendès France, head from r. Gambetta to pl. de la République, then turn left on av. de Champagne to reach the **tourist office,** 7 av. de Champagne. (☎03 26 53 33 00; www.ot-epernay.fr. Open Mar. 23 to mid-Oct. M-Sa 9:30am-12:30pm and 1:30-7pm, Su 11am-4pm; mid-Oct. to Easter M-Sa 9:30am-12:30pm and 1:30-5:30pm.) **Postal Code:** 51200.

ALSACE-LORRAINE AND FRANCHE-COMTÉ

STRASBOURG ☎03 88

Just a few kilometers from the Franco-German border, Strasbourg (pop. 270,000) is a city with true international character. *Winstubs* (wine-bar restaurants specializing in local dishes) sit peacefully beside *pâtisseries* in the *vieille ville*, while German and French conversations mingle in the street.

BIG BUCKS FOR BIGWIGS. Prices rise during EU plenary sessions. To take in the city's sights without going broke, avoid visiting (during these dates in 2009) Jan. 12-15, Feb. 2-5, Mar. 9-12 and 23-26, Apr. 21-24, May 4-7, July 14-16, Sept. 14-17, Oct. 19-22, Nov. 23-26, and Dec. 14-17.

TRANSPORATION AND PRACTICAL INFORMATION. **Trains** leave from Pl. de la Gare. to Frankfurt, Germany (2-4hr., 13 per day, €52); Luxembourg (2-3hr., 10 per day, €33); Paris (4hr., 24 per day, €47; TGV 2hr., €63); Zurich, Switzerland (3hr., 4 per day, €40-47). SNCF **buses** run to surrounding towns from the station. The **Compagnie des Transports Strasbourgeois** (CTS), 14 rue de la Gare aux Marchandises (☎77 70 11, bus and tram info 77 70 70; www.cts-strasbourg.fr) has 5 tram lines which run 4:30am-12:30am. Find tickets (€1.30, round-trip €2.50) on board and *carnets* of 10 (€11.50) and day passes (€3.50) at **CTS,** 56 rue du Jeu des Enfants. Open M-F 8:30am-6:30pm, Sa 9am-5pm.) The **tourist office** is at 17 pl. de la Cathédrale. (☎03 88 52 28 28; www.ot-strasbourg.fr. Open daily 9am-7pm. There's also a branch at pl. de la Gare. (☎03 88 32 51 49. Open M-Sa 9am-12:30pm and 1:45-7pm.) **Postal Code:** 67000.

ACCOMMODATIONS AND FOOD. Great deals on hotels are all over the city, especially around the train station. Wherever you stay, make reservations early. Hotel prices often drop on weekends and when the EU Parliament is not in session. Near the train station, **Hôtel le Grillon ❷,** 2 r. Thiergarten, this offers the best value. (☎03 88 32 71 88; www.grillon.com. Breakfast €7.50. Internet €1 per 15min; free Wi-Fi. Reception 24hr. Singles €33, with shower €43-58; doubles €40/50-65. Extra bed €13. MC/V.) The scenic **La Petite France** neighborhood, especially along r. des Dentelles, is full of *winstubs* with Alsatian specialties.

SIGHTS. The **Cathédrale de Strasbourg** is a Gothic cathedral with a tower that stretches 142m skyward; young Goethe scaled its 332 steps to cure his fear of heights. Inside, the **Horloge Astronomique** demonstrates 16th-century Swiss clockmaking wizardry. Also check out the **Pilier des Anges** (Angels' Pillar), a depiction of the Last Judgment. (Cathedral open M-Sa 7-11:40am and 12:40-7pm, Su 12:45-6pm. Tower open daily July-Aug. 9am-7:15pm; Apr.-June and Sept. 9am-6pm; Mar. and Oct. 9am-5:30pm; Nov.-Feb. 9am-4:30pm. Clock tickets sold at the northern entrance; €1. Tower €4.60, students €2.30.) The Palais Rohan houses three excellent museums. The Musée des Beaux-Arts displays 14th- to 19th-century art, including works by Botticelli, Giotto, Goya, Raphaël, and Rubens. The **Musée des Arts Décoratifs,** refurbished for Napoleon in 1805, features pistachio-green rooms encrusted with gold and marble, including the emperor's bedroom and library. The **Musée Archéologique** illustrates Alsace's history through relics and a slew of skeletons. (2 pl. du Château. All open M and W-Su 10am-6pm. €6 each, students €3; free 1st Su of every month.)

NIGHTLIFE. Strasbourg specializes in friendly bars rather than throbbing clubs. **Place Kléber** attracts a student scene, while **rue des Frères** fills up quickly after 10pm with a diverse crowd. **Bar Exils,** 28 r. de l'Ail, boasts over 40 beers, leather couches, and an unflagging spirit that buzzes into the early morning. (☎03 88 35 52 70. Beer from €2; after 10pm €2.50. Open M-F noon-4am, Sa-Su 2pm-4am. MC/V min. €6.) Rock all night at **Le Tribord,** Ponts Couverts, a lively gay and lesbian club. (☎03 88 36 22 90. Beer from €2.50. Mixed drinks from €4. Open Th-Sa 10pm-4am.)

LA ROUTE DU VIN

The vineyards of Alsace flourish in a 150km corridor along the foothills of the Vosges from Strasbourg to Mulhouse—a region known as the Route du Vin. The Romans were the first to ferment Alsatian grapes, and today Alsatians sell over 150 million bottles annually. Consider staying in **Colmar** (p. 218) or **Sélestat** (p. 218), larger towns that anchor the southern Route, and daytripping to the smaller (and pricier) towns. The best source of info on regional *caves* is the **Centre d'Information du Vin d'Alsace,** 12 av. de la Foire aux Vins, at the Maison du Vin d'Alsace in Colmar. (☎03 89 20 16 20. Open M-F 9am-noon and 2-5pm.)

TRANSPORTATION

Buses, the cheapest option, run frequently from Colmar to surrounding towns, though smaller northern towns are difficult to reach. **Car rental** from Strasbourg or Colmar resolves transportation problems, albeit at a steep cost. Despite well marked trails, only those with stamina should bike the lengthy and often hilly roads from Colmar. **Trains** connect Sélestat, Molsheim, Barr, Colmar, and Mulhouse. Minimal sidewalks make country roads difficult to walk along.

SÉLESTAT ☎03 88

Sélestat (pop. 17,500), between Colmar and Strasbourg, is a haven of good wines and good vibes that is often overlooked by tourists on their way to more "authentic" Route cities. The **Maison du Pain,** on r. du Sel, reveals the history of breadmaking from 12,500 BC to the present. View models of ancient and modern bakeries before taking history into your own hands: a workshop in the ground-floor patisserie allows visitors to twist and bake their own **pretzels.** (Open Dec. daily 10am-7pm; Jan. and Mar.-Nov. Tu-F 9:30am-12:30pm and 2-6pm, Sa 9am-12:30pm and 2-6pm, Su 9am-12:30pm and 2:30-6pm. Closed Dec. 25-Jan. 7 and mid-Jan. to Feb. €4.60, students €3.80, ages 16-18 €1.60.) Founded in 1452, the **Bibliothèque Humaniste,** 1 r. de la Bibliothèque, contains a fascinating collection of illuminated manuscripts and meticulously handwritten books produced during Sélestat's 15th-century Humanist heyday. (Open July-Aug. M and W-F 9am-noon and 2-6pm, Sa 9am-noon and 2-5pm, Su 2-5pm; Sept.-June M-F 9am-noon and 2-6pm, Sa 9am-noon. €3.80, students €2.30.)

Hôtel de l'Ill ❸, 13 r. des Bateliers, has 15 rooms with shower and TV. (☎03 88 92 91 09. Breakfast €5. Reception 7am-9pm. Check-out 10am. Singles €33; doubles €42; triples €50. AmEx/MC/V.) **JP Kamm ❶,** 15 r. des Clefs, has outdoor dining and a large selection of mouthwatering desserts. (☎03 88 92 11 04. Pizzas and quiches €3.80-5.40. Ice cream from €4.60. Open Tu and Th-F 8am-7pm, W 8:30am-7pm, Sa 8am-6pm, Su 8am-1pm. Terrace service Tu-F until 6:30pm, Sa until 5:30pm. MC/V min. €8.) From pl. de la Gare, **trains** run to Colmar (15min., 38 per day, €4) and Strasbourg (30min., 54 per day, €7). (Ticket office open M 6am-7pm, Tu-F 7am-7pm, Sa 8:30am-5pm, Su 11:20am-6:50pm.) The **tourist office** is at bd. Général Leclerc. (☎03 89 58 87 20; www.selestat-tourisme.com. Open July-Aug. M-F 9:30am-12:30pm and 1:30-6:30pm, Sa 9am-12:30pm and 2-5pm, Su 10:30am-3pm; Sept.-June reduced hours.) **Postal Code:** 67600.

COLMAR ☎03 89

Colmar (pop. 68,000) is a great base for exploring smaller Route towns. The **Musée Unterlinden,** 1 r. d'Unterlinden has a collection ranging from Romanesque to Renaissance, including Grünewald's Issenheim Altarpiece, an Alsatian treasure. (Open May-Oct. daily 9am-6pm; Nov.-Apr. M and W-Su 9am-noon and 2-5pm. €7, students €5. MC/V min. €8.) The **Église des Dominicains,** pl. des Dominicains, is a bare-bones showroom for Colmar's other masterpiece, Schongauer's ornate *Virgin in the Rose Bower.* (Open June-Oct. M-Th and Su 10am-1pm and 3-6pm, F-Sa 10am-6pm; Apr.-May and Nov.-Dec. daily 10am-1pm and 3-6pm. €1.50, students €1.) The 10-day **Foire aux Vins d'Alsace** is the region's largest wine fair, with concerts, free tastings, and exhibitions. (Mid-Aug. ☎03 90 50 50 50; www.foire-colmar.com. 11:30am-1:30pm €1, 1:30pm-5pm €4, after 5pm €6. Concerts €20-43.) To reach the **Auberge de Jeunesse (HI) ❶,** 2 r. Pasteur, take bus #4 (dir.: Europe) to Pont Rouge. On Sundays take Bus B (dir.: Ingershiem) to Pont

Rouge. (☎03 89 80 57 39. Breakfast included. Linens €4. Reception Nov. to mid-Dec. and mid-Jan. to Feb. 7-10am and 5-11pm; Apr.-Sept. 7-10am and 5pm-10:30pm. Lockout 10am-5pm. Curfew in summer midnight, in winter 11pm. Open mid-Jan. to mid-Dec. Dorms €13; singles €17; doubles €26. HI discount €3. MC/V.) **Trains** depart pl. de la Gare for Lyon (4-5hr., 9 per day, €42), Paris (5hr., 2 per day, €52), and Strasbourg (30min., 12 per day, €10). The **tourist office** is at 4 r. d'Unterlinden. (☎03 89 20 68 92; www.ot-colmar.fr. Open July-Aug. M-Sa 9am-7pm, Su 10am-1pm; Sept.-June reduced hours.) **Postal Code:** 68000.

NANCY ☎03 83

Nancy (pop. 106,000) the intellectual heart of modern Lorraine with its many museums and beautiful architecture. The works on display at the **Musée de L'École de Nancy,** 36-38 r. du Sergent Blandan, reject straight lines, instead using organic forms to recreate aspects of the natural landscape. Take bus #122 (dir.: Villers Clairlieu) or 123 (dir.: Vandoeuvre Cheminots) to Painlevé. (☎03 83 40 14 86; www.ecole-de-nancy.com. Open W-Su 10:30am-6pm. €6, students €4. W students free. €8 pass to all museums.) The recently renovated **place Stanislas** houses three Neoclassical pavilions, including place de la Carrière, a former jousting ground that Stanislas Leszczynski—Duke of Lorraine from 1737 to 1766—refurbished with Baroque architecture, golden angel sculptures, and wrought-iron ornaments. The place's beauty can be absorbed over a large cup of coffee at one of its many cafes. **Rue Stanislas** and **Grand Rue** are great places to grab a drink. Suave, smoky **Blitz,** 76 r. St-Julien, is decorated in red velvet. (Beer from €2.30. Mixed drinks from €5. Open M 5:30pm-2am, Tu-Sa 2pm-2am. July-Aug. also open Su 5:30pm-1am. AmEx/MC/V min. €7 charge.)

Don't let the exterior of **Hôtel de L'Académie ❷**, 7 r. des Michottes, deter you; it has large, clean rooms in a convenient location. (☎03 83 35 52 31. Breakfast €3.50. Reception 7am-11pm. Singles €20-28; doubles €28-39. AmEx/MC/V.) Immerse yourself in the cheesy delights of **Le Bouche à Oreille ❷**, 42 r. des Carmes (☎03 83 35 17 17. Fondues €14-15. Lunch *menu* €11. Dinner *menu* €18. Open M, Sa 7-10:30pm, Tu-F noon-1:30pm and 7-10:30pm. AmEx/MC/V.). Restaurants also line **rue des Maréchaux, place Lafayette,** and **place St-Epvre.**

Trains depart from the station at 3 pl. Thiers for Paris (3 hr., 27 per day, €42-50) and Strasbourg (1hr., 20 per day, €23). The new **TGV** Est line also connects Nancy to Paris.. **Postal Code:** 54000.

FRANCE

RHÔNE-ALPES AND MASSIF CENTRAL

LYON ☎04 78

Ultra-modern, ultra-friendly, and undeniably gourmet, Lyon (pop. 453,000) elicits cries of "Forget Paris!" from backpackers. Its location—at the confluence of the Rhône and Saône rivers and along an Italian road—earned Lyon (then Lugdunum) its place as Roman Gaul's capital. A transportation hub, Lyon is now better known for its beautiful parks, modern financial center, well-preserved Renaissance quarter, and fantastic restaurants.

TRANSPORTATION

Flights: Aéroport Lyon-St-Exupéry (**LYS;** ☎08 26 80 08 26). Satobuses/Navette Aéroport (☎72 68 72 17) **shuttles** to Gare de la Part-Dieu, Gare de Perrache, and subway stops Grange-Blanche, Jean Macé, and Mermoz Pinel (every 20min., €8.60). **Air France,** 10 q. Jules Courmont, 2*ème* (☎08 20 32 08 20), has 10 daily flights to Paris's **Orly** and **Charles de Gaulle airports** (from €118). Open M-Sa 9am-6pm.

Trains: The convenient **TGV,** which stops at the airport, is cheaper than daily flights to Paris. Trains passing through stop at **Gare de la Part-Dieu,** 5 pl. Béraudier (M: Part-Dieu), on the Rhône's east bank. Info desk open daily 5am-12:45am. Ticket window open M-Th and Sa 5:15am-11pm, F and Su 5:15am-midnight. Trains terminating in Lyon continue to Gare de Perrache, pl. Carnot (M: Perrache). Open daily 4:45am-12:30am. Ticket window open M 5am-10pm, Tu-Sa 5:30am-10pm, Su 7am-10pm. **SNCF trains** go from both stations to: **Dijon** (2hr., 1 per hr., €26); **Grenoble** (1hr., 1 per hr., €18); **Marseille** (1hr., 1 per hr., €44); **Nice** (6hr., 3 per day, €62); **Paris** (2hr., 17 per day, €60); **Strasbourg** (5hr., 6 per day, €49); **Geneva, SWI** (4hr., 6 per day, €23). The **SNCF Boutique** is at 2 pl. Bellecour. Open M-F 9am-6:45pm, Sa 10am-6:30pm.

Buses: On the Gare de Perrache's lowest level and at Gorge de Loup in the 9*ème* (☎72 61 72 61). It's almost always cheaper and faster to take the train. Domestic companies include **Philibert** (☎72 75 06 06). **Eurolines** (☎72 56 95 30; www.eurolines.fr) travels out of France; office on the main floor of Perrache open M-Sa 9am-9pm.

Local Transportation: TCL (☎08 20 42 70 00; www.tcl.fr) has information offices at both bus stations and all major metro stops. *Plan de Poche* (pocket map) available from any TCL branch. Tickets valid for all forms of mass transport. (Tickets €1.60, carnet of 10 €12.80; student discount includes 10 passes valid for 1 month €11.10. Pass valid 1hr. in 1 dir., connections included.)

ORIENTATION AND PRACTICAL INFORMATION

Lyon is divided into nine *arrondissements* (districts). The 1*er*, 2*ème*, and 4*ème* lie on the *presqu'île* (peninsula), which juts toward the Saône River to the west and the Rhône to the east. Starting in the south, the 2*ème* (the centre ville) includes the Gare de Perrache and place Bellecour. The nocturnal **Terreaux** neighborhood, with its sidewalk cafes and lively, student-packed bars, makes up the 1*er*. Farther north, the *presqu'île* widens into the 4*ème* and the famous **Croix-Rousse.** The main pedestrian roads on the *presqu'île* are **rue de la République** and **rue Victor Hugo West** of the Saône, Fourvière Hill and its basilica overlook **Vieux Lyon** (5*ème*). East of the Rhône (3*ème* and 6-8*ème*) lie the **Gare de la Part-Dieu** and most of the city's population.

Tourist Office: Located in the Pavilion at pl. Bellecour, 2*ème* (☎04 72 77 69 69; www.lyon-france.com). M: Bellecour. The **Lyon City Card** authorizes unlimited public transportation along with admission to museums, tours, and river boat cruises. 1-day pass €19; 2-day €29; 3-day €39. Open June-Sept. M-Sa 9:30am-6:30pm, Su 10am-5:30pm; Oct.-May M-Sa 10am-5:30pm. MC/V.

Police: 47 r. de la Charité, ☎04 78 42 26 56. M: Perrache.

Hospital: Hôpital Hôtel-Dieu, 1 pl. de l'Hôpital, 2*ème*, near q. du Rhône, is the most central. City hospital line ☎04 78 08 20 69.

Post Office: pl. Antonin Poncet, 2*ème* (☎04 72 40 65 22), near pl. Bellecour. **Postal Code:** 69001-69009; last digit indicates *arrondissement.*

FRANCE

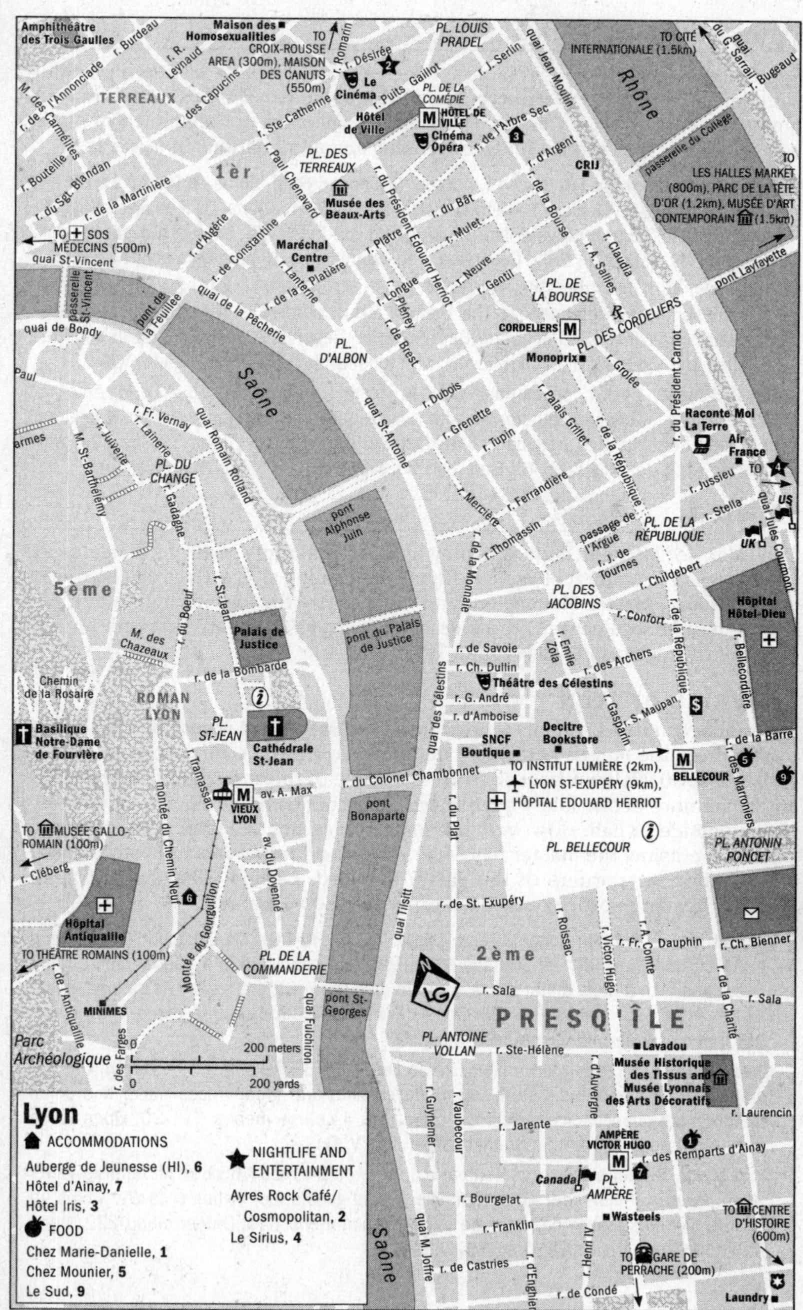

Lyon
ACCOMMODATIONS
Auberge de Jeunesse (HI), 6
Hôtel d'Ainay, 7
Hôtel Iris, 3
FOOD
Chez Marie-Danielle, 1
Chez Mounier, 5
Le Sud, 9
NIGHTLIFE AND ENTERTAINMENT
Ayres Rock Café/ Cosmopolitan, 2
Le Sirius, 4
Amphithéâtre des Trois Gaulles
Maison des Homosexualities
TO CROIX-ROUSSE AREA (300m), MAISON DES CANUTS (550m)
PL. LOUIS PRADEL
TO CITÉ INTERNATIONALE (1.5km)
Rhône
TERREAUX
Le Cinéma
Hôtel de Ville
HÔTEL DE VILLE
PL. DE LA COMÉDIE
Cinéma Opéra
PL. DES TERREAUX
1èr
CRIJ
Musée des Beaux-Arts
TO LES HALLES MARKET (800m), PARC DE LA TÊTE D'OR (1.2km), MUSÉE D'ART CONTEMPORAIN (1.5km)
TO SOS MÉDECINS (500m)
Maréchal Centre
quai St-Vincent
passerelle St-Vincent
pont de la Feuillée
quai de Bondy
quai de la Pêcherie
PL. DE LA BOURSE
CORDELIERS
PL. DES CORDELIERS
pont Lafayette
Monoprix
PL. D'ALBON
Saône
quai St-Antoine
quai Romain Rolland
Raconte Moi La Terre
Air France
PL. DU CHANGE
pont Alphonse Juin
US
UK
PL. DE LA RÉPUBLIQUE
5ème
PL. DES JACOBINS
Hôpital Hôtel-Dieu
Palais de Justice
pont du Palais de Justice
Théâtre des Célestins
ROMAN LYON
PL. ST-JEAN
Cathédrale St-Jean
Basilique Notre-Dame de Fourvière
SNCF Boutique
Decitre Bookstore
BELLECOUR
TO INSTITUT LUMIÈRE (2km), LYON ST-EXUPÉRY (9km), HÔPITAL EDOUARD HERRIOT
VIEUX LYON
pont Bonaparte
TO MUSÉE GALLO-ROMAIN (100m)
PL. BELLECOUR
PL. ANTONIN PONCET
Hôpital Antiquaille
TO THÉATRE ROMAINS (100m)
PL. DE LA COMMANDERIE
2ème
MINIMES
pont St-Georges
PRESQ'ÎLE
Parc Archéologique
0 200 meters
0 200 yards
PL. ANTOINE VOLLAN
Lavadou
Musée Historique des Tissus and Musée Lyonnais des Arts Décoratifs
AMPÈRE VICTOR HUGO
Canada
PL. AMPÈRE
Wasteels
TO CENTRE D'HISTOIRE (600m)
TO GARE DE PERRACHE (200m)
Laundry

FRANCE

ACCOMMODATIONS

September is Lyon's busiest month; it's easier and cheaper to find a place in summer but still wise to reserve ahead. Rooms under €30 are rare. Low-end hotels are east of place Carnot. There are inexpensive options north of place des Terraux. Watch out for budget-breaking accommodations in *vieux* Lyon.

Auberge de Jeunesse (HI), 41-45 montée du Chemin Neuf, 5*ème* (☎04 78 15 05 50, www.fuaj.org). M: Vieux Lyon. A terrace and bar draw international backpackers. English-speaking staff. Breakfast and linens included. Laundry €4.05. Internet €5 per hr. Max. 6-night stay. Reception 24hr. Reserve ahead. Dorms €16. HI members only. MC/V. ❶

Hôtel Iris, 36 r. de l'Arbre Sec, 1er (☎04 78 39 93 80, ☎04 72 00 89 91; www.hoteliris.freesurf.fr). M: Hôtel de Ville. This tranquil former convent is in a prime location near Terreaux. Breakfast €5. Reception 8am-8:30pm. Reserve 2 weeks ahead in summer. Singles and doubles with sink €35-42, with toilet and shower €48-50. MC/V ❸

Hôtel d'Ainay, 14 r. des Remparts d'Ainay, 2*ème* (☎04 78 42 43 42). M: Ampère-Victor Hugo. Offers spacious rooms with private bath. Travelers enjoy the great location between Perrache and Bellecour. Breakfast €4.50. Reception 24hr. Singles €27, with shower €42; doubles €32/48. Extra bed €8. MC/V. ❸

FOOD

The galaxy of Michelin stars adorning Lyon's restaurants confirms its status as the gastronomic capital of France. Equally appealing alternatives can be found on **rue St-Jean, rue des Marronniers,** and **rue Mercière** for less during lunchtime. Ethnic restaurants center on **rue de la République.** There are markets on the *quais* of the **Rhône** and **Saône** (open Tu-Su 8am-1pm).

THE PRIDE OF LYON

The pinnacle of the Lyonnais food scene is **Restaurant Paul Bocuse ❺,** 4km out of town, where the *menus* (€120-195) definitely cost more than your hotel room. (☎04 72 42 90 90; www.bocuse.fr. MC/V.) Some of these restaurants occasionally have more accessible weekend buffet brunches hovering around €30-40; check outside or call. However, gourmands need not sell their souls to enjoy Bocusian cuisine; the master has several **spin-off restaurants** in Lyon, themed around the four corners of the earth: Le Nord, Le Sud, L'Est and L'Ouest. Whether heading north, south, east, or west, reserve ahead.

Le Sud, 11 pl. Antonin Poncet, 2*ème* (☎04 72 77 80 00). M: Bellecour. Specializing in "la cuisine du soleil," Le Sud serves up Mediterranean fare in a casual dining room decorated with a huge metal sun. A seafood dish (from €15) is worth the splurge. Pasta dishes from €12. *Menus* €19-22. Open daily noon-2:30pm and 7-11pm, F-Sa noon-2:30pm and 7pm-midnight. AmEx/MC/V. ❹

Chez Mounier, 3 r. des Marronniers, 2*ème* (☎04 78 37 79 26). M: Bellecour. Despite small portions, a friendly staff, top-notch cuisine, and great prices make this small restaurant a good choice. Afternoon *menu* €8. 4-course *menus* €11-20. Open Tu-Sa noon-2pm and 7-11pm, Su noon-1:30pm. MC/V. ❸

Chez Marie-Danielle, 29 r. des Remparts d'Ainay (☎04 78 37 65 60). M: Ampère-Victor Hugo. Award-winning chef Marie-Danielle makes guests feel at home as she whips up superb *lyonnais* fare in her intimate eatery. Lunch *menu* €15. Dinner *menu* €22. Open M-F noon-2pm and 7:30-10pm. MC/V. ❹

SIGHTS

VIEUX LYON

Stacked against the Saône at the foot of the Fourvière hill, *vieux* Lyon's narrow streets are home to lively cafes, hidden passageways, and magnificent medieval and Renaissance homes. The striking *hôtels particuliers*, with their delicate carvings and ornate turrets, sprang up between the 15th and 18th centuries when Lyon was the center of Europe's silk and printing industries.

TRABOULES. The distinguishing features of vieux Lyon townhouses are their *traboules*, tunnels connecting parallel streets through a maze of courtyards, often with vaulted ceilings and exquisite spiral staircases. Although their original purpose is debated, the *traboules* were often used to transport silk from looms to storage rooms. During WWII, the passageways proved invaluable as info-gathering and escape routes for the Resistance. Many are open to the public. A 2hr. tour beginning at the tourist office is the ideal way to see them. The tourist office has a list of open *traboules* and their addresses. *(English-language tours in summer every few days at 2:30pm; winter hours vary. €9, students €5.)*

CATHÉDRALE ST-JEAN. The cathedral's soaring columns dominate the southern end of *vieux* Lyon. It was here that Henri IV met and married Maria de Médici in 1600. Inside, every hour between noon and 4pm, mechanical angels pop out of the 14th-century **astronomical clock** in a reenactment of the Annunciation. *(Open M-F 8am-noon and 2-7:30pm, Sa-Su 8am-noon and 2-7pm. Free.)*

FOURVIÈRE AND ROMAN LYON

Fourvière Hill, the nucleus of Roman Lyon, is accessible via the rose-lined **Chemin de la Rosaire** (garden open daily 6am-9:30pm) and, for the more sedentary, *la ficelle* (funicular), which leaves from the *vieux* Lyon Metro station.

BASILIQUE NOTRE-DAME DE FOURVIÈRE. During the Franco-Prussian War, the people of Lyon prayed fervently to the Virgin Mary for protection; afterward, they erected this magnificent basilica in her honor. *(Behind the esplanade at the top of the hill. Chapel open daily 7am-7pm. Basilica open daily 8am-7pm.)*

MUSÉE GALLO-ROMAIN. Taking up five mostly underground floors, this expansive museum educates and fascinates. Both history buffs and novices will appreciate a collection of mosaics and statues. *(☎72 38 81 90; www.musees-gallo-romains.com. Open Tu-Su 10am-6pm. €3.80, students €2.30; under 18 and Th free.)*

PARC ARCHÉOLOGIQUE. While the Musée Gallo-Romain provides a wonderful collection of artifacts, the Roman experience in Lyon isn't complete without a walk through this ancient park. Next to the Minimes/Théâtre Romain funicular stop, the Parc holds the well-restored 2000-year-old **Théâtre Romain** and the **Odéon,** discovered when modern developers dug into the hill. On summer evenings, relax and enjoy the show; the **Nuits de Fourvière festival** plays in both venues. *(Open daily mid-Apr. to mid-Sept. 7am-9pm; mid-Sept. to mid-Apr. 7am-7pm. Free.)*

LA PRESQU'ÎLE AND LES TERREAUX

Monumental squares, statues, and fountains are the *presqu'île's* trademarks. At its heart, **place Bellecour** links Lyon's two main pedestrian arteries. Boutique-lined **rue Victor Hugo** runs south. To the north, crowded **rue de la République,** or "la Ré," is Lyon's urban aorta. It continues through **place de la République,** ending at **place Louis Pradel** in the 1*er*, at the tip of the **Terreaux district.** Once a marshy wasteland, it was filled with soil, creating a neighborhood of dry *terreaux* (terraces) where today chic bars keep things hopping long into the night.

MUSÉE HISTORIQUE DES TISSUS. Clothing and textile fanatics will enjoy the rows of extravagant 18th-century dresses and 4000-year-old Egyptian tunics displayed here. The neighboring **Musée des Arts Décoratifs,** housed in an 18th-century *hôtel* has rooms showcasing clocks and silverware from the Renaissance to the present. *(34 r. de la Charité, 2ème. M: Ampère Victor Hugo. ☎04 78 38 42 00, www.musee-des-tissus.com. Tissus open Tu-Su 10am-5:30pm. Arts Décoratifs open Tu-Su 10am-noon and 2-5:30pm. €5, students €3.50, under 18 free; includes both museums.)*

LA CROIX-ROUSSE AND THE SILK INDUSTRY

Though mass silk manufacturing is based elsewhere today, Lyon is proud of its historical dominance of the industry in Europe. The city's **Croix-Rousse district,** a steep, uphill walk from pl.Terreaux, houses the vestiges of its silk-weaving days; Lyon's few remaining silk workers still create delicate handiwork, reconstructing and replicating rare patterns for museum and château displays.

LA MAISON DES CANUTS. The silk industry lives on at this Croix-Rousse workshop, which provides the best intro to Lyon's *canuts* (silk weavers). Scarves cost €32 or more, but silk enthusiasts can purchase a handkerchief for €9. *(10-12 r. d'Ivry, 4ème. ☎04 78 28 62 04. Open Tu-Sa 10am-6:30pm. €5, students €2.50, under 12 free. English-language tours daily at 11am and 3:30pm.)*

EAST OF THE RHÔNE AND MODERN LYON

Lyon's newest train station and monstrous space-age mall form the core of the ultra-modern Part-Dieu district. Locals call the **Tour du Crédit Lyonnais** "le Crayon" for its unintentional resemblance to a giant pencil standing on end. Next to it, the shell-shaped **Auditorium Maurice Ravel** hosts major cultural events.

CENTRE D'HISTOIRE DE LA RÉSISTANCE ET DE LA DÉPORTATION. Housed in a building where Nazis tortured detainees during the Occupation, the museum presents documents, photos, and films about Lyon's role in the Resistance. *(14 av. Bertholet, 7ème. M: Jean Macé. ☎04 78 72 23 11. Open W-F 9am-5:30pm, Sa-Su 9:30am-6pm. €4, students €2, under 18 free; includes audio tour in 3 languages.)*

MUSÉE D'ART CONTEMPORAIN. This extensive mecca of modern art, video, and high-tech installations resides in the futuristic **Cité International de Lyon,** a super-modern complex with shops, theaters, and Interpol's world headquarters. All of its exhibits are temporary—even the walls are rebuilt for each display. *(Q. Charles de Gaulle, next to Parc de la Tête d'Or, 6ème. Take bus #4 from M: Foch. ☎04 72 69 17 17; www.moca-lyon.org. Open W-Su noon-7pm. €5, students €3 under 18 free.)*

FRANCE

NIGHTLIFE

At the end of June, the two-week **Festival Jazz à Vienne** welcomes jazz masters to Vienne, a sleepy river town south of Lyon, accessible by bus or train. (www.jazzavienne.com. Tickets free-€30.) In June and July, **Les Nuits de Fourvière** music festival features classical concerts, dance, movies, plays, and popular performers in the ancient Théâtre Romain and Odéon. (☎04 72 32 00 00; www.nuitsdefourviere.fr. Tickets and info at the Théâtre Romain and the FNAC shop on r. de la République. Tickets from €12.) Nightlife in Lyon is fast and furious; the city's vast array of pubs, **GLBT establishments,** riverboat nightclubs, and student bars make going out an adventure. The most accessible late-night spots are a strip of riverboat clubs docked by the east bank of the Rhône. Students buzz in and out of tiny, intimate bars on **rue Ste-Catherine** (1*er*) until 1am, before hitting up the clubs. For a more mellow (and more expensive) evening, head to the jazz and piano bars on the streets off **rue Mercerie.** *Lyon Libertin* (€2) lists hot nightlife venues. For superb tips about gay nightlife, pick up *Le Petit Paumé.*

Ayers Rock Café, 2 r. Désirée, 1er (☎08 20 32 02 03, www.ayersrockcafe.com). M: Hôtel de Ville. This Aussie bar is a cacophony of loud rock music and wild bartenders drumming on the hanging lights for 20-somethings. Open daily 6pm-3am, summer opens at 9pm, closes at 10pm on Su. Next door slightly more chic **Cosmopolitan,** 4 r. Désirée (☎08 20 32 02 03) serves New York-themed drinks. Tu student nights; happy hour 8pm-3am. Open M-Sa 8pm-3am, opens at 9pm in summer. MC/V.

Le Sirius, across from 4 q. Augagneur, 3*ème* (☎04 78 71 78 71; www.lesirius.com). M: Guillotière. A young, international crowd packs the lower-level dance floor and bar of this cargo ship-themed riverboat. Open Tu-Sa 6pm-3am.

Q Boat, across from 17 q. Augagneur, 3*ème* (☎04 72 84 98 98, www.actunight.com). M: Guillotière. Formerly Le Fish, this club plays electronic and house music on a swanky boat. Chic Europeans crowd its 2 bars and top-floor deck. Dress well; admission at bouncer's discretion. Open W-Sa 5pm-5am, Su 2pm-5am. AmEx/MC/V.

GRENOBLE ☎04 76

Young scholars from all corners of the globe and sizable North and West African populations meet in Grenoble (pop. 168,000), a dynamic city whose surrounding snow-capped peaks are cherished by both athletes and aesthetes. *Téléphériques* (cable cars) depart from q. Stéphane-Jay every 10min. for the 16th-century **Bastille,** a fort perched 475m above the city. (Open July-Aug. M 11am-12:15am, Tu-Su 9:15am-12:15am; Sept.-June reduced hours. €4.15 one way, 6.10 round-trip; students €3.35/4.85.) After enjoying the views from the top, you can walk down the Parc Guy Pape, through the other end of the fortress, to the **Jardin des Dauphins** (1hr.). Cross the Pont St-Laurent and go up Montée Chalemont to reach the **Musée Dauphinois,** 30 r. Maurice Gignoux, which has exhibits on the history of skiing. (Open M and W-Su June-Sept. 10am-7pm; Oct.-May 10am-6pm. Free.) The **Musée de Grenoble,** 5 pl. de Lavelette, houses one of France's most prestigious art collections. (☎04 76 63 44 44; www.museedegrenoble.fr. Open M and W-Su 10am-6:30pm. €5, students €2, free under 18.) The biggest and most developed ski areas are to the east in Oisans; the **Alpe d'Huez** has 250km of trails. (Tourist office ☎04 76 11 44 44, ski area ☎04 76 80 30 30.) The **Belledonne region,** northeast of Grenoble, is at a lower altitude and lower prices; its most popular ski area is **Chamrousse.** Grenoble's funky night scene is found between **place St-André** and **place Notre-Dame.** International students and 20-somethings mix it up at **Le Couche-Tard,** 1 r. du Palais. (Mixed drinks €2.50. Student prices offered M-W. Open M-Sa 7pm-2am. AmEx/MC/V.)

From the tourist office, follow pl. Ste-Claire to pl. Notre-Dame and take r. du Vieux Temple on the right to reach **Le Foyer de l'Étudiante ❶**, 4 r. Ste-Ursule. This stately building serves as a student dorm during most of the year, but opens its large rooms to co-ed travelers from June to August, though the shortest stay offered is one week. (☎04 76 42 00 84. Laundry €2.20. Free Wi-Fi. Singles €118 per week; doubles €80 per week per person.) Grenoblaise restaurants cater to locals around **place de Gordes** and **pl. St. Andre,** while cheap pizzerias line **quai Perrière** across the river. Pâtisseries and North African joints center on **rue Chenoise** and **rue Lionne,** between the pedestrian area and the river. Cafes cluster around place **Notre-Dame** and place **St-André,** in the heart of the *vieille ville.*

Trains leave pl. de la Gare for: Lyon (1hr., 30 per day, €18); Marseille (4-5hr., 15 per day, €37); Nice (5-6hr., 5 per day, €57); Paris (3hr., 9 per day, €70). **Buses** leave from left of the train station for Geneva, SWI (3hr., 1 per day, €26). You can find the **tourist office** at 14 r. de la République. (☎04 76 42 41 41; www.grenoble-isere.info. Open Oct.-Apr. M-Sa 9am-6:30pm, Su 10am-1pm; May-Sept. M-Sa 9am-6:30pm, Su 10am-1pm and 2-5pm.) **Postal Code:** 38000.

AQUITAINE AND PAYS BASQUE

BORDEAUX ☎05 56

Though its name is synonymous with wine, the city of Bordeaux (bohr-doh; pop. 235,000) has more to offer than most lushes would expect. Everyone from punks to tourists gather on the elegant streets of the shop- and cafe-filled city center, while in the surrounding countryside, the vineyards of St-Émilion, Médoc, Sauternes, and Graves are internationally renowned.

TRANSPORTATION AND PRACTICAL INFORMATION. **Trains** leave Gare St-Jean, r. Charles Domercq, for: Lyon (8-10hr., 7 per day, €61-154); Marseille (6-7hr., 10 per day, €73); Nice (9-12hr., 2 per day, €105); Paris (3hr., 15-25 per day, €55); Toulouse (2-3hr., 10 per day, €32). From the train station, take tramway line C to pl. Quinconces (€1.30) and cross the street to reach the **tourist office,** 12 cours du 30 juillet, which arranges **winery tours.** (☎05 56 00 66 00; www.bordeaux-tourisme.com. Open July-Aug. M-Sa 9am-7:30pm, Su 9:30am-6:30pm; May-June and Sept.-Oct. M-Sa 9am-7pm, Su 9:30am-6:30pm; Nov.-Apr. M-Sa 9am-6:30pm, Su 9:45am-4:30pm.) **Postal Code:** 33000.

ACCOMMODATIONS AND FOOD. A favorite among backpackers, **Hôtel Studio** ❷, 26 r. Huguerie, has tiny, clean rooms with bath, phone, and TV. (☎05 56 48 00 14; www.hotel-bordeaux.com. Breakfast €5. Reserve ahead. Singles €19-29; doubles €25-35. AmEx/MC/V.) Find rooms decorated in metallic and bright colors at **Auberge de Jeunesse Barbey (HI)** ❷, 22 cours Barbey, four blocks from the Gare St-Jean in the run-down red light district. Visitors, especially those traveling alone, should exercise caution at night. (☎05 56 33 00 70; fax 33 00 71. Breakfast and linens included. Free Internet. Max. 3-night stay. Lockout 10am-4pm. Curfew 2am. 2- to 6-bed dorms €21. MC/V.)

The Bordelais's flair for food rivals their vineyard expertise. Hunt around rue St-Remi and place St-Pierre for regional specialties: oysters, *foie gras*, and *lamproie à la bordelaise* (eel braised in red wine). Busy **L'Ombrière** ❸, 13 pl. du Parlement, serves perfectly prepared French cuisine in one of the city's most beautiful squares. (Menu €15-23. Open daily noon-2pm and 7-11pm. MC/V.) Dine at **La Fromentine** ❷, 4 r. du Pas St-Georges, near pl. du Parlement, for galettes (€6-8) with imaginative names. (☎05 56 79 24 10. 3-course menu €10-15. Open M-F noon-2pm and 7-10pm, Sa 7-10pm. MC/V.)

SIGHTS AND ENTERTAINMENT. Nearly nine centuries after its consecration, the **Cathédrale St-André,** in pl. Pey-Berland, sits at the heart of Gothic Bordeaux. Its bell tower, the **Tour Pey-Berland,** rises 66m. (Cathedral open M 2-7pm, Tu-F 7:30am-6pm, Sa 9am-7pm, Su 9am-6pm. Tower open June-Sept. daily 10am-1:15pm and 2-6pm; Oct.-May Tu-Su 10am-12:30pm and 2-5:30pm. €5, 18-25 and seniors €3.50, under 18 with an adult free.) For the best cityscape of Bordeaux, look down from the 114m bell tower of the **Église St-Michel.** (Open June-Sept. daily 2-7pm. €2.50, under 12 free.) Back at ground level, a lively **flea market** sells anything from Syrian *narguilas* (hookahs) to African specialties. (Open daily 9am-1pm.) Note that this area, like around the train station, should not be frequented alone at night. On pl. de Quinconces, the elaborate **Monument aux Girondins** commemorates guillotined Revolutionary leaders from towns bordering the Gironde. Bordeaux's opera house, the **Grand Théâtre,** conceals a breathtaking interior behind its Neoclassical facade and houses concerts, operas, and plays in fall and winter. (☎05 56 00 85 95; www.

opera-bordeaux.com. Tours M-Sa 11am-6pm. Concert tickets from €8. Opera tickets up to €80. 50% discount for students and under 26.)

Bordeaux has a varied, vibrant nightlife. For an overview, check out the free *Clubs and Concerts* brochure at the tourist office. Year-round, students and visitors pack the bars in **Place de la Victoire, Place Gambetta,** and **Place Camille Julian.** Popular but cheesy **El Bodegon,** on pl. de la Victoire, draws students with cheap drinks, theme nights, and weekend giveaways. (Beer €3. Happy hour 6-8pm. Open M-Sa 7am-2am, Su 2pm-2am.)

BAYONNE ☎05 59

In Bayonne (pop. 42,000), the self-proclaimed chocolate capital of France, visitors wander along the Nive River's banks and admire the small bridges, petite streets, and colorful shutters. The **Musée Bonnat,** 5 r. Jacques Laffitte, showcases works by Bayonnais painter Léon Bonnat alongside others by Degas, van Dyck, Goya, Rembrandt, and Rubens. (Nov.-Apr. daily 10am-12:30pm and 2-6pm; May-Oct. M and W-Su 10am-6:30pm; July-Aug., open Tu as well at the regular hours and W 10am-9:30pm for a free 'nocturne'. €5.50, students €3, under 18 free; Sept.-June 1st Su of the month and July-Aug. W 6:30-9:30pm free.) Starting the first Wednesday in August, let loose for five days during the **Fêtes Traditionnelles** (Aug. 5-9; www.fetes-de-bayonne.com).

The **Hôtel Paris-Madrid ❷,** pl. de la Gare, has clean rooms and knowledgeable proprietors at rock-bottom prices. (☎05 59 55 13 98. Breakfast €4. Reception daily from 6:30am-12:30am. Singles and doubles €20, with shower €28, with shower and toilet €35; triples and quads with bath €49-59. MC/V.) A **Monoprix** supermarket is at the corner of r. Pont Neuf and r. Orbe. (Open M-Sa 8:30am-8pm.) **Trains** depart from pl. de la Gare for: Biarritz (10min.; at least 15per day; €2.30, TGV €3); Bordeaux (2hr., at least 10 per day, € 22-28); Paris (5hr.,at least 8 per day, € 40-81); San Sebastián, SPA via Hendaye (30min., 15 per day, €8); Toulouse (4hr., 5 per day, €37). Local STAB buses (☎05 59 59 04 61) depart from the Hôtel de Ville for Biarritz (buses #1, 2, and 6 run M-Sa 6:30am-8pm, Lines A and B run Su 6:30am-7pm. €1.20). From the train station, take the middle fork onto pl. de la République, veer right over pont St-Esprit, pass through pl. Réduit, cross pont Mayou, and turn right on r. Bernède, which becomes av. Bonnat. The **tourist office,** pl. des Basques, is on the left. (☎05 59 42 64 64; www.bayonne-tourisme.com. Open July-Aug. M-Sa 9am-7pm, Su 10am-1pm; Sept.-June M-F 9am-6:30pm, Sa 10am-6pm.) **Postal Code:** 64100.

FRANCE

PARC NATIONAL DES PYRÉNÉES

Riddled with sulfurous springs and unattainable peaks, the Pyrénées change dramatically and impressively with the seasons. To get a full sense of the mountains' breadth, hikers should experience both the lush French and barren Spanish sides of the Pyrénées (a 4- to 5-day round-trip hike from Cauterets).

CAUTERETS ☎05 62

Nestled in a valley on the edge of the **Parc National des Pyrénées Occidentales** is Cauterets (pop. 1300). Its *sulfuric thermes* (hot springs) have long been instruments of healing. **Thermes de César,** av. du Docteur Domer, offers treatments. (☎05 62 92 51 60. Information/Reservation desk open M-Sa 8:30am-noon and 2-6pm and treatments available Open Sept.-June M-Sa 4-8pm and some Su; June-Sept. M-Sa 5-8pm. Hours may vary.) Most visitors come to ski and hike. **Hotel le Chantilly ❸,** 10 r. de la Raillère, one street away from the town center, is owned by a charming Irish couple. (☎05 62 92 52 77; www.hotel-cauterets.com. Breakfast €6. Reception 7am-10pm. Open late Dec. to Oct. July-Sept. Singles and doubles €34, with shower €42; triples from €52. Oct.-June €30/34/38. MC/V.) SNCF **buses** run from pl. de la Gare to Lourdes (1hr., 8 per day, €6.60). Rent **bikes** at Le Grenier, 4 av. du Mamelon Vert. (☎05 62 92 55 71. €23 per half day, €32 per day. Open daily 9am-7pm.) The **tourist office** is in pl. Foch. (☎05 62 92 50 50; www.cauterets.com. Open July-Aug. M-Sa 9am-12:30pm and 2-7pm, Su 9am-noon and 3-6pm; Sept.-June reduced hours.) **Postal Code:** 65110.

OUTDOOR ACTIVITIES

The **Parc National des Pyrénées Occidentales** shelters hundreds of endangered species in its snow-capped mountains and lush valleys. Touch base with the friendly **Parc National Office,** Maison du Parc, pl. de la Gare, in Cauterets, before braving the park's ski paths or 14 hiking trails. (☎05 62 92 52 56; www.parc-pyrenees.com. Open July-Aug. M-Sa 9:30am-noon and 2:30-7pm; Sept.-June M-F 9:30am-noon and 3-6pm. Maps €7-9.) Appropriate for a variety of skill levels, the trails begin and end in Cauterets. From there, the **GR10** (a.k.a. **circuit de Gavarnie)**, which intersects most other hikes in the area, winds through Luz-St-Saveur, over the mountain, and then on to Gavarnie, another day's trek up the valley. One of the most spectacular trails follows the GR10 past the turquoise Lac de Gaube to the end of the glacial valley (2hr. past the lac), where you can spend the night at the **Refuge des Oulettes ❶.** (☎05 62 92 62 97. Open Mar.-Sept. Dorms €19.) Other *gîtes* (shelters) located in the park, usually located in towns along the GR10, cost about €11 per night.

LANGUEDOC-ROUSSILLON

With reasonable prices all over, Languedoc-Rousillon provides a great opportunity for travelers to see the south of France on a budget. Though it has been part of France since the 12th century, Languedoc preserves its rebellious spirit: its *joie de vivre* shows up in impromptu street performances and large neighborhood parties. Between the peaks of the Pyrénées, Roussillon inspired Matisse and Picasso and now attracts a mix of sunbathers and backpackers.

FRANCE

TOULOUSE ☎05 61

Vibrant, zany Toulouse (pop. 435,000) is known as *la ville en rose* (the pink city). It's the place to visit when all French towns begin to look alike. Exuberant yet laid-back, clean yet gritty, Toulouse is a university town whose graduating students don't want to leave. Its quality museums and concert halls makes it southwest France's cultural capital.

TRANSPORTATION AND PRACTICAL INFORMATION. Trains leave Gare Matabiau, 64 bd. Pierre Sémard, for: Bordeaux (2-3hr., at least 10 per day, €33); Lyon (4hr., at least 5 per day, €70); Marseille (4hr., at least 10 per day, €50); Paris (6hr., at least 10 per day, €90). The ticket office is open daily 7am-9:10pm. Eurolines, 68-70 bd. Pierre Sémard, sends **buses** to major cities. (☎05 61 26 40 04; www.eurolines.fr. Open M-F 9am-12:30pm and 1:30-6:30pm, Sa 9am-12:30pm and 1:30-6pm.) Get map and information at the **tourist office,** r. Lafayette in pl. Charles de Gaulle. (☎05 61 11 02 22; www.ot-toulouse.fr. Open June-Sept. M-Sa 9am-7pm, Su 10:30am-12:30pm and 2-5:15pm; Oct.-May M-Sa 9am-6pm, Su 10:30am-12:30pm and 2-5pm.) **Postal Code:** 31000.

NOTHING TOU-LOUSE. Those visiting Toulouse for longer than a day or two should pick up a Carte Privilège at the tourist office. For a mere €13, cardholders get 30% discounts at museums and participating hotels. As a final bonus, cardholders receive free *apéritifs* at many Toulouse restaurants. The tourist office has a list of participating establishments.

ACCOMMODATIONS AND FOOD. A member of the French League of Youth Hostels, **Résidence Jolimont ❶**, 2 av. Yves Brunaud, doubles as a long-term *résidence sociale* for 18- to 25-year-olds. A basketball court and ping-pong tables bring excitement to large, plain double rooms. (☎05 34 30 42 80; www.residence-jolimont.com. Breakfast M-F €2.50. Dinner daily €7.90. Linens included. Reception 24hr. Doubles €16. €1 HI member discount. AmEx/MC/V.) **Hôtel Beauséjour ❷**, 4 r. Caffarelli, near the station, has clean, bright rooms with new beds, making it a great value. (☎/fax 05 61 62 77 59. Free Wi-Fi. Reception 7am-11pm. Singles €33, with bath €35; doubles €39/41; triples €44/46. MC/V.)

Cheap eateries on **rue du Taur,** in the student quarter. Markets (open Tu-Su 6am-1pm) line place des Carmes, place Victor Hugo, and place St-Cyprien. Neighborhood favorite **Jour de Fête ❷**, 43 r. du Taur, is a relaxed brasserie with tastes as creative as the local art decorating its brick walls. (☎05 61 23 36 48. *Plat* du jour €7. Open daily noon-midnight. Cash only.)

SIGHTS AND NIGHTLIFE. The **Capitole,** a brick palace next door to the tourist office, is Toulouse's most prominent monument. The building was home to the *bourgeois capitouls* (unofficial city magistrates) in the 12th century. (Open daily 9am-7pm in the summer. Free.) Rue du Taur leads to the **Basilique St-Sernin,** the longest Romanesque structure in the world. Its crypt houses holy relics from the time of Charlemagne. (☎05 61 21 80 45. Church open July-Sept. daily 8:30am-6:30pm; Oct.-June daily 8:30-noon and 2-6pm. Crypt open July-Sept. M-Sa 10am-5pm, Su 2:30am-5pm; Oct.-June M-Sa 10-11:30am and 2:30-5pm, Su 11:30-5pm. €2.) The 13th-century southern **Gothic Jacobin church,** 69 r. Pargaminières, entrance on r. Lakanal, houses the remains of St. Thomas Aquinas. (☎05 61 22 21 92; www.jacobins.mairie-toulouse.fr. Open daily 9am-7pm.) Across the river, **Les Abbatoirs,** 76 allées Charles-de-Fitte, previously an old slaughterhouse, presents intermittent exhibits by up-and-coming artists. (☎05 62 48 58 00. Open Tu-Su 11am-7pm. €6, students €3.)

Toulouse has something to please almost any nocturnal whim. Numerous cafes flank place **St-Georges, place St-Pierre,** and **place du Capitole,** and late-night bars line **rue de la Colombette** and **rue des Filatiers.** For cheap drinks and a rambunctious atmosphere, try **Café Populaire,** 9 r. de la Colombette, where you can polish off 13 glasses of beer for only €20, €13 on Mondays 9:30pm-12:45am. (☎05 61 63 07 00. Happy hour 7:30-8:30pm. Every 13th of the month beer €1. Open M-F 11am-2am, Sa 2pm-4am. Cash only.)

MONTPELLIER ☎04 67

Occasional live music brings each street corner to life in Montpellier (pop. 225,000), southern France's most lighthearted city. The gigantic, beautifully renovated **Musée Fabre,** 39 bd. Bonne Nouvelle, holds one of the largest collections of 17th- to 19th-century paintings outside Paris, with works by Delacroix, Ingres, and Poussin. (☎04 68 14 83 00. Open Tu, Th-F, and Su 10am-6pm, W 1-9pm, Sa 11am-6pm. €6, with temporary exhibits €7; students €4/5.)

The friendly owner of **Hôtel des Étuves ❷**, 24 r. des Étuves, keeps 13 plain, comfortable rooms, all with toilet and shower. (☎04 68 60 78 19; www.

FRANCE

LOST IN TRANSLATION

Hollywood movies and American television may have captivated a market in France, but there's often little rhyme or reason regulating the translation of their titles:

Lolita in Spite of Myself *(Mean Girls):* Vladimir Nabokov and Lindsay Lohan: the perfect pop-culture union.

The Counterattack of the Blondes *(Legally Blonde):* Perhaps a little aggressive for a movie about Reese Witherspoon and Harvard Law School.

The Little Champions *(Mighty Ducks):* From the Flying V to the quack chant, the *canard* is the heart and soul of this film.

Rambo *(Rambo):* Some words just transcend linguistic and cultural barriers.

The Man Who Would Murmur at the Ears of Horses *(The Horse Whisperer):* Just in case there was any ambiguity in the original title.

A Day with No End *(Groundhog Day):* If you don't get the Groundhog Day reference, this is going to be a long movie.

La Grande Évasion *(The Great Escape):* If they didn't translate this literally, Steve McQueen would've taken everyone down.

The Big Lebowski *(The Big Lebowski):* The French recognize that The Dude does not appreciate name changes.

Lost in Translation *(Lost in Translation):* Apparently one title that wasn't.

—Vinnie Chiappini

hoteldesetuves.fr. Breakfast €5. Reception M-Sa 6:30am-11pm, Su 7am-noon and 6-11pm. Reserve 1 week ahead. Singles €23, with TV €35; doubles €37; singles and doubles with bath €45. Cash only.) Standard French cuisine dominates Montpellier's *vieille ville*, while a number of Indian and Lebanese restaurants are on **rue des Écoles Laïques.** On pl. de la Comédie, **Crêperie le Kreisker ❶,** 3 passage Bruyas, serves 80 kinds of crepes (€1.90-6.80) topped with everything from buttered bananas to snails. (☎04 68 60 82 50. Open M-Sa 11:30am-3pm and 6:30-11pm. AmEx/MC/V.) At dusk, **rue de la Loge** fills with vendors, musicians, and stilt-walkers. The liveliest bars are in **place Jean Jaurès,** which lights up at night. **Le Rebuffy Pub,** 2 Rebuffy, is packed with local regulars and international students and always has something to do and someone to meet. (☎04 67 66 32 76. Beer €2.60-5.90. Open in summer M-F 9am-2am, Sa 11am-2am, Su 10pm-2am; in winter M-Sa 11am-1am, Su 10pm-1am. MC/V €8 min.) Gay nightlife is around **place du Marché aux Fleurs.**

Trains leave pl. Auguste Gibert (☎08 92 35 35 35) for: Avignon (2hr., at least 10 per day, €14.50-17.50); Marseille (2-3½hr., at least 10 per day, €24-28); Nice (4hr., 2 per day, €40-60); Paris (3hr., at least 10 per day, €66-130); Toulouse (2½ hr., at least 10 per day, €30-34). The **tourist office** is at 30 allée Jean de Lattre de Tassigny. (☎04 68 60 60 60; www.ot-montpellier.fr. Open July-Sept. M-F 9am-7:30pm, Sa 10am-6pm, Su 9:30am-1pm and 2:30-6pm; Oct.-June M-F 9am-6:30pm, Sa 10am-6pm, Su 10am-1pm and 2-5pm.) **Postal Code:** 34000.

PROVENCE

If Paris boasts world-class paintings, it's only because Provence inspired them. Mistral winds cut through olive groves in the north, while pink flamingoes, black bulls, and unicorn-like white horses gallop freely in the marshy south. From the Roman arena and cobblestone of Arles to Cézanne's lingering footsteps in Aix-en-Provence, Provence provides a taste of *La Vie en Rose.*

MARSEILLE ☎04 91

Dubbed "the meeting place of the entire world" by Alexandre Dumas, Marseille (pop. 821,000) is a jumble of color and commotion. A walk through its side streets is punctuated by the vibrant hues of West African fabrics, the sounds of Arabic music, and the smells of North African cuisine. A true immigrant city, Marseille offers visitors a taste of multiple cultures.

TRANSPORTATION

Flights: Aéroport Marseille-Provence (**MRS;** ☎04 42 14 14 14; www.marseille.aeroport.fr). Flights to **Corsica, ITA, Lyon,** and **Paris.** Shuttle **buses** run to **Gare St-Charles** (3 per hr.; €9). **Taxis** from the *centre-ville* to airport cost €40-50.

Trains: Gare St-Charles, pl. Victor Hugo (☎08 92 35 35 35). To **Lyon** (1hr., 21 per day, €54), **Nice** (2hr., 21 per day, €28.50), and **Paris** (3hr., 18 per day, €92.50).

Buses: Gare Routière, pl. Victor Hugo, near the train station. M: Gare St-Charles. To **Aix-en-Provence** (2-6 per hr., €4.80), **Cannes** (2-3hr., 4 per day, €19-26), and **Nice** (2hr., 1 per day, €19-27). Ticket windows are open M-F 6:15am-7:30pm, Sa 6:30am-6:30pm, Su 7:30am-noon and 12:45-6pm.

Ferries: SNCM, 61 bd. des Dames (☎08 25 88 80 88; www.sncm.fr). To **Corsica, ITA** (11hr.; €39-53) and **Sardinia, ITA** (14hr., €62-70). Open M-F 8am-6pm, Sa 8:30am-noon and 2-5:30pm. Prices higher June-Sept. Student discount €5-10.

Local Transportation: RTM, 6 r. des Fabres (☎04 91 91 92 10; www.rtm.fr). Tickets sold at bus and Metro stations (€1.70, day pass €4.50, 3-day pass €10). The **Metro** runs M-Th 5am-9pm, F-Su 5am-12:30am.

Taxis: Marseille Taxi (☎04 91 02 20 20). 24hr. €20-30 from Gare St-Charles.

ORIENTATION AND PRACTICAL INFORMATION

Marseille is divided along major streets into 16 *quartiers* (neighborhoods). **La Canebière** is the main artery, funneling into the **vieux port** (old port) to the west and becoming urban sprawl to the east. North of the *vieux port* and west of rue de la République lies **Le Panier**, the city's oldest neighborhood. Surrounding La Canebière are several *maghreb* (North African and Arabic communities), including the **Belsunce quartier,** which has many markets. The area around **rue Curiol** should be avoided late at night.

Tourist Office: 4 la Canebière (☎04 91 13 89 00; www.marseille-tourisme.com). M: Vieux Port. Sells the **Marseille City Pass,** which includes an RTM day pass, tourist office walking tours, the ferry to Île d'If, and admission to 14 museums (€20 for 1 day, €27 for 2 days). Open M-Sa 9am-7pm, Su 10am-5pm.

Consulates: UK, pl. Varian Fry (☎04 91 15 72 10). **US,** 12 bd. Paul Peytral (☎04 91 54 92 00). Both open by appointment M-F 9:30am-noon and 2-4:30pm.

Currency Exchange: ID SUD, 3 pl. Général de Gaulle (☎04 91 13 09 00). Open M-F 9am-6pm, Sa 9am-5pm. Also at the post office.

Police: 2 r. du Antoine Becker (☎04 91 39 80 00). Also found in the train station on esplanade St-Charles (☎04 96 13 01 88).

Emergency: SOS Traveler, Gare St-Charles (☎04 91 62 12 80).

Hospital: Hôpital Timone, 264 r. St-Pierre (☎04 91 38 00 00). M: Timone. SOS Médecins (☎04 91 52 91 52) and SOS Dentist (☎04 91 85 39 39). Doctors on call.

Post Office: 1 pl. Hôtel des Postes (☎04 91 15 47 00). Currency exchange at main branch only. Open M-F 9:30am-12:30pm and 1:30-6pm. **Postal Code:** 13001.

ACCOMMODATIONS

Marseille has a range of options, from pricey hotels in the *vieux port* to Belsunce's less reputable but cheap lodgings. Listings here prioritize safety and location. The tourist office also provides a list of **recommended safe accommodations.**

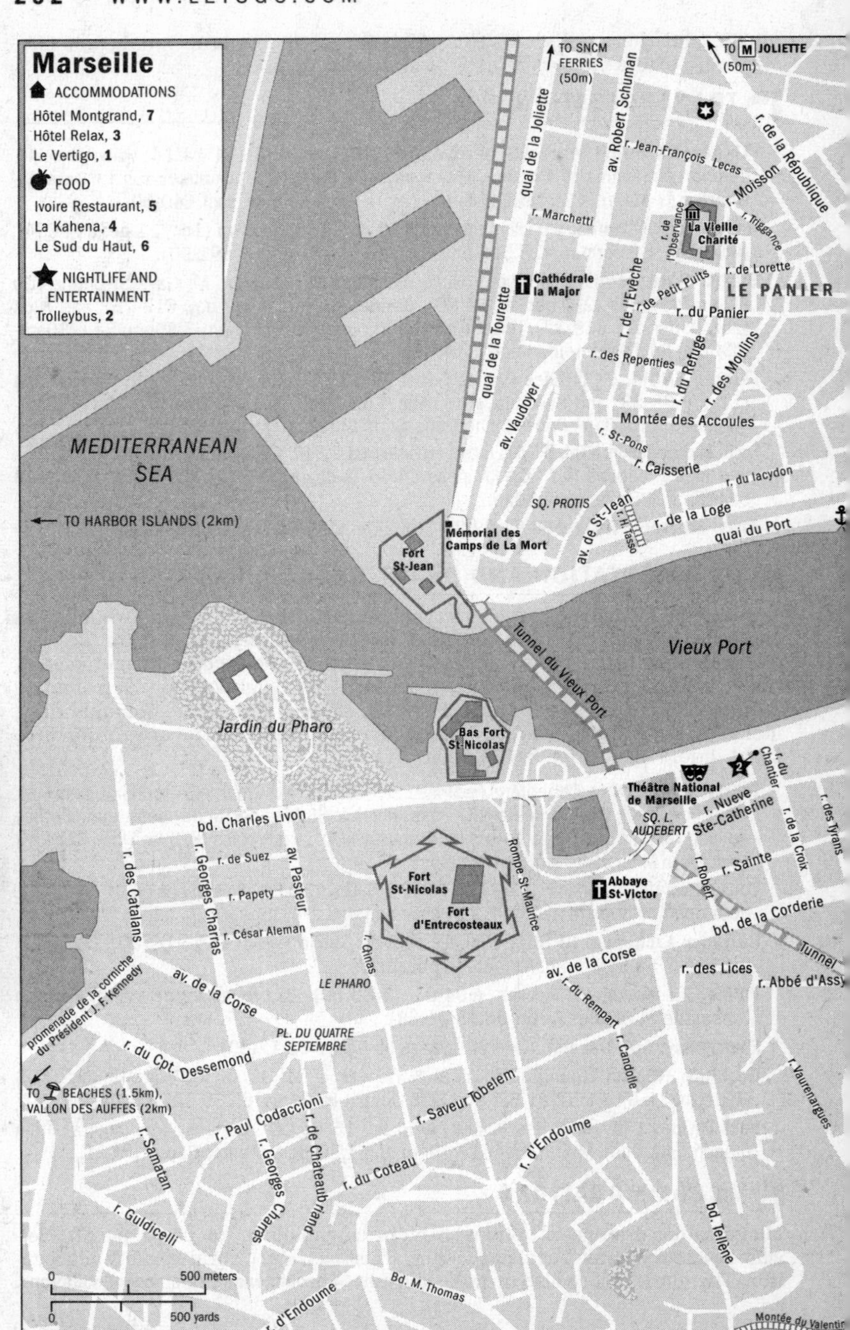
Marseille
ACCOMMODATIONS
Hôtel Montgrand, 7
Hôtel Relax, 3
Le Vertigo, 1
FOOD
Ivoire Restaurant, 5
La Kahena, 4
Le Sud du Haut, 6
NIGHTLIFE AND ENTERTAINMENT
Trolleybus, 2
TO SNCM FERRIES (50m)
TO M JOLIETTE (50m)
MEDITERRANEAN SEA
TO HARBOR ISLANDS (2km)
quai de la Joliette
av. Robert Schuman
r. Jean-François Lecas
r. de la République
r. Moisson
r. Marchetti
r. de l'Observance
La Vieille Charité
r. Triggance
r. de Lorette
Cathédrale la Major
quai de la Tourette
r. de l'Evêche
r. de Petit Puits
LE PANIER
r. du Panier
r. des Repenties
r. du Refuge
r. des Moulins
av. Vaudoyer
Montée des Accoules
r. St-Pons
r. Caisserie
r. du lacydon
SQ. PROTIS
av. de St-Jean
r. H. Tasso
r. de la Loge
quai du Port
Mémorial des Camps de La Mort
Fort St-Jean
Tunnel du Vieux Port
Vieux Port
Jardin du Pharo
Bas Fort St-Nicolas
Théâtre National de Marseille
r. du Chantier
r. des Tyrans
bd. Charles Livon
SQ. L. AUDEBERT
r. Nueve Ste-Catherine
r. de la Croix
r. de Suez
r. Papety
r. César Aleman
r. des Catalans
r. Georges Charras
av. Pasteur
Fort St-Nicolas
Fort d'Entrecosteaux
Rompe St-Maurice
Abbaye St-Victor
r. Robert
r. Sainte
bd. de la Corderie
Tunnel
r. des Lices
r. Abbé d'Assy
av. de la Corse
r. Otnas
LE PHARO
r. du Rempart
promenade de la corniche du Président J. F. Kennedy
PL. DU QUATRE SEPTEMBRE
r. Candolle
r. Vaurenargues
r. du Cpt. Dessemond
TO BEACHES (1.5km), VALLON DES AUFFES (2km)
r. Saveur Tobelem
r. Paul Codaccioni
r. Samatan
r. de Chateaubriand
r. d'Endoume
r. du Coteau
bd. Tellène
r. Guldicelli
0
500 meters
500 yards
Bd. M. Thomas
Montée du Valentin

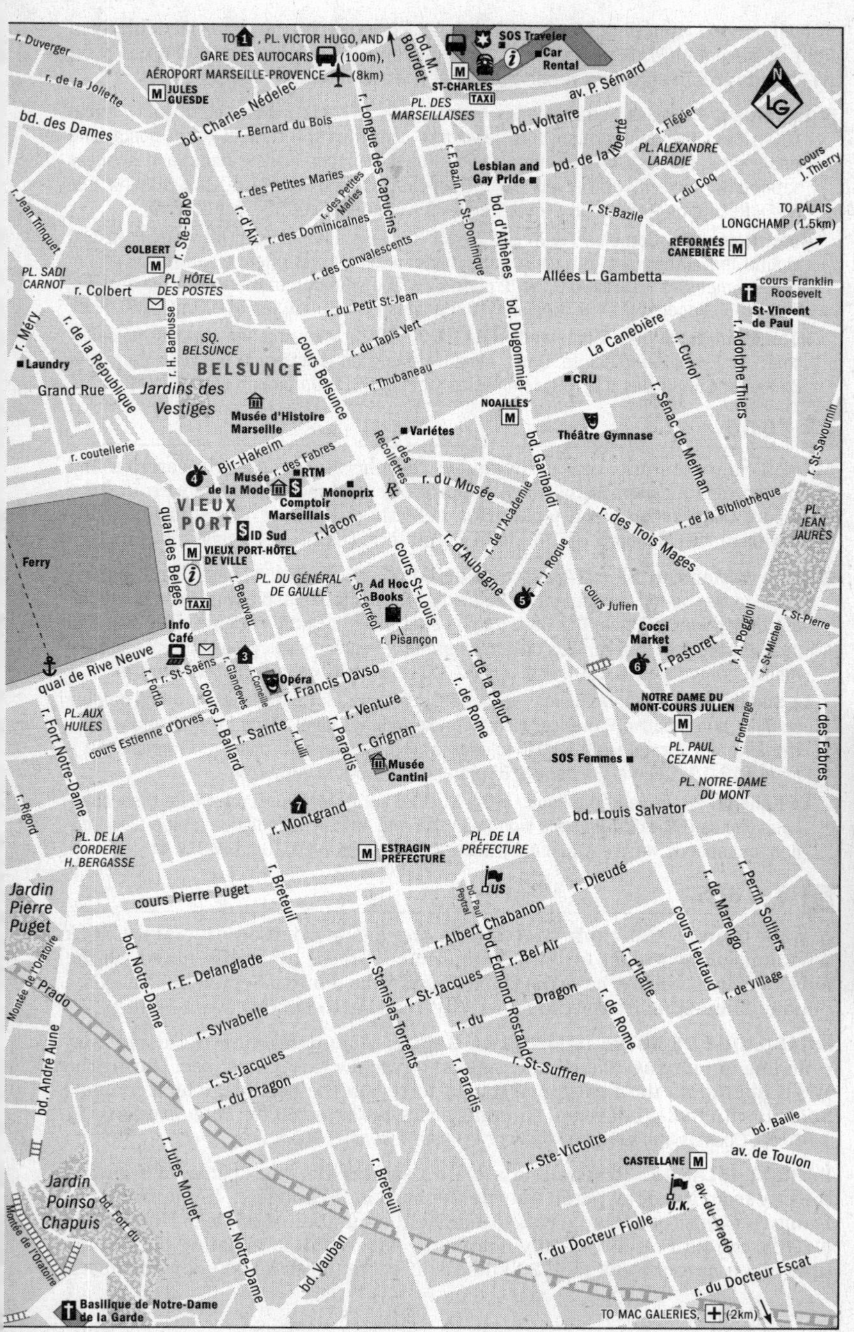
TO 1, PL. VICTOR HUGO, AND
GARE DES AUTOCARS (100m),
AÉROPORT MARSEILLE-PROVENCE (8km)
SOS Traveler
Car Rental
ST-CHARLES
JULES GUESDE
COLBERT
RÉFORMÉS CANEBIÈRE
TO PALAIS LONGCHAMP (1.5km)
St-Vincent de Paul
Laundry
BELSUNCE
Jardins des Vestiges
Musée d'Histoire Marseille
Lesbian and Gay Pride
CRIJ
NOAILLES
Variétes
Théâtre Gymnase
Musée de la Mode
RTM
Monoprix
VIEUX PORT
Comptoir Marseillais
ID Sud
VIEUX PORT-HÔTEL DE VILLE
Ferry
Ad Hoc Books
Info Café
Opéra
Cocci Market
NOTRE DAME DU MONT-COURS JULIEN
SOS Femmes
Musée Cantini
ESTRAGIN PRÉFECTURE
US
CASTELLANE
U.K.
Basilique de Notre-Dame de la Garde
TO MAC GALERIES, (2km)
Jardin Pierre Puget
Jardin Poinso Chapuis
La Canebière
Allées L. Gambetta
cours Belsunce
cours St-Louis
bd. Garibaldi
bd. Dugommier
bd. d'Athènes
r. Longue des Capucins
r. d'Aix
r. de Rome
r. Paradis
r. Breteuil
quai de Rive Neuve
quai des Belges
cours Pierre Puget
bd. Notre-Dame
bd. Louis Salvator
av. de Toulon
av. du Prado
r. du Docteur Fiolle
r. du Docteur Escat
r. d'Aubagne
r. des Trois Mages
cours Julien
cours Lieutaud
cours J. Ballard
r. Sainte
r. Grignan
r. Montgrand
r. Francis Davso
r. Sylvabelle
r. St-Jacques
r. du Dragon
bd. Edmond Rostand
r. Stanislas Torrents
r. Jules Moulet
bd. Vauban
bd. André Aune
PL. DU GÉNÉRAL DE GAULLE
PL. DE LA PRÉFECTURE
PL. JEAN JAURÈS
PL. PAUL CEZANNE
PL. NOTRE-DAME DU MONT
PL. AUX HUILES
PL. DE LA CORDERIE H. BERGASSE
PL. SADI CARNOT
PL. HÔTEL DES POSTES
SQ. BELSUNCE
PL. DES MARSEILLAISES
PL. ALEXANDRE LABADIE
FRANCE

The HI hostel is quiet but inconveniently far from the city center—particularly in light of infrequent bus service and early curfews. Most places fill up quickly on weekends and in summer; reserve at least a week ahead.

Le Vertigo, 42 r. des Petites Maries (☎04 91 91 07 11; www.hotelvertigo.fr). About 100m from the train station, this newcomer combines the best of youth hostel and small hotel. Its English-speaking owners, attractive decor, inviting beds, and spotless bathrooms make it worth every cent. Breakfast €5. Internet €1.50 per 30min.; free Wi-Fi. Reception 24hr. 2- to 6-bed dorms €23.90; doubles €55-65. MC/V. ❷

Hôtel Relax, 4 r. Corneille (☎04 91 33 15 87; www.hotelrelax.fr). M: Vieux Port. Just around the corner from the *vieux port,* this charming hotel offers clean rooms at fair prices. Amenities include A/C, bath, phone, TV, and soundproof windows. Breakfast €6. Free Wi-Fi. Reception 24hr. Singles €40; doubles €50-60; triples €70. AmEx/MC/V. ❷

Hôtel Montgrand, 50 r. Montgrand (☎04 91 00 35 20; www.hotel-montgrand-marseille.com). M: Estragin-Préfecture. Quiet, recently renovated rooms near the *vieux port.* A/C. Breakfast €5. Singles €52-59; family-size rooms €69. Extra person €8. MC/V. ❸

FOOD

Marseille's restaurants are as diverse as its inhabitants. African eateries and kebab stands line **cours St-Louis,** while outdoor cafes pack the streets around the **vieux port. Cours Julien** has a wonderful, eclectic collection of restaurants. Buy groceries at the **Monoprix** on bd. de la Canebière. (Open M-Sa 8:30am-9pm.)

Ivoire Restaurant, 57 r. d'Aubagne (☎04 91 33 75 33). M: Noailles. Loyal patrons come to this no-frills restaurant for authentic African cuisine and advice from its exuberant owner, Mama Africa. The Côte d'Ivoire specialties include *maffé* (a meat dish with peanut sauce; €7.50) and *jus de gingembre* (a refreshingly spicy ginger drink and West African aphrodisiac; €3.50). *Plats* €8.50-12. Open daily noon-4am. Cash only. ❷

Le Sud du Haut, 80 cours Julien (☎04 91 92 66 64). M: Cours Julien. Inviting, outdoor seating, and creative Provençal cuisine make this the ideal place for a leisurely meal. The **lunch formule** (€11.50) includes a *plat,* coffee, and dessert. Entrees €8-11. *Plats* €13-19. Open M-Sa noon-2:30pm and 8-10:30pm. MC/V. ❸

La Kahena, 2 r. de la République (☎04 91 90 61 93). M: Vieux Port. Offers tasty couscous dishes (€9-16) garnished with fresh fish and African ingredients, a blue-tiled interior, and speedy service. Open daily noon-2:30pm and 7-10:30pm. MC/V. ❸

SIGHTS

A walk through the city's streets tops any sights-oriented itinerary. Check www.museum-paca.org for info on museums. Unless otherwise noted, all the museums listed below have the same hours: from June to September Tuesday-Sunday 11am-6pm; from October to May Tuesday to Sunday 10am-5pm.

BASILIQUE DE NOTRE DAME DE LA GARDE. A stunning view of the city, surrounding mountains, and island-studded bay make this a must-see. During the WWII liberation, the Resistance fought to regain the basilica, which remains pocked with bullet holes and shrapnel scars. *(Take bus #60, dir.: Notre Dame. ☎04 91 13 40 80. Open daily in summer 7am-7pm; in winter 7:30am-5:30pm. Free.)*

HARBOR ISLANDS. Resembling a child's sandcastle, the **Château d'If** guards the city from its rocky perch outside the harbor. Its dungeon, immortalized in Dumas's *Count of Monte Cristo,* once held a number of hapless Huguenots. Nearby, the Île Frioul was only marginally successful in isolating plague victims when an outbreak in 1720 killed half of the city's 80,000 citizens. *(Boats* *depart from q. des Belges for numerous islands in the bay. ☎08 25 13 68 00. Round-trip 1½hr. Boats leave at 10, 11:30am, 1:30, 3, and 4:30pm. Adults €15, students €13.50.)*

ABBAYE ST-VICTOR. Fortified against invaders, this medieval abbey's **crypt**—still holding the remains of two martyrs—is one of Europe's oldest Christian sites. Its fifth-century construction brought Christianity to the pagan *Marseillais.* *(On r. Sainte at the end of q. de Rive Neuve. ☎04 96 11 22 60. Festival info ☎04 91 05 84 48. Open daily 9am-7pm. Crypt €2. Festival tickets €33, students €15.)*

MUSÉE CANTINI. This memorable museum chronicles the region's 20th-century artistic successes, with major Cubist, Fauvist, and Surrealist collections, including works by Matisse and Signac. *(19 r. Grignan. M: Estragin-Préfecture. ☎04 91 54 77 75. €2.50, students €1.50, over 65 and under 10 free.)*

OTHER SIGHTS. The **Musée de la Mode**'s rotating exhibits feature international clothing from different eras. *(Espace Mode Méditerranée, 11 La Canebière. M: Vieux Port-Hôtel de Ville. ☎04 96 17 06 00. €3, students €1, seniors free.)* At the nearby **Musée d'Histoire de Marseille,** Greek, Phoenician, and modern artifacts reveal Marseille's rich past. A museum ticket also gives access to the **Jardin des Vestiges,** just next door. *(Enter through the Centre Bourse mall's lowest level. ☎04 91 90 42 22. Open Tu-Sa noon-7pm. €2, students €1, under 10 free.)* Bus #83 (dir.: Rond-Point du Prado) goes from the *vieux port* to Marseille's main **public beaches.** Get off the bus just after it rounds the David statue (20-30min.). Both the north and south **plages du Prado** offer views of Marseille's surrounding cliffs.

NIGHTLIFE

Late-night restaurants and a few nightclubs center around **place Thiers,** near the *vieux port.* On weekends, tables from the bars along the **quai de Rive Neuve** spill out into the sidewalk. A more counter-culture crowd unwinds along the **cours Julien.** Tourists should exercise caution at night, particularly in Panier and Belsunce, and near the Opera on the *vieux port.* Night buses are scarce, taxis are expensive, and the metro closes early (M-Th and Su 9pm, F-Sa 12:30am). **Trolleybus,** 24 q. de Rive Neuve (M: Vieux Port), is a mega-club in an 18th-century warehouse with three separate rooms for pop-rock, techno, and soul-funk-salsa. Prize-winning French and international DJs have been spinning here for 15 years. (Beer from €5. Mixed drinks €4-8. Cover Sa €10; includes 1 drink. Open July-Aug. W-Sa 11pm-6am; Sept.-June Th-Sa 11pm-6am. MC/V.)

FRANCE

AIX-EN-PROVENCE ☎04 42

Famous for festivals, fountains, and former residents Paul Cézanne and Émile Zola, Aix-en-Provence ("X"; pop. 141,000) caters to tourists without being ruined by them. The **chemin de Cézanne,** 9 av. Paul Cézanne, features a 2hr. self-guided tour that leads to the artist's birthplace and favorite cafes. (Open daily July-Aug. 10am-6pm; Apr.-June and Sept. 10am-noon and 2-6pm; Oct.-Mar. 10am-noon and 2-5pm. €5.50, ages 13-25 €2.) The **Fondation Vasarely,** av. Marcel-Pagnol, in nearby Jas-de-Bouffan, is a must-see for Op-Art fans. (Open Tu-Sa 10am-1pm and 2-6pm. €7, students €4.) The **Cathédrale St-Sauveur,** r. Gaston de Saporta, fell victim to misplaced violence during the Revolution; angry Aixois mistook the apostle statues for statues of royalty and defiantly chopped off their heads. The statues were re-capitated in the 19th century, but remain sans neck. (Open daily 8am-noon and 2-6pm.) In June and July, famous performers and rising stars descend on Aix for the **Festival d'Aix-en-Provence**. (☎04 42 16 11 70; www.festival-aix.com. Tickets from €8.)

July travelers should reserve rooms in March. **Hôtel Paul ❸,** 10 av. Pasteur, has relatively cheap, clean rooms and serves breakfast in a quiet garden. (☎04 42

23 23 89; hotel.paul@wanadoo.fr. Breakfast €5. Check-in before 6pm. Singles and doubles with bath €43, with garden-facing windows €53; triples €65; quads €76. Cash only.) Charming restaurants pack **rue Verrerie** and the roads north of **cours Mirabeau. Rue Verrerie,** off r. des Cordiliers, has bars and clubs.

Trains, at the end of av. Victor Hugo, run to Marseille (45min., 27 per day, €7), Nice (3-4hr., 25 per day, €35), and Paris (TGV 3hr., 10 per day, €77-131). **Buses** (☎08 91 02 40 25) leave av. de l'Europe for Marseille (30min., 6 per hr., €5). The **tourist office** is at 2 pl. du Général de Gaulle. (☎04 42 16 11 61; www.aixenprovencetourism.com. Open July-Aug. M-Sa 8:30am-9pm, Su 10am-8pm; Sept.-June M-Sa 8:30am-8pm, Su 10am-1pm and 2-6pm.) **Postal Code:** 13100.

FRENCH RIVIERA (CÔTE D'AZUR)

Between Marseille and the Italian border, sun-drenched beaches and warm Mediterranean waters combine to form the fabled playground of the rich and famous. Chagall, F. Scott Fitzgerald, Matisse, Picasso, and Renoir all flocked to the coast in its heyday. Now, the Riviera is a curious combination of high-rolling millionaires and low-budget tourists. In May, high society makes its yearly pilgrimage to the Cannes Film Festival and the Monte-Carlo Grand Prix, while Nice's February Carnaval and summer jazz festivals draw budget travelers.

NICE ☎04 93

Classy, colorful Nice (NIECE; pop. 340,000) is the Riviera's unofficial capital. Its non-stop nightlife, top-notch museums, and packed beaches are tourist magnets. During February Carnaval, visitors and *Niçois* alike ring in spring with revelry. When visiting Nice, prepare to have more fun than you'll remember.

TRANSPORTATION

Flights: Aéroport Nice-Côte d'Azur (NCE; ☎08 20 42 33 33). Air France, 10 av. de Verdun (☎08 02 80 28 02). To: **Bastia, Corsica** (€116; under 25 and couples €59) and **Paris** (€93/50). **Buses** on the Ligne d'Azur (€4, 3-4 per hr.) leave for the airport from the train station (#99), bus station (#98); before 8am, take bus #23 (€1, 3-4 per hr.).

Trains: Gare SNCF Nice-Ville, av. Thiers (☎14 82 12). Open daily 5am-12:00am. To: **Cannes** (40min., 3 per hr., €6.30); **Marseille** (2hr., 16 per day, €28.50); **Monaco** (15min., 2-6 per hr., €2.80-4); **Paris** (5hr., 9 per day, €136.10).

Buses: 5 bd. Jean Jaurès (☎04 93 85 61 81). Info booth open M-F 8:30am-5:30pm, Sa 9am-4pm. To **Cannes** (2hr., 2-3 per hr.) and **Monaco** (1hr., 3-6 per hr.). All ligne d'Azur buses are now €1 for any destination.

Ferries: Corsica Ferries (☎04 92 00 42 93; www.corsicaferries.com). Bus #1 or 2 (dir.: Port) from pl. Masséna. To **Corsica** (€20-40, bikes €10, cars €40-65). MC/V.

Public Transportation: Ligne d'Azur, 10 av. Félix Faure (☎93 13 53 13; www.lignedazur.com), near pl. Leclerc. Buses run daily 7am-8pm. Tickets €1, 1-day pass €4, 7 day pass €15, and 10 trip pass €10. Purchase tickets and day passes on board the bus; *carnet* passes from the office. **Noctambus** (night service) runs 4 routes daily 9:10pm-1:10am. Completed in 2009, the Nice **tram** runs along Jean Médecin and Place Massena, connecting the northern reaches of the city to the eastern edge. The 8.7 km line is wheelchair-accessible, air-conditioned, and stops about every 5 minutes along its L shaped route from 6am to 2am. Prices and tickets are the same as the buses.

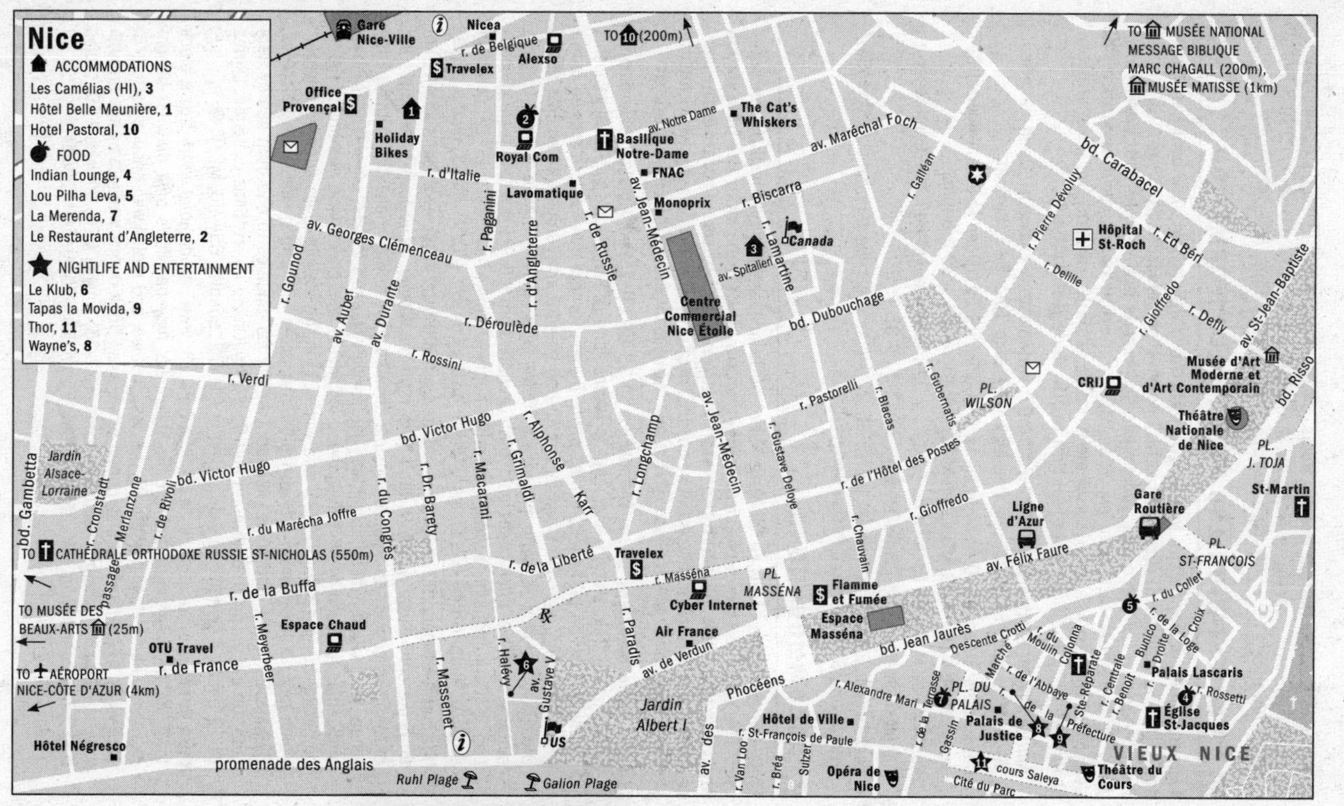
Nice
ACCOMMODATIONS
Les Camélias (HI), 3
Hôtel Belle Meunière, 1
Hotel Pastoral, 10
FOOD
Indian Lounge, 4
Lou Pilha Leva, 5
La Merenda, 7
Le Restaurant d'Angleterre, 2
NIGHTLIFE AND ENTERTAINMENT
Le Klub, 6
Tapas la Movida, 9
Thor, 11
Wayne's, 8
TO MUSÉE NATIONAL MESSAGE BIBLIQUE MARC CHAGALL (200m), MUSÉE MATISSE (1km)
TO 10 (200m)
TO CATHÉDRALE ORTHODOXE RUSSIE ST-NICHOLAS (550m)
TO MUSÉE DES BEAUX-ARTS (25m)
TO AÉROPORT NICE-CÔTE D'AZUR (4km)
Gare Nice-Ville
Nicea
Alexso
Travelex
Office Provençal
Holiday Bikes
Royal Com
Lavomatique
Basilique Notre-Dame
FNAC
Monoprix
The Cat's Whiskers
Canada
Centre Commercial Nice Étoile
Hôpital St-Roch
CRIJ
Musée d'Art Moderne et d'Art Contemporain
Théâtre Nationale de Nice
Gare Routière
St-Martin
Ligne d'Azur
Flamme et Fumée
Espace Masséna
Cyber Internet
Air France
Espace Chaud
OTU Travel
Hôtel Négresco
US
Palais Lascaris
Église St-Jacques
Théâtre du Cours
Palais de Justice
Hôtel de Ville
Opéra de Nice
Jardin Albert I
Jardin Alsace-Lorraine
Ruhl Plage
Galion Plage
promenade des Anglais
VIEUX NICE
PL. MASSÉNA
PL. WILSON
PL. J. TOJA
PL. ST-FRANCOIS
PL. DU PALAIS
av. Jean-Médecin
bd. Victor Hugo
bd. Dubouchage
bd. Carabacel
av. Maréchal Foch
av. Georges Clémenceau
av. Félix Faure
bd. Jean Jaurès
av. de Verdun
bd. Gambetta
r. de France
r. de la Buffa
r. Paradis
r. Masséna
r. Alphonse Karr
r. de la Liberté
r. Grimaldi
r. Macarani
r. Dr. Barety
r. du Congrès
r. Massenet
r. Halévy
av. Gustave V
r. Meyerbeer
r. Verdi
r. Rossini
r. Déroulède
r. Paganini
r. d'Italie
r. d'Angleterre
r. de Russie
r. de Belgique
r. Lamartine
r. Biscarra
r. Gustave Deloye
r. Chauvain
r. Blacas
r. Gubernatis
r. Pastorelli
r. de l'Hôtel des Postes
r. Gioffredo
r. Longchamp
r. Pierre Dévoluy
r. Delille
r. Galléan
r. Ed Béri
r. Defly
av. St-Jean-Baptiste
bd. Risso
r. du Collet
r. de la Loge
r. Droite
r. Croix
r. Rossetti
r. Benoit
r. Centrale
Ste-Réparate
r. Colonna
r. du Moulin
Marché
Descente Crotti
r. de l'Abbaye
r. de la Préfecture
r. de la Terrasse
r. Gassin
cours Saleya
Cité du Parc
r. Alexandre Mari
r. St-François de Paule
r. Sulzer
r. Bréa
r. Van Loo
av. des Phocéens
av. Durante
av. Auber
r. Gounod
r. du Marécha Joffre
r. de Rivoli
passage Merlanzone
r. Cronstadt
av. Notre Dame
av. Spitalieri
FRANCE

Bike and Scooter Rental: Holiday Bikes, 34 av. Auber (☎04 93 16 01 62; nice@holiday-bikes.com), near the train station. Bikes €18 per day, €75 per week; €230 deposit. Scooters €40/175; €500 deposit. Open M-Sa 9am-6:30pm. AmEx/MC/V.

ORIENTATION AND PRACTICAL INFORMATION

Avenue Jean Médecin, on the left as you exit the train station, and **boulevard Gambetta,** on the right, run directly to the beach. **Place Masséna** is 10min. down av. Jean Médecin. On the coast, **promenade des Anglais** is a people-watcher's paradise. To the southeast, past av. Jean Médecin and toward the bus station, is **vieux Nice.** Everyone should exercise caution at night, around the train station, along the port, in *vieux* Nice, and on promenade des Anglais.

Tourist Office: av. Thiers (☎08 92 70 74 07; www.nicetourisme.com). Open June-Sept. M-Sa 8am-8pm, Su 9am-7pm; Oct.-May M-Sa 8am-7pm, Su 9am-6pm.

Consulates: Canada, 10 r. Lamartine (☎04 93 92 93 22). Open M-F 9am-noon. **US,** 7 av. Gustave V (☎88 89 55). Open M-F 9-11:30am and 1:30-4:30pm.

Police: 1 av. Maréchal Foch (☎04 92 17 22 22), opposite end from bd. Jean Médecin.

Hospital: St-Roch, 5 r. Pierre Dévoluy (☎04 92 03 33 75).

Post Office: 23 av. Thiers (☎04 93 82 65 22), found near the train station. Open M-F 8am-7pm, Sa 8am-noon. **Postal Code:** 06033.

ACCOMMODATIONS

Make reservations before visiting Nice; beds are elusive particularly in summer. The city has two clusters of budget accommodations: near the **train station** and near **vieux Nice.** Those by the station are newer but more remote; the surrounding neighborhood has a deservedly rough reputation, so exercise caution at night. Hotels closer to *vieux* Nice are more convenient but less modern.

Hôtel Belle Meunière, 21 av. Durante (☎04 93 88 66 15; www.bellemeuniere.com), opposite the train station. According to legend, one of Napoleon's generals gave this stunning mansion to his mistress as a gift. Budget favorite now hosts a relaxed crowd in private rooms with baths and in 4- to 5-bed co-ed dorms, some with ensuite baths. Breakfast included in dorm prices, €3.50 for those renting private rooms. Luggage storage available after check-out (€2). Laundry from €6. Parking available. Reception 7:30am-midnight; access code after hours. Dorms in summer €17-22, in winter €15-20; doubles €44-57; triples €48-63; quads €64-84. MC/V with €1 surcharge. ❷

Villa Saint-Exupéry, 22 av. Gravier (toll free ☎0800 30 74 09; www.vsaint.com), 5km from the *centre-ville* and less than 1km from the Comte de Falicon tram stop. One of Europe's coolest backpacker hostels, located in a former monestary. Outstanding amenities include a beatiful outdoor garden with France's longest bio-wall, canyoning and sailing tours led by staff (call ahead for prices), and cheap food and drink (nightly dinner €6.50; pizza €5.50; beer and wine €1) in the stained-glass-adorned "chapel," which morphs into a lively bar at night. Most rooms with baths, some with balconies. Breakfast, internet, and Wi-Fi included. Laundry €5. Shuttles to and from nearby tram stop run every 15min. 8am-noon and 6pm-2am. Online reservations preferred. Dorms (4-12 beds) in summer €18-30, in winter €16-22; doubles €54-90. MC/V. ❷

Hôtel Paradis, 1 rue Paradis (☎04 93 87 71 23; www.paradishotel.com). Just a block from the Mediterranean, the 7 dorm-style beds may be Nice's best deal for beachheads on a budget. Also offers airy singles, doubles, and triples with ensuite bath. A/C. Free Wi-Fi; free internet at sister hotel 5min. away. Book dorms well in advance through www.hostelbookers.com. In summer dorms €22-25; singles €75; doubles €90; triples €120. In winter singles €50; doubles €60-65; triples €90. AmEx/MC/V. ❷

FOOD

Mediterranean spices flavor Niçois cuisine. Try crusty *pan bagnat*, a round loaf of bread topped with tuna, sardines, vegetables, and olive oil, or *socca*, a thin, olive-oil-flavored chickpea bread. Famous *salade niçoise* combines tuna, olives, eggs, potatoes, tomatoes, and a spicy mustard dressing. Save your euro for olives, cheese, and produce from the **markets** at cours Saleya and avenue Maché de la Libération (both open Tu-Su 7am-1pm). **Avenue Jean Médecin** features reasonable brasseries, panini vendors, and kebab stands.

La Merenda, 4 rue Bosio. Savor the work of a culinary master, Dominique Le Stanc, who turned his back on one of Nice's best-known restaurants to open this 12-table gem. Outstanding *plats* (€11-16) rotate based on the availability of ingredients. *Ratatouille* and pizza €11. Wine €8 per glass. Open M-F noon-1:30pm and 7-9pm. Reserve in person for lunch and dinner. Cash only. ❸

Lou Pilha Leva, 10-13 rue du Collet (☎04 93 13 99 08), in vieux Nice. Lively staff dishes out plate after plate of excellent local pub-style grub, including *socca* (€2.50), *pissaladière* (€3), and *salade niçoise* (€8), to patrons seated at long wooden outdoor tables. The assortment *niçois* (€8) offers a hearty sampling of the area's typical fare. Pizza €4. Lasagna €8. Open daily 10:30am-midnight. MC/V over €10. ❷

Le Restaurant d'Angleterre, 25 rue d'Angleterre (☎04 93 88 64 49), near the train station. Local favorite known for traditional French and English favorites. €16 *menù* includes starter, *plat,* side dish, and dessert. €27 gourmet *menu* includes cheese course and gourmet options like Burgundy snails. Open Tu-Sa 11:45am-2pm and 6:45-9:50pm, Su 11:45am-2pm. MC/V. ❸

SIGHTS

One look at Nice's waves and you may be tempted to spend your entire stay stretched out on the sand. As the city with the second-most museums in France, however, Nice offers more than azure waters and topless sunbathers.

VIEUX NICE. Although vieux Nice, the oldest part of the city, lacks museums and other sights of the traditional sort, its hand-painted awnings, beautiful churches, and lively squares more than justify a meander down its winding and largely pedestrian streets. Filled with the inevitable slew of souvenir shops, vieux Nice still remains the heart of the city. Bilingual street signs introduce you to Niçard, a dialect of the Occitan language still spoken by half a million people in France. In summer, the streets of vieux Nice pulse with commerce: as shop owners ply their wares along cramped sidewalks, vendors selling fresh and dried flowers take over **cours Saleya,** and crafts merchants occupy the square fronting Nice's imposing neoclassical **Palais de Justice.** *(Guided tours of vieux Nice start at the tourist office Sa 9:30am. €12, under 10 €6, under 5 free.)*

MUSÉE D'ART MODERNE ET D'ART CONTEMPORAIN. Located just blocks from vieux Nice and spread over four levels, Nice's Museum of Modern and Contemporary Art is a true gem. Its minimalist galleries pay homage to French New Realists and American pop artists like Lichtenstein, Oldenberg, Dine, and Warhol. Changing contemporary exhibits showcase artists from around the world in considerable depth. *(Promenade des Arts, near av. St-Jean-Baptiste. Tram: Cathédrale. ☎04 93 62 61 62; www.mamac-nice.org. Open Tu-Su 10am-6pm. Tours in English available July-Aug. by reservation. Free. Tours €3, students €1.50, under 18 free. Cash only.)*

MUSÉE NATIONAL MESSAGE BIBLIQUE MARC CHAGALL. This impressive museum was founded by Chagall to showcase an assortment of biblically themed pieces that he gave to the French government in 1966. The museum includes an auditorium that hosts concerts and other events (check the schedule online); it is decorated with stained-glass panels by Chagall depicting the creation story. *(Av. du Docteur Ménard. Walk 15min. northeast from the train station or take bus #22, dir.: Rimiez, to Musée Chagall. ☎04 93 53 87 20; www.musee-chagall.fr. Open May-Oct. M and W-Su 10am-6pm; Nov.-Mar. M and W-Su 10am-5pm. Last entry 30min. before closing. €9.50, under 25 €7.50; art students and EU citizens free. Free 1st Su of month. When there is no temporary exhibition, prices fall to €7.50/5.50.)*

LE CHÂTEAU. The remains of an 11th-century fort located on a hilltop overlooking vieux Nice, Le Château marks the city's birthplace. Celto-Ligurian tribes called the spot home until they were ousted by the Romans in 154 BC. Centuries later, Provençal nobles built a castle and the Cathédrale Ste-Marie on top of the hill as a symbol of their authority over the developing village below. Louis XIV methodically destroyed the château and fortress in 1706; all that remains today is a green park, stone ruins, and Nice's best view at the highest point, **Terrace Nietzsche.** Those looking to avoid the lengthy but manageable walk to the summit can take an elevator most of the way, though some climbing is still required to reach the very top. *(Elevator open daily June-Aug. 9am-8pm; Sept. and Apr.-May 10am-7pm; Oct.-Mar. 10am-6pm. €0.90 one way, €1.20 round trip.)* Those overheated from the ascent should seek out the manmade waterfall just below the peak of the hill—a refreshing breeze emanates from its base. *(☎04 93 85 62 33. Park open daily June-Aug. 9am-8pm; Sept. 10am-7pm; Oct.-Mar. 8am-6pm; Apr.-May 8am-7pm. Info booth open July-Aug. Tu-F 9:30am-12:30pm and 1:30-6pm. Free.)*

ENTERTAINMENT AND NIGHTLIFE

Nice's **Jazz Festival,** at the Parc et Arènes de Cimiez, attracts world-famous performers. (mid-July; ☎08 20 80 04 00; www.nicejazzfest.com. €31-51.) The **Carnaval** gives Rio a run for its money with three weeks of confetti, fireworks, parades, and parties. (☎04 92 14 46 46; www.nicecarnaval.com.) Bars and nightclubs around **rue Masséna** and **vieux Nice** pulsate with dance and jazz but have a strict dress code. To experience Nice's nightlife without spending a euro, head down to the **promenade des Anglais,** where street performers, musicians, and pedestrians fill the beach and boardwalk. Hard to find *Le Pitchoun* provides the lowdown on trendy bars and clubs (in French; free; www.lepitchoun.com). Exercise caution after dark; men have a reputation for harassing lone women on the promenade, in the Jardin Albert I, and near the train station, while the beach sometimes becomes a gathering place for prostitutes and thugs.

FRANCE

Wayne's, 15 rue de la Préfecture (☎04 93 13 46 99; www.waynes.fr). Huge crowd every night in and around one of vieux Nice's most popular bars. English-speaking bartenders serve travelers while a rowdier crew dances to pop-rock on packed tabletops and benches downstairs. Rock posters and plasma TVs complete the decor. Pints €6-7. Mixed drinks €7.50. Live music or DJ. Th Ladies Night in low season. Happy hour 5-9pm; beer €3.90. Open daily noon-2am. AmEx/MC/V.

Tapas la Movida, 2 bis rue de l'Abbaye. Once a tapas bar, this hole-in-the-wall doesn't serve food anymore. Instead, it doles out some of Nice's cheapest drinks to a young, alternative crowd. Figure out how to crawl home before attempting the **bar-o-mètre** (€18), a meter-long box of shots. Live reggae, rock, and ska concerts M-F (M-Tu free, W-F €2). Open M-Th and Su 8:30pm-1am, F-Sa 8:30pm-2:30am. Cash only.

Smarties, 10 rue Défly (☎04 93 62 30 75; nicesmarties.free.fr). This sleek, orange-and-silver "bar electro lounge," decked out in rainbow flags, is one of Nice's trendiest spots to begin a night on the town. Open Tu-Su 5pm-12:30am. Cash only.

Le Six, 6 rue Bosio (☎04 93 62 66 64). Part nightclub and part piano bar, gay-friendly Le Six draws 20- to 40-somethings to its beautiful 19th-century space (think crystal chandeliers and elaborate moldings) to dance to drag queens belting out American top 40 hits. Climb the metal ladder to the small lounge and dance space upstairs for a great view of the antics below. Champagne €8. Mixed drinks €10. Open M-Tu and Th 10pm-4am, F-Sa 10pm-5am, Su 10pm-4am. AmEx/MC/V.

MONACO AND MONTE-CARLO ☎04 93

In 1297, François Grimaldi of Genoa established his family as Monaco's rulers, staging a coup aided by henchmen disguised as *monaco* (Italian for monk). The tiny principality jealously guarded its independence ever since. Monaco (pop. 7100) brashly displays its tax-free wealth with surveillance cameras, high-speed luxury cars, multi-million-dollar yachts, and Monte-Carlo's famous casino.

CALLING TO AND FROM MONACO

Monaco's country code is 377. To call Monaco from France, dial 00377, then the eight-digit Monaco number. To call France from Monaco, dial 0033 and drop the first zero of the French number.

TRANSPORTATION AND PRACTICAL INFORMATION. **Trains** run from Gare SNCF, pl. Ste-Dêvote, to Antibes (1hr., 2 per hr., €6.50), Cannes (1hr., 2 per hr., €8-8.40), and Nice (25min., 2 per hr., €3.10). **Buses** (☎04 93 85 64 44) leave bd. des Moulins and av. Princesse Alice for Nice (45min., 4 per hr., €1). The enormous **Rocher de Monaco** (Rock of Monaco) looms over the harbor. At the city's top, Monaco-Ville, the historical and legislative heart, is home to the **Palais Princier,** the **Cathédrale de Monaco,** and narrow cafe-lined pedestrian avenues. **La Condamine quarter,** Monaco's port, sits below Monaco-Ville, with a morning market, spirited bars, and lots of traffic. Monaco's famous glitz is concentrated in **Monte-Carlo,** whose casino draws international visitors. Bus #4 links the Ste-Dêvote train station entrance to the casino; buy tickets on board (€1). The **tourist office** is at 2A bd. des Moulins. (☎04 92 16 61 16. Open M-Sa 9am-7pm, Su and holidays 11am-1pm.) **Postal Code:** MC 98000 Monaco.

ACCOMMODATIONS AND FOOD. Rather than stay in expensive Monaco, the nearby town of **Beausoleil, FRA,** only a 10min. walk from the casino, offers several budget accommodations. The modest rooms at **Hôtel Diana ❸,** 17 bd. du Général Leclerc, come with A/C and TV. (☎04 93 78 47 58; www.monte-carlo.mc/hotel-diana-beausoleil. Singles €40-60; doubles €40-70; triples €75. Reservations recommended. AmEx/MC/V.) Unsurprisingly, Monaco has little in the way of cheap fare. Try the narrow streets behind the **place du Palais** for affordable sit-down meals, or, better yet, fill a picnic basket at the **market** on pl. d'Armes at the end of av. Prince Pierre. (Open daily 6am-1pm.)

SIGHTS AND ENTERTAINMENT. At the notorious **Monte-Carlo Casino,** pl. du Casino, Richard Burton wooed Elizabeth Taylor and Mata Hari shot a Russian spy. Optimists tempt fate at blackjack, roulette (daily from noon), and slot machines (July-Aug. daily from noon; Sept.-June M-F from 2pm, Sa-Su from noon). French games like *chemin de fer* and *trente et quarante* begin at noon in the exclusive salons privés (€20 extra cover). (Cover €10. Coat and tie required.) Next door, the relaxed **Café de Paris** opens at 10am and has no cover. All casinos have dress codes at night (no sandals, shorts, sneakers, or jeans). Guards are strict about the age requirement (18+); bring a passport as proof. On a seaside cliff, **Palais Princier** is the occasional home of Monaco's tabloid-darling royal family. Visitors can tour the small but lavish palace. (Open daily

June-Sept. 10am-7pm; Oct. 10am-5:30pm. €7, students €3.50.) The venue for Prince Rainier and Grace Kelly's 1956 wedding, nearby **Cathédrale de Monaco,** pl. St-Martin, is the burial site for 35 generations of the Grimaldi family. Princess Grace lies behind the altar in a tomb marked with her Latinized name, "Patritia Gracia"; Prince Rainier is buried on her right. (Open daily Mar.-Oct. 8am-7pm; Nov.-Feb. 8am-6pm. Mass Sa 6pm, Su 10:30am. Free.) The **Private Collection of Antique Cars of His Serene Highness Prince Rainier III,** les Terraces de Fontvieille, showcases 100 sexy cars. (Open daily 10am-6pm. €6, students €3.)

Monaco's nightlife offers fashionistas a chance to see and be seen. Speckled with cheaper venues, **La Condamine,** near the port, caters to a young clientele while glitzy trust-funders frequent pricier spots near the casino. Vintage decor, video games, and the latest pop and techno beats draw young, international masses to **Stars N' Bars,** 6 q. Antoine 1. (☎04 97 97 95 95; www.starsnbars.com. Open June-Sept. daily 9:30am-3am; Oct.-May Tu-Su 11am-3am. AmEx/MC/V.)

ANTIBES ☎04 93

Blessed with beautiful beaches and a charming *vieille ville*, Antibes (pop. 80,000) is less touristy than Nice and more relaxed than St-Tropez. It provides much-needed middle ground on the glitterati-controlled coast. The **Musée Picasso,** in the Château Grimaldi on pl. Mariejol, displays works by the former Antibes resident and his contemporaries. The two main public beaches in Antibes, **plage du Ponteil** and neighboring **plage de la Salis,** are crowded all summer. Cleaner and slightly more secluded, the rocky beaches on Cap d'Antibes have white cliffs and blue water perfect for snorkeling.

For the cheapest accommodations in Antibes, grab a bunk at **The Crew House ❷,** 1 av. St-Roch. From the train station, walk down av. de la Libération; just after the roundabout, make a right onto av. St-Roch. (☎04 92 90 49 39; workstation_fr@yahoo.com. Luggage storage €1.50. Internet €4.80 per hr. Reception M-F 9am-8pm, Sa-Su 10am-6pm. Dorms Apr.-Oct. €25; Nov.-Mar. €20. MC/V.) A variety of restaurants set up outdoor tables along **boulevard d'Aguillon,** behind the *vieux port*. For cheaper eats, you're better off at **place Nationale,** a few blocks away. The **Marché Provençal,** on cours Masséna, is one of the best fresh produce markets on the Côte d'Azur. (Open Tu-Su 6am-1pm.)

Come summer, the hip neighboring town Juan-les-Pins is synonymous with wild nightlife. **Pam Pam Rhumerie,** 137 bd. Wilson, is a hot Brazilian sit-down bar. Bikinied showgirls take the stage at 9:30pm to dance and down flaming drinks. (☎04 93 61 11 05. Open daily mid-Mar. to early Nov. 2pm-5am. MC/V.) Brave long lines to attend one of the popular Mexican fiestas held in **Le Village.** (☎04 92 93 90 00. Ladies free M-Th midnight-12:30am. Cover €16; includes 1 drink. Open July-Aug. daily midnight-5am; Sept.-June F-Sa midnight-5am. MC/V.)

Frequent **buses** (10min., 2 per hr., €1) and **trains** (5min., 1-2 per hr., €1.20) run from Antibes, although walking between the two towns along bd. Wilson is also an option. Although touristy, the **petit train** (☎06 03 35 61 35) leaves r. de la République and serves as both a guided tour of Antibes and a means of transportation to Juan-les-Pins. (30min.; 1 per hr. July-Aug. 10am-10pm, May-Oct. 10am-7pm.; round-trip €8, 3-10 €3.50. Buy tickets on board. Cash only.) **Trains** leave pl. Pierre Semard in Antibes, off av. Robert Soleau, for Cannes (15min., 23 per day, €2.50), Marseille (2hr., 12 per day, €26.70), and Nice (15min., 25 per day, €4.40-5.40). RCA **buses** leave pl. de Gaulle for Cannes (20min.) and Nice (45min.). All buses depart every 20min. and cost €1. The **tourist office** is at 11 pl. de Gaulle. (☎04 97 23 11 11; www.antibes-juanlespins.com. Open July-Aug. daily 9am-7pm; Sept.-June M-F 9am-5pm.) **Postal Code:** 06600.

CANNES ☎04 93

Stars compete for camera time at Cannes's annual, world-famous and invite only **Festival International du Film** (May 15-26, 2009). During the rest of the year, Cannes (pop. 67,000) rolls up all but its most famous red carpet—leaving one at the Palais for your tacky photographic pleasure. During this downtime, it also becomes the most accessible of all the Riviera's glam towns. Of the town's three prestigious casinos, the least exclusive is **Le Casino Croisette,** 1 Lucien Barrière, next to the Palais des Festivals. (No shorts, jeans, or T-shirts. Jackets required for men in gaming rooms. 18+. Open daily 10am-4am; table games 8pm-4am.)

Hotel Mimont ❸, 39 r. de Mimont, is Cannes's best budget hotel. English-speaking owners maintain basic, clean rooms two streets behind the train station. (☎04 93 39 51 64; canneshotelmimont65@wanadoo.fr. Free Wi-Fi. Singles €34-40; doubles €40-47; triples €60. Prices about 15% higher July-Aug. Ask about €30 petites chambres for *Let's Go* readers. MC/V.) The zone around **rue Meynadier** has inexpensive restaurants. Cafes and bars near the waterfront stay open all night and are a great alternative to the expense of gambling and posh clubs. Nightlife thrives around **rue Dr. G. Monod.** Try **Morrison's,** 10 r. Teisseire, for casual company in a literary-themed pub. (☎04 92 98 16 17. Beer from €5.30. Happy hour 5-8pm. Open daily 5pm-2am. MC/V.) Coastal **trains** depart from 1 r. Jean Jaurès for: Antibes (15min., €2.50); Marseille (2hr., 6:30am-11:03pm, €25); Monaco (1hr., €8); Nice (40min., €5.80); St-Raphaël (25min., €6.10). **Buses** go to Nice (1hr., 3 per hr., €6) from the pl. de l'Hôtel de Ville (☎04 93 48 70 30) and Grasse (50min., 1 per hr., €1) from the train station. The **tourist office** is at 1 bd. de la Croisette. (☎04 93 39 24 53; www.cannes.fr. Open July-Aug. daily 9am-8pm; Sept.-June 9am-7pm.) Get Internet at **Cap Cyber,** 12 r. 24 Août. (€3 per hr. Open in summer 10am-11pm; in winter 10am-10pm. MC/V.) **Postal Code:** 06400.

ST-TROPEZ ☎04 94

Hollywood stars, corporate giants, and curious backpackers congregate on the spotless streets of St-Tropez (pop. 5400), where the Riviera's glitz and glamor shines brightest. The young, beautiful, and restless flock to this "Jewel of the Riviera" to flaunt tans and designer clothing on notorious beaches and in posh nightclubs. The best beaches are difficult to reach without a car, but the *navette municipale* (shuttle) leaves pl. des Lices for Les Salins, a secluded sunspot, and **plage Tahiti** (Capon-Pinet stop), the first of the famous plages des Pampelonne. (M-Sa 5 per day, €1. Tourist office has schedule.) Take a break from the sun at the **Musée de l'Annonciade,** pl. Grammont, which showcases Fauvist and neo-Impressionist paintings. (Open M and W-Su June-Sept. 10am-noon and 2-6pm; Oct.-May 10am-1pm and 4-7pm. €6, students €4.)

Budget hotels do not exist in St-Tropez. Camping is the cheapest option, but is only available outside the city. Prices remain shockingly high, especially in July and August. To reach **Les Prairies de la Mer ❸,** a social campground on the beach, take a *bateau vert* (☎04 94 49 29 39) from the *vieux* port to Port Grimaud (Apr. to early Oct., 5min., 1 per hr., round-trip €11). Bowling, supermarkets, tennis courts and other facilities are available. (☎04 94 79 09 09; www.riviera-villages.com. Open late Mar. to early Oct. July to mid-Aug. €8 per person, €45 per tent; Apr.-June and late Aug. €3/20; Sept. to mid-Oct. €3/20. Electricity €5. MC/V.) To eat cheap, stop by the snack stands and cafes near **place des Lices,** the center of St-Tropez's wild nightlife. Sodetrav **buses** (☎04 93 97 88 51) leave av. Général Leclerc for St-Raphaël (2hr., 10-12 per day, €11.30). **Ferries** (☎04 93 95 17 46; www.tmr-saintraphael.com), at the *vieux* port, serve St-Tropez from St-Raphaël (1hr., 4-5 per day, €13 one-way, 22 round-trip). The **tourist office** is on q. Jean Jaurès. (☎04 93 97 45 21. Open daily 9:30am-8pm; hours vary seasonally.) **Postal Code:** 83990.

GERMANY (DEUTSCHLAND)

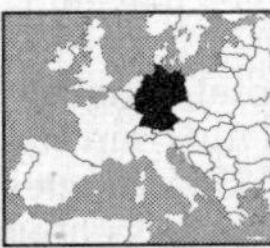

Encounters with history are unavoidable in Germany, as changes in outlook, policy, and culture are manifest in the country's architecture, landscape, and customs. Glass skyscrapers rise from former concrete wastelands; towns crop up from fields and forests, interspersed with medieval castles and industrial structures. World-class music rings out from sophisticated city centers, while a grittier youth culture flourishes in quite different neighborhoods. Such divisions echo the entrenched Cold War separation between East and West. Today, over 20 years after the fall of the Berlin Wall, Germans have fashioned a new identity for themselves. Visitors will find flowing beer and wondrous sights from the darkest corners of the Black Forest to the shores of the Baltic Sea.

DISCOVER GERMANY: SUGGESTED ITINERARIES

THREE DAYS. Enjoy 2 days in **Berlin** (p. 253): stroll along **Unter den Linden** and the **Ku'damm,** gape at the **Brandenburger Tor** and the **Reichstag,** and explore the **Tiergarten.** Walk along the **East Side Gallery** and visit **Checkpoint Charlie** for a history of the **Berlin Wall,** then spend an afternoon at **Schloß Sanssouci**. Overnight it to **Munich** (p. 299) for a Stein-themed last day.

ONE WEEK. After scrambling through **Berlin** (3 days), head north to racy **Hamburg** (1 day; p. 282). Then, take in the cathedral of **Cologne** (1 day; p. 290). End your trip Bavarian-style with the beer gardens, castles, and cathedrals of **Munich** (1 day).

TWO WEEKS. Begin in fun and famous **Berlin** (3 days). Party in **Hamburg** (2 days), then zip to **Cologne** (1 day) and glitzy **Frankfurt** (1 day; p. 294). Finally, trot over to **Munich** (2 days), marvel at **Neuschwanstein** (1 day; p. 310), and see the beauty of the **Romantic Road** (2 days; p. 309).

LIFE AND TIMES

HISTORY

EARLY HISTORY AND THE FIRST REICH (UNTIL 1400). Germany's recent history has been one of cyclical unity and fracture, and its early history was no different. The **Roman Empire** conquered the tribes that had occupied the area; Roman ruins can still be seen in **Trier** and **Cologne** (p. 290). After the collapse of the empire, the Germanic tribes separated again, only to be reunified in the AD 8th century by **Charlemagne** (Karl der Große) into what is now known as the **First Reich,** or first empire. Charlemagne established his capital at **Aachen,** where his remains still reside. After his death, the former empire disintegrated into a system of decentralized **feudalism.** Visit **Rothenburg** (p. 310) for a glimpse into a medieval walled city typical of the period.

THE NORTHERN RENAISSANCE (1400-1517). Inspired by the ideas of the Italian Renaissance, northern philosophers developed a tradition of **humanism,**

with a particular focus on religious reform and a return to classical authors. **Johannes Gutenberg** paved the way for widespread dissemination of ideas by inventing the **printing press** in Mainz. Rapid production of books led to increased literacy, putting info—and power—into the hands of laypeople.

RELIGION AND REFORM (1517-1700). On All Saints' Day, 1517, **Martin Luther** nailed his *95 Theses* to the door of Wittenberg's church (p. 491). His treatises, which condemned the extravagances of the Catholic hierarchy, sparked the Protestant Reformation, and his translation of the Bible into German crystallized the various German dialects into a standard literary form and allowed ordinary people to access the text without mediation. Tensions brewing between Catholics and Protestants across the continent eventually led to the long and costly **Thirty Years' War** (1618-1648), which dissolved Germany into small, independent fiefdoms ruled by local princes.

RISE OF BRANDENBURG-PRUSSIA (1700-1862) AND THE SECOND REICH (1862-1914). The 18th and early 19th centuries saw the rise of Prussian power, the conquest of Germany by **Napoleon Bonaparte,** and, after Napoleon's fall, the formation of the Austrian-led **German Confederation.** The relative peace following the establishment of the Confederation came to an end when worldly aristocrat **Otto von Bismarck** was named chancellor of Prussia in 1862. A great practitioner of *Realpolitik* ("the ends justify the means"), Bismarck worked to consolidate the disunited German states through a complex series of political and military maneuvers. These efforts culminated in the **Franco-Prussian War** in 1870, in which the technologically superior Prussians easily swept through France. After the German victory, the king of Prussia, **Wilhelm I,** crowned himself **Kaiser of the German Reich** at Versailles. Bismarck's unification of Germany under an authoritarian ruler made the country a formidable and ambitious neighbor. Anxiety over Germany's rising power soon caused Britain, France, and Russia to band together in the **Triple Entente.**

WORLD WAR I (1914-1918). The growing polarization of Europe resulted in war when, in 1914, a Serbian nationalist assassinated Archduke **Franz Ferdinand,** heir to the Austrian throne. Russia's loyalty to Serbia and Germany's to Austria led this obscure act to plunge the entire continent into the **First World War.** After four agonizing years of trench warfare, Germany and its allies were defeated.

THE WEIMAR REPUBLIC (1918-1933). The harsh peace agreement in the **Treaty of Versailles** drastically reduced the size of the German army and required Germany to make staggering reparation payments. The defeated nation had little choice but to accept these conditions. The constitution for a new republic was written in **Weimar;** its parliament met in the **Reichstag** in Berlin (p. 253). Outstanding war debts and the burden of reparations produced staggering hyperinflation from 1922 to 1923 during which paper money was worth more as fuel in the fireplace than as currency. Already suffering from the Treaty of Versailles, Germany needed any sort of change, which the charismatic Austrian **Adolf Hitler** seemed to promise. His party, the National Socialist German Workers (or **Nazis**), offered an über-nationalist platform.

Hitler's first attempt to seize power, the November 1923 **Beer Hall Putsch** in Munich, failed and ended in his arrest. As hardship worsened, however, Nazi promises of prosperity and community appealed to more Germans, and by 1930, party membership exceeded one million. Hitler failed in his 1932 presidential bid against the nearly senile war hero **Paul von Hindenburg,** but since Hitler's party won a legislative majority, Hindenburg reluctantly appointed Hitler to the position of chancellor on January 30, 1933.

UNDER THE THIRD REICH (1933-1939). Hitler's platform, set out clearly in his early book **Mein Kampf** (My Struggle), used the Jews as a scapegoat for Germany's defeat in WWI. His government instituted a boycott of Jewish enterprises and expelled Jews from professional and civil service. Rival parties were outlawed or dissolved, and after Hindenburg's death in 1934, Hitler appropriated presidential powers. That year also saw the first **Nuremberg Laws,** depriving Jews of German citizenship and preventing intermarriage between Jewish and Aryan residents. Nazis destroyed Jewish businesses, burned synagogues, and killed and deported thousands of Jews on the **Kristallnacht** (Night of Broken Glass), November 9, 1938. With the help of **Joseph Goebbels,** his minister of propaganda, Hitler consolidated his power by saturating media with Nazi ideology. The Nazis burned books by Jewish and other "subversive" authors at Bebelplatz in Berlin, banned American art, and relentlessly destroyed "degenerate" art in favor of propagandist paintings and statues.

Hitler went beyond attacking his own country and began invading others. In 1938, he annexed Austria in an infamous maneuver known as the **Anschluß.** Other nations, hoping to avert another world war, next sanctioned his invasion of the Sudetenland, now part of the Czech Republic, at the **Munich Accords.**

WORLD WAR II (1939-1945). Despite Hitler's promises at Munich that he would not seek to acquire further territories, German tanks rolled into Poland on September 1, 1939. Britain and France immediately declared war on Germany, dragging most of the world into conflict. Germany's **Blitzkrieg** (lightning war) overwhelmed Poland; Belgium, Denmark, France, the Netherlands, and Norway were soon swallowed up as well.

Soon the Nazis had opened two fronts, attacking westward with an airborne offensive in the **Battle of Britain** and eastward with the invasion of the USSR, which had not yet joined the Allies. Daily air raids spurred the British to fight back tooth and nail, and the *Blitzkrieg* on the eastern front faltered in the Russian winter; Hitler sacrificed thousands of his soldiers by refusing to retreat. The bloody **Battle of Stalingrad** (1942-1943), won by the Soviets, marked a critical turning point on the eastern front. The western front was punctured by the Allied landing in Normandy on **D-Day** (June 6, 1944) and followed by an arduous advance eastward. The Soviet Army finally took Berlin in April 1945. The Third Reich, which Hitler boasted would endure for 1000 years, had lasted only 12.

THE HOLOCAUST. At the center of Nazi ideology was **genocide,** Hitler's "final solution" to the "Jewish question." By 1940, Jews had lost all rights and had to wear yellow Star of David patches. By 1945, nearly six million Jews—two-thirds of those living in Europe—had been gassed, shot, starved, and worked to death in these camps. Six death camps carried out this mass extermination; dozens of "labor" camps, including **Dachau** (p. 309), held Jews and other undesirables. Millions of others, including other religious minorities, prisoners of war, Slavs, Roma (gypsies), homosexuals, mentally disabled persons, and political dissidents, also died in Nazi camps.

OCCUPATION AND DIVISION (1945-1949). In July 1945, the United States, Great Britain, and the Soviet Union met at **Potsdam** to partition Germany into zones of occupation. The East went to the Soviets and the West to the British and Americans; Berlin was likewise divided. Despite rising Western animosity toward the Soviets, their plan of democratization, demilitarization, and de-Nazification proceeded apace. In 1948, the Allies welded their zones into a single economic unit, and, with huge infusions of cash granted by the American **Marshall Plan,** they began to rebuild a market economy in Western Germany. Afterward, and especially after the Allies' introduction of the **Deutschmark,** Germany's twin halves became increasingly disparate.

THE FEDERAL REPUBLIC OF GERMANY (1949-1989). Western Germany established the Federal Republic of Germany *(Bundesrepublik Deutschland)* as its provisional government on May 23, 1949. Its **Basic Law** safeguarded individual rights and established a system of freely elected parliamentary assemblies. One of its most visionary paragraphs established a **Right of Asylum,** which guaranteed refuge to any person escaping from persecution.

As the only party untainted by the Third Reich, the **Social Democratic Party (SDP)** seemed poised to dominate postwar politics, but the **Christian Democratic Union (CDU)** was able to gain power in the new Federal Republic by uniting Germany's historically fragmented conservatives and centrists under one platform. Helmed by former Cologne mayor **Konrad Adenauer,** the CDU won a small majority of seats in the Federal Republic's first general election. As chancellor, Adenauer tirelessly worked to integrate Germany into a unified Europe. West Germany aligned in 1955 with the **North Atlantic Treaty Organization (NATO)** and became a charter member of the European Coal and Steel Community, precursor to the **European Union (EU).** Speedy fiscal recovery consolidated the position of the CDU. In 1982, the CDU's **Helmut Kohl** became chancellor and pursued a policy of tight monetary policy and military cooperation with the US.

THE GERMAN DEMOCRATIC REPUBLIC (1949-1989). Despite pledges to the contrary, the Soviets ended free elections in their sector in 1949. On October 7, they established the **German Democratic Republic,** with Berlin as its capital. Constitutional promises of civil liberties and democracy were empty: East Germany became a satellite of the Soviet Union. The **Stasi,** or secret police, strove to monitor every citizen from their Berlin headquarters using spy networks—one in seven East Germans was a paid informant.

Many chose to escape oppression by immigrating to West Germany. By 1961, more than three million had crossed the border illegally, and the East German government decided to stop the exodus of young skilled workers. Overnight, on August 12, the first foundations of the **Berlin Wall** were laid; barbed wire and guns dissuaded further attempts to escape.

REUNIFICATION (1989). Following his policy of **glasnost** (openness), Soviet President **Mikhail Gorbachev** announced in October 1989 that the USSR would not interfere with East Germany's domestic affairs. Citizens began to demand free elections and freedom of press and of travel. The entire East German government resigned on November 8, 1989, and the next day the Central Committee announced all borders open to the West. Both West and East Germans began climbing over and dismantling the Berlin Wall in what would become the symbolic and most profound end of the Cold War.

On September 12, 1990, the two halves and the four occupying powers signed the **Four-Plus-Two Treaty,** which spelled the **end of a divided Germany.** On October 3, Germany became a united sovereign nation for the first time in 45 years. East and West Germany did not come together on equal terms, however. The collapse of East Germany's inefficient industries brought with it massive unemployment in the East and ushered in the West's worst-ever recession. Many Westerners resented the inflation and taxes brought on by reunification, while Easterners missed the generous social benefits associated with communism. Economic frustrations led to the scapegoating of foreigners, especially immigrant workers and asylum-seekers from Eastern Europe, leading Germany to abolish its uncategorical right to asylum. Germany has recently begun to implement economic and social reforms that seek to address this issue.

TODAY

After the demolition of the Berlin Wall in 1989, Helmut Kohl and his CDU party seemed invincible, scoring a victory in the first all-German elections. Kohl had difficulties managing the reunification, however, and his popularity plummeted to the point that Easterners pelted him with eggs during campaign visits. In 1998, left-wingers ousted the CDU and elected **Gerhard Schröder** chancellor.

Given the past, many continue to be uneasy about Germany's participation in military operations. Germans have recently promoted peace, however, with a hand in peacekeeping missions in Yugoslavia and flood relief operations in Africa. Germany was also initially an outspoken critic of aggressive Anglo-American foreign policy after the terrorist attacks of September 11, 2001. Rioters greeted American President George W. Bush's visit to Berlin in May 2002 with protests significant enough to necessitate the largest police presence since the end of WWII. Relations, however, have recently improved; in February 2004, Schröder issued a joint statement with Bush on "The German-American Alliance for the 21st Century." Ties to America were strengthened with the election of Germany's current and first female chancellor, CDU-affiliated **Angela Merkel**—so strengthened that US President George W. Bush felt the urge to give her an impromptu shoulder rub at a 2006 G-8 Summit. Merkel has also made waves for having the highest approval rating recorded for a German chancellor since 1949, although the failure of her plan to reform national healthcare in 2007 has lowered her notable popularity.

In recent years, major symbols have marked Germany's reconciliation with its other WWII antagonists. Schröder attended the 60th anniversary of the D-Day invasion in France in 2004 and was present at the opening of Berlin's **Holocaust Memorial** in 2005. Even German architecture shows signs of the nation's healing: the cross now atop Dresden's Frauenkirche was built by the son of a RAF pilot who took part in the Allied firebombing of the city.

PEOPLE AND CULTURE

DEMOGRAPHICS AND RELIGION. Germany is home to roughly 82 million people. Most of Germany's population growth in recent years has come from a rise in immigration. The group of Turkish immigrants is the largest, followed by groups from various Southern and Eastern European countries; together, these groups account for nearly 10% of the population. In terms of religion, Germany has developed as a Christian country, with the Protestant North and the Roman Catholic South each currently representing about one-third of the country's inhabitants. The total Jewish population in Germany today has risen to approximately 100,000; the largest Jewish congregations are in Berlin and Frankfurt. A small Islamic community has also developed as a result of the steady Turkish and Bosnian immigration.

LANGUAGE. Younger Germans and residents of Western Germany are usually proficient in English. For some basic German, see **Phrasebook: German,** p. 598.

ESSENTIALS

WHEN TO GO

Germany's climate is temperate. The mild months of May, June, and September are the best time to go, as there are fewer tourists and enjoyable weather. In July, Germans head en masse to summer spots. Winter sports gear up from November to April; ski season takes place from mid-December to March.

DOCUMENTS AND FORMALITIES

EMBASSIES. All foreign embassies are in Berlin (p. 253). German embassies abroad include: **Australia,** 119 Empire Circuit, Yarralumla, Canberra, ACT 2600 (☎02 6270 1911; www.germanembassy.org.au); **Canada,** 1 Waverly St., Ottawa, ON, K2P OT8 (☎613-232-1101; www.ottawa.diplo.de); **Ireland,** 31 Trimleston Ave., Booterstown, Blackrock, Co. Dublin (☎01 269 3011; www.dublin.diplo.de); **New Zealand,** 90-92 Hobson St., Thorndon, Wellington 6001 (☎04 473 6063; www.wellington.diplo.de); **UK,** 23 Belgrave Sq., London, SW1X 8PZ (☎020 7824 1300; www.london.diplo.de); **US,** 4645 Reservoir Rd. NW, Washington, D.C., 20007 (☎202-298-4000; www.germany-info.org).

FACTS AND FIGURES

OFFICIAL NAME: Federal Republic of Germany.	**RELIGIONS:** Protestant (34%), Roman Catholic (34%), Muslim (2%).
CAPITAL: Berlin.	**PERCENTAGE OF EUROPEAN BEER PRODUCTION:** 26.5%.
MAJOR CITIES: Cologne, Frankfurt, Hamburg, Munich.	**LAND AREA:** 349,200 sq. km.
POPULATION: 82,401,000	**TIME ZONE:** GMT +1.

VISA AND ENTRY INFORMATION. EU citizens do not need a visa. Citizens of Australia, Canada, New Zealand, and the US do not need a visa for stays of up to 90 days, beginning upon entry into any of the countries in the EU's freedom-of-movement zone. For more info, see p. 8. For stays longer than 90 days, all non-EU citizens need visas (around €100), available at German consulates.

TOURIST SERVICES AND MONEY

EMERGENCY	**Ambulance** and **Fire:** ☎112. **Police:** ☎110.

TOURIST OFFICES. The **National Tourist Board** website (www.germany-tourism.de) links to regional info and provides dates of national and local festivals. Every city in Germany has a tourist office, usually near the *Hauptbahnhof* (main train station) or *Marktplatz* (central square). All are marked by a sign with a thick lowercase "i," and many book rooms for a small fee.

MONEY. The **euro (€)** has replaced the **Deutschmark (DM)** as the unit of currency in Germany. For more info, see p. 10. As a general rule, it's cheaper to exchange money in Germany than at home. Costs for those who stay in hostels and prepare their own food may range anywhere from €25-50 per person per day. **Tipping** is not practiced as liberally in Germany as elsewhere—most natives just round up €1. Tips are handed directly to the server with payment of the bill—if you don't want any change, say *"Das stimmt so"* (das SHTIMMT zo; "so it stands"). Germans rarely bargain except at flea markets.

BUSINESS HOURS. Offices and stores are open from 9am-6pm, Monday through Friday, often closing for an hour lunch break. Stores may be open on Saturday in cities or shopping centers. Banks are also open from approximately 9am-6pm and close briefly in the late afternoon, but they may stay open late on Thursday nights. Many museums are closed on Monday.

TRANSPORTATION

BY PLANE. Most international flights land at **Frankfurt Airport (FRA;** ☎069 6900; www.airportcity-frankfurt.com); **Berlin (BML), Munich (MUC),** and **Hamburg (HAM)** also have international airports. **Lufthansa,** the national airline, is not always the best-priced option. For cheaper domestic travel by plane than by train; check out **Air Berlin** (www.airberlin.com), among other options.

BY TRAIN. The **Deutsche Bahn (DB;** www.bahn.de) network is Europe's best—and one of its most expensive. Luckily, all trains have clean and comfy second-class compartments, and there are a wide variety of train lines to choose from. **RegionalBahn (RB)** trains include rail networks between neighboring cities and connects to **RegionalExpress (RE)** lines. **InterRegioExpress (IRE)** trains, covering larger networks between cities, are speedy and comfortable. **S-Bahn** trains run locally within large cities and high density areas. Some S-Bahn stops also service speedy **StadtExpress (SE)** trains, which directly connects city centers. **EuroCity (EC)** and **InterCity (IC)** trains zoom between major cities every 1-2hr. **InterCityExpress (ICE)** trains approach the luxury and kinetics of airplanes, barreling along the tracks at speeds up to 300kph, and service international destinations including Austria, Belgium, the Netherlands, and Switzerland. For overnight travel, choose between the first-class **DB Autozug** or cheaper **DB Nachtzug** lines.

Eurail is valid in Germany. The **German Rail Pass** allows unlimited travel for four to 10 days within a one-month period, including Basel, SWI and Salzburg, AUT. Non-EU citizens can purchase German Rail Passes at select major train stations in Germany (5- or 10-day passes only) or through travel agents (2nd class 4-day pass €169, 10-day €289; under 26 €139/199). A Schönes-Wochenende-Ticket (€33) gives up to five people unlimited travel on any of the slower trains (RE or RB) from 12:01am Saturday or Sunday until 3am the next day; single travelers often find larger groups who will share their ticket.

BY BUS. Bus service runs from the local **ZOB** *(Zentralomnibusbahnhof)*, usually close to the main train station. Buses are more expensive than trains. Rail passes are not valid on buses, except for a few run by Deutsche Bahn.

BY CAR AND BY BIKE. Given generally excellent road conditions, Germans drive fast. The rumors are true: the *Autobahn* does not have a speed limit, only a recommendation of 130kph (80 mph). Watch for signs indicating the right-of-way (usually a yellow triangle). Signs with an "A" denote the *Autobahn;* signs bearing a "B" accompany secondary highways, which typically have a 100kph (60mph) speed limit. In cities and towns, speed limits hover around 30-60kph (20-35 mph). Seat belts are mandatory, and police strictly enforce driving laws. Germany has designated lanes for **bicycles**.

BY THUMB. Hitchhiking on the Autobahn is illegal. In some parts of Germany, hitchhiking does occur. *Let's Go* does not recommend hitchhiking.

KEEPING IN TOUCH

PHONE CODES	**Country code:** 49. **International dialing prefix:** 00. For more info on how to place international calls, see **Inside Back Cover.**

TELEPHONE. Most public phones will accept only a phone card (Telefonkarte), which can be purchased at post offices, kiosks, and some Deutsche Bahn counters. **Mobile phones** are an increasingly popular and economical alternative (p. 21). Phone numbers have no standard length. Direct-dial access numbers for calling out of Germany include: **AT&T USADirect** (☎0800 225 5288); **Canada Direct** (☎0800 888 0014); **MCI WorldPhone** (☎0800 888 8000); **Telecom New Zealand** (☎0800 080 0064); and **Telstra Australia** (☎0800 080 0061); most of these services require a calling card or credit card. For more info, see p. 21.

MAIL. Airmail (*Luftpost* or *par avion*) usually takes three to six days to Ireland and the UK, and four to 10 days to Australia and North America. *Let's Go* lists addresses for mail to be held **Poste Restante** *(Postlagernde Briefe)* in the **Practical Information** sections of big cities. Mail will go to the main post office unless you specify a subsidiary by street address. Address mail to be held as follows: First name Last name, *Postlagernde Briefe*, Postal code, City, GERMANY.

ACCOMMODATIONS AND CAMPING

GERMANY	❶	❷	❸	❹	❺
ACCOMMODATIONS	under €15	€15-25	€26-33	€34-50	over €50

Germany currently has more than 600 **youth hostels**—more than any other nation. Official hostels in Germany are overseen by **DJH** *(Deutsches Jugendherbergswerk)*, Bismarckstr. 8, D 32756 Detmold, Germany (☎05231 740 10; www.jugendherberge.de). A growing number of **Jugendgästehäuser** (youth guesthouses) have more facilities than hostels and attract slightly older guests. DJH publishes *Jugendherbergen in Deutschland*, a guide to federated German hostels. Most charge €15-25 for dorms. The cheapest **hotel-style** accommodations are places that have *Pension*, *Gasthof*, or *Gästehaus* in the name. Hotel rooms start at €20 for singles and €30 for doubles; in large cities, expect to pay nearly twice as much. *Frühstück* (breakfast) is almost always available, if not included. The best bet for a cheap bed is often a **Privatzimmer** (room in a family home), where a basic knowledge of German is very helpful. Prices can be as low as €15 per person. Reservations are made through the local tourist office or through a *Zimmervermittlung* (private booking office), sometimes for a small fee. Over 2500 **campsites** dot the German landscape. Bathrooms, a restaurant or store, and showers generally accompany a campground's well-maintained facilities. Camping costs €3-12 per tent site and €4-6 per extra person, with additional charges for tent and vehicle rental. Blue signs with a black tent on a white background indicate official campsites.

GERMANY

FOOD AND DRINK

GERMANY	❶	❷	❸	❹	❺
FOOD AND DRINK	under €4	€4-8	€9-12	€13-20	over €20

A typical breakfast *(Frühstück)* consists of coffee or tea with **rolls** *(Brötchen)*, **cold sausage** *(Wurst)*, and **cheese** *(Käse)*. Germans' main meal, lunch *(Mittagessen)*, includes soup, broiled sausage or roasted meat, potatoes or dumplings, and a salad or vegetable. Dinner (*Abendessen* or *Abendbrot*) is a reprise of breakfast, with beer in place of coffee and a wider selection of meats and cheeses. Many older Germans indulge in a daily ritual of coffee and cake *(Kaffee und Kuchen)* at 3 or 4pm. Another common dinner option is *schnitzel*, veal, pork or chicken pounded into flat cutlets. Often seasoned and breaded, it is served with a variety of topping including peppers, brown gravy, mushrooms, and lemon. To eat cheaply, stick to a restaurant's daily menu *(Tagesmenü)*, buy food in supermarkets, or head to a **university cafeteria** *(Mensa)*. Fast-food stands *(Imbiß)* also offer cheap, often foreign eats. The average German beer is maltier and more "bread-like" than Czech or American beers; a common nickname for German brew is liquid bread *(flüßiges Brot)*.

BERLIN ☎030

Berlin is bigger than Paris, up later than New York, and wilder than Amsterdam. Dizzying and electric, this city of 3.4 million has such an increasingly diverse population that it can be difficult to keep track of which *Bezirk* (neighborhood) is currently the trendiest. Traces of the past century's Nazi and Communist regimes remain etched in residents' minds, and a psychological division between East and West Germany—the problem dubbed *Mauer im Kopf* ("wall in the head")—still exists nearly two decades after the Berlin Wall's destruction. Restless and contradictory, Germany's capital shows no signs of slowing down its rapid, self-motivated reinvention. With such a dynamic character, the Berlin of next year may be radically different from the Berlin of today.

INTERCITY TRANSPORTATION

Flights: The city is now transitioning from 3 airports to 1 (Flughafen Schönefeld will become the Berlin-Brandenburg International Airport, BBI), but at least until 2011, **Flughafen Tegel (TXL)** will remain West Berlin's main international airport. For info on all 3 of Berlin's airports, call ☎0180 500 0186 (www.berlin-airport.de). Take express bus #X9 from Bahnhof Zoo, bus #109 from Jakob-Kaiser-Pl. on U7, bus #128 from Kurt-Schumacher-Pl. on U6, or bus TXL from Potsdamer Pl. or Bahnhof Zoo. **Flughafen Schönefeld (BER),** southeast of Berlin, is used for intercontinental flights and travel to developing countries. Take S9 or 45 to Flughafen Berlin Schönefeld, or ride the Schönefeld Express train, which runs 2 per hr. through most major S-Bahn stations, including Alexanderpl., Bahnhof Zoo, Friedrichstr., Hauptbahnhof, and Ostbahnhof. **Flughafen Tempelhof (THF)** was slated to close October 31, 2008.

Trains: Berlin's massive new **Hauptbahnhof,** which opened in time for the 2006 World Cup, is the city's major transit hub, with many international and domestic trains continuing to **Ostbahnhof** in the East. Hauptbahnhof currently connects to the S-Bahn and a U55 line. **Bahnhof Zoologischer Garten** (a.k.a. Bahnhof Zoo), formerly the West's main station, now connects only to regional destinations. Many trains also connect to **Schönefeld Airport.** A number of U- and S-Bahn lines stop at **Oranienburg, Potsdam,** and **Spandau.** Trains in the Brandenburg regional transit system tend to stop at all major stations, as well as Alexanderpl. and Friedrichstr.

Buses: ZOB (☎030 301 03 80; www.zob-reisebuero.de), the "central" bus station, is actually at the western edge of town, by the Funkturm near Kaiserdamm. U2 to Kaiserdamm or S41/42 to Messe Nord/ICC. Open M-F 6am-9pm, Sa-Su 6am-3pm. **Gullivers,** at ZOB (☎030 890 660; www.gullivers.de), and **Berlin Linien Bus** (☎030 851 9331; www.berlinlinienbus.de) often have good deals on bus fares. Open in summer daily 8am-9pm; in winter reduced hours. Check website for more information.

Mitfahrzentralen (Ride-Share): Citynetz, Joachimstaler Str. 14 (☎030 194 44; www.citynetz-mitfahrzentrale.de), has a ride-share database. U9 or 15 to Kurfürstendamm. To **Hamburg, Hanover** (€18.50), and **Frankfurt** (€31). Open M-F 9am-8pm, Sa-Su 10am-6pm. Other ride share bulletins at www.mitfahrzentrale.de and www.mitfahrgelegenheit.de. Check *030, Tip,* and *Zitty* for addresses and phone numbers.

ORIENTATION

Berlin's landmarks include the **Spree River,** which flows through the city from west to east, and the narrower **Landwehrkanal** that spills into the Spree from the south. The vast central park, **Tiergarten,** stretches between the waterways. Two radio towers loom above the city: the pointed **Funkturm,** in the west, and the globed **Fernsehturm,** rising above **Alexanderplatz** in the east. In the west, the major thoroughfare **Kurfürstendamm** (a.k.a. Ku'damm) is lined with department stores and leads to the **Bahnhof Zoologischer Garten,** West Berlin's transportation hub. Nearby is the elegant wreck of the **Kaiser-Wilhelm Gedächtniskirche,** as well as one of Berlin's few real skyscrapers, the **EuropaCenter.** Tree-lined **Straße des 17. Juni** runs east-west through the Tiergarten, ending at the **Brandenburger Tor,** the park's eastern border gate. The **Reichstag** (Parliament) is north of the gate; several blocks south, **Potsdamer Platz** bustles beneath the glittering Sony

Center and the headquarters of the Deutsche Bahn. Heading east, Straße des 17. Juni becomes **Unter den Linden** and travels past most of Berlin's imperial architecture. In the east, **Karl-Marx-Allee, Prenzlauer Allee**, and **Schönhauser Allee** fan out from the central meeting point of Alexanderplatz.

Berlin is rightly considered a collection of towns, not a homogeneous city; each neighborhood has a strong sense of its individual history. **Mitte** is currently its commercial heart. The neighboring eastern districts of **Friedrichshain** and **Prenzlauer Berg** are the city's liveliest and most youthful, while **Kreuzberg** is the outpost of counterculture in the west. **Charlottenburg** in the west has a more staid, upscale character, while **Schöneberg** is in between Kreuzberg and Charlottenburg, both in geography and in spirit.

LOCAL TRANSPORTATION

Public Transportation: The **BVG** (www.bvg.de) is one of the world's most efficient transportation systems. The extensive **bus, Straßenbahn** (streetcar or tram), **U-Bahn** (subway), and **S-Bahn** (surface rail) networks will get you to your destination quickly. Almost all the reconstruction and expansion of the pre-war transit grid has been completed; service disruptions are rare, causing at most an extra 20min. wait.

Orientation and Basic Fares: Berlin is divided into 3 transit zones. **Zone A** encompasses central Berlin, including Flughafen Tempelhof. The rest of Berlin is in **Zone B,** while **Zone C** consists of the outlying areas, including Potsdam and Oranienburg. An AB ticket is the best deal, as you can buy extension tickets for the outlying areas. An **Einzelfahrausweis** (1-way ticket) is good for 2hr. after validation. Zones A and B €2.10; B and C €2.50; A, B, and C €2.80. Under 6 free with an adult; children under 14 reduced fare. Within the validation period, the ticket may be used on any S-Bahn, U-Bahn, bus, or tram. A **Tageskarte** (1-day unlimited ticket; A and B €6.10; A, B, and C €6.50) is the best deal if you're planning to travel a lot in a single day.

Night Transport: U- and S-Bahn lines generally don't run M-F 1-4am. On F-Sa nights, all trains except for the U4, S45, and S85 continue but less frequently. An extensive system of **night buses** runs 2-3 per hr. and tends to follow major transit lines; pick up the free *Nachtliniennetz* map at a Fahrscheine und Mehr office. The letter N precedes night bus numbers. Trams run at night.

Taxis: (☎080 02 63 00 00). Call at least 15min. ahead. Female travelers can request female drivers. Trips within the city can cost up to €21. Patrons should request a *Kurzstrecke* to travel up to 2km in any direction for a flat €3 fee.

LIFE (OR, UH, DEATH) IN THE FAST LANE. When you're walking on Berlin's sidewalks, make sure you don't step onto a bike path. Lanes usually run through the middle of walkways and are marked with subtle, reddish lines. Bikers usually don't tolerate wandering tourists, so stay clear.

Bike Rental: Fahrradstation, Dorotheenstr. 30 (☎20 45 45 00; www.fahrradstation.de), near the Friedrichstr. S-Bahn station. Turn in at the parking lot next to STA. €15 per day for a standard mountain bike. Open M-F 9am-8pm, Sa 10am-6pm, Su 10am-4pm. Less central **Orange Bikes,** Kollwitzstr. 35, is a youth community project. Bikes €2.50 per 3hr., €5 per day. Open M-F 2:30-7pm, Sa 10am-7pm.

PRACTICAL INFORMATION

Tourist Offices: Euraide (www.euraide.com), in the Hauptbahnhof. Sells phone cards, rail- and walking-tour tickets. Arrive early—the office is often packed and doesn't accept phone calls. Open June-Oct. daily 8am-noon and 1-6pm; Nov.-May M-F 8am-noon and 1-4:45pm. **Berlin Tourismus Marketing (BTM),** in the EuropaCenter, on Budapester

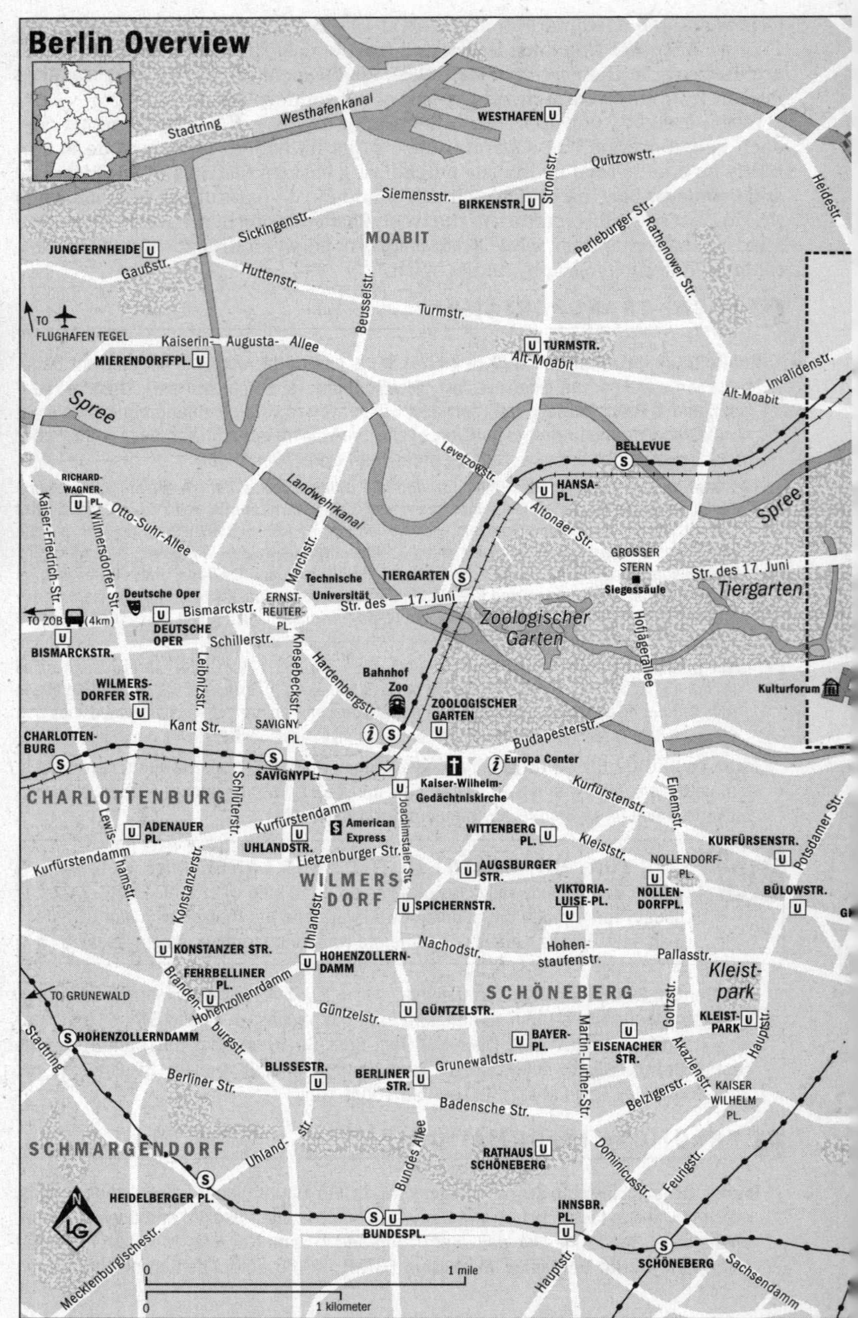
Berlin Overview
Stadtring
Westhafenkanal
WESTHAFEN
Quitzowstr.
Heidestr.
Stromstr.
Siemensstr.
BIRKENSTR.
Sickingenstr.
MOABIT
Perleburger Str.
Rathenower Str.
JUNGFERNHEIDE
Gaußstr.
Huttenstr.
Beusselstr.
Turmstr.
TO FLUGHAFEN TEGEL
Kaiserin- Augusta- Allee
MIERENDORFFPL.
TURMSTR.
Alt-Moabit
Invalidenstr.
Spree
Levetzowstr.
BELLEVUE
RICHARD-WAGNER-PL.
HANSA-PL.
Landwehrkanal
Otto-Suhr-Allee
Altonaer Str.
Kaiser-Friedrich-Str.
Wilmersdorfer Str.
Marchstr.
GROSSER STERN
Siegessäule
Str. des 17. Juni
Tiergarten
TIERGARTEN
Deutsche Oper
Technische Universität
ERNST-REUTER-PL.
TO ZOB (4km)
Bismarckstr.
DEUTSCHE OPER
Schillerstr.
BISMARCKSTR.
Zoologischer Garten
Hofjägerallee
Hardenbergstr.
Bahnhof Zoo
WILMERS-DORFER STR.
Leibnizstr.
Knesebeckstr.
ZOOLOGISCHER GARTEN
Kulturforum
Kant Str.
SAVIGNY-PL.
Budapesterstr.
CHARLOTTEN-BURG
Europa Center
SAVIGNYPL.
Kaiser-Wilhelm-Gedächtniskirche
CHARLOTTENBURG
Schlüterstr.
Joachimstaler Str.
Kurfürstenstr.
Einemstr.
Potsdamer Str.
Lewis-hamstr.
ADENAUER PL.
Kurfürstendamm
American Express
WITTENBERG PL.
Kleiststr.
KURFÜRSENSTR.
UHLANDSTR.
Lietzenburger Str.
NOLLENDORF-PL.
Konstanzerstr.
AUGSBURGER STR.
WILMERSDORF
VIKTORIA-LUISE-PL.
NOLLEN-DORFPL.
BÜLOWSTR.
Uhlandstr.
SPICHERNSTR.
Nachodstr.
Hohen-staufenstr.
Pallasstr.
KONSTANZER STR.
HOHENZOLLERN-DAMM
FEHRBELLINER PL.
Hohenzollerndamm
Kleist-park
TO GRUNEWALD
Brandenburgstr.
SCHÖNEBERG
Güntzelstr.
GÜNTZELSTR.
Goltzstr.
KLEIST-PARK
Stadtring
HOHENZOLLERNDAMM
BAYER-PL.
EISENACHER STR.
Hauptstr.
Akazienstr.
Martin-Luther-Str.
Grunewaldstr.
BLISSESTR.
BERLINER STR.
Berliner Str.
Belzigerstr.
KAISER WILHELM PL.
Badensche Str.
Uhland-str.
Bundes Allee
Dominicusstr.
Feurigstr.
SCHMARGENDORF
RATHAUS SCHÖNEBERG
HEIDELBERGER PL.
INNSBR. PL.
BUNDESPL.
Mecklenburgischestr.
SCHÖNEBERG
Sachsendamm
0
1 mile
1 kilometer

GERMANY

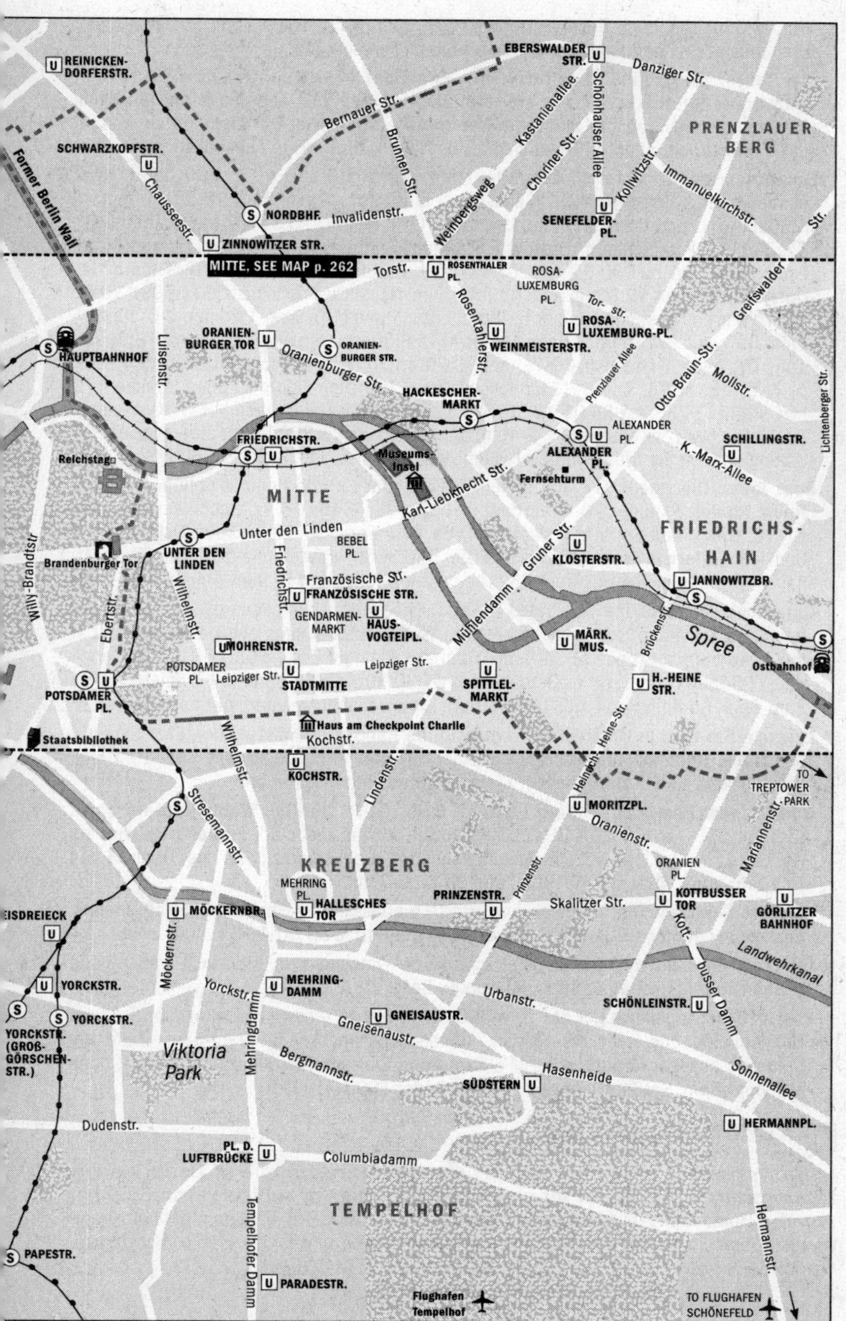
REINICKEN-DORFERSTR.
EBERSWALDER STR.
Danziger Str.
Bernauer Str.
Brunnen Str.
Kastanienallee
Schönhauser Allee
PRENZLAUER BERG
SCHWARZKOPFSTR.
Former Berlin Wall
Chausseestr.
Choriner Str.
Weinbergsweg
Kollwitzstr.
Immanuelkirchstr.
SENEFELDER-PL.
NORDBHF.
Invalidenstr.
ZINNOWITZER STR.
MITTE, SEE MAP p. 262
Torstr.
ROSENTHALER PL.
ROSA-LUXEMBURG PL.
Tor-str.
Greifswalder Str.
Rosenthalerstr.
ROSA-LUXEMBURG-PL.
WEINMEISTERSTR.
ORANIEN-BURGER TOR
ORANIEN-BURGER STR.
Luisenstr.
HAUPTBAHNHOF
Oranienburger Str.
Prenzlauer Allee
Otto-Braun-Str.
Mollstr.
HACKESCHER-MARKT
ALEXANDER PL.
FRIEDRICHSTR.
Museums-Insel
ALEXANDER PL.
SCHILLINGSTR.
K.-Marx-Allee
Lichtenberger Str.
Reichstag
Karl-Liebknecht Str.
Fernsehturm
MITTE
FRIEDRICHS-HAIN
Unter den Linden
BEBEL PL.
Gruner Str.
KLOSTERSTR.
Brandenburger Tor
UNTER DEN LINDEN
Friedrichstr.
Willy-Brandtstr.
Wilhelmstr.
Französische Str.
FRANZÖSISCHE STR.
JANNOWITZBR.
GENDARMEN-MARKT
HAUS-VOGTEIPL.
Mühlendamm
Ebertstr.
MOHRENSTR.
MÄRK. MUS.
Brückenstr.
Spree
POTSDAMER PL.
Leipziger Str.
STADTMITTE
SPITTEL-MARKT
Ostbahnhof
H.-HEINE STR.
Haus am Checkpoint Charlie
Kochstr.
Staatsbibliothek
Heinrich-Heine-Str.
KOCHSTR.
TO TREPTOWER PARK
Stresemannstr.
Lindenstr.
MORITZPL.
Oranienstr.
Mariannenstr.
KREUZBERG
ORANIEN PL.
MEHRING PL.
Prinzenstr.
PRINZENSTR.
Skalitzer Str.
KOTTBUSSER TOR
GÖRLITZER BAHNHOF
HALLESCHES TOR
MÖCKERNBR.
EISDREIECK
Kottbusser Damm
Landwehrkanal
Möckernstr.
YORCKSTR.
Yorckstr.
MEHRING-DAMM
Urbanstr.
SCHÖNLEINSTR.
GNEISAUSTR.
Gneisenaustr.
YORCKSTR. (GROß-GÖRSCHEN-STR.)
Viktoria Park
Mehringdamm
Bergmannstr.
Hasenheide
Sonnenallee
SÜDSTERN
Dudenstr.
HERMANNPL.
PL. D. LUFTBRÜCKE
Columbiadamm
TEMPELHOF
Hermannstr.
Tempelhofer Damm
PAPESTR.
PARADESTR.
Flughafen Tempelhof
TO FLUGHAFEN SCHÖNEFELD

Str., in Charlottenburg. Reserves rooms (€3). Open M-Sa 10am-7pm, Su 10am-6pm. Branches at Brandenburger Tor and Alexanderpl. Fernsehturm.

City Tours: The guides at **Terry Brewer's Best of Berlin** (☎177 388 1537p; www.brewersberlintours.com) are legendary for their vast knowledge and engaging personalities. 8hr. tours €12. Shorter **free tours** leave daily at 10:30am from in front of the Bandy Brooks shop on Friedrichstr. (S5, 7, 9, or 75 or U6 to Friedrichstr.)

Embassies and Consulates: Australia, Mitte, Wallstr. 76-79 (☎030 880 0880; www.australian-embassy.de). U2: "Märkisches Museum". Open M-Th 8:30am-5pm, F 8:30am- 4:15pm. **Canada,** Mitte, Leipziger Pl. 17 (☎030 20 31 20; www.canada.de). S1, 2 or U2: "Potsdamer Pl." Open M-F 8:30am-12:30pm and 1:30-5pm. **Ireland,** Mitte, Friedrichstr. 200 (☎030 22 07 20; www.embassyofireland.de). U2 or 6: "Stadtmitte." Open M-F 9:30am-12:30pm and 2:30-4:45pm. **NZ,** Mitte, Friedrichstr. 60 (☎030 20 62 10; www.nzembassy.com). U2 or 6: "Stadtmitte." Open M-Th 9am-1pm and 2-5:30pm, F 9am-1pm and 2-4:30pm. Summer hours M-Th 8:30am-1pm and 2-5:30pm, F 8:30am-1pm. **UK,** Mitte, Wilhelmstr. 70-71 (☎030 20 45 70; www.britischebotschaft.de). S1-3, 5, 7, 9, 25, or 75, or U6: "Friedrichstr." Open M-F 9am-5:30pm. **US,** Clayallee 170 (☎030 832 9233; fax 83 05 12 15). U1: Oskar-Helene-Heim. Open M-F 8:30am-noon. Telephone advice available M-F 2-4pm; after hours, call ☎830 50 for emergencies. The visiting address for the United States Embassy is Pariser Pl. 2 (☎030 238 5174).

GERMANY

Boat Tours: The extensive canal system makes boat tours a popular option. **Reederei Heinz Riedel,** Planufer 78, Kreuzberg (☎030 693 4646; U8 to "Schönleinstr.") Tours €7-16. Open Mar.-Sept. M-F 6am-9pm, Sa 8am-6pm, Su 10am-3pm; Oct.-Feb. M-F 8am-4pm. **Stern & Kreisschiffahrt** (☎030 536 3600; www.sternundkreis.de), Puschkinallee 15, Treptow. Crusies from €5 (1hr. mini-tour). Open M-Th 9am-4pm, F 9am-2pm.

Currency Exchange: The best rates are usually found in large squares, at most major train stations, and at exchange offices with **Wechselstube** signs outside. **ReiseBank** at the *Hauptbahnhof* (open M-Sa 8am-10pm), at Bahnhof Zoo (☎030 881 7117; open daily 7:30am-10pm) and at Ostbahnhof (☎030 296 4393; open M-F 7am-10pm, Sa 8am-8pm, Su 8am-noon and 12:30-4pm), is conveniently located, but has poor rates.

Luggage Storage: In **DB Gepäck Center,** in the Hauptbahnhof, 1st floor, East Side. €4 per day. In **Bahnhof Zoo.** Lockers €3-5 per day. Max 72hr. Open daily 6am-10:30pm. 24hr. lockers also at **Ostbahnhof, Alexanderplatz** and bus station.

Crisis Lines: American Hotline (☎0177 814 1510). **Berliner Behindertenverband,** Jägerstr. 63D (☎030 204 3847), has advice for the disabled. **Frauenkrisentelefon** (☎030 615 42 43; www.frauenkrisentelefon.de) is a women's crisis line. Open M and Th 10am-noon, Tu-W and F 7-9pm, and Sa-Su 5-7pm.

Medical Services: The American and British embassies list English-speaking doctors. **Emergency doctor:** ☎31 00 31. **Emergency dentist:** ☎89 00 43 33. Both 24hr.

Internet: Inexpensive Internet cafes cluster on Oranienstr. in Kreuzberg and around U-Bahn stop Ebenswalder Str. in Prenzlauer Berg.

Post Offices: Joachimstaler Str. 7 (☎030 88 70 86 11), down Joachimstaler Str. from Bahnhof Zoo and near the Kantstr. intersection. Open M-Sa 9am-8pm. There are branches at **Tegel Airport,** open M-F 8am-6pm, Sa 8am-noon, and **Ostbahnhof,** open M-F 8am-8pm, Sa-Su 10am-6pm. **Postal Code:** 10001-14199.

ACCOMMODATIONS

Longer stays are most conveniently arranged through one of Berlin's many **Mitwohnzentrale,** which can set up house-sitting gigs or sublets (from €250 per month). **Home Company Mitwohnzentrale,** Joachimstaler Str. 17, has a useful placement website. (☎0421 792 6293; www.homecompany.de. U9 or 15 to Ku'damm. Open M-Th 9am-6pm, F 9am-5pm, Sa 11am-2pm. MC/V.)

MITTE

Mitte's Backpacker Hostel, Chausseestr. 102 (☎030 28 39 09 65; www.backpacker.de). U6 to "Zinnowitzer Str." The apex of hostel hipness, with a gregarious English-speaking staff and themed rooms, from "Aztec" to "skyline" (of Berlin, of course). The social common room is lined with antique theater sets. A pickup spot for Terry Brewer's Tours and Insider Tours bike tours. Sheets €2.50. Laundry €7. Internet €3 per hr. Bike rental €10 per day. Reception 24hr. Dorms €14-19; singles €30-34; doubles €48-54; quads €80-84. AmEx/MC/V. ❷

Circus, Weinbergersweg 1A (☎030 28 39 14 33; www.circus-berlin.de). U8 to "Rosenthaler Platz." Designed with the English-speaking traveler in mind. Nightly happy hours and W karaoke. Breakfast €2-5 until 1pm. Free laundry. Wi-Fi in rooms; internet €0.05 per min. Wheelchair-accessible. Reception and bar 24hr. 4- to 8-bed dorms €19-23; singles €40, with bath €50; doubles €56/70; triples €75. MC/V. ❷

BaxPax Downtown Hostel/Hotel, Ziegelstr. 28 (☎030 251 52 02; www.baxpax-downtown.de). S1, S2, or S25 to "Oranienburger Str." or U6 to "Oranienbuger Tor." The sleeker sibling of the Kreuzberg branch has all the usual amenities plus a bar/lounge with fireplace and a rooftop bar with a huge kiddie pool. All-female dorm rooms available. Breakfast €5.50. Laundry facilities available. Internet €3 per hr. Dorms €13-17; singles €29-45; doubles €60-65; triples €70. MC/V. ❷

GERMANY

CHARLOTTENBURG

Berolina Backpacker, Stuttgarter Pl. 17 (☎030 32 70 90 72; www.berolinabackpacker.de). S3, S5, S7, S9, or S75 to "Charlottenburg." This quiet hostel with an ivy-laced facade keeps things elegant with print art in the bunk-free dorms and daisies on the breakfast table. Surrounding cafes and proximity to the S-Bahn make up for its distance from the rush of the city. Communal and private kitchens (communal €1 per day, private €9.50) available for use. Breakfast buffet €7; "backpackers' breakfast" (a roll with cheese and coffee) €3.50. Internet €0.50 per 15min. Reception 24hr. Check-out 11am. 5-bed dorms €10-13.50; singles €29.50-35.50; doubles €37-47; triples €39-64; quads €46-60. AmEx/MC/V. ❶

SCHÖNEBERG AND WILMERSDORF

Jugendhotel Berlincity, Crellestr. 22 (☎030 7870 2130; www.jugendhotel-berlin.de). U7 to "Kleistpark" or "Yorckstr." The high ceilings and enormous windows in this former factory provide guests with spacious, airy rooms. Funky light fixtures shaped like fried eggs illuminate the hallways, which are lined with dark hard wood. Request a room with a view of the TV tower. Breakfast and linens included. Wi-Fi €1 per 20min., €5 per day. Reception 24hr. Singles €38, with bath €52; doubles €60/79; triples €87/102; quads €112/126; quints €124/150; 6-person room €146/168. MC/V. ❺

JetPAK, Pücklerstr. 54, Dahlem (☎030 8325 011; www.jetpak.de). U3 to "Fehrbelliner Pl." or U9 to "Güntzelstr.," then bus #115 (dir.: Neuruppiner Str.) to "Pücklerstr." Follow sign to Grunewald and turn left on Pücklerstr. Turn left again when the JetPAK sign directs you at the edge of the forest. Hidden in an old *Wehrmacht* military complex in the Grunewald forest, this casual hostel has a summer-camp feel that belies its history and makes up for the distance. Ping-pong table and basketball hoop outside. Common room with computers and foosball. Breakfast and linens included. Free internet. Dorms €14-18; singles €30; doubles €50. Additional €1 charge on F-Sa. Cash only. ❷

KREUZBERG

Bax Pax, Skalitzer Str. 104 (☎030 69 51 83 22; www.baxpax-kreuzberg.de). U1 or U15 to "Görlitzer Bahnhof," right across the street. Run by the same friendly people as Mitte's

Backpacker Hostel. Around the corner from Oranienstr., with a pool table, roomy common spaces, walls painted with film reels, and a bed inside an antique VW Bug (ask for room 3). Kitchen facilities and an outdoor terrace. Breakfast €4.50. Linens €2.50. Internet €2 per 30min. Bike rental 1st day for €12, 2nd €10, additional days €5. Reception 24hr. Big dorms in high season €16, in low season €15; 7- to 8-bed dorms €17/15; 5- to 6-bed rooms €18/17; singles €31/30; doubles €48/46, with bath €60/56; triples €63/60; quads €76/72. AmEx/MC/V. ❷

Hostel X Berger, Schlesische Str. 22 (☎030 69 53 18 63; www.hostelxberger.com). U1 or U15 to "Schlesisches Tor," or night bus #N65 to "Taborstr." This social hostel is a good launching pad for the one Kreuzberg area that might be more fun at night than Oranienstr. The colorful graffiti outside is more exciting than the basic, roomy dorms. Female-only dorms available. Sheets €2, towel €1. Free internet. Reception 24hr. Dorms €11-15; singles €28-32; doubles €36-40; triples €36-38. Cash only. ❶

PRENZLAUER BERG

East Seven Hostel, Schwedter Str. 7 (☎030 93 62 22 40; www.eastseven.de). U2 to "Senefelderpl." No bunks in the well-lit, beautifully painted dorms. The grill area in the garden out back is friendly and social. Kitchen available. Linens €3. Towels €1. Laundry €4. Internet €0.50 per 20min; free Wi-Fi. Reception 7am-midnight. Dorms €13-17; singles in low-season €30, in high season €37; doubles €42/50; triples €52.50/63; quads €66/76. Cash only. ❷

Pfefferbett, Christinenstraße 18-19 (☎030 93 93 58 58; www.pfefferbett.de). U2 to "Senefelderpl." Juxtaposing its original 19th-century brick walls with contemporary design, this hostel has a roof deck and some of the best deals in Berlin. Named after the nearby beer garden. Breakfast buffet €4. Linens €2.50. Free Wi-Fi. Reception and bar open 24hr. 6- to 8-bed dorms with shared bath from €12; 4- to 6-bed dorms with private bath from €17.50. Doubles with private bath, TV, and telephone €27. Cash only. ❶

Alcatraz, Schönhauser Allee 133A (☎030 48 49 68 15; www.alcatraz-backpacker.de). U2 to "Eberswalder Str." Tucked away in a spray-painted courtyard. 80 beds in small but carefully decorated rooms. The "chill out room" is quite the hangout after dark. Kitchen facilities. Linens €2. Free internet and Wi-Fi. Bike rental €5. Reception 24hr. 8-bed dorms in summer €16, in winter €13; singles €40/30; doubles €50/42; triples €66/54; quads €72/60. 5% discount per night with ISIC Card. MC/V. ❷

FRIEDRICHSHAIN

Sunflower Hostel, Helsingforser Str. 17 (☎030 44 04 42 50; www.sunflower-hostel.de). This relaxed, eclectic hostel features a vine-hung bright orange lounge. Spotless dorms are a marked contrast to the studied chaos of the common areas. The staff knows the nightlife scene well. Breakfast buffet €3. Locks and linens €3 deposit each. Laundry €4.50. Internet €0.50 per 10min.; free Wi-Fi. Reception 24hr. 7- to 8-bed dorms €10-14.50; 5- to 6-bed dorms €12.50-16.50; singles €30-36.50; doubles €38-46.50; triples €51-61.50; quads €60-79.50. 7th night free. MC/V. ❶

Eastern Comfort Hostelboat, Mühlenstr. 73-77 (☎030 66 76 38 06; www.eastern-comfort.com). Enter through the first opening in the East Side Gallery (p. 270). Those willing to brave narrow corridors and cramped quarters will be rewarded with Berlin's most adventurous hostel: a docked boat. The truly bold can sleep outside on the deck in summer for the cheapest view of the river in town. Breakfast €4. Linens €5. Laundry €5 per load. Internet €2 per hr. Tent/open-air €12; dorms €16; 1st-class singles €64, 2nd-class €50; doubles €78/58; triples €69; quads €76. 2-night bookings only on weekends. The new sister ship, Western Comfort, is docked on the opposite side of the Spree and rents pricier rooms and no dorms. MC/V. ❶

FOOD

Berlin's cuisine is quite diverse thanks to its Middle Eastern and Southeast Asian populations. Seasonal highlights include the beloved *Spargel* (white asparagus) in early summer, Pfifferling mushrooms in late summer, and *Federweiße* (young wine) in September. Perhaps the dearest culinary tradition is breakfast; Germans love to wake up late over a *Milchkaffee* (bowl of coffee with foamed milk) and a sprawling brunch buffet. Vendors of currywurst or bratwurst are perfect for a quick bite; or, find a 24hr. Turkish *Imbiß* (snack food stand) to satisfy any midnight craving. **Aldi, Edeka, Penny Markt,** and **Plus** are the cheapest supermarket chains (all typically open M-F 9am-8pm, Sa 9am-4pm). Stores at Ostbahnhof are an exception to Sunday closing laws. Almost every neighborhood has an **open-air market;** the market on Winterfeldtpl., is particularly busy on Saturday mornings. In Kreuzberg along Maybachufer, on the Landwehrkanal, the **Turkish market** sells cheap veggies and huge wheels of *Fladenbrot* every Tuesday and Friday. Take U8 to Schönleinstr. Also popular is the more upscale, largely **organic market** that takes over Prenzlauer Berg's Kollwitzpl. on Thursday and Friday (U2 to Senefelder Pl).

GERMANY

MITTE

Schwarzwaldstuben, Tucholskystr. 48, (☎030 28 09 80 84). S-Bahn to "Oranienburger Str." Fitted out like a rustic southern German restaurant with sofas between the tables and stuffed boar heads on the wall, this is the best place for a schnitzel and Rothaus beer, made in the only state brewery left in Germany. Reserve on weekends, or drop by during the day for a *Flammkuchen* (€4.50-8), a sort of German pizza, and to read by the light of the fringed lamps. Entrees €8-18. ❹

Tadshickische Teestube, Am Festungsgraben 1, (☎030 204 1112). S3, 5, 7, 9, or 75 to "Hackescher Markt." Dating back to the Soviet days, this Tajik teahouse is a hidden haven of oriental carpets, tea served in samovars (€2-6), and sour cream covered meat pierogi (€5). Take off your shoes before settling cross-legged onto the cushions around the low tables. Open M-F 5pm-midnight, Sa-Su 3pm-midnight. Cash only. ❷

Monsieur Vuong, Alte Schönhauser Str. 46 (☎030 99 29 69 24; www.monsieurvuong.de). U8 to "Weinmeisterstr." or U2 to "Rosa Luxembourg Pl." Gallerists, artists, and, yes, tourists perch on the red cube seats in this extremely popular Vietnamese restaurant. Fresh fruit drinks €3.40. Entrees €6-9. Open daily noon-midnight. Cash only. ❷

Cafe Fleury, Weinbergsweg 20 (☎030 044 03 41 44). U8 to Rosenthaler Platz. One Berlin-dweller imported some blue-and-white wallpaper, photographs, and knickknacks from her native France and turned her hobby into a job, opening this gorgeous cafe. Unbeatable croque monsieur and fresh soups and snacks. Entrees €5-6. Open M-F 8am-10pm, Sa-Su 10am-10pm. Cash only. ❷

CHARLOTTENBURG

Schwarzes Cafe, Kantstr. 148 (☎030 313 8038). S3, S5, S7, S9, or S75 to "Savignypl." The most popular boho cafe in the area for a reason: absinthe all night in the dimly lit, frescoed space, followed by delicious breakfast when the sun comes up. Weekly specials served 11:30am-8pm (€7-10). Breakfast always available (€5-8.50). Open 24hr., (except Tu 3am-11am). Cash only. ❸

Am Nil, Kaiserdamm 114 (☎30 321 44 06) U2 to "Sophie-Charlotte Platz." Recline on the Oriental carpets and enjoy platters of spiced Egyptian food (€7-14). Belly dancer F and Sa 9pm. Open Tu-Su 3pm-1am. Cash only. ❸

Kuchi, Kochstr. 30 (☎030 31 50 78 15). S5, S7, S9 or S75 to "Savignypl." A bit more pricey than the sushi *Imbisse*, but you can be sure you are eating real fish in this trendy

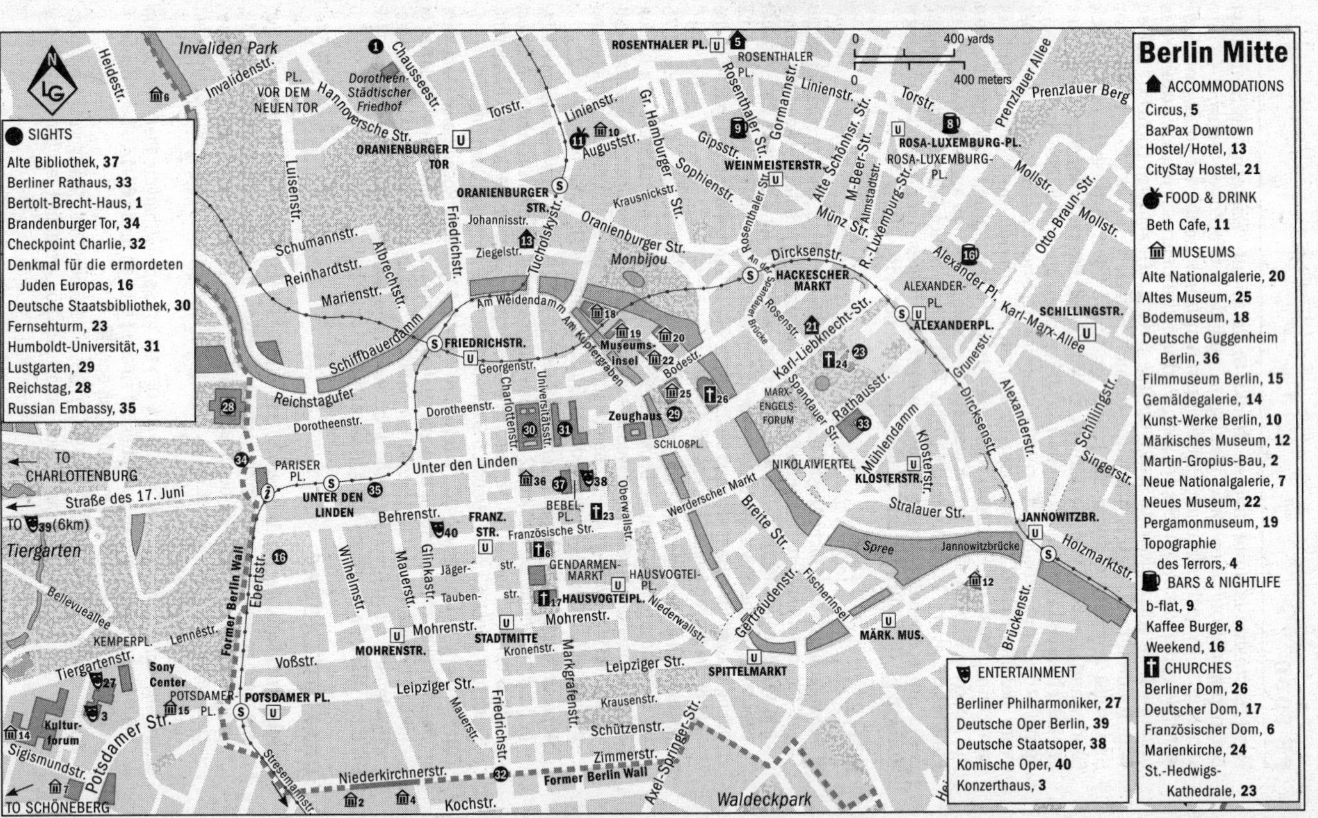
Berlin Mitte
ACCOMMODATIONS
Circus, 5
BaxPax Downtown Hostel/Hotel, 13
CityStay Hostel, 21
FOOD & DRINK
Beth Cafe, 11
MUSEUMS
Alte Nationalgalerie, 20
Altes Museum, 25
Bodemuseum, 18
Deutsche Guggenheim Berlin, 36
Filmmuseum Berlin, 15
Gemäldegalerie, 14
Kunst-Werke Berlin, 10
Märkisches Museum, 12
Martin-Gropius-Bau, 2
Neue Nationalgalerie, 7
Neues Museum, 22
Pergamonmuseum, 19
Topographie des Terrors, 4
BARS & NIGHTLIFE
b-flat, 9
Kaffee Burger, 8
Weekend, 16
CHURCHES
Berliner Dom, 26
Deutscher Dom, 17
Französischer Dom, 6
Marienkirche, 24
St.-Hedwigs-Kathedrale, 23
SIGHTS
Alte Bibliothek, 37
Berliner Rathaus, 33
Bertolt-Brecht-Haus, 1
Brandenburger Tor, 34
Checkpoint Charlie, 32
Denkmal für die ermordeten Juden Europas, 16
Deutsche Staatsbibliothek, 30
Fernsehturm, 23
Humboldt-Universität, 31
Lustgarten, 29
Reichstag, 28
Russian Embassy, 35
ENTERTAINMENT
Berliner Philharmoniker, 27
Deutsche Oper Berlin, 39
Deutsche Staatsoper, 38
Komische Oper, 40
Konzerthaus, 3
0 400 yards
0 400 meters
Invaliden Park
Heidestr.
Invalidenstr.
PL. VOR DEM NEUEN TOR
Hannoversche Str.
Dorotheen-Städtischer Friedhof
Chausseestr.
Torstr.
ORANIENBURGER TOR
ORANIENBURGER STR.
Linienstr.
Auguststr.
Tucholskystr.
Johannisstr.
Ziegelstr.
Friedrichstr.
Luisenstr.
Schumannstr.
Reinhardtstr.
Albrechtstr.
Marienstr.
Schiffbauerdamm
Reichstagufer
Dorotheenstr.
Am Weidendamm
Am Kupfergraben
FRIEDRICHSTR.
Georgenstr.
Charlottenstr.
Universitätsstr.
Museumsinsel
Bodestr.
Zeughaus
SCHLOßPL.
Krausnickstr.
Oranienburger Str.
Monbijou
Gr. Hamburger Str.
Sophienstr.
Gipsstr.
ROSENTHALER PL.
ROSENTHALER PL.
Rosenthaler Str.
Gormannstr.
WEINMEISTERSTR.
Alte Schönhsr. Str.
M-Beer-Str.
Almstadtstr.
R.-Luxemburg-Str.
Münz Str.
ROSA-LUXEMBURG-PL.
ROSA-LUXEMBURG-PL.
Prenzlauer Allee
Prenzlauer Berg
Mollstr.
Otto-Braun-Str.
Dircksenstr.
HACKESCHER MARKT
An der Spandauer Brücke
Rosenstr.
Karl-Liebknecht-Str.
Alexander Pl.
ALEXANDER-PL.
ALEXANDERPL.
Karl-Marx-Allee
SCHILLINGSTR.
Grunerstr.
Alexanderstr.
Schillingstr.
Singerstr.
MARX-ENGELS-FORUM
Spandauer Str.
Rathausstr.
Mühlendamm
Klosterstr.
KLOSTERSTR.
NIKOLAIVIERTEL
Stralauer Str.
JANNOWITZBR.
Holzmarktstr.
Spree
Jannowitzbrücke
Brückenstr.
MÄRK. MUS.
Fischerinsel
Gertraudenstr.
SPITTELMARKT
Breite Str.
Werderscher Markt
Niederwallstr.
Oberwallstr.
HAUSVOGTEI-PL.
HAUSVOGTEIPL.
GENDARMEN-MARKT
BEBEL-PL.
Französische Str.
FRANZ. STR.
Jäger-str.
Tauben-str.
Mohrenstr.
STADTMITTE
Kronenstr.
Markgrafenstr.
Krausenstr.
Schützenstr.
Zimmerstr.
Leipziger Str.
Axel-Springer-Str.
Waldeckpark
Former Berlin Wall
Kochstr.
Niederkirchnerstr.
Mauerstr.
Glinkastr.
Wilhelmstr.
MOHRENSTR.
Voßstr.
Behrenstr.
Unter den Linden
UNTER DEN LINDEN
PARISER PL.
TO CHARLOTTENBURG
Straße des 17. Juni
TO 39 (6km)
Tiergarten
Ebertstr.
Bellevueallee
KEMPERPL.
Lennéstr.
Tiergartenstr.
Sony Center
POTSDAMER PL.
POTSDAMER PL.
Kulturforum
Potsdamer Str.
Sigismundstr.
Stresemannstr.
TO SCHÖNEBERG

little restaurant. Sushi rolls from €4. Hot Japanese entrees. Open M-Th noon-midnight, F-Su 12:30pm-1am. Cash only. ❷

SCHÖNEBERG

Café Bilderbuch, Akazienstr. 28 (☎030 78 70 60 57; www.cafe-bilderbuch.de). U7 to "Eisenacher Str." While fringed lamps, oak bookcases, and velvety couches give this cafe a Venetian library feel, the "Bilderbuch Sudoku Puzzle" on the menu brings diners back to the twenty-first century. Daily tasty brunch baskets and sumptuous Sunday buffet (€8). Weekly dinner specials €5-8.50. Open M-Th 9am-1am, F-Sa 9am-2am, Su 10am-1am. Kitchen open 9am-11pm. Cash only. ❷

Café Berio, Maaßenstr. 7 (☎030 216 19 46; www.cafe-berio.de). U1, U2, U4, or U15 to "Nollendorfpl." Always jam-packed with locals, this 2-fl. Viennese-style cafe tempts passersby off the street with its unbeatable breakfast menu (€3-11). Entrees €5-9. Happy hour cocktails 2 for 1 M-Th and Su 7-9pm and F-Sa 7pm-midnight. Open M-Th and Su 8am-midnight, F-Sa 8am-1am. Kitchen closes at 11pm. Cash only. ❷

Die Feinbäckerei, Vorbergstr. 2 (☎030 81 49 42 40; www.feinbaeck.de). U7 to "Kleistpark." Like Die Feinbäckerei's pub-like interior, its Swabian cuisine is unassuming and traditional. Try the delectable *Spätzle* (noodles; €6.90). Keep a look out for the occasional all-you-can-eat specials. Sa-Su breakfast served noon-4pm. Open daily noon-1am. Cash only. ❷

KREUZBERG

Maroush, Adalbertstr. 93 (☎030 69 53 61 71). U1 or U15 to Kotbusser Tor. Tourists flock to Turkish Hasir, across the street, which claims to have invented the *Döner* kebab, but this Lebanese *Imbiss* is cozier and much cheaper. Favorite choices from the menu, handwritten in Arabic and German, are chicken shawarma wrap (€2.50) and a vegetarian platter with falafel and salads (€6). Open 11am-2am. Cash only. ❷

Wirtshaus Henne, Leuschnerdamm 25 (☎030 614 7730; www.henne-berlin.de). U1, or U15 to Kottbusser Tor. Though this slightly out-of-the-way German restaurant does serve other dishes (€2.50-6), virtually everyone orders the famous *Brathähnchen* (fried chicken), arguably the best in Berlin. It has a small beer garden, but the real charm is in its dark wood interior, with plaid tablecloths and antique lanterns. Always packed, so reserve in advance. Open Tu-Sa from 7pm, Su from 5pm. Cash only. ❷

THE BEST WURST

So you're finally in Germany and itching to sink your teeth into your first authentic German Wurst. With over 1500 varieties, you'll have plenty of choices. All have one thing in common: German law mandates that sausages can only be made of meat and spices. If it has cereal filling, it's not wurst.

Bockwurst: This tasty sausage is commonly roasted or grilled at street stands, and is served dripping with ketchup and mustard in a *Brötchen* (roll). Although *Bock* means billy-goat, this wurst is made of ground veal with parsley and chives. Complement your *Bockwurst* with some *Bock* beer.

Thüringer Bratwurst: Similar to the *Bockwurst*, the *Bratwurst* has a little pork too, plus ginger and nutmeg.

Frankfurter: Unlike the American variety, the German *Frankfurter* can only have this name if made in Frankfurt. It's made of lean pork ground into a paste and then cold smoked, which gives it that orange-yellow coloring.

Knockwurst: Short and plump, this sausage is served with sauerkraut. It's made of lean pork and beef, with a healthy dose of garlic.

Weißwurst: Cream and eggs give this "white sausage" its pale coloring. *Weißwurst* goes with rye bread and mustard.

Currywurst: A great late-night snack, this pork *Bratwurst* is smothered in a tomato sauce and sprinkled with paprika and curry.

FRIEDRICHSHAIN AND PRENZLAUER BERG

Hans Wurst, Dunckerstr. 2A (☎030 41 71 78 22). U2 to "Eberswalderstr.," M10 to "Husemannstr." This cafe/restaurant-on-a-mission serves only organic, vegan foods with no flavor enhancers. Readings, DJs, and acoustic concerts in the evenings. The menu changes daily, with seasonal offerings and fresh creations (€3.70-8). Free Wi-Fi. Brunch Sa-Su 11am-5pm. Open Tu-Th noon-midnight, F-Sa noon-late. ❷

Cafe-Restaurant Miró, Raumerstr. 29 (☎030 44 73 30 13; www.miro-restaurant.de). U2 to "Eberswalder Str." A Mediterranean cafe whose candelit, pillowed back room and fresh entrees (€8-11) capture the region's essence perfectly. Breakfast €4.50-8.25. Soups €3.20-3.70. Large appetizers and salads €4-9. Open daily 10am-late. Kitchen closes at midnight. ❸

The Bird, Am Falkplatz 5 (☎0305 105 3283). U8 to "Voltastr." One of the few, if not the only, places to get an honest-to-goodness burger in Berlin, cooked by 2 gruff New York transplants in their exposed-brick restaurant. Everything is made from scratch daily, including the sauce for the aptly named "napalm wings" (€6). Burgers €9-12. Angry hour (buy 1 beer get 1 free) 6-8pm. Open M-Sa 6pm-late, Su noon-late. Cash only. ❸

Frittiersalon, Boxhagener Straße 104 (☎030 25 93 39 06). U5 to "Frankfurter Tor." Multicultural, all-organic "frying salon" serves french fries and organic burgers with all kinds of fusion twists, including a meatless currywurst. The cheery place has won prizes for Berlin's best currywurst and best hangover breakfast, among other honors. Everything €2.20-9. Open M 6pm-late, Tu-F noon-late, Sa-Su 1pm-late. Cash only. ❷

W-Imbiss, Kastanienallee 49 (☎030 4849 2657). U8 to "Rosenthaler Pl." Look for the upside-down McDonald's sign and crowded outdoor seating at this casual spot. Naan cooked fresh to order and covered with your choice of toppings. Entrees €2.50-6. Open daily in summer noon-midnight, in winter 12:30-11:30pm. Cash only. ❷

SIGHTS

Most of central Berlin's major sights lie along the **bus #100** route which runs every 5min. from Bahnhof Zoo to Prenzlauer Berg. It passes the **Siegessäule**, breathtaking **Brandenburger Tor** (p. 264) and **Unter den Linden,** the **Berliner Dom** (p. 267), and **Alexanderplatz** (p. 267). Remnants of the **Berlin Wall** still survive in a few places: in **Potsdamer Platz** (p. 266); near the **Haus Am Checkpoint Charlie** (p. 273); in **Prenzlauer Berg,** next to the sobering **Documentation Center** (p. 271); and in altered form at the **East Side Gallery** (p. 270) in Friedrichshain.

MITTE

The sights of Mitte alone could keep a tourist busy for weeks. The most efficient approach is to start at the Brandenburg Gate and either walk due east on Unter den Linden or take the #100 bus to do a drive-by of Imperial Berlin.

UNTER DEN LINDEN

This famous street was named "under the linden trees" for the 18th-century specimens that still line what was the spine of Imperial Berlin and what has become the nerve center of tourist Berlin. During the DDR days, it was known as the "idiot's mile," because it was often all that visitors saw, giving them little idea of what the eastern part of the city was really like. Originating in Pariser Platz, dominated by Brandenburger Tor, the street runs east through Bebelpl. and the Lustgarten, passing most of what remains of the city's still-impressive imperial architecture. *(S1, S2, or S25 to "Unter den Linden." Bus #100 runs the length of the street every 4-6min.)*

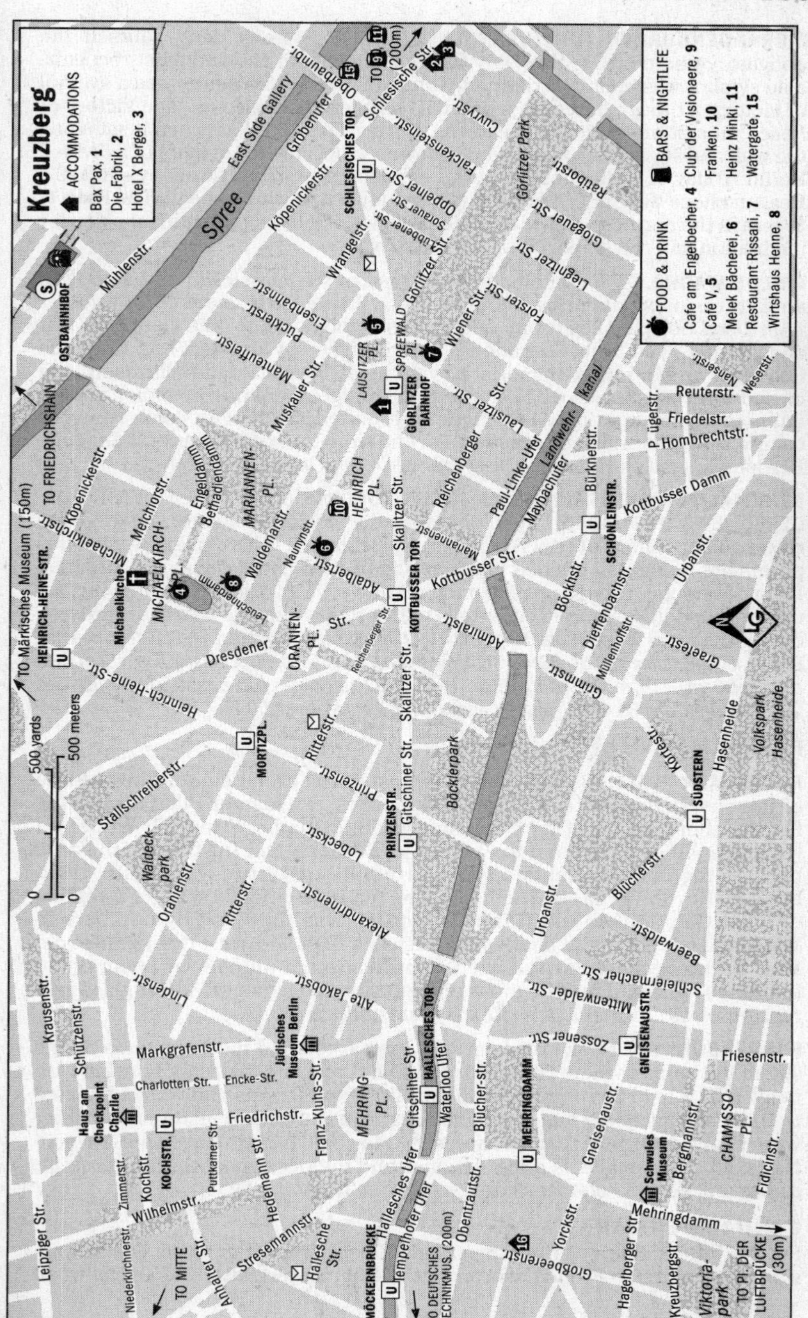

Kreuzberg
ACCOMMODATIONS
Bax Pax, 1
Die Fabrik, 2
Hotel X Berger, 3
FOOD & DRINK
Cafe am Engelbecher, 4
Café V, 5
Melek Bächerei, 6
Restaurant Rissani, 7
Wirtshaus Henne, 8
BARS & NIGHTLIFE
Club der Visionaere, 9
Franken, 10
Heinz Minki, 11
Watergate, 15
0 500 yards
0 500 meters
TO Märkisches Museum (150m)
TO FRIEDRICHSHAIN
OSTBAHNHOF
Spree
East Side Gallery
Mühlenstr.
Köpenickerstr.
Michaelkirchstr.
HEINRICH-HEINE-STR.
Heinrich-Heine-Str.
Michaelkirche
MICHAELKIRCH-PL.
Melchiorstr.
Engeldamm
Bethaniendamm
MARIANNEN-PL.
Waldemarstr.
Leuschnerdamm
Dresdener Str.
ORANIEN-PL.
Naunynstr.
Adalbertstr.
HEINRICH PL.
Reichenberger Str.
KOTTBUSSER TOR
Skalitzer Str.
Mariannenstr.
Kottbusser Str.
Kottbusser Damm
SCHÖNLEINSTR.
Manteuffelstr.
Muskauer Str.
Pücklerstr.
Eisenbahnstr.
Wrangelstr.
Köpenickerstr.
Gröbenufer
Oberbaumbr.
SCHLESISCHES TOR
Schlesische Str.
TO (200m)
Falckensteinstr.
Oppelner Str.
Sorauer Str.
Lübbener Str.
Görlitzer Str.
Görlitzer Park
Cuvrystr.
Ratiborstr.
Glogauer Str.
Liegnitzer Str.
Forster Str.
Wiener Str.
LAUSITZER PL.
SPREEWALD PL.
GÖRLITZER BAHNHOF
Lausitzer Str.
Reichenberger Str.
Paul-Linke-Ufer
Landwehr-kanal
Maybachufer
Bürknerstr.
Pflügerstr.
Reuterstr.
Friedelstr.
Hombrechtstr.
Nansestr.
Weserstr.
Urbanstr.
Böckhstr.
Dieffenbachstr.
Müllenhoffstr.
Admiralstr.
Grimmstr.
Graefestr.
Volkspark Hasenheide
Hasenheide
Körtestr.
SÜDSTERN
Blücherstr.
Urbanstr.
Baerwaldstr.
Schleiermacher Str.
Mittenwalder Str.
Zossener Str.
GNEISENAUSTR.
Friesenstr.
Gneisenaustr.
Bergmannstr.
Schwules Museum
CHAMISSO-PL.
Fidicinstr.
Mehringdamm
MEHRINGDAMM
Yorckstr.
Hagelberger Str.
Kreuzbergstr.
Viktoria-park
TO PL. DER LUFTBRÜCKE (30m)
Großbeerenstr.
Obentrautstr.
Blücher-str.
Waterloo Ufer
HALLESCHES TOR
Gitschiner Str.
Böcklerpark
PRINZENSTR.
Prinzenstr.
Ritterstr.
MORITZPL.
Stallschreiberstr.
Waldeck-park
Oranienstr.
Lobeckstr.
Alexandrinenstr.
Lindenstr.
Alte Jakobstr.
Jüdisches Museum Berlin
Markgrafenstr.
Krausenstr.
Schützenstr.
Charlotten Str.
Encke-Str.
Haus am Checkpoint Charlie
Friedrichstr.
KOCHSTR.
Kochstr.
Zimmerstr.
Puttkamer Str.
Hedemann str.
Franz-Kluhs-Str.
MEHRING-PL.
Leipziger Str.
Niederkirchnerstr.
Wilhelmstr.
TO MITTE
Anhalter Str.
Stresemannstr.
Hallesche Str.
Hallesches Ufer
Tempelhofer Ufer
MÖCKERNBRÜCKE
TO DEUTSCHES TECHNIKMUS. (200m)

BRANDENBURGER TOR (BRANDENBURG GATE). Don't deny yourself the obligatory photo op. Berlin's only remaining city gate and and most recognizable symbol was built by Friedrich Wilhelm II in the 18th century as a symbol of victory, although in recent years this has been rephrased as "The Victory of Peace" in a fit of political correctness. During the Cold War, when it sat along the wall and served as a barricaded gateway, it became the symbol of a divided Berlin. Today, it is the most powerful emblem of reunited Germany—in 1987, Reagan chose this spot to make his "Tear down this wall" speech. The **Room of Silence** in the northern end of the gate provides a non-denominational place for meditation and reflection. *(Open daily 11am-6pm.)*

NEUE WACHE. The combination of Prussian Neoclassicism and a copy of an Expressionist statue by Käthe Kollwitz, *Mutter mit totem Sohn* (*Mother with Dead Son*), makes for an oddly moving memorial to "the victims of war and tyranny." The "New Guardhouse" was designed by architect Karl Friedrich Schinkel, turned into a memorial to victims of "fascism and militarism," and closed after reunification. Now the remains of an unknown soldier and an unknown concentration camp victim are buried inside with earth from the camps at Buchenwald and Mauthausen and from the battlefields of Stalingrad, El Alamein, and Normandy. *(Unter den Linden 4. Open daily 10am-6pm.)*

GERMANY

DENKMAL FÜR DIE ERMORDETEN JUDEN EUROPAS (MEMORIAL FOR THE MURDERED JEWS OF EUROPE). Just looking at the block of concrete stelae—large rectangular columns of concrete varying in height—it is hard to know what this prominent memorial, opened in the spring of 2005 and designed by architect Peter Eisenman, represents. Most agree, however, that it is quite moving. An underground information center tells the stories of specific families murdered during the Holocaust. *(Cora-Berliner-Str. 1, at the corner of Behrenstr. and Ebertstr. near the Brandenburg Gate. ☎030 26 39 43 36; www.stiftung-denkmal.de. Open daily 10am-8pm. Last entry Apr.-Sept. 7:15pm, Oct.-Mar. 6:15pm. Free audio tour. Guided public tours Sa-Su 11am and 2pm in German and Su 4pm in English. Admission €3, students €2.50.)*

POTSDAMER PLATZ

POTSDAMER PLATZ. Both Berlin's shiniest commercial center and the site of its most high-profile architectural failures, Potsdamer Platz is amazing for the sheer speed of its construction. Built under Friedrich Wilhelm I (in imitation of Parisian boulevards) as a launch pad for troops, the area became the commercial and transportation hub of pre-war Berlin, regulated by Europe's first traffic lights (the massive clock is set into a replica of what they looked like). But the square was flattened by bombers in WWII and caught in the death strip between East and West during the Cold War. In the decade that followed reunification, a number of commercial buildings sprouted up, the most recognizable being an off-kilter glass recreation of Mt. Fuji. *(U2, or S1, S2, or S25 to "Potsdamer Pl.")*

FÜHRERBUNKER. Near Potsdamer Pl., unmarked and inconspicuous, is the site of the bunker where Hitler married Eva Braun and then shot himself. During WWII, it held 32 rooms including private apartments and was connected to Hitler's chancellery building (since destroyed). Plans to restore the bunker were shelved for fear that the site would become a pilgrimage spot for neo-Nazis; all that remains is a dirt expanse and the occasional tourist. *(Under the parking lot at the corner of In den Ministergärten and Gertrud-Kolmar-Str.)*

GENDARMENMARKT

Several blocks south of Unter den Linden, Berlin's most typically Old Europe square became the French quarter in the 18th century after the arrival of an influx of Huguenots fleeing persecution by Louis XIV. During the last week of June and the first week of July, the square becomes an outdoor stage for open-air classical concerts. *(U6 to "Französische Str." or U2 or U6 to "Stadtmitte.")*

MUSEUMSINSEL (MUSEUM ISLAND)

There are more than a handful of reasons to set aside a good chunk of time for Museum Island, the entirety of which is a **UNESCO World Heritage Sight.** After crossing the Schloßbrücke over the Spree, Unter den Linden becomes Karl-Liebknecht-Str. and cuts through the Museumsinsel, which is home to five major museums (p. 271) and the **Berliner Dom.** *(Take S3, S5, S7, S9, or S75 to "Hackescher Markt" and walk toward the Dom. Alternatively, pick up bus #100 along Unter den Linden and get off at "Lustgarten." For more information, see Museums, p. 271.)*

BERLINER DOM. One of Berlin's most recognizable landmarks, this elegantly bulky, multiple-domed cathedral proves that Protestants can design buildings as dramatically as Catholics. Built during the reign of Kaiser Wilhelm II in a faux-Renaissance style, the cathedral suffered severe damage in a 1944 air raid and took 20 years to fully reconstruct. Look for the Protestant icons (Calvin, Zwingli, and Luther) that adorn the decadent interior, or soak up the glorious view of Berlin from the top of the cupola. *(☎030 20 26 91 19; www.berlinerdom.de. Open M-Sa 9am-8pm, Su noon-8pm, closed during services 6:30-7:30pm. Free organ recitals W-F 3pm. Frequent concerts in summer; buy tickets in the church or call ahead. Combined admission to Dom, crypt, tower, and galleries €5, students €3. Audio tour €3.)*

SCHLOSSPLATZ. Known as Marx-Engels-Pl. during the days of the DDR, the "palace square" is at the heart of Berlin's biggest architectural and urban-planning controversy. The Berliner Schloß, the Hohenzollern Imperial palace, used to stand here, but was torn down in 1950 by the East German authorities to overwhelming (mostly West Berliner) protest. The Schloß was replaced by the concrete Palast der Republik, where the East German parliament met. After reunification, the Palast was knocked down to make way for a replica of, you guessed it, the Schloß, to enormous (mostly East Berliner) protest. *(Across the street from the Lustgarten.)*

ALEXANDERPLATZ AND NIKOLAIVIERTEL

Formerly the heart of Weimar Berlin, **Alexanderplatz** became the center of East Berlin, an urban wasteland of fountains, pre-fab concrete apartment buildings, and—more recently—chain stores and malls. **Karl-Liebknecht-Strrasse,** which divides the Museuminsel, leads into the monolithic Alexanderplatz, a former cattle market. Behind the Marx-Engels-Forum, the preserved cobblestone streets of **Nikolaiviertel** (Nicholas' Quarter) stretch toward Mühlendamm. *(Take U2, U5, or U8, or S3, S5, S7, S9, or S75 to "Alexanderpl.")*

FERNSEHTURM (TV TOWER). The tremendous and bizarre tower, the tallest structure in Berlin (368m0, was originally intended to prove East Germany's technological capabilities, though Swedish engineers were ultimately brought in when construction faltered. As a result, the tower has acquired some colorful, politically infused nicknames, among them "Walter Ulbricht's Last Erection." Look at the windows when the sun is out to see the cross-shaped glint pattern known as the *Papsts Rache* (Pope's Revenge), so named because it defied the Communist government's attempt to rid the city of religious symbols. An elevator whisks tourists up to the magnificent view from the spherical node (203m) and a slowly rotating cafe one floor up serves international meals for €8-16. *(☎030 242 3333; www.berlinerfernsehturm.de. Open daily Mar.-Oct. 9am-midnight, Nov.-Feb. 10am-midnight. €10, under 16 €4.50.)*

MARIENKIRCHE. The non-bombed and non-reconstructed church (Berlin's second oldest) is Gothic, the altar and pulpit Rococo, and the tower Neo-Romantic thanks to centuries of additions to the original structure. Knowledgeable guides explain the artifacts as well as the painting collection, which features works from the Dürer and Cranach schools. *(☎030 242 4467. Open daily in summer 10am-9pm, in winter 10am-6pm.)*

NEUE SYNAGOGE. This huge building, modeled after the Alhambra, was designed by Berlin architect Eduard Knoblauch in the 1850s. The synagogue, which seated 3200, was used for worship until 1940, when the Nazis occupied it and used it for storage. Amazingly, the building survived *Kristallnacht*—the SS torched it, but a local police chief bluffed his way past SS officers to order the fire extinguished. The synagogue was later destroyed by bombing, but its restoration, largely financed by international Jewish organizations, began in 1988 and was completed in 1995. Too big for Berlin's remaining Jewish community, the striking building is no longer used for services and instead houses an exhibit chronicling its history as well as that of the Jewish community that once thrived in the surrounding neighborhood. *(Oranienburger Str. 29. ☎030 88 02 83 00; www.cjudaicum.de. Open Apr.-Sept. M and Su 10am-5pm, Tu-Th 10am-6pm, F 10am-5pm; Mar. and Oct. M and Su 10am-2pm, Tu-Th 10am-8pm, F 10am-6pm; Nov.-Feb. M and Su 10am-2pm, Tu-F 10am-6pm. Last entry 30min. before closing. Permanent exhibition "Open Ye the Gates" €3, students €2. Dome €1.50/1. Temporary exhibition €3/2.)*

GERMANY

THE MISSING HOUSE. Across the street from the Jewish Cemetery is a 1990 art installation by Christian Boltanski in the space where a house was bombed during WWII. Boltanski researched the apartment's earlier inhabitants—Jews and non-Jews alike—and put plaques on the walls of the surrounding buildings at the approximate height of their apartment floors with their names, dates of birth and death, and professions. *(Große Hamburger Strasse.)*

TIERGARTEN

Stretching from Bahnhof Zoo in the west to the Brandenburg Gate in the east, this vast landscaped park was formerly used by Prussian monarchs as a hunting and parade ground. Today, it is frequented by strolling families, elderly couples. **Straße des 17. Juni** bisects the park from west to east, connecting Ernst-Reuter-Pl. to the Brandenburg Gate. The street is the site of many demonstrations and parades, including Barack Obama's 2008 speech, which attracted over 200,000 viewers.

THE REICHSTAG. The current home of Germany's governing body, the **Bundestag,** the Reichstag has seen some critical historical moments in its day. Philipp Scheidemann proclaimed "*Es lebe die Deutsche Republik*" ("Long live the German Republic") here in 1918. In 1933 Adolf Hitler used a fire at the Reichstag as an excuse to declare a state of emergency and seize power. In 1997, a glass dome was added to the top, built around the upside-down solar cone that powers the building. A walkway spirals up the inside of the dome, providing visitors with information about the building, panoramic views of the city, and a view of the parliament meeting inside—a powerful symbol of government transparency. Braving the line is worth it. *(☎030 22 73 21 52; www.bundestag.de. Open daily 8am-midnight. Last entry 10pm. Free.)*

CHARLOTTENBURG

During the city's division, West Berlin centered around Bahnhof Zoo, the station that inspired U2's "Zoo TV" tour. The area around the station is dominated by department stores and peep shows intermingled with souvenir shops and more G-rated attractions.

ZOOLOGISCHER GARTEN. Germany's oldest zoo houses around 14,000 animals of 1500 species, most in open-air habitats. The southern entrance is the famous **Elefantentor** (across from Europa-Center), a decorated elephant pagoda standing at Budapester Str. 34. You had better visit the world-famous polar bear **Knut;** otherwise he might go berserk. Originally deemed the cutest polar bear alive, Knut has been diagnosed by animal specialists as a psychopath who is addicted to human attention. *(☎030 25 40 10; www.zoo-berlin.de. Park open daily 9am-7:30pm, animal houses open 9am-6pm; entrance closes at 6:30pm. €12, students €9, children €6. Combination ticket to zoo and aquarium €18/14/9.)*

SCHLOSS CHARLOTTENBURG (CHARLOTTENBURG PALACE). The broad Baroque palace, which was commissioned by Friedrich I in the 17th century for his second wife, Sophie-Charlotte, stands impassively at the end of a beautiful, tree-lined esplanade in northern Charlottenburg. The *Schloß*'s extensive grounds include the **Altes Schloß,** underneath the iconic dome topped with a stature of Fortuna; the **Große Orangerie,** which contains rooms filled with historic furnishings (much of it reconstructed as a result of war damage) and gratuitous gilding; the **Neuer Flügel,** which includes the marble receiving rooms and the more sober royal chambers; the **Neuer Pavillon,** a museum dedicated to Prussian architect Karl Friedrich Schinkel; the **Belvedere,** a small building housing the royal family's porcelain collection; and the **Mausoleum,** the final resting place for most of the family. Stroll the **Schloßgarten** behind the main buildings, an elysium of small lakes, footbridges, fountains, and meticulously manicured trees. *(Spandauer Damm 10-22. Take bus #M45 from Bahnhof Zoo to "Luisenpl./Schloß Charlottenburg" or U2 to "Sophie-Charlotte Pl." ☎030 320 9275. Altes Schloß open Tu-Su Apr.-Oct. 10am-6pm, Nov.-Mar. 10am-5pm. Neuer Flügel open M and W-Su Apr.-Oct. 10am-6pm, Nov.-Mar. 10am-5pm. Belvedere and Mausoleum open daily Apr.-Oct. 10am-6pm, Nov.-Mar. noon-5pm. Altes Schloß €10, students €7; Neuer Flügel €6/5; Belvedere €2/1.50; Mausoleum €2/1.50. Audio tours, available in English, are included.)*

OLYMPIA-STADION. This massive Nazi-built stadium comes in a close second after Tempelhof Airport in the list of monumental Third Reich buildings in Berlin. It was erected for the infamous 1936 Olympic Games, in which African-American Jesse Owens won four gold medals. Hitler refused to congratulate Owens, a legendary runner who now has a Berlin street (Jesse-Owens-Allee) named after him. Film buffs will recognize the complex from Leni Riefenstahl's terrifying film *Olympia* (1938) while others will recognize it as the sight of the 2006 World Cup final. The **Glockenturm** (bell tower) provides a great lookout point and houses an exhibit on the history of German athletics. *(S5, S7, or U2 to "Olympia-Stadion." For Glockenturm, S5 or S7 to "Pichelsburg." ☎030 25 00 23 22; www.olympiastadion-berlin.de. Open daily Mar. 20-May 9am-7pm, Jun.-Sept. 15 9am-8pm, Sept. 16-Oct. 31 9am-7pm, Nov.-Mar. 19 9am-4pm. €4, students €3. Tour with guide €8, students €7; children under 6 free. Audio tour €2.50.)*

KREUZBERG

Kreuzberg sights are mostly devoted to the area's hybrid history as a hub for both punks and immigrants.

SOUTHERN KREUZBERG. The cobblestone streets and pre-war ornamented apartment blocks just east of Mehringdamm form the most gentrified area of Kreuzberg—witness the outdoor organic food market on Saturdays in Chamissopl. The spine of of the area is **Bergmannstraße,** a stretch of cafes, secondhand clothing and record stores, and bookshops. West of Mehringdamm, forested Viktoria Park is the highest natural point in Berlin at 66m. A huge neo-Gothic memorial commemorating the Napoleonic Wars provides a great view of Berlin. Vineyards first planted by the Knights Templar and a number of small restaurants and beer gardens—including philosopher Georg Friedrich Hegel's favorite watering hole—are tucked away in the park near the artificial waterfall. Farther south down Mehringdamm is **Tempelhof Airport,** built by Nazi architect Albrecht Speer but most famous as the site of the Berlin Airlift, 1948-1949, one of the most dramatic crises of the Cold War. The German government closed the airport in 2008, but still visible in a flower-ringed field is a monument known as the **Hungerharke** (hunger rake) representing the three air corridors and dedicated to the 78 pilots who lost their lives in the 328 days of the airlift. *(U6 to "Platz der Luftbrücke" or U6 or U7 to "Mehringdamm.")*

EASTERN KREUZBERG. The **Landwehrkanal,** a channel bisecting Kreuzberg, is a lovely place to take a stroll, with moored boats doubling as on-the-water cafes. Its history is less pleasant: it is where the conservative, nationalist Freikorps threw the body of left-wing activist and communist revolutionary Rosa Luxemburg after murdering her in 1919. The Berlin Wall once ran near **Schlesisches Tor,** a nightlife hotspot with a huge Turkish and Balkan influence and arguably the best street art and graffiti in the city—especially around Wrangelstraße. The **Oberbaumbrücke,** an iconic double-decker brick bridge, spans the Spree River. It was once a border crossing into East Berlin, and now connects Kreuzberg to Friedrichshain. Residents of the rival neighborhoods duke it out in a "water fight" on the bridge each July 27, with up to a thousand people throwing water and rotten vegetables at one another. *(U1 or U15 to "Schlesisches Tor.")*

ORANIENSTRASSE. This strip's colorful mix of cafes, bars, and stores is home to the city's punk and radical elements. May Day parades, which start on Oranienpl., were the scene of violent riots in the 1980s, although May 1 has since become a family holiday complete with a big block party. The street's **Heinrichplatz** boasts, in addition to great cafes, a women-only Turkish-style bath, **Schoko Fabrik,** which doubles as a community center (www.schokofabrik.de; open M 3-11pm, Tu-Su noon-11pm). Squatters still occupy the **Bethanien Kunsthaus** in Marienplatz (www.bethanien.de), which hosts frequent exhibitions and an open-air cinema in summer. *(U1 or U15 to "Kottbusser Tor" or "Görlitzer Bahnhof."*

FRIEDRICHSHAIN AND LICHTENBERG

EAST SIDE GALLERY. The longest remaining portion of the Berlin Wall, this 1.3km stretch of cement slabs also serves as the world's largest open-air art gallery. The murals are not remnants of Cold War graffiti, but rather the organized efforts of an international group of artists who gathered here in 1989 to celebrate the end of the city's division. One of the most famous is artist Dmitri Vrubel's depiction of a wet kiss between Leonid Brezhnev and East German leader Eric Honecker. The stretch of street remains unsupervised and, on the Warschauer Str. side, open at all hours. *(Along Mühlenstr. Take U1 or U15 or S3, S5-S7, S9, or S75 to "Warschauer Str." or S5, S7, S9, or S75 to "Ostbahnhof" and walk back toward the river. www.eastsidegallery.com.)*

STASI MUSEUM. The Lichtenberg suburb harbors perhaps the most hated and feared building of the DDR regime: the headquarters of the East German secret police, the *Staatssicherheit* or Stasi. During the Cold War, the Stasi kept dossiers on some six million of East Germany's own citizens, an amazing feat and a testament to the huge number of civilian informers in a country of only 16 million people. On January 15, 1990, a crowd of 100,000 Berliners stormed and vandalized the building to celebrate the demise of the police state. Since a 1991 law returned the records to the people, the "Horror Files" have rocked Germany, exposing millions of informants—and wrecking careers, marriages, and friendships—at every level of German society. Officially known today as the **Forschungs- und Gedenkstätte Normannenstraße,** the building maintains its oppressive Orwellian gloom and much of its worn 1970s aesthetic. The exhibit displays the extensive offices of Erich Mielke, the loathed Minister for State Security from 1957 to 1989, a large collection of tiny microphones and hidden cameras used for surveillance by the Stasi, and a replica of a Stasi prison cell. *(Ruschestr. 103, Haus 1. U5 to "Magdalenenstr." ☎ 030 553 6854; www.stasimuseum.de. Exhibits in German. English info booklet €3. Open M-F 11am-6pm, Sa-Su 2-6pm. €4, students €3.)*

PRENZLAUER BERG

BERLINER MAUER DOKUMENTATIONSZENTRUM (BERLIN WALL DOCUMENTATION CENTER). A museum, a chapel, and an entire city block of the preserved Berlin Wall—two concrete barriers separated by the open *Todesstreife* (death strip)—come together in a memorial to "victims of the communist tyranny." The museum has assembled a comprehensive collection of all things Wall. Exhibits include photos, film clips, and sound bites. The collection here is both cheaper and more informative than the private museum at Checkpoint Charlie covering similar material. *(Bernauer Str. 111; www.berliner-mauer-dokumentationszentrum.de. ☎ 030 464 1030. U8 to "Bernauer Str.", switch to S1 or S2 to "Nordbahnhof." Open Apr.-Oct. Tu-Su 10am-6pm, Nov.-Mar. Tu-Su 10am-5pm. Free.)*

JÜDISCHER FRIEDHOF (JEWISH CEMETERY). Prenzlauer Berg was one of the major centers of Jewish Berlin during the 19th and early 20th centuries. The ivy-covered Jewish cemetery on Schönhauser Allee contains the graves of composer Giacomo Meyerbeer and painter Max Liebermann. *(Enter by the "Lapidarium." Open M-Th 8am-4pm, F 8am-1pm. Men must cover their heads.)* Nearby, **Synagoge Rykestraße,** Rykestr. 53, is one of Berlin's loveliest synagogues. It was spared on *Kristallnacht* thanks to its inconspicuous location. Unfortunately, visitors are currently not allowed in, as the synagogue is a still-operational school.

MUSEUMS

With over 170 museums, Berlin is one of the world's great museum cities. Collections range from every epoch; the *Berlin Programm* (€1.60) lists them all.

SMB MUSEUMS

Staatliche Museen zu Berlin (SMB) runs over 20 museums in four major areas of Berlin—the **Museumsinsel, Tiergarten-Kulturforum, Charlottenburg,** and **Dahlem**—and elsewhere in Mitte and the Tiergarten. (www.smb.museum; ☎ 030 209 055 77.) All museums sell single-admission tickets (€8, students €4) and the three-day card (*Drei-Tage-Karte;* €19, students €9.50). Admission is free the first Sunday of every month and on Thursdays after 6pm. Unless otherwise noted, all SMB museums are open Tuesday through Sunday 10am-6pm and Thursday 10am-10pm. All offer free English-language audio tours.

MUSEUMSINSEL (MUSEUM ISLAND)

The Museumsinsel holds five separate museums on an area cordoned off from the rest of Mitte by two arms of the Spree. The museums were built in the 19th- and 20th centuries, suffered bombing during World War II and isolation and neglect afterwards, but have all been recently and extensively renovated. *(S3, S5, S7, S9, or S75 to "Hackescher Markt" or bus #100 to "Lustgarten." ☎ 030 266 3666. All national museums, unless otherwise noted, open Tu-W and F-Su 10am-6pm, Th 10am-10pm. Free audio tours in English. Admission to each €8, students €4. All sell a 3-day card good for admission to every museum; €14, students €7.)*

PERGAMONMUSEUM. One of the world's great ancient history museums, the Pergamon dates from the days when Heinrich Schliemann and other zealous

19th-century German archaeologists dismantled the remnants of collapsed empires the world over and sent them home for reassembly. Named for Pergamon, the city in present-day Turkey from which the enormous **Altar of Zeus** (180 BC) was taken, the museum features gargantuan pieces of ancient Mediterranean and Near Eastern civilizations from as far back as the 10th century BC. The colossal blue **Ishtar Gate** of Babylon (575 BC) and the **Roman Market Gate** of Miletus are just two more massive pieces in a collection that also includes Greek, Assyrian, and Far Eastern art. *(Bodestr. 1-3. ☎030 2090 5577. Open M-Su 10am-6pm, Th 10am-10pm. Last entry 30min. before closing. €8, students €4.)*

BODE-MUSEUM. The island's most attractive museum, which looks like it rises straight up from the water, reopened in 2006 after six years of renovations. It houses a hodgepodge of classical sculpture, Byzantine art, and oil painting. Its numismatic collection (coins and monies) is one of the world's largest. *(Monbijoubrücke. ☎030 266 3666. Open Tu-W and F-Su 10am-6pm. Th 10am-10pm. €8, students €4.)*

ALTE NATIONALGALERIE (OLD NATIONAL GALLERY). After extensive renovations, this museum is open to lovers of 19th-century art, showcasing everything from German Realism to French Impressionism. Camille Pisarro leads the all-star cast of featured artists. *(Am Lustgarten. ☎030 2090 5577. Open Tu-W and F-Su 10am-6pm. Th 10am-10pm. €8, students €4.)*

ALTES MUSEUM. At the far end of the Lustgarten, the museum in the stately columned building designed by Karl Friedrich Schinkel is surprisingly untouristed. The lower level contains a permanent collection of ancient Greco-Roman (especially Etruscan) decorative art. The highlight of the upstairs Egyptian collection, and probably the whole museum, is the amazingly realistic bust of Nefertiti. *(AmLustgarten. ☎030 266 3660. Open M-W and F-Su 10am-6pm. Th 10am-10pm. €8, students €4. Free audio tour.)*

TIERGARTEN-KULTURFORUM

The Tiergarten-Kulturforum is a complex of museums at the eastern end of the Tiergarten, near the Staatsbibliothek and Potsdamer Pl. Students and local fine arts aficionados swarm throughout the buildings and on the multi-leveled courtyard in front. *(S1, S2, or S25 or U2 to "Potsdamer Pl." and walk down Potsdamer Str.; the museums will be on your right on Matthäikirchpl. ☎030 20 90 55 55.)*

GEMÄLDEGALERIE (PICTURE GALLERY). This is the place to come in Berlin, and arguably in Germany, for painting. The city's most famous museum houses a collection of 2700 13th- to 18th-century masterpieces by Dutch, Flemish, German, and Italian masters, including works by Botticelli, Bruegel, Dürer, Gainsborough, Raphael, Rembrandt, Rubens, Titian, Velazquez, and many, many others. *(Matthäikirchplatz 4-6. ☎030 266 2951. Open Tu-W and F-Su 10am-6pm, Th 10am-10pm.)*

NEUE NATIONALGALERIE (NEW NATIONAL GALLERY). This sleek building, designed by **Mies van der Rohe** at the height of 1960s Minimalism, contains often wacky temporary exhibits in the glass entrance hall and gallery downstairs. The real draw is its formidable permanent collection of 20th-century art, including works by Warhol, Munch, Kirchner, and Beckmann. *(Potsdamer Str. 50. ☎030 266 2651. Open Tu-W and F 10am-6pm, Th 10am-10pm, Sa-Su 11am-6pm.€8, students €4.)*

OTHER MUSEUMS IN MITTE AND TIERGARTEN

HAMBURGER BAHNHOF: MUSEUM FÜR GEGENWART (MUSEUM FOR THE PRESENT). With a colossal 10,000 sq. m of exhibition space, this converted train station houses Berlin's foremost collection of contemporary art. The museum features several whimsical works by Warhol, as well as pieces by Twombly and Kiefer and some more puzzling exhibits in its vast white spaces. *(Invalidenstr. 50-51. S3, S5, S7, S9, or S75 to "Hauptbahnhof" or U6 to "Zinnowitzer Str." ☎ 030 3978 3411; www.hamburgerbahnhof.de. Open Tu-F 10am-6pm, Sa 11am-8pm, Su 11am-6pm. €8, students €4; Th 2-6pm free.)*

DEUTSCHE HISTORISCHES MUSEUM (GERMAN HISTORY MUSEUM). The oldest building on Unter den Linden, a baroque former military arsenal dating to 1730, the museum now houses a thorough exploration of German history, from Neanderthals to the Nazis to the fall of the Wall. Temporary exhibitions focus on the last 50 years, with plenty of depictions of smiling workers from the DDR era. Behind the main building stands its modern counterpart, a new wing designed by I. M. Pei that further bolster Berlin's reputation for cutting-edge architecture. *(Unter den Linden 2. S3, 5, 7, 9, or 75 to "Hackescher Markt." ☎ 030 2030 4444; www.dhm.de. Open daily 10am-6pm. €5, 18 and under free. Audio tour €3.)*

HAUS AM CHECKPOINT CHARLIE. Checkpoint Charlie, the border crossing between former East and West Berlin has become one of Berlin's most popular attractions, with tour buses, stands selling DDR memorabilia, actors clad as soldiers, and a table where you can get your passport "stamped." Perhaps the biggest rip off (those actors only charge €1 per photo) in the area is the **Haus am Checkpoint Charlie,** a two-bedroom apartment turned private museum. The exhibits detail how women curled up in loudspeakers, students dug tunnels with their fingers, and others found ingenious ways of getting into the West. Much of the same information can be gleaned for free by reading the placards along **Kochstraße,** where the wall used to run. *(Friedrichstr. 43-45. U6 to "Kochstr." ☎ 030 253 7250; www.mauer-museum.de. Museum open daily 9am-10pm. German-language films with English subtitles every 2hr. from 9:30am. €12.50, students €9.50. Audio tour €3.)*

GERMANY

CHARLOTTENBURG

Charlottenburg's museums range from high culture to smut and house one of the strongest collections of Picasso outside of Barcelona.

MUSEUM BERGGRUEN. This intimate three-floor museum exhibits some wonderful Picassos alongside works that influenced the artist, including African masks and late French Impressionist paintings by Matisse. The top floor showcases paintings by Bauhaus teacher Paul Klee and Alberto Giacometti's surreally elongated sculptures. *(Schloßstr. 1. Near the Schloß Charlottenburg. Take bus #M45 from "Bahnhof Zoo" to "Luisenpl./Schloß Charlottenburg" or U2 to "Sophie-Charlotte-Pl." ☎ 030 3269 580. Open Tu-Su 10am-6pm. €6, students €3, children free. Audio guide free.)*

KÄTHE-KOLLWITZ-MUSEUM. Through both World Wars, Käthe Kollwitz, a member of the Berlin *Sezession* (Secession) movement and one of Germany's most prominent 20th-century artists, protested war and the condition of the working class through her haunting depictions of death, poverty, and suffering. The artist's biographical details—her son died in World War II and she withdrew into so-called inner migration during the DDR—provide context for her depictions of death, pregnancy, and starvation and for her somber self-portraits shown in what used to be a private home. *(Fasanenstr. 24. U1 to "Uhlandstr." ☎ 030 882 5210; www.kaethe-kollwitz.de. Open daily 11am-6pm. €5, students €2.50. Audio guide €3.)*

BEATE UHSE EROTIK MUSEUM. The world's largest sex museum contains over 5000 sex artifacts from around the world. Attracting a quarter of a million visitors per year, it is Berlin's fifth-most popular tourist attraction. Visitors come to see erotica ranging from naughty carvings on a 17th-century Italian deer-hunting knife to a 1955 calendar featuring Marilyn Monroe in the nude. A small exhibit describes the life of Beate Uhse, a pilot-turned-entrepreneur who pioneered Europe's first and largest sex shop chain. *(Joachimstalerstr. 4. ☎030 886 0666; www.erotikmuseum.de. Museum open daily 9am-midnight. €6, students €5. Gift store open M-Sa 9am-9pm, Su 1-10pm.)*

INDEPENDENT (NON-SMB) MUSEUMS

JÜDISCHES MUSEM (JEWISH MUSEUM). Architect Daniel Libeskind's design for the zinc-plated Jewish Museum is fascinating even as an architectural experience. No two walls are parallel, creating a sensation of perpetual discomfort. Underground, three symbolic hallways—the **Axis of the Holocaust,** the **Axis of Exile,** and the **Axis of Continuity**—are intended to represent the trials of death, escape, and survival. The labyrinthine "Garden of Exile" replicates the dizzying effects of dislocation and the eerie "Holocaust Tower," a giant, asymmetrical concrete room nearly devoid of light and sound, encourages reflection. Exhibits feature works by contemporary artists, memorials to victims of the Holocaust, and a history of Jews in Germany. Enter at the top of the stairs from the Axis of Continuity. *(Lindenstr. 9-14. U6 to "Kochstr.," or U1, U6, or U15 to "Prinzenstr." ☎030 25 99 33 00. Open M 10am-10pm, Tu-Su 10am-8pm. Last entry 1hr. before closing. €5, students €2.50. Special exhibits €4. Audio tour €2.)*

BAUHAUS-ARCHIV MUSEUM FÜR GESTALTUNG (BAUHAUS ARCHIVE MUSEUM FOR DESIGN). A must-visit for design fans, this building was conceived by Bauhaus founder **Walter Gropius** and houses rotating exhibits of paintings, sculptures, and of course, the famous furniture. *(Klingelhöferstr. 14. Bus #100, 187, 200, or 341 to "Nordische Botschaften/Adenauer-Stifteng" or U1, U2, U3, or U4 to "Nollendorfpl." ☎030 254 0020; www.bauhaus.de. Open M and W-Su 10am-5pm. M-Tu and Sa-Su €7, students €4; W-F €6/3. Audio tour free.)*

GERMANY

ENTERTAINMENT

Berlin has one of the world's most vibrant cultural scenes. Numerous festivals celebrating everything from Chinese film to West African music enrich the regular offerings; posters advertising special events plaster the city well in advance. Despite recent cutbacks, the city still generously subsidizes its art scene, and tickets are usually reasonably priced. Most theaters and concert halls offer up to 50% discounts for students who purchase tickets at the *Abendkasse* (evening box office), which generally opens 1hr. before shows. Other ticket outlets charge 15-18% commissions and do not offer student discounts. The **KaDeWe** has a ticket counter. (☎030 217 7754. Open M-F 10am-8pm, Sa 10am-4pm.) Theaters generally accept credit cards, but many ticket outlets do not—so bring cash just in case. Most theaters and operas close from mid-July to late August. The monthly pamphlets *Konzerte und Theater in Berlin und Brandenburg* (free) and *Berlin Programm* (€1.75) list concerts, film, and theater info, as do the biweekly *030*, *Kultur!news*, *Tip*, and *Zitty*.

NIGHTLIFE

Berlin's nightlife is world-renowned absolute madness—a teeming cauldron of debauchery that bubbles around the clock. Bars typically open at 6pm and get crowded around 10pm, just as the clubs open their doors. Bar scenes wind down anywhere between midnight and 6am; meanwhile, around 1am, dance floors fill up and the lights flash at clubs that keep pumping beats until dawn, when a variety of after-parties keep up the perpetual motion. In summer months it's only dark from 10:30pm to 4am, so it's easy to be unintentionally included in the early morning crowd, watching the sun rise on Berlin's landmarks and waiting for the cafes to open. From 1-4am on weekdays, 70 night buses operate throughout the city, and on Friday and Saturday nights the U- and S-Bahn run on a limited schedule throughout the night. The best sources of information about bands and dance venues are the bi-weekly magazines *Tip* (€2.70) and the superior *Zitty* (€2.70), available at all newsstands, or the free *030*, distributed in hostels, cafes, shops, and bars.

Berlin's most touristed bar scene sprawls down pricey, packed **Hackescher Markt** and **Oranienburger Straße** in Mitte. Prices fall only slightly around yuppie **Kollwitzplatz** and **Kastanienallee** in Prenzlauer Berg, but areas around Schönhauser Allee and **Danziger Straße** still harbor a somewhat edgier scene. The most serious clubbing takes place near the river in Friedrichshain, with a growing presence on the Kreuzberg side of the river. Bars line **Simon-Dach-Straße, Gabriel-Max-Straße,** and **Schlesiche Straße.** Businessmen and middle-aged tourists drink at bars along the Ku'damm. Gay nightlife centers on Nollendorfplatz, in the west, and lesbian nightlife has its stronghold in Kreuzberg.

GERMANY

MITTE

The Mitte nightlife scene centers on **Hackescher Markt** and **Oranienburger Straße** (also, incidentally, the city's most conspicuous prostitution drag). The pricey, packed strip offers a mixture of both world-renowned and touristy bars and clubs. If you'd prefer to get off the beaten track, head to the outskirts of Mitte or its eastern neighborhoods.

Week-End, Alexanderpl. 5 (☎030 24 63 16 76; www.week-end-berlin.de), on the 12th and 15th fl. of the building with the "Sharp" sign overlooking the city. A staple of the Berlin club scene, where techno fuels the floor until the sun rises over the block-housing of East Berlin. Wheelchair-accessible. Cover €8-12. Open F-Su 11pm-late. Cash only.

Tape, Heidestr. 14 (☎030 848 4873; www.tapeberlin.de), near a few art galleries along a strip close to the Hauptbahnhof. This converted warehouse is worth the trip. The walls, the entrance, and ravers' hands are all stamped with images of cassette tapes, the club's symbol. An artsy crowd dances in the enormous main room and hangs out on couches in the silver lounge. Cover varies. Open F-Sa 11pm-late.

Clärchen's Ballhouse, Auguststr. 24 (☎030 282 92 95; www.ballhaus.de). This odd-looking building was a ballroom before WWI, and now it is again. Older couples gather to tango and swing, while younger groups attempt to join in or enjoy beer in the flower-filled courtyard. Free introductory "swing tease" lesson W. Classical concerts and chacha brunch W. Open daily noon-late.

Bang Bang Club, Neue Promenade 10 (☎030 60 40 53 10; www.bangbang-club.de). Twiggy look-alikes run around a dance floor while guys in fedoras nod and smile. Grab your best tight jeans and ankle boots for "Death by Britpop" on F. Opening days and times vary. Check website or show up after midnight.

KREUZBERG

Although clubs are emerging throughout the rest of eastern Berlin (especially Friedrichshain), Kreuzberg is still a nightlife stronghold, full of options for virtually every demographic. Although there is no shortage of bars, **Oranienstraße** has the densest and coolest stretches of nightlife offerings. A unique row of bars along the water on **Schlesisches Straße** allow travelers to watch the sun set and then sip drinks until it rises again.

Club der Visionaere, Am Flutgraben 1 (☎030 69 51 89 42; www.clubdervisionaererecords.com). U1 or U15 to "Schlesisches Tor" or night bus #N65 to "Heckmannufer." Lounging around on their torch-lit raft in the canal in summer is the single most pleasant bar experience in Berlin. Legend has it that bargoers occasionally fall into the water, but more common activities include dancing to house music or downing a pizza (€5-8) along with your drink. Beer €3. Open M-F 2pm-late, Sa-Su noon-late. Cash only.

Monarch Bar, Skalitzer Str. 134. U1 or U15 to "Kotbusser Tor." Don't be put off by the urine smell in the staircase that leads up to this small, unmarked bar above Kaiser's supermarket. Some of the cheapest beer (€1 and up) around, a panoramic view of the raised S-Bahn thundering by, and a nightly DJ spinning electronica. Open 10pm-late.

Watergate, Falckensteinstr. 49 (☎030 61 28 03 96; www.water-gate.de). U1 or U15 to "Schlesisches Tor." Depending on who is spinning, this can be the best party in the city on any given night. Polka-dot light show on the ceiling and the unbeatable view of the Spree from the "Water Floor" lounge and terrace. Crowds pick up at 2am. Cover W €6, F-Sa €10. Open W and F 11pm-late and Sa midnight-late. Cash only.

PRENZLAUER BERG

Prenzlauer Berg is the place to go for a slightly more relaxed, less techno oriented scene than the elsewhere in Berlin. Trendy bars and late-night cafes cluster around **Kastanienallee** (U2 to "Eberswalder Str.") while the areas around **Helmholtzplatz** (SBahn to "Prenzlauer Allee") are your best bet for the neighborhood's trademark shabby chic.

The Weinerei, Veteranenstr. 14 (☎030 440 6983). The unmarked wine bar has gone from local secret to local legend, based on comfortable elegance and a strange pricin-system. Pay €1 for a glass, sample all of the wines, sample again, and again, and before leaving pay however much you think you owe. Open 10am-very late. Cash only.

Klub Der Republik (KDR Bar), Pappelallee 81. U2 to "Eberswalderstr.," M10, N2, N42. Turn into what looks like a deserted parking lot and climb the stairs of a dance studio to find a totally preserved DDR ballroom turned favorite post-wall watering hole. Cheap drinks for the neighborhood (€2-4). Open in summer from 9pm, in winter from 8pm. Cash only.

Wohnzimmer, Lettestr. 6 (☎030 445 5458). U2 to "Eberswalder Str." The name means living room, and they aren't kidding. With wood-beam floors, the bar resembles an old-fashioned kitchen, and glassware cabinets line the walls. You'll feel right at home as you settle into a velvet armchair with a matching mixed drink. Damn good mojito €5. Open daily 9am-4am. Cash only.

Solsi e Morsi, Marienburger Str. 10. Owner Johnny Petrongolo flits around his always packed familial wine bar opening bottles and bestowing plates of free *parma* ham, cheese, and olives. The young clientele love their Galouises: Solsi e Morsi is not for the faint of lung. Open 6pm-late.

FRIEDRICHSHAIN

When people think of Berlin techno clubs, they're thinking of Friedrichshain. There are more legendary converted factory or warehouse clubs in this neighborhood than you can shake a stick at. Raging dance venues are scattered between the car dealerships and empty lots on **Mühlenstrasse.**

Berghain/Panorama Bar, Am Wriezener Bahnhof (☎030 29 00 05 97; www.berghain.de). S3, S5, S7, S9, or S75 to "Ostbahnhof." Heading up Str. der Pariser Kommune, take the 3rd right into what looks like a parking lot. The granddaddy of Berlin's "it" clubs deserves its reputation as a must-visit. Beneath the towering ceilings of this former power plant, spaced-out techno-fiends pulse to the reverberating music. Cover generally €12. Open F-Sa and occasionally W from midnight. Cash only.

Maria am Ostbahnhof, Am der Schillingbrücke (☎030 21 23 81 90; www.clubmaria.de). S-Bahn to "Ostbahnhof." From Stralauer Pl. exit, take Str. der Pariser Kommune to Stralauer Pl., follow it right along the wall, turn left at the bridge, and look for the red lights by the water. Tucked away by the river in an old factory, this club embodies the industrial legacy of Friedrichshain's scene. Sizable—and usually full—dance floor. Mostly electronic music, occasional punk, and reggae. Beer €2.50-3.50. Cover €10-12. Open F-Sa 11pm-late, weekdays for concerts and events only. Cash only.

Sanitorium 23, Frankfurter Allee 23 (☎030 42 02 11 93; www.sanatorium23.de). Large windows look into a sterile yet hip interior of this sleek break from converted warehouses. Hang your coat on the overturned gurney and try the "Moscow Mule" (€5). Open daily 2pm-late. Chic rooms available above. Singles €40; doubles €55. Cash only.

Häbermeyer, Gärtnerstr. 6 (☎030 29 77 18 87). U5 to "Samariterstr." Retro stylings and soft red lighting from funky lamps complement the New Wave DJ sessions. Foosball table in back lends a competitive edge to the otherwise relaxed atmosphere. Mixed drinks €5.90-7.40. Open daily 7pm-late. Cash only.

GERMANY

GLBT NIGHTLIFE

Berlin is definitely one of Europe's most gay-friendly cities. Thousands of homosexuals flocked to Berlin during the Cold War to take part in the city's left-wing activism and avoid West Germany's *Wehrpflicht* (mandatory military service). In the gay mecca of **Schöneberg, Akazienstraße, Goltzstraße,** and **Winterfeldtstraße** have mixed bars and cafes, while the **"Bermuda Triangle"** of Eisenacherstr., Fuggerstr., and Motzstr. is more exclusively gay. *Gay-yellowpages, Sergej,* and *Siegessäule* have GLBT entertainment listings. **Mann-o-Meter,** Bülowstr. 106, at the corner of Else-Lasker-Schüler-Str., provides counseling, info on gay nightlife, and long-term accommodations, in addition to **Internet** access. (☎030 216 8008; www.mann-o-meter.de. Open M-F 5-10pm, Sa-Su 4-10pm.) **Spinnboden-Lesbenarchiv,** Anklamer Str. 38, has hip lesbian offerings, including exhibits, films, and other cultural info. Take U8 to "Bernauer Str." (☎030 448 5848. Open W and F 2-7pm.) The **Christopher Street Day (CSD)** parade, a 6hr. street party with ecstatic, champagne-soaked floats, draws over 250,000 participants annually in June. Nollendorfpl. hosts the **Lesbisch-schwules Stadtfest** (Lesbian-Gay City Fair) the weekend before the parade.

SCHÖNEBERG

Schöneberg is Berlin's unofficial "gay district" and teems with GLBT nightlife.

Hafen, Motzstr. 19 (☎030 211 4118; www.hafen-berlin.de). U1-U4 to "Nollendorfpl." Nearly 20 years old, this bar has become a landmark for Berlin's gay community. The sign outside specifically invites in "drop dead gorgeous looking tourists," but there are plenty of locals here, too. The mostly male crowd jams the surrounding sidewalk in summer. Weekly pub quiz M 8pm (1st M of the month in English). New DJs W. Open daily 8am-4am. Cash only.

Connection, Fuggerstr. 33 (☎030 218 1432; www.connection-berlin.de). U1 or U2 to "Wittenbergpl." The name says it all. Find your soulmate (or one-night stand) in the disco, then go next door to the labyrinthine **Connection Garage** to get acquainted. First F of the month mixed; otherwise, men only. Cover €7, includes 1st drink. Club open F-Sa 11pm-late; Garage open M-Sa 10am-1am, Su and holidays 2pm-1am. AmEx/MC/V.

Begine, Potsdamer Str. 139 (☎030 215 1414; www.begine.de). U2 to "Bülowstr." In a neighborhood dominated by sceney gay clubs, this is a welcome retreat for women. Named after a now-defunct lesbian squat, Berlin's biggest lesbian community center has a popular, low-key cafe/bar with live music and readings at night. No cover. Open M-F 6pm-late, Sa-Su 9:30pm-late.

Heile Welt, Motzstr. 5 (☎030 2191 7507). U1-U4 to "Nollendorfpl." Despite the addition of 2 enormous, quiet inner sitting rooms, the 20-something clientele still pack the bar and spill into the street. Aside from a fur-covered wall and single tiara hanging above the bar, both the decor and mood are reserved. Mostly male crowd during "prime time;"

more women in the early evening, on weekdays, and in the early morning. Open daily 6pm-4am, sometimes later. Cash only.

KREUZBERG

Rose's, Oranienstr. 187 (☎615 65 70). U1 to "Görlitzer Bahnhof." Marked only by "Bar" over the door. It's Liberace meets Cupid meets Satan. A friendly, gay and lesbian clientele packs this intense and claustrophobic party spot all night. The voluptuous dark-red interior is accessorized madness, boasting hearts, glowing lips, furry ceilings, feathers, and glitter. The small menu covers the basics with whiskey (€5) and schnapps (€2). Open M-Th and Su 11pm-6am, F-Sa 11pm-8am. Cash only.

SchwuZ, Mehringdamm 61 (☎030 629 0880; www.schwuz.de). U6 or U7 to "Mehringdamm." Enter through Melitta Sundström, a popular gay and lesbian cafe. The city's longest-running gay bar features 2 dance floors and a loungy underground area lined with pipes and its own DJ and disco lights. Crowd varies from young to very young. Lesbian night every 2nd F of the month. Cover F €5 before midnight, €6 after; Sa €6/7. Open F-Sa 11pm-late. Cash only.

POTSDAM ☎0331

Visitors disappointed by Berlin's distinctly unroyal demeanor can get their Kaiserly fix by taking the S-Bahn to Potsdam (pop. 146,000), the glittering city of Friedrich II (the Great). While his father, Friedrich Wilhelm I (the "Soldier King"), wanted to turn Potsdam into a huge garrison of the tall, tall men he had kidnapped to serve as his toy soldiers, the more aesthetically-minded Friedrich II beautified the city. His additions include Schloß Sanssouci and the surrounding park, and the nearby Neues Garten with its Marmorpalais. Potsdam was Germany's "Little Hollywood" in the 1920s and 30s, when the suburb of Babelsberg played a critical role in the early film industry. A 20min. air raid in April 1945 brought Potsdam's cinematic glory days to an end. As the site of the 1945 Potsdam Conference, in which the Allies divvied up the country, Potsdam's name became synonymous with German defeat. After hosting Communist Party fat cats for 45 years, the 1000-year-old city gained independence from Berlin in 1991, recovering its eminent status as capital of the Land. Much of the residential city has been renovated to create long boulevards adorned with gateways and historic buildings. Today, the city moves at a leisurely pace, its palaces and avenues swelling with curious visitors.

TRANSPORTATION

Trains: S7 runs to Potsdam's Hauptbahnhof, as does the RE1 from Berlin's Friedrichstr., Alexanderplatz, and other major stations (40min. or 25min., €2.80). Trains every hr. to: **Dessau** (2hr., €32); **Leipzig** (1¾hr., €44); **Magdeburg** (1¼hr., €19.20).

Public Transportation: Potsdam is in Zone C of Berlin's BVG transit network. It is also divided into its own subdivisions of A, B, and C; special Potsdam-only tickets can be purchased on any bus or tram (€1.20, valid 1hr.; all-day €3.70-5.50). The **Berlin Welcome Card** (€18-24.50) is also valid in Potsdam.

Bike Rental and Tours: Potsdam is best seen by bike, and bike rental places often map out the best way to see all the sights. **Potsdam Per Pedales** (☎0331 748 0057; www.pedales.de) rents them out from their main location at Rudolf-Breitscheid-Str. 201, in the Griebnitzsee S-Bahn station or on the S-Bahn platform at Potsdam Hauptbahnhof. From the former, pay to take your bike on the S-Bahn (special bike pass €1.20-1.80 at any BVG ticket office). Bike tours in English (reserve ahead) and German (€10.50, students €8.50; €6 audio guide.) **Canoe** and **kayak** rental €28-30 per day. Griebnitzsee Station open Good Friday-Oct. daily 9am-6:30pm; Potsdam Hauptbahnhof open May-Sept. daily 9am-7pm. **Cityrad** rents **bikes** right across from the Babelsbergerstr. exit of the Hauptbahnhof. (☎0177 825 4746; www.cityrad-rebhan.de. €11 per day. Open Apr. 1-Oct. 31 M-F 9am-7pm, Sa-Su 9am-8pm).

PRACTICAL INFORMATION

Tourist Office: Brandenburger Str. 3 (☎0331 27 55 80; www.potsdamtourismus.de) by Brandenburg Gate. Buy city maps and book a room (from €15). Open Apr.-Oct. M-F 9:30am-6pm Sa-Su 9:30am-4pm; Nov.-Mar. M-F 10am-6pm, Sa-Su 9:30am-2pm.

Tours: The tourist office runs 2hr. tours of the city; inquire at the office (€8, departs May-Sept. daily 3pm). Original Berlin Walks has 5-6hr. walking tours that leave from the taxi stand outside Berlin's Bahnhof Zoo Apr.-Oct., Th and Su 9:50am. €15, under age 26 €11.50. Double-decker buses from **Potsdam City Tours** leave daily on the hour from Hauptbahnhof 10:45am-3:45pm. €14, students €11.

Post Office: Platz der Einheit. Open M-F 9am-6:30pm, Sa 9am-1pm. **Postal Code:** 14476.

GERMANY

ACCOMMODATIONS AND CAMPING

Budget options are limited in Potsdam. The tourist office finds private rooms and has a list of campgrounds in the area. Consider staying in Wannsee, 10min. away by S-Bahn, or at one of the many hostels in central Berlin.

Jugendherberge Potsdam (HI), Schulstr. 9 (☎030 264 9520; www.jh-potsdam.de), located in Babelsberg just one S-Bahn stop from the Potsdam Hauptbahnhof. Head left out of the S-Bahn station and take the 1st left. Breakfast and sheets included. Internet €0.50 for 10min. Dorms €15, over 27 €18; singles €31.50/34.50; doubles €26.50/29.50. Nov.-Feb. all rooms €15 per person. Cash only. ❷

Campingplatz Sanssouci-Gaisberg, An der Pirschheide 41 (☎0331 951 0988; www.campingpark-sanssouci-potsdam.com) on the scenic banks of the Templiner See. Take S7 to Potsdam Hauptbahnof, then tram #91 to Bahnhof Pirschheide. Call 8:45am-9pm for free shuttle to campsite. Phone reception 8am-1pm and 3-8pm. €10.50 per person. Internet available for €2 per day. Laundry €4. ❶

FOOD

Bright, renovated **Brandenburger Str.,** the local pedestrian zone, encompasses many of the city's restaurants, fast-food stands, and markets. The dozens of cafes near Brandenburger Tor are lovely but pricey, as are the cafes and restaurants along parts of Friedrich-Ebert-Str. and the **Holländisches Viertel.** Head to the **flea market** on Bassinplatz for fresh produce. (Open M-F 9am-6pm.) In the Hauptbahnhof is a massive **Kaufland** grocery store. (Open daily 6am-8pm.)

Siam, Friedrich-Ebert-Str. 13 (☎0311 200 9292), prepares tasty Thai food (€5-8) right before your eyes in a bamboo-laden interior. Open daily 11:30am-11pm. Cash only. ❷

Kashmir Haus, Jägerstr. 1 (☎0331 870 9580), offers Indian food in a tapestry-draped setting removed from the tourist bustle. The weekday lunch special (€4.50-6.50, 11am-4pm) includes vegetarian options and is an unbeatable deal. Open M-F 11am-11pm, Sa-Su 11am-midnight. Cash only. ❸

Cafe Heider, Friedrich-Ebert-Str. 29 (☎0331 270 5596). Heider is a beautiful outdoor cafe, located right on the border of the Hollandisches Viertel. Entrees €8-12. Open M-F from 8am, Sa from 9am, Su from 10am. ❸

SIGHTS

A **Premium Day Ticket** (€15, students €10) is a good investment for anyone interested in serious sightseeing. It is valid and available at all castles in Potsdam, including Sanssouci, which requires separate admission.

PARK AND SCHLOSS SANSSOUCI

PARK SANSSOUCI. Schloß Sanssouci's 600-acre "backyard," a testament to the size of Friedrich II's treasury and the diversity of his aesthetic tastes, has two distinct areas to explore. Half of the park is done in the Baroque style, with straight paths intersecting at topiaries and statues of nude nymphs arranged in geometrically pleasing patterns. The other half is in the rambling, rolling style of English landscape gardens. The sheer magnitude of the park—encompassing wheat fields, rose trellises, and lush, immaculate gardens—makes it a compelling place to spend an afternoon. For information on the park's many attractions, from Rococo sculptures to beautiful fountains, head to the visitors center next to the windmill, behind the *Schloß*. *(☎0331 969 4200. Open daily Mar.-Oct. 8am-10pm; Nov.-Feb. 9am-8pm.)*

SCHLOSS SANSSOUCI. The park's main attraction, the very-Versailles *Schloß*, sits atop a landscaped hill. Designed by Georg Wenzeslaus von Knobelsdorff in 1747, the yellow palace is small and airy, adorned with rich depictions of Dionysus and other Greek gods. Inside Sanssouci (French for "without worry"), the style is cloud-like French Rococo—all pinks and greens with gaudy gold trim. Friedrich, an unrepentant Francophile until his death, built the exotic **Voltairezimmer** (Voltaire Room), decorated with carved reliefs of parrots and tropical fruit, in honor of Voltaire, though the writer never stayed here. The library reveals another of Friedrich's eccentricities: whenever he wanted to read a book, he had a copy printed for each of his palaces—*en français*, of course. Also on display in the palace is Andy Warhol's modern interpretation of the king's portrait. *(Bus #695 or X15 to Schloß Sanssouci. ☎0331 969 42 00. Open Tu-Su Apr.-Oct. 10am-6pm, last entry 5:30pm; Nov.-Mar. 10am-5pm, last entry 4:30. Price of admission for Schloß Sanssouci and Buldergalerie together: €12, students €8. Audio guide included.)*

NEUES PALAIS. At the opposite end of the park, the New Palace is the largest and latest of the park's four castles. Commissioned by Friedrich the Great to emphasize Prussia's power after the Seven Years' War, this 200-room ornate pink *Schloß* features royal apartments, festival halls, and the impressive Grottensaal, whose shimmering walls are literally coated with seashells. *(☎0331 96 94 361. Open Apr.-Oct. M and W-Su 10am-6pm, last entry 5:30pm; Nov.-Mar. and 10am-5pm, last entry 4:30.. €5, students €4. Tours €1 extra in summer.)*

OTHER BUILDINGS IN THE PARK. Next to the Schloß Sanssouci, the **Bildergalerie's** collection of Caravaggio, van Dyck, and Reubens crowd a long hall of massive and elaborate canvases. *(☎0331 969 4181. Open Apr. 1-Oct. 31. Tu-Su 10am-5:30pm. €3, students €2.50. Audio Guide €1.)* The **Neue Kammern** (New Chambers) are former the *Schloß*'s guesthouse and recital hall. The ball and festival rooms are symbolically decorated with Baroque circumstance. The wall gildings depict Ovid's *Metamorphosis* while a painting of Venus looks down for the carefully painted ceiling in order to emphasize the importance of beauty. *(Open Apr 1-Apr 30 Sa-Su 10am-6pm; May 1-Oct 31 Tu-Su 10am-6pm. Last entry 5:30pm. €4, students €3. Audioguide included. Tour €1.)* The stunning **Sizilianer Garten** (Sicilian Garden) is next door. Overlooking the park from the north, the pseudo-Italian **Orangerie** is famous for its 67 dubious Raphael imitations that replace originals swiped by Napoleon. *(Open from mid-May to mid-Oct. Tu-Su 10am-12:30pm and 1-5pm. Mandatory tours €3, students €2.50. Tower only €2.)* Romantic **Schloß Charlottenhof,** whose park surroundings were a Christmas gift from Friedrich Wilhelm III to his son Friedrich Wilhelm IV, melts into landscaped gardens and grape arbors to the south. *(Open May-Oct. Tu-Su 10am-6pm. €4, students €3.)* Nearby are the **Römische Bäder** (Roman baths), alongside a reedy pond with a miniature bridge. Meant to provide a contrast to the Italian villas, the gold-plated **Chinesisches Teehaus** stands complete with a parasol-wielding rooftop Buddha and 18th-century *chinois* porcelain inside. *(Open May-Oct. Tu-Su 10am-6pm. €3, students €2.50)* The almost industrial-looking **Friedenskirche** at the east entrance of the park contains the graves of Friedrich Wilhelm IV and his wife Elizabeth below glittering mosaics.

GERMANY

OTHER SIGHTS

NEUER GARTEN. Running alongside the Heiliger See, Potsdam's second park contains several royal residences. **Schloß Cecilienhof,** built in the image of an English Tudor manor, houses exhibits on the **Potsdam Treaty,** signed at the palace in 1945. Visitors can see numerous Potsdam Conference items, including the table at which the Big Three bargained over Europe's fate, and can stand in the very room Stalin used as his study. *(☎ 0331 969 4244. Open Tu-Su Apr.-Oct. 10am-6pm; Nov.-Mar. 10am-5pm. €5, students €4. Tours in summer €1 extra.)* The garden also contains the centerpiece of the park, the **Marmorpalais** (Marble Palace). One of the quirkier buildings is a replica of an Egyptian pyramid formerly used for food storage. *(Take bus #692 to Schloß Cecilienhof. Marmorpalais open Apr.-Oct. Tu-Su 10am-6pm; Nov.-Mar. Sa-Su 10am-5pm. €4, students €3. Tour extra €1 in summer.)* At the far end of the park, beachgoers bare all by the lake. Another palace-park, **Schloßpark Glienicke** contains a casino and **Schloß Glienicke,** built by Karl Friedrich Schinkel in 1828 for Prince Karl of Prussia. The nearby **Mauerweg** (Wall Path) follows the 160km route along which the Wall separated West Berlin from the surrounding DDR territory. *(Take tram #93 to Glienicker Brücke and continue along Berliner Str. to the bridge; the castle is just on the other side to the left. Open from mid-May to mid-Oct. Sa-Su 10am-5pm).* A walk back on Berliner Str. leads to the **Glienicker Brücke** (a.k.a. "The James Bond Bridge"), swallowed up by the death strip between the DDR and West Berlin. Closed to traffic until 1989, it was instead used for the exchange of spies and known ironically as the "Bridge of Unity."

RUSSISCHE KOLONIE. In the beginning of the 19th century, General Yorck brought 500 Russian soldiers to Prussia. Friedrich Wilhelm III, a great fan of Russian culture and handsome soldiers, discovered that many of them had singing talent. Unfortunately, only 12 of the original group were left by the 1820s. To mitigate the depressing atmosphere, Friedrich III built each soldier a small, shingled wooden house trimmed with ornate carvings. The nearby pink, onion-domed Kapelle Alexander Newski, designed by Schinkel, was also intended as compensation. *(Tram #90, 92, or 95 to Puschkinalle; follow the street north.)*

FILMMUSEUM. Housed in an old orangerie that once held Friedrich's stables, this museum documents Potsdam's days as a film mecca, with artifacts like Marlene Dietrich's costumes, as well as a silent film archive and a small **movie theater.** *(On the corner of Breite Str. and Schloßstr. ☎ 0331 271 8112; www.filmmuseum-potsdam.de. Open daily 10am-6pm. €3.50, students €2.50. Movies from M-W 6 and 8pm, Th-Su 6pm, 8pm, and 10pm. Theater open daily noon-1am. €5, students €4. €3 on M.)*

HOLLÄNDISCHES VIERTEL. Friedrich's attempt to import Dutch craftsmen to beautify the city produced the Dutch Quarter, which lies in the center of the town around Friedrich-Ebert-Str. Though it fell into disrepair during the mid-20th century, the neighborhood was revitalized when entrepreneurs converted the beautiful old buildings into a row of shops and restaurants in 1990.

NIKOLAIKIRCHE. Toward the waterfront, the impressive dome of the Nikolaikirche rises above its neighbors. With closer inspection, the dome and the granite cube upon which it sits don't seem to match. While the cap is light and spacious, the interior was renovated à la DDR with glass and sound-tiles that somehow dampen the aesthetic impact. An obelisk decorated with sphinxes and ram skulls, dedicated to Schinkel, stands in front. *(Am Alten Markt. ☎0331 270 8602; www.nikolaipotsdam.de. Open daily 10am-7pm, in winter 10am-5pm.)*

FILMPARK BABELSBERG. Back in the Golden Age of European cinema, the UFA-Fabrik in Babelsberg was *the* German studio, giving Marlene Dietrich, Hans Albers, and Leni Riefenstahl their first big breaks. Fritz Lang also made *Metropolis* here. That said, this amusement park has little to do with film, and little beyond the lunch-counter wurst is particularly German. Still, the park is fun and very family-conscious, with rides and huge walk-through exhibits geared toward children. *(August-Bebel-Str. 26-53. Take S7 to Babelsberg, then bus #690 to Filmpark or take bus #601 or 690 to the same stop from Potsdam Hauptbahnhof. ☎0331 721 2750; www.filmpark.de. Open daily Mar 18-Nov 2 10am-6pm. Closed M and F in Jun. and Sept. €19, students €15.50. Tickets purchased 2½hr. before close discounted €12, students €10.50.)*

NORTHERN GERMANY

HAMBURG ☎040

Germany's largest port city and the second largest city in Europe, Hamburg (pop. 1,800,000) radiates an inimitable recklessness. Its skyline is punctuated by ancient church towers, modern skyscrapers, and masts of ships carrying millions of containers of cargo. Hamburg gained the status of Free Imperial City in 1618 and now retains its autonomy as one of Germany's three city-states. Riots and restorations have defined the post-WWII landscape. Today, Hamburg is a haven for artists, intellectuals, and revelers who live it up in Germany's self-declared capital of lust.

TRANSPORTATION

Trains: The **Hauptbahnhof** has connections every hour to: **Berlin** (1.5hr., €52); **Frankfurt** (5hr., €819); **Hanover** (1.5hr., €34); **Munich** (7hr., €108); **Copenhagen, DEN** (5hr., €72). DB Reisezentrum ticket office open M-F 5:30am-10pm, Sa-Su 7am-10pm; or purchase at ticket machines in the station anytime. The **Dammtor** train station is near the university; **Harburg** station is south of the Elbe; **Altona** station is to the west of the city's center; and **Bergedorf** is to the southeast. **Lockers** (€2-6 per day) are available at stations. Check www.bahn.de for more information.

Buses: The **ZOB** is on Steintorpl. across from the Hauptbahnhof, just past the Museum für Kunst und Gewerbe. Open M-Th and Su 5am-10pm, F-Sa 5am-midnight. **Autokraft** (☎40 280 8660) runs to **Berlin** (3hr., every 2hr. 7am-9pm, €25). **Touring Eurolines** (☎69 7903 501) runs to **Amsterdam, NTH** (8hr., M-Sa, €39); **London, UK** (daily, connecting in **Brussels,** €89); and **Paris, FRN** (11hr., daily, €69). Student discounts.

Public Transportation: HVV operates an efficient U-Bahn, S-Bahn, and bus network. One-way tickets within the downtown area €1.65; prices vary with distance and network. 1-day pass €5.10 (valid only after 9am); 3-day pass €15. Buy tickets at Automaten (machines), or consider buying a **Hamburg Card** (p. 288).

Bike Rental: Fahrradstation Dammtor/Rothebaum, Schlüterstr. 11 (☎41 46 82 77), rents bikes for just €3 per day. Open M-F 9am-6pm. **Fahrradladen St. Georg,** Schmilinskystr. 6 (☎40 24 39 08), is off Lange Reihe toward the AuBenalster. €8 per day, €56 per week with €50 deposit. Open M-F 10am-7pm, Sa 10am-1pm.

ORIENTATION AND PRACTICAL INFORMATION

Hamburg's city center sits between the **Elbe River** and two lakes: **Außenalster** and **Binnenalster.** The arc of the **Alsterfleet** canal, separating the *Altstadt* on the east from the *Neustadt* on the west, echoes the arch of the impressive system of parks and gardens just above it. Most major sights lie between the **St. Pauli Landungsbrücken** port area in the west and the *Hauptbahnhof* in the east. **Mönckebergstraße,** Hamburg's most famous shopping street, runs all the way to **Rathausmarkt,** the seat of the sumptuous town hall. North of downtown, the **university** dominates the **Dammtor** area, sustaining a community of students and intellectuals. To the west of the university, the **Schanzenviertel** hums with artists, squatters, and a sizeable Turkish population, similar to the atmosphere in Altona, still further west. At the south end of town, an entirely different atmosphere reigns in **St. Pauli,** where the raucous **Fischmarkt** (fish market) is surpassed only by the wilder **Reeperbahn,** home to Hamburg's best discos.

Tourist Offices: The **Hauptbahnhof** office, in the Wandelhalle near the Kirchenallee exit (☎30 05 12 01; www.hamburg-tourism.de), books rooms for €4, as does the **Hamburg hotline** (☎30 05 13 00. Open M-Sa 8am-9pm, Su 10am-6pm). The **St. Pauli Landungsbrücken** office (☎30 05 12 03), between piers 4 and 5 is less crowded (Open Oct.-Mar. daily 10am-5:30pm; Apr.-Sept. M, W and Su 8am-6pm, Tu and Th-Sa 8am-7pm). Both supply free English-language **maps** and city guides; they also sell the **Hamburg Card,** which provides unlimited access to public transportation, reduced admission to museums, and discounts on restaurants, tickets, souvenirs, some hotels, and bus and boat tours. 1-day card €8, 3-day €18, 5-day €33. The **Group Card** provides the same benefits for up to 5 people; 1-day €11.80, 3-day €29.80, 5-day €51.

Consulates: Canada, Ballindamm 35 (☎40 460 0270). S1 or 3 or U1 to Jungfernstieg; between Alstertor and Bergstr. Open M-F 9:30am-12:30pm. **Ireland,** Feldbrunnenstr. 43 (☎44 18 61 13). U1 to Hallerstr. Open M-F 9am-1pm. **New Zealand,** Domstr. 19, Zürich-Haus, block C, 3rd fl. (☎40 442 5550). U1 to Messberg. Open M-Th 9am-1pm and 2-5:30pm, F 9am-1pm and 2-4:30pm. **UK,** Harvestehuder Weg 8a (☎40 448 03 20). U1 to Hallerstr. Open M-Th 9am-4pm, F 9am-3pm. **US,** Alsterufer 27-28, 20354 Hamburg (☎40 4117 1422).

Currency Exchange: ReiseBank, on the 2nd fl. of the *Hauptbahnhof* near the Kirchenallee exit (☎40 32 34 83), has Western Union services, cashes traveler's checks, and exchanges currency. Open daily 7:30am-10pm. Watch out for steep hidden fees and consider trying one of the many exchange bureaus or banks downtown.

GLBT Resources: The neighborhood of St. Georg is the center of the gay community. Pick up the free *Hinnerk* magazine and *Friends: The Gay Map* from **Cafe Gnosa** or from the tourist office. Organizations include **Hein und Fiete,** Pulverteich 21, which gives advice on health and entertainment in the area (☎40 24 03 33). Walk down Steindamm away from the *Hauptbahnhof,* turn right on Pulverteich; it's the building with the rainbow flag. Open M-F 4-9pm, Sa 4-7pm.

Pharmacy: Senator-Apotheke, Hachmannpl. 14 (☎40 32 75 27 or ☎40 33 92 92). Turn right from the station's Kirchenallee exit. Open M-F 8am-6:30pm, Sa 9am-1pm.

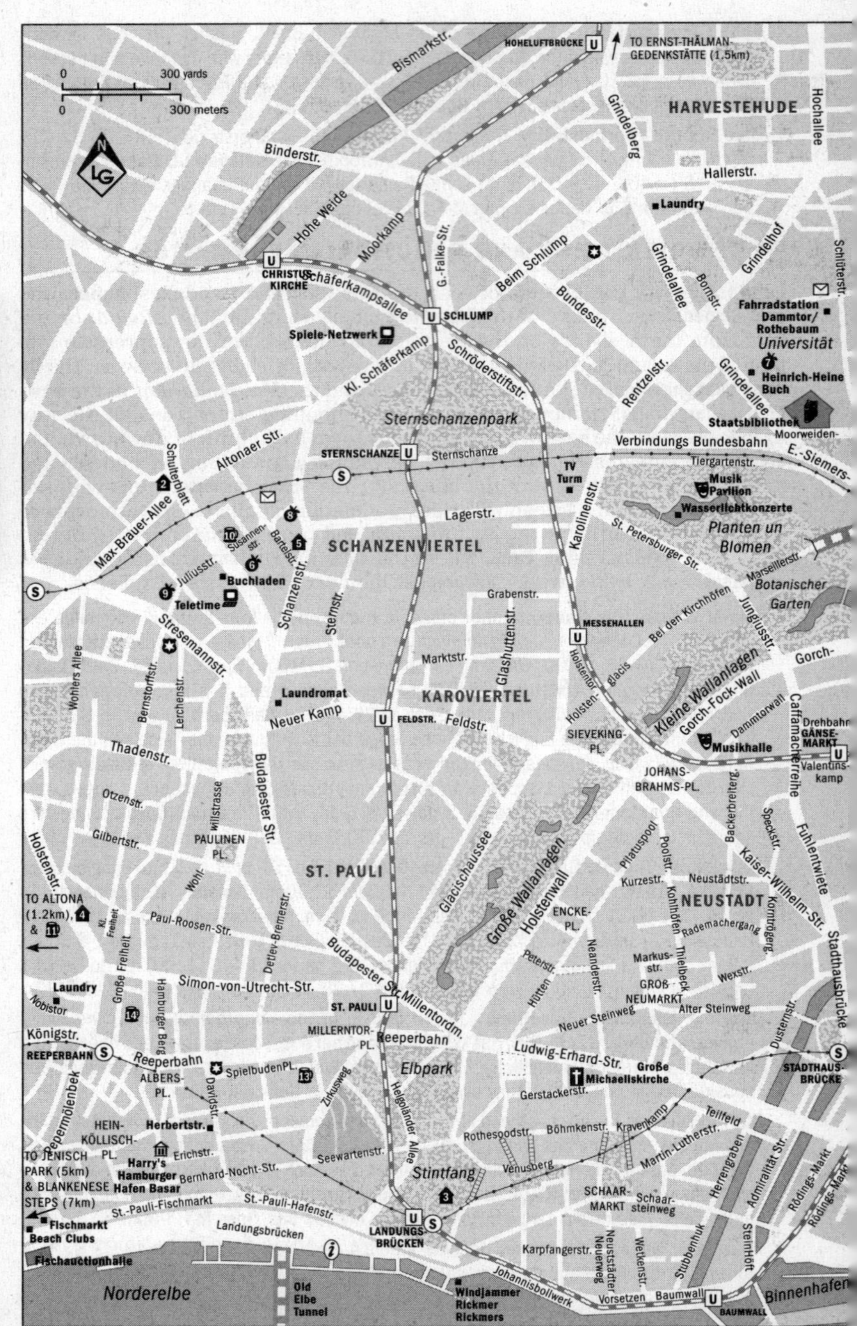

HARVESTEHUDE
SCHANZENVIERTEL
KAROVIERTEL
ST. PAULI
NEUSTADT
Sternschanzenpark
Planten un Blomen
Botanischer Garten
Kleine Wallanlagen
Große Wallanlagen
Elbpark
Stintfang
Norderelbe
Binnenhafen
Universität
HOHELUFTBRÜCKE
TO ERNST-THÄLMAN-GEDENKSTÄTTE (1.5km)
CHRISTUS KIRCHE
SCHLUMP
STERNSCHANZE
MESSEHALLEN
FELDSTR.
ST. PAULI
REEPERBAHN
LANDUNGS-BRÜCKEN
BAUMWALL
STADTHAUS-BRÜCKE
GÄNSE-MARKT
Spiele-Netzwerk
Laundry
Fahrradstation Dammtor/ Rothebaum
Heinrich-Heine Buch
Staatsbibliothek
TV Turm
Musik Pavilion
Wasserlichtkonzerte
Buchladen
Teletime
Laundromat
Musikhalle
Große Michaeliskirche
Herbertstr.
Harry's Hamburger Hafen Basar
Fischmarkt
Beach Clubs
Fischauctionhalle
Old Elbe Tunnel
Windjammer Rickmer Rickmers
TO ALTONA (1.2km), 4 & 11
TO JENISCH PARK (5km) & BLANKENESE STEPS (7km)
SIEVEKING-PL.
JOHANS-BRAHMS-PL.
PAULINEN PL.
ENCKE-PL.
GROß NEUMARKT
MILLERNTOR-PL.
ALBERS-PL.
HEIN-KÖLLISCH-PL.
SCHAAR-MARKT
Bismarkstr.
Binderstr.
Hohe Weide
Moorkamp
Schäferkampsallee
Kl. Schäferkamp
G.-Falke-Str.
Beim Schlump
Bundesstr.
Schröderstiftstr.
Grindelberg
Grindelallee
Grindelhof
Hallerstr.
Hochallee
Schlüterstr.
Bornstr.
Rentzelstr.
Verbindungs Bundesbahn
Moorweiden-
E.-Siemers-
Tiergartenstr.
Sternschanze
Altonaer Str.
Schulterblatt
Max-Brauer-Allee
Lagerstr.
Karolinenstr.
St. Petersburger Str.
Marseillerstr.
Jungiusstr.
Bei den Kirchhöfen
Holstenglacis
Gorch-Fock-Wall
Dammtorwall
Caffamacherreihe
Drehbahn
Valentinskamp
Susannenstr.
Bartelsstr.
Schanzenstr.
Juliusstr.
Sternstr.
Grabenstr.
Glashüttenstr.
Marktstr.
Stresemannstr.
Wohlers Allee
Bernstorffstr.
Lerchenstr.
Neuer Kamp
Feldstr.
Thadenstr.
Budapester Str.
Otzenstr.
Wohlwillstrasse
Gilbertstr.
Holstenstr.
Detlev-Bremerstr.
Glacischaussee
Holstenwall
Pilatuspool
Poolstr.
Backerbreitergang
Speckstr.
Kaiser-Wilhelm-Str.
Fuhlentwiete
Kurzestr.
Neustädtstr.
Kohlhöfen
Thielbeck
Rademachergang
Kornträgergang
Stadthausbrücke
Kl. Freiheit
Paul-Roosen-Str.
Peterstr.
Neanderstr.
Markusstr.
Wexstr.
Große Freiheit
Hamburger Berg
Simon-von-Utrecht-Str.
Millentordm.
Hütten
Neuer Steinweg
Alter Steinweg
Laundry
Nobistor
Königstr.
Reeperbahn
Davidstr.
SpielbudenPl.
Zirkusweg
Helgoländer Allee
Ludwig-Erhard-Str.
Dusterstr.
Gerstackerstr.
Pepermölenbek
Erichstr.
Seewartenstr.
Rothesoodstr.
Böhmkenstr.
Kravenkamp
Teilfeld
Martin-Luther-Str.
Herrengraben
Admiralität Str.
Rödings-Markt
Venusberg
Bernhard-Nocht-Str.
St.-Pauli-Fischmarkt
St.-Pauli-Hafenstr.
Schaarsteinweg
Landungsbrücken
Karpfangerstr.
Neustädter Neuerweg
Wetkenstr.
Stubbenhuk
Steinhöft
Johannisbollwerk
Vorsetzen
Baumwall
0
300 yards
0
300 meters
N
LG

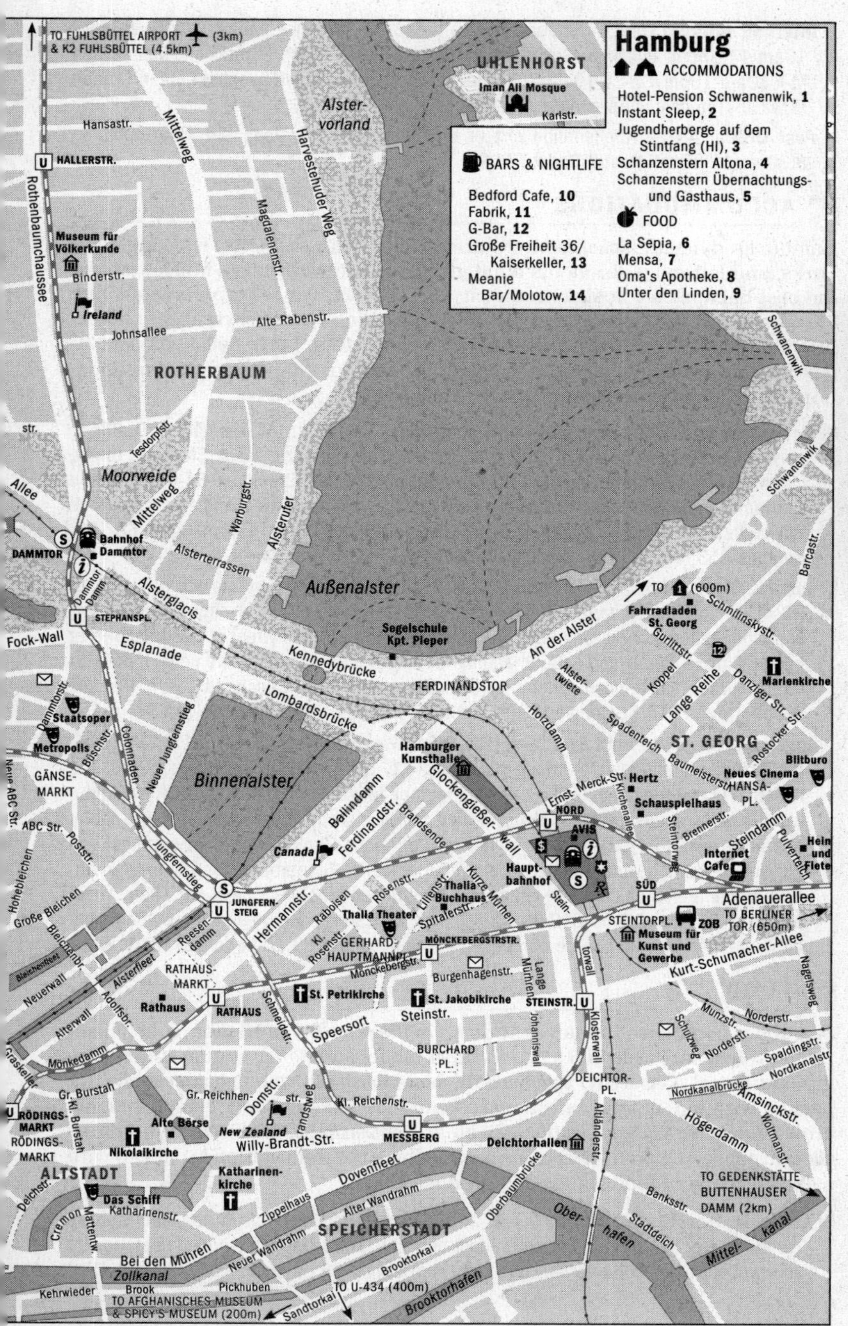
Hamburg
ACCOMMODATIONS
Hotel-Pension Schwanenwik, 1
Instant Sleep, 2
Jugendherberge auf dem Stintfang (HI), 3
Schanzenstern Altona, 4
Schanzenstern Übernachtungs- und Gasthaus, 5
FOOD
La Sepia, 6
Mensa, 7
Oma's Apotheke, 8
Unter den Linden, 9
BARS & NIGHTLIFE
Bedford Cafe, 10
Fabrik, 11
G-Bar, 12
Große Freiheit 36/ Kaiserkeller, 13
Meanie Bar/Molotow, 14
TO FUHLSBÜTTEL AIRPORT (3km) & K2 FUHLSBÜTTEL (4.5km)
UHLENHORST
Iman Ali Mosque
Karlstr.
Alster-vorland
Hansastr.
Mittelweg
HALLERSTR.
Harvestehuder Weg
Magdalenenstr.
Rothenbaumchaussee
Museum für Völkerkunde
Binderstr.
Ireland
Johnsallee
Alte Rabenstr.
ROTHERBAUM
Schwanenwik
Tesdorpfstr.
Moorweide
Warburgstr.
Alsterufer
Allee
Bahnhof Dammtor
DAMMTOR
Alsterterrassen
Dammtor Damm
Alsterglacis
Außenalster
TO (600m)
Barcastr.
Fahrradladen St. Georg
Schmilinskystr.
STEPHANSPL.
Fock-Wall
Esplanade
Segelschule Kpt. Pieper
Kennedybrücke
An der Alster
Gurlittstr.
Koppel
Lange Reihe
Marienkirche
Danziger Str.
FERDINANDSTOR
Alster-twiete
Lombardsbrücke
Holzdamm
Spadenteich
ST. GEORG
Rostocker Str.
Dammtorstr.
Staatsoper
Metropolis
Büschstr.
Colonnaden
Neuer Jungfernstieg
Binnenalster
Hamburger Kunsthalle
Glockengießer-wall
Baumeisterstr.
Biltburo
Neues Cinema HANSA-PL.
GÄNSE-MARKT
Neue ABC Str.
ABC Str.
Poststr.
Ballindamm
Ferdinandstr.
Brandsende
Ernst-Merck-Str.
NORD
Hertz
Schauspielhaus
Kirchenallee
AVIS
Steintorweg
Brennerstr.
Steindamm
Pulverteich
Hein und Fiete
Internet Cafe
Canada
Hohebleichen
Jungfernstieg
Haupt-bahnhof
Stein-
SÜD
Adenauerallee
TO BERLINER TOR (650m)
Große Bleichen
JUNGFERN-STEIG
Hermannstr.
Raboisen
Rosenstr.
Lilienstr.
Thalia Buchhaus
Kurze Mühren
Spitalerstr.
Thalia Theater
STEINTORPL.
ZOB
Museum für Kunst und Gewerbe
Bleichenbr.
Reesen-damm
Kl. Rosenstr.
GERHARD-HAUPTMANNPL.
MÖNCKEBERGSTRSTR.
Kurt-Schumacher-Allee
Nagelsweg
Neuerwall
Alsterfleet
RATHAUS-MARKT
Mönckebergstr.
Burgenhagenstr.
Lange Mühren
torwall
Rathaus
RATHAUS
St. Petrikirche
St. Jakobikirche
STEINSTR.
Norderstr.
Munzstr.
Adolfsbr.
Alterwall
Schmiedestr.
Steinstr.
Speersort
Klosterwall
Schultzweg
Spaldingstr.
Nordkanalstr.
Mönkedamm
BURCHARD PL.
Johanniswall
Graskeller
Gr. Burstah
Gr. Reichhen-str.
DEICHTOR-PL.
Nordkanalbrücke
Amsinckstr.
Domstr.
Kl. Reichenstr.
RÖDINGS-MARKT
Kl. Burstah
Alte Börse
New Zealand
Högerdamm
Woltmanstr.
Nikolaikirche
Willy-Brandt-Str.
MESSBERG
Deichtorhallen
Altländerstr.
ALTSTADT
Katharinen-kirche
Dovenfleet
TO GEDENKSTÄTTE BUTTENHAUSER DAMM (2km)
Deichstr.
Das Schiff
Katharinenstr.
Zippelhaus
Alter Wandrahm
Oberbaumbrücke
Ober-hafen
Banksstr.
Stadtdeich
Cremon
Mattentw.
SPEICHERSTADT
Mittel-kanal
Bei den Mühren
Neuer Wandrahm
Brooktorkai
Zollkanal
Kehrwieder
Brook
Pickhuben
TO U-434 (400m)
TO AFGHANISCHES MUSEUM & SPICY'S MUSEUM (200m)
Sandtorkai
Brooktorhafen

Internet: Internet Cafe, Adenauerallee 10 (☎28 00 38 98). €1.50 per hr. Open daily 10am-11:55pm. **Teletime,** Schulterblatt 39 (☎41 30 47 30). €0.50 per 15min. Open M-F 10am-10pm, Sa-Su 10am-7pm. Free Wi-Fi available at **Wildwechsel,** Beim Grünen Jäger 25. The cafe is open daily 4pm-close.

Post Office: At the Kirchenallee exit of the *Hauptbahnhof.* Open M-F 8am-6pm, Sa 8:30am-12:30pm. **Postal Code:** 20099.

ACCOMMODATIONS

Hamburg's dynamic **Schanzenviertel** area—filled with students, working-class Turks, and left-wing dissidents amid graffiti-splattered walls—houses two of the best backpacker hostels in the city. Small, relatively cheap *pensions* line **Steindamm** and the area around the *Hauptbahnhof*, where several safe hotels provide respite from the area's unsavory characters. **Lange Reihe** has equivalent lodging options in a cleaner neighborhood. More expensive accommodations line the **Binnenalster** and eastern **Außenalster.**

Schanzenstern Übernachtungs und Gasthaus, Bartelsstr. 12 (☎ 40 439 8441; www.schanzenstern.de). S21 or 31, or U3 to "Sternschanze." Near St. Pauli, bright, clean, and comfortable rooms in a renovated pen factory. Breakfast €4-6. Reception 6:30am-2am. Free Internet available between the reception area and the restaurant. Wheelchair-accessible. Laundry €4.50. Reserve ahead. Dorms €19; singles €37.50; doubles €53; triples €63; quads €77; quints €95. Cash only. ❷

Instant Sleep, Max-Brauer-Allee 277 (☎43 18 23 10; www.instantsleep.de). S21 or 31 or U3 to "Sternschanze." Helpful, bilingual staff, as well as an improvised library, communal kitchen, and long-term guests contribute to a family feel at this backpacker hostel. Close to the U-and S-Bahn and right above a busy bar, it's convenient—if noisy at times. Lockers €5 deposit. Linens €3. Reception 8am-2am. Check-out 11am. Reserve ahead. Dorms €15.50; singles €30; doubles €44; triples €60. Cash only. ❷

Jugendherberge auf dem Stintfang (HI), Alfred-Wegener-Weg 5 (☎40 31 34 88, www.djh.de/jugendherbergen/hamburg-stintfang). S1, S3, or U3 to Landungsbrücke. The hostel is above the Landungsbrücke station; look for stairs on the left side. Newly renovated and expanded with futuristic, backlit plexiglass and brushed-steel in the lobby, this huge hostel has an incredible view of the harbor. Bunks, checkered curtains, and gaggles of young travelers spilling over from the nearby Reeperbahn contribute to youthful summer feel. Breakfast and linens included. Reception 24hr. Check-out 10am. Lockout 2am-6:30am. Dorms €18.80-20.30, over 27 €3 extra per night. HI members only, although membership can be purchased at the hostel for €3.10 per night. MC/V. ❷

FOOD

Seafood is common—but never boring—in the port city of Hamburg. In Schanzenviertel, avant-garde cafes and Turkish falafel and *döner* stands entice hungry and frugal passersby. **Schulterblatt, Susannenstraße,** and **Schanzenstraße** are packed with hip, unique cafes and restaurants, while cheaper establishments crowd the **university** area, especially along **Rentzelstraße, Grindelhof,** and **Grindelallee.** In **Altona,** the pedestrian zone approaching the train station is packed with a diverse array of food stands and produce shops.

La Sepia, Schulterblatt 36 (☎40 432 2484; www.lasepia.de). This Portuguese-Spanish restaurant serves some of the city's most delicious and reasonably-priced seafood. For your wallet's sake, come for lunch (11am-5pm), when €5 buys you a big plate of grilled salmon with scalloped carrots and potatoes, a basket of fresh bread, and a bowl of soup. Lunch €3.50-6. Dinner €7.50-22. Open daily noon-3am. AmEx/MC/V. ❷

Unter den Linden, Juliusstr. 16 (☎40 43 81 40). Read complimentary German papers over *Milchkaffee* (coffee with foamed milk; €2.90-3.40), breakfast (€4.60-7.30), or a simple salad or pasta (€3.70-6.90) in a relaxed atmosphere; perfect for quiet conversation underneath the linden trees. Open daily 9:30am-1am. Cash only. ❷

Oma's Apotheke, Schanzenstr. 87 (☎40 43 66 20). With its retro wall decorations, pub-like atmosphere, and namesake apothecary drawers, the causal eatery is popular with a mixed crowd. German, Italian, and American cuisine. Schnitzel €7.50. Hamburger with 1lb. fries €6.60. Open M-Th and Su 9am-1am, F-Sa 9am-2am. Cash only. ❷

Mensa, Von-Melle-Park 5 (☎41 90 22 02). S21 or 31 to Dammtor, then bus #4 or 5 to Staatsbibliothek (1 stop). Turn right into the courtyard past the bookstore, Heinrich-Heine Buchhandlung, on Grindelallee. Big portions of cafeteria food and listings of university events. Meals €2-2.50, up to €1 extra for non-students. Open M-Th 10am-4pm, F 10am-3:30pm. Limited summer hours. Cash only. ❶

SIGHTS

ALTSTADT

RATHAUS. Built between 1886 and 1897, the city's town hall is one of *Altstadt's* most impressive buildings. The city and state governments both convene amid intricate mahogany carvings and spectacular two-ton chandeliers. Its 647 stunning and varied rooms should not be missed. In front, the **Rathausmarkt** hosts festivities ranging from political demonstrations to medieval fairs for excited locals and visitors alike. *(☎428 312 470. English-language tours every 2hrs. M-Th 10:15am-3:15pm, F 10:15am-1:15pm, Sa 10am-5pm, Su 10am-4pm. Building open daily 8am-6pm. Rooms accessible only through tours. €3, €2 with Hamburg Card.)*

NIKOLAIKIRCHE. The blackened spire of this Neo-Gothic ruin, bombed in 1943, serves as a haunting memorial for the victims of war and persecution. The church itself, built first in 1195, took nearly 700 years to complete, but now stands as a stone skeleton with empty frames for stained glass windows and half-ruined walls. A glass **elevator** takes visitors up 76m, and a small documentation center underneath the glass pyramid details the 1943 bombing of Hamburg. *(U3 to Rödingsmarkt. Exhibition open M-F 10:30am-5:30pm. Elevator open daily Jan.-Mar. 10am-5:30pm; Apr. 10am-7pm; May-Aug. 10:30am-8pm; Sept.-Oct 10am-7pm; Nov-Dec. 10:30am-5:30pm. €2, students €1.50, children €1. One ticket pays for both.)*

GROßE MICHAELSKIRCHE. The 18th-century Michaelskirche, named after the archangel Michael, who stands guard over the main entrance, is arguably the best-recognized symbol of Hamburg. The church, battered repeatedly by lightning, fire, and allied bombs, was fully restored in 1996. A panoramic view of Hamburg awaits those who climb the 462 stairs of the spire (and those who opt for the elevator). There is daily organ music Apr.-Aug. at noon, and multimedia presentations on the church's history on weekends in the crypt. *(U-Bahn to Baumwall, S-Bahn to Stadthausbrücke. ☎37 67 81 00. Church open daily May-Oct. 9am-8pm; Nov.-Apr. 10am-5pm. Crypt open June-Oct. daily 11am-4:30pm; Nov.-May Sa-Su 11am-4:30pm. Church suggested donation €2. Crypt and tower €2.50.)*

MÖNCKEBERGSTRAßE. Two spires punctuate Hamburg's glossiest shopping zone, which stretches from the *Rathaus* to the *Hauptbahnhof.* Closest to the Rathaus is **St. Petrikirche,** the oldest church in Hamburg, which also has the highest climbable tower, first dated back to 1195. *(☎40 325 7400; www.samlt-petri.de. Open M-Sa 10am-6:30pm, Su 9am-9pm. Tower €2, under 15 €1, under 10 free. Frequent free* *concerts.)* The other, **St. Jakobikirche,** is known for its 17th-century *arpschnittger* organ with almost 1000 pipes. *(☎40 303 7370. Open M-Sa 10am-5pm.)*

BEYOND THE ALTSTADT

PLANTEN UN BLOMEN. West of the Außenalster, this huge expanse of manicured flower beds and trees includes the largest Japanese garden in Europe, complete with a teahouse built in Japan. *(S21 or 31 to Dammitor. www.plantenunblomen.hamburg.de. Open May-Sept. daily 7am-11pm, Oct.-Apr. 7am-8pm. Free.)* Exotic botanical garden and plenty of children's attractions, including a small water park and a mini-golf course. In summer, performers in the outdoor **Musikpavillon** range from Irish step-dancers to Hamburg's police choir. *(May-Sept. most performances 3pm. See garden website for performance listings)* At night, opt for the **Wasserlichtkonzerte,** a choreographed play of fountains and underwater lights set to music. *(Daily May-Aug. 10pm, Sept. 9pm.)* To the north, the tree-lined paths bordering the two **Alster lakes** provide refuge from the city crowds.

GERMANY

ST. PAULI LANDUNGSBRÜCKEN. The harbor lights up at night with ships from all around the world. Go during the day for a clearer view or heat out on a river tour with Kapitän Prüsse, HADAG, or the HVV **ferry.** Look for the 426m **Elbtunnel,** completed in 1911 and still active. *(Free for pedestrians. Behind pier 6 in the building with the copper cupola.)* At the **Fischmarkt,** eager vendors hawk fish, produce, beer, and pastries. *(S1, S3, or U3 to Landungsbrücken or S1 or S3 to Königstr. or Reeperbahn. Open Su Apr.-Oct. 5-9:30am, Nov.-Mar. 7-9:30am).* The museum ship **Windjammer Rickmer Rickmeers** has been painstakingly restored to the original 1890s decor, with an added exhibit space and cafe. *(☎319 59 59. Open daily 10am-5:30pm. €3, students €2.50, families €7. Discounts with Hamburg Card.)*

MUSEUMS

The **Hamburg Card** provides free or discounted access to nearly all museums. *Museumswelt Hamburg*, a free newspaper available at tourist offices, lists exhibits and events. Most museums are closed on Mondays and open 10am-6pm the rest of the week, and until 9pm on Thursdays. Usually museums also house a "Kultur Kompact," a small kiosk or display that contains info and brochures for most other museums in the city.

HAMBURGER KUNSTHALLE. It would take days to fully appreciate every work in this sprawling fine arts museum. The oldest building presents the Old Masters and extensive special exhibits, including impressionist works by the likes of Degas, Monet, and Renoir. In the connected four-level **Galerie der Gegenward,** find inspiring contemporary art that takes a stand in a mix of temporary and permanent exhibits. *(Glockengieberwall 1. Turn right from Spitalerstr. City exit to the Hauptbahnahof and cross the street. ☎428 131 200; www.hamburger.kunsthalle.de. Open Tu-W and F-Su 10am-6pm, Th 10am-9pm. €8.50, students €5, families €14.)*

MUSEUM FÜR KUNST UND GEWERBE. Handicrafts, china, and furnishings from all corners of the earth fill this arts and crafts museum. A huge exhibit chronicles the evolution of the modern piano with dozens of the world's oldest harpsichords, clavichords, and *Hammerklaviers*, a monument to the lost art of exquisite craftsmanship. Be sure to visit the **Hall of Mirrors,** a beautiful reconstruction of a room in the home of a Hamburg banker. *(Steintorpl. 1., 1 block south of the Hauptbahnhof. ☎40 428 134; www.mkg-hamburg.de. Open Tu-W and F-Su 10am-6pm, Th 10am-9pm. €8, students, Hamburg card holders, and seniors €5, under 18 free.)*

DEICHTORHALLEN HAMBURG. Hamburg's contemporary art scene thrives inside these two airplane hangar-sized fruit markets, with painting and photography installations, as well as video displays. *(Deichtorstr. 1-2. U1 to Steinstr. Follow signs from the U-Bahn. ☎32 10 20; www.deichtorhallen.de. Open Tu-Su 11am-6pm. Each building €7, students €5, families €9.50. Combo ticket to both halls €12/8/16.50. Under 18 free.)*

ENTERTAINMENT

The **Staatsoper,** Große Theaterstr. 36, houses one of the premier **opera** companies in Germany; the associated John Neumeier **ballet** company is one of the nation's best. (U2 to Gänsemarkt. ☎40 35 68 68. Open M-Sa 10am-6:30pm and 90min. before performances.) **Orchestras** include the Philharmonie, the Norddeutscher Rundfunk Symphony, and Hamburg Symphonia, which all perform at the **Musikhalle** on Johannes-Brahms-Pl. (U2 to Gänsemarkt. ☎40 34 69 20; www.musikhalle-hamburg.de. Box office open M-F 10am-4pm.) Live music also thrives in Hamburg. Superb traditional jazz swings at the **Cotton Club** and **Indra** (Große Freiheit 64). Early on Sundays, talented musicians (and not- so-talented hopefuls), play at the rowdy **Fischmarkt** while free organ concerts echo through the churches. The **West Port Jazz Festival** runs in mid-July; for info, call the Konzertkasse (ticket office ☎32 87 38 54).

NIGHTLIFE

Hamburg's unrestrained nightlife scene heats up in the **Schanzenviertel** and **St. Pauli** areas. The infamous **Reeperbahn** runs through the heart of St. Pauli; lined with sex shops, strip joints, and peep shows, it's also home to the city's best bars and clubs. Though the Reeperbahn is generally safe, it is unwise to stray alone into less crowded sidestreets. Parallel to the Reeperbahn lies **HerbertstraBe,** Hamburg's official prostitution strip, where licensed sex entrepreneurs flaunt their flesh (only those over the age of 18 allowed.) Potential patrons should be warned, however, that engaging with streetwalkers is something of a game of venereal Russian roulette. Students head north to the streets of the Schanzenviertel and west to Altona, where cafes and trendy bars create an atmosphere more leftist than lustful. The **St. Georg** district, near Berliner Tor and along Lange Reihe, is the center of Hamburg's **gay scene.** In general, clubs open and close late, with some techno and trance clubs remaining open well into the morning. *Szene* (€3), available at newsstands, lists events.

GroBe Freiheit 36/Kaiserkeller, GroBe Freiheit 36 (☎40 317 7780). Big names from Ziggy Marley to Prince have performed upstairs, home to popular concerts and hip club music orchestrated by DJs. **Kaiserkeller,** downstairs, caters to the rock contingent with its dungeonlike quarters and harsher music. F-Sa club nights. Cover €5-6. Concerts 7-8pm, 10pm-5am. Frequent free entry until 11pm.

Fabrik, Barnerstr. 36 (☎40 39 10 70; www.fabrik.de). From Altona station, head toward Offenser Hauptstr. and go right on Bahrenfelderstr. This former weapons factory now cranks out raging beats to crowds wanting to hear an eclectic mix of names in music, with styles ranging from Latin to punk to rock. Music nearly every night at 9pm. Every 2nd Sa of the month, "Gay Factory" attracts a mixed crowd. Live DJ 10pm most Sa; cover €7-8. Cover for live music €18-30, but check the website to be sure. Cash only.

Meanie Bar/Molotow, Spielbudenpl. 5 (☎40 31 08 45; www.molotowclub.com), parallel to the Reeperbahn. The **Molotow,** in the basement of the retro Meanie Bar, keeps it hip with fashionable crowds, live bands; abundant standing, dancing, and schmoozing room. The bar upstairs has a more relaxed atmosphere. **Meanie Bar** open daily from 9pm. No cover. Molotow cover for club nights and other events €3-4, live bands €8-15. Open from 8pm when there are concerts, and from 11pm F-Sa for disco. Cash only.

CENTRAL AND WESTERN GERMANY

COLOGNE (KÖLN) ☎0221

Although 90% of historic Cologne (pop. 991,000) crumbled to the ground during WWII, the magnificent Gothic *Dom* amazingly survived 14 bombings and is still one of Germany's main attractions. Today, the city is the largest in North Rhine-Westphalia, offering first-rate museums, theaters, and nightlife.

TRANSPORTATION

Flights: Planes depart from **Köln-Bonn Flughafen (CGN).** Flight info ☎022 03 40 40 01 02; www.koeln-bonn-airport.de. Airport shuttle S13 leaves the train station M-F, 3-6 per hr.; Sa-Su, 2 per hr. Shuttle to Berlin, 24 per day, 6:30am-8:30pm.

Trains: Cologne's **Hauptbanhof** has trains that leave for **Berlin** (4-5hr., 1-2 per hr., €86-104); **Düsseldorf** (1hr., 5-7 per hr., €10-18); **Frankfurt** (1-2hr., 2-3 per hr., €34-63); **Hamburg** (4hr., 2-3 per hr., €74-86); **Munich** (4-5hr., 2-3 per hr., €91-124); **Amsterdam, NTH** (2-3hr., 1-3 per hr., €40-56); **Paris, FRA** (4hr., 3 per hr., €87-120).

Ride Share: Citynetz Mitfahrzentrale, Krefelderst. 21 (☎0221 194 44). Turn left from the back of the train station, left at the intersection onto Eigelstein, then another left onto Weidengasse, which becomes Krefelderst. Open M-F 9am-8pm, Sa-Su 10am-6pm.

Public Transportation: KVB offices have free **maps** of the S- and U-Bahn, bus, and streetcar lines; branch downstairs in the *Hauptbahnhof.* Major terminals include the **Hauptbahnhof, Neumarkt,** and **Appellhofplatz.** Single-ride tickets from €1.50, depending on distance. Day pass from €5.20. The Minigruppen-Ticket (from €5.60) allows up to 4 people to ride M-F 9am-midnight and all day Sa-Su. Week tickets from €13.70. The WelcomeCard allows visitors to use all forms of public transportation in Cologne and Bonn (1-day €9, 2-day €14, 3-day €19).

Bike Rental: Kölner Fahrradverleih, Markmannsg. (☎0171 629 87 96), in the *Altstadt.* €2 per hr., €10 per day, €40 per week; €25 deposit. Open daily 10am-6pm.

ORIENTATION AND PRACTICAL INFORMATION

Cologne extends across the Rhine, but the city center and nearly all sights are located on the western side. The *Altstadt* splits into **Altstadt-Nord,** near the **Hauptbahnhof,** and **Altstadt-Süd,** just south of the **Severinsbrücke** bridge.

Tourist Office: KölnTourismus, Unter Fettenhennen 19 (☎0221 22 13 04 10; www.koelntourismus.de), across from the main entrance to the *Dom,* books rooms for a €3 fee and sells the **Welcome Card** (€9), which provides a day's worth of free public transportation and museum discounts. Open M-F 9am-10pm, Sa and Su 10am-5pm.

Currency Exchange: A **Reisebank** can be found in the train station. Open daily 7am-10pm. Also at the tourist office.

Internet: Telepoint Callshop & Internet C@fe, Komödenstr. 19 (☎0221 250 9930), by the *Dom.* €1.50 per hr. Open M-F 9am-10pm, Sa-Su 10am-10pm.

Laundromat: Waschsalon, at the corner of Händelst. and Richard-Wagner-St. Take U1, 7, 12, 15, 16, or 18 to Rudolfpl. Wash 6-10am €1.90, 10am-11pm €2.50. Soap €0.50. Dry €0.50 per 10min. Open M-Sa 6am-11pm.

Gay and Lesbian Resources: SchwIPS Checkpoint, Pipinstr. 7, just around the corner from Hotel Timp (☎0221 92 57 68 68/69; www.checkpoint-koeln.de). Emergency help-line (☎0221 192 28).

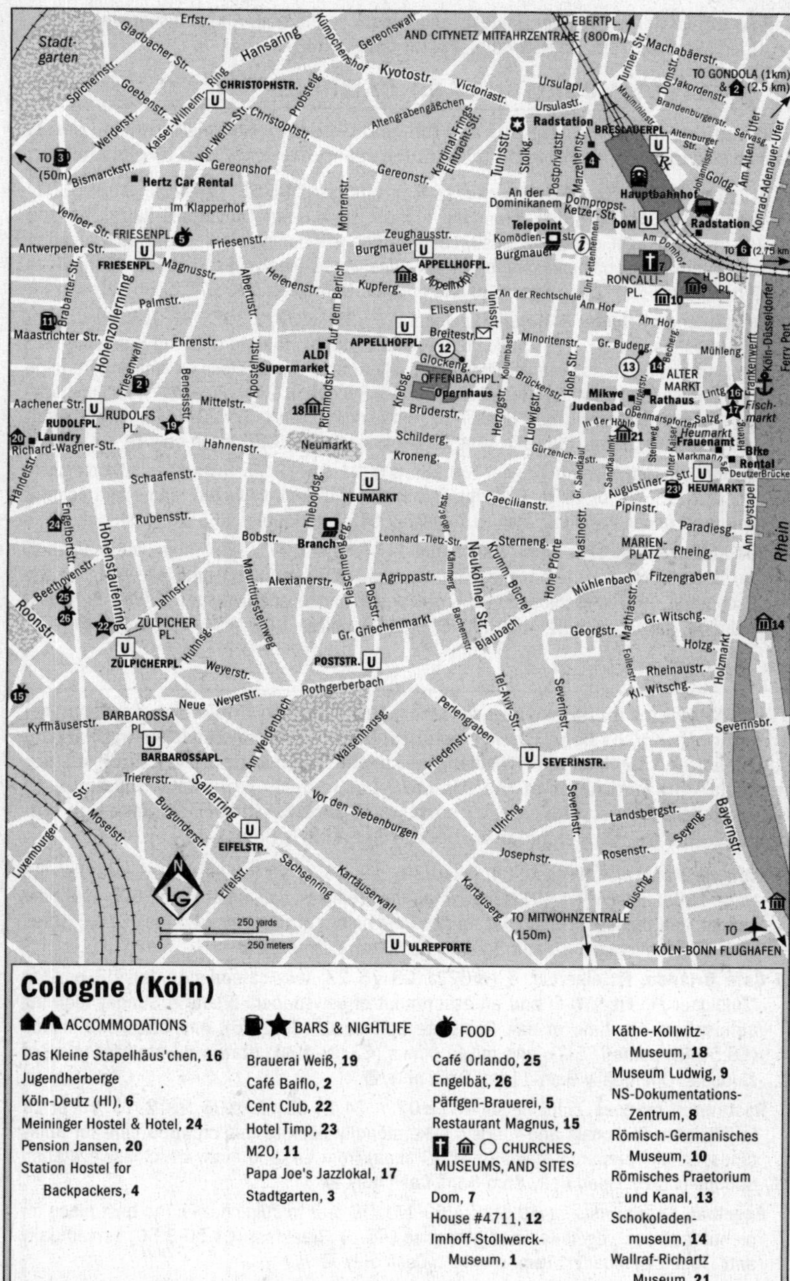
Cologne (Köln)
ACCOMMODATIONS
Das Kleine Stapelhäus'chen, 16
Jugendherberge Köln-Deutz (HI), 6
Meininger Hostel & Hotel, 24
Pension Jansen, 20
Station Hostel for Backpackers, 4
BARS & NIGHTLIFE
Brauerai Weiß, 19
Café Baiflo, 2
Cent Club, 22
Hotel Timp, 23
M20, 11
Papa Joe's Jazzlokal, 17
Stadtgarten, 3
FOOD
Café Orlando, 25
Engelbät, 26
Päffgen-Brauerei, 5
Restaurant Magnus, 15
CHURCHES, MUSEUMS, AND SITES
Dom, 7
House #4711, 12
Imhoff-Stollwerck-Museum, 1
Käthe-Kollwitz-Museum, 18
Museum Ludwig, 9
NS-Dokumentations-Zentrum, 8
Römisch-Germanisches Museum, 10
Römisches Praetorium und Kanal, 13
Schokoladen-museum, 14
Wallraf-Richartz Museum, 21
Stadt-garten
Erfstr.
Gladbacher Str.
Hansaring
Kümpchenshof
Gereonswall
TO EBERTPL. AND CITYNETZ MITFAHRZENTRALE (800m)
Machabäerstr.
Tunnisstr.
Domstr.
TO GONDOLA (1km), & 2 (2.5 km)
Jakordenstr.
Spichernstr.
Goebenstr.
Kaiser-Wilhelm-Ring
CHRISTOPHSTR.
Kyotostr.
Victoriastr.
Ursulapl.
Ursulastr.
Maximinstr.
Brandenburgerstr.
Servasg.
Am Alten Ufer
Konrad-Adenauer-Ufer
Werderstr.
Von-Werth-Str.
Christophstr.
Probsteig.
Altengrabengäßchen
Kardinal-Frings-Str.
Eintracht-Str.
Radstation
BRESLAUERPL.
Altenburger Str.
Johannisstr.
TO 3 (50m)
Bismarckstr.
Gereonshof
Hertz Car Rental
Gereonstr.
Tunisstr.
Stolkg.
Postprivatstr.
Marzellenstr.
Hauptbahnhof
Goldg.
Im Klapperhof
Mohrenstr.
An der Dominikanern
Dompropst-Ketzer-Str.
Venloer Str.
FRIESENPL.
Telepoint
DOM
Radstation
Antwerpener Str.
Friesenstr.
Zeughausstr.
Komödienstr.
Am Domhof
TO 6 (2.75 km)
Burgmauer
APPELLHOFPL.
Burgmauer
Unt. Fettenhennen
FRIESENPL.
Magnusstr.
Helenenstr.
Appellhofpl.
RONCALLI-PL.
H.-BOLL-PL.
Brabanter-Str.
Albertusstr.
Auf dem Berlich
Kupferg.
An der Rechtsschule
Am Hof
Palmstr.
Elisenstr.
Köln-Düsseldorfer Ferry Port
Hohenzollernring
Breitestr.
Maastrichter Str.
Ehrenstr.
APPELLHOFPL.
Minoritenstr.
Gr. Budeng.
Mühleng.
ALDI Supermarket
Glockeng.
Becherg.
Friesenwall
Apostelnstr.
OFFENBACHPL.
Kolumbastr.
Brückenstr.
ALTER MARKT
Frankenwerft
Opernhaus
Mikwe Judenbad
Rathaus
Aachener Str.
RUDOLFS PL.
Mittelstr.
Richmodstr.
Krebsg.
Brüderstr.
Hohe Str.
Lintg.
Fischmarkt
RUDOLFPL.
Laundry
Benesisstr.
Herzogstr.
Ludwigstr.
Obenmarspforten
Salzg.
Richard-Wagner-Str.
Hahnenstr.
Neumarkt
Schilderg.
In der Höhle
Heumarkt
Frauenamt
Kroneng.
Gürzenichstr.
Unter Kaiser
Unter Markmann
Bike Rental
Handelstr.
Schaafenstr.
Sandkaulstr.
Steinweg
Hateng.
Deutzer Brücke
NEUMARKT
Augustinerstr.
HEUMARKT
Engelbertstr.
Rubensstr.
Thieboldsg.
Jabachstr.
Caecilienstr.
Gr. Sandkaul
Pipinstr.
Am Leystapel
Hohenstaufenring
Bobstr.
Branch
Leonhard-Tietz-Str.
Sterneng.
Kasinostr.
Paradiesg.
Rhein
Neuköllner Str.
Krumm. Büchel
Hohe Pforte
MARIEN-PLATZ
Rheing.
Beethovenstr.
Mauritiussteinweg
Fleischmengerg.
Alexianerstr.
Agrippastr.
Kämmerg.
Mühlenbach
Filzengraben
Jahnstr.
Poststr.
Bachemstr.
Mathiasstr.
Roonstr.
ZÜLPICHER PL.
Gr. Griechenmarkt
Blaubach
Georgstr.
Gr. Witschg.
Huhnsg.
Holzg.
ZÜLPICHERPL.
Weyerstr.
POSTSTR.
Follerstr.
Rheinaustr.
Holzmarkt
Tel-Aviv-Str.
Rothgerberbach
Kl. Witschg.
Severinstr.
Neue Weyerstr.
Perlengraben
Kyffhäuserstr.
BARBAROSSA PL.
Am Weidenbach
Waisenhausg.
Severinsbr.
Friedenstr.
BARBAROSSAPL.
SEVERINSTR.
Triererstr.
Salierring
Vor den Siebenburgen
Luxemburger Str.
Burgunderstr.
Ulrichg.
Severinstr.
Landsbergstr.
Moselstr.
EIFELSTR.
Bayernstr.
Seyeng.
Josephstr.
Rosenstr.
Sachsenring
Eifelstr.
Kartäuserwall
Kartäuserg.
Buschg.
250 yards
250 meters
TO MITWOHNZENTRALE (150m)
ULREPFORTE
TO KÖLN-BONN FLUGHAFEN

GERMANY

Post Office: At the corner of Breitestr. and Tunisstr. in the WDR-Arkaden shopping gallery. Open M-F 9am-7pm, Sa 9am-2pm. **Postal Code:** 50667.

ACCOMMODATIONS AND CAMPING

Conventions fill hotels in spring and fall, and Cologne's hostels often sell out. If you're staying over a weekend in summer, reserve at least two weeks ahead.

Station Hostel for Backpackers, Marzellenstr. 44-56 (☎0221 912 5301; www.hostel-cologne.de). From the station, walk down Dompropst-Ketzer-Str. and take the 1st right on Marzellenstr. Large dorms without bunks and an ideal location attract crowds of backpackers. Breakfast price varies. Free Wi-Fi. Reception 24hr. 4- to 6-bed dorms €17-21; singles €30-37; doubles €45-52; triples €72. Cash only. ❷

Meininger City Hostel & Hotel, Engelbertst. 33-35 (☎0221 355 332 014; www.meininger-hostels.de). U1, 7, 12, 15, 16, or 18 to Rudolfpl., then turn left on Habsburgerst., right on Lindenst., and left on Engelbertst. A bar and lounge close to amazing Rudolpl. and Zülpicherpl. nightlife. Breakfast included. Reception 24hr. Free Wi-Fi, lockers, towels, and linens. Dorms (max. 8) €17-22; small dorms (max. 6) €20-24; multi-bed room (4-6) €24-32; triples €28-36; twins €34-44; singles €43-56. Cash only. ❷

Pension Jansen, Richard-Wagner-Str. 18 (☎0221 25 18 75; www.pensionjansen.de). U1, 6, 7, 15, 17, or 19 to Rudolfpl. Family-run with high-ceilinged rooms and colorful walls and decor. Breakfast included. Singles €45-80; doubles €65-90. Cash only. ❸

Das Kleine Stapelhäus'chen, Fischmarkt 1-3 (☎0221 272 7777; www.koeln-altstadt.de/stapelhaeuschen). From the Rathaus, cross the Altenmarkt and take Lintg. to the Fischmarkt. An old-fashioned, richly decorated inn overlooking the Rhine. Breakfast included. Singles €39-52, with bath €52-82; doubles €64-74/90-121. MC/V. ❹

FOOD

The *Kölner* diet includes *Rievekoochen* (fried potato dunked in applesauce) and smooth *Kölsch* beer. Cheap restaurants converge on **Zülpicherstraße** to the southeast and **Eigelstein** and **Weidengasse** in the Turkish district. Ethnic restaurants line the perimeter of the *Altstadt*, particularly from **Hohenzollernring** to **Hohenstaufenring.** German eateries surround **Domplatz.** An **open-air market** on Wilhelmspl. fills the Nippes neighborhood. (Open M-Sa 8am-1pm.)

Päffgen-Brauerei, Friesenstr. 64. Take U3-5, 12, 16, or 18 to Friesenpl. A local favorite since 1883. *Kölsch* (€1.40) is brewed on the premises, consumed in the 600-seat beer garden, and refilled until you put your coaster on top of your glass. Entrees €7-15. Open daily 10am-midnight. Sa and Su until 12:30am. Cash only. ❸

Café Orlando, Engelbertstr. 7 (☎0221 23 75 23; www.cafeorlando.de). U8 or 9 to "Zülpicher Pl." Free Wi-Fi and an assortment of newspapers create a Sunday morning atmosphere any time of day. Complete breakfasts (€3.10-6), omelettes and salads (€5.50-8), pasta (€5-7), and mixed drinks (€3.50-4.80) draw a devoted following of students. Open daily 9am-11pm. Cash only. ❷

Restaurant Magnus, Zülpicherstr. 48 (☎0221 24 14 69). Take U8, 9, 12, 15, 16, or 18 to Zülpicher Pl. Locals and tourists alike steadily flock to this crowded cafe for funky tunes, artfully prepared meals (mostly Italian) from €4, and many delicious vegetarian options (€5-8). Open daily 8pm-3am. Cash only. ❷

Engelbät, Engelbertst. 7 (☎0221 24 69 14). U8 or 9 to Zülpicher Pl. The best place for plentiful crepes, vegetarian and otherwise (€5-8). Breakfast (€1.50-3.50) served daily until 3pm. Open daily 11am-midnight. Cash only. ❶

SIGHTS

DOM. Germany's greatest cathedral, the *Dom*, is a perfect realization of High Gothic style. Built over the course of six centuries, it was finally finished in 1880 and miraculously escaped destruction during WWII. Today, its colossal spires define the skyline of Cologne. A chapel on the inside right houses a 15th-century **triptych** depicting the city's five patron saints. Behind the altar in the center of the choir is the **Shrine of the Magi,** the cathedral's most sacred compartment, which allegedly holds the remains of the Three Kings and was once a pilgrimage site for a number of European monarchs. Before exiting the choir, stop in the **Chapel of the Cross** to admire the 10th-century **Gero crucifix,** which is the oldest intact sculpture of a crucified Christ. It takes about 15min. to scale the 509 steps of the **Südturm** (south tower); catch your breath at the **Glockenstube,** a chamber with the tower's nine bells three-quarters of the way up. *(Cathedral open daily 6am-7:30pm. 45min. English-language tours M-Sa 10:30am and 2:30pm, Su 2:30pm. Tower open daily May-Sept. 9am-6pm; Nov.-Feb. 9am-4pm; Mar.-Apr. and Oct. 9am-5pm. Cathedral free. Tour €6, children €4. Tower €3.50, students €1.)*

MUSEUMS. Gourmands will want to head straight for the **Schokoladenmuseum,** which is best described as Willy Wonka's factory come to life. It presents every step of chocolate production, from the rainforests to the gold fountain that spurts streams of free samples. *(Rheinauhafen 1A, near the Severinsbrücke. ☎ 0221 931 8880; www.schokoladenmuseum.de. From the train station, head for the Rhine, and walk to the right along the river; go under the Deutzer Brücke, and take the 1st footbridge. Open Tu-Sa 10am-6pm, Su 11am-7pm. €6.50, students €4.)* Masterpieces from the Middle Ages to the Post-Impressionist period are gathered in the **Wallraf-Richartz Museum.** *(Martinstr. 39. From the Heumarkt, take Gürzenichtstr. 1 block to Martinstr. ☎ 0221 276 94; www.museenkoeln.de/wrm. Open Tu-W and F 10am-6pm, Th 10am-10pm, Sa-Su 11am-6pm. €7.50, students €5.)* The collection of the **Museum Ludwig** focuses on 20th-century and contemporary art. *(Bischofsgartenstr. 1, behind the Römisch-Germanisches Museum. ☎ 0221 22 12 61 65. Open Tu-Su 10am-6pm, 1st F of each month 10am-10pm. €9, students €6.)* The **Römisch-Germanisches Museum** displays artifacts documenting the daily lives of Romans in ancient Colonia. *(Roncallipl. 4, beside the Dom. Open Tu-Su 10am-5pm. €6, students €3.50.)* The **NS-Dokumentations-Zentrum,** Appellhofpl. 23-25, includes a former Gestapo prison with inmates' wall graffiti intact. *(☎ 0221 22 12 63 32. U3-6 or 19 to Appelhofpl. Open Tu-W and F 10am-4pm, Th 10am-6pm. €3.60, students €1.50.)* The **Käthe-Kollwitz-Museum** houses the world's largest collection of sketches, sculptures, and prints by the 20th-century artist-activist. *(Neumarkt 18-24. On the top fl. in the Neumarkt-Passage. Take U1, 3-4, 6-9, or 19 to Neumarkt. ☎ 0221 227 2363. Open Tu-F 10am-6pm, Sa-Su 11am-6pm. German-language tours Su 3pm. €3, students €1.50.)*

ENTERTAINMENT AND NIGHTLIFE

Cologne explodes in celebration during **Karneval** (late Jan. to early Feb.), a week-long pre-Lenten festival made up of 50 neighborhood processions. **Weiberfastnacht** (late January) is the first major to-do: the mayor mounts the platform at Alter Markt and surrenders leadership to the city's women, who then hunt down their husbands at work and chop off their ties. The weekend builds to the out-of-control parade on **Rosenmontag** (Rose Monday; early Feb.), when thousands of merry participants sing and dance their way through the city center while exchanging *Bützchen* (kisses on the cheek). While most revelers nurse their hangovers on **Shrove Tuesday,** pubs and restaurants set fire to the straw scarecrows hanging out their windows. For more info, pick up the Karneval booklet at the tourist office. For summer visitors, Cologne offers the huge **C/O**

Pop Festival in mid-August, a multi-day event that draws some 200 electronic and independent musicians for 40 shows. (www.c-o-pop.de. €49.)

Roman mosaics dating back to the 3rd century record the wild excesses of the city's early residents. The monthly *Kölner* (€1), sold at newsstands, lists clubs, parties, and concerts. The closer to the Rhine or *Dom* you venture, the faster your wallet will empty. After dark in **Hohenzollernring**, crowds of people move from theaters to clubs and finally to cafes in the early morning. The area around **Zülpicherpl.** is a favorite of students and the best option for an affordable good time. Radiating westward from Friesenpl., the **Belgisches Viertel** (Belgian Quarter) has slightly more expensive bars and cafes.

Papa Joe's Jazzlokal, Buttermarkt 37 (☎0221 257 7931). Papa Joe has a legendary reputation for providing good jazz and good times. Add your business card or expired ID to the collage that adorns the bar. *Kölsch* (€3.60) in 0.4L glasses, not the usual 0.2L. Live jazz M-Sa 10:30pm-12:30am. Su "4 o'clock Jazz"–8hours of, nonstop jazz from two bands starting at 3:30pm (not June-Sept.). Open daily 8pm-3am. Cash only.

Cent Club, Hohenstaufenring 25-27 (www.centclub.de). Near Zülpicher Pl. Take U8 or 9 to Zülpicher. This student disco features more dance (to R&B, pop, dance classics) and less talk, with the appeal of low-priced drinks. Shots €0.50. Beer €1-2. Mixed drinks from €3. Cover W-Sa €5. Open W-Sa 9pm-3am.

Hotel Timp, Heumarkt 25 (☎0221 258 1409; www.timp.de). Across from the Heumarkt U-Bahn stop. This club/hotel has become an institution in Cologne. Gay and straight crowds come for the gaudy and glitter-filled cabarets. Drag shows daily 1-4am. No cover. 1st drink M-Th and Su €8, F-Sa €13. Open daily 10am-late. AmEx/MC/V.

M20, Maastrichterstr. 20 (☎0221 51 96 66; www.m20-koeln.de). U1, 6, or 7 to Rudolfpl. DJs deliver some of the city's best drum'n'bass and punk to a local crowd. Cocktails €5. Beer €1.50-3.20. Open daily from 8pm-late. Cash only.

GERMANY

FRANKFURT AM MAIN ☎069

International offices, shiny skyscrapers, and expensive cars can be found at every intersection in Frankfurt (pop. 660,000), best known as the home of the EU's Central Bank and a major international airport. Don't let Frankfurt's reputation as a transportation center fool you–from shopping to museums to great nightlife, there's always something to see and do in this international city.

TRANSPORTATION

INTERCITY TRANSPORTATION

Flights: The largest and busiest airport in Germany, Frankfurt's **Flughafen Rhein-Main** (**FRA;** ☎01805 37 24 36) is connected to the *Hauptbahnhof* by S-Bahn trains S8 and 9 (2-3 per hr.) Buy tickets (€3.60) from the green machines marked "Fahrkarten" before boarding. Taxis to the city center cost around €20.

Trains: Trains run from the **Hauptbahnhof** to: **Amsterdam, NTH** (4hr., 1 per 2hr., €150); **Berlin** (4hr., 2 per hr., €90-105); **Cologne** (1hr., 1 per hr., €38-60); **Hamburg** (3-5hr., 2 per hr., €78-98); **Munich** (3hr., 1 per hr., €64-81). For schedules, reservations, and info call ☎01805 19 41 95; www.bahn.de. Note: there is no English help option.

LOCAL TRANSPORTATION

Public Transportation: Frankfurt's public transportation system runs daily 4am-1:30am. Single-ride tickets (€2.20; reduced fares available) are valid for 1hr. in 1 direction. **Eurail** is valid only on S-Bahn trains. The **Tageskarte** (day pass; €5.60) provides unlim-

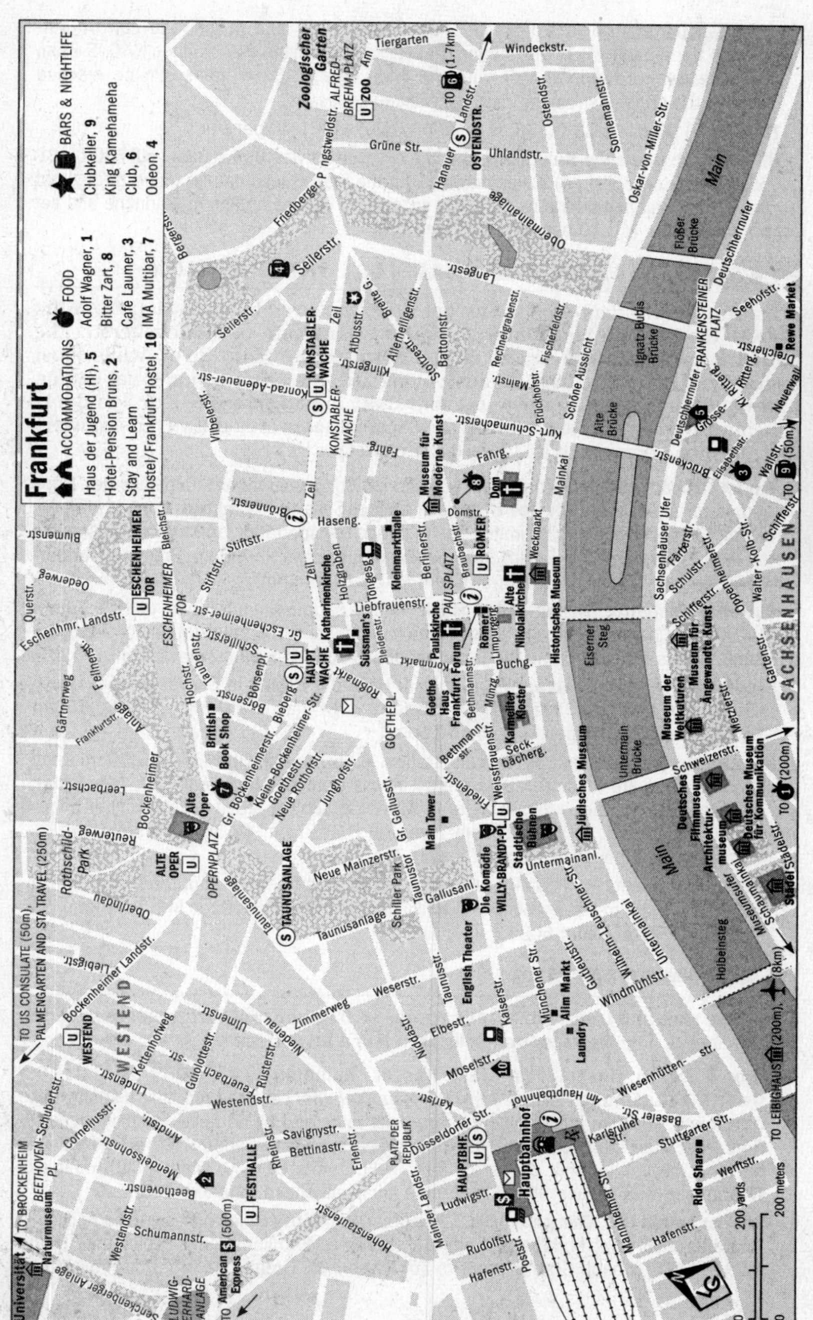
Frankfurt
ACCOMMODATIONS
Haus der Jugend (HI), 5
Hotel-Pension Bruns, 2
Stay and Learn Hostel/Frankfurt Hostel, 10
FOOD
Adolf Wagner, 1
Bitter Zart, 8
Cafe Laumer, 3
IMA Multibar, 7
BARS & NIGHTLIFE
Clubkeller, 9
King Kamehameha Club, 6
Odeon, 4
Zoologischer Garten
ZOO
OSTENDSTR.
KONSTABLER-WACHE
ESCHENHEIMER TOR
HAUPTWACHE
Katharinenkirche
Kleinmarkthalle
Museum für Moderne Kunst
Dom
RÖMER
PAULSPLATZ
Paulskirche
Alte Nikolaikirche
Historisches Museum
Goethe Haus
Frankfurt Forum
Karmeliter Kloster
Alte Oper
ALTE OPER
OPERNPLATZ
British Book Shop
Main Tower
TAUNUSANLAGE
Die Komödie
WILLY-BRANDT-PL.
Städtische Bühnen
Jüdisches Museum
English Theater
Alim Markt
Laundry
WESTEND
FESTHALLE
HAUPTBHF.
Hauptbahnhof
Ride Share
American Express
Naturmuseum
Universität
SACHSENHAUSEN
Museum der Weltkulturen
Museum für Angewandte Kunst
Deutsches Filmmuseum
Architekturmuseum
Deutsches Museum für Kommunikation
Städel
Alte Brücke
Ignatz Bubis Brücke
Flößer Brücke
Eiserner Steg
Untermain Brücke
Holbeinsteg
Main
Rewe Market
TO US CONSULATE (50m), PALMENGARTEN AND STA TRAVEL (250m)
TO BROCKENHEIM
TO LEIBIGHAUS (200m)
200 yards
200 meters

GERMANY

ited transportation on the S-Bahn, U-Bahn, streetcars, and buses, and can be purchased from machines in any station. Ticketless passengers can be fined €40. S-Bahn trains leave the *Hauptbahnhof* from the lower level; U-Bahn trains can be reached through the primary shopping passage *(Einkaufspassage)*.

Taxis: ☎23 00 01, ☎23 00 33, or ☎25 00 01. From €1.40 per km.

Bike Rental: Deutsche Bahn (DB) runs the citywide service **Call a Bike** (☎0700 05 22 55 22; www.callabike.de). Bikes marked with the red DB logo can be found throughout the city for your immediate rental. To do so, call the service hotline or go online and set up an account. (€0.10 per min., €15 per day.)

ORIENTATION AND PRACTICAL INFORMATION

Frankfurt's *Hauptbahnhof* opens onto the city's red-light district; from the station, the *Altstadt* is a 20min. walk down Kaiserstr. or Münchenerstr. The tourist heavy **Römerberg** square is just north of the Main River, while most commercial stores lie farther north along **Zeil**, the city's commercial center. Cafes and services cluster near the university in **Bockenheim** (U6 or 7 to Bockenheimer Warte). Across the river, the **Sachsenhausen** area draws pub-crawlers and museum-goers (take U1, 2, or 3 to Schweizer Pl.).

Tourist Office: in the *Hauptbahnhof* (☎21 23 88 00; www.frankfurt-tourismus.de). Book rooms for a €3 fee or for free if you call ahead. Sells the **Frankfurt Card** (1-day €8, 2-day €12), which allows unlimited use of public transportation and provides discounts on many sights. Open M-F 8am-9pm, Sa-Su and holidays 9am-6pm. Branch in **Römerberg** square (open M-F 9:30am-5:30pm, Sa-Su 10am-4pm).

Currency Exchange: At the **Reise Bank** in the *Hauptbahnhof* (open daily 7:30am-10:30pm). Cheaper exchange rates can be found outside the train station. Try **Deutsche Bank,** across the street from the *Hauptbahnhof.* (Open M-F 9am-1pm, 2-5pm.)

Laudromat: SB Waschsalon, Wallstr. 8, near Haus der Jugend in Sachsenhausen. Wash €3.50 for a small machine (6 kg) or €5 for a large machine (12 kg). Dry €0.50 per 15min. Soap €0.50. Open M-Sa 6am-11pm.

Internet: In the basement of the train station. €2.50 per hr. Open M-Sa 8:30am-1am. Internet cafes are located on Kaiserstr., across from the *Hauptbahnhof*. **CybeRyder,** Tongesg. 31, near Ziel, offers a more comfortable setting, albeit slightly higher prices (€1.60 per 15min. on M-F 9:30am-7pm, Sa 10am-7pm; €1.30 per 15min. on Su. noon-10pm; €1 per 15min. on M-Sa after 7pm.)

Post Office: Goethe Pl. 7. Walk 10min. down Taunusstr. from the *Hauptbahnhof,* or take the U- or S-Bahn to Hauptwache and walk south to the square. Open M-F 7am-8pm, Sa 8am-2pm. **Postal Code:** 60313.

ACCOMMODATIONS

Deals are rare and trade fairs make rooms scarce in Frankfurt; reserve several weeks ahead. The **Westend/University** area has a few cheap options.

Stay & Learn Hostel/Frankfurt Hostel, Kaiserstr. 74 (☎069 247 5130; www.frankfurt-hostel.com). Near the *Hauptbahnhof* (and the red-light district), this convenient, sociable hostel organizes free city tours and holds free bi-weekly dinners. 24hr. reception located on the 4th fl. Luggage storage included. Free breakfast. €2 beers at the bar. Internet €1 per hr. Free Wi-Fi. Dorms €17-20; singles €50; doubles €60; triples €66. Higher rates during trade fairs; call ahead for prices. MC/V. ❷

Haus der Jugend (HI), Deutschhermufer 12 (☎069 610 0150; www.jugendherberge-frankfurt.de). Take bus #46 (dir.: Mühlberg) from the station to Frankensteiner Pl., or take tram #16 (dir.: Offenbach Stadtgrenze) to *Lokalbahnhof.* Great location along the Main

and in front of Sachsenhausen's pubs and cafes. A good find despite the groups of noisy schoolchildren. Some private baths. Breakfast and linens included. Check-in 1pm, check-out 9:30am; curfew 2am. Dorms from €21.50; under 27 from €17; singles €39-43; doubles €56-76. HI discount €3.10. MC/V. ❷

Hotel-Pension Bruns, Mendelssohnstr. 42, 2nd fl. (☎069 74 88 96; www.brunsgallus-hotel.de). U4: Festhalle/Messe. Exit onto Beethovenstr. and turn left. At the traffic circle, continue on Mendelssohnstr.; the hotel is on the right. In the wealthy but quiet Westend area, Bruns has 9 Victorian rooms with cable TV. Breakfast in bed included. Call ahead. Singles €40-45; doubles €50-55; triples €65-70; quads €88-95. Cash only. ❹

FOOD

Town specialties include Frankfurter Wurst, Schlachplate, and Binding Beer. The most reasonably priced meals can be found in **Sachsenhausen** or near the university in **Bockenheim.** One of two grocery stores, **Tengelmann Supermarkt** and **HL-Markt,** can be found in virtually every neighborhood, including near the *Hauptbahnhof,* at Karlstr. 4, and in Westend, at Arntstr. 22 (open M-F 7am-9pm and Sa 8am-9pm). **Kleinmarkthalle,** on Haseng. between Berlinerstr. and Töngesg., is a three-story warehouse with bakeries, butchers, fruits, nuts, cheese, and vegetable stands. (Open M-F 8am-6pm, Sa 8am-4pm.)

GERMANY

Cafe Laumer, Bockenheimer Landstr. 67 (☎069 72 79 12). U6 or U7 to "Westend." Dine like a local on the outdoor patio or in the backyard garden of this celebrated cafe in the Westend, only blocks from the uni. Young businessmen on their lunch break enjoy the hearty special of the day (€6.70), while neighborhood residents read the newspaper, drink coffee (€2.20), and eat generous slices of cake (from €2.40). Open M-F 8am-7pm, Sa 8:30am-7pm, Su 9:30am-7pm. AmEx/MC/V. ❷

Adolf Wagner, Schweizer Str. 71 (☎069 61 25 65). Saucy German dishes (€5-17) and some of the region's most renowned *Äpfelwein* (€1.40 per 0.3L) keep the patrons of this famous corner of old Sachsenhausen jolly and packed. Sit elbow-to-elbow with storied regulars and taste traditional regional specialties like *Gruene Sosse* or *Handkaese mit Musik.* Open daily 11am-midnight. Cash only. ❸

IMA Multibar, Klein Bockenheimer Str. 14 (☎069 90 02 56 65). This fast-paced and hip bar/cafe combo, on the back streets (off Zeil), offers hungry patrons delicious smoothies (€3.50) and wraps (€4-7.30) by day, and a great selection of beer, wine, and mixed drinks by night. Drinks from €7. MC/V. ❷

SIGHTS

Beneath the daunting skyscrapers that define the Frankfurt landscape are several historic sights, all of which have undergone some degree of reconstruction since the old city's unfortunate destruction in 1944. The **Museumsufer** along the southern bank of the Main includes some of the city's most vital cultural institutions. If you plan on touring any of them, consider buying a **Frankfurt Card** (p. 296) or a **Museum Card** for discounted rates.

STÄDEL. The *Städel's* impressive collection comprises seven centuries of art and includes notable works by Old Masters, Impressionists, and Modernists. **Holbein's,** the first floor cafe, is a widely celebrated destination for visitors and locals alike. *(Schaumainkai 63, between Dürerstr. and Holbeinstr. ☎605 0980; www.staedelmuseum.de. Open Tu and F-Su 10am-6pm, W-Th 10am-9pm. €10, students €8, under 12 and last Sa of each month free. English-language audio tour €4, students €3.)*

MUSEUM FÜR MODERNE KUNST. The modern architecture of this triangular "slice of cake" building complements the art within. This museum houses a permanent collection of European and American art from the 1960s to the present and stages large-scale temporary exhibitions. *(Domstr. 10. ☎21 23 04 47; www.mmk-frankfurt.de. Open Tu and Th-Su 10am-5pm, W 10am-8pm. €7, students €3.50.)*

RÖMERBERG. This plaza, at the heart of Frankfurt's *Altstadt*, is surrounded on all four sides by exciting things to see and do. With its picturesque **Fachwerkhaeuser** (half-timbered houses) and daunting **Statue of Justice** fountain at the center of the square, the Römerberg is justifiably the most heavily-touristed spot in town. Across from the Römerberg, **Paulskirche** (St. Paul's Church), the birthplace of Germany's 19th-century attempt at constitutional government, now memorializes the trials of German democracy with an acclaimed mural. At the west end of the Römerberg, the gables of **Römer** have marked the site of Frankfurt's city hall since 1405. The **Kaisersaal,** upstairs, is a former imperial banquet hall adorned with dignified portraits of 52 German emperors, from Charlemagne to Franz II. Emperors were once crowned in the **Gothic Dom,** the lone survivor of catastrophic WWII bombings. An attached museum features large paintings and elaborate altarpieces. (*St. Paul's Church: ☎21 23 85 26. Open daily 10am-5pm. Free. Römer enter from Limpurgerg. Open daily 10am-1pm and 2-5pm. €2. Gothic Dom: church open M-Th and Sa-Su 9am-noon and 2:30-6pm. Museum open Tu-F 10am-5pm and Sa-Su 11am-5pm. Church free. Museum €2, students €1.)*

NIGHTLIFE

Though Frankfurt lacks a centralized nightlife scene, a number of techno clubs lie between **Zeil** and **Bleichstraße.** Wait until midnight or 1am for things to really heat up. Visit www.nachtleben.de for more information on Frankfurt's nightlife options. For drinks, head to the cobblestone streets of the **Sachsenhausen** district, between Brückenstr. and Dreieichstr., where there are many rowdy pubs and beer gardens serving specialty *Aepfelwein.*

Odeon, Seilerstr. 34 (☎069 28 50 55). Whitewashed medieval villa with cut-out octopi on the door and ornate pillars. The party changes daily, with M night hip-hop, and Th-Sa thumping house music. F 27+, Sa Wild Card. M and Th-F drinks half-price until midnight. Cover from €5, students €3 on Th only. Open M-Sa from 10pm. Cash only.

King Kamehameha Club, Hanauer Landstr. 192 (☎069 48 00 370; www.king-kamehameha.de). Take the U6 to "Ostbahnhof" and walk down Hanauer Landstr. With intricate timber rafters, exposed brick, and a raging dance floor, this club lures Frankfurt's hip 20-somethings to its weekend dance parties. Partygoers drink vodka and Red Bull (€8) and dance to loud pop. Open Th-Sa from 10pm. Cover from €10. Cash only.

Clubkeller, Textorstr. 26 (☎069 66 37 26 97; www.clubkeller.com). A small bar/club with low brick-arched ceilings, cheap beer (€2-2.50), hard liquor (vodka shots €2), and lively clientele. Local DJs play a mix of rock and indie most nights, and live bands use the space for concerts during the week. Dress casually and come with good friends. Cover from €4. Open daily from 8:30pm. Cash only.

BAVARIA (BAYERN)

MUNICH (MÜNCHEN) ☎089

Bavaria's capital and cultural center, Munich (pop. 1,245,000) is a sprawling, liberal metropolis where world-class museums, handsome parks, colossal architecture, and a genial population create a thriving city.

TRANSPORTATION

Flights: Flughafen München (**MUC;** ☎089 97 52 13 13). **Buses** S1 and 8 run from the airport to the *Hauptbahnhof* and Marienpl. (40min., 3 per hr., €8.80 or 8 strips on the *Streifenkarte*). For all-day travel, buy a **Gesaskamtnetz** day pass that covers all zones (€10). The Lufthansa **shuttle bus** goes to the *Hauptbahnhof* (40min., 3 per hr., €10) but is slower and more expensive than taking the train.

Trains: Munich's **Hauptbahnhof** (☎118 61) is the hub of southern Germany with connections to: **Berlin** (6hr., 2 per hr., €110); **Cologne** (4½hr., 2 per hr., €122); **Frankfurt** (3hr., 2 per hr., €85); **Füssen** (2hr., 2 per hr., €20); **Hamburg** (6hr., 1 per hr., €115); **Amsterdam, NTH** (7-9hr., 17 per day, €140); **Budapest, HUN** (7-9hr., 8 per day, €98); **Copenhagen, DEN** (11-15hr., 8 per day, €156); **Paris, FRA** (8-10hr., 6 per day, €124-152); **Prague, CZR** (6-7hr., 4 per day, €55); **Rome, ITA** (10-11hr., 5 per day, €126); **Salzburg, AUT** (1-2hr., 1 per hr., €29); **Venice, ITA** (7-10hr., 6 per day, €92); **Vienna, AUT** (4-6hr., 1-2 per hr., €73); **Zürich, SWI** (4-5hr., 4-5 per day, €70). The train goes through Austria, so make sure you've included Austria in the list of countries the pass covers if you have a Eurail pass—otherwise pay a small nominal fee (under €10) before you board the train. Purchase a **Bayern-Ticket** (€21, 2-5 people €29) for unlimited train transit daily 9am-3am in Bavaria and to Salzburg. **EurAide,** in the station, sells tickets. **Reisezentrum** ticket counters at the station are open daily 7am-9:30pm.

GERMANY

Ride Share: Mitfahrzentrale, Lämmerstr. 6 (☎089 194 40; www.mifaz.de/muenchen). Arranges intercity rides with drivers going the same way. See **Transportation,** p. 251.

Public Transportation: MVV (☎089 41 42 43 44; www.mvv-muenchen.de) operates **buses**, **trains**, the **S-Bahn** (underground trains), and the **U-Bahn** (subway). Most run M-Th 5am-12:30am, F-Sa 5am-2am. S-Bahn trains run until 2 or 3am daily. Night buses and trams ("N") serve Munich's dedicated clubbers. Eurail, Inter Rail, and German rail passes are valid on the S-Bahn but not on buses, trams, or the U-Bahn.

Tickets: Buy tickets at the blue vending machines and validate them in the blue boxes before entering the platform; otherwise, risk a €40 fine.

Prices: Single-ride tickets €2.20 (valid 2hr.). **Kurzstrecke** (short-trip) tickets €1.10 (1hr. or 2 stops on the U- or S-Bahn, 4 stops on a tram or bus). A **Streifenkarte** (10-strip ticket; €10.50) can be used by more than 1 person. Cancel 2 strips per person for a normal ride, or 1 strip for a short trip; for rides beyond the city center, cancel 2 strips per zone. A **Single-Tageskarte** (single-day ticket; €5) for *Innenraum* (the city's central zone) is valid until 6am the next day; the **partner** day pass (€9) is valid for up to 5 people. **3-day** single pass €13; 5-person pass €21. The **XXL Ticket** (single €6.70, partner €12) gives day-long transit in Munich's 2 innermost zones, white and green. Single **Gesamtnetz** (day ticket for all zones) €10; 5-person pass €18.

Taxis: Taxi-München-Zentrale (☎089 216 10 or 089 194 10).

Bike Rental: Mike's Bike Tours, Bräuhausstr. 10 (☎089 25 54 39 87; after hours ☎0172 852 0660). €12 per 1st day; €9 per day thereafter. 50% discount with tour (below). Open daily mid.-Apr. to mid-Oct. 10am-8pm; Mar. to mid-Apr. and mid-Oct. to mid-Nov. 10:30am-1pm and 4:30-5:30pm. **Radius Bikes** (☎089 59 61 13), in the *Hauptbahnhof,* behind the lockers opposite tracks 30-36. €3-4 per hr., €15-18 per day. €50 deposit. Open daily mid-Apr. to mid-Oct. 10am-6pm. 10% student discount.

ORIENTATION

Downtown Munich is split into quadrants by thoroughfares running east-west and north-south. These intersect at Munich's central square, **Marienplatz,** and link the traffic rings at **Karlsplatz** (called Stachus by locals) in the west, **Isartorplatz** in the east, **Odeonsplatz** in the north, and **Sendlinger Tor** in the south. In the east beyond the Isartor, the Isar River flows north-south. The *Hauptbahnhof* is beyond Karlspl., to the west of the ring. To get to Marienpl. from the station, take any eastbound S-Bahn or use the main exit and make a right on Bahnhofpl., a left on Bayerstr. heading east through Karlspl., and continue straight. The **university** is to the north amid the **Schwabing** district's budget restaurants; to the east of Schwabing is the **English Garden** and to the west, **Olympiapark.** South of downtown is the **Glockenbachviertel,** filled with nightlife hot spots and gay bars. Here, travelers can find many hostels and fast food options, although the area can be dimly lit at night. Oktoberfest takes place on the large, open **Theresienwiese,** southeast of the train station on the U4 and 5 lines.

PRACTICAL INFORMATION

The most comprehensive list of services, events, and museums can be found in the English-language monthly *Munich Found* for €3 at the tourist office.

Tourist Offices: Main office (☎089 23 39 65 55) on the front side of the *Hauptbahnhof,* next to Yorma's on Bahnhofpl. Books rooms for free with a 10-15% deposit, and sells English-language city **maps** (€0.30). Open M-Sa 9am-6pm, Su 10am-6pm. **Branch office,** on Marienpl. at the entrance to the Neues Rathaus tower, is open M-F 10am-8pm, Sa 10am-4pm, Su noon-4pm, and accepts MC/V. **EurAide** (☎089 59 38 89), counter at the Reisezentrum in the *Hauptbahnhof,* books train tickets for free, English-language city tours, and explains public transportation. Open June-Sept. M-Sa 7:45am-noon and 2-6pm, Su 8am-noon; Oct.-May reduced hours.

Tours: Mike's Bike Tours, Bräuhausstr. 10 (☎089 25 54 39 87; www.mikesbiketours.com). If you only have 1 day in Munich, take this tour. Starting from the Altes Rathaus on Marienpl., the 4hr., 6km city tour includes a *Biergärten* break. Tours leave daily mid-Apr. to Aug. 11:30am and 4pm; Sept. to mid-Nov. and Mar. to mid-Apr. 12:30pm. €24. Look for coupons on biking tours at youth hostels.

Consulates: Canada, Tal 29 (☎089 219 9570). Open M-F 9am-noon; 2-4pm by appointment only. **Ireland,** Dennigerstr. 15 (☎089 20 80 59 90). Open M-F 9am-noon. **UK,** Möhlstr. 5 (☎089 21 10 90). Open M-Th 8:30am-noon and 1-5pm, F 8:30am-noon and 1-3:30pm. **US,** Königinstr. 5 (☎089 288 80). Open M-F 1-4pm.

Currency Exchange: ReiseBank (☎089 551 0813), at the front of the *Hauptbahnhof.* Slightly cheaper than other banks. Open daily 7am-11pm.

Laundromat: SB Waschcenter, Lindwurmstr. 124. Wash €3.50, dry €0.60 per 10min. Detergent €0.30. Open daily 7am-11pm. A **branch** is located at Untersbergstr. 8 (U2, 7, or 8 to Untersbergstraße) provides free Wi-Fi.

Medical Emergency: ☎112 or 192 22.

Post Office: Bahnhofpl. In the yellow building opposite the Hauptbahnhof exit. Open M-F 7:30am-8pm, Sa 9am-4pm. **Postal Code:** 80335.

ACCOMMODATIONS AND CAMPING

Lodgings in Munich tend to be either seedy, expensive, or booked solid. During mid-summer and Oktoberfest, book at least a week ahead or start calling before noon; rooms are hard to find and prices jump 10% or more.

Euro Youth Hotel, Senefelderstr. 5 (☎089 59 90 88 11; www.euro-youth-hotel.de). Friendly, well-informed staff offers helpful info and spotless rooms. Fun and noisy travelers' bar serves *Augustinerbräu* (€2.90) daily 6pm-4am, lending this alpine lodge a frat-house atmosphere. Happy hour 6-9pm, beer €2. Breakfast €3.90. Free storage lockers (€10 deposit). Larger lockers available; locks €1.50 or bring your own. Laundry: wash €3, dry €1.50. Internet €1 per 30min. Free Wi-Fi. Reception

GERMANY

GERMANY

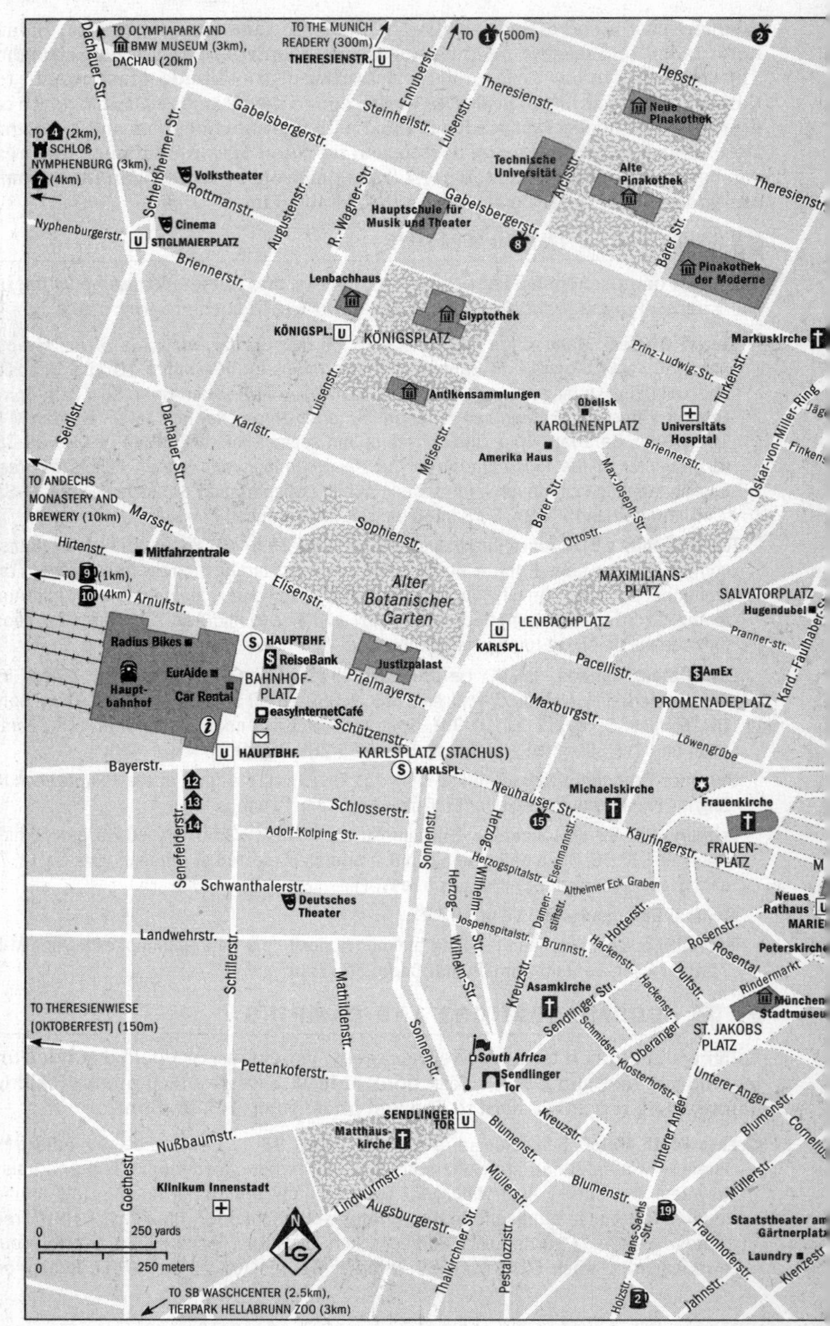

TO OLYMPIAPARK AND BMW MUSEUM (3km), DACHAU (20km)
TO THE MUNICH READERY (300m)
THERESIENSTR.
TO 1 (500m)
2
TO 4 (2km), SCHLOß NYMPHENBURG (3km), 7 (4km)
Dachauer Str.
Heßstr.
Theresienstr.
Neue Pinakothek
Gabelsbergerstr.
Steinheilstr.
Enhuberstr.
Luisenstr.
Technische Universität
Alte Pinakothek
Arcisstr.
Schleißheimer Str.
Volkstheater
Rottmanstr.
Augustenstr.
R.-Wagner-Str.
Hauptschule für Musik und Theater
Cinema
Nyphenburgerstr.
STIGLMAIERPLATZ
Briennerstr.
8
Barer Str.
Pinakothek der Moderne
Lenbachhaus
Glyptothek
KÖNIGSPL.
KÖNIGSPLATZ
Markuskirche
Prinz-Ludwig-Str.
Türkenstr.
Antikensammlungen
Obelisk
KAROLINENPLATZ
Universitäts Hospital
Oskar-von-Miller-Ring
Seidlstr.
Karlstr.
Meiserstr.
Amerika Haus
Max-Joseph-Str.
Finkenstr.
TO ANDECHS MONASTERY AND BREWERY (10km)
Marsstr.
Sophienstr.
Ottostr.
Hirtenstr.
Mitfahrzentrale
TO 9 (1km), 10 (4km)
Arnulfstr.
Elisenstr.
Alter Botanischer Garten
MAXIMILIANSPLATZ
SALVATORPLATZ
Hugendubel
LENBACHPLATZ
KARLSPL.
Pranner-str.
Radius Bikes
HAUPTBHF.
ReiseBank
Justizpalast
Pacellistr.
AmEx
EurAide
Hauptbahnhof
Car Rental
BAHNHOFPLATZ
Prielmayerstr.
easyInternetCafé
Maxburgstr.
PROMENADEPLATZ
Kard.-Faulhaber-Str.
Schützenstr.
Löwengrube
HAUPTBHF.
KARLSPLATZ (STACHUS)
KARLSPL.
Bayerstr.
12
13
14
Neuhauser Str.
Michaelskirche
Frauenkirche
Schlosserstr.
15
Adolf-Kolping Str.
Sonnenstr.
Herzog-Wilhelm-Str.
Eisenmannstr.
Kaufingerstr.
FRAUENPLATZ
Senefelderstr.
Herzogspitalstr.
Altheimer Eck
Graben
Schwanthalerstr.
Deutsches Theater
Damenstiftstr.
Neues Rathaus
MARIEN
Josephspitalstr.
Hotterstr.
Rosenstr.
Landwehrstr.
Brunnstr.
Hackenstr.
Rosental
Peterskirche
Schillerstr.
Mathildenstr.
Kreuzstr.
Dultstr.
Rindermarkt
Asamkirche
Sendlinger Str.
Münchener Stadtmuseum
TO THERESIENWIESE [OKTOBERFEST] (150m)
Schmidstr.
Oberanger
ST. JAKOBS PLATZ
South Africa
Pettenkoferstr.
Sendlinger Tor
Klosterhofstr.
Unterer Anger
SENDLINGER TOR
Matthäuskirche
Blumenstr.
Nußbaumstr.
Goethestr.
Lindwurmstr.
Müllerstr.
Klinikum Innenstadt
Augsburgerstr.
19
Hans-Sachs-Str.
Fraunhoferstr.
Staatstheater am Gärtnerplatz
0
250 yards
250 meters
N
LG
Thalkirchner Str.
Pestalozzistr.
Laundry
Klenzestr.
Holzstr.
2
Jahnstr.
TO SB WASCHCENTER (2.5km), TIERPARK HELLABRUNN ZOO (3km)

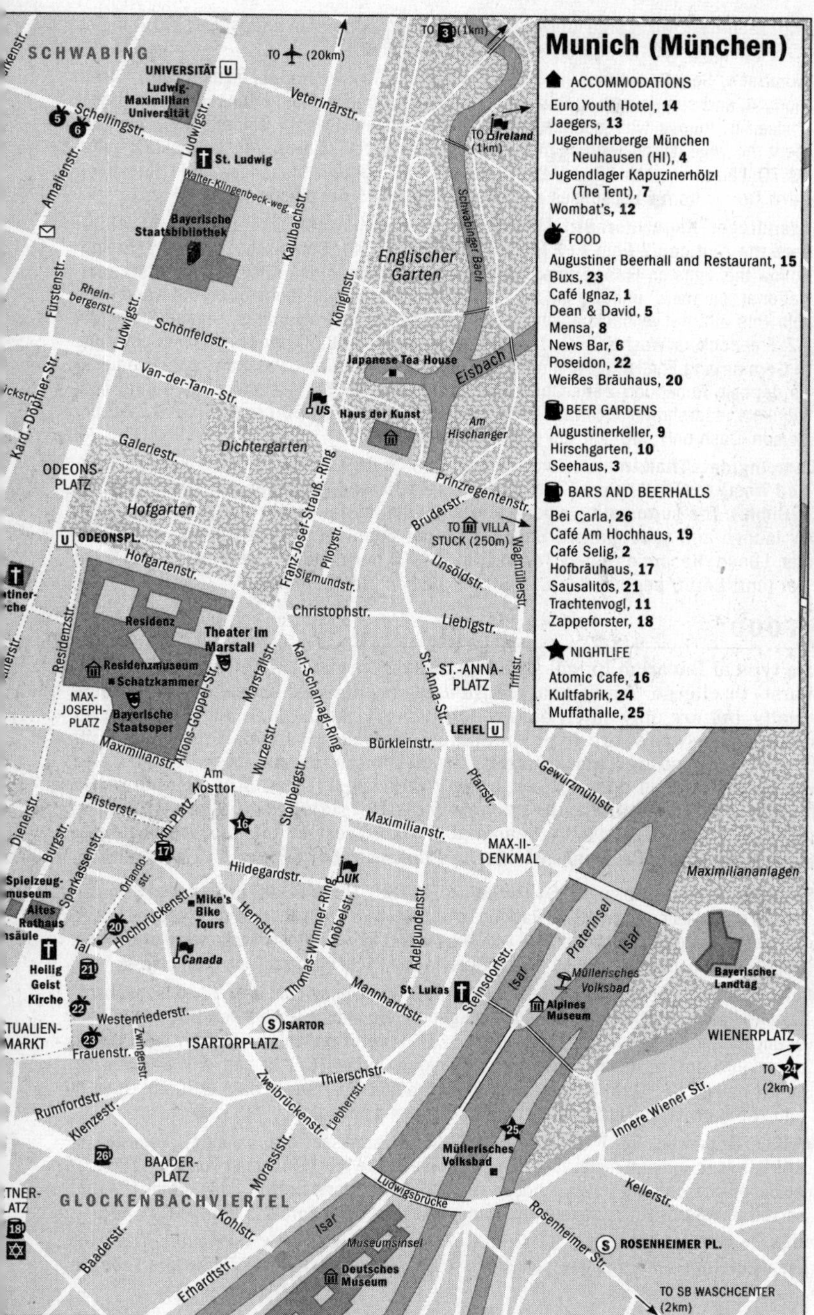

Munich (München)
ACCOMMODATIONS
Euro Youth Hotel, 14
Jaegers, 13
Jugendherberge München Neuhausen (HI), 4
Jugendlager Kapuzinerhölzl (The Tent), 7
Wombat's, 12
FOOD
Augustiner Beerhall and Restaurant, 15
Buxs, 23
Café Ignaz, 1
Dean & David, 5
Mensa, 8
News Bar, 6
Poseidon, 22
Weißes Bräuhaus, 20
BEER GARDENS
Augustinerkeller, 9
Hirschgarten, 10
Seehaus, 3
BARS AND BEERHALLS
Bei Carla, 26
Café Am Hochhaus, 19
Café Selig, 2
Hofbräuhaus, 17
Sausalitos, 21
Trachtenvogl, 11
Zappeforster, 18
NIGHTLIFE
Atomic Cafe, 16
Kultfabrik, 24
Muffathalle, 25
SCHWABING
UNIVERSITÄT
Ludwig-Maximilian Universität
St. Ludwig
Bayerische Staatsbibliothek
Englischer Garten
Japanese Tea House
Haus der Kunst
Dichtergarten
Hofgarten
ODEONSPLATZ
ODEONSPL.
Residenz
Residenzmuseum
Schatzkammer
Theater im Marstall
Bayerische Staatsoper
MAX-JOSEPH-PLATZ
ST.-ANNA-PLATZ
LEHEL
MAX-II-DENKMAL
Maximiliananlagen
Bayerischer Landtag
Mike's Bike Tours
Spielzeug-museum
Altes Rathaus
Heilig Geist Kirche
ISARTOR
ISARTORPLATZ
St. Lukas
Müllerisches Volksbad
Alpines Museum
Praterinsel
Isar
WIENERPLATZ
ROSENHEIMER PL.
TO SB WASCHCENTER (2km)
Deutsches Museum
Museumsinsel
Ludwigsbrücke
BAADER-PLATZ
GLOCKENBACHVIERTEL
TO VILLA STUCK (250m)
TO Ireland (1km)
TO (20km)
US
UK
Canada
Schellingstr.
Veterinärstr.
Ludwigstr.
Amalienstr.
Kaulbachstr.
Schwabinger Bach
Königinstr.
Schönfeldstr.
Van-der-Tann-Str.
Eisbach
Am Hischanger
Galeriestr.
Prinzregentenstr.
Franz-Josef-Strauß-Ring
Hofgartenstr.
Sigmundstr.
Christophstr.
Liebigstr.
Unsöldstr.
Maximilianstr.
Bürkleinstr.
Gewürzmühlstr.
Thomas-Wimmer-Ring
Steinsdorfstr.
Mannhardtstr.
Westenriederstr.
Frauenstr.
Zweibrückenstr.
Innere Wiener Str.
Kellerstr.
Rosenheimer Str.
Erhardtstr.
Kohlstr.
Baaderstr.
Rumfordstr.
Klenzestr.
Morassistr.
Hochbrückenstr.
Tal
Hildegardstr.
Hernstr.
Knöbelstr.
Adelgundenstr.
Pfisterstr.
Am Kosttor
Stollbergstr.
Wurzerstr.
Marstallstr.
Alfons-Goppel-Str.
Residenzstr.
Karl-Scharnagl-Ring
St.-Anna-Str.
Pilotystr.
Bruderstr.
Wagmüllerstr.
Triftstr.
Pfarrstr.
Thierschstr.
Liebherrstr.
Zwingerstr.
Sparkassenstr.
Burgstr.
Dienerstr.
Fürstenstr.
Rheinbergerstr.
Kard.-Döpfner-Str.
Walter-Klingenbeck-weg.
Am Platz
Orlando-str.

GERMANY

and security 24hr. Large dorms €17.50; 3- to 5-person dorms €21.50; singles €35; doubles €60-70; quads €84. AmEx/MC/V. ❷

Wombat's, Senefelderstr. 1 (☎089 59 98 91 80; www.wombats-hostels.com). Sleek, modern, and surprisingly sophisticated. Enjoy your free welcome drink in the ultra-cool glassed-in lounge with beanbags and lounge chairs. Swanky colored walls complement the large rooms, lending this relaxed hostel a cool, laid-back feel. Breakfast buffet €3.70. Laundry: wash €2, dry €2.50. Internet €0.50 per 20min. Free Wi-Fi. Reception 24hr. Dorms from €18; singles and doubles from €35 per person. MC/V. ❷

Jugendlager Kapuzinerhölzl (The Tent), In den Kirschen 30 (☎089 141 4300; www.the-tent.com). Tram #17 (dir.: Amalienburgstr.) to "Botanischer Garten" (15min.). Follow the signs on Franz-Schrank-Str. and turn left on In den Kirschen. Join 250 international "campers" under a gigantic tent in a series of bunk beds or on the wood floor. Join this alternative backpacking community at evening campfires. Organic breakfast €2. Free lockers. Wash €2.50, dry €2. Internet access €0.50 per 15min. Free city tours in German and English on W mornings. Free kitchen facilities. Passport or €25 required as deposit. Reception 24hr. Open June to mid-Oct. €7.50 gets you a foam pad, wool blankets, and shower facilities. Beds €10.50; camping €5.50 per site plus €5.50 per person. Cash only; MC/V if you book online. ❶

Campingplatz Thalkirchen, Zentralländstr. 49 (☎089 723 1707). U3 (dir.: Fürstenried West) to "Thalkirchen," change to bus #135, and get off at the "Campingplatz" (20min.). The surrounding woods and meandering paths give the site a rural feel. TV lounge and supermarket. Showers €1 per 6min. Laundry: wash €5, dry €0.50 per 10min. Reception open 7am-11pm. €4.70 per person, under 14 €1.50; €3-8 per tent; €4.50 per car. RVs €11.50 per person. Cash only. ❶

GERMANY

FOOD

For a typical Bavarian lunch, spread a *Brez'n* (pretzel) with *Leberwurst* (liverwurst) or cheese. Traditional *weißwürste* (white veal sausages) are a local specialty, but are only eaten before noon. Don't eat the skin; slice them open instead. *Leberknödel* are liver dumplings. Just south of Marienpl., vendors gather in the bustling **Viktualienmarkt** to sell flowers, meats, fresh veggies, and specialty dishes, but don't expect budget groceries. (Open M-F 10am-8pm, Sa 8am-4pm.) Off **Ludwigstraße,** the university district supplies students with inexpensive yet filling meals. Many reasonably priced restaurants and cafes cluster around **Schellingstraße, Amalienstraße,** and **Türkenstraße** (U3 or 6 to Universität).

Schelling Salon, Schellingstr. 54 (☎089 272 0788), U3 or U6 to "Universität." Bavarian *Knödel* and billiards since 1872. Rack up at tables where Lenin, Rilke, and Hitler once played (€7 per hr.). A great spot to unwind with a beer and friends after a hectic week of drinking. Breakfast €3-5. German entrees €4-11. Open M and Th-Su 6:30am-1am. Cash only. ❸

Cafe Ignaz, Georgenstr. 67 (☎089 27 16 093; www.ignaz-cafe.de). U2 to "Josephspl." Take Adelheidstr. 1 block north and turn right on Georgenstr. Have a heart-healthy dinner of anything from crepes to stir-fry dishes (€5-9) at this rockin' eco-friendly cafe, before diving into one of its many desserts. Breakfast buffet (€7) M and W-F 8-11:30am. Lunch buffet (€7.50) M-F noon-2pm. Brunch buffet (€9) Sa-Su 9am-1:30pm. Open M and W-F 8am-10pm, Tu 11am-11pm, Sa-Su 8am-11pm. AmEx/MC/V. ❷

Weißes Bräuhaus, Tal 7 (☎089 290 1380; www.weisses-brauhaus.de). Founded in 1490, this traditional restaurant cooks up dishes like the *Münchener Voressen* (€6.50) made of calf and pig lungs. Choose from 40-50 options on the daily menu (€3-17) served by waitresses in classic Bavarian garb. Open daily 8am-12:30am. MC/V. ❸

Dukatz Kaffee, Maffeistr. 3a (☎089 710 40 73 73; www.dukatz.de). The center of literary events in Munich since 1997. Gourmet food (€7-12) and creative drinks (€2-4) in this modern glass and steel triangle. Sip a coffee and people-watch—you'll be observing the city's trendiest writers. Open M-Sa 8:30am-1am, Su 9:30am-7pm. Cafe cash only; restaurant MC/V. ❸

SIGHTS

RESIDENZ. The richly decorated Residenz is the most visible presence of the Wittelsbach dynasty, whose state rooms now make up the **Residenzmuseum.** The luxurious apartments reflect the Renaissance, Baroque, Rococo, and Neoclassical styles. Also on display are collections of porcelain, gold and silverware, and a 17th-century court chapel. Highlights include the Rococo **Ahnengalerie,** hung with over 100 family portraits tracing the royal lineage, and the spectacular **Renaissance Antiquarium,** the oldest room in the palace, replete with stunning frescoes and statuary. *(Max-Joseph-Pl. 3. U3-6 to "Odeonspl." ☎089 29 06 71; www.residenz-muenchen.de. Open daily from Apr. to mid-Oct. 9am-6pm; from late Oct. to Mar. 10am-4pm. Last admission 30min. before closing. German-language tours meet outside the museum entrance Su at 11am. €6, students €5, under 18 free.)*

HOFGARTEN. Behind the Residenz, the beautifully landscaped Hofgarten shelters a small temple where couples gather on Sunday afternoons for free swing dancing. The **Schatzkammer** (treasury), which shares the same entrance as the Residenz, contains the most precious religious and secular symbols of Wittelsbach power: crowns, swords, crosses, and reliquaries collected during the Counter-Reformation to increase the dynasty's Catholic prestige. A comprehensive free audio tour of both the Schatzkammer and the Residenz is available in five languages. A collection of **Egyptian art** is also housed on the premises. *(Treasury open same hours as Residenzmuseum. €6; students, seniors, and group members €5; under 18 free. Combination ticket to Schatzkammer and Residenzmuseum €9, students and seniors €8. Art collection ☎089 28 92 76 30. Open Tu-F 9am-5pm, Sa-Su 10am-5pm. €5, students and seniors €4, under 18 free, Su €1.)*

ENGLISCHER GARTEN. Stretching majestically along the city's western border, the Englischer Garten (English Garden) is the largest metropolitan public park in the world, dwarfing both New York's Central Park and London's Hyde Park, offering everything from nude sunbathing and bustling beer gardens to pick-up soccer games and shaded bike paths. On sunny days, all of Munich turns out to fly kites, ride horses, and tan. Nude sunbathing areas are designated **FKK** (Frei Körper Kultur, or Free Body Culture) on signs and park maps. The main park ends with the **Kleinhesseloher See,** a large artificial lake, but the park extends much further and becomes ever more wild. If you look carefully you might see a roaming flock of sheep. There are several beer gardens on the grounds as well as a Japanese tea house, a Chinese pagoda, and a Greek temple. Daring Müncheners surf the white-water rapids of the Eisbach, the artificial river that flows through the park.

FRAUENKIRCHE. A vestige of the city's Catholic past and a symbol of Munich, the Frauenkirche towers were topped with their now-iconic domes in the mid-16th century. See the final resting place of Kaiser Ludwig der Bayer and take a German-language tour (€5) or ride the elevator to the top of the tower for the highest vantage point in the old city. *(Frauenplatz 1. Church open daily 7am-7pm. Free. Towers open Apr.-Oct. M-Sa 10am-5pm. Tours Apr.-Oct. Tu, Th, Su 2pm, €3.50, students €1.50, under 6 free.)*

ASAMKIRCHE. This small Rococo masterpiece commemorates Prague's patron saint, **John of Nepomuk,** who was thrown in the Moldau River on the orders of the Emperor for allegedly refusing to violate the confidentiality of confession. Gold, silver, and rich marble glimmer on almost every surface of this tiny, 11-pew marvel. Mesmerizing ceiling frescoes narrate the story in detail. To either side of the church stand the residences of the two Asam brothers, Cosmas Damian and Egid Quirin, who financed its construction. Their houses are still connected to the church balcony. *(Sendlinger Str. 32; 4 blocks down Sendlinger Str. from the Marienpl. Open daily 9am-5:30pm.)*

MARIENPLATZ. Sacred stone spires tower above the Marienpl., a major S- and U-Bahn junction and the social nexus of the city at the center of Munich's large pedestrian zone. The plaza, formerly known as Marktplatz, takes its name from the ornate 17th-century monument to the Virgin Mary at its center, the **Mariensäule,** which was built in 1638 and restored in 1970 to celebrate the city's near-miraculous survival of both the Swedish invasion and the plague. At the neo-Gothic **Neues Rathaus** (built in medieval style at the dawn of the 20th century), a **Glockenspiel** chimes with a display of a victorious Bavarian jouster. (Chimes daily 11am and noon; summer also 5pm.) At 9pm a mechanical watchman marches out and the Guardian Angel escorts the *Münchner Kindl* ("Munich Child," a symbol of the city) to bed. All of Munich's coats of arms are on the face of the **Altes Rathaus** tower, to the right of the Neues Rathaus, with the notable exception of the Nazi swastika-bearing shield. Hitler commemorated his failed 1923 Putsch in the ballroom, which is still in use for official functions. *(Tower open daily 10am-7pm. €2, under 18 €1, under 6 free.)*

MUSEUMS

Many of Munich's museums would require days to explore completely. All state-owned museums, including the three **Pinakotheken,** are €1 on Sunday.

PINAKOTHEKEN. Designed by *Münchener* Stephan Braunfels, the beautiful **Pinakothek der Moderne** is four museums in one. Subgalleries display architecture, design, drawings, and paintings by artists ranging from Picasso to contemporary masters. *(Barerstr. 40. U2 to Königspl or tram #27 to Pinakotheken. ☎089 23 80 53 60. Open Tu-W and Sa-Su 10am-5pm, Th-F 10am-8pm. €9.50, students €6. Audio tour free.)* Commissioned in 1826 by King Ludwig I, the **Alte Pinakothek** houses 500 years of art, works by 19th- and 20th-century artists including works by Leonardo da Vinci, Rembrandt, and Rubens. *(Barerstr. 27. ☎089 23 80 52 16; www.alte-pinakothek.de. Open Tu 10am-8pm, W-Su 10am-6pm. €5.50, students €4.)* Next door, the **Neue Pinakothek** displays fascinating work of famous artists including Cézanne, Monet, and van Gogh. *(Barerstr. 29. ☎089 23 80 51 95; www.neue-pinakothek.de. Open M and Th-Su 10am-5pm, W 10am-8pm. €5.50, students €4; includes audio tour.)*

DEUTSCHES MUSEUM. The Deutsches Museum is one of the world's most comprehensive museums of science and technology. Exhibits include an early telephone, the work bench on which Otto Hahn first split an atom, and a recreated subterranean labyrinth of mining tunnels. The museum's 50+ departments cover over 17km. An English guidebook (€4) thoroughly explains all exhibits, though many signs have English translations. The **planetarium** shows educational films (4 shows per day; €2). Don't miss the aviation display featuring full-sized prop-planes and Leonardo da Vinci-esque flying machines, or the over 50 try-it-yourself (but not at home) experiments in the physics department. Finally, stroll through the fascinating sundial garden with a panoramic city view on the roof next to the planetarium. The museum also maintains an impressive **flight museum** in a WWI hangar in Schleißheim and a **transportation museum.** *(Museumsinsel 1. S1-S8 to "Isartor" or tram #18 to "Deutsches Museum." ☎089 21 791; www.deutsches-museum.de. Open daily 9am-5pm. €8.50, students €3, under 6 free. Flight museum: Effnerstr. 18. ☎089 315 71 40. S-Bahn to "Oberschleißheim," then follow signs. Open daily 9am-5pm. €5, students and seniors €3. Transportation museum: Theresienhöhe 14a. ☎089*

500 8067 62. U4-5 to "Schwanthalerhöhe." Open daily 9am-5pm. €5, students and seniors €3. Combined admission to flight, transportation, and science museums €17.)

ENTERTAINMENT

Munich deserves its reputation as a world-class cultural center. Sixty theaters are scattered generously throughout the city staging productions that range from dramatic classics at the **Residenztheater** and **Volkstheater** to comic opera at the **Staatstheater am Gärtnerplatz** to experimental works at the **Theater im Marstall.** Munich's numerous fringe theaters, cabaret stages, and art cinemas in **Schwabing** reveal its bohemian spirit. *Monatsprogramm* (free) and *Munich Found* (free at the tourist office) list schedules for festivals, museums, and performances. In July, a magnificent **opera festival** arrives at the **Bayerische Staatsoper** (Bavarian National Opera), Max-Joseph-Pl. 2. (☎089 21 85 01; www.bayerische.staatsoper.de. U3-6 to Odeonspl. or tram #19 to Nationaltheater.) For €8-10, students can buy tickets for performances marked "Young Audience Program" two weeks in advance. Snag leftover tickets—if there are any—at the **evening box office,** Max-Joseph-Pl. 2, near the theater, for €10. (Opens 1hr. before curtain.) Standing-room tickets are half-price and can be purchased at any time. The **daytime box** office is at Marstallpl. 5. (☎089 21 85 19 20. Open M-F 10am-6pm, Sa 10am-1pm. Performances Oct.-July.)

GERMANY

NIGHTLIFE

Munich's nightlife is a mix of Bavarian *Gemütlichkeit* (coziness) and chic trendiness. A typical odyssey begins at a beer hall, which usually closes around midnight. Cafes and bars close their taps at 1am (later on weekends), while discos and dance clubs, sedate before midnight, throb until 4am. Trendsetters head to **Leopoldstraße** in **Schwabing** or **Glockenbachviertel,** near Gärnterpl. Many venues require partiers to dress up.

BEER HALLS AND GARDENS

Bavaria agreed to become a part of a larger Germany on one condition: that it be allowed to maintain its beer purity laws. Since then, Munich has remained loyal to six great labels: **Augustiner, Hacker-Pschorr, Hofbräu, Löwenbräu, Paulaner,** and **Spaten-Franziskaner,** which together provide Müncheners and tourists alike with all the fuel they need for late-night revelry. Four main types of beer are served in Munich: *Helles* (standard light beer with a crisp, sharp taste); *Dunkles* (dark beer with a heavier, fuller flavor); *Weißbier* (smooth, cloudy blond beer made from wheat instead of barley); and *Radler* or *Russ'n* ("shandy" or "cyclist's brew": half beer and half lemon soda with a light, fruity taste). Munich's beer is typically 5% alcohol, though in **Starkbierzeit** (the first two weeks of Lent), Müncheners traditionally drink *Starkbier*, a dark beer that is 8-10% alcohol. Daring travelers can go for a full liter of beer, known as a **Maß** (€5-7). Specify if you want a *halb-Maß* (.5L, €3-4); Weißbier is almost exclusively served in 0.5L sizes. While some beer gardens offer veggie dishes, vegetarians may wish to eat elsewhere before a post-meal swig. It's traditional to bring your own food to outdoor beer halls—drinks, however, must be bought at the *Biergarten*. Bare tables usually indicate cafeteria-style *Selbstbedienung* (self-service).

Augustiner Bräustuben, Landsberger Str. 19 (☎089 50 70 47; www.augustiner-braustuben.de). S1-S8 to "Hackerbrücke." Walk to the far side of the bridge to Landsberger Str. and take a right. In the Augustiner brewery's former horse stalls. With a candlelit interior and some of the cheapest beer in the city (*Maß*; €5.10), this relatively undiscovered beer hall is the perfect place to share laughs over heaps of Bavarian food at great prices (€5-9) either inside or on the recently completed roof terrace. Devoted carnivores should try the *Bräustüberl* (duck, two cuts of pork, *Kraut,* and two types of dumplings; €10). Open daily 10am-midnight; kitchen open daily 11am-11pm. MC/V.

Hirschgarten, Hirschgarten 1 (☎089 17 999 119, www. hirschgarten.de). Tram #17 (dir.: Amalienburgstr.) to "Romanpl." Walk south to the end of Guntherstr. The largest *Biergarten* in Europe (seating 8000), tucked away in a small park just outside the city center, is boisterous and always crowded. Families come for the grassy park and carousel, and to see the deer still kept on the premises. Entrees €6-18. *Maß* €6. Open daily 9am-midnight; kitchen open until 10:30pm. MC/V.

Zum Flaucher, Isarauen 8 (☎089 723 2677; www.zum-flaucher.de), U3 to "Brudermühlstr." Walk down Brudermühlstr, follow street signs to "Nürnberg," and take a right just over the bridge onto the wooded path. At the next bridge, turn left and follow signs to "Zum Flaucher"; it's on the right. Gorgeous 2000-seat *Biergarten* near the banks of the Isar and riverside bike path. Lift a *Maß* (€6.50-6.80) with locals relaxing near the water, or join one of the pickup soccer games. Try the individually made *Leberkäse* (€3.80). Open May-Oct. daily 10am-midnight, Nov.-Apr. Sa-Su 10am-9pm. Cash only.

GERMANY

BARS AND CLUBS

K & K Klub, Reichenbachstr. 22 (☎089 20 20 74 63; www.kuk-club.de). U1-U2 to "Frauenhoferstr." Subdued walls, cube seats, and a large projection screen playing art films attract a young, artsy crowd. Sip a beer (€3.40) against the orange glow of the illuminated tribal symbols and retro video games (€0.50). Local DJs play electro, indie, and house M-Sa. Open M-W and Su 8pm-2am, Th-Sa 8pm-5am. Cash only.

Cafe Am Hochhaus, Blumenstr. 29 (☎089 058 152, www.cafeamhochhaus.de). U1-U3 or U6 to "Sendlinger Tor." Sometimes a dance party, sometimes a relaxed cafe with quirky wallpaper, the mood changes nightly with the crowd. Live DJs spin everything from funk to house starting at 10pm. Open daily 8pm-3am or even later. Cash only.

GLBT NIGHLTIFE

Morizz, Klenzestr. 43 (☎089 201 6776). U1 or U2 to "Frauenhofer Str." Subdued ambient lighting and stylish decor create an intimate interior that attracts a mixed crowd. Settle into the chic low chairs for a mixed drink (€7.60-8.50) and upscale Thai dishes (€6-15), served until 12:30am. Open M-Th and Su 7pm-2am, F-Sa 7pm-3am. MC/V.

Bau, Müllerstr. 41 (☎089 26 92 08; www.bau-munich.de). U1 or U2 to "Fraunhoferstr." Broad rainbow stripes on the door and posters of leather-clad men on the walls suit the heavy-duty construction theme of this gay club and bar. No mixed drinks—only beer (€2.70) and liquor (€2.50). Drinks buy 1 get 1 free M 8-10pm; €1 shots every Th 8-10pm and 1-3am. Open daily 8pm-4am. AmEx/MC/V.

Cafe Selig, Hans-Sachs Str. 3 (☎089 23 88 88 78; www.einfachselig.de). U1 or U2 to "Fraunhoferstr." Sleek wooden tables and striking red contemporary art attract a diverse crowd (all sexual orientations by day, mostly gay Sa-Su and at night) to this chic locale. The modern cafe and bar also serves international coffees, homemade cakes, and strudel (€3-7). Open M and W-Sa 9am-late. AmEx/MC/V.

OKTOBERFEST

Every fall, hordes of tourists make an unholy pilgrimage to Munich to drink and be merry in true Bavarian style. From the penultimate Saturday of September through early October (Sept. 19-Oct. 4, 2009), beer consumption prevails. The numbers for this festival have become truly mind-boggling: participants chug five million liters of beer, but only on a full stomach of 200,000 *Würste.* What began in 1810 as a celebration of the wedding of Ludwig I has become the world's largest folk festival. Representatives from all over Bavaria met outside the city gates for a week of horse racing on fields they named **Theresienwiese** in honor of Ludwig's bride (U4 or U5 to Theresienwiese). The bash was such fun that Munich's citizens have repeated the revelry (minus the horses) ever since. An agricultural show, inaugurated in 1811, is still held every three years.

DAYTRIPS FROM MUNICH

DACHAU. *Arbeit Macht Frei* (Work Will Set You Free) was the first message prisoners saw as they passed through the **Jourhaus** gate into Dachau, where over 206,000 "undesirables" were interned between 1933 and 1945. Dachau, the Third Reich's first concentration camp, was primarily a work rather than a death camp like Auschwitz; the SS reserved it for the construction of armaments knowing the Allies would not bomb prisoners of war. Restored in 1962, the crematorium, gates, and walls now form a **memorial** to the victims. *(Open Tu-Su 9am-5pm. Free.)* In former administrative buildings, the **museum** examines pre-1930s anti-Semitism, the rise of Nazism, the establishment of the concentration camp system, and the lives of prisoners. A short **English-language film** (22min., free) screens at 11:30am, 2, and 3:30pm. Displays in the barracks, the former prison and the torture chamber chronicle prisoners' lives and SS guards' barbarism. A 2hr. English-language **tour** covers the entire camp. *(May-Sept. Tu-F at 1:30pm, Sa-Su at noon and 1:30pm; Oct.-Apr. Th-Su at 1:30pm. €3.)* A brief **introduction** (30min.) gives a general overview of the complex. *(May-Sept. Tu-F 12:30pm, Sa-Su 11am and 12:30pm; Oct.-Apr. Th-Su 12:30pm. €1.50.)* Or, purchase the worthwhile audio tour (€3, students €2) for a self-directed tour of the camp. Food and beverages are not available at Dachau; pack your own lunch. (*Take the S2 (dir.: Petershausen) to Dachau (20min.), then bus #726 (dir.: Saubachsiedlung) to KZ-Gedenkstätte (10min.); a €6.70 XXL day pass covers the trip.*)

ROMANTIC ROAD

Groomed fields of sunflowers, vineyards, and hills checker the landscape between Würzburg and Füssen. Officially christened *Romantische Straße* (the Romantic Road) in 1950, the road is dotted with almost a hundred castles, helping to make it one of the most traversed routes in Germany.

TRANSPORTATION

Train travel is the most flexible, economical way to visit the Romantic Road. Deutsche Bahn operates a **bus** route along the Romantic Road, shuttling tourists from Frankfurt to Munich (13hr., €99), stopping in Würzburg (2hr., €22), Rothenburg (4hr., €35), and Füssen (11hr., €80). A Castle Road **bus** route connects Rothenburg with Nuremburg by bus (3hr., €14). Both buses run once a day in each direction. For reservations and more detailed information, see www.romanticroadcoach.de. There is a 10% student and under 26 discount, and a 60% Eurail and German Rail Pass discount.

FÜSSEN ☎08362

Füssen ("feet") seems an apt name for a little town at the foot of the Bavarian Alps. Füssen is the ideal basecamp for some of Germany's best daytrips; the town is mere minutes from King Ludwig's famed **Königsschlößer,** one of the best hiking, biking, and boating regions in the country. Above the pedestrian district, the town's own **Hohes Schloß** (High Castle) stands as a reminder of the power that Bavaria once wielded. The only way to enter the Schloß is by paying a visit to the **Staatsgalerie** (municipal gallery), which displays mostly religious art from the 15th to the 19th century. (☎08362 90 31 46. Open Tu-Su Apr.-Oct. 11am-4pm; Nov.-Mar.1 noon-4pm. €2.50, students €2.) The **Annakapelle,** which commemorates bubonic plague victims, has paintings depicting everyone swept up in the *Todestanz,* the dance of death. Entry to the Annakapelle is included in a ticket to the **Museum der Stadt** (City Museum), which details Füssen's history. (☎08362 90 31 46. Open Tu-Su Apr.-Oct. 11am-5pm; Nov.-Mar. 1-4pm. €2.50, students €2.) A combined ticket to the Stadtmuseum and the Staatsgalerie (€3) can be purchased at either museum.

Although Füssen's best accommodations are pensions, the tourist office keeps a list of *Privatzimmer* with vacant rooms. **Jugendherberge (HI) ❷,** Mariahilfer Str. 5, lies in a residential area 15min. from the town center. Turn right from the station and follow the railroad tracks. (☎08362 77 54. Laundry €1.60. Reception daily Mar.-Sept. 7am-noon and 5-10pm; Oct. and Dec.-Apr. 5-10pm. Lockout 11pm-6:30am; keycode available. Dorms €17.50. MC/V.) Bakeries, butcher shops, and *Imbiße* (snack bars) stand among the pricey cafes on **Reichenstraße,** particularly off the Luitpold Passage. The **Plus** supermarket is on the right toward the rotary from the station. (Open M-Sa 8:30am-8pm.)

Trains run to Augsburg (1hr., every hr., €17) and Munich (2hr., every hr., €21). From the train station to the **tourist office,** Kaiser-Maximilian-Pl. 1, walk the length of Bahnhofstr. and head across the roundabout to the big yellow building on your left. (☎938 50; www.fuessen.de. Open June-Sept. M-F 9am-6pm, Sa 10am-2pm; Oct.-May M-F 9am-5pm, Sa 10am-noon.) **Postal Code:** 87629.

DAYTRIP FROM FÜSSEN: KÖNIGSSCHLÖSSER. King Ludwig II, a frenzied visionary, built fantastic castles soaring into the alpine skies. In 1886, a band of nobles and bureaucrats deposed Ludwig, declared him insane, and imprisoned him; three days later, the king was mysteriously discovered dead in a lake. The fairy-tale castles that Ludwig created and the enigma of his death captivate tourists. The glitzy **Schloß Neuschwanstein** inspired Disney's Cinderella Castle, and is one of Germany's iconic attractions. Its chambers include an artificial grotto and an immense Wagnerian opera hall. Hike 10min. to the **Marienbrücke,** a bridge that spans the gorge behind the castle. Climb the mountain on the other side of the bridge for the enchantment without the crowds. Ludwig spent his summers in the bright yellow **Schloß Hohenschwangau** across the valley. While you're there, spend the extra money to see both castles. Each one is amazing in its own right. From the Füssen train station, take **bus** #73 or 78, marked "Königsschlößer" (10min.; 1-2 per hr.; €1.70, round-trip €3.20) or **walk** the 4km along beautiful, winding roads. Tickets for both castles are sold at the **Ticket-Service Center,** about 100m uphill from the bus stop. Arrive before 10am to escape long lines. *(☎08362 93 08 30. Both castles open daily Apr.-Sept. 9am-6pm, ticket windows open 8am-5pm; Oct.-Mar. castles 10am-4pm, tickets 9am-3pm. Mandatory tours of each castle €9, students €8; 10 languages available. Combination ticket €17/15.)*

ROTHENBURG OB DER TAUBER ☎09861

Possibly the only walled medieval city without a single modern building, Rothenburg (pop. 12,000) is *the* Romantic Road stop. After the Thirty Years' War, without money to modernize, the town remained unchanged for 250 years. Tourism later brought economic stability and another reason to preserve the medieval *Altstadt.* The English-language tour led by the **night watchman** gives a fast-paced and entertaining introduction to Rothenburg history. (Starts at the

Rathaus on Marktpl. Easter-Dec. 25 daily 8pm. €6, students €4.) A long climb up the narrow stairs of the 60m **Rathaus Tower** leads to a panoramic view of the town's red roofs. (Open Apr.-Oct. daily 9:30am-12:30pm and 1-5pm; Dec. daily noon-3pm; Nov. and Jan.-Mar. Sa-Su noon-3pm. €2.) According to proud local lore, during the Thirty Years' War, the conquering Catholic general Johann Tilly offered to spare the town from destruction if any local could chug a keg containing 3.25L of wine. Mayor Nusch successfully met the challenge, passed out for several days, then lived to a ripe old age. His saving **Meistertrunk** (Master Draught) is reenacted with great fanfare each year (May 29-June 1, 2009).

For private rooms unregistered at the tourist office (€15-45), look for the *Zimmer frei* (free room) signs in restaurants and stores. The 500-year-old **Pension Raidel ❷**, Wengg. 3, will make you feel like you're sleeping in the past. (☎9861 31 15; www.romanticroad.com/raidel. Breakfast included. Singles €24, with bath €42; doubles €49/59. Cash only.) Dine on sinfully good food at **Zur Höll ❷**, Burgg. 8. Originally built as a home in AD 980, Zur Höll (To Hell) still serves Franconian fare (€4-18) by dim candlelight. (☎9861 42 29. Bratwurst with sauerkraut €6. Open daily 5pm-midnight. Cash only.)

Trains run to Steinach (15min., 1 per hr., €1.90), which has transfers to Munich (€32) and Würzburg (€12). The **Europabus** leaves from the *Busbahnhof* by the train station. The **tourist office,** Marktpl. 2, has great resources that will make your trip to Rothenburg much more organized, and offers 15min. of free **Internet**. From the train station, head left before taking a right on Ansbacherstr.. (☎9861 404 800. Open May-Oct. M-F 9am-6pm, Sa-Su 10am-3pm; Nov.-Apr. M-F 9am-noon and 1-5pm, Sa 10am-1pm.) **Postal Code**: 91541.

GREECE (Ελλάδα)

With sacred monasteries as mountainside fixtures, standard three-hour siestas, and circle dancing and drinking until daybreak, Greece revels in its epic past. Renaissance men long before the Renaissance, the ancient Greeks sprung to prominence with their intellectual prowess and athletic mastery. Today, the Greek lifestyle remains a mix of high speed and sun-inspired lounging.

DISCOVER GREECE: SUGGESTED ITINERARIES

THREE DAYS. Spend it all in **Athens** (p. 319). Roam the **Acropolis,** gaze at treasures in the **National Archaeological Museum,** and pay homage to the goddess Athena at the **Parthenon.** Visit the ancient **Agora,** then take a trip down to **Poseidon's Temple** at Cape Sounion.

ONE WEEK. Begin your sojourn in **Athens** (3 days). Seek rest on **Santorini** (1 day; p. 332), the god Apollo's advice on **Delos** (1 day; p. 332), and sun on **Mykonos** (1 day; p. 331). Lastly, brush up on your Byzantine history in **Thessaloniki** (2 days; p. 327).

LIFE AND TIMES

HISTORY

BRONZE AGE (3200-1150 BC). The first Aegean island civilization, the **Cycladic** population flourished on the Cyclades (p. 331) between 3000 and 1100 BC, leaving a legacy of miniature marble sculptures. Around the same time, the seafaring **Minoans** of Crete (p. 333) created grand palaces and a syllabic writing system before they disappeared around 1500 BC, presumably in a volcanic eruption in Santorini. On the mainland, the warring **Mycenaean** princes allied for the storied attack on Troy and further developed Linear B, a written language based on Minoan hieroglyphs. The Mycenaean civilization ended abruptly around 1150 BC when the Dorians invaded from the north.

THE RISE OF THE CITY-STATE (800-500 BC). Around 800 BC, a discernibly Greek culture coalesced, unified by the Greek language and religious rites. The **polis,** or city-state, emerged as the major Greek political structure. At the heart of each city was the **acropolis,** a fortified citadel and religious center atop the highest point, and the **agora,** the marketplace and center of commercial and social life. Greek unity grew during the **Persian Wars** (490-449 BC), when Athens and Sparta led the Greeks against overwhelming odds to defeat the Persians in the legendary battles at Marathon, Plataea, and Salamis. The victories ushered in the Classical period: a time of unprecedented prosperity as well as artistic, commercial, and political success.

CLASSICAL GREECE (479-323 BC). Athens created the **Delian League** of Greek states to defend against Persian aggression. The league established Athens as a colonial power by requiring all members to pay dues and swear loyalty to Athens. This expansion brought the city, which prided itself on its com-

mercial, democratic, and cultural achievements, into direct conflict with the agricultural, monarchical, and martial Sparta for control of Greece. During the **Peloponnesian War** (431-404 BC), the Athenians proved no match for the military prowess of the Spartans, whose soldiers entered the army at age 7. Classical Greece dissolved as bickering between warring *poles* became heated.

MACEDONIAN RULE (323-20BC). After the Peloponnesian War, Macedonia's **King Philip II** took advantage of the weakened city-states and invaded from the north in 338 BC. His later assassination left his 20-year-old son, Alexander, in command. The young king spent the rest of his life at war, establishing a stranglehold on the Greek city-states before sweeping into Persia and Egypt. At the time of his sudden death, **Alexander the Great,** 33, ruled much of the known world, having widely spread Greek culture and language. His extensive empire's dissolution restored some independence to the Greek city-states. The Romans invaded in 146 BC; by 20 BC Greece was part of the Roman Empire.

ROMAN EMPIRE: EAST SIDE (20 BC-1000 AD). As Rome slowly declined, competing halves began to dominate the empire: an eastern half, centered in Anatolia, the Levant, and Greece; and a western half, centered in Rome. This unusual political arrangement ended in a scramble for power won by **Constantine** in AD 312. He later legalized Christianity and gave the Roman Empire a new capital in AD 324 with the founding of **Constantinople,** built over the ancient city of Byzantium in modern-day Turkey. While Western Europe was overrun by barbarian invaders, the eastern **Byzantine Empire** became an unrivaled center of learning, trade, and influence.

NASTY NEIGHBORS (1000-1800 AD). From 1200 to 1400, the Byzantine Empire was plagued by crusaders who conquered and looted Constantinople in 1204 and imposed Catholicism upon the city. In 1453, the Ottoman Turks overran the much-reduced city, renaming it **İstanbul.** The Muslim Turkish rulers treated their Greek subjects as members of a *millet*—a separate community ruled by its own religious leaders. The Greek Orthodox Church became the moderator of culture and the foundation of Greek autonomy. By the 19th century, Greeks were pushing for independence from the Ottoman Empire.

GREEK NATIONALIST REVOLT (1800-1833 AD). In 1821, **Bishop Germanos** of Patras raised a Greek flag at the monastery of Agia Lavra, sparking an empire-wide rebellion. Disorganized but impassioned guerrillas on the Peloponnese and in the Aegean Islands waged war on the Turkish government for nearly a decade, although the revolt never gained support from the peasants. Finally, in 1829, with help from various European powers, Greece won its **independence.** The borders of the new Greece were narrow, including only a fraction of the six million Greeks living under Ottoman rule. For the next century, Greek politics centered around the **Megali Idea** (Great Idea): freeing İstanbul from the Turks and uniting all Greeks into one state.

GREECEY SITUATION (1833-1923 AD). In 1833, after the assassination of **Ioannis Kapodistrias,** the first democratically elected Greek president, the European powers intervened, declared Greece a monarchy, and handed the crown to a succession of Germanic princes. Democracy prevailed in 1864 when the constitution established an elected prime minister as the head of state. **Eleftherios Venizelos,** elected in 1910, employed these powers to expand Greece's territory to **Crete, Thessaloniki** (p. 327), **Epirus,** and a portion of **Macedonia** on the Aegean coast. Despite the Ottoman Empire's defeat in WWI, Greece did not receive land in Asia Minor, and in 1919 Venizelos ordered an invasion of Turkey. A young Turkish general, Mustafa Kemal, later called **Atatürk,** crushed the invasion and ordered the slaughter of ethnic Greeks along the Turkish coast. This continued until the **Treaty of Lausanne** (1923) enacted a population exchange that brought 1.5 million Greeks from Asia Minor to Greece and sent 400,000 Turkish Muslims from Greece to Turkey, effectively ending the *Megali Idea.*

WORLD WAR II AND THE MODERN GREEK STATE (1923-1980 AD). The 1930s were rocked by political turmoil as brief intervals of democracy gave way to a succession of monarchies and military rule. The extreme nationalist General John Metaxas succeeded Venizelos as prime minister, notably rejecting Mussolini's request to bring Italian troops through neutral Greece with a resounding *"Oci!"* (No!). Greeks now celebrate Okhi Day on October 28. Although they drove back the Italians who invaded anyway, Greece fell to the Axis in 1941 and endured four years of bloody and brutal occupation, during which 65,000 Greek Jews perished in Nazi camps. Resistance was split between the popular communist-led movement and the US-backed royalist movement. This struggle for influence turned violent in 1944 as the devastating Greek Civil War, marked by purges and starvation, became one of the early battles in the Cold War. The left-wing, Soviet-backed Democratic Army finally lost to the anti-communist coalition in 1949. The US played a visible role in Greek politics through the subsequent decades of turmoil. A new constitution was drawn up in 1975, establishing the current parliamentary government with a ceremonial president appointed by the country's legislature.

TODAY

On January 1, 1981, Greece became the European Union's 10th member. The nation's Prime Minister throughout the 1980s and mid-1990s, **Andreas Papandreou,** founded the leftist **Panhellenic Socialist Movement (PASOK)** and pioneered the passage of women's rights legislation. **Costas Simitis** succeeded him, successfully pursuing economic reforms. Under his guidance, Greece finally met the qualifying standards for adoption of the **euro (€)** in January 2001. In the same month, foreign minister **George Papandreou** traveled to Turkey, the first such visit in 37 years. Officially, Greece supports Turkey's bid for EU membership, but Cyprus remains a stumbling block in Greek-Turkish relations. A UN-sponsored plan to reunify the Greek and Turkish areas of the island passed in the Turkish North in 2004 but was voted down in the Greek region. Regardless, Greek Cyprus was admitted into the EU later that year. National power shifted back to the right-wing New Democracy party following the 2004 parliamentary elections. Prime Minister **Kostas Karmanlis,** new to office, finished preparing Athens for the 2004 Summer Olympics. His ascension returned PASOK to the opposition. Greece's Communist Party (KKE) forms a vocal minority, occasionally channeling passionate anti-Americanism.

HOLIDAYS AND FESTIVALS

Holidays: Feast of St. Basil/New Year's Day (Jan. 1); Epiphany (Jan. 6); Clean Monday (Mar. 10); Independence Day (Mar. 25); St. George's Day (Apr. 23); Orthodox Good Friday (Apr. 2, 2010); Orthodox Easter (Apr. 4-5, 2010); Labor Day (May 1); Pentecost (May 11-12); Day of the Holy Spirit (June 16); Assumption (Aug. 15); Feast of St. Demetrius (Oct. 26); Okhi Day (Oct. 28); All Saints' Day (Nov. 1); Christmas (Dec. 25-26).

Festivals: 3 weeks of Carnival feasting and dancing (from mid-Feb. to early Mar.) precede Lenten fasting. April 23 is St. George's Day, when Greece honors the dragon-slaying knight with horse races, wrestling matches, and dances. The Feast of St. Demetrius (Oct. 26) is celebrated with particular enthusiasm in Thessaloniki.

ESSENTIALS

FACTS AND FIGURES

OFFICIAL NAME: Hellenic Republic.
CAPITAL: Athens.
MAJOR CITIES: Thessaloniki, Patras.
POPULATION: 10,723,000.
LAND AREA: 131,900 sq. km.
TIME ZONE: GMT +2.
LANGUAGE: Greek.
RELIGION: Eastern Orthodox (98%).
HIGHEST PEAK: Mt. Olympus (2917m).
LENGTH OF NATIONAL ANTHEM: 158 verses.

WHEN TO GO

July through August is peak season; it is best to visit in May, early June, or September, when smaller crowds enjoy the gorgeous weather. Visiting during low season ensures lower prices, but many sights and accommodations have shorter hours or close altogether.

DOCUMENTS AND FORMALITIES

EMBASSIES. Foreign embassies in Greece are in Athens (p. 319). Greek embassies abroad include: **Australia,** 9 Turrana St., Yarralumla, Canberra, ACT, 2600 (☎62 7330 11); **Canada,** 80 MacLaren St., Ottawa, ON, K2P 0K6 (☎613-238-6271; www.greekembassy.ca); **Ireland,** 1 Upper Pembroke St., Dublin, 2 (☎31 676 7254, ext. 5); **New Zealand,** 5-7 Willeston St., 10th fl., Wellington (☎4 473 7775, ext. 6); **UK,** 1a Holland Park, London, W11 3TP (☎020 72 21 64 67; www.greekembassy.org.uk); **US,** 2217 Massachusetts Ave., NW, Washington, DC, 20008 (☎202-939-1300; www.greekembassy.org).

VISA AND ENTRY INFORMATION. EU citizens do not need a visa. Citizens of Australia, Canada, New Zealand, and the US do not need a visa for stays of up to 90 days, beginning upon entry into any of the countries in the EU's freedom-of-movement zone. For more info, see p. 8. For stays longer than 90 days, all non-EU citizens need Schengen visas, available at Greek embassies and online at www.greekembassy.org. Processing a tourist visa takes about 20 days.

TOURIST SERVICES AND MONEY

TOURIST OFFICES. Two national organizations oversee tourism in Greece: **Greek National Tourist Organization** (GNTO; known as the EOT in Greece) and the **tourist police** *(touristiki astinomia)*. The GNTO, Tsoha 7, Athens supplies general info about Grecian sights and accommodations. (☎2108 70 70 00; www.gnto.gr. Open M-F 8am-3pm.) In addition to the "Tourist Police" insignia decorating their uniforms, white belts, gloves, and cap bands help identify the tourist police. The **Tourist Police Service** and **General Police Directorate**, P. Kanellopoulou 4, Athens (☎2106 92 8510, 24hr. general emergency 171) deal with local and immediate problems concerning bus schedules, accommodations, and lost passports. Offices are willing to help, but their staff's English may be limited.

EMERGENCY	**Ambulance:** ☎166. **Fire:** ☎199. **Police:** ☎100. **General Emergency:** ☎112.

MONEY. The **euro (€)** has replaced the Greek **drachma** as the unit of currency in Greece. For more info, see p. 11. It's generally cheaper to change money in Greece than at home. When changing money in Greece, try to go to a bank (trpeza; TRAH-peh-za) with at most a 5% margin between its buy and sell prices. A bare-bones day in Greece costs €40-60. A day with more comforts runs €55-75. While all restaurant prices include a 15% gratuity, **tipping** an additional 5-10% for the assistant waiters and busboys is considered good form. Taxi drivers do not expect tips although patrons generally round their fare up to the nearest euro. Generally, **bargaining** is expected for street wares and at other informal venues, but when in doubt, wait and watch to avoid offending merchants. Bargaining for cheaper *domatia* (rooms to let) and at small hotels, as well as for unmetered taxi rides is also common.

Greece has a 19% **value added tax (VAT),** a sales tax applied to goods and services sold in mainland Greece and 13% VAT on the Aegean islands. Both are included in the listed price. The prices given in *Let's Go* include VAT. In the airport upon exiting the EU, non-EU citizens can claim a refund on the tax paid for goods purchased at participating stores. In order to qualify for a refund in a store, you must spend at least €120; make sure to ask for a refund form when you pay. For more info on qualifying for a VAT refund, see p. 13.

TRANSPORTATION

BY PLANE. International flights land in **Athens International Airport** (**ATH;** ☎21035 30 000; www.aia.gr), though some also serve Corfu (CFU), Heraklion (HER), Kos (KSG), and Thessaloniki (SKG). **Olympic Airlines,** 96 Syngrou Ave., Athens, 11741 (☎21092 691 11; www.olympicairlines.com), offers domestic service. A 1hr. flight from Athens (€60-100) can get you to almost any Grecian island.

BY TRAIN. Greece is served by a number of international train routes that connect Athens and Thessaloniki to most European cities. Train service within Greece, however, is limited and sometimes uncomfortable. The new air-conditioned, intercity express trains, while a bit more expensive and less frequent, are worth the price. **Eurail** is valid on all Greek trains. **Hellenic Railways Organization** (**OSE;** ☎1110; www.osenet.gr) connects Athens to major Greek cities.

BY BUS. Few buses run directly from European cities to Greece, except for chartered tour buses. Domestic bus service is extensive and fares are cheap. **KTEL** (www.ktel.org) operates most domestic buses; check with an official source about scheduled departures, as posted schedules are often outdated.

BY FERRY. Boats travel from Bari, ITA, to Corfu, Durres, Igoumenitsa, Patras, and Sami and from Ancona, ITA, to Corfu, Igoumenitsa, and Patras. Ferries also run from Greece to various points on the Turkish coast. There is frequent ferry service to the Greek islands, but schedules are irregular and incorrect info is common. Check schedules at the tourist office, the port police, or at www.ferries.gr. Make reservations and arrive at least 1hr. before your departure time. In addition to conventional service, **Hellenic Seaways** (☎21041 99 000; www.hellenicseaways.gr) provides high-speed vessels between the islands at twice the cost and speed of ferries. Student and children receive reduced fares; travelers buying tickets up to 15 days before intended departure date receive a 15% **Early Booking Discount** on ferries leaving Tuesday through Thursday.

BY CAR AND MOPED. You must be 18 to drive in Greece, and 21 to rent a car; some agencies require renters to be at least 23 or 25. Rental agencies may quote low daily rates that exclude the 18% tax and **collision damage waiver (CDW)** insurance. Foreign drivers must have an **International Driving Permit** and an **International Insurance Certificate.** The **Automobile and Touring Club of Greece (ELPA),** Messogion 395, Athens, 15343, provides help and offers reciprocal membership to members of foreign auto clubs like AAA. (☎21060 68 800, 24hr. emergency roadside assistance 104, infoline 174; www.elpa.gr.) **Mopeds,** while great for exploring, are extremely dangerous—wear a helmet.

KEEPING IN TOUCH

PHONE CODES	**Country code:** 30. **International dialing prefix:** 00. For more info on how to place international calls, see **Inside Back Cover.**

EMAIL AND THE INTERNET. The availability of the Internet in Greece is rapidly expanding. In all big cities, most small cities and large towns, and on most islands, you'll be able to find Internet cafes. Expect to pay €2-6 per hr.

TELEPHONE. Whenever possible use a calling card for international phone calls, as long-distance rates for national phone services are often very high. **Pay phones** in Greece use prepaid **phone cards,** sold at *peripteros* (streetside kiosks) and OTE offices. **Mobile phones** are an increasingly popular, economical option. Major mobile carriers include Q-Telecom, Telestet, and Vodaphone. Direct-dial access numbers for calling out of Greece include: **AT&T Direct** (☎00 800 1311); **British Telecom** (☎00 800 4411); **Canada Direct** (☎00 800 1611); **Sprint** (☎00 800 1411); **NTL** (☎00 800 4422); For more info on calling from Europe, see p. 21.

MAIL. Airmail is the best way to send mail home from Greece. To send a letter (up to 20g) anywhere from Greece costs €0.65. To receive mail in Greece, have it delivered **Poste Restante.** Mail will go to the main post office unless you specify a subsidiary by street address. Address mail to be held as follows: First name LAST NAME, Town Post Office, Island, Greece, Postal Code, POSTE RESTANTE. Bring a passport to pick up your mail; there may be a small fee.

ACCOMMODATIONS AND CAMPING

GREECE	❶	❷	❸	❹	❺
ACCOMMODATIONS	under €22	€22-33	€34-45	€46-60	over €70

Local tourist offices usually have lists of inexpensive accommodations. A **hostel** bed averages €15-30. Those not endorsed by HI are usually still safe and reputable. In many areas, **domatia** are a good option; locals offering cheap lodging may approach you as you enter town, a common practice that is illegal. It's usually a better bet to go to an official tourist office. Prices vary; expect to pay €15-35 for a single and €25-45 for a double. Always see the room and negotiate with *domatia* owners before settling on a price; never pay more than you would to stay in a hotel. If in doubt, ask the tourist police; they may set you up with a room and conduct the negotiations themselves. **Hotel** prices are regulated, but proprietors may push you to take the most expensive room. Budget hotels start at €20 for singles and €30 for doubles. Check your bill carefully, and threaten to contact the tourist police if you think you're being cheated. Greece has plenty of official **campgrounds,** which cost €2-3 per tent plus €4-8 per person. Though common in summer, camping on public beaches—sometimes illegal—may not be the safest option.

FOOD AND DRINK

GREECE	❶	❷	❸	❹	❺
FOOD	under €6	€6-12	€13-19	€19-25	over €25

Penny-pinching carnivores will thank Zeus for lamb, chicken, or pork **souvlaki,** stuffed into a pita to make **gyros** (YEE-ros). **Vegetarians** can also find cheap eateries; options include *horiatiki* (Greek salad), and savory pastries like *tiropita* (cheese pie) and *spanakopita* (spinach and feta pie). Frothy iced coffee milkshakes take the edge off the summer heat. **Ouzo** (a powerful licorice-flavored spirit) is served with *mezedes* (snacks of octopus, cheese, and sausage). Breakfast, served only in the early morning, is generally very simple: a piece of toast with *marmelada* or a pastry. Lunch, a hearty and leisurely meal, can begin as early as noon but is more likely eaten sometime between 2 and 5pm. Dinner is a drawn-out, relaxed affair served late. Greek restaurants are known as *tavernas* or *estiatorios;* a grill is a *psistaria.*

BEYOND TOURISM

Doing more than just sightseeing on a trip to Greece is as easy (and as challenging) as offering some of one's own time. Though considered wealthy by international standards, Greece has an abundance of aid organizations to combat the nation's very real problems. For more info on opportunities across Europe, see **Beyond Tourism,** p. 45.

American School of Classical Studies at Athens (ASCSA), 54 Souidias St., GR-106 76 Athens (☎21072 36 313; www.ascsa.edu.gr). Provides study-abroad opportunities in Greece for students interested in archaeology and the classics. US$2950-17,000 including tuition, room, and partial board.

Archelon Sea Turtle Protection Society, Solomou 57, 10432 Athens (☎/fax 21052 31 342; www.archelon.gr). Non profit group devoted to studying and protecting sea turtles on the beaches of Zakynthos, Crete, and the Peloponnese. Opportunities for seasonal field work and year-round work at the rehabilitation center. €100 participation fee.

Conservation Volunteers Greece, Veranzerou 15, 10677 Athens (☎21038 25 506; www.cvgpeep.gr; phones answered M-F 9am-2pm). Offers 2- to 3-week summer programs in environmental and cultural conservation, as well as courses in leadership and first aid. Participants must be 19-29 and speak English. €120 participation fee.

GREECE

ATHENS (Αθήνα) ☎210

An illustrious past invigorates Athens. The ghosts of antiquity peer down from its hilltops, instilling residents with a sense of the city's historic importance. Home to 3.7 million people—a third of Greece's population—Athens is daring and modern; its patriotic citizens pushed their capital into the 21st century with massive clean-up and building projects before the 2004 Olympic Games. International menus, hipster bars, and large warehouse performance spaces crowd Byzantine churches, traditional *tavernas*, and toppled columns.

TRANSPORTATION

Flights: Eleftherios Venizelou (ATH; ☎210 353 0000; www.aia.gr). Greece's international airport operates as one massive, yet navigable terminal. Arrivals are on the ground floor, departures on the 2nd. The **Suburban Rail** services the airport from the city center in 30min. 4 bus lines run to Athens, Piraeus, and Rafina. Budget airlines **SkyEurope** (www.skyeurope.com) and **Wizz Air** (www.wizzair.com) fly to Athens.

Ferries: Most leave from the **Piraeus** port. Ferry schedule changes daily; check ahead at the tourist office (☎1440; www.openseas.gr or www.ferries.gr). Ferries sail directly to all major Greek **islands** except for the Sporades and Ionians. To Crete: **Hania** (11hr., €30-33); **Heraklion** (11hr., €27-35); **Rethymno** (11hr., €21-29). Others to: **Ios** (7hr., €25.50-32); **Kos** (13hr., €36-45.50); **Lesvos** (12hr., €26); **Mykonos** (6hr., €21); **Naxos** (6hr., €24-30); **Paros** (5hr., €25-29); **Patmos** (8hr., €33-34); **Rhodes** (14hr., €43-53); **Santorini** (9hr., €27-34). International ferries head to **Turkey** (€30).

Trains: Hellenic Railways (OSE), Sina 6 (☎1110 362 7947; www.ose.gr). **Larisis Train Station** (☎210 529 8837) serves northern Greece. Ticket office open daily 5am-midnight. Trolley #1 from El. Venizelou in Pl. Syndagma (5 per hr., €1) or the Metro to Larisis Station. Trains go to **Thessaloniki** (7hr., 5 per day, €15; express 4¼hr., 2 per day, €48).

Buses: Terminal A, Kifissou 100 (☎210 512 4910). Take blue bus #051 from the corner of Zinonos and Menandrou near Pl. Omonia (4 per hr. from 5am-midnight, €0.80). Buses to: **Corfu** (9½hr., 2-3 per day, €39.50); **Corinth** (1½hr., 1 per hr., €7.50); **Patras** (3hr., 2 per hr., €17; express 2hr., 9 per day); **Thessaloniki** (6hr., 12-13 per day, €35). **Terminal B,** Liossion

260 (☎210 831 7153). Take blue bus #024 from Amalias, outside the National Gardens (45min., 3 per hr. 5:10am-11:40pm, €0.80). Buses to **Delphi** (3hr., 6 per day, €13.60).

THE WHEELS ON THE BUS GO... Getting to and from Athens by bus can be incredibly confusing as there are two intercity bus terminals (Terminal A and Terminal B) and yet another terminal (Mavromateon) serving destinations outside of Athens but within the prefecture of Attica (including Cape Sounion). The larger Terminal A is more difficult to reach than Terminal B, as the bus to the terminal departs from a random intersection in Omonia, but taking a local bus to the bus station is much cheaper than taking a taxi and is still the best bet.

Public Transportation: Yellow **KTEL** buses travel all around Attica from orange bus stops throughout the city. Other buses in Athens and its suburbs are blue and designated by 3-digit numbers. Electrical antennae distinguish **trolleys** from buses. Public transport tickets (valid for bus, trolley, tram, and metro connections) are available at blue **OASA (Athens Urban Transport Organization)** booths and some kiosks, and may be used for up to 90min. after validation. Travelers without validated tickets face a fine of 60 times the ticket price. A standard public transport ticket costs €0.80. 24hr. tickets (€3) and 7-day tickets (€10) are also available. The modern Athens **metro** consists of 3 lines running from 5:30am to midnight. The green **M1** line runs from northern Kifissia to Piraeus, the red **M2** from Ag. Antonios to Ag. Dimitrios, the blue **M3** from Egaleo to the airport via Doukissis Plakentias. Buy tickets (€0.70 for trips in 1-2 successive zones of M1, €0.80 for trips in all 3 zones of M1 and for combined trips between M1, M2, and M3) in any station.

Taxis: Ikaros (☎210 515 2800); **Hermes** (☎210 411 5200); **Kosmos** (☎1300). Base fare €1; €0.34 per km, midnight-5am €0.65 per km. €3.20 surcharge from airport, €0.86 surcharge for trips from port, bus, and railway terminals, plus €0.32 for each piece of luggage over 10kg. Minimum fare €2.65. Call for pickup (€1.60-2.65 extra).

ORIENTATION AND PRACTICAL INFORMATION

Most travelers hang around the **Acropolis** and **Agoras,** while guide-bearing foreigners flood central **Plaka,** Athens's old town. Marked by the square and flea market, **Monastiraki** (Little Monastery) is a hectic, exciting neighborhood where crowded *tavernas* and Psiri's trendy bars keep pedestrian traffic flowing late into the night. In the heart of Athens, **Syntagma Square** is the transportation center. On the opposite side of Stadiou, bustling **Omonia Square** bursts with ethnic and ideological diversity. A short walk north on **Em. Benaki** leads to the hip, student-filled neighborhood of **Exarhia,** where a young, alternative vibe enlivens graffiti-painted streets lined with relaxed cafes, independent bookshops, and record stores. The **Larisis** train station is to the northwest of town, while most museums are on **Vas Sofias** to the east. The fashionable neighborhood of **Kolonaki** attracts a posh Athenian crowd and is situated below Lycavittos Hill. Take the M1 (green line) south to its end or bus #040 from Filellinon and Mitropoleos, in Syntagma (4 per hr.), to reach Athens's port city, **Piraeus.** The metro also travels east to several beaches. If you get lost, just look for Syntagma or the Acropolis, Athens's clearest reference points.

Tourist Office: Information Office, Amalias 26 (☎210 331 0392 or 210 331 0716; www.gnto.gr). Has tons of useful literature, up-to-date bus schedules, and the most detailed city map. Open M-F 9am-7pm, Sa-Su 10am-4pm.

Budget Travel: STA Travel, Voulis 43 (☎210 321 1188). Open M-F 9am-5pm, Sa 10am-2pm. **Consolas Travel,** Eolou 100 (☎210 321 9228), on the 9th fl. above the post office. Open M and Sa 9am-2pm, Tu-F 9am-5pm.

Bank: National Bank, Karageorgi Servias 2 (☎210 334 0500), in Pl. Syntagma. Open M-Th 8am-2:30pm, F 8am-2pm; open for **currency exchange** M-F 3:30-5pm, Sa

9am-2pm, Su 9am-1pm. Commission about 5%. 24hr. currency exchange at the airport, but commissions there are usually exorbitant.

Emergencies: Poison control ☎210 779 3777. **AIDS Help Line** ☎210 722 2222.

Tourist Police: Dimitrakopoulou 77 (☎171). English spoken. Open 24hr.

Pharmacies: Check *Athens News* for a current list of 24hr. pharmacies.

Hospitals: Duty hospitals and **clinics** ☎1434. Free emergency health care for tourists. Geniko Kratiko; **Public General Hospital,** Mesogion 154 (☎210 777 8901). Near Kolonaki is the public hospital **Evangelismos,** Ypsilantou 45-47 (☎210 720 1000).

Internet: Athens has many Internet cafes. Expect to pay around €3 per hr. **Bits and Bytes,** Kapnikareas 19 (☎210 325 31; www.bnb.gr), in Plaka. 9am-midnight €5 per hr., midnight-9am €3 per hr. Open 24hr. **2nd location** in Exarhia, Akadamias 78 (☎210 381 3830). **C@FE4U,** Ippokratous 44 (☎210 361 1981; www.cafe4u.gr). Open 24hr. Free **city Wi-Fi** at Syntagma Sq., Thesseion Sq., Kotzia Sq., and across the Evangelismos Metro Station at the National Hellenic Research Foundation (SSID: athenswifi).

Post Office: Syntagma (☎210 323 7573, 210 331 9501), on the corner of Mitropoleos. Open M-F 7:30am-8pm, Sa 7:30am-2pm, Su 9am-1:30pm. **Postal Code:** 10300.

ACCOMMODATIONS

Many budget accommodations exist in Athens, but prices generally increase toward the city center at Pl. Syntagma.The reception desk at **Youth Hostel #5** (otherwise known as Pagration Youth Hostel), Damareos 75 in Pagrati, acts as the Athens branch of the **Greek Youth Hostel Association,** which has 10 other affiliated hostels in Thessaloniki, Patra, and Olympia as well as on Santorini and Crete that share common (and very reasonable) rates. (☎21075 19 530. Open M-F 9am-3pm.) The **Hellenic Chamber of Hotels,** Stadiou 24, provides info and reservations for hotels throughout Greece. (☎21033 10 022; www.grhotels.gr. Open May-Nov. M-F 8:30am-1:30pm.)

Athens Backpackers, Makri 12 (☎21092 24 044; www.backpackers.gr). Ⓜ Acropolis; walk down Ath. Diakou away from the Acropolis and take the 1st left onto Makri. While its proximity to the city's major sights is a huge plus, the real draw here is the spectacular view of the Acropolis from the rooftop, where cold beer (€1.50), cheap cocktails (€3), and karaoke flow nightly during summer. Plenty of space between bunks in tidy, spacious rooms. Breakfast, luggage storage, A/C, and the friendly Aussies at the front desk sweeten the deal. Some rooms have bath and patio. Also offers weekend daytrips to sites near Athens, complete with tours and lunch (€40-50). Laundry €5. Free Wi-Fi. 6- or 8-bed dorms €18-25. AmEx/MC/V. ❶

Hotel Acropolis House, 6-8 Kodrou (☎21032 22 344 or 26 241; www.acropolishouse.gr), across from Adonis Hotel. This 19th-century mansion-turned-guesthouse has been run by the same family since 1965. While the rooms are a tad small and very basic—bed, desk, TV, and not much else—the high ceilings, Neoclassical architectural detailing, and floor-to-ceiling art collection add charm. A/C. Some rooms have bath, others have a bathroom on the hall. Breakfast included. Doubles €60-79. Reservations recommended in the high season. ❹

Hotel Orion, Em. Benaki 105 (☎21033 02 387; www.orion-dryades.com). Walk up Em. Benaki toward the Strefi Hill, or take bus #230 from Pl. Syntagma. Orion's rooms might charitably be described as "cozy," but its array of amenities and funky 70s decor more than make up for the small size. All rooms have A/C and TVs. Exquisite rooftop canopy, kitchen, and killer view of the Acropolis. Breakfast €6, but the bakery around the corner has great pastries for less. Internet €1 per day. Singles €30; doubles with private baths €40-45. MC/V. ❷

GREECE

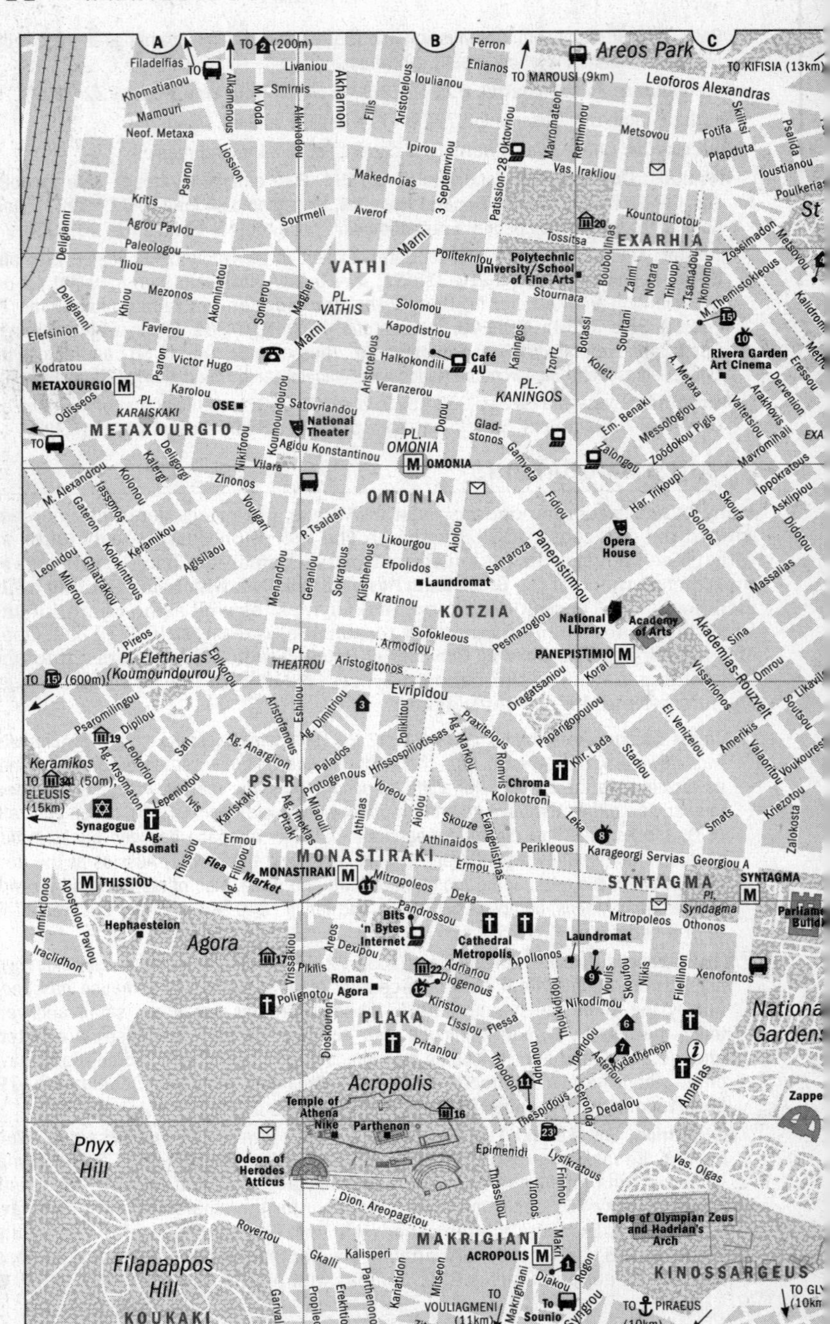
A
B
C
TO 2 (200m)
Areos Park
TO MAROUSI (9km)
TO KIFISIA (13km)
Leoforos Alexandras
Filadelfias
Khomatianou
Mamouri
Neof. Metaxa
Livaniou
Smirnis
Alkamenous
M. Voda
Liossion
Akharnon
Alkiviadou
Fillis
Aristotelous
Ioulianou
Ferron
Enianos
Patission-28 Oktovriou
Mavromateon
Rethimnou
Metsovou
Fotifa
Skilitsi
Psalida
Plapduta
Ioustianou
Poulkeria
Ipirou
Makednoias
Vas. Irakliou
3 Septemvriou
Psaron
Kritis
Agrou Pavlou
Paleologou
Sourmeli
Averof
Kountouriotou
Tossitsa
EXARHIA
20
Delligianni
Iliou
Marni
VATHI
Politekniou
Polytechnic University/School of Fine Arts
Stournara
Bouboulinas
Zaimi
Notara
Trikoupi
Tsamadou
Ikonomou
Zossimadon
M. Themistokleous
15
10
Rivera Garden Art Cinema
Mezonos
Khiou
Akominatou
Sonierou
Magher
PL. VATHIS
Solomou
Kapodistriou
Elefsinion
Favierou
Halkokondili
Café 4U
Kaningos
Tzortz
Botassi
Koleti
Soultani
A. Metaxa
Eressou
Dervenion
Kodratou
Victor Hugo
Karolou
Veranzerou
PL. KANINGOS
Arakhovis
Valtetsiou
METAXOURGIO
PL. KARAISKAKI
Odisseos
OSE
Koumoundourou
Satovriandou
National Theater
Glad-stonos
Em. Benaki
Messologiou
Zoodokou Pigis
Mavromihali
EXA
TO
METAXOURGIO
Nikiforou
Agiou Konstantinou
Vilara
PL. OMONIA
OMONIA
Dorou
Gamveta
Zalongou
Ippokratous
Deligiorgi
Kategi
Kolonou
M. Alexandrou
Iassonos
Gateron
Zinonos
OMONIA
Fidiou
Har. Trikoupi
Skoufa
Asklipiou
Leonidou
Kolokinthous
Keramikou
Agisilaou
Voulgari
P. Tsaldari
Likourgou
Aiolou
Santaroza
Panepistimiou
Opera House
Solonos
Didotou
Milerou
Ghiatrakou
Menandrou
Geraniou
Sokratous
Klisthenous
Efpolidos
Laundromat
Massalias
Kratinou
KOTZIA
Pesmazoglou
National Library
Academy of Arts
Akademias-Rouzvelt
Sina
Pireos
Pl. Eleftherias (Koumoundourou)
Epikorou
Sofokleous
Armodiou
PL. THEATROU
Aristogitonos
PANEPISTIMIO
Omirou
TO 15 (600m)
Evripidou
Dragatsaniou
Korai
Vissarionos
Likavitou
Soutsou
Psaromilingou
Dipliou
Aristofanous
Eshilou
Ag. Dimitriou
3
Polikitou
Praxitelous
Papanigopoulou
El. Venizelou
Amerikis
Valaoritou
Voukourestiou
19
Leokoriou
Sari
Ag. Anargiron
Hrissospiliotissas
Ag. Markou
Romvis
Khr. Lada
Stadiou
Keramikos
Ag. Asomaton
Palados
TO ELEUSIS (15km)
(50m)
PSIRI
Protogenous
Lepeniotou
Ivis
Kariskaki
Ag. Pitaki
Ag. Theklas
Miaouli
Athinas
Voreou
Aiolou
Chroma
Kolokotroni
Evangelistrias
Leka
Kriezotou
Smats
Zalokosta
Synagogue
Ag. Assomati
Ermou
Skouze
Athinaidos
Perikleous
8
Karageorgi Servias
Georgiou A
MONASTIRAKI
Thissiou
Flea Market
Ag. Filipou
MONASTIRAKI
Mitropoleos
11
Ermou
SYNTAGMA
SYNTAGMA
Pl. Syndagma
Parliament Building
THISSIOU
Amfiktionos
Apostolou Pavlou
Deka
Pandrossou
Bits 'n Bytes Internet
Cathedral Metropolis
Mitropoleos
Othonos
Hephaesteion
Agora
Iraclidhon
Areos
Dexipou
Laundromat
Apollonos
Vrissakiou
17
Pikilis
22
Adrianou
Diogenous
Xenofontos
Roman Agora
12
9
Voulis
Skoufou
Nikis
Filellinon
Polignotou
Kiristou
Nikodimou
National Gardens
PLAKA
Lissiou
Flessa
6
Dioskouron
Pritaniou
Tripodon
Adrianou
Thoukididou
Ipeiridou
7
Asteriou
Kydatheneon
Amalias
Acropolis
Thespidous
Geronda
Dedalou
Zappe
Temple of Athena Nike
16
Parthenon
23
Pnyx Hill
Epimenidi
Odeon of Herodes Atticus
Lysikratous
Vas. Olgas
Thrasillou
Vironos
Frinhou
Dion. Areopagitou
Temple of Olympian Zeus and Hadrian's Arch
Rovertou
MAKRIGIANI
Kalisperi
Gkalli
ACROPOLIS
Makri
1
Diakou
Rogon
KINOSSARGEUS
Filapappos Hill
Karatidon
Mitseon
Parthenonos
Erekhtiou
Propileon
Garivaldi
TO VOULIAGMENI (11km)
Makrighiani
To Sounio
Syngrou
TO PIRAEUS (10km)
TO GLY (10km)
KOUKAKI
Zitrou

thens
ACCOMMODATIONS
ens Backpackers, 1 B6
stel Aphrodite (HI), 2 A1
tel Cecil, 3 B4
tel Orion, 4 C2
gration Athens outh Hostel, 5 F6
aedra Hotel, 6 C5
dent and raveller's Inn, 7 C5
FOOD
Chroma Chroma, 8 C4
Noodle Bar, 9 C5
O Barba Giannis, 10 C2
Thanasis, 11 B4
NIGHTLIFE
Bretto's, 12 B6
The Daily, 13 E3
Hoxton, 14 A3
Wunderbar, 15 C2
MUSEUMS
New Acropolis Museum, 16 B5
Agora Museum, 17 A5
Byzantine & Christian Museum, 18 D4
Benaki Museum of Islamic Art, 19 A4
National Archaeolgical Museum, 20 C1
Oberlaender Museum, 21 A4
Popular Musical Instruments Museum, 22 B5
D
E
F
1
2
3
4
5
6
NEAPOLI
AMBELOKIPI
KOLONAKI
PANGRATI
Lycavittos Hill
Alsos Syngrou
Lycavittos Theater
Chapel of St. George
St. Andrew's
Lycavittos Funicular
Evangelismos Hospital
EVANGELISMOS
MEGARO MOUSSIKIS
PL. DEXAMENI
PL. KOLONAKI
PL. RIGILIS
TRUMAN SQ.
Athens Conservatory
Royal Palace
Panathenaic Stadium
PL. STADIOU
PL. PLASTIRA
Ardittos
Pangratiou Park
Veropoulos
Leoforos Alexandras
Vasilisis Sofias
Vasileos Konstantinou
Vasileos Alexandrou
TO RAFINA (20km)
TO NATIONAL CEMETERY (150m)
TO (14km), LAVRIO (30km)
TO 5 (200m)
300 yards
300 meters

GREECE

Pagration Athens Youth Hostel, Damareos 75 (☎21075 19 530). From Omonia or Pl. Syndagma, take trolley #2 or 11 to Filolaou (past Imittou) or walk through the National Garden, down Eratosthenous, then 3 blocks down Efthidiou to Frinis and down Frinis until you come to Damareos; it's on your right. There's no sign for this cheery, family-owned hostel—just the number 75 and a green door. The charming common spaces and ultra-helpful staff make this out-of-the-way hostel worth the 20-25min. walk to the city center. TV lounge and full kitchen. Hot showers €0.50. Laundry €4 to wash, with dryer €7; or line-dry on the roof for free. Quiet hours 2:30-5pm and 11pm-7am. High-season dorms €12. When the hostel fills up, the owner opens the roof (€10 per person) to travelers; bring a sleeping bag. Cash only. ❶

FOOD

Athens offers a mix of fast-food stands, open-air cafes, side-street *tavernas*, and upscale restaurants. On the streets, vendors sell dried fruits and nuts or fresh coconut (€1-2), and you can find *spanakopita* (cheese and spinach feta pies) at any local bakery (€1.50-2). Diners on a budget can choose from the many *souvlaki* spots in **Monastiraki,** at the end of **Mitropoleos.** Places in **Plaka** tend to advertise "authentic Greek for tourists." If you really want to eat like a local, head to the simple *tavernas* uphill on Em. Benaki in Exarhia.

GREECE

O Barba Giannis,Em. Benaki 94 (☎21038 24 138). From Exarchia, take Metaxa to Benaki and walk 3 blocks toward the Strefi Hill; it's the yellow building on the corner with tall green doors. "Uncle John's" is informal, and that's how the locals like it—at 3pm, when other cafes sit empty, Giannis is bustling. The place has a French feel, but the food is pure Greek. So is the staff: only Tony speaks English. Stewed veal with pasta €7. Open M-Sa noon-1:30am. Cash only. ❷

Matsoukas, Karageorgi Servias 3 (☎21032 52 054). Shelves packed floor to ceiling with delicious sugary treats. Dried fruit, chocolate, cookies, and colorful marzipan abound. Try a chunk of nougat (€12 per kilo) or a ball of marzipan rolled in pistachios (€15 per kilo). Ouzo and *metaxa* €9-15. Open daily 8am-midnight. MC/V.❶

Taverna Platanos, Diogenous 4 (☎21032 20 666), near the Popular Musical Instruments Museum and Roman Agora. An oasis of cool and quiet minutes away from Plaka's most crowded streets. Fresh, traditional Greek fare. Stuffed grape leaves, grilled dishes, and foods cooked with ample amounts of olive oil, as well as a selection of fruit, cheese, and a few desserts. Enjoy it on the outdoor patio, or inside the cozy *taverna.* Spinach pie €3.80. Greek salad €6.30. Moussaka €7.40. Open M-Sa noon-4:30pm and 7:30pm-midnight, Su noon-4:30pm. Cash only. ❷

Stamatopoulos, Lissiou 26 (☎21032 28 722). Walking north on Adrianou, turn left at Eat at Milton's. Family-owned since 1882, this popular restaurant tucked in a corner just off 1 of Plaka's busiest streets has a bright outdoor terrace, lively Greek music, and dancing every night. Grilled *haloumi* cheese with tomatoes €5. Veal in a clay pot with white sauce €10. Open M and W-Su 7pm-3am. Cash only. ❷

Cook-cou Food, Themistokleous 66 (☎21038 31 955). This cafe's zebra-print booths and pulsing techno-pop might feel out of place in other neighborhoods, but in Exarhia it fits right in. The kitchen fashions typical Greek ingredients into creative treasures, such as lentils with mango (€5.50) and chicken breast stuffed with *manouri* cheese (€7). The menu changes daily, but the house wine (€1 per glass) is always a steal. Vegetarian entrees €4.50-€6. Meat entrees €6.80-€7.50. Open in summer M-Sa 7am-7pm, in winter M-Sa 1pm-1am. Cash only. ❷

Derlicious, Tsakalof 14 (☎21036 30 284), tucked between boutiques on the southern-most block of Tsakalof. The sign is written in Greek letters, but you'll know it by the open coals just behind the counter. Such low-priced fare is rare in Kolonaki, and although the staff might be brisk, the cheap and "derlicious" food is worth every penny. Try the *flaouto* (big tortilla) with chicken (€3.22). Open M-W and Su 1pm-4am, Th 1pm-5am, F-Sa 1pm-6am. Cash only. ❶

Taverna Kiouri, Filikis Eterias 4 (☎21036 14 033). Look for it below street level. A bastion of homespun simplicity in slick Pl. Kolonaki, Kiouri sells traditional Greek food for modest prices. Try meatballs with egg and lemon sauce (€8) or daily specials like sardines cooked with tomatoes and vegetables (€8). No matter what you choose, you'll be taken care of by the welcoming staff. M-Sa 8am-10pm. Cash only. ❷

Cucina Povera, Eforionos 13 (☎21075 66 008; www.cucinapovera.gr). Walk east from the Panathenaic Stadium (away from the Acropolis) on Vas. Konstandinou, then turn right on Eratosthenous and left onto Eforionos. Cucina Povera whips up elegant dishes from simple ingredients, such as *aubergine millefeuille* with creamy cheese (€8.50) and stuffed rooster with vegetables and Gruyère (€12.50). The menu changes daily, but the house burger stuffed with olives, *metsovone* cheese, and potatoes is always on the menu for €12. Open M-Sa noon-3pm and 8-11pm, Su noon-3pm. Cash only. ❷

SIGHTS

ACROPOLIS

The Acropolis has stood over the heart of Athens since the fifth century BC. Although each Greek city-state had an *acropolis* (high point), the buildings atop Athens's peak outshine their imitators and continue to awe visitors. Visit as early or as late in the day as possible to avoid large crowds and the broiling midday sun. *(Enter on Dionissiou Areopagitou or Theorias. ☎210 321 0219. Open daily in summer 8am-7pm; in winter 8am-2:30pm. Admission includes access to the Acropolis, the Agora, the Roman Agora, the Temple of Olympian Zeus, Keramikos, and the Theater of Dionysos, within a 4-day period; purchase tickets at any of the sights. €12, students and EU seniors over 65 €6, under 19 free. Cash only.)*

PARTHENON. The **Temple of Athena Parthenos** (Athena the Virgin), commonly known as the Parthenon, watches over Athens. Ancient Athenians saw their city as the capital of civilization; the **metopes** (scenes in the spaces above the columns) on the sides of the temple celebrate Athens's rise. The architect Iktinos successfully integrated the Golden Mean, about a four-to-nine ratio, in every aspect of the temple.

NEW ACROPOLIS MUSEUM. Recently completed after a protracted €130 million construction process, the New Acropolis Museum, 300m southeast of the Acropolis at 2-4 Makriyianni, houses a superb collection of statues, including five of the original **Caryatids** that supported the southern side of the Erechtheion. The carvings of a lion devouring a bull and of a wrestling match between Herakles and a sea monster display the ancient mastery of anatomical and emotional detail. Notice the empty space where room has been left for the British to return the missing Elgin Marbles. *(☎210 924 1043; www.newacropolismuseum.gr. Visitors can tour the ground floor 10am-noon. Expected to open early 2009.)*

TEMPLE OF ATHENA NIKE. Currently undergoing renovation, this tiny temple was first raised during the Peace of Nikias (421-415 BC), a respite from the Peloponnesian War. Ringed by eight miniature Ionic columns, it housed a winged statue of Nike, the goddess of victory. Athenians, afraid Nike might abandon them, clipped the statue's wings. The remains of the 5m thick **Cyclopean wall** that once circled the Acropolis now lie below the temple.

ERECHTHEION. Completed in 406 BC, just before Sparta defeated Athens in the Peloponnesian War, the Erechtheion lies to the left of the Parthenon, supported by copies of the famous Caryatids in the museum. The building is named after a snake-bodied hero, whom Poseidon speared during a dispute. When Poseidon

GREECE

struck a truce with Athena, he was allowed to share her temple—the eastern half is devoted to the goddess of wisdom and the western part to the god of the sea.

OTHER SIGHTS

NATIONAL ARCHAEOLOGICAL MUSEUM. Almost every artifact in this collection is a masterpiece. The museum's highlights include the **Mask of Agamemnon,** in fact excavated from the tomb of a king who lived at least three centuries before Agamemnon, as well as the colorful 16th-century BC "Spring Fresco," from the Akrotiri settlement on Santorini (Thira), which depicts swallows floating above undulating red lilies. *(Patission 44. Take trolley #2, 4, 5, 9, 11, 15, or 18 across from the National Gardens in Syntagma, or trolley #3 or 13 from the north side of Vas. Sofias. Metro stop Victoria on the green line (M1). ☎210 821 7717. Open M 1-7:30pm, Tu-Su 8am-7:30pm. €7, students and EU seniors €3, EU students and under 19 free.)*

BENAKI MUSEUM OF ISLAMIC ART. Built on the ruins of ancient Athenian fortifications, the building's glass windows, marble staircases, and white walls showcase a collection of brilliant tiles, metalwork, and tapestries documenting the history of the Islamic world until the 19th-century. Its exhibits include an inlaid marble reception room brought from a 17th-century Cairo mansion and pottery with Kufic inscriptions. *(Ag. Asomaton 22 & Dipilou, in Psiri. M: Thisso. ☎210 325 1311; www.benaki.gr. Open Tu and Th-Su 9am-3pm, W 9am-9pm. €5, students free. W free.)*

AGORA. The Agora served as Athens's marketplace, administrative center, and focus of daily life from the sixth century BC to the AD sixth century. Many of Athenian democracy's greatest debates were held here; Socrates, Aristotle, Demosthenes, Xenophon, and St. Paul all lectured in the Agora. The 415 BC **Hephaesteion,** on a hill in the Agora's northwest corner, is Greece's best-preserved Classical temple, with friezes depicting Theseus's adventures. The **Stoa of Attalos,** an ancient shopping mall, played host to informal philosophers' plentiful gatherings. Reconstructed in the 1950s, it now houses the **Agora Museum.** *(Enter the Agora off Pl. Thission, from Adrianou, or as you descend from the Acropolis. ☎210 321 0185. Agora open daily 8am-7:30pm. Museum open Tu-Su 8am-7:20pm. €4, students and EU seniors €2, under 19 and with Acropolis ticket free.)*

ENTERTAINMENT AND NIGHTLIFE

The weekly *Athens News* (€1) lists cultural events, as well as news and ferry info. Summertime performances are staged in venues throughout the city, including the ancient **Odeon of Herodes Atticus,** as part of the **Athens Festival** (May-Sept.; www.greekfestival.gr). Chic Athenians head to the seaside clubs in **Glyfada,** enjoying the breezy night air. **Psiri** and **Gazi** are the bar and club districts. Get started on **Miaouli,** where young crowds gather after dark. For an alternative to bar hopping, follow the guitar-playing local teens and couples that pack **Pavlou** at night.

Psira, Miaouli 19 (☎21032 44046), half a block from Pl. Iroön. On a street full of relaxed and funky pubs, Psira is the most relaxed and funkiest. Its tiny interior is wallpapered with images of the South Seas and hung with photos of James Dean and lots of tinsel. There's room for all on the sidewalk outside. Beer €4. Mixed drinks €6. Open daily noon-4am or later. Cash only.

Brettos, Kydatheneon 41 (☎21032 32 110). Serves its own ouzos (€3-4) straight from the barrel. Offers over 90 different varieties of Greek wine. Backlit shelves of colorful glass bottles line the walls from from counter to ceiling, converting Brettos into a cathedral of liquor for its devout clientele. Red wine €2 per glass. Ouzo €2.50-€19 per bottle. Open daily 10am-midnight. Cash only.

GREECE

Wunderbar, Themistokleous 80 (☎21038 18 577), on Pl. Exarhia. A pop oasis in Exarhia's alternative desert. Late-night revelers lounge under large umbrellas outside, enjoying one of Wunderbar's signature specialty chocolate drinks (€5). Mixed drinks €8. Champagne €9. Open M-Th 9am-3am, F-Su 9am-dawn. Cash only.

Flower, Dorylaou 2 (☎21064 32 111), in Pl. Mavili. An intimate little dive, Flower offers drinks and snacks in a casual, mellow setting. Additional seating outside in the square. Shots €4. Mixed drinks €7. Open daily 7pm-late. Cash only.

THESSALONIKI Θεσσαλονίκη ☎2310

Thessaloniki (a.k.a. Salonica; pop. 364,000), the Balkans' trade center, has historically been one of the most diverse cities in Greece, and is second in size only to Athens. The city is an energetic bazaar of clothing shops and fashionable cafes, while its churches and mosques provide a material timeline of the region's restless past. Thessaloniki's current lack of tourism infrastructure and subway construction through 2012 may frustrate some travelers.

TRANSPORTATION

Flights: Macedonia Airport (**SKG;** ☎2310 985 000), 16km east of town. Take bus #78 from the KTEL station or Pl. Aristotelous (2 per hr., €0.50 at kiosks, €0.60 onboard) or taxi (€15). **Olympic Airlines,** Kountouriotou 3 (☎2310 368 311; www.olympicairlines.com; open M-F 8am-4pm), and **Aegean Airlines,** 1 Nikis, off Venizelou (☎2310 239 225; www.aegeanair.com; open M-F 8am-3pm, Sa 8am-2pm), fly to: **Athens** (1hr., 24 per day, €72); **Corfu** (1hr., 5 per week, €116); **Chania** (1hr., 9 per week, €144); **Ioannina** (35min., 4 per week, €130); **Heraklion** (1hr., 15 per week, €85); **Lesvos** (1hr., 15 per day, €96); **Rhodes** (2hr., 11 per week, €110).

Ferries: Buy tickets at **Karacharisis Travel and Shipping Agency,** Kountouriotou 8 (☎2310 513 005). Open M-F 8:30am-8:30pm, Sa 8:30am-2:30pm. Most destinations are pretty far from Thessaloniki (and more easily accessible via Athens), but if you must depart from this city, ferries leave once per week for: **Heraklion** (21-24hr., €38) via **Skiathos** (5hr., €19); **Mykonos** (13hr., €42); **Mytilini** (14 hr., €44); **Naxos** (14hr., €39) via **Syros** (12hr., €38); **Santorini** (17-18hr., €45).

Trains: To reach the **main terminal,** Monastiriou 28, (☎2310 517 517), in the western part of the city, take any bus down Egnatia (€0.50 at kiosks, €0.60 onboard). Trains go to: **Athens** (7hr., 3 per day, €15; express 5hr., 4 per day, €28); **Istanbul, TUR** (14hr., 1 per day, €25); **Skopje, MAC** (4hr., 2 per day, €11); **Sofia, BUL** (7hr., 2 per day, €16). Timetables are available online at www.ose.gr. All trains are run by OSE. It's wise to book a day in advance for trains to Athens.

Buses: Most **KTEL** buses leave from the central, dome-shaped **Macedonia Bus Station** 3km west of the city center (☎2310 595 408). Because Thessaloniki is a major transportation hub, each destination city has its own "platform" or parking spot, and its own ticketing booth. To: **Athens** (6hr., 8 per day, €24); **Corinth** (7hr., 1 per day, €37); **Ioannina** (6hr., 6 per day, €28); **Patras** (7hr., 4 per day, €33). Schedules are subject to change.

Local Transportation: Local buses run often throughout the city. Buy tickets at *periptera* (newsstands; €0.50) or on board (€0.60).

Taxis: (☎2310 551 525) run down Egnatia, Mitropoleos, and Tsimiski with stands at Ag. Sophia and the intersection of Mitropoleos and Aristotelous.

ORIENTATION AND PRACTICAL INFORMATION

Thessaloniki stretches along the Thermaic Gulf's northern shore from the iconic **White Tower** in the east to the prominent western **harbor.** Its rough grid layout makes it nearly impossible to get lost. Its most important arteries run parallel to the water. Closest to shore is **Nikis,** which goes from the harbor to the White Tower and is home to the city's main cafes. Farthest from shore is **Egnatia,** the city's busiest thoroughfare, a six-lane avenue; the Arch of Galerius stands at its intersection with D. Gounari. Inland from Egnatia are **Agios Dimitriou** and the **Old Town.** The city's main square, Aristotelous, has numerous banks, businesses, and restaurants.

Tourist Offices: EOT (☎23109 85 215), at the airport. Open M-F 8am-8pm, Sa 8am-2pm. **GNTO,** Tsimiski 136 (☎2310 2 21 100), at the eastern end of Tsimiski, north of the White Tower. Open M-F 8am-2:50pm, Sa 8:30am-2pm.

Banks: Citi Bank, Tsimiski 21 (☎23103 73 300). Open M-Th 8am-2:30pm, F 8am-2pm. **HSBC,** Tsimiski 8 (☎23102 86 044). Open M-Sa 8am-2:30pm, Su 8am-2pm. No bank accepts Bulgarian or Albanian currencies; travelers coming from these countries must head to the exchange booths at El. Venizelou's intersection with Ermou. All the above banks have **24hr. ATMS.**

Police: (☎23105 53 800). **Tourist police,** 5th fl., Dodekanisou 4 (☎23105 54 871). Free maps and brochures. Open daily 8am-10pm.

Hospital: Acepa Hospital, Kiriakidi 1 (☎23109 93 111). **Hippokratio General Hospital,** A. Papanastassiou 50 (☎23108 92 000). Some doctors speak English. On weekends and at night call ☎1434 to find which hospital has emergency care.

Internet Access: E-Global, Vas. Irakliou 40 (☎23102 52 780; www.e-global.gr), behind the American Consulate. Internet €2.20 per hr., min. €1. Open 24hr.

Post Office: Aristotelous 26 (☎2310 2 68 954), just below Egnatia. Open M-F 7:30am-8pm, Sa 7:30am-2pm, Su 9am-1:30pm. Poste Restante. **Postal Code:** 54101.

ACCOMMODATIONS

Budget options are available, but be prepared to get what you pay for. Thessaloniki's less expensive, slightly run-down hotels are along the western end of **Egnatia** between **Plateia Dimokratias** (500m east of the train station) and **Aristotelous.** Most face the chaotic road on one side and squalid back streets on the other. Hotels fill up quickly during high season, April through September.

Hotel Augustos, El. Svoronou 4 (☎23105 22 550; www.augustos.gr). Clean Rooms with wooden floors and high ceilings. Some have A/C and TVs. Free Wi-Fi. Reception 24hr. Singles €25, with bath €30; doubles €40/50; triples €50/60. Cash only. ❷

Hotel Kastoria, Egnatia 24 and L. Sofou 17 (☎23105 36 280). Most buses stop right outside at the Kolombou stop on Egnatia. The cheapest available option sports cracked linoleum floors and water-stained ceilings. Sinks in each room; communal bathrooms. Reception 24hr. Singles €20; doubles €30; triples €40. Cash only. ❶

Hotel Atlantis, Egnatia 14 (☎2310 5 40 131; www.atlantishotel.com.gr), by the Kolombou bus stop. Underwent renovations last year. Clean and stylish, the standard rooms have sinks and well-maintained shared baths. Only the pricier rooms have A/C and fridges. Hospitable English-speaking staff. Breakfast €4. Free Wi-Fi. Reception and bar 24hr. Singles €27, with bath €33; doubles €40; triples €50. AmEx/MC/V. ❷

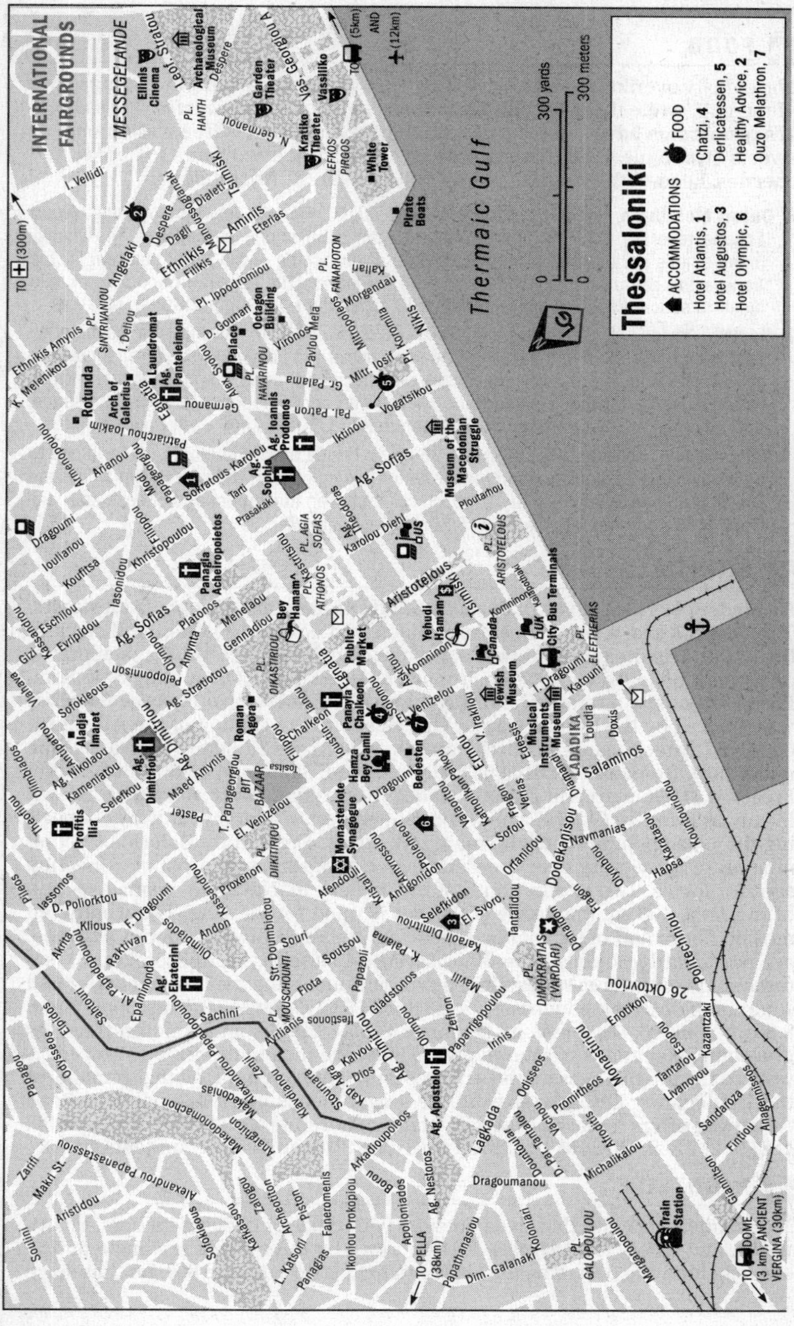

Thessaloniki

ACCOMMODATIONS

Hotel Atlantis, 1
Hotel Augustos, 3
Hotel Olympic, 6

FOOD

Chatzi, 4
Derlicatessen, 5
Healthy Advice, 2
Ouzo Melathron, 7

0 — 300 yards
0 — 300 meters

Thermaic Gulf

FOOD

The old city overflows with *tavernas* and restaurants providing sweeping views of the gulf, while the lovely **Bit Bazaar** has characteristic *ouzeries*. Thessaloniki's restaurants have a delightful custom of giving patrons free watermelon or sweets after a meal, but if you crave anything from dried fruits to apple-sized cherries, head to the bustling public **market,** right off Aristotelous.

Ouzeri Melathron, Karypi 21-34 (☎23102 75 016). From El. Venizelou, walking toward Egnatia take the 1st right after Ermou into the cobblestone passageway. The cheeky menu at this secluded gem features a little of everything and a lot of chicken. Try the Transvestite Lamb (actually chicken; €5.94) or Maria's Tits (smoked pork chop in mild mustard sauce; €6.16). Free drink with ISIC. Open daily 12:30pm-2:30am. MC/V. ❷

Healthy Advice, Al. Svolou 54 (☎23102 83 255). Already missing your ecofriendly-health-food fix? The friendly French-Canadian owner will personally serve you innovative sandwiches and salads, even concocting unique creations (€3.50-7) using the freshest ingredients. Ask for Theo's salad (blue cheese with corn, jalapenos, arugula, hot sauce, and a homemade mustard dressing). Open daily 11:30am-2am. Cash Only. ❶

Delicatessen, Kouskoura 7 (☎23102 36 367). Hands down the most popular place to eat souvlaki (€2), and for good reason: after tasting it here, you won't want to eat the Greek staple anywhere else. Try lamb, chicken, or even mushroom and cheese souvlaki. Open M-W noon-4am, Th-Sa noon-5:30am. Cash only. ❶

SIGHTS

Reminders of Thessaloniki's Byzantine and Ottoman might pervade its streets. The **Roman Agora,** a second-century odeon and covered market, still rests at the top of Aristotelous. Its lower square once held eight *caryatids*, sculptures of women believed to have been magically petrified. (Open daily 8am-8pm. Free.) Originally a temple honoring Jupiter, the **Rotunda** (now **Agios Georgios**) was erected by the Roman Caesar Galerius at the beginning of the AD fourth century. It later became a church honoring martyred Christians, then a mosque under the Ottomans. (☎2310 968 860. Open Tu-F 8am-7pm, Sa-Su 8:30am-3pm. Free.) At D. Gounari and Egnatia stands the striking **Arch of Galerius,** known locally as *Kamara* (Arch), which constituted part of a larger gateway connecting the palace complex to the main city street. Erected by Galerius to commemorate his victory over the Persians, it now serves as a popular meeting spot for locals. Two blocks south of the arch, in Pl. Navarino, a small section of the once 150 sq. km **Palace of Galerius** is open for viewing. The weathered mosaic floors and octagonal hall, believed to have housed Galerius's throne, are particularly notable. The **Archaeological Museum,** M. Andronikou 6, features some of the area's most prized artifacts, including the Derveni krater and sculptures of Greek goddesses. (☎2310 830 538. Open M 10:30am-5pm, Tu-Su 8:30am-3pm. €6, students and seniors €3, EU students and children free.) Its gruesome executions earned the **White Tower** the nickname "Bloody Tower." A walk to the top of Thessaloniki's most prominent landmark, all that remains of the 15th-century Ottoman seawall, no longer means inevitable death; instead the tower offers a view of the city and its shoreline. (Bus #3, 5, 6, 33, or 39. ☎2310 267 832. Open M 12:30pm-7pm, Tu-Su 8:30am-7pm. €2, students free.)

NIGHTLIFE

Thessaloniki is a city that lives outside, with citizens packing its bars, boardwalks, and cafes. The **Ladadika** district, a two-by-three-block rectangle of *tavernas* behind the port, was the city's red-light strip until the 80s, but has since transformed into a sea of dance clubs. The heart of the city's social life during the winter, it shuts down almost entirely in summer, when everyone moves to the open-air discos around the airport. As Thessaloniki's popular clubs change frequently, ask the locals for an update. The waterfront cafes and the **Aristotelous** promenade are always packed, as is the student-territory **Bit Bazaar,** a cobblestoned square of *ouzeries* and wine and tapas bars. For a unique experience, drink and dance to music on one of the three **pirate boats** that leave from behind the White Tower for 30min. harbor tours.

CYCLADES Κυκλάδες

MYKONOS Μύκονος ☎22890

Coveted by 18th-century pirates, Mykonos still attracts revelers and gluttons. Although Mykonos is a fundamentally chic sophisticates' playground, you don't have to break the bank to have a good time. Ambling down **Mykonos Town's** colorful alleyways at dawn or dusk, surrounded by tourist-friendly pelicans, is the cheapest, most exhilarating way to experience the island. Drinking and sunbathing are Mykonos's main forms of entertainment. While the island's beaches are nude, bathers' degree of bareness varies; in most places, people prefer to show off their designer bathing suits rather than their birthday suits. **Platis Yialos** and **Super Paradise** appeal to more brazen nudists, while **Elia** beach attracts a tamer crowd. The super-famous **Paradise** beach is so crowded with hungover Italians and overpriced sun beds that you can barely see its gorgeous water. The **Skandinavian Bar,** inland from the waterfront towards Little Venice, is a two-building party complex. (☎22890 22 669. Beer €4-6. Mixed drinks from €8. Open daily 9pm-5am.) After drinking all night, usher in a new day at **Cavo Paradiso,** on Paradise beach. Considered one of the world's top dance clubs, it hosts internationally renowned DJs and inebriated crowds. Take the bus to Paradise beach and follow the signs; it's a 10min. walk. (☎22890 27 205. Drinks from €10. Cover €25, after 2am €40; includes 1 drink. Open daily 3-11am.)

Like everything else on Mykonos, accommodations are prohibitively expensive. Camping is the best budget option. The popular **Paradise Beach Camping ❶,** 6km from Mykonos Town, has decent facilities, plenty of services, and proximity to the beach. (☎22890 22 129; www.paradisemykonos.com. Free pickup. Breakfast included. Internet €4.50 per hr. €5-10 per person, €2.50-4 per small tent, €4.50-7 per large tent; 1- to 2-person cabin €15-50. 3-person tent rental €8-18.) At **Hotel Philippi ❹,** Kalogera 25, in Mykonos Town, rooms with A/C, bath, and fridge center around a garden. (☎22890 22 294. Open Apr.-Oct. Singles €55-85; doubles €70-110; triples €84-132. AmEx/MC/V.) The colorful **Kalidonios ❸,** Dilou 1, off Kalogera, serves a range of Greek and Mediterranean dishes. (☎22890 27 606. Entrees €8-15. Open daily noon-12:30am. MC/V.) For a cheap meal, head to **Pasta Fresca ❶,** on Georgouli, near the Skandinavian Bar. Its streetside take-out window is the place to grab the best *gyros* (€2) and chicken pitas (€2) that Mykonos has to offer. (☎22890 22 563. Open daily 4pm-late.)

Ferries run from the New Port, west of town, to Naxos (3hr., 1 per week, €9.50), Paros (3hr., 1 per day, €8.40), and Piraeus (6hr., 1 per day, €26). The **tourist police** are at the ferry landing. (☎22890 22 482. Open daily 8am-9pm.) **Buses** run south from Mykonos Town to Platis Yialos and Paradise (20min., 2 per hr., €1.20-1.50) and to Elia (30min., 8 per day, €1.10). Windmills Travel, on Xenias, around the corner from South Station, has a number of **GLBT resources.** (☎2290 26 555; www.windmillstravel.com. Open daily 8am-10pm.) **Postal Code:** 84600.

GREECE

DAYTRIP FROM MYKONOS: DELOS (Δήλος). Delos was the ancient sacred center of the Cyclades. Though the archaeological site covers the whole island, its highlights can be seen in 3hr. *(Open Tu-Su 8:30am-3pm. €5, students and EU seniors €3, EU students free.)* From the dock, head straight to the **Agora of the Competaliasts;** go in the same direction and turn left on the wide **Sacred Road** to reach the **Sanctuary of Apollo,** a group of temples that date from Mycenaean times to the fourth century BC. On the right is the famous **Temple of Apollo.** Continue 50m past the end of the Sacred Road to the beautiful **Terrace of the Lions.** The museum, next to the cafeteria, contains an assortment of archaeological finds. *(Open Tu-Su 8:30am-3pm. €5, students and seniors €3.)* From the museum, a path leads to the summit of **Mount Kythnos** (112m), from which Zeus supposedly watched Apollo's birth. Temples dedicated to Egyptian gods, including the **Temple of Isis,** line the descent. **Excursion boats** (30min.; 4 per day; round-trip €13, with tour €30) leave for Delos from Mykonos Town's Old Port, past Little Venice. Buy tickets at Hellas or Blue Star Ferries on the waterfront.

SANTORINI Σαντορίνη ☎22860

Whitewashed towns sitting delicately on cliffs, black-sand beaches, and deeply scarred hills make Santorini's landscape nearly as dramatic as the volcanic cataclysm that created it. Despite the overabundance of expensive boutiques and glitzy souvenirs in touristy **Fira** (pop. 2500), the island's capital, nothing can ruin the pleasure of wandering the town's cobbled streets or browsing its craft shops. At Santorini's northern tip, the town of **Oia** (*EE-ah;* pop. 700) is the best place in Greece to watch the sunset, though its fame draws crowds hours in advance. To catch a glimpse of the sun, and not of someone taking a picture of it, walk down the hill from the village and settle alone near the many windmills and pebbled walls. To get to Oia, take a **bus** from Fira (25min., 23 per day, €1.20). **Red Beach,** and the impressive archaeological excavation site of the Minoan city **Akrotiri,** entirely preserved by lava (but currently closed for repairs), lie on Santorini's southwestern edge. Buses run to Akrotiri from Fira (30min., 15 per day, €1.60). Buses also leave Fira for the black-sand beaches of **Kamari** (20min., 32 per day, €1.20), **Perissa** (30min., 32 per day, €1.90), and **Perivolos** (20min., 21 per day, €1.90). The bus stops before Perissa in Pyrgos; from there, **hike** (2hr.) across a rocky mountain path to the ruins of **Ancient Thira.** Stop after 1hr. on a paved road at **Profitis Ilias Monastery,** for an island panorama. (Open M and W 4-5pm, Sa 4:30-8:30pm. Dress modestly. Free.)

Close to Perissa's beach, **Youth Hostel Anna ❶** has colorful rooms and loads of backpackers hanging out on its streetside veranda. (☎22860 82 182. Port pickup and drop-off included. Reception 9am-5pm and 7-10pm. Check-out 11:30am. Reserve ahead. June-Aug. 10-bed dorms €12; 4-bed dorms €15; doubles €50; triples €60. Sept.-May €6/8/22/30. MC/V.) At night, head to **Murphy's** in Fira, which claims to be Greece's first Irish pub. (Beer €5. Mixed drinks €6.50. Cover €5 after 10pm. Open Mar.-Oct. daily 11:30am-late.)

Olympic Airways (☎22860 22 493) and **Aegean Airways** (☎22860 28 500) fly from Fira's airport to Athens (50min., 4-7 per day, €85-120) and Thessaloniki (1hr., 1-2 per day, €125). **Ferries** depart from Fira to: Crete (4hr., 4 per week, €16); Ios (1hr., 1-3 per day, €7); Naxos (3hr., 1-2 per day, €16); Paros (4hr., 1-4 per day, €17); Piraeus (10hr., 2-3 per day, €33). Most ferries depart from Athinios Harbor. Frequent **buses** (25min., €1.70) with changing daily schedules connect to Fira, but most hostels and hotels offer **shuttle** service as well. Check bus and ferry schedules at any travel agency for up-to-date information, and be aware that the self-proclaimed **tourist offices** at the port are actually for-profit agencies. **Postal Codes:** 84700 (Fira); 84702 (Oia).

IRELAND

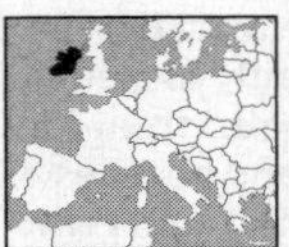

The green, rolling hills of Ireland, dotted with Celtic crosses, medieval monasteries, and Norman castles, have inspired poets and musicians from Yeats to U2. Today, the Emerald Isle's jagged coastal cliffs and untouched mountain ranges balance the country's thriving urban centers. Dublin pays tribute to the virtues of fine brews and the legacy of resisting British rule, while Galway offers a vibrant arts scene. In the past few decades, the computing and tourism industries have raised Ireland out of the economic doldrums, and current living standards are among the highest in Western Europe. Despite fearing the decline of traditional culture, the Irish language lives on in secluded areas known as the *gaeltacht*, and village pubs still echo with reels and jigs.

DISCOVER IRELAND: SUGGESTED ITINERARIES

THREE DAYS. Spend it all in **Dublin** (p. 345). Wander through **Trinity College,** admire the ancient **Book of Kells,** and sample the whiskey at the **Old Jameson Distillery.** Take a day to visit the **National Museums,** shop on **O'Connell Street** and get smart at the **James Joyce Cultural Centre.** Work your pubbing potential by night in **Temple Bar.**

ONE WEEK. After visiting the sights and pubs of **Dublin** (3 days), return to the urban scene in the cultural center of **Galway** (3 days; p. 357).

TWO IRELANDS. The Republic of Ireland is separate from Northern Ireland, which is part of the United Kingdom. See **Britain** (see p. 91) for travel information about Northern Ireland.

LIFE AND TIMES

HISTORY

EARLY CHRISTIANS AND VIKINGS (AD 450-1200). The pre-Christian inhabitants of Ireland left behind stone monuments like **Newgrange,** the Neolithic tomb outside of present-day Dublin, and adopted the language and customs of **Celtic** groups from mainland Europe. Beginning with **St. Patrick** in the 5th century AD, a series of hopeful missionaries began piecemeal Christianization of the island. **Vikings** raided the Irish coast in the 9th century and established settlements and a ruling dynasty. After the **Dal Cais** clan defeated the Vikings in the epic **Battle of Clontarf** in 1014, Ireland was divided between competing chieftains **Tiernan O'Rourke** and **Dermot MacMurrough.** MacMurrough unwisely sought the assistance of the Norman earl, **Richard de Clare,** popularly known as **Strongbow,** who arrived from England in 1169 and cut a bloody swath through Leinster (eastern Ireland). After MacMurrough's death in 1171, Strongbow married MacMurrough's daughter Aoife, poised to proclaim an independent Norman kingdom. Instead, the turncoat affirmed his loyalty to King Henry II and offered to govern Leinster on his behalf. This betrayal began English domination of Irish land.

FEUDALISM (1200-1641). The subsequent feudal period saw constant struggles between the English government, based in the area around Dublin known as the Pale, and the lords in other parts of the island who increasingly adopted Irish customs. When **Henry VIII** formed the Church of England in the 16th century, the Dublin Parliament passed the **Irish Supremacy Act** of 1537, which declared Henry VIII head of the Protestant Church of Ireland and effectively made the island property of the Crown. Ulster earl **Hugh O'Neill** raised an army of thousands in open rebellion during the **Nine Years War** of the late 1590s. His forces were demolished, and the rebels fled Ireland in 1607 in what became known as the **Flight of the Earls,** leaving a power vacuum in the area.

ULSTER PLANTATION AND CROMWELL (1641-88). The English embarked on a project of dispossessing Catholics of their land and "planting" Ulster with

Protestants. The plan succeeded most notably in the province of Ulster in the north, where the **Ulster Plantation** was established. The landless Irish revolted in 1641, leading to the formation of the **Confederation of Kilkenny,** an uneasy alliance between lords of English and Irish descent who took power over two-thirds of Ireland. The Confederation entered into negotiations with England's King Charles I, but the talks ended when parliamentary forces ousted Charles in the **English Civil War** (1642-49). The new English Commonwealth's despotic leader, **Oliver Cromwell,** led his army to Ireland in 1649 to take back the island from the Confederation. Cromwell's army destroyed everything in its path, and after the bloody conquest, the majority of Irish land fell to Protestant control.

THE PROTESTANT ASCENDANCY (1688-1798). Thirty years after the English Civil War, English political disruption again resulted in Irish bloodshed. Deposed Catholic monarch **James II,** driven from England by the **Glorious Revolution** of 1688, came to Ireland to gather military support. His war with **William of Orange,** the new Protestant king of England, ended with James's defeat and exile at the famous **Battle of the Boyne** in 1690. New **Penal Laws** enforced at the turn of the 18th century banned the practice of Catholicism in Ireland. The term **"Ascendancy"** was coined to describe the elite Anglicans who rose to prominence in Dublin and controlled Irish land. **Trinity College,** founded in 1592, came to be the quintessential institution of the **Ascendancy Protestants.**

UNION AND THE FAMINE (1798-1870). The 1800 **Act of Union** dissolved the Dublin Parliament, creating the United Kingdom of Great Britain and Ireland and the United Church of England and Ireland. During this time, the potato was the wonder-food of the rapidly growing Irish population. When potato blight wiped out the crop during the **Great Famine** (1845-52), an estimated one million people died and a million more emigrated. Meanwhile, in 1858 the **Irish Republican Brotherhood (IRB),** commonly known as the **Fenians,** was founded, a secret society aimed at the violent removal of the British.

CULTURAL NATIONALISM (1870-1914). In 1870, **Isaac Butt** founded the **Irish Home Rule League** to try to secure Ireland's autonomous rule. Meanwhile, various groups tried to revive a traditional Irish culture unpolluted by foreign influence. **Arthur Griffith** began the **Sinn Féin** (SHIN FAYN; translated as "ourselves alone") movement in 1905 advocating Irish abstention from British politics. Between 1910 and 1913, in opposition to this growing movement for independence, thousands of Protestants from the northern region joined a paramilitary organization named the **Ulster Volunteer Force.** Nationalists led by university professor **Eoin MacNeill** in Dublin responded by creating the **Irish Volunteers.**

EASTER RISING (1914-16). In 1914, the British Parliament passed a **Home Rule Act** granting self-government to Ireland within the United Kingdom, but implementation was delayed as Britain fought **World War I.** Fenian leaders adopted the ideology of "blood sacrifice," believing that the deaths of martyrs would generate public support for Irish independence. On Monday, April 24, more than 1000 rebels seized the Dublin General Post Office on **O'Connell St.** (p. 346) and proclaimed an independent **Irish Republic.** This launched the **Easter Rising,** six days of fighting in which 450 people were killed. The British authorities put down the insurrection and executed 15 of the ringleaders, but the event swung public opinion in favor of the rebels and the fortified anti-British movement.

INDEPENDENCE AND CIVIL WAR (1917-23). The Sinn Féin party, incorrectly linked to the Easter Rising, rose to newfound fame in Ireland and won the 1918 elections under leader **Éamon de Valera.** The Irish Volunteers reorganized under Fenian bigwig **Michael Collins** and became known as the **Irish Republican Army**

(IRA), Sinn Féin's military arm. De Valera proclaimed an Irish government and Parliament, and between 1919 and 1921 the IRA fought the guerrilla-style **War of Independence** against the British. Hurried negotiations produced the **Anglo-Irish Treaty** in 1921, which created a 26-county **Irish Free State,** an independent republic whose members were required to take an oath of allegiance to the king. Sinn Féin, the IRA, and the population were split over whether to accept the Treaty. Although it also partitioned Northern Ireland, opposition to the treaty was focused on the oath. Collins said yes; de Valera disagreed. When the representative parliament voted in favor, de Valera resigned from the presidency and party elder **Arthur Griffith** took office. In 1922, a portion of the IRA that opposed the Treaty, led by **General Rory O'Connor,** occupied the **Four Courts** in Dublin. The ensuing civil war lasted until the following year, when the pro-Treaty government emerged victorious.

THE DE VALERA ERA (1923-60). In 1927, de Valera founded his own political party, **Fianna Fáil (Soldiers of Destiny).** The party won the 1932 election, and de Valera held power for much of the next 20 years. In 1937, voters approved the **Irish Constitution.** It declared the state's name to be **Éire** and established a government with a prime minister (Taoiseach; TISH-ek), a ceremonial president, and a two-chamber parliament. Ireland stayed neutral during **World War II,** known as the **Emergency** in Ireland, though many Irish citizens identified with the Allies and approximately 50,000 volunteered in the British army. In 1948, Taoiseach **John Costello** took the British by surprise when he declared to a reporter that the Irish Free State would leave the British Commonwealth and become the free **Republic of Ireland.** The UK recognized the Republic in 1949 but retains control over Northern Ireland, a region tied to the Crown since the settlement of Protestants in the Ulster Plantation.

RECENT HISTORY (1960-2005). Ireland's post-war boom began in the early 1960s, but economic mismanagement and poor governmental policies kept it brief. In search of economic upturn, the Republic entered the European Economic Community (EEC), now the **European Union** (EU), in 1973. EEC funds were crucial in helping Ireland out of recession in the mid-80s and reducing its dependence on the UK. In 1990, the Republic broke social and political ground by electing its first female president, **Mary Robinson.** Social reform continued when the leftist **Labour Party** enjoyed success in the 1992 elections. The new Taoiseach, **Albert Reynolds,** declared that his priority was to stop violence in Northern Ireland. During the period known as **the Troubles** between the 1960s and 90s, periodic conflict broke out in Northern Ireland and the Republic between opposing paramilitary groups: the Catholic, republican IRA and the Protestant, loyalist UVF. In August 1994, Reynolds announced a cease-fire agreement between Nationalists and Unionists. In April 1998, Taoiseach **Bertie Ahern** helped to negotiate the **Good Friday Accord,** under which the political parties would share power in the Northern Ireland Assembly. The following month, in the first island-wide election since 1918, 94% of voters in the Republic and 71% in Northern Ireland supported the enactment of the accord.

While many felt that a lasting peace was finally in reach, a few controversial issues remained unresolved, such as the disbanding of the largely Protestant **Royal Ulster Constabulary (RUC).** British Prime Minister Tony Blair declared the RUC would continue to exist, but appointed **Chris Patten,** former governor of Hong Kong, to review the RUC's practices. However, all was not peaceful for long: from May to July of 1998, a series of marches and parades instigated violence and destruction in Garvaghy Road and West Belfast. In 2001, the RUC was reformed into the **Police Service of Northern Ireland.** During the elections of November 2003, Ian Paisley's Democratic Unionists and Sinn Féin outpolled more moderate parties. Despite communication issues, there is widespread hope that the joint government will lead to a lasting era of peace.

TODAY

With money coming to Ireland from the European Union, increased computer software development, and a thriving tourism industry, the Irish economy has flourished under Ahern's tenure. In the spring of 2006, Ireland had the highest per capita gross domestic product in the EU, and its educated workforce continues to lure foreign investment. The fast-growing nation was nicknamed the **Celtic Tiger,** and its powerful roar prompted the return of Irish expatriates and Irish-Americans from the US, as well as the arrival of immigrants from Eastern Europe and other parts of the world.

However, in recent times, Ireland's progress has been slowing down. Ahern resigned in May 2008 after a corruption controversy damaged his reputation. With the economy stalling, and the Celtic Tiger in hibernation, his replacement, current Taoiseach **Brian Cowen,** faces many economic and political challenges.

PEOPLE AND CULTURE

CUSTOMS AND ETIQUETTE. In Ireland, when the occasion warrants it, people form orderly lines (or queues) that are considered sacred. "Jumping the queue" will earn you disapproving stares and often verbal confrontations. Another easy way to anger the locals is to flip someone **the fingers.** Yes, fingers: the Irish flip both their middle finger and their index finger, forming a V shape. Flipping the birds is only insulting if your palm is facing inward. In addition, avoid jokes or references to leprechauns, Lucky Charms, pots of gold, and the "wee" people. Such comments will not earn you friends at the local pub.

LANGUAGE. The English language came to Ireland with the Normans in the 12th century. Since then, it has become the island's primary language, but like many things British, the Irish have molded the language to make it their own. The Irish accent, or "lilt," differs throughout the country, but is particularly thick and guttural in the southern and western counties. In Dublin and in the North, expect clearer pronunciation and a sing-song style of conversation. Northern Irish accents also bear the mark of Scottish settlement.

Because English is overwhelmingly spoken in Ireland, the average traveler is often unaware of the strong legacy of the **Irish language.** It is the official language of Ireland (declared in the constitution), as well as an official language of the EU. There are about 85,000 individuals who live in the Irish-speaking region, or **Gaeltacht** (GAYL-tacht), in the western part of Ireland. Still, many households in this region no longer speak Irish fluently, and government studies suggest that the language may become extinct within several generations.

RELIGION. Over 92% of the population of the Republic of Ireland is Catholic, and the Church has been tightly woven into everyday life. Though divorce was legalized in 1995, the Republic remains solidly anti-abortion. Public schools have mandatory religion classes and Sunday Mass is a family event. Most of the nation's Protestants belong to the Anglican Church of Ireland; small Muslim, Jewish, and Buddhist populations can be found in the cities.

LITERATURE. Irish bards (from the Irish *baird*), whose poetry told the stories of battles and kings, wrote the largest collection of European folklore. In the 17th century, wit and satire characterized the emerging modern Irish literature, especially in the biting works of **Jonathan Swift** (1667-1745). In addition to his masterpiece *Gulliver's Travels* (1726), Swift penned political essays decrying English cruelty to the Irish. While Dublin continued to breed talent over the following centuries, some gifted young writers like **Oscar Wilde** (1854-1900) headed to London to make their names. Wilde wrote his best-known play, *The Importance of Being Earnest*, in 1895. Fellow playwright **George Bernard Shaw** (1856-1950) also moved to London, where he became an active socialist and won the Nobel Prize for Literature in 1925.

Near the end of the 19th century, during the **Irish Literary Revival,** a crop of young Irish writers turned to their homeland for inspiration. The early poems of **William Butler Yeats** (1865-1939) evoked the picturesque Ireland of a mythical past, earning him worldwide fame and a Nobel Prize in 1923. Other authors, including the nation's most famous expatriate, **James Joyce** (1882-1941), found Ireland too insular to suit their literary aspirations. Though Joyce spent most of his adult life in continental Europe, he still wrote about Ireland. In his first novel, *A Portrait of the Artist as a Young Man* (1916), protagonist Stephen Dedalus's experiences reflect Joyce's own youth in Dublin. Dedalus reappears in *Ulysses*, Joyce's revolutionary novel of 1922, loosely based on Homer's *Odyssey*. **Samuel Beckett** (1906-89) wrote world-famous plays during the mid-20th century, including *Waiting for Godot* and *Endgame*, convey a darkly comic, pessimistic vision. He won the Nobel Prize in 1969 but refused to attend the ceremony because Joyce had never received the prize.

The grit of Ireland continues to provide fodder for new generations of writers. **Roddy Doyle** (1956-present) displays his trademark humor but also tackles serious themes in his works, including the *Barrytown* trilogy about family life in down-and-out Dublin and the Booker Prize-winning *Paddy Clarke Ha Ha Ha* (1993). **Frank McCourt** (1930-present) won the Pulitzer Prize in 1997 for *Angela's Ashes*, a memoir about his poverty-stricken childhood in Limerick. Not to be outdone, his brother **Malachy McCourt** (1931-present) published his own memoir, *A Monk Swimming* (1998). Dublin native **John Banville** (1945-present) has explored metaphysical themes in his award-winning novels such as *The Book of Evidence* (1989) and *The Sea* (2005). The most prominent living Irish poet, **Seamus Heaney** (1939-present), grew up in rural County Derry in Northern Ireland and received the Nobel Prize in 1995. Heaney's works have directly addressed the violence in his homeland.

MUSIC. Traditional Irish music, or **trad,** is an array of dance rhythms, cyclical melodies, and embellishments passed down through generations of musicians. Traditional musicians train by listening to and building on the work of others. A typical **pub session** will showcase a variety of styles, including reels, jigs, hornpipes, and slow airs. Beginning with the early recordings of the **Chieftains** and their mentor **Sean O'Riada** (1931-71) in the 1960s, trad has been resurrected from near-extinction to become a national art form. In addition to the best-selling recording artists **Altan** and **De Danann,** some excellent trad groups include the **Bothy Band** and **Planxty** of the 1970s, and more recently—**Nomos, Solas, Dervish,** and **Deanta.** For the best trad, head to a **fleadh** (FLAH), a festival at which musicians' scheduled sessions often spill over into nearby pubs.

Many of Ireland's most popular musical exports draw upon elements of traditional Irish music, including **Van Morrison, Sinéad O'Connor,** and **Enya**. The members of **U2** came together in Dublin in 1976 and have since catapulted to international superstardom. The band's 1983 song "Sunday Bloody Sunday" decried sectarian violence in Northern Ireland. Lead singer **Bono** has also become a prominent advocate of humanitarian causes. Formed in 1984, **My Bloody Valentine** spearheaded "shoegazing" rock, a sound based on shimmery, textured guitar landscapes. Irish artists who achieved mainstream success in the 1990s include **The Corrs, The Cranberries,** and the teen groups **Boyzone** and **B*witched.**

VISUAL ARTS. Hollywood discovered Ireland after **John Ford** (1894-1973) directed the *The Quiet Man* (1952), giving an international audience their first view of the island's beauty. Art-filmmakers like **Robert Flaherty** (1884-1951), who employed cinematic realism in his classic documentary *Man of Aran* (1934), have tried to capture a more accurate version of Ireland.

Beginning in the late 20th century, the government has encouraged a truly Irish film industry. Director **Jim Sheridan** (1949-present) helped kick off the cinematic renaissance with his universally acclaimed adaptation of Christy Brown's autobiography *My Left Foot* (1989). Sheridan also worked with Irish actor **Daniel Day-Lewis** (1957-present) in two films that compassionately examine the lives of Catholics and Protestants during the Troubles: *In the Name of the Father* (1993) and *The Boxer* (1997). Sheridan's more recent film, *In America* (2002), is a personal tale of emigration and loss.

English director **John Boorman's** (1930-present) saga *The General* (1998) describes the rise and fall of notorious criminal Martin Cahill. The Ireland of fairy tales has been captured with exquisite cinematography in **Mike Newell's** *Into the West* (1992) and **John Sayles's** *The Secret of Roan Inish* (1994). Acclaimed Irish director **Neil Jordan** (1950-present) and actor **Liam Neeson** (1952-present) teamed up on *Michael Collins* (1996), chronicling the life of the Irish revolutionary, and *Breakfast on Pluto* (2005), based on Pat McCabe's novel about an Irish foster child.

Peter O' Toole (1932-present) has been nominated for eight Academy Awards during his long acting career, for his work in such classics as *Lawrence of Arabia* (1962) and *The Lion in Winter* (1968). Dublin native **Colin Farrell** (1976-present), who starred in the Irish gangster film *Ordinary Decent Criminal* (2000), has achieved Hollywood hunk status. The success of the darkly comic *I Went Down* (1997) demonstrates the growing overseas popularity of Irish independent film. *The Magdalene Sisters* (2002), which depicts three Irish women in a Catholic asylum, and *Adam and Paul* (2004), about Irish junkies, both won numerous awards at European film festivals. **Cillian Murphy** (1976-present) has captivated an international audience with his brooding characters in *28 Days Later* (2002), *Batman Begins* (2005), and *Redeye* (2005). He was recently praised for his role as an Irish revolutionary in **Ken Loach's** *The Wind that Shakes the Barley* (2006).

HOLIDAYS AND FESTIVALS

Holidays: New Year's Day (Jan. 1); St. Patrick's Day (Mar. 17); Good Friday and Easter Monday (Apr. 2-3); and Christmas (Dec. 25). There are 4 bank holidays, which will be observed on May 3, June 7, Aug. 2, and Oct. 25 in 2010. Northern Ireland also observes Orangemen's Day (July 12).

Festivals: All of Ireland goes green for St. Patrick's Day (Mar. 17). On Bloomsday (June 16), Dublin celebrates James Joyce's Ulysses. In mid-July, the Galway Arts Festival offers theater, trad, rock, and film. Tralee crowns a lucky young lady "Rose of Tralee" at a festival in late August, and many return happy from the Lisdoonvarna Matchmaking Festival in the Burren in early September.

ESSENTIALS

FACTS AND FIGURES

OFFICIAL NAME: Republic of Ireland.

CAPITAL: Dublin.

MAJOR CITIES: Cork, Galway, Limerick.

POPULATION: 4,156,000.

RELIGIONS: Roman Catholic 88%, Church of Ireland 3%.

TIME ZONE: GMT.

LANGUAGES: English, Irish.

LONGEST PLACE NAME IN IRELAND: Muckanaghederdauhaulia, in Galway County.

LEASE ON THE ORIGINAL GUINNESS BREWERY IN DUBLIN: 9000 years.

WHEN TO GO

Ireland has a consistently cool, wet climate, with average temperatures ranging from around 4°C (39°F) in winter to 16°C (61°F) in summer. Travelers should bring raingear in any season. Don't be discouraged by cloudy, foggy mornings—the weather usually clears by noon. The southeastern coast is the driest and sunniest, while western Ireland is considerably wetter and cloudier. May and June offer the most sun; July and August are warmest. December and January have short, wet days, but temperatures rarely drop below freezing.

DOCUMENTS AND FORMALITIES

EMBASSIES AND CONSULATES. Foreign embassies are in Dublin (p. 345). Irish embassies abroad include: **Australia,** 20 Arkana St., Yarralumla, Canberra, ACT 2600 (☎06 273 3022; irishemb@cyberone.com.au); **Canada,** Ste. 1105, 130 Albert St., Ottawa, ON K1P 5G4 (☎613-233-6281; www.irishembassyottawa.com); **New Zealand,** Level 7, Citigroup Building, 23 Customs Street E., Auckland (☎09 977 2252; www.ireland.co.nz); **UK,** 17 Grosvenor Pl., London (☎020 72 35 21 71; www.ireland.embassyhomepage.com); **US,** 2234 Massachusetts Ave., NW, Washington, D.C., 20008 (☎202-462-3939; www.irelandemb.org).

VISA AND ENTRY INFORMATION. EU citizens do not need a visa. Citizens of Australia, Canada, New Zealand, and the US do not need a visa for stays of up to 90 days, beginning upon entry into any of the countries in the EU's freedom-of-movement zone. For more info, see p. 8. For stays longer than 90 days, non-EU citizens must register with the **Garda National Immigration Bureau,** 13-14 Burgh Quay, Dublin, 2 (☎01 666 9100; www.garda.ie/gnib).

TOURIST SERVICES AND MONEY

EMERGENCY	Ambulance, Fire, and Police: ☎999. Emergency: ☎112.

TOURIST OFFICES. Bord Fáilte (Irish Tourist Board; ☎1850 23 03 30; www.ireland.ie) operates a nationwide network of offices. Most tourist offices book rooms for a small fee (around €4) and a 10% deposit, but many hostels and B&Bs are not on the board's central list.

MONEY. The **euro (€)** has replaced the **Irish pound (£)** as the unit of currency in the Republic of Ireland. For more info, p. 11. Northern Ireland uses the **pound sterling (£).** As a general rule, it is cheaper to exchange money in Ireland than at home. ATMs are the easiest way to retrieve money and are much more common than bureaux de change. Mastercard and Visa are almost universally accepted.

If you stay in hostels and prepare your own food, expect to spend about €30 per person per day; a slightly more comfortable day (sleeping in B&Bs, eating one meal per day at a restaurant, going out at night) would cost €60. Most people working in restaurants do not expect a tip, unless the restaurant is targeted exclusively toward tourists. In that case, consider leaving 10-15%. Tipping is very uncommon for other services, such as taxis and hairdressers. In most cases, people are happy if you simply round up the bill to the nearest euro.

SAFETY AND SECURITY. Although sectarian violence is at an all-time low since the height of the Troubles, some neighborhoods and towns still experience unrest during sensitive political times. It's best to remain alert and cautious while traveling in Northern Ireland, especially during Marching Season, which reaches its peak July 4-12. August 12, when the Apprentice Boys march in Derry/Londonderry, is also a testy period. Despite these concerns, Northern Ireland has one of the lowest tourist-related crime rates in the world. The **Irish Tourist Assistance Service,** Block 1 Garda Headquarters, Harcourt St., in Dublin can assist travelers during crises. (☎01 478 5295; www.itas.ie. Open M-Sa 10am-6pm, Su noon-6pm.) Unattended luggage is always considered suspicious and is often confiscated. It is generally unsafe to hitch a ride in Northern Ireland. *Let's Go* does not recommend hitchhiking.

BUSINESS HOURS. Offices are generally open Monday through Friday 9am-4pm. Banks are open M-F 10am-4pm. Stores are open M-Sa 9am-6pm.

TRANSPORTATION

BY PLANE. A popular carrier to Ireland is national airline **Aer Lingus** (☎081 836 5000, US 800-474-7424; www.aerlingus.com), with direct flights to London, Paris, and the US. **Ryanair** (☎081 830 3030; www.ryanair.com) offers low fares from Cork, Dublin, and Shannon to destinations across Europe. **British Airways** (Ireland ☎890 626 747, UK 0844 493 0787, US 800-247-9297; www.ba.com) flies into most major Irish airports daily.

BY FERRY. Ferries run between Britain and Ireland many times per day. Fares for adults generally cost €15-30, with additional fees for cars. **Irish Ferries** (Ireland ☎01 818 300 400, UK 8705 17 17 17, US 772-563-2856; www.irishferries.com) and **Stena Line** (☎01 204 7777; www.stenaline.ie/ferry) typically offer discounts to students, seniors, and families. Ferries run from Dublin to Holyhead, BRI; from Cork to Roscoff, FRA; and from Rosslare Harbour to Pembroke, Wales, Cherbourg, FRA, and Roscoff, FRA.

BY TRAIN. **Iarnród Éireann** (Irish Rail; www.irishrail.ie) is useful for travel to urban areas. The **Eurail Global** pass is accepted in the Republic but not in Northern Ireland. The **BritRail** pass does not cover travel in anywhere in Ireland, but the **BritRail+Ireland** pass (€289-504) offers five or 10 days of travel in a one-month period as well as ferry service between Britain and Ireland.

BY BUS. **Bus Éireann** (☎01 836 6111; www.buseireann.ie), Ireland's national bus company, operates Expressway buses that link larger cities as well as local buses that serve the countryside and smaller towns. One-way fares between cities generally range €5-25; student discounts are available. Bus Éireann offers the **Irish Rover** pass, which also covers the Ulsterbus service in Northern Ireland (3 of 8 consecutive days €76, under 16 €44; 8 of 15 days €172/94). The **Emerald Card,** also available through Bus Éireann, offers unlimited travel on Expressway and other buses, Ulsterbus, Northern Ireland Railways, and local services (8 of 15 consecutive days €248, under 16 €124; 15 of 30 days €426).

Bus Éireann works in conjunction with ferry services and the bus company **Eurolines** (www.eurolines.com) to connect Ireland with Britain and the Continent. Eurolines passes for unlimited travel between major cities range €199-439. Discounts are available in the low season and for people under 26 or over 60. A major route runs between Dublin and Victoria Station in London; other stops include Birmingham, Bristol, Cardiff, Glasgow, and Liverpool, with services to Cork, Derry/Londonderry, Galway, Tralee, and Waterford.

BY CAR. Drivers in Ireland use the left side of the road. Be particularly cautious at roundabouts—give way to traffic from the right. **Dan Dooley** (☎062 53103, UK 0800 282 189, US 800-331-9301; www.dandooley.com) and **Enterprise** (☎UK 0870 350 3000, US 800-261-7331; www.enterprise.ie) will rent to drivers between 21 and 24, though such drivers must pay an additional daily surcharge. Fares are €85-200 per week (plus VAT), including insurance and unlimited mileage. If you plan to drive a car in Ireland for longer than 90 days, you must have an **International Driving Permit (IDP).** If you rent, lease, or borrow a car, you will need a **green card** or an **International Insurance Certificate** to certify that you have liability insurance that applies abroad. It is always significantly less expensive to reserve a car from the US than from within Europe.

BY BIKE, FOOT, AND THUMB. Ireland's countryside is well suited to **biking,** as many roads are not heavily traveled. Single-digit "N" roads are more trafficked and should be avoided. Ireland's mountains, fields, and hills make **walking** and **hiking** arduous joys. The **Wicklow Way,** a 132km hiking trail in the mountains southeast of Dublin, has hostels within a day's walk of each other. Some locals caution against **hitchhiking** in County Dublin and the Midlands, where it is not very common. *Let's Go* does not recommend hitchhiking.

KEEPING IN TOUCH

PHONE CODES	**Country code:** 353. **International dialing prefix:** 00. For more info on how to place international calls, see **Inside Back Cover.**

TELEPHONE. Whenever possible, use a calling card for international phone calls, as long-distance rates for national phone services are often very high. Mobile phones are an increasingly popular and economical option, and carriers Vodafone and O2 offer the best service. Direct-dial access numbers for calling out of Ireland include: **AT&T Direct** (☎800 550 000); **British Telecom** (☎800 890 353); **Canada Direct** (☎800 555 001); **MCI WorldPhone** (☎800 55 10 01); **Telecom New Zealand Direct** (☎800 55 00 64).

MAIL. Postcards and letters up to 50g cost €0.55 within Ireland and €0.82 to Europe and other international destinations. Airmail parcels take four to nine days between Ireland and North America. Dublin is the only place in the Republic with Postal Codes (p. 347). To receive mail in Ireland, have mail delivered **Poste Restante.** Mail will go to the main post office unless you specify a subsidiary by street address. Address mail to be held according to the following example: First name LAST NAME, Poste Restante, City, Ireland. Bring a passport to pick up your mail; there may be a small fee.

ACCOMMODATIONS AND CAMPING

IRELAND	❶	❷	❸	❹	❺
ACCOMMODATIONS	under €17	€17-26	€27-40	€41-56	over €56

A **hostel** bed will average €13-20. **An Óige** (an OYJ), the **HI** affiliate, operates 27 hostels countrywide. (☎01 830 4555; www.irelandyha.org. One-year membership €20, under 18 €10.) Many An Óige hostels are in remote areas or small villages and are designed to serve nature-seekers. They therefore do not offer the same social environment typical of other European hostels. Over 100 hostels in Ireland belong to **Independent Holiday Hostels** (**IHH;** ☎01 836 4700; www.hostels-ireland.com). Most IHH hostels have no lockout or curfew, accept all ages, require no membership card, and have a less institutional feel than their An Óige counterparts; all are Bord Fáilte-approved. In virtually every Irish town, **B&Bs** can provide a luxurious break from hosteling. Expect to pay €30-35 for singles and €45-60 for doubles. "Full Irish breakfasts" are often filling enough to last until dinner. Camping in Irish State Forests and National Parks is not allowed. **Camping** on public land is permissible only if there is no official campsite nearby. Sites cost €5-13. For more info, see www.camping-ireland.ie.

FOOD AND DRINK

IRELAND	❶	❷	❸	❹	❺
FOOD	under €6	€6-10	€11-15	€16-20	over €20

Food in Ireland can be expensive, but the basics are simple and filling. Find quick and greasy staples at **chippers** (fish and chips shops) and **takeaways.** Most pubs serve Irish stew, burgers, soup, and sandwiches. Cafes and restaurants have begun to offer more vegetarian options to complement the typical meat-based entrees. **Soda bread** is delicious, and Irish **cheddars** are addictive. **Guinness,** a rich, dark stout, is revered with a zeal usually reserved for the Holy Trinity. Known as "the dark stuff" or "the blonde in the black skirt," a proper pint has a head so thick that you can stand a match in it. **Irish whiskey,** which Queen Elizabeth once said was her only true Irish friend, is sweeter than its Scotch counterpart. "A big one" (a pint of Guinness) and "a small one" (a glass of whiskey) are often ordered alongside one another. When ordering at an Irish **pub,** one individual in a small group will usually approach the bar and buy a round of drinks for everyone. Once those drinks are downed, another individual will buy the next round. It's considered poor form to refuse someone's offer to buy you a drink. The legal age in Ireland to purchase alcohol is 18.

ACT LIKE YOU OWN THE PLACE. The Heritage Card, a VIP pass for anyone, provides admission year-round to 80 historical sites throughout the Republic. With individual admission costing up to €10, this card (€21, students €8) is well worth the investment, even if you only get to visit 2 or 3 sites. Cards can be purchased at most sites, all of which are managed by the Office for Public Works or the Department of the Environment, Heritage and Local Government. For more info, call ☎647 6000, or visit www.heritageireland.ie.

BEYOND TOURISM

To find opportunities that accommodate your interests and schedule, check with national agencies such as Volunteering Ireland (www.volunteeringireland.com). For more info on opportunities in Europe, see **Beyond Tourism,** p. 45.

L'Arche Ireland, "Seolta," Warrenhouse Rd., Baldoyle, Dublin, 13 (☎01 839 4356; www.larche.ie). Assistants can join residential communities in Cork, Dublin, or Kilkenny to live with, work with, and teach people with learning disabilities. Room, board, and small stipend provided. Commitment of 1-2yr. expected.

Sustainable Land Use Company, Doorian, Glenties, Co. Donegal (☎074 955 1286; www.donegalorganic.ie). Offers opportunities to assist with organic farming, forestry, habitat maintenance, and wildlife in the northern county of Donegal.

Focus Ireland, 9-12 High St., Dublin, 8 (☎01 881 5900; www.focusireland.ie). Advocacy and fundraising for the homeless in Dublin, Limerick, and Waterford.

DUBLIN ☎01

In a country known for its rural landscapes, the international flavor and frenetic pace of Dublin stick out like the 120m spire in the city's heart. Ireland's capital since the Middle Ages, Dublin offers all the amenities of other world-class cities on a more manageable scale, with all buildings topping off at five stories. Prestigious Trinity College holds treasures of Ireland's past, while Temple Bar has become one of Europe's hottest nightspots. The city's musical, cultural, and drinkable attractions continue to draw droves of visitors.

TRANSPORTATION

Flights: Dublin Airport (**DUB;** ☎01 814 1111; www.dublinairport.com). Dublin **buses** #41 and 41B run from the airport to Eden Quay in the city center (40-45min., every 10min., €1.80). Airlink **shuttle** (☎01 703 3092) runs nonstop to Busáras Central Bus Station and O'Connell St. (20-25min., every 10-20min. 5:45am-11:30pm, €6), and to Heuston Station (50min., €6). A **taxi** to the city center costs roughly €25.

Trains: The **Irish Rail Travel Centre,** 35 Lower Abbey St. (☎01 836 6222; www.irishrail.ie), sells train tickets. Open M-F 8:30am-6pm, Sa 9:30am-6pm.

Pearse Station, Pearse St. (☎01 828 6000). Ticketing open M-Sa 7:30am-9:50pm, Su 9am-9:50pm. Receives southbound trains from Connolly Station and serves as a departure point for **Dublin Area Rapid Transit (DART)** trains serving the suburbs and coast (4-6 per hr., €2-6.70).

Connolly Station, Amiens St. (☎01 703 2358), north of the Liffey and close to Busáras. Bus #20b heads south of the river and #130 goes to the city center, while the DART runs to Tara Station on the south quay. Trains to: **Belfast** (2hr.; M-Sa 9 per day, Su 5 per day; €36), **Sligo** (3hr., M-Sa 8 per day, Su 6 per day per day, €29), and **Wexford and Rosslare** (3hr., 3 per day, €20.50).

Heuston Station (☎01 703 2132), south of Victoria Quay and west of the city center (a 25min. walk from Trinity College). Buses #78 and 79 run to the city center. Trains to: **Cork** (3hr., M-Sa 15 per day, Su 11 per day, €59.50); **Galway** (2hr.; M-Sa 7 per day, Su 6 per day; €31.50 M-Th and Sa, €44 F and Su); **Limerick** (2hr.; M-Sa 10, Su 7 per day; €45.50); **Waterford** (2hr.; M-Sa 6 per day, Su 4 per day; €24.50 M-Th and Sa, €31.50 F and Su).

Buses: Intercity buses to Dublin arrive at **Busáras Central Bus Station,** Store St. (☎01 836 6111; www.buseireann.ie), next to Connolly Station. Buses to: **Belfast** (3hr., 24 per day, €15); **Cork** (4½hr., 6 per day, €12); **Derry/Londonderry** (4hr., 9 per day, €20); **Donegal** (4hr., 10 per day, €18); **Galway** (3hr., 17 per day, €15); **Limerick** (3½hr., 13 per day, €10); **Rosslare** (3hr., 13 per day, €16.80); **Sligo** (4hr., 5-6 per day, €18); **Tralee** (6hr., 9 per day, €23); **Wexford** (2hr.; M-Sa 17 per day, Su 10 per day; €13.50).

Ferries: Irish Ferries, 2-4 Merrion Row, (☎0818 300 400; www.irishferries.com) off St. Stephen's Green. Open M-F 9am-5pm, Sa 9am-1pm. Stena Line ferries arrive from Holyhead at the **Dún Laoghaire** ferry terminal (☎01 204 7777; www.stenaline.com).

Public Transportation: Info on local buses available at **Dublin Bus Office,** 59 Upper O'Connell St. (☎01 873 4222; www.dublinbus.ie). Open M 8:30am-5:30pm, Tu-F 9am-5:30pm, Sa 9am-2pm, Su 9:30am-2pm. **Rambler** passes offer unlimited rides for a day (€6) or a week (€23). Dublin Bus runs the **NiteLink** service to the suburbs (M-Th 12:30 and 2am, F-Sa every 20min. 12:30-4:30am; €5; passes not valid). The **Luas** (☎01 461 4910 or ☎1800 300 604; www.luas.ie; phone line open M-F 7am-7pm, Sa 10am-2pm), Dublin's **Light Rail Tram System,** is the city's newest form of mass transit.

Taxis: Blue Cabs (☎01 802 2222), **ABC** (☎01 285 5444), and **City Cabs** (☎01 872 7272) have wheelchair-accessible cabs (call ahead). Available 24hr.

Car Rental: Europcar, Dublin Airport (☎01 812 0410; www.www.europcar.ie). Economy around €50 per day, €200 per wk. Ages 24-70.

Bike Rental: Cycle Ways, 185-6 Parnell St. (☎01 873 4748). Rents quality hybrid or mountain bikes. €20 per day, €80 per wk. with €200 deposit. Open M-W and F-Sa 9:30am-6pm, Th 9:30am-8pm, Su 11am-5pm. AmEx/MC/V.

ORIENTATION AND PRACTICAL INFORMATION

Although Dublin is compact, getting lost is not much of a challenge. Street signs, when posted, are located high up on the sides of buildings at most intersections. The essential *Dublin Visitor Map* is available for free at the Dublin Bus Office. The **Liffey River** forms a natural boundary between Dublin's North and South Sides. Heuston Station and the more famous sights, posh stores, and upscale restaurants are on the **South Side,** while Connolly Station, the majority of hostels, and the bus station are on the **North Side.** The North Side is less expensive than the more touristed South Side, but it also has a reputation for being rougher, especially after dark. The streets running alongside the Liffey are called **quays** (pronounced "keys"); the name of the quay changes with each bridge. **O'Connell Street,** three blocks west of the Busáras Central Bus Station, is the primary link between northern and southern Dublin. On the North Side, **Henry** and **Mary Streets** constitute a pedestrian shopping zone, intersecting with O'Connell St. two blocks from the Liffey at the **General Post Office.** On the South Side, a block from the river, **Fleet Street** becomes **Temple Bar,** an area full of music centers and galleries. **Dame Street** runs parallel to Temple Bar and leads east to **Trinity College,** Dublin's cultural center.

Tourist Office: Main Office, Suffolk St. (☎01 605 7700; www.visitdublin.com). Near Trinity College in a converted church. Open M-Sa 9am-5:30pm, Su 10:30am-3pm; July-Aug. M-Sa 9am-7pm; Su 10:30am-5pm. **Northern Ireland Tourist Board,** 16 Nassau St. (☎01 679 1977 or ☎1850 230 230). Open M-F 9:15am-5:30pm, Sa 10am-5pm.

Embassies: Australia, Fitzwilton House, Wilton Terr., 7th fl. (☎01 664 5300; www.ireland.embassy.gov.au); **Canada,** 7-8 Wilton Terr. (☎01 234 4000; www.canada.ie); **UK,** 29 Merrion Rd. (☎01 205 3700; www.britishembassy.ie); **US,** 42 Elgin Rd. (☎01 668 8777; http://dublin.usembassy.gov). Citizens of **New Zealand** should contact their embassy in London.

Banks: Branches with currency exchange and 24hr. **ATMs** cluster on Lower O'Connell St., Grafton St., and near Suffolk and Dame St. Most are open M-W and F 10am-4pm, Th 10am-5pm.

Luggage Storage: Connolly Station: Small lockers €4, large lockers €6. Open daily 5am-midnight. **Busáras:** Lockers €6/8. Open 24hr.

Laundromat: All-American Launderette, 40 South Great Georges St. (☎01 677 2779). Self-service €8.50; full-service €9.50. Open M-Sa 8:30am-7pm, Su 10am-6pm.

Police (Garda): Dublin Metro Headquarters, Harcourt Terr. (☎01 666 9500); Store St. Station (☎01 666 8000); Fitzgibbon St. Station (☎01 666 8400); Pearse St. Station (☎01 666 9000). **Police Confidential Report Line:** ☎800 666 111.

Pharmacy: Hickey's, 56 Lower O'Connell St. (☎01 873 0427). Convenient to bus routes. Open M-F 7:30am-10pm, Sa 8am-10pm, Su and bank holidays 10am-10pm. Other branches scattered about the city, including locations on Grafton St. and Henry St.

Hospital: St. James's Hospital, James St. (☎01 410 3000). Bus #123. **Mater Misericordiae Hospital,** Eccles St. (☎01 803 2000). Buses #3, 10, 11, 16, 22 36, 121. **Beaumont Hospital,** Beaumont Rd. (☎01 809 3000). Buses #103, 104, 27b, 42a.

Internet: The Internet Exchange at Cecilia St. (☎01 670 3000) in Temple Bar. €3 per hr. Open M-F 8am-2am, Sa-Su 10am-2am. There are numerous other Internet cafes with comparable rates around the city.

Post Office: General Post Office, O'Connell St. (☎01 705 7000). **Poste Restante** pickup at the Poste Restante window (see Mail, p. 343). Open M-Sa 8am-8pm. Smaller post offices, including one on Suffolk St. across from the tourist office, are typically open M-Tu and Th-F 9am-6pm, W 9:30am-6pm. **Postal Codes:** Dublin is the only place in the Republic that uses postal codes. The city is organized into regions numbered 1-18, 20, 22, and 24; even-numbered codes are for areas south of the Liffey, while odd-numbered ones are for the north. The numbers radiate out from the city center: North City Centre is 1, South City Centre is 2.

ACCOMMODATIONS

Because Dublin is an incredibly popular destination, it is necessary to book accommodations at least one week in advance, particularly around holidays and in the summer. If the following accommodations are full, consult Dublin Tourism's annual *Sleep!* Guide (€2.50), or ask hostel staff for referrals.

HOSTELS

Four Courts Hostel, 15-17 Merchants Quay (☎01 672 5839). On the south bank of the river. Bus #748 from the airport stops next door. 230-bed hostel with pristine, well-lit rooms and hardwood floors. Quiet lounge and a combination TV/game room provide plenty of space to wind down. Continental breakfast included. In-room lockers. Free Wi-Fi; computer use €1 per 15min. Laundry €7.50. 8- to 16-bed dorms €17-21.50; 4- to 6-bed €25-38; doubles €64-72; triples around €90. ❶

Abbey Court Hostel, 29 Bachelor's Walk (☎01 878 0700; www.abbey-court.com). Corner of O'Connell St. and Bachelor's Walk near bridge. Hostel boasts clean, narrow rooms overlooking the Liffey. Hidden apartments each have lounge, TV, and courtyard. Internet €1 per 15min., €2 per 40min. Continental breakfast at **NYStyle cafe** next door included. Free luggage storage; security box €1. Full-service laundry €8. 12-bed dorms €19-23; 6-bed €24-27; 4-bed €27-31; doubles €78-89. Long-term rate €108-126 per week includes breakfast. Apartments from €89 per night. ❷

Avalon House (IHH), 55 Aungier St. (☎01 475 0001; www.avalon-house.ie). Performers get free accommodation if they spend 1hr. teaching other guests. Wheelchair-accessible with elevator. Light continental breakfast included. Lockers and smaller lockboxes €1 per day; €8-10 deposit. Laundry €7. Free Wi-Fi. 24hr. reception. Large dorms €14-20; 4- to 6-bed dorms €24-31; singles €32-41; doubles €30-39. MC/V. ❶

Barnacles Temple Bar House, 19 Temple Ln. (☎01 671 6277). Patrons can nearly jump into bed from Temple Bar pubs, including the actual Temple Bar, next door. Spacious, sky-lit lounge with fireplace and TV. Breakfast included. Free luggage storage. Laundry €7. Free Wi-Fi; Internet on house computers €1 per 15min. 11-bed dorms €19-21; 6-bed €27-29.50; quads €28.50-31.50; doubles €80-87. ❶

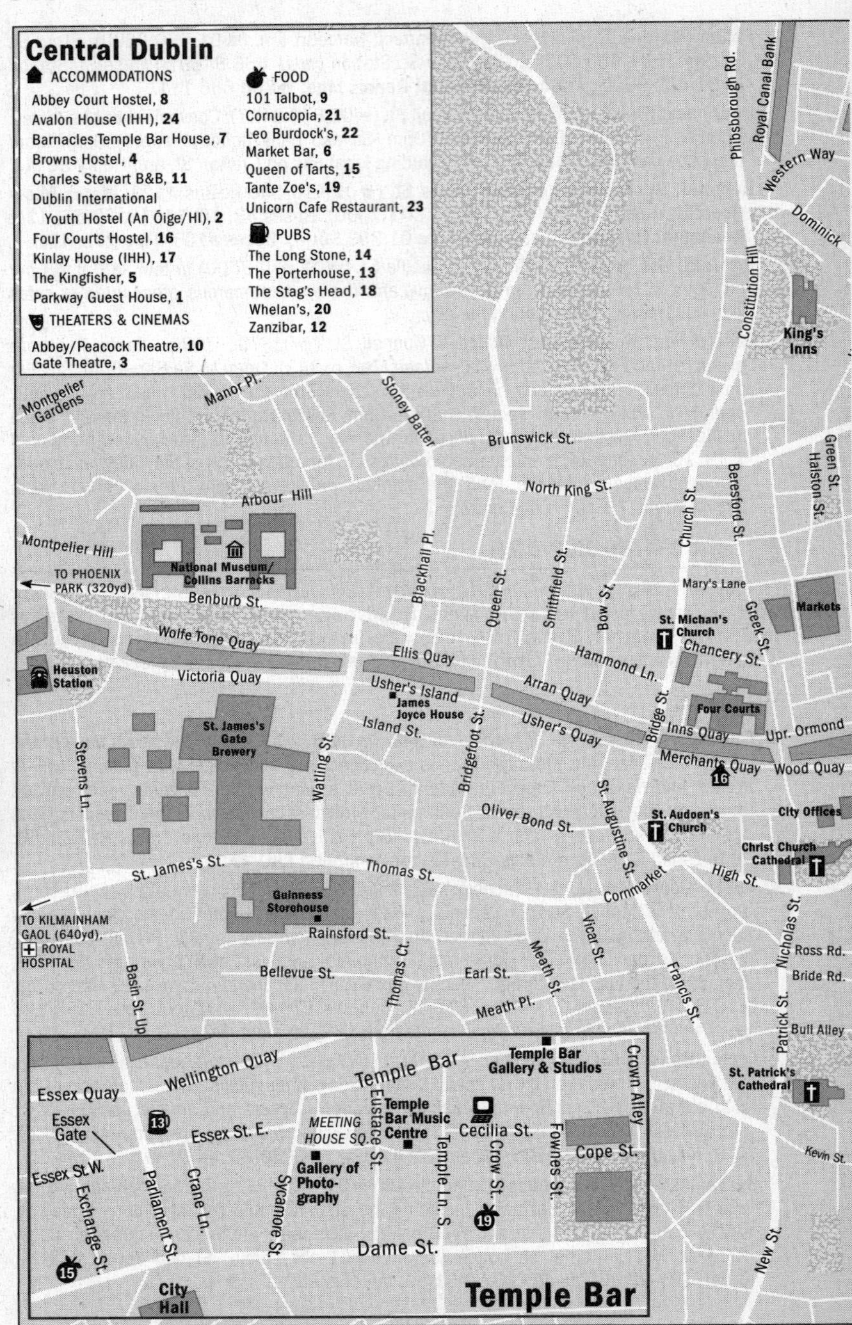

Central Dublin
ACCOMMODATIONS
Abbey Court Hostel, 8
Avalon House (IHH), 24
Barnacles Temple Bar House, 7
Browns Hostel, 4
Charles Stewart B&B, 11
Dublin International Youth Hostel (An Óige/HI), 2
Four Courts Hostel, 16
Kinlay House (IHH), 17
The Kingfisher, 5
Parkway Guest House, 1
THEATERS & CINEMAS
Abbey/Peacock Theatre, 10
Gate Theatre, 3
FOOD
101 Talbot, 9
Cornucopia, 21
Leo Burdock's, 22
Market Bar, 6
Queen of Tarts, 15
Tante Zoe's, 19
Unicorn Cafe Restaurant, 23
PUBS
The Long Stone, 14
The Porterhouse, 13
The Stag's Head, 18
Whelan's, 20
Zanzibar, 12
Phibsborough Rd.
Royal Canal Bank
Western Way
Dominick
Constitution Hill
King's Inns
Montpelier Gardens
Manor Pl.
Stoney Batter
Brunswick St.
Green St.
Halston St.
Beresford St.
North King St.
Church St.
Arbour Hill
Blackhall Pl.
Smithfield St.
Queen St.
Montpelier Hill
National Museum/ Collins Barracks
TO PHOENIX PARK (320yd)
Mary's Lane
Bow St.
Benburb St.
St. Michan's Church
Markets
Greek St.
Wolfe Tone Quay
Hammond Ln.
Chancery St.
Ellis Quay
Heuston Station
Victoria Quay
Usher's Island
James Joyce House
Arran Quay
Four Courts
Island St.
Usher's Quay
Bridge St.
Inns Quay
Upr. Ormond
St. James's Gate Brewery
Stevens Ln.
Watling St.
Bridgefoot St.
Merchants Quay
16
Wood Quay
St. Augustine St.
Oliver Bond St.
St. Audoen's Church
City Offices
Christ Church Cathedral
St. James's St.
Thomas St.
Cornmarket
High St.
Guinness Storehouse
TO KILMAINHAM GAOL (640yd).
ROYAL HOSPITAL
Rainsford St.
Vicar St.
Nicholas St.
Ross Rd.
Bride Rd.
Meath St.
Francis St.
Basin St. Up.
Bellevue St.
Thomas Ct.
Earl St.
Meath Pl.
Patrick St.
Bull Alley
St. Patrick's Cathedral
Kevin St.
New St.
Temple Bar
Wellington Quay
Temple Bar
Temple Bar Gallery & Studios
Crown Alley
Essex Quay
Essex Gate
13
Essex St. E.
MEETING HOUSE SQ.
Eustace St.
Temple Bar Music Centre
Cecilia St.
Cope St.
Essex St.W.
Exchange St.
Parliament St.
Crane Ln.
Sycamore St.
Gallery of Photo-graphy
Temple Ln. S.
Crow St.
Fownes St.
19
Dame St.
15
City Hall

IRELAND

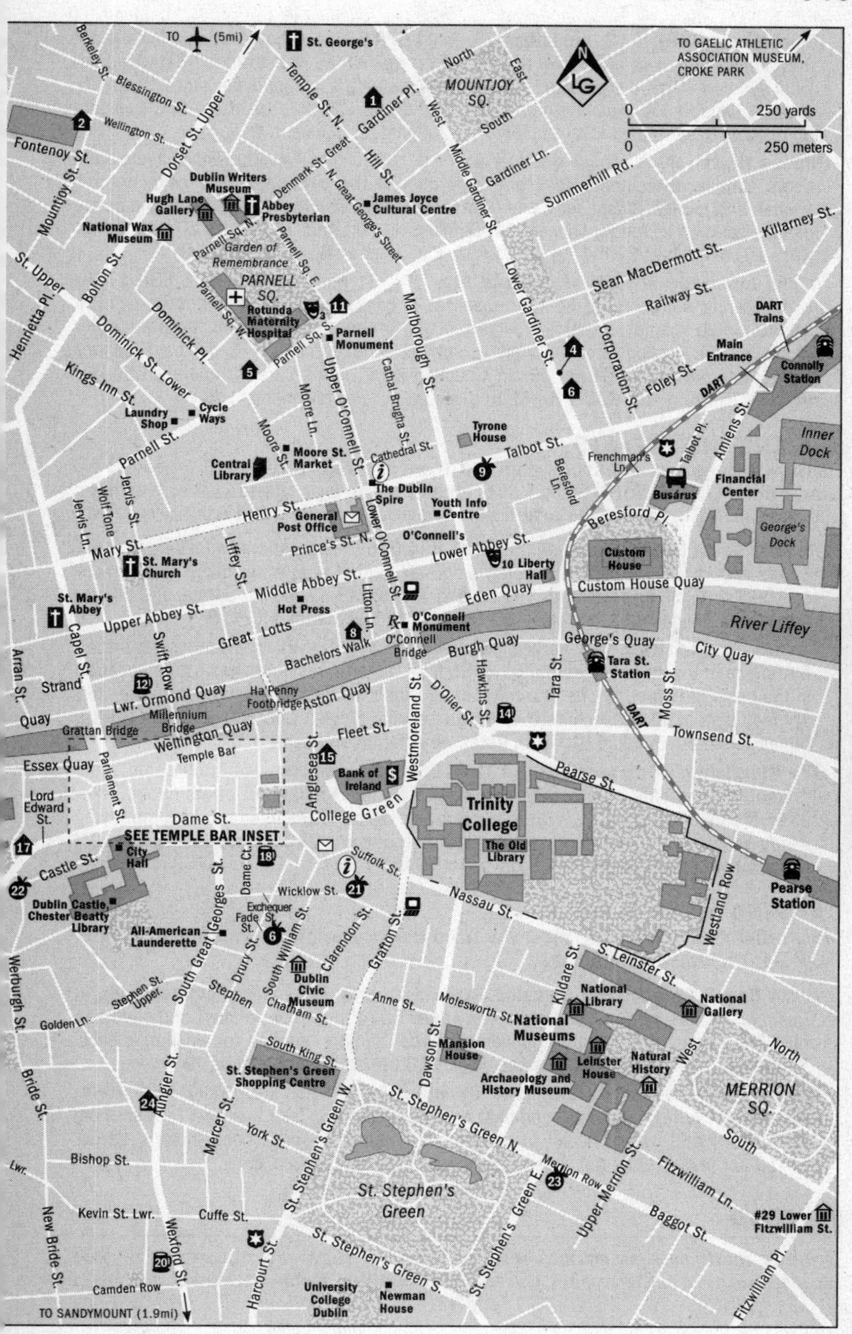
TO (5mi)
St. George's
TO GAELIC ATHLETIC ASSOCIATION MUSEUM, CROKE PARK
MOUNTJOY SQ.
250 yards
250 meters
Dublin Writers Museum
Hugh Lane Gallery
Abbey Presbyterian
James Joyce Cultural Centre
National Wax Museum
Garden of Remembrance
PARNELL SQ.
Rotunda Maternity Hospital
Parnell Monument
DART Trains
Main Entrance
Connolly Station
Laundry Shop
Cycle Ways
Tyrone House
Inner Dock
Moore St. Market
Central Library
The Dublin Spire
Youth Info Centre
Busáras
Financial Center
General Post Office
O'Connell's
George's Dock
Custom House
St. Mary's Church
10 Liberty Hall
St. Mary's Abbey
Hot Press
O'Connell Monument
River Liffey
O'Connell Bridge
Tara St. Station
Ha'Penny Footbridge
Millennium Bridge
Grattan Bridge
Temple Bar
Bank of Ireland
Trinity College
The Old Library
SEE TEMPLE BAR INSET
City Hall
Dublin Castle, Chester Beatty Library
All-American Launderette
Exchequer St.
Dublin Civic Museum
Pearse Station
National Library
National Gallery
National Museums
Mansion House
Leinster House
Natural History
Archaeology and History Museum
St. Stephen's Green Shopping Centre
MERRION SQ.
St. Stephen's Green
#29 Lower Fitzwilliam St.
University College Dublin
Newman House
TO SANDYMOUNT (1.9mi)

IRELAND

Kinlay House (IHH), 2-12 Lord Edward St. (☎01 679 6644). Great location a few blocks from Temple Bar. If you don't get a room with a view of the Christ Church Cathedral, at least you can watch the plasma TV. Continental breakfast included. Lockers €1 with €5 deposit. Laundry €8. Free Internet. 4- to 6-bed dorms €22-33; 16- to 24-bed €18-24; doubles €30-38; triples €32-41. Min. stay 2 nights on weekend. ❶

Browns Hostel, 89-90 Lower Gardiner St. (☎01 855 0034; www.brownshostelireland.com). Long-term residents cook and play pool in the cavernous wine cellar turned kitchen and lounge. Closet, A/C, and TV in most rooms. Communal showers in the basement. Breakfast included. Lockers €1. Blankets €2. Internet €3 per hr. 20-bed dorms €15; 10- to 14-bed €20; 4- to 6-bed €25. €100 per week. AmEx/MC/V. ❶

Dublin International Youth Hostel (An Óige/HI), 61 Mountjoy St. (☎01 830 1766; www.irelandyha.org). Huge hostel housed in a converted convent and 18th-century school. Complimentary breakfast served in the former chapel. Wheelchair-accessible. Towels €1.25. In-room storage; luggage storage at reception €1.25 per day. Laundry €2.50. Internet access €1 per 40min. Check-in 2pm. Dorms €20-27; doubles €50-60; triples €75-85; quads €90-110. €2 HI discount per person per night. ❷

BED AND BREAKFASTS

B&Bs with a green shamrock sign out front are registered and approved by Bord Fáilte. On the North Side, B&Bs cluster along Upper and Lower Gardiner St., on Sheriff St., and near Parnell Sq. All prices include a full Irish breakfast.

Parkway Guest House, 5 Gardiner Pl. (☎01 874 0469; www.parkway-guesthouse.com). Sports fans bond with the proprietor, a former hurling star, while those less athletically inclined still appreciate his great eye for interior design, sound advice, and all-star breakfasts. Singles €40; doubles €60-80, €80-100 with bath. MC/V. ❸

Charles Stewart B&B, 5-6 Parnell Sq. E. (☎01 878 0350; www.charlesstewart.ie). Birthplace of the infamous author Oliver St. John Gogarty, this home has a great location in the oasis of Parnell Sq. Its proximity to the Dublin Writer's Museum adds to the literary feel. Irish breakfast included. All rooms ensuite. Singles €45-63; doubles €69-89; triples €99-120, quads €120-140. Rates vary greatly with season. MC/V. ❹

The Kingfisher, 166 Parnell St. (☎01 872 8732; www.kingfisherdublin.com). Inn, restaurant, and cafe in one. Irish breakfast included. Restaurant offers cheap takeaway. Free Wi-Fi in cafe. TV/VCR in each room; kitchenettes in some. Accompanying 4-course dinner in restaurant from €12 per person. 24hr. reception. €45. 10% discount for stays longer than 5 days. AmEx/MC/V. ❸

IRELAND

CAMPING

Most official campsites are far away from the city center. Camping in Phoenix Park is both illegal and unsafe.

North Beach Caravan and Camping Park (☎01 843 7131; www.northbeach.ie), in Rush. Accessible by bus #33 from Lower Abbey St. (45min., 25 per day) and suburban rail. Quiet, beachside location outside the urban jumble. Kitchen for washing dishes. Showers €2. Electricity €3. Open Apr.-Sept. €10 per adult, €5 per child. ❶

Camac Valley Tourist Caravan and Camping Park, Naas Rd. (☎01 464 0644; www.camacvalley.com), in Clondalkin near Corkagh Park. Take bus #69 (45min. from city center) and ask to be let off at Camac. Wheelchair-accessible. Showers €1.50. €9-10 per person; €22 per 2 people with car; €24 per caravan. ❶

FOOD

Dublin's many **open-air markets** sell fresh food at relatively cheap prices. The later in the week, the livelier the market. Bustling **Moore St. Market,** between

Henry St. and Parnell St., is a great place to get fresh veggies. (Open M-Sa 10am-5pm.) The **Thomas Street Market,** along the continuation of Dame St., is a calmer alternative. (Generally open Th-Sa 11am-5pm, although some stalls are open during the week; drop by to check.) Produce can be found every day along Wexford Sreet. The best value for supermarkets around Dublin is in the **Dunnes Stores** chain, with full branches at St. Stephen's Green (☎01 478 0188; open M-W and F 8:30am-8pm, Th 8:30am-9pm, Sa 8:30am-7pm, Su 10am-7pm), the ILAC Centre off Henry St., and N. Earl St. off O'Connell; a smaller version is on South Great Georges St.

Queen of Tarts, Dame St. (☎01 670 7499), across from City Hall (and new, bigger location on Cow's Lane, Temple Bar). Pastries, light meals, and coffee in a supremely feminine hideaway. Delectable tarts €10 (savory) and €5.50 (sweet). Breakfast €3.50-10. Sandwiches €8. Open M-F 7:30am-7pm, Sa-Su 9am-7pm. MC/V. ❶

Market Bar, Fade St. (☎01 613 9094; www.tapas.ie). Right off S. Great Georges after Lower Stephen St. Huge sausage factory given a classy makeover; now serves tapas in heaping portions. Small tapas €8; large tapas €12. Kitchen open M-Th noon-11:30pm, F-Sa noon-12:30am, Su 3-11pm. ❶

Cornucopia, 19 Wicklow St. (☎01 671 9449). If there's space, sit down in this cozy spot for a delicious meal (€11-12) or a cheaper salad smorgasbord (€4.25-9.25 for choice of 2, 4, or 6 salads). Accommodates many dietary restrictions. Open M-F 8:30am-9pm, Sa 8:30am-8pm, Su noon-7pm. ❷

Leo Burdock's, 2 Werburgh St. (☎01 454 0306), behind The Lord Edward Pub across from Christ Church Cathedral. Additional location on Lower Liffey St. Fish and chips served the right way—in brown paper. A nightly pilgrimage for many Dubliners. Takeaway only. Fish €4.50-7; chips €3. Open daily noon-midnight. ❶

Tante Zoe's, 1 Crow St. (☎01 670 7559), across from the back entrance of the Foggy Dew pub. Fresh flowers and creamy linens complement the Cajun-Creole menu. Jambalayas €17.50-20.50; entrees €18-28. 2-course lunch €17. Open M-Sa noon-4pm and 5:30pm-midnight, Su 4-10pm. ❸

Unicorn Café Restaurant, 12B Merrion Ct. (☎01 676 2182; www.unicornrestaurant.com). Left off Merrion Row, behind Unicorn Food Store and Café. Legendary Italian restaurant serves classic dishes with panache. Lunch €16-30; dinner €20-32. Open M-Sa noon-11pm. ❸ **Unicorn Food Store and Café,** Merrion Row (☎01 662 4757), offers food from the same kitchen, at a fraction of the price, for sit-down or takeaway. Panini €8.20; pasta €8-10. Open daily 8am-7pm. ❷

101 Talbot, 101 Talbot St. (☎01 874 5011), between Marlborough and Gardiner St., 1 flight up through the red doors. Excellent Mediterranean food catered to Abbey Theatre-goers. Large windows look onto Talbot St. Menu changes frequently. Book ahead. Entrees €14.50-24. Early-bird 5-7:45pm €22. Open Tu-Sa 5-11pm. AmEx/MC/V. ❷

SIGHTS

TRINITY COLLEGE. The British built **Trinity College** in 1592 as a Protestant seminary that would "civilize the Irish and cure them of Popery." The college became part of the path on which members of the Anglo-Irish elite trod on their way to high positions: it has educated such luminaries as Jonathan Swift, Robert Emmett, Thomas Moore, Oscar Wilde, and Samuel Beckett. The Catholic Church deemed it a cardinal sin to attend Trinity until the 1960s; when the Church lifted the ban, the size of the student body tripled. Today, it's a celebrated center of learning, located steps away from the teeming center of a cosmopolitan capital, and an unmissable stop on the tourist trail. *(Between Westmoreland and Grafton St., South Dublin. Main entrance fronts the traffic circle now called College*

Green. Pearse St. runs along the north edge of the college, Nassau St. the south. ☎ 01 608 1724; www.tcd.ie. Grounds always open. Free.)

THE NATIONAL GALLERY. This collection of over 2500 canvases, only 800 of which are on display, contains a comprehensive mix of internationally and locally renowned artists. Paintings by Brueghel, Goya, Caravaggio, Vermeer, and Rembrandt can be seen in the European exhibits, while a major part of the collection is dedicated to the Irish tradition. The works of Jack Yeats—brother of poet W.B. and Ireland's most celebrated artist of the 20th century—are of particular interest. The new **Millennium Wing** houses a 20th-century Irish art exhibit, a Yeats archive which celebrates the combined talents of father John B. and his four children, and computer stations that give "virtual tours" of the museum. Summertime brings concerts, lectures, and art classes; inquire at the front desk for schedules. *(Merrion Sq. W. ☎ 01 661 5133; www.nationalgallery.ie. Open M-W and F-Sa 9:30am-5:30pm, Th 9:30am-8:30pm, Su noon-5:30pm. Free guided tours Sa 3pm, Su 2, 3, 4pm; July also daily 3pm. Admission free. Temporary exhibits €10, students and seniors €6.)*

THE NATIONAL MUSEUM OF ARCHAEOLOGY AND HISTORY. Dublin's largest museum has incredible artifacts spanning the last two millennia to illustrate the history of Ireland. One room gleams with the **Tara Brooch,** the **Ardagh Hoard,** and other Celtic goldwork. Another section is devoted to the Republic's founding years and flaunts the bloody vest of nationalist hero **James Connolly.** *(Kildare St., next to Leinster House. ☎ 01 677 7444; www.museum.ie. Open Tu-Sa 10am-5pm, Su 2-5pm. Guided tours €2; call for times. Museum free.)*

TEMPLE BAR MUSIC CENTRE. The TBMC houses a concert venue (the Button Factory), teaching space and studio, and cafe (M-Sa noon-6pm). A diverse lineup takes the stage 5-6 times a week beginning at 7:30pm.The space becomes a hip club W-Su 11pm-3am. *(Curved St. ☎ 01 670 9202; www.tbmc.ie. For lineups, check with box office or www.buttonfactory.ie. Cover usually €5-15.)*

CHESTER BEATTY LIBRARY. Honorary Irish citizen **Alfred Chester Beatty** was an American mining magnate who amassed a beautiful collection of Asian and Middle Eastern art, sacred scriptures, and illustrated texts. He donated this collection to Ireland upon his death, and a new library behind Dublin Castle houses his abundance of cultural artifacts. It's no wonder that the library was European Museum of the Year in 2002. This collection of truly fascinating objects, from intricate Chinese snuff bottles to some of the earliest fragments of the Biblical Gospels, is arranged on the first floor by region of the world. The second floor contains Beatty's extensive collection of texts from nearly every major world religion. On the roof, a specially designed garden incorporates surfaces of plant life and stones to create a serene space suspended above the urban landscape. *(Behind Dublin Castle. ☎ 01 407 0750; www.cbl.ie. 45min. tours W 1pm, Su 3 and 4pm. Open May-Sept. M-F 10am-5pm, Sa 11am-5pm, Su 1-5pm; Oct.-Apr. Tu-F 10am-5pm, Sa 11am-5pm, Su 1-5pm. Free.)*

DUBLINIA. This three-story interactive exhibition, which gets its name from one of the ancient Latin terms for the city, is housed on the site of the medieval parish of St. Michael the Archangel. Figures come to life as visitors are ushered through Dublin's medieval history, from AD 1170 to 1540. *(Across from Christ Church Cathedral. ☎ 01 679 4611; www.dublinia.ie. Open Apr.-Sept. daily 10am-5pm; Oct.-Mar. M-F 11am-4pm, Sa-Su 10am-4pm. Last admission 45min. before closing. €6.25, students €5.25, seniors and unemployed €5. Combined admission with Christ Church Cathedral €10.)*

DUBLIN CASTLE. Norman King John built the castle in 1204 on top of the Viking settlement Dubh Linn ("black pool"); more recently, a series of structures from the 18th and 19th centuries has covered the site, culminating in an uninspired

20th-century office complex. But for 700 years, Dublin Castle was the seat of British rule in Ireland, and its state apartments—open to the public for tours—still host important state functions. Next door, the intricate inner dome of **Dublin City Hall** (designed as the Royal Exchange in 1779) shelters statues of national heroes like **Daniel O'Connell.** *(Dame St., at the intersection of Parliament and Castle St. ☎ 01 677 7129; www.dublincastle.ie. State Apartments open M-F 10am-5pm, Sa-Su and holidays 2-4:45pm; closed during official functions. €4.50, students and seniors €3.50, children €2. Grounds free.)*

CHRIST CHURCH CATHEDRAL. Built in the name of the universal Church, Irish cathedrals were forced to convert to the Church of Ireland in the 16th century. Stained glass sparkles above the raised crypts, one of which supposedly belongs to **Strongbow.** In merrier times, the cavernous crypt held shops and drinking houses, but nowadays cobwebs hang from the ceiling, fragments of ancient pillars lie about, and in every corner a looming stone memorial serves as an eerie reminder of the human history captured within its walls. The entrance fee includes admission to the **"Treasure of Christ Church,"** a rotating exhibit that displays the church's hoard of medieval manuscripts, gleaming gold vessels, and funereal busts. *(At the end of Dame St., uphill and across from the Castle. A 10min. walk from O'Connell Bride, or take bus #50 from Eden Quay or 78A from Aston Quay. ☎ 01 677 8099. Open daily 9am-5pm except during services. €6, students and seniors €4.)*

ST. PATRICK'S CATHEDRAL. This church dates back to the 12th century, although Sir Benjamin Guinness remodeled much of the building in 1864. At 100m long, it's Ireland's largest cathedral. Richard Boyle, father of scientist Robert, has a memorial here, and the writer Jonathan Swift spent his last years as Dean of St. Patrick's; his grave is marked on the floor of the south nave. *(From Christ Church, Nicholas St. runs south and downhill, eventually becoming Patrick St. Take bus #49, 49A, 50, 54A, 56A, 65, 65B, 77, or 77A from Eden Quay. ☎ 01 475 4817; www.stpatrickscathedral.ie. Open Mar.-Oct. daily 9am-6pm; Nov.-Feb. Sa 9am-5pm, Su 9am-3pm. Church closed to visitors Su half hr. before services which begin 8:30am, 11:15am, 3:15pm, although visitors are welcome to attend. €5.50, students and seniors €4.20.)* **Marsh's Library,** beside the cathedral, is Ireland's oldest public library. A peek inside reveals elegant wire alcoves, a collection of early maps, and exhibits of its holdings. *(☎ 01 454 3511. Open M and W-F 10am-1pm and 2-5pm, Sa 10:30am-1pm. €2.50, students and seniors €1.50.)*

GUINNESS STOREHOUSE. The abundance of stout-stamped paper bags hanging from the arms of tourists are a good indication of Ireland's number one tourist attraction. Most can't resist the chance to discover the ins and outs of the famed black magic. Forward-looking Arthur Guinness ensured that his original 1759 brewery would become the success that it is today by signing a 9000-year lease, which is dramatically set into the floor of the massive reception hall. Seven floors of glass and suspended metal catwalks coax you through the production and legacy of Ireland's most famous brew. The self-guided tour ends with a complimentary pint in the top floor's **Gravity Bar,** a modern, light-filled space that commands a stunning panoramic view of the city. *(St. James's Gate. From Christ Church Cathedral, follow High St. west through its name changes—Cornmarket, Thomas, and James. Or, take bus #51B or 78A from Aston Quay or #123 from O'Connell St. ☎ 01 408 4800; www.guinness-storehouse.com. Open daily July-Aug. 9:30am-7pm; Sept.-June 9:30am-5pm. €14, students over 18 and seniors €10, students under 18 €8, ages 6-12 €5, under 6 free.)*

KILMAINHAM GAOL. Almost all the rebels who fought in Ireland's struggle for independence between 1792 and 1921 spent time here; the jail's last occupant was Éamon de Valera, the former leader of Éire. It was built on raised land outside of the city, and its open-barred windows left prisoners exposed to the elements with the belief that the air would dispel disease. The prison's dark history echoes through its frigid, eerie passages. The ghastly, compelling stories of the prisoners are dealt out in two doses, first in the comprehensive museum that sets the jail in the context of its socio-political history, and then in a 1hr. tour of the dank chambers that ends in the haunting wasteland of an execution yard. *(Inchicore Rd. Take bus #51b, 51c, 78a, or 79 from Aston Quay. ☎01 453 5984. Open Apr.-Sept. daily 9:30am-6pm; Oct.-Mar. M-Sa 9:30am-5:30pm, Su 10am-6pm. Last admission hr. before close. Tours every 30min. €5.30, seniors €3.70, students €2.10, families €11.50. Small museum, separate from tour, is free of charge.)*

O'CONNELL STREET. This shopping thoroughfare starts at the Liffey and leads to Parnell Square. At 45m, it was once the widest street in Europe. In its pre-Joycean heyday, it was known as Sackville St., but its name was changed in honor of "The Liberator" Joseph Parnell. The central traffic islands contain monuments to Irish leaders like James Larkin—who organized the heroic Dublin general strike of 1913—O'Connell, and Parnell. O'Connell's **statue** faces the Liffey and O'Connell Bridge; the winged women aren't angels but Winged Victories, although one has a bullet hole from 1916 in a rather inglorious place. Parnell's statue points toward nearby Parnell Mooney's pub, while the engraved words at his feet proclaim: "Thus far and no further." In front of the General Post Office stands the recently erected 120m **Dublin Spire.** Originally planned as a Millennium Spire, it wasn't actually completed until early 2003. The spire and the recently planted trees lining the lower part of the street are the first steps to restoring the area to its former glory.

THE DUBLIN WRITERS MUSEUM. Sure to delight wordsmiths, this enthralling museum documents Dublin's rich literary heritage and the famous figures who played a part. Manuscripts, rare editions, and memorabilia of giants like Swift, Shaw, Wilde, Yeats, Beckett, Behan, Kavanagh, and O'Casey share space with caricatures and paintings. Don't miss the **Gallery of Writers** upstairs, an ornate, bust-lined room that harbors one of the most personal items of the collection: James Joyce's piano. Also worth checking out is the one-man performance titled **"The Writers Entertain,"** which focuses on some of Ireland's most famous literary figures. *(18 Parnell Sq. N. ☎01 872 2077; www.writersmuseum.com. Open June-Aug. M-F 10am-6pm, Sa 10am-5pm, Su 11am-5pm; Sept.-May M-Sa 10am-5pm, Su 11am-5pm. €7.25, students and seniors €6.10, children €4.55, families €21. Combined ticket with the Shaw birthplace €12.50, students and seniors €10.30.)* The **Irish Writers Centre,** adjacent to the museum, is the hub of Ireland's living community of writers, providing today's aspiring writers with frequent fiction and poetry readings. It is not a museum, but it does provide information about Dublin's literary happenings. *(19 Parnell Sq. N. ☎01 872 1302; www.writerscentre.ie. Open M-F 10am-5:30pm.)*

JAMES JOYCE CULTURAL CENTRE. Mock-ups reveal insight into Joyce's life, love, and labor, while intriguing items like the original door to his home at 7 Eccles St., a map tracing Stephen Dedalus' and Leopold Bloom's relative movements, and a 1921 Ulysses schema pique literary interest. *(35 N. Great Georges St., up Marlborough St. and past Parnell Sq. ☎01 878 8547; www.jamesjoyce.ie. Open year-round Tu-Sa 10am-5pm; Apr.-Oct. additionally Su noon-5pm. Guided tour every Sa 11am and 2pm; Jul.-Aug. additionally Tu and Th 11am and 2pm; €10, students and seniors €8. Admission to the center €5, students and seniors €4.)*

THE CUSTOM HOUSE. Dublin's greatest architectural triumph, the Custom House was designed and built in the 1780s by London-born James Gandon, who gave up the chance to be Russia's state architect so that he could settle in Dublin. The Roman and Venetian columns and domes give the cityscape a taste of what the city's 18th-century Anglo-Irish brahmins wanted Dublin to become. Carved heads along the frieze represent the rivers of Ireland; the sole woman is the Liffey. *(East of O'Connell St. at Custom House Quay, where Gardiner St. meets the river. ☎01 878 7660. Visitors Centre open mid-Mar.-Oct. M-F 10am-5pm, Sa-Su 2-5pm; Nov. to mid-Mar. W-F 10am-5pm, Su 2-5pm. €1, families €3, students free.)*

OLD JAMESON DISTILLERY. Learn how science, grain, and tradition come together to form liquid gold. The tour walks visitors through the creation of whiskey, although the stuff is really distilled in Co. Clare. Not to disappoint those hankering for a taste after all that talking, the tour ends at the bar with a free drink (or soft drinks for the uninitiated). Volunteer in the beginning to get the chance to taste-test a tray of six different whiskeys from around the world. *(Bow St. From O'Connell St., turn onto Henry St. and continue straight as the street narrows to Mary St., then Mary Ln.; the warehouse is on a cobblestone street on the left. Buses #68, 69, and 79 run from city center to Merchant's Quay. ☎01 807 2355. Tours daily 9:30am-6pm, typically every 45min. €12.50, students and seniors €9, children €6.)*

PHOENIX PARK AND DUBLIN ZOO. Europe's largest enclosed public park is most famous for the "Phoenix Park murders" of 1882. The Invincibles, a Republican splinter group, stabbed Lord Cavendish, Chief Secretary of Ireland, and his Under Secretary a mere 180m from the Phoenix Column. Complications ensued when a Unionist journalist forged a series of letters linking Parnell to the murderers. The column itself, which is capped with a phoenix rising from flames, is something of an inside joke—the park's name actually comes from the Irish Fionn Uísce, meaning "clean water." The 714 hectares also harbor the **President's Residence** (Áras an Uachtaraín), the US Ambassador's residence, cricket pitches, polo grounds, and lots of red deer. To view all the sights without all the hikes, see the friendly owners of **Phoenix Park Bike Hire,** located at the Conyngham Rd. entrance. *(☎086 265 6258. Bikes €5 per hr., €10 for 3hr., €20 per day; tandem €10/20/40.)* Even though it is also home to one of the Garda's largest headquarters, the park is still not safe to travel in at night, especially alone. *(☎01 677 0095. Take bus #10 from O'Connell St. or #25 or 26 from Middle Abbey St. west along the river.)* The most notable attraction within its grounds is **Dublin Zoo,** one of the world's oldest and Europe's largest. It contains 700 critters and the world's biggest egg. The habitats are large for an urban zoo and the animals tend to move around—the elephants even have room to swim. *(Bus #10 from O'Connell St.; #25 or 26 from Wellington Quay. ☎01 474 8900. Open M-Sa 9:30am-6pm, Su 10:30am-6pm. Last admission 5pm. Zoo closes at dusk in winter. €14.50, students and seniors €12, children €10.)*

IRELAND

ENTERTAINMENT

Whether you seek poetry, punk, or something in between, Dublin is ready to entertain. The free *Event Guide* is available at music stores and hotels throughout the city. The glossier *In Dublin* (free at Tower Records, the tourist office) comes out every two weeks with feature articles and listings for music, theater, art exhibitions, comedy shows, clubs, museums, and movie theaters. Go to www.visitdublin.com for the latest hot spots.

Abbey Theatre, 26 Lower Abbey St. (☎01 878 7222; www.abbeytheatre.ie). The theater was founded by W.B. Yeats and Lady Gregory in 1904 to promote the Irish cultural revival and Modernist theater, a combination that didn't go over well with audiences. The Abbey's 1907 premiere of J. M. Synge's *Playboy of the Western World* led to storms of protest. Today, the Abbey (and Synge) have gained respectability. Ireland's National Theatre is on the cutting edge of international drama. Tickets €22-35; Sa 2:30pm matinee €18-22, students and seniors with ID €14. Box office open M-Sa 10:30am-7pm.

Peacock Theatre, 26 Lower Abbey St. (☎01 878 7222). The Abbey's experimental downstairs studio theater. Evening shows, plus occasional lunchtime plays, concerts, and poetry. Doors open M-Sa at 7:30pm. Tickets €15-22; Sa 2:30pm matinees €18, students/seniors €15. Available at Abbey box office.

Gate Theatre, 1 Cavendish Row (☎01 874 4045; www.gate-theatre.ie). Contemporary Irish and classic international dramas in intimate, elegant setting. Wheelchair-accessible. Box office open M-Sa 10am-7:30pm. Tickets €16-30; M-Th student ticket at curtain €15 with ID, subject to availability.

PUBLIN

James Joyce proposed that a "good puzzle would be to cross Dublin without passing a pub." When a local radio station once offered £100 to the first person to solve the puzzle, the winner explained that any route worked—you'd just have to stop in each one along the way. Dublin's pubs come in all shapes, sizes, and specialties. Ask around or check the publications *In Dublin*, *Hot Press*, or *Event Guide* for music listings. Normal pub hours in Ireland end at 11:30pm Sunday through Wednesday and 12:30am Thursday through Saturday. The laws that dictate these hours are subject to yearly changes—patrons often get about a half-hour after "closing" to finish off their drinks. An increasing number of pubs have late permits that allow them to remain open until at least 2am; drink prices tend to rise around midnight to cover the permit's cost (or so they claim). Bars that post their closing time as "late" mean after midnight and, sometimes, after what is legally mandated. ID-checking almost always happens at the door rather than at the bar. A growing number of bars are blurring the distinction between pub and club by hosting live music and staying open late into the night on weekdays.

The Stag's Head, 1 Dame Ct. (☎01 679 3687). Atmospheric Victorian pub with stained glass, marble-topped round tables, and evidence of deer decapitation front and center above the bar. Student crowd dons everything from T-shirts to tuxes. Pub grub, like bangers and mash, runs €6-12. Kitchen open M-Sa noon-4pm. Bar open M-Th 10:30am-11:30pm, F-Sa 10:30am-12:30am, Su 12:30-11pm.

The Porterhouse, 16-18 Parliament St. (☎01 679 8847). Way, way more than 99 bottles of beer on the wall, including 9 self-brewed porters, stouts, and ales. The Porterhouse Red is a must. 3 floors fill nightly with great crowd for trad, blues, and rock. Open M-W 11:30am-11:30pm, Th-F 11:30am-2am, Sa 11:30am-2:30am, Su 12:30-11pm.

Whelan's, 25 Wexford St. (☎01 478 0766; www.whelanslive.com). Pub hosts big-name trad, rock, and everything in between in attached music venue. Live music nightly starting at 8:30pm (doors open at 8pm). Th DJ takes the floor. Cover for shows next door €8-16. Open for lunch (€8-12) 12:30-2pm. Open M-W until 2am and Th-Sa until 3am.

Zanzibar, at the Ha'penny Bridge (☎01 878 7212). Dances between club and pub with explosive results. Unique private rooms on the balcony, one overlooking the Liffey. Th-Su DJ plays R&B, blues, and chart-toppers. Cover after 11pm F €5, Sa €7. Kitchen open until 10pm. 21+. Open Th-Sa 5pm-2:30am, Su noon-11:30pm.

The Long Stone, 10-11 Townsend St. (☎01 671 8102). Multi-level maze of comfortable booths. Frequent live bands. Heated beer garden. Kitchen open M-Su 12-9pm. Open M-Th and Su 11am-11:30pm, F-Sa 11am-12:30am.

CLUBLIN

As a rule, clubs open at 10 or 10:30pm, but they don't heat up until the pubs empty around 12:30am. Clubbing is an expensive end to the evening; covers run €5-20 and pints can surpass €5. To save some money, find a club with an expensive cover but cheap drink prices and stay all night. A handful of smaller clubs on Harcourt and Camden Streets are basic but fun. Most clubs close between 1:30 and 3am, but a few have been known to stay open until daybreak. To get home after 11:30pm, when Dublin Bus stops running, take the **NiteLink bus** (M-W 12:30am and 2am, Th-Sa every 20min. from 12:30am to 4:30am; €5), which runs designated routes from the corner of Westmoreland and College St. to Dublin's suburbs. Taxi stands are sprinkled throughout the city, the most central being in front of Trinity, at the top of Grafton St. Be prepared to wait 30-45min. on weekend nights. For info on clubs, check the *Event Guide*.

The PoD, 35 Harcourt St. (☎01 476 3374; www.pod.ie), corner of Hatch St., in an old train station. Stylishly futuristic, orange interior. Serious about its music. Upstairs is **The Red Box** (☎478 0225), a huge, separate club with brain-crushing music and a crowd at the bar so deep it seems designed to winnow out the weak. Mellow train-station-turned-bar **Crawdaddy** hosts musical gigs, including some world stars. Cover €10-20; Th students €5; can rise fast when big-name DJs perform. Open until 2:30am on weekends.

The Mezz (The Hub), 21-25 Eustace St. (☎01 670 7655). Live bands rock nightly right inside the entrance of this poster-plastered, atmospheric club—try not to knock over a drum set as you make your way toward the bar. Quiet pub by afternoon (M-Sa 5pm-2:30am, Su 5pm-1am) transforms into a loud, live-music cauldron at night. No cover. It shares the building with **The Hub,** which, as one of the only 18+ clubs in Temple Bar, attracts the younger crowd. Cover at The Hub €5-10 or more, depending on the band—doors 8pm, dancing 11:30pm. Open Tu-Sa until 2:30am.

The Dragon, S. Great Georges St. (☎01 478 1590), a few doors down from The George. Packed to its trendy rafters on weekend nights. Quieter lounge area in front gives way to a DJ spinning house by the dance floor in back. Massive sculpture of Hercules wrestling a snake floats above the crowd. 18+. Open M and Th 5pm-2:30am, Tu-W 5-11:30pm, F-Sa 5pm-3:30am, Su 5-11pm. The upstairs bar is the drinking quarters for the Emerald Warriors, Ireland's gay rugby team.

The Village, 26 Wexford St. (☎01 475 8555). Posh ground-floor bar. Occasional live music below a popular upstairs weekend club. Th-Sa bands play 7-10:30pm (about €15), then DJs spin chill-out, jungle, and house downstairs. Tickets for live bands available next door. Club F €8, Sa €10. Bar open until 1:30am; club open Th-Sa until 3am.

WESTERN IRELAND

Even Dubliners will say that the west is the "most Irish" part of Ireland; in remote areas you may hear Irish being spoken almost as often as English. The potato famine was most devastating in the west—entire villages emigrated or died—and the current population is still less than half of what it was in 1841.

GALWAY ☎091

With its youthful, exuberant spirit, Galway (pop. 80,000) is one of the fastest growing cities in Europe. Performers dazzle crowds on the appropriately named Shop St., locals and tourists lounge in outdoor cafes, and hip crowds pack the pubs and clubs at night. In addition to its peaceful quay-side walks, Galway is only a short drive away from beautiful Connemara.

TRANSPORTATION. **Trains** leave from Eyre Sq. (☎091 537 521) for Dublin (3hr., 6-8 per day, €31.50) via Portarlington (€33.50); transfer at Portarlington for all other lines. **Buses** also leave from the Eyre Sq. station (☎091 562 000) for Belfast, UK (7hr., 2 per day., €30), Donegal (4hr., 3-4 per day, €17.10), and Dublin (4hr., every hr., €13.10).

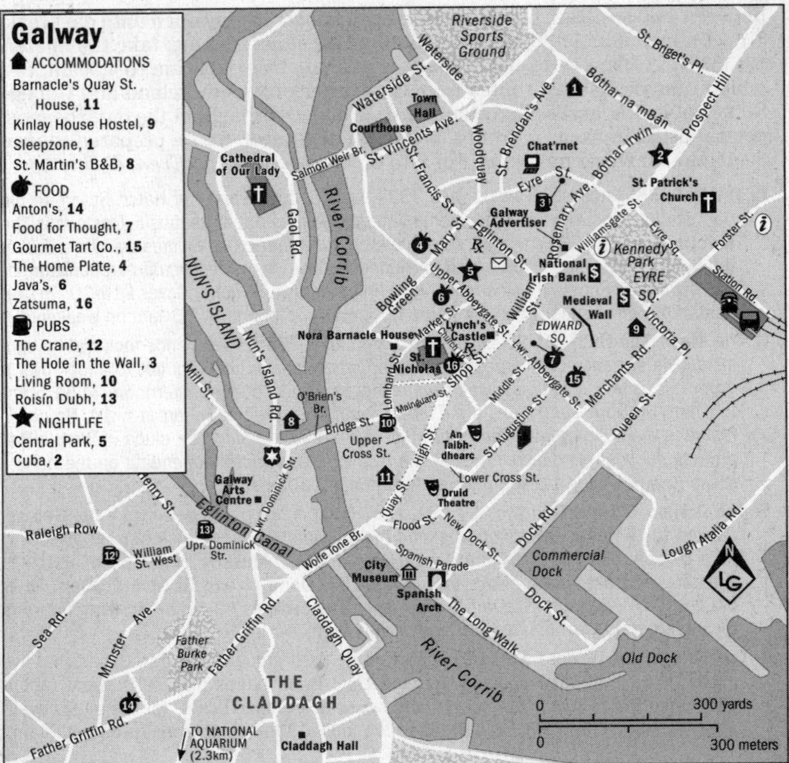

ORIENTATION AND PRACTICAL INFORMATION. Galway's train and bus stations are on a hill to the northeast of **Eyre Square,** a recently renovated block of lawns and monuments. A string of small, cheap B&Bs are north of the square along **Prospect Hill.** The western corner of the square is the gateway to the pedestrian center, filled with shoppers seeking cups of coffee or pints of stout. From the square, **Shop Street** becomes **High Street,** which then becomes **Quay Street.** The **Wolfe Tone Bridge** spans the River Corrib and connects the city center to the bohemian left bank. The **tourist office** is on Forster St. near the train and bus stations. (☎091 537 700; www.irelandwest.ie. Open Apr.-Oct. daily 9am-5:45pm; Nov.-Mar. M-Sa 9am-5:45pm.) For **Internet,** head to **Chat'rnet,** 5 Eyre St, across from The Hole in the Wall pub. (☎091 539 912. €4 per hr. Open M-Sa 9am-11pm, Su 10am-11pm. Cash only.) A 24hr. **ATM** and currency exchange are at the **National Irish Bank,** 20 Eyre Sq. (☎890 882 545. Open M-T and F 10am-4pm, W 10:30am-4pm, Th 10am-5pm.) The **post office** is at 3 Eglinton St. (☎091 534 727. Open M and W-Sa 9am-5:30pm, Tu 9:30am-5:30pm.)

ACCOMMODATIONS AND FOOD. The number of accommodations in Galway has recently skyrocketed, but reservations are still necessary in summer. Most B&Bs are concentrated in **Salthill** or on **College Road.** **Barnacle's Quay Street House (IHH) ❶**, 10 Quay St., is the most conveniently located hostel in

Galway. Its bright, spacious rooms are perfect for crashing after a night on the town. (☎091 568 644; www.barnacles.ie. Light breakfast included. Laundry €8. Kitchen. Free towels. Free Wi-Fi. Computer use €1 per 15min. Single-sex dorms available. Check-in 11am; check-out 10:30am. 4- to 12-bed dorms €13-20.50; doubles €56-68. MC/V.) **Sleepzone ❷,** Bóthar na mBán (BO-her na-MAHN), Woodquay, a left off Prospect Hill, has large rooms and top-notch facilities. (☎091 566 999; www.sleepzone.ie. Laundry €7. Free Wi-Fi. Single-sex dorms available. Dorms from €16-24; singles €30-55; doubles €50-76. Weekend and low-season rates vary. MC/V.) **Kinlay House ❶,** at the corner of Eyre Sq. and Merchant's Rd., has 220 beds in a convenient and clean location. From the bus station, walk down Station Rd. towards Square and turn left. (☎091 565 244; www.kinlaygalway.ie. Breakfast included. Free luggage room and safe. Towels €1. Free Wi-Fi; computer use €3 per hr. Reception 24hr. Check-out 10:30am. Dorms €15.50-22, doubles €56-63. MC/V.) At **St. Martin's B&B ❸,** 2 Nun's Island Rd., on the west bank of the river at the end of O'Brien's Bridge, the gorgeous back garden features a waterfall cascading into the river. This friendly B&B caters to young travelers and the owner greets every guest with coffee. (☎091 568 286; stmartins@gmail.com. Singles €35; doubles €70. Cash only.)

The cafes and pubs around Quay, High, and Shop Streets are good options for budget dining. On Saturdays, an **open-air market** on Market St. sells fruit and ethnic foods. (Open 8am-4pm.) How the stylish **Gourmet Tart Co. ❶,** 7 Lower Abbeygate St., manages to sell its sumptuous creations at such low prices remains a mystery, but be sure to take advantage of the best deal in Galway. (Sandwiches under €4, salad buffet €13 per kg., pastries €1-2. Open M-Su 7:30am-7pm. Cash only.) At **The Home Plate ❷,** on Mary St., diners enjoy large sandwiches (€7) and entrees (€7.50-10) on tiny wooden tables. (☎091 561 475. Open M-Sa noon-9pm, Su noon-6:30pm. Cash only.) **Zatsuma ❷,** 27 Shop St., produces delicious crepes with a skilled assembly line as salivating customers look on. Savory varieties, like the chicken- and bacon-filled Connemara Combo, run €5-6.75, while sweet ones, like Parisian Pear with hazelnut spread, cost €3.25-4. (☎091 895 877; www.zatsuma.ie. Open daily 11am-3am. MC/V.) Cross Wolfe Tone Bridge and walk 3min. up Father Griffin Rd. to reach **Anton's Cafe and Art Space ❷** and its homemade fare. The walls feature the work of local artists. (☎091 582 067; www.antonscafe.com. Sandwiches €6-6.50. Open M-F 8am-6pm. Cash only.) Take a left just before Shop St. for **Food For Thought ❶,** Lower Abbeygate St., a student hangout with wallet-friendly prices. (☎091 565 854. Moussaka €6.50. Open M-F 7:30am-6pm, Sa 8am-6pm, Su 11:30am-4pm. Cash only.) Artsy students flock to **Java's ❶,** 17 Upper Abbeygate St., for *amuse-gueules* (€7) and *tartines* (€9-10.50). (☎091 532 890. Open M-W and Su 10am-8pm, Th-Sa 10pm-4am. MC/V.)

SIGHTS AND ENTERTAINMENT. The best *craic* in Galway is people-watching: Eyre Square and Shop St. are full of street performers, some unknowing. At the **Church of Saint Nicholas** on Market St., a stone marks the spot where Columbus supposedly stopped to pray to the patron saint of travelers before sailing the ocean blue. (Open daily Apr.-Sept. 8:30am-8pm, Oct.-Mar. 9am-5pm. Free.) On Shop St., **Lynch's Castle** is a well-preserved 16th-century merchant's residence than now houses a bank. From Quay St., head across Wolfe Tone Bridge to the **Claddagh,** an area that was an Irish-speaking, thatch-roofed fishing village until the 1930s. The famous **Claddagh rings** are today's mass-produced reminders of yesteryear. The **Nora Barnacle House,** 8 Bowling Green, off Market St., has hardly changed since James Joyce's future wife Nora lived there with her family at the turn of the 20th century. Check out Joyce's love letters to his life-long companion. (☎091 564 743 www.norabarnacle.com. Open mid-May to mid-Sept. M-Sa 10am-1pm and 2-5pm, or by appointment. €2.50, students €2.) Hang with sea creatures for an afternoon at the **National Aquarium of Ireland,** on the Salt Hill Promenade. (☎091 585 100; www.nationalaquarium.ie. Open Apr.-Sept. M-F 9am-6pm, Sa-Su 9am-7pm; Oct.-Mar. M-F 9am-5pm, Sa-Su 9am-6pm. €9.75, students €7. MC/V.) Event listings are published in the free *Galway Advertiser*, available at the tourist office and most accommodations. In mid-July, the **Galway Arts Festival** (☎091 566 577) attracts droves of filmmakers, rock groups, theater troupes, and trad musicians.

NIGHTLIFE. With approximately 650 pubs and 80,000 people, Galway maintains a low person-to-pub ratio. Pubs on Quay St., High St., and Eyre Sq. cater primarily to tourists, while locals stick to the more trad-oriented pubs on Dominick Street across the river. Fantastic trad fills two floors at **The Crane,** 2 Sea Rd. (☎091 587 419. Open M-Th 2:30-11:30pm, F-Sa 12:30pm-12:30am, Su 12:30-11pm. Downstairs free, upstairs cover €10-22.50. Cash only.) Nearby, at the **Roisín Dubh (The Black Rose),** on Dominick St., a bookshelved front hides some of Galway's hottest live music. (☎091 586 540; www.roisindubh.net. Pints €4.20. Live music 6 nights a week, W stand-up comedy 9pm. Cover €5-25 most nights for music in the back room; front room and bar free. Open daily 3pm-2am. Cash only.) At **Living Room,** Bridge St., weekend DJs keep the young crowd drinking and dancing at the red-lit bar. (☎091 563 804; www.thelivingroom.ie. No cover. Open M-W 10:30am-11pm, Th-Su 10:30am-2am. MC/V.) **The Hole in the Wall,** Eyre St., is a student hangout with a beer garden. (☎091 564 677. DJ nightly 9:30pm. Open M-Th and Su 10:30am-11:30pm, F-Sa 10:30am-12:30am.)

Between 11:30pm and 12:30am, the pubs drain out, and the young and tireless go dancing. The crowd usually ends up at **Central Park,** 36 Upper Abbeygate St. With five bars and a huge dance floor, this is the place to be in Galway. (☎091 565 976; www.centralparkclub.com. Cover €5-10. Open daily 11pm-late.) **Cuba,** on Prospect Hill, past Eyre Sq., is second only to Central Park in popularity and features danceable live music on two floors. (☎091 565 991; www.cuba.ie. Su stand-up comedy 8:30pm; free admission to club afterward. Cover €6-13. Many hostels give out 50% discount cards. Open daily 11pm-2am.)

NORTHERN IRELAND

The calm tenor of everyday life in Northern Ireland has long been overshadowed by headlines about riots and bombs. While the majority of violence has been subdued, the divisions in civil society continue to some extent. Protestants and Catholics usually live in separate neighborhoods, attend separate schools, and patronize separate stores and pubs. The 1998 Good Friday Accord (p. 337) began a slow march toward peace, and all sides have renewed their efforts to make their country as peaceful as it is beautiful.

BELFAST (BÉAL FEIRSTE) ☎028

The second-largest city on the island, Belfast (pop. 276,000) is the center of Northern Ireland's cultural, commercial, and political activity. **Queen's University** testifies to the city's rich academic history—luminaries such as Nobel Laureate Seamus Heaney once roamed its halls, and Samuel Beckett taught the young men of **Campbell College.** The Belfast pub scene ranks among the best in the world, combining the historical appeal of old-fashioned watering holes with more modern bars and clubs. While Belfast has suffered from the stigma of its violent past, it has rebuilt itself, surprising most visitors with its neighborly, urbane feel. Progress is slow to take root in the still-divided West Belfast area, home to separate communities of Protestants and Catholics.

TRANSPORTATION

Flights: Belfast is served by 2 airports.

Belfast International Airport (☎028 9448 4848; www.belfastairport.com) in Aldergrove. **Aer Lingus** (☎087 0876 5000; www.aerlingus.com); **Air Transat** (☎028 9031 2312; www.airtransat.com); **BMI** (☎087 0264 2229; www.flybmi.com); **Continental** (☎012 9377 6464; www.continental.com); **Easyjet** (☎087 1244 2366; www.easyjet.com); **Flyglobespan** (☎087 0556 1522; www.flyglobespan.com); **Jet2** (☎087 1226 1737; www.jet2.com); **Manx2** (☎087 0242 2226; www.manx2.com); **Wizz Air** (☎482 2351 9499; www.wizzair.com) operate from here. Translink Bus 300 has 24hr. **bus** service from the airport to Europa bus station in the city center M-F every 10min. 6:50am-6:15pm, every 15-40min. otherwise; Sa every 20min. 7:35am-6:40pm, at least once per hr. otherwise; Su every 30min. 8:15am-10:40pm, at least once per hr. otherwise. Call ☎9066 6630 or visit www.translink.co.uk for full timetables. £6, round-trip £9 if you return within 1 month. **Taxis** (☎028 9448 4353) get you there for £25-30.

Belfast City Airport (☎028 9093 9093; www.belfastcityairport.com), is located at the harbor. **Flybe** (☎087 1700 0535; www.flybe.com); **BMI** (☎087 0607 0555; www.flybmi.com); **Ryanair** (☎00353 1249 7791; www.ryanair.com); **Aer Arann** (☎080 0587 2324; www.aerarann.ie); **Manx2** (☎087 0242 2226; www.manx2.com) operate from here. To get from City Airport to Europa bus station, take **Translink Bus 600.** M-F every 20-30min., 8:35am-10:05pm, Sa every 20-30min. 8:05am-9:50pm, Su every 45min. 7:30am-9:50pm. Single £1.30, return £2.20.

Trains: For **train** and **bus** info, contact **Translink** (☎028 9066 6630; www.translink.co.uk; inquiries daily 7am-8pm). Trains depart from several of Belfast's stations **(Great Victoria Street, City Hospital, Botanic, Central)** for Derry/Londonderry (2hr.; M-F 9 per day, Sa 8 per day, Su 4 per day; £10.50 single, £15 return) and leave **Central Station,** E. Bridge St. to Dublin (2hr.; M-Sa 8 per day, Su 5 per day; £25 single, £36 return). The **Metro** buses are free with rail tickets.

Buses: Europa Bus Terminal, off Great Victoria St., behind the Europa Hotel (☎028 9043 4424; ticket office open M-Sa 7:35am-8:05pm, Su 9:15am-6:15pm). Buses to Derry/Londonderry (1hr.; M-F 39 per day, Sa 20 per day, Su 11 per day; £10 single, £15 return) and Dublin (3hr.; M-Su 24 per day; buses at midnight, 1, 2, 3, 4, 5am depart Glengall St.; £10 single, £14 return). The **Centrelink bus** connects the station with the city center.

Ferries: Norfolk Ferries (☎01 819 2999; www.norfolkline-ferries.co.uk) operates out of the **SeaCat** terminal and runs to Liverpool, England (8hr., fares seasonal, starting at £99 with car and £20 without). Book online and before the day of travel to avoid a £10 booking fee. **Stena Line** (☎028 087 0570 7070; www.stenaline.com), up the Lagan River, has the quickest service to Scotland, docking in Stranraer (1hr.; book online, fares seasonal, starting at £55).

ORIENTATION

Buses arrive at the **Europa Bus Station** on Great Victoria Street. To the northeast is **City Hall** in Donegall Square. Donegall Pl. turns into Royal Avenue and runs from Donegall Sq. through the shopping area. To the east, in Cornmarket, pubs in narrow entries (small alleyways) offer an escape. The stretch of Great Victoria St. between the bus station and Shaftesbury Sq. is known as the **Golden Mile** for its highbrow establishments and Victorian architecture. Botanic Avenue and Bradbury Place (which becomes University Road) extend south from Shaftesbury Sq. into **Queen's University** turf. The city center, Golden Mile, and the University are relatively safe areas. Although locals advise caution in the east and west, central Belfast is safer for tourists than most European cities.

Westlink Motorway divides working-class West Belfast, more politically volatile than the city center, from the rest of Belfast. The **Protestant district** stretches along Shankill Rd., just north of the **Catholic neighborhood,** centered around Falls

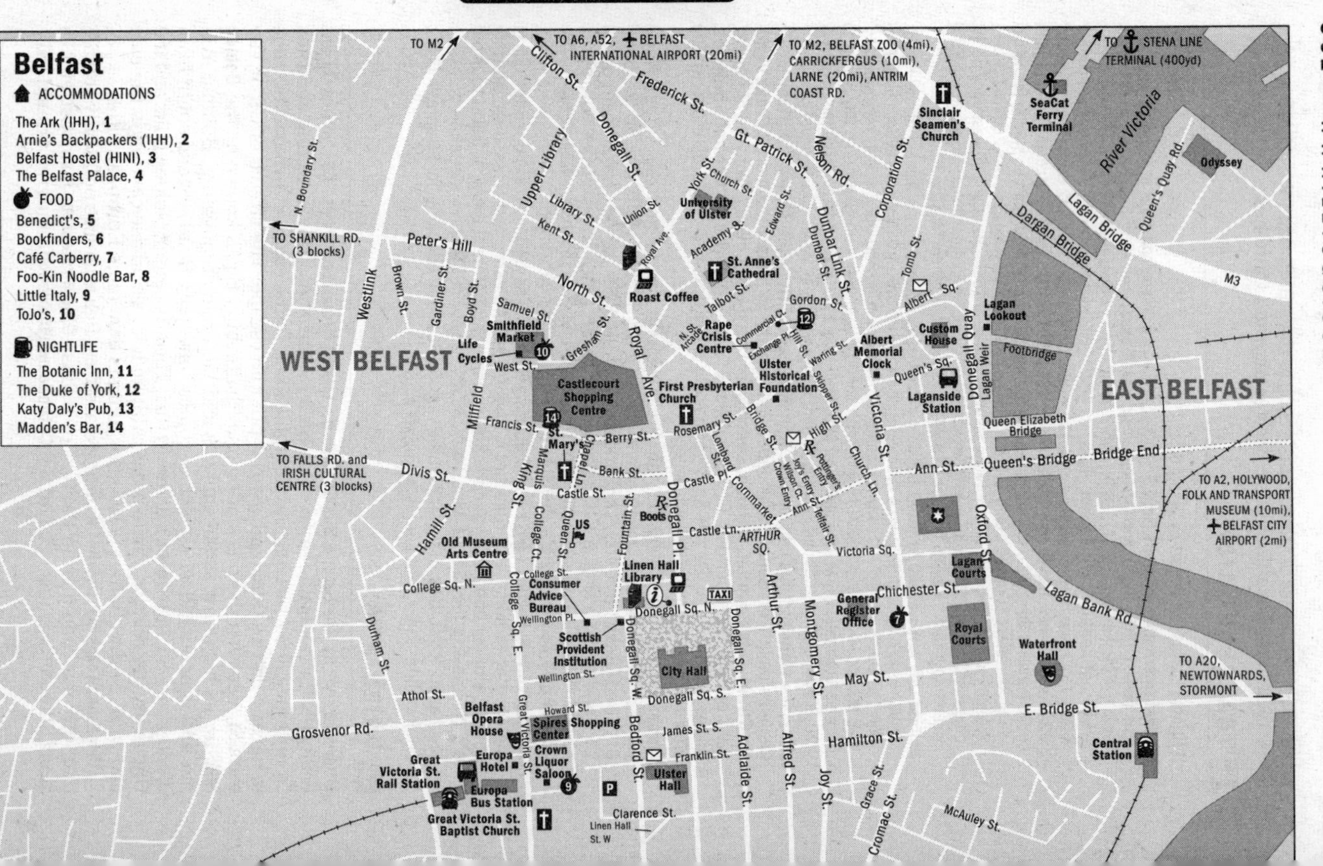
Belfast
ACCOMMODATIONS
The Ark (IHH), 1
Arnie's Backpackers (IHH), 2
Belfast Hostel (HINI), 3
The Belfast Palace, 4
FOOD
Benedict's, 5
Bookfinders, 6
Café Carberry, 7
Foo-Kin Noodle Bar, 8
Little Italy, 9
ToJo's, 10
NIGHTLIFE
The Botanic Inn, 11
The Duke of York, 12
Katy Daly's Pub, 13
Madden's Bar, 14
WEST BELFAST
EAST BELFAST
TO M2
TO A6, A52, BELFAST INTERNATIONAL AIRPORT (20mi)
TO M2, BELFAST ZOO (4mi), CARRICKFERGUS (10mi), LARNE (20mi), ANTRIM COAST RD.
TO STENA LINE TERMINAL (400yd)
TO SHANKILL RD. (3 blocks)
TO FALLS RD. and IRISH CULTURAL CENTRE (3 blocks)
TO A2, HOLYWOOD, FOLK AND TRANSPORT MUSEUM (10mi), BELFAST CITY AIRPORT (2mi)
TO A20, NEWTOWNARDS, STORMONT
SeaCat Ferry Terminal
River Victoria
Odyssey
Queen's Quay Rd.
Lagan Bridge
Dargan Bridge
M3
Sinclair Seamen's Church
Clifton St.
Frederick St.
Gt. Patrick St.
Nelson Rd.
Corporation St.
Donegall St.
Upper Library
Library St.
Kent St.
Union St.
Royal Ave.
York St.
Church St.
University of Ulster
Academy St.
Edward St.
Dunbar St.
Dunbar Link St.
Tomb St.
Albert Sq.
N. Boundary St.
Peter's Hill
Westlink
Brown St.
Gardiner St.
Boyd St.
Samuel St.
North St.
Roast Coffee
St. Anne's Cathedral
Talbot St.
Gordon St.
Lagan Lookout
Custom House
Donegall Quay
Lagan Weir
Footbridge
Smithfield Market
Life Cycles
West St.
Gresham St.
N. St. Arcade
Rape Crisis Centre
Commercial Ct.
Exchange Pl.
Hill St.
Waring St.
Albert Memorial Clock
Queen's Sq.
Laganside Station
Castlecourt Shopping Centre
Ulster Historical Foundation
First Presbyterian Church
Skipper St.
Victoria St.
Queen Elizabeth Bridge
Milfield
Francis St.
St. Mary's
Chapel Ln.
Berry St.
Rosemary St.
Bridge St.
High St.
Pottinger's Entry
Joy's Entry
Wilson Ct.
Crown Entry
Church Ln.
Ann St.
Queen's Bridge
Bridge End
Divis St.
King St.
Marquis
Bank St.
Castle St.
Castle Pl.
Lombard St.
Cornmarket
Fountain St.
Donegall Pl.
Boots
Telfair St.
Ann St.
Oxford St.
Hamill St.
Old Museum Arts Centre
College Ct.
Queen St.
US
Castle Ln.
ARTHUR SQ.
Victoria Sq.
Lagan Courts
Lagan Bank Rd.
College Sq. N.
College St.
Consumer Advice Bureau
Wellington Pl.
Linen Hall Library
TAXI
Donegall Sq. N.
Chichester St.
General Register Office
Royal Courts
Waterfront Hall
Durham St.
College Sq. E.
Scottish Provident Institution
Donegall Sq. W.
City Hall
Donegall Sq. E.
Arthur St.
Montgomery St.
Wellington St.
May St.
Athol St.
Donegall Sq. S.
E. Bridge St.
Grosvenor Rd.
Belfast Opera House
Howard St.
Great Victoria St.
Spires Shopping Center
Bedford St.
James St. S.
Adelaide St.
Alfred St.
Hamilton St.
Central Station
Great Victoria St. Rail Station
Europa Hotel
Crown Liquor Saloon
Franklin St.
Ulster Hall
Joy St.
Grace St.
Europa Bus Station
Great Victoria St. Baptist Church
Clarence St.
Linen Hall St. W
Cromac St.
McAuley St.

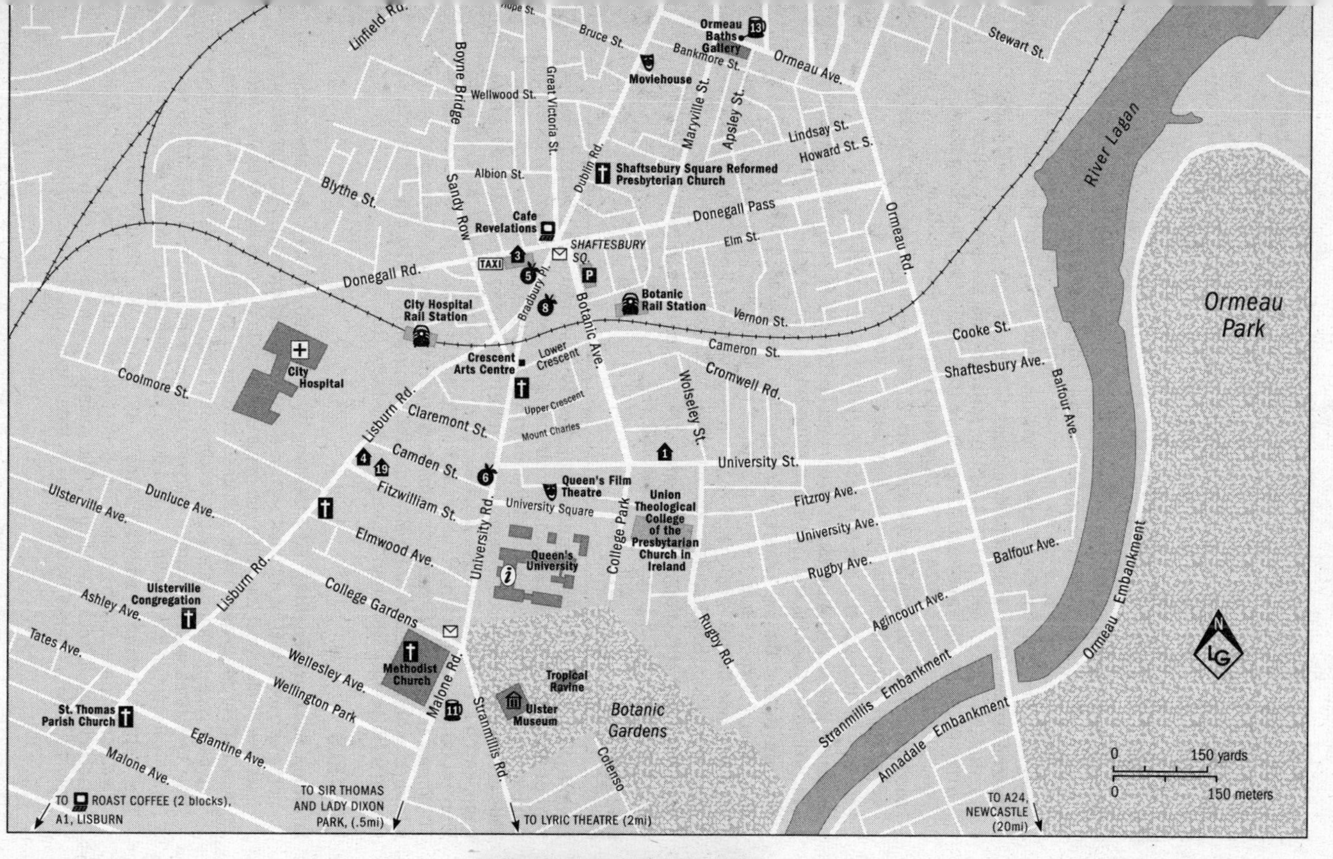

Linfield Rd.
Bruce St.
Ormeau Baths Gallery
Stewart St.
Boyne Bridge
Great Victoria St.
Moviehouse
Bankmore St.
Ormeau Ave.
Wellwood St.
Maryville St.
Apsley St.
Lindsay St.
Howard St. S.
River Lagan
Albion St.
Dublin Rd.
Shaftesbury Square Reformed Presbyterian Church
Blythe St.
Sandy Row
Cafe Revelations
Donegall Pass
Ormeau Rd.
Elm St.
SHAFTESBURY SQ.
TAXI
Donegall Rd.
Bradbury Pl.
Botanic Ave.
Botanic Rail Station
Vernon St.
Ormeau Park
City Hospital Rail Station
Cooke St.
Cameron St.
City Hospital
Crescent Arts Centre
Lower Crescent
Cromwell Rd.
Shaftesbury Ave.
Coolmore St.
Wolseley St.
Balfour Ave.
Lisburn Rd.
Claremont St.
Upper Crescent
Mount Charles
Camden St.
University St.
Queen's Film Theatre
Union Theological College of the Presbyterian Church in Ireland
Ulsterville Ave.
Dunluce Ave.
Fitzwilliam St.
University Square
Fitzroy Ave.
University Rd.
College Park
University Ave.
Elmwood Ave.
Queen's University
Rugby Ave.
Balfour Ave.
Ulsterville Congregation
Lisburn Rd.
Ashley Ave.
College Gardens
Rugby Rd.
Agincourt Ave.
Ormeau Embankment
Tates Ave.
Wellesley Ave.
Methodist Church
Malone Rd.
Tropical Ravine
Stranmillis Embankment
Wellington Park
Ulster Museum
Botanic Gardens
St. Thomas Parish Church
Stranmillis Rd.
Annadale Embankment
Eglantine Ave.
Colenso
Malone Ave.
0
150 yards
0
150 meters
TO ROAST COFFEE (2 blocks), A1, LISBURN
TO SIR THOMAS AND LADY DIXON PARK, (.5mi)
TO LYRIC THEATRE (2mi)
TO A24, NEWCASTLE (20mi)

IRELAND

Rd. The River Lagan splits industrial East Belfast from Belfast proper. The shipyards and docks extend north on both sides of the river as it grows into Belfast Lough. During the week, the area north of City Hall is essentially deserted after 6pm. Streets remain quiet even during the weekend, belying the boisterous pub/club scene. Although muggings are infrequent in Belfast, it's wise to use taxis after dark, particularly near pubs and clubs in the northeast.

PRACTICAL INFORMATION

Tourist Information Centre: Belfast Welcome Centre, 47 Donegall Pl. (☎028 9024 6609; www.gotobelfast.com). Offers comprehensive free booklet on Belfast and info on surrounding areas. Books reservations in Northern Ireland (£2) and the Republic (£3). Open M-Sa 9am-5:30pm, Su 11am-4pm, and June-Sept. M-Sa 9am-7pm.

Financial Services: ATMs at: **Ulster Bank** locations, 140 Great Victoria St (☎028 9024 2686); 11 Donegall Sq. E. (☎028 9024 4112); **Alliance and Leicester,** 63 Royal Ave, (☎028 9024 1957); **First Trust,** 92 Ann St. (☎028 9032 5599); **Northern Bank,** 14 Donegall Sq. W. (☎028 9024 5277). Most banks open M-F 9am-4:30pm.

Launderette: Globe Drycleaners & Launderers, 37-39 Botanic Ave. (☎028 9024 3956). £5 per load. Open M-F 8am-9pm, Sa 8am-6pm, Su noon-6pm.

Police: 6-18 Donegall Pass and 65 Knock Rd. (☎028 9065 0222).

Hospitals: Belfast City Hospital, 91 Lisburn Rd. (☎028 9032 9241). From Shaftesbury Sq., follow Bradbury Pl., and take a right at the fork for Lisburn Rd.

Internet: Belfast Central Library, 122 Royal Ave. (☎028 9050 9150). Open M-Th 9am-8pm, F 9am-5:30pm, Sa 9am-4:30pm. £1.50 per 30min. for nonmembers. **Belfast Welcome Centre,** 47 Donegall Pl., is the most central. £1 per 20min. Open M-Sa 9:00am-5:30pm, Su 11am-4pm, and June-Sept. M-Sa 9am-7pm.

Post Office: Central Post Office, on the corner of High St. and Bridge St. (☎084 5722 3344). Open M-Sa 10am-5:30pm. **Postal Code:** BT2 7FD.

ACCOMMODATIONS

Despite fluctuating tourism and rising rents, Belfast provides a healthy selection of hostels for travelers. Almost all are near Queen's University, close to the city's pubs and restaurants, and a short walk or bus ride to the city center. This area is by far the best place to stay in Belfast. If you are hindered by baggage, catch Metro Bus 8A, 8B, 8C, 9A, 9B, or 9C from Donegall Sq. E or from Europa on Great Victoria St. to areas in the south. Walking to the area takes 10-20min. from bus or train stations. Reservations are necessary during the summer, when hostels and B&Bs often fill to capacity. B&Bs cluster south of Queen's University between Malone and Lisburn Rds.

HOSTELS

Arnie's Backpackers (IHH), 63 Fitzwilliam St. (☎028 9024 2867; www.arniesbackpackers.co.uk). Look for a cutout sign of a sky-gazing backpacker. Arnie, the hostel's jovial owner, may greet you with a cup of tea and check in on you daily. The hostel offers bunk beds in small, clean rooms, a kitchen, common room with television and fireplace, and back garden. Immaculate shared bathrooms. Library of travel info includes bus and train timetables, bulletin board in entryway posts work opportunities, and staff is very friendly. Reception 8:30am-9pm. 8-bed dorms £9; 4-bed £11. Cash only. ❶

The Belfast Palace (Paddy's Palace), 68 Lisburn Rd. (☎028 9033 3367; www.paddyspalace.com). Call it The Belfast Palace in public: Paddy has Catholic associations, and could cause upset. This sociable new hostel offers free Wi-Fi (daily 8am-11:30pm), satellite TV, and videos in the spacious lounge, continental breakfast, a kitchen, and laundry (£5 per load). Young travelers pack into the well-kept rooms. Book ahead in summer. Reception M-Th and Su 8am-8pm, F-Sa 8am-10pm. Dorms £9.50-13.50. Singles £27, doubles £37. Pay for 4 nights, stay free on the 5th. MC/V. ❶

The Ark (IHH), 44 University St. (☎028 9032 9626; www.arkhostel.com). You'll find large, sunny dorms and a kitchen stocked with free tea and coffee. Guests make good use of the dining room, TV area, and computers (Internet £3 per hour). Compete for free laundry on one machine. Lockers in rooms and weekend luggage storage available. Helpful staff provide info on work opportunities. Curfew 2am. Book ahead for holidays and summer. Reception daily 8am-2am. Co-ed 4- to 15-bed dorms £11. Cash only. ❶

Belfast Hostel (HINI), 22 Donegall Rd. (☎028 9031 5435; www.hini.org.uk), off Shaftesbury Sq. A large, modern hostel fills its many beds with tourists. Groups socialize in the large common room. **The Causeway Cafe** is open daily 8-11am (full breakfast; £4). Self-service kitchen. Wheelchair-accessible. Internet and Wi-Fi £1 per 20min. Laundry £3.50. Reception 24hr. Check-in after 1:30pm; check-out before 11am. M-Th and Su 4- to 6-bed dorms £9.50, F-Sa £10.50; ensuite upgrade £1. MC/V. ❶

BED AND BREAKFASTS

Windermere Guest House, 60 Wellington Park (☎028 9066 2693; www.windermereguesthouse.co.uk). Leather couches provide comfortable seating in the living room of this Victorian house. Each room is well equipped with TV and tea/coffee maker. Singles £31-42; doubles £56-60. Cash only. ❸

Camera Guesthouse, 44 Wellington Park (☎028 9066 0026; www.cameraguesthouse.com). Quiet, pristine Victorian house makes an appealing choice. Breakfasts offer wide selection of organic foods and herbal teas that cater to specific dietary concerns. Singles £34, with bath £48; doubles £45/52. 3% commission. MC/V. ❹

Avenue Guest House, 23 Eglantine Ave. (☎028 9066 5904; www.avenueguesthouse.com). Four large, airy rooms equipped with TV and Wi-Fi. Comfortable living room has free DVDs and books. The walk to City Centre is a little over a mile. Dorms £28-30. ❸

FOOD

Dublin Road, Botanic Avenue, and the **Golden Mile** around **Shaftesbury Square** have the most restaurants. The **Tesco** supermarket is at 2 Royal Ave. (☎028 9032 3270. Open M-W and Sa 8am-7pm, Th 8am-9pm, F 8am-8pm, Su 1-5pm.)

Little Italy, 13 Amelia St. (☎028 9031 4914). A little Mediterranean kitchen tucked in Belfast's city center. Customers watch at the brick counter as the industrious staff make their pizzas to order, or linger hungrily on the sidewalk—there are no tables here. Call ahead to avoid a wait, or savor the aromas of the Italiano, Vegetarian Special, Fabio, and Hawaiian pizzas. 9" £4-6, 10" £4-7, 12" £5-8. Open M-Sa 5pm-midnight. ❶

Tojo's, Smithfield Market (☎028 9032 4122). Offers some of Belfast's lowest prices for honest food. While it may look like a cafeteria, the chalkboard full of sandwich options like the Tunatastic (tuna, corn, peppers; £3) fulfills its promise of "homemade food with a modern twist." Open M-F 8am-4pm, Sa 8am-5pm. Cash only. ❶

Bookfinders, 47 University Rd. (☎028 9032 8269). Find it one block from the University, on the corner of Camden St. Read, eat, and use free Wi-Fi amid cluttered bookshelves. A favorite with the University crowd because of its proximity, low prices, and disheveled character, Bookfinders hosts occasional poetry readings and features student art upstairs. Vegan soup and bread £3; sandwiches £3. Open M-Sa 10am-5:30pm. ❶

Cafe Carberry, 153 Victoria St. (☎028 9023 4020). An urban oasis for the crowd-weary traveler. Clean, quiet, and stylish, Café Carberry provides a bright spot in which to refuel with daily specials like soup, baked potato, or salad (£3-5), plus more elaborate fare.

Enjoy a selection of standard and exotic coffees and teas (£1.60-3) while enjoying the local art for sale on the walls. AmEx/MC/V. ❶

Foo-Kin Noodle Bar, 38 Bradbury Place (☎028 9023 2889). Sit down at one of the long dark benches at Foo-Kin and you may soon find yourself sharing condiments with a new friend. Opt for the all-you-can-eat buffet (lunch M-F 12-2pm £7, student £6; dinner M-Sa 5-10pm, £10, students £9), order a noodle dish (£8-9), or try a Cantonese specialty from the menu (£7-9). ❷

Benedict's, 7-21 Bradbury Pl. (☎028 9059 1999; www.benedictshotel.co.uk). This swanky hotel restaurant offers a "Beat the Clock" deal, with selections from the menu daily 5-7:30pm for £5-10. Dress smartly to fit in. Lunches £7.50-12. Dinners £12-16. Open M-Sa 12-2:30pm and 5-10pm, Su 12-5pm and 5-9pm. 21+ to drink. ❸

TOURS

BLACK CAB TOURS. Black Cab tours provide commentary on the murals and sights on both sides of the **Peace Line.** Most drivers have been personally affected by the Troubles, but remain staunchly impartial. The tours provide impassioned yet even-handed commentary, and one of the five Protestant and five Catholic drivers will answer any question. Contact them directly, or ask your hostel to book a tour with a favorite driver. Walter, one of the original drivers, has charmed travelers for over 12 years with insight and wry humor. *(☎077 2106 7752. 1hr. tour from £10 per person.)*

BAILEY'S HISTORICAL PUB TOURS OF BELFAST. A departure from recreational pubbing, this tour is really a primer in Pint Studies. The tour leads visitors through seven or more of Belfast's oldest and best pubs. *(☎028 9268 3665; www.belfastpubtours.com. 2hr. tour departs from Crown Dining Rooms, above the Crown Liquor Saloon, May-Oct. Th 7pm, Sa 4pm. £6, £5 for groups of 10 or more; excludes drinks, although a complimentary tumbler of Bailey's Irish Cream is included.)*

BIKE TOURS. In addition to bike rental, **Life Cycles** (see Bike Rental, p. 343) and **Irish Cycle Tours,** 27 Belvoir View Pk., offer tours of Belfast for £12-16 per day. *(☎028 9064 2222; www.irishcycletours.com)*

BUS TOURS. **Mini-Coach** conducts tours of Belfast *(☎028 9031 5333. 1hr.; departs M-F noon; £10, children £5)* and the Giant's Causeway *(M-Su 9:45am-6:45pm; £25 adults, £22 students, £17.50 children).* Tours depart from the Belfast International Youth Hostel. Tickets available at Belfast Welcome Centre.

SIGHTS

BELFAST CITY HALL. The city hall is currently under renovation, and will not re-open until late 2009, although the grounds remain open. The most dramatic and impressive piece of architecture in Belfast is also its administrative and geographic center. Dominating the grassy square that serves as the locus of downtown Belfast, its green copper dome is visible from nearly any point in the city. Inside, a grand staircase ascends to the second floor, where portraits of the city's Lord Mayors line the halls. The City Council's oak-paneled chambers, used only once per month, are deceptively austere, considering the Council's reputation for rowdy meetings (fists have been known to fly). The interior of City Hall is only accessible by guided tours, which are suspended until the renovation is complete. *(☎028 9027 0477.)*

THE BELFAST WHEEL. This oversized ferris wheel offers unrivaled views of City Hall, Belfast, and the immediately surrounding countryside. Weekends and holidays are the busiest time. Popular with stag and hen parties, tourists, and celebrities. *(Open M-Th and Su 10am-9pm, F 10am-10pm, Sa 9am-10pm. £6.50, children £4.50. Book for VIP capsule, £55.)*

QUEEN'S UNIVERSITY BELFAST. Charles Lanyon designed the beautiful Tudor Gothic brick campus in 1849, modeling it after Magdalen College at Oxford. The **Visitors Centre,** in the Lanyon Room to the left of the main entrance, offers Queen's-related exhibits and merchandise, as well as a **free pamphlet** detailing a walking tour of the grounds. Upstairs, the **Naughton Gallery** displays rotating exhibits of contemporary art. *(University Rd. Visitors Centre. ☎028 9097 5252; www.qub.ac.uk/vcentre. Wheelchair-accessible. Open May-Sept. M-Sa 10am-4pm, tour £5, children free; Oct.-Mar. M-F 10am-4pm, tours by request. Gallery open M-Sa 11am-4pm. Free)*

ODYSSEY. The poster child of Belfast's riverfront revival, this attraction packs five distinct sights into one entertainment center. *(2 Queen's Quay. ☎028 9045 1055; www.theodyssey.co.uk.)* The **Odyssey Arena,** with 10,000 seats, is the largest indoor arena in Ireland. When the Belfast Giants hockey team isn't on the ice, big-name performers heat up the stage. *(Box office ☎028 9073 9074; www.odysseyarena.com. Hockey ☎028 9059 1111; www.belfastgiants.com.)* The **W5 Discovery Centre** (short for "whowhatwherewhenwhy?") is a playground for curious minds and hyperactive schoolchildren. Design your own racecar, waltz up the musical stairs, build a wind turbine, or stage a space rescue mission. *(☎028 9046 7700; www.w5online.co.uk. Workshops run throughout the summer. Wheelchair-accessible. Open M-Sa 10am-6pm; closes at 5pm when school is in session, Su noon-6pm; last admission 1hr. before closing. £7, children £5. Family discounts available.)* The **Sherbidan IMAX Cinema** plays 2D and 3D films on its enormous 62 by 82 ft. screen, while Warner Village Cinemas shows Hollywood blockbusters on its own 12 screens. *(IMAX ☎028 9046 7014; www.belfastimax.com. £5; students £4.50, children £4. Multiplex ☎028 9073 9134; www.stormcinemas.co.uk/belfast. £6/4/3.80. Tu tickets £2.50 all day; Sa-Su kids' tickets £2.50 at 11:30am.)* The **Pavilion** contains shops, bars, and restaurants—including a tourist mecca, the **Hard Rock Cafe.** *(Hard Rock Cafe ☎028 9076 6990. Open M-Sa noon-1am, Su noon-midnight.)*

GRAND OPERA HOUSE. The opera house was cyclically bombed by the IRA, restored to its original splendor at enormous cost, and then bombed again. Visitors today enjoy its grandeur, and tours offer a look behind the ornate facade and include a complimentary coffee and danish at the cafe, **Luciano's.** *(☎028 9023 1919; www.goh.co.uk. Office open M-F 8:30am-9pm, Sa 8:30am-6pm. Tours begin across the street at the office W-Sa 11am. Times vary, so call ahead. £3, seniors/students/children £2.)*

BELFAST CASTLE. Built in 1870 by the Third Marquis of Donegall, the castle sits atop Cave Hill, long the seat of Ulster rulers, and offers the best panoramas of the Belfast port—on a clear day, views extend as far as Scotland and the Isle of Man. The ancient King Matudan had his McArt's Fort here (where more recently the United Irishmen plotted rebellion in 1795) although these days the castle sees more weddings than skirmishes. Marked trails lead north from the fort to five caves in the area, which historians postulate are ancient mines. Only the lowest is accessible to tourists. For those on foot, the small path to the right of the gate makes for a far shorter and prettier walk than the road. *(☎028 9077 6925; www.belfastcastle.co.uk. Open M-Sa 9am-10pm, Su 9am-5:30pm. Free.)*

ST. ANNE'S CATHEDRAL. This Church of Ireland cathedral was begun in 1899, and to keep from disturbing regular worship, it was built around a smaller church already on the site. Upon completion of the new exterior, builders extracted the earlier church brick by brick. Each of the cathedral's 10 interior pillars names one of Belfast's professional fields: Science, Industry, Healing, Agriculture, Music, Theology, Shipbuilding, Freemasonry, Art, and Womanhood. In an enclave called the Chapel of Unity, visitors pray for understanding among Christians of all denominations. *(Donegall St., a few blocks from the city center. Open M-Sa 10am-4pm, Su before and after services at 10am, 11am, 3:30pm.)*

SINCLAIR SEAMEN'S CHURCH. Designed to accommodate the hordes of sinning sailors landing in Belfast port, this quirky church does things its own way—the minister delivers his sermons from a pulpit carved in the shape of a ship's prow, collections are taken in miniature lifeboats, and the choir uses an organ from a Guinness barge with port and starboard lights. *(Corporation St., down from the SeaCat terminal. ☎028 9071 5997. Open W 2-5pm; Su service at 11:30am and 7pm.)*

SIR THOMAS AND LADY DIXON PARK. The most stunning of Belfast's parks sits removed from Belfast Centre, on Upper Malone Rd. Rambling paths and 20,000 flowering rose bushes belie the proximity to the city. The gardens were founded in 1836 and include stud China roses, imported between 1792 and 1824. They now feature a prodigious trial collection of other international varieties. *(☎028 9091 8768. Open M-Sa 7:30am-dusk, Su 9am-dusk.)*

BELFAST ZOO. Set in the hills alongside Cave Hill Forest Park, the zoo's best attribute is its natural setting—catching sight of a lumbering elephant against the backdrop of Belfast lough can be a surreal experience. The recommended route includes the standard lineup of tigers, giraffes, camels, zebras, and the acrobatic spider monkey. *(4 mi. north of the city on Antrim Rd. Take Metro bus 1A, 1B, 1C, 1D, 1E, 1F, 1G, or 2A from City Centre. ☎028 9077 6277. www.belfastzoo.co.uk. Open daily Apr.-Sept. 10am-7pm, last admission 5pm; Oct.-Mar. 10am-4pm, last admission 2:30pm. Apr.-Sept. £8.10, children £4.30; Oct.-Mar. £6.70/3.40. Seniors, children under 4, and disabled free.)*

WEST BELFAST AND THE MURALS

West Belfast has historically been at the heart of political tensions in the North. The Troubles reached their peak in the 1970s; the particularly violent year of 1972 saw 1000 bomb explosions and over 400 murders. While there have not been any large-scale outbreaks of violence in recent years, tensions remain high. The **Catholic area** (centered on the **Falls**) and the **Protestant neighborhood** (centered on the **Shankill**) are separated by the peace line, a grim, gray barricade with a number of gates that close at nightfall. Along the wall, scorch marks, abandoned buildings and fortified homes testify to a tumultuous history and an uneasy future. One bit of the peace line, near **Lanark Way,** connecting the Falls and Springfield roads, contains symbolic paintings and signatures—left mostly by tourists—promoting hope for peaceable relations. West Belfast is not a tourist site in the traditional sense, although the walls and houses along the streets display political murals which speak to Belfast's religious and political divide. These murals are the city's most popular attraction. Those traveling to these sectarian neighborhoods often take **black taxis,** community shuttles that take residents to the city center along set routes. Some black taxis can also be booked for tours of the Falls or Shankill (p. 369). *Let's Go* offers two neighborhood maps (see **Catholic and Protestant Murals**, at right and left) of the Catholic and Protestant murals and memorials, to facilitate a self-guided tour.

It's safest to visit the Falls and Shankill during the day, when the neighborhoods are full of locals and the murals are visible. Do not visit the area during **Marching Season** (the weeks around July 12) when the parades are characterized by mutual antagonism that can lead to violence (see **History and Politics,** p. 334). As the area around the peace line remains politically charged, travelers should be wary of visiting outside of daylight hours. Travelers are advised not to wander from one neighborhood to the other, but to return to the city center between visits to Shankill and the Falls.

New murals in the Falls and Shankill constantly appear, so the descriptions below and the neighborhood maps describe only a fraction of what is there. Before taking a camera, ask about the current political climate. Taking pictures is not advised during Marching Season. However, photography is acceptable on black cab tours; drivers have agreements with the communities.

THE FALLS. This Catholic and Republican neighborhood is larger than Shankill, following Castle St. west from the city center. As Castle St. continues across A12/ Westlink, it becomes Divis Street. A high-rise apartment building marks **Divis Tower,** an ill-fated housing development built by optimistic social planners in the 1960s. The project soon became an IRA stronghold and saw some of the worst of Belfast's Troubles in the 1970s. The British Army still occupies the top floors of the building.

Continuing west, Divis St. turns into Falls Road. The **Sinn Féin office** is easily spotted: one side of it is covered with an enormous portrait of Bobby Sands (see **The Troubles,** p. 337) and an advertisement for the Sinn Féin newspaper, *An Phoblacht*. Continuing down Falls Rd., murals appear on the side streets. In the past, both the Falls and Shankill contained many militaristic representations of the past, but newer murals, which sometimes replace the old ones, feature less charged historical and cultural themes. The newest Falls murals recall Celtic myths and legends, and depict **The Great Hunger,** the phrase Northern Catholics use to refer to the Famine. Earlier militant murals still exist, including a few that depict the Republican armed struggle.

Falls Rd. soon splits into Andersonstown Road and Glen Road, one of the few urban areas with a predominately Irish-speaking population. On the left are the Celtic crosses of **Milltown Cemetery,** the resting place of many fallen Republicans. Inside the entrance, a memorial to Republican casualties is bordered by a low, green fence on the right; the grave of Bobby Sands lies here. Nearby, Bombay Street was the first street to be burned down during the Troubles. There, **Clonard Martyrs Memorial Garden** commemorates the event and lists the names of the dead. Another mile along Andersontown Rd. lies a housing project that was formerly a wealthy Catholic neighborhood—and more murals. The **Springfield Rd. Police Service of Northern Ireland station,** previously named the RUC station, was the most attacked police station in Ireland and the UK. It was recently demolished. The **Andersonstown Barracks,** at the corner of Glen and Andersonstown Rd., are still heavily fortified.

SHANKILL. Shankill Rd. begins at the Westlink and turns into Woodvale Rd. as it crosses Cambrai St. The Ardoyne roundabout is at the intersection of Woodvale Rd. and Crumlin Rd. and can be taken back into the city center. The **Shankill Memorial Garden** honors 10 people who died in a bomb attack on Fizzel's Fish Shop in October 1993; the garden is on Shankill Rd., facing Berlin St. Farther on the road toward the city center, is a mural of **James Buchanan,** the 15th President of the United States (1857-1861), who was a descendant of Ulster Scots (known in the US as the "Scots-Irish"). Other cultural murals depict the 50th Jubilee of the coronation of Queen Elizabeth in 1952 and the death of the Queen Mother in 2002. These are at the beginning of the Shankill near the Rex Bar. Historical murals include a **memorial** to the UVF who fought at the Battle of the Somme in 1916 during WWI, also near the Rex Bar. In the **Shankill Estate,** some murals represent Cromwell suppressing the 1741 Rebellion against the Protestant plantation owners. The densely decorated **Orange Hall** sits on the left. **Brookmount St. McClean's Wallpaper** on the right occupies the space that Fizzel's Fish Shop did before the blast. Through the estate, Crumlin Rd. heads back to the city center, passing an army base, the courthouse, and the jail.

SANDY ROW AND NEWTOWNARDS ROAD. This area's Protestant population is growing steadily, partly due to the redevelopment of the Sandy Row area, and also because many working-class residents are leaving the Shankill. This stretch is a turn off Donegall Rd. at Shaftesbury Sq. An orange arch topped with King William once marked its start. Nearby murals show the **Red Hand of Ulster,** a bulldog, and William crossing the Boyne. East Belfast is a secure, growing Protestant enclave. Murals line Newtownards Rd. On the Ballymacart road, which runs parallel to Newtownards Rd., is a **mural** of local son C.S. Lewis' *The Lion, the Witch, and the Wardrobe.*

ENTERTAINMENT

Belfast's many cultural events and performances are covered in the monthly *Arts Council Artslink*, free at the tourist office, while the bimonthly *Arts Listings* covers arts and entertainment throughout Northern Ireland. Listings appear daily in the *Belfast Telegraph* (which also has a Friday "Arts" supplement) and in Thursday's issue of the *Irish News*. July and August are slow months for arts as the city shuts down for Marching Season, but check *What About?*, *The Big List*, and *Fate* for summer events and concerts. See also the **The Black Box** (see opposite page).

The Crescent Arts Centre, 2 University Rd. (☎028 9024 2338). Hosts concerts and art exhibits. Also supplies some general Belfast arts info. Classes £40-60, children £24-32. Open in term time M-F 10am-10pm, Sa 10am-7pm; otherwise M-Sa 10am-5pm.

The Grand Opera House, 4 Great Victoria St. (☎028 9024 0411, tickets 9024 1919; www.goh.co.uk). Presents opera, ballet, musicals, and drama. Tickets £9-27. Open M-F 8:30am-9pm, Sa 8:30am-6pm.

The Lyric Theatre, 55 Ridgeway St. (☎028 9038 5685; www.lyrictheatre.co.uk). Puts up a mix of classical and contemporary plays with an emphasis on Irish productions. Counts Liam Neeson among its esteemed alums. Tickets M-W £14, concessions £11; Th-Sa £17. Open M-Sa 10am-7pm.

Waterfront Hall, 2 Lanyon Pl. (☎028 9066 8798; www.ulster-orchestra.org.uk). One of Belfast's newest concert centers, hosting a variety of performances throughout the year. Its concourse features visual arts exhibitions. The Ulster Orchestra plays concerts at Waterfront Hall. Tickets £8-24; student discounts available.

SPORTS

Take a cab to the **Odyssey Arena** to catch the **Coors Belfast Giants** battle it out on the ice with county competitors (☎028 9073 9074; www.belfastgiants.com). Football (soccer) fanatics can catch a game at the **Windsor Park** pitch on Donegall Ave. (☎028 9024 4198). Gaelic footballers run to **Andersonstown,** West Belfast, to enjoy Sunday afternoon matches. (Contact the Gaelic Athletic Association at ☎028 9038 3815; www.gaa.ie.) Belfast is crazy about horse racing; see the action down at the **Maze** (☎028 9262 1256; www.downroyal.com) in Lisburn. Just 10 mi. from Belfast, the racecourse has events throughout the year, including **Mirror May Day** and the **Ulster Harp Derby** in June. Ulster Rugby, former winners of the European Cup, play at **Ravenhill Stadium** (☎028 9049 3222).

NIGHTLIFE AND PUBS

Pubs in Belfast are the place to experience the city's *craic* and meet its colorful characters. Pubs were targets for sectarian violence at the height of the Troubles, so most are new or restored, although many retain their historic charm. Those in the city center and university area are now relatively safe.

Bushmills Irish Pub Guide, by Sybil Taylor, relates the history of Belfast pubs (£7; available at local bookstores). For a full list of entertainment options, grab a free copy of *The Big List* or *Fate*, available in tourist centers, hostels, and certain restaurants and pubs.

- **The Duke of York,** 7-11 Commercial Ct. (☎028 9024 1062). Take first left off Hill St. to reach this old boxing venue turned Communist printing press. Rebuilt after it was bombed by the IRA in the 60s, today it is one of Belfast's favorite pubs. Serves the city's largest selection of Irish whiskeys and draws a diverse crowd with cheer and live music—a weekly lineup includes trad (Th 10pm), acoustic guitar (F 10:30pm), and disco (Sa, £5; 18+). Kitchen serves sandwiches and toasties daily until 2:30pm. Open M 11:30am-11pm, Tu-F 11:30am-1am, Sa 11:30am-2am, Su 2-9pm.
- **Madden's Bar,** 74 Berry St. (☎028 9024 4114). You might hear Gaelic among the local crowd, and you'll definitely hear live music—if none is scheduled, a local musician will likely strike up a tune. W beginners' language class, 8:30pm, followed by Irish step-dancing, 9:30pm. Th beginners' piping class followed by pipers' session and open mic. F folk night downstairs, trad upstairs. Sa blues, jazz, or electric folk downstairs, trad upstairs. Lunch M-F noon-2pm. Open daily 11am-1am.
- **Katy Daly's Pub,** 17 Ormeau Ave. (☎028 9032 5942; www.the-limelight.co.uk). Behind City Hall, head toward Queen's, take a left on Ormeau Ave., and you'll find this stalwart of the Belfast music and nightlife scene. Students and young people, tourists included, congregate in this ultimate party spot (the Limelights, Spring and Airbrake clubs are connected). M pub quiz, Tu student night then disco, Th headbangers' ball (1st of the month), Th school disco (2nd), Th live local act (3rd), F disco, Sa rock/current. Lunch served M-F noon-2:30pm. Bar open M-F until 1am, Sa 3pm-1am, Su 8pm-midnight. Open M-Sa 3pm-1am, Su 8pm-midnight.
- **The Black Box,** 18 Hill St. (☎028 9024 4400; www.blackboxbelfast.com). Visit this hip and vibrant committee-owned, publicly-funded arts venue during the day to lounge in a sunlit room with plenty of tables and sofas, and enjoy a sandwich or salad (£3-4) and coffee or tea (£1-2). In the evening, you may catch a book-signing, seminar, or film-screening in the cafe. The Black Box itself (with a stage, bar, and seating or standing room for up to 250 guests) features shows which include: plays, national musical acts, burlesque shows, and balls. Most performances 18+. Cafe open M-F 10am-5pm.

The Botanic Inn, 23 Malone Rd. (☎028 9050 9740). Standing in as the unofficial student union, the hugely popular "Bot" is packed nightly with raucous groups of friends and die-hard sports fans. M live music, W traditional, Th-F soft rock, Sa choose-your-music. Su 70's-80's disco. 19+. Kitchen serves pub grub daily noon-8pm. Open M-Sa 11:30am-1am, Su noon-midnight. MC/V.

The John Hewitt, 51 Lower Donegall St. (☎028 9023 3768; www.thejohnhewitt.com), around the corner from the Duke of York. Half the profits go to the Unemployment Resource Centre, so drink up. Open mic singer/songwriter M at 9:30pm, Tu trad session 9:30pm, Th Nevada Blues (blues/soul) 9:30pm, F Panama Jazz Band 8:30pm, Sa trad session 6pm, Su Silver Cloud Lounge with Lee Rogers (acoustic). 18+. Open M-F 11:30am-1am, Sa noon-1am, Su 7pm-midnight.

Kelly's Cellars, 30 Bank St. (☎028 9024 6058; www.kellyscellars.com). Turn right at St. Mary's Chapel, and you'll find Kelly's, the pub that the others are emulating. Its mottled plaster walls, sloping floors, and arched doorways honor its 1720 pedigree. You'll never find it empty: locals and tourists, young and old, drink here together. No cover. 18+.

The Crown, 46 Great Victoria St. (☎028 9027 9901). As any friendly Belfast resident will claim, you can't visit without seeing The Crown. Duck into a snug (a fully enclosed booth) and you'll be transported back in time. It's safe to say bars no longer see this kind of craftsmanship: gargoyles atop snug posts, stained glass windows, etched mirrors, and scaly pillars. Well-stocked bar. Open M-Sa 11:30am-midnight, lunch noon-3pm. Su 12:30-10:30pm, Sunday lunch 12:30-5pm.

ITALY (ITALIA)

With offspring from Michelangelo to Armani, Italy has carved a distinct path through the centuries, consistently setting a world standard for innovation and elegance. Defined by the legacy of the Roman Empire and the prominence of the Catholic Church, Italy carried artistic, intellectual, and cultural developments forward from ancient times to form the foundations of a modern civilization. Steep Alpine peaks in the north, lush olive trees in the interior, and aquamarine waters along the Riviera provide only a few of the country's breathtaking vistas. Indulging in daily *siestas* and frequently hosting leisurely feasts, Italians seem to possess a knowledge of and appreciation for life's pleasures, while their openness lets travelers ease into Italy's relaxed lifestyle.

DISCOVER ITALY: SUGGESTED ITINERARIES

THREE DAYS. Don't even think about leaving **Rome,** *La Città Eterna* (p. 380). Go back in time at the **Ancient City:** become a gladiator in the **Colosseum,** explore the **Roman Forum,** and stand in the well-preserved **Pantheon.** Spend a day to admiring the fine art in the **Capitoline Museums** and the **Galleria Borghese,** and then satiate your other senses in a *discoteca.* The next morning, redeem your debauched soul in **Vatican City,** gazing at the glorious ceiling of the **Sistine Chapel,** gaping at **St. Peter's Cathedral,** and enjoying the **Vatican Museums.**

ONE WEEK. Spend 3 days taking in the sights in **Rome** before heading north to **Florence** (2 days; p. 418) to immerse yourself in Italy's amazing Renaissance art at the Uffizi Gallery. Move to **Venice** (2 days; p. 408) to float along the canals.

BEST OF ITALY, 2 WEEKS. Begin by savoring the sights and history of **Rome** (3 days), Then move on to **Florence** (3 days). Visit cosmopolitan **Milan** (2 days; p. 402) for shopping. Paddle through canals and peer into delicate blown-glass in **Venice** (2 days) before flying south to **Naples** (2 days; p. 430). Be sure to check out the ash casts and preserved frescoes at ancient **Pompeii** (1 day; p. 436).

LIFE AND TIMES

HISTORY

FROM INFANT TO EMPIRE (1200 BC-AD 476). Although archaeological excavations at Isernia date the earliest inhabitants of Italy to the Paleolithic Era (100,000-70,000 BC), legendary **Aeneas** did not lead his tribe from the ruins of Troy to the Tiber valley to found the city of Alba Longa until 1200 BC. According to Roman tradition, two of Aeneas's descendants, **Remus** and **Romulus,** founded the city of Rome in 753 BC (p. 380) before their brotherly love deteriorated into fratricide. The **Tarquin dynasty** ruled tyrannically for centuries until **Lucius Brutus** expelled the King, Sextus Tarquinius, after he raped the Roman Lucretia. Brutus then established the Roman Republic in 509 BC. A string of military vic-

tories brought near total unification of the Italian peninsula in 474 BC, and victory in the **Punic Wars** made Rome the undisputed ruler of the Mediterranean, with control over all of Carthage's vast empire. The perceived corruption of the goals of the Republic set the stage for **Julius Caesar** to name himself dictator, a rule which lasted only one year before he was assassinated on the Ides of March (Mar. 15), 44 BC. Power eluded would-be successors Brutus and Marc Antony, and Octavian, Caesar's adopted heir, emerged victorious and took the name **Augustus** in 27 BC. His rule spread the *Pax Romana* (Roman Peace) throughout the Mediterranean, the republic morphed into an empire, and the era became known as the **Golden Age of Rome.** The Empire persecuted Christians until Constantine's **Edict of Milan** granted religious tolerance in AD 313. The symbolic end of the Roman Empire came with the sacking of Rome by the Visigoths in AD 410. While the East continued to thrive as the **Byzantine Empire** expanded, the West fell into the **Dark Ages.**

OUT OF THE DARK (476-1500). Rome's fall reverberated throughout the region for a millennium until artistic and literary culture was revived in the 14th century. Fueled by the rediscovery of Greek and Latin texts and art, the **Renaissance** sparked new interest in the Classical conception of humanistic education (rhetoric, grammar, and logic). As the medieval church's monopoly on knowledge gradually eroded, a new merchant middle class arose, epitomized by the exalted **Medici family** in Florence (p. 418). They rose from obscurity and eventually boasted three popes, a couple of cardinals, and a queen or two. Their power in Florence was consolidated under Cosimo and Lorenzo *(il Magnifico)*, who broadened the family's activities from banking and warring to patronizing the arts. Meanwhile, the **Borgia family** brought new heights of corruption and decadence to the papacy, based in Rome since the Dark Ages.

TO THE VICTOR GO THE SPOILS (1500-1815). The 16th-18th centuries were difficult times for Italy: the peninsula was no longer able to support the economic demands placed upon it by the Holy Roman Empire. **Charles II,** the last Spanish **Hapsburg** ruler, died in 1700, sparking the **War of the Spanish Succession.** Italy, weak and decentralized, became the booty in battles between the Austrian Hapsburgs and the French and Spanish Bourbons. A century later, **Napoleon** decided to solve the battles by taking everything for himself; in doing so, he united much of northern Italy into the Italian Republic, conquered Naples, fostered national sovereignty, and declared himself monarch of the newly united **Kingdom of Italy** in 1804. After Napoleon's fall in 1815 at the **Battle of Waterloo,** the **Congress of Vienna** carved up Italy, granting considerable control to Austria.

TOGETHER AGAIN (1815-1945). Reaction against the arbitrary divisions of Italy catalyzed the establishment of the nationalist **Risorgimento** unification movement, led by **Giuseppe Mazzini, Giuseppe Garibaldi,** and **Camillo Cavour.** In 1861, Italy's first Parliament met in Turin. Once the elation of unification wore off, however, age-old provincial differences reasserted themselves. The North wanted to protect its money from the needs of the agrarian South, and cities were wary of surrendering power to a central administration. The Pope, who had lost power to the kingdom, threatened to excommunicate Catholics who participated in politics. Disillusionment increased as Italy became involved in **World War I.** The nationalism of war paved the way for the rise of fascism under the control of **Benito Mussolini,** *Il Duce*, who promised order and stability for the young nation. Mussolini established the world's first fascist regime in 1924, expelling all opposing parties from his government. As Mussolini initiated domestic development programs and an aggressive foreign policy, support for the fascist leader ran from intense loyalty to increasing discontent. In 1940, Italy entered **World War II** on the side of its Axis ally, Germany. Axis success was short-lived: the Allies landed in Sicily in 1943, pushing Mussolini from power. As a final indignity, he and his mistress were captured and executed by infuriated citizens, their naked bodies left hanging upside down in a public square. By the end of 1943, Italy had formally withdrawn its support from Germany. The Nazis responded promptly, invading their former ally. In 1945, Italy was freed from German domination, and was divided between those supporting the monarchy and those favoring a return to fascism.

POST-WAR POLITICS AND RECOVERY (1945-1983). The end of WWII highlighted the intense factionalism of Italy. The **Constitution,** adopted in 1948, established the **Republic;** instead of Caesar, Augustus, and warring lords, this modern republic had a prime minister, a bicameral parliament, and an independent judiciary. The **Christian Democratic Party (DC),** bolstered by Marshall Plan money and American military aid, soon overtook the **Socialist Party (PSI)** as the primary force in the government. More than 300 political parties, working in tenuous coalitions, composed the minority government, resulting in instability and nearly constant political change. Economic recovery, primarily in the North, began with 1950s industrialization. Despite the **Southern Development Fund** to build roads, construct schools, and finance industries, the South lagged behind. The 1969 *autunno caldo* (hot autumn), a season of strikes, demonstrations, and riots (mainly instigated by students and factory workers), ushered in the violence of the 1970s. The most shocking episode was the 1978 kidnapping and murder of former Prime Minister **Aldo Moro** by a group of left-wing militant terrorists. The horrors of the 1970s were offset by a few reforms, such as the legalization of divorce and the expansion of women's rights. In 1983, **Bettino Craxi** became Italy's first Socialist premier.

CORRUPTION AND REFORM (1983-1999). Oscar Luigi Scalfaro, elected in 1992, set out to reform Italy's corrupt government. Shortly thereafter, in the *Mani Pulite* (Clean Hands) campaign, Scalfaro and **Judge Antonio di Pietro** uncovered the *Tangentopoli* (Bribesville) scandal. This unprecedented political crisis implicated over 1200 politicians and businessmen. Reactions to the investigation included the May 1993 bombing of Florence's **Uffizi** (p. 425), the "suicides" of 10 indicted officials, and the murders of anti-Mafia investigators. The 1996 election brought the center-left coalition, the **l'Ulivo** (Olive Tree), to power, with **Romano Prodi,** a Bolognese economist, as prime minister. For the first time in modern history, Italy was dominated by two stable coalitions: the center-left l'Ulivo and the center-right **Il Polo.** Prodi's coalition returned a vote of no confidence in October 1998; his government collapsed, and **Massimo D'Alema** became prime minister. D'Alema and **Carlo Ciampi** instituted fiscal reform that qualified Italy for entrance into the European Monetary Union (EMU) in January 1999.

TODAY

Italy's tendency toward partisan schisms was tempered, momentarily at least, by its faith in one individual: **Silvio Berlusconi.** The allure and nonstop drive of Italy's richest man secured his re-election as prime minister in May 2001, although he was widely criticized outside of Italy for alleged corruption. (He had served briefly as prime minister from 1994-96.) Berlusconi led the longest serving government since WWII with his **Forza Italia** party, but resigned in May 2006 following the loss of his center-right coalition in the April elections to **Romano Prodi,** once again. The fragile government lived up to its reputation for instability when Prodi resigned in February 2007. After only a few days, Prodi returned to office upon the request of Italian president, **Giorgio Napolitano.**

HOLIDAYS AND FESTIVALS

Holidays: New Year's Day (Jan. 1); Epiphany (Jan. 6); Good Friday (Apr. 10, 2010); Easter Sunday and Monday (Apr. 4-5, 2010); Liberation Day (Apr. 25); Labor Day (May 1); Feast of the Assumption (Aug. 15); All Saints' Day (Nov. 1); Immaculate Conception (Dec. 8); Christmas (Dec. 25); St. Stephen's Day (Dec. 26).

Festivals: The most common reason for a local festival in Italy is the celebration of a religious event—everything from a patron saint's holy day to the commemoration of a special miracle counts. **Carnevale,** a country-wide celebration, is held during the 10 days leading up to Lent. In Venice, costumed Carnevale revelers fill the streets and canals. During **Scoppio del Carro,** held in Florence's P. del Duomo on Easter Sunday, Florentines set off a cart of explosives in keeping with medieval tradition. The **Spoleto Festival** (known as the Festival dei Due Mondi, or Festival of Two Worlds) is one of the world's most prestigious international arts events. Each June and July it features concerts, operas, ballets, film screenings, and modern art shows (www.spoletofestival.it). For a complete list of festivals, contact the Italian Government Tourist Board (p. 376).

ESSENTIALS

FACTS AND FIGURES

OFFICIAL NAME: Italian Republic.

CAPITAL: Rome.

MAJOR CITIES: Florence, Milan, Naples, Venice.

POPULATION: 58,145,000.

TIME ZONE: GMT +1.

LANGUAGE: Italian; some German, French, and Slovene.

RELIGION: Roman Catholic (90%).

LONGEST SALAMI: Made by Rino Parenti in Zibello, displayed on Nov. 23, 2003; 486.8m in length.

WHEN TO GO

Traveling to Italy in late May or early September, when the temperature averages a comfortable 77°F (25°C), will ensure a calm, cool vacation. When planning, keep in mind festival schedules and weather patterns in northern and southern areas. Tourism goes into overdrive in June, July, and August: hotels are booked solid and prices know no limits. In August, Italians flock to the coast for vacationing, but northern cities are filled with tourists.

DOCUMENTS AND FORMALITIES

EMBASSIES AND CONSULATES. Foreign embassies in Italy are in Rome (p. 380). Italian embassies abroad include: **Australia,** 12 Grey St., Deakin, Canberra ACT 2600 (☎61 262 733 333; www.ambcanberra.esteri.it); **Canada,** 275 Slater St., 21st fl., Ottawa, ON K1P 5H9 (☎613-232-2401; www.ambottawa.esteri.it); **Ireland,** 63/65 Northumberland Rd., Dublin 4 (☎353 16 60 17 44; www.ambdublino.esteri.it); **New Zealand,** 34-38 Grant Rd., Wellington (☎64 44 735 339; www.ambwellington.esteri.it); **UK,** 14 Three Kings Yard, London, W1K 4EH (☎44 20 73 12 22 00; www.embitaly.org.uk); **US,** 3000 Whitehaven St., N.W., Washington, D.C., 20008 (☎202-612-4400; www.ambwashingtondc.esteri.it).

VISA AND ENTRY INFORMATION. EU citizens do not need a visa. Citizens of Australia, Canada, New Zealand, and the US do not need a visa for stays of up to 90 days, beginning upon entry into any of the countries within the EU's freedom-of-movement zone. For more info, see p. 8. For stays longer than 90 days, all non-EU citizens need visas (around €60).

TOURIST SERVICES AND MONEY

EMERGENCY	**Ambulance:** ☎118. **Fire:** ☎115. **Police:** ☎112. **General Emergency:** ☎113.

TOURIST OFFICES. The **Italian Government Tourist Board** (**ENIT;** www.italiantourism.com) provides useful info about many aspects of the country, including the arts, history, and activities. The main office in Rome (☎06 49 71 11; sedecentrale@cert.enit.it) can help locate any local office that is not listed online.

MONEY. The **euro (€)** has replaced the **lira** as the unit of currency in Italy. For more info, see p. 11. At many restaurants, a **service charge** *(servizio)* or **cover** *(coperto)* is included in the bill. Most locals do not tip, but it is appropriate for foreign visitors to leave an additional €1-2 at restaurants. Taxi drivers expect a 10-15% tip. Bargaining is common in Italy, but use discretion. It is appropriate at markets, with vendors, and unmetered taxi fares (settle the price before getting in). Haggling over prices elsewhere is usually inappropriate.

Italy has a 20% **value added tax (VAT,** or **IVA** in Italy), a sales tax applied to most goods and services. The prices given in *Let's Go* include VAT. In the airport upon exiting the EU, non-EU citizens can claim a refund on the tax paid for goods purchased at participating stores. In order to qualify for a refund in a store, you must spend at least €155; make sure to ask for a refund form when you pay. For more info on qualifying for a VAT refund, see p. 13.

BUSINESS HOURS. Nearly everything closes around 1-3pm for *siesta.* Most museums are open 9am-1pm and 3-6pm; some are open through lunch, however. Monday is often a *giorno di chiusura* (day of closure).

TRANSPORTATION

BY PLANE. Most international flights land at Rome's international airport, known as both **Fiumicino** and **Leonardo da Vinci** (**FCO;** ☎06 65 951; www.adr.it). Other hubs are Florence's **Amerigo Vespucci** airport **(FLR)** and Milan's **Malpensa (MXP)** and **Linate (LIN)** airports. **Alitalia** (☎800-223-5730; www.alitalia.com) is Italy's national airline. Budget airlines **Ryanair** (☎353 12 49 77 91; www.ryanair.com) and **easyJet** (☎0871 244 2366; www.easyjet.com) offer inexpensive fares to cities throughout the country; reserve ahead to get the best deals.

BY FERRY. Sicily, Sardinia, Corsica, and smaller islands along the coast are connected to the mainland by **ferries** *(traghetti)* and **hydrofoils** *(aliscafi).* Italy's largest private ferry service, **Tirrenia** (www.tirrenia.it), runs ferries to Sardinia, Sicily, and Tunisia. Other lines, such as the **SNAV** (tickets and special offers available online at www.aferry.to/snav-ferry.htm), have hydrofoil services from major ports such as Ancona, Bari, Brindisi, Genoa, La Spezia, Livorno, Naples, and Trapani. Ferry service is also prevalent in the Lake Country. Reserve well ahead, especially in July and August.

BY TRAIN. The Italian State Railway **Ferrovie dello Stato,** or **FS** (national info line ☎89 20 21; www.trenitalia.com), offers inexpensive, efficient service and Trenitalia passes, the domestic equivalent of the Eurail Pass. There are several types of trains: the *locale* stops at every station on a line, the *diretto* makes fewer stops than the *locale,* and the *espresso* stops only at major stations. The air-conditioned *rapido,* an **InterCity (IC)** train, zips along but costs more. Tickets for the fast, pricey **Eurostar** trains require reservations. **Eurail Passes** are valid without a supplement on all trains except Eurostar. Always validate your ticket in the orange or yellow machine before boarding to avoid a €120 fine.

BY BUS. Bus travel within Italy has its own benefits and disadvantages; in remote parts of the country private companies offer cheap fares and are often the only option, though schedules may be unreliable. Intercity buses serve points inaccessible by train. For city buses, buy tickets in *tabaccherie* or kiosks. Validate your ticket immediately after boarding to avoid a €120 fine. Websites www.bus.it and www.italybus.it are helpful resources for trip planning.

BY CAR. To drive in Italy, you must be 18 or older and hold an **International Driving Permit (IDP)** or an EU license. There are four kinds of roads: *autostrada* (superhighways; mostly toll roads; usually 130km per hr. speed limit); *strade statali* (state roads); *strade provinciali* (provincial); and *strade communali* (local). Driving in Italy is frightening; congested traffic is common in large cities and in the north. On three-lane roads, the center lane is for passing. **Mopeds** (€30-40 per day) can be a great way to see the more scenic areas but can be disastrous in the rain and on rough roads. Always exercise caution. Practice in empty streets and learn to keep up with traffic. Drivers in Italy—especially in the south—are notorious for ignoring traffic laws.

BY BIKE AND BY THUMB. While cycling is a popular sport in Italy, bike trails are rare. Rent bikes where you see a *noleggio* sign. Hitchhiking can be unsafe in Italy, especially in the south. *Let's Go* does not recommend hitchhiking.

KEEPING IN TOUCH

PHONE CODES	**Country code:** 39. **International dialing prefix:** 00. For more info on how to place international calls, see **Inside Back Cover.**

EMAIL AND THE INTERNET. While **Internet** is a relatively common amenity throughout Italy, **Wi-Fi** is not, and as a general rule, the prevalence of both decreases the further you travel from urban areas. A new Italian law requires a passport or driver's license to use an Internet cafe. Rates are €2-6 per hr. For free Internet access, try local universities and libraries.

TELEPHONE. Almost all **public phones** require a prepaid card *(scheda)*, sold at *tabaccherie*, Internet cafes, and post offices. Italy has no area codes, only regional prefixes that are incorporated into the number. **Mobile phones** are widely used in Italy; buying a prepaid SIM card for a GSM phone can be a good, inexpensive option. Of the service providers, **TIM** and **Vodafone** have the best networks. International direct dial numbers include: **AT&T Direct** (☎800 17 24 44); **Canada Direct** (☎800 17 22 13); **Telecom New Zealand Direct** (☎800 17 26 41); **Telstra Australia** (☎800 17 26 10).

MAIL. Airmail letters sent from Australia, North America, or the UK to Italy take anywhere from four to 15 days to arrive. Since Italian mail is notoriously unreliable, it is usually safer to send mail priority *(prioritaria)* or registered *(raccomandata)*. It costs €0.85 to send a letter worldwide. To receive mail in Italy, have mail delivered **Poste Restante.** Mail will go to the main post office unless you specify a subsidiary by street address. Address mail to be held according to the following example: First name LAST NAME, *Fermo Posta*, City, Italy. Bring a passport to pick up your mail; there may be a small fee.

ACCOMMODATIONS AND CAMPING

ITALY	❶	❷	❸	❹	❺
ACCOMMODATIONS	under €16	€16-25	€26-40	€41-60	over €60

Associazione Italiana Alberghi per la Gioventù (AIG), the Italian hostel federation, is a **Hostelling International (HI)** affiliate. A full list of AIG hostels is available online at www.ostellionline.org. Prices in Italy average around €15-25 per night for **dorms.** Hostels are the best option for solo travelers (single rooms are relatively scarce in hotels in the country), but curfews, lockouts, distant locations, and less-than-perfect security can detract from their appeal. Italian **hotel** rates are set by the state. A single room in a hotel *(camera singola)* usually starts at €25-50 per night, and a double *(camera doppia)* starts at €40-90 per room. A room with a private bath *(con bagno)* usually costs 30-50% more. Smaller **pensioni** are often cheaper than hotels. Be sure to confirm charges before checking in; Italian hotels are notorious for tacking on additional costs at check-out time. **Affittacamere** (rooms for rent in private houses) are an inexpensive option for longer stays. For more info, inquire at local tourist offices. There are over 1700 **campgrounds** in Italy; tent sites average €4.20. The **Federazione Italiana del Campeggio e del Caravaning** (www.federcampeggio.it) has a complete list of sites.

FOOD AND DRINK

ITALY	❶	❷	❸	❹	❺
FOOD	under €7	€7-15	€16-20	€21-25	over €25

Breakfast is the simplest meal in Italy: at most, *colazione* consists of coffee and a *cornetto* or *brioche* (croissant). For *pranzo* (lunch), locals grab panini or salads, or dine more calmly at an inexpensive *tavola calda* (cafeteria-style snack bar), *rosticceria* (grill), or *gastronomia* (snack bar with hot dishes for takeout). *Cena* (dinner) usually begins at 8pm or later. In Naples, it's not unusual to go for a midnight **pizza.** Traditionally, dinner is the longest meal of the day, usually lasting much of the evening and consisting of an *antipasto* (appetizer), a *primo piatto* (starch-based first course like pasta or risotto), a *secondo piatto* (meat or fish), and a *contorno* (vegetable side dish). Finally comes the *dolce* (dessert or fruit), then *caffè* (espresso), and often an after-dinner liqueur.

Lunch is usually the most important meal of the day in rural regions where daily work comes in two shifts and is separated by a long lunch and **siesta.** Many restaurants offer a fixed-price *menù turistico* including *primo*, *secondo*, bread, water, and wine. While food varies regionally—seafood in the South and on the coast, heartier selections in the North, pesto in Liguria, *gnocchi* in Trentino-Alto Adige, parmesan and balsamic vinegar in Emilia-Romagna, and rustic stews in Tuscany—the importance of relaxing and having an extended meal does not. **La bella figura** (a good figure) is another social imperative, and the after-dinner **passeggiata** (walk) is as much a tradition as the meal itself. Dense **gelato** is a snack, a dessert, and even a budget meal in itself. **Coffee** and **wine** are their own institutions, each with their own devoted followers.

BEYOND TOURISM

From harvesting grapes on vineyards in Siena to restoring and protecting marine life in the Mediterranean, there are diverse options for working for a cause. Those in search of a more lucrative experience might consider working as an intern for the Italian press or teaching English in Italian schools. For more info on opportunities across Europe, see **Beyond Tourism,** p. 45.

Associazione Culturale Linguista Educational (ACLE), V. Roma 54, 18038 San Remo, Imperio (☎01 84 50 60 70; www.acle.org). Non-profit association that works to bring theater, arts, and English language instruction to Italian children. Employees create theater programs in schools and teach English at summer camps.

Cook Italy, (☎34 90 07 82 98; www.cookitaly.com). Region- or dish-specific cooking classes. Venues include Bologna, Cortona, Florence, Lucca, Rome, and Sicily. Courses 3- to 6- nights from €950. Housing, meals, and recipes included.

Aegean Center for the Fine Arts, Paros 84400, Cyclades, Greece (☎30 22 84 02 32 87; www.aegeancenter.org). Italian branch located in Pistoia. Instruction in arts, literature, creative writing, voice, and art history. Classes taught in English. Fees cover housing in 16th-century villa, meals, and excursions to Rome, Venice, and Greece. University credit on individual arrangement. 14-week program in the fall €8500.

ROME (ROMA) ☎06

Rome (pop. 2.8 million), *La Città Eterna,* is a concentrated expression of Italian spirit. Whether flaunting the Italian 2006 World Cup victory or retelling the mythical story of the city's founding, Romans exude a fierce pride for the Rome that was and the Rome that will be. Crumbling pagan ruins form the backdrop for the center of Christianity's largest denomination, and hip clubs and bars border grand cathedrals. Augustus once boasted that he found Rome a city of brick and left it a city of marble. No matter how you find it, you'll undoubtedly leave with plenty of memories and a new appreciation for *la dolce vita.*

INTERCITY TRANSPORTATION

Flights: Da Vinci International Airport (FCO; ☎06 65 21 01), known as **Fiumicino,** handles most flights. The **Termini** line runs nonstop to Rome's main station, **Stazione Termini** (30min., 2 per hr., €11). After hours, take the blue COTRAL **bus** (☎06 80 01 50 008) to Tiburtina from outside the main doors after customs (4 per day, €5). From Tiburtina, take bus #175 or 492, or metro B to Termini. A few domestic and budget flights, including Ryanair, arrive at **Ciampino (CIA;** ☎06 65 951). To get to Rome, take the COTRAL bus (2 per hr., €1) to **Anagnina** station, or the **Terravision Shuttle** (www.terravision.it) to V. Marsala at the Hotel Royal Santina (40min., €8).

Trains: Trains leave Stazione Termini for: **Bologna** (2-3hr., €33-42); **Florence** (1-3hr., €14-33); **Milan** (4-8hr., €30-50); **Naples** (1-2hr., €10-25); **Venice** (4-5hr., €33-50). Trains arriving in Rome between midnight and 5am arrive at **Stazione Tiburtina** or **Stazione Ostiense,** which are connected to Termini by bus #175.

ORIENTATION

Because Rome's winding streets are difficult to navigate, it's helpful to orient yourself to major landmarks and main streets. The **Tiber River,** which snakes north-south through the city, is also a useful reference point. Most trains arrive at Stazione Termini east of Rome's historical center. **Termini** and **San Lorenzo** to the east are home to the city's largest university and most of its budget accommodations. **Via Nazionale** originates two blocks northwest of Termini Station in **Piazza della Repubblica** and leads to **Piazza Venezia,** the focal point of the city, recognizable by the immense white **Vittorio Emanuele II monument.** From P. Venezia, **Via dei Fori Imperiali** runs southeast to the Ancient City, where the **Colosseum** and the **Roman Forum** attest to former glory. **Via del Corso** stretches north from P. Venezia to **Piazza del Popolo,** which has an obelisk in its center. The **Trevi Fountain, Piazza Barberini,** and the fashionable streets around **Piazza di Spagna** and the **Spanish Steps** lie to the east of V. del Corso. **Villa Borghese,** with its impressive gardens and museums, is northeast of the Spanish Steps. West of V. del Corso is the *centro storico,* the tangle of streets around the **Pantheon, Piazza Navona, Campo dei Fiori,** and the old **Jewish Ghetto.** West of P. Venezia, **Largo Argentina** marks the start of **Corso Vittorio Emanuele II,** which runs through the *centro storico* to the Tiber River. Across the river to the northwest is **Vatican City** and the **Borgo-Prati** neighborhood. South of the Vatican is **Trastevere** and residential **Testaccio.** Pick up a free **map** in English at the tourist office (see **Practical Information,** p. 381).

LOCAL TRANSPORTATION

Public Transportation: The A and B **Metropolitana subway** lines (www.metroroma.it) meet at Termini and usually run 5:30am-11:30pm; however, due to construction on the forthcoming C line, the subway now closes at 10pm. **ATAC buses** (www.atac.roma.it) run 5am-midnight (with limited late-night routes); validate your ticket in the machine when you board. Buy tickets (€1) at *tabaccherie,* newsstands, and station machines; they're valid for 1 metro ride or unlimited bus travel within 1hr. of validation. **BIG daily tickets** (€4) and **CIS weekly tickets** (€16) allow for unlimited public transport. Beware: **pickpocketing** is rampant on buses and trains.

Taxis: Radiotaxi (☎06 35 70). Taxis are expensive. Ride only in yellow or white taxis, and make sure your taxi has a meter (if not, negotiate the price before riding). **Surcharges** apply at night (€2.60), on Su (€1), and when heading to or from Fiumicino (€7.25) or Ciampino (€5.50). Fares run about €11 from Termini to Vatican City, around €35 between the city center and Fiumicino.

Bike and Moped Rental: Bikes generally cost €5 per hr. or €10 per day while scooters cost €35-55 per day. Try **Bici & Baci,** V. del Viminale 5 (☎06 48 28 443; www.bicibaci.com). 16+. Open daily 8am-7pm. AmEx/MC/V.

PRACTICAL INFORMATION

Tourist Office: Enjoy Rome, V. Marghera 8/A (☎06 44 56 890; www.enjoyrome.com). From the middle concourse of Termini, exit right, with the trains behind you; cross V. Marsala and follow V. Marghera for 3 blocks. The helpful, English-speaking staff makes reservations at museums, shows, and accommodations. They also lead walking tours (€27, under 26 €22). Pick up their detailed map and a *When in Rome* booklet. Open Apr.-Oct. M-F 8:30am-7pm, Sa 8:30am-2pm; Nov.-Mar. M-F 9am-6pm, Sa 9am-2pm.

Embassies: Australia, V. Antonio Bosio 5 (☎06 85 27 21; www.italy.embassy.gov.au). Open M-F 9am-5pm. **Canada,** V. Zara 30 (☎06 85 44 41; www.canada.it). Open M-F 9am-5pm. **Ireland,** P. di Campitelli 3 (☎06 69 79 121). **New Zealand,** V. Zara 28 (☎06 44 17 171). Open M-F 8:30am-12:45pm and 1:45-5pm. **UK,** V. XX Settembre 80a (☎06 42 20 00 01). Consular section open M-F 9:15am-1:30pm. **US,** V. Vittorio Veneto 119/A (☎06 46 741; www.usembassy.it/mission). Open M-F 8:30am-5:30pm.

Currency Exchange: Banca di Roma and **Banca Nazionale del Lavoro** have good rates, but the ubiquitous **ATMs** are an even better option. Open M-F 8:30am-1:30pm.

American Express: P. di Spagna 38 (☎06 67 641; lost cards 800 87 20 00). Open M-F 9am-5:30pm, Sa 9am-12:30pm.

Luggage Storage: In Termini Station, underneath track #24. €3.80 for first 5hr., €0.60 per hr. up to 12hr., €0.20 per hr. thereafter.

Lost Property: Oggetti Smarriti (☎06 58 16 040). On buses (☎06 58 16 040); Metro A (☎06 48 74 309); Metro B (☎06 57 53 22 65).

GLBT Resources: ARCI-GAY, V. Goito 35/B (☎06 64 50 11 02; www.arcigayroma.it). Open M-F 4-8pm. **Circolo Mario Mieli di Cultura Omosessuale,** V. Efeso 2/A (☎06 54 13 985; www.mariomieli.org). **Libreria Babele,** V. d. Banchi Vecchi. (☎06 68 76 628; www.libreriababeleroma.it). Library focusing on gay literature. Open M-Sa 11am-7pm.

Laundromat: Splashnet, V. Varese 33 (☎06 49 38 04 50; www.splashnetrome.com), 3 blocks from Termini. *Let's Go* discount. Open daily 8:30am-11pm.

Pharmacies: Farmacia Piram, V. Nazionale 228 (☎06 48 80 754). Open 24hr. MC/V.

Hospitals: International Medical Center, V. Firenze 47 (☎06 48 82 371; www.imc84.com). Call ahead. Referral service to English-speaking doctors. General visit €100. Open

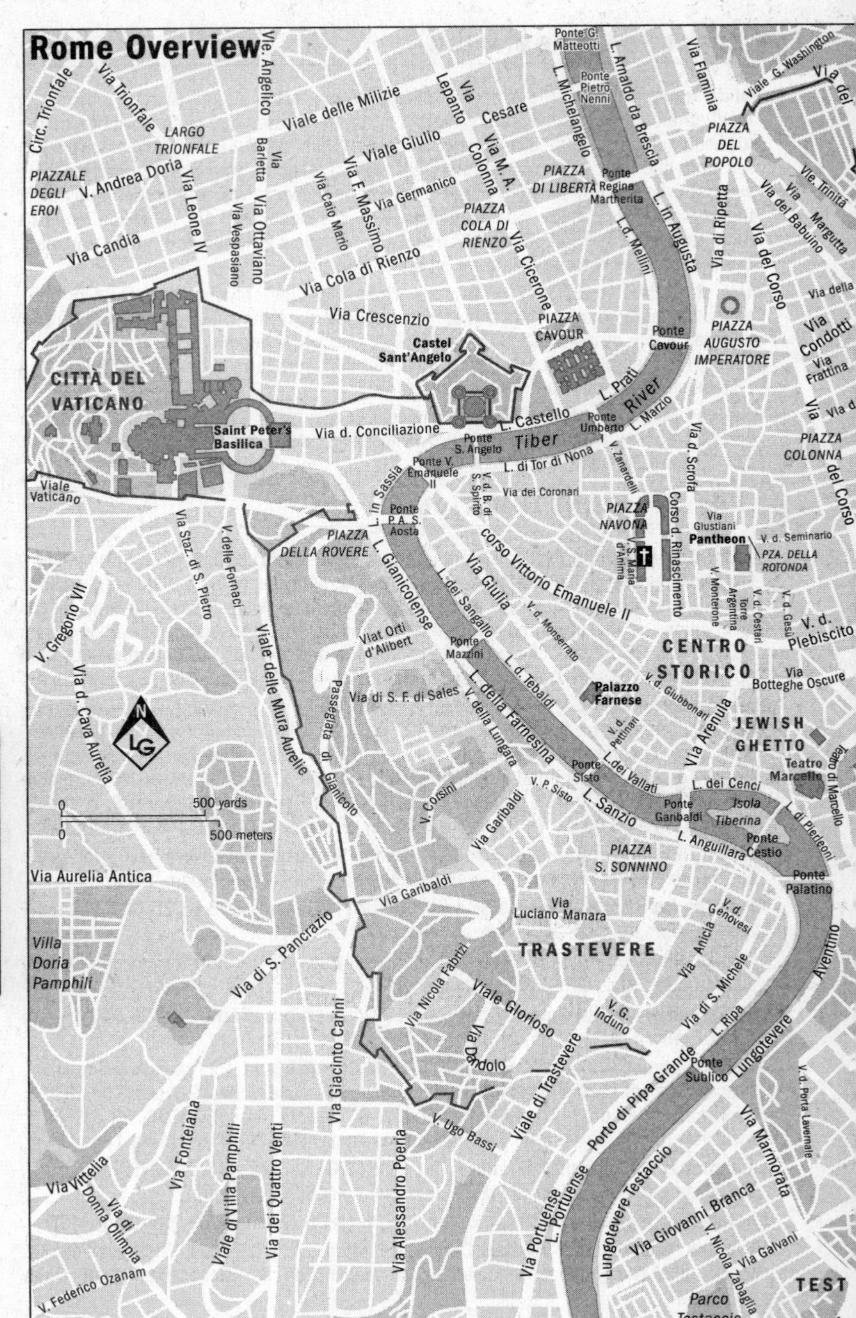
Rome Overview
CITTÀ DEL VATICANO
Saint Peter's Basilica
Castel Sant'Angelo
Tiber River
CENTRO STORICO
JEWISH GHETTO
TRASTEVERE
Pantheon
Palazzo Farnese
PIAZZA DEL POPOLO
PIAZZA AUGUSTO IMPERATORE
PIAZZA CAVOUR
PIAZZA DI LIBERTÀ
PIAZZA COLA DI RIENZO
PIAZZA NAVONA
PIAZZA COLONNA
PZA. DELLA ROTONDA
PIAZZA DELLA ROVERE
PIAZZA S. SONNINO
PIAZZALE DEGLI EROI
LARGO TRIONFALE
Isola Tiberina
Villa Doria Pamphili
Parco Testaccio
Teatro Marcello
Via Crescenzio
Via Cola di Rienzo
Via d. Conciliazione
Corso Vittorio Emanuele II
Via del Corso
Viale delle Mura Aurelie
Via Aurelia Antica
Via Garibaldi
Via di S. Pancrazio
Viale di Trastevere
Via Marmorata
Lungotevere Testaccio
Ponte Cavour
Ponte Sisto
Ponte Garibaldi
Ponte Cestio
Ponte Palatino
Ponte Sublicio
Ponte Mazzini
Ponte Umberto
Ponte S. Angelo
Ponte Regina Martherita
Ponte Pietro Nenni
Ponte G. Matteotti
500 yards
500 meters
ITALY

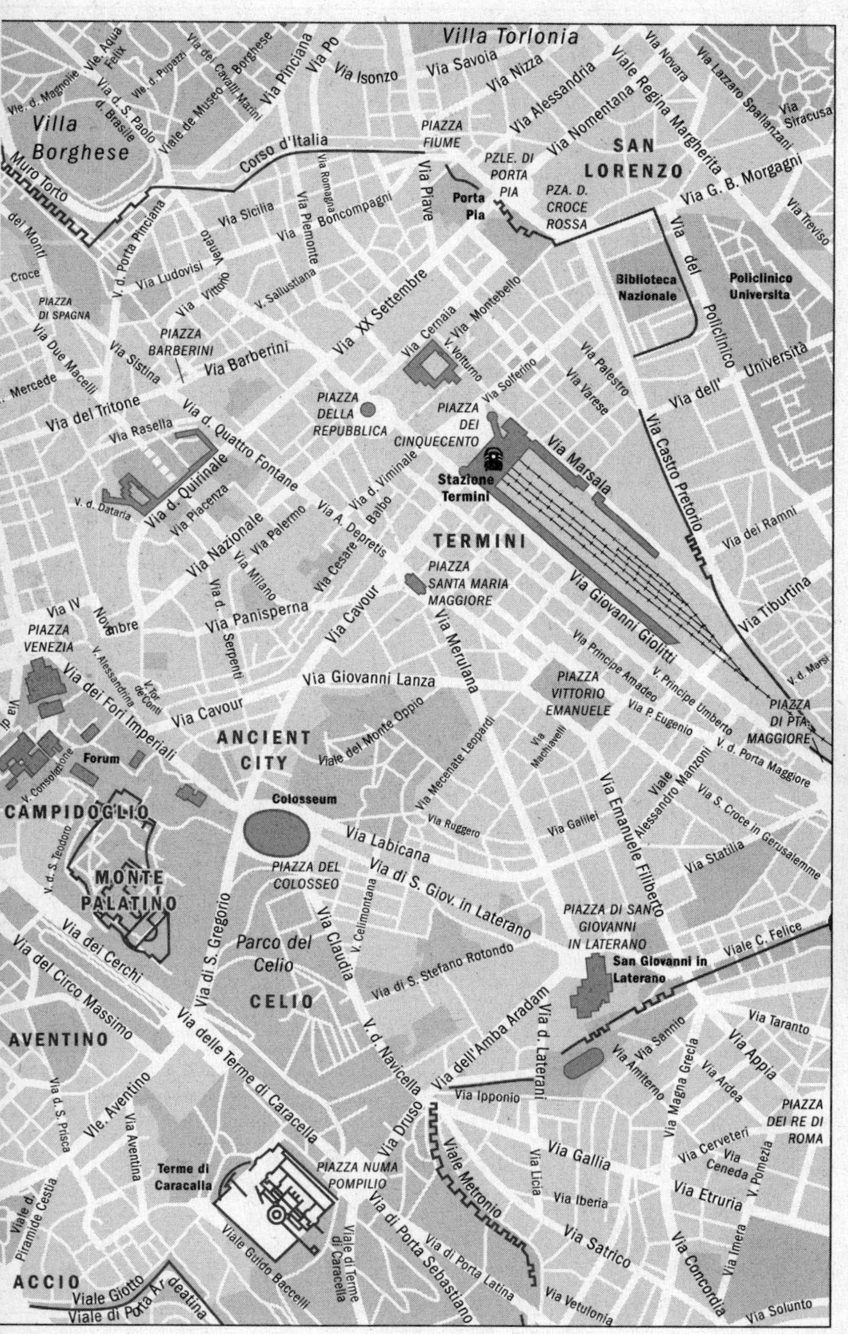

Villa Torlonia
Villa Borghese
Via Po
Via Pinciana
Via Isonzo
Via Savoia
Via Nizza
Via Alessandria
Viale Regina Margherita
Via Nomentana
Via Novara
Via Lazzaro Spallanzani
Via Siracusa
SAN LORENZO
PIAZZA FIUME
Corso d'Italia
Muro Torto
Porta Pia
PZLE. DI PORTA PIA
PZA. D. CROCE ROSSA
Via G. B. Morgagni
Via Treviso
Via Piave
Via Sicilia
Via Boncompagni
Via Piemonte
Via Romagna
Via Veneto
Via Vittorio
Via Ludovisi
V. d. Porta Pinciana
V. Sallustiana
Via XX Settembre
Via Montebello
Biblioteca Nazionale
Policlinico Universita
Via del Policlinico
Via dell' Università
PIAZZA DI SPAGNA
Via Due Macelli
Via Sistina
PIAZZA BARBERINI
Via Barberini
Via del Tritone
Via Rasella
Via d. Quattro Fontane
Via Cernaia
V. Volturno
Via Solferino
Via Palestro
Via Varese
PIAZZA DELLA REPUBBLICA
PIAZZA DEI CINQUECENTO
Via Marsala
Via Castro Pretorio
Stazione Termini
TERMINI
Via d. Quirinale
V. d. Dataria
Via Piacenza
Via Nazionale
Via Palermo
Via Milano
Via d. Viminale
Via A. Depretis
Via Cesare Balbo
PIAZZA SANTA MARIA MAGGIORE
Via dei Ramni
Via Tiburtina
Via Giovanni Giolitti
Via Panisperna
Via d. Serpenti
Via Cavour
Via Merulana
Via IV Novembre
PIAZZA VENEZIA
V. Alessandrina
Via dei Fori Imperiali
V. Tor de' Conti
Via Giovanni Lanza
PIAZZA VITTORIO EMANUELE
Via Principe Amadeo
V. Principe Umberto
Via P. Eugenio
V. d. Marsi
PIAZZA DI PTA. MAGGIORE
V. d. Porta Maggiore
ANCIENT CITY
Viale del Monte Oppio
Via Mecenate Leopardi
Via Machiavelli
Via Emanuele Filiberto
Viale Alessandro Manzoni
Via S. Croce in Gerusalemme
Forum
V. Consolazione
CAMPIDOGLIO
Colosseum
Via Ruggero
Via Galilei
Via Labicana
Via Statilia
V. d. S. Teodoro
MONTE PALATINO
PIAZZA DEL COLOSSEO
Via di S. Giov. in Laterano
V. Celimontana
Via Claudia
Via di S. Gregorio
Parco del Celio
CELIO
Via dei Cerchi
Via del Circo Massimo
Via di S. Stefano Rotondo
PIAZZA DI SAN GIOVANNI IN LATERANO
San Giovanni in Laterano
Viale C. Felice
AVENTINO
Via delle Terme di Caracella
V. d. Navicella
Via dell'Amba Aradam
Via d. Laterani
Via Sannio
Via Amiterno
Via Magna Grecia
Via Ardea
Via Taranto
Via Appia
Via Ipponio
Via d. S. Prisca
Vle. Aventino
Via Aventina
Via Druso
Viale Metronio
Via Licia
Via Gallia
Via Cerveteri
Via Ceneda
V. Pomezia
PIAZZA DEI RE DI ROMA
Terme di Caracalla
PIAZZA NUMA POMPILIO
Via Iberia
Via Etruria
Viale d. Piramide Cestia
Viale Guido Baccelli
Viale di Terme di Caracella
Via di Porta Sebastiano
Via di Porta Latina
Via Satrico
Via Concordia
Via Imera
ACCIO
Viale Giotto
Viale di Porta Ardeatina
Via Vetulonia
Via Solunto
ITALY

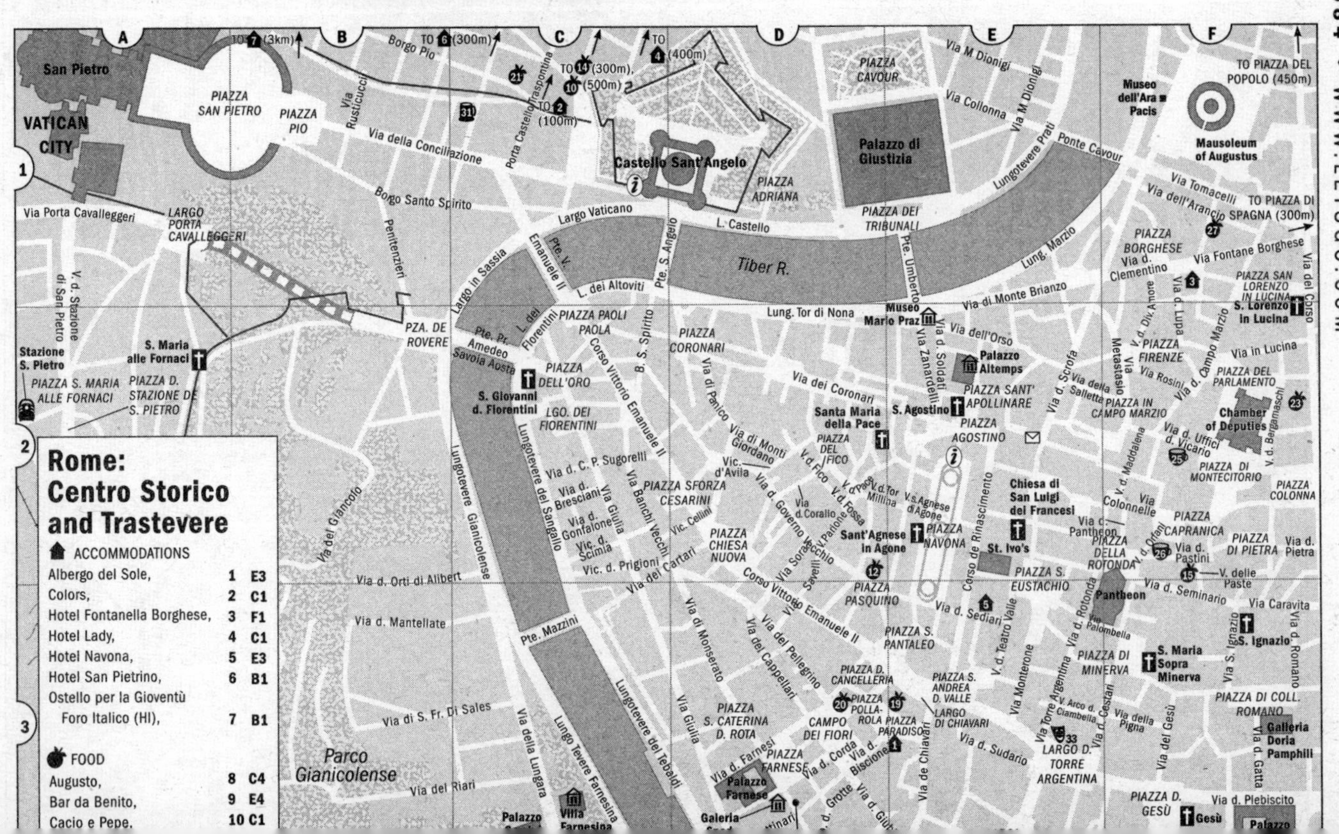

Rome: Centro Storico and Trastevere
ACCOMMODATIONS
Albergo del Sole, 1 E3
Colors, 2 C1
Hotel Fontanella Borghese, 3 F1
Hotel Lady, 4 C1
Hotel Navona, 5 E3
Hotel San Pietrino, 6 B1
Ostello per la Gioventù Foro Italico (HI), 7 B1
FOOD
Augusto, 8 C4
Bar da Benito, 9 E4
Cacio e Pepe, 10 C1
A
B
C
D
E
F
1
2
3
VATICAN CITY
San Pietro
PIAZZA SAN PIETRO
PIAZZA PIO
Castello Sant'Angelo
PIAZZA ADRIANA
Palazzo di Giustizia
PIAZZA CAVOUR
Tiber R.
Mausoleum of Augustus
Museo dell'Ara Pacis
Chamber of Deputies
Palazzo Altemps
Chiesa di San Luigi dei Francesi
Pantheon
St. Ivo's
S. Maria Sopra Minerva
S. Ignazio
Galleria Doria Pamphili
Gesù
Sant'Agnese in Agone
S. Agostino
Santa Maria della Pace
Museo Mario Praz
PIAZZA NAVONA
CAMPO DEI FIORI
Palazzo Farnese
Villa Farnesina
Parco Gianicolense
S. Giovanni d. Fiorentini
S. Maria alle Fornaci
Stazione S. Pietro
TO PIAZZA DEL POPOLO (450m)
TO PIAZZA DI SPAGNA (300m)
Corso Vittorio Emanuele II
Lungotevere Gianicolense
Via della Conciliazione
Via Giulia

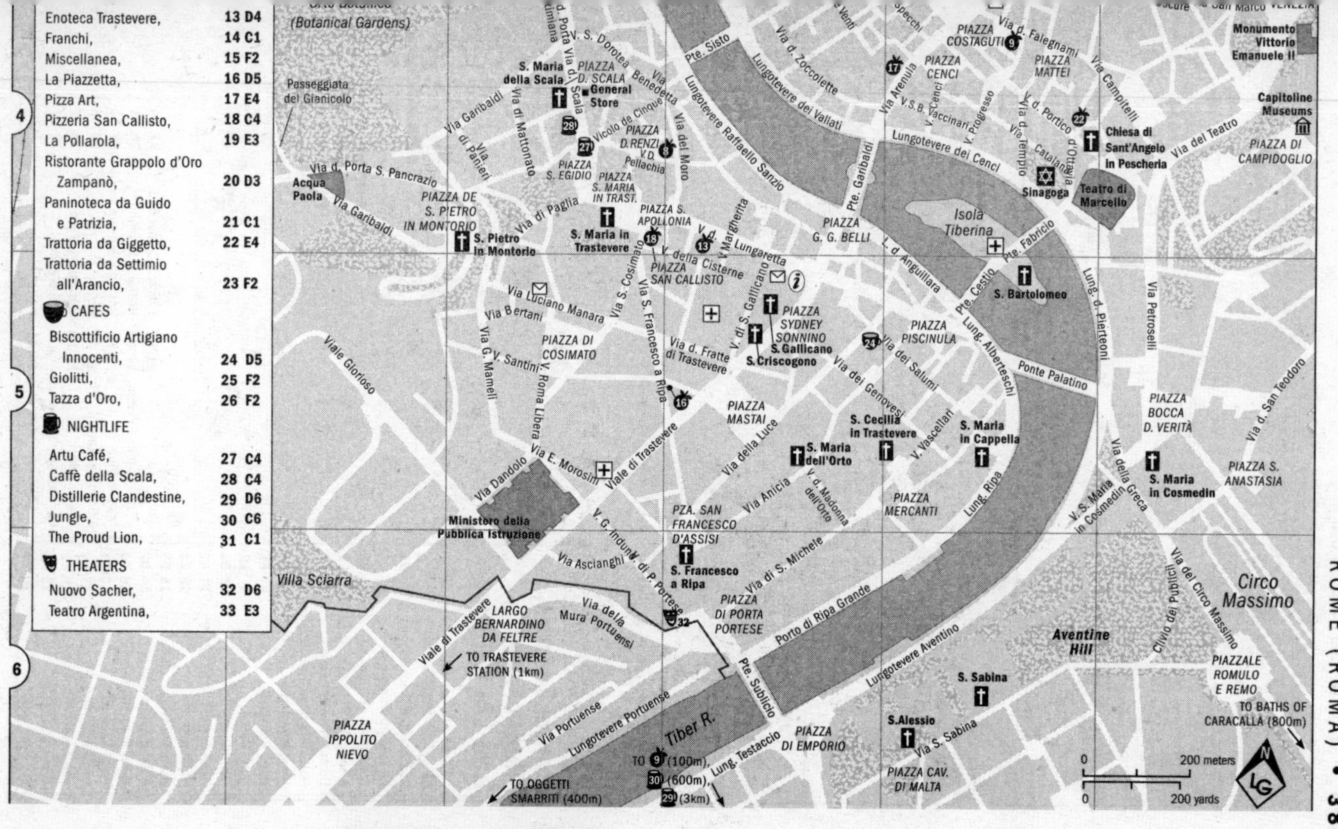
Enoteca Trastevere, 13 D4
Franchi, 14 C1
Miscellanea, 15 F2
La Piazzetta, 16 D5
Pizza Art, 17 E4
Pizzeria San Callisto, 18 C4
La Pollarola, 19 E3
Ristorante Grappolo d'Oro Zampanò, 20 D3
Paninoteca da Guido e Patrizia, 21 C1
Trattoria da Giggetto, 22 E4
Trattoria da Settimio all'Arancio, 23 F2
CAFES
Biscottificio Artigiano Innocenti, 24 D5
Giolitti, 25 F2
Tazza d'Oro, 26 F2
NIGHTLIFE
Artu Café, 27 C4
Caffè della Scala, 28 C4
Distillerie Clandestine, 29 D6
Jungle, 30 C6
The Proud Lion, 31 C1
THEATERS
Nuovo Sacher, 32 D6
Teatro Argentina, 33 E3
4
5
6
(Botanical Gardens)
Passeggiata del Gianicolo
Acqua Paola
Via d. Porta S. Pancrazio
Via Garibaldi
PIAZZA DE S. PIETRO IN MONTORIO
S. Pietro in Montorio
Via di Paglia
Via di Mattonato
S. Maria della Scala
PIAZZA D. SCALA
General Store
Via S. Dorotea
Via Benedetta
Vicolo de Cinque
PIAZZA D.RENZI
V.D. Pellachia
PIAZZA S. EGIDIO
PIAZZA S. MARIA IN TRAST.
S. Maria in Trastevere
PIAZZA S. APOLLONIA
PIAZZA SAN CALLISTO
Via del Moro
Lungotevere Raffaello Sanzio
Lungotevere dei Vallati
Via d. Zoccolette
Pte. Sisto
Pte. Garibaldi
PIAZZA G. G. BELLI
Lungaretta
V. della Cisterne
Via S. Cosimato
Via S. Francesco a Ripa
Via Luciano Manara
Via Bertani
PIAZZA DI COSIMATO
Via G. Mameli
V. Santini
V. Roma Libera
Viale Glorioso
Via E. Morosini
Via Dandolo
Ministero della Pubblica Istruzione
Viale di Trastevere
Via d. Fratte di Trastevere
V. di S. Gallicano
PIAZZA SYDNEY SONNINO
S. Gallicano
S.Criscogono
PIAZZA MASTAI
Via della Luce
S. Maria dell'Orto
V. d. Madonna dell'Orto
Via Anicia
PZA. SAN FRANCESCO D'ASSISI
S. Francesco a Ripa
Via di S. Michele
PIAZZA DI PORTA PORTESE
V. G. Induno
V. di P. Portese
Via Ascianghi
Villa Sciarra
LARGO BERNARDINO DA FELTRE
Via della Mura Portuensi
Viale di Trastevere
TO TRASTEVERE STATION (1km)
PIAZZA IPPOLITO NIEVO
Via Portuense
Lungotevere Portuense
Tiber R.
TO (100m), (600m), (3km)
TO OGGETTI SMARRITI (400m)
Pte. Sublicio
Porto di Ripa Grande
Lung. Testaccio
PIAZZA DI EMPORIO
PIAZZA PISCINULA
Via dei Salumi
Via dei Genovesi
S. Cecilia in Trastevere
V. Vascellari
S. Maria in Cappella
PIAZZA MERCANTI
Lung. Ripa
Lungotevere Aventino
S. Sabina
S.Alessio
Via S. Sabina
PIAZZA CAV. DI MALTA
Aventine Hill
L. d. Anguillara
Pte. Cestio
Lung. Alberteschi
Ponte Palatino
Isola Tiberina
Pte. Fabricio
S. Bartolomeo
Lungotevere dei Cenci
PIAZZA COSTAGUTI
Via d. Falegnami
PIAZZA MATTEI
PIAZZA CENCI
Via Arenula
V.S.B. Vaccinari
V. Progresso
V. d. Portico d'Ottavia
Via d. Tempio
Catalana
Sinagoga
Teatro di Marcello
Chiesa di Sant'Angelo in Pescheria
Via Campitelli
Via del Teatro
Monumento Vittorio Emanuele II
Capitoline Museums
PIAZZA DI CAMPIDOGLIO
Lung. d. Pierteoni
Via Petroselli
PIAZZA BOCCA D. VERITÀ
S. Maria in Cosmedin
Via della Greca
V. S. Maria in Cosmedin
PIAZZA S. ANASTASIA
Via d. San Teodoro
Clivio dei Publici
Via del Circo Massimo
Circo Massimo
PIAZZALE ROMULO E REMO
TO BATHS OF CARACALLA (800m)
0
200 meters
200 yards

Rome: Termini, San Lorenzo, and Via del Corso
ACCOMMODATIONS
Affittacamere Aries, 1 D1
Alessandro Downtown, 2 D4
Alessandro Legends, 3 D2
Alessandro Palace, 4 E2
Domus Nova Bethlehem, 5 C3
Hotel and Hostel des Artistes, 6 E2
Hotel Boccaccio, 7 B2
Hotel Bolognese, 8 E1
Hotel Cervia, 9 E2
Hotel Cortorillo, 10 D4
Hotel Fontanella Borghese, 11 A1
Hotel Galli, 12 E3
Hotel Giù Giù, 13 D3
Hotel Papa Germano, 14 D2
Hotel Scott House, 15 D4
Hotel Suisse, 16 B1
Pensione di Rienzo, 17 D4
Pensione Fawlty Towers, 18 E3
Pensione Panda, 19 A1
Pensione Rosetta, 20 B4
FOOD
Africa, 21 E2
L'Antica Birreria Peroni, 22 B2
Arancia Blu, 23 F5
Il Brillo Parlante, 24 A1
I Buoni Amici, 25 D6
Centro Macrobiotico Italiano Naturist Club, 26 A1
Enoteca Cavour 313, 27 B4
Hostaria da Bruno, 28 E3
Hostaria Romana da Dino, 29 E2
Luzzi, 30 C5
Trimani Wine Bar, 31 D2
Vini e Buffet, 32 A1
TO PIAZZA DEL POPOLO
(250m)
(400m)
(600m)
TO VILLA BORGHESE (1km)
PIAZZA BORGHESE
PIAZZA S. LORENZO IN LUCINA
S. Lorenzo in Lucina
PIAZZA DI SPAGNA
Via Condotti
Via Borgognona
Via Frattina
Via della Vite
Via Mercede
Via del Corso
Via Sistina
Via Veneto
Palazzo Margherita
L'Immacolata Concezione
BARBERINI
PIAZZA BARBERINI
Via del Tritone
LARGO D. TRITONE
Chamber of Deputies
PIAZZA DI MONTECITORIO
PIAZZA COLONNA
Trevi Fountain
Palazzo Barberini
Galleria Nazionale d'Arte Antica
Palazzo del Quirinale
PIAZZA QUIRINALE
Four Fountains
S. Andrea al Quirinale
Via XX Settembre
Ministero Difesa Esercito
S. Susanna
Pantheon
S. Maria Sopra Minerva
S. Ignazio
Palazzo delle Esposizioni
Via Nazionale
Galleria Doria Pamphili
Galleria Colonna
Gesù
Palazzo Venezia
PIAZZA VENEZIA
Trajan's Column
Markets of Trajan
Forum of Trajan
Forum of Augustus
Vittorio Emanuele II Monument
Museo del Risorgimento
Ministero d. Interno
Teatro Nazionale
S. Prudenziana
Via Panisperna
Capitoline Museums
Via dei Fori Imperiali
Via Cavour
CAVOUR
S. Pietro in Vincoli
Roman Forum
COLOSSEO
PIAZZA DEL COLOSSEO
Colosseum
Palatine Hill
Colle Oppio
Parco di Traiano
Domus Aurea
Parco Oppio
Teatro Colosseo
PIAZZA SAN CLEMENTE

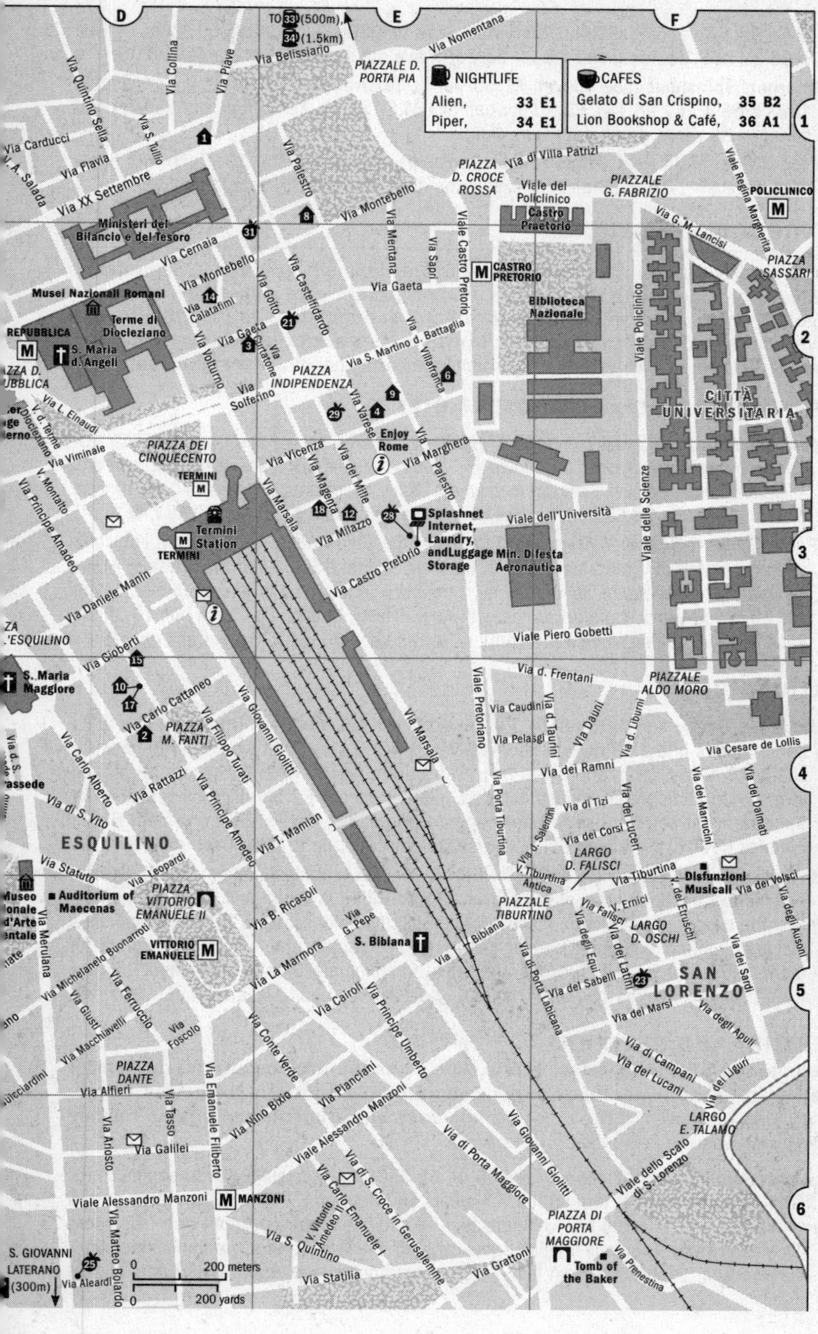
D
E
F
1
2
3
4
5
6
TO 33 (500m), 34 (1.5km)
NIGHTLIFE
Alien, 33 E1
Piper, 34 E1
CAFES
Gelato di San Crispino, 35 B2
Lion Bookshop & Café, 36 A1
Via Nomentana
PIAZZALE D. PORTA PIA
Via Belissiario
Via Collina
Via Piave
Via Quintino Sella
Via S. Tullio
Via Carducci
Via Flavia
Via XX Settembre
Ministeri del Bilancio e del Tesoro
Via Palestro
Via Montebello
Via Cernaia
Musei Nazionali Romani
Terme di Diocleziano
REPUBBLICA
S. Maria d. Angeli
Via Calatafimi
Via Goito
Via Castelfidardo
Via Gaeta
Via Curtatone
Via Volturno
Via Solferino
PIAZZA INDIPENDENZA
Via S. Martino d. Battaglia
Via Villafranca
Via Mentana
Via Sapri
Viale Castro Pretorio
CASTRO PRETORIO
PIAZZA D. CROCE ROSSA
Via di Villa Patrizi
Viale del Policlinico
Castro Pretorio
PIAZZALE G. FABRIZIO
POLICLINICO
Viale Regina Margherita
Via G. M. Lancisi
PIAZZA SASSARI
Biblioteca Nazionale
Viale Policlinico
CITTÀ UNIVERSITARIA
Via L. Einaudi
V. d. Terme Diocleziano
PIAZZA DEI CINQUECENTO
Via Viminale
Via Vicenza
Via Varese
Enjoy Rome
Via Marghera
Via Magenta
Via dei Mille
Via Palestro
TERMINI
Termini Station
V. Montalto
Via Principe Amadeo
Via Marsala
Via Milazzo
Splashnet Internet, Laundry, and Luggage Storage
Via Castro Pretorio
Viale dell'Università
Min. Difesta Aeronautica
Viale delle Scienze
Via Daniele Manin
Viale Piero Gobetti
L'ESQUILINO
Via Gioberti
S. Maria Maggiore
Via Carlo Cattaneo
PIAZZA M. FANTI
Via Filippo Turati
Via Giovanni Giolitti
Via d. Frentani
PIAZZALE ALDO MORO
Viale Pretoriano
Via Caudini
Via d. Taurini
Via Dauni
Via d. Liburni
Via Pelasgi
Via Cesare de Lollis
Via Carlo Alberto
Via Rattazzi
Via Principe Amedeo
Via dei Ramni
Via Porta Tiburtina
Via di Tizi
Via dei Luceri
Via dei Marrucini
Via dei Dalmati
Via di S. Vito
ESQUILINO
Via T. Mamiani
Via d. Salentini
Via dei Corsi
LARGO D. FALISCI
V. Tiburtina Antica
Via Tiburtina
Disfunzioni Musicali
Via dei Volsci
Via Statuto
Via Leopardi
Auditorium of Maecenas
PIAZZA VITTORIO EMANUELE II
Via B. Ricasoli
Via G. Pepe
PIAZZALE TIBURTINO
Via Falisci
V. Ernici
V. dei Etruschi
LARGO D. OSCHI
Via degli Ausoni
Museo Nazionale d'Arte Orientale
Via Merulana
VITTORIO EMANUELE
Via Michelangelo Buonarroti
Via La Marmora
S. Bibiana
Via Bibiana
Via degli Equi
Via dei Latini
SAN LORENZO
Via dei Sardi
Via Ferruccio
Via Giusti
Via Macchiavelli
Via Foscolo
Via Cairoli
Via Principe Umberto
Via di Porta Labicana
Via del Sabelli
Via dei Marsi
Via degli Apuli
Via Conte Verde
Via di Campani
Via dei Lucani
Via dei Liguri
PIAZZA DANTE
Via Alfieri
Via Tasso
Via Emanuele Filiberto
Via Nino Bixio
Via Pianciani
Viale Alessandro Manzoni
Via Giovanni Giolitti
LARGO E. TALAMO
Via Ariosto
Via Galilei
Via di Porta Maggiore
Via Carlo Emanuele I
Via di S. Croce in Gerusalemme
Viale dello Scalo di S. Lorenzo
Viale Alessandro Manzoni
MANZONI
V. Vittorio Amedeo II
PIAZZA DI PORTA MAGGIORE
Via S. Quintino
Via Matteo Boiardo
Tomb of the Baker
Via Prenestina
S. GIOVANNI LATERANO (300m)
Via Aleardi
Via Statilia
Via Gratton
0 200 meters
0 200 yards

ITALY

M-Sa 9am-8pm; on-call 24hr. **Rome-American Hospital,** V.E. Longoni 69 (24hr. service ☎06 22 551, appointments 06 22 55 290; www.rah.it). Visits average €100-200.

Internet: Splashnet (see above). €1.50 per hr. **Yex Internet Points,** C. V. Emmanuele 106 (☎06 45 42 98 18). €2.90 per half hr., €4.80 per hr. Also offers wire transfer and currency exchange. Open daily 8am-9pm.

Post Office: Main Post Office (Posta Centrale), P. San Silvestro 19. Open M-F 8am-7pm, Sa 8am-1:15pm. Branch at V. d. Terme di Diocleziano 30, near Termini.

ACCOMMODATIONS

Rome swells with tourists around Easter, May through July, and in September. Prices vary widely with the seasons, and proprietors are sometimes willing to negotiate rates. Termini swarms with hotel scouts. Many are legitimate and have IDs issued by tourist offices; however, beware of impostors with fake badges directing travelers to run-down locations charging exorbitant rates.

CENTRO STORICO AND ANCIENT CITY

Pensione Rosetta, V. Cavour 295 (☎06 47 82 30 69; www.rosettahotel.com), past the Fori Imperiali. Buzz at the large, wooden front doors and walk through the Vespa and palm-filled courtyard. Affordable for the location. Spacious rooms have baths, TVs, phones, and fans. A/C €5-10. Free Wi-Fi in lounge. Singles €50-60; doubles €85; triples €95; quads €120. AmEx/MC/V. ❸

Rome Student House, V. Merulana 117. From the Colosseum, walk down V. Labicana and make a left at V. Merulana. Buzz at the front and take Scala II to the 3rd floor. Make reservations beforehand so the owner, who occasionally cooks guests dinner, is not out when you arrive. Colorful rooms with fans, linens, and Wi-Fi. Check-out 10:30am. Reserve online (www.hostelworld.com). 4- to 6-person dorms €20-25. Cash only. ❷

VATICAN CITY

Colors, V. Boezio 31 (☎06 68 74 030; www.colorshotel.com). ⓂA-Ottaviano. True to its name, Colors offers 18 beds in rooms painted with a verve that would put Raphael to shame. 2 hostel floors and a 3rd floor with private rooms. A/C. Kitchens and tranquil terraces on all floors. Breakfast included. Internet access €2 per hr. Reserve dorms by 9pm the night before; wise to book earlier. Dorms €27; singles €90, with bath €105; doubles €100/130; triples €120. Low season discount up to 30%. Cash only. ❷

Orange Hotel, V. Crescenzio 86 (☎06 68 68 969; www.orangehotelrome.com). Stylish, eco-friendly boutique hotel offers a lovely terrace with a solarium and a panoramic view over the cupola of San Pietro. Points for guessing the color scheme. Delightful amenities include a rooftop restaurant, parking garage, terrace hot tub, and in-hotel laundromat. All rooms with bathtubs, A/C, TVs, internet, safes, and minibars. Breakfast included. Doubles €93-174, junior suites 154-214; triples 158-218; extra beds available. AmEx/MC/V. ❺

TERMINI AND ENVIRONS

Welcome to budget traveler central. The accommodations around the **Termini station** are some of the least expensive and most centrally located in Rome. They also play host to the most backpackers and students, so look no further if a fun atmosphere is what you crave.

Alessandro Palace, V. Vicenza 42 (☎06 44 61 958; www.hostelalessandropalace.com). From Termini's track 1, turn left on V. Marsala and right on V. Vicenza. Renovated dorms with baths and A/C. Fun bar with flatscreen TV and cheap drinks (happy hour; €3 beers daily 10-11pm). Fantastic English-speaking staff. Breakfast and pizza dinners included. Lockers free; supply your own lock. Internet (computer lounge and Wi-Fi) free 30min.

per day; €1 per hr. thereafter. Check-in 3pm. Check-out 10am. 4- to 8-person dorms €25-35; doubles €110; triples and quads €44 per person. MC/V. ❷

Hotel Papa Germano, V. Calatafimi 14/A (☎06 48 69 19; www.hotelpapagermano.com). From Termini, turn left on V. Marsala, which becomes V. Volturno, and take 4th right on V. Calatafimi. Clean, simple rooms with TVs. Helpful, English-speaking staff. Continental breakfast included. A/C €5; free fans. Free internet on 3 computers. Reception 24hr. 4-bed dorms €21-28; singles €35-50; doubles €50-80, with bath €60-105; triples €60-90/80-120; quads €85-120/95-140. AmEx/D/MC/V. ❷

The Yellow, V. Palestro 44 (☎06 49 38 26 82; www.the-yellow.com). From Termini, exit on V. Marsala, head down V. Marghera, and take the 4th left. Look no farther if you want to party hearty with people from all over the world. Huge rooms with stenciled *Blues Brothers* and *Pussy Wagon* logos accent this modern, chic youth hostel. Rocking hostel bar next door caters to guests. Lockers, linens, luggage storage, and fans included. A/C in rooms with bath. Breakfast €2. Free Wi-Fi in lounge. 4- to 12- person dorms with shared bath €10-30; 4- and 6-person dorms with private bath €10-34. €5 cash discount. AmEx/D/MC/V. ❶

Fawlty Towers Hotel and Hostel, V. Magenta 39, 5th fl. (☎06 44 50 374; www.fawltytowers.org). From Termini, cross V. Marsala onto V. Marghera and turn right on V. Magenta. Relaxed, bohemian feel. Brightly colored rooms. Comfortable common room with stained glass, TV, A/C, DVD player, book exchange, and free internet on 1 computer. Most rooms have A/C—ask for it when reserving, at no extra cost. Free lockers, linens, and towels. Kitchen with stocked fridge available for snacking. Free BBQs 2-3 F per month in summer on the sweet outdoor terrace. Reception 24hr. 3-bed dorms €25-30; 4-bed dorms €18-25; singles €30-55, with shower or full bath €35-60; doubles €45-70/50-85; triples €70-95/75-99; quads €80-100/80-110. Cash only; pay in advance. ❷

FOOD

Traditional Roman cuisine includes *spaghetti alla carbonara* (egg and cream sauce with bacon), *spaghetti all'amatriciana* (thin tomato sauce with chiles and bacon), *carciofi alla giudia* (deep-fried artichokes, common in the Jewish Ghetto), and *fiori di zucca* (stuffed, fried zucchini flowers). Pizza is often a good and inexpensive option; like elsewhere in Italy, it is eaten with a fork and knife. Try *pizza romana,* which is like foccaccia: a flat bread with olive oil, sea salt, rosemary, and sometimes more toppings. Lunch is typically the main meal of the day, though some Romans now enjoy panini on the go during the week. Restaurants tend to close between 3 and 6:30pm.

CENTRO STORICO AND ANCIENT CITY

The area around the Forum and the Colosseum is home to some of Italy's finest tourist traps. Avoid the main streets.

Cul de Sac, P. Pasquino 73 (☎06 68 80 10 94), off P. Navona. One of Rome's first wine bars. Substantial list of reasonably priced wines by the glass (from €2.50). At aperitif time, pair your pick with a snack like tuna, tomato and green bean salad, or the tasty *baba ghanoush.* Primi €7-8. Secondi €7-9. Open daily noon-4pm and 6pm-12:30am. AmEx/MC/V. ❷

L'Antica Birreria Peroni, V. San Marcello 19 (☎06 67 95 310; www.anticabirreriaperoni.it). From the Vittorio Emmanuele monument, turn right on V. Cesare Battisti and left into P. dei Santissimi Apostoli. 2 blocks down on the left. Energetic *enoteca* with a German twist and backlit beers tempting you from a ledge on the wall. Wash down a *wurstel* (€6-7) with 1 of 4 delicious Peroni beers on tap (€2-5). Fantastic *fiori di zucca* €1. Primi €6-7. Cover €1. Open M-Sa noon-midnight. AmEx/D/MC/V. ❷

Luzzi, V. San Giovanni in Laterano 88 (☎06 70 96 332), just down V. dei Fori Imperiali from the Colosseum. No-fuss *osteria* packed with locals. Specials like *pennette al sal-*

mone (€7) will leave you wanting more. Enjoy inexpensive seafood (shrimp and prawns €10) and enough cheap wine to scuttle a liner (€4 per L). Primi €5-7. Secondi €7-11. Dessert €4. Open M-Tu and Th-Su noon-3pm and 7pm-midnight. AmEx/MC/V. ❷

Pizza Art, V. Arenula 76 (☎06 68 73 16 03 78). From C. V. Emanuele II, cut through Largo di Torre Argentina and walk toward the river. Counter seating only. Thick focaccia pizza topped with arugula, goat cheese, and fried treats including *suppli* (fried rice balls) and *crochette*. Most pizza €11-13 per kg; average slice €2.50. Open daily 8am-10pm. Cash only. ❶

VATICAN CITY

Cacio e Pepe, V. Giuseppe Avezzana 11 (☎06 32 17 268). From ⓂA-Ottaviano, take the V. Barletta exit; right onto V. de Milizie, then left onto V. Avezzana. Worth the walk. In summer, rub elbows with locals at the close-packed tables outside. Namesake specialty is perfectly *al dente*, topped with olive oil, grated cheese, and fresh-ground pepper (€6). Open M-F 12:30-3pm and 7:30-11pm, Sa 12:30-3pm. Cash only. ❷

La Tradizione, V. Cipro 8/e (☎06 39 72 03 49; www.latradizione.it). This gourmet store, steps from ⓂA-Cipro, has been educating palates for nearly 3 decades with a broad selection of fine meats, wines, and over 300 cheeses. Beautifully-prepared foods (including regional specialties) sold by the kg. A large meal €15. Open M 3-8:15pm, Tu-Sa 8am-2pm and 4:30-8:15pm. AmEx/MC/V. ❷

TRASTEVERE

Giorgiagel, V. di San Francesco a Ripa 130 (☎32 01 65 02 66 or 33 32 70 59 18). Turn right on V. de San Francesco a Ripa from Vle. Trastevere. Large portions of amazing Sicilian pastries and gelato that is right up there with Rome's best. Unbelievably decadent *cioccolato fondente* (dark chocolate) and intense *frutti di bosco* (forest fruit) make a great pair. Ingredients listed. Gelato €1.50-3. *Frappè* €2.50. Open daily 1pm-9pm. Cash only. ❶

Da Simone, V. Giacinto Carini 50 (☎06 58 14 980). From Acqua Paola on the Gianicolo hill, walk behind the fountain and down V. Giacomo Medici to the end of the street. Turn right, walk under the arches to V. Carini; it's behind the bus stop to the left. Treats you to fantastic pizza and prepared foods with only the best ingredients—fine extra virgin olive oil, buffalo mozzarella, and no animal fat. Priced by weight. Open M-Sa 7:30am-8:15pm. Cash only. ❶

Siven, V. di San Francesco a Ripa 137 (☎06 58 97 110). Northwest on V. de San Francesco a Ripa from Vle. Trastevere. A hole in the wall that sells tasty pizza and prepared pastas and meats (priced by weight) to a constant stream of locals, all of whom treat the chefs like old friends. Amazing spicy chicken and lasagna. Sizeable portion around €4. No seating. Open M-Sa 9am-10pm. Cash only. ❶

ITALY

TERMINI AND ENVIRONS

San Lorenzo offers inexpensive food with local character to the budget-conscious student with a discriminating palate. There's a **Conad** supermarket on the lower floor of Termini Station (open daily 6am-midnight).

LET'S NOT GO. Termini and the surrounding areas are unsafe at night. Stay alert and avoid walking alone in the neighborhood after dark.

Hostaria da Bruno, V. Varese 29 (☎06 49 04 03). Take V. Milazzo from V. Marsala and turn right on V. Varese. A bastion of authenticity in a sea of tourist traps. Try *tortellini al sugo* (meat tortellini) or *fettuccine alla gricia* (white amatriciana; €7) as you check

out the pictures of founder Bruno with Pope John Paul II hang noon-3pm and 7-10pm, Sa 7-10pm. AmEx/MC/V. ❷

Hostaria Romana da Dino, V. dei Mille 10 (☎06 49 14 25 left on V. Marsala, right on V. Vicenza, and left on V. dei cheap prices. Loyal local following. Delectable pizza €1.50 per ¼L. Open M-Tu and Th-Su 11:30am-3pm and

AVENTINE AND TESTACCIO

P. Testaccio is just past V. Luca della Robbia. In the *piazza*, you **cio Market,** a small market set up in metal huts. Numerous vendors fruit, vegetables, meat, fish, pasta, candy, nuts, and a variety of prepare (Prices vary, most by weight. Open M-Sa 6am-2pm. Cash only.)

Il Volpetti Più, V. Alessandro Volta 8 (☎06 57 44 306; www.volpetti.com). Turn left on V. A. Volta, off V. Marmorata. Relive high school as you slide down the lunch line at this *tavola calda* (cafeteria)—but replace day-old sloppy joes with authentic Italian fare. Primi €6-7.50. Secondi €4-7.50. Fresh fish F €6-8. Desserts €4. Open M-Sa 10:30am-3:30pm and 5:30-9:30pm. AmEx/D/MC/V. ❷

Giacomini, V. Aventino 104-106 (☎06 57 43 645). Ⓜ B-Circo Massimo. South on V. Aventino from the metro stop, past V. Licinia. Inside this *alimentari,* owner Claudio, certified *Maestro Salumiere Gastronomio,* prepares indescribably wonderful *panini* to order (€4-8) with the highest quality ingredients, as he has done for over 50 years. Wide selection of hand-picked meats and cheeses from only the best producers, priced by weight. Next door, his wife and daughter create similarly wonderful pizza. Open M-Sa 7:30am-2pm and 4:45-6:30pm. AmEx/MC/V. ❶

SIGHTS

From ancient temples, medieval churches, and Renaissance basilicas to Baroque fountains and modern museums, *La Città Eterna* bursts with masterpieces. Travelers planning to visit many Roman monuments should consider the **Archeologica Card** (☎06 39 96 77 00; 7-day €22), valid at the Colosseum, Palantine Hill, and Baths of Caracalla, among other sites.

ANCIENT CITY

COLOSSEUM. This enduring symbol of the Eternal City—a hollowed-out marble structure that dwarfs every other ruin in Rome—once held as many as 50,000 spectators. Within 100 days of its AD 80 opening, some 5000 wild beasts perished in the arena. The floor once covered a labyrinth of brick cells, ramps, and elevators used to transport animals from cages up to arena level. Men were also infamously pitted against each other in gladiator competitions. *(Ⓜ B-Colosseo or bus 75 from Termini. ☎06 70 05 469. Open daily 8:30am-7:15pm. Last entry 6:15pm. Tour with archaeologists in Italian Sa-Su, English and Spanish daily every 30 min.-1 hr. 9:45am-5:15pm. Tours €4. Audio tour €4.50. Video tour €5.50. Combined tickets with Palatine Hill and Roman Forum €12, EU citizens 18-24 €7.50, EU citizens over 65 or under 18 free. Cash only.)*

PALATINE HILL. Legend has it that the Palatine Hill was home to the she-wolf who suckled brothers Romulus and Remus, the mythical founders of Rome. The best way to attack the Palatine is from the stairs near the Forum's **Arch of Titus** (where ticket lines are shorter than at the Colosseum), which lead to gardens and lookouts. On the southwest side of the hill is an ancient village with the **Casa di Romulo,** alleged home of Romulus, and the podium of the **Temple of Cybele.** The stairs to the left lead to the **Casa di Livia,** home of Augustus's wife, which once connected to the **Casa Augusto** next door. Around the corner, the spooky **Cryptoporticus** tunnel ties Tiberius's palace to nearby buildings. **Domus**

ITALY

...a was the emperors' private space; sprawling **Domus Flavia,** to its right, ...gigantic octagonal fountain. Between them stands the **Stadium Palatinum,** ...podrome, a sunken space once used as a riding school that is now a ...eum with artifacts excavated from the hill. *(South of the Forum. Same hours and ...es as Colosseum. Guided English-language tour daily 12:15pm. €3.50.)*

IMBIBE THIS! Remember that Rome's water is *potabile* (drinkable), and many fountains or spigots run throughout the city. Take a drink, or fill up your water bottle from these free sources of cold, refreshing *acqua naturale.*

ROMAN FORUM. Etruscans and Greeks used the Forum as a marketplace before early Romans founded a thatched-hut shanty town here in 753 BC. Enter through **Via Sacra,** Rome's oldest street, which leads to the **Arch of Titus.** The broad space in front of the Curia was the **Comitium,** where male citizens came to vote and representatives gathered for public discussion. Bordering the Comitium is the large brick **Rostra** (speaker's platform), erected by Julius Caesar in 44 BC. The **market square** holds a number of shrines and sacred precincts, including the *Lapis Niger* (Black Stone), where Romulus was supposedly murdered by Republican senators; below are the underground ruins of a 6th-century BC altar and the oldest known Latin inscription in Rome. In the square, the **Three Sacred Trees of Rome**—olive, fig, and grape—have been replanted. The **Lower Forum** holds the 5th-century BC **Temple of Saturn,** which achieved mythological status during Rome's Golden Age, when it hosted Saturnalia, a raucous winter party. At the end of Vicus Tuscus stands the **Temple of Castor and Pollux,** built to celebrate the 499 BC Roman defeat of the Etruscans. The **Temple of Vesta,** where Vestal Virgins kept the city's sacred fire lit for more than 1000 years, is next to the **House of the Vestal Virgins,** where they lived for 30 secluded years beginning at the ripe old age of seven. *(Main entrance on V. dei Fori Imperiali, at Largo Corrado Ricci, halfway between P. Venezia and the Colosseum. ⓂB-Colosseo or bus to P. Venezia. Open in summer daily 8:30am-6:15pm; hours reduced in winter. Audio tour €4. Cash only.)*

FORI IMPERIALI. Closed indefinitely for excavations, the **Fori Imperiali,** across the street from the Ancient Forum, is a complex of temples, basilicas, and public squares constructed in the first and second centuries, still visible from the railing at V. dei Fori Imperiali. Built between AD 107 and 113, the **Forum of Trajan** included a colossal equestrian statue of Trajan and an immense triumphal arch. At one end of the now-destroyed Forum, 2500 carved legionnaires march their way up the almost perfectly preserved **Trajan's Column,** one of the greatest specimens of Roman relief-sculpture. The crowning statue is St. Peter, who replaced Trajan in 1588. The gray rock wall of the **Forum of Augustus** commemorates Augustus's victory over Caesar's murderers in 42 BC. The only remnant of **Vespasian's Forum** is the mosaic-filled **Chiesa della Santi Cosma e Damiano** across V. Cavour, near the Roman Forum. *(Reservations ☎06 67 97 702. English tour given Su at 4:30pm. €7. Inquire within the visitor's information center on V. dei Fori Imperiali.)*

CAPITOLINE HILL. Home to the original capitol, **Monte Capitolino** still serves as the seat of the city government. Michelangelo designed its **Piazza di Campidoglio,** now home to the **Capitoline Museums** (p. 398). Stairs lead up to the rear of the 7th-century **Chiesa di Santa Maria in Aracoeli.** *(Santa Maria open daily 9am-12:30pm and 3-6:30pm. Donation requested.)* The gloomy **Mamertine Prison,** consecrated as the **Chiesa di San Pietro in Carcere,** lies down the hill from the back stairs of the Aracoeli. Imprisoned here, St. Peter baptized his captors with the waters that flooded his cell. *(Prison open daily in summer 9am-7pm; in winter 9am-12:30pm and 2-5pm. Donation requested.)* At the far end of the *piazza,* opposite the stairs, lies the turreted **Palazzo dei Senatori,** the home of Rome's mayor. *(Take any bus to P. Venezia. From P. Venezia, walk around to P. d'Aracoeli and take the stairs up the hill.)*

VELABRUM. The Velabrum area is in a Tiber flood plain, south of the Jewish Ghetto. At the bend of V. del Portico d'Ottavia, a shattered pediment and a few columns are all that remain of the once magnificent **Portico d'Ottavia.** The **Teatro di Marcello** next door was the model for the Colosseum's facade. One block south along V. Luigi Petroselli, the **Chiesa di Santa Maria in Cosmedin,** currently undergoing renovations, harbors the **Bocca della Verità,** a drain cover made famous by the film *Roman Holiday*. *(Chiesa open daily 9:30am-5:50pm.)*

DOMUS AUREA. Take a break from the relentless sun and enjoy the cacophony of birds chirping in the shady trees. Joggers, wild flowers, and ruins of a palatial estate now occupy Oppian Hill. This park houses a portion of Nero's "Golden House," which once covered a huge chunk of Rome. After deciding that he was a god, Nero had architects build a house worthy of his divinity. The Forum was reduced to a vestibule of the palace; Nero crowned it with the 35m *Colossus*, a huge statue of himself as the sun. *(Open daily 6:30am-9pm. Free.)*

CENTRO STORICO

VIA DEL CORSO AND PIAZZA VENEZIA. Shopping thoroughfare **Via del Corso,** so named because of its days as Ancient Rome's premier race course, runs between P. del Popolo and busy P. Venezia. **Palazzo Venezia** was one of the first Renaissance *palazzi* built in the city. Mussolini used it as an office and delivered his famous orations from its balcony, but today it's little more than a glorified roundabout dominated by the massive **Vittorio Emanuele II monument.** Off V. del Corso, the picturesque **Piazza Colonna** was named for the **Colonna di Marco Aurelio,** which imitated Trajan's column. Off the northwestern corner of the Piazza Colonoa is the **Piazza di Montecitorio,** home to Bernini's **Palazzo Montecitorio,** which is now the seat of the Chamber of Deputies.

THE PANTHEON. Architects still wonder how this 2000-year-old temple was erected. Its dome—a perfect half-sphere made of poured concrete without the support of vaults, arches, or ribs—is the largest of its kind. The light that enters the roof was used as a sundial; it also indicates the dates of equinoxes and solstices. In AD 606, it was consecrated as the **Chiesa di Santa Maria ad Martyres.** *(In P. della Rotonda. Open M-Sa 8:30am-7:30pm, Su 9am-6pm. Free.)*

PIAZZA NAVONA. Originally an AD first-century stadium, the *piazza* hosted wrestling matches, track and field events, and mock naval battles in which the stadium was flooded and filled with fleets. Each of the river god statues in Bernini's **Fountain of the Four Rivers** represents one of the four continents of the globe (as known in 1651): Ganges for Asia, Danube for Europe, Nile for Africa, and Río de la Plata for the Americas. *(Open daily 9am-noon and 4-7pm.)* C. V. Emanuele II runs to **Il Gesu,** inside which Andrea Pozzo's **Chapel of S. Ignazio** and Bernini's **Monument to S. Bellarmino** are must-sees. *(Open daily 6:45am-12:45pm and 4-7:45pm.)*

CAMPO DEI FIORI. Across C. Vittorio Emanuele II from P. Navona, Campo dei Fiori hosts a bustling, colorful, and quintessentially Italian open-air market. At night, the area transforms into a hot spot. You can find the Renaissance **Palazzo Farnese,** built by Alessandro Farnese (the first Counter-Reformation pope) in nearby P. Farnese, south of the Campo.

THE JEWISH GHETTO

Rome's Jewish community is the oldest in Europe—Israelites came in 161 BC as ambassadors from Judas Maccabei, asking for help against invaders. The

Ghetto, a tiny area to which Pope Paul IV confined the Jews in 1555, was dissolved in 1870, but it still remains the center of Rome's Jewish population. In the center are **Piazza Mattei** and the 16th-century **Fontana delle Tartarughe.** Nearby is the **Chiesa di Sant'Angelo in Pescheria,** where Jews forced to attend mass resisted by stuffing wax in their ears. *(V. de Funari, after P. Campitelli. Church under restoration indefinitely.)* The **Sinagoga Ashkenazita,** on the Tiber near the Theater of Marcellus, was bombed in 1982; guards now search all visitors. Inside is the **Jewish Museum,** which has ancient copies of the Torah and Holocaust artifacts. *(Synagogue open for services only. Museum open Oct.-May M-Th and Su 10am-10pm, F 10am-4pm; June-Sept. M-Th and Su 10am-7pm, F 9am-4pm. €7.50, students €3.)*

PIAZZA DI SPAGNA AND ENVIRONS

FONTANA DI TREVI. The bombastic **Fontana di Trevi** has enough presence to turn even the most jaded visitor into a romantic mush. Legend has it that a traveler who throws a coin into the fountain is ensured a speedy return to Rome; one who tosses two will fall in love there. Opposite is the Baroque **Chiesa dei Santi Vincenzo e Anastasio.** The crypt preserves the hearts and lungs of popes who served from 1590 to 1903. *(Open daily 7am-noon and 4-7pm.)*

SCALINATA DI SPAGNATHE (SPANISH STEPS). Designed by an Italian, paid for by the French, named for the Spaniards, occupied by the British, and currently featuring the American great Ronald McDonald, the **Spanish Steps** exude worldliness. The house to the right is where John Keats died; it's now the **Keats-Shelley Memorial Museum.** *(Open M-F 9am-1pm and 3-6pm, Su 11am-2pm and 3-6pm. €3.50.)*

PIAZZA DEL POPOLO. In the center of the "people's square"–once the venue for the execution of heretics–is the 3200-year-old **Obelisk of Pharaoh Ramses II** that Augustus brought back from Egypt in AD 10. The **Church of Santa Maria del Popolo** contains Renaissance and Baroque masterpieces. *(Open M-Sa 7am-noon and 4-7pm, Su 8am-1:30pm and 4:30-7:30pm.)* Two exquisite Caravaggios, *The Conversion of St. Paul* and *Crucifixion of St. Peter*, are in the **Cappella Cerasi,** which Raphael designed. *(Open M-Sa 7am-noon and 4-7pm, Su 7:30am-1:30pm and 4:30-7:30pm.)*

VILLA BORGHESE. To celebrate his purchase of a cardinalship, Scipione Borghese built the **Villa Borghese** north of P. di Spagna and V. V. Veneto. Its huge park houses three fantastic art museums: world-renowned **Galleria Borghese** (p. 397), airy **Galleria Nazionale d'Arte Moderna,** and intriguing **Museo Nazionale Etrusco di Villa Giulia.** North of the Borghese are the **Santa Priscilla catacombs** and the **Villa Ada** gardens. *(M: A-Spagna. Open M-F 9:30am-6pm, Sa-Su 9:30am-7pm. €8.50.)*

ITALY

VATICAN CITY

Once the mightiest power in Europe, the administrative and spiritual center of the Roman Catholic Church now lies on 108 autonomous acres within Rome. The Vatican has symbolically preserved its independence by minting coins, running a separate press and postal system, maintaining an army of Swiss Guards, and hoarding art in the **Musei Vaticani.** *(M: A-Ottaviano. Or catch bus #64, 271, or 492 from Termini or Largo Argentina, #62 from P. Barberini, or #23 from Testaccio.)*

BASILICA DI SAN PIETRO (ST. PETER'S). A famous colonnade by Bernini leads from **Piazza San Pietro** to the church. The **obelisk** in the *piazza*'s center is framed by two fountains; stand on the round discs set in the pavement and the quadruple rows of the colonnade will visually resolve into one perfectly aligned row. Above the colonnade are 140 statues of saints; those on the basilica represent Christ, John the Baptist, and the Apostles (except for Peter). The pope opens the **Porta Sancta** (Holy Door) every 25 years by knocking on the bricks with a silver hammer; on warm Wednesday mornings, he holds papal audiences on a platform in the *piazza.* The basilica itself rests on the reputed site of St. Peter's tomb. Inside, metal lines mark the lengths of other major world churches. To the right, Michelangelo's *Pietà* has been protected by bullet-proof glass since 1972, when an axe-wielding fiend smashed Christ's nose and broke Mary's hand. The climb to the top of the **dome** might very well be worth the heart attack it could cause. An elevator will take you up about 300 of the 350 stairs. *(Modest dress required. Multilingual confession available. Church: open daily Apr.-Sept. 7am-7pm; Oct.-Mar. 7am-6pm. Mass M-Sa 8:30, 9, 10, 11am, noon, 5pm; Su 9, 10:30, 11:30am, 12:15, 1, 4, 5, 5:30pm. Free. Dome: From inside the basilica, exit the building and re-enter the door to the far left. Open daily Apr.-Sept. 8am-5pm; Oct.-Mar. 8am-4pm. Stairs €4, elevator €7.)*

SISTINE SIGHTSEEING. The Sistine Chapel is at the end of the standard route through the Vatican Museums (p. 397), and it's usually extremely crowded. Go straight to the Sistine Chapel to enjoy Michelangelo's masterpiece, and then backtrack. It's relatively empty early in the morning.

SISTINE CHAPEL. Since its completion in the 16th century, the Sistine Chapel (named for its founder, Pope Sixtus IV) has served as the chamber in which the College of Cardinals elects new popes. Michelangelo's glorious ceiling, which depicts stories from Genesis, gleams post-restoration. *The Last Judgment* fills the altar wall; the figure of Christ, as judge, sits in the upper center surrounded by saints and Mary. Michelangelo painted himself as a flayed human skin hanging between heaven and hell. The cycle was completed in 1483 by artists under Perugino, including Botticelli, Ghirlandaio, Roselli, Pinturicchio, Signorelli, and della Gatta. The frescoes on the side walls predate Michelangelo's ceiling. *(Admission included with Vatican Museums, p. 397.)*

CASTEL SANT'ANGELO. Built by Hadrian (AD 117-138) as a mausoleum for himself and his family, this mass of brick and stone has been a fortress, prison, and palace. When the plague struck Rome, Pope Gregory the Great saw an angel at its top; the plague soon abated, and the edifice was rededicated to the angel. The fortress offers an incomparable view of Rome. *(Walk along the river from St. Peter's toward Trastevere. Open daily 9am-7pm. €5. Audio tour €4.)*

TRASTEVERE

Right off the **Ponte Garibaldi** stands the statue of the famous dialect poet G. G. Belli. On V. di Santa Cecilia, through the gate and beyond the courtyard, is the **Basilica di Santa Cecilia in Trastevere.** Carlo Maderno's famous statue of Santa Cecilia lies under the altar. *(Open daily 9:30am-12:30pm and 4-6:30pm. Donation requested. Cloisters open M-F 10:15am-12:15pm, Sa-Su 11:15am-12:15pm. Cloisters €2.50. Crypt €2.50.)* From P. Sonnino, V. della Lungaretta leads west to P. S. Maria in Trastevere, home to stray dogs, expatriates, and the **Chiesa di Santa Maria in Trastevere,** built in the 4th century. *(Open M-Sa 9am-5:30pm, Su 8:30-10:30am and noon-5:30pm.)* North of the *piazza* are the Rococo **Galleria Corsini,** V. della Lungara 10, and the **Villa Farnesina** (p. 398), once home to Europe's wealthiest man. Atop the Gianicolo Hill is the **Chiesa di San Pietro in Montorio,** built on the spot believed to be the site of St. Peter's upside-down crucifixion. The church contains del Piombo's *Flagellation.* Next door is Bramante's tiny **Tempietto,** characterized by a combination of ancient and Renaissance architecture; it commemorates St. Peter's martyrdom. Rome's **botanical gardens** have a rose garden that holds the bush from which all the world's roses are supposedly descended. *(Church and Tempietto open Tu-Su May-Oct. 9:30am-12:30pm and 4-6pm; Nov.-Apr. 9:30am-12:30pm and 2-4pm. Gardens open M-Sa Oct.-Mar. 9:30am-5:30pm; Apr.-Oct. 9:30am-6:30pm.)*

ITALY

NEAR TERMINI

PIAZZA DEL QUIRINALE. At the southeast end of V. del Quirinale, this *piazza* occupies the summit of one of Ancient Rome's seven hills. In its center, the enormous statues of Castor and Pollux stand on either side of an obelisk from the Mausoleum of Augustus. The President of the Republic resides in the **Palazzo del Quirinale,** its Baroque architecture by Bernini, Maderno, and Fontana. Farther along the street lies the facade of Borromini's **Chiesa di San Carlo alle Quattro Fontane.** Bernini's **Four Fountains** are built into the intersection of V. delle Quattro Fontane and V. del Quirinale. *(Palazzo closed to the public. Chiesa open daily 8:30am-12:30pm and 3:30-6pm.)*

BASILICA OF SANTA MARIA MAGGIORE. Crowning the Esquiline Hill, this gigantic basilica is officially part of Vatican City. To the right of the altar beneath the stunning coffered ceiling, a marble slab marks **Bernini's tomb.** The 14th-century mosaics in the **loggia** *(open daily with guided tour at 1pm; €5)* depict the August snowfall that showed the pope where to build the church; the snowstorm is re-enacted each August with white flower petals. *(Modest dress required. Open daily 7am-7pm. Museum open 9:30am-6:30pm. Suggested donation €4. Audio tour €4.)*

SOUTHERN ROME

The area south of the center, a mix of wealthy and working-class neighborhoods, is home to the city's best nightlife and some of its grandest churches.

APPIAN WAY. The Appian Way was the most important thoroughfare of Ancient Rome. Early Christians secretly constructed maze-like catacombs under the ashes of their persecutors. On Sundays, when the street is closed to traffic, take a break from the city to bike through the countryside. *(M: B-S. Giovanni to P. Appio; take bus #218 from P. di S. Giovanni to V. Appia Antica and get off at the info office.)* **San Callisto** is the largest catacomb in Rome. Its four levels once held 16 popes, St. Cecilia, and 500,000 other Christians. *(V. Appia Antica 126, entrance on road parallel to V. Appia. Open M-Tu and Th-Su 9am-noon and 2-5pm. €5.)* Catacomb **Santa Domitilla** houses an intact 3rd-century portrait of Christ and the Apostles. *(V. delle Sette Chiese 282. Facing V. Ardeatina from the San Callisto exit, cross the street and walk right up V. Sette Chiese. Open Feb.-Dec. M and W-Su 9am-noon and 2-5pm. €5. Cash only.)*

CAELIAN HILL. Southeast of the Colosseum, the Caelian was the hill where elite Romans made their home in ancient times. The **Chiesa di San Giovanni in Laterano** was the seat of the papacy until the 14th century; founded by Constantine in AD 314, it is Rome's oldest Christian basilica. Outside to the left, **Scala Santa** has what are believed to be the 28 steps used by Jesus outside Pontius Pilate's home. *(Modest dress required. M: A-S. Giovanni or bus #16. Open daily 7am-6:30pm. €2, students €1.)* The **Chiesa di San Clemente** is split into three levels, each from a different era. A fresco cycle by Masolino dating from the 1420s graces its **Chapel of Santa Caterina.** *(M: B-Colosseo. Turn left down V. Labicana away from the Forum. Open M-Sa 9am-12:30pm and 3-6pm, Su 10am-12:30pm and 3-6pm. €5, students €3.50.)*

AVENTINE HILL. The **Roseto Comunale,** a public rose garden, is host to the annual Premio Roma, the worldwide competition for the best blossom. *(V. d. Valle Murcia, across the Circus Maximus from the Palatine Hill. Open May-June daily 8am-7:30pm.)* Just before the crest of the hill, stroll among orange trees at **Giardini degli Aranci.** *(Open daily dawn-dusk.)* The top left-hand panel of the wooden front doors at nearby **Chiesa di Santa Sabina** is one of the earliest-known representations of the Crucifixion. V. S. Sabina runs along the crest of the hill to **Piazza dei Cavalieri di Malta,** home of the order of the Knights of Malta. Look through the **keyhole** in the arched gate: there is a perfectly framed view of the dome of St. Peter's Cathedral.

EUR. South of the city is a residential area that remains as a memento of the second Roman Empire that never was. EUR (AY-oor) is the Italian acronym for Universal Exposition of Rome, the 1942 World's Fair that Mussolini intended to be a showcase of Fascist achievement–apparently, this involved the ability to build lots of identical square buildings. **Via Cristoforo Colombo,** EUR's main street, runs north from the metro station to **Piazza Guglielmo Marconi** and its 1959 **obelisk.** There is also a scenic artificial lake surrounded by jogging paths. The nearby hills are a popular lounging spot. *(M: B-EUR Palasport or take bus #714.)*

MUSEUMS

Etruscans, emperors, and popes have been busily stuffing Rome with artwork for several millennia, leaving behind a city teeming with collections. Museums are generally closed on Mondays, Sunday afternoons, and holidays.

GALLERIA BORGHESE. Upon entering, don't miss Mark Antonio's **ceiling,** which depicts the Roman conquest of Gaul. **Room I,** on the right, houses Canova's steamy statue of **Paolina Borghese** portrayed as Venus triumphant, reclining with Paris's golden apple. The next rooms display some of Bernini's most monumental sculptures: a striking **David,** crouching with his slingshot; **Apollo and Daphne;** the weightless body in **Rape of Proserpina;** and weary-looking Aeneas in **Eneo e Anchise.** The dark paintings in the **Caravaggio Room** include *Self Portrait as Bacchus* and *David and Goliath.* The collection continues in the **pinacoteca** upstairs, which is accessible from the gardens around the back by a winding staircase. **Room IX** holds Raphael's **Deposition** while Sodoma's *Pietà* graces **Room XII.** Look for del Conte's *Cleopatra and Lucrezia*, Rubens's *Pianto sul Cristo Morto*, and Titian's *Amor Sacro e Amor Profano. (Vle. del Museo Borghese. M: A-Spagna; take the Villa Borghese exit. ☎06 32 810. Open Tu-Su 8:30am-7:30pm. Entrance every 2hr. Reserve ahead, especially for large groups. Tickets €8.50. Audio tour €5.)*

VATICAN MUSEUMS. The Vatican Museums constitute one of the world's greatest art collections; plan to spend at least four hours exploring them. Ancient, Renaissance, and modern statues and paintings are rounded out with papal odds and ends. The **Museo Pio-Clementino** has the world's greatest collection of antique sculpture. Two Molossian hounds guard the entrance to the **Stanza degli Animali,** a marble menagerie. Other gems include the **Apollo Belvedere** and **Hercules.** From the last room, the Simonetti Stairway climbs to the **Museo Etrusco,** filled with artifacts from Tuscany and northern Lazio. Back on the landing of the Simonetti Staircase is the **Stanza della Biga** (ancient marble chariot room) and the **Galleria della Candelabra** (chandelier). The long trudge to the Sistine Chapel begins here, passing through the **Galleria degli Arazzi** (tapestries), the **Galleria delle Mappe** (maps), the **Apartamento di Pio V** (where there is a sneaky shortcut to *la Sistina*), the **Stanza Sobieski,** and the **Stanza della Immaculata Concezione.** A door leads into the first of the four **Stanze di Rafaele,** apartments built for Pope Julius II in the 1510s. One *stanza* features Raphael's **School of Athens,** painted as a trial piece for Julius, who was so impressed that he fired his other painters and commissioned Raphael to decorate the entire suite. From here, there are two paths: a staircase leading to the brilliantly frescoed Borgia Apartments, which house the **Museum of Modern Religious Art,** and another route leading to the Sistine Chapel (p. 395). On the way out of the Sistine Chapel, take a look at the **Room of the Aldobrandini Marriage,** which contains a series of rare, ancient Roman frescoes. Finally, the Vatican's painting collection, the **pinacoteca,** spans eight centuries and is one of the best in Rome. It includes Perugino's *Madonna and Child*, Titian's *Madonna of San Nicoletta dei Frari*, and Raphael's *Transfiguration. (Walk north from P.S. Pietro along the wall of the Vatican City for 10 blocks. ☎06 69*

88 49 47; www.vatican.va. Open M-Sa 8:30am-6pm. Last entrance 2hr. before closing. €13, with ISIC €8. Also open last Su of the month 8:30am-12:30pm. Free.)

ARE WE THERE YET? Lines for the Vatican Museums begin forming around 6:30am and become increasingly unbearable as the hours pass. It's not a bad idea to drag yourself out of your rock-hard hostel bed at an ungodly hour if you want to avoid the long wait.

MUSEI CAPITOLINI. This collection of ancient sculpture is the world's first public museum of ancient art. Pope Clemente XII bought the *palazzo* in 1733 to exhibit Cardinal Alessandro Albani's ancient sculptures. The Palazzo dei Conservatori's courtyard contains fragments of the frightening **Colossus of Constantine.** The original statue of **Marcus Aurelius,** Bernini's interesting **Head of Medusa,** and the famous **Capitoline Wolf**—a statue that has symbolized the city of Rome since antiquity—occupy the first floor. At the top of the stairs, the **pinacoteca's** masterpieces include Bellini's *Portrait of a Young Man*, Caravaggio's *St. John the Baptist and Gypsy Fortune-Teller*, Rubens's *Romulus and Remus Fed by the Wolf*, and Titian's *Baptism of Christ*. *(On Capitoline Hill behind the Vittorio Emanuele II monument. ☎06 82 05 91 27. Open Tu-Su 9am-8pm. €6.50-8, students with ISIC €4.50-6.)*

VILLA FARNESINA. The villa was the sumptuous home of Europe's one-time wealthiest man, Agostino "il Magnifico" Chigi. To the right of the entrance lies the breathtaking **Sala of Galatea,** a vault displaying astrological signs and showing the stars as they were at 9:30pm on November 29, 1466, the moment of Agostino's birth. The room's masterpiece is Raphael's **Triumph of Galatea.** The ceiling of the **Loggia di Psiche** depicts the marriage of Cupid and Psyche. Returning to the entrance, a stucco-ceilinged stairway, with gorgeous perspective detail, ascends to Peruzzi's **Salone delle Prospettive,** which incorporates five different colored marbles in the floor design and offers views of Rome between columns. The adjacent bedroom, known as the **Stanza delle Nozze** (Marriage Room), is a highlight. A maze of stolen commissions between Raphael and Il Sodoma led to the latter's creating a masterful fresco of Alexander the Great's marriage to Roxane. *(V. della Lungara 230. Across from Palazzo Corsini on Lungotevere della Farnesina. Bus #23, 271, or 280; get off at Lungotevere della Farnesina or Ponte Sisto. ☎06 68 02 72 67. Open M-Sa 9am-1pm; 1st Su of the month 9am-1pm. Last entry 12:40pm. €5.)*

MUSEO NAZIONALE D'ARTE ANTICA. This collection of 12th- through 18th-century art is split between Palazzo Barberini and Palazzo Corsini. **Palazzo Barberini** contains paintings from the medieval through Baroque periods, and **Palazzo Corsini** features works by Caravaggio, El Greco, and Raphael. *(V. Barberini 18. M: A-Barberini. Bus #62 or 492. ☎06 48 14 591. Open Tu-Su 8:30am-7:30pm. €5.)* **Galleria Corsini** holds works by 17th- and 18th-century painters, from Rubens to Caravaggio. *(V. della Lungara 10. Opposite Villa Farnesina in Trastevere. Take bus #23 to between Ponte Mazzini and Ponte Sisto. ☎06 22 58 24 93. Open Tu-Su 8:30am-7:30pm. €4.)*

GALLERIA SPADA. Cardinal Bernardino Spada bought an imposing assortment of paintings and sculpture and commissioned an even more impressive set of rooms to house them. Time and good luck have left the palatial 17th-century apartments nearly intact; a visit to the gallery offers a glimpse of the luxury surrounding Baroque courtly life. In **Room 1,** the modest cardinal hung portraits of himself by Cerini, Guercino, and Reni. In **Room 2,** look for paintings by Venetians Tintoretto and Titian and a frieze by Vaga, originally intended for the Sistine Chapel. **Room 4** has three canvases by the father-daughter team of Orazio and Artemisia Gentileschi. *(P. Capo d. Ferro 13, in the Palazzo Spada. Bus #64. ☎06 68 32 409. Open Tu-Su 8:30am-7:30pm. Guided tour Su 10:45am from museum bookshop. €5.)*

MUSEI NAZIONALI ROMANI. The fascinating **Museo Nazionale Romano Palazzo Massimo alle Terme** is devoted to the history of art during the Roman Empire, and features the *Lancellotti Discus Thrower* and a rare Nero-era mosaic. *(Largo di V. Peretti 1, in P. dei Cinquecento. Open Tu-Su 9am-7:45pm.)* Nearby, the **Museo Nazionale Romano Terme di Diocleziano,** a beautifully renovated complex partly housed in the huge **Baths of Diocletian,** has exhibits on ancient epigraphy (writing) and a Michelangelo cloister. *(V. Enrico de Nicola 78. Open Tu-Su 9am-7:45pm.)* The **Aula Ottogonale** holds classical sculptures. *(V. Romita 8. Open daily 9am-1pm. Free.)* Across town, the **Museo Nazionale Romano Palazzo Altemps** displays the 5th-century *Ludovisi Throne. (P. Sant'Apollinare 44, just north of P. Navona. Open Tu-Su 9am-7:45pm. €5. Audio tour €4. Combo ticket for Diocleziano, Crypta Balbi, and Palazzo Altemps €9.)*

ENTERTAINMENT

The weekly *Roma C'è* and *Time Out*, both available at newsstands, have comprehensive and up-to-date club, movie, and event listings.

THEATER AND CINEMA

The **Festival Roma-Europa** (www.romaeuropa.net) in late summer brings a number of world-class acts to Rome. **Teatro Argentina,** Largo di Torre Argentina 52, is the matriarch of all Italian theater venues, with year-round performances. (☎06 684 00 01 11. Box office open M-F 10am-2pm and 3-7pm, Sa 10am-2pm. Tickets €14-26, students €12-21. AmEx/MC/V.) **Teatro Colosseo,** V. Capo d'Africa 5/A, usually features work by foreign playwrights translated into Italian, but also hosts an English-language theater night. (☎06 70 04 932. M: B-Colosseo. Box office open Sept.-Apr. Tu-Sa 6-9:30pm. Tickets €10-20, students €8.)

Most English-language films are dubbed in Italian; for films in their original languages, check newspapers for listings marked **v.o.** or **l.o.** The theater of Italian director Nanni Moretti, **Nuovo Sacher,** Largo Ascianghi 1, shows independent films. (☎06 58 18 116. Films in the original language M-Tu. €7, matinee €4.50.)

MUSIC

Founded by Palestrina in the 16th century, the **Accademia Nazionale di Santa Cecilia,** V. Vittoria 6, off V. del Corso (☎06 36 11 064 or 800 90 70 80; www.santacecilia.it), remains the best in classical music performance. Concerts are held at the **Parco della Musica,** V. Pietro di Coubertin 30, near P. del Popolo (www.musicaperroma.it. Tickets at Parco della Musica. Regular season runs Sept.-June. €15, students €8.) Known as one of Europe's best jazz clubs, **Alexanderplatz Jazz Club,** V. Ostia 9, is decorated with messages left on its walls by old greats. The club moves outside to the Villa Celimontana during summer. (☎06 39 74 21 71; www.alexanderplatz.it. M: A-Ottaviano. Required membership €10. Open daily Sept.-May 9pm-2am. Shows start at 10pm.) The **Cornetto Free Music Festival Roma Live** (www.cornettoalgida.it) has attracted the likes of Pink Floyd and the Black Eyed Peas; it takes place at various venues during the summer.

SPECTATOR SPORTS

Though May brings tennis and equestrian events, sports revolve around *calcio*, or football. Rome has two teams in *Serie A*, Italy's prestigious league: **S.S. Lazio** and **A.S. Roma.** Matches are held at the **Stadio Olimpico,** in Foro Italico, almost every Sunday from September to June. Tickets (from €16) can be bought at team stores like **A.S. Roma,** P. Colonna 360 (☎06 67 86 514; www.asroma.it.

Tickets sold daily 10am-6:30pm. AmEx/MC/V), and **Lazio Point,** V. Farini 34/36, near Termini. (☎06 48 26 688. Open daily 9am-7pm. AmEx/MC/V.) Tickets can also be obtained at the stadium before games, but beware of long lines. If you're buying last minute, watch out for overpriced or fake tickets.

NIGHTLIFE

Romans find nighttime diversion at the pubs of San Lorenzo, the clubs of Testaccio, and everywhere in between. Pick up *Roma C'è* for updates on clubs' openings and closings. *Time Out* covers Rome's sparse but solid collection of gay nightlife listings, many of which require an **ARCI-GAY pass** (1 year. €10). Also check with **Circolo di Cultura Omosessuale Mario Mieli** (☎06 54 13 985).

ANCIENT CITY

Oppio Caffè, V. delle Terme de Tito 72 (☎06 47 45 262; www.oppiocaffe.it). ⓂB-Colosseo. Step into a neon paradise. Color-changing lights and funky art surround a pit with translucent tables in this hip bar overlooking one of history's bloodiest arenas. Check out your dreads in the reflective metal ceiling and get your thump on as DJs pump out indie-electronic beats. Mixed drinks €7. M, W, F-Su DJs. Live music 1 Th per month. Wheelchair-accessible. Open daily 7am-2am. AmEx/D/MC/V over €15.

Tree Folk's, V. Capo d'Africa 29 (☎ 06 97 61 52 72). ⓂB-Colosseo. The music and decor is a cocktail of American, German, and British classics in this creative pub that caters to your inner beer connoisseur with 10 delectable taps (€5). You'll have to be drunk to understand why the special Summer Lightning beer is only imported during the winter. Mutton €7-12. Massively delicious salads €7-10. Wine €5 per glass. Wheelchair-accessible. Open daily 7pm-2am. D/MC/V.

CENTRO STORICO

Société Lutèce, Vco. di Montevecchio 17 (☎06 68 30 14 72). Take V. di Parione from V. del Governo Vecchio; bear straight and then make a left onto Vco. di Montevecchio. Effortlessly hip. The perfect place for a pre- or post-dinner drink. Wine €6 per glass. Mixed drinks €7-8. The vaguely Middle Eastern apertif buffet is fresh, yummy, substantial, and included. Wheelchair accessible. Open daily 6pm-2am. MC/V.

Sloppy Sam's, P. Campo dei Fiori 9 (☎06 68 80 26 37). This popular pub is packed with visiting students even on a Tuesday. Numerous drink specials and a window on the action on Campo dei Fiori. Wheelchair accessible. Happy hour M-F 4pm-8pm; bottled beer and pints €4, mixed drinks €6.50, house win €3 per glass. Other specials nightly, some requiring student ID. Open daily 4pm-2am. AmEx/MC/V.

Rialto Santambrogio, V. de Sant' Ambrogio 4 (☎06 68 13 36 40; www.rialto.roma.it). Easiest to approach from V. del Portico. Tucked away in the Jewish Ghetto in a more or less unmarked building; pay close attention to the street numbers. Rialto isn't a bar, pub, club, or *discotheque:* it's a *centro sociale*, where serious scenesters meet to hear music, dance to visiting DJs, see art, and talk left politics. No such thing as regular hours—your best bet's to check the website for a schedule of events.

TRASTEVERE

Bir & Fud, V. Benedetta 23 (☎06 58 94 016; www.birefud.it), behind the P. Trilussa fountain. Delicious, frequently changing Italian craft beers flow from about 20 taps and all organic food graces plates in this taste bud heaven. Co-owner and brewmaster Leonardo takes a break from perfecting his own highly original and uniformly amazing beers at the Birra del Borgo brewery (birradelborgo.it) to come by and engage other beer connoisseurs on weekends. Try the Ke-To Re-Porter (a lighter porter spiced with fermented Kentucky tobacco), the My Antonia (a savory brew originating from a partnership between Leonardo and the Dogfish Head brewmaster), the Rubus (a refreshing raspberry beer with all the fruit but none of the heaviness of a lambic), or the Opperbacco TripIIpa (a cross between a Belgian triple and an IPA with amarillo accents). Beer €5-70. Pizza €5-12. Open daily 7pm-2am. AmEx/D/MC/V.

Ma Che Siete Venuti A Fà, V. Benedetta 25 (☎06 97 27 52 18; www.football-pub.com), behind the P. Trilussa fountain. Owned by the same beer luminaries as Bir & Fud, this smaller counterpart across the street specializes in unpasteurized, unfiltered beers handpicked from international breweries on beer scouting trips. There is absolutely nothing but the 16 taps, 100+ bottled beers, and their fans in the tiny wooden shack of an interior, filled with soccer memorabilia and kegs, and no loud music to take the focus off of malt beverages and good conversation. Try the Montegioco Makkestout, a dry stout with excellent mouth feel brewed especially for the bar. Pints and 33cl bottles €5, 75cl bottles €15. Open daily 3pm-2am. Cash only.

TESTACCIO AND OSTIENSE

L'Oasi della Birra, P. Testaccio 38/41 (☎06 57 46 122; www.ristorantidiroma.com/oasi.htm). From V. Marmorata, turn left on V. A. Manuzio and right on P. Testaccio. You'll think it's a mirage in the middle of the club desert until you pay the bill. Enjoy affordable, incredibly delicious drinks and food before getting sloshed on expensive, bad selections on the dance floors in the area. The beer catalog boasts over 500 types from all over the world, arranged by region and type (most bottles €4.50), and there is a selection of wines (€10+ per bottle) and grappa in the quadruple digits. Gourmet meats and cheeses are similarly numerous and delectable (try 6 types for €15.50, 8 for €18.50). Happy hour daily 5-8:15pm; food and a drink €10. Open daily 5pm-midnight. AmEx/D/MC/V.

Akab, V. di Monte Testaccio 69 (☎06 57 25 05 85; www.akabcave.com). One of Rome's most famous clubs has the potential for entirely different scenes every night on each of 3 dance floors. Advanced ventilation and an expensive permit allow smoking on the primary floor, a large area covered by a metal roof and flanked by a blue-lit bar on one side and a red-lit private table area on the other. Tu techno; Th hip-hop, R&B, and rap; F-Sa pop and mix. If you get in, get ready to rub elbows with tons of Rome's hippest club-goers doing their thing and possibly some famous musical talents (50 Cent and

TOP TEN PLACES TO SMOOCH IN ROMA

While you may be close enough to pucker up with strangers on the subway, save your saliva for these dreamy destinations.

1. Stroll through **Villa Borghese (p. 394)**, find a secluded, shaded spot, and go in for the kill.
2. Bottle of red. Bottle of white. **Trevi Fountain** (p. 394) at night.
3. With the sun setting behind St. Peter's and the swirling Tiber beneath you, **Ponte Sisto** is the perfect place to lay it on. Hard.
4. St. Peter's Square (p. 394). Just try to keep it PG—his Holiness may be looking.
5. Look out over **Circus Maximus** (p. 396) from Palatine Hill: imagine thousands of fans cheering on you and your sweetie.
6. The terrace of the **Vittorio Emanuele II** monument (p. 393). There's a reason people call this spot the "wedding cake."
7. Top of the **Spanish Steps** (p. 394). If it fails, you can always push the person down them.
8. Waiting for the **Metro.** You'd be surprised—it can get pretty steamy. Plus you'll make a stranger's day.
9. Chiesa di Santa Maria in Cosmedin (p. 406). Forget chocolates and roses; the skull and relics of St. Valentine are the key ingredient in any love potion.
10. Over a shared bowl of spaghetti, *Lady and the Tramp* style.

Fabolous performed here in 2009). Drinks €10. Cover €10-15 includes 1 drink. Open Tu and Th-Sa 10:30pm-4:30am. AmEx/D/MC/V.

MILAN (MILANO) ☎02

Unlike Rome, Venice, or Florence, which wrap themselves in veils of historic allure, Milan (pop. 1,400,000), once the capital of the western half of the Roman Empire, presents itself simply as it is: rushed, refined, and cosmopolitan. This urban center also hides many artistic treasures, including da Vinci's *Last Supper*. Milan owes much of its heritage to the medieval Visconti and Sforza families, and its culture to Austrian, French, and Spanish occupiers. Now that Italians run the show, the city flourishes as the country's producer of cutting-edge style, hearty risotto, and die-hard football fans.

TRANSPORTATION

Flights: Malpensa Airport (MXP), 48km from the city, handles intercontinental flights. **Malpensa Express** train leaves from Stazione Nord for the airport. Accessible via Cadorna Metro station (40min., onboard €11/13). **Linate Airport (LIN),** 7km away, covers domestic and European flights. From there, take **Starfly buses** (20min., €2.50) to Stazione Centrale, which is quicker than bus #73 (€1) to San Babila Metro station.

Regional Hubs: Orio al Serio Airport (**BGY;** ☎035 32 63 23; www.sacbo.it) in Bergamo is a hub for budget airlines **Ryanair, SkyEurope,** and **Wizz Air.**

Trains: Stazione Centrale (☎02 89 20 21; www.trenitalia.com), in P. Duca d'Aosta on M2. Trains run hourly to: **Bergamo** (1hr., €4.10); **Florence** (3hr., €15-36); **Rome** (7hr., €52-73); **Turin** (2hr., €8.75); **Venice** (2hr., €29.50).

Buses: Stazione Centrale. Intercity buses tend to be less convenient and more expensive than trains. **Autostradale, SAL, SIA,** and other carriers leave from P. Castello (M1: Cairoli) and Porta Garibaldi for **Bergamo,** the **Lake Country, Trieste,** and **Turin.**

Public Transportation: The **Metro** (Metropolitana Milanese, or **M**) runs 6am-midnight. Line #1 (red) stretches from the *pensioni* district east of Stazione Centrale through the center of town. Line #2 (green) connects Milan's 3 train stations. Use the **bus** system for trips outside the city proper. Metro tickets can be purchased at *tabaccherie,* ticket booths, and station machines. Single-fare tickets €1, 1-day pass €3, 10 trips €9.20.

ORIENTATION AND PRACTICAL INFORMATION

Milan resembles a giant bull's-eye, defined by its ancient concentric city walls. In the outer rings lie suburbs built during the 50s and 60s to house southern immigrants. In the inner circle are four squares: **Piazza del Duomo,** where **Via Orefici, Via Mazzini,** and **Corso Vittorio Emanuele II** meet; **Piazza Castello** and the attached **Largo Cairoli,** near the Castello Sforzesco; **Piazza Cordusio,** connected to Largo Cairoli by **Via Dante;** and **Piazza San Babila,** the entrance to the business and fashion district. The **duomo** and **Galleria Vittorio Emanuele** are roughly at the center of the circles. The **Giardini Pubblici** and the **Parco Sempione** radiate from the center. From the huge **Stazione Centrale,** northeast of the city, take M3 to the *duomo.*

Tourist Office: IAT, P. Duomo 19A. (☎02 72 52 43 01; www.milanoinfotourist.com), in P. del Duomo. Pick up helpful *Hello Milano.* Open M-Sa 8:45am-1pm and 2-6pm, Su 9am-1pm and 2-5pm. **Branch** in Stazione Centrale (☎02 77 40 43 18) has shorter lines. Open M-Sa 9am-6pm, Su 9am-1pm and 2-5pm.

American Express: V. Larga 4 (☎02 72 10 41), on the corner of V. Larga and S. Clemente. Exchanges currency, handles wire transfers, and holds mail for up to 1 month for AmEx cardholders for free. Open M-F 9am-5:30pm, Sa 9am-12:30pm.

Lost Property: Ufficio Oggetti Smarriti Comune, V. Fruili 30 (☎02 88 45 39 00). Open M-F 8:30am-4pm.

Hospital: Ospedale Maggiore di Milano, V. Francesco Sforza 35 (☎02 55 031).

24hr. Pharmacy: (☎02 66 90 735). In Stazione Centrale's 2nd fl. *galleria.*

Internet: Internet Enjoy, Vle. Tunisia 11 (☎02 36 55 58 05). M1: Porta Venezia. €2-3 per hr. Open M-Sa 9am-midnight, Su 2pm-midnight.

Post Office: P. Cordusio 4 (☎02 72 48 21 26), near P. del Duomo. Currency exchange and **ATM.** Open M-F 8am-7pm, Sa 8:30am-noon. **Postal Code:** 20100.

ACCOMMODATIONS

Every season is high season in fashionable Milan—except during August, when many hotels close. Prices rise in September, November, March, and April due to theater season and business conventions. For the best deals, try the hostels on the city periphery or in the areas east of Stazione Centrale.

Hotel Eva and Hotel Arno, V. Lazzaretto 17, 4th fl. (☎02 67 06 093; www.hotelevamilano.com or www.hotelarno.com). M1: Pta. Venezia. Follow V. Felice Casati, then take a right on V. Lazzaretto. Ring bell. Quirky, mirrored decor and spiral staircases make for an intriguing and inviting atmosphere. Note the life-size porcelain snow leopard. 18 large rooms with wood floors, TV, and phone. Shared bathroom. Free luggage storage. Free Internet. Singles €30-45; doubles €50-100; triples €65-90. AmEx/MC/V. ❸

La Cordata Ostello, V. Burigozzo 11 (☎02 58 31 46 75; www.ostellimilano.it). M3: Missori. From P. Missori, take tram #15 2 stops to Italia San Luca; continue in the same direction for 1 block and turn right on V. Burigozzo. Entrance around the corner on V. Aurispa. Close to the Navigli area, a lively crash pad for a young, international crowd ready to party. Colorful, plant-filled common rooms with TV and large kitchens. Laundry €3. Free Internet and Wi-Fi. 7-night max. stay. Reception 24hr. except 1-2:30pm. Check-out 11am. Closed Aug. 10-20 and Dec. 23-Jan 2. Single-sex dorms €21-25; doubles €70-100; triples €90-110; quads €100-140. MC/V. ❷

Hotel Cà Grande, V. Porpora 87 (☎02 26 14 52 95; www.hotelcagrande.it), 7 blocks from Ple. Loreto. Tram #33 stops 50m from the hotel. Though a bit far, it is a pleasant option with English-speaking owners and a pleasant garden. All rooms have A/C, TV, sink, and phone. Breakfast included. Singles €40-65, with bath €45-80; doubles €55-85/60-110. AmEx/D/MC/V. ❹

Albergo Villa Mira, V. Sacchini 19 (☎02 29 52 56 18). Despite the barbed wire over the entrance, the small rooms in this family-run hostel are colorful. A few of the rooms overlook the garden patio. Singles €26-35; doubles €45-62; triples €70-85. Cash only. ❷

Hotel San Tomaso, Vle. Tunisia 6, 3rd fl. (☎02 29 51 47 47; www.hotelsantomaso.com). M1: Porta Venezia. Exit at C. Buenos Aires; turn left on Vle. Tunisia. Rooms with TV and phone. Elevator. Singles €30-65; doubles €50-100; triples €70-150. AmEx/MC/V. ❸

FOOD

Choose between chowing down on focaccia with the lunch-break crowd, clinking crystal glasses, or taking your palate on a world tour through the city's ethnic neighborhoods. Old-style trattorie still follow Milanese culinary traditions with *risotto alla milanese* (rice with saffron), *cotoletta alla milanese* (breaded veal cutlet with lemon), and *osso buco* (lamb, beef, or veal shank). Many local bars offer happy-hour buffets of focaccia, pasta, and risotto that come free with drink purchase. In the *centro*, weary tourists near the *duomo* often succumb to P. del Duomo's pricey and mediocre offerings, but cheap and delicious rewards await those who look a little harder.

Big Pizza: Da Noi 2, V. Giosué Borsi 1 (☎02 83 96 77). Takes its name seriously. Beer and house wine flow liberally at this riverfront location, which has a restaurant feel but the prices of a small pizza joint. The *pizza della casa* is topped with pasta (€8). If not in the mood for pizza, try the crab pasta (€5). Calzoni €5-7. Pizza €4-8.50. Cover €1. Open M-Sa 10am-2:30pm and 7pm-midnight. MC/V. ❶

Il Forno dei Navigli, Alzaia Naviglio Pavese 2 (☎02 83 23 372). Some of the most delicious pastries in the city, fresh out of "the oven of Navigli." The *cestini* (pear tart with Nutella; €2.25) defines decadence. Pastries and breads €0.50-6. Open M-Sa 7am-2pm and 6pm-1am, Su 6pm-1am. Cash only. ❶

Princi, V. Speronari 6 (☎02 87 47 97; www.princi.it), off P. del Duomo. Take V. Torino and make 1st left. Stone walls and glass countertops make this more zen than you imagined an Italian bakery could be. Local favorite for authentic food on-the-go. Pastries €1-4. Pizza €3.50-5. Primi and secondi €5. Open M-Sa 7am-8pm. Cash only. ❶

Z2, Corso di Porta Ticinese 32 (☎02 89 42 02 41). Savvy, minimalist decor contributes to a relaxing and elegant atmosphere. Watch chefs in glassed-in kitchen prepare dishes such as *gnocchi agli spinaci* (€10). Primi €9-10. Secondi €10-19. Dessert €7-8. ❸

Fratelli la Bufala, Corso di Porta Ticinese 16 (☎02 83 76 529; www.fratellilabufala.com). Relax in the lively atmosphere of this buffalo-meat inspired pizzeria. Don't miss out on the lunch *menù,* with 2 courses, 1 side, and water (€10). Pizza €5.50-9.50. ❷

Trattoria Milanese, V. S. Marta 11 (☎02 86 45 19 91). M1/3: Duomo. From P. del Duomo, take V. Torino; turn right on V. Maurilio and again on V. S. Marta. Serves *costolette alla milanese* (breaded veal; €18) and *mondeghili milanesi* (breaded meatballs; €14) under brick arches. Primi €6-11. Secondi €8-23. Cover €2. Open M-F noon-3pm and 7-11:30pm. Closed last 2 weeks of July. AmEx/MC/V. ❸

Peck, V. Spadari 9 (☎02 80 23 161; www.peck.it). Aromas from the ground floor spread from the wine cellar in the basement to the deli and cafe above. Open M 3:30-7:30pm, Tu-F 9:15am-7:30pm, Sa 8:45am-7:30pm. AmEx/MC/V. ❷

SIGHTS

NEAR THE DUOMO AND IN THE GIARDINI PUBBLICI

DUOMO. The geographical and spiritual center of Milan and a good starting point for any walking tour of the city, the *duomo*—the third-largest church in the world—was begun in 1386 by **Gian Galeazzo Visconti,** who hoped to persuade the Virgin Mary to grant him a male heir. Work proceeded over the next centuries and was completed in 1809 at Napoleon's command. The marble tomb of **Giacomo de Médici** in the south transept was inspired by the work of Michelangelo. Climb (or ride) to the **roof walkway** for prime views of the city and the Alps. *(M1/3: Duomo. Cathedral open daily 7am-7pm. Modest dress required. Free. Roof open daily 9:30am-9:30pm. €5, elevator €7.)*

PINACOTECA AMBROSIANA. The 23 palatial rooms of the Ambrosiana display exquisite works from the 14th through 19th centuries, including Botticelli's circular *Madonna of the Canopy,* Caravaggio's *Basket of Fruit* (the first Italian still life), Raphael's wall-sized *School of Athens,* Titian's *Adoration of the Magi,* and da Vinci's *Portrait of a Musician.* The statue-filled courtyard is enchanting. *(P. Pio XI 2. M1/3: Duomo. Open Tu-Su 10am-5:30pm. €8, under 18 and over 65 €5.)*

TEATRO ALLA SCALA. Founded in 1778, La Scala has established Milan as the opera capital of the world. Its understated Neoclassical facade and lavish interior set the stage for premieres of works by Mascagni, Puccini, Rossini, and Verdi, performed by virtuosos like Maria Callas and Enrico Caruso. The **Museo Teatrale alla Scala** is replete with portraits, pianos, and porcelain figu-

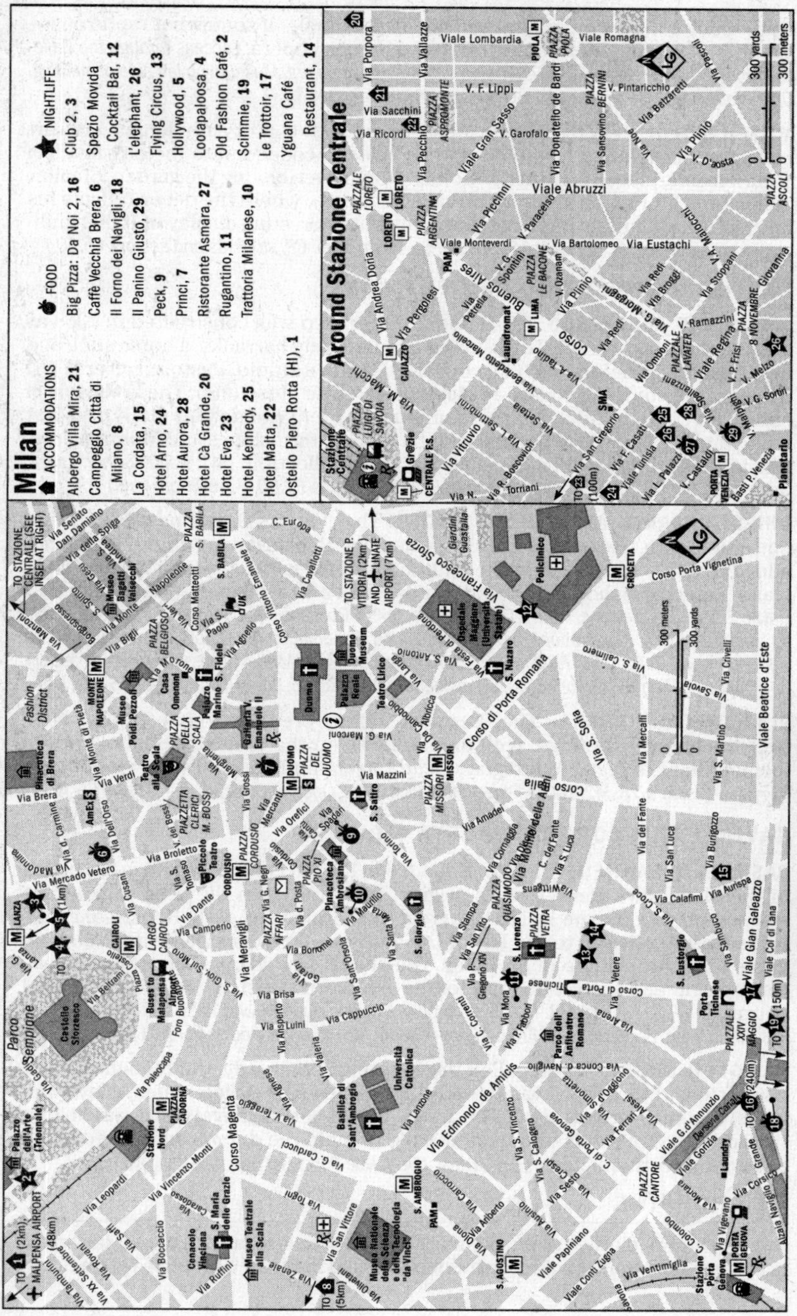

Milan

ACCOMMODATIONS

- Albergo Villa Mira, 21
- Campeggio Città di Milano, 8
- La Cordata, 15
- Hotel Arno, 24
- Hotel Aurora, 28
- Hotel Cà Grande, 20
- Hotel Eva, 23
- Hotel Kennedy, 25
- Hotel Malta, 22
- Ostello Piero Rotta (HI), 1

FOOD

- Big Pizza: Da Noi 2, 16
- Caffè Vecchia Brera, 6
- Il Forno dei Navigli, 18
- Il Panino Giusto, 29
- Peck, 9
- Princi, 7
- Ristorante Asmara, 27
- Rugantino, 11
- Trattoria Milanese, 10

NIGHTLIFE

- Club 2, 3
- Spazio Movida Cocktail Bar, 12
- L'elephant, 26
- Flying Circus, 13
- Hollywood, 5
- Loolapaloosa, 4
- Old Fashion Café, 2
- Scimmie, 19
- Le Trottoir, 17
- Yguana Café Restaurant, 14

Around Stazione Centrale

ITALY

rines. Look for the compelling and highly personal—if somewhat rapturous—account of Maria Callas' contribution to modern opera. *(Access through the Galleria Vittorio Emanuele from P. del Duomo. www.teatroallascala.org. Museum on left side of building. Open daily 9am-12:30pm and 1:30-5:30pm. €5, students €4.)*

MUSEO POLDI PEZZOLI. Poldi Pezzoli, an 18th-century nobleman and art collector, bequeathed his house and its eclectic collection to the city in 1879. Today, masterpieces hang in the Golden Room overlooking the garden. Smaller collections fill Pezzoli's former private chambers, where the decor reflects his fine taste. Particularly impressive is a tiny but interesting display of Italian military armaments. *(V. Manzoni 12. Open Tu-Su 10am-6pm. €8, students and seniors €5.50.)*

CASTELLO SFORZESCO AND ENVIRONS

CASTELLO SFORZESCO. The Castello Sforzesco was constructed in 1368 as a defense against Venice. Later, it was used as army barracks, a horse stall, and a storage house before da Vinci converted it into a studio. Restored after WWII damage, the complex houses 10 **Musei Civici** (Civic Museums). The **Museum of Ancient Art** contains Michelangelo's unfinished *Pietà Rondanini* (1564), his last work, and the **Museum of Decorative Art** has ornate furnishings and Murano glass. The underground level has a small Egyptian collection. *(M1: Cairoli or M2: Lanza. Open Tu-Su 9am-5:30pm. Combined admission €3, students €1.50, F 2-5:30pm free.)*

CHIESA DI SANTA MARIA DELLA GRAZIE. The church's Gothic nave is dark and patterned with frescoes, contrasting the airy Renaissance tribune Bramante added in 1497. To the left of the church entrance is the **Cenacolo Vinciano** (Vinciano Refectory), home to Leonardo da Vinci's **Last Supper.** *(P di S. Maria della Grazie 2. M1: Conciliazione. From P. Conciliazione, take V. Boccaccio and then go right onto V. Ruffini for about 2 blocks. Reservations ☎02 89 42 11 46. Reservation fee €1.50. Church open M-Sa 7am-noon and 3-7pm, Su 7:30am-12:15pm and 3:30-9pm. Modest dress required. Refectory open Tu-Su 8:15am-6:45pm. €6.50, EU residents 18-25 €3.25, under 18 and over 65 free.)*

PINACOTECA DI BRERA. The Brera Art Gallery presents a collection of 14th- to 20th-century paintings, with an emphasis on the Lombard School. Works include Bellini's *Pietà*, Mantegna's *Dead Christ*, and Raphael's *Marriage of the Virgin*. *(V. Brera 28. M2: Lanza. Wheelchair-accessible. Open Tu-Su 8:30am-7:15pm. €5.)*

NAVIGLI AND CORSO DI PORTA TICINESE

BASILICA DI SANT'EUSTORGIO. Founded in the 4th century to house the bones of the Magi, the church lost its original function when the dead sages were spirited off to Cologne in 1164. A great masterpiece of early Renaissance art is the **Portinari Chapel,** to the left of the entrance. Frescoes below the rainbow dome illustrate the life of St. Peter. The chapel stands on a **Paleochristian cemetery;** pagan and early Christian tombs are down the steps before the chapel entrance. *(P. S. Eustorgio 3. M2: S. Ambrogio. Basilica open M and W-Su 8:30am-noon and 3:30-6pm. Free. Cappella open Tu-Su 10am-6:30pm. €6, students and seniors €3.)*

NAVIGLI DISTRICT. Often called the Venice of Lombardy, the Navigli district, complete with canals, elevated footbridges, open-air markets, cafes, alleys, and trolleys, comes alive at night. The area was part of a medieval canal system that transported thousands of tons of marble to build the *duomo* and linked Milan to various northern cities and lakes. *(From M2: Porta Genova, take V. Vigevano.)*

SHOPPING

In a city where clothes really do make the man (or woman), fashionistas arrive in spring and summer to watch models dressed in the newest styles glide down the runway. When the music has faded and the designers have bowed, world-famous **saldi** (sales) in July and January usher the garb into the real world. The **Quadrilatero della Moda** (fashion district) has become a sanctuary in its own right. This posh land, where limos transport poodles dressed to impress and jean jackets can sell for €2000, is formed by **Via Monte Napoleone, Borgospresso, Via della Spiga,** and **Via Gesu.** On these streets, Giorgio and Donatella not only sell their styles, they live in the suites above their stores and nightclubs. Even though most stores close at 7:30pm, have no fear; you can shop around the clock at the touch screens outside the Ralph Lauren Store, so long as you don't mind waiting for delivery until the next morning. Designer creations are available to mere mortals at the trendy boutiques along **Corso di Porta Ticinese.** Small shops and affordable staples from brand names can be found on **Via Torino** near the *duomo* and on **Corso Buenos Aires** near M1: Porta Venezia. Those who don't mind being a season behind can purchase famous designer wear from *blochisti* (stocks or wholesale clothing outlets), such as the well-known **Il Salvagente,** V. Bronzetti 16, off C. XXII Marzo (M1: S. Babila), or **Gruppo Italia Grandi Firme,** V. Montegani #7/A (M2: Famagosta), which offers designer duds at 70% off. True bargain hunters cull the bazaars on **Via Faucé** (M2: Garibaldi; Tu and Sa) and **Viale Papinian** (M2: Agnostino; Sa mornings).

NIGHTLIFE

The nightlife in **Navigli** is popular with students and centers around V. Sforza. The **Brera** district invites tourists and Milanese to test their singing skills while sipping mixed drinks at one of its piano bars. **Corso di Porta Ticinese** is the sleek land of the all-night happy hour buffet, where the price of a mixed drink (€6-8) also buys dinner. A block of **Corso Como** near **Stazione Garibaldi** is home to the most exclusive clubs. Bars and clubs cluster around **Largo Cairoli,** where summer brings Milan's hottest outdoor dance venues. Southeast of **Stazione Centrale** is home to an eclectic mix of bars and much of Milan's gay and lesbian scene.

Yguana Café Restaurant, V. Papa Gregorio XIV 16 (☎89 40 41 95), just off P. Vetra, a short walk down V. E. de Amicis and V. Molino delle Armi. Beautiful people sip fruity mixed drinks (€8-10). Lounge on a couch outside, or groove to hip hop downstairs. Su brunch noon-4pm. Happy-hour buffet (M-Sa 5:30-9:30pm, Su 5:30-10pm) with 50 rotating dishes makes other bars' offerings look downright pedestrian. Open M-Th and Su 5:30pm-2am, F-Sa 5:30pm-3am. Kitchen open M-F 12:30-3pm.

Le Trottoir, P. XXIV Maggio 1 (☎/fax 02 83 78 166; www.letrottoir.it). Located in the center of P. XXIV Maggio as its own island in a sea of roads. This self-proclaimed *"Ritrovo d'Arte, Cultura, e Divertimento"* (House of Art, Culture, and Diversions) may be the Navigli's loudest, most crowded bar and club. A young, alternative crowd comes nightly to get down to live underground music 10:30pm-3am on ground fl., while upstairs features a DJ or jazz (M and W). Check schedule for weekly roster and other music nights. Mixed drinks €6-9. Pizza and sandwiches €8. Cover depends on act; usually €8, includes 1 drink. Happy hour daily 6-8pm with beer €4. Open daily 11am-3am. AmEx/MC/V.

Old Fashion Café, Vle. Emilio Alemagna 6 (☎02 80 56 231; www.oldfashion.it). M1/2: Cadorna F. N. Walk up V. Paleocapa next to the station, and turn right on Vle. Alemagna before the bridge. Club is to left of Palazzo dell'Arte along a dirt path. Summer brings stylish clubgoers to couches encircling an outdoor dance floor and stage, with live music and DJ. Tu is the most popular night, with mixed music. Su brunch noon-6pm; €20. Appetizer buffet 7:30-10pm; €13. Open M-Tu and Th-Sa 10:30pm-4:30am, W 10:30pm-4am, Su 11am-4pm and 7:30pm-midnight.

L'elephant, V. Melzo 22 (☎02 29 51 87 68; www.lelephant.it). M2: Pta. Venezia. From C. Buenos Aires turn right on V. Melzo and walk 5 blocks. An almost entirely male crowd socializes at tables under chandeliers, and on the street corner. Gay- and lesbian-friendly. Mixed drinks €7-8. Happy hour 6:30-9:30pm; €6. Open Tu-Su 6:30pm-2am.

Club 2, V. Formentini 2 (☎02 86 46 48 07), down V. Madonnina from V. Fiori Chiari. This bar sets the mood with red lights and a grand piano on the ground floor and a maze of cushions in its dark downstairs "discopub." Loud bass downstairs. F-Sa DJ and karaoke. Basement open daily in winter. Beer €6. Mixed drinks €10. Open daily 8:30pm-3am.

Loolapaloosa, C. Como 15 (☎02 65 55 693). Guests are invited to dance on the bar while the bartenders entertain by swinging lamps and ringing bells. Mixed drinks €6-8. Cover from €6. Buffet 6:30-10:30pm. Open M-Sa noon-4am, Su 2pm-4am.

VENICE (VENEZIA) ☎041

In Venice (pop. 60,000), palaces stand tall on a steadily sinking network of wood, and the waters of age-old canals creep up the mossy steps of abandoned homes. People flock here year-round to float down labyrinthine canals, peer into delicate blown-glass, and gaze at the masterworks of Tintoretto and Titian. While dodging hoards of tourists and pigeons will prove inevitable, the city is nonetheless a worthwhile wonder.

TRANSPORTATION

The **train station** is on the northwest edge of the city; be sure to get off at **Santa Lucia,** not at Mestre. Buses and boats arrive at **Piazzale Roma,** across the Canal Grande from the train station. To get from either station to **Piazza San Marco,** take *vaporetto* (water bus) #1, 2, 51, or 52 or follow signs for a 25-30min. walk.

Flights: Aeroporto Marco Polo (VCE; ☎041 26 09 260; www.veniceairport.it), 10km north of the city. Take the **ATVO shuttlebus** (☎042 13 83 671) from the airport to Ple. Roma on the main island (30min., 1 per hr. 8am-midnight, €3).

Trains: Stazione Santa Lucia (☎041 89 20 21). Ticket windows open M-F 8:30am-7:30pm, Sa-Su 9am-1:30pm and 2-5:30pm. **Information office** (☎041 89 20 21) to the left as you exit the platforms. Trains go to: **Bologna** (2hr., 32 per day, €8.20); **Florence** (3hr., 19 per day, €23.50); **Milan** (3hr., 26 per day, €13.75); **Rome** (4hr., 23 per day, €41.50). **Luggage storage** by track #14.

Buses: Local **ACTV** buses (☎041 24 24; www.hellovenezia.it), in Ple. Roma. Open daily 7:30am-8pm. **ACTV long-distance carrier** runs buses to **Padua** (1hr., 2 per hr., €4).

Public Transportation: The **Canal Grande** can be crossed on foot only at the Scalzi, Rialto, and Accademia *ponti* (bridges). **Traghetti** (gondola ferry boats) traverse the canals at 7 locations, including Ferrovia, San Marculola, Cà d'Oro, and Rialto (€0.50). **Vaporetti** (V; water buses) provide 24hr. service around the city, with reduced service midnight-5am (single-ride €6.50; 24hr. *biglietto turistico* pass €16, 3-day €31). Buy tickets at *vaporetti* stops. Stock up on tickets by asking for a pass *non timbrato* (unvalidated), then validate before boarding by inserting tickets into one of the yellow boxes at each stop. **Lines #1** (slow) and **2** (fast) run from the station down Canal Grande and Canale della Giudecca; lines **#41** and **51** circumnavigate Venice from the station to Lido; **#42** and **52** do the reverse; line **LN** runs from F. Nuove to Burano, Murano, and Lido, and connects to Torcello.

ITALY

ORIENTATION

Venice is composed of 118 islands in a lagoon, connected to the mainland by a thin causeway. The city is a veritable labyrinth and can confuse even natives, most of whom simply set off in a general direction and patiently weave their way. If you unglue your eyes from the map and go with the flow, you'll discover some unexpected surprises. Yellow signs all over the city point toward the following landmarks: **Ponte di Rialto** (in the center), **Piazza San Marco** (central south), **Ponte Accademia** (southwest), **Ferrovia** (the train station, in the northwest), and **Piazzale Roma** (south of the station). The **Canal Grande** winds through the city, creating six *sestieri* (sections): **Cannaregio** is in the north and includes the train station, Jewish ghetto, and Cà d'Oro; **Castello** extends east toward the Arsenale; **Dorsoduro,** across the bridge from S. Marco, stretches the length of Canale della Giudecca and up to Campo S. Pantalon; **Santa Croce** lies west of S. Polo, across the Canal Grande from the train station; **San Marco** fills in the area between the Ponte di Rialto and Ponte Accademia; and **San Polo** runs north from Chiesa S. Maria dei Frari to the Ponte di Rialto. In each *sestiere,* addresses are not specific to a particular street—every building is given a number, and jumps between numbers are unpredictable. If *sestiere* boundaries prove too vague, Venice's **parrochie** (parishes) provide a more defined idea of where you are.

PRACTICAL INFORMATION

Tourist Office: APT, Cal. della Ascensione, S. Marco 71/F (☎041 52 98 740; www.doge.it), directly opposite the basilica. Open daily 9am-3:30pm. Avoid the mobbed branches at the train and bus stations. The **Rolling Venice Card** (€4) offers discounts on transportation and at over 200 restaurants, cafes, hotels, museums, and shops for ages 14-29. Cards are valid for 1 year from date of purchase and can be purchased at APT, which provides a list of participating vendors, or at the **ACTV VeLa** office (☎041 27 47 650) in Ple. Roma. Open daily 7am-8pm. **VeneziaSi** (☎800 84 30 06), next to the tourist office in the train station, books rooms for a €2 fee. Open daily 8am-9pm. Branches in Ple. Roma (☎041 52 28 640) and the airport (☎041 54 15 133).

Budget Travel: CTS, F. Tagliapietra, Dorsoduro 3252 (☎041 52 05 660; www.cts.it). From Campo S. Barnaba, cross the bridge closest to the church and follow the road through the *piazza.* Turn left at the foot of the large bridge. Sells discounted plane tickets and issues ISICs. English spoken. Open M-F 9:30am-1:30pm and 2:30-6pm. MC/V.

Pharmacy: Farmacia Italo-Inglese, Cal. della Mandola, S. Marco 3717 (☎041 52 24 837). Follow Cal. Cortesia out of Campo Manin. Open Apr.-Nov. M-F 9am-1:30pm and 2:30-7:30pm, Sa 3:30-7:30pm; Dec.-Mar. M-F 9am-12:30pm and 3:45-7:30pm, Sa 3:30-7:30pm. MC/V. Pharmacies rotate late-night and weekend hours; check the list posted in the window of any pharmacy.

Hospital: Ospedale Civile, Campo S. S. Giovanni e Paolo, Castello (☎041 52 94 111).

Internet: ABColor, Lista di Spagna, Cannaregio 220 (☎041 52 44 380). Look for the "@" symbol on a yellow sign, left off the main street heading from the train station. €6 per hr., students €4. Printing €0.15 per page. Open M-Sa 10am-8pm. **Internet Station,** Cannaregio 5640. Just over the bridge toward S. Marco from C. Apostoli. €4 per 30min., €7 per hr. 20% student discount with ID. Open M-Sa 10am-1pm and 3-8pm.

Post Office: Poste Venezia Centrale, Salizzada Fontego dei Tedeschi, S. Marco 5554 (☎041 27 17 111), off Campo S. Bartolomeo. Open M-Sa 8:30am-6:30pm. **Postal Codes:** 30121 (Cannaregio); 30122 (Castello); 30123 (Dorsoduro); 30135 (S. Croce); 30124 (S. Marco); 30125 (S. Polo).

ACCOMMODATIONS AND CAMPING

Hotels in Venice are often more expensive than those elsewhere in Italy, but savvy travelers can find cheap rooms if they sniff out options early in summer. Agree on a price before booking, and reserve one month ahead. **VeneziaSi** (see **Tourist Offices,** p. 376) finds rooms on the same day, but not cheap ones. If you're looking for a miracle, try religious institutions, which often offer rooms in summer for €25-110. Options include: **Casa Murialdo,** F. Madonna dell'Orto,

ITALY

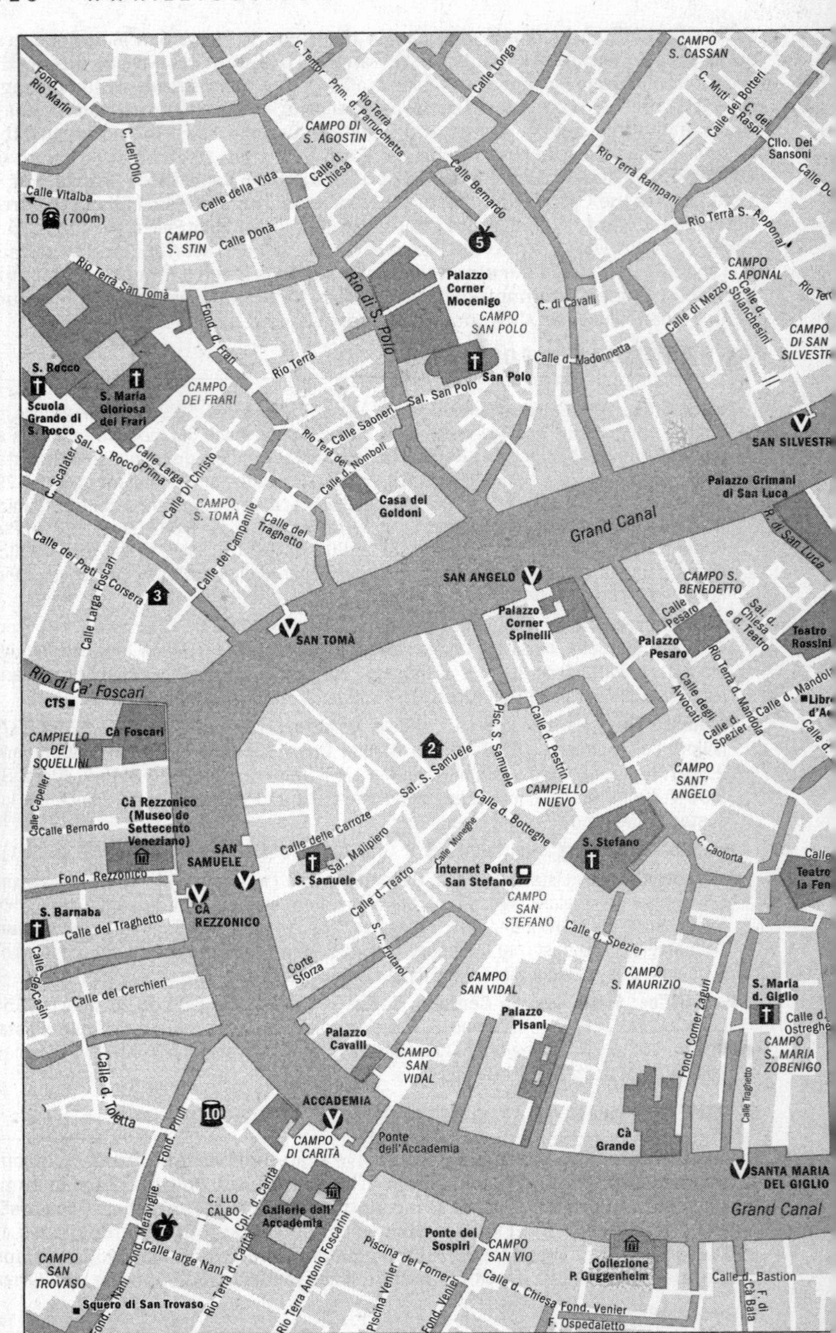

CAMPO S. CASSAN
Fond. Rio Marin
C. Tentor
Prim. d. Parrucchetta
Rio Terrà
Calle Longa
C. Muti
Calle dei Botteri
C. dei Raspi
Cllo. Dei Sansoni
CAMPO DI S. AGOSTIN
C. dell'Olio
Calle d. Chiesa
Calle Bernardo
Rio Terrà Rampani
Calle della Vida
Calle Vitalba
TO (700m)
CAMPO S. STIN
Calle Donà
Rio Terrà S. Aponal
CAMPO S.APONAL
Rio Terrà San Tomà
Palazzo Corner Mocenigo
CAMPO SAN POLO
C. di Cavalli
Calle di Mezzo
Calle d. Sbianchesini
CAMPO DI SAN SILVESTR
Rio di S. Polo
Fond. d. Frari
Rio Terrà
Calle d. Madonnetta
S. Rocco
CAMPO DEI FRARI
San Polo
Sal. San Polo
Scuola Grande di S. Rocco
S. Maria Gloriosa dei Frari
Calle Saoneri
Rio Terrà dei Nomboli
SAN SILVESTR
Sal. S. Rocco
Calle Larga Prima
Calle Di Christo
Calle d. Nomboli
C. Scalater
Casa del Goldoni
Palazzo Grimani di San Luca
CAMPO S. TOMÀ
Calle dei Campanile
Calle dei Traghetto
Grand Canal
R. di San Luca
Calle dei Preti
Corsera
Calle Larga Foscari
SAN ANGELO
CAMPO S. BENEDETTO
Palazzo Corner Spinelli
Calle Pesaro
Sal. d. Chiesa e d. Teatro
Teatro Rossini
SAN TOMÀ
Palazzo Pesaro
Rio Terrà d. Mandola
Rio di Ca' Foscari
Calle degli Avvocati
Calle d. Mandola
Libr d'A
CTS
Calle d. Pestrin
Calle d. Spezier
Cà Foscari
CAMPIELLO DEI SQUELLINI
Pisc. S. Samuele
Sal. S. Samuele
CAMPO SANT' ANGELO
CAMPIELLO NUEVO
Calle d. Botteghe
Calle Capeller
Cà Rezzonico (Museo de Settecento Veneziano)
Calle Bernardo
Calle delle Carroze
Sal. Malipiero
Calle Muneghe
S. Stefano
C. Caotorta
SAN SAMUELE
Internet Point San Stefano
Teatro la Fen
Fond. Rezzonico
S. Samuele
Calle d. Teatro
CAMPO SAN STEFANO
CÀ REZZONICO
S. Barnaba
Calle del Traghetto
S. C. Frutarol
Calle d. Spezier
Calle de Casin
Corte Sforza
CAMPO SAN VIDAL
CAMPO S. MAURIZIO
S. Maria d. Giglio
Calle del Cerchieri
Palazzo Pisani
Fond. Corner Zaguri
Calle d. Ostreghe
CAMPO S. MARIA ZOBENIGO
Palazzo Cavalli
CAMPO SAN VIDAL
Calle d. Toletta
ACCADEMIA
Calle Traghetto
Fond. Priuli
CAMPO DI CARITÀ
Ponte dell'Accademia
Cà Grande
SANTA MARIA DEL GIGLIO
Cpl. d. Carità
C. LLO CALBO
Gallerie dall' Accademia
Grand Canal
Fond. Meraviglie
Ponte dei Sospiri
CAMPO SAN VIO
Calle large Nani
Piscina del Forner
CAMPO SAN TROVASO
Collezione P. Guggenheim
Calle d. Bastion
Calle d. Chiesa
Fond. Venier
Squero di San Trovaso
Fond. Nani
Rio Terrà d. Carità
Rio Terra Antonio Foscarini
Piscina Venier
Fond. Venier
F. Ospedaletto
F di Cà Bala

ITALY

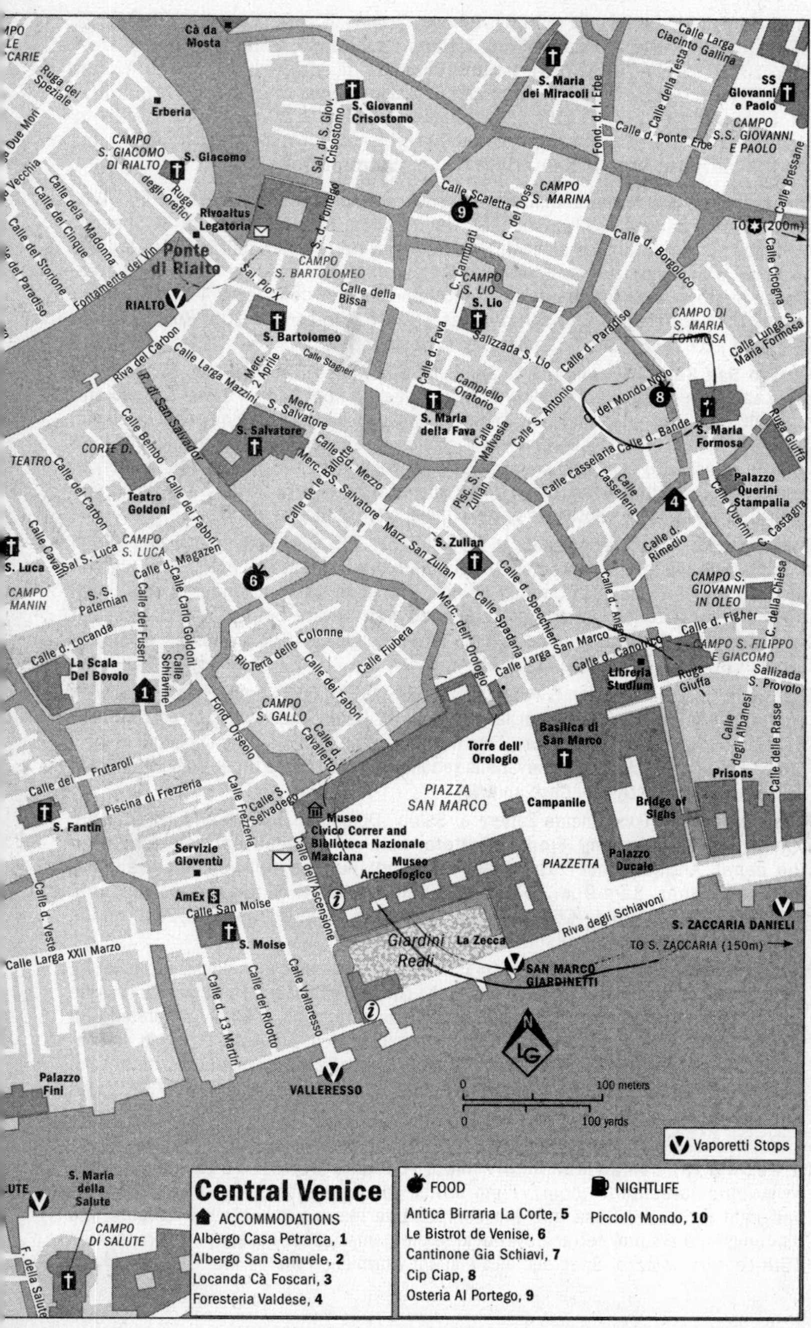
Central Venice
ACCOMMODATIONS
Albergo Casa Petrarca, 1
Albergo San Samuele, 2
Locanda Cà Foscari, 3
Foresteria Valdese, 4
FOOD
Antica Birraria La Corte, 5
Le Bistrot de Venise, 6
Cantinone Gia Schiavi, 7
Cip Ciap, 8
Osteria Al Portego, 9
NIGHTLIFE
Piccolo Mondo, 10
Vaporetti Stops
Cà da Mosta
Erberia
S. Giovanni Crisostomo
S. Maria dei Miracoli
SS Giovanni e Paolo
CAMPO S.S. GIOVANNI E PAOLO
CAMPO S. GIACOMO DI RIALTO
S. Giacomo
Rivoaltus Legatoria
Ponte di Rialto
RIALTO
CAMPO S. BARTOLOMEO
S. Bartolomeo
CAMPO S. MARINA
CAMPO S. LIO
S. Lio
CAMPO DI S. MARIA FORMOSA
S. Maria Formosa
S. Maria della Fava
S. Salvatore
CORTE D.
TEATRO
Teatro Goldoni
CAMPO S. LUCA
S. Luca
CAMPO MANIN
S. Zulian
Palazzo Querini Stampalia
CAMPO S. GIOVANNI IN OLEO
CAMPO S. FILIPPO E GIACOMO
La Scala Del Bovolo
CAMPO S. GALLO
Libreria Studium
Torre dell' Orologio
Basilica di San Marco
Prisons
PIAZZA SAN MARCO
Campanile
Bridge of Sighs
Palazzo Ducale
PIAZZETTA
Museo Civico Correr and Biblioteca Nazionale Marciana
Museo Archeologico
S. Fantin
Servizie Gioventù
AmEx
S. Moise
Giardini Reali
La Zecca
SAN MARCO GIARDINETTI
S. ZACCARIA DANIELI
TO S. ZACCARIA (150m)
TO (200m)
VALLERESSO
Palazzo Fini
S. Maria della Salute
CAMPO DI SALUTE
100 meters
100 yards
Riva degli Schiavoni
Calle Larga XXII Marzo
Calle Larga San Marco
Calle Larga Mazzini
Calle dei Fabbri
Calle Frezzeria
Calle Vallaresso
Calle dei Ridotto
Calle d. 13 Martiri
Calle dell'Ascensione
Calle San Moise
Piscina di Frezzeria
Calle dei Frutaroli
Fond. Orseolo
Calle d. Locanda
Calle dei Fuseri
Calle Carlo Goldoni
Calle Schiavine
Calle Cavalli
Sal S. Luca
Calle del Carbon
Calle Bembo
Riva del Carbon
R. di San Salvador
Merc. S. Salvatore
Marz. San Zulian
Merc. dell' Orologio
Calle Spadaria
Calle d. Specchieri
Calle Fiubera
Rio Terrà delle Colonne
Calle d. Canonica
Ruga Giuffa
Sallizada S. Provolo
Calle degli Albanesi
Calle delle Rasse
C. della Chiesa
Calle d. Figher
Calle d. Rimedio
Calle Casselleria
Calle Casselarie
Calle d. Bande
C. del Mondo Novo
Calle d. Paradiso
Calle S. Antonio
Salizzada S. Lio
Campiello Oratorio
Calle Malvasia
Calle d. Fava
C. Carminati
Calle della Bissa
Calle Stagneri
Merc. 2 Aprile
Sal. Pio X
Fontamenta dei Vin
Calle del Paradiso
Calle del Storione
Calle dei Cinque
Calle della Madonna
Ruga degli Orefici
Ruga dei Speziale
Calle Scaletta
C. del Dose
Calle d. Borgoloco
Calle Cicogna
Calle Bressane
Calle Lunga S. Maria Formosa
Ruga Giuffa
C. Castagna
Calle Querini
Calle d. Ponte Erbe
Calle della Testa
Calle Larga Ciacinto Gallina
Fond. d. l. Erbe
Sal. di S. Giov. Crisostomo
S. d. Fontego
Calle d. Veste
F. della Salute

Cannaregio 3512 (☎041 71 99 33); **Domus Cavanis,** Dorsoduro 896 (☎041 52 87 374), near the Ponte Accademia; **Istituto Canossiano,** F. delle Romite, Dorsoduro 1323 (☎041 24 09 713); **Istituto Ciliota,** Cal. Muneghe S. Stefano, San Marco 2976 (☎041 52 04 888); **Patronato Salesiano Leone XIII,** Cal. S. Domenico, Castello 1281 (☎041 52 87 299). For **camping,** plan on a 20min. boat ride from Venice. In addition to camping options listed here, Litorale del Cavallino, on the Lido's Adriatic side, has multiple beach campgrounds.

Alloggi Gerotto Calderan, Campo San Geremia, Cannaregio 283 (☎041 71 55 62 or 041 71 53 61; www.283.it). From the train station, turn left on Lista di Spagna; continue for 5min. until you reach C.S. Geremia. Half hostel, half hotel in a great location. All rooms have bath. Internet €4 per hr. Wi-Fi available, 1st 15min. free. Check-in 2pm. Lockout for dorms 10:30am-2pm. Curfew 1am. 4- to 6-person dorms €23-25; singles €35-60; doubles €50-90; triples €75-105. Rolling Venice discount 10%; discounts for longer stays. Cash only. ❷

Albergo San Samuele, Salizada S. Samuele, San Marco 3358 (☎041 52 28 045; www.albergosansamuele.it). Follow C. delle Botteghe from Campo Santo Stefano and turn left on Salizada San Samuele. Spacious and simple rooms on a quiet street 10min. from P. S. Marco, including several family suites with kitchens. Smaller rooms only have fan. Breakfast (€5) served 5min. away at Ribo Restaurant. Free Wi-Fi. 24hr reception. Reserve 1-2 months ahead. Singles with shared bath €45-65; doubles €65-85, with bath €85-120. Check website as prices change often. AmEx/MC/V. ❹

Hotel Arcadia, Cannaregio 1333/D (☎041 717 355 www.hotelarcadia.net). From Campo Geremia, cross Ponte delle Guglie and follow the road. Look for the sign on the left. Housed in a 17th-century palace, this hotel offers luxurious rooms 5min. from the train station. Rooms are equipped with private baths, TV, and safe, but (sigh) no A/C. Breakfast included. Free Wi-Fi. Singles €45-80; doubles €80-120; triples €80-150; quads €90-160. MC/V. ❹

Best B&B, Calle del Capeler, S. Polo 1575 (☎349 00 70 508). From Ponte Rialto walk northwest on Ruga D. Oresi, turn left on Calle D. Boteri and left again on Calle Del Capeler. Simple B&B in the center of the city with dorm-style rooms and a super friendly owner. Breakfast included. Reservations required. Dorms €18-28 per person; doubles €60-80; triples €100-120. Cash only. ❷

Pensione Seguso, Fondamente Zattere ai Saloni, Dorsoduro 779 (☎041 52 86 858; www.pensioneseguso.com). From V: Zattere, walk right. Great real estate right on the canal. Antique decor. Breakfast included; ½- and full-pension available. Reception open 8am-9pm. Open Jan. and Mar.-Nov. Singles €40-122, with bath €50-160; doubles €65-180/70-190; triples €150-235/160-245; quads €190-255. Prices vary seasonally. AmEx/MC/V. ❺

Foresteria Valdese, Castello 5170 (☎041 52 86 797; www.diaconiavaldese.org/venezia). From Campo Santa Maria Formosa, take Calle Lunga Santa Maria Formosa; it's over the 1st bridge. An 18th-century house run by a Protestant church. Ornately decorated with a gorgeous fresco on the ceiling and river views to match. Breakfast included. Reception 8:30am-8pm. Lockout 10am-1pm. Reservations required for bedrooms, though not possible for dorms. Dorms €27 for 1-night stays, €24 otherwise; doubles €78-88, with kitchen €85-91; triples €90-99, with bath €96-102; quads with bath €114-126; quints with bath €132-147. Rolling Venice discount €1. MC/V. ❺

La Residenza, Campo Bandiera e Moro, Castello 3608 (☎041 52 85 315; www.venicelaresidenza.com). From V: Arsenal, turn left on Riva degli Schiavoni and right on C. del Dose into the *campo.* Live like a prince: lavish carpets and paintings and a sunny terrace overlooking the *campo* greet guests in this renovated 15th-century *palazzo.* Spacious and elegantly furnished rooms with TV, A/C, private

ITALY

bathroom, safe, and minibar. Breakfast included. Free Wi-Fi. Reception 24hr. Singles €50-100; doubles €80-180. Extra bed €35. MC/V. ❹

FOOD

With few exceptions, the best restaurants lie in alleyways, not along the canals around San Marco that advertise a *menù turistico*. Venetian cuisine is dominated by fish, like *sarde in saor* (sardines in vinegar and onions), available only in Venice and sampled cheaply at most bars with other types of *cicchetti* (tidbits of seafood, rice, and meat; €1-3). **Wines** of the Veneto and Friuli regions include the whites *Prosecco della Marca*, *Bianco di Custoza*, and dry *Tocai*, as well as the red *Valpolicella*. Venice's renowned Rialto **markets** spread between the Canal Grande and the San Polo foot of the Rialto every Monday through Saturday morning. A **BILLA supermarket,** Str. Nuova, Cannaregio 5660, is near Campo S. Fosca. (Open M-Sa 8:30am-8:30pm, Su 9am-8:30pm. AmEx/MC/V.

Le Bistrot de Venise, C. dei Fabbri, San Marco 4685 (☎041 52 36 651; www.bistrotdevenise.com). From P. San Marco, head through 2nd Sottoportego dei Dai under the awning. Follow road over two bridges and turn right. Scrumptious Venetian dishes and over 50 wines, based on medieval and Renaissance recipes. Only restaurant with an in-house librarian scouring for *renascimento* delicacies. Share the tasting *menù* (€45) or try dishes like marinated *umbrine* in black grape sauce with yellow garlic and almond pudding (€28). Check the website for cultural events and wine tastings on the schedule. *Enoteca: cicchetti* €3-4, meat/cheese plates €12-24. Restaurant: primi €12-24; secondi €18-32. Wine from €5 per glass. Open daily 10:30am-midnight. Rolling Venice discount 10%. AmEx/MC/V. ❹

Trattoria da Fiore, Santo Stefano 3461 (☎041 52 35 310; www.trattoriadafiore.com). Take Calle de le Boteghe from Campiello San Stefano. Neighbors claim this is the only true *bacaro* left in San Marco. Serves a simple menu with wine (from €2 per glass) and tasty *cicchetti* (from €0.50). Try *spaghetti pinoli* with fresh tomatoes and basil (€10). Brush up on your Italian; this place is filled with locals. Plates €9-15. Open M and W-Su 8:30am-12:30am. Cash only. ❷

Gam Gam, Canale di Cannaregio, Cannaregio 1122 (☎041 71 52 84). From Campo S. Geremia, cross the bridge and turn left. Canal-side tables, friendly owners, and a unique mix of Italian and Jewish cuisines. Bars from the old Jewish ghetto preserved for all to see. Try their *Pasticcio Gam Gam* (vegetable lasagna; €9) or their special Israeli appetizer plates (€9.80). Main courses €7.50-15. Kosher. Open M-Th and Su noon-10pm, F noon-4pm. *Let's Go* discount 10%. Cash only. ❷

Antica Birraria La Corte, Campo S. Polo, San Polo 2168 (☎041 27 50 570; www.birrarialacorte.it). The expansive interior of this former brewery houses a large restaurant and bar as well as outdoor tables on the large peaceful *campo*. Head inside for a fun beer-hall atmosphere. Filling salads (€10) hit the spot in the summer heat. Pizza €5.50-9. Primi €11-15. Secondi €13.50-19. Cover €2. Restaurant open daily noon-2:30pm and 7-10:30pm. Pizzeria open summer 10am-midnight. AmEx/MC/V. ❸

Cantinone Gia Schiavi, Fondamenta Meraviglie, Dorsoduro 992 (☎041 52 30 034). From the Frari, follow signs for the Accademia bridge. Just before Ponte Meraviglie, turn toward the Chiesa di San Trovaso. Cross the 1st bridge. Choose from hundreds of wines (€2-5) and dozens of fresh *cicchetti* (€1) with toppings like pumpkin cream in this old *enoteca*. Standing room only. Open M-Sa 8am-11pm, Su 8am-noon. Cash only. ❶

Cip Ciap, C. del Mondo Novo, Castello 5799/A (☎041 52 36 621). From Campo S. Maria Formosa, follow C. del Mondo Novo. Perhaps Venice's best value pizzeria. Uses fresh ingredients on Sicilian slices sold by weight (€1.20 per 100g). Their best deals are the huge prosciutto-filled calzones and margherita pies (€2.50). No seating; nab a bench in the nearby *campo.* Open M and W-Su 9am-9pm. Cash only. ❶

Frary's, Fondamenta dei Frari, San Polo 2559 (☎041 72 00 50). Across from entrance to S. Maria Gloriosa dei Frari. Right on the river. Serves Greek and Arab cuisine with many vegetarian options. Try the lunch *menù* (€12), which includes 1 appetizer and 1 main course, or the tasting *menù* (€9). Appetizers €4-6. Main courses €8.50-14. Cover €1.50. Open M and W-Su noon-3:15pm and 6-10:30pm. AmEx/MC/V. ❷

Gelati Nico, Zattere, Dorsoduro 922 (☎041 52 25 293). From V: Zattere, walk west along the waterfront. Grab a quick, freshly made gelato (€1.20) before a long walk along the waterfront. Open M-Sa 6:45am-12pm and 7:30-11:30pm. Cash only. ❶

Pizza and Kebab Toletta, Dorsoduro 1215 (☎041 24 13 324). From Ponte Accademia head west on C. Contarini Corfu, cross the bridge and follow C. Tolleta. Skip overpriced restaurants next to the museums and grab a huge slice of pizza (€1.80) or falafel sandwich (€3) at this simple pizzeria just a few blocks away. Pies €3.50-7. Open daily 11am-4pm and 5:30pm-midnight. Cash only. ❶

SIGHTS

Venice's layout makes sightseeing a disorienting affair. Most sights center around the **Piazza San Marco.** Museum passes (€18, students €12), sold at participating museums, grant one-time admission to each of 10 museums over the course of six months. The Foundation for the Churches of Venice (☎041 27 50 462; www.chorusvenezia.org) sells the **Chorus Pass** (€9, students €6), which provides admission to all of Venice's churches.

AROUND PIAZZA SAN MARCO

Venice's only official *piazza*, **Piazza San Marco** is an un-Venetian expanse of light, space, and architectural harmony. Enclosing the *piazza* are rows of cafes and expensive shops along the Renaissance **Procuratie Vecchie.** The 96m brick **campanile** (bell tower; open daily 9am-9pm, €6) provides one of the best views of the city; on clear days, the panorama spans Croatia and Slovenia.

BASILICA DI SAN MARCO. The symmetrical arches and incomparable mosaics of Venice's crown jewel grace Piazza San Marco. To avoid the long lines at Basilica di San Marco, visit early in the morning; still, late afternoon visits profit from the best natural light. Begun in the 9th century to house the remains of St. Mark, which had been stolen from Alexandria by Venetian merchants, the church now sparkles with 13th-century Byzantine and 16th-century Renaissance mosaics. Behind the altar, the **Pala d'Oro** relief frames a parade of saints in gem-encrusted gold. The rose-adorned tomb of St. Mark rests at the altar. The **tesoro** (treasury) contains precious relics from the Fourth Crusade. Steep stairs in the atrium lead to the **Galleria della Basilica,** which affords intimate views of the tiny golden tiles in the basilica's vast ceiling mosaics, as well as the original bronze **Cavalli di San Marco** (Horses of St. Mark). A balcony overlooks the *piazza. (Basilica open M-Sa 9:45am-5pm, Su 2-4pm. Modest dress required. Free. Pala d'Oro and treasury open in summer M-F 9:45am-5pm, Sa-Su 2-4:30pm, in winter M-F 9:45am-4pm, Sa-Su 2-4pm. €3/2. Galleria open M-Sa 9:45am-4:45pm. €4.)*

PALAZZO DUCALE (DOGE'S PALACE). Once the home of Venice's *doge* (mayor), the Palazzo Ducale is now a museum. Veronese's *Rape of Europa* is among its spectacular works. In the courtyard, Sansovino's enormous sculptures, *Mars* and *Neptune*, flank the **Scala dei Giganti** (Stairs of the Giants), upon which new *doges* were crowned. The Council of Ten, the *doge*'s administrators, would drop the names of suspected criminals into the **Bocca di Leone** (Lion's Mouth), on the balcony. Climb the **Scala d'Oro** (Golden Staircase) to the

Sala delle Quattro Porte (Room of the Four Doors) and the **Sala dell'Anticollegio** (Antechamber of the Senate), whose decorations depict myths about Venice. Courtrooms of the Council of Ten and the Council of Three lead to the **Sala del Maggior Consiglio** (Great Council Room), dominated by Tintoretto's *Paradise*, the largest oil painting in the world. Near the end, thick stone lattices line the **Ponte dei Sospiri** (Bridge of Sighs), named after the mournful groans of prisoners who walked it on their way to the prison's damp cells. *(Wheelchair-accessible. Open daily Apr.-Oct. 9am-7pm; Nov.-Mar. 9am-5pm. €16, students €10.)*

CHIESA DI SAN ZACCARIA. Designed in the late 1400s by Coducci and others, and dedicated to John the Baptist's father, this Gothic-Renaissance church holds S. Zaccaria's corpse in a sarcophagus along the nave's right wall. Nearby is Bellini's *Virgin and Child Enthroned with Four Saints*, a Renaissance masterpiece. *(S. Marco. V: S. Zaccaria. Open daily 10am-noon and 4-6pm. Free.)*

AROUND THE PONTE RIALTO

THE GRAND CANAL. The Grand Canal is Venice's "main street." Over 3km long and nearly 50m wide, it loops through the city and passes under three bridges: the **Ponte Scalzi, Rialto,** and **Accademia.** The *bricole*, candy-cane posts used for mooring boats on the canal, are painted with the colors of the family whose *palazzo* adjoins them. *(For great facade views, ride V. #1 or 2 from the train station to P. S. Marco. The facades are lit at night and produce dazzling reflections.)*

RIVOALTUS LEGATORIA. Step into the book-lined Rivoaltus shop on any given day and hear Wanda Scarpa greet you from the attic, where she has been sewing leatherbound, antique-style **journals** for an international cadre of customers and faithful locals for more than three decades. Though Venice is now littered with shops selling journals, Rivoaltus was the first and remains the best. *(Ponte di Rialto 11. Notebooks €19-39. Photo albums €37-79. Open daily 10am-7:30pm.)*

PONTE RIALTO. This structure is named after Rivo Alto, the first colony built in Venice. The original wood bridge collapsed in the 1500s; the stone replacement is strong enough to support the plethora of shops that line it today.

SAN POLO

The second-largest *campo* in Venice, **Campo San Polo** once hosted bloody bull-baiting matches during *Carnevale*. Today, the *campo* is dotted with elderly women and trees, and there is no blood spilled on the ground—only gelato.

BASILICA DI SANTA MARIA GLORIOSA DEI FRARI. Titian's corpse and two of his paintings reside within this Gothic church, known as *I Frari* and begun by Franciscans in 1340. **Assumption** (1516-18), on the high altar, marks the height of the Venetian Renaissance. The golden Florentine chapel, to the right of the high altar, frames Donatello's gaunt wooden sculpture, **St. John the Baptist.** Titian's tomb is an elaborate lion-topped triumphal arch with bas-relief scenes of Paradise. *(S. Polo. V: S. Tomà. Open M-Sa 9am-6pm, Su 1-6pm. €3.)*

CHIESA DI SAN GIACOMO DI RIALTO. Between the Rialto and nearby markets stands Venice's first church, diminutively called "San Giacometto." Across the *piazza*, a statue called *Il Gobbo* (The Hunchback) supports the steps, once used for announcements. At the foot of the statue, convicted thieves would collapse after being forced to run naked from P. S. Marco. *(V: Rialto. Cross bridge and turn right. Church open M-Sa 10am-6pm. Free.)*

DORSODURO

COLLEZIONE PEGGY GUGGENHEIM. Guggenheim's Palazzo Venier dei Leoni displays works by Dalí, Duchamp, Kandinsky, Klee, Magritte, Picasso, and Pollock. The Marini sculpture *Angel in the City*, in front of the *palazzo*, was designed with a detachable penis so that Ms. Guggenheim could avoid offending her more prudish guests. *(F. Venier dei Leoni, Dorsoduro 701. V: Accademia. Turn left and follow the yellow signs. Open M and W-Su 10am-6pm. €10; students and Rolling Venice €5.)*

GALLERIE DELL'ACCADEMIA. The Accademia houses the world's most extensive collection of Venetian art. Among the enormous altarpieces in **Room II,** Giovanni Bellini's *Madonna Enthroned with Child, Saints, and Angels* stands out with its soothing serenity. **Rooms IV** and **V** have more Bellinis plus Giorgione's enigmatic *La Tempesta.* In **Room VI,** three paintings by Tintoretto, *The Creation of the Animals, The Temptation of Adam and Eve,* and *Cain and Abel,* grow progressively darker with age. **Room X** displays Titian's last painting, a *Pietà* intended for his tomb. In **Room XX,** works by Bellini and Carpaccio depict Venetian processions and cityscapes so accurately that scholars use them as "photos" of Venice's past. *(V: Accademia. Open M 8:15am-2pm, Tu-Su 8:15am-7:15pm. €6.50. English-language tours F-Su 10am and 3:30pm, €7.)*

CHIESA DI SANTA MARIA DELLA SALUTE. The *salute* (Italian for "health") is a hallmark of the Venetian skyline: perched on Dorsoduro's peninsula just southwest of San Marco, the church and its graceful domes are visible from everywhere in the city. In 1631, the city had **Baldassarre Longhena** build the church for the Virgin Mary, who they believed would end the current plague. Next to the *salute* stands the *dogana*, the customs house, where ships sailing into Venice were required to pay duties. *(Dorsoduro. V: Salute. ☎041 52 25 558. Open daily 9am-noon and 3-5:30pm. Free. The inside of the dogana is closed to the public.)*

CASTELLO

CHIESA DI SANTISSIMI GIOVANNI E PAOLO. This brick structure, also called San Zanipolo, is built primarily in the Gothic style but has a Renaissance portal and an arch supported by Greek columns. Inside, monumental walls and ceilings enclose the tombs and monuments of the *doges*. An altarpiece by Bellini depicts St. Christopher, St.Sebastian, and St. Vincent Ferrer. The equestrian statue of local mercenary Bartolomeo Colleoni stands on a marble pedestal outside; he left Venice his inheritance on the condition that his monument stand in San Marco, but the city chose this more modest spot. *(Castello. V: Fond. Nuove. Turn left, then right on Fond. dei Mendicanti. ☎041 52 35 913. Open M-Sa 9am-6:30pm, Su noon-6:30pm. €2.50, students €1.25.)*

CHIESA DI SANTA MARIA DEI MIRACOLI. The Lombardi family designed this small Renaissance jewel in the late 1400s. Inside the tiny pink-, white-, and blue-marble exterior sits a fully functional parish with a golden ceiling and pastel walls interrupted only by the vibrant window above the apse. *(Cross the bridge directly in front of S. Giovanni e Paolo, and continue down Cal. Larga Gallina over 2 bridges. Open July-Aug. M-Sa 10am-5pm; Sept.-June M-Sa 10am-5pm, Su 1-5pm. €3.)*

CANNAREGIO

JEWISH GHETTO. In 1516, the *doge* forced Venice's Jewish population into the old cannon-foundry area, creating the first Jewish ghetto in Europe and coining the word "ghetto," the Venetian word for foundry. In the Campo del Ghetto Nuovo, the **Schola Grande Tedesca** (German Synagogue), the area's oldest synagogue, and the **Museo Ebraica di Venezia** (Hebrew Museum of Venice) now share a building. *(Cannaregio 2899/B. V: S. Marcuola. Museum open M-F and Su June-Sept. 10am-7pm; Oct.-May 10am-4:30pm. Enter synagogue by 40min. tour every hr. daily June-Sept. 10:30am-5:30pm; Oct.-May 10:30am-4:30pm. Museum €3, students €2. Museum and tour €8.50/7.)*

CHIESA DELLA MADONNA DELL'ORTO. Tintoretto's 14th-century parish church, the final resting place of the painter and his children, contains 10 of his largest paintings, as well some works by Titian. Look for Tintoretto's *Last Judgment* and *The Sacrifice of the Golden Calf* near the high altar. There is a light switch for illuminating the works. *(V: Madonna dell'Orto. Open M-Sa 10am-5pm. €3.)*

ISLANDS OF THE LAGOON

LIDO. The breezy resort island of Lido provided the setting for Thomas Mann's haunting novella, *Death in Venice.* Visonti's film version was also shot here at the Hotel des Bains, Lungomare Marconi 17. Today, people flock to Lido to enjoy the surf at the popular public beach. An impressive shipwreck looms at one end, while a casino, horseback riding, and the fine Alberoni Golf Club add to the island's charm. *(V #1 and 2: Lido. Beach open daily 9am-8pm. Free.)*

MURANO. Famous since 1292 for its glass (Venice's artisans were forced off Venice proper because their kilns started fires), the six-island cluster of Murano affords visitors the opportunity to witness resident artisans blowing crystalline creations for free. Quiet streets are lined with shops and boutiques with jewelry, vases, and delicate figurines for a variety of prices; for demonstrations, look for signs directing to the *fornace*, concentrated around the Colona, Faro, and Navagero *vaporetto* stops. Some studios let visitors blow their own glass creations. The collection at the **Museo Vetrario** (Glass Museum) ranges from funereal urns to a sea-green octopus presumably designed by Carlo Scarpa in 1930. *(V #DM, LN, 5, 13, 41, 42: Faro from either S. Zaccaria or F Nuove. Museo Vetrario, F. Giustian 8. Open M-Tu and Th-Su Apr.-Oct. 10am-6pm; Nov.-Mar. 10am-5pm. €5.50, students and Rolling Venice €3. Basilica open daily 8am-7pm. Modest dress required. Free.)*

BURANO. Postcard-pretty Burano is a traditional fishing village where hand-tatted lace has become a community art. The small and somewhat dull **Scuola di Merletti di Burano** (Lace Museum), once the home of the island's professional lace-making school, features strips from the 16th century and yellowing lace-maker diplomas. From October to June, ask to see the lace-makers at work. *(40min. by boat from Venice. V #LN: Burano from F. Nuove. Museum in P. Galuppi.)*

TORCELLO. Torcello, a safe haven for early fishermen fleeing barbarians on the mainland, was the most powerful island in the lagoon before Venice usurped its inhabitants and its glory. The island's cathedral, **Santa Maria Assunta,** contains *Psychosis*, a mosaic in the nave, which depicts both a peaceful heaven and a scorching hell. The *campanile* affords splendid views of the outer lagoon. *(45min. by boat from Venice. V #T: Torcello from Burano. Cathedral open daily 10:30am-6pm; ticket office closes at 5:30pm. Modest dress required. €3; church, campanile, and museum €8.)*

ISOLA DI SAN MICHELE. You'll face only small crowds on Venice's cemetery island, San Michele, home to Coducci's tiny **Chiesa di San Michele in Isola,** the first Renaissance church in Venice. Enter the grounds through the church's right-hand portal and look up to see a relief depicting St. Michael slaying the dragon. Poet and fascist sympathizer Ezra Pound is buried in the Protestant cemetery, while Russian composer Igor Stravinsky and choreographer Sergei Diaghilev are entombed in the Orthodox graveyard. *(V: Cimitero from F. Nuove. Church and cemetery open daily Apr.-Sept. 7:30am-6pm; Oct.-Mar. 7:30am-4pm. Free.)*

ENTERTAINMENT AND FESTIVALS

Admire Venetian houses and *palazzi* via their original canal pathways. **Gondola** rides are most romantic about 50min. before sunset and most affordable if shared by six people. The rate that a gondolier quotes is negotiable, but expect to pay €80-100 for a 40min. ride. The most price-flexible gondoliers are those standing by themselves rather than those in groups at "taxi-stands."

Banned by the church for several centuries, Venice's famous **Carnevale** was successfully reinstated in the early 1970s. During the 10 days preceding Ash Wednesday, masked figures jam the streets while outdoor performances spring up all over. For **Mardi Gras,** the population doubles. Contact the tourist office for details, and make lodging arrangements well ahead. Venice's second-most colorful festival is the **Festa del Redentore** (3rd weekend in July), originally held to celebrate the end of the 16th-century plague. On Sunday, craftsmen build a bridge across the Giudecca Canal, connecting **Il Redentore** to the **Zattere.**

NIGHTLIFE

While pubs and bars are not uncommon in Venice, most residents agree that a vibrant nightlife is virtually nonexistent. The majority of locals prefer an evening spent sipping wine in a *piazza* to grinding in a disco, but the island's fluctuating population means that new establishments spring up (and wither and die) regularly. Student nightlife is concentrated around **Campo Santa Margherita** in Dorsoduro, and tourists swarm **Lista di Spagna** in Cannaregio.

Café Blue, Campo S. Pantalon, Dorsoduro 3778 (☎041 52 27 613, www.cafebluevenezia.com). Popular, laid-back local hangout that is busy any time of day. Grab a glass of wine (€1.50-3.20) or a distinctly Venetian "sex on the bridge" (€6). F live jazz and blues. Free Wi-Fi. Open M-F 10am-2am, Sa-Su 6pm-2am. Cash only.

Orange, Campo S. Margherita, Dorsoduro 3054/A (☎041 52 34 740; www.orangebar.it). The painted bar seems to be on fire at this crowded spot, where an attentive staff serves everything from *panini* (€4) to mixed drinks (€3.50-7). Humming during the day and hopping later. For a break from the orange, retreat to the quiet garden out back or the white umbrella seats in front. Beer €3-6. Wine from €2.50. Open daily 9am-2am. Cash only.

Bistrot ai Do Draghi, Campo S. Margherita 3665 (☎041 52 89 731). Maybe not as fierce as the name implies ("Bistro of the Two Dragons" in Venetian dialect), but certainly more artsy than its neighbors. A cozy spot for a late night drink with old-fashioned, wood decor and dim lighting. Extensive wine list (€1.20-1.80). Famous spritz €1.20. Open daily 8am-2am. Cash only.

Sotto Sopra, Dorsoduro 3740/1 (☎041 52 42 177). From C. Santa Margherita, follow C. della Chiesa, cross bridge and continue towards the right until you reach C. San Pantalon. Keep going until you hear the music. Funky bar features 2 fl. of stained-glass windows, Pop art, and rock music near student nightlife. Bar downstairs. Cozy upstairs seating. Beers €2-5.50. Mixed drinks €5. Wine €1.20. Open M-Sa 10am-2am. MC/V.

FLORENCE (FIRENZE) ☎055

Florence (pop. 400,000) is the city of the Renaissance. By the 14th century, it had already become one of the most influential cities in Europe. In the 15th century, Florence overflowed with artistic excellence as the Medici family amassed a peerless collection, supporting masters like Botticelli, Donatello, and Michelangelo. These days, the tourists who flood the streets are captivated by Florence's distinctive character, creative spirit, and timeless beauty.

TRANSPORTATION

Flights: Aeroporto Amerigo Vespucci (**FLR;** main line ☎055 30 615, 24hr. automated flight info line 30 61 700; www.aeroporto.firenze.it) in the suburb of Peretola. Mostly domestic and charter flights.

Trains: Stazione Santa Maria Novella, across from S. Maria Novella. Trains run 1 per hr. to: **Bologna** (1hr., €20); **Milan** (2½hr., €47); **Rome** (3hr., €44); **Siena** (1½hr., €14); **Venice** (3hr., €44).

Buses: SITA, V. S. Caterina da Siena 17 (☎800 37 37 60; www.sita-on-line.it), runs buses to **San Gimignano** (1hr., 14 per day, €5.90) and **Siena** (1hr., 2 per day, €6.50). **LAZZI,** P. Adua 1-4R (☎35 10 61; www.lazzi.it), runs to **Pisa** (1 per hr., €6.30). Both offices are near S. Maria Novella.

Public Transportation: ATAF (☎800 42 45 00; www.ataf.net), outside the train station, runs orange city buses 6am-1am. Tickets 1hr. €1.30; 24hr. €5; 3-day €12. Buy them at any newsstand, *tabaccheria,* or ticket dispenser. You cannot purchase tickets on the bus. Validate your ticket using the orange machine on board or risk a €50 fine.

Taxis: ☎43 90, 47 98, or 42 42. Outside the train station.

ORIENTATION

From the train station, a short walk on V. Panzani and a left on V. dei Cerretani leads you to the **duomo,** in the center of Florence. The bustling **Via dei Calzaiuoli** runs south from the *duomo* to **Piazza della Signoria.** V. Roma leads from the *duomo* through **Piazza della Repubblica** to the **Ponte Vecchio** (Old Bridge), which crosses from central Florence to **Oltrarno,** the district south of the **Arno River.** Note that most streets change names unpredictably.

PRACTICAL INFORMATION

Tourist Office: Informazione Turistica, P. Della Stazione 4 (☎055 21 22 45; turisimo3@comune.fi.it), across the *piazza* from the station's main exit. Info in major foreign languages on tourist attractions, events, directions, available tours, and general emergency information. Open M-Sa 8:30-7pm, Su and holidays 8:30am-2pm.

Laundromats: Wash and Dry (☎055 58 04 480; www.washedry.it). Self-service locations throughout the city. Wash and dry €3.50 each. Detergent €1.

Emergency: ☎113 or ☎055 31 80 00

Police: Tourist Police, Ufficio Stranieri,V. Zara 2 (☎055 49 771). For visa or work-permit problems. Open M-F 9:30am-1pm. To report lost or stolen items, go around the corner to **Ufficio Denunce,** V. Duca d'Aosta 3 (☎055 49 771). Open M-Sa 8am-8pm.

Municipal Police: ☎055 32 831, in emergency ☎055 32 85.

Pharmacies: Farmacia Comunale (☎055 28 94 35), by track 16 at the train station.

Medical Services: Tourist Medical Services, V. Lorenzo il Magnifico 59 (☎055 47 54 11). English-, German-, and French-speaking doctors with 70 specialists. In P. Duomo (☎055 21 22 21). Open M-F 8am-8pm, doctors on-call 24hr. **Ospedale Santa Maria Nuova,** P. Santa Maria Nuova 1 (☎055 27 581), near the Duomo.

Internet Access: Internet Train, V. Guelfa 54/56 (☎055 26 45 146), V. dell'Oriolo 40r (☎055 26 38 968), Borgo San Jacopo 30r (☎055 265 7935), V. Giacomini 9 (☎055 50 31 647), V. de'Benci 36r (☎055 26 38 555), V. Alamanni 5a (☎055 28 69 92), V. Porta Rossa 38r (☎055 27 41 037), Lungarno B. Cellini 43r (☎055 38 30 921). Internet €3.20-4.30 per hr. Wi-Fi €2.50 per hr. Open daily 10am-10:30pm.

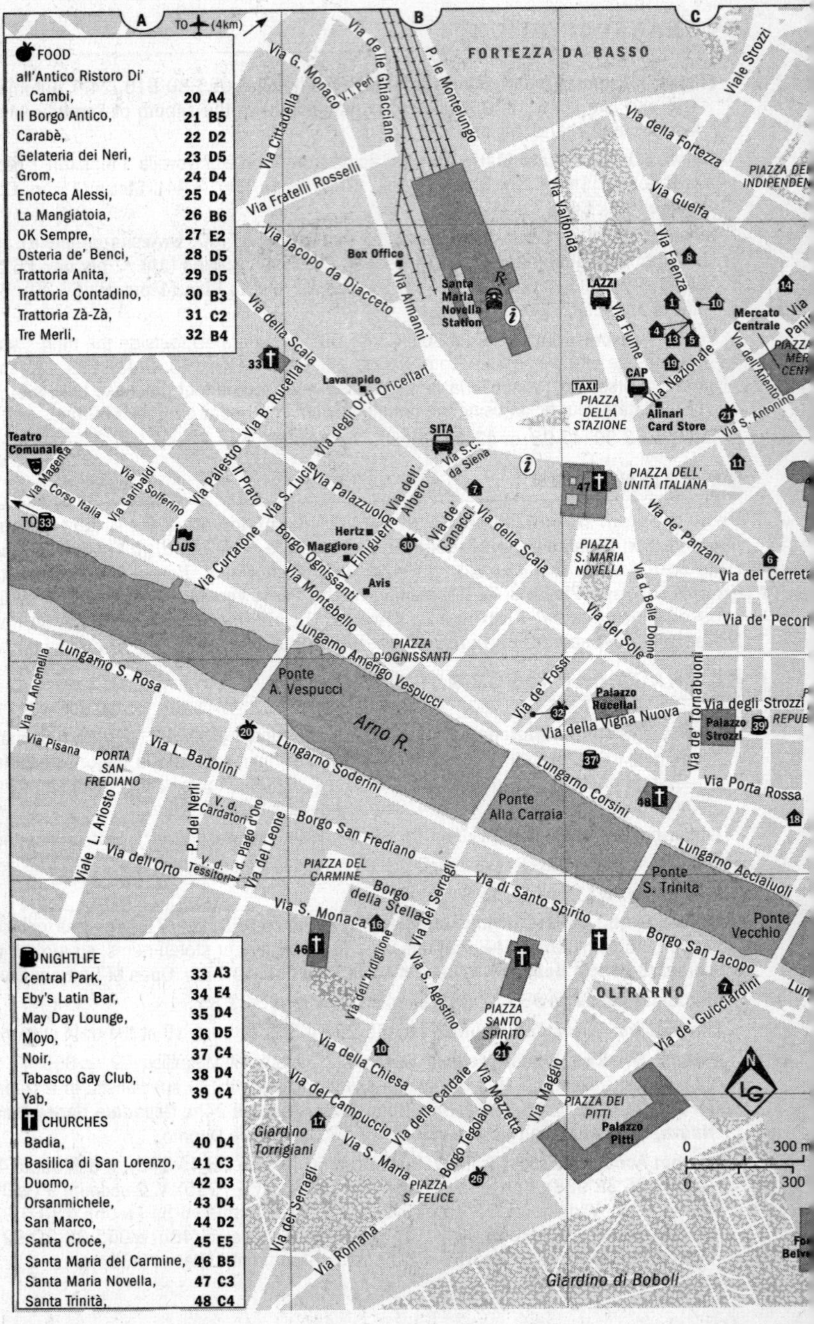
A
B
C
TO (4km)
FOOD
all'Antico Ristoro Di' Cambi, 20 A4
Il Borgo Antico, 21 B5
Carabè, 22 D2
Gelateria dei Neri, 23 D5
Grom, 24 D4
Enoteca Alessi, 25 D4
La Mangiatoia, 26 B6
OK Sempre, 27 E2
Osteria de' Benci, 28 D5
Trattoria Anita, 29 D5
Trattoria Contadino, 30 B3
Trattoria Zà-Zà, 31 C2
Tre Merli, 32 B4
NIGHTLIFE
Central Park, 33 A3
Eby's Latin Bar, 34 E4
May Day Lounge, 35 D4
Moyo, 36 D5
Noir, 37 C4
Tabasco Gay Club, 38 D4
Yab, 39 C4
CHURCHES
Badia, 40 D4
Basilica di San Lorenzo, 41 C3
Duomo, 42 D3
Orsanmichele, 43 D4
San Marco, 44 D2
Santa Croce, 45 E5
Santa Maria del Carmine, 46 B5
Santa Maria Novella, 47 C3
Santa Trinità, 48 C4
FORTEZZA DA BASSO
Via G. Monaco
V. I. Peri
Via delle Ghiacciane
P. le Montelungo
Viale Strozzi
Via della Fortezza
PIAZZA DELL' INDIPENDENZA
Via Cittadella
Via Fratelli Rosselli
Via Valfonda
Via Guelfa
Via Jacopo da Diacceto
Box Office
Via Alamanni
Santa Maria Novella Station
LAZZI
Via Faenza
Via Fiume
Mercato Centrale
Via della Scala
Lavarapido
Via B. Rucellai
Via degli Orti Oricellari
TAXI
CAP
PIAZZA DELLA STAZIONE
Via Nazionale
Alinari Card Store
Via dell'Ariento
Via S. Antonino
Teatro Comunale
Via Magenta
SITA
Via S.C. da Siena
Via Palestro
Via Solferino
Via Garibaldi
Corso Italia
Il Prato
Via S. Lucia
Via Palazzuolo
Via dell' Albero
PIAZZA DELL' UNITÀ ITALIANA
TO 33
BUS
Via Curtatone
Borgo Ognissanti
Hertz
Maggiore
V. Finiguerra
Via de' Canacci
Via della Scala
Via de' Panzani
PIAZZA S. MARIA NOVELLA
Avis
Via Montebello
Via d. Belle Donne
Via dei Cerretani
Via del Sole
Via de' Pecori
PIAZZA D'OGNISSANTI
Lungarno Amerigo Vespucci
Ponte A. Vespucci
Lungarno S. Rosa
Via d. Ancenella
Via de' Fossi
Palazzo Rucellai
Via de' Tornabuoni
Via degli Strozzi
Palazzo Strozzi
Arno R.
Via della Vigna Nuova
Via Pisana
PORTA SAN FREDIANO
Via L. Bartolini
Lungarno Soderini
Lungarno Corsini
Via Porta Rossa
P. dei Neri
V. d. Cardatori
V. d. Tessitori
V. d. Piago d'Oro
Via del Leone
Ponte Alla Carraia
Borgo San Frediano
Viale L. Ariosto
Via dell'Orto
Lungarno Acciaiuoli
PIAZZA DEL CARMINE
Borgo della Stella
Via dei Serragli
Via di Santo Spirito
Ponte S. Trinita
Via S. Monaca
Ponte Vecchio
Via dell'Ardiglione
Borgo San Jacopo
Via S. Agostino
OLTRARNO
PIAZZA SANTO SPIRITO
Via de' Guicciardini
Via della Chiesa
Via del Campuccio
Via delle Caldaie
Via Mazzetta
Via Maggio
PIAZZA DEI PITTI
Palazzo Pitti
Giardino Torrigiani
Via S. Maria
Borgo Tegolaio
PIAZZA S. FELICE
Via dei Serragli
Via Romana
Giardino di Boboli
0
300 m
0
300
N
LG

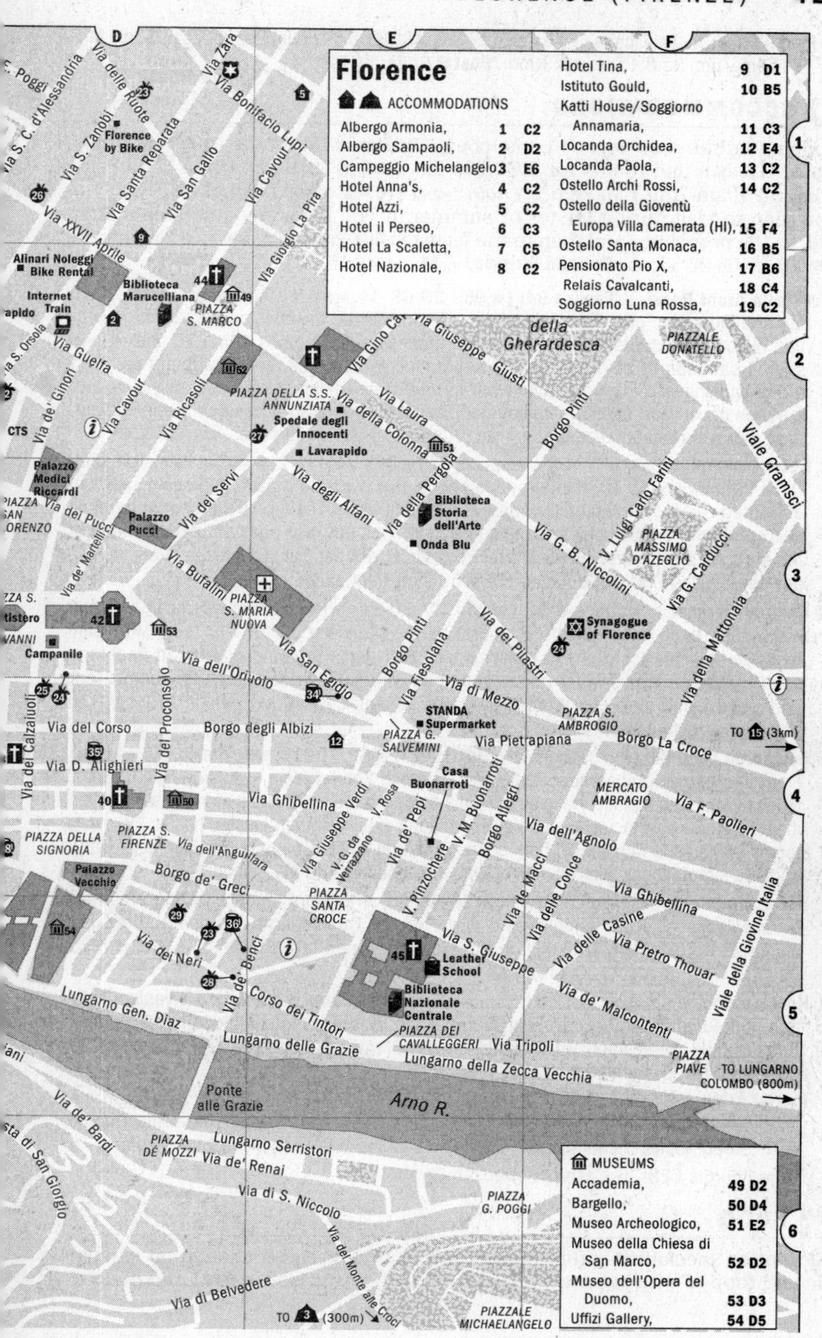
D
E
F
Florence
ACCOMMODATIONS
Albergo Armonia, 1 C2
Albergo Sampaoli, 2 D2
Campeggio Michelangelo 3 E6
Hotel Anna's, 4 C2
Hotel Azzi, 5 C2
Hotel il Perseo, 6 C3
Hotel La Scaletta, 7 C5
Hotel Nazionale, 8 C2
Hotel Tina, 9 D1
Istituto Gould, 10 B5
Katti House/Soggiorno Annamaria, 11 C3
Locanda Orchidea, 12 E4
Locanda Paola, 13 C2
Ostello Archi Rossi, 14 C2
Ostello della Gioventù Europa Villa Camerata (HI), 15 F4
Ostello Santa Monaca, 16 B5
Pensionato Pio X, 17 B6
Relais Cavalcanti, 18 C4
Soggiorno Luna Rossa, 19 C2
MUSEUMS
Accademia, 49 D2
Bargello, 50 D4
Museo Archeologico, 51 E2
Museo della Chiesa di San Marco, 52 D2
Museo dell'Opera del Duomo, 53 D3
Uffizi Gallery, 54 D5
1
2
3
4
5
6
Via delle Ruote
Via S. C. d'Alessandria
Via Zara
Via Bonifacio Lupi
Florence by Bike
Via S. Zanobi
Via Santa Reparata
Via San Gallo
Via Cavour
Via XXVII Aprile
Via Giorgio La Pira
Alinari Noleggi Bike Rental
Biblioteca Marucelliana
Internet Train
PIAZZA S. MARCO
Via Guelfa
Via de' Ginori
Via Ricasoli
PIAZZA DELLA S.S. ANNUNZIATA
Spedale degli Innocenti
Lavarapido
Via della Colonna
Via Laura
Via Gino Capponi
Via Giuseppe Giusti
della Gherardesca
PIAZZALE DONATELLO
Borgo Pinti
Viale Gramsci
CTS
Palazzo Medici Riccardi
PIAZZA SAN LORENZO
Via dei Pucci
Palazzo Pucci
Via dei Servi
Via degli Alfani
Via della Pergola
Biblioteca Storia dell'Arte
Onda Blu
Via G. B. Niccolini
V. Luigi Carlo Farini
PIAZZA MASSIMO D'AZEGLIO
Via G. Carducci
Via de' Martelli
Via Bufalini
PIAZZA S. MARIA NUOVA
Campanile
Synagogue of Florence
Via dei Pilastri
Via della Mattonaia
Via dell'Oriuolo
Via San Egidio
Borgo Pinti
Via Fiesolana
Via di Mezzo
STANDA Supermarket
PIAZZA G. SALVEMINI
PIAZZA S. AMBROGIO
Via Pietrapiana
Borgo La Croce
TO (3km)
Via del Calzaiuoli
Via del Corso
Borgo degli Albizi
Via del Proconsolo
Via D. Alighieri
Casa Buonarroti
Via Ghibellina
Via Giuseppe Verdi
V. Rosa
Via de' Pepi
V. M. Buonarroti
Borgo Allegri
MERCATO AMBRAGIO
Via F. Paolieri
Via dell'Agnolo
PIAZZA DELLA SIGNORIA
PIAZZA S. FIRENZE
Via dell'Anguillara
Palazzo Vecchio
Borgo de' Greci
V. G. da Verrazzano
V. Pinzochere
Via de Macci
Via delle Conce
Via Ghibellina
Viale della Giovine Italia
PIAZZA SANTA CROCE
Via delle Casine
Via Pretro Thouar
Via S. Giuseppe
Leather School
Via dei Neri
Via de' Benci
Biblioteca Nazionale Centrale
Via de' Malcontenti
Lungarno Gen. Diaz
Corso dei Tintori
PIAZZA DEI CAVALLEGGERI
Via Tripoli
Lungarno delle Grazie
Lungarno della Zecca Vecchia
PIAZZA PIAVE
TO LUNGARNO COLOMBO (800m)
Ponte alle Grazie
Arno R.
Via de' Bardi
PIAZZA DÉ MOZZI
Lungarno Serristori
Via de' Renai
Via di S. Niccolo
PIAZZA G. POGGI
Via del Monte alle Croci
Via di Belvedere
TO (300m)
PIAZZALE MICHAELANGELO

Post Office: V. Pellicceria 3 (☎055 27 36 480), off P. della Repubblica. Open M-F 8:15am-7pm, Sa 8:15am-12:30pm. **Postal Code:** 50100.

ACCOMMODATIONS

Lodging in Florence doesn't come cheap. **Consorzio ITA,** in the train station by track #16, can find rooms for a €3-8.50 fee. (☎066 99 10 00. Open M-Sa 8am-8pm, Su 10am-7pm.) Make a *prenotazioni* (reservation) ahead, especially if you plan to visit during Easter or summer. If you have any complaints, first talk to the proprietor and then to the **Tourist Rights Protection Desk,** V. Cavour 1R (☎055 29 08 32 33), or **Servizio Turismo,** V. Manzoni 16 (☎055 27 60 552).

Ostello Archi Rossi, V. Faenza 94r (☎055 29 08 04; www.hostelarchirossi.com). You'll feel the Florentine creative vibe as soon as you see the frescoes painted in the reception by local art students. Each of the 30 spotless rooms comes with a PC, locker, and shared bathroom. Archi Rossi boasts a romantic garden, free Wi-Fi, computer use, and a free walking tour every morning with an English-speaking guide. Breakfast included; features bacon and eggs. Complimentary pasta dinners also occasionally served. Luggage storage available. Reception 24hr. Dorms €18-25; singles €25-35. MC/V. ❶

Hotel Consigli, Lungarno Amerigo Vespucci 50 (☎055 21 41 72; www.hotelconsigli.com). Once the playground of a Renaissance prince, this riverside palace is a sunlit sanctum of vaulted ceilings, sweeping frescoes, and marble stairs. The rooms are enormous, cool, and quiet, and the balcony and breakfast room look out over postcard-perfect views of the Arno. A/C. Breakfast included. Wi-Fi €3 per hr., €5 per 2hr., €7 per 3hr. Parking €15 per day. Singles €60-90; doubles €60-150. AmEx/MC/V. ❸

Holiday Rooms, V. Nazionale 22 (☎055 28 50 84; www.marcosplaces.com). Owner Marco has been known to meet guests at the train station to help them with their baggage—a small taste of the conveniences and perks to come. Hardwood beds and satin curtains adorn 8 quiet rooms equipped with satellite flatscreen TVs, computers, Wi-Fi, and laundry access. Kitchen available. Rooms €25-40 per person. Discounts at some local restaurants. ❶

Soggiorno Luna Rossa, V. Nazionale 7, 3rd fl. (☎328 62 51 017; www.marcosplaces.com). From the Piazza Stazione near Santa Maria Novella Station, walk to V. Nazionale until you reach Marco's other place. Wake up in a brightly-decorated room to the morning sun streaming through the spectacular stained-glass windows of this centrally located hostel. 18 private rooms available, 3 with shared bathrooms. Each with Wi-Fi, computer, satellite flatscreen TV, and free international calls. Kitchen available. Rooms €25-40 per person. ❷

Hotel Medici, V. dei Medici 6 (☎055 28 48 18). A 6-story student favorite. Top-floor terrace looks out over unbelievable views of the Duomo and Campanile. Breakfast included; we recommend dining on the aforementioned terrace. No A/C. Singles €50; doubles €75; quads €100. MC/V. ❸

Hotel Abaco, V. dei Banchi 1 (☎055 23 81 919; www.abaco-hotel.it). Convenient location, helpful staff, and extravagant rooms. Each room is a masterpiece named after a Renaissance great. Each with phone and TV. Breakfast included. Wi-Fi. Singles €60; doubles €70-95; triples €110. MC/V. ❸

Hostel AF19, V. Ricasoli 9 (☎055 23 98 665; www.academyhostels.com). A bright and spacious hostel with multi-floor suites and a location literally steps from the Duomo. A/C. Safety lockers. Laundry €5. Free Wi-Fi in the lobby. Lockout 11am-2pm. 2- to 6-bed dorms €28-36. Cash preferred. AmEx/MC/V. ❶

FOOD

Florentine specialties include *bruschetta* (grilled bread soaked in oil and garlic and topped with tomatoes, basil, and anchovy or liver paste) and *bistecca alla Fiorentina* (thick sirloin). The best local cheese is *pecorino*, made from sheep's milk. A liter of house wine usually costs €3.50-6 in a *trattoria*, but stores sell bottles of chianti for as little as €2.50. The local dessert is *cantuccini di prato* (almond cookies) dipped in *vinsanto* (a rich dessert wine). Florence's own Buontalenti family supposedly invented gelato; extensive sampling is a must. For lunch, visit a *rosticceria gastronomia*, peruse the city's pushcarts, or pick up fresh produce and meats at the **Mercato Centrale,** between V. Nazionale and S. Lorenzo. (Open June-Sept. M-Sa 7:30am-2pm; Oct.-May M-F 7am-2pm, Sa 7am-2pm and 4-8pm.) To get to **STANDA** supermarket, V. Pietrapiana 1R, turn right on V. del Proconsolo, take the first left on Borgo degli Albizi, and continue straight through P. G. Salvemini. (Open M-Sa 8am-9pm, Su 9am-9pm. MC/V.)

Grom, V. del Campanile (☎055 21 61 58), off P. del Duomo to the left of the Campanile. The kind of gelato you'll be talking about in 50 years. As fresh as it gets; sublimely balanced texture. Large store is standing-room only and flooded with tourists and locals. Cups €2-5, cones €2-4. Open daily Apr.-Sept. 10:30am-midnight, Oct.-Mar. 10:30am-11pm. ❶

Trattoria Le Mossacce, V. del Proconsolo 55r (☎055 29 43 61; www.trattorialemossacce.it). The sort of place that you just don't expect near the Duomo, Mossacce seats strangers shoulder-to-shoulder and whips out Tuscan specialties. Primi €5-8.50. Secondi €5.50-10. Cover €1. Open daily noon-2:30pm and 7-9:30pm. ❷

Gelateria del Neri, V. dei Neri 20-22r (☎055 21 00 34). Follow the street between Uffizi and Palazzo Vecchio. Just big enough for a counter and the waiting line, this gelateria is the locals' favorite. Serves generous scoops of creative flavors like *crema giotto* (a blend of coconut, almond, and hazelnut) and equally delicious classics like pistachio. Cones and cups from €1.50. Open daily 11am-midnight. Cash only. ❶

Teatro del Sale, V. dei Macci 111r (☎055 20 01 492). It's "members only" at this private club, but the slight fee and mission statement ensure that the pretensions end here. In a high-arched, hardwood theatre, Fabio Picchi picks the freshest ingredients and announces each delicious course from his open kitchen. Once the last piece of mouthwatering dessert has been snatched off the plate, the entertainment begins, ranging from music lessons to theatrical performances—but many shows are in Italian, so plan ahead. Breakfast €7; lunch €20. Membership fee €5. Open Tu-Sa 9-11am, noon-2:15pm, and from 7:30pm until the end of the show. Reservations required. AmEx/MC/V. ❹

Ruth's Kosher Vegetarian Restaurant, V. Luigi Carlo Farini 2A (☎055 24 80 888). Carnivorous Christians, be not afraid! There are plenty options for you, as well. Photos of Woody Allen and Kafka look on as wise owner Simcha makes everyone feel part of the community, serving hummus (€6), pasta (€7), and couscous (€13-15). Students enjoy special dinners W nights for €10. Free Wi-Fi. Open M-Th and Su noon-2:30pm and 7:30-10:30pm, F noon-2:30pm. AmEx/MC/V. ❷

Buongustai, V. dei Cerchi 15 (☎055 29 13 04). Walk north from Palazzo Vecchio . After a day at the nearby Duomo, Bargello, and P. della Signoria, relax at this quirky and casual spot. Make sure to try the house special *Piatto del Buongustai* (Tuscan salami, cheese, and pickled vegetables; €10). Primi €4.50-6.50. Secondi €6.50-10. Open M-Th 9:30am-3:30pm, F-Sa 8:30-11pm. Cash only. ❷

Amon Specialità e Panini Egiziani, V. Palazzuolo 26-28r (☎055 29 31 46). This Egyptian alleyway take-out whips up kebabs (€3.50-3.90), falafel (€3), hummus (€2.80), and kofta for hungry Florentines on the go. Kebab sandwiches are stuffed with generous heaps of juicy shaved meat. Open daily noon-3pm and 6-11pm. Cash only. ❶

Trattoria Mario, V. Rosina 2r, near P. del Mercato Centrale. Despite the 45min. wait, this family-run restaurant has proven its worth. Be prepared to share tables with other parties. ½ portions are available on select dishes, and all courses are created with entirely fresh ingredients; there isn't a freezer in the whole place. Try the *ribollita* (soup with beans, bread, vegetables; €4.50), the *pollo fritto* (fried chicken) on M, or come for fish F. Be sure to arrive early in the afternoon before ingredients run out and some dishes stop being served. Open M-Sa 12-3:30pm. Cover €0.50. Cash only. ❷

Antica Gelateria Florentina, V. Faenza 2A. Every day, some of the best gelato in the Duomo area is prepared at this *gelateria* using fresh milk and fruit. The painted walls and the knowledgeable staff impart some of the treat's rich history. Enjoy nearly 30 flavors like *nocciola* (hazelnut) and *napole,* a fruit native to Italy. Cones and cups €1.60-4. Open daily noon-1am. Cash only. ❶

SIGHTS

For a list of museum openings, check out www.firenzeturismo.it. For museum reservations, call **Firenze Musei** (☎055 29 48 83; www.firenzemusei.it). There are **no student discounts** at museums and admission can be expensive. Choose destinations carefully and plan to spend a few hours at each landmark.

THE DUOMO

DUOMO (CATTEDRALE DI SANTA MARIA DEL FIORE). In 1296, the city fathers commissioned Arnolfo di Cambio to erect a cathedral so magnificent that it would be "impossible to make it either better or more beautiful with the industry and power of man." Di Cambio succeeded, designing a massive nave with the confidence that by the time it was completed (1418), technology would have advanced enough to provide a solution to erect a dome. **Filippo Brunelleschi** was called in for this task: after studying long-neglected classical methods, he came up with his double-shelled, interlocking-brick construction. The *duomo* claims the world's third longest nave, trailing only St. Peter's in Rome and St. Paul's in London. *(Open M-W and F 10am-5pm, Th 10am-4pm, Sa 10am-4:45pm, Su 1:30-4:45pm. Mass daily 7am, 12:30, 5-7pm. Free.)* Climb the 463 steps inside the dome to **Michelangelo's lantern,** which offers an expansive view of the city from the 100m high external gallery. *(Open M-F 8:30am-7pm, Sa 8:30am-5:40pm. €6.)* The climb up the 82m **campanile** next to the *duomo*, also called "Giotto's Tower," reveals views of the *duomo*, the city, and the **battistero** (baptistry), whose bronze doors, forged by Ghiberti, are known as the **Gates of Paradise.** Byzantine-style mosaics inside the baptistry inspired details of the *Inferno* by Dante, who was christened here. *(Campanile open daily 8:30am-7:30pm. €6. Baptistry open M-Sa noon-7pm, Su 8:30am-2pm. €3.)* Most of the *duomo*'s art resides behind the cathedral in the **Museo dell'Opera del Duomo.** Up the first flight of stairs is a late *Pietà* by Michelangelo; according to legend, he broke Christ's left arm in a fit of frustration. *(P. del Duomo 9, behind the duomo. ☎055 23 02 885. Open M-Sa 9am-6:50pm, Su 9am-1pm. €6.)*

ORSANMICHELE. Built in 1337 as a granary, the Orsanmichele became a church after a fire convinced officials to move grain operations outside the city. The ancient grain chutes are still visible outside. Within, tenacious visitors will discover Ghiberti's *St. John the Baptist* and *St. Stephen*, Donatello's *St. Peter and St. Mark*, and Giambologna's *St. Luke*. *(V. Arte della Lana, between the duomo and P. della Signoria. Open Tu-Su 10am-5pm. Free.)*

PIAZZA DELLA SIGNORIA

From P. del Duomo, **Via dei Calzaiuoli,** one of the city's oldest streets, runs south past crowds, street vendors, *gelaterie*, and chic shops to **Piazza della Signoria,** a 13th-century *piazza* bordered by the Palazzo Vecchio and the Uffizi. With the construction of the Palazzo Vecchio in 1299, the square became Florence's civic and political center. In 1497, religious zealot Girolamo Savonarola lit the **Bonfire of the Vanities** here, barbecuing some of Florence's best art. Today P. della

ITALY

Signoria fills daily with photo-snapping tourists who later return for drinks and dessert in its upscale cafes. Monumental sculptures stand in front of the *palazzo* and inside the 14th-century **Loggia dei Lanzi.** *(Free.)*

NO ART FOR YOU. To avoid disappointment at the Uffizi, keep in mind that a few rooms are usually closed each day and famous pieces often go on temporary loan, so not all works are always on display. A sign outside the ticket office lists the rooms that are closed for the day.

THE UFFIZI. Giorgio Vasari designed this palace in 1554 for the offices *(uffizi)* of Duke Cosimo's administration; today, the gallery holds one of the world's finest art collections. Beautiful statues overlook the walkway from niches in the columns; play "spot the Renaissance man" and try to find Leonardo, Machiavelli, Petrarch, and Vespucci among them. Botticelli, Caravaggio, Cimabue, Duccio, Fra Angelico, della Francesca, Giotto, Michelangelo, Raphael, del Sarto, Titian, da Vinci, even Dürer, Rembrandt, Rubens—you name it, it's here. Be sure to look at the rare sketches in the **Cabinet of Drawings and Prints** on the first floor before confining yourself to the U-shaped corridor of the second floor. A few rooms are usually closed each day, and some works may be on loan. A sign at the ticket office lists the rooms that are closed. *(From P. B. S. Giovanni, take V. Roma past P. della Repubblica, where the street turns into V. Calimala. Continue until V. Vaccereccia and turn left. ☎055 23 88 651. Open Tu-Su 8:15am-6:35pm. €10; EU citizens 18-25 €5. Reserve ahead for €4 fee. Audio tour €4.70.)*

MAKE FRIENDS WITH THE UFFIZI. If you plan on visiting 3 or more museums in Florence, consider obtaining an **Amici degli Uffizi card.** Students under 26 pay €25 for the card (regularly €60) and receive free admission to the Uffizi and all state museums in Florence (including the Accademia and Bargello). It includes one visit to each of the museums and gets you to the front of the line. For more information, call Amici degli Uffizi, V. Lorenzo il Magnifico 1, ☎055 47 94 422, or email amicidegliuffizi@waf.it.

PALAZZO VECCHIO. Arnolfo del Cambio designed this fortress-like *palazzo* in the late 13th century to be the seat of government. It included apartments which functioned as living quarters for members of the city council while they served two-month terms. After the *palazzo* became the Medici's home in 1470, Michelozzo decorated the courtyard. The **Monumental Apartments,** which house the *palazzo*'s extensive art collections, are now an art and history museum. The worthwhile **Activities Tour** includes the "Secret Routes," which reveal hidden stairwells and chambers tucked behind exquisite oil paintings. The ceiling of the **Salone del Cinquecento,** where the Grand Council of the Republic met, is so elaborately decorated that the walls can hardly support its weight. The tiny **Studio di Francesco I** is a treasure trove of Mannerist art. *(☎055 27 68 224. Open M-W and F-Sa 9am-7pm, Su 9am-1pm. Palazzo and Monumental Apartments each €6, ages 18-25 €4.50. Activities tour €8/5.50. Courtyard free. Reserve ahead for tours.)*

BARGELLO. The heart of medieval Florence is in this 13th-century fortress, once the residence of the chief magistrate and later a brutal prison with public executions in its courtyard. It was restored in the 19th century and now houses the largely untouristed **Museo Nazionale.** Donatello's bronze *David,* the first free-standing nude since antiquity, stands opposite the two bronze panels of the *Sacrifice of Isaac,* submitted by Ghiberti and Brunelleschi in the baptistry door competition. Michelangelo's early works, including *Bacchus*, *Brutus*, and *Apollo*, are on the ground floor. *(V. del Proconsolo 4, between the duomo and P. della Signoria. ☎055 23 88 606. Open daily 8:15am-6pm. Closed 2nd and 4th M of each month. €7.)*

PONTE VECCHIO. From the Uffizi, follow V. Georgofili left and turn right along the river to reach the Ponte Vecchio, Florence's oldest bridge, built in 1345. In the 1500s, the Medici gentrified: they kicked out the butchers and tanneries and installed goldsmiths and diamond-carvers in their place. Today, the boutiques of the shop owners' descendants make the bridge glitter with chic necklaces, brooches, and charms; tourists and street performers make up the bulk of its traffic. Don't miss the **sunset view** from neighboring **Ponte alle Grazie.**

BADIA. The site of medieval Florence's richest monastery, the Badia church is now buried in the interior of a residential block. Filippino Lippi's *Apparition of the Virgin to St. Bernard*, one of the most famous paintings of the 15th century, hangs in eerie gloom to the left of the church. Be sure to glance up at the intricately carved dark wood ceiling. Some say Dante may have first glimpsed his beloved Beatrice here. Visitors are asked to walk silently among the prostrate, white-robed worshippers. *(Entrance on V. Dante Alighieri, off V. Proconsolo. ☎055 26 44 02. Open to tourists M 3-6pm, but visitors can walk through at any time.)*

SANTA MARIA NOVELLA

The largest open space in Florence, the P. della Repubblica teems with crowds, overpriced cafes, restaurants, and *gelaterie*. In 1890, it replaced the Mercato Vecchio as the site of the city market, but has since traded stalls for more fashionable vendors. The inscription "*antico centro della città, da secolare squalore, a vita nuova restituito*" ("ancient center of the city, squalid for centuries, restored to new life") makes a derogatory reference to the *piazza*'s location in the old Jewish ghetto. The area around Mercato Nuovo and V. Tornabuoni was Florence's financial capital in the 1400s. Now it's residential, but still touristy.

CHIESA DI SANTA MARIA NOVELLA. The chapels of the wealthiest 13th- and 14th-century merchants are part of this church. Santa Maria Novella was home to an order of Dominicans, or *Domini canes* (Hounds of the Lord), who took a bite out of sin and corruption. The facade of the *chiesa* is made of Florentine marble and is considered one of the great masterpieces of early Renaissance architecture. The Medicis commissioned Vasari to paint new frescoes over the 13th-century ones on the walls, but the painter spared Masaccio's **Trinity,** the first painting to use geometric perspective. In the **Gondi Chapel** is Brunelleschi's *Crucifix*, designed in response to Donatello's, in Santa Croce, which Brunelleschi found too full of "vigorous naturalism." Donatello was supposedly so impressed by his rival's creation that he dropped the bag of eggs he was carrying. *(Open M-Th 9am-5pm, F-Su 1-5pm. €2.70.)*

ITALY

CHIESA DI SANTA TRINITÀ. Hoping to spend eternity in elite company, the most fashionable *palazzo* owners commissioned family chapels in this church. The facade, designed by Bernardo Buontalenti in the 16th century, is almost Baroque in its elaborate ornamentation. Scenes from Ghirlandaio's *Life of St. Francis* decorate the **Sassetti Chapel** in the right arm of the transept. The famous altarpiece, Ghirlandaio's *Adoration of the Shepherds*, resides in the Uffizi—this one is a copy. *(In P. S. Trinità. Open M-Sa 7am-noon and 4-7pm, Su 7-noon. Free.)*

MERCATO NUOVO. The *loggie* (guilds) of the New Market have housed gold and silk traders since 1547. Today, faux designer gear dominates vendors' wares. Rubbing the snout of Pietro Tacca's plump statue, *Il Porcellino* (The Little Pig), is reputed to bring luck, but don't wait for that purse you covet to become real leather. *(Off V. Calimala, between P. della Repubblica and the Ponte Vecchio. Open dawn-dusk.)*

SAN LORENZO

ACCADEMIA. It doesn't matter how many pictures of him you've seen—when you come around the corner to see Michelangelo's triumphant **David** towering in self-assured perfection, you will be blown away. The statue's base was struck by lightning in 1512, the figure was damaged by anti-Medici riots in 1527, and David's left wrist was broken by a stone, after which he was moved here from P. della Signoria in 1873. In the hallway leading to *David* are Michelangelo's four *Slaves* and a *Pietà*. The master purposely left these statues unfinished, staying true to his theory of "releasing" figures from the living stone. Botticelli's Madonna paintings and Uccello's works are worth seeing. *(V. Ricasoli 60, between the churches of S. Marco and S. S. Annunziata. ☎055 23 88 609. Open Tu-Su 8:15am-6:50pm. Reserve ahead €4 extra. May-Sept. €10; Oct.-Apr. €7.)*

BASILICA DI SAN LORENZO. Because the Medicis lent the funds to build this church, they retained artistic control over its construction and decided to add Cosimo dei Medici's grave to Brunelleschi's spacious basilica. They cunningly placed it in front of the high altar to make the entire church his personal mausoleum. Michelangelo began the exterior, but, disgusted by Florentine politics, he abandoned the project, leaving the plain facade. *(Open M-Sa 10am-5pm, Mar.-Oct. also Su 1:30-5pm. €2.50.)* While the **Cappelle dei Medici** (Medici Chapels) offer a rare glimpse of the Baroque in Florence, the **Cappella dei Principi** (Princes' Chapel) emulates the baptistry in P. del Duomo. Michelangelo sculpted the **Sacrestia Nuova** (New Sacristy) to hold two Medici tombs. On the tomb of Lorenzo he placed the female Night and the muscular male Day; on Giuliano's sit the more androgynous Dawn and Dusk. *(Walk around to the back entrance in P. Madonna degli Aldobrandini. Open daily 8:15am-5pm. Closed 1st and 3rd M and 2nd and 4th Su. €6.)*

PIAZZA SANTA CROCE

CHIESA DI SANTA CROCE. The Franciscans built this church as far as possible from their Dominican rivals at S. Maria Novella. Ironically, the ascetic Franciscans produced what is arguably the most splendid church in the city. Luminaries buried here include Galileo, Machiavelli, Michelangelo (whose tomb was designed by Vasari), and humanist Leonardo Bruni. Check out Donatello's *Crucifix* (so irksome to Brunelleschi) in the Vernio Chapel, and his gilded *Annunciation*, by Bruni's tomb. At the end of the cloister next to the church is the perfectly proportioned **Cappella Pazzi,** whose decorations include Luca della Robbia's *tondi* of the apostles and Brunelleschi's moldings of the evangelists. *(Open M-Sa 9:30am-5:30pm, Su 1-5:30pm. €5.)*

SYNAGOGUE OF FLORENCE. This synagogue, also known as the **Museo del Tempio Israelitico,** is resplendent with arches and Sephardic domes. David Levi, a wealthy Florentine Jewish businessman, donated his fortune in 1870 to build "a monumental temple worthy of Florence," recognizing the Jews' new freedom to live and worship outside the old Jewish ghetto. *(V. Farini 4, at V. Pilastri. ☎055 24 52 52. Free tours every hr.; reserve ahead. Open M-Th and Su 10am-6pm, F 10am-2pm. €4.)*

CASA BUONARROTI. This museum houses Michelangelo memorabilia and two of his crucial early works, *The Madonna of the Steps* and *The Battle of the Centaurs.* Both works were completed when he was 16, and indicate his shift from relief to sculpture in the round. *(V. Ghibellina 70. ☎055 25 17 52. From P. S. Croce, follow V. dei Pepi and turn right on V. Ghibellina. Open M and W-Su 9:30am-2pm. €6.50, students €4.)*

OLTRARNO

Historically disdained by downtown Florentines, the far side of the Arno remains a lively and unpretentious quarter, filled with students and relatively few tourists. Head back on Ponte S. Trinità after dallying in P. San Spirito.

PALAZZO PITTI. Luca Pitti, a 15th-century banker, built his *palazzo* east of P. S. Spirito against the Boboli hill. The Medicis acquired the *palazzo* in 1550 and expanded it in every way possible. Today, it houses six museums, including the **Galleria Palatina.** Florence's most important art collection after the Uffizi, the gallery has works by Caravaggio, Raphael, Rubens, and Titian. Other museums display Medici family costumes, porcelain, and **Royal Apartments**—reminders of the time when the *palazzo* was the living quarters of the royal House of Savoy. The **Galleria d'Arte Moderna** hides one of Italian art history's big surprises, the proto-Impressionist works of the Macchiaioli group. *(Open Tu-Su 8:15am-6:50pm. Ticket for Galleria Palatina, Royal Apartments, and Galleria d'Arte Moderna €8.50.)*

SAN MINIATO AL MONTE. An inlaid marble facade and 13th-century mosaics provide a prelude to the floor inside, patterned with doves, lions, and astrological signs. Visit at 5:40pm to hear the monks chant. *(Take bus #13 from the station or climb the stairs from Piazzale Michelangelo. ☎055 23 42 731. Open daily Mar.-Nov. 8am-7pm; Dec.-Feb. 8am-1pm and 2:30-6pm. Free.)*

BOBOLI GARDENS. With geometrically sculpted hedges, contrasting groves of holly and cypress trees, and bubbling fountains, the elaborate gardens are an exquisite example of stylized Renaissance landscaping. A large oval lawn is just up the hill from the back of the Palazzo Pitti, with an Egyptian obelisk in the middle and marble statues dotting the perimeter. Spend an afternoon wandering through the grounds and the small on-site museums. *(Open daily June-Aug. 8:15am-7:30pm; Apr.-May and Sept.-Oct. 8:15am-6:30pm; Nov.-Mar. reduced hours. €6.)*

PIAZZALE MICHELANGELO. A visit to Piazzale Michelangelo is a must. At sunset, waning light casts a warm glow over the city. Views from here are even better (and certainly cheaper) than those from the top of the *duomo*. Make the challenging uphill trek at around 8:30pm during the summer to arrive at the *piazzale* in time for sunset. Unfortunately, the *piazzale* doubles as a large parking lot, and is home to hordes of tour buses during summer days. *(Cross the Ponte Vecchio to the Oltrarno and turn left, walk through the piazza, and turn right up V. de Bardi. Follow it uphill as it becomes V. del Monte alle Croci. A staircase to the left heads to the piazzale.)*

NIGHTLIFE

For info, consult the city's entertainment monthly, *Firenze Spettacolo* (€2). **Piazza Santo Spirito** has live music in summer. When going to bars that are far from the *centro*, keep in mind that the last bus may leave before the fun winds down, and taxis are rare in the area with the most popular discos.

Mago Merlino Tea House, V. Pilastri 31r (☎055 24 29 70). Always ready to share his wisdom, expert Rocco serves steaming cups of sophisticated tea in his Moroccan-inspired cafe. Choose from a variety of specialty brews (€7-9 a pot) containing everything from amber and saffron to homemade orange water and fresh mint. Take your shoes off and lounge among the floor pillows in the back room, or hit the hookah (€15 per group) in the small courtyard. Come during Happy hour (6:30-9pm) and have organic vegetarian food as you sip on a tea cocktail (€5); Rocco will make it with absinthe if you ask. Open daily 6:30pm-2am. Cash only.

Las Palmas, P. Ghiberti (☎347 27 60 033). Each summer, P. Ghiberti is transformed into a neighborhood block party with the help of Las Palmas. Drinks, live music, and an outdoor dance floor ensure fun-filled nights. Serves tasty dishes. Tables fill quickly, so make reservations. Happy hour 6:30-9pm; drinks €4. Beer €4. Mixed drinks €7. Shots €3. Open daily from the 2nd week of May to the 2nd week of Aug. 6:30pm-1:30am.

Caffè Sant'Ambrogio, P. Sant'Ambrogio 7 (☎055 24 10 35). Hip red lights and pulsating techno pop. People begin pouring in for *aperitivi* 6-9pm, but during the rest of the night, most just come in to buy their drinks before heading back into the warm night air of the *piazza*. Wine €4-6. Beer €2.50-5. Open M-Sa 10am-2am, Su 6pm-2am. MC/V.

Central, V. del Fosso Macinante 2 (☎055 35 35 05), in Parco delle Cascine. Four open-air dance floors pulse with hip-hop, reggae, and Italian "dance rock." Favored by teens and university students. Well-dressed bouncers and management keep things under control. All drinks €10. Cover €20, foreign students €3 until 1am. Open in summer Tu-Su 8pm-3am. AmEx/MC/V.

Aquarama Meccanò, Vle. degli Olmi 1 (☎055 33 13 71), near Parco delle Cascine. One of Florence's most popular discos; caters to a slightly older crowd than Central. Open-air dance floors and sparkling grounds make for sophisticated fun. Drinks €10. Cover €10-16; includes 1 drink. Open Tu-Sa 11pm-4am. AmEx/MC/V.

PISA ☎050

Millions of tourists arrive in Pisa (pop. 85,400) each year to marvel at the famous "Leaning Tower," forming a gelato-slurping, photo-snapping mire. Commanding a beautiful stretch of the Arno River, Pisa has a diverse array of cultural and artistic diversions, as well as three universities. The **Piazza del Duomo,** also known as the **Campo dei Miracoli** (Field of Miracles), is a grassy expanse that contrasts with the white stone of the tower, baptistry, *duomo*, and surrounding museums. Begun in 1173, the famous **Leaning Tower** began to tilt when the soil beneath it suddenly shifted. The tilt intensified after WWII, and thanks to the tourists who climb its steps daily, the tower slips 1-2m each year, though it's currently considered stable. Tours of 30 visitors are permitted to ascend the 294 steps once every 30min. (Tours depart daily June-Aug. 8:30am-11pm; Sept.-May 8:30am-7:30pm. Assemble next to info office 10min. before tour. €15. Cash only.) Also on the Campo is the **Battistero** (Baptistry), whose precise acoustics allow an unamplified choir to be heard 2km away. An acoustic demonstration occurs every 30min. (Open daily Apr.-Sept. 8am-7:30pm; Oct. 9am-5:30pm; Nov.-Feb. 9am-4:30pm; Mar. 9am-5:30pm. €5.) The dazzling **duomo** next door, considered one of the finest Romanesque cathedrals in the world, has a collection of splendid art, including a mosaic by Cimabue. (Open daily Apr.-Sept. 10am-8pm; Oct. and Mar. 10am-7pm; Nov.-Feb. 10am-1pm and 3-5pm. €2.) The **Camposanto,** a cloistered cemetery, is filled with Roman sarcophagi and covered with earth that Crusaders brought from Golgotha, the site of Jesus's crucifixion (same hours as *Battistero*). Occasional concerts take place in the adjacent *duomo;* call **Opera della Primaziale Pisana,** P. Duomo 17 (☎050 38 72 210; www.opapisa.it). An **all-inclusive ticket** to the Campo's sights costs €10.50 and is available at the two *biglietterie* (ticket booths) on the Campo (at the Museo del Duomo and next to the tourist office adjacent to the tower).

Two minutes from the *duomo*, the **Albergo Helvetia ❸,** V. Don Gaefano Boschi 31, off P. Archivescovado, has large, clean rooms, small shared baths, a multilingual staff, and a welcoming downstairs bar. (☎050 55 30 84. Reception 8am-midnight. Reserve ahead. Singles €35, with bath €50; doubles €45-62. Cash only.) In the heart of Pisa, the newly opened **Pisa Tower Hostel ❹,** P. Garibaldi 9, 2nd floor, offers small rooms with steel frame beds and long windows. (Free bed linens and towels. 4-bed female-only dorms €49; singles €55; doubles with shared bath €80. Cash payment on arrival.) Steer clear of the countless touristy pizzerias near the tower and head for the river, where the restaurants offer a more authentic ambience and consistently high quality. Try one of the many *primi* offerings, including various *sfogliate* (quiche) at **Il Paiolo ❶**, V. Curtatone e Montanara 9. (*Primi* and *secondi* €5-8. Open M-F 12:30-3pm and 8pm-1am, Sa-Su 8pm-2am. MC/V.) Get groceries at **Pam,** V. Giovanni Pascoli 8, just off C. Italia. (Open M-Sa 7:30am-8:30pm, Su 9am-1pm. Cash only.)

Trains (☎89 20 21) run from P. della Stazione, in the southern end of town, to Florence (75min., 2 per hr., €5.40), Genoa (2hr., 1 per hr., €8), and Rome (4hr., 1-2 per day, €23-29). To reach the **tourist office,** walk straight out of the train station and go left in P. Vittorio Emanuele. (☎050 42 291; www.turismo.toscana.it. Open M-F 9am-7pm, Sa 9am-1:30pm.) Take bus marked LAM ROSSA (€0.85) from the station to the Campo. **Postal Code:** 56100.

NAPLES (NAPOLI) ☎081

Naples (pop. 1 million), Italy's third largest city, is also its most chaotic—Naples moves a million miles per minute. Locals spend their waking moments out on the town, eating, drinking, shouting, laughing, and pausing in the middle of busy streets to finish conversations. The birthplace of pizza and the modern-day home of tantalizing seafood, Naples boasts unbeatable cuisine. Once you submit to the city's rapid pulse, everywhere else will just seem slow.

TRANSPORTATION

Flights: Aeroporto Capodichino, V. Umberto Maddalena (**NAP;** ☎081 78 96 259; www.gesac.it). Connects to major Italian and European cities. **Alibus** (☎081 53 11 706) goes to P. Municipio and P. Garibaldi (20min., 6am-11:30pm, €3.10).

Trains: Trenitalia (www.trenitalia.it) goes from Stazione Centrale in P. Garibaldi to **Milan** (8hr., 15 per day, €39-50) and **Rome** (2hr., 31 per day, €11-38). **Circumvesuviana** (☎800 05 39 39) runs to **Herculaneum** (€1.80) and **Pompeii** (€2.40).

Ferries: Depart from **Stazione Marittima,** on Molo Angioino, and **Molo Beverello,** at the base of P. Municipio. From P. Garibaldi, take the R2, 152, 3S, or the Alibus to P. Municipio. **Caremar,** Molo Beverello (☎081 55 13 882), runs frequently to **Capri** and **Ischia** (both 1hr., €4.80-10). **Tirrenia Lines,** Molo Angioino (☎199 12 31 199), goes to **Cagliari** (16hr.) and **Palermo** (11hr.). **Hydrofoils** are generally faster and more expensive. The daily newspaper *Il Mattino* (€1) lists up-to-date ferry schedules.

Public Transportation: The **UnicoNapoli** (www.napolipass.it) ticket is valid on the buses, funicular, Metro, and trains in Naples (€1.10 per 90min., full-day €3.10). Route info for the **Metro** and funiculars is at www.metro.na.it.

Taxis: Consortaxi (☎081 20 20 20); **Napoli** (☎081 44 44 44). Only take metered taxis, and always ask about prices up front. Meter starts at €3; €0.05 per 65m thereafter. €2.50 surcharge 10pm-7am.

ORIENTATION AND PRACTICAL INFORMATION

The main train and bus terminals are in the immense **Piazza Garibaldi** on the east side of Naples. From P. Garibaldi, a left on **Corso Garibaldi** leads to the waterfront district; **Piazza Guglielmo Pepe** is at the end of C. Garibaldi. Access **Piazza Plebiscito** by walking down **Via Nuova Marina** with the water on your left. **Via Toledo,** a chic pedestrian shopping street, links the waterfront to the Plebiscito district, where the well-to-do hang out, and the maze-like **Spanish Quarter.** Along V. Toledo, **Piazza Dante** lies on the western extreme of the **Spaccanapoli** *(centro storico)* neighborhood. Walking away from the waterfront, a right on any of the streets leads to the historic district.

Tourist Offices: EPT (☎081 26 87 79; www.eptnapoli.info), at Stazione Centrale. Free maps. Grab **Qui Napoli,** a bimonthly publication full of listings and events. Open M-Sa 9am-7pm, Su 9am-1pm. **Branch** at P. Gesù Nuovo (☎081 55 12 701).

Consulates: Canada, V. Carducci 29 (☎081 40 13 38). **UK,** V. dei Mille 40 (☎081 42 38 911). **US,** P. della Repubblica (☎081 58 38 111, emergency 033 79 45 083).

Currency Exchange: Thomas Cook, at the airport and in P. Municipio 70 (☎081 55 18 399, branch 081 55 18 399). Open M-F 9:30am-1pm and 3-7pm.

Police: ☎113. **Ambulance:** ☎118.

Hospital: Incurabili (☎081 25 49 422). M: Cavour (Museo).

Post Office: P. Matteotti (☎081 552 42 33), at V. Diaz on the R2 line. Unreliable *fermo-posta.* Open M-F 8:15am-6pm, Sa 8:15am-noon. **Postal Code:** 80100.

ACCOMMODATIONS

Avoid hotels that solicit customers at the station, never give your passport until you've seen the room, agree on the price before unpacking, and be alert for hidden costs.

Hostel Pensione Mancini, V. Pasquale Stanislao Mancini 33, 2nd fl. (☎081 55 36 731; www.hostelpensionemancini.com), off far end of P. Garibaldi, 5min. walk to station. Attentive owners share their extensive knowledge of Naples. Clean and spacious rooms. New common room and kitchen. English spoken. Breakfast included. Free luggage storage, lockers, and Wi-Fi. Reception 24hr. Excellent for late-night arrivals. Co-ed and female dorms €14-18; singles €30-35, with bath €40-50; doubles €40-50/50-60; triples €60-75/70-80; quads €70-80/76-90. 10% *Let's Go* discount. AmEx/MC/V. ❶

6 Small Rooms, V. Diodato Lioy 18, 3rd fl. (☎081 79 01 378; www.6smallrooms.com). From P. Dante, turn left on V. Toledo, left on V. Senise, and right on V. Lioy. Huge, beautiful rooms defy the name. Frescoed kitchen open until 10:30pm and English video collection available. Resident cat and dogs. Breakfast included. Wash and dry €5. Free lockers, internet, and Wi-Fi. Some private rooms have A/C. Dorms €18-20; small singles or doubles with bath and A/C €25-45; doubles €50-55, with bath €55-65; triples €60-75; quad 80-95. 10% *Let's Go* discount. MC/V. ❶

Hostel and Hotel Bella Capri, V. Melisurgo 4 (☎081 55 29 494; www.bellacapri.it). Take R2 bus from station, exit at V. De Pretis. Top-notch hostel offers clean, safe, and fun accommodations for all. Laid-back atmosphere and helpful owner who likes to organize pizza outings. All rooms have A/C and TVs; some have bay views. Flatscreen satellite TV and DVDs in the common room. Common kitchen. English spoken. Breakfast included. Free lockers, luggage storage, and high-speed Internet access. Wash and dry €4. Reception 24hr. Mixed and all-female dorms €15-20; singles €40-50, with bath €50-70; doubles €50-60/60-80; triples €70-80/80-100; quads €80-90/90-110; quints and 6-person rooms with bath €20-29 per person. 10% *Let's Go* discount. AmEx/MC/V. ❶

Hostel of the Sun, V. Melisurgo 15 (☎081 42 06 393; www.hostelnapoli.com). Take R2 bus from station, exit at V. De Pretis. Buzz #51. Surefire entertainment and comfort are provided by the exuberant staff, who give out free maps and advice, organize outings once or twice a week, and cook for guests one night a week. Colorful, bright common room has A/C, satellite TV, DVDs, Skype phone, and tons of pictures of happy customers. All private rooms have TV, DVD, and A/C. Wheelchair accessible facilities. Kitchen and fridge available. Breakfast included. Free small lockers, internet, and Wi-Fi in most rooms. Wash €3, dry €3; free with 3 nights' stay. Reception 24hr. 5-7 bed dorms €16-20; doubles €55-60, with bath €60-70; triples €75-80/70-90; quads €80-90, with bath €85-100. 10% *Let's Go* discount. D/MC/V. ❷

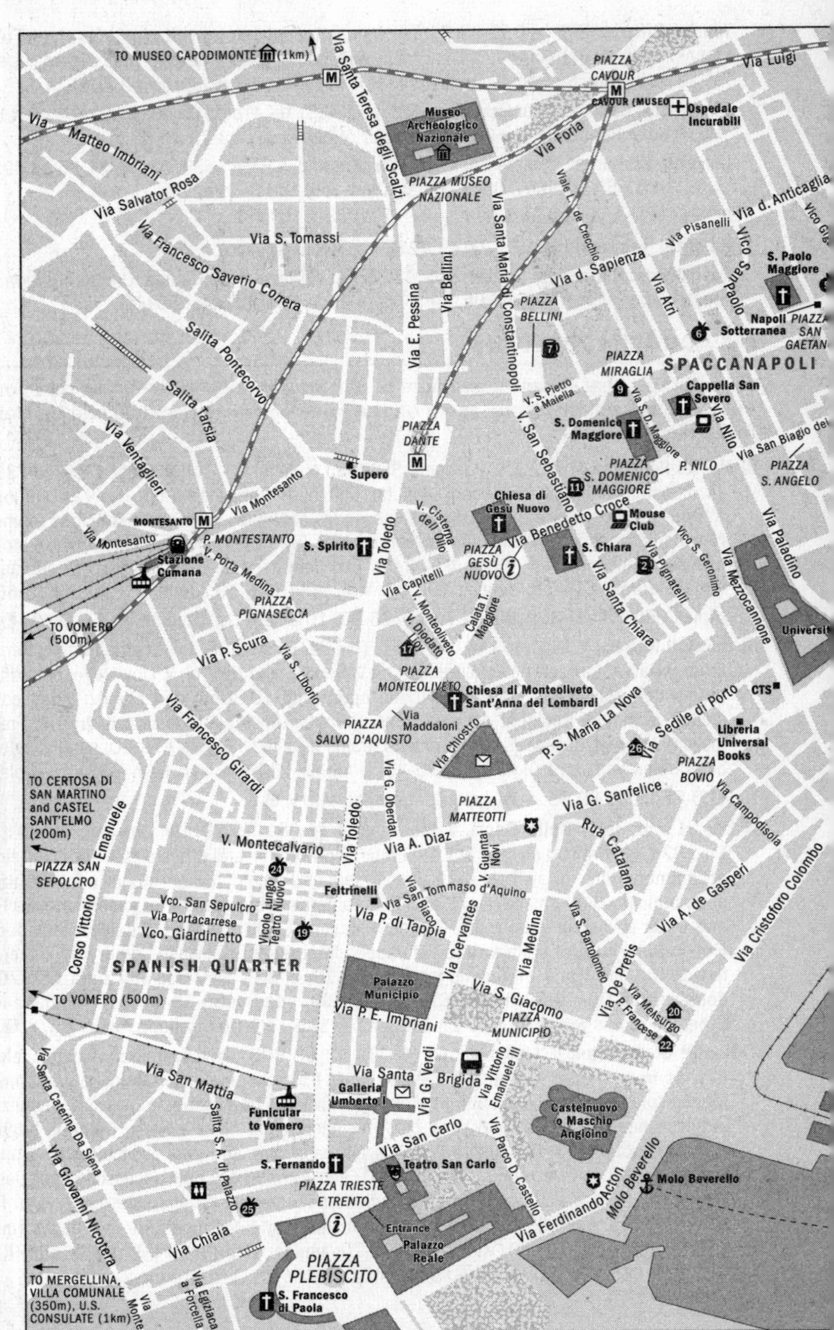
TO MUSEO CAPODIMONTE (1km)
Via Santa Teresa degli Scalzi
PIAZZA CAVOUR
CAVOUR (MUSEO)
Via Luigi
Ospedale Incurabili
Museo Archeologico Nazionale
Via Matteo Imbriani
Via Foria
PIAZZA MUSEO NAZIONALE
Via Salvator Rosa
Via Santa Maria di Costantinopoli
Viale L. de Crecchio
Via d. Anticaglia
Via Pisanelli
Via Francesco Saverio Correra
Via S. Tomassi
Via Bellini
Via d. Sapienza
Vico San Paolo
S. Paolo Maggiore
Via Atri
Via E. Pessina
PIAZZA BELLINI
Napoli Sotterranea
Salita Pontecorvo
SPACCANAPOLI
PIAZZA MIRAGLIA
Cappella San Severo
Salita Tarsia
V. S. Pietro a Maiella
S. Domenico Maggiore
Via S. D. Maggiore
Via Nilo
Via Ventaglieri
PIAZZA DANTE
V. San Sebastiano
Via San Biagio dei
Supero
PIAZZA S. DOMENICO MAGGIORE
P. NILO
PIAZZA S. ANGELO
Via Montesanto
Chiesa di Gesù Nuovo
MONTESANTO
V. Cisterna dell'Olio
Via Benedetto Croce
Mouse Club
Via Paladino
Via Montesanto
P. MONTESTANTO
S. Spirito
Via Toledo
PIAZZA GESÙ NUOVO
S. Chiara
Vico S. Geronimo
Via Pignatelli
Stazione Cumana
V. Porta Medina
Via Capitelli
Via Santa Chiara
Via Mezzocannone
PIAZZA PIGNASECCA
V. Monteoliveto
Calata T. Maggiore
TO VOMERO (500m)
V. Diodato Lioy
Via P. Scura
Via S. Liborio
PIAZZA MONTEOLIVETO
Chiesa di Monteoliveto Sant'Anna dei Lombardi
CTS
Via Sedile di Porto
Via Francesco Girardi
PIAZZA SALVO D'AQUISTO
Via Maddaloni
Via Chiostro
P. S. Maria La Nova
Libreria Universal Books
PIAZZA BOVIO
TO CERTOSA DI SAN MARTINO and CASTEL SANT'ELMO (200m)
Corso Vittorio Emanuele
Via G. Oberdan
PIAZZA MATTEOTTI
Via G. Sanfelice
Via Campodisola
Rua Catalana
PIAZZA SAN SEPOLCRO
V. Montecalvario
Via A. Diaz
V. Guantai Novi
Via Cristoforo Colombo
Feltrinelli
Via San Tommaso d'Aquino
Via A. de Gasperi
Vco. San Sepulcro
Via Portacarrese
Vco. Giardinetto
Vicolo Lungo Teatro Nuovo
Via P. di Tappia
Via Biaco
Via Cervantes
Via Medina
Via S. Bartolomeo
SPANISH QUARTER
Palazzo Municipio
Via S. Giacomo
Via De Pretis
Via Melsurgo
P. Francese
TO VOMERO (500m)
Via P. E. Imbriani
PIAZZA MUNICIPIO
Via Santa Brigida
Via G. Verdi
Via Vittorio Emanuele III
Via San Mattia
Galleria Umberto I
Castelnuovo o Maschio Angioino
Funicular to Vomero
Salita S. A. di Palazzo
Via San Carlo
Via Parco D. Castello
Via Santa Caterina Da Siena
S. Fernando
Teatro San Carlo
Molo Beverello
Via Giovanni Nicotera
PIAZZA TRIESTE E TRENTO
Via Ferdinando Acton
Via Chiaia
Entrance
Palazzo Reale
PIAZZA PLEBISCITO
TO MERGELLINA, VILLA COMUNALE (350m), U.S. CONSULATE (1km)
Via Monte
Via Egiziaca a Forcella
S. Francesco di Paola

ITALY

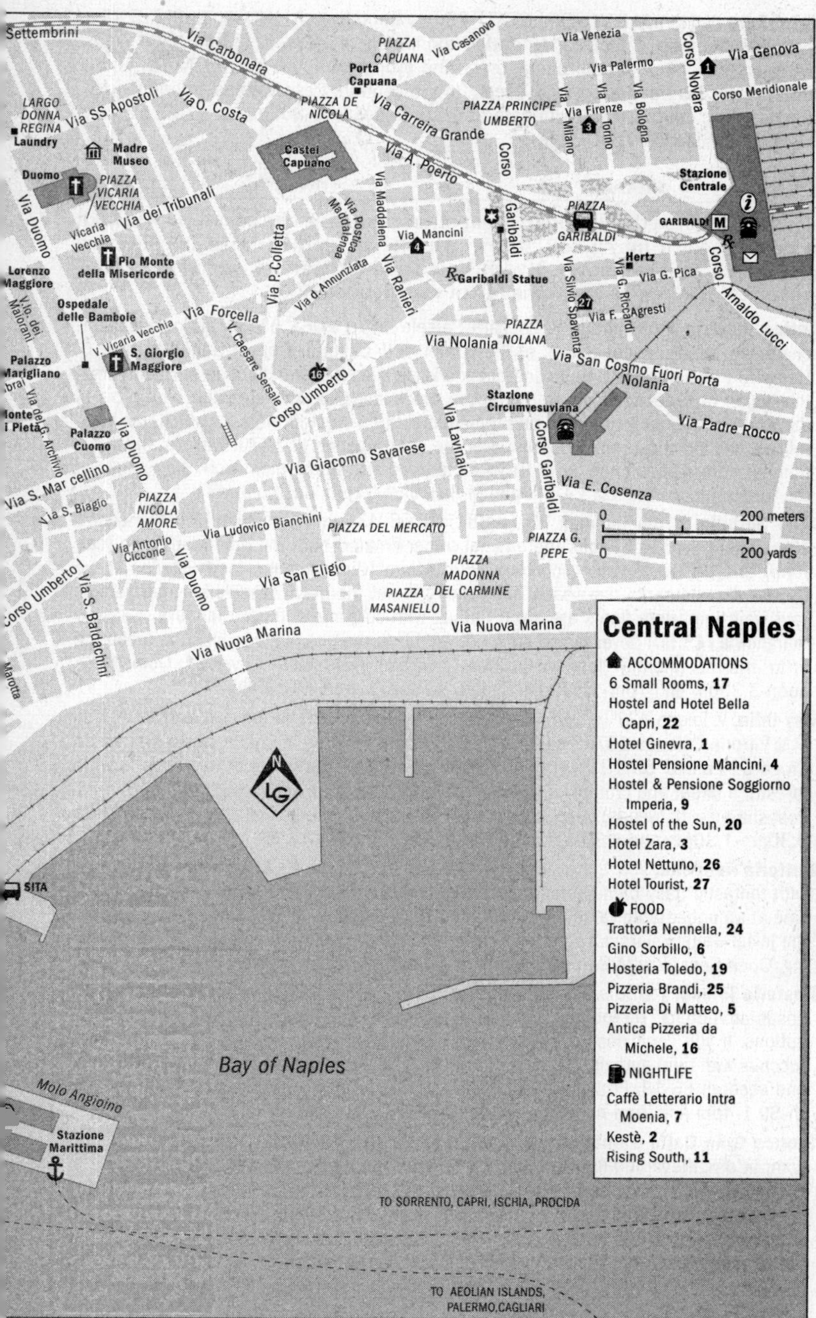
Central Naples
ACCOMMODATIONS
6 Small Rooms, 17
Hostel and Hotel Bella Capri, 22
Hotel Ginevra, 1
Hostel Pensione Mancini, 4
Hostel & Pensione Soggiorno Imperia, 9
Hostel of the Sun, 20
Hotel Zara, 3
Hotel Nettuno, 26
Hotel Tourist, 27
FOOD
Trattoria Nennella, 24
Gino Sorbillo, 6
Hosteria Toledo, 19
Pizzeria Brandi, 25
Pizzeria Di Matteo, 5
Antica Pizzeria da Michele, 16
NIGHTLIFE
Caffè Letterario Intra Moenia, 7
Kestè, 2
Rising South, 11
Settembrini
Via Carbonara
PIAZZA CAPUANA
Via Casanova
Porta Capuana
Via Venezia
Corso Novara
Via Genova
Via Palermo
Corso Meridionale
LARGO DONNA REGINA
Laundry
Via SS Apostoli
Via O. Costa
PIAZZA DE NICOLA
Via Carreira Grande
PIAZZA PRINCIPE UMBERTO
Via Milano
Via Firenze
Via Torino
Via Bologna
Madre Museo
Castel Capuano
Via A. Poerto
Corso Garibaldi
Stazione Centrale
Duomo
PIAZZA VICARIA VECCHIA
Via Duomo
Via dei Tribunali
Vicaria Vecchia
Via Postica Maddalena
Via Maddalena
Via Mancini
PIAZZA GARIBALDI
GARIBALDI
Pio Monte della Misericorde
Via P. Colletta
Via d. Annunziata
Via Ranieri
Garibaldi Statue
Hertz
Via Silvio Spaventa
Via G. Riccardi
Via G. Pica
Corso Arnaldo Lucci
Lorenzo Maggiore
V.lo. dei Maiorani
Ospedale delle Bambole
Via Forcella
Via F. Agresti
V. Vicaria Vecchia
V. Caesare Sersale
PIAZZA NOLANA
Via Nolania
Palazzo Marigliano
S. Giorgio Maggiore
Via San Cosmo Fuori Porta Nolania
Corso Umberto I
Stazione Circumvesuviana
Via del G. Archivio
Palazzo Cuomo
Via Lavinaio
Via Padre Rocco
Via S. Mar cellino
Via Giacomo Savarese
Via E. Cosenza
Via S. Biagio
PIAZZA NICOLA AMORE
Via Ludovico Bianchini
PIAZZA DEL MERCATO
0
200 meters
200 yards
Via Antonio Ciccone
PIAZZA G. PEPE
PIAZZA MADONNA DEL CARMINE
Via San Eligio
PIAZZA MASANIELLO
Via S. Baldachini
Via Nuova Marina
Marotta
N
LG
SITA
Bay of Naples
Molo Angioino
Stazione Marittima
TO SORRENTO, CAPRI, ISCHIA, PROCIDA
TO AEOLIAN ISLANDS, PALERMO,CAGLIARI

Hotel Zara, V. Firenze 81 (☎081 28 71 25; www.hotelzara.it; info@hotelzara.it). Near Stazione Centrale. Spacious, renovated rooms, all with TVs, A/C, and baths; most with terraces. International book library and exchange. Breakfast €5. No Wi-Fi, but internet access free for *Let's Go* users. 24h. reception. Reservations recommended. Singles €35; doubles €45, with bath €50-70; triples €75-80; quads €100. 5% *Let's Go* discount. AmEx/D/MC/V. ❷

FOOD

If you ever doubted the legendary Neapolitan pizza, the city's pizzerie will take that doubt, beat it into a ball, throw it in the air, spin it on their collective finger, punch it down, cover it with sauce and mozzarella, and serve it *alla margherita*. The *centro storico* is full of excellent choices.

Antica Pizzeria da Michele, V. Caesare Sersale 1/3 (☎081 55 39 204; www.damichele.net; info@damichele.net), at the corner of V. Colletta. From P. Garibaldi, take C. Umberto I and turn right. Huge line outside is an even better indication of quality than the legion of reviews, which are correct in proclaiming da Michele's the best pizza in the world. Serves only marinara and margherita, the perfect formula for which has been refined and practiced since shortly after the shop opened in 1870. Walk in and get a number from a pizza chefs or order your pie to go and watch them work their magic at the wood-fired oven. Pizza €4-5. Open M-Sa 10am-11pm. Cash only. ❶

Gino Sorbillo, V. dei Tribunali 35 (☎081 44 66 43; www.sorbillo.eu), in the *centro storico* near Vco. San Paolo. The original owner created both the *ripieno al forno* (calzone) and 21 pizza-making children, 3 of whom (Gino, Antonio, and Esterina) have "Sorbillo" restaurants near each other along V. dei Tribunali. Reservation may reduce your wait time. Both floors are always abuzz with customers. Basic marinara (€3) and margherita (€3.50) never tasted so good, yet this is the one place to feast on a calzone *fritto al forno* (literally "fried in the oven"; €6.50). Pizza €3-7. Cover €1. Open M-Sa noon-3:30pm and 7pm-11:30pm. Closed 3 weeks in Aug. MC/V. ❶

Gay-Odin, V. Toledo 427 (☎081 55 13 491; www.gay-odin.it), in the *centro storico*. Also at V. Vittoria Colonna 15/B (☎081 41 82 82) off P. Amedeo in Chiaia, and V. Benedicto Croce 61 (☎081 55 10 794) near P. Plebiscito. Chocolate treats at this shop include *foresta,* a sweet and crumbly chocolate stalk (from €1 for a small twig to €9 for a trunk best shared with friends). Also offers 12 flavors of gourmet chocolate gelato. Open M-Sa 9:30am-1:30pm and 4:30-8pm, Su 10am-2pm. AmEx/MC/V. ❶

Trattoria Nennella, Vco. Lungo Teatro Nuovo 105 (☎081 41 43 38). Family-run trattoria with fantastic daily *menù* (primo, secondo, *contorno,* fruit, and wine; €10). Local cuisine at an unbeatable value attracts hordes of Neapolitans nightly. Don't be surprised if the jovial waiters slam a watermelon down and chop it up in front of you, without warning. Open Sept.-July M-Sa noon-3pm and 7-10:30pm. Cash only. ❷

Hosteria Toledo, Vco. Giardinetto 78/A (☎081 42 12 57; www.hosteriatoledo.it; info@hosteriatoledo.it). Neapolitan comfort food. Tons of antipasti, pasta, and seafood options. If you can't decide, try the chef's surprise—it rarely disappoints. Try the fried zucchini with mint and vinegar (€3), a favorite passed down from Mamma Sosora. Primi and secondi €6-18. Pizza from €5. Cover €2; €1 for pizza. Service 10%. Open M and Th-Su 1-4pm and 7pm-midnight, Tu 1pm-4pm. D/MC/V. ❸

Storico Gran Caffè Gambrinus, V. Chiaia 1/2 (☎081 41 75 82; www.caffegambrinus.com; info@caffegambrinus.com), off P. del Plebiscito. No visit to the impressive *piazza* is complete without a stop at this equally grand coffee spot. Established in 1860 and renovated in the Liberty style in 1890, the *caffè* still prepares hazelnut cream coffee (€2, €4.50 with table service), historically sipped by Ernest Hemingway, Oscar Wilde, Italian presidents, and Neapolitans alike. Frozen desserts from its spectacular *gelateria* start at €5.50. Beware the large differences in price between counter and table service. Open Su-Thu 7am-1am, F 7am-2am, Sa 7am-3am. AmEx/MC/V. ❶

SIGHTS

MUSEO ARCHEOLOGICO NAZIONALE. Situated in a 16th-century *palazzo* and former military barracks, one of the world's oldest archaeological museums contains treasures from Pompeii, Herculaneum, and the personal collection of Charles Bourbon. Unreliable labeling makes a guidebook, tour, or audio tour a good investment. The mezzanine has a mosaic room; one design features a fearless Alexander the Great routing the Persian army. Check out the Farnese Bull, the largest extant ancient statue. The *Gabinetto Segreto* (secret cabinet) of Aphrodite grants glimpses into the goddess's life. *(M: P. Cavour. Turn right from the station and walk 2 blocks. ☎081 44 22 149. Open M and W-Su 9am-7:30pm. €6.50, EU students €3.25, under 18 and over 65 free. Audio tour in English, French, or Italian €4.)*

MUSEO AND GALLERIE DI CAPODIMONTE. Housed in another 16th-century *palazzo*, the museum resides inside a park often filled with locals. A plush royal apartment and the Italian National Picture Gallery lie within the palace. Among its impressive works are Bellini's *Transfiguration*, Masaccio's *Crucifixion*, and Titian's *Danae*. *(Take bus #178, C64, R4, M4, or M5 from the Archaeological Museum and exit at the gate to the park, on the right. 2 entrances: Porta Piccola and Porta Grande. ☎081 74 99 109. Open M-Tu and Th-Su 8:30am-7:30pm. €7.50, after 2pm €6.50.)*

PALAZZO REALE AND MASCHIO ANGIONO. The 17th-century Palazzo Reale contains opulent royal apartments, the **Museo di Palazzo Reale,** and a view from the terrace of the **Royal Chapel.** *(P. Plebescito 1. Take the R2 bus from P. Garibaldi to P. Trieste e Trento and walk around the palazzo to the entrance on P. Plebiscito. ☎081 40 05 47; www.pierreci.it. Open M-Tu and Th-Su 9am-7pm. €4, EU students €2, under 18 and over 65 free.)* The **Biblioteca Nazionale** stores 1½ million volumes, including the scrolls from the **Villa dei Papiri** in Herculaneum. *(☎081 78 19 231. Open M-F 10am-1pm. Reservations required.)* The **Teatro San Carlo**'s acoustics are reputed to top those of Milan's La Scala. *(Theater entrance on P. Trieste e Trento. ☎081 79 72 331; www.teatrosancarlo.it. Open daily 9am-7pm.)* It's impossible to miss **Maschio Angiono,** whose five turrets shadow the Bay of Naples. Built in 1284 by Charles II of Anjou as his royal residence, the fortress's most stunning feature is its entrance, where reliefs depict the arrival of Alphonse I of Aragon in 1443. The castle also holds the magnificent **Hall of the Barons,** where King Ferdinand once trapped rebellious barons. Bullet holes from WWII are visible on the northern wall. *(P. Municipio. Take the R2 bus from P. Garibaldi. ☎081 42 01 241. Open M-Sa 9am-7pm. €5.)*

NAPOLI SOTTERRANEA (CATACOMBS AND THE UNDERGROUND). The catacombs of S. Gennaro, S. Gaudioso, and S. Severo all date back to the early centuries AD. Tours of the subterranean alleys beneath the city are fascinating: they involve crawling through narrow underground passageways, spotting Mussolini-era graffiti, and exploring Roman aqueducts. Napoli Sotterranea runs below the historic center. *(P. S. Gaetano 68. Take V. dei Tribunali and turn left right before S. Paolo Maggiore. ☎081 29 69 44; www.napolisotterranea.org. Tours every 2hr. M-F noon-4pm, Sa-Su 10am-6pm. €9.30, students €8.)*

NIGHTLIFE

Content to groove at small clubs and discos during the winter, Neapolitans take to the streets and *piazze* in summer. **Piazza Vanvitelli** is accessible by the funicular from V. Toledo or the bus C28 from P. Vittoria. **Via Santa Maria La Nova** is another hot spot. Outdoor bars are popular in **Piazza Bellini,** near P. Dante. **ARCI-GAY/Lesbica** (☎081 55 28 815) has info on gay and lesbian club nights.

Rising South, V. San Sebastiano 19 (☎081 33 36 53 42 73; www.risingsouth.it), near P. Gesù Nuovo. *Enoteca,* bar, cultural association, cinema—this club does it all. Plush, Oriental carpets, vintage chandeliers, and a soundproof main hall carved from tufa set the scene at this student favorite for term-time fun. Mixed drinks €3-6. Open as a bar Sept.-May Tu-Su 10pm-3am (depending on weather) and for special events in summer.

Caffè Letterario Evaluna, P. Bellini 72 (☎081 29 23 72; www.evaluna.it). Appeals to an intellectual crowd or those who have always wanted to drink in a library (for whatever reason), with books laid out for skimming and rotating photo and painting exhibitions; focus on feminist literature. Secluded outdoor courtyard holds theater performances. Beer from €3. Spirits and mixed drinks €5-7. Wine €4. Open M-Sa in summer 7pm-1am, in winter 5-11pm. AmEx/MC/V.

Lemme Lemme By Internet Bar, P. Bellini 74 (☎081 29 52 37). Located in 1 of Naples's more peaceful *piazze,* this bar has art expos, internet access, and outdoor seating. The music is as soft as the relaxed atmosphere. Internet and Wi-Fi €0.05 per min. Beer €3-5. Mixed drinks €5. *Aperitivo* daily 6pm-7pm. F Oct.-Apr. live jazz and blues. Open daily in summer 9am-2am; in winter 6pm-2am. AmEx/D/MC/V.

DAYTRIPS FROM NAPLES

HERCULANEUM. Buried by volcanic ash, Herculaneum is less excavated than its famous neighbor, Pompeii. A modern city sits on the remains of the ancient town. Don't miss the **House of Deer.** (Open daily 8:30am-7:30pm. €11.) As its name suggests, the **House of the Mosaic of Neptune and Amphitrite** is known for its mosaics. The **tourist office** (☎081 78 81 243) is at V. IV Novembre 84. *(Take the Circumvesuviana train, ☎081 77 22 444, from Naples to the Ercolano Scavi stop, dir.: Sorrento. 20min. The city is 500m downhill.)*

POMPEII. On the morning of August 24, AD 79, a deadly cloud of volcanic ash from Mt. Vesuvius settled over the Roman city of Pompeii, catching the 12,000 prosperous residents by surprise and engulfing the city in suffocating black clouds. Mere hours after the eruption, stately buildings, works of art, and human bodies were sealed in hardened casts of ash. These natural tombs would remain undisturbed until 1748, when excavations began to unearth a stunningly well-preserved picture of daily Roman life. Walk down V. della Marina to reach the colonnaded **Forum,** which was once the civic and religious center of the city. Exit the Forum through the upper end by the cafeteria and head right on V. della Fortuna to reach the **House of the Faun,** where a bronze dancing faun and the spectacular Alexander Mosaic (today in the Museo Archeologico Nazionale) were found. Continue on V. della Fortuna and turn left on V. dei Vettii to reach the **House of the Vettii** and the most vivid frescoes in Pompeii. Backtrack on V. dei Vettii, cross V. della Fortuna to V. Storto, turn left on V. degli Augustali, and take a quick right to reach a small frescoed brothel (the *Lupenare*). V. dei Teatri, across the street, leads to the oldest standing **amphitheater** in the world (80 BC). To get to the **Villa of the Mysteries,** the ancient city's best-preserved villa, head west on V. della Fortuna, right on V. Consolare, and all the way up Porta Ercolano and V. della Tombe. *(Take the Circumvesuviana train, ☎081 77 22 444, from Naples to the Pompeii Scavi stop, dir.: Sorrento. 40min., 2 per hr., round-trip €2.30. Archaeological site open daily Apr.-Oct. 8:30am-7:30pm; Nov.-Mar. 8:30am-5pm. €11.)*

CASERTA. Few palaces, no matter how opulent, can hold a candle to Caserta's **La Reggia,** often referred to as "The Versailles of Naples." A world apart from the stark brutality of Pompeii, the palace and grounds resonate with a passion for art and beauty. When King Charles III commissioned the palace in 1751, he intended it to rival Louis XIV's spectacular abode. The vast lawns filled with fountains and sculptures culminate in a 75m manmade waterfall—the setting for the final scene of *Star Wars* (1977). To the right are the **English Gardens,** with fake ruins inspired by Pompeii and Paestum. The **palazzo** boasts 1200 rooms, 1742 windows, 34 staircases, and grandiose furnishings. *(Trains run from Naples to Caserta. 40min., 98 per day. Open M and W-Su 9am-7:30pm. Palazzo and gardens €6.)*

THE NETHERLANDS (NEDERLAND)

The Dutch take great pride in their country, in part because they effectively created vast stretches of it, claiming land from the ocean using an extensive system of dikes and canals. With most of their country's land area below sea level, the task of keeping their iconic tulips and windmills on dry ground has become something of a national pastime. Over the centuries, planners built dikes higher and higher to hold back the sea, culminating in a new "flexible coast" policy that depends on spillways and reservoirs to contain potentially disastrous floods. For a people whose land constantly threatens to become ocean, the staunch Dutch have a deeply grounded culture and a down-to-earth friendliness. Time-tested art, ambitious architecture, and dynamic nightlife make the Netherlands one of the most popular travel destinations in Western Europe.

HISTORY

FROM ROMANS TO HABSBURGS (100 BC TO AD 1579). Romans under **Julius Caesar** invaded the region in the first century BC, displacing Celtic and Germanic tribes. The native Germanic tribes had the last laugh in the AD fourth century as their retaliating forces swept through Roman lands in the Low Countries, the Netherlands, Belgium, and Luxembourg. Freedom was short-lived: the **Franks** supplanted the Romans from the fifth to the eighth century. During this period, towns rose as powerful, independent centers. The **House of Burgundy** infiltrated the region in the 14th century to establish a centralized yet truncated monarchy. By the 15th century, the Austrian **Habsburgs** had seized the Dutch crown by marriage. When **Philip I** of the Habsburgs married into the Spanish royal family, the Netherlands was subjected to another foreign power.

UTRECHT AND THE START OF THE GOLDEN AGE (1579-1651). The Netherlands was officially founded in 1579 under the **Union of Utrecht,** which aimed to form an independent group of provinces and cities led by a **States-General.** Under Prince **William of Orange,** the Dutch declared independence from Spain in 1580. This sparked a prolonged struggle and religious debate between the Protestant Netherlands and Catholic Spain. The conflict was settled in 1609 by the **Twelve Years' Truce,** which recognized the Netherlands' sovereignty. But the feisty Spanish kept fighting until Dutchman **Frederick Henry** defeated them on land, while the Dutch navy near Cuba and along the English coast stopped them at sea. An embarrassed Spain offered the **Peace of Westphalia** (1648), which acknowledged Dutch independence and pushed for an alliance against growing France.

During the 17th-century **Age of Exploration,** also known as the **Dutch Golden Age,** Dutch conquerors fanned out over the globe and gained control of all the major trade routes across Europe. This generated incredible prosperity for the Dutch—the **Dutch East India Company** was responsible for much of this economic surge—but also trod on the toes of the British, who resented invasion of their commercial spheres. To protect trade routes, the company colonized the **Cape of Good Hope** and other strategic posts. Meanwhile, the **Dutch West India Company**

explored the New World, creating colonies such as **New Amsterdam** (now New York). This global activity spurred the growth of Dutch wealth and trade.

WAR GAMES AND POWER STRUGGLES (1651-1780). Neighboring European powers hotly resented the domestic and foreign success of the Dutch. England sought recompense by passing **Navigation Acts** in 1651 and 1660 aimed at severely limiting Dutch incursions on English trade, then by attacking the Dutch navy. The vastly stronger Brits prevailed, forced peace, and secretly drafted the **Act of Seclusion,** forever banning the independence-seeking Prince of Orange from Dutch politics. Grand Pensionary **Johan de Witt** managed to rebuild the Netherlands' military and economy, but bitterness between English and the Dutch remained paramount. With the restoration of **King Charles II** of England in 1660, the Dutch carefully negotiated an alliance with the French and sabotaged the English fleet in 1667 in the **Raid on the Medway.**

In 1667, France reneged and invaded the Netherlands, threatening the interests of both the English and the Dutch, who in turn formed an unlikely coalition. Betrayed, **King Louis XIV** of France proposed an alliance with the English, heavily subsidized by the French. When England accepted in 1672, the Netherlands found itself in an impossible situation, at war against both countries. Against all odds, under the leadership of **William III,** the country repeatedly managed to defeat the Franco-English fleets. However, the glory of winning was quickly undermined by a strategic marriage: William wed his first cousin **Mary,** daughter of English king James II, and ascended the throne in England with the 1688 **Glorious Revolution,** subjecting the Netherlands to England. The Dutch entered a period of decline, with international trade dwindling in the 18th century as that of neighboring countries steadily grew.

FRENCH RULE AND INDEPENDENCE (1780-1914). The Netherlands was the second country, after France, to recognize the American Revolution—sparking English anger, another attack, and yet another war. In 1795, French forces under **Napoleon Bonaparte** invaded, conquering a Netherlands weakened by war and perhaps overly sympathetic to the French Revolution. After Napoleon's defeat at Waterloo, the **Treaty of Vienna** (1815) established the Kingdom of the Netherlands, which included Belgium and Luxembourg. Although this new union did not last, with Belgium revolting and gaining independence in 1839, King **William I of Orange** still managed to rebuild the economy and trade routes. Under William, the Dutch created a constitution establishing the Netherlands as a **constitutional monarchy** in which parliament held most of the power, leading to the formation of modern political parties. **Queen Wilhelmina** succeeded to the throne in 1890, breaking the tradition of male ascendancy.

THE WORLD WARS (1914-1945). When **World War I** broke out, the Dutch remained neutral, focusing on trade and economy. Surrounded by combatting nations, their country suffered deprivation as intense as that of WWI's active participants. **World War II** again breached Dutch neutrality: the Nazis invaded in May 1940 and occupied the nation for five years. The Dutch suffered horribly. All acts of resistance were punished severely, and the population nearly starved. Jews, including **Anne Frank** and her family, were sent to concentration camps. Frank's diary is now a quintessential account of life under Nazi rule and her home was made into a museum in Amsterdam (p. 461).

THE POST-WAR ERA (1945-1990). After the war, Wilhelmina supported sweeping democratic changes for the nation, creating proportional representation in government. The nation also abandoned its policy of neutrality, joining **NATO** and creating the **Benelux** economic union with Belgium and Luxembourg. To recover from the devestation of WWII, the government started an economic policy that focused on industrial and commercial expansion.

While the nation experienced relative peace in the 1950s, the economic and political problems of the 1960s brought rioting students and workers. In the 1980s, Dutch politics saw the disintegration of old parties and alliances. The recent rise of the **Christian Democratic Appeal (CDA)** has provided a new outlet for major Christian factions. Though centrist, the CDA supports limiting drug legality, prostitution, and abortion. The center-left **Labour Party (PvdA)** has managed to avoid ties with extreme groups and allied with the CDA in 1989. The **Liberal Party (VVD)** supports private business and hands-off economic policy.

TODAY

The Netherlands is an integral member of the **European Union (EU).** The government is a parliamentary democracy with a constitutional monarchy: parliament has all legislative power while **Queen Beatrix,** who has been queen since 1980, holds a symbolic role. Immigration has become a central issue in politics. On both the right and the left, people fear the influx of conservative newcomers who might threaten their open Dutch society. In 2002 elections, populist politician **Pim Fortuyn** and his new **Lijst Pim Fortuyn (LPF)** party, which advanced a platform with many anti-immigration tenets, seemed on their way to a victory. Fortuyn was dramatically assassinated just before the parliamentary election. The CDA won the election, attracting many who might have supported Fortuyn. Although the party was leaderless, the LPF still gained seats in parliament. **Jan Peter Balkenende,** the leader of the CDA, has been prime minister since 2002 and is currently at the head of a coalition, formed following the 2006 elections, between the CDA, the PvdA, and the **Christian Union (CU)** party.

Long known for its relaxed drug policies, the Netherlands has been trying to crack down, especially in order to diminish its role as European entry point for cocaine and ecstasy. The Netherlands continues to play a disproportionately large role in global politics, having taken on the role of international arbiter. The **International Court of Justice,** housed in the Vredespaleis (Peace Palace) in **The Hague,** oversees disputes between sovereign nations.

ESSENTIALS

FACTS AND FIGURES

OFFICIAL NAME: Kingdom of the Netherlands.

CAPITAL: Amsterdam; The Hague is the seat of government.

MAJOR CITIES: The Hague, Rotterdam, Utrecht.

POPULATION: 16,645,000.

LAND AREA: 41,500 sq. km.

TIME ZONE: GMT +1.

LANGUAGE: Dutch; English is spoken almost universally.

RELIGIONS: Catholic (31%), Protestant (20%), Muslim (6%).

LAND BELOW SEA LEVEL: One-third of the country, kept dry by an extensive network of dikes 2400km (1500 miles) long.

WHEN TO GO

July and August are lovely for travel in the Netherlands, which results in crowded hostels and lengthy lines. If you fancy a bit more elbow room, you may prefer April, May, and early June, as tulips and fruit trees furiously bloom and temperatures hover around 12-20°C (53-68°F). The Netherlands is famously drizzly year-round, so travelers should bring raingear.

DOCUMENTS AND FORMALITIES

EMBASSIES AND CONSULATES. Foreign embassies and consulates are in The Hague. Both the UK and the US have consulates in Amsterdam (p. 449). Dutch embassies abroad include: **Australia,** 120 Empire Circuit, Yarralumla Canberra, ACT, 2600 (☎262 20 94 00; www.netherlands.org.au); **Canada,** 350 Albert St., Ste. 2020, Ottawa, ON, K1R 1A4 (☎613-237-5030; www.netherlandsembassy.ca); **Ireland,** 160 Merrion Rd., Dublin, 4 (☎12 69 34 44; www.netherlandsembassy.ie); **New Zealand,** P.O. Box 840, at Ballance and Featherston St., Wellington (☎044 71 63 90; www.netherlandsembassy.co.nz); **UK,** 38 Hyde Park Gate, London, SW7 5DP (☎20 75 90 32 00; www.netherlands-embassy.org.uk); **US,** 4200 Linnean Ave., NW, Washington, DC, 20008 (☎202-244-5300; www.netherlands-embassy.org).

VISA AND ENTRY INFORMATION. EU citizens do not need a visa. Citizens of Australia, Canada, New Zealand, and the US do not need a visa for stays of up to 90 days, beginning upon entry into any of the countries in the EU's freedom of movement zone. For more info, see p. 8. For stays longer than 90 days, all non-EU citizens need visas (around US$80), available at Dutch embassies and consulates or online at www.minbuza.nl/en/home, the website for the Dutch Ministry of Foreign Affairs. It normally takes approximately two weeks after application submission to receive a visa.

TOURIST SERVICES AND MONEY

EMERGENCY **Ambulance, Fire,** and **Police:** ☎112.

TOURIST OFFICES. **VVV** (vay-vay-vay) tourist offices are marked by triangular blue signs. The website www.visitholland.com is also a useful resource. The **Holland Pass** (www.hollandpass.com, €25) grants free admission to five museums or sites of your choice and gives discounts at restaurants and attractions.

MONEY. The **euro (€)** has replaced the **guilder** as the unit of currency in the Netherlands. As a general rule, it's cheaper to exchange money in the Netherlands than at home. A bare-bones day in the Netherlands will cost €35-40; a slightly more comfortable day will run €50-60. Hotels and restaurants include a service charge in the bill; additional tips are appreciated but not necessary. Taxi drivers are generally tipped 10% of the fare.

The Netherlands has a 19% **value added tax (VAT),** a sales tax applied to retail goods. The prices given in *Let's Go* include VAT. In the airport upon exiting the EU, non-EU citizens who have stayed in the EU fewer than 180 days can claim a refund on the tax paid for purchases at participating stores. In order to qualify for a refund in a store, you must spend at least €130; make sure to ask for a refund form when you pay. For more info on VAT refunds, see p. 13.

TRANSPORTATION

BY PLANE. Most international flights land at **Schiphol Airport** in Amsterdam (**AMS;** ☎800 72 44 74 65, info ☎900 724 4746; www.schiphol.nl). Budget airlines, like **Ryanair** and **easyJet,** fly out of **Eindhoven Airport** (**EIN;** ☎314 02 91 98 18; www.eindhovenairport.com), 10min. away from Eindhoven, and Schiphol Airport, to locations around Europe. The Dutch national airline, **KLM** (☎020 474 7747, US ☎800-447-4747, UK ☎08705 074 074; www.klm.com), offers student discounts. For more info on traveling by plane around Europe, see p. 33.

BY TRAIN. The national rail company is the efficient **Nederlandse Spoorwegen** (**NS;** Netherlands Railways; www.ns.nl). **Sneltreinen** are the fastest, while **stoptreinen** make many local stops. One-way tickets are called *enkele reis*. Same-day, round-trip tickets *(dagretour)* are valid only on the day of purchase, but are roughly 15% cheaper than normal round-trip tickets. *Weekendretour* tickets are not quite as cheap, but are valid from 7pm Friday through 4pm Monday. A day pass *(dagkaart)* allows unlimited travel throughout the country for one day, for the price equivalent to the most expensive one-way fare across the country. **Eurail** and **InterRail** have passes that are valid in the Netherlands. **Holland Rail** passes are good for three or five travel days in any one-month period. Although available in the US, the Holland Rail pass is cheaper in the Netherlands at DER Travel Service or RailEurope offices. Overall, train service tends to be faster than bus service. For more detailed informaton about traveling by train throughout the countries in Europe, see p. 37.

ALL ABOARD. Nederlandse Spoorwegen is the Dutch national rail company, operating the country's intercity train service. Their website, www.ns.nl, has a user-friendly English-language section with train times, prices, and door-to-door directions for all stops in the Netherlands.

BY BUS. With transportation largely covered by the extensive rail system, bus lines are limited to short trips and travel to areas without rail lines. A **nationalized fare system** covers city buses, trams, and long-distance buses. The country is divided into zones: a trip between destinations in the same zone costs two strips on a *strippenkaart* (strip card); a trip in two zones will set you back three strips. On buses, tell the driver your destination and he or she will cancel the correct number of strips; on trams and subways, stamp your own in either a yellow box at the back of the tram or in the subway station. Drivers sell cards with two, three, and eight strips, but it's much more cost efficient to buy 15-strip or 45-strip cards at tourist offices, post offices, and some newsstands. Day passes *(dagkaarten)* are valid for travel throughout the country and are discounted as special summer tickets *(zomerzwerfkaarten)* June through August. Riding without a ticket can result in a fine.

BY CAR. Normally, tourists with a driver's license valid in their home country can drive in the Netherlands for fewer than 185 days. The country has well-maintained roadways, although drivers may cringe at high fuel prices, traffic, and scarce parking near Amsterdam, The Hague, and Rotterdam. The yellow cars of the **Royal Dutch Touring Club** (**ANWB;** toll-free ☎08 00 08 88) patrol many major roads, and offer roadside assistance in the case of a breakdown.

BY BIKE AND BY THUMB. **Cycling** is the way to go in the Netherlands—distances between cities are short, the countryside is absolutely flat, and most streets have separate bike lanes. Bike rentals run €6-10 per day and €30-40 per week. For a database of bike rental shops and other cycling tips and information, visit www.holland.com/global/discover/active/cycling. **Hitchhiking** is illegal on motorways but common elsewhere. *Let's Go* does not recommend hitchhiking.

KEEPING IN TOUCH

EMAIL AND THE INTERNET. Internet cafes are plentiful throughout the Netherlands. Travelers with Wi-Fi-enabled computers may be able to take advantage of an increasing number of hot spots, which offer Wi-Fi for free or for a small nominal fee. Websites like www.jiwire.com, www.wi-fihotspotlist.com, and www.locfinder.net can help you locate hot spots.

PHONE CODES	**Country code:** 31. **International dialing prefix:** 00. For more info on how to place international calls, see **Inside Back Cover.**

TELEPHONE. Some pay phones still accept coins, but **phone cards** are the rule. KPT and Telfort are the most widely accepted varieties, the former available at post offices and the latter at train stations (from €5). Whenever possible, use a calling card for international phone calls, as long-distance rates for national phone services are often very high. **Mobile phones** are an increasingly popular and economical option. Major mobile carriers include Vodafone, KPN, T-Mobile, and Telfort. For directory assistance, dial ☎09 00 80 08, for collect calls ☎08 00 01 01. Direct-dial access numbers for calling out of the Netherlands include: **AT&T Direct** (☎0800 022 9111); **British Telecom** (☎0800 022 0444); **Canada Direct** (☎0800 022 9116); **Telecom New Zealand** (☎0800 022 4464). For more info on calling home from Europe, see p. 20.

MAIL. Post offices are generally open Monday through Friday 9am-5pm, Thursday or Friday nights, and Saturday mornings in some larger towns. Amsterdam and Rotterdam have 24hr. post offices. Mailing a postcard or letter within the EU costs €0.69 and up to €0.85 outside of Europe. To receive mail in the Netherlands, have mail delivered **Poste Restante.** Mail will go to the main post office unless you specify a subsidiary by street address. Address mail to be held according to the following example: First Name, Last Name, Poste Restante, followed by the address of the post office. Bring a passport to pick up your mail from the office. There may be a small nominal fee.

ACCOMMODATIONS AND CAMPING

NETHERLANDS	❶	❷	❸	❹	❺
ACCOMMODATIONS	under €36	€36-55	€56-77	€78-100	over €100

VVV offices around the country supply travelers with accommodation listings and can almost always reserve rooms for a €2-5 fee. **Private rooms** cost about two-thirds the price of a hotel, but are harder to find; check with the VVV. During July and August, many cities add a tourist tax (€1-2) to the price of all rooms. The country's 30 **Hostelling International (HI) youth hostels** are run by **Stayokay** (www.stayokay.com) and are dependably clean and modern. There is camping across the country, although sites tend to be crowded during the summer months; **CityCamps Holland** has a network of 17 well-maintained sites. The website www.strandheem.nl has camping information.

FOOD AND DRINK

NETHERLANDS	❶	❷	❸	❹	❺
FOOD	under €8	€8-12	€13-17	€18-22	over €22

Traditional Dutch cuisine is hearty, heavy, and meaty. Expect bread for breakfast and lunch, topped with melting *hagelslag* (flaked chocolate topping) in the morning and cheese later in the day. Generous portions of meat and fish make up dinner, traditionally the only hot meal of the day. Seafood, from various grilled fish and shellfish to fish stews and raw herring, is popular. For a truly authentic Dutch meal (most commonly available in May and June), ask for *spargel* (white asparagus), served with potatoes, ham, and eggs. Light snacks include *tostis* (hot grilled-cheese sandwiches, sometimes with ham) and *broodjes* (light, cold sandwiches). The Dutch colonial legacy has brought Surinamese and Indonesian cuisine to the Netherlands, bestowing cheaper and lighter dining options and a wealth of falafel stands in cities. Wash down meals with brimming glasses of Heineken or Amstel.

BEYOND TOURISM

Volunteer and work opportunities often revolve around international politics or programs resulting from liberal social attitudes. Studying in the Netherlands can entail in-depth looks at sex and drugs. For more info on opportunities across Europe, see the **Beyond Tourism** chapter p. 45.

COC Amsterdam, Rozenstr. 14, Amsterdam (☎626 3087; www.cocamsterdam.nl). The world's oldest organization dedicated to the support of homosexuals and their families. Contact for involvement in support groups, gay pride activities, and publications.

University of Amsterdam, Spui 21, Amsterdam (☎525 8080 or 525 3333; www.uva.nl/english). Amsterdam's largest university offers degree programs in Dutch. Open to college and graduate students. The Summer Institute on Sexuality, Culture, and Society (www.ishss.uva.nl/summerinstitute) examines sexuality in various cultures. Tuition €1445-10,000 per year, depending on the program. Discounts offered for EU citizens.

AMSTERDAM ☎020

Amsterdam's reputation precedes it—and what a reputation it is. Born out of a murky bog and cobbled together over eight centuries, the "Dam on the River Amstel" (pop. 743,000) tempts visitors with its blend of hedonism and grandeur. Thick clouds of marijuana smoke waft from subdued coffee shops, and countless bicycles zip past blooming tulip markets. Yet there's much more to Amsterdam than its stereotypes. Against the legacy of Vincent van Gogh's thick swirls and Johannes Vermeer's luminous interiors, gritty street artists spray graffiti in protest. Politicians have sought to curb some of Amsterdam's excesses in recent years, closing over 700 coffee shops and half of the famous red-lit windows, yet the city's rebellious attitudes seems to have grown more pronounced in response.

INTERCITY TRANSPORTATION

Flights: Schiphol Airport (AMS; ☎0800 72 447 465, flight info ☎0900 724 4746; www.schiphol.nl). **Sneltraihen** connects the airport to Centraal Station (20min., €5.40).

Trains: Centraal Station, Stationspl. 1 (☎0900 9292, €0.50 per min.; www.ns.nl). To: **Groningen** (2-3hr., 2 per hr., €26.60); **Haarlem** (20min., 6 per hr., €3.80); **The Hague** (50min., 1-6 per hr., €10.10); **Rotterdam** (1hr., 1-5 per hr., €13.30); **Utrecht** (30min., 3-6 per hr., €6.70); **Brussels, BEL** (2-3hr.; every hr.; €32, under 26 €24).

ORIENTATION

Let the canals guide you through Amsterdam's cozy but confusing neighborhoods. In the city center, water runs in concentric half-circles, beginning at Centraal Station. The **Singel** runs around **Centrum,** which includes the **Oude Zijd** (Old Side), the infamous **Red Light District,** and the **Nieuwe Zijd** (New Side), which, oddly enough, is older than the Oude Zijd. Barely a kilometer in diameter, the Centrum overflows with bars, brothels, clubs, and tourists wading through wafts of marijuana smoke. The next three canals—the **Herengracht,** the **Keizersgracht,** and the **Prinsengracht**—constitute the **Canal Ring.** Nearby **Rembrandtplein** and **Leidseplein** are full of classy nightlife, spanning from flashy bars to traditional *bruin cafes.* Just over the **Singelgracht, Museumplein** is home to the city's most renowned art museums. The verdant, sprawling **Vondelpark** also houses more of the city's reputable art musuems. Farther out lie the more residential Amsterdam neighborhoods: to the north and west, the **Scheepvaartbuurt, Jordaan, Westerpark,** and **Oud-West;** to the south and east, **Jodenbuurt, Plantage, De Pijp,** and far-flung **Greater Amsterdam.** These districts are densely populated and boast excellent restaurants and museums.

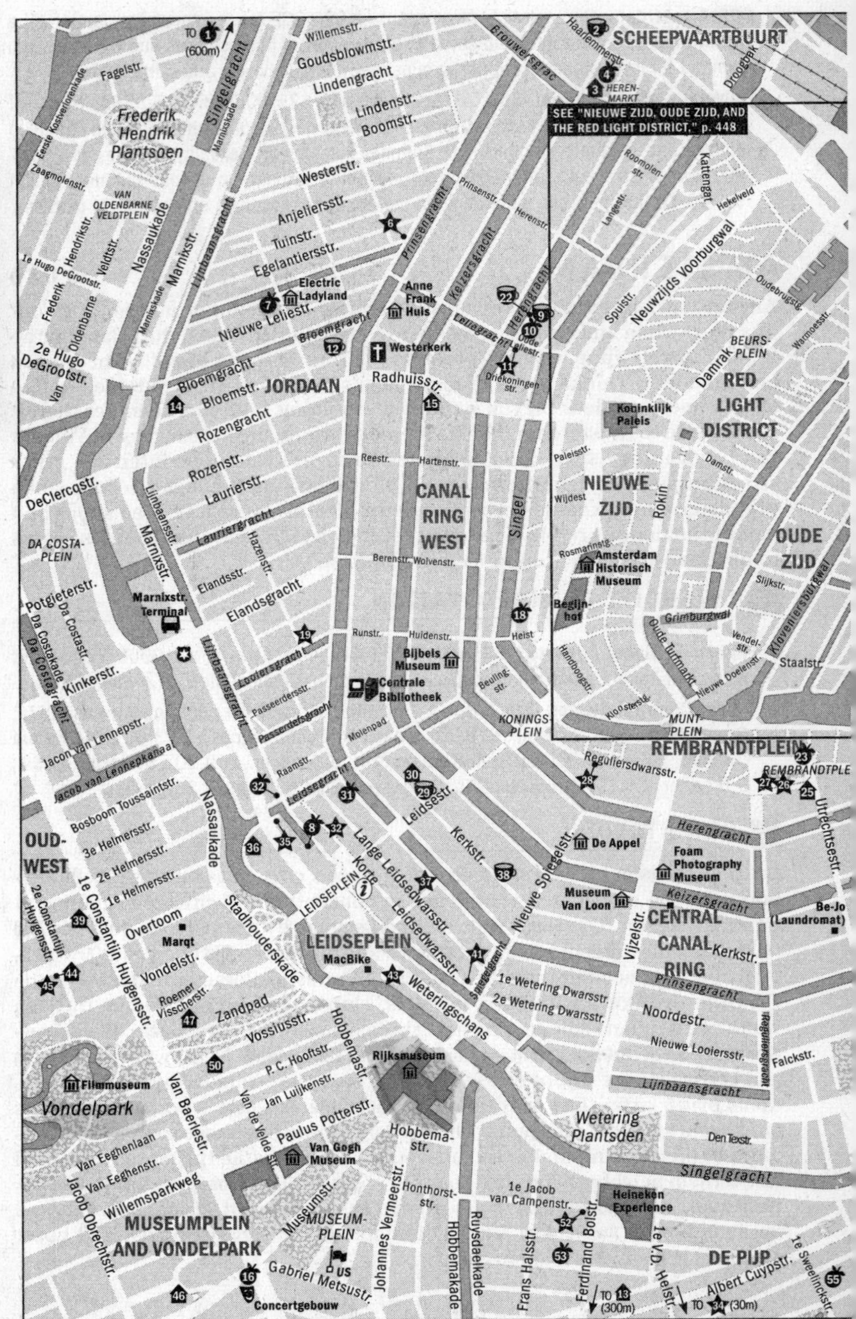

SCHEEPVAARTBUURT
SEE "NIEUWE ZIJD, OUDE ZIJD, AND THE RED LIGHT DISTRICT," p. 448
TO 1 (600m)
Willemsstr.
Goudsblowmstr.
Lindengracht
Lindenstr.
Boomstr.
Westerstr.
Anjeliersstr.
Tuinstr.
Egelantiersstr.
Brouwersgracht
Haarlemmerstr.
HERENMARKT
Droogbak
Fagelstr.
Frederik Hendrik Plantsoen
Singelgracht
Marnixkade
Eerste Kostverlorenkade
Zaagmolenstr.
VAN OLDENBARNE VELDTPLEIN
Nassaukade
Marnixstr.
Lijnbaansgracht
Frederik Hendrikstr.
Veldtstr.
1e Hugo DeGrootstr.
Oldenbarne
2e Hugo DeGrootstr.
Van
Electric Ladyland
Anne Frank Huis
Nieuwe Leliestr.
Bloemgracht
Westerkerk
Prinsengracht
Prinsenstr.
Herenstr.
Keizersgracht
Herengracht
Leliegracht
Oude Leliestr.
Driekoningenstr.
Roomolenstr.
Langestr.
Kattengat
Hekelveld
Spuistr.
Nieuwezijds Voorburgwal
Oudebrugstr.
Warmoesstr.
BEURSPLEIN
Damrak
RED LIGHT DISTRICT
JORDAAN
Radhuisstr.
Bloemstr.
Rozengracht
Rozenstr.
Lauierstr.
Lauriergracht
Hazenstr.
Elandsstr.
Elandsgracht
Koninklijk Paleis
Paleisstr.
Damstr.
Wijdest
NIEUWE ZIJD
Rokin
OUDE ZIJD
Reestr.
Hartenstr.
CANAL RING WEST
Singel
Berenstr.
Wolvenstr.
Rosmarinstg.
Amsterdam Historisch Museum
Begijnhof
Slijkstr.
Grimburgwal
Oude Turfmarkt
Vendelstr.
Kloveniersburgwal
Staalstr.
Handboogstr.
Nieuwe Doelenstr.
Kloosterstg.
MUNTPLEIN
DeClercqstr.
DA COSTAPLEIN
Potgieterstr.
Da Costastr.
Da Costakade
Da Costagracht
Marnixstr. Terminal
Lijnbaansstr.
Kinkerstr.
Lijnbaansgracht
Looiersgracht
Passeerdersstr.
Passeerdersgracht
Runstr.
Huidenstr.
Bijbels Museum
Centrale Bibliotheek
Heist
Beulingstr.
KONINGSPLEIN
Molenpad
REMBRANDTPLEIN
Reguliersdwarsstr.
Jacob van Lennepstr.
Jacob van Lennepkanaal
Bosboom Toussaintstr.
Raamstr.
Leidsegracht
Leidsestr.
Herengracht
Utrechtsestr.
OUD-WEST
3e Helmersstr.
2e Helmersstr.
1e Helmersstr.
Lange Leidsedwarsstr.
Korte Leidsedwarsstr.
Kerkstr.
Nieuwe Spiegelstr.
De Appel
Foam Photography Museum
Museum Van Loon
Keizersgracht
Be-Jo (Laundromat)
2e Constantijn Huygensstr.
1e Constantijn Huygensstr.
Overtoom
Marqt
LEIDSEPLEIN
Stadhouderskade
LEIDSEPLEIN
MacBike
Spiegelgracht
Vijzelstr.
CENTRAL CANAL RING
Kerkstr.
Prinsengracht
Vondelstr.
Roemer Visscherstr.
Zandpad
Weteringschans
1e Wetering Dwarsstr.
2e Wetering Dwarsstr.
Noordestr.
Nieuwe Looiersstr.
Reguliersgracht
Falckstr.
Vossiusstr.
Hobbemastr.
Rijksmuseum
P. C. Hooftstr.
Lijnbaansgracht
Filmmuseum
Vondelpark
Van Baerlestr.
Jan Luijkenstr.
Van de Veldestr.
Paulus Potterstr.
Hobbemastr.
Wetering Plantsden
Den Texstr.
Van Eeghenlaan
Van Eeghenstr.
Van Gogh Museum
Singelgracht
Jacob Obrechtstr.
Willemsparkweg
Museumstr.
Honthorststr.
1e Jacob van Campenstr.
Heineken Experience
MUSEUMPLEIN AND VONDELPARK
MUSEUMPLEIN
Johannes Vermeerstr.
Hobbemakade
Ruysdaelkade
Frans Halsstr.
Ferdinand Bolstr.
1e V.D. Helstr.
DE PIJP
1e Sweelinckstr.
Albert Cuypstr.
US
Gabriel Metsustr.
Concertgebouw
TO 13 (300m)
TO 34 (30m)

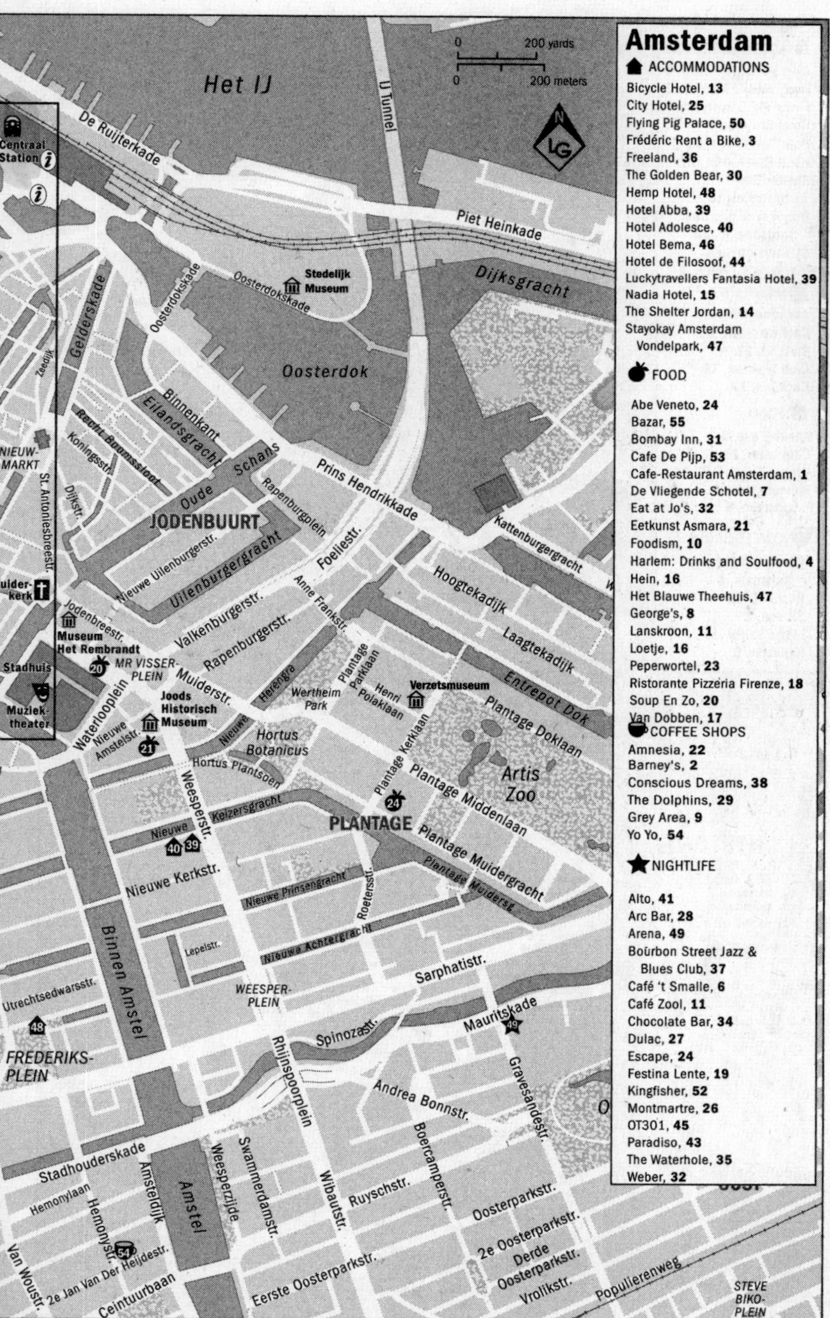
Amsterdam
ACCOMMODATIONS
Bicycle Hotel, 13
City Hotel, 25
Flying Pig Palace, 50
Frédéric Rent a Bike, 3
Freeland, 36
The Golden Bear, 30
Hemp Hotel, 48
Hotel Abba, 39
Hotel Adolesce, 40
Hotel Bema, 46
Hotel de Filosoof, 44
Luckytravellers Fantasia Hotel, 39
Nadia Hotel, 15
The Shelter Jordan, 14
Stayokay Amsterdam Vondelpark, 47
FOOD
Abe Veneto, 24
Bazar, 55
Bombay Inn, 31
Cafe De Pijp, 53
Cafe-Restaurant Amsterdam, 1
De Vliegende Schotel, 7
Eat at Jo's, 32
Eetkunst Asmara, 21
Foodism, 10
Harlem: Drinks and Soulfood, 4
Hein, 16
Het Blauwe Theehuis, 47
George's, 8
Lanskroon, 11
Loetje, 16
Peperwortel, 23
Ristorante Pizzeria Firenze, 18
Soup En Zo, 20
Van Dobben, 17
COFFEE SHOPS
Amnesia, 22
Barney's, 2
Conscious Dreams, 38
The Dolphins, 29
Grey Area, 9
Yo Yo, 54
NIGHTLIFE
Alto, 41
Arc Bar, 28
Arena, 49
Boûrbon Street Jazz & Blues Club, 37
Café 't Smalle, 6
Café Zool, 11
Chocolate Bar, 34
Dulac, 27
Escape, 24
Festina Lente, 19
Kingfisher, 52
Montmartre, 26
OT301, 45
Paradiso, 43
The Waterhole, 35
Weber, 32
0 200 yards
0 200 meters
Het IJ
IJ Tunnel
De Ruijterkade
Piet Heinkade
Dijksgracht
Centraal Station
Stedelijk Museum
Oosterdokskade
Oosterdok
Gelderskade
Zeedijk
Binnenkant
Eilandsgracht
Recht Boomssloot
Koningsstr.
NIEUW-MARKT
St. Antoniesbreestr.
Dijkstr.
Oude Schans
Prins Hendrikkade
Kattenburgergracht
Rapenburgplein
JODENBUURT
Nieuwe Uilenburgerstr.
Uilenburgergracht
Foeliestr.
Hoogtekadijk
Laagtekadijk
Entrepot Dok
Anne Frankstr.
Zuider-kerk
Jodenbreestr.
Museum Het Rembrandt
Valkenburgerstr.
Rapenburgerstr.
Stadhuis
MR VISSER-PLEIN
Muziek-theater
Waterlooplein
Muiderstr.
Joods Historisch Museum
Nieuwe Amstelstr.
Herengra
Wertheim Park
Plantage Parklaan
Henri Polaklaan
Verzetsmuseum
Plantage Doklaan
Hortus Botanicus
Hortus Plantsoen
Artis Zoo
Plantage Kerklaan
Plantage Middenlaan
PLANTAGE
Weesperstr.
Nieuwe Keizersgracht
Plantage Muidergracht
Nieuwe Kerkstr.
Nieuwe Prinsengracht
Roetersstr.
Binnen Amstel
Lepelstr.
Nieuwe Achtergracht
Sarphatistr.
WEESPER-PLEIN
Utrechtsedwarsstr.
Mauritskade
FREDERIKS-PLEIN
Spinozastr.
Rhijnspoorplein
Andrea Bonnstr.
Gravesandestr.
Stadhouderskade
Amsteldijk
Amstel
Weesperzijde
Swammerdamstr.
Wibautstr.
Boerhaavestr.
Ruyschstr.
Oosterparkstr.
2e Oosterparkstr.
Derde Oosterparkstr.
Eerste Oosterparkstr.
Vrolikstr.
Populierenweg
Hemonylaan
Hemonystr.
Van Woustr.
2e Jan Van Der Heijdestr.
Ceintuurbaan
STEVE BIKO-PLEIN

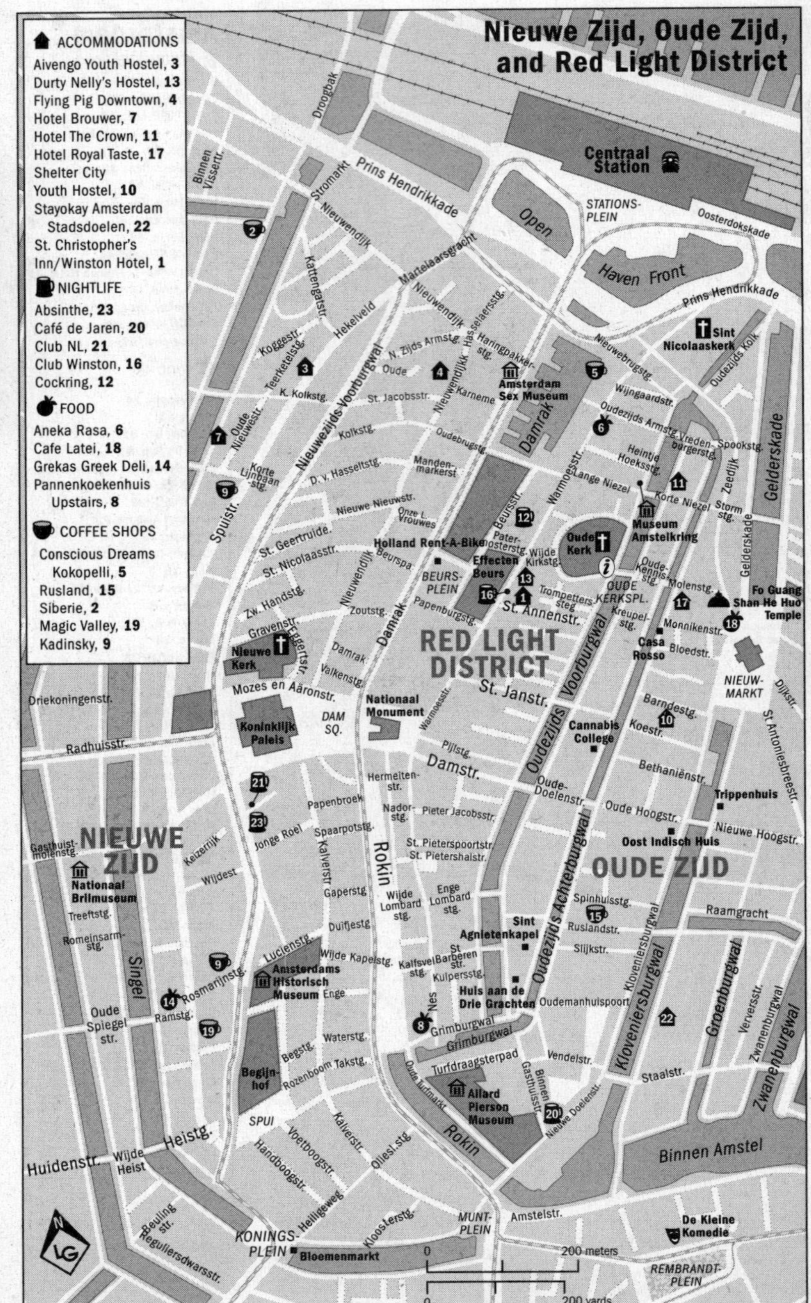

Nieuwe Zijd, Oude Zijd, and Red Light District
ACCOMMODATIONS
Aivengo Youth Hostel, 3
Durty Nelly's Hostel, 13
Flying Pig Downtown, 4
Hotel Brouwer, 7
Hotel The Crown, 11
Hotel Royal Taste, 17
Shelter City Youth Hostel, 10
Stayokay Amsterdam Stadsdoelen, 22
St. Christopher's Inn/Winston Hotel, 1
NIGHTLIFE
Absinthe, 23
Café de Jaren, 20
Club NL, 21
Club Winston, 16
Cockring, 12
FOOD
Aneka Rasa, 6
Cafe Latei, 18
Grekas Greek Deli, 14
Pannenkoekenhuis Upstairs, 8
COFFEE SHOPS
Conscious Dreams Kokopelli, 5
Rusland, 15
Siberie, 2
Magic Valley, 19
Kadinsky, 9
Centraal Station
STATIONS-PLEIN
Open Haven Front
Prins Hendrikkade
Oosterdokskade
Sint Nicolaaskerk
Amsterdam Sex Museum
Damrak
RED LIGHT DISTRICT
Oude Kerk
Museum Amstelkring
Holland Rent-A-Bike
Effecten Beurs
BEURS-PLEIN
OUDE KERKSPL.
Fo Guang Shan He Huo Temple
Casa Rosso
NIEUW-MARKT
Nieuwe Kerk
Koninklijk Paleis
DAM SQ.
Nationaal Monument
Cannabis College
Trippenhuis
Oost Indisch Huis
NIEUWE ZIJD
OUDE ZIJD
Nationaal Brilmuseum
Sint Agnietenkapel
Amsterdams Historisch Museum
Huis aan de Drie Grachten
Begijnhof
SPUI
Allard Pierson Museum
Binnen Amstel
Rokin
Singel
Kalverstr.
Spuistr.
Nieuwezijds Voorburgwal
Oudezijds Voorburgwal
Oudezijds Achterburgwal
Kloveniersburgwal
Groenburgwal
Zwanenburgwal
Gelderskade
Damstr.
Radhuisstr.
Raamgracht
Huidenstr.
Wijde Heist
Heistg.
KONINGS-PLEIN
Bloemenmarkt
MUNT-PLEIN
Amstelstr.
De Kleine Komedie
REMBRANDT-PLEIN
0 200 meters
0 200 yards

LOCAL TRANSPORTATION

Public Transportation: GVB (☎020 460 6060; www.gvb.nl), on Stationspl. in front of Centraal Station. Open M-F 7am-9pm, Sa-Su 10am-6pm. **Tram, metro,** and **bus** lines radiate from Centraal Station. Trams are the most convenient for city-center travel; the metro leads into the area's many outlying neighborhoods. Both run daily 6am-12:30am. **Night buses** traverse the complex city roads 12:30am-7:30am; pick up a schedule and map at the GVB (€3 per trip). Two strips (€1.60) gets you to nearly every sight within the city center and includes unlimited transfers for 1hr.

Buses: Trains are much quicker, but the GVB will direct you to a bus stop for domestic destinations not included on a rail line. **Muiderpoort** (2 blocks east of Oosterpark) sends buses east; **Marnixstation** (at the corner of Marnixstr. and Kinkerstr.) west; and the **Stationsplein** head both north and south.

Bike Rental: Frédéric Rent a Bike, Brouwersgr. 78 (☎020 624 5509; www.frederic.nl), in the Scheepvaartbuurt. Bikes €10 per day, €40 per week. Passport or credit card deposit. Lock and theft insurance included. **Maps** and advice are liberally dispensed by the attendants. Open daily 9am-6pm. Cash only. **Bike City,** Bloemgr. 68-70 (☎020 626 3721; www.bikecity.nl). €13.50 per day, €43.50 for 5 days. Bring a government-issued ID. Deposit €25. Open daily 9am-6pm.

GETTING AROUND. The best way to get around Amsterdam is by bike. Get a single-speed bike that has lights in the front and back–you can be ticketed for not using both at night. Get 2 locks–one for each wheel–and secure your bike to something sturdy. You'll inevitably see people biking down the wrong side of a street, running red lights, and playing chicken with trucks, but that doesn't mean you should join in the fun. Always bike perpendicular to tram rails (so your wheels don't get caught in them) and, finally, use hand signals. Canal boats are another great way to get around Amsterdam. Try taking advantage of the "Hop on, Hop off" tours where you can ride and check out different museums at the stops all day.

PRACTICAL INFORMATION

Tourist Office: VVV, Stationspl. 10 (☎0900 400 4040; www.amsterdamtourist.nl), opposite Centraal Station. Books rooms and sells maps for €2. Internet €0.40 per min. Open daily 8am-9pm. Branches at Stadhouderskade 1, Schiphol Airport, and inside Centraal. Sells **I Amsterdam card,** which gives you free public transit, parking, boat trip, and discounts. 24hr. pass €33, 48hr. pass €43, 72hr. pass €53.

Consulates: All foreign embassies in the Netherlands are based in **The Hague. UK,** Koningslaan 44 (☎020 676 4343). Open M-F 8:30am-1:30pm. **US,** Museumpl. 19 (☎020 575 5309; http://amsterdam.usconsulate.gov). Open M-F 8:30-11:30am. Closed last W of every month. Passport issues can be addressed at the Amsterdam offices.

Currency Exchange: American Express, Damrak 66 (☎020 504 8777). Offers the best rates, no commission on American Express Traveler's Cheques, and a €4 flat fee for all non-Euro cash and non-AmEx traveler's checks. Open M-F 9am-5pm, Sa 9am-noon.

Library: Openbare Bibliotheek Amsterdam, Prinsengr. 587 (☎020 523 0900). Reserve free internet for 30min. at the information desk. Adequate English selection. Open Apr.-Sept. M 1-9pm, Tu-Th 10am-9pm, F-Sa 10am-5pm; Oct.-Mar. M 1-9pm, Tu-Th 10am-9pm, F-Sa 10am-5pm, Su 1-5pm.

GLBT Resources: Pink Point (☎020 428 1070; www.pinkpoint.org). A kiosk located in front of the Westerkerk. Provides info on GLBT life in Amsterdam. Open daily noon-6pm. **Gay and Lesbian Switchboard** (☎020 623 6565; www.switchboard.nl) takes calls M-F noon-10pm, Sa-Su 4-8pm.

Laundromat: Rozengracht Wasserette, Rozengr. 59 (☎020 638 5975), in the Jordaan. You can do it yourself (wash €6, with dry €7 per 5kg load) or have it done for you (€8 for 5kg). Open daily 9am-9pm. Cash only.

Police: Headquarters at Elandsgr. 117 (☎020 559 9111). The national non-emergency line, ☎0900 8844, connects you to the nearest station or the rape crisis department.

Crisis Lines: General counseling at **Telephone Helpline** (☎020 675 7575). Open 24hr. Rape crisis hotline (☎020 612 0245) staffed M-F 10:30am-11pm, Sa-Su 3:30-11pm. Drug counseling at the **Jellinek Clinic** (☎020 570 2378). Open M-F 9am-5pm.

24hr. Pharmacy: A **hotline** (☎020 694 8709) gives you the nearest 24hr. pharmacy.

Medical Services: For hospital care, **Academisch Medisch Centrum,** Meibergdreef 9 (☎020 566 9111), is easily accessible on subway #50 or 54 (dir.: Gein; stop: Holendrecht). **Tourist Medical Service** (☎020 592 3355) offers 24hr. referrals for visitors.

Internet: Many of the city's coffee shops and hostels offer internet for customers and guests. **easyInternetcafé,** Damrak 33 (☎020 320 8082). €1 per 22min., €6 per day, €10 per week, €22 for 20 days. Open daily 9am-10pm. **The Mad Processor,** Bloemgracht 82 (☎020 421 1482). Provides a relaxed setting to those hoping to surf the net. €2 per hr. Open Tu-Su 2pm-midnight.

Post Office: Singel 250, at Raadhuisstr. Open M-W and F 9am-6pm, Th 9am-8pm, Sa 10am-1:30pm.

ACCOMMODATIONS

The chaos of the **Red Light District** prompts accommodations in the **Centrum** to enforce strong security measures, while hostels and hotels in the **Canal Ring** and the **Singelgracht** are more carefree. Lodgings in the Red Light District are often bars with beds over them. Before signing up, consider how much noise and drug use you can tolerate from your neighbors. Places near the train station may be a convenient walk, but are often expensive and lacking in facilities. Amsterdam's canal-side accommodations offer affordable hotels and hostels with beautiful views, though they can be a bit cramped.

CENTRUM

Flying Pig Downtown, Nieuwendijk 100 (☎020 420 6822; www.flyingpig.nl). Knockout location and stylish decor matched with a welcoming party environment. A perennial favorite among young, energetic backpackers. Stoner-friendly lounge in reception area and drinking matches every Tu, Th, and Sa. Pitchers €10. Breakfast and linens included. Free Internet. Key deposit with locker €5. Dorms €28-29. Queen-sized dorms (holds 2 people): 32-bed €44.80, 20-bed €43.40. Weekends rates go up €3 per night. ISIC holders get a free beer in summer and a 5% discount in winter. Online booking up to a week in advance is recommended. AmEx/MC/V. ❶

Shelter City, Barndesteeg 21 (☎020 625 3230; www.shelter.nl). In the heart of the Red Light District, this clean Christian youth hostel, staffed by volunteers, is a comforting resting place for any backpacker. Activities organized by staff most nights. Breakfast and linens included. Travelers can choose to clean for 1 month for free room and board. Lockers €5 deposit. Internet €0.30 for 10min. Dorms June-Aug. €24-30. ❶

St. Christopher's Inn/Winston Hotel, Warmoesstr. 129 (☎020 623 2380; www.winston.nl). Each room is decorated by a different artist. Popular outdoor garden for those looking to imbibe. Be sure to head to **Club Winston** next door for live music. Free Wi-Fi. Dorms €29-35; singles €75-87. MC/V. ❶

Stayokay Amsterdam Stadsdoelen, Kloveniersburgwal 97 (☎020 624 6832; www.stayokay.com/stadsdoelen). This branch of the chain sleeps 176 and provides clean, drug-free lodgings in a (relatively) quiet environment. Great temporary housing choice for large younger groups. Breakfast, lockers, and linens included. Locker deposit €20 or passport. Internet €10 per 3hr. Rent bikes €10 per day. Reception 24hr. Co-ed or single-sex 8- to 20-bed dorms €19-30; singles €76. €2.50 HI discount. AmEx/MC/V. ❶

Hotel Brouwer, Singel 83 (☎020 624 6358; www.hotelbrouwer.nl). 8 gorgeously restored rooms, each with private bath and canal view. Breakfast included. Free Wi-Fi. Singles €63; doubles €100. No smoking. Cash or traveler's checks only. ❸

Hotel Royal Taste, Oudezijds Achterburgwal 47 (☎020 623 2478; www.hotelroyaltaste.nl). You'll find clean, comfortable, almost fancy accommodations at reasonable prices at Hotel Royal Taste in the heart of the red-light district. Breakfast €7.50. Free internet. Singles €50, with bath €60, with canal view €120; triples €150-165; quads €190. AmEx/MC/V. ❷

Hotel The Crown, Oudezijds Voorburgwal 21 (☎020 626 9664; www.hotelthecrown.com). Dependable rooms in a fun, if rowdy, environment. Loads of British tourists call this a temporary home because of its proximity to the action. Canal views available upon request. Singles €50-85; doubles €70-115. AmEx/MC/V. ❷

CANAL RING AND REMBRANDTPLEIN

Hemp Hotel, Frederikspl. 15 (☎020 625 4425; www.hemp-hotel.com). Take tram line #4 to Frederiksplein. Each room is designed and decorated according to a different cultural theme. Revel in all things hemp including wines, beers, and candies. Breakfast—featuring yummy hemp bread—included. Singles €60; doubles €70, with private shower €75. MC/V with 5% surcharge. ❷

Nadia Hotel, Raadhuisstr. 51 (☎020 620 1550; www.nadia.nl). Each comfortable room includes fridge, safe, and TV. Nice interior garden. Breakfast included. Free Wi-Fi. Weekday high-season singles €65; doubles €90-120; triples €135-165. Higher prices for balcony or rooms with canal views, and on weekends. AmEx/MC/V. ❸

City Hotel, Utrechtsestr. 2 (☎020 627 2323; www.city-hotel.nl). Take tram #4 to Rembrandtplein. Clean, spacious, and above a pub on vibrant Rembrandtpl. Breakfast €5. Reception 24hr. 2- to 8-bed rooms €45 per person; singles and doubles €100; triples €135. MC/V. ❷

The Golden Bear, Kerkstr. 37 (☎020 624 4785; www.goldenbear.nl). Claim to fame as Amsterdam's oldest openly gay hotel. Rooms include a phone, safe, fridge, TV, VCR, and DVD. Continental breakfast included. Free Wi-Fi. Internet €2 per 30min. Reception 8am-10pm; ask for a key. Singles from €63 (furnished with double beds), with bath €103; doubles €73-118. ❸

WEST OF TOWN

☒ **Frédéric Rent a Bike,** Brouwersgr. 78 (☎020 624 5509; www.frederic.nl). 3 cheerful rooms in the back of a bike shop—each named after a different painter. Bikes €10. Reception 9am-6pm. Singles €40-50; doubles €60-100; houseboats for 2-4 people €100-160. Apartments available for short-term stays from €140 for 2 people to €225 for 6. Cash only; AmEx/MC/V required for reservation. See **Local Transportation,** p. 449. ❶

The Shelter Jordan, Bloemstr. 179 (☎020 624 4717; www.shelter.nl). Well-run Christian hostel in the upscale Jordaan district. No obligation to participate in any of the hostel's religious activities. Best suited to those under 35. Breakfast included. Lockers with padlocks for sale. Cafe with internet (€1 per 20min.) and a piano. 1-month max. stay. Free room and board for those willing to clean; inquire at the desk. Dorms June-Aug. €24-28, Nov.-Feb. €17-21, Sept.-Oct. and Mar.-May €19-23. No drugs or alcohol. MC/V. ❶

Hotel Abba, Overtoom 122 (☎020 618 3058; www.abbabudgethotel.com), near Leidsepl. You can dance, you can jive, having the time of your life. Small, clean rooms, each with TV, table, and chairs. Breakfast included. Wi-Fi €3 per hr. Reception 8am-11pm. Rooms €25-40 per person. during high season. Cash only. ❶

Hotel de Filosoof, Anna Vondelstr. 6 (☎020 683 3013; www.hotelfilosoof.nl). The name gives away the theme—each room is dedicated to a different philosopher or culture. There is a library as well as several gorgeous gardens (including nearby Vondelpark) just a few steps away. All rooms come with cable TV, Wi-Fi, phone, and bath. Breakfast €15. Singles €80-125; doubles €95-150. AmEx/MC/V. ❹

LEIDSEPLEIN AND MUSEUMPLEIN

Hotel Bema, Concertgebouw 19B (☎020 679 1396; www.bemahotel.com). Luxury at an affordable price. Friendly staff and beautifully decorated, airy rooms, right off the Museumplein. Breakfast included. Reception 8am-midnight. Singles €40-45; doubles and twins €65-70, with shower €85-90; triples €85-90/95-105; quads with shower €110-120. AmEx/MC/V with 5% surcharge. ❶

Flying Pig Downtown, Vossiusstr. 46-47 (☎020 400 4187; www.flyingpig.nl). Communal feeling in a tranquil setting. Bar open from 3pm. Ample breakfast included (8:30-10:30am). Free linens, internet, and Skype. Computers available for loan with deposit. Fully equipped kitchen. Reception 24-hr. High-season dorms €27-28; doubles €40. For long-term stays, ask about working in exchange for rent. Reserve ahead for discounts. AmEx/MC/V. ❶

Freeland, Marnixstr. 386 (☎020 622 7511; www.hotelfreeland.com). This GLBT-friendly establishment boasts exceptionally clean and cheery rooms. Rooms have DVD player; most have A/C and private bath. Breakfast included. Free internet in lobby, and Wi-Fi throughout the hotel. Singles €60-75; doubles €90-120; triples €150. Book early. AmEx/MC/V. ❸

Stayokay Amsterdam Vondelpark, Zandpad 5 (☎020 589 8996; www.stayokay.com/vondelpark). Between music in the lobby, a pool table (€1), foosball (€0.50), and a bar, this spotless hostel is a favorite with younger travelers. Well-suited for large groups and school trips. Breakfast and linens included; towels €3. Internet €1.50 per 15min. or €3 per hr. 7-night max stay. Reception 24hr. Dorms €24-34; doubles €80-93; quads €130-146. €2.50 HI discount. MC/V. ❶

DE PIJP, JODENBUURT, AND PLANTAGE

Hotel Adolesce, Nieuwe Keizersgr. 26 (☎020 626 3959; www.adolesce.nl). Pristine, quiet, unique, and completely angst-free 10-room hotel in an old canal house. All rooms come with sinks, TVs, and phones; many have sofas, desks, and views of the canal. Coffee, tea, chocolate, fruit, and biscuits served all day. Reception 8:30am-1am. Singles €60-70; doubles €85-100; triples €130. No drugs allowed. MC/V. ❷

Bicycle Hotel, Van Ostadestr. 123 (☎020 679 3452; www.bicyclehotel.com). Clean digs with a large, airy, common room and a leafy garden in the beautiful De Pijp area make this a favorite among backpackers. Sink and TV in all rooms. Breakfast included. Free safe and internet. Bike rental €7.50 per day. 3-night min. weekend stay. Singles €40-70; doubles €50-85, with private shower toilet €80-115; triples €80-105/100-150. 4-person canal house in the Plantage €130. AmEx/MC/V; 4% surcharge. ❷

MUNCHIES

Cheap restaurants cluster around **Leidseplein, Rembrandtplein,** and **De Pijp.** Cafes, especially in the **Jordaan,** serve inexpensive sandwiches (€2-5) and good Dutch fare (€6-10). Bakeries line **Utrechtsestraat,** south of **Prinsengracht.** Fruit, cheese, flowers, and even live chickens are sold at markets on **Albert Cuypstraat** in De

Pijp (open M-Sa 9am-5pm). **Albert Heijn** supermarkets are plentiful; two of the most popular can be found in Dam Sq. and underneath Museumpl. **Lange Leidsedwarsstracht** and **Korte Leidsedwarsstracht** have a line of inexpensive pizzerias. You'll also find a good variety of spicy Indonesian restaurants and delightful Greek cuisine. Just to the left of Centraal Station on **Zeedijk,** Asian buffets offer filling yet budget-friendly meals.

CENTRUM

Cafe Latei, Zeedijk 143 (☎020 625 7485; www.latei.net), near Nieuw Markt. At this unique cafe and curiosity shop, everything except the stray cat is for sale—even your plate. Sandwiches around €3. All-day continental breakfast €7.50. Fresh juices €2-4. Th-Sa home-style Indian food. Vegetarian dishes €8. Filling meaty meals €12. Open M-F 8am-6pm, Sa 9am-6pm, Su 11am-6pm. Cash only. ❶

Greenwoods, Singel 103 (☎020 623 7071). Known for its cakes and breads, this restaurant serves high tea every Su for those looking for low-priced elegance with a canal view (€13). Breakfast (€8) served all day. Sandwiches €5. Open M-Th 9:30am-6pm, F-Su 9:30am-7pm. Cash only. ❶

Aneka Rasa, Warmoesstr. 25-29 (☎020 626 1560; www.finerestaurant.nl). Palm trees and murals make this relaxing restaurant a wonderful oasis on a rainy Dutch afternoon. Partake of the fruits of the Netherland's colonial past with dishes combining Dutch technique and Indonesian ingredients. Vegetarian plates €9-11. Meat dishes €12-14. Dinner for 2 €17-33.50. Open daily 5-10:30pm. AmEx/MC/V. ❷

In de Waag, Nieuwmarkt 4 (☎020 422 7772; www.indewaag.nl). Eat by candlelight in this upscale restaurant, an old weigh house from 1488, complete with stone walls, long wooden tables, and sleek stainless steel decor. Comfortable outdoor seating available in the Nieuwmarkt. Lunch sandwiches €5-10. Vegetarian dishes €19-21. Main courses €21-23. Complete 3-course meal €34.50. Open daily 10am-1am. Kitchen open 10am-10:30pm. MC/V. ❹

Pannenkoekenhuis Upstairs, Grimburgwal 2 (☎020 626 5603). Adorned with vintage photos of Dutch royalty. Traditional pancakes (€11), said to be among the best in Amsterdam. Open F noon-7pm, Sa noon-6pm, Su noon-5pm. ❷

Eat Mode, Zeedijk 105-107 (☎020 330 0806; www.eatmode.nl). Delicious Asian restaurant serving veggie entrees €3-6. Sushi €1.50. Rice dishes €6.50-11. Noodles €8-10. Open M-Th and Su noon-10pm, F-Sa noon-midnight. MC/V. ❶

BICYCLE BUILT FOR YOU

Even if you've experienced the Red Light District or clouded yourself in smoke at all of Amsterdam's coffeeshops, you can't say you've truly conquered this city unless you've ridden a bike here. The red bike lanes and special bike lights, as well as a multitude of cheap and convenient rental companies, permit tourists to whiz around as if they were locals.

A horseshoe-shaped path along any of the canals of the Central Canal Ring—Prinsengracht is prettiest—passes near the Anne Frank Huis, the Rijksmuseum, the van Gogh Museum, and the Heineken Brewery. Westerpark has wide-open biking lanes and smaller crowds than Vondelpark.

Take advantage of your mobility to explore farther afield. Leave Amsterdam to ride along the Amstel River, glimpsing windmills, houseboats, and quintessentially Dutch rolling hills. Cycle east along green trails to the seaside town of Spaarndam (20-25km). Or, use the canals as racetracks, leaving mellow locals in the dust.

MacBike, Weteringsschans 2 (☎528 76 88; www.macbike.nl), in Leidseplein, rents bikes and sells reliable bike-tour maps.

Holland-Rent-A-Bike, Damrak 247 (☎622 32 07), just minutes from Centraal Station, rents unmarked bikes to help you blend in with the locals.

Grekas Greek Deli, Singel 311 (☎020 620 3890). Take a break from the busy city and dine at this cozy, old-fashioned deli on the Singel canal. Starters €3-6. Salads €4-7. Entrees €12-15. Take-out items €2-10. Open W-Su 1-9pm. Cash only. ❸

CANAL RING AND REMBRANDTPLEIN

Lanskroon, Singel 385 (☎020 623 7743). Traditional Dutch pastries like *stroopwafels* (honey-filled cookies; €2), fresh fruit pies (€3.50), and exotic flavors of sorbet made on-site. Open M-F 8am-5:30pm, Sa 9am-5:30pm, Su 10am-5:30pm. Cash only. ❶

Ristorante Pizzeria Firenze, Halvemaansteeg. 9-11 (☎020 627 3360; www.pizzeria-firenze.nl). Delightful Italian restaurant and pizzeria, complete with murals of the Italian countryside, friendly service, and unbeatable prices. 25 types of pizza (€4.60-13) and pasta (€5.30-11). Lasagna €9. Glass of house wine €2.50. Open daily 1-11pm. MC/V. ❶

Foodism, Oude Leliestr. 8 (☎020 627 6424; www.foodism.nl). Bright green walls, red tables, and an alternative air. The warm staff encourages second helpings of healthy snacks and tasty smoothies (€4). Panini €5. Omelettes €6. Vegetarian and pasta platters €10-13. Breakfast (served all day) €9.50. Open M-Sa noon-10pm, Su noon-6pm. MC/V. ❷

Eetsalon Van Dobben, Korte Reguliersdwarsstr. 5-9 (☎020 624 4200; www.vandobben.com), right off Rembrandtplein. No-frills food on the go in a diner. Choose from the large selection of sandwiches (under €4), including roast beef and ham. Open M-Th 9:30am-1am, F-Sa 9:30am-2am, Su 11:30am-8pm. Cash only. ❶

WEST OF TOWN

Those who venture just west of the train station along Haarlemmerstr. will find bountiful dining opportunities with higher quality, lower prices, and better ambience than the smoke-filled interiors suggest.

Harlem: Drinks and Soulfood, Haarlemmerstr. 77 (☎020 330 1498). Down-home soul food infused with a unique mix of Cajun and Caribbean flavors. The outdoor seating is perfect for a lazy Sunday. Lunch €5-9. Dinner entrees €11-17. Open M-Th 10am-1am, F-Sa 10am-3am, Su 11am-1am. Kitchen open 10am-10pm. Cash only. ❸

Vennington, Prinsenstr. 2 (☎020 625 9398). Dirt-cheap, delicious food in low-key setting just outside the Centrum. Let a real fruit shake (€3.50) accompany your towering club sandwich (€6.50). Sandwiches €2.50-6.50. Open daily 8am-5:30pm. Cash only. ❶

Cafe-Restaurant Amsterdam, Watertorenpl. 6 (☎020 682 2667; www.cradam.nl). A great lunch spot, this surprisingly casual restaurant with high ceilings and a spacious dining room has a seasonal menu of meat, fish, and vegetable entrees (€13-23). Free Wi-Fi. Open M-Th 11am-midnight, F-Sa 11am-1am. Kitchen open M-Th 11am-10:30pm, F-Sa 11am-11:30pm. AmEx/MC/V. ❸

De Vliegende Schotel, Nieuwe Leliestr. 162-168 (☎020 625 2041; www.vliegendeschotel.com). Organic vegetarian food. Look for the delicious daily specials (under €10). Soups and starters from €3.50. Entrees from €9.40. Open daily 6-11:30pm. Kitchen open 6-9:30pm. AmEx/MC/V. ❷

LEIDSEPLEIN AND MUSEUMPLEIN

Loetje, Johannes Vermeerstr. 52 (☎020 662 8173). Known to have the juiciest steak in all of Amsterdam. Typical Dutch decor with wood furnishings, chalkboard menus, and crowds of hungry professionals. Hamburger €6.50. Steaks €16. Beer €4. Open M-F 11am-10pm, Sa 5:30pm-10pm. Cash only. ❷

Eat at Jo's, Marnixstr. 409 (☎020 638 3336; www.eatatjos.com). Locals rave about the the freshly prepared fusion food on the menu. Bands often grab a bite to eat after a performance at Melkweg, located inside. Menus change weekly. Open W-Su noon-9pm. Dinner starts at 5:30pm. Cash only. ❷

Bombay Inn, Lange Leidsedwarsstr. 46 (☎020 624 1784). Delicately spiced dishes at excellent value. Generous "tourist menu" includes 3 courses (chicken menu €8.50; lamb menu €9.50). Veggie sides €5.50. Open daily 5-10pm. AmEx/MC/V. ❷

Village Bagels, Vijzelstr. 137 (☎020 468 5286; www.vilagebagels.nl). Enjoy a quiet brunch with a wide assortment of bagels and bagel sandwiches. The avocado-chicken bagel (€5.35) makes a hearty lunch. Bagels sandwiches €3.30-5.60. Open M-F 7:30am-6pm, Sa-Su 9am-6pm. Cash only. ❶

De Binnen Pret, Amstelveenseweg 134 (☎020 679 0712; www.binnenpret.org). Take tram 1 to end of Vondelpark. The menu changes every day at this one-of-a-kind restaurant where it's all you can eat for €5. Plenty of vegetarian and vegan options. Reservations are a must. Hours vary depending on volunteer participation, reduced during summer. ❶

DE PIJP, JODENBUURT, AND PLANTAGE

Bazar, Albert Cuypstr. 182 (☎020 664 7173; www.bazaramsterdam.nl). Fantastic Turkish decor housed in the open space of a former church. Extensive menu features inexpensive cuisine from North Africa, Lebanon, and Turkey. Lunch special €10 per person (min. 2 people). Breakfast (Algerian pancakes and Turkish yogurt) and lunch start from €5. Open M-Th 9am-1am, F-Sa 9am-2am, Su 9am-midnight. Reserve ahead for dinner. ❷

Cafe De Pijp, Ferdinand Bolstr. 17-19 (☎020 670 4161). A hip and sociable restaurant in the heart of De Pijp with sleek black tables against a faux-wood background and a terrace. Mediterranean-influenced food and a laid-back atmosphere. Popular tapas €2.50-8. Mixed drinks €6. Open M-Th 4pm-1am, F 3:30pm-3am, Sa noon-2am, Su noon-1am. Cash only. ❸

Eetkunst Asmara, Jonas Daniel Meijerpl. 8 (☎020 627 1002). Enjoy specially prepared East African specialties, like beef with an assortment of mild herbs (€9). Served on *injera,* a spongy bread. Vegetarian options. Open daily 6-11pm. Cash only. ❷

Soup En Zo, Jodenbreestr. 94A (☎020 422 2243; www.soupenzo.nl). Let your nose guide you to the amazing broth at this tiny soupery, great for snacks on-the-go. Several soups and sizes (€2.70-6) with free bread and delicious toppings like coriander, dill, cheese, and nuts. Salads under €7. Open M-F 11am-8pm, Sa-Su noon-7pm. Another take-out only location in Leidseplein at Nieuwe Spiegelstraat 54 (☎020 330 7823). ❶

SIGHTS

Amsterdam is not a city of traditional sights; if you want to join the sweating masses in endless lines to catch a glimpse of a postcard monument, you've come to the wrong place. But don't be fooled. This city—a collection of nearly 100 interlocking islands—is a sight in itself. Amsterdam is fairly compact, so tourists can easily explore on foot or by bike. When you get tired, the tram system will get you to any of the city's major sights within minutes. For a peaceful view of the city from the water, contract the **Saint Nicolaas Boat Club** (www.amsterdamboatclub.com), which organizes tours that offer unique views of the canal system.

CENTRUM

DAM SQUARE AND KONINKLIJK PALEIS. Next to the Nieuwe Kerk on Dam Sq. is one of Amsterdam's most impressive architectural accomplishments, the Koninklijk Paleis, . The building's exterior bursts with history, while the interior tells the story of Amsterdam's rise as a commercial power. The building was opened in 1655 and fully completed 10 years later. It originally served as the town hall, but it was no ordinary municipal building. In a city at the center of burgeoning worldwide trade, governed by a group of magistrates, the town hall became the most important government building in the region. The interior holds the opulent history of Amsterdam, including government offices and the Balcony Room where death sentences were proclaimed to the public. Architect Jacob van Campen aimed to replace the entrenched Amsterdam Renaissance style with a more Classic one. Across Dam Sq. is the Dutch **Nationaal Monument,** unveiled on May 4, 1956, to honor Dutch victims of WWII. Inside the 22m white stone obelisk is soil from all 12 of the Netherlands's provinces and the Dutch East Indies. Along the back of the monument, you'll find the provinces' crests bordered by the years 1940 and 1945. In addition to this reminder of Dutch suffering during the war, the monument is one of Amsterdam's central meeting and people-watching spots. *(Tram #5, 13, 17, or 20 to Dam. Paleis. ☎020 620 4060; www.paleisamsterdam.nl. Open daily June-Aug. 11am-5pm, Sept-May Tu-Su noon-5pm. €7.50, reduced €6.50. Audio tour included. AmEx/MC/V.)*

NIEUWMARKT. Nieuwmarkt is one of Amsterdam's most beloved squares. It is lined with cafes, restaurants, markets, and coffee shops. On warm summer days, crowds pack the area late into the evening. Be sure to stop and take a look at the **Waag,** Amsterdam's largest surviving medieval building. Dating back to the 15th century, then known as *Sint Antoniespoort,* the Waag came into existence as one of Amsterdam's fortified city gates. As Amsterdam expanded, it was converted into a house for public weights and measures. At the end of the 17th century, the Surgeon's Guild built an amphitheater at the top of the central tower to house public dissections as well as private anatomy lessons—famously depicted in **Rembrandt van Rijn's** *The Anatomy Lesson of Dr. Tulp.* The Waag has also housed a number of other sites, including the Jewish Historical Museum and the Amsterdam Historical Museum. *(Metro to Nieuwmarkt.)*

BEGIJNHOF. This secluded courtyard was the 14th-century home of the **Beguines,** a sect of free-thinking and religiously devoted laywomen. The casual visitor will be rewarded with access to one of the area's most attractive sights. The peaceful Begijnhof's rosy gardens, beautifully manicured lawns, gabled houses, and tree-lined walkways afford a much-needed respite from the excesses of the Nieuwe Zijd. While there, visit the court's two churches, the **Engelsekerk** and the **Begijnhofkapel.** *(From Dam, take Nieuwezijds Voorburgwal south 5min. to Spui, turn left, and then go left again on Gedempte Begijnensloot; the gardens are on the left. Alternatively, follow signs to Begijnhof from Spui. No guided tours, bikes, or pets. Open daily 9am-5pm. Free.)* One of the oldest houses in Amsterdam, **Het Houten Huys** (The Wooden House), can also be found on the premises. *(☎020 623 5554. Open M-F 10am-4pm.)* Red Light District. No trip to Amsterdam would be complete without witnessing the spectacle that is the Red Light District. Sex theaters and peep shows throw open their doors to eager patrons, and the streets are thick with people gawking at lingerie-clad prostitutes pressing themselves against windows. Despite closing half of the windows in Amsterdam, wall-to-wall brothels crowd **Warmoesstraat** and **Oudezijds Achterburgwal.** There are also **sex shows,** in which actors perform strictly choreographed and often ridiculous fantasies on stage; the most famous takes place at **Casa Rosso.** *(Oudezijds Achterburgwal 106-108. ☎020 627 8954; www.janot.com. Open M-Th 8pm-2am, F-Sa 8pm-3am. €30, with 4 drinks €45.)*

FLESH PHOTOGRAPHY. Do not take pictures in the Red Light District, especially of prostitutes. Taking pictures is considered incredibly rude and will get you into trouble.

OUDE KERK. Located right in the middle of the otherwise lurid Red Light District, the Old Church may be the only church in the world completely bounded by whorehouses. Erected in 1306, the Oude Kerk was the earliest parish church built in Amsterdam. It is now a cultural center that hosts photography and modern art exhibits. At the head of the church is the massive **Vater-Müller organ,** built in 1724, and still played for public concerts. The massive Gothic church has seen hard times: it was stripped of its artwork and religious artifacts during the Alteration. The Protestant church has since served a number of functions: a home for vagrants, a theater, a market, and a space for fishermen to mend broken sails on the rough hewn cobblestones that make up the church's floor. Today, there is still an empty, spare feeling inside the building, but the church is nevertheless one of the most impressive and prominent structures in the city. *(Oudekerkspl. 23. ☎020 625 8284; www.oudekerk.nl. Open M-Sa 11am-5pm, Su 1-5pm. €5, students and over 65 €4, under 12 free. I Amsterdam cardholders free. Tower €6. Additional charge for exhibits.)*

SINT NICOLAASKERK. Above the impressive columned altar, a burst of color emanates from the stained-glass windows of this relatively new Roman Catholic church that resembles the interior of a massive sailing vessel. Completed in 1887 to honor the patron saint of sailors, it replaced a number of Amsterdam's secret Catholic churches from the era of the Alteration. The walls of the church are art themselves, lined with magnificent murals depicting the life and story of St. Nicolaas. *(Prins Hendrikkade 73. ☎020 624 8749. Daily service 12:30pm; Su mass 10:30am Dutch, 1pm Spanish. Organ festival July-Sept. Sa 8:15pm. Contemporary and classical organ concerts occasionally Sa 3pm—call ahead. Open M 1-4pm, Tu-F 11am-4pm, Sa noon-3pm. Organ festival €6.)*

SPUI. Pronounced "spow," this square was originally a body of water that constituted the southernmost point of the city until 1420. In 1882, the Spui was filled in and became the tree-lined, cobblestone square—perfect for quiet lounging on summer afternoons. The area, surrounded by bookstores, is home to an art market on Sundays and a book market on Fridays. Look out for **Het Lievertje** (The Little Urchin), a small bronze statue by Carel Kneulman that became a symbol for the Provos, a Dutch counter-culture movement of the 1960s. *(Tram #1, 2, 4, 5, 9, 14, 16, 24, or 25 to Spui.)*

CANAL RING AND REMBRANDTPLEIN

WESTERKERK. This stunning Protestant church was designed by Roman Catholic architect Hendrick de Keyser and completed in 1631. The blue and yellow imperial crown of Maximilian of Austria—the Hapsburg ruler of the Holy Roman Empire in the late 15th century—rests atop the 87m tower, which has become a patriotic symbol for the citizens of Amsterdam. Rembrandt is believed to be buried here, but no one knows for sure, because he was moved when his family could no longer pay his debts. In contrast to the decorative exterior, the Protestant church remains properly sober and plain inside; it is still used by a Presbyterian congregation. Make sure to climb the **Westerkerkstoren** as part of a 30min. guided tour for an awe-inspiring view of the city. *(Prinsengr. 281. ☎020 624 7766. Open Apr.-Sept. M-F 11am-5:30pm, July-Aug. M-Sa 11am-3pm. Tower tours Apr.-Sept. every 30min. 10am-5:30pm. €6.)*

HOMOMONUMENT. Since 1987, the Homomonument has stood as a testament to the strength and resilience of the homosexual community in Amsterdam. Conceived by Karin Daan, the monument consists of pale-pink granite triangles that allude to the symbols homosexuals were required to wear in Nazi concentration camps. The raised triangle points to the **COC,** the oldest gay rights organization in the world; the ground-level triangle points to the **Anne Frank Huis;** and the triangle with steps into the canal points to the **Nationaal Monument** on the Dam, a reminder that homosexuals were among those sent to concentration camps. On Queen's Day (Apr. 30) and Liberation Day (May 5), celebrations surround the monument. *(Next to Westerkerk. www.homomonument.nl.)*

CENTRAL CANAL RING. You haven't seen Amsterdam until you've spent some time wandering in the Central Canal Ring, the city's most expensive district and arguably its most beautiful. The **Prinsengracht** (Prince's Canal), **Keizersgracht** (Emperor's Canal), and **Herengracht** (Gentleman's Canal) are collectively known as the *grachtengordel* (canal girdle). In the 17th century, residents of Amsterdam were taxed according to the width of their homes, and houses could not be more than one plot (a few meters) wide. To encourage investment in construction, the city government allowed its elite to build homes that were twice as wide on a stretch now known as the **Golden Bend,** on Herengr. between Leidsegr. and Vijzelstr. Across the Amstel is the **Magere Brug** (Skinny Bridge), which sways precariously above the water. It is the oldest of the city's many pedestrian drawbridges and the only one still operated by hand.

REMBRANDTPLEIN. Rembrandtpl. is a disorganized grass rectangle surrounded by haphazard flower beds, criss-crossed by pedestrian paths, and populated with half-dressed locals lazing about (when weather permits, of course). A bronze likeness of the famed master Rembrandt van Rijn and a 3D version of his famous painting *Night Watch* overlook the scene. By night, Rembrandtpl. competes with Leidsepl. for Amsterdam's hippest nightlife, with a particularly rich concentration of GLBT hot spots in the area. South and west of the square lies **Reguliersdwarsstraat,** dubbed by locals "the gayest street in Amsterdam." *(In the northeast corner of the Canal Ring, just south of the Amstel.)*

LEIDSEPLEIN AND MUSEUMPLEIN

VONDELPARK. With meandering walkways, green meadows, and several ponds, this leafy park—the largest within the city center—is a lovely meeting place, constantly full of skaters, bikers, and sunbathers. In addition to a few good outdoor cafes, Vondelpark has an open-air theater where visitors can enjoy free music and dance concerts Thursday through Sunday during the summer. Every Friday, the **Friday Night Skate** takes place at the round bench by the Filmmuseum. It starts around 8:30pm and continues for 15-20km until about 10:30pm. *(www.fridaynightskate.com.)* Rent skates at Snoephuisje (near Amstelveenseweg entrance). For the less daring, try wandering around the beautifully maintained rose gardens or have a picnic lunch on any of the park's expanses of grass. *(In the southwestern corner of the city, outside the Singelgr. www.vondelpark.org. Theater ☎020 673 1499; www.openluchttheater.nl.)* If you get the munchies, try the pub-slash-restaurant **'t Blauwe Treehuis,** Vondelpark 5, a cylindrical tower situated inside the park that is surrounded by trees and lush greenery. *(☎020 662 0254. Lunch sandwiches €5. Dinner entrees €13. Finger food €4. Open 9am-1am. MC/V.)*

LEIDSEPLEIN. Leidsepl. is a clash of cacophonous street musicians, blaring neon lights, and clanging trams. During the day, the square is packed with countless shoppers, smokers, and drinkers lining the busy sidewalks. When night falls, tourists and street performers flock here. A slight respite is available just east of Leidsepl. along Weteringschans at **Max Euweplein.** The square sports a giant chess board with oversized pieces where older men hang out all day pondering the best moves. One of Amsterdam's more bizarre public spaces, it is notable both for the tiny park across the street (where bronze iguanas provide amusement) and for the motto inscribed above its pillars: Homo sapiens non urinat in ventum ("a wise man does not pee into the wind").

DE PIJP, JODENBUURT, AND PLANTAGE

HORTUS BOTANICUS. With over 6000 plants and 4000 species, this outstanding botanical garden is the perfect place to get lost. Originally a medicinal garden founded in 1638, visitors can now wander past lush palms, flowering cacti, and working beehives. Take an enlightening stroll through simulated ecosystems, a rock garden, a rosarium, an herb garden, a three-climate greenhouse, and a butterfly room. Many of the garden's more exceptional specimens, including a smuggled Ethiopian coffee plant whose clippings spawned the Brazilian coffee empire, were gathered during the 17th and 18th centuries by several members of the Dutch East India Company. *(Plantage Middenlaan 2A. ☎020 625 9021; www.dehortus.nl. Open Sept.-June M-F 9am-5pm, Sa-Su 10am-5pm.; July-Aug. M-F 9am-7pm, Sa-Su 10am-7pm. Guided tours in English Su 2pm, €1. €7, ages 5-14, City card holders, and seniors €3.50. Cafe open M-F 10am-5pm, Sa-Su 11am-5pm; in summer also daily until 7pm.)*

HEINEKEN EXPERIENCE. Since Heineken stopped producing here in 1988, it has turned the factory into an altar devoted to the green bottle. Visitors guide themselves past holograms, virtual-reality machines, and other multimedia treats in this orgy of brand loyalty. Some of the attractions can get absurd, but it's all in fun—after a few drinks. A visit includes two beers (or soft drinks), a tasting, and a wristband. To avoid the crowds, come before 11am and take your alcohol before noon like a true fan. New attractions will include a mini brewery, tasting bar, and the "Stable Walk," where visitors can access the nearby stables and view Heineken's iconic Shire horses. *(☎020 523 9222; www.heinekenexperience.com. Open daily 11am-5:30pm. €15, €11.25 with I Amsterdam Card. AmEx/MC/V.)*

PORTUGEES-ISRAELIETISCHE SYNAGOGE. Amsterdam's early Sephardic Jewish community, mainly refugees fleeing religious persecution in Spain, founded this large synagogue, known as the *Esnoga* (the Portuguese word for synagogue), in 1675. One of the few tangible remnants of Amsterdam's once-thriving Jewish community, the synagogue features a plain but beautiful *chuppah* (a Jewish wedding canopy). Visitors are free to walk through the large worship hall, which has massive brass candelabras and arches reminiscent of those of Amsterdam's canal houses. A video presentation provides background on Amsterdam's Jewish community. After you leave, take a look at **The Dockworker,** a bronze statue just behind the synagogue. *(Mr. Visserpl. 1-3. ☎020 624 5351; www.esnoga.com. Open Apr.-Oct M-F and Su 10am-4pm.; Nov.-Mar. M-Th and Su 10am-4pm, F 10am-2pm. €6.50, students, seniors, and Museumjaarkaart holders €5, 13-17 €4, under 13 free. Combined pass with the Jewish History Museum €10, children €5.)*

HOLLANDSCHE SCHOUWBURG. A poignant memorial to Amsterdam's Holocaust victims, Hollandsche Schouwburg opened at the end of the 19th century as a Dutch theater on the edge of the old Jewish quarter and became a deportation center for Jews during WWII. A stone monument now occupies the space where the theater's stage once was. A memorial room reminds visitors of the extraordinary toll of WWII. *(Plantage Middenlaan 24. ☎020 531 0430; www.hollandscheschouwburg.nl. Open daily 11am-4pm; closed on Yom Kippur. Free.)*

ARTIS ZOO. Artis is the oldest zoo and park in the Netherlands; it is also a zoological museum, an aquarium, and a planetarium. A day of good weather is enough to make the Artis complex worth a visit. The zoo's got all the big guns: a polar bear, several massive gorillas, elephants, giraffes, an entire building full of scary bugs, and hundreds of free-roaming schoolchildren—be careful not to trip over any as you stroll the grounds. *(Plantage Kerklaan 38-40. ☎020 523 3400; www.artis.nl. Open daily 9am-5pm, during daylight saving time 9am-6pm, Sa 9am-10pm. €18.50, seniors €17, ages 3-9 €15, under 3 free. Guidebooks €2.50. AmEx/MC/V.)*

MUSEUMS

Whether you crave Rembrandts and van Goghs, cutting-edge photography, WWII history, or erotica, Amsterdam has a museum for you. The useful www.amsterdammuseums.nl has plenty of info for easy planning.

> TIP **MAJOR MOOCHING ENCOURAGED.** Visitors planning to see even a handful of museums may want to invest in a **Museumjaarkaart.** The pass (€35, under 25 €20) entitles the holder to admission at most of the major museums in the Netherlands. Cards are good for a year, but are still a value for those staying only for a week. To purchase the pass, bring a passport photo to any participating museum. For more information, check the Dutch-language-only www.museumjaarkaart.nl.

CENTRUM

NIEUWE KERK. The New Church, an extravagant 15th-century brick-red cathedral at the heart of the Nieuwe Zijde, now plays three roles as religious edifice, historical monument, and art museum. **Commemorative windows** have been given to the church to honor royal inaugurations and other events. The church, which has been rebuilt several times after fires, is still used for weddings and other ceremonial events. Check the website before you go; the church closes for two weeks between art exhibits. *(Adjacent to Dam Sq., beside Koninklijk Paleis. ☎ 638 6909; www.nieuwekerk.nl. Open daily 10am-5pm. Organ recitals June-Sept. Th 12:30pm, Su 8pm. Call ahead for exact times. €4, I Amsterdam Card holders free.)*

AMSTERDAMS HISTORISCH MUSEUM. Even though nothing beats a walk around the city itself, this archival museum offers an eclectic introduction to Amsterdam's historical development by way of ancient archaeological findings, medieval manuscripts, Baroque paintings, and multimedia displays. The section of the museum that features artistic accounts of gory Golden Age anatomy lessons is particularly interesting. Catch one of the Historical Museum's hidden surprises: in the covered passageway between the museum and the Begijnhof, there is an extensive collection of large 17th-century paintings of Amsterdam's civic guards that used to hang in the Palais. *(Kalverstr. 92 and Nieuwezijds Voorburgwal 357. ☎ 020 523 1822; www.ahm.nl. Open M-F 10am-5pm, Sa-Su 11am-5pm; closed Queen's Day. €10, seniors €7.50, ages 6-18 €5.)*

MUSEUM AMSTELKRING "ONS' LIEVE HEER OP SOLDER." The continued persecution of Catholics after the Alteration led Jan Hartmann, a wealthy Dutch merchant, to build this secret church in 1663. The chapel is housed in the attics of three separate canal houses and includes a fantastic 18th-century Baroque altar. The large antique organ, specially designed in 1794 to maintain this secret church's covertness, is equally impressive. Small exhibitions and period rooms re-create life during the Dutch Reformation, augmented by the museum's small collection of Dutch painting and antique silver. The church is still active, holding mass six times per year and performing marriages on request; check the website for information on either. *(Oudezijds Voorburgwal 40, at Heintje Hoekssteeg. ☎ 020 624 6604; www.opsolder.nl. Open M-Sa 10am-5pm, Su and holidays 1-5pm. €7, students €5, ages 5-18 €1, under 5 and I Amsterdam Card holders free. AmEx/MC/V.)*

CANNABIS COLLEGE. Don't let the word college ward you off; this staggering think tank is informative and totally non-academic. The staff of volunteers is unbelievably friendly, knowledgeable, and eager to answer any questions about the establishment. If you think you're enough of an expert and want to spread your reefer know-how, don't be afraid to ask about lending a hand (or a lighter). *(Oudezijds Achterburgwal 124. ☎020 423 4420; www.cannabiscollege.com. Open daily 11am-7pm. Free. €3 to see the weed garden downstairs.)*

AMSTERDAM SEX MUSEUM. This almost requisite museum will likely disappoint those looking for a sophisticated examination of sexuality, but it does claim to be the first and oldest sex museum. The first of four floors features amusing life-size mannequins of pimps, prostitutes, and even a flasher. The museum also has ancient artifacts such as a stone phallus from the Roman age, but the exhibits are hardly informative; the majority is composed of photograph after photograph of sexual acts, some more familiar than others. The gallery of fetishes, however, is not for the weak of stomach. *(Damrak 18. ☎020 622 8376; www.sexmuseumamsterdam.com. Open daily 9:30am-11:30pm. €3.)*

CANAL RING AND WEST OF TOWN

ANNE FRANK HUIS. In 1942, the Nazis began deporting all Jews to ghettos and concentration camps, forcing Anne Frank's family and four other Dutch Jews to hide in the *Achterhuis*, or annex, of this warehouse on the Prinsengracht. All eight refugees lived in this secret annex for two years, during which time Anne kept her famous diary, which can be found at the end of the tour. Displays of various household objects, text panels mounted with pages from the diary, and video footage of the rooms as they looked during WWII give some sense of life in that tumultuous time. The original bookcase used to hide the entrance to the secret annex remains, cracked open for visitors to pass through. The endless line stretching around the corner attests to the popularity of the Anne Frank Huis: your best bet is to arrive before 10am or after 7pm, or to book tickets online. *(Prinsengr. 267. ☎020 556 7100; www.annefrank.nl. Open daily Mar.-Jun. 9am-9pm; Jul.-Aug. 9am-10pm; Sept.-Mar. 9am-7pm; closed on Yom Kippur. Last entry 30min. before closing. €8.50, 10-17 €3, under 10 free. Reservations can be made online. MC/V.)*

FOAM PHOTOGRAPHY MUSEUM. Housed in a traditional canal house, the Foam Photography Museum fearlessly explores every aspect of modern photography. All genres of the image are welcome here, regardless of message or content. The museum hosts as many as 20 exhibits per year, bringing fanfare and curiosity to an otherwise subdued neighborhood. *(Keizersgr. 609. ☎020 551 6500; www.foam.nl. Open M-W, Sa-Su 10am-6pm. Th-F 10am-9pm. €7.50, students with ID €5, under 12 and I Amsterdam Card holders free.)*

MUSEUM VAN LOON. The Museum Van Loon provides an exciting look at the history of Amsterdam. Built in 1672, the house eventually fell into the hands of the Van Loon family. Their portraits, along with the family crest commemorating their connection with the East Indies, adorn the walls of this exquisite residence. Numerous other heirlooms and antique furniture decorate each room. *(Keizersgr. 672, between Vijzelstr. and Reguliersgr. ☎020 624 5255; www.museumvanloon.nl. Open M and W-Su 11am-5pm. €6, students and ages 6-18 €4, I Amsterdam card/Museumcard holders free. Cash only.)*

BIJBELS MUSEUM. Inside two canal houses, this museum presents information on both the contents and history of the Bible and the cultural context in which it was written. Opened in 1851 with a display of the ancient Israeli Tabernacle, it includes the first Bible ever printed in the Netherlands and a scale replica of King Solomon's temple. The house, a monument in itself, contains artistic designs that demonstrate the Bible's influence on culture and society as well as a small outdoor sculpture garden. *(Herengr. 366-8. ☎020 624 2436; www.bijbelsmuseum.nl. Open M-Sa 10am-5pm, Su 11am-5pm. €7.50, students and ages 13-18 €4.50, under 13 free.)*

MUSEUMPLEIN

RIJKSMUSEUM AMSTERDAM. Even though the main building of the museum is closed for renovations, the Rijksmuseum is still a mandatory Amsterdam excursion. Originally opened in 1885, the Rijks—or "state"—museum settled into its current monumental quarters, designed by the architect of Centraal Station. It houses masterpieces by Rembrandt van Rijn, Johannes Vermeer, Frans Hals, and Jan Steen. Of this tour-de-force collection, **Rembrandt's** gargantuan and complicated militia portrait *Night Watch* is the crème de la crème. Equally astounding is the museum's collection of paintings by Vermeer. *(Stadhouderskade 42. Visitors must enter instead through the Philips Wing, around the corner at the intersection of Hobbemastr. and Jan Luijkenstr. ☎020 674 7000; www.rijksmuseum.nl. Open M-Th and Sa-Su 9am-6pm, F 9am-8:30pm. Maps available at the ticket counters. €10, students and I Amsterdam Card holders €8, under 18 free. Audio tour €4.)*

VAN GOGH MUSEUM. The Van Gogh Museum is one of Amsterdam's biggest cultural tourist attractions. Suffer the shortest wait and go around 10:30am or after 4pm. The permanent collection, including many of Van Gogh's masterpieces, is on the first floor. The second and third floors hold a substantial collection of important 19th-century art by Impressionist, post-Impressionist, Realist, and Surrealist painters and sculptors. The partially subterranean exhibition wing is the venue for the museum's top-notch traveling exhibitions. *(Paulus Potterstr. 7 ☎020 570 5200; www.vangoghmuseum.nl. Open M-Th and Sa 10am-6pm, F 10am-10pm. €10, ages 13-17 €2.50, under 12 free. Audio tours €4. AmEx/MC/V over €25.)*

TGIF. The Rijksmuseum and the Van Gogh Museum are open late on Fridays. Take advantage of the relative lack of tourists and spend some personal time with the world's greatest painters.

STEDELIJK MUSEUM FOR MODERN AND CONTEMPORARY ART. As the Stedelijk's building on Museumplein undergoes extensive renovations, its collection can be found in seemingly random spaces throughout the city, most notably the Van Gogh Museum. *(☎020 573 2745; www.stedelijk.nl. Check the website for construction and opening information.)*

JODENBUURT AND PLANTAGE

MUSEUM HET REMBRANDT. Dutch master Rembrandt van Rijn's house at Waterloopl. has become the happy home of the artist's impressive collection of 250 etchings (of which only a selection are on display). In the upstairs studio, Rembrandt produced some of his most important works. You'll also find some of his tools and plates, including a pot he used to mix paint. *(Jodenbreestr. 4, at the corner of Oude Schans. ☎020 520 0400; www.rembrandthuis.nl. Open daily 10am-5pm. €8, students €5.50, ages 6-15 €1.50, under 6 free. Special exhibits more expensive. AmEx/MC/V.)*

VERZETSMUSEUM. The Resistance Museum traces life under the Nazi occupation and the steps the Dutch took to oppose the German forces. Visitors can track the occupation and resistance chronologically, from an exhibit on Dutch colonial resistance to one on post-war Dutch regeneration. *(Plantage Kerklaan 61. ☎020 620 2535; www.verzetsmuseum.org. Open M, Sa, and Su 11am-5pm, Tu-F 10am-5pm, public holidays 11am-5pm. €6.50; ages 7-15 €3.50; under 7, Museum Card holders free. Tour of neighborhood available by phone or email appointment; €9 per person.)*

JOODS HISTORISCH MUSEUM. In the heart of Amsterdam's traditional Jewish neighborhood, the Jewish Historical Museum connects four different 17th- and 18th-century Ashkenazi synagogues. Through exhibits by Jewish artists and galleries of historically significant Judaica, the museum presents the Netherlands's most comprehensive picture of Jewish life. *(Jonas Daniel Meijerpl. 2-4. ☎ 020 531 0310; www.jhm.nl. Open daily 11am-5pm, Th 11am-9pm; closed on Yom Kippur and Rosh Hashanah. Free audio tour. €7.50; seniors, ages 7-16, ISIC holders €4.50; I Amsterdam Cardholders and under 13 free.)*

GREATER AMSTERDAM

COBRA MUSEUM. This museum pays tribute to the 20th-century CoBrA art movement: the name is an abbreviation of the capital cities of the group's founding members (Copenhagen, Brussels, and Amsterdam). The beautiful, modern museum presents the movement's work from Karel Appel's experimentation with sculpture to Corneille's developing interest in color and non-Western worlds. *(Sandbergpl. 1-3, south of Amsterdam in Amstelveen. Tram #5 or bus #170, 171, or 172. The tram stop is a 10min. walk from the museum; after a 15min. ride, the bus will drop you off in bus depot adjacent to the museum. ☎ 020 547 5050, tour reservations ☎ 020 547 5045; www.cobra-museum.nl. Open Tu-Su 11am-5pm. €9.50, students, seniors, and 6-18 discounted prices. AmEx/MC/V.)*

COFFEE SHOPS

"Soft" drugs, including marijuana, are tolerated in the Netherlands. **Let's Go does not recommend drug use (or hitchhiking),** though many travelers report having a great time smoking with their friends.

DON'T BOGART OUR CITY. On July 1, 2008, Amsterdam banned smoking indoors. This means that marijuana consumption is only permitted in certain designated rooms inside of coffee shops. Please secure your own jay before attempting to roll one for a friend, and keep all joints, spliffs, bongs, spoons, apples, edibles, one-hitters, and Sherlock Holmes pipes inside the designated areas at all times. Thank you and enjoy your flight.

Amsterdam's coffee shops sell hashish, marijuana, and "space" goodies. As a general rule, the farther you travel from the touristed spots, the better value and higher quality the establishments you'll find. Look for the green-and-white **BCD** sticker that certifies a shop's credibility. When you move from one coffee shop to another, you must buy a drink in the next shop, even if you already have weed. While it's alright to smoke on the outdoor patio of a coffee shop, don't go walking down the street smoking a joint: it is considered déclassé. Not only is this an easy way for pickpockets and con artists to pick out a tourist, but locals also consider it offensive. Note that Europeans only smoke joints. When pipes or bongs are provided, they are usually for tourists.

Coffee shop menus have more variety than most might assume. **Hashish** comes in three varieties: blonde (Moroccan), black (Indian), and Dutch (Ice-o-Lator), all of which can cost €4-35 per gram. Typically, cost is proportional to quality and strength. Black hash hits harder than blonde, and Ice-o-Lator can send even a seasoned smoker off his or her head.

Centrum coffee shops are notorious for higher prices and poor quality product. Avoid the super touristy and commercialized places in Amsterdam and opt for smaller, more cozy shops.

Amnesia, Herengr. 133 (☎020 427 7874, www.myspace.com/amnesiahigh). Slightly larger and significantly more elegant than other coffee shops. Wide selection of drinks, milkshakes, and snacks. Buy 5 joints (€4-6 each) and get 1 free. For an extra treat, try the Amnesia Haze (€13 per g), a 2004 Cannabis Cup winner. Open daily 9:30am-1am. Cash only.

Rusland, Rusland 16 (☎020 627 9468). More than just a drug store: choose from over 40 varieties of herbal tea or refreshing yogurt shakes (€4). Pre-rolled joints €2.50-4.50. Tasty Afghan bud €7 per g. Space muffins €5. White space muffins €1.80. Milkshakes €4. Mixed drinks with fresh fruit €2. Open M-Th and Su 10am-midnight, F-Sa 10am-1am. Cash only.

Kadinsky, Rosmarijnstg. 9 (☎020 624 7023; www.kadinsky.nl). One of the city's friendliest, hippest, and most comfortable stoneries. Joints €3.40-4. Weed €7-11 per g. 20% off 5g purchases. Open daily 9:30am-1am. Cash only.

Paradox, 1e Bloemdwarsstraat 2 (☎020 623 5639, www.paradoxcoffeeshop.com). Get blazed in this relaxed coffee shop that locals call home. The African-themed interior and steady influx of regulars provides an authentic coffee-shop experience. Pre-rolled joints €3. Hash €6.50-10. Open daily 10am-8pm. Cash only.

Yo Yo, 2e Jan van der Heijdenstr. 79 (☎020 664 7173). One of the few coffee shops where neighborhood non-smokers can relax. Apple pie (€1.80), *tostis* (grilled sandwiches), soup, and (normal) brownies served. All weed is organic and sold in bags for €5 or €10, with a monthly €3.50 special. Joints €2.50. Open M-Sa noon-8pm.

Grey Area, Oude Leliestr. 2 (☎020 420 4301; www.greyarea.nl). Last American-run coffee shop in Amsterdam. A single sticker-adorned room that is usually packed, this locale has a good reputation and a friendly staff more than happy to help novices. Borrow a glass bong or vaporizer to smoke, or hit one of Amsterdam's cheapest pure marijuana joints (€3.50). Juice (€1.50) is also available. Open daily noon-8pm.

Siberië, Brouwersgr. 11 (☎020 623 5909; www.siberie.nl). Over 25 years old, Siberie has an extensive menu of coffees and an assortment of teas. Pre-rolled joints (€2-5) are especially popular. Features unique art exhibitions, arcade, and internet. Hash €3-11. Cannabis €3-11. Open M-Th and Su 11am-11pm, F and Sa 11am-midnight. Cash only.

The Dolphins, Kerkstr. 39 (☎020 774 3336). Smoke with the fishes at this underwater-themed coffee shop. Free Wi-Fi. Pre-rolled joints €4. Try the White Dolphin reefer (€10 per g; pure joint €6.50) for an uplifting high. Vaporizers and bongs available with €10 deposit. Open M-Th and Su 10am-1am, F-Sa 10am-1am.

Abraxas, Jonge Roelensteeg 12-14 (www.abraxasparadise.nl). Try this upscale coffeeshop right in the heart of Amsterdam for potent space cakes and muffins (€3.90). Glass floors and winding staircases makes this well-decorated 2-story shop a great place to chill out. The helpful staff will tell you what type of high you will get with each strain. Highs range from "friendly" to "clear-stoned." Pre-rolled joints €3-8. Pure €4.50. Get 3 joints for €10. Open 10am-1am.

ENTERTAINMENT

The **Amsterdams Uit Buro (AUB),** Leidsepl. 26, is stuffed with free monthly magazines, pamphlets, and tips to help you sift through seasonal offerings. It also sells tickets and makes reservations for just about any cultural event in the city for a commission. **Last Minute Ticket Shop,** part of the AUB, offers some of the best deals for half-off tickets. Visit the office for a list of same-day performances at 50% off. (☎0900 0191; www.amsterdamsuitburo.nl or www.lastminuteticketshop.nl. AUB open M-Sa 10am-7:30pm, Su noon-7:30pm. Last Minute Ticket Shop begins selling tickets daily at noon.) The theater desk at the **VVV,** Stationspl. 10, can also make reservations for cultural events. (☎0900 400 4040, €0.40 per min.; www.amsterdamtourist.nl. Open F-Sa 9am-8pm.)

Filmmuseum, Vondelpark 3 (☎020 589 1400; www.filmmuseum.nl). At least 4 screenings per day, many of them older classics. Also houses an extensive information center, with 1900 periodicals and over 30,000 books on film theory and history as well as screenplays. Box office open daily 9am-10:15pm.

Boom Chicago, Leidsepl. 12 (☎020 530 0232; www.boomchicago.nl). For a laugh, head to the English-language improv comedy show M-Th and Su 8:15pm (€20). Dinner (appetizers from €5, entrees around €15) starts at 6:30pm. Open M-Th and Su 10am-1am, F-Sa 10am-3am.

Concertgebouw, Concertgebouwpl. 2-6 (☎020 671 8345; www.concertgebouw.nl). Home to the Royal Concertgebouw Orchestra. Hosts 650 events per year in its 16 beautiful venue halls. Su morning concerts with guided tours before the performance are cheaper options (€12; tours 9:30am, €3.50). Rush tickets for persons age 26 and under from €7.50. Free lunchtime concerts during fall, winter, and spring W 12:30pm. Ticket office open daily 10am-7pm; until 8:15pm for same-day ticketing. Telephone reservations until 5pm. AmEx/MC/V.

THE NETHERLANDS

NIGHTLIFE

Leidseplein and **Rembrandtplein** remain the busiest areas for nightlife, with coffee shops, loud bars, and tacky clubs galore. Amsterdam's most traditional spots are the old, dark, wood-paneled *bruin cafes* (brown cafes). The concept of completely "straight" versus "gay" nightlife does not really apply; most establishments are gay-friendly and happily attract a mixed crowd. Rembrandtpl. is the hub for gay bars geared almost exclusively toward men. For an authentic Dutch experience, you should venture beyond the tourist bars of the Centrum.

CENTRUM

Club NL, Nieuwezijds Voorburgwal 169 (☎020 622 7510; www.clubnl.nl). Posh seating under dim red lighting in this smoky club, reminiscent of the movie *Sin City*. Celebs like Kate Moss, P. Diddy, and Mick Jagger are said to have partied at this joint. Enjoy the pricey mixed drinks while listening to the latest house music. Strict door policy to keep ratio of men to women equal. 21+. Cover F-Su €7, includes coat check. Open M-Th and Su 10pm-3am, F-Sa 10pm-4am. AmEx/MC/V.

Café de Jaren, Nieuwe Doelenstr. 20-22 (☎020 625 5771). The air of sophistication and beautiful river patio at this 2-floor riverside cafe don't quite mesh with its budget-friendly prices. Popular with students and staff from the nearby University of Amsterdam. Mixed drinks and beer €3.10). Open M-Th and Su 10am-1am, F-Sa 10am-2am. Kitchen open M-Th and Su 10am-10:30pm, F-Sa 10am-midnight. AmEx/MC/V.

Kingdom, Warmoesstr. 129 (☎020 625 3912; www.winston.nl). Small eclectic club with a packed crowd and deceptively large dance floor. Live music and DJs every day of the week. Cover varies but usually €3-7. Open M-Th 9pm-3am, F-Su 9pm-4am. MC/V.

Cockring, Warmoesstr. 96 (☎020 623 9604; www.clubcockring.com). "Amsterdam's Premier Gay Disco." Straddles the line between a dance venue and a hard-core sex club. Live strip shows Th-Su from 1am. Special "SafeSex" parties 1st and 3rd Su of the month (€8, with free condoms; dress code "shoes only" or naked; 3-7pm). Men only. Cover M-W €2.50, Th-F and Su €4.50, Sa €5. Open M-Th and Su 11pm-4am, F-Sa 11pm-5am.

Cuckoo's Nest, Nieuwezijds Kolk 6 2. (☎020 627 1752; www.cuckoosnest.nl). Small but popular men-only gay bar. Some outside seating. Wine €3. Beer €2.70. Hours vary, check online. Cash only.

CANAL RING AND REMBRANDTPLEIN

Escape, Rembrandtpl. 11 (☎020 622 1111; www.escape.nl). One of Amsterdam's hottest clubs, with 6 bars, a breezy upstairs lounge, and a hip cafe on the 1st fl. Lines grow long through 2am. Beer €2.70. Mixed drinks €6.60. Cover Th-Sa €10-16, students Th €6. Club open Th 11pm-4am, F-Sa 11pm-5am, Su 11pm-4:30am. Cash only.

Cafe Hoppe, Spui 18-20 (☎020 420 4420; www. cafehipe.com). Built in the 1670s, Hoppe serves traditional Dutch drinks from barrels straight out of a Rembrandt painting. Friendly owner will happily talk about Amsterdam for hours. Open M-Th 8pm-1am, F-Su 8pm-2am. MC/V.

Arc.., Reguliersdwarsstr. 44 (☎020 689 7070; www.bararc.com). This gay-friendly establishment in the heart of Amsterdam's GLBT area hosts a young, trendy crowd that overtakes the bar weekend nights. DJs spin nightly to an eager crowd that gets started around 6pm on the weekends. Mixed drinks €7.50-9. Open M-Th and Su 4pm-1am, F-Sa 4pm-3am. MC/V.

Montmartre, Halvemaanstg. 17 (☎020 625 5565,). Voted best gay bar by local gay mag *Gay Krant* 8 years in a row, but the crowd is straight-friendly. Trendy and popular, with transgendered revelers on any night. Open M-Th and Su 5pm-4am, F-Sa 5pm-3am. Cash only.

WEST OF TOWN

Festina Lente, Looiersgr. 40 (☎020 638 1412; www.cafefestinalente.nl). Charming bar and cafe that continues to attract a young, fashionable, and friendly crowd. Multi-level old-fashioned interior filled with books. Ask the staff for board games on Su afternoons. Wine and beer from €2.20. Open M noon-midnight, Tu-Th 10:30am-1am, F 10:30am-3am, Sa 11am-3am, Su noon-1am. AmEx/MC/V.

Dulac, Haarlemmerstr. 118 (☎020 624 4265). Popular with locals and university students. with its pool table, booths, ample nooks, and dimly-lit interior. Entrees €7.50-17; half-price with student ID. Pint €3.90. Mixed drinks €7. DJ spins Th-Sa 8pm-3am. Open M-Tu 4pm-1am, W and Su noon-1am, F-Sa noon-3am. Kitchen open daily until 10:30pm. AmEx/MC/V.

Sound Garden, Marnixstr. 164 (☎020 620 285; www.cafesoundgarden.nl). Enjoy a pint on the canal patio in this alternative bar popular with locals. Pints €3.70. Open M-Th 1am-1pm, F 1pm-3am, Sa 3pm-3am, Su 3pm-1am. Cash only.

OT301, Overtoom 301 (www.squat.net/ot301). Frequent weekend nights fill this basement art-space with young, open-minded people ready to dance. Cover free-€5. Beer €2. Check the website in advance for events and opening hours.

LEIDSEPLEIN

Alto, Korte Leidsedwarsstr. 115. (☎020 626 3249). The vibe is subdued, but the live jazz performances are sizzling. Arrive early to get a table up front or listen from the bar. Cover W €5. Free jazz on other nights (and occasionally blues) M-Th and Su 10pm-2am, F-Sa 10pm-3am. Open M-Th and Su 9pm-3am, F-Sa 9pm-4am. Cash only.

The Waterhole, Korte Leidsedwarsstr. 49 (☎020 620 8904; www.waterhole.nl). Shoot a round of pool with the locals over a lager (€4.80) in this live-music bar with a southern theme. Music varies by night, with performances ranging from reggae to classic rock. M-W and Su are jam nights, and Th-Sa mostly feature local bands. Music starts around 9pm. Happy Hour 6-9pm, pints €3. Open M-Th and Su 4pm-3am, F-Sa 4pm-4am. Cash only.

Paradiso, Weteringschans 6-8 (☎020 626 8790; www.paradiso.nl). In the summer, this popular concert hall hosts a full lineup of big-name rock, punk, New Wave, hip-hop, and reggae acts. After concerts, it becomes a nightclub with multiple dance halls for a variety of music styles. Concert tickets €5-50; additional mandatory monthly membership fee €2.50. W-Th club cover €6-8, F-Su €13. Open until 4am. Cash only.

Bourbon Street Jazz & Blues Club, Leidsekruisstr. 6-8 (☎020 623 3440; www.bourbonstreet.nl). A slightly older tourist crowd dances with abandon to blues, funk, rock, and soul bands. Beer €2.80. M-Th and Su live music 10:30pm-3am, F-Sa 11pm-4am. Cover Th and Su €3, F-Sa €5. Open M-Th and Su 10pm-4am, F-Sa 10pm-5am. AmEx/MC/V.

Occii, Amstelveenseweg 134. (☎020 671 7778; www.occii.org). This eclectic club has a great underground punk scene and a laid-back clientele. Staffed by volunteers. Hours vary-check website for events. Often closed in summer. Cash only.

DE PIJP, JODENBUURT, AND PLANTAGE

Canvas, Wibautstr. 150, 7th fl. (☎020 716 3817; www.canvasopde7e.nl). Right across from the Wibautsraat Metro stop. From the metro, cross the street and enter the high-rise and take the elevator to the 7th floor. This (figuratively) underground bar inhabits the 7th floor of an abandoned newspaper office. Provides pristine views of the sunset over Amsterdam from the rooftop terrace and an alternative vibe (astroturf and neon flamingos). Beer €2. Mixed drinks €6.50. Open M-Th 10am-1am, F-Sa 10am-3am. AmEx/MC/V.

Trouw, Wibautstr. 127 (☎020 463 7788; www.TrouwAmsterdam.nl). Next to the Wibautsraat Metro stop. This converted newspaper printing facility (note the motif) plays host to a gourmet restaurant during the week and a hopping dance club on the weekends. House, trance and electronica pulse late into the night in a building where printing presses once thundered away. Cover from €10. Restaurant open Tu-W 5-11pm. Club open Th-Sa 9pm-4am. Cash only.

Kingfisher, Ferdinand Bolstr. 24 (☎020 671 2395). A modern take on the traditional Dutch "brown cafe" that is hipper and more stylish than its neighbors but remains low-key and unpretentious. The terrace is open in summer, perfect for nursing a drink and enjoying the famed Dutch sunset. Global beer selections €2-4. Mixed drinks €6. Club sandwiches €6. Open M-Th 11am-1am, F-Sa 11am-3am, Su noon-1am. Cash only.

Chocolate Bar, 1e Van Der Helststr. 62A (☎020 675 7672; www.chocolate-bar.nl). In summer, 20-somethings relax on terrace sofas amid sauntering pedestrians. Sa-Su DJs spin lounge music indoors. Mixed drinks €6-7. Open M-Th and Su 10am-1am, F-Sa 10am-3am. AmEx/MC/V.

COFFEE ONLY?

Amsterdam is commonly identified as the world capital of tolerance. Chilled-out people puff thick clouds of smoke filling infamous coffeeshops, while popular smartshops sell everything from sex stimulants to mushrooms. Recent governmental trends, however, may soon dampen this international perception.

Customers must be 18 to enter a coffeeshop and may only buy 5g per visit per shop. The shops themselves cannot advertise, sell hard drugs, export soft drugs, or have more than 500g on stock. In April 2007, shops had to declare themselves a "bar" or a "coffeeshop," forcing them to make a choice between selling cannabis or alcohol. And, because of the ambiguity of how much THC is in smoothies and other food/drink items, the only legal "space" items available for purchase are cakes. Most recently (July 2008), mushrooms were banned by the government, which was a huge blow to smartshop shelves.

This may not be the end to the controversial decrees being passed in the Netherlands. Rumors over banning the purchase of cannabis by foreigners have been widespread ever since France, Germany, and other nearby countries have complained of their citizens crossing the border predominantly to buy drugs.

Will Amsterdam's tolerant reputation fade? Only time will tell, so puff away... for now.

ULTIMATE PARTY. For a touristy good time, try Amsterdam's most famous Pub Crawl. The staff always gets the crowd going, taking you to 6 different bars, with a free drink and shot at each local hotspot along the trail. M-F and Su 8:30pm. Tram 1, 2, 5, 6, 7, 10 to Leidseplein. €20.

DAYTRIPS FROM AMSTERDAM

AALSMEER

Take bus #172 across from the Victoria Hotel near Centraal Station to the flower auction (Bloemenveiling Aalsmeer) and then on to the town of Aalsmeer. The first bus leaves at 5am (45min.; every 15min.; 6 strips to the flower auction, 2 more to the town).

The reason to visit Aalsmeer is the **Bloemenveiling Aalsmeer** (Aalsmeer flower auction). This massive warehouse and trading floor hosts thousands of traders every day representing some of the world's largest flower-export companies. Nineteen million flowers and over two million plants are bought and sold daily, with an annual turnover of almost US$2 billion. All of the flowers, often flown overnight from across the globe, go through Aalsmeer's massive trading floor (the largest commercial trading space in the world) in a beautifully choreographed dance of global commerce. Since the flowers have to make it to their final destination by the end of the day, almost all the trading is finished by 11am. To see the most action, go between 7 and 9am. Thursday is the least busy day, with trading finishing as early as 8am. The trading floor is visible to tourists via a large catwalk along the ceiling. This self-guided tour takes approximately an hour to complete. *(Legmeerdijk 313, ☎020 739 2185; www.aalsmeer.com. Open M-F 7-11am. €5, ages 6-11 €3, €4 per person for groups of 15+. Guides available to hire for €75.)*

MARCH MADNESS. Visit the Netherlands between March and May to experience *Keufkenhof:* the millions of colorful tulips in bloom are just as pretty as they sound. (www.keukenhof.nl.)

HAARLEM ☎023

Haarlem's (pop. 150,000) narrow cobblestone streets, rippling canals, and fields of tulips in spring make for a great escape from the urban frenzy of Amsterdam. Still, the city beats with a relaxed energy that befits its size.

TRANSPORTATION AND PRACTICAL INFORMATION. **Trains** depart for Amsterdam every few minutes (20min., €3.60). The **VVV,** Stationspl. 1, sells **maps** (€2) and finds accommodations for a €5 fee. It also sells discounted passes to museums. (☎0900 616 1600, €0.50 per min.; www.vvvzk.nl. Open Oct.-Mar. M-F 9:30am-5pm, Sa 10am-3pm; Apr.-Sept. M-F 9am-5:30pm, Sa 10am-4pm.)

ACCOMMODATIONS AND FOOD. The best place to stay is the **Stayokay Haarlem ❶,** Jan Gijzenpad 3, 3km from the train station. Rooms are spare (but cheery) and clean with bath. (☎023 537 1176; www.stayokay.com/haarlem. Breakfast included. Wheelchair-accessible. Dorms in high-season €29; doubles €102. €2.50 HI discount. AmEx/MC/V.) Ideally located right in the town square is **Hotel Carillon ❷,** Grote Markt 27. Bright, clean rooms all have TV, shower, and phone. (☎023 531 0591; www.hotelcarillon.com. Breakfast included. Reception and bar daily in summer 7:30am-1am; in winter daily 7:30am-midnight. Singles €40, with bath €60; doubles €65/80; triples €102; quads €110. MC/V.)

The Indonesian **Toko Nina ❶**, Koningstr. 48, has delicious prepared foods behind the deli counter. (☎023 531 7819; www.tokonina.nl. Combo meals €5.80-8.80. Open M 11am-7pm, Tu-F 9:30am-7pm, Sa 9:30am-6pm, Su 1-6pm. Cash only.) **Fortuyn ❶**, Grote Markt 23, one of the smaller grandcafes in Grote Markt, has more personal service. Sandwiches (€5-8) and snacks are served until 5pm, dinner (€18-23) until 10pm. (☎023 542 1899; www.grandcafefortuyn.nl. Open M-W and Su 10am-midnight, Th-Sa 10am-1am. Cash only.)

SIGHTS. The action in Haarlem centers on Grote Markt, its vibrant main square. Its main attraction is the **Grote Kerk,** whose interior glows with light from the enormous stained-glass windows and houses the splendid, mammoth **Müller organ,** once played by both Handel and Mozart. Also known as St. Bavo's, it holds many historical artifacts and the graves of Jacob van Ruisdael, Pieter Saenredam, and Frans Hals. (☎023 553 2040; www.bavo.nl. Open Nov.-Feb. M-Sa 10am-4pm, Mar.-Oct. Tu-Sa 10am-4pm. €2, children €1.30. Guided tours by appointment €0.50. Organ concerts Tu 8:15pm, June-Sept. also Th 3pm; www.organfestival.nl. €2.50.) These painters' masterpieces can be found in the **Frans Hals Museum,** Groot Heiligland 62. Spread through recreated period rooms, the paintings are displayed as they might have been in the Golden Age. Hals's work reveals casual brush strokes that are now understood as an early move toward Impressionism. (☎023 511 5775; www.franshalsmuseum.com. Wheelchair-accessible. Open Tu-Sa 11am-5pm, Su noon-5pm. €7, under 19 free, groups €5.30 per person.) The **Corrie ten Boomhuis,** Barteljorisstr. 19, served as a secret headquarters for the Dutch Resistance in WWII. It is estimated that Corrie ten Boom saved the lives of over 800 people by arranging to have them hidden in houses, including her own. (☎023 531 0823; www.corrietenboom.com. Open daily Apr.-Oct. 10am-4pm, last tour 3:30pm; Nov.-Mar. 11am-3pm, last tour 2:30pm. Tours every 30min., alternating between Dutch and English; call or check the clock outside for times. Free, but donations accepted.)

DAYTRIP FROM HAARLEM: ZANDVOORT AND BLOEMENDAAL AAN ZEE.

From Zandvoort, take a train to Amsterdam (30min., 3 per hr., €4.70) or Haarlem (10min., round-trip €3.20). Bloemendaal is a 30min. walk north of Zandvoort. You can also take bus #81 to Haarlem from both.

A mere 11km from Haarlem, the seaside town of Zandvoort aan Zee draws sun-starved Dutch and Germans to its miles of sandy beaches. You can stake out a spot on the sand for free, but most locals catch their rays through the comfort of beach clubs, wood pavilions that run along the shore with enclosed restaurants and outdoor patios. These clubs open early each morning, close at midnight, and are only in service during the summer. Nearby Bloemendaal aan Zee does not even qualify as a town; instead, it's a purely hedonistic collection of fashionable and fabulous beach clubs. Local club **Woodstock 69** is the granddaddy of them all, clocking in at almost 15 years old. There is a distinct hippie feel here with hammocks, tiki torches, and lots of loose clothing. *(☎023 573 8084.)* **Bloomingdale** tends to be the favorite of most locals. *(☎023 573 7580; www.bloomingdaleaanzee.com. Open daily 10am-midnight.)* Zandvoort's **VVV,** Schoolpl. 1, is about eight minutes from the beach and train station. The friendly staff can provide a guide to the beaches and accommodations, a map of hiking and biking trails in nearby **Kennemerland National Park,** and lots of information on the city. (☎023 571 7947; www.vvvzk.nl. Open Oct.-Mar. M-F 9am-12:30pm and 1:30-4:30pm, Sa 10am-2pm; Apr.-Sept. M-F 9am-12:30pm and 1:30-4:30pm, Sa 10am-4pm.)*

THE HAGUE (DEN HAAG) ☎070

Whereas Amsterdam is the cultural and commercial center of the Netherlands, The Hague (pop. 480,000) is without a doubt its political nucleus; all of the Netherlands's important governmental institutions are housed here. World-class art museums (the stunning Mauritshuis in particular), a happening city center, high-class shopping, and a tons of open green space combine to make this political hub anything but boring.

TRANSPORTATION AND PRACTICAL INFORMATION. **Trains** run from Amsterdam (55min., 1-6 per hr., €10) and Rotterdam (30min., 1-6 per hr., €4.30) to both of The Hague's major stations, Den Haag Centraal and Holland Spoor. The **VVV,** Hofweg 1, across from the Parliamentary buildings next to Dudok, has an extensive selection of city guides, bicycle **maps,** and guidebooks for sale in their shop, and the desk can arrange canal, carriage, and city tours. (☎070 340 3505; www.denhaag.com. Open M-F 10am-6pm, Sa 10am-5pm, Su noon-5pm.)

ACCOMMODATIONS AND FOOD. **Stayokay City Hostel Den Haag ❷,** Scheepmakerstr. 27, near Holland Spoor, is one of the best hostels in the Netherlands, with sparkling rooms, private baths, spacious lounging areas, and library. From Centraal Station take tram 1, 9, 12 or 16 to Spoor or tram 17 to Rijswijkseplein. Or walk 20 minutes down Lekstr., making a right on Schenkviaduct. The hostel is behind the pink building. (☎070 315 7888; www.stayokay.com/denhaag. Breakfast included 7:30-9:30am. Lockers €2 per 24hr. Linens included. Internet €5 per hr. Reception 7:30am-10:30pm. Wheelchair-accessible4- to 8-bed dorms €27.50; singles €56; doubles €67-78; quads €122. €2.50 HI discount. €2.50 weekend surcharge. MC/V.) **Hotel 't Centrum ❹,** Veenkade 5-6, has simple, airy, and elegant rooms. From either station take tram 17 (dir: Statenkwartier) to Noodrwal. (☎070 346 3657; www.hotelhetcentrum.nl. Check-in 2-11:30pm. Breakfast buffet €12.50; with champagne €15. Singles €49, Su €39, with bath €75/€65; doubles with bath €95/85; 1-person apartments including breakfast €90/85; 2-person €115/105; 3-person €125/115. AmEx/MC/V.) **HNM Café ❶,** Molenstr. 21A, has floor-to-ceiling windows, brightly colored chairs and walls, and a large bowl of Thai noodle soup (€7) on the menu. (☎070 365 6553. Salads €8.50. Dinner €10-14. Open M-W noon-midnight, Th-Sa noon-1am, Su noon-6pm. Cash only.) The excellent **Tapaskeuken Sally ❷,** Oude Molstr. 61, is great for tapas (☎070 345 1623. Open W-Sa 5:30-10:30pm. Cash only.)

SIGHTS AND ENTERTAINMENT. The opulent home of the International Court of Justice and the Permanent Court of Arbitration, the **Peace Palace,** Carnegiepl. 2, has served as the site of international arbitrations, peace-treaty negotiations, and high-profile conflict resolutions. Take a walk around the gardens and enjoy the magnificence of the Grand Hall. Although the Permanent Court of Arbitration is closed to the public, hearings of the International Court of Justice are free to attend (☎070 302 4242, guided tours ☎070 302 4137; www.vredespaleis.nl. Tours M-F 10, 11am, 2, 3, 4pm. Book one week ahead. No tours when the court is in session. €5, under 13 €3. Cash only.) With only two modest stories, the **Mauritshuis,** Korte Vijverberg 8, is one of the most beautiful small museums anywhere, with a near-perfect collection of Dutch Golden Age art. Not counting the precious selection of paintings by Peter Paul Rubens, Jacob van Ruisdael, and Jan Steen, the museum has several excellent

Rembrandts, including his famous *The Anatomy Lesson of Dr. Tulp.* Their showstopping pieces are *Girl with a Pearl Earring* and *View of Delft*, both by Johannes Vermeer. (☎070 302 3456; www.mauritshuis.nl. Open Tu-Sa 10am-5pm, Su 11am-5pm. Free audio tour. €9.50, under 18 and Museum Card holders free. AmEx/MC/V.) Show up at the **Binnenhof**, Binnenhof 8A, for a guided tour that covers both the historic **Ridderzaal** (Hall of Knights) and the **Second Chamber of the States-General**, the Netherlands's main legislative body. Tours don't run when Parliament is in session. The Binnenhof's courtyard is one of The Hague's best photo-ops. Take tram 2, 3, 6 or 10 to Binnenhof or walk about 15min. from Centraal; follow the signs. (☎070 364 6144; www.binnenhofbezoek.nl. Open M-Sa 10am-4pm. Last tour 3:45pm. Parliament is often in session Tu-Th. You can enter the Second Chamber only with a passport or driver's license. Entrance to courtyard free. Admission to Hall of Knights or Second Chamber €6; €8 for both. Tours €5, seniors and children €4.30. Cash only.)

In late June, the Hague hosts what the Dutch consider the largest free public pop concert in Europe, **Parkpop**, on 3 large stages in Zuiderpark with top big-name acts. (☎070 523 9064; www.parkpop.nl.) **De Paas**, Dunne Bierkade 16A, has 11 unusually good beers on tap, about 170 available in bottles, and nearly as many friendly faces around the bar. (☎070 360 0019; www.depaas.nl. Beer from €1.70. Open M-Th and Su 3pm-1am, F-Sa 3pm-1:30am. MC/V.)

DAYTRIP FROM THE HAGUE: DELFT. Lily-lined canals and stone footbridges still line the streets of picturesque Delft (pop. 100,000), the birthplace of the 17th-century Dutch painter **Johannes Vermeer** and the home of the famous blue-and-white ceramic pottery known as **Delftware.** The best of the three factories that produce it is **De Candelaer**, Kerkstr. 13, where everything is made from scratch, and visitors can listen to a free explanation of the process. *(☎070 213 1848; www.candelaer.nl. Open daily 9am-6pm. Will ship to the US. AmEx/MC/V.)* William of Orange, father of the Netherlands, used **Het Prinsenhof**, St. Agathapl. 1, as his headquarters during the Dutch resistance to Spain in the 16th century. The gorgeous old building now houses a museum chronicling his life as well as a collection of paintings, Delftware, and other artifacts from the Dutch Golden Age. *(☎070 260 2358; www.prinsenhof-delft.nl. Open Tu-Sa 10am-5pm, Su 1-5pm. €6, ages 12-16 €5, under 12 and Museum card holders free.)* A long stretch of a canal leads up to the 27 stained-glass windows at the monumental **Oude Kerk**, Heilige Geestkerkhof 25. The three antique organs are worth an examination, and the church is also Vermeer's final resting place. Its tower is about 75m high and leans a staggering—and slightly unnerving—1.96m out of line. *(☎070 212 3015; www.oudekerk-delft.nl. Open Apr.-Oct. M-Sa 9am-6pm; Nov.-Mar. M-F 11am-4pm, Sa 10am-5pm. Entrance to both Nieuwe Kerk and Oude Kerk €3, seniors €2, ages 3-12 €1.50.)* You can catch the **train** to either of the two train stations in The Hague (8min., 5 per hr., €2.30) or to Amsterdam (1hr., 5 per hr., €11.30) The **Tourist Information Point**, Hippolytusbuurt 4, has free **Internet** terminals as well as free **maps** and information on sights and events. You can also purchase a "hop-on, hop-off" city pass for the Hague and Delft, allowing you to use public transit. €13 for 24hr., €20 for 48hr. *(☎070 215 4051; www.delft.nl. Open M 10am-4pm, Tu-F 9am-6pm, Sa 10am-5pm, Su 10am-3pm.)*

ROTTERDAM ☎010

Marked by a razor-sharp skyline, countless steamships, and darting high-speed trains, Rotterdam (pop. 590,000) is the busiest port in Europe. It's also the country's most exciting multicultural capital, with the largest traditional immigrant population in the Netherlands. Festivals, art galleries, and an extremely dynamic nightlife make Rotterdam a busy center of cultural activity and the hippest, most up-and-coming city in the Netherlands.

TRANSPORTATION AND PRACTICAL INFORMATION. Trains roll out of Rotterdam Centraal to Amsterdam (1hr., 1-5 per hr., €13) and The Hague (30min., 1-5per hr., €4.30). Rotterdam has a network of **buses, trams,** and **two Metro lines** (**Calandlijn** and **Erasmuslijn**) that intersect in the center of the city at Beurs station. Metro tickets, equivalent to two strips, are valid for two hours. The **VVV,** Coolsingel 5, has free **maps** of public transportation as well as maps of the city. (☎0900 271 0120, €0.40 per min.; from abroad ☎010 414 0000; www.vvvrotterdam.nl. Open M-Th 9:30am-6pm, F 9:30am-9pm, Sa 9:30am-5pm.) Stop by the backpacker-oriented **Use-it Rotterdam,** Conradstr. 2, where you will find great money-saving tips and useful info. (☎010 240 9158; www.use-it.nl.)

ACCOMMODATIONS AND FOOD. For true backpackers, the clean, simple, and fun hostel **Sleep-in De Mafkees ❶,** Schaatsbaan 41-45, is a great place to stay. A "honeymoon suite" is available for guests in love and willing to kiss in public. (☎010 281 0459; www.only10euroanight.nl. Dorms available end of June-Aug. €10. Breakfast included. Personal locker €1 per day. Internet €0.80 per 15min. Must bring own sleeping bag or sheets; limited rentals. Reception closed 5:15pm-11:30am. Check-in at Use-It and store luggage in lockers.) Expect knowledgeable staff and clean, comfortable rooms at the commercial **Stayokay Rotterdam ❶,** Rochussenstr. 107-109, a hostel that's great for large groups. (☎010 436 5763; www.stayokay.com/rotterdam. Internet €5 per hr. Reception 24hr. Dorms €20-31; singles €40-45; doubles €56-65. €2.50 HI discount. AmEx/MC/V.) **Bazar ❷,** attracts nightly crowds with glittering colored lights, bright blue tables, and satisfying Mediterranean and Middle Eastern fusion cuisine. (☎010 206 5151. Sandwiches €4. Special dinner €8. Breakfast and lunch served all day. Reservations recommended for dinner. Open M-Th 8am-1am, F 8am-2am, Sa 10am-2am, Su 10am-midnight. AmEx/MC/V.) **Bagel Bakery ❶,** Schilderstr. 57A-59A, a popular stop for students, serves artfully-topped bagels in a well-lit, hip environment. Try their freshly-baked *liefdesbrood*, "true love bread." (☎010 412 1413. Open Tu-Th 9am-9pm, F-Sa 9am-10pm, Su 10am-9pm. Cash only).

SIGHTS AND ENTERTAINMENT. Only the extremely ambitious should attempt to see all of the **Museum Boijmans van Beuningen,** Museumpark 18-20, in one day. On the ground floor, you'll find post-war work by artists like Andy Warhol. The second floor is home to a large selection of Surrealist paintings as well as Expressionist pieces, plus several Monets and an impressive collection of Dutch and Flemish art by the like of Hans Memling, Anthony van Dyck, Jan Steen, Frans Hals, and Rembrandt van Rijn. (☎010 441 9400; www.boijmans.nl. Open Tu-Su 11am-5pm. €9, students €4.50, under 18 and Museum Card holders free. Wheelchair-accessible. Library open Tu-Su 11am-4:30pm; free with entrance ticket.) The **Nederlands Architectuurinstituut (NAI),** Museumpark 25, boasts one of the most extraordinary designs in all of Rotterdam. The multi-level glass and steel construction—which traverses a manmade pool and looks out onto Museumpark—is home to several exhibition spaces, a world-class archive, and 39,500 books. (☎010 440 1200; www.nai.nl. Open Tu-Sa 10am-5pm, Su 11am-5pm. Library and reading room open Tu-Sa 10am-5pm, Su 11am-5pm. €8, age 12-18, students, and seniors €5, ages 4-12 €1, Museum Card holders free.) Ascending the tallest structure in the Netherlands, the popular **Euromast,** Parkhaven 20, is the best way to take in a panoramic view of Rotterdam's jagged skyline. From the 112m viewing deck, you can take an elevator to the 185m mark, where you'll see all the way to Delft and The Hague.

(☎010 436 4811; www.euromast.nl. Open daily Apr.-Sept. 9:30am-11pm; Oct.-Mar. 10am-11pm. Platforms open until 10pm. €8.30, ages 4-11 €5.40.)

Coffee shops line **Oude** and **Nieuwe Binnenweg.** At **Off_Corso,** Kruiskade 22, art exhibitions share the bill with regular dance parties and live DJs at this very popular club. (☎010 280 7359; www.offcorso.nl.) **Dizzy,** 's-Gravendijkwal 127, Rotterdam's premier jazz cafe for 25 years, hosts frequent jam sessions. (☎010 477 3014; www.dizzy.nl. Take tram 4 to Dijkzicht. Beer €1.80. Whiskey €5.20. Open M-Th noon-1am, F-Sa noon-2am, Su noon-midnight. AmEx/MC/V.)

UTRECHT ☎030

Smack-dab in the center of the Netherlands lies Utrecht (pop. 290,000), a mecca for history buffs, thesis writers, and student revelers. The swarms of fraternity boys that fill the city's outdoor cafes are a visible testament to Utrecht's status as the Netherlands's largest university town. Utrecht is also a cultural hub: visitors come here for action-packed festivals, nightlife, and tree-lined canals.

TRANSPORTATION AND PRACTICAL INFORMATION. Take **train** to Amsterdam (30min., 3-6 per hr., €6.60). The **VVV,** Dompl. 9, is in a building called the RonDom, a **visitor's center** for cultural history, across from the Domkerk. Pick up a free **map** of the city and a complete listing of museums and sights. (☎0900 128 8732, €0.50 per min.; www.utrechtyourway.nl. Open Apr.-Sept. M-Sa 10am-5pm, Su noon-5pm; Oct.-Mar. M-F and Su noon-5pm, Sa 10am-5pm.)

ACCOMMODATIONS AND FOOD. **Strowis Hostel ❶,** Boothstr. 8, has a laid-back staff, a convenient location, and unbeatable prices. This former squat feels more like a welcoming country villa. (☎030 238 0280; www.strowis.nl. Breakfast €6. Free lockers. Linens and blanket €1.25. Free Internet. Bike rental €6 per day. Curfew M-Th and Su 2am, F-Sa 3am. Max. 2-week stay. 14-bed dorms €15; 8-bed €16; 6-bed €17; 4-bed €18; singles/doubles €57.50; triples €69.) The three-story **B&B Utrecht City Centre ❶,** Lucasbolwerk 4, is geared towards free-spirited backpackers looking for a welcoming community. Hostel includes beds, a fully-stocked kitchen with edible food (open 24hr.), a music corner full of instruments, and an extensive movie collection. Take bus # 3, 4 or 11 to Stadsschouwburg or walk down Lange Viestr. for 10min.; it's to the left on the corner of Lucasbolwerk and Nobelstr. (☎065 043 4884; www.hostelutrecht.nl. Mandatory sheet rental €2.50. Towel €1. Free Wi-Fi and plenty of computers. Bike rental €5 per day. Private rooms located in separate building. Dorms €17.50; singles €55; doubles €65; triples €90; quads €120. MC/V.) **Het Nachtrestaurant ❷,** Oudegr. 158, has a decadent, pillow-lined cellar dining room, while the flashier clientele crowd the canal-side terrace. (☎030 230 3036. Tapas €3-6. Nightclub Sa 11pm-close. Open M-W 11am-midnight, Th-F 11am-1am, Sa 11am-10:30pm. Su noon-midnight. AmEx/MC/V.)

SIGHTS AND NIGHTLIFE. **Utrecht's Domtoren,** Achter de Dom 1, is impossible to ignore: the city's most beloved landmark is also the highest church tower in the Netherlands. The 112m tower presides over the province with magnificent spires and 26,000kg of bronze bells. The brick-red *Domkerk* was attached to the tower until an errant tornado blew away the nave in 1674. During the tour, you'll learn about the history of the church and get a glimpse of the church's bells. (☎030 231 0403. Open Oct.-Apr. M-F 11am-4:30pm, Sa 11am-3:30pm, Su 2-4pm; May-Sept. M-F 10am-5pm, Sa 10am-3:30pm, Su 2-4pm. Free concert every Sa 3:30pm. *Domtoren* accessible only through 1hr. tours daily Oct.-Mar. M-F noon, 2, 4pm, Sa 1 per hr. 10am-5pm, Su 1 per hr. noon-5pm; Apr.-Sept. M-Sa 1 per hr. 10am-5pm, Su 1 per hr. noon-5pm. Domkerk free.

Domtoren €7.50, students and over 65 €6.50, ages 4-12 €4.50.) At the **Centraal Museum,** Nicolaaskerkhof 10, visitors enter a labyrinth of pavilions to experience Dutch art. The museum oversees the world's largest collection of work by De Stijl designer Gerrit Rietveld, but many of these objects have been transferred to the avant-garde **Rietveld Schroderhuis,** a UNESCO World Heritage Site. The museum is accessible only by guided tour, so call ahead for reservations. (☎030 236 2362; 030 236 2310 for Rietveld Schroderhuis; www.centraalmuseum.nl. Open Tu-Su 11am-5pm, F noon-9pm. Audio tour free. €8, students, over age 65 and ages 13-17 €6, under 12 €2.)

At **'t Oude Pothuys,** Oudegr. 279, uninhibited patrons have been known to jump off the bar's terrace into the canal after a long night of festivities. (☎030 231 8970. Beer €2. Live music nightly 11pm. Open M-W and Su 3pm-2am, Th-Sa 3pm-3am. AmEx/MC.) A former squat turned political and cultural center, **ACU Politiek Cultureel Centrum,** Voorstr. 71, hosts live music (W, F cover €5-6), a political discussion group (M 8pm-2am), and a Su movie night. (☎030 231 4590; www.acu.nl. Beer €1.70. Vegetarian Tu, Th, Su 6pm-8:30pm. Organic and vegan dining W 3-5pm. Cash only. Open M-Th and Su 5pm-2am. F-Sa 9pm-4am.) Utrecht's theater school, **Hofman,** Janskerkhof 17A, is packed with students and twentysomethings throughout the week. Take advantage of student-friendly events and live music nights. (☎030 230 2470; www.hofman-cafe.nl. Beer €2. Open M-Th and Su 11am-2am, F-Sa 11am-3:30am. Cash only.)

PORTUGAL

While Portugal is small, its imposing forests and mountains, scenic vineyards, and almost 2000km of coastline rival the attractions of Spain. Portugal's capital, Lisbon, offers marvelous museums, castles, and churches. The country experienced international glory and fabulous wealth 400 years ago during the Golden Age of Vasco da Gama. Despite suffering under the dictatorship of Salazar for 30 years in the 20th century, Portugal has reemerged as a European cultural center with a growing economy. Extremes of fortune have contributed to the unique Portuguese concept of *saudade*, a yearning for the glories of the past and a dignified resignation to the fact that the future can never compete. Visitors may experience *saudade* through a *fado* singer's song or over a glass of port, but Portugal's attractions are more likely to inspire delight than nostalgia.

DISCOVER PORTUGAL: SUGGESTED ITINERARIES

THREE DAYS. Make your way through **Lisbon** (1 day; p. 482): venture through its famous Moorish district, the Alfama, Castelo de São Jorge, and the Parque das Nações. By night, listen to *fado* and hit the clubs in Bairro Alto. Daytrip to **Sintra's** fairytale castles (1 day), then sip wine in **Porto** (1 day).

ONE WEEK. After wandering the streets of **Lisbon** (2 days) and **Sintra** (1 day), lounge on the beaches of **Lagos** (1 day) and admire the cliffs of **Sagres** (1 day). Move on to the university town of **Coimbra** (1 day) before ending your week in **Porto** (1 day).

BEST OF PORTUGAL, TWO WEEKS. After taking in the sights, sounds, and cafes of **Lisbon** (4 days), daytrip to enchanting **Sintra** (1 day). Head down to the infamous beaches and bars of **Lagos** (2 days), where hordes of visitors dance the night away. Take an afternoon in **Sagres** (1 day), once considered the edge of the world. Check out the macabre bone chapel in **Évora** (1 day) before heading north to vibrant **Coimbra** (2 days). The incredible selection of port should keep you occupied in **Porto** (2 days). Finish your tour in the impressive gardens and plazas of **Braga** (1 day).

LIFE AND TIMES

HISTORY

EARLY HISTORY (UNTIL AD 1139). Settlement of Portugal began around 8000 BC when Neolithic hunters and fishermen arrived from Andalucía. Several tribes, including the Celts, Phoenicians, Greeks, and Carthaginians, began to populate the Iberian Peninsula in the first millennium BC. After their victory over Carthage in the Second Punic War (218-201 BC) and their defeat of the Celts in 140 BC, the Romans gained control of central and southern Portugal. Six centuries of Roman rule Latinized Portugal's language and customs.

The decline of the Roman Empire in the third and fourth centuries permitted the ascendance of the **Visigoths,** a nomadic Germanic tribe who arrived

in AD 469 and dominated the peninsula for the next two centuries. In AD 711, however, the **Moors** invaded Iberia, toppling the Visigoth monarchy. They established Muslim communities called *al-Gharb* (Algarve) along the southern coast. After nearly four centuries of rule, the Moorish legacy of agricultural advances, architectural landmarks, and linguistic and cultural customs continues to influence the region.

THE CHRISTIAN RECONQUISTA AND THE BIRTH OF PORTUGAL (1139-1385). The **Reconquista** picked up steam in the 11th century when **Fernando I** united Castilla and León, thereby providing a base from which to reclaim territory for Christendom from the Moors. In 1139, **Dom Afonso Henriques** (Afonso I), a noble from the territory around Porto, declared independence from Castilla and León. Soon thereafter, he named himself the first king of Portugal. The division between Spain and Portugal is the oldest established border in Europe. With the help of Christian military groups like the **Knights Templar,** the new monarchy battled Muslim forces, capturing Lisbon in 1147. By 1249, the Reconquista under **Afonso III** defeated the remnants of Muslim power through successful campaigns in the Alentejo and the Algarve. The Christian kings, led by **Dinis I** (1279-1325), promoted the Portuguese language over Spanish, and, with the **Treaty of Alcañices** (1297), settled border disputes with neighboring Castilla. It was at this time that Portugal's identity as Europe's first unified, independent nation was confirmed.

THE AGE OF DISCOVERY (1385-1580). The reign of **João I** (1385-1433), the first king of the **House of Avis,** ushered in a period of unity and prosperity. **João** increased the power of the crown, establishing a strong base for future Portuguese expansion and economic success. Under the leadership of João's son, **Prince Henry the Navigator,** Portugal also established itself as a world leader in maritime science and exploration. Portuguese adventurers captured the Moroccan city of Ceuta in 1415, discovered Madeira in 1419, happened upon the uninhabited Açores in 1427, and began to plunder the African coast for slaves and riches. Lagos became Europe's first slave market in 1441.

The Portuguese monarchs, while refusing to sponsor Christopher Columbus's expedition, did fund a number of momentous voyages. **Bartolomeu Dias** rounded Africa's Cape of Storms (later renamed the Cape of Good Hope) in 1488, opening the route to the East and paving the way for Portuguese entrance into the spice trade. In 1497, the royal family supported **Vasco da Gama,** who led the first European naval expedition to India. Three years later, **Pedro Álvares Cabral** claimed Brazil for Portugal. Portugal's international power peaked during the reign of **Manuel I** (1495-1521), the "King of Gold," who controlled a spectacular commercial empire. During his rule, Fernão de Magalhães, known as **Magellan,** completed the first circumnavigation of the globe in 1521. Concurrently, other European powers began developing their own routes to the East, and Portuguese dominance of trade waned by the end of the 16th century.

BRING ON THE BRAGANÇA (1580-1807). In 1580, Hapsburg **King Felipe II** of Spain forcibly claimed the Portuguese throne, and the Iberian Peninsula was briefly ruled by one monarch. Over the next 60 years, the Habsburgs dragged Portugal into several ill-fated battles, including the failed **Spanish-Portuguese Armada** in 1588. By the end of Hapsburg rule, Portugal had lost much of its once-vast empire. In 1640, the **House of Bragança** engineered a nationalist rebellion against **King Felipe IV.** After a brief struggle, they assumed control, asserting Portuguese independence from Spain. To secure sovereignty, the Bragança dynasty re-established ties with England, beginning to restore prosperity to Portugal. However, the momentous **earthquake of 1755** devastated far more than the economies of Lisbon and southern Portugal; as many as 60,000 people died in the quake and during the subsequent tsunami and fire. A mass grave containing the bodies of 3000 Portuguese who died in the tragedy was recently found in the cloisters of a Franciscan convent. Despite the damage, dictatorial minister **Marquês de Pombal** rebuilt Lisbon and instituted national economic reform.

NAPOLEON MAKES IT PERSONAL (1807-1910). Napoleon took control of France in 1799 and soon set his sights on the rest of Europe. When he reached Portugal in 1807, his army met with little resistance. Rather than risk death, the Portuguese royal family fled to Brazil. The **Constitution of 1822,** drawn up during their absence, severely limited the power of the monarchy, and soon the ultimate sibling rivalry exploded into the **War of the Two Brothers** (1826-1834). Constitutionalists supported Pedro, the new king of Brazil, and monarchists supported Miguel, Pedro's brother. Continued tensions between the constitutionalists and the monarchists marked the next 75 years.

FROM THE "FIRST REPUBLIC" TO SALAZAR (1910-1970). Portugal spent the first decade of the 20th century trying to recover from the political discord of the 19th century. On October 5, 1910, 20-year-old **King Manuel II** fled to England seeking amnesty from civil unrest. Portugal's new government, the **First Republic,** received worldwide disapproval for its expulsion of the Jesuits and other religious orders. Conflict between the government and labor movements heightened tensions. Portugal's decision to enter **World War I** on the side of the Allies proved economically draining and internally divisive, despite eventual victory. The weak republic wobbled and eventually fell in a 1926 military coup. The provisional military government that took control named **General António Óscar de Fragoso Carmona** its leader, and appointed **António de Oliveira Salazar,** a prominent economics professor, minister of finance. In 1932, Salazar became prime minister, the position soon devolving into a dictatorship. His **Estado Novo** (New State) granted suffrage to women but did little else to end the country's authoritarian tradition. While Portugal's international economic standing improved, the regime laid the cost of progress squarely on the shoulders of the working class, the peasantry, and colonial subjects in Africa. A terrifying secret police **(PIDE)** crushed domestic opposition to Salazar's rule, and African rebellions were subdued in bloody battles that drained the nation's economy.

FROM IMPERIALISM TO SOCIALISM (1970-1999). The slightly more liberal **Marcelo Caetano** dragged on the unpopular African wars after Salazar's death in

1970, but international disapproval of Portuguese imperialism and the army's dissatisfaction with colonial entanglements led **General António Spinola** to call for decolonization. On April 25, 1974, a left-wing military coalition calling itself the **Armed Forces Movement** overthrew Caetano in a coup. The **Revolution of the Carnations** sent citizens dancing into the streets; today, every town in Portugal seems to have its own Rua 25 de Abril. When the new government took over, Marxist-dominated armed forces established civil and political liberties; Portugal also withdrew its claims on African colonies by 1975, resulting in a deluge of refugees. In 1976, the country's first elections brought Socialist prime minister **Mario Soares** to power. Soares improved the economy, and in 1986 the country entered the European Economic Community (now the European Union).

TODAY

The **European Union** declared Portugal a full member of the EU Economic and Monetary Union (EMU) in 1999, and the nation continues its quest to close the economic gap with the rest of Western Europe. Political integration was furthered during Portugal's tenure as President of the Council of the European Union in 2007. In 1999, Portugal ceded Macau, its last overseas territory, to the Chinese. Portugal and Indonesia have agreed to cooperate over the reconstruction of East Timor, formerly a Portuguese colony.

Jorge Sampaio returned to the presidency after the January 2001 parliamentary elections, but Socialist prime minister **António Guterres** resigned in December 2001, just after overseeing Portugal's successful transition to the euro. President Sampaio then appointed Social Democrat **Jose Manuel Durão Barroso** as prime minister. Barroso resigned the post in July 2004 to accept the Presidency of the European Commission. **Pedro Santana Lopez** took his place, but lost the post to **José Sócrates** (the leader of the Socialist party) in March 2005. The presidential elections of 2006 named **Aníbal Cavaco Silva,** who had lost to President Sampaio in the 1996 presidential elections, as the next head of state.

ESSENTIALS

WHEN TO GO

FACTS AND FIGURES

OFFICIAL NAME: The Portuguese Republic.

CAPITAL: Lisbon.

MAJOR CITIES: Coimbra, Porto.

POPULATION: 10,463,000.

LAND AREA: 92,000 sq. km.

TIME ZONE: GMT.

LANGUAGES: Portuguese, Mirandese.

RELIGION: Roman Catholic (85%).

NUMBER OF GRAPE VARIETALS AUTHORIZED FOR MAKING PORT: 48.

Summer is high season, but the southern coast draws tourists between March and November. In the low season, many hostels slash their prices, and reservations are seldom necessary. While Lisbon and some of the larger towns (especially the university town of Coimbra) burst with vitality year-round, many smaller towns virtually shut down in winter, and sights reduce their hours.

DOCUMENTS AND FORMALITIES

EMBASSIES AND CONSULATES. Foreign embassies in Portugal are in Lisbon. Portuguese embassies abroad include: **Australia,** 23 Culgoa Circuit, O'Malley,

Canberra, ACT 2606 (☎612 6290 1733); **Canada,** 645 Island Park Dr., Ottawa, ON K1Y 0B8 (☎613-729-2270); **Ireland,** Knocksinna Mews, 7 Willow Park, Foxrock, Dublin, 18 (☎353 289 4416); **UK,** 11 Belgrave Sq., London, SW1X 8PP (☎020 7235 5331); **US,** 2012 Massachusetts Ave. NW, Washington, D.C., 20036 (☎202-350-5400). **NZ** citizens should contact the embassy in Australia.

VISA AND ENTRY INFORMATION. EU citizens do not need a visa. Citizens of Australia, Canada, New Zealand, the UK, and the US do not need a visa for stays up to 90 days, beginning upon entry into any of the countries within the EU's freedom-of-movement zone. For more info, see p. 8. For stays over 90 days, non-EU citizens need visas, available at Portuguese consulates.

TOURIST SERVICES AND MONEY

TOURIST OFFICES. For general info, contact the Portuguese Tourism Board, (☎+1 646 723 02 00; www.portugal.org). When in Portugal, stop by tourist offices, listed in the Practical Information section of each city and town.

EMERGENCY	**General Emergency:** ☎112.

MONEY. The **euro (€)** has replaced the **escudo** as the unit of currency in Portugal. For more info on the euro, see p. 11. Generally, it's cheaper to exchange money in Portugal than at home. **ATMs** have the best exchange rates. Credit cards also offer good rates and may sometimes be required to reserve hotel rooms or rental cars; **MasterCard** (known in Portugal as **Eurocard**) and **Visa** are the most frequently accepted. Tips of 5-10% are customary only in fancy restaurants or hotels. Some cheaper restaurants include a 10% service charge; if they don't and you'd like to leave a tip, round up to the nearest euro and leave the change. Taxi drivers do not expect tips except for especially long trips. **Bargaining** is not customary in shops, but you can give it a shot at the local market *(mercado)* or when looking for a private room *(quarto)*.

BUSINESS HOURS. Shops are open M-F from 9am to 6pm, although many close for a few hours in the afternoon. Restaurants serve lunch from noon to 3pm and dinner from 7 to 10pm—or later. Museums are often closed on Monday, and many shops are closed over the weekend. Banks usually open around 9am M-F and close in the afternoon.

TRANSPORTATION

BY PLANE. Most international flights land at **Portela Airport** in Lisbon (**LIS;** ☎218 41 35 00); some also land at **Faro** (**FAO;** ☎289 80 08 00) or **Porto** (**OPO;** 229 43 24 00). **TAP Air Portugal** (Canada and the US ☎800-221-7370, Portugal ☎707 20 57 00, UK ☎845 601 0932; www.tap.pt) is Portugal's national airline, serving domestic and international locations. **Portugália** (☎218 93 80 70; www.flypga.pt) is smaller and flies between Faro, Lisbon, Porto, major Spanish cities, and other Western European destinations. For more information, see p. 33.

BY TRAIN. **Caminhos de Ferro Portugueses** (☎213 18 59 90; www.cp.pt) is Portugal's national railway. Lines run to domestic destinations, Madrid, and Paris. For travel outside of the Braga-Porto-Coimbra-Lisbon line, buses are better. Lisbon, where local trains are fast and efficient, is the exception. Trains often leave at irregular hours, and posted schedules *(horários)* aren't always accurate; check ticket booths upon arrival. Fines for riding without a ticket *(sem* *bilhete)* are high. Those under 12 or over 65 get half-price tickets. Youth discounts are available only to Portuguese citizens. Train passes are usually not worth buying, as tickets are inexpensive. For more information, see p. 37.

BY BUS. Buses are cheap, frequent, and connect to just about every town in Portugal. **Rodoviária** (☎212 94 71 00), formerly the national bus company, has recently been privatized. Each company name corresponds to a particular region of the country, such as Rodoviária Alentejo or Minho e Douro, with a few exceptions, such as EVA in the Algarve. Private regional companies, including **AVIC, Cabanelas,** and **Mafrense,** also operate buses. Beware of non-express buses in small regions like Estremadura and Alentejo, which stop every few minutes. Express service *(expressos)* between major cities is good, and inexpensive city buses often run to nearby villages. Portugal's main Euroline (p. 37) affiliates are Internorte, Intercentro, and Intersul. **Busabout** coaches stop in Portugal at Lisbon, Lagos, and Porto. Every coach has a guide on board to answer questions and to make travel arrangements en route.

BY CAR. A **driver's license** from one's home country is required to rent a car; no International Driving Permit is necessary. Portugal has the **highest automobile accident rate** per capita in Western Europe. The highway system *(itinerarios principais)* is easily accessible, but off the main arteries, the narrow roads are difficult to negotiate. Speed limits are ignored, recklessness is common, and lighting and road surfaces are often inadequate. Parking space in cities is nonexistent. In short, buses are safer. The national automobile association, the **Automóvel Clube de Portugal (ACP),** (☎800 50 25 02; www.acp.pt), has breakdown and towing service, as well as first aid.

BY THUMB. In Portugal, **hitchhiking** is rare. Beach-bound locals occasionally hitchhike in summer, but more commonly stick to the inexpensive bus system. Rides are easiest to come by between smaller towns and at gas stations near highways and rest stops. *Let's Go* does not recommend hitchhiking.

KEEPING IN TOUCH

PHONE CODES	**Country code:** 351. **International dialing prefix:** 00. Within Portugal, dial city code + local number. For more info on placing international calls, see **Inside Back Cover.**

TELEPHONE. Whenever possible, use a calling card for international phone calls, as long-distance rates for national phone services are often very high. Mobile phones are an increasingly popular and economical option. Major mobile carriers include: TMN, Optimus Telecom SA, and Vodafone. Direct-dial access numbers for calling out of Portugal include: **AT&T Direct** (☎800 80 01 28); **British Telecom** (☎800 80 04 40); **Canada Direct** (☎800 80 01 22); **Telecom New Zealand Direct** (☎800 80 06 40); **Telstra Australia** (☎800 80 06 10). For more info on calling home from Europe, see p. 20.

MAIL. Mail in Portugal is somewhat inefficient. **Airmail** *(via aerea)* takes one to two weeks to reach Canada or the US, and longer to get to Australia and New Zealand. **Surface mail** *(superficie)*, for packages only, takes up to two months. **Registered** or blue mail takes five to eight business days for roughly three times the price of airmail. **EMS** or **Express Mail** will most likely arrive overseas in three to four days, though it costs more than double the blue mail price. To receive mail in Portugal, have mail delivered **Poste Restante.** Mail will go to the main post office unless you specify a subsidiary by street address. Address mail to be held according to the following example: Last Name, First Name, Posta Restante, Postal code City, PORTUGAL; AIRMAIL.

ACCOMMODATIONS AND CAMPING

PORTUGAL	❶	❷	❸	❹	❺
ACCOMMODATIONS	under €16	€16-20	€21-30	€31-40	over €40

Movijovem, R. Lúcio de Azevedo 27, 1600-146 Lisbon (☎707 20 30 30; www.pousadasjuventude.pt), the **Portuguese Hostelling International** affiliate, oversees the country's HI hostels. All bookings can be made through them. A bed in a *pousada da juventude* costs €9-15 per night, including breakfast and linens, slightly less in the low season. Though often the cheapest option, hostels may lie far from the town center. To reserve rooms in the high season, get an **International Booking Voucher** from Movijovem (or your country's HI affiliate) and send it to the desired hostel four to eight weeks in advance. In the low season (Oct.-Apr.), double-check to see if the hostel is open. **Hotels** in Portugal tend to be pricey. Rates typically include breakfast and showers, and most rooms without bath or shower have a sink. When business is slow, try bargaining in advance—the "official price" is just the maximum. **Pensões,** also called **residencias,** are a budget traveler's mainstay, cheaper than hotels and only slightly more expensive (and much more common) than crowded youth hostels. Like hostels, *pensões* generally provide linens and towels. Many do not take reservations in high season; for those that do, book a week ahead. **Quartos** are rooms in private residences, similar to Spain's *casas particulares.* These may be the cheapest option in cities and the only option in town; tourist offices can help find one. Prices are flexible and bargaining expected. Portugal has 150 **official campgrounds** *(parques de campismo)*, often beach-accessible and equipped with grocery stores and cafes. Urban and coastal parks may require reservations. Police are cracking down on illegal camping—don't try it. Tourist offices stock *Portugal: Camping and Caravan Sites*, a free guide to campgrounds.

FOOD AND DRINK

PORTUGAL	❶	❷	❸	❹	❺
FOOD	under €6	€6-10	€11-15	€16-20	over €20

Portuguese dishes are seasoned with olive oil, garlic, herbs, and sea salt, but few spices. The fish selection includes *choco grelhado* (grilled cuttlefish), *linguado grelhado* (grilled sole), and *peixe espada* (swordfish). Portugal's renowned *queijos* (cheeses) are made from cow, goat, and sheep milk. For dessert, try *pudim flan* (egg custard). A hearty *almoço* (lunch) is eaten between noon and 2pm; *jantar* (dinner) is served between 8pm and midnight. *Meia dose* (half-portions) cost more than half-price but are often more than adequate. The *prato do dia* (special of the day) and the set *menú* of appetizer, bread, entree, and dessert, are also filling choices. Cheap, high-quality Portuguese *vinho* (wine) is astounding. Its delicious relative, *vinho do porto* (port), is a dessert in itself. Coffees include *bica* (black espresso), *galão* (with milk, in a glass), and *café com leite* (with milk, in a cup). *Mini-Preço* and *Pingo Doce* are good supermarkets for cheap groceries.

LISBON (LISBOA)

At sunset, the scarlet glow cast over the Rio Tejo is matched by the ruby red shimmer inside your glass of *vinho do porto*. Welcome to Lisbon. A magnificent history has left its mark upon this ancient city: illustrious bronze figures stand proud in open plazas, Roman arches and columns inspire reverence in visitors, and a towering 12th-century castle keeps watch from atop one of the city's infamous seven hills. Lisbon is quickly becoming one of the most talked-about capitals in Europe, driven by cutting-edge fashion, flourishing art and music scenes, and enthusiastic nightlife. Graffiti adorns the time-worn walls of Bairro Alto, and at night the cobblestone sidewalks echo with the modern rhythms of local clubs. A monumental past may loom over every corner of the city, but Lisbon is thriving in the present. Immigrants and visitors from all around the world give Lisbon an international feel that is hard to come by anywhere else in Portugal. Crowds of unique people—street performers, break dancers, and peddlers of various sorts—line the streets of Baixa and Bairro Alto, giving the city its diverse and distinctive flavor.

Complexity is not new to Lisbon. Half a dozen civilizations claim parenthood of the city, beginning with the Phoenicians, Greeks, and Carthaginians. The Romans arrived in 205 BC and ruled for 600 years. Under Julius Caesar, Lisbon became one of the most important port cities in Lusitania, and in 1255, Lisbon was made the capital of Portugal. The city, along with the empire, reached its zenith at the end of the 15th century, when Portuguese navigators pioneered the exploration of Asia, Africa, and South America during the Age of Discovery. A catastrophic earthquake on November 1, 1755 catalyzed the nation's fall from glory—close to one-fifth of the population died, and two-thirds of Lisbon was destroyed in the resulting fires. Immediately, the Prime Minister Marquês de Pombal began a massive reconstruction effort, an overhaul that explains the contrast between the neat, grid-like layout of Baixa (entirely destroyed in the earthquake) and the hilly mazes of the surrounding areas that at least partially survived. Twentieth-century Lisbon saw plenty of change, as new technologies complemented the traditions of the past. Temples, castles, and cathedrals stand next to crowded plazas, buzzing cafes, and blaring *discotecas*, giving Lisbon a life of its own.

INTERCITY TRANSPORTATION

BY PLANE

All flights land at **Aeroporto de Lisboa** (☎218 41 35 00 or 41 37 00 for departures and arrivals) near the city's northern edge. Major **airlines** have offices at Pr. Marquês de Pombal and along Av. da Liberdade. The cheapest way into town is by bus: walk out of the terminal, turn right, and go straight across the street to the bus stop, marked by yellow metal posts with arrival times of incoming buses. Take bus #44, 45, or 745 (15-20min., every 12-25min. 6am-12:15am, €1.40) to Pr. dos Restauradores; the bus stops in front of the tourist office, located inside the Palácio da Foz. The express AeroBus #91 runs to the same locations (15min.; every 20min. 7am-11pm; €3.50, TAP passengers free); it's a good option during rush hour. The bus stop is in front of the terminal exit. A **taxi** downtown costs about €10-15 (plus a €1.60 baggage fee) at low traffic, but you're billed by time, not distance. Beware that some drivers may keep your change or take a longer route.

PRE-PAY YOUR WAY. Ask at the airport tourist office (☎218 450 660; open 7am-midnight) about the voucher program, which allows visitors to pre-pay for cab rides from the airport (€21).

BY TRAIN

Train service in and out of Lisbon routinely confuses newcomers, as there are four stations in Lisbon and one across the river in Barreiro, each serving different destinations. Portugal's affordable, express **Alfa Pendular** line offers the easiest connections between Lisbon and Braga, Porto, Coimbra, and Faro. Regional trains make frequent stops; buses, although more expensive and lacking toilets, are faster and more comfortable. Suburban train lines, which offer service to Cascais and Sintra (and stops along the way), are efficient and reliable. Contact **Caminhos de Ferro Portugueses** for further info. (☎808 20 82 08; www.cp.pt.)

Estação do Barreiro, across the Rio Tejo. Southbound trains. Accessible by ferry from the Terreiro do Paço dock off Pr. do Comércio (30min., 2 per hr., €2.10). Trains go to **Pinhal Novo** (25min., 1-2 per hr., €1.30) and **Setúbal** (20min., 1-2 per hr., €1.70).

Estação Cais do Sodré, just beyond the end of R. do Alecrim, beside the river; a 5min. walk from Baixa. M: Cais do Sodré or take any tram 28E from Bairro Alto or Alfama. Serves the southwestern suburbs. Take trains labeled "Cascais Todos" or "Oeiras" to **Belém** (10min., 3-4 per hr. 5:30am-1:30am, €1.20). Take trains labeled "Cascais Todos" or "Cascais" to **Estoril** (30-35min., 3-4 per hr. 5:30am-1:30am, €1.70). Take any trains to **Cascais** (35-40min., 6 per hour 5:30am-1:30am, €1.70) and the youth hostel in **Oeiras** (20min., 6 per hr. 5:30am-1:30am, €1.30).

Estação Rossio, M: Rossio. Cross the *praça* for 2 blocks until you see the station on your right. Alternatively, you can get off at M: Restauradores and walk down Av. da Liberdage; the station will be on your right. Serves the northwestern suburbs. Trains to **Queluz** (20min., every 20min., €1.20) and **Sintra** (40min., every 20min., €1.70).

Estação Santa Apolónia, Av. Infante Dom Henrique. M: Santa Apolónia. Runs international, northern, and eastern lines. All trains stop at **Estação Oriente** (see below). The ticket office is open M-F 5:30am-1030pm and Sa-Su 6am-10:30pm. There is a **currency exchange** station and an **information desk** (English spoken). To: **Aveiro** (2½hr., 16 per day 6am-9:30pm, €16-35); **Braga** (3½hr.; 7am, 1, 4, 7pm; €22-43); **Coimbra** (2hr., 19 per day 6am-9:30pm, €19.50-30); **Madrid** (10hr., 10:30pm, €59); **Porto** (3-4hr., 16 per day 6am-9:30pm, €19.50-39.50).

Estação Oriente, M: Oriente, by the **Parque das Nações.** Offers service to the south. Trains to **Évora** (2hr.; 8:10am, 2:10pm, and 6:10pm; €10); **Faro** (3¼-3¾hr., 6 per day, €18-19.50), with connections to other destinations in the Algarve.

BY BUS

The **bus station** in Lisbon is close to the Jardim Zoológico metro stop, but it can be tricky to find. Once at the metro stop, follow the exit signs to Av. C. Bordalo Pinheiro. Exit the metro and go around the corner. Walk ahead 100m and then cross left in front of Sete Rios station. The stairs to the station are on the left.

Rede Expressos (☎707 22 33 44; www.rede-expressos.pt). To: **Braga** (5hr., 14-16 per day 7am-12:15am, €18); **Coimbra** (2hr., 24-32 per day 7am-12:15am, €13); **Évora** (2hr., 20-25 per day 7am-10:30pm, €11.50); **Faro** (4hr., 9-11 per day 7am-1am, €18-19); **Lagos** (4hr., 9-14 per day 7:30am-1am, €18-19); **Peniche** (1½-2hr., 9-10 per day 7am-10pm, €8); **Portalegre** (4hr., 7-8 per day 7:30am-8pm, €13); **Porto** (3½hr., 20-24 per day 7am-12:15am, €17.50); **Tavira** (5hr., 9 per day 7am-1am, €18-19).

ORIENTATION

Lisbon's historic core has four main neighborhoods: commercial **Baixa** (the low district), museum-heavy **Chiado,** nightlife-rich **Bairro Alto** (the high district), and hilly, labyrinthine **Alfama.** The last, Lisbon's famous medieval Moorish neighborhood, was the lone survivor of the 1755 earthquake. The city's oldest district is a maze of narrow alleys, unmarked alleyways, and *escandinhas* stairways that seem only to lead to more unindentifiable streets. Expect to get lost repeatedly without a detailed map. The street-indexed *For Ways* maps (including Sintra, Cascais, and Estoril) are good, though expensive (sold at newsstands; â,¬5). The maps at the tourist offices are also reliable and free. Visitors exhausted from treks up and down the historic center's many hills can hop aboard tram 28E, which runs East-West through these neighborhoods, connecting most of their major sights. The *bairros* extending in both directions along the river are some of the fastest-growing sections of the city, offering pulsing nightlife and stunning architectural beauty, both ancient and contemporary.

THE BAIRROS OF LISBON

BAIXA

Baixa, Lisbon's old business hub, is the city's historic center, with restaurants and trendy apparel stores lining its streets. The neighborhood grid begins at **Praça Dom Pedro IV** (better known as **Rossio**) and ends at **Praça do Comércio** on the Rio Tejo. The *praças* (squares) function as decorative bookends to the new Lisbon that took shape following the earthquake of 1755, which destroyed most of the city. (If Mr. Richter's scale had been available at the time, the quake would probably have reached an 8.9.) Pr. do Comércio was built on the site of the former Royal Palace, which toppled in the quake, and hence bears the nickname Terreiro do Paço (Palace Lot). Expect to meet many travelers in Baixa: the tourist offices, cheap *pensões*, and stylish hostels concentrated here make Rossio the city's tourist hub. Linked to Rossio is **Praça dos Restauradores,** an urban transit hub and the main drop-off for airport buses. Pr. dos Restauradores lies just above Baixa; Avenida da Liberdade runs uphill from it to the modern business district surrounding **Praça do Marquês de Pombal.**

BAIRRO ALTO AND CHIADO

As Lisbon's most famous neighborhood, Bairro Alto means something different to everyone. To thousands of natives, the upper floors and laundry-covered balconies of the neighborhood's many colorful buildings are home. To music lovers, it's a must-see for *fado*. And to night owls, it's the best place to party. Cobblestone sidewalks lead to inexpensive cafes filled with locals enjoying *bacalhau assado* (grilled codfish), and graffiti-covered walls separate the quirky shops selling shoes and T-shirts from bars that bustle every night of the week. Bairro Alto has budget delights as well, such as the bargain-filled shopping center at the end of **Rua Garrett,** and better yet, the beautiful churches and museums around cultured **Chiado,** which abuts Baixa below. At night, *fado* singers perform traditional Portuguese songs of longing as the well-to-do enjoy fine meals and red wine. Meanwhile, hip young *Lisboetas* grab drinks at the bars between **Rua do Norte** and **Rua da Atalaia** before taking the party to the hilly streets. Get your beer or caipirinha in a plastic cup so you can take it with you as you wander from place to place; the night never ends in Bairro Alto.

ALFAMA

Hilly Alfama, Lisbon's medieval quarter, was the lone neighborhood to survive the infamous 1755 earthquake. The **Castelo de São Jorge,** with its commanding view of Baixa and Bairro Alto, sits at the neighborhood's peak. Around and below it, layers of houses, shops, and restaurants descend to the Rio Tejo. Between Alfama and Baixa is the **Mouraria** (Moorish quarter), ironically established by Dom Afonso Henriques after the expulsion of the Moors in 1147. This labyrinth of alleys, small stairways, and unmarked streets is a challenge to navigate and poorly lit after dark, so be careful at night.

GRAÇA

If the climb to Graça doesn't take your breath away, the incredible *miradouros* (lookout points) you'll find there will. The neighborhood is one of the oldest in Lisbon, and in addition to great views of the city and river, Graça offers several impressive historical sights that keep tourists trekking up its hilly streets day after day. Graça is a mainly residential area and is easily accessible by tram 28E, making it a quick and convenient trip from Baixa or Bairro Alto.

AROUND PRAÇA DO MARQUÊS DE POMBAL

Lisbon's modern business center, the area around Pç. do Marquês de Pombal abounds in department stores, shopping centers, and office complexes. Amid this sea of commerce, peaceful **São Sebastião** houses two of the finest museums in all of Portugal, legacies of oil tycoon Calouste Gulbenkian.

FARTHER AFIELD

Lisbon calms down as you move west from Bairro Alto into **Estrela** and **Prazeres,** where cobblestone streets give way to leafy parks and peaceful manicured cemeteries. South of these neighborhoods, the docks of riverfront **Alcântara** house Lisbon's most vibrant club scene. Several kilometers downriver, architecturally stunning **Belém** celebrates the glory of Portugal's imperial past. Northeast of the historic core, the **Parque das Nações,** built to host the 1998 World Exposition, is home to a fantastic oceanarium and Santiago Calatrava's soaring Gare do Oriente.

LOCAL TRANSPORTATION

CARRIS, Lisbon's efficient public transportation system, runs subways, buses, trams, funiculars throughout Lisbon and its surroundings (☎213 61 30 00; www.carris.pt). Short-term visitors should consider a 24-hour **bilhete combinado** (€3.50), good for unlimited travel on all CARRIS transports. Those planning a longer stay, or who intend to take the metro, should acquire a rechargeable **viva viagem** card. The pass itself costs €0.50 and can be purchased and charged in all metro stations. When entering buses, trams, or the metro, hold the card against the magnetic reader; your trip will cost only €0.79. CARRIS booths, located in most train and major metro stations (including Baixa-Chiado, Restauradores, and Marquês de Pombal), sell day passes and dispense information. (Open daily 6:30am-1pm.)

Buses: €1.40 within the city, or €0.79 with a viva viagem card. Pay on the bus; exact change not required.

Metro: (☎213 50 01 00; www.metrolisboa.pt). €0.79 with a viva viagem card (required for travel on the metro). 4 lines traverse downtown and the business district. A red "M" marks metro stops. Trains run daily 6:30am-1am, though some stations close earlier.

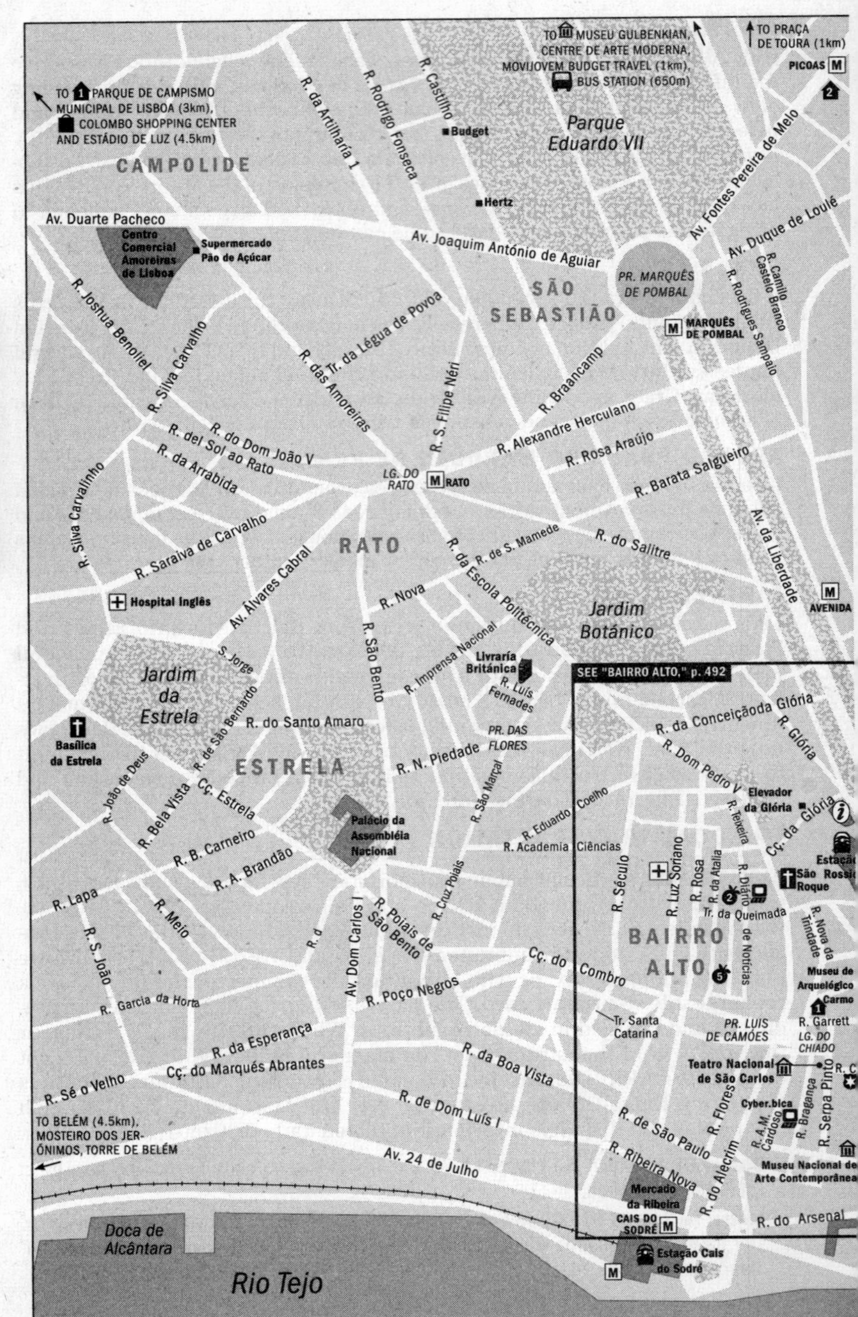

TO MUSEU GULBENKIAN, CENTRE DE ARTE MODERNA, MOVIJOVEM BUDGET TRAVEL (1km), BUS STATION (650m)
TO PRAÇA DE TOURA (1km)
PICOAS
TO PARQUE DE CAMPISMO MUNICIPAL DE LISBOA (3km), COLOMBO SHOPPING CENTER AND ESTÁDIO DE LUZ (4.5km)
CAMPOLIDE
Parque Eduardo VII
Budget
Hertz
R. Castilho
R. Rodrigo Fonseca
R. da Artilharía 1
Av. Fontes Pereira de Melo
Av. Duque de Loulé
Av. Duarte Pacheco
Av. Joaquim António de Aguiar
Centro Comercial Amoreiras de Lisboa
Supermercado Pão de Açúcar
PR. MARQUÊS DE POMBAL
SÃO SEBASTIÃO
MARQUÊS DE POMBAL
R. Camilo Castelo Branco
R. Rodrigues Sampaio
R. Joshua Benoliel
R. Silva Carvalho
Tr. da Légua de Povoa
R. das Amoreiras
R. S. Filipe Néri
R. Braancamp
R. Alexandre Herculano
R. Rosa Araújo
R. Barata Salgueiro
R. do Dom João V
R. del Sol ao Rato
R. da Arrabida
LG. DO RATO
RATO
R. Silva Carvalinho
R. Saraiva de Carvalho
RATO
R. de S. Mamede
R. do Salitre
Av. da Liberdade
AVENIDA
Av. Álvares Cabral
R. Nova
R. da Escola Politécnica
Jardim Botánico
Hospital Inglês
S. Jorge
R. São Bento
R. Imprensa Nacional
Livraría Británica
R. Luís Fernades
Jardim da Estrela
SEE "BAIRRO ALTO," p. 492
R. de São Bernardo
R. do Santo Amaro
PR. DAS FLORES
R. da Conceiçãoda Glória
R. Glória
Basílica da Estrela
R. João de Deus
R. Bela Vista
Cç. Estrela
ESTRELA
R. N. Piedade
R. São Marçal
R. Dom Pedro V
Elevador da Glória
Cç. da Glória
R. Eduardo Coelho
R. Teixeira
Palácio da Assembléia Nacional
R. B. Carneiro
R. A. Brandão
R. Academia Ciências
R. Século
R. Luz Soriano
R. Rosa
R. da Atalia
R. Diário de Notícias
Estação Rossio
São Roque
Tr. da Queimada
R. Nova da Trindade
R. Lapa
R. Meio
R. S. João
R. d
Av. Dom Carlos I
R. Poiais de São Bento
R. Cruz Poiais
Cç. do Combro
BAIRRO ALTO
Museu de Arquelógico Carmo
R. Garcia da Horta
R. Poço Negros
Tr. Santa Catarina
PR. LUIS DE CAMÕES
R. Garrett
LG. DO CHIADO
R. da Esperança
Cç. do Marqués Abrantes
R. da Boa Vista
Teatro Nacional de São Carlos
R. Sé o Velho
R. de Dom Luís I
R. de São Paulo
R. Flores
Cyber.bica
R. A.M. Cardoso
R. Bragança
R. Serpa Pinto
TO BELÉM (4.5km), MOSTEIRO DOS JERÓNIMOS, TORRE DE BELÉM
Av. 24 de Julho
R. Ribeira Nova
R. do Alecrim
Museu Nacional de Arte Contemporânea
Mercado da Ribeira
CAIS DO SODRÉ
R. do Arsenal
Doca de Alcântara
Estação Cais do Sodré
Rio Tejo

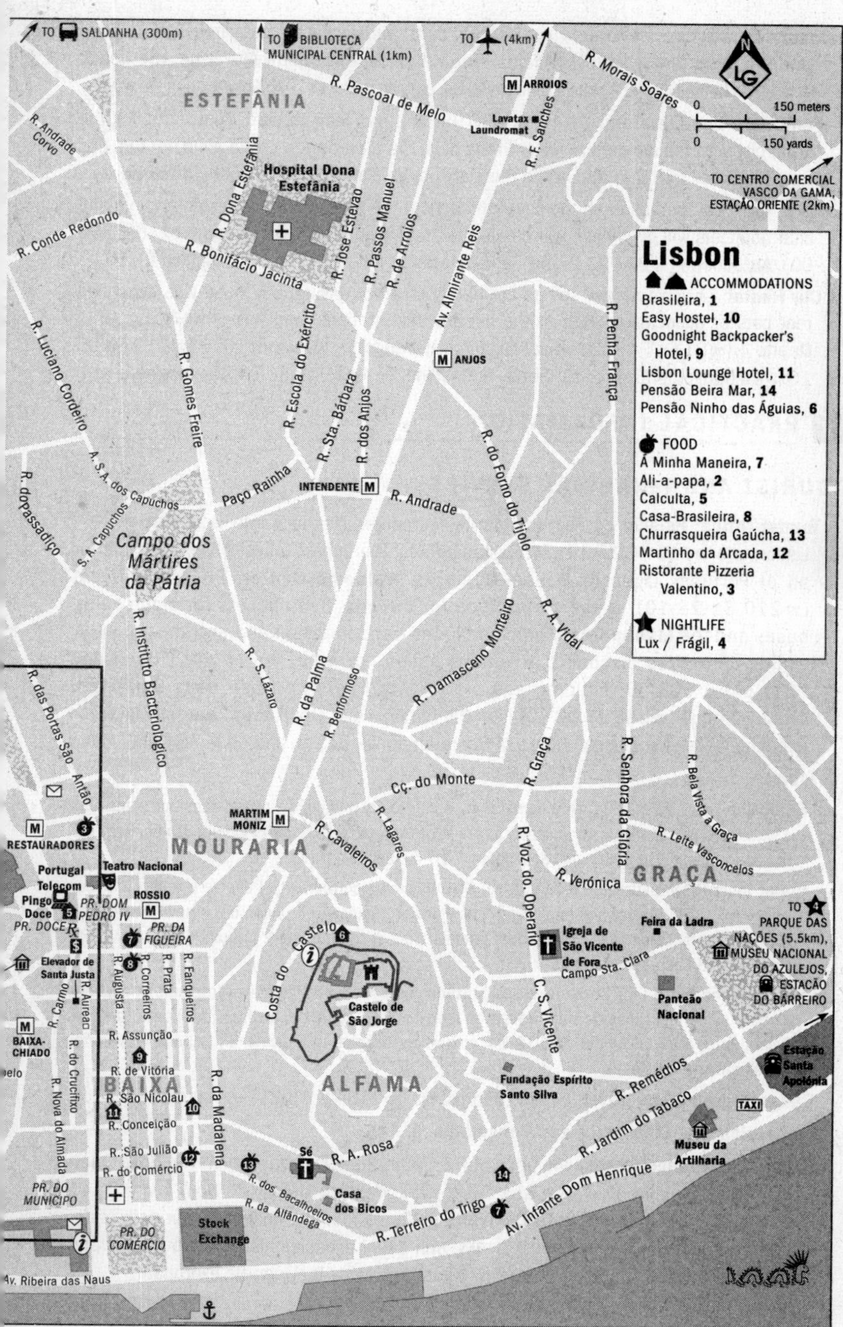
Lisbon
ACCOMMODATIONS
Brasileira, 1
Easy Hostel, 10
Goodnight Backpacker's Hotel, 9
Lisbon Lounge Hotel, 11
Pensão Beira Mar, 14
Pensão Ninho das Águias, 6
FOOD
À Minha Maneira, 7
Ali-a-papa, 2
Calculta, 5
Casa-Brasileira, 8
Churrasqueira Gaúcha, 13
Martinho da Arcada, 12
Ristorante Pizzeria Valentino, 3
NIGHTLIFE
Lux / Frágil, 4
TO SALDANHA (300m)
TO BIBLIOTECA MUNICIPAL CENTRAL (1km)
TO (4km)
150 meters
150 yards
TO CENTRO COMERCIAL VASCO DA GAMA, ESTAÇÃO ORIENTE (2km)
ESTEFÂNIA
MOURARIA
GRAÇA
ALFAMA
BAIXA
ARROIOS
ANJOS
INTENDENTE
MARTIM MONIZ
RESTAURADORES
ROSSIO
BAIXA-CHIADO
Lavatax Laundromat
Hospital Dona Estefânia
Campo dos Mártires da Pátria
Teatro Nacional
Portugal Telecom
Pingo Doce
Elevador de Santa Justa
Castelo de São Jorge
Igreja de São Vicente de Fora
Feira da Ladra
Panteão Nacional
Fundação Espírito Santo Silva
Sé
Casa dos Bicos
Stock Exchange
Museu da Artilharia
Estação Santa Apolónia
TAXI
TO PARQUE DAS NAÇÕES (5.5km), MUSEU NACIONAL DO AZULEJOS, ESTAÇÃO DO BARREIRO
PR. DOM PEDRO IV
PR. DA FIGUEIRA
PR. DO MUNICIPO
PR. DO COMÉRCIO
R. Morais Soares
R. Pascoal de Melo
R. F. Sanches
R. Andrade Corvo
R. Dona Estefânia
R. Conde Redondo
R. Bonifácio Jacinta
R. Jose Estevão
R. Passos Manuel
R. de Arroios
Av. Almirante Reis
R. Penha França
R. Luciano Cordeiro
R. Gomes Freire
R. Escola do Exército
R. Sta. Bárbara
R. dos Anjos
R. do Forno do Tijolo
S.A. dos Capuchos
S.A. Capuchos
R. dopassadiço
Paço Rainha
R. Andrade
R. Instituto Bacteriológico
R. S. Lázaro
R. da Palma
R. Benformoso
R. Damasceno Monteiro
R. A. Vidal
R. das Portas São Antão
R. Graça
R. Senhora da Glória
R. Bela Vista à Graça
Cç. do Monte
R. Lagares
R. Cavaleiros
R. Leite Vasconcelos
R. Verónica
R. Voz. do. Operario
Costa do Castelo
Campo Sta. Clara
C. S. Vicente
R. Augusta
R. Correeiros
R. Prata
R. Fanqueiros
R. Carmo
R. Aurea
R. Assunção
R. de Vitória
R. do Crucifixo
R. Nova do Almada
R. São Nicolau
R. Conceição
R. São Julião
R. do Comércio
R. da Madalena
R. A. Rosa
R. dos Bacalhoeiros
R. da Allândega
R. Terreiro do Trigo
Av. Infante Dom Henrique
R. Jardim do Tabaco
R. Remédios
Av. Ribeira das Naus

PORTUGAL

Trams: €1.40, or €0.79 with a viva viagem card. Many vehicles date from before WWI. Line 28E runs through Graça, Alfama, Baixa, Chiado, and Bairro Alto. Line 15E heads from Pr. do Comércio and Pr. da Figueira to Belém, passing the clubs of Alcântara along the way.

Funiculars and Elevators: €1.40, or €0.79 with a viva viagem card. Funiculars link the lower city with the residential areas in the hills. The Elevador da Glória goes from Pr. dos Restauradores to Bairro Alto, while the Elevador de Santa Justa links Chiado to Baixa.

Taxis: Cabs can be hailed on the street throughout the historic center. Restauranteurs and club bouncers will gladly call you a cab after dark. **Rádio Táxis de Lisboa** (☎218 11 90 00), **Autocoope** (☎217 93 27 56), and **Teletáxis** (☎218 11 11 00). Luggage €1.60.

Car Rental: Lisbon's narrow streets are hardly ideal for driving, but those who insist can rent cars at agencies located at the airport, train stations, and downtown. **Avis,** Av. D. Duarte 4 (☎213 17 42 31; www.avis.com.pt); **Budget,** R. Castilho, 167B (☎213 86 05 16; www.budgetportugal.com); **Hertz,** R. Castilho, 72A (☎213 81 24 30; www.hertz.pt).

PORTUGAL

PRACTICAL INFORMATION

TOURIST AND FINANCIAL SERVICES

Tourist Office: Palácio da Foz, Pr. dos Restauradores (Portugal info ☎213 46 63 07, Lisbon info ☎213 46 33 14). M: Restauradores. The largest tourist office, with info for all of Portugal. Open daily 9am-8pm. The **Welcome Center,** Pr. do Comércio (☎210 31 28 10), is the main office for the city. Sells tickets for sightseeing buses and the **Lisboa Card,** which includes transportation and entrance to most sights, as well as discounts at various shops, for a flat fee (1-day €16, 2-day €27, 3-day €33.50; children age 5-11 €9.50/14/17). Open daily 9am-8pm. **Airport branch** (☎218 45 06 60) near the terminal exit. Open daily 7am-midnight. For info, check "Ask Me Lisboa" kiosks in Santa Apolónia, Belém, and on R. Augusta.

Tours:

CARRISTur (☎213 58 23 34; www.carristur.pt), a subsidiary of the city's public transit provider, runs 1½hr. tours of Lisbon's historic center in pre-WWI tram cars. Tours depart every 30min. from the Pç. do Comércio 10am-8pm. €18, children 4-10 €9, under 4 free.

GoCar Tours R. Douradores, 16 (☎210 96 50 30; www.gocartours.pt). Reserve a yellow mini-car online for a GPS-guided self-tour along 1 of 4 Lisbon routes. A bit pricey, but a novel way to see the city and focus on sites of individual interest. Cars accommodate 2 people. €25 1st hr., €20 2nd hr., €18 each additional hr.

Inside Lisbon (☎968 41 26 12; www.insidelisbon.com). A wide range of walking tours throughout Lisbon; some tours include tram rides and food tastings. Tours depart from the Rossio daily at 10am. Tours €14-18, under 26 €10-14. Also offers daytrips to Cascais, Sintra, and elsewhere; check website for details.

Budget Travel: Tagus Travel, Pç. de Londres, 9C (☎218 49 15 31; www.taguseasy.pt).

Embassies: See **Embassies and Consulates,** p. 478.

Currency Exchange: Banks are open M-F 8:30am-3pm. Exchange money at **Nova Câmbios,** Praça D. Pedro IV, 42 (☎213 24 25 53). **Western Union,** Pr. Dom Pedro IV, 41 (☎213 22 04 80), inside **Cota Câmbios,** performs money transfers. Open daily 8pm-10pm. The main post office, most banks, and travel agencies also change money, and exchanges line the streets of Baixa. Ask about fees first—they can be exorbitant.

LOCAL SERVICES

English-Language Bookstore: FNAC, Armazéns do Chiado, 4th fl., R. do Carmo, 2 (☎213 22 18 00). Large section just for English books, but they can be found throughout the store in the regular sections as well. Open daily 10am-10pm.

Libraries: Biblioteca Municipal Central, Palácio Galveias (☎217 80 30 20). M: Campo Pequeno. Open M and Sa 1-7pm, Tu-F 10am-7pm. **Biblioteca Municipal Camões,** Largo do Calhariz 17 (☎213 42 21 57). Free internet. Open M and W-F 10:30am-6pm, 2nd and 4th M and Sa of every month 10:30am-6pm.

Shopping Centers:

Armazéns do Chiado, R. do Carmo 2 (☎213 21 06 00; www.armazensdochiado.com). Food court at the top. Open daily 10am-10pm, restaurants close at 11pm.

El Corte Inglés (☎213 71 17 00; www.elcorteingles.pt), between Av. António Augusto de Agular and Marquês da Fronteira e Sidónio Pais. M: São Sebastião. Portugal's 1st branch of the Spanish department store. Open M-Th 10am-10pm, F-Sa 10am-11:30pm, Su 10am-1pm. MC/V.

Colombo, Av. Lusíada (☎217 11 36 00; www.colombo.pt), in front of Benfica stadium. M: Colégio Militar-Luz. Over 400 shops, a 10-screen cinema (adult ticket €5), and a small amusement park. Open daily 9am-midnight.

Centro Comercial Amoreiras de Lisboa, Av. Eng. Duarte Pacheco (☎213 81 02 00; www.amoreiras.com), near R. Carlos Alberto da Mota Pinto. M: Marquês de Pombal. Towers house 383 shops, including a huge **Pão de Açúcar** supermarket and cinema. Open daily 10am-11pm.

Centro Comercial Vasco da Gama, Av. Dom João II (☎218 93 06 01; www.centrovascodagama.pt). M: Oriente. Open daily 10am-midnight.

PORTUGAL

EMERGENCY AND COMMUNICATIONS

Police: Tourism Police Station, Palácio Foz in Restauradores (☎213 42 16 24), and at R. Capelo, 13 (☎213 46 61 41 or 42 16 34). English spoken.

Late-Night Pharmacy: 24hr. pharmacy rotates, check the listings in the window of any pharmacy. Look for a lighted green cross, or check listings at **Farmácia Azevedos,** Pr. Dom Pedro IV, 31 (☎213 43 04 82), at the base of Rossio in front of the metro. Regular hours 8:30am-7:40pm.

Medical Services: ☎112 in case of emergency. **Hospital de Saint Louis,** R. Luz Soriano, 182 (☎213 21 65 00) in Bairro Alto. Open daily 9am-8pm. **Hospital de São José,** R. José António Serrano (☎218 84 10 00 or 261 31 28 57).

Telephones: Portugal Telecom, Pr. Dom Pedro IV, 68 (☎808 21 11 56). M: Rossio. Pay the cashier after your call or use a phone card. Also has pre-paid internet (€2 per hr.). Office open daily 8am-11pm. Portugal Telecom phone cards (50 units €3) available at the office or at bookstores and stationers. Local calls cost at least 2 units. Minutes per unit vary. PT cards should only be purchased for local use; better deals on non-local calls can be found elsewhere.

Internet Access: Portugal Telecom (see above). **The Instituto Portuges da Juventude,** Av. Liberdade 194 (☎213 17 92 00; juventude.gov.pt). 30min. of free internet and assistance for students. Open Tu-Sa 9am-8pm. **Web C@fé,** R. Diário de Notícias 126 (☎213 421 181) in Bairro Alto. Doubles as a bar. €0.75 per 15min. Open daily 7pm-2am.

Post Office: Main office, Pr. dos Restauradores (☎213 23 89 71). Open M-F 8am-10pm, Sa-Su 9am-6pm. To avoid the lines, go to the branch at Pr. do Comércio (☎213 22 09 20). Open M-F 8:30am-6:30pm. Cash only. **Postal Code:** 1100.

ACCOMMODATIONS AND CAMPING

Lisbon has seen an explosion of tourism in recent years, and with it, a rapid growth in accommodations catering to student travelers on a budget. The result is a remarkable selection of fresh, funky, comfortable, and even occasionally elegant hostels, all at prices travelers to Paris or Madrid could only dream of. These hostels are concentrated in Baixa and Bairro Alto and tend to be very similar in setup: mixed four- to eight-person dorms, shared bathrooms, a common living room, and free internet. They do differ slightly in amenities, but most are comfortable and run €18-20 in the summer. Thanks to online booking, they fill up fast, so reserve ahead. Unless otherwise stated, assume that linens and towels are included but that internet is not.

Pensões and budget hotels abound in Lisbon, but room quality varies significantly—ask to see the room before paying. During the summer, expect to pay €20-30 for a single and €35-45 for a double, depending on amenities. You can usually find a room in the summer with little or no notice, but you may want to book in advance during mid-June for the Festa de Santo Antonio. In the low season (Oct.-Apr.), prices generally drop €5 or more, so try bargaining. Many establishments only have rooms with double beds and charge per person. Several hotels can be found in the center of town on Av. da Liberdade, while cheaper *pensões* cluster in Baixa and Bairro Alto. Avoid those surrounding Rossio: while they're very convenient, they're usually around €10 more than the norm. Look around Baixa's **Rua da Prata, Rua dos Correiros,** and **Rua do Ouro** for cheaper accommodations. Lodgings near **Castelo de São Jorge** are quieter and closer to the sights, but more difficult to reach. Be careful at night thoughout the historic center and be particularly mindful walking alone through the poorly lit, winding streets of Alfama and in Bairro Alto.

Camping is reasonably popular in Portugal, but campers can be prime targets for thieves. Stay at an enclosed campsite and ask ahead about security. There are 30 campgrounds within a 45min. radius of the capital. The most popular, **Lisboa Camping,** is inside the 900-acre *parque florestal*, and has a four-star rating. (☎217 62 82 00; www.lisboacamping.com. €6, children under 12 €3, tents €6-7, cars €4. Prices fall in winter. Bungalows available.)

BAIXA

Baixa may not offer much in the way of fine dining or nightlife, but its prime location between Alfama and Bairro Alto makes the neighborhood an excellent home base. Hostels here are among the best designed and most inviting in the city; as a result, they fill quickly in the summer, so book well ahead. The neighborhood's many *pensões*—less luxurious and more expensive than its hostels—may have last-minute availability, even during the high season. Prices tend to be a bit higher than in surrounding neighborhoods. Be advised that most accommodations are located on upper floors, a hassle for travelers with heavy luggage.

Kitsch Hostel, Pr. Dos Restauradores 65 (☎213 46 73 32; www.kitschhostel.com). M: Restauradores. Opened in March 2009, this centrally located hostel is every bit as quirky as the name would suggest. Enter through the Tabacaria Restauradores into an energetic world of reflective ceilings, celebrity collages, and delightfully tacky furniture. All rooms with shared bath. Breakfast included. Towels €1. Free internet and Wi-Fi. Key deposit €10. 4- to 12-bed dorms M-Th and Su €14-16, F-Sa €16-18; doubles from €50; triples from €60. AmEx/MC/V. ❶

Living Lounge Hostel, R. do Crucifixo 116 (☎213 46 10 78; www.lisbonloungehostel.com), and **Lisbon Lounge Hostel**, R. de São Nicolau 41 (213 462 061; www.lisbonloungehostel.com). M: Baixa-Chiado (Baixa exit). Under joint ownership, both of these hostels feature excellent contemporary design, with bold colors and cool touches like chandeliers made from teacups. Free city tours Tu and F. Nightly dinners (€8) include wine and dessert. All rooms with shared bath; singles at Living Lounge only. Breakfast included. Laundry €7. Free internet and Wi-Fi. Key deposit €5. 4- to 8-bed dorms Oct. 15-Apr. 14 €18,

Apr. 15-May 31 and Sept. 16-Oct. 14 €20, June 1-Sept. 15 €22; singles €30/35/35; doubles €50/60/60. AmEx/MC/V. ❶

Goodnight Backpacker's Hostel, R. dos Correeiros, 113, 2nd fl. (☎213 43 01 39; www.goodnighthostel.com). M: Baixa-Chiado (Baixa exit). Exposed stone, offbeat wallpaper, and dozens of little black birds adorn this lively hostel spread over 4 fl. (no elevator). Breakfast included. Towels €1. Free internet and Wi-Fi. Key deposit €5. Dorms €16-20; doubles with shared bath €50. Cash only. ❶

BAIRRO ALTO AND CHIADO

Although less central than Baixa, the many budget accommodations in Bairro Alto and Chiado offer the most direct access to nightlife and museums.

Oasis Backpackers Mansion, R. de Santa Catarina, 24 (☎213 47 80 44; www.oasislisboa.com). From M: Baixa-Chiado, follow directions to the Miradouro de Santa Catarina (p. 496). Facing the river, turn to your right; the hostel is the yellow house at the bottom of the hill. True to its name, funky Oasis is a backpacker's haven. A diverse range of travelers gather for home-cooked dinners in the classy dining room (M-Sa, €5) or for drinks in the patio bar (open daily 6pm-midnight). Breakfast included. Laundry €7. Free internet and Wi-Fi. Key deposit €5. Co-ed dorms €18-20; doubles with private bath €44. AmEx/MC/V. ❶

Lisbon Poets Hostel, R. Nova da Trinidade 2 (☎213 46 10 58; www.lisbonpoetshostel.com), on the 5th fl. Decked out in soothing earth tones and beanbag chairs, this ideally located newcomer to Lisbon's hostel scene features a small book exchange and spacious 2- to 6-bed dorms named for famous writers. Breakfast included. Laundry €7. Free internet and Wi-Fi. Key deposit €5. Co-ed dorms mid-Oct. to mid-Apr. €18, mid-Apr. to June €20, Jul. to mid-Oct. €22; doubles mid-Oct to mid-Apr. €42-65, mid-Apr. to mid-Oct. €45-70. MC/V over €50. ❷

ALFAMA

Alfama has few lodging options and they're generally a bit more expensive, but staying here is a nice change of pace (especially after hectic Baixa). The steep, unmarked streets can make each trip back to the *pensão* a grueling workout, but hikes frequently pay off with postcard views of downtown Lisbon.

Pensão Ninho das Águias, Costa do Castelo, 74 (☎218 85 40 70). Perched at the top of Alfama, Ninho das Águias towers above Lisbon's other *pensões,* literally and metaphorically. Beautiful common spaces, garden patio, family vibe, and fantastic views, especially from rooms 5, 6, 12-14, and the small tower at the top of the stairs. English and French spoken. Reserve ahead in summer. Singles €30; doubles €45, with bath €50; triples (some with bath) €60. Sept.-Apr. prices drop by €10. Cash only; prices may be flexible with bargaining. ❸

Pensão Beira Mar, Largo Terreiro do Trigo, 16 (☎218 86 99 33; www.guesthousebeiramar.com), near the Sta. Apolonia train station. Avoid the 4-story climb by entering through the back where there are only 2 flights of stairs. 7 brightly decorated rooms with showers and sinks, some with TVs. Living room and kitchen for guest use. Breakfast included. Free internet. Singles €20-25; doubles €35-45; triples €60; quads €70. Oct.-May prices drop by €5. Cash only. ❷

AROUND MARQUÊS DE POMBAL

Black and White Hostel, R. Alexandre Herculano, 39, 1st fl. (☎213 46 22 12; www.costta.com). M: Marquês de Pombal. From the station, walk away from the statue down Av. da Liberdade and turn right on R. Alexandre Herculano; the hostel is 3 blocks down on your left. 15min. walk to both Baixa and Bairro Alto. One of the most artistic hostels in town—rooms are boldly painted with murals of psychedelic spirals and Andy

PORTUGAL

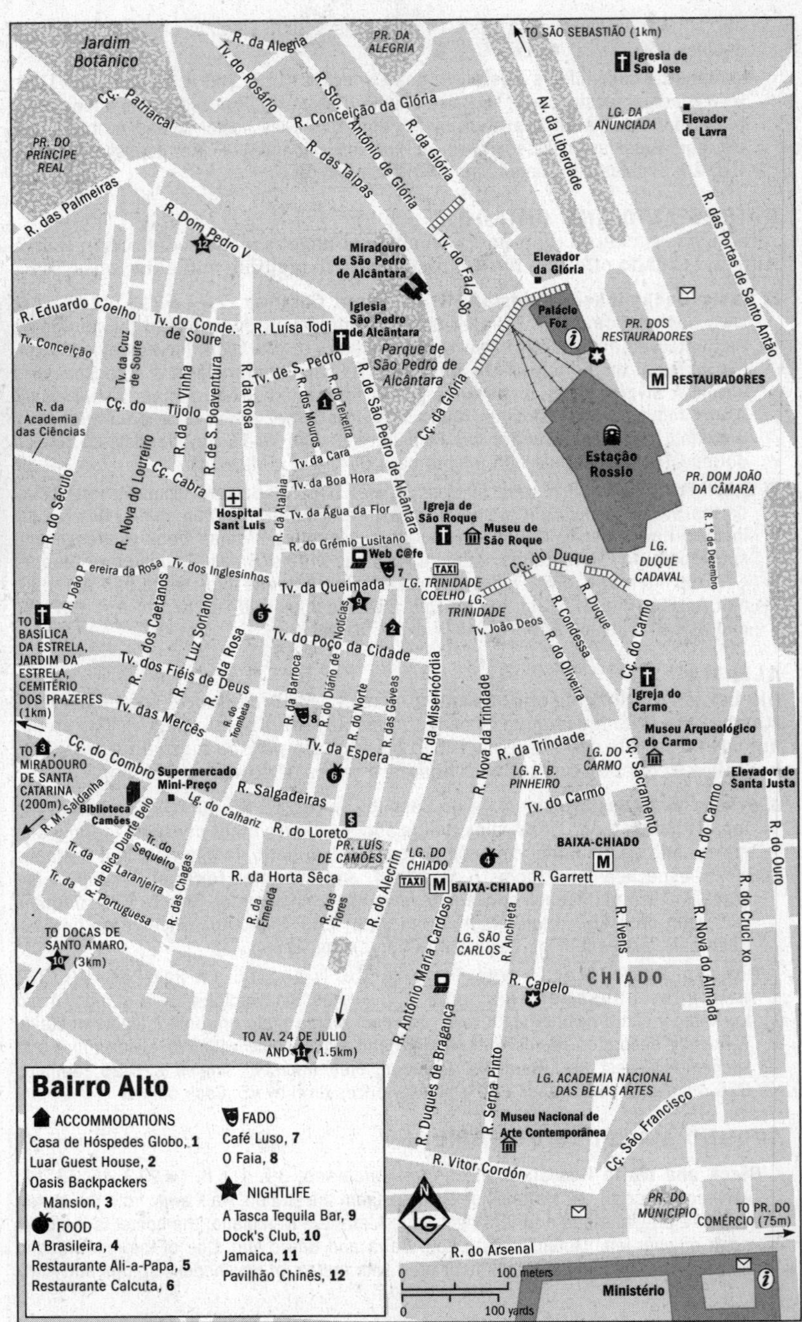

Bairro Alto
ACCOMMODATIONS
Casa de Hóspedes Globo, 1
Luar Guest House, 2
Oasis Backpackers Mansion, 3
FOOD
A Brasileira, 4
Restaurante Ali-a-Papa, 5
Restaurante Calcuta, 6
FADO
Café Luso, 7
O Faia, 8
NIGHTLIFE
A Tasca Tequila Bar, 9
Dock's Club, 10
Jamaica, 11
Pavilhão Chinês, 12
Jardim Botânico
PR. DO PRÍNCIPE REAL
PR. DA ALEGRIA
TO SÃO SEBASTIÃO (1km)
Igresia de Sao Jose
LG. DA ANUNCIADA
Elevador de Lavra
Miradouro de São Pedro de Alcântara
Iglesia São Pedro de Alcântara
Parque de São Pedro de Alcântara
Elevador da Glória
Palácio Foz
PR. DOS RESTAURADORES
RESTAURADORES
Estação Rossio
PR. DOM JOÃO DA CÂMARA
Hospital Sant Luis
Igreja de São Roque
Museu de São Roque
Web C@fe
LG. TRINIDADE COELHO
LG. TRINIDADE
LG. DUQUE CADAVAL
Igreja do Carmo
Museu Arqueológico do Carmo
LG. DO CARMO
LG. R. B. PINHEIRO
Elevador de Santa Justa
Supermercado Mini-Preço
Biblioteca Camões
PR. LUÍS DE CAMÕES
LG. DO CHIADO
BAIXA-CHIADO
LG. SÃO CARLOS
CHIADO
LG. ACADEMIA NACIONAL DAS BELAS ARTES
Museu Nacional de Arte Contemporânea
PR. DO MUNICIPIO
TO PR. DO COMÉRCIO (75m)
Ministério
TO BASÍLICA DA ESTRELA, JARDIM DA ESTRELA, CEMITÉRIO DOS PRAZERES (1km)
TO MIRADOURO DE SANTA CATARINA (200m)
TO DOCAS DE SANTO AMARO, (3km)
TO AV. 24 DE JULIO AND (1.5km)
0 100 meters
0 100 yards
R. da Alegria
Tv. do Rosário
R. Sto. António de Glória
R. Conceição da Glória
R. da Glória
R. das Taipas
Cç. Patriarcal
R. das Palmeiras
R. Dom Pedro V
Av. da Liberdade
R. das Portas de Santo Antão
Tv. do Fala Só
R. Eduardo Coelho
Tv. do Conde. de Soure
R. Luísa Todi
Tv. Conceição
Tv. da Cruz de Soure
R. da Vinha
R. de S. Boaventura
R. da Rosa
Tv. de S. Pedro
R. dos Mouros
R. do Teixeira
R. de São Pedro de Alcântara
Cç. da Glória
R. da Academia das Ciências
Cç. do Tijolo
R. Nova do Loureiro
Cç. Cabra
R. do Século
Tv. da Cara
Tv. da Boa Hora
Tv. da Água da Flor
R. da Atalaia
R. do Grémio Lusitano
R. João Pereira da Rosa
Tv. dos Inglesinhos
Tv. da Queimada
Cç. do Duque
R. Duque
R. Condessa
R. do Oliveira
Tv. João Deos
Cç. do Carmo
R. 1° de Dezembro
R. dos Caetanos
R. Luz Soriano
Tv. do Poço da Cidade
Tv. dos Fiéis de Deus
R. da Barroca
R. do Diário de Notícias
R. do Norte
R. das Gáveas
R. da Misericórdia
R. Nova da Trindade
Tv. das Mercês
R. do Trombeta
Tv. da Espera
R. da Trindade
Cç. Sacramento
Cç. do Combro
R. Salgadeiras
Tv. do Carmo
R. M. Saldanha
Lg. do Calhariz
R. do Loreto
R. da Bica Duarte Belo
Tr. do Sequeiro
Tr. da Laranjeira
Tr. da Portuguesa
R. das Chagas
R. da Horta Sêca
R. Garrett
R. do Carmo
R. do Ouro
R. da Emenda
R. das Flores
R. do Alecrim
R. António Maria Cardoso
R. Anchieta
R. Ivens
R. Nova do Almada
R. do Cruci xo
R. Capelo
R. Duques de Bragança
R. Serpa Pinto
Cç. São Francisco
R. Vitor Cordón
R. do Arsenal

Warhol prints. Breakfast included. Free internet. Key deposit €10. 4-, 6-, and 14-person dorms €15-20. Sa-Su all rooms €17. Cash only. ❶

Pousada de Juventude de Lisboa (HI), R. Andrade Corvo, 46 (☎213 53 26 96). M: Picoas. Exit the metro station onto R. Andrade Corvo; the hostel is marked by a large banner directly in front of you. A large hostel worth looking into if others are booked. Breakfast included; lunch and dinner €6 each. Reserve ahead. 4- and 6-bed dorms €16-18; doubles with bath and TVs €43-45. MC/V. ❶

FOOD

Calorie-counters beware: Lisbon has some of the cheapest, most irresistible restaurants of the western European capitals, not to mention the best wine. A full dinner costs about €9-11 per person and the *prato do dia* (daily special) is often only €5-7. Between lunch and dinner, snack on cheap, filling, and addictive Portuguese pastries. Lisbon boasts almost as many *pastelarias* as Spain has tapas bars, and the city abounds with seafood specialties such as *pratos de caracois* (snail dishes), *creme de mariscos* (seafood chowder with tomatoes), and *bacalhau cozido com grão e batatas* (cod with chickpeas and boiled potatoes, doused in olive oil). For a more diverse selection, head up to the winding streets of Bairro Alto where you'll find many international restaurants.

MARKETS

Pingo Doce and **Mini-Preço supermarkets** have locations throughout the city; most locations are open 9am-8pm. Check www.clubeminipreco.website.pt for specific locations. Two convenient locations are R. 1 de Dezembro, 81-83, just outside Pr. do Dom Pedro IV, and R. do Loreto.

Supermercado Pão de Açúcar, Av. Duarte Pacheco (☎213 82 66 80), in the Amoreiras Shopping Center de Lisboa. Take bus #11 from Pr. dos Restauradores or Pr. da Figueira. A large supermarket with a wide selection. Open daily 9am-11pm.

Mercado da Ribeira, Av. 24 de Julho (☎213 46 29 66). M: Cais de Sodré. Accessible by bus #40 or tram #15. This vast, century-old, picturesque market complex is located inside a warehouse just outside Estação Cais do Sodré. Go early for the freshest selection of fruit, fish, and a variety of other foods. Prices on produce can't be beat. Produce market open Tu-Sa 5am-2pm. Flower market open M-Sa 5am-7pm. Cash only.

BAIXA

Baixa is not a gourmand's paradise. **Rua das Portas, Rua Augusta,** and **Rua dos Correeiros** are lined with restaurants promising authentic Portuguese cuisine, although the menus in nine languages posted outside tell a different story. To eat affordably, look for restaurants offering appealing *pratos do dia* or set *menus*.

Ristorante-Pizzaria Valentino, R. Jardim do Regedor 37-45 (☎213 46 17 27). A slice of Italy on the Pr. Dos Restauradores. Watch chefs prepare Italian classics in the open kitchen, and keep your eyes peeled for the Portuguese soccer stars known to swing by. Try the crunchy-crusted Pizza Caprese (€8.50). Homemade pasta €7-15. Pizzas €4-9. Open daily noon-midnight. MC/V. ❷

Casa Brasileira, R. Augusta 267-269. A great place to grab a pastry and a drink while sightseeing. Huge selection of baked goods €1-3.50. Large salads and basic entrees (hamburgers, omlettes, etc.) all €8. Open M-Sa 7am-1am, Su 8am-1am. Cash only. ❷

Martinho da Arcada, Pr. do Comércio 3 (☎218 87 92 59). Enjoy the one-of-a-kind ambience at the oldest restaurant in Lisbon, founded in 1782. Guests can read poems on the walls by Portuguese poet Fernando Pessoa, a regular during his lifetime. Outside seating available. Fish options less expensive than grilled meats or chicken, though still pricey. Entrees €17-38. Open M-Sa noon-4pm and 7-11pm. AmEx/MC/V. ❸

BAIRRO ALTO AND CHIADO

The narrow streets of Bairro Alto are lined with cozy international restaurants and *fado* houses, while Chiado is home to trendy date spots and sleek cafes. Those in search of cheap, traditional places should not lose hope—although not immediately apparent, Portuguese holes-in-the-wall can be found on the side streets off Cç. do Combro.

noo bai café, Miradouro de Santa Catarina (☎213 46 50 14; www.noobaicafe.com). Follow directions to the Miradouro de Santa Catarina (p. 496). Its sandwiches (€3-5) may be excellent and its coffee (€1-2.50) and beer (€2-4) surprisingly affordable, but it's the patio's commanding view of the Tagus and the dramatic, burnt-orange 25 de Abril bridge that draws a crowd. If you see an open table by the railing, spring for it—and stay the whole day. Internet €3 per hr., free with €5 purchase. Open M-Sa noon-midnight, Su noon-10pm. MC/V over €5. ❶

A Brasileira, R. Garrett 120-22 (☎213 46 95 41). This beautiful wood- and marble-filled cafe has been a Lisbon institution since poet Fernando Pessoa started coming here in the early 20th century. (He's still hanging around—that's his statue planted on the patio.) Light sandwiches and croissants €2-4; entrees €8-20. Open daily 8am-2am. Kitchen open noon-3pm and 7-11pm. AmEx/MC/V. ❷

Pastelaria Rigoleto, R. Capelo 12 (☎213 47 04 62). A typical and always-packed Portuguese lunch spot with prices well below the Chiado average. Daily fish and meat specials (€5-6.50) are simple but delicious. Open daily 7:30am-8pm. MC over €5. ❷

PORTUGAL

ALFAMA

The winding streets of Alfama conceal a number of small and simple restaurants, often packed with locals. The **Rua da Padaria** and the area around its intersection with **Rua dos Bacalhoeiros** offers the cheapest options in Lisbon.

Flôr da Sé, Largo Santo António da Sé, 9-11 (☎218 87 57 42), next to the Santo Antonio church. This *pastelaria* is clean, brightly lit, and serves quality food at notably low prices. The lunchtime *prato do dia* (€4.50) is scrumptious, and homemade desserts and candies taste as good as they look. Open M-F and Su 7am-8pm. Cash only. ❶

À Minha Maneira, Largo do Terreiro do Trigo 1 (☎218 86 11 12; www.a-minha-maneira.pt). Once a bank, the old vault has been revamped into a wine closet. Various meat and fish dishes with little choice for vegetarians. Free Wi-Fi. Entrees €8-15. Open daily noon-3pm and 7-11:30pm. Cash only. ❷

Churrasqueira Gaúcha, R. dos Bacalhoeiros, 26C-D (☎218 87 06 09). Portuguese food cooked to perfection in a comfortable, cavernous setting. Incredibly fresh meat, poultry, and fish. No vegetarian options. Entrees €8-12. Open M-Sa 10am-midnight. AmEx/MC/V. ❷

GRAÇA

Good, cheap eats are easy to find in the area around the Lg. da Graça; stop by a view of the many *pastelarias* lining the square to compare *pratos do dia* (€4-6). To get there, take any tram 15E one stop beyond the large white Igreja de São Vicente de Fora. Those in search of a snack or light lunch with an incredible view should head to the **Esplanada Igreja de Graça,** where two kiosks serve tea (€1.50) and sandwiches (€2-4) atop Lisbon's most dramatic hills. (Open daily 11:30am-2am. Cash only.) To get there from the tram stop, climb the stairs to your right and follow Lg. de Graça past the large, white building to your right; the Esplanada is just behind the small park on your left. Things heat up after dark, when churches and markets recede and thumping beats take center stage.

O Pitéu, Lg. da Graça, 95-6 (☎218 87 10 67). *Azulejo*-lined walls and wine-inspired decorations. Serves a few Brazilian dishes in addition to traditional Portuguese dishes of fish, chicken, pork, and steak. Entrees €8-12. Open M-F noon-3pm and 7-10pm, Sa noon-3pm. Cash only. ❷

Pastelaria Estrela da Graça, Lg. da Graça, 98 (☎218 87 24 38). Try an affordable *prato do dia* (€4-6) or a delicious homemade pastry, accompanied by a large glass of jaw-droppingly underpriced house wine (€0.50-0.90). Open daily 7am-10pm. Cash only. ❶

SIGHTS

With 3000 years of history, Lisbon is constantly gesturing to the past. Moorish *azulejos* (painted tiles) adorn the Alfama district; the 12th-century Sé cathedral maintains a tough Romanesque stone facade; the elaborate Manueline monastery in Belém features excessive ornamentation reflective of Portugal's glory during the Age of Discovery. The Neoclassical design of Praça do Comércio's triumphal Roman arch marks a return to the simpler forms favored by the Marquês de Pombal's post-earthquake rebuilding. But Lisbon's beauty speaks of the present as well, from the sleek, modern Parque das Nações to the expressive, graffitied streets of Bairro Alto. Those planning to do a lot of sightseeing in a few days should consider purchasing the Welcome Center's **Lisboa Card** for a flat fee (p. 488). Many museums and sites are closed on Mondays and free on Sundays before 2pm.

PORTUGAL

BAIXA

Although Baixa claims few historical sights, the lively pedestrian traffic and dramatic history surrounding the neighborhood's three main *praças* make it a monument on its own. Beware Baixa's softly cooing pigeons, well-trained by countless statues of distinguished leaders on which they've made their mark.

AROUND ROSSIO. Begin your historical tour of 18th-century Lisbon at its heart: **Rossio,** or **Praça Dom Pedro IV** as it is more formally known. The city's main square was once a cattle market, public execution stage, bullring, and carnival ground. Today, it is the fast-paced domain of tourists and ruthless local drivers circling Pedro's enormous statue, and shadier characters by night. Another statue, this one of Gil Vicente, Portugal's first great dramatist, peers from atop the **Teatro Nacional de Dona Maria II** (easily recognized by its large, Parthenon-esque columns) at one end of the *praça*.

AROUND PRAÇA DOS RESTAURADORES. In Praça dos Restauradores, a giant obelisk celebrates Portugal's hard-earned independence from Spain, achieved in 1640 after 60 years of Spanish rule. The obelisk stands by a bronze sculpture of the "Spirit of Independence," a reminder of the centuries-old Spanish-Portuguese rivalry. The tourist office is housed at Palácio da Foz, and shops line the *praça* and C. da Glória, the hill that leads to Bairro Alto. Pr. dos Restauradores is also the start of **Avenida da Liberdade,** one of Lisbon's most elegant promenades. Modeled after the boulevards of 19th-century Paris, this mile-long thoroughfare ends at **Praça do Marquês de Pombal.** There, an 18th-century statue of the Marquês still watches over the city he whipped into shape 250 years ago.

AROUND PRAÇA DO COMÉRCIO. After the earthquake of 1755 leveled this section of Lisbon, the Marquês de Pombal designed the new streets to serve as a conduit for goods from the ports on the Rio Tejo to the city center. The grid formed perfect blocks, with streets designated for specific trades: *sapateiros* (shoemakers), *douradores* (gold workers), and *bacalhoeiros* (cod merchants) each had their own avenue. The roads lead to Praça do Comércio, on the banks of the Tejo. Today the *praça*, watched over by a 9400 lb. statue of **Dom João I,**

serves as a tourist hub, providing a wide and inviting space between the Tejo's many boats and the city's buzzing crowds.

BAIRRO ALTO AND CHIADO

Cultured Chiado is home to many of Lisbon's finest museums, while Bairro Alto offers some of the best views in the city. Lively **Praça Luís de Camões,** where the two meet, is a prime spot for people watching.

MUSEU ARQUELÓGICO DO CARMO. Built around the ruins of a medieval church destroyed in the 1755 earthquake, this museum features archeological remains from four millennia. Strengths of the small collection include mummies from 16th-century Peru and ancient Egypt, but the highlight is undoubtedly the museum building itself. At its heart is a stunning open-air courtyard framed by the soaring stone arches of the collapsed church, and its galleries occupy a set of beautifully restored gothic rooms. *(On Lg. do Carmo. ☎213 47 86 29. Open M-Sa Oct.-May 10am-6pm, Apr.-Feb. 10am-7pm. €2.50, students and seniors €1.50, under 14 free.)*

IGREJA E MUSEU DE SÃO ROQUE. When the Plague descended on Lisbon in 1505, King Manuel I begged the residents of Venice to send him a relic of São Roque, to whom legend assigned miraculous healing powers. The plague went on to kill thousands in Portugal, but the Jesuits nonetheless began to construct a splendid church in São Roque's honor in 1555. The church, under construction for more then two centuries, reflects a diverse range of architectural and decorative styles. Particularly notable are the dozens of creepy wooden angel-children emerging from the gilded walls of the **Chapel of Our Lady of Piety** (third on the left) and the Italianate **Chapel of Saint John the Baptist** (fourth on the left), considered a masterpiece of neoclassical art. Astounding **gold candlesticks** and other accoutrements originally displayed in this chapel have been moved to the adjacent museum, which also includes permanent exhibits on Jesuit history and Eastern art. *(On Lg. Trinidade Coelho. ☎213 23 53 80. Church open M 2-6pm; Tu-W, and F-Su 9am-6pm; Th 9am-9pm. Museum open T, W, and F-Su 10am-6pm; Th 2-9pm. Church free. Museum €2.50; students, seniors, and under 14 free; free Su until 2pm.)*

MUSEU DO CHIADO. With just a small permanent collection of Portuguese art from the late 19th century to the present, the recently rebuilt Museu do Chiado, home of the National Museum of Contemporary Art, welcomes large new temporary exhibitions every three months. As a result, the art filling its sleek, soaring galleries can range from Romanian avant-garde painting to recent Portuguese photography. *(R. Serpa Pinto 4. ☎213 43 21 48; www.museudochiado-ipmuseus.pt. Open Tu 2-6pm, W-Su 10am-6pm. €4, under 25 and over 65 €2, under 14 free; free Su until 2pm.)*

VIEWS. With a name like "High Neighborhood," it's no surprise that Bairro Alto deals in dramatic vistas. The **Parque São Pedro de Alcântara,** located two blocks behind the Igreja de São Roque, offers a beautifully maintained garden terrace along with a panorama of Baixa and Alfama. Behind the Museo do Carmo on R. Santa Justa, the towering Victorian **Elevador de Santa Justa,** part of the CARRIS network, whisks tourists and commuters alike between Bairro Alto and Baixa. The **Miradouro de Santa Catarina** overflows with locals drinking cheap beer (available at a nearby kiosk) as they take in the Taugus below. To get there from Pr. Luís de Camões, walk down R. do Loreto (it changes name twice after leaving the *praça*), turn left on R. Marechal Saldanha, and follow it to the end.

WEST OF BAIRRO ALTO

Lisbon grows substantially greener as you head west from Bairro Alto. The area's most notable attractions are in the pleasant residential neighborhoods of Estrela and Prazeres.

CEMITÁRIO DOS PRAZERES. Lisbon's most famous cemetery is not only the final resting place of some of Lisbon society's biggest names, but one of the most pleasant places to spend a peaceful afternoon. Thousands of elaborate mausoleums constitute a veritable city of the dead, replete with tree-lined "avenues" and its own small chapel and museum of death-related artifacts. *(Pr. S. João Bosco. ☎213 96 15 11. Take tram 28E (but only cars labeled "Prazeres") from Pr. Do Comércio or Pr. Luís de Camões to the end of the line; the large granite structure in front of you is the entrance. Cemetery open daily May-Sept. 9am-6pm, Oct.-Apr. 9am-5pm. Museum open Tu-Su 10am-4:30pm. Free.)*

BASÍLICA DA ESTRELA. Queen Dona Maria I in 1796 promised God anything for a son. When she finally gave birth to a baby boy, she built this church as a small token of her gratitude. After taking in the baroque interior rich in pink and green marble, check out the ancient *presépio*, or crib, at the center of the beautiful nativity scene to the right of the main altar. If you're visiting on a Wednesday or Friday afternoon, ask in the vestry for permission to ascend to the rooftop terrace; you'll be rewarded with a fantastic view. *(Pr. da Estrela. ☎213 96 09 15. Take any tram 28E from Pr. Do Comércio or Pr. Luís de Camões to Estrela, where you'll see a large white church on your left and a park on your right. Open daily 7:45am-8pm. Presépio open M-Sa 10-11:45am and 1:30-5pm, Su 2-5pm. Terrace open W and F 2-5pm. Free.)*

SÃO SEBASTIÃO

MUSEU DO ORIENTE. Just opened in 2008, this new museum documents Portugal's more than five centuries of involvement in the East with detailed permanent exhibitions of artifacts from across Asia. Not to be missed are the room-sized Indian Altar to Durga and the dramatic Indonesian Barong, included in the "Gods of Asia" exhibit. *(Av. Brasilia at the Doca de Alcântara. ☎213 58 52 00; www.museudooriente.pt. Take tram 15E in the direction of Belém; get off when you see a large warehouse covered in black cloth on your left. Open M, W-Th, Sa-Su 10am-6pm; F 10am-10pm. €4, seniors €2.50, ages 6-12 and students €2, under 6 free. Free F 6-10pm.)*

FUNDACION CALOUSTE GULBENKIAN. Perhaps Portugal's biggest fan ever, native Armenian Calouste Gulbenkian was so charmed when he visited in 1942 that he stayed in the same hotel in Lisbon for 13 years, until his death in 1955. In his will, the millionaire left his extensive art collection (some of it purchased from the Hermitage in St. Petersburg, Russia) to Portugal. The collection, which offers a survey of Western art from ancient Egypt through the early 20th century, forms the core of the Museu Caloueste Gulbenkian. Although it lacks any true blockbusters, the worthwhile museum's highlights include excellent French Neoclassical decorative arts, intricate Art Nouveau jewelry, and paintings by Monet, Rodin, and Fantin-Latour. Across a lush sculpture garden from the Museu stands the Fundacion's second project, the smaller **Centro de Arte Moderno José de Azeredo Perdigão.** The Centro hosts temporary exhibitions of contemporary art and houses a small permanent collection focused on artists from Portugal and its former colonies. *(Av. Berna, 45A. ☎217 82 30 00; www.gulbenkian.pt. M: São Sebastião. From the main entrance of El Corte Inglés, follow the main road, Av. Augusto Antonio de Aguiar, downhill until you see the sign for the "Fundação Calouste Gulbenkian." Take a right up the staircase, climb another set of stairs, and the Museu is across the parking lot. Open Tu-Su 10am-6pm. Museums €4 each, €7 together. Students, teachers, and seniors 50% discount. Free Su until 2pm.)*

ALFAMA

CASTELO DE SÃO JORGE. Built by the Moors in the 11th century, the castle was conquered by Don Alfonso Enriquez, first king of Portugal, then converted into a playground for the royal family between the 14th and 16th centuries. The towers and castle walls allow for a spectacular panoramic view of Lisbon and the Rio Tejo. Also inside the walls are a small museum, cafe, and gallery. *(☎218 80 06 20; www.egeac.pt. Open daily Mar.-Oct. 9am-9pm; Nov.-Feb. 9am-6pm. Last entry 30min before closing. €5, students €2.50, with Lisboa card €3.50, under 10 or over 65 free.)*

LOWER ALFAMA. The small white **Igreja de Santo António** was built in 1812 over the saint's alleged birthplace. The construction was funded with money collected by the city's children, who fashioned altars bearing saintly images to place on doorsteps. The custom is reenacted annually on June 13, the saint's feast day and Lisbon's biggest holiday, which draws out thousands and involves a debaucherous festival the night before. The church is located on R. da Alfândeo, which begins two blocks away from Pr. do Comércio and connects Baixa and lower Alfama. *(Veer right when you see Igreja da Madalena in Lg. da Madalena on the right. Take R. de Santo António da Sé and follow the tram tracks. ☎218 86 91 45. Open daily 8am-7pm. Mass daily 11am, 5, and 7pm.)* In the square beyond the church is the 12th-century **Sé de Lisboa.** The cathedral's interior lacks the ornamentation of the city's other churches, but its age, treasury (containing a small collection of religious objects and manuscripts), and cloister (an archeological site and small museum) make for a worthwhile visit. *(☎218 86 67 52. Open daily 9am-7pm except during mass, held Tu-Sa 6:30pm, Su 11:30am and 7pm. Free. Treasury open M-Sa 10am-1pm and 2-5pm. €2.50, students €1.50. Cloister open M-Sa 10am-6:30pm, Su 2-6:30pm. €2.50, students €1.25.)*

PORTUGAL

GRAÇA

PANTEÃO NACIONAL. The National Pantheon was originally meant to be the Igreja da Santa Engrácia; the citizens of Graça started building the church in 1680 to honor their patron saint. Their ambitions outstripped their finances, however, and they abandoned the project before completing the dome, leaving a massive hole in the top. General Salazar's military regime eventually took over construction, dedicating it as the National Pantheon, a burial ground for important statesmen, in 1966. In a twist of irony, when democracy was restored in 1975, the new government relocated the remains of prominent anti-Fascist opponents to the building and prohibited those who had worked with Salazar from entering. The dome juts out above the Graça skyline, providing an amazing view of Lisbon from its outdoor terrace. Highlights include the tombs of presidents as well as cenotaphs (honorary tombs for people buried elsewhere) for explorers. The Pantheon houses the remains of Amália Rodrigues, the queen of *fado*, and the cenotaphs of Vasco da Gama, the famous Portuguese explorer, and Luis de Camoes, the 17th-century poet. *(To reach the Panteão, take any #28E tram from R. Do Loreto or R. Garrett. ☎218 85 48 20. Open Tu-Su 10am-5pm. €2.50, seniors €1.25, under 14 free. Free Su and holidays until 2pm.)*

IGREJA AND MOSTEIRO DE SÃO VICENTE DE FORA. Built between 1582 and 1629, the Igreja is dedicated to St. Vincent, Lisbon's official patron saint, though Lisbon tends to celebrate its adopted patron saint, St. Antony, much more. The church sanctuary is closed indefinitely for restoration, but in the meantime, the attached Mosteiro offers a small museum detailing the history of the church, offering access to the beautiful chapel inlaid with four colors of marble and displaying some of the church's excellent collection of *azulejo* tile. *(From the bottom of R. dos Correeiros in Baixa, take bus #12 or any tram #28E in the direction of the castle;*

hop off when you see the large white church on your right. ☎218 85 56 52. Mosteiro open Tu-Su 10am-6pm; last entry 5pm. €4, students and seniors €2, under 13 free.)

FEIRA DA LADRA. Every Tuesday and Saturday between the Panteão and Igreja de São Vicente, local vendors hit the streets in the early morning for the Graça "thieves market." Merchants bring piles of goods, from Beatles paraphernalia to African sculptures, and passersby are encouraged to bargain. Get steals on old wristwatches and cameras, dig through piles of jewelry, or admire handmade chandeliers and crucifixes. *(Tu and Sa 8am-late afternoon.)*

FESTIVALS AND ENTERTAINMENT

Those who love to mingle with locals will want to visit Lisbon in June. Open-air *feiras*—festivals of eating, drinking, live music, and dancing—fill the streets. After savoring *farturas* (huge Portuguese pastries whose name means "abundance") and Sagres beer, join in traditional Portuguese dancing. On the night of June 12, the streets explode into song and dance in honor of St. Anthony during the **Festa de Santo António.** Banners are strung between streetlights and confetti falls in buckets during a parade along Av. da Liberdade. Young crowds pack the streets of Alfama and the neighborhoods of Bairro Alto and Santa Catarina, and grilled *sardinhas* (sardines) and *ginja* (wild cherry liqueur) are sold everywhere. Lisbon also has a number of commercial *feiras*. From late May to early June, bookworms burrow for three weeks in the outdoor **Feira do Livro** in Parque Eduardo VII, behind Pr. Marquês de Pombal. The **Feira Internacional de Lisboa** occurs every few months in the Parque das Nações; in July and August, the **Feira de Mar de Cascais** and **Feira de Artesanato de Estoril** (celebrating famous Portuguese pottery) take place near the casino. Year-round *feiras* include the **Feira de Oeiras** (sells antiques on the fourth Sunday of each month) and the **Feira de Carcanelos** (sells clothes Th 8am-2pm) in Rato. Packrats should catch the **Feira da Ladra,** a large flea market held every Tuesday and Sunday (see above).

Agenda Cultural and *Follow Me Lisboa*, free at the tourist office and at kiosks in the Rossio on R. Portas de Santo Antão, have information on concerts, *fado*, movies, plays, and bullfights as well as lists of museums, gardens, and libraries.

FADO

A mandatory experience for visitors, Lisbon's trademark entertainment is the traditional *fado*, an expressive art combining elements of singing and narrative poetry. *Cantadeiras de fado*, cloaked in black dresses and shawls, relate emotional tales of lost loves and faded glory. Numerous *fado* houses lie in the small streets of Bairro Alto and near R. de São João da Praça in Alfama. Some have both *fado* and folk dance performances. To avoid making a tragedy of your budget, explore nearby streets; various bars and small venues often offer free shows with less notable performers. Those in town during the **Festa do Fado** (June 5-27) should check out the free evening performances at the Castelo de São Jorge (details at www.egeac.pt). Book in advance for dinner performances, especially on weekends, and arrive at *fado* houses 30-45min. early. Minimum consumption requirements tend to run €10-20, but ask ahead of time as they may only apply to the second show, which starts around 11pm and typically does not require reservations. The following places are quite touristy and tend to draw and older crowd, but they do feature Portugal's biggest names.

Café Luso, Travessa da Queimada, 10 (☎213 42 22 81; www.cafeluso.pt). Pass below the club's glowing neon-blue sign to reach *fado* nirvana. Open since 1927, Lisbon's premier *fado* club combines the best in Portuguese music, cuisine, and atmosphere. Fixed menu

PORTUGAL

€25. Entrees €22-39. Min. €25. *Fado* and folkloric dance 8:30-10pm; the *fado* continues until 2am. Make reservations for F and Sa nights. Open daily 7:30pm-2am. AmEx/MC/V.

O Faia, R. Barroca, 54-56 (☎213 42 67 42; www.ofaia.com). Performances by famous *fadistas* like Anita Guerreiro and Lenita Gentil, as well as very fine Portuguese cuisine, make O Faia worth your time and money. 4 singers. Entrees €20-35. Min. €20, includes 2 drinks. *Fado* starts at 9:30pm. 2nd show starts at 11:45pm. Open M-Sa 8pm-2am. AmEx/MC/V.

BULLFIGHTING

Portuguese bullfighting differs from the Spanish variety in that the bull is typically not killed in the ring, but butchered afterwards, a tradition that dates back to the 18th century. These spectacles take place most Thursdays from late June to late September at **Praça de Touros de Lisboa,** Campo Pequeno. (☎217 93 21 43; www.campopequeno.com.) The newly renovated *praça* doubles as a shopping center during the day and also features the distinctly Portuguese *toureio equestre,* or horseback bullfighting at night. Aficionados should include **Santarém** in their travel plans—it's the capital of Portuguese bullfighting and hosts the most celebrated *cavaleiros.*

PORTUGAL

FUTEBOL

Futebol is the lifeblood of many a Portuguese citizen. *Futebol* fever became an epidemic during the 2006 World Cup, and after a month of nail-biting, shop-closing, crowd-gathering soccer mania, the Portuguese team returned from Germany national heroes after reaching the semifinal round for the first time in 40 years. These days, the Portuguese get riled up for the popular Euro Cup and regional games. If you are in Lisbon when Portugal is playing, go to **Marques de Pombal** (M: Marques de Pombal), where you will see hundreds of fans screaming at a giant TV screen. If they win, follow the fans to the main *praça,* where they will stop traffic, clamber onto random cars, and sometimes flip them over. Lisbon's two main teams are **Benfica** and **Sporting,** both of which feature some of the world's finest players. (Benfica at Estádio da Luz. ☎707 200 100; www.slbenfica.pt. M: Colégio Militar-Luz. Ticket office open daily 10am-7pm. Sporting at Alvalade Stadium. ☎707 20 44 44; www.sporting.pt. M: Campo Grande. Ticket office open M-F 10am-7pm.) Benfica made headlines with its magical rise to the semifinal round of the 2006 UEFA Champions League, the most prestigious club tournament in Europe, for the first time in over a decade. Benfica and Sporting are bitter rivals—be careful whom you support, since both have diehard fans who won't care that you're "just a tourist." Check the newspaper *A Bola* for games.

NIGHTLIFE

Bairro Alto is one giant street party every night until 2am, and is a good first stop for nightlife. **Rua do Norte, Rua do Diário de Notícias, Rua da Rosa,** and **Rua Atalaia**, which run parallel to each other, pack many small bars and clubs into three short blocks, making bar-hopping as easy as crossing the street. Several gay and lesbian establishments lie in this area; there are also some in **Rato** near the edge of Bairro Alto, past Pr. Príncipe Real. The options south of Bairro Alto near the water are larger, flashier, and generally more diverse. The **Docas de Santo Amaro** host a strip of waterfront bars, clubs, and restaurants, while the **Avenida 24 de Julho** and the parallel **Rua das Janelas Verdes** (Street of Green Windows), in the **Santos** area, have some of the most popular clubs and discotecas. Beneath the bridge stands the new **LX Factory,** a hipster haven featuring trendy restaurants, design shops, cafes, bars, and performance spaces. Check out www.lxfactory.com for details. Newer expansions include the area along the river across from the Santa Apolónia train station, home to glitzy club Lux. The Bairro Alto bar scene is very casual, but sandals, sneakers, and jeans (excepting the highest-end designer pairs) are generally not allowed in clubs—some places have uptight fashion police at the door. Inside, beer runs €3-5, and it gets more expensive as the night wears on. Some clubs also charge a cover (generally €5-13), which usually includes two to four free drinks. Entrance is often free for women. There's no reason to show up before midnight; crowds flow in around 2am and stay past dawn.

BAIRRO ALTO

From tiny bars to punk clubs to posh *fado* restaurants, the Bairro Alto and nearby districts can't be beat for nightlife and entertainment.

BAIRRO ALTO AND NORTH TO THE JARDIM BOTANICO

Pavilhão Chinês, R. Dom Pedro V 89 (☎213 424 729). Ring the doorbell and a red-vested waiter will usher you into this delightful cross between classic and kitsch. Sip a drink or play pool in lounges dripping with Chinese paper fans, model airplanes, and anything else that happened to strike the owner's eclectic fancy. Huge range of teas (€4) and throwback mixed drinks like the Tom Collins and Sidecar (€7.50 each) presented in a 50+ page menu-cum-graphic novel. Open M-Sa 6pm-2am, Su 9pm-2am. AmEx/MC/V.

Portas Largas, R. da Atalaia 105 (☎213 46 63 79). Thanks to daily live music, this Bairro Alto classic is a safe bet any night of the week, even during the low-season. Gay-friendly with a mixed, welcoming crowd. Beer €2-4. *Caipirinhas* €4. Open daily July-Sept. 7pm-2am, Oct.-June 8pm-2am. Cash only.

Discoteca Trumps, R. da Imprensa Nacional 104 (☎213 97 10 59; www.trumps.pt). This always-packed "hetero-friendly" club is ideal for anyone in search of an unpretentious place to dance. 2 underground dance floors (one plays pop, the other house) lined with black-and-white photographs of buff male and female torsos. More relaxed upstairs lounge. Mostly male clientele, but all are welcome. €10 cover buys equivalent drink credit. Open F-Sa 11:45pm-6am. AmEx/MC/V.

SOUTH OF BAIRRO ALTO: ALCÂNTARA AND THE RIVERFRONT

A visit to any of these clubs will most likely involve a cab ride (about €6 from Rossio or Bairro Alto). Tram 15E runs the length of the Rio Tejo but stops at 1am; the area along the river is not ideal for a late-night stroll.

op art, Doca de Santo Amaro (☎213 95 67 87; www.opartcafe.com). During the week, trendy op art is a relaxed spot to grab a light meal or a drink; on F and Sa, it morphs from cafe to club as guest DJs pack the small all-glass structure to capacity. Beer €2.50, mixed drinks €5. Cover typically €5-10, includes 1 drink, €10-20 for special events. Open Tu-Th 3pm-2am, F 3pm-6am, Sa 1pm-6am, Su 1pm-2am. AmEx/MC/V.

Dock's Club, R. da Cintura do Porto de Lisboa 226 (☎213 95 08 56). This large club plays great hip hop, latino, and house music, and starts to fill up around 2am. 2 bars inside, with a pleasant patio-bar out back. €14 buys equivalent drink credit. Girls' night Tu: women pay no cover and get €14 in free drinks. Open Tu, F-Sa midnight-6am. AmEx/MC/V.

Kapital, Av. 24 de Julho 68 (☎213 95 71 01). One of the classiest clubs in Lisbon, Kapital's ruthless door policy makes admission a competitive sport. Dress nicely; this is definitely the time to break out your designer duds. Don't expect to get in, especially if you're an unaccompanied male or if it's clear you're a tourist. Those who make it past the door earn access to a sleek, multi-level space with a panoramic view of the Rio Tejo. Drinks €5. Cover €12-20; includes 2 drinks. Open M-Sa 11:30pm-6am. MC/V.

ALFAMA AND GRAÇA

Restô, R. Costa do Castelo, 7 (☎218 86 73 34). Don't be surprised to see a flying trapeze or tightrope act—Restô is on the grounds of a government-funded clown school, Chapitô. Upstairs serves Argentine steaks (€17-30) and Spanish tapas (€4-8). Huge, colorful patio with a carnival atmosphere. Downstairs bar open W-Su 10pm-2am. Shows most evenings; check the schedule online. Open M-F noon-3pm and 7:30pm-1:30am, Sa-Su noon-1:30am. Cash only.

Lux, Av. Infante D. Henrique A, (☎218 82 08 90; www.luxfragil.com). Across from the Sta. Apolónia train station; take a taxi (€5-6 from Baixa or Bairro Alto). One-of-a-kind view from the roof of this enormous 3-story complex, which many deem the best club in Lisbon. Lounge at the bar upstairs or descend into the maelstrom of light, sound, and dancing downstairs. Bouncers are very selective and tend not to look kindly on pushy tourists, so smile, be very polite, speak in Portuguese if possible, and dress well—the stylish hipster look works better than suiting up. Arrive after 2am. Cover is typically €12, though you get an equivalent amount in free drinks. Open Tu-Sa 11pm-6am. AmEx/MC/V.

Ondajazz Bar, Arco de Jesus, 7 (☎ 218 87 30 64, www.ondajazz.com). Visit the Ondajazz Bar for a wide selection of performances including jazz, blues, world music, and poetry readings. Relaxed coffee shop atmosphere. Open mic W. Cover €5-7 most nights; no cover W. Dinner and concert package (€30-37) includes starter, entree and a drink. Open M-Th and Su 8pm-2am, F-Sa 8pm-3am. Kitchen open until 11pm. MC/V.

SPAIN (ESPAÑA)

The fiery spirit of flamenco; the energy of artistic genius; the explosive merging of urban style and archaic tradition—this is Spain. Here, dry golden plains give way to rugged coastline, and modern architectural feats rise from ancient plazas. Explore winding medieval alleyways that lead to bustling city centers, or watch from a sidewalk cafe as mulleted youth pass by. In Spain, there is always a reason to stay up late, and there is always time for an afternoon *siesta*.

DISCOVER SPAIN: SUGGESTED ITINERARIES

THREE DAYS. Soak in **Madrid's** (p. 512) art and culture as you walk through the **Retiro's** gardens and peruse the halls of the **Prado, Thyssen-Bornemisza,** and **Nacional Centro de Arte Reina Sofía.** By night, move from the *tapas* bars of Santa Ana to Malasaña and Chueca. Daytrip to **Segovia** or **El Escorial.**

ONE WEEK. Begin in southern Spain, exploring the **Alhambra's** Moorish palaces in **Granada** (1 day; p. 541) and the mosque in **Córdoba** (1 day). After 2 days in **Madrid,** travel northeast to **Barcelona** (2 days) and the beaches of **Costa Brava** (1 day).

THREE WEEKS. See the beautiful cathedral of **León** (1 day), then head to **Madrid** (3 days), with daytrips to **El Escorial** (1 day) and **Segovia** (1 day). Take the train to **Córdoba** (2 days), and on to **Seville** (2 days; p. 533). Take in the incredible gorge in **Ronda** (1 day) before heading south to charming **Málaga,** on the **Costa del Sol** (1 day p. 546). Head inland to **Granada** (2 days), then seaward again to **Valencia** (1 day) before traveling up the coast to **Barcelona** (3 days). Daytrip to the **Costa Brava** (1 day), taking in the **Teatre-Museu Dalí** and the **Casa-Museu Salvador Dalí.** From Barcelona, head to the beaches and tapas bars of **San Sebastián** (1 day) and **Bilbao** (1 day; p. 568), home of the world-famous **Guggenheim Museum.**

LIFE AND TIMES

HISTORY

RULE HISPANIA (PREHISTORY TO AD 711). Spain played host to a succession of civilizations—**Basque, Celtiberian,** and **Greek**—before the Romans came for an extended visit in the third century BC. Over the next seven centuries, the Romans infused Spanish culture with their language, architecture, roads, and food (particularly grapes, olives, and wheat). Following the Romans, a slew of Germanic tribes swept through Iberia, and the **Visigoths**—newly converted Christians—emerged victorious. In AD 419, they established their court at Barcelona and ruled Spain for the next 300 years.

PLEASE, SIR, MAY I HAVE SOME MOORS? (711-1492). A small force of **Arabs, Berbers,** and **Syrians** invaded Spain in AD 711 following Muslim unification. The **Moors** encountered little resistance from the divided **Visigoths,** and the peninsula fell to the caliph of Damascus, the spiritual leader of Islam. The Moors established their Iberian capital at **Córdoba,** which by the 10th century was the larg-

est city in Western Europe with over 500,000 inhabitants. During Abderramán III's rule (929-961), many considered Spain the wealthiest and most cultivated country in the world. Abderramán III's successor, **Al-Mansur,** snuffed out opposition in his court and undertook a series of military campaigns that culminated in AD 997 with the destruction of **Santiago de Compostela** and the kidnapping of its bells. It took the Christians 240 years to get them back, and centuries more to retake Spain.

LOS REYES CATÓLICOS (1469-1516). The marriage of **Fernando de Aragón** and **Isabel de Castilla** in 1469 joined Iberia's two mightiest Christian kingdoms. During their half-century rule, these Catholic monarchs established Spain as the prime European exponent of Catholicism, and as an international power. They introduced the brutal **Inquisition** in 1478, which mandated execution or burning of heretics, principally Jews. The policy prompted a mass exodus, as Jews and Muslims who stayed faced conversion to Christianity or imprisonment and death. In 1492, the royal couple captured Granada from the Moors, ending the centuries-long *Reconquista* and uniting Spain under Catholic rule. This dominance continued with lucrative conquests in the Americas, beginning in 1492 when they financed **Christopher Columbus's** first adventure.

ENTER THE HAPSBURGS (1516-1713). The daughter of Fernando and Isabel, **Juana la Loca** (the Mad), married **Felipe el Hermoso** (the Fair) of the powerful Hapsburg dynasty. When Felipe died in a game of *jai alai*, La Loca took the news badly, dragging his corpse through the streets screaming. Juana and Felipe had secured their legacy with the birth of **Carlos I,** better known as Holy Roman Emperor Charles V. He eventually retired to a monastery, leaving **Felipe II** a handful of rebellious territories in the Protestant Netherlands. The 1554 marriage of Felipe II to Mary Tudor, Queen of England, created an international Catholic alliance; Felipe believed his life's purpose was to create a Catholic empire. In 1581, the Dutch declared their independence from Spain, starting a war and spurring antagonism with England's new Protestant Queen, Elizabeth I. The conflict with the British heralded Spain's downfall; **Sir Francis Drake** decimated Spain's "invincible" **Armada** in 1588. With much of his empire lost and his wealth from the Americas depleted, Felipe retreated to **El Escorial** (p. 528), sulking in its monastery until his death. In 1609, Felipe III (r. 1598-1621) expelled nearly 300,000 of Spain's remaining Moors. After him, **Felipe IV** (r. 1621-65) painstakingly held the country together through a long, tumultuous reign, while fostering the arts (painter **Diego Velázquez** graced his court). Defending Catholicism began to drain Spain's resources after the outbreak of the **Thirty Years' War** (1618-48), which ended in the marriage of Felipe IV's daughter María Teresa to **Louis XIV** of France. However, their son was not fit to succeed to the throne. **Carlos II el Hechizado** (the Bewitched; r. 1665-1700), the product of generations of inbreeding, was known to fly into fits of rage and suffered from seizures. From then on, little went right: Carlos II died without heirs, Spain fell into economic depression, and cultural bankruptcy ensued. Rulers battled for the crown in the **War of the Spanish Succession** (1701-14).

THE REIGN IN SPAIN (1713-1931). The 1713 Treaty of Utrecht ended the ordeal (and Spain's possession of Gibraltar, which went to the English) and landed **Felipe V** (r. 1713-1746), a Bourbon grandson of **Louis XIV,** on the Spanish throne. Though the new king cultivated a flamboyant, debaucherous court, he competently administered the empire, at last regaining control of Spanish-American trade. The next century was dominated by the Bourbon effort to create a modern state, as the crown centralized power and stripped the different regions of their historical privileges. Finally, in 1808, **Napoleon** invaded Spain as part of his bid for world domination, inaugurating an occupation as short as the general himself. In the midst of the upheaval, most of Spain's Latin American empire threw off the colonial yoke, and those still beyond Napoleon's reach penned the progressive **Constitution of 1812**, which established Spain as a parliamentary monarchy. The violence ended when the Protestant Brits defeated the Corsican troops at Waterloo (1815), placing the reactionary **Fernando VII** (r. 1814-1833) on the throne.

Parliamentary liberalism was restored in 1833 upon Fernando VII's death, and survived the conservative challenge of the first **Carlist War** (1833-39), a dispute over the monarchy of **Queen Isabel II** (r. 1843-68). Her successor, **King Amadeo I** (1870-73), enjoyed a short reign before the **First Spanish Republic** was proclaimed. After a coup d'etat in 1875, the monarchy was restored under **King Alfonso XII** (1875-85), and the last two decades of the 19th century were marked by rapid industrialization. However, Spain's 1898 loss to the US in the **Spanish-American War** cost it the Philippines, Puerto Rico, Cuba, and any remaining dreams of colonial wealth.

Closer to home, Moroccan tribesmen rebelled against Spanish troops in northern Africa beginning in 1917, resulting in a series of embarrassing military defeats. These events further weakened Spanish morale and culminated in the massacre of 14,000 royal troops in 1921, threatening the very survival of the monarchy. The search for someone to blame for the disaster occupied aristocrats, bureaucrats, and generals for the next decade, throwing the country into chaos. In 1923, **General Miguel Primo de Rivera** sought to bring order to the situation in the form of Spain's first dictatorship.

REPUBLIC AND REBELLION (1931-39). **King Alfonso XIII** (1902-31) abdicated the throne in April 1931, giving rise to the **Second Spanish Republic** (1931-39). Republican Liberals and Socialists established safeguards for farmers and industrial workers, granted women's suffrage, assured religious tolerance, and chipped away at traditional military dominance. National euphoria, however, faded fast. The 1933 elections split the Republican-Socialist coalition, increasing the power of right-wing and Catholic parties in parliament. Military dissatisfaction led to a heightened profile of the **Fascist Falange** (founded by Primo de Rivera's son, José Antonio), which further polarized national politics. By 1936, radicals, anarchists, Socialists, and Republicans had formed a **Popular Front** coalition to win the February elections. Their victory, however, was short lived. After increasing polarization, **Generalísimo Francisco Franco** led a militarist uprising and the nation plunged into war, as the infectious ideology of **La Guerra Civil** (**The Spanish Civil War;** 1936-39) diffused across the globe. Germany and Italy readily supplied Franco with troops and munitions, while the US and liberal European states instituted the Non-Intervention Treaty. The Soviet Union organized the **International Brigades,** an amalgamation of Communists and other leftist volunteers from all over Europe and the US, to battle Franco's fascism. Foreign aid waned as Stalin began to see the benefits of an alliance with Hitler. Bombings, executions, combat, starvation, and disease took nearly 600,000 lives and forced almost one million Spaniards to emigrate. In April 1939, Franco bid a "farewell to arms," marching into Madrid and ending the war.

FRANCO AND THE NATIONAL TRAGEDY (1939-75). Franco's dictatorship was largely centered around the church, the army, and the Falange. Thousands of scientists, artists, intellectuals, and sympathizers were exiled, imprisoned, or executed in the name of order and purity. Franco initially pursued an isolationist economic policy, but stagnant conditions eventually forced him to adopt a more open policy. With prosperity came unrest. Dissatisfied workers and students engaged in protests, hoping to draw attention to the dark underside of Franco's reign. Groups like the Basque **ETA** also provided resistance throughout the dictatorship, often via terrorist acts, producing turmoil that undermined the legitimacy of the regime. In his old age, the general tried to smooth international relations by joining NATO, courting the Pope, and encouraging tourism. However, the **"national tragedy,"** as the tense period under Franco was later called, did not officially end until Franco's death in 1975. **King Juan Carlos I** (r. 1975-), grandson of Alfonso XIII and nominally a Franco protégé, carefully set out to undo Franco's damage.

DEMOCRACY RISES (1975-2005). In 1978, under centrist Prime Minister **Adolfo Suárez,** Spain adopted a new constitution and restored parliamentary government and regional autonomy. The post-Franco years have been marked by progressive social change in the economic and political arenas. The period was also characterized by a movement known in Madrid as "La Movida," which saw an unprecedented outburst of artistic, cultural, and social expression after decades of censorship and inhibition. Suárez's resignation in early 1981 left the country ripe for an attempted coup on February 23 of that year, when a group of rebels took over parliament in an effort to impose a military-backed government. King Juan Carlos I used his personal influence to convince the rebels to stand down, paving the way for the charismatic **Felipe González** to lead the PSOE (Spanish Socialist Worker's Party) to victory in the 1982 elections. González opened the Spanish economy and championed consensus policies, overseeing Spain's integration into the European Community (now the EU) four years later. Despite unpopular economic policies, González was reelected in 1986 and continued a program of massive public investment to rejuvenate the nation's economy. By the end of 1993, however, recession and revelations of large-scale corruption led to a resounding Socialist defeat at the hands of the Popular Party (PP) in the 1994 European parliamentary elections. The leader of the PP, **José María Aznar,** managed to maintain a fragile coalition with the support of the Catalan and Islas Canarias regional parties. He won an absolute majority in 2000. Since then Spain has moved in a more liberal direction. On July 1, 2005 the government legalized gay marriage, eliminating all legal distinctions between same-sex and heterosexual couples.

GLOBAL TERRORISM. Under the conservative Aznar, Spain became one of the US's most prominent allies in the war on terror, but the relationship has since been strained. On **March 11, 2004,** days before the national elections, the country suffered its own grievous attack, often referred to as **11-M** *(el once eme).* In an attack linked to Al-Qaeda, 10 bombs exploded on four trains heading to Madrid from the suburbs, killing 191 passengers and injuring more than 1800. Immediately thereafter, the conservatives lost the election to **José Luis Rodríguez Zapatero** of the PSOE. Many attributed the loss to the popular reaction against Aznar's attempt to shirk responsibility for the attacks. Under the new government, Spain withdrew its troops from Iraq in 2004.

ESSENTIALS

FACTS AND FIGURES

OFFICIAL NAME: Kingdom of Spain.

CAPITAL: Madrid.

GOVERNMENT: Parliamentary monarchy.

MAJOR CITIES: Barcelona, Granada, Seville, Valencia.

POPULATION: 40,448,000.

LAND AREA: 500,500 sq. km.

TIME ZONE: GMT +1.

LANGUAGES: Spanish (Castilian), Basque, Catalan, Galician.

RELIGION: Roman Catholic (94%).

LARGEST PAELLA EVER MADE: 20m in diameter, this *paella* fed 100,000 people in 1992.

WHEN TO GO

Summer is high season in Spain, though in many parts of the country, *Semana Santa* and other festivals are particularly busy. Tourism peaks in August, when the coastal regions overflow while inland cities empty out. Winter travel has the advantage of lighter crowds and lower prices, but sights reduce their hours.

DOCUMENTS AND FORMALITIES

EMBASSIES. Foreign embassies in Spain are in Madrid. Spanish embassies abroad include: **Australia:** 15 Arkana St., Yarralumla, ACT 2600; mailing address: P.O. Box 9076, Deakin ACT 2600 (☎+612 6273 35 55; www.mae.es/Embajadas/Canberra/es/Home). Consulates: Level 24, St. Martin's Tower, 31 Market St., Sydney, NSW 2000 (☎+612 9261 24 33; cog.sydney@maec.es); 146 Elgin St., Carlton, VIC 3053 Melbourne (☎+613 9347 1966; cog.melbourne@maec.es).

Canada: 74 Stanley Ave., Ottawa, ON K1M 1P4 (☎+1-613-747-2252; www.embaspain.ca). Consulates: 1 Westmount Sq., Ste. 1456, Ave. Wood, Montreal, QC H3Z 2P9 (☎+1 -14-935-5235; conspmontreal@mail.mae.es); 2 Bloor St. East. St. 1201, Toronto, ON M4W 1A8 (☎+1 416 977 1661; cog.toronto@mae.es). **Ireland:** 17 Merlyn Park, Ballsbridge, Dublin 4 (☎+353 1 269 1640; www.mae.es/embajadas/dublin). **New Zealand:** 56 Victoria Street, P.O.B. 24-150, Wellington 6142 (☎+64 4 913 1167; emb.wellington@maec.es). **UK:** 39 Chesham Pl., London SW1X 8SB (☎ +44 207 235 5555; embaspuk@mail.mae.es). Consulates: 20 Draycott Pl., London SW3 2RZ (☎+44 207 589 8989; www.conspalon.org); Ste. 1A, Brook House, 70 Spring Gardens, Manchester M2 2BQ (☎+44 161 236 1262; consmanchester@btconnect.com); 63 North Castle St., Edinburgh EH2 3LJ (☎+44 131 220 1843; cog.edimburgo@maec.es.) **US:** 2375 Pennsylvania Ave. NW, Washington, D.C. 20037 (☎+1-202-728-2330; www.spainemb.org). **Consulates:** 150 E. 58th St., 30th fl., New York, NY 10155 (☎+1-212 355-4080; cog.nuevayork@mae.es); branches in Boston, Chicago, Houston, Los Angeles, Miami, New Orleans, San Francisco, and San Juan, PR.

VISA AND ENTRY INFORMATION. EU citizens do not need visas. Citizens of Australia, Canada, New Zealand, the US, and many Latin American countries do not need visas for stays of up to 90 days, beginning upon entry into the EU's freedom-of-movement zone. For more info, see p. 8. For stays over 90 days, all non-EU citizens need visas, available at Spanish consulates (€100).

TOURIST SERVICES AND MONEY

TOURIST OFFICES. For general info, contact the **Instituto de Turismo de España,** Jose Lazaro Galdiano 6, 28071 Madrid (☎913 433 500; www.tourspain.es).

EMERGENCY	**Ambulance:** ☎061. **Fire:** ☎080. **Local Police:** ☎092. **National Police:** ☎091. **General Emergency:** ☎112.

MONEY. The **euro (€)** has replaced the **peseta** as the unit of currency in Spain. For more info, see p. 10. As a general rule, it's cheaper to exchange money in Spain than at home. **ATMs** usually have good exchange rates. In restaurants, all prices include a service charge. Satisfied customers occasionally toss in some spare change—usually no more than 5%—and while it is purely optional, **tipping** is becoming increasingly widespread in restaurants and other places that cater to tourists. Many people give train, airport, and hotel porters €1 per bag, while taxi drivers sometimes get 5-10%. **Bargaining** is only common at flea markets and with street vendors.

BUSINESS HOURS. Almost all museums, shops, and churches close from 2-4pm or longer for an afternoon **siesta.** Most Spaniards eat lunch during their *siesta* (as well as nap), so restaurants open in the late afternoon. Shops and sights re-open at 3pm, and some may stay open until 8pm. Most restaurants will start serving dinner by 9pm, although eating close to midnight is very common in Spain. After midnight, the clubhopping commences. Increasingly, some large chains and offices are open all day, in large part due to an effort by the Spanish government to encourage a stronger economy and more "normal" business hours. It's still a safe bet that nearly every store will be closed on Sundays.

TRANSPORTATION

BY PLANE. Flights land mainly at **Barajas Airport** in Madrid (**MAD;** ☎913 93 60 00) and the **Barcelona International Airport** (**BCN;** ☎932 98 39 25). Contact AENA

(☎902 40 47 04; www.aena.es) for info on flight times at most airports. See p. 33 for info on flying to Spain.

BY FERRY. Spain's islands are accessible by ferry. Ferries are also the least expensive way of traveling between Spain and Tangier or the Spanish enclave of **Ceuta** in Morocco. See p. 43.

BY TRAIN. Direct trains are available to Madrid and Barcelona from several European cities, including Geneva, SWI; Lisbon, POR; and Paris, FRA. Spanish trains are clean, relatively punctual, and reasonably priced. However, most train routes do tend to bypass small towns. Spain's national railway is **RENFE** (☎902 24 02 02; www.renfe.es). When possible, avoid *transvía*, *semidirecto*, or *correo* trains, as they are very slow. *Estrellas* are slow night trains with bunks and showers. *Cercanías* (commuter trains) go from cities to suburbs and nearby towns. There is no reason to buy a Eurail Pass if you plan to travel only within Spain. Trains are cheap, so a pass saves little money; moreover, buses are the most efficient means of traveling around Spain. Several Rail Europe passes cover travel within Spain. See www.raileurope.com for more info on the following passes. The **Spain Flexipass** ($155) offers three days of unlimited travel in a two-month period. The **Spain Rail 'n' Drive Pass** ($307) is good for three days of unlimited first-class train travel and two days of unlimited mileage in a rental car. The **Spain-Portugal Pass** offers three days or more of unlimited first-class travel in Spain and Portugal over a two-month period (from $289).

JUST SAY NO. If you are planning on traveling only within Spain (and Portugal), do not buy a **Eurail Pass.** Bus travel is usually the best option, and trains are less expensive than in the rest of Europe. A Eurail Pass makes sense only for those planning to travel in other European countries as well.

SPAIN

BY BUS. In Spain, buses are cheaper and have far more comprehensive routes than trains. Buses provide the only public transportation to many isolated areas. For those traveling primarily within one region, **buses are the best method of transportation.** Spain has numerous private companies, and the lack of a centralized bus company may make itinerary planning difficult. Companies' routes rarely overlap, so it is unlikely that more than one will serve your intended destination. **Alsa** (☎913 27 05 40; www.alsa.es) serves Asturias, Castilla and León, Galicia, and Madrid, as well as international destinations including France, Germany, Italy, and Portugal. **Auto-Res** (☎902 02 00 52; www.auto-res.net) serves Castilla y León, Extremadura, Galicia, Valencia, and Portugal.

BY CAR. Spain's highway system connects major cities by four-lane *autopistas*. Speeders beware: police can "photograph" the speed and license plate of your car and issue a ticket without pulling you over. If you are pulled over, fines must be paid on the spot. **Gas** prices, €0.80-1.10 per liter, are lower than in many European countries but high by North American standards. Renting a car is cheaper than elsewhere in Europe. Spain accepts Canadian, EU, and US driver's licenses; otherwise, an International Driving Permit (IDP) is required. Try **Atesa** (☎902 10 01 01; www.atesa.es), Spain's largest rental agency. The automobile association is **Real Automóvil Club de España** (RACE; ☎902 40 45 45; www.race.es). For more on renting and driving a car, see p. 40.

BY THUMB. Hitchhikers report that Castilla and Andalucía are long, hot waits, and hitchhiking out of Madrid is virtually impossible. The Mediterranean coast and the islands are more promising; remote areas in the Balearics, Catalonia, or Galicia may be best accessible by hitchhiking. Although approaching people for rides at gas stations near highways and rest stops purportedly gets results, *Let's Go* does not recommend hitchhiking.

KEEPING IN TOUCH

PHONE CODES	**Country code:** 34. **International dialing prefix:** 00. Within Spain, dial city code + local number, even when dialing inside the city. For more info on how to place international calls, see **Inside Back Cover.**

TELEPHONE. Whenever possible, use a prepaid phone card for international phone calls, as long-distance rates for national phone service are often very high. Find them at tobacconists. However, some public phones will only accept change. Mobile phones are an increasingly popular and economical option, costing as little as €30 (not including minutes). Major mobile carriers include Movistar and Vodafone. Direct-dial access numbers for calling out of Spain include: AT&T Direct (☎900 990 011); British Telecom (☎900 96 4495); Canada Direct (☎900 990 015); Telecom New Zealand Direct (☎900 990 064).

MAIL. Airmail *(por avión)* takes five to eight business days to reach Canada or the US; service is faster to the UK and Ireland and slower to Australia and New Zealand. Standard postage is €0.78 to North America. Surface mail *(por barco)* can take over a month, and packages take two to three months. Certified mail *(certificado)* is the most reliable way to send a letter or parcel and takes four to seven business days. Spain's overnight mail is not actually overnight, and is thus not worth the expense. To receive mail in Spain, have it delivered **Poste Restante.** Mail will go to the main post office unless you specify a subsidiary by street address. Address mail to be held according to the following example: Last Name, First Name; **Lista de Correos;** City; Postal Code; SPAIN; AIRMAIL.

ACCOMMODATIONS AND CAMPING

SPAIN	❶	❷	❸	❹	❺
ACCOMMODATIONS	under €18	€18-24	€25-34	€35-45	over €45

The cheapest and most basic options are *refugios*, *casas de huéspedes*, and *hospedajes*, while *pensiones* and *fondas* tend to be a bit nicer. All are essentially boarding houses with basic rooms, shared bath, and no A/C. Higher up the ladder but not necessarily more expensive, *hostales* generally have sinks in bedrooms and provide linens and lockers, while *hostal-residencias* are similar to hotels in overall quality. The government rates *hostales* on a two-star system; even establishments receiving one star are typically quite comfortable. The system also fixes *hostal* prices, posted in the lounge or main entrance. Prices invariably dip below the official rates in the low season (Sept.-May), so bargain away. **Red Española de Albergues Juveniles** (REAJ), the Spanish **Hostelling International** (HI) affiliate (www.reaj.com), runs more than 200 hostels year-round. Prices depend on season, location, and services offered, but are generally €9-15 for guests under 26 and higher for those 26 and over. Breakfast is usually included; lunch and dinner are occasionally offered at an additional charge. Hostels usually have lockouts around 11am and have curfews between midnight and 3am. As a rule, don't expect much privacy—rooms typically have from 4 to 20 beds in them. To reserve a bed in the high season (July-Aug. and during festivals), call at least a few weeks in advance. **Campgrounds** are generally the cheapest choice for two or more people. Most charge separate fees per person, per tent, and per car; others charge for a *parcela* (a small plot of land), plus per-person fees. Pick up the informative *Guía de Campings.*

FOOD AND DRINK

SPAIN	❶	❷	❸	❹	❺
FOOD	under €6	€6-10	€11-15	€16-20	over €20

Fresh, local ingredients are still an integral part of Spanish cuisine, varying according to each region's climate, geography, and history. The old Spanish saying holds true: "*Que comer es muy importante, porque de la panza, ¡nace la danza!*" (Eating is very important, because from the belly, dance is born!)

Spaniards start the day with a light breakfast *(desayuno)* of coffee or thick, hot chocolate, and a pastry. The main meal of the day *(comida)* consists of several courses and is typically eaten around 2 or 3pm. Dinner at home *(cena)* tends to be light. Dining out begins anywhere between 8pm and midnight. Barhopping for *tapas* is an integral part of the Spanish lifestyle. Some restaurants are "open" from 8am until 1 or 2am, but most serve meals only from 1pm or 2pm to 4pm and 8pm to midnight. Many restaurants offer a *plato combinado* (main course, side dish, bread, and sometimes a beverage) or a *menú del día* (two or three set dishes, bread, beverage, and dessert) for roughly €5-9. If you ask for a *menú*, this is what you may receive; *carta* is the word for menu.

Tapas (small dishes of savory meats and vegetables cooked according to local recipes) are quite tasty, and in most regions they are paired with beer or wine. *Raciones* are large *tapas* served as entrees; *bocadillos* are sandwiches. Spanish specialties include *tortilla de patata* (potato omelet), *jamón serrano* (smoked ham), *calamares fritos* (fried squid), *arroz* (rice), *chorizo* (spicy sausage), *gambas* (shrimp), *lomo de cerdo* (pork loin), *paella* (steamed saffron rice with seafood, chicken, and vegetables), and *gazpacho* (cold tomato-based soup). Vegetarians should learn the phrase "*yo soy vegetariano*" (I am a vegetarian) and specify this means no *jamón* (ham) or *atún* (tuna). A normal-sized draft beer is a *caña de cerveza;* a *tubo* is a little bigger. A *calimocho* is a mix of Coca-Cola and red wine, while *sangria* is a drink of red wine, sugar, brandy, and fruit. *Tinto de verano* is a lighter version of *sangria:* red wine and Fanta. *Café solo* means black coffee; add a touch of milk for a *nube;* a little more and it's a *café cortado;* half milk and half coffee makes a *café con leche.*

SPAIN

BEYOND TOURISM

Spain offers volunteer opportunities from protecting dolphins on the Costa del Sol to fighting for immigrants' rights. Universities in major cities host thousands of foreign students every year, and language schools are a good alternative to university study if you desire a deeper focus on language or a slightly less rigorous courseload. Those seeking long-term work in Spain should consider teaching English. Short-term jobs are widely available in the restaurant, hotel, and tourism industries, and are typically held by those without permits. For more info on opportunities across Europe, see **Beyond Tourism,** p. 45.

Enforex, Alberto Aguilera, 26, 28015 Madrid, Spain (☎915 943 776; www.enforex.com). Offers 20 Spanish programs in Spain, ranging from 1 week to a year in duration. Opportunities in 12 Spanish cities, including Granada, Sevilla, Barcelona, and Madrid.

Ecoforest, Apdo. 29, Coin, 29100 Málaga, Spain (☎661 07 99 50; www.ecoforest.org). Fruit farm and vegan community in southern Spain that aims for a sustainable lifestyle. Visitors are welcome to stay, contributing €5-15 per day towards operating costs.

Ecos do Sur, C. Ángel Senra 25, 15007 La Coruña, Spain (☎981 15 01 18; www.ecosdosur.org). Works to ease recent immigrants' transitions into Galician society with English, Spanish, and Gallego classes and support services. Teach, assist with HIV/AIDS prevention programs, conduct tuberculosis tests, or do other community outreach.

MADRID ☎91

After Franco's death in 1975, young *Madrileños* celebrated their liberation from totalitarian repression with raging all-night parties across the city. This revelry became so widespread that it defined an era, and *la Movida* (the Movement) is now recognized as a world-famous nightlife renaissance. The newest generation has kept the spirit of *la Movida* alive—Madrid is truly a city that never sleeps. While neither as funky as Barcelona nor as charming as Seville, Madrid is the political, intellectual, and cultural capital of Spain, balancing its history and heritage with the festive insomnia it has come to embrace.

SPAIN

INTERCITY TRANSPORTATION

Flights: All flights land at **Aeropuerto Internacional de Barajas** (☎902 404 704; www.aena.es.), 16km northeast of Madrid. The **Bus-Aeropuerto #200** leaves from the national terminal T2 and runs to the city center via the metro station Avenida de América. (☎902 50 78 50. Look for "EMT" signs just outside the airport doors. Daily every 10-15min. 5:20am-11:30pm. €1.) **Line 204** leaves from T4 and goes to Avenida de América as well. **Line 101** leaves from T1, 2, and 3 and goes to Canillejas. Fleets of **taxis** swarm the airport. Taxi fare to central Madrid should cost €35-40, including the €5.50 airport surcharge, depending on traffic and time of day.

Trains: Two largo *recorrido* (long-distance) **RENFE** stations, **Atocha** and **Chamartín,** connect Madrid to surrounding areas and the rest of Europe. Both stations are easily accessible by metro. Call RENFE (☎902 24 02 02; www.renfe.es) for reservations and info. Buy tickets at the station or online.

Estación Atocha, Av. Ciudad de Barcelona (☎915 066 137). M: Atocha Renfe. The cast-iron atrium of the original station has been turned into an urban rainforest, with lush plants, a small marsh with a colony of turtles, and the occasional bird. Galleries, boutiques, and restaurants provide more commercial diversions. There is a **tourist office** (☎913 15 99 76) in the station. Open M-Sa 8am-8pm, Su 9am-2pm. **RENFE information office** (☎902 24 02 02) located in the main terminal. Open daily 7am-11pm. **Luggage storage** (*consignas automáticas;* €2.40-4.50), at the back right corner of the atrium. Open daily 6:30am-10pm. Ticket windows open daily 6:30am-9pm; buy tickets at vending machines outside these hours. No international service. **AVE** (☎91 506 63 29) offers high-speed service to southern Spain, including **Barcelona** (3hr., 20-26 per day 5:45am-9pm, €110-130), **Sevilla** (2½hr., 24-20 per day 6:30am-11pm, €70-78) via **Córdoba** (1¾hr., €58-64), and **Valladolid** (1hr., 14-15 per day 6:35am-9pm, €21-34).

Estación Chamartín, C. Agustín de Foxa (☎913 00 69 69). M: Chamartín. Bus #5 runs to and from **Puerta del Sol** (45min.); the stop is just beyond the lockers. Alternatively, get off at M: Atocha Renfe and take a red Cercanías train (15min., every 5-10min., €1.20) to Chamartín. Be sure to keep your ticket, or you won't be able to exit the turnstiles. Chamartín is a mini-mall of useful services, including a **tourist office** (*Vestíbulo,* Puerta 14; ☎913 15 99 76; open M-Sa 8am-8pm, Su 9am-2pm), **currency exchange, accommodations service, post office, car rental, police,** and **luggage storage** (*consignas;* €2.40-4.50; open daily 7am-11pm). Call RENFE at ☎902 24 34 02 for international destinations and ☎902 24 02 02 (Spanish only) for domestic. Ticket windows open daily 6:30am-9pm; buy tickets at vending machines outside these hours. Chamartín serves both international and domestic destinations to the northeast and south. Most Cercanías (local) trains stop at both Chamartín and Atocha. Major destinations include: **Barcelona** (9½hr., daily 10pm, €41); **Bilbao** (5hr., 1-2 per day, €47); **Lisboa** (9hr., daily 10:25pm, €59); **Paris, FRA** (13½hr., 7pm, €115-130).

Buses: Numerous private companies serve Madrid, each with its own station and set of destinations. Most buses pass through **Estación Sur de Autobuses** or **Estación de Moncloa,** both easily accessible by metro. The Pl. Mayor tourist office and any other branch in the city has information on the most relevant intercity buses.

Estación Sur de Autobuses: C. Méndez Álvaro (☎914 68 42 00; www.estacionautobusesmadrid.com). M: Méndez Álvaro; inside station. Info booth open daily 6:30am-1am. **ATMs, food,** and **luggage storage** (€1.30 per bag per day; open M-F 6:30am-10:30pm, Sa 6:30am-3pm). Serves 40+ private bus companies. National destinations include: **Algeciras, Alicante, Aranjuez, Benidorm, Cartagena, A Coruña, Gijón, Lugo, Murcia, Oviedo, Santiago de Compostela,** and **Toledo.** Check at the station or online or call for specific info on routes and schedules.

LOCAL TRANSPORTATION

Metro: Safe, speedy, spotless, and almost always under *obras* (improvements), Madrid's Metro puts most major subway systems to shame. Free Metro maps (available at any ticket booth) and the wall maps showing surrounding streets are clear and helpful. Fare and schedule info is posted in every station; trains run daily 6am-2am, with the last inbound train leaving most terminal stations around 1:30am. An individual metro ticket costs €1, or €2 if you leave the city limits; children under the age of four travel free. Frequent riders opt for the **Metrobus** (10 rides valid for both the Metro and bus system; €7.40). Buy them at machines in Metro stops, *estancos* (tobacco shops), or newsstands. Remember to keep your ticket until you leave the metro—riding without one can subject you to outrageous fines. In addition, **abonos mensuales,** or monthly passes, grant unlimited travel within the city proper for €46, while **abonos turísticos** (tourist passes) come in various lengths (1, 2, 3, 5, or 7 days) and sell for €5-24. These are available at all metro stations or online. For information, call **Metro info** (☎902 44 44 03) or visit www.metromadrid.es.

SPAIN

Bus: Buses cover areas inaccessible by Metro and are a great way to see the city. Bus and Metro fares are equivalent, and tickets are interchangeable. Buses run 6am-11pm, generally every 10 to 15 minutes. From midnight-6am, the **Búho** (owl), or night bus, travels from Pl. de Cibeles and other marked routes to the outskirts of the city (M-Th and Sa every 30min. midnight-3am, every hr. 3-6am; F-Sa every 20min.) These buses, marked on the essential *Red de autobuses nocturnos,* available at any tourist office or from www.emtmadrid.es, run along 26 lines covering regular daytime routes. For info, call **Empresa Municipal de Transportes.** (☎902 50 78 50 or 914 06 88 10; www.emtmadrid.es. Open M-F 8am-2pm.)

Taxi: Call **Radio Taxi Madrid** (☎915 47 32 32), **Radio-Taxi Independiente** (☎914 05 55 00 or 914 05 12 13; www.radiotaxiindependiente.com), or **Teletaxi** (☎913 71 21 31; www.tele-taxi.es). A *"libre"* sign or a green light indicates availability. Base fare is €2.05 (or €2.20 M-F after 10pm and €3.10 Sa-Su after 10pm), plus €0.98 per km 6am-10pm and €1.15 10pm-6am. **Teletaxi** charges a flat rate of €1 per km. Fare supplements include airport (€5.50) and bus and train stations (€2.95). Official taxis are white with a red stripe on the door; avoid impostors.

ORIENTATION

Marking the epicenter of both Madrid and Spain, **Kilómetro 0** in **Puerta del Sol** ("Sol" for short) is within walking distance of most sights. To the west are the **Plaza Mayor,** the **Palacio Real,** and the **Ópera district.** East of Sol lies **Huertas,** the heart of cafe, museum, and theater life. The area north of Sol is bordered

A
B
C
Centro Cultural Conde Duque
TO C. GALILEO (650m)
TO MONCLOA, MUSEO DE AMERICA (1.4km), AND EL PARDO
VENTURA RODRÍGUEZ
TO 1 (300m)
TO HOSPITAL DE MADRID (600m)
PL. DEL DOS DE MAYO
C. Velarde
Motocicletas Antonio Castro
Iglesia de San Marcos
Princesa
ARGÜELLES
Torre de Madrid
Edificio de España
NOVICIADO
Museo Cerralbo
TO TEMPLO DE DEBOD (225m)
PL. DE ESPAÑA
PLAZA DE ESPAÑA
Atesa Car Rental
Jardines Ferraz
MALASAÑA
Gran Vía
GRAN VÍA
TO CAMPO DEL MORO (400m)
Jardines de Sabatini
PL. DE LA MARINA ESPAÑOLA
Convento de la Encarnación
SANTO DOMINGO
PL. DE SANTO DOMINGO
CALLAO
PL. DEL CALLAO
Casa del Libro
Jardines Cabo Noval
Convento de las Descalzas Reales
Palacio Real
PL. DEL ORIENTE
Teatro Real
PL. DE ISABEL II
ÓPERA
PL. SAN MARTÍN
PL. DE LAS DESCALZAS
PL. DEL CARMEN
El Corte Inglés
SOL
PUERTA DEL SOL
Jardines Lepanto
PL. SAN GINES
CENTRO
Catedral de Ntra. Sra. de la Almudena
Torre de los Lujanes
PL. DE SAN MIGUEL
PL. MAYOR
Ayuntamiento
PL. DE LA VILLA
Casa de los Lujanes
Casa de Cisneros
PL. DE SANTA CRUZ
Santa Cruz
PL. JACINTO BENAVENTE
Jardines de las Vistillas
PL. DE LA PAJA
Iglesia de San Pedro
PL. SEGOVIA NUEVA
Champion Supermarket
Catedral de San Isidro
TIRSO DE MOLINA
PL. TIRSO DE MOLINA
Filmoteca Española
San Andrés
Museo de San Isidro
LA LATINA
PL. DE HUMILLADERO
PL. DE LA CEBADA
PL. DE CASCORRO
LA LATINA
PL. DEL GENERAL VARA DEL RAY
El Rastro
TO GLORIETA PUERTA DE TOLEDO (190m), ESTADIO VICENTE CALDERON (1.6km)
Gran Vía de San Francisco
C. de Bailén
C. Mayor
C. de Arenal
C. de Toledo
C. de Segovia
C. de Ferraz
Cuesta de San Vicente
C. de la Princesa
C. de San Bernardo
C. de Alcalá

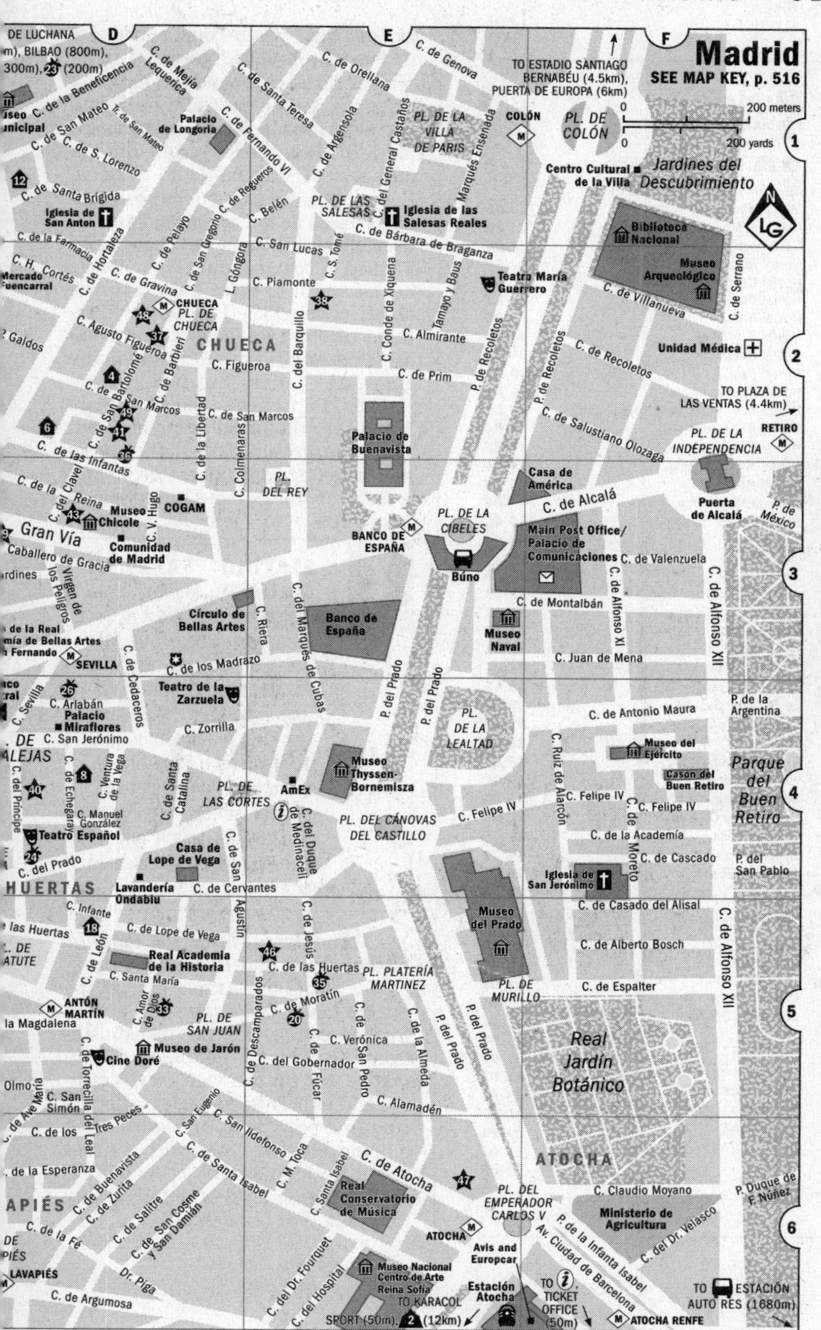
Madrid
SEE MAP KEY, p. 516
0
200 meters
0
200 yards
D
E
F
1
2
3
4
5
6
DE LUCHANA
m), BILBAO (800m),
300m), 23 (200m)
TO ESTADIO SANTIAGO
BERNABÉU (4.5km),
PUERTA DE EUROPA (6km)
C. de Genova
C. de Orellana
C. de Santa Teresa
C. de Mejía Lequerica
C. de la Beneficencia
C. de San Mateo
Tr. de San Mateo
C. de S. Lorenzo
C. de Santa Brígida
C. de Fernando VI
C. de Argensola
C. del General Castaños
Marqués Ensenada
PL. DE LA VILLA DE PARIS
COLÓN
PL. DE COLÓN
Palacio de Longoria
useo Municipal
Centro Cultural de la Villa
Jardines del Descubrimiento
Iglesia de San Anton
C. de Regueros
C. Belén
PL. DE LAS SALESAS
Iglesia de las Salesas Reales
C. de Bárbara de Braganza
Biblioteca Nacional
Museo Arqueológico
C. de Serrano
C. de la Farmacia
C. H. Cortés
Mercado Fuencarral
C. de Hortaleza
C. de Pelayo
C. de San Gregorio
L. Góngora
C. San Lucas
C. S. Tomé
C. Piamonte
C. Conde de Xiquena
Tamayo y Baus
Teatro María Guerrero
C. de Villanueva
C. de Gravina
CHUECA
PL. DE CHUECA
C. Agusto Figueroa
Galdos
CHUECA
C. del Barquillo
C. Almirante
P. de Recoletos
C. de Recoletos
Unidad Médica
C. Figueroa
C. de Prim
C. de Barbieri
C. de San Bartolomé
C. de San Marcos
C. de San Marcos
C. de la Libertad
C. Colmenaras
Palacio de Buenavista
TO PLAZA DE LAS VENTAS (4.4km)
RETIRO
PL. DE LA INDEPENDENCIA
C. de Salustiano Olozaga
C. de las Infantas
C. de la Reina
C. del Clavel
C. V. Hugo
PL. DEL REY
Casa de América
C. de Alcalá
Puerta de Alcalá
P. de México
Museo Chicole
COGAM
Gran Vía
Comunidad de Madrid
Caballero de Gracia
PL. DE LA CIBELES
BANCO DE ESPAÑA
Main Post Office/ Palacio de Comunicaciones
C. de Valenzuela
Búho
rdines
Virgen de los Peligros
C. del Marqués de Cubas
C. de Alfonso XI
C. de Alfonso XII
Círculo de Bellas Artes
C. Riera
Banco de España
C. de Montalbán
Museo Naval
de la Real
mía de Bellas Artes
Fernando
SEVILLA
C. de los Madrazo
C. de Cedaceros
C. Juan de Mena
C. Sevilla
C. Arlabán
Teatro de la Zarzuela
P. del Prado
P. del Prado
PL. DE LA LEALTAD
C. de Antonio Maura
P. de la Argentina
Palacio Miraflores
C. Zorrilla
C. San Jerónimo
. DE
ALEJAS
C. de Echegaray
C. Ventura de la Vega
C. de Santa Catalina
Museo Thyssen-Bornemisza
C. Ruiz de Alarcón
Museo del Ejército
Casón del Buen Retiro
Parque del Buen Retiro
C. del Príncipe
C. Manuel González
PL. DE LAS CORTES
AmEx
C. del Duque de Medinaceli
C. Felipe IV
C. Felipe IV
C. Felipe IV
C. de Moreto
Teatro Español
Casa de Lope de Vega
C. de San Agustín
PL. DEL CÁNOVAS DEL CASTILLO
C. de la Academia
C. del Prado
C. de Cascado
P. del San Pablo
HUERTAS
Lavandería Ondabiu
C. de Cervantes
Iglesia de San Jerónimo
C. de Casado del Alisal
C. Infante
las Huertas
C. de Lope de Vega
C. de Jesús
Museo del Prado
C. de Alberto Bosch
C. de León
Real Academia de la Historia
C. de las Huertas
PL. PLATERÍA MARTINEZ
C. de Alfonso XII
C. Santa María
C. de Descamparados
C. de Moratín
PL. DE MURILLO
C. de Espalter
ANTÓN MARTÍN
C. Amor de Dios
PL. DE SAN JUAN
C. de San Pedro
C. de la Almeda
P. del Prado
P. del Prado
la Magdalena
Museo de Jarón
C. Verónica
Real Jardín Botánico
C. de Torrecilla del Leal
Cine Doré
C. del Gobernador
C. de Fúcar
Olmo
C. de Ave María
C. San Simón
C. San Eugenio
C. Alamadén
C. de los Tres Peces
C. San Ildefonso
C. de Santa Isabel
C. M. Toca
C. de Atocha
ATOCHA
de la Esperanza
C. de Buenavista
C. de Zurita
C. Santa Isabel
Real Conservatorio de Música
PL. DEL EMPERADOR CARLOS V
C. Claudio Moyano
Ministerio de Agricultura
P. Duque de F. Núñez
APIÉS
C. de Salitre
C. de San Cosme y San Damián
ATOCHA
P. de la Infanta Isabel
C. del Dr. Velasco
C. de la Fé
Av. Ciudad de Barcelona
DE
PIÉS
Dr. Piga
C. del Dr. Fourquet
C. del Hospital
Museo Nacional Centro de Arte Reina Sofía
Avis and Europcar
LAVAPIÉS
C. de Argumosa
TO KARACOL SPORT (50m), 2 (12km)
Estación Atocha
TO TICKET OFFICE (50m)
ATOCHA RENFE
TO ESTACIÓN AUTO RES (1680m)

SPAIN

Madrid

SEE MAP, p. 514-515

ACCOMMODATIONS

Albergue Juvenil Santa Cruz de Marcenado (HI),	1	B1
Camping Alpha,	2	E6
Cat's Hostel,	3	C5
Hostal Bianco,	4	D4
Hostal Concepción Arenal,	5	C2
Hostal Don Juan,	6	D2
Hostal Gran,	7	C3
Hostal R. Arantza,	8	D2
Hostal Oriente,	9	B3
Hostal Paz,	10	B3
Hostal Real Valencia,	11	A3
Hostal Residencia Domínguez,	12	D1
Hostal Residencia Luz,	13	B4
Hostal Santillan,	14	B2
Hostel Miguel Ángela,	15	C4
Mad Hostel,	16	C5
Pension Magdalena,	17	D5
La Posada de Huertas,	18	D5

FOOD

Almendro 13,	19	B5
Arrocería Gala,	20	E5
Café-Botillería Manuela,	21	C1
Casa Alberto,	22	D5
Casa Maravilla,	23	D1
Cervecería Alemana,	24	D4
El Estragón Vegetariano,	25	A5
La Finca de Susana,	26	D4
La Granja de Said,	27	C1
Inshala,	28	A4
El Mejillón de Madrid,	29	C4
Museo del Jamon,	30	C4
Osteria Il Regno de Napoli,	31	D1
Restaurante Casa Granada,	32	C5
La Sanabresa,	33	D5
Shapla,	34	C6
Taberna Maceira,	35	E5
El Tigre,	36	D2

NIGHTLIFE

Bar Nike,	37	D2
El Clandestino,	38	E2
Costello Club,	39	D3
Cuevas de Sésamo,	40	D4
l'levn	41	D2
Joy Eslava,	42	B4
De Las Letras Restaurante,	43	D3
Ocho y Medio Club,	44	C3
Reinabruja,	45	B3
Teatro Kapital,	46	E5
Trocha,	47	E6
El Truco,	48	D2
Why Not?,	49	D2

by **Gran Vía,** which runs northwest to **Plaza de España.** North of Gran Vía are three club- and bar-hopping districts, linked by Calle de Fuencarral: **Malasaña, Bilbao,** and **Chueca.** Modern Madrid is beyond Gran Vía and east of Malasaña and Chueca. East of Sol, the tree-lined thoroughfares **Paseo de la Castellana, Paseo de Recoletos,** and **Paseo del Prado** split Madrid in two, running from **Atocha** in the south to **Plaza Castilla** in the north, passing the Prado, the fountains of **Plaza de Cibeles,** and **Plaza de Colón.** Madrid is safer than many European cities, but Sol, Pl. de España, Pl. Chueca, and Pl. Dos de Mayo are still intimidating at night. Travel in groups, avoid the parks and quiet streets after dark, and watch for thieves and pickpockets in crowds.

STAYING SAFE IN MADRID. Madrid is just as safe as most major European cities, but Pta. del Sol, Pl. de España, Pl. Chueca, C. Gran Vía, and southern Malasaña can be intimidating late at night. As a general rule, avoid parks and quiet residential streets after dark and always watch out for thieves and pickpockets in crowds.

The free *Plano de Madrid* (street map) and *Plano de Transportes* (public transport map) are fantastic. Pick them up at any tourist office. Public transportation info is also available by phone (☎012) or on the web (www.ctm-madrid.es). **El Corte Inglés** offers a free one-page map of Madrid. For a comprehensive map with a street index, pick up an *Almax* map (€2-8 depending on level of detail) at any newsstand or bookstore.

PRACTICAL INFORMATION

Tourist Offices: English and French are spoken at most tourist offices. Those planning trips outside the Comunidad de Madrid can visit region-specific offices within the city; ask for their addresses at any tourist office.

Regional Office of the Comunidad de Madrid, C. del Duque de Medinaceli, 2 (☎914 29 49 51, info 902 10 00 07; www.turismomadrid.es). M: Banco de España. Brochures, transportation info, and maps for the Comunidad. Extremely helpful; if you are planning to travel beyond the city itself, make this your first stop. Open M-Sa 8am-8pm, Su 9am-2pm.

Madrid Tourism Centre, Pl. Mayor, 27 (☎915 88 16 36; www.esmadrid.com). M: Sol. Hands out indispensable city and transportation maps and a complete guide to accommodations as well as *In Madrid,* a monthly activity and information guide in English. Branches at Estación Chamartín (p. 512), Estación Puerta de Atocha (p. 512), and the airport (p. 512), also at Plaza de Cibeles, Plaza de Callao, and Plaza de Felipe II. All open daily 9:30am-8pm.

General Info Line: Linea Madrid (☎010). Info on all things Madrid, from police stations to zoo hours. Ask for *inglés* for an English-speaking operator.

Tours: Tours can be informative but pricey, so read the fine print before signing on. The *Ayuntamiento* offers walking tours in English and Spanish called **Descubre Madrid** (☎915 88 29 06. €3.90; students, children, and seniors €3.12); the tours leave from the municipal tourist office, where you can get more info. **Madrid Vision** (☎917 79 18 88; www.madridvision.es) operates double-decker bus tours. There are 2 routes (Madrid Histórico and Moderno) each of which makes 15-20 stops around the city, featuring monuments and museums. Get on and off the bus as you please. €19, ages 7-16 and seniors €10; discounts available online.

Budget Travel: TIVE, C. Fernando el Católico, 88 (☎915 43 74 12). M: Moncloa. Walk straight down C. Arcipreste de Hita (one street over, parallel to C. Princesa) and turn left on C. Fernando el Católico. A great resource for long-term visitors. Lodging, tourism, and student residence info. Organizes group excursions as well as language classes and cheap trips to other European cities. Some English spoken. Some services only for Spanish nationals. Sells cheap **ISIC** cards (€6) and **Hostelling International (HI)** memberships (€21), along with discount memberships for teachers and people above 26. Open M-F 9am-2pm. Arrive early to avoid lines. Another smaller branch is located at Paseo de Recoletos, 7 (☎917 20 13 24). M: Banco de España. Open M-F 9am-2pm.

Embassies: Australia, Pl. del Descubridor Diego de Ordás 3, 2nd fl. (☎91 353 6600; www.spain.embassy.gov.au). **Canada,** Núñez de Balboa 35 (☎91 423 3250; www.canada-es.org). **Ireland,** Po. Castellana 46, 4th fl. (☎91 436 4093). **New Zealand,** Pl. de la Lealtad 2, 3rd fl. (☎91 523 0226). **UK,** Po. de Recoletos 7-9 (☎91 524 9700; www.ukinspain.com). **US,** C. Serrano 75 (☎91 587 2200; www.embusa.es).

Luggage Storage: At the airport (€3.70 for the 1st day, €4.78 per day for the next 2 weeks) and bus and train stations (€2.40-4.50 per bag per day).

Women's Resources: For general information on women's services in Spain or to report an incident, call **Instituto de la Mujer,** C. Genova, 11 (24hr. information line ☎900 19 10 10; www.mtas.es/mujer). M: Colón or Alonso Martinez. Open M-F 9am-2pm.

GLBT Resources: Most establishments in Chueca carry *Shangay,* a free guides to gay nightlife in Spain, also available online at www.shangay.com. The guide also offers detailed listings and maps of the many gay establishments in and around Madrid. Alternatively, you can purchase *Zero* magazine (€5) at any kiosk, or check it out for free online at www.zero-web.com.

Colectivo de Gais y Lesbianas de Madrid (COGAM), C. Puebla, 9 (☎915 22 45 17; www.cogam.org). M: Callao. Provides a wide range of services and organizes activities; call or check the website for a schedule. Reception open M-Th 10am-2pm and 5-8pm, F 10am-2pm.

GAY-INFORM/Línea Lesbos (☎915 23 00 70). A gay info line and hotline provides counseling from 5-9pm every night. Th 7-9pm in English. F staffed by and for lesbians, but takes all calls. Also provides information about gay associations, activities, health issues, sports, and dinners.

Laundromat: Central Madrid is tragically devoid of self-service laundromats. Try to arrange for laundry service through your hotel, or call **Tintorería La Plancha Veloz,** C. Doctor Esquerdo, 96 (☎915 73 36 76; www.laplanchaveloz.com); they'll pick up and return your clothing right to your door for no additional charge. M: Conde de Casal. Open M-F 9am-2pm and 5-8pm, Sa 9am-2pm.

Police: C. de los Madrazo, 9 (☎913 22 11 60 or 900 15 00 00). M: Sevilla. Largely administrative. English forms available. Open daily 9am-2pm. **Policía Municipal,** C. Montera 18, has staff 24hr. **Servicio de Atención al Turista Extranjero (SATE),** C. Leganitos, 19, are police who deal exclusively with tourists; they help with administrative formalities, reporting crimes, canceling credit cards, contacting embassies and family members, finding lost objects, and finding counseling. (☎915 48 85 37 for the office or ☎902 102 112 to report a crime. M: Plaza de España. Open daily 9am-midnight.)

24hr. Pharmacy: Farmacia Ortopedia, C. Mayor, 13 (☎913 664 616), off Pta. del Sol. Dial ☎098 for additional rotating locations.

Hospitals: Emergency rooms are the best option for immediate attention. US insurance is not accepted, but if you get a receipt your insurance may pay. For non-emergency concerns, **Unidad Médica Angloamericana,** C. del Conde de Aranda, 1, 1st fl. (☎914 35 18 23; www.unidadmedica.com). M: Serrano or Retiro. Regular English-speaking personnel on duty M-F 9am-8pm, Sa 10am-1pm. English-speaking specialists in every branch of medicine do non-urgent consultations. Appointments required. AmEx/MC/V. Embassies and consulates keep lists of English-speaking doctors.

Emergency Clinics: In a medical emergency, dial ☎061 or 112. **Hospital de Madrid,** Pl. del Conde del Valle Suchil, 16 (☎914 47 66 00; www.hospitaldemadrid.com). M: Bilbao. **Hospital Ramón y Cajal,** Ctra. Colmenar Viejo, km 9100 (☎913 36 80 00). M: Begoña or Bus #135 from Pl. de Castilla. **Red Cross** (☎915 22 22 22, info 902 22 22 92). **Centro Sanitorio Sandoval,** C. Sandoval, 7 (☎914 48 57 58). M: Bilbao. Free, confidential government clinic specializing in HIV/AIDS and other STIs; call ahead to arrange a visit.

Telephones: Directory services ☎11822. (See **Keeping in Touch,** p. 510.)

Internet Access: Hundreds of internet cafes are spread across the city, and most hostels provide free internet access as well. Rates are generally consistent (roughly €1-1.50 per 30min. and €2 per hr.). **Kioscocity,** C. Montera 47. Internet and Wi-Fi €1 for 15min., €1.50 for 30min., €2 per hr. Domestic and international fax services available. Open daily 24hr.

Post Office: Palacio de Comunicaciones, C. Alcalá, 51, on Pl. de Cibeles (☎902 19 71 97). M: Banco de España. Enormous palace on the far side of the plaza from the metro. Info (main vestibule) open M-Sa 8:30am-9:30pm. Windows open M-Sa 8:30am9:30pm, Su 8:30am-2pm for stamp purchases. To find a more convenient location near you, check the website at www.correos.es. **Postal Code:** 28080.

ACCOMMODATIONS

Make reservations for summer visits. Expect to pay €15-50 per person, depending on location, amenities, and season.

EL CENTRO: SOL, ÓPERA, AND PLAZA MAYOR

Miguel Ángel Residencia Comunitaria, Pl. Celenque, 1, 4th fl. (☎915 22 23 55; www.hostelmiguelangel.com), 1 block up off C. Arenal. The cleanest, classiest "backpacker hostel" around and the best deal in the *centro*. Immaculate air-conditioned rooms have bright curtains and comforters. Communal bathrooms are big and very clean. English spoken. Breakfast included. Free internet and Wi-Fi. Reserve in advance. Dorms €17-21; triples €78. ❶

Hostal Oriente, C. de Arenal, 23, 1st fl. (☎915 48 03 14). Rooms have magnificently clean white tile and creamy peach walls and bedspreads. Balconies at this elegant *hostal* add breeze but unexciting views. 17 rooms have TV, phone, A/C, and bath. Free internet. Reserve ahead. Singles €45; doubles €65; triples €85. MC/V. ❹

HUERTAS

Way Hostel, C. Relatores 17 (☎914 20 05 83; reservas@wayhostel.com). M: Tirso de Molina. The sleek black-and-white lounge and inviting kitchen at this cozy, 70-bed hostel lend it a relaxed, friendly feel. Clean, spacious 6- to 10-bed dorms are a fantastic value; most come with A/C. Breakfast included. Towels €1. Free internet and Wi-Fi. Dorms €15-22. AmEx/MC/V. ❶

Cat's Hostel, C. Cañizares, 6 (☎913 69 28 07; www.catshostel.com). M: Antón Martín. This renovated 18th-century palace stands among Europe's most beautiful hostels, although some travelers complain that its size (200 beds) makes for an institutional vibe and its unfriendly staff make for a less than pleasant stay. Basic dorms (2-14 beds) and small doubles with private baths open onto a restored Moorish patio replete with plants, fountain, and luxurious cushions. Wood-paneled pub and cave-like basement bar draw crowds, especially after the courtyard closes at midnight. No kitchen. A/C and breakfast included. Laundry €5. Free internet and Wi-Fi. Reserve ahead, as it often fills quickly. Dorms M-Th and Su €17-20, F-Sa 18-22; doubles with bath €38-42. MC/V. ❶

GRAN VÍA

Hostal Santillan, Gran Vía, 64, 8th fl. (☎915 48 23 28; www.hostalsantillan.com). M: Pl. de España. Take the glass elevator to the top of this gorgeous building. Leaf-patterned curtains and wooden furniture give rooms a homey feel. All have shower, sink, TV, and fan. A little more cash can you get you a bath and much bigger room; explore the options. Laundry €1-3 per piece. Free Wi-Fi. Singles €30-35; doubles €50-55; triples €70-75. MC/V. ❸

Hostal Concepción Arenal, C. Concepción Arenal, 6, 3rd fl. (☎915 22 68 83). M: Callao. Breezy and just far enough from Gran Vía to be tranquil. Brown decor. Quiet rooms have short but soft beds and well-scrubbed showers. Rooms come with shower and TV, some with full bath. Free Wi-Fi. Singles €29, with full bath €35; doubles €40/50; triples with ½-bath €60. MC/V. ❸

TAPAS A TO Z

Food on toothpicks and in small bowls? The restaurant isn't being stingy, and your food isn't shrinking; you're experiencing an integral part of the Spanish lifestyle. The *tapas* tradition is one of the oldest in Spain. These tasty little dishes are Spain's answer to hors d'oeuvres, but they have more taste, less pretension, and they're eaten instead of meals.

To the untrained tourist, *tapas* menus are often indecipherable, if the bar has even bothered to print any. In order to avoid awkward encounters with tentacles or parts of the horse you rode in on, keep the following things in mind before *tapeando* (eating tapas).

Servings come in three sizes: *pinchos* (eaten with toothpicks), *tapas* (small plate), and *raciónes* (meal portion). On any basic menu you'll find: *Aceitunas* (olives), *albóndigas* (meatballs), *callos* (tripe), *chorizo* (sausage), *gambas* (shrimp), *jamón* (ham), *patatas bravas* (fried potatoes with spicy sauce), *pimientos* (peppers), *pulpo* (octopus), and *tortilla española* (onion and potato omelette). The more adventurous should try *morcilla* (blood sausage), or *sesos* (cow's brains). Often, bartenders will offer tastes of *tapas* with your drink and strike up a conversation. Ask for a *caña* (glass) of the house *cerveza* (beer) to guarantee the full respect of the establishment.

MALASAÑA AND CHUECA

Hostal Don Juan, Pl. Vasquez de Mella, 1, 2nd fl. (☎915 22 31 01). M: Chueca. Luxury fit for the romancing namesake himself. Chinese vases, tapestries, and antique candlesticks fill the lobby and adjacent common room. Rooms come with beautiful wooden flooring and hand-carved furniture, A/C, TV, and gleaming bath; many have small balconies. Free internet and Wi-Fi. Singles €38; doubles €53; triples €71. AmEx/MC/V. ❹

Hostal Condestable, C. Puebla, 15, 2nd fl. (☎915 31 62 02; www.hostalcondestable.com). M: Callao. Pastel-hued, fully-carpeted lobby fronts tranquil rooms with tall ceilings, solid-wood furniture, TV, and A/C; some with full bath. Communal baths are clean and bright. Singles €30, with bath €38; doubles €40/48; triples with bath €60. ❸

FOOD

In Madrid, it's not hard to fork it down without forking over too much. Most restaurants offer a *menú del día* (€9-11), which includes bread, one drink, and a choice of appetizer, main course, and dessert. Many small eateries cluster on **Calles Echegaray, Ventura de la Vega,** and **Manuel Fernández González** in Huertas. **Chueca** is filled with *bars de cañas* (small beer from the tap), which serve complimentary *tapas*. The streets west of **Calle Fuencarral** in Gran Vía are lined with cheap restaurants, while **Bilbao** has affordable ethnic cuisine. Linger in Madrid's cafes to absorb the sights of the city; you won't be bothered with the check until you ask. Keep in mind the following words for quick, cheap *madrileño* fare: *bocadillo* (a sandwich on half a baguette; €2-3); *ración* (a large *tapa* served with bread; €3-6); and *empanada* (a puff pastry with meat fillings; €1.30-2). The *Guía del Ocio* has a complete listing of Madrid's vegetarian options under the section "Otras Cocinas." **Dia%** and **Champion** are the cheapest supermarket chains; smaller markets are open later but are more expensive.

EL CENTRO: SOL ÓPERA AND PLAZA MAYOR

El Mejillón de Madrid, Pasaje de Matheu, 4, just off Espoz y Mina. No-frills seafood under umbrellas right on Madrid's shellfish row. Try the heaping plate of mussels (€8), the restaurant's namesake, or the plate of paella (€25) for 2 or more. Order 4 *raciones* (€4-11) and you'll get a free jug of sangria for up to 4 people—the best deal in the *centro*. Open M-Th, Su 11:30am-12:30am, F-Sa 11:30am-1:30am. Cash only. ❷

Sobrino del Botín, C. Cuchilleros, 17 (☎913 66 42 17; www.botin.es), off Pl. Mayor. Advertising itself as the oldest restaurant in the world, Sobrino del Botín has seen its share of the famous since it opened in 1725. Goya washed dishes here when he was 19, and Hemingway, a regular customer, mentions it by name in *The Sun Also Rises* (as the sign out front won't let passers-by forget). Ancient wooden doors and patterned red walls with gold filigree lend the kind of class that only age can bring. Entrees €8-20. Suckling pig €22.50. Open daily 1-4pm and 8pm-midnight. AmEx/MC/V. ❹

TAPAS BARS AND CAFES

Chocolatería San Ginés, Pl. San Ginés (☎913 66 54 31). M: Sol. Tucked into a small plaza behind Joy Eslava, this beautifully-tiled *chocolatería* is a legend among early-risers and clubgoers alike, both for its unbeatable *chocolate con churros* (€4) and for its steadfast refusal to close. Open daily 24hr. Cash only. ❶

Casa Labra, C. de Teután, 11 (☎915 310 081). A Madrid classic since the 19th century. No frills, just excellent tapas served at the small wood-paneled bar (*bocadillos* €4-6; *raciones* €8-16.50). *Cañas* €1.10. More elaborate (and expensive) dishes in the attached dining room. Open daily noon-11pm, dining room open daily 1:30-3:30pm and 8:30-11pm. Cash only. ❷

LA LATINA AND LAVAPIÉS

El Estragón Vegetariano, Pl. de la Paja, 10 (☎913 65 89 82). M: La Latina. This unobtrusive restaurant, with its quiet decor and patio feel, would blush at any superlatives we might give it, but its vegetarian delights could convince even the most die-hard carnivores to switch teams. Lunch *menús* M-F €8-12. Sa-Su special entrees €9. Open M-F 1:30-4pm and 8pm-midnight, Sa-Su 8pm-midnight. AmEx/MC/V. ❸

TAPAS BARS AND CAFES

Almendro 13, C. Almendro, 13 (☎913 65 42 52). M: La Latina. Locals dive into plates of *huevos rotos* (eggs and ham over fried potatoes; €8.40) and the tomato salad (€5). Shout over the clamor to order *manzanilla alemondro* (almond liquer, €1.50). Open M-F 1-4pm and 7:30pm-12:30am, Sa-Su 1-5pm and 8pm-1am. Cash only. ❷

Casa Amadeo, Pl. de Cascorro, 18 (☎913 65 94 39). M: La Latina. The owner of 68 years supervises the preparation of his renowned *caracoles* (snails; €6). Good stop after a day at El Rastro. *Caña* €1.20. Open daily 8am-midnight. Cash only. ❷

HUERTAS

La Finca de Susana, C. Arlaban, 4 (☎913 69 35 57; www.lafinca-restaurant.com). M: Sevilla. Simple, elegant dining at jaw-droppingly low prices. The beef and arugula sushi (€7.80) is one of countless top-notch plates. M-F lunch *menú* with wine an amazing €9.50. Arrive early to avoid the ever-present line down the street. Open daily 1-3:45pm and 8:30-11:45pm. AmEx/MC/V. ❷

Arrocería Gala, C. de Moratín, 22 (☎914 29 25 62; www.paellas-gala.com). M: Antón Martín. Pastoral Spanish scenes of bulls on hillsides are gracefully overlaid in vine and shadows from the gorgeous chandeliers. The specialty made-to-order paellas (€15-20 per person, minimum 2 people) are 2nd to none. Tasty sangria €10 per pitcher. Reserve ahead on weekends. Open Tu-Su 1-5pm and 9pm-1:30am. Cash only. ❸

TAPAS BARS AND CAFES

Restaurante Casa Granada, C. Doctor Cortezo, 17, 6th fl. (☎914 20 08 25). The door (on the left side of C. Doctor Cortezo as you head downhill) is unmarked; ring the bell for the 6th fl. and then head up the elevators at the back of the modest lobby. Though easy to miss, the experience of a sunset meal on the rooftop terrace is hard to forget. Put your name on the outdoor seating list when you arrive; you'll be vying with lots of other *madrileños*-in-the-know for a table. *Cañas* of beer (€2.40) come with tapas. *Raciones* €6.50-14. Open daily noon-1am. MC/V. ❷

Casa Alberto, C. de las Huertas, 18 (☎914 29 93 56; www.casaalberto.es). M: Antón Martín. The manual-wash bar and shanks hanging from the walls are throwbacks to the early days of this bar, founded in 1827. Very popular; getting a table during bustling meal hours can be difficult. Sweet vermouth (€1.70) is served with original house tapas. Try the delicious cod and lamb omelette (€4) or the *patatas ali-oli* (garlic potatoes; €4.50). Open Tu-Sa noon-5:30pm and 8pm-1:30am. MC/V. ❷

GRAN VÍA

Root, C. Virgen de los Peligros, 1 (☎912 75 81 18). M: Gran Vía. Sophisticated white leather mixes with soft light diffused through lots of glass walls to create a mellow environment. A professional crowd comes in for the lunch *menú* (M-F 1-3pm, €13.50) and the desserts. "Death by Chocolate" €5. Open M-Th and Su 1:30-4pm and 8:3011:30pm, F-Sa 1:30-4pm and 9pm-12:30am. MC/V. ❸

El Jamonal, Mesonero Romanos, 7 (☎915 31 51 04). M: Gran Vía or Callao. Skip the metal bar that runs the perimeter of the cramped, littered interior and sit in the peaceful, tree-shaded area outside; it may be just a block from the heat and bustle of Gran Vía, but it feels like miles. *Menú* €10 on the terrace, €8.60 inside. Open daily 7am-midnight. Cash only. ❷

CHUECA

Bazaar, C. de la Libertad, 21 (☎915 23 39 05; www.restaurantbazaar.com). M: Chueca. Another fantastic and shockingly affordable bistro from the team behind La Fince de Susana. Bright dining room with white leather banquettes and funky wine glasses. Elegant entrees an amazing €6-9. M-F lunch *menú* €10. Open daily 1:15-4pm and 8:30-11:45pm. MC/V. ❷

Al-Jaima, Cocina del Desierto, C. de Barbieri, 3 (☎915 23 11 42). M: Gran Vía or Chueca. Ambience is a serious business here—waiters in Moroccan *djellabas* scurry through the heavily incensed air, bringing tea and Maghrebi dishes to patrons seated on cushions beside low tables. Try the *pollo con higos y miel* (chicken with figs and honey; €6.90). Dinner entrees €12-18. Couscous €6-9. Open daily 1:30-4pm and 9pm-midnight. Reserve ahead for dinner. MC/V. ❹

TAPAS BARS AND CAFES

BAires Café, C. Gravina, 4 (☎915 32 98 79), corner of Pelayo. M: Chueca. What its ties are to Buenos Aires is unclear but this is a laid-back cafe with soft music playing and artwork covering the black-and-white walls. Sit down and take a load off with your *caña* (€2.20) or wine (€2-2.50), or try a traditional *café española* (coffee with aniseed liquor; €2.70). Open M-W and Su 3pm-1am, Th-Sa 3pm-2:30am. ❶

El Tigre, C. Infantas, 30 (☎915 32 00 72). Bursting with boars' heads, antlers, and other assorted animal parts, El Tigre Chueca's most happening *cañas* spot. The marvelous, salty tapas—included with your drink—get tastier with each sip. Beer €1.80. *Raciones* €4-7. Open daily 10:30am-1am or later. Cash only. ❶

MALASAÑA

La Granja de Said, C. de San Andrés, 11 (☎915 32 87 93). M: Tribunal or Bilbao. Moorish designs in the doorways, beautiful tiling, and the dim glow of light through lamps and tapestries bring the Middle East to Malasaña. Dine well, then puff peacefully on hookah (€8). *Tabouleh* salad €6. Delicious falafel plate €7. Open Tu-Su 1pm-5pm and 8pm-2am. MC/V. ❷

Olokun, C. Fuencarral, 105 (☎914 45 69 16). M: Bilbao. From the Gl. de Bilbao exit, walk south on Fuencarral. Beach scenes, tropical mixed drinks (€5-7), and delicacies like *tostones* (fried plantains; €6) served on wooden barrels bring Cuba to Malasaña. *Menú* €11.90. Salsa Th 5:30pm. Open daily noon-5pm and 9pm-2am; kitchen open until 1am. MC/V. ❷

TAPAS BARS AND CAFES

Lolina Vintage Cafe, C. Espíritu Santo, 9 (☎667 20 11 69; www.lolinacafe.com). This quirky cafe's mismatched armchairs, geometric wallpaper, and eccentric lamps could have come from a Brooklyn thrift store, but they fit perfectly into the trendy Malasaña scene. Great selection of teas (try the Green Earl Grey) in super-cool pots that detach to reveal cups hidden underneath (€2). Large salads €8. Hot dogs €5. Keeps bustling into the night, when mojitos are €6. Wi-Fi available. Open M-Tu and Su 9:30am-1am, W-Th 9:30am-2am, F-Sa 9:30-2:30am. MC/V. ❶

ARGÜELLES AND MONCLOA

Subiendo al Sur, C.Ponciano, 5 (☎915 48 11 47; www.subiendoalsur.org). M: Noviciado. From the colorful Central American decor to the warm, friendly waitstaff to the knowledge that 100% of proceeds from your meal will go to support development projects in the global South, it's hard not to feel good eating at this cafe and restaurant. Lunch *menú* €9.50. *Caña* €1. Open M 1:45-4:30pm 1:45-4:30pm and 9pm-midnight. Cash only. ❷

SIGHTS

Two dynasties, a dictatorship, and a cultural rebirth have bequeathed Madrid a broad, diverse, and fantastic collection of parks, palaces, plazas, cathedrals, and art museums. While Madrid is small enough to walk in a day, its sights are enough to keep you for weeks. Soak it all in, strolling from Sol to Cibeles and Pl. Mayor to the Palacio Real.

HAPSBURG MADRID

In the 16th century, Hapsburgs of the Austrian dynasty funded the construction of **Plaza Mayor** and the **Catedral de San Isidro.** After moving the seat of Castilla from Toledo to Madrid (then only a town of 20,000) in 1561, Felipe II and his descendants commissioned the court architects (including **Juan de Herrera,** the master behind El Escorial) to update many of Madrid's buildings, creating a distinctive set of churches and palaces with wide central patios and scrawny black towers—the "Madrid style."

PLAZA MAYOR. Juan de Herrera, the architect of **El Escorial** (p. 528), also designed this plaza. Its elegant arcades, spindly towers, and open verandas, built for Felipe III in 1620, are defining elements of the "Madrid style," which inspired architects nationwide. Toward evening, Pl. Mayor awakens as *Madrileños* resurface, tourists multiply, and cafes fill up. Live *flamenco* performances are a common treat. While the cafes are a nice spot for a drink, food is overpriced. *(M: Sol. Walk down C. Mayor. The plaza is on the left.)*

BOURBON MADRID

Weakened by plagues and political losses, the Hapsburg era in Spain ended with the death of Carlos II in 1700. Felipe V, the first of Spain's Bourbon monarchs, ascended to the throne in 1714 after the 12-year War of the Spanish Succession. Bankruptcy, economic stagnation, and disillusionment compelled Felipe V to embark on a crusade of urban renewal, and his successors pursued the same ends with astounding results. Today, their lavish palaces, churches, and parks are the most spectacular (and touristed) in Madrid.

PALACIO REAL. Palacio Real. The luxurious Palacio Real lies at the western tip of central Madrid, overlooking the Río Manzanares. Felipe V commissioned Giovanni Sachetti to replace the Alcázar, which burned down in 1734, with a palace that would dwarf all others—he succeeded. Today, King Juan Carlos and Queen Sofía use the palace only on special occasions. The **Salón del Trono** (Throne Room) contains the two magnificent Spanish thrones, supported by golden lions. The room also features a ceiling fresco painted by Tiepolo, outlining the qualities of the ideal ruler. The **Salón de Gasparini,** site of the king's ceremonial dressing before the court, houses Goya's portrait of Carlos IV. Perhaps most beautiful is the **Chinese Room,** whose walls swirl with green tendril patterns. The **Real Oficina de Farmacia** (Royal Pharmacy) has crystal and china receptacles used to hold royal medicine. Also open to the public is the **Real Armería** (Armory), which has an entire floor devoted to knights' armor. *(From Pl. de Isabel II, head toward the Teatro Real. M: Ópera. ☎914 54 87 88. Open Apr.-Sept. M-Sa 9am-6pm, Su 9am-3pm; Oct.-Mar. M-Sa 9:30am-5pm, Su 9am-2pm. Arrive early to avoid lines. Changing of the guard Sept.-May 1st W of every month at noon. €8, with tour €10; students, seniors, and children ages 5-16 €3.50/6; under 5 free. EU citizens free W.)*

TRA SEÑORA DE LA ALMUDENA. Begun in 1879 and inau- century later in 1993, this cathedral's simple forms and ass windows stand in stark contrast to the cherub-filled narble of most major Spanish churches. Even today, the roversial, as gray stone walls clash with the ceiling pan- and sharp geometric shapes that verge on Art Deco. *(C. o Real on C. Bailén. M: Ópera. ☎915 422 200. Open daily Sept.-June m-2pm and 5-9pm. Closed during mass. €1 donation requested. Call a telephonic guided tour of the church.)* The blindingly white **crypt** below is worth a visit, but make sure you aren't interrupting any nuptials—oddly enough, it's a popular wedding spot. *(C. Mayor, 92; enter from the side facing away from the Palacio. Open daily 10am-1pm and 5-8pm. €2)* Visitors can also take in a **museum** that details the construction of the church; admission includes a trip up into the cupola, which affords spectacular views of the Campo del Moro, the Palace, and the city below. *(Behind the church, on the side facing the Palacio. ☎915 592 894; www.archimadrid.es. Open M-Sa 10am-2:30pm. €4.)*

OTHER SIGHTS

PARQUE DEL BUEN RETIRO. Join an array of vendors, palm-readers, football players, and sunbathers in the area Felipe IV converted from a hunting ground into a *buen retiro* (nice retreat). The 300-acre park is centered around a magnificent monument to King Alfonso XII and a lake, the **Estanque Grande.** Around the lake, all manner of mimes, puppeteers, and street performers show off for the benefit of the crowd (and a few coins). *(The Estanque can be reached by following Av. de Méjico from the park's Pl. de la Independencia entrance. Boats for up to 4 people €4.55 per 45min.)*

EL RASTRO (FLEA MARKET). For hundreds of years, *El Rastro* has been a Sunday-morning tradition in Madrid. The market begins in La Latina at Pl. Cascorro off C. Toledo and ends at the bottom of C. Ribera de Cortidores. El Rastro sells everything from zebra hides to jeans to antique tools to pet birds. Whatever price you're thinking (or being offered), it can probably be bargained in half. The flea market is a pickpocket's paradise, so leave your camera behind, bust out the money belt, and turn that backpack into a frontpack. Police (p. 518) are available if you need them. (Open Sundays and holidays 9am-3pm.)

MUSEUMS: AVENIDA DEL ARTE

Considered to be among the world's best art galleries, the Museo del Prado, Museo Thyssen-Bornemisza, and the Museo Nacional Centro de Arte Reina Sofía form the impressive "Avenida del Arte."

MUSEO DEL PRADO. One of Europe's finest centers for 12th- to 17th-century art, the Prado is Spain's most prestigious museumhome to the world's greatest collection of Spanish paintings. Its 7000 pieces are the result of hundreds of years of collecting by the Hapsburgs and Bourbons. The museum provides an indispensable guide for each room. English-language **audio tours** are available for €3. On the first floor, keep an eye out for the unforgiving realism of **Diego Velázquez** (1599-1660). His technique of "illusionism" is on display in the magnificent **Las Meninas,** considered by some art historians to be the best painting ever made. Deaf and alone, **Goya** painted the *Pinturas Negras* (Black Paintings), so named for the darkness of both their color and their subject matter. The Prado also displays many of **El Greco's** religious paintings, characterized by luminous colors, elongated figures, and mystical subjects. On the second floor are works by other Spanish artists, including **Murillo** and **Ribera.** *(Po. del Prado at Pl.*

Cánovas del Castillo. M: Banco de España or Atocha. ☎91 330 2800; www.museoprado.es. Open Tu-Su 9am-8pm €6, students €3, under 18 and over 65 free. Tu-Sa 6-8pm and Su 5-8pm free.)

MUSEO NACIONAL CENTRO DE ARTE REINA SOFÍA. Since Juan Carlos I decreed this renovated hospital a national museum in 1988, the Reina Sofía's collection of **twentieth-century art** has grown steadily. Rooms dedicated to **Salvador Dalí, Juan Gris,** and **Joan Miró** display Spain's vital contributions to the Surrealist movement. **Picasso's** masterpiece, **Guernica,** is the highlight. *(Pl. Santa Isabel 52. ☎91 774 1000; www.museoreinasofia.es. M: Atocha. Open M and W-Sa 10am-9pm, Su 10am-2:30pm. €3, students €1.50. Sa after 2:30pm, Su, holidays, under 18, over 65 free.)*

MUSEO THYSSEN-BORNEMISZA. The Thyssen-Bornemisza exhibits works ranging from 14th-century paintings to 20th-century sculptures. The museum's collection constitutes the world's most extensive private showcase. The top floor is dedicated to the **Old Masters** collection, which includes such notables as Hans Holbein's austere *Portrait of Henry VIII* and El Greco's *Annunciation.* The Thyssen-Bornemisza's Baroque collection, with pieces by Caravaggio, Claude Lorraine, and Ribera, rivals the Prado's. The **Impressionist** and **Post-Impressionist** collections demonstrate the evolution toward modern art forms. The ground floor of the museum houses the extensive **twentieth-century** collection. The showcased artists include Chagall, Dalí, Hopper, O'Keeffe, Picasso, Pollock, and Rothko. *(Paseo del Prado, 8, on the corner of Po. del Prado and C. Manuel González. M: Banco de España or Atocha. ☎91 369 0151; www.museothyssen.org. Open Tu-Su 10am-7pm. Last entry 6:30pm. €6, students with ISIC and seniors €4, under 12 free. Audio guides €4.)*

ENTERTAINMENT

EL RASTRO (FLEA MARKET)

For hundreds of years, El Rastro has been a Sunday-morning tradition in Madrid. The market begins in La Latina at Pl. Cascorro off C. Toledo and ends at the bottom of C. Ribera de Cortidores. El Rastro sells everything from zebra hides to jeans to antique tools to pet birds. As crazy as the market seems, it is actually organized thematically; for many it's a weekly stop. The main street is a labyrinth of clothing, cheap jewelry, leather goods, incense, and sunglasses, branching out into side streets, each with its own repertoire of vendors and wares. As you descend further into the market, the typical shoe stands disappear and more eclectic stalls appear, selling back-issues of pornographic comic books, tarnished old silver tea services, and animal hides. Fantastic collections of old books and LPs are sold in Pl. del Campillo del Mundo at the bottom of C. Carlos Arnides. Whatever price you're thinking (or being offered), it can probably be bargained in half. The flea market is a pickpocket's paradise; so leave your camera behind, bust out the money belt, and turn that backpack into a frontpack. Always keep your hand on your bag while walking. Police (p. 518) are available if you need them. (Open Su and holidays 9am-3pm.)

FÚTBOL

Real Madrid plays at **Estadio Santiago Bernabéu,** Av. Cochina Espina, 1. (☎914 57 11 12. M: Santiago Bernabéu.) In the summer, the club offers tours of the stadium. (☎902 29 17 09; www.realmadrid.com. Tours on non-game days, M-Sa 10am-7pm, Su 10:30am-6:30pm. €15, under 14 €10.) Atlético de Madrid plays at **Estadio Vicente Calderón,** Po. de la Virgen del Puerto, 67. (☎913 64 22 34; www.clubatleticodemadrid.com. M: Pirámides or Marqués de Vadillos.) Getafe plays at **Coliseum Alfonso Pérez,** Av. Teresa de Calcuta s/n. (☎916 95 97 71. M: Los Espartales.) Tickets for Real games sell out well in advance and will probably run €50-100; tickets for Atlético are a little cheaper, and lower still for Getafe.

BULLFIGHTS

Some call it animal torture, others tradition; either way, bullfighting remains one of Spain's most cherished traditions, and it is at its brightest (or its darkest) at the **Plaza de las Ventas,** C. Alcalá, 237, the most important bullfighting arena in the world since its opening in 1931. (☎913 56 22 00; www.las-ventas.com or www.taquillatoros.com. M: Ventas.) The ring plays host to the real professionals; you can also catch a summer *Novillada* (beginner) show, when a younger and less experienced bullfighter takes on smaller bulls. Seats costs €2-115, depending on their location in the *sol* (sun) or *sombra* (shade).

Tickets are available, in person only, the Friday and Saturday before and Sunday of a bullfight. There are bullfights every Sunday from March to October and less frequently during the rest of the year. From early May to early June, the **Fiestas de San Isidro** in Pl. de las Ventas stages a daily *corrida* (bullfight) with top *toreros* and the fiercest bulls. Look for posters in bars and cafes for upcoming *corridas* (especially on C. Victoria, off C. San Jerónimo). **Plaza de Toros Palacio de Vistalegre** also hosts bullfights and cultural events. (☎914 22 07 80. M: Vista Alegre. Call for schedule and prices.) To watch amateurs, head to the **Escuela de Tauromaquia de Madrid,** a training school with its own *corridas* on Saturdays at 7:30pm. (At the Casa de Campo, Avda. de Portugal Lago. ☎914 70 19 90. Open M-F 10am-2pm. €7, children €3.50.)

FESTIVALS

The city bursts with dancing and processions during **Carnaval** in February, culminating on Ash Wednesday with the beginning of Lent and the **Entierro de la Sardina** (Burial of the Sardine), which commemorates the arrival of a shipload of rotting sardines to Madrid during the reign of Carlos III, who ordered them promptly buried. Goya's painting of these popular feasts and festivals hangs in the **Real Academia de Bellas Artes.** In March, the city gets dramatic for the renowned **International Theater Festival.** The Comunidad de Madrid celebrates its struggle against the French invasion of 1808 during the **Fiestas del 2 de Mayo** with bullfights and concerts. Starting May 15, the week-long **Fiestas de San Isidro** honor Madrid's patron saint with concerts, parades, and Spain's best bullfights. In the last week of May, the small but wonderful **Fería de la Tapa** sees restaurants and chefs putting out their best for Madrid with fantastically cheap, exquisite tapas and beer. In the last week of June or the first week of July, Madrid goes mad with **Orgullo Gay** (Gay Pride). Outrageous floats filled with drag queens, muscle boys, and rambunctious lesbians shut down traffic between El Retiro and Puerta del Sol on the festival's first Saturday. Free concerts in Pl. Chueca and bar crawls among the congested streets of Chueca are popular weekend activities. Last year over three million people poured through Chueca during the course of the week. Throughout the summer, the city sponsors the **Veranos de la Villa.** Movies play nightly at 10:30pm in Parque de la Bombilla, Av. de Valladolid. (M: Príncipe Pío; June 29-Sept. 3. Ticket office opens 9:30pm. €5, students €4.50; schedule at tourist office.) The **Festivales de Otoño** (Autumn Festivals), from September to November, offer more refined music, theater, and film events. In November, an **International Jazz Festival** entices great musicians to Madrid. On New Year's Eve, *El Fin del Año,* crowds gather at Puerta del Sol to count down to the new year. The brochure *Madrid en Fiestas,* available at tourist offices, contains comprehensive details on Spain's festivals. The *Guía de Fiestas* details all the festivals for the whole year in *La Comunidad de Madrid,* another thing worth picking up.

NIGHTLIFE

Indulging in Madrid's world-renowned, mind-melting nightlife, especially in the summer months, is not an optional part of your visit—it's required. This city does nightlife bigger and better, later and harder, with more bars, clubs, and discos than nearly anywhere else on earth. People hit the streets around 10 or 11 when music and liquor begin pouring out of bars and *cervecerías*, and revelers don't go to bed until they've "killed the night" and, usually, a good part of the following morning. Proud of their nocturnal offerings, *madrileños* will tell you with a straight face that they were bored in Paris or New York—how can a city be truly exciting if the traffic isn't as heavy at 2am on a Saturday as it is at 5pm on a Monday?

Cool, C. Isabel la Católica, 6 (☎902 49 99 94). M: Santo Domingo. Madrid's aptly named club-of-the-moment draws a beautiful, fashionable crowd of gay and straight people with its crisp design and pounding house beats. Small lounge and dance floor upstairs overlook the main room below. Men dominate "Royal Club" Sa, Madrid's best gay night. Lines can be long and the bouncers particularly difficult, so dress well and be polite. Cover €12-18, includes 1 drink. Call ahead to add youself to the list for dicounted entry. Open Th and Su midnight-5:30am, F-Sa midnight-6am. AmEx/MC/V.

Cuevas de Sésamo, C. del Príncipe, 7 (☎914 296 524). M: Antón Martín. "Descend into these caves like Dante!" (Antonio Machado) is one of the many colorful literary tidbits that welcome you to this packed, smoky, underground gem. Charmingly worn plush seats, live jazz from an unassuming upright piano (Tu-Su), and strong, cheap sangria (large pitcher €10, small pitcher €6) bring in Madrid's bohemian youth. Open daily 7pm-2am. Cash only.

Why Not?, C. de San Bartolomé, 7. M: Chueca. A super-hip, wood-paneled underground bunker playing Europop and salsa. Well-dressed patrons sip drinks under a domed ceiling and the gazes of black-and-white Hollywood stars of olden days. Beer €7. Mixed drinks €10-15. Cover €10 when crowded, includes 1 drink. Open daily M-Th and Su 9pm-3:30am, F-Sa 9pm-6am. MC/V.

Café-Botillería Manuela, C. de San Vicente Ferrer, 29 (☎915 31 70 37). M: Tribunal. Gleaming marble, mirrors, and antique brass fixtures fill this Old World Parisian cafe. Player piano stacked high with classic board games. Enjoy conversation over a glass of *rioja* (€2.50). Tapas €3-8. Mixed drinks €6. Live music last Sa of every month at 9:30pm. Open June-Aug. daily 6pm-2am; Sept.-May daily 4pm-2am. Cash only.

Reinabruja, C. Jacometrezo, 6 (☎915 42 81 93). M: Callao. A sinuous, subterranean jungle of stenciled pillars and curving, color-changing illuminated honeycombed walls surrounding a bumping central dance floor packed with trendy 20- to 30-year-olds. Come ready and raring to dance to house music—there's practically nowhere to sit down. Wine €7. Mixed drinks €9. Cover €12, includes 1 drink. Open Th-Sa 11pm-6am. MC/V.

Teatro Kapital, C. de Atocha, 125 (☎91 420 29 06). M: Atocha. 7 fl. of justly famed *discoteca* insanity. From hip hop to house, cinemas to karaoke, Kapital offers countless ways to lose yourself, your dignity, and your money in the madness. Special-effects insanity on the massive main dance floor (converted from an old theater) include digital projections and a giant nitrogen-spray cannon. For a change of pace, ascend up through the surrounding 4-story maze of balconies to the palm- and fountain-filled rooftop *terraza,* where you can relax with a hookah (€30) or a game of pool under the open sky. Drinks €11. Cover Th €15, F €18, Sa €22, all with 1 drink included; keep your eyes peeled for flyers that will get you a 2nd drink free. Open Th midnight-5:30am, F-Sa midnight-6am. AmEx/MC/V.

El Café de Schérezad, C. Santa Maria, 18 (☎ 913 694 140). M: Antón Martín. Young *madrileños* lie on plush cushions smoking hookah and relaxing to soothing Moroccan

SPAIN

music. Delicious herbal teas come with fresh fruit and small pastries. Tea €3.50; hookah €7-10. Open daily 5pm-3am. Cash only.

Bar Nike, C. Augusto Figueroa, 22 (☎915 21 07 51). M: Chueca. A colorless *cafetería* where half of Chueca comes to drink before clubbing. Absolutely packed from wall to wall. Fight your way to the bar for an enormous, sticky *calimocho* (red wine and cola; €4.50). Beer €4.80. Sangria €5. Open daily noon-3am. Cash only.

El Sitio de Malasaña, C. Manuela Malasaña, 7 (☎914 46 68 76). M: Bilbao. From the Gl. de Bilbao exit, walk just a few feet down C. Fuencarral before turning right on C. Manuela Malasaña. Green and red-orange walls breathe life into this simple cafe offering cheap wine (from €1.90 per glass), Irish coffee (€5) and a wide selection of mixed drinks (€7). Delicious *tostas* (€4.90) include brie with fruit-infused honey. Open Tu-F 6:30pm-2am, Sa 1pm-2:30am, Su 1pm-1am. MC/V.

La Cabra en el Tejado, C. Santa Ana, 31, just off C. Toledo. M: La Latina. A funky place, packed as local acts stand on rickety wooden tables and sing Spanish favorites. Mediterranean tapas offers a break from the usual fare (hummus and *tzatziki;* €3.50). Beer €2.50. Cheap glass of *rioja* €1.30. Check the posters outside for concerts. Open M-Th 6pm-midnight, F-Sa 6pm-2am, Su 1pm-midnight. Cash only.

SPAIN

DAYTRIP FROM MADRID

EL ESCORIAL

(Autocares Herranz buses run between El Escorial and Moncloa Metro; 50min., 2-6 per hr., €3.20. Complex ☎918 90 59 03. Open Tu-Su Apr.-Sept. 10am-7pm; Oct.-Mar.10am-6pm. Last entry 1hr. before closing. Monastery €7, with guide €9; students and seniors €3.50.)

This enormous complex was described by Felipe II as "majesty without ostentation." The Monasterio de San Lorenzo del Escorial was a gift from Felipe II to God, the people, and himself, commemorating his victory over the French at the battle of San Quintín in 1557. Near the town of San Lorenzo, El Escorial is filled with artistic treasures, a church, a magnificent library, two palaces, and two pantheons. To avoid crowds, enter via the gate on C. Floridablanca, on the western side. The adjacent **Museo de Arquitectura y Pintura** has an exhibit comparing El Escorial's construction to that of similar structures. The **Palacio Real** is lined with 16th-century *azulejo* tiles and includes the majestic **Salón del Trono**.

CASTILLA LA MANCHA

TOLEDO ☎925

Cervantes called Toledo (pop. 75,000) "the glory of Spain and light of her cities." The city is a former capital of the Holy Roman, Visigoth, and Muslim Empires, and its churches, synagogues, and mosques share twisting alleyways. Toledo is known as the "City of Three Cultures," symbol of a time when Spain's three religions coexisted peacefully, although as one might expect, locals will tell you the history is somewhat romanticized.

TRANSPORTATION AND PRACTICAL INFORMATION. From the station on Po. de la Rosa, just over Puente de Azarquiel, **trains** (RENFE info ☎902 24 02 02) run to Madrid (30min., 9-11 per day, €9). **Buses** run from Av. Castilla La Mancha (☎925 21 58 50), 10min. from **Puerta de Bisagra** (the city gate), to Madrid (1hr., 2 per hr., €4.53) and Valencia (5hr., 1 per day, €25). Within the city, buses #8.1 and #8.2 serve the bus station and buses #1-7 run from the Pl. de Zocodóver to points outside the old city. Buses (€1; at night €1.30) stop to the right of the train station, underneath and across the street from the bus station. Though Toledo's streets are well labeled, it's easy to get lost; pick up a map at the **tourist office,** at Pta. de Bisagra. (☎925 22 08 43. Open July-Sept. M-F 9am-7pm, Sa 10am-6pm, Su 10am-2pm; Oct.-June M-F 9am-6pm, Sa 10am-6pm, Su 10am-2pm.) **Postal Code**: 45001.

ACCOMMODATIONS AND FOOD. Toledo is full of accommodations, but finding a bed in summer can be a hassle, especially on weekends. Reservations are strongly recommended. Spacious rooms among suits of armor await at the **Residencia Juvenil San Servando (HI) ❶,** Castillo San Servando, uphill on Subida del Hospital from the train station, in a 14th-century castle with a pool, TV room, and Internet. (☎925 22 45 54. Dorms €11, with breakfast €15; under 30 €9.20/11. MC/V.) To reach **Hostal Alfonso XII ❹,** C. Alfonso XII, 18 (☎925 25 25 09; www.hostal-alfonso12.com), turn off C. Santo Tomé up Campana and follow it to C. Alfonso XII. Scented herbs and flowers fill the halls and rooms with good aromas. Wooden beams traverse the ceilings and add the finishing note to an elegant, deceptively rustic place with modern amenities. Rooms with TV, A/C, Wi-Fi. (Singles €40; doubles €55; triples €70. MC/V.) To reach **Pensión Castilla ❷,** C. Recoletos 6, go down C. Las Armas from Pl. de Zocodóver and turn left on C. Recoletos. The *pensíon* has a great price and location. (☎925 22 45 54; reservations ☎925 22 16 78. Midnight curfew. Reserve ahead. Singles €18; doubles €26, with bath €29. Cash only.) Take bus #7 from Pl. de Zocodóver to get to **Camping El Greco ❶**, 1.5km from town on Ctra. CM-4000. The shady, wooded site features a bar, pool, restaurant, and supermarket. (☎925 22 00 90. €5.94 per person, per tent, and per car. VAT not included. MC/V.)

SPAIN

Pastelería windows beckon with *mazapán* (marzipan) of every shape and size. For the widest array, stop by the **market** in Pl. Mayor, behind the cathedral. (Open M-Sa 9am-8pm.) To reach **La Abadía ❷,** Pl. de San Nicolás, 3, bear left when C. de la Sillería splits; Pl. de San Nicolás is on the right. Dine on the regional lunch *menú* (€10) in a maze of underground rooms. Combo *tapas* plates €5-10.(☎925 25 11 40. Open daily 8am-midnight. AmEx/MC/V.) **Restaurante Gambrinus ❷,** C. Santo Tomé, 10 (☎925 21 44 40). has the shadiest outdoor seating in the old city, which is perfect for people-watching as you slowly conquer a hearty traditional Spanish meal. Has big soups (€6) as well as the whole partridge (€19.80) for the hungry. (Meat dishes €10-11. Open daily 11am-4pm and 8pm-midnight. MC/V.)

SIGHTS AND NIGHTLIFE. Within the fortified walls, Toledo's attractions form a belt around its middle. Many sights are closed Mondays. At Arco de Palacio, up C. del Comercio from Pl. de Zocodóver, Toledo's **cathedral** boasts five naves, delicate stained glass, and unapologetic ostentation. Behind the altar is the **Capilla de la Descensión,** which supposedly holds the stone that the Virgin tread on when imposing the priest's robes on St. Ildefonso, Toledo's patron saint. The **sacristía** holds 18 works by El Greco (including *El espolio*), as well as paintings by other notable Spanish and European masters. (☎925 22 22 41. Open M-Sa 10am-6:30pm, Su 2-6:30pm. €8, students €6. Audio tour €3. Dress modestly.) Greek painter Doménikos Theotokópoulos, better known as El Greco, spent most of his life in Toledo. Though the majority of his masterpieces have been carted off to the Prado (p. 524), some are still displayed throughout town. The best place to start is the **Casa Museo de El Greco**, on C. Samuel Leví 2, which contains 19 of his works. (☎925 22 44 05. Open in summer Tu-Sa 10am-2pm and 4-9pm, Su 10am-2pm; in winter Tu-Sa 10am-2pm and

4-6pm, Su 10am-2pm. €2.40; students, under 18, Sa afternoon, and Su free. Closed for renovations until at least 2009.) Up the hill and to the right is the **Iglesia de Santo Tomé**, which still houses one of his most famous and recognized works, **El Entierro del Conde de Orgaz** (The Burial of Count Orgaz). The stark figure staring out from the back is El Greco himself, and the boy is his son, Jorge Manuel, architect of Toledo's city hall. Arrive early to beat the tour groups. Pl. del Conde, 4. (☎925 25 60 98; www.santotome.org. Open daily Mar.-Oct. 15 10am-7pm; Oct.16-Feb. 10am-6pm. €2.30, students and over 65 €1.80.)

On the same street as Museo El Greco is the **Sinagoga del Tránsito**, one of two remaining synagogues in Toledo's *judería* (Jewish quarter). Inside, the **Museo Sefardí** documents early Jewish history in Spain. Look up at the Hebrew letters carved into the *mudéjar* plasterwork and a stunning coffered wood ceiling. (☎711 35 52 30; www.museosefardi.net. Open Mar.-Nov. Tu-Sa 10am-2pm and 4-9pm, Su 10am-2pm; Dec.-Feb. Tu-Sa 10am-2pm and 4-6pm, Su 10am-2pm. €2.40, students, seniors, and under 18 free. Sa after 4pm and Su free.)

At the western edge of the city stands the **Monasterio de San Juan de los Reyes,** a Franciscan monastery commissioned by Fernando and Isabel to commemorate their 1476 victory over the Portuguese in the Battle of Toro. The peaceful cloister centers around a quiet garden with blossoms and orange trees.(☎925 22 38 02. Open daily Apr.-Sept. 10am-7pm; Oct.-Mar. 10am-6pm. €2.30.)

Nestling in the middle of the city, the **Iglesia de Los Jesuitas** is a Jesuit church that has **amazing views** from its towers. Located at one of the highest points in the city, the roof offers a panorama of all the towers and tiled roofs in the old city and the hills for miles around. It's breezy, so hold on to your hat. (Pl. Padre Juan de Mariana, 1, up C. Nuncio Viejo from the cathedral, and then a left on Alfonso X El Sabio. ☎925 25 15 07. Open daily April -Sept. 10am-6:45pm, Oct.-Mar. 10am-5:45pm. €2.30.)

For nightlife, head through the arch and to the left from Pl. de Zocodóver to **Calle Santa Fé**, which brims with beer and local youth. For upscale bars and clubs, try **Calle de la Sillería** and **Calle los Alfileritos**, west of Pl. de Zocodóver. To escape the raucous noise, check out the chill **Café Teatro Pícaro**, C. Cadenas, 6, where lights play on abstract art, and *batidos* (milkshakes, €3, with Bailey's, €4) and mixed drinks abound. (☎925 22 13 01; www.picarocafeteatro.com. Mixed drinks €5. Beer €1.50-2.50. Open M-F 4pm-3am, Sa-Su 4pm-5am.)

CASTILLA

SALAMANCA ☎923

Salamanca "la blanca" (pop. 163,000), city of royals, saints, and scholars, glows with the yellow stones of Spanish Plateresque architecture by day and a vivacious club scene by night. The prestigious Universidad de Salamanca, grouped in medieval times with Bologna, Oxford, and Paris as one of the "four leading lights of the world," continues to add youthful energy to the city.

TRANSPORTATION AND PRACTICAL INFORMATION. Trains go from Po. de la Estación (☎923 24 02 02) to Madrid (2hr., 6-7 per day, €15) and Lisbon, POR (6hr., 1 per day, €47). **Buses** leave from the station (☎923 23 67 17) on Av. Filiberto Villalobos 71-85 for: Barcelona (11hr., 2 per day, €47); León (2hr., 4-7 per day, €13); Madrid (2hr., 16 per day, €12-17); Segovia (2hr., 2 per day, €10). Majestic **Plaza Mayor** is the center of Salamanca. From the train station, catch bus #1 (€0.80) to Gran Vía and ask to be let off at Pl. San Julián, a block from

Pl. Mayor. The **tourist office** is at Pl. Mayor 32. (☎923 21 83 42. Open June-Sept. M-F 9am-2pm and 4:30-8pm, Sa 10am-8pm, Su 10am-2pm; Oct.-May M-F 9am-2pm and 4:30-6:30pm, Sa 10am-6:30pm, Su 10am-2pm.) *DGratis*, a free weekly newspaper about events in Salamanca, is available from newsstands, tourist offices, and around Pl. Mayor. Free **Internet** is available at the **public library,** C. Compañía 2, in Casa de las Conchas. (☎923 26 93 17. Limit 30min. Open July to mid-Sept. M-F 9am-3pm, Sa 9am-2pm; mid-Sept. to June M-F 9am-9pm, Sa 9am-2pm.) **Postal Code**: 37001.

ACCOMMODATIONS AND FOOD. Reasonably priced *hostales* and *pensiones* cater to the floods of student visitors, especially off Pl. Mayor and C. Meléndez. **Hostal Las Vegas Centro ❷,** C. Meléndez 13, 1st fl., has friendly owners and spotless rooms with terrace and TV. (☎923 21 87 49; www.lasvegascentro.com. Singles €20, with bath €24; doubles €30 MC/V.) At nearby **Pensión Barez, ❶,** C. Meléndez 19, 1st fl., clean rooms overlook the street. (☎923 21 74 95. Rooms €14. Cash only.) **Pensión Los Ángeles ❷,** Pl. Mayor 10, 2nd-3rd fl., has spectacular views and clean, bright rooms. (☎ 923 21 81 66; www.pensionlosangeles.com. Breakfast €4. Singles €15-25; doubles €25-60; triples €45-80. MC/V). **Albergue Juvenil Salamanca ❷,** on C/ Escoto 13-15 has cool, friendly owners and the good company of students and tourists, making this a good place for social travelers. The location is slightly inconvenient; Plaza Mayor is a ten minute walk. (☎923 26 91 41; Singles €25; doubles €36; dormitories with up to 20 beds €12.90. Storage for valuables €1 per night.) **Camping Regio ❶,** which offers first-class campsites with hot showers, is 4km toward Madrid on Ctra. Salamanca. (Buses run from Gran Vía; 2 per hr., €0.80. ☎923 13 88 88; www.campingregio.com. Laundry €3. €3.20 per person, €2.80 per tent, car, or for electricity. MC/V.)

Many cafes and restaurants are in Pl. Mayor. Pork is the city's specialty, with dishes ranging from *chorizo* (spicy sausage) to *cochinillo* (suckling pig). Funky **Restaurante Delicatessen Café ❷,** C. Meléndez 25, serves a wide variety of *platos combinados* (€10.50-11) and a lunch *menú* (€11) in a colorful solarium. (☎923 28 03 09. Open daily 1:30-4pm and 9pm-midnight. MC/V.) *Salamantinos* crowd **El Patio Chico ❷**, C. Meléndez 13, but the hefty portions are worth the wait. (☎923 26 51 03. Entrees €5.5-17. *Menú* €14. Open daily 1-4pm and 8pm-midnight. MC/V). At **El Ave Café ❷,** C. Libreros 24, enjoy your lunch (*menú* €11) on the terrace or take a peek at the colorful murals inside. (☎923 26 45 11. Open daily 8am-midnight. MC/V.) **Carrefour,** C. Toro 82, is a central supermarket. (☎923 21 22 08. Open M-Sa 9:30am-9:30pm.)

SIGHTS AND NIGHTLIFE. From Pl. Mayor, follow R. Mayor, veer right onto T. Antigua, and left onto C. Libreros to reach **La Universidad de Salamanca** (est. 1218), the city's focal point. Hidden in the delicate Plateresque filigree of the entryway is a tiny frog perched on a skull. According to legend, those who can spot him without assistance will be blessed with good luck. The old lecture halls inside are open to the public, but to get into the library you'll need to befriend a professor. The 15th-century classroom **Aula Fray Luis de León** has been left in its original state, more or less. Located on the second floor atop a Plateresque staircase is the **Biblioteca Antigua**, one of Europe's oldest libraries. The staircase is thought to represent the ascent of the scholar through careless youth, love, and adventure on the perilous path to true knowledge. Don't miss the 800-year-old scrawlings on the walls of the **Capilla del Estudiante** and the benches of the **Sala Fray Luis de Leon.** Across the street and through the hall on the left corner of the patio is the **University Museum**. The reconstructed **Cielo de Salamanca,** the library's famous 15th-century ceiling fresco of the zodiac, is preserved here. (University ☎923 29 45 00 ext 1225,

SPAIN

NAKED TRUTH

Civil liberties have come a long way in Spain since Franco died; a fact that became clear to me as I walked through the Plaza de Oriente one day.

Traffic stopped, and a din arose from down C. Bailén, which runs in front of the Palacio Real. Then hundreds—perhaps thousands—of naked protesters rode by slowly on bicycles. What they wanted was unclear at first. Some chanted *"Gasolina es asesina"* (gas is an assassin), others merely *"Coches = mierda"* (cars are shit). Whatever it was, they were out in force, with their children, wives, and coworkers, drinking beer and taking pictures as they rode.

I stopped and talked to a few of the unclad riders. "We're protesting for urban transport," one said, patting his bicycle. He told me that riding your bicycle in Madrid is often dangerous because drivers don't care about cyclists. The protestors rode on, followed by a police escort, ostensibly protecting the group from traffic.

Enjoying the irony, I paused and saw the mass of naked riders being escorted past one of the most beautiful royal palaces in the world, an image that will stay with me. Riding naked in my puritanical country, much less past the Capitol or the home of the President, would not be tolerated. *Madrileños* cherish their rights, and that's the naked truth.

- Russell Rennie

museum ext 1150. Museum open M-Sa 10am-2pm and 4-8pm, Su 10am-2pm. University open M-F 9:30am-1:30pm and 4-7:30pm, Sa 9:30am-1:30pm and 4-7pm, Su 10am-1:30pm. €4, students and seniors €2.).

It's not surprising it took 220 years to build the stunning **Catedral Nueva,** in Pl. de Anaya. Be sure to climb the tower to get a spectacular **view** from above. The route through the tower connects the old and new cathedrals. Admission includes an exhibit contrasting the architecture of the two structures. Architects of modern renovations have also left their marks; look for an astronaut and a **dragon** eating an ice cream cone on the left side of the main door. (Open daily Apr.-Sept. 9am-8pm; Oct.-Mar. 9am-1pm and 4-6pm. Tower open daily 10am-8pm, last entry 7:45pm. Cathedral free. Tower €3, see www.ieronimus.com.) The smaller **Catedral Vieja** was built in the Romanesque style in AD 1140. The cupola, assembled from intricately carved miniature pieces, is one of the most detailed in Spain. Students and tourists congregate on the Patio Chico for a view of both cathedrals. (Enter through the Catedral Nueva. Museum ☎923 21 74 76. Cathedral open daily Oct.-Mar. 10am-12:30pm and 4-5:30pm; Apr.-Sept. 10am-7:30pm. €4.25, students €3.50 children €2.75.) According to *salamantinos*, Salamanca is the best place in Spain to party. It is said that there is one bar for every 100 people living in the city. There are *chupiterías* (shot bars), *bares*, and *discotecas* on nearly every street. Nightlife centers on **Plaza Mayor,** where troubadours serenade women, then spreads out to **Gran Vía**, **Calle Bordadores,** and side streets. **Calle Prior** and **Rúa Mayor** are also full of bars, while intense partying occurs off **Calle Varillas.** After a few shots (€1-2) at **Bar La Chupitería,** Pl. de Monterrey, wander from club to club on C. Prior and C. Compañía, where tipsy Americans mingle with tireless *salamantinos*. Once you get past the bouncers, **Niebla,** C. Bordadores 14 (☎923 26 86 04), **Gatsby,** C. Bordadores 16 (☎923 21 73 62), **Camelot,** C. Bordadores 3 (☎923 21 21 82), and **Cum Laude,** C. Prior 5-7 (☎923 26 75 77), all offer a party that doesn't peak until 2:30-3:30am and stays strong for another 2hr. (Dress to impress. All clubs have no cover and are cash only.)

SOUTHERN SPAIN

SEVILLE (SEVILLA) ☎954

Site of a Roman acropolis, capital of the Moorish empire, focal point of the Spanish Renaissance, and guardian of traditional Andalusian culture, romantic Seville (pop. 700,000) represents a fusion of cultures. Bullfighting, flamenco, and tapas are at their best here, and Seville's cathedral is among the most impressive in Spain. The city offers more than historical sights: its **Semana Santa** and **Feria de Abril** celebrations are among the most elaborate in Europe.

INTERCITY TRANSPORTATION

Flights: All flights arrive at **Aeropuerto San Pablo,** Ctra. de Madrid (☎954 449 000; www.aena.es), 12km outside town. A taxi from the center costs about €25. **Los Amarillos** (☎954 989 184) runs a bus from outside the Prado de San Sebastián bus stop across from the university. (M-Sa every 15-30min. 5:15-12:15am; Su every 30min-1hr. 6:15am-11:15pm; €2.10. Also stops at the train station). **Iberia,** C. Guadaira, 8 (☎954 228 901, nationwide 902 400 500; open M-F 9am-1:30pm) runs daily flights to Barcelona (55min.) and Madrid (45min.).

Trains: Estación Santa Justa, Av. de Kansas City. (☎902 240 202. Info and reservations open daily 4:30am-12:30am.) Services include **luggage storage, car rental,** and **ATM.** In town, the RENFE office, C. Zaragoza, 29, posts prices and schedules on the windows and also handles bookings. (☎954 54 02 02. Open in summer 9:30am-2pm and 5:30-8pm, in winter M-F 9am-1:15pm and 4-7pm.) To get to Santa Cruz from the station, take bus C-2 and transfer to C-3 at the Jardines del Valle; it will drop you off on C. Menéndez Pelayo at the **Jardines de Murillo.** Turn right and walk 1 block past the gardens; C. Santa María la Blanca is on the left. Without the bus, it's a 15-20min. walk. To reach El Centro from the station, catch bus #32 to **Plaza de la Encarnación,** several blocks north of the cathedral.

Altaria and **Talgo** trains to: **Barcelona** (12½hr., 8:20am, €60); **Córdoba** (1hr., 8 per day 6:50am-9:35pm, €15); **Málaga** (2hr., 4-6 per day 6:05am-7:35pm, €35) and **Valencia** (9hr., 8:20am, €50). **AVE** trains to **Barcelona** (5½hr., 4pm, €134), **Córdoba** (45min., 12-18 per day 6:15am-9:45pm, €26-30), **Madrid** (2½hr., 12-18 per day 6:15am-9:45pm, €70-78), and **Zaragoza** (3½hr, 4pm, €104) **Regionales** trains to: **Almería** (5½hr., 4 per day 7am-5:40pm, €36); **Antequera** (2½hr., 6 per day 6:50am-7:35pm, €28); **Cádiz** (2hr., 11 per day 6:35am-9:35pm, €10); **Córdoba** (1½hr., 6 per day 7:50am-8:15pm, €8.60); **Granada** (3hr., 4 per day 7am-5:40pm, €23); **Huelva** (1hr.; 9:10am, 4:30, 8:40pm; €7.85); **Jaén** (2-3hr.; 1:25, 3, 7:52pm; €18-23); **Málaga** (2½hr., 5-6 per day 7:35am-8:10pm, €18).

Buses: Estación Prado de San Sebastián, C. Manuel Vázquez Sagastizábal (☎954 41 71 11), serves most of Andalucía and sits adjacent to its namesake. It's a five-minute walk (right on C. Diego Riaño, right on Av. Carlos V) to the Puerta de Jerez in Santa Cruz. (Open daily 5:30am-1am.) **Estación Plaza de Armas,** Av. Cristo de la Expiración (☎954 90 80 40), sends buses outside of Andalucía, including to many international destinations. (Open daily 5am-1:30am.) Bus C-4 connects the station to Prado de San Sebastián.

Estación Prado De San Sebastián: Alsina Graells (☎913 270 540; www.alsa.es). Open daily 6:30am-11pm. To: **Almería** (7hr.; 7, 8am, 5pm; €32); **Córdoba** (2-3hr., 10 per day 7:30am-10pm, €10); **Granada** (3hr., 10 per day 8am-11pm, €19-25); **Jaén** (4hr., 1:30pm, €19); **Málaga** (2-3hr., 9 per day 7am-7:30pm, €16); **Murcia** (7½hr;, 3 per day 8, 11am, 11pm; €38). **Los Amarillos** (☎902 210 317; www.touristbus.es). Open M-F 7:30am-2pm and 2:309pm, Sa-Su 7:30am-2pm and 2:30-8:30pm. To: **Arcos de la Frontera** (2½hr.; 8am, 2:30pm; €7); **Marbella** (3hr.; 8am, 4pm; €16);

SPAIN

Ronda (2½hr., 8am, noon, 5pm; €11); **Sanlúcar de Barrameda** (2hr., 5-9 per day 8am-8pm, €7). **Transportes Comes** (☎902 199 208; www.tgcomes.es). Open daily 6:30am-10pm. To: **Algeciras** (3½hr., 4 per day 9:30am-7:30pm, €18); **Cádiz** (1hr., 9 per day 7am-10pm, €11.40); **Jerez de la Frontera** (1½hr., 7 per day 10:45am-10pm, €7.50); **Tarifa** (3hr., 4 per day 9:30am-7:30pm, €17).

Estación Plaza De Armas: ALSA (☎913 270 540; www.alsa.es). Open M-F 5:45am-10:30pm, Sa-Su 7:30am-10:45pm. To: **Cáceres** (4-4½hr., 7 per day 7am-8:30pm, €33); **León** (11hr.; 7, 11:30am, 8:30pm; €43); **Lisbon, POR** (6hr.; 3pm, midnight; €45); **Salamanca** (7hr., 6 per day 7am-8:30pm, €31); **Valencia** (9-11hr., 3 per day 9:30am, 4, 10pm, €50-57).**Damas** (☎954 908 040; www.damas-sa.es). Open daily 6am-10pm. To: **Badajoz** (3hr., 5 per day 6:45am-8pm, €13.25); **Faro, POR** (4hr.; 4 per day 7:30am, 4:15pm; €16); **Lagos, POR** (7hr.; 7:30am, 6:15pm; €20); **Huelva** (1hr., 16-20 per day 7:30am-9:30pm, €7).**Socibus** (☎902 229 292; www.socibus.es). Open daily 7:30-10:30am and 11-12:45am. To **Madrid** (6hr., 7 per day 8am-midnight, €19.40).

Public Transportation: TUSSAM (☎900 71 01 71; www.tussam.es). Most bus lines run daily every 10min. 6am-11:15pm and converge in Pl. Nueva, Pl. de la Encarnación, and at the cathedral. Night service departs from Pl. Nueva (every hr. M-Th and Su midnight-2am; F-Sa all night). C-3 and C-4 circle the center and #34 hits the HI-affiliated hostel, university, cathedral, and Pl. Nueva. €1.20. *Bonobús* (10 rides) €6. 30-day pass €30.

Taxis: TeleTaxi (☎954 622 222). **Radio Taxi** (☎954 580 000). Base rate €1.19 plus €0.83 per km; M-F after 9pm and all day Sa-Su €1.45 base plus €1.01 per km. Extra charge for luggage.

SPAIN

ORIENTATION AND PRACTICAL INFORMATION

The **Río Guadalquivir** flows north to south through the city, bordered by Po. de Cristóbal, which becomes Po. de las Delicias by the municipal tourist office. Most of Sevilla's touristy areas, including **Santa Cruz** and **El Arenal,** are on the east bank. The historic *barrios* (neighborhoods) of **Triana, Santa Cecilia,** and **Los Remedios** lie on the western bank. **Avenida de la Constitución,** home of the *Andaluz* tourist office, runs along the cathedral. **El Centro,** a busy commercial pedestrian zone, starts at the intersection of Av. de la Constitución, **Plaza Nueva,** and **Plaza de San Francisco,** site of the *Ayuntamiento* (city hall). **Calle Tetuán** and **Calle Sierpes,** both popular shopping areas, run north from Pl. Nueva through El Centro.

Tourist Offices: Centro de Información de Sevilla Laredo, Pl. de San Francisco, 19 (☎954 592 915; www.turismo.sevilla.org). Main municipal office. English spoken. Open M-F 9am-7:30pm, Sa-Su 10am-2pm. **Naves del Barranco,** C. Aronja, 28 (☎954 221 714), near the bridge to Triana. Secondary municipal office. Open M-F 9am-7:30pm. **Turismo de la Provincia,** Pl. del Triunfo, 1-3 (☎954 210 005; www.turismodesevilla.org). Info on daytrips and specific themed itineraries. Open daily 10:30am-2:30pm and 3:30-7:30pm.**Turismo Andaluz,** Av. de la Constitución, 21B (☎954 221 404; www.andalucia.org). English spoken. Info on all of Andalucía. Free maps of the region. Open M-F 9am-7:30pm, Sa-Su 9:30am-3pm.

Budget Travel: Barceló Viajes, C. de los Reyes Católicos, 11 (☎954 226 131; www.barceloviajes.com). Open June-Sept. M-F 9:30am-1:30pm and 5-8:30pm, Sa 10am-1pm; Oct.-May M-F 9:30am-1:30pm and 4:30-7:30pm, Sa 10am-1pm.

Currency Exchange: Banco Santander Central Hispano, C. Tetuán, 10, and C. Martín Villa, 4 (☎902 24 24 24). Open M-F 8:30am-2pm, Sa 8:30am-1pm;. Apr.-Sept. closed Sa. Banks and *casas de cambio* (currency exchange) crowd Av. de la Constitución, El Centro, and the sights in Santa Cruz.

Luggage Storage: Estación Prado de San Sebastián. (€0.90 per day; open 6:30am-10pm); **Estación Plaza de Armas** (€3.50 per day); **train station** (€3.50 per day).

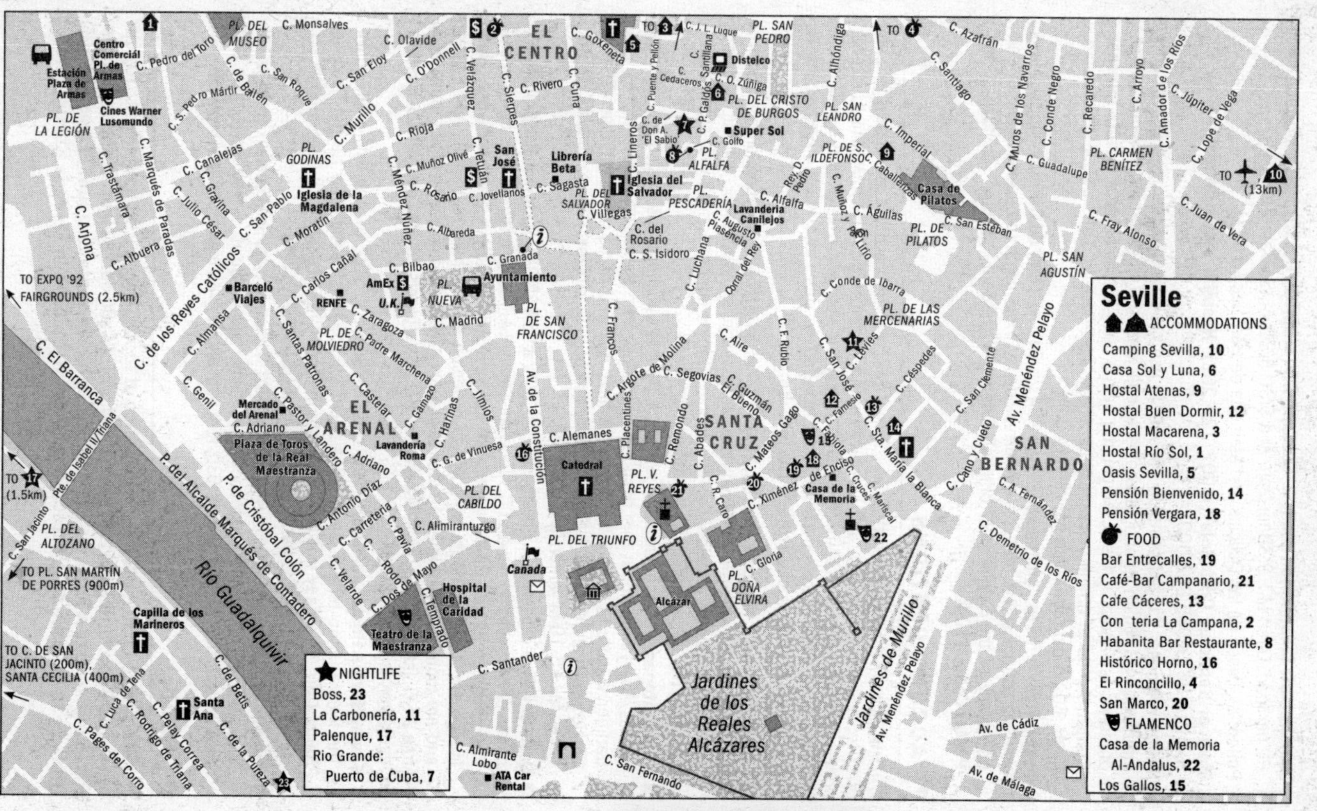
Seville
ACCOMMODATIONS
Camping Sevilla, 10
Casa Sol y Luna, 6
Hostal Atenas, 9
Hostal Buen Dormir, 12
Hostal Macarena, 3
Hostal Río Sol, 1
Oasis Sevilla, 5
Pensión Bienvenido, 14
Pensión Vergara, 18
FOOD
Bar Entrecalles, 19
Café-Bar Campanario, 21
Cafe Cáceres, 13
Con teria La Campana, 2
Habanita Bar Restaurante, 8
Histórico Horno, 16
El Rinconcillo, 4
San Marco, 20
FLAMENCO
Casa de la Memoria
Al-Andalus, 22
Los Gallos, 15
NIGHTLIFE
Boss, 23
La Carbonería, 11
Palenque, 17
Rio Grande:
Puerto de Cuba, 7
EL CENTRO
SANTA CRUZ
SAN BERNARDO
EL ARENAL
Río Guadalquivir
Jardines de los Reales Alcázares
Jardines de Murillo
Catedral
Alcázar
Ayuntamiento
Plaza de Toros de la Real Maestranza
Casa de Pilatos
Iglesia del Salvador
Iglesia de la Magdalena
Hospital de la Caridad
Teatro de la Maestranza
Estación Plaza de Armas
Centro Comercial Pl. de Armas
Cines Warner Lusomundo
Capilla de los Marineros
Santa Ana
Mercado del Arenal
Librería Beta
Super Sol
Distelco
Lavandería Canilejos
Lavandería Roma
Barceló Viajes
RENFE
AmEx
U.K.
Canada
ATA Car Rental
Av. de la Constitución
Av. Menéndez Pelayo
P. de Cristóbal Colón
P. del Alcalde Marqués de Contadero
C. de los Reyes Católicos
TO EXPO '92 FAIRGROUNDS (2.5km)
TO PL. SAN MARTÍN DE PORRES (900m)
TO C. DE SAN JACINTO (200m), SANTA CECILIA (400m)

SPAIN

Laundromat: Lavandería Roma, C. Castelar, 2C (☎954 210 535). Wash, dry, and fold €6 per load. Open M-F 9:30am-2pm and 5:30-8:30pm, Sa 9am-2pm.

Police: Av. Paseo de las Delicias and Alameda de Hércules (☎091).

Medical Services: Cruz Roja (☎902 222 292). **Hospital Virgen Macarena,** Av. Dr. Fedriani, 56 (☎955 008 000).

Internet Access: It is substantially cheaper to use pre-paid minutes; most places offer internet *bonos,* which amount to wholesale bulk minutes (most come with a min. of 2hr. or more). Ask about *bonos* at the counter before using the computers. **Sevilla Internet Center,** Av. de la Constitucion at Almirantazgo (☎954 347 108; www.internetsevilla.com). €0.05 per min. Open daily 9am-10pm.

Post Office: Av. de la Constitución, 32 (☎954 21 64 76). **Lista de Correos** and fax. Have your mail addressed to the *Lista de Correos de la Constitución* (otherwise mail may end up at any of the Sevilla post offices). Open M-F 8:30am-8:30pm, Sa 9:30am2pm. **Postal Code:** 41080.

ACCOMMODATIONS

During *Semana Santa* and the *Feria de Abril,* vacant rooms vanish and prices double; reserve several months in advance. The tourist office has lists of *casas particulares* (private residences) that open for visitors on special occasions. Outside of these weeks, you should reserve a few days in advance and about a week ahead if you're staying for the weekend.

Pensión Vergara, C. Ximénez de Enciso, 11, 2nd fl. (☎954 215 668; www.pensionvergara.com). Above a souvenir shop at C. Mesón del Moro. Quirky, antique decor, colorful common spaces, and perfect location. Singles, doubles, triples, and quads, all with shared bath and A/C. No internet. €20 per person. Cash only. ❷

Hostal Atenas, C. Caballerizas 1 (☎954 21 80 47; www.hostal-atenas.com), off Pl. de Pilatos. Everything about this hostel is appealing, from the *mudéjar*-style arches and traditional patio to the cheery rooms. All have A/C and baths Internet €1 per 30min. Singles M-Th and Su €43, F-Sa €48; doubles €55/70; triples €70/79; quads €79/86. Prices fall €5-10 in winter. MC/V. ❹

Oasis Sevilla, reception at Pl. Encarnación, 29 1/2 (☎954 29 37 77; www.hostelsoasis.com), rooms above reception and at C. Alonso el Sabio, 1A. Young, international crowd packs this energetic hostel. Co-ed dorms are centrally located above the guests-only **Hiro** lounge. On C. Alonso doubles and 4- to 6-person dorms share bathrooms and fridges and are roomier and quieter. All rooms with A/C. Terrace pool, weekly tapas tours, and free Wi-Fi, internet, and breakfast (served 8-11am). Towels €1. Key deposit €5. Reserve early. Dorms €20; doubles €46. MC/V. ❷

Samay Sevilla Hostel, Menéndez Pelayo, 13 (☎955 100 160; www.samayhostels.com). The lively rooftop terrace at this 2-year-old backpackers' hostel may be the finest in Santa Cruz. Free daily walking tours, internet, and Wi-Fi. Laundry €8. Key deposit €5. 8-bed dorms €15-19, 6-bed €16-20, 4-bed €17-22. MC/V. ❶

Pensión Macarena, C. San Luis, 91 (☎954 37 01 41; www.hostalmacarena.es). Large yellow and green rooms with A/C surround a sunny inner atrium. Quiet, relaxed atmosphere and friendly staff. Singles €20; doubles €30, with bath and TV €40; triples €45/51. MC/V. ❷

FOOD

Seville, which claims to be the birthplace of *tapas,* keeps its cuisine light. *Tapas* bars cluster around **Plaza San Martín** and along **Calle San Jacinto.** Popular venues for *el tapeo* (tapas barhopping) include **Barrio de Santa Cruz** and **El Arenal.** Find produce at **Mercado de la Encarnación,** near the bullring in Pl. de la Encarnación.

(Open M-Sa 9am-2pm.) There is a supermarket below **El Corte Inglés,** in Pl. del Duque de la Victoria. (☎954 27 93 97. Open M-Sa 9am-10pm. AmEx/MC/V.)

San Marco, C. Mesón del Moro, 6 (☎954 564 390). Branches at C. del Betis, 68 (☎954 28 03 10) and C. Santo Domingo de la Calzada, 5 (☎954 583 343). Entrees and Italian desserts in vaulted basement rooms that once housed Arab baths. A full menu of creative salads (€4.30-9.25), pizza (€7.50-8.90), and meat and fish entrees (€9.60-16.50). Open daily 1-4:15pm and 8pm-12:15am. MC/V. ❸

El Rinconcillo, C. Gerona, 40 (☎954 223 183). Founded in 1670 in an abandoned convent, this *bodega* is the epitome of a local hangout, teeming with gray-haired men deep in conversation and locals stopping in for a quick glass of wine or a delicious tapas spread. The bartender tallies up your tab in chalk on the wooden counter. Tapas €1.80-3.20. *Raciones* €6-14.50. Open daily 1:30pm-1:30am. AmEx/MC/V. ❶

Confitería La Campana, C. Sierpes 1 and 3 (☎954 223 570). Founded in 1885, Sevilla's most famous cafe has twice made an appearance in Spanish short stories, and it continues to serve up *granizadas de limón* (lemon-flavored crushed ice), ice cream (€2-2.50), and an astounding variety of homemade pastries (€1.50-3.40). Open daily 8am-11pm. AmEx/MC/V. ❶

Bar Entrecalles, Ximenez de Enciso, 14 (☎617 86 77 52). Situated at the center of the tourist buzz, but the reggae music and relaxed atmosphere help maintain a local following. Tapas (only available inside, €2) and delicious gazpacho (meal-sized potion €6) are unusually generous. Open daily 1pm-2am. Kitchen closed 3:30-8pm. Cash only. ❶

Levíes Café-Bar, C. San José, 15 (☎954 215 308). The bar at this tapas restaurant predominates, pouring out deliciously liberal and refreshing glasses of *tinto de varano* (€1.45) and gazpacho (€3.30). Tapas €2.60-3.90. Entrees €6-12. Open M-F 7:30am2am, Sa-Su 11am-2am. ❶.

SIGHTS

While any visit to Seville should include the Catedral and Alcázar, there is much more to the city than Santa Cruz. Around these central icons are winding streets full of tapas joints, *artesanía*, and quirky finds. The **Plaza de Toros** is nestled on the riverbank to the east and serves as an ideal place to begin a scenic tour along the Guadalquivir. North of Santa Cruz, the bustling Centro, home to some of the city's finest museums, constrasts with the peaceful churches of La Macarena. Heading south toward the **Torre del Oro,** garden oases offer a breezy respite from the summer heat. There, the private gardens behind the Alcázar are flanked by the public **Jardines de Murillo,** near to the monumental **Plaza de España** and beautiful **Parque de María Luisa.**

CATEDRAL

Entrance by Pl. de la Virgen de los Reyes. ☎954 21 49 71; www.catedralsevilla.com. Open M-Sa 11am-5pm, Su 2:30-6pm. Last entry 1hr. before closing. €7.50, seniors and students under 26 €2, under 16 free. Audio tour €3. Mass held in the Capilla Real M-Sa 8:30, 10:30am, noon; Su 8:30, 10:30, 11am, noon, and 1pm. Free.

Legend has it that the *reconquistadores* wanted to demonstrate their religious fervor by constructing a church so great that "those who come after us will take us for madmen." Sevilla's immense cathedral does appear to be the work of an extravagant madman—with 44 individual chapels, it is the third largest in the world, after St. Peter's Basilica in Rome and St. Paul's Cathedral in London, and it is the biggest Gothic edifice ever constructed.

In 1402, a 12th-century Almohad mosque was destroyed to clear space for the cathedral. All that remains is the **Patio de Los Naranjos,** where the faithful washed before prayer, the **Puerta del Perdón** entryway from C. Alemanes, and **La**

SPAIN

Giralda minaret, built in 1198. The tower and its twins in Marrakesh and Rabat are the oldest and longest-surviving Almohad minarets in the world. The 35 ramps leading to the tower's top were installed to replace the stairs that once stood there, allowing a disabled *muezzín* to ride his horse up to issue the call to prayer. Climbing the ramps will leave you breathless, as will the views from the top—the entire city of Sevilla lies just on the other side of the iron bells. (Be warned that these bells sound every 15min., and they are very loud.)

The 42m central **nave,** decorated with 3 tons of gold leaf, is considered one of the greatest in the Christian world—take a good look at its four tiers via a well-placed mirror on the nave's floor. In the center of the cathedral, the Renaissance-style **Capilla Real** stands opposite choir stalls made of mahogany recycled from a 19th-century Austrian railway. The **retablo mayor,** one of the largest in the world, is an intricately wrought portrayal of saints and disciples. Nearby, the bronze **Sepulcro de Cristóbal Colón** (Columbus's tomb) is supported by four heralds that represent the ancient kingdoms of Spain united by Fernando and Isabel. The coffin holds Columbus' remains, brought back to Sevilla from Cuba in 1898. Farther on stands the **Sacristía Mayor,** which holds works by Ribera, Zurbarán, Goya, and Murillo, and a glittering Corpus Cristi icon.

SPAIN

ALCÁZAR

Pl. del Triunfo, 7. ☎954 50 23 23. Open daily Apr.-Sept. 9:30am-7pm; Oct.-Mar. 9:30am5pm. Tours of private residence every 30min. Aug.-May 10am-1:30pm and 3:30-5:30pm; June-July 10am-1:30pm. Max. 15 people per tour, so buy tickets in advance. €7.50, students, over 65, and under 16 free. Tours €4.20. English audio tours €3.

The oldest European palace still used as a private residence for royals, Sevilla's Alcázar exudes extravagance. The palace, built by the Moors in the seventh century and embellished in the 17th century, is a mix of Moorish, Gothic, Renaissance, and Baroque architectural elements, but its intricacies are most prominently displayed in the *mudéjar* style of many of its many arches, tiles, and geometic ceiling designs. Fernando and Isabel, the Catholic monarchs of *reconquista* fame, are the palace's best known former residents; Carlos V lived here after marrying his cousin Isabel of Portugal in the **Salón Techo Carlos V.**

The Alcázar is a network of splendid patios and courtyards, around which court life revolved. From the moment you step through the **Patio de la Montería,** the melange of cultures is apparent; an Arabic inscription praising Allah is carved in Gothic script. Through the archway is the **Patio del Yeso,** an exquisite geometric space first used by Moorish governors. The center of public life at the Alcázar, however, was the **Patio de las Doncellas** (Patio of the Maids), a colonnaded quadrangle encircled by tiled archways. The **Patio de las Muñecas** (Patio of the Dolls), served as a private area for Moorish kings; the room had an escape path so that the king would not have to cross a wide-open space during an attack. The columns are thought to have come from the devastated **Madinat Al-Zahra**, built at the height of the caliph period. Look for the little faces at the bottom of one column for a hint at how the patio got its name.

The palace's interior is a sumptuous labyrinth where even the walls are works of art. In the **Sala de los Azulejos del Alcázar,** history's stain is literally visible—the room was the stage of a bloody duel between 14th-century King Pedro I and his half-brother Fadrique, and even today the traces of unlucky Fadrique's blood can be seen on the floor. On a more peaceful note, the golden-domed **Salón de los Embajadores** (Ambassadors' Room) is rumored to be the site where Fernando and Isabel welcomed Columbus back from the New World. Their son, Juan, was born in the red-and-blue tiled **Cuarto del Príncipe.** The private residences upstairs, the official home of the King and Queen on their visits to Sevilla, have been renovated and redecorated throughout the years, and most of the furniture today dates from the 18th and 19th centuries. These rooms are accessible only by 25min. guided tours.

MUSEO PROVINCIAL DE BELLAS ARTES. This museum contains Spain's finest collection of works by painters of the Sevillana School, most notably Murillo, Valdés Leal, and Zurbarán, as well as El Greco and Dutch master Peter Brueghel. Much of the art was cobbled together from convents in the mid-1800s, finding a stately home amid the traditional tiles and courtyards of this impressive building. Not to be missed are **Gallery V** (formerly a church, it's a splendid setting for Baroque art) and José Villegas Cordro's somber 1913 canvas *La muerte del maestro* upstairs. *(Pl. del Museo, 9. ☎954 786 500; www.museosdeandalucia.es. Open Tu-Sa 9am-8:30pm, Su 9am-2:30pm. €1.50, students and EU citizens free.)*

NIGHTLIFE

Seville's reputation for hoopla is tried and true—most clubs don't get going until well after midnight, and the real fun often starts only after 3am. Popular bars can be found around **Calle Mateos Gago** near the cathedral, **Calle Adriano,** and **Calle del Betis** in Triana. Gay clubs cluster around **Plaza de Armas.**

La Carbonería, C. Levies, 18 (☎954 22 99 45). A gigantic cellar bar frequented by students and young summer travelers. Agua de Sevilla pitchers €20 (M-W and Su €15). Sangria pitchers €8.50. Free live flamenco shows nightly at 11pm. Open daily 8pm-3 or 4am. Cash only.

Antique (www.antiquetheatro.com), to the left of the Pte. de la Barqueta facing away from La Macarena. A monumental outdoor playground for Sevilla's rich and beautiful. Egyptian-stye columns preside over a lush outdoor dance space complete with VIP cabanas and a waterfall. Dress well and come before 2am to avoid a long line. Mixed drinks €8. No cover. Open in summer Tu-Su midnight-7am. MC/V.

Puerto de Cuba, C. del Betis (www.riogrande-sevilla.com), immediately to the right of the Pte. de San Telmo as you cross into Triana. Right on the bank of the river, it's hard to believe this palmy oasis has no cover charge. Recline in a wicker couch or curl up in a pillow-strewn beached dingy. Th-Sa dance parties. Dressy casual will get you past the bouncers and to the bar (beer €3.50; mixed drinks from €6.50). Open only in summer daily 10:30pm-4am.

Terraza Chile, Po. de las Delicias at Av. de Chile. A 5min. walk from the Puente de San Telmo along the riverside Po. de las Delicias, away from the Torre del Oro. This popular, unpretentious bar-cafe transforms into a packed dance club Th-Sa, when loud salsa and pop bring together young *sevillanos,* foreign students, and tourists. Beer from €2; mixed drinks from €5. Open June-Sept. M-W 9am-3am, Th-Sa 9am-5am; Oct.-May M-Th 9am-1am, F-Sa 9am-4am. MC/V.

Ritual (www.todounritoalacopa.com), to the right of the Pte. de la Barqueta facing away from La Macarena. Dancers in shimmering outfits and silky tents hung with North African lamps lend this upscale outdoor lounge and dance club a desert-oasis feel. Well-dressed 20-somethings dance to American hip hop, Latin favorites, and lots of reggaeton. Wine and mixed drinks from €6. Typically 21+. No cover. Open in summer daily 10pm-late. AmEx/MC/V.

Noveccento, C. Julio Cesar, 10 (☎954 229 102; www.noveccento.com). A predominantly lesbian crowd sips mojitos (€6) and chills in this cozy, relaxed bar. Open in summer M-Th and Su 8pm-3am, F-Sa 8pm-4am; in winter M-Th and Su 5pm-3am, F-Sa 5pm-4am. Cash only.

ENTERTAINMENT

The tourist office distributes *El Giraldillo* and its English counterpart, *The Tourist,* two free monthly magazines with listings on music, art exhibits, theater, dance, fairs, and film. It can also be found online at www.elgiraldillo.es.

FLAMENCO

Sevilla would not be Sevilla without flamenco. Born of a *gitano* (gypsy) musical tradition, flamenco consists of dance, guitar, and songs characterized by spontaneity and passion. Rhythmic clapping, intricate fretwork on the guitar, throaty wailing, and rapid foot-tapping accompany the swirling dancers.

Signs advertising *tablao* shows are everywhere, from souvenir shops to internet cafes, and the majority of flamenco *tablaos* in Sevilla cater to the tourist crowd rather than to true flamenco aficionados. Many *tablaos* are *tablao-restaurantes*, so you can eat while watching the show, but dinner tends to be very expensive. Less expensive alternatives are the impressive one-hour shows at the cultural center **Casa de la Memoria Al-Andalus,** C. Ximénez de Enciso, 28, in the middle of Santa Cruz. Ask at the tourist office or swing by their ticket office for a schedule of different themed performances, including traditional Sephardic Jewish concerts. (☎954 560 670; www.casadelamemoria.es. Shows nightly 9pm, in summer also 10:30pm; seating is very limited, so reserve your tickets a day or two ahead and up to four days in advance for weekend shows. €15, students €13, under 10 €9.)

La Carbonería, C. Levies, 18, fills with students and backpackers. **El Tamboril,** Pl. de Santa Cruz, hosts a primarily middle-aged tourist crowd for midnight singing and dancing. (☎954 561 590. Open daily June-Sept. 5pm-3am; Oct.-May noon-3am.) Bar-filled Calle del Betis, across the river, houses several other *tabernas:* **Lo Nuestro, El Rejoneo,** and **Taberna Flamenca Triana.**

SPAIN

BULLFIGHTING

Sevilla's bullring hosts bullfights from *Semana Santa* through October. The cheapest place to buy tickets is at the ring on Po. Alcalde Marqués de Contadero. When there's a good *cartel* (line-up), buy tickets at booths on **Calle Sierpes, Calle Velázquez,** and **Plaza de Toros.** Prices can run from €20 for a *grada de sol* (nosebleed seat in the sun) to €75+ for a *barrera de sombra* (front-row seat in the shade). The two main options are *corridas de toros* (traditional bullfights) or *novilladas* (fights with apprentice bullfighters and younger bulls). During July and August, *corridas* occasionally occur on Thursday at 9pm; check posters around town. (Pl. de Toros ticket office ☎954 50 13 82; www.plazadetorosdelamaestranza.com.)

FESTIVALS

Sevilla swells with tourists during its fiestas, and with good reason: the parties are world-class. If you're in Spain during any major festivals, head straight to Sevilla—you won't regret it. Reserve a room a few months in advance, and expect to pay at least twice what you would normally.

Semana Santa, from Palm Sunday to Easter Sunday. In each neighborhood, thousands of penitents in hooded cassocks guide *pasos* (huge, extravagantly-decorated floats) through the streets, illuminated by hundreds of candles; the climax is Good Friday, when the entire city turns out for a procession along the bridges and through the oldest neighborhoods. Book rooms well in advance. The tourist office stocks a helpful booklet on accommodations and food during the festivities.

Feria De Abril, the final week in April. The city rewards itself for its Lenten piety with the *Feria de Abril,* held in the southern end of Los Remedios. Begun as part of a 19th-century revolt against foreign influence, the Feria has grown into a massive celebration of all things Andalucian, with circuses, bullfights, and flamenco. A spectacular array of flowers and lanterns decorates over 1000 kiosks, tents, and pavilions, known as *casetas,* which each have a small kitchen, bar, and dance floor. Most *casetas* are private, however, and the only way to get invited is by making friends with locals. The city holds bullfights daily during the festival; buy tickets in advance.

GRANADA

☎958

The splendors of the Alhambra, the magnificent palace which crowns the highest point of Granada (pop. 238,000), have fascinated both prince and pauper for centuries. Legend has it that in 1492, when the Moorish ruler Boabdil fled the city, the last Muslim stronghold in Spain, his mother berated him for casting a longing look back at the Alhambra. "You do well to weep as a woman," she told him, "for what you could not defend as a man." The Albaicín, an enchanting maze of Moorish houses, is Spain's best-preserved Arab quarter. Granada has grown into a university city infused with youthful energy.

TRANSPORTATION

Trains: RENFE, Av. Andaluces (☎902 24 02 02. www.renfe.es). Take bus #3-6, 9, or 11 from Gran Vía to the Constitución 3 stops and turn left onto Av. Andaluces. To: **Algeciras** (4-5hr., 3 per day 7:15am-5pm, €18.35); **Almería** (2hr., 4 per day 10:03am-9:06pm, €14.45); **Barcelona** (12hr.; 9:45pm; €52.10-57.40); **Madrid** (5-6hr.; 6:42am, 6pm; €61.80); **Sevilla** (4-5hr., 4 per day 8:18am-8:24pm, €21.65).

Buses: All major intercity bus routes start at the bus station (☎958 18 54 80) on the outskirts of Granada on **Ctra. de Madrid,** near C. Arzobispo Pedro de Castro. Take bus #3 or 33 from Gran Vía de Colón or a **taxi** (€6-7). Services reduced on Su.

ALSA (☎902 42 22 42 or 958 15 75 57; www.alsa.es.) to: **Alicante** (6hr., 6 per day 2:31am-11:30pm, €26.69); **Barcelona** (14hr., 5 per day 2:31am-11:30pm, €65.96); **Valencia** (9hr., 5 per day 2:31am-11:30pm, €40.23); **Algeciras** (3hr., 6 per day 9am-8:15pm, €20.20); **Almería** (2hr., 8 per day 6:45am-7:30pm, €11.50); **Antequera** (1hr., 4 per day 9am-7pm, €7.20); **Cádiz** (5hr., 4 per day 3am-6:30pm, €29.52); **Córdoba** (3hr., 8 per day 7:30am-7pm, €12.04); **Madrid** (5-6hr., 15 per day 7am-1:30am, €15.66); **Málaga** (2hr., 16 per day 7am-9pm, €9.38); **Marbella** (2hr., 8 per day 8am-8:15pm, €14.35); **Sevilla** (3hr., 7 per day 8am-8pm, €18.57).

Public Transportation: Local **buses** (☎900 71 09 00). Pick up the bus map at the tourist office. Important buses include: "Bus Alhambra" #30 from Gran Vía de Cólon or Pl. Nueva to the Alhambra; #31 from Gran Vía or Pl. Nueva to the Albaicín; #10 from the bus station to the youth hostel, C. de Ronda, C. Recogidas, and C. Acera de Darro; #3 from the bus station to Av. de la Constitución, Gran Vía, and Pl. Isabel la Católica. €1.10, *bonobus* (9 tickets) €5.45.

ORIENTATION AND PRACTICAL INFORMATION

The center of Granada is small **Plaza Isabel la Católica,** at the intersection of the city's two main arteries, **Calle de los Reyes Católicos** and **Gran Vía de Colón.** Just off Gran Vía, you'll find the cathedral; farther down Gran Vía by Pl. de la Trinidad is the university area. Uphill from Pl. Isabel la Católica on C. Reyes Católicos sits **Plaza Nueva,** and the **Alhambra** rises on the hill above. From Pl. Nueva, **Calle Elvira,** lined with bars and eateries, runs parallel to Gran Vía. Downhill, the pedestrian streets off C. de los Reyes Católicos comprise the shopping district.

Tourist Offices: Junta de Andalucía, C. Santa Ana, 2 (☎958 57 52 02). Open M-F 9am-7:30pm, Sa 9:30am-3pm, Su 10am-2pm. Posts bus and train schedules and provides a list of accommodations. Use this office for information about all of Andalucía. **Oficina Provincial,** Pl. Mariana Pineda, 10 (☎958 24 71 28). Walk up to the left past plaza

Isabel and make a right on Pineda. Walk until the square. English spoken. Great for all questions concerning Granada. Open M-F 9am-8pm, Sa 10am-7pm, Su 10am-3pm.

Currency Exchange: Banco Santander Central Hispano, Gran Vía, 3 (☎902 24 24 24). Open Apr.-Sept. M-F 8:30am-2pm.

Luggage Storage: 24hr. storage at the train and bus stations (€3). Frequently sold out.

English-Language Bookstore: Metro, C. Gracia, 31, off Veronica de la Magdelana, off C. Recogidas, which begins where Reyes Católicos hits Puerta Real. (☎958 26 15 65). Vast foreign language section. Open M-F 10am-2pm and 5-8:30pm, Sa 11am-2pm.

Gay and Lesbian Resources: Juvenós, C. Lavadero de las Tablas, 15, organizes weekly activities for gay youth. **Información Homosexual Hotline** (☎958 20 06 02).

Laundromat: C. de la Paz, 19, off Veronica de la Magdelena. Wash €8, dry €2 per 10min.; detergent included. Open M-F 10am-2pm and 5-8pm.

Police: C. Duquesa, 21 (☎091). English spoken.

Medical Services and Pharmacy: Hospital Universitario de San Cecilio, C. Dr. Olóriz, 16 (☎958 02 30 00). **Farmacia Gran Vía,** Gran Vía, 6 (☎958 22 29 90). Open M-F 9:30am-1:30pm and 5-8:30pm, Sa 9:30am-1:30pm and 5:30-9pm

Internet: Locutorio Cyber Alhambra, C. Joaquin Costa, 4 (☎958 22 43 96). €1.20 per hour; €5 *bono* for 6hr., €10 *bono* for 13hr. Open daily 9:30am-10:30pm. Second alley to left on Reyes Católicos walking away from Plaza Isabel.

Post Office: Pta. Real (☎958 22 48 35). *Lista de Correos* and fax service. Open M-F 8:30am-8:30pm, Sa 9:30am-2pm. **Postal Code:** 18009.

SPAIN

ACCOMMODATIONS

Hostels line Cuesta de Gomérez, Plaza Trinidad, and Gran Vía. Be sure to call ahead during Semana Santa (Apr. 5-12, 2009).

Funky Backpacker's, Cuesta de Rodrigo del Campo, 13 (☎958 22 14 62; funky@alternativeacc.com). From Pl. Nueva, go uphill on Cuchilleros 20m to find Cuesta de Rodrigo on the right. Sizable dorms surround a central atrium over the funky lobby. Take in the view of the Alhambra, mountains, and rooftops from the bar atop the hostel. The friendly staff hangs out with travelers. Outings to nearby thermal baths (€10), tapas bars and *flamenco* shows (€21). A/C, breakfast, and lockers included. Laundry (wash, dry and fold) €7. Free Internet. Dinner €4.50-6. Dorms €16.50-17; doubles €40. MC/V. ❶

Hostal Venecia, Cuesta de Gomérez, 2, 3rd fl. (☎958 22 39 87). Eccentrically decorated with bright colors and Granada paraphernalia, this small, homey hostel has the most character per square meter in town. Homemade herbal tea and conversation available any time of day. Reserve early, especially in summer, since the secret is out. Dorms €19; doubles €34; triples €45. MC/V. ❶

Hospedaje Almohada, C. Postigo de Zárate, 4 (☎958 20 74 46; www.laalmohada.com;). Follow C. Trinidad out of Pl. Trinidad to the T-intersection, then make a right and walk down the short street ahead. Look for double red doors with hand-shaped knockers. Lounge in the TV area, use the kitchen to cook your own meal, and peruse the communal music collection and travel guides. Laundry (wash and hang-dry) €5 for 8kg. Four-bed dorms €15; singles €19; doubles €35; triples €50. Cash only. ❶

Oasis Granada, Placeta Correo Viejo, 3 (☎958 21 58 48; from Spain free at ☎9001 OASIS; www.hostelsoasis.com). Frequented by the under-30 crowd. Weekly parties and daily activities like *tapas* tours and pub crawls. Breakfast included. Free Internet, common kitchen, ping-pong table on outdoor patio, rooftop lounge. Dinner *menús,* all-you-can-eat €4. Dorms €18; doubles €40. If hostel is "full," try showing up early in the morning for a spot as they usually hold about 10 beds for walk-ins. MC/V. ❷

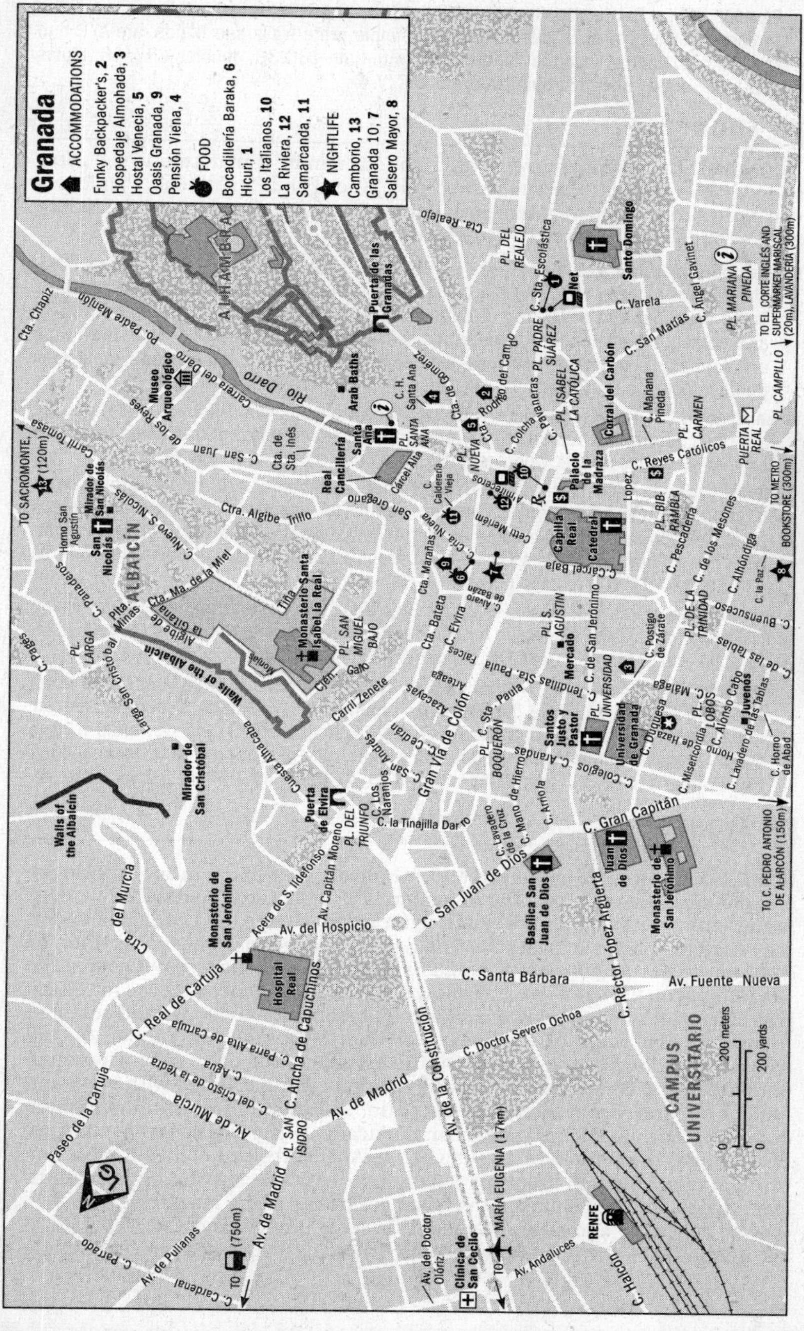

Granada
ACCOMMODATIONS
Funky Backpacker's, 2
Hospedaje Almohada, 3
Hostal Venecia, 5
Oasis Granada, 9
Pensión Viena, 4
FOOD
Bocadillería Baraka, 6
Hicuri, 1
Los Italianos, 10
La Riviera, 12
Samarcanda, 11
NIGHTLIFE
Camborio, 13
Granada 10, 7
Salsero Mayor, 8
ALHAMBRA
Puerta de las Granadas
Arab Baths
Río Darro
Carrera del Darro
Museo Arqueológico
Mirador de San Nicolás
San Nicolás
ALBAICÍN
Walls of the Albaicín
Monasterio Santa Isabel la Real
Mirador de San Cristóbal
Real Cancillería
Santa Ana
PL. SANTA ANA
PL. NUEVA
Capilla Real
Catedral
Palacio de la Madraza
Corral del Carbón
Santo Domingo
PL. DEL REALEJO
PL. ISABEL LA CATÓLICA
PL. BIB-RAMBLA
PL. DE LA TRINIDAD
PL. DEL CARMEN
PUERTA REAL
PL. MARIANA PINEDA
Mercado
Santos Justo y Pastor
Universidad de Granada
PL. UNIVERSIDAD
Gran Vía de Colón
Puerta de Elvira
PL. DEL TRIUNFO
Basílica San Juan de Dios
Monasterio de San Jerónimo
Hospital Real
C. San Juan de Dios
C. Gran Capitán
C. Reyes Católicos
C. Real de Cartuja
Av. de la Constitución
Av. de Madrid
Av. Fuente Nueva
C. Santa Bárbara
C. Doctor Severo Ochoa
C. Rector López Argüeta
Paseo de la Cartuja
PL. SAN ISIDRO
CAMPUS UNIVERSITARIO
RENFE
Clínica de San Cecilio
TO SACROMONTE, (120m)
TO METRO BOOKSTORE (300m)
TO EL CORTE INGLÉS AND SUPERMARKET MARISCAL (20m), LAVANDERÍA (300m)
TO C. PEDRO ANTONIO DE ALARCÓN (150m)
TO MARÍA EUGENIA (17km)
TO (750m)
200 meters
200 yards

SPAIN

Pensión Viena, C. Hospital Santa Ana, 2 (☎958 22 18 59; www.hostalviena.com). The greatest selling points of this hostel, with simple white walls and blinds, are A/C and proximity to central Granada. Singles €25, with bath €30-38; doubles €37/48; triples €50/65; quads €60/75; quint €65/95. MC/V. ❷

FOOD

North African cuisine and vegetarian options can be found around the Albaicín, while more typical *menús* await in Pl. Nueva and Pl. Trinidad. Picnickers can gather fresh fruit, vegetables, and meat for an outdoor feast at the indoor market on Pl. San Agustín. (Open M-Sa 9am-3pm.)

Bocadillería Baraka, C. Elvira, 20 (☎958 22 97 60). Stands out among many Middle Eastern eateries for being the cheapest and the tastiest. Proud that their meat is home prepared and never frozen, Baraka serves delicious traditional pitas (€2.50-4) and addictive homemade lemonade infused with *hierbabuena* (€1). Hedi, the owner and formerly in the travel business, also organizes week long, all-inclusive excursions through Morocco (☎649 11 41 71). Open daily 1pm-2am. Cash only. ❶

La Riviera, C. Cetti Meriem, 7 (☎958 22 79 69), off C. Elvira. The best place to score delicious, free *tapas*. You can't go wrong with the extensive list of traditional fare. Beer or *tinto de verano* €1.80. Open daily 12:30-4pm and 8pm-midnight. ❶

Hicuri, C. Santa Escolástica, 12 (☎653 78 34 22), on corner of Pl. de los Girones. Walk uphill past Pl. Isabela about 200m. Your search for healthy, affordable cuisine stops here. This popular eatery's huge selection of tasty vegetarian and vegan dishes will satisfy any tofu craving. Entrees €5.80-6.50. Menú €12. Open M-Fr 8:30am-4:30pm, Sa and Su 8:30-11:30pm. Cash only. ❷

Los Italianos, Gran Vía, 4 (☎958 22 40 34). Don't just gape at the ridiculously cheap ice-cream prices; get in line and try another flavor. No seating. *Barquillos* (cones) €1-2; *tarrinas* (cups) from €1. Mar.-Oct. open daily 9am-2am. Cash only. ❶

Samarcanda, C. Calderería Vieja, 3 (☎958 21 00 04), walking away from Nueva down Elvira, up to the right where the road forks around a kiosk. Outdoor seating in a small, quiet plaza; interior is a calm Middle Eastern setting. For €43, you can order a huge *Mesa Libanesa* platter to share, complete with a bottle of Lebanese wine. Menu in English. Entrees €8-12.50. Open M-Tu and Th-Su 1-4:30pm and 7:30-11:30pm. MC/V. ❸

SPAIN

SIGHTS

THE ALHAMBRA. From the streets of Granada, the Alhambra appears blocky and practical. But up close, the Alhambra is an elaborate and detailed work of architecture, one that unites water, light, wood, stucco, and ceramics to create a fortress-palace of aesthetic grandeur. The age-old saying holds true: "*Si mueres sin ver la Alhambra, no has vivido.*" (If you die without seeing the Alhambra, you have not lived.) Follow signs to the Palacio Nazaries to see the **Alcázar,** a 14th-century royal palace full of stalactite archways and sculpted fountains. The walls of the Patio del Cuarto Dorado are topped by the shielded windows of the harem. Off the far side of the patio, archways open onto the **Cuarto Dorado,** whose carved wooden ceiling is inlaid with ivory and mother-of-pearl. From the top of the patio, glimpse the 14th-century **Fachada de Serallo,** the palace's intricately carved facade. In the **Sala de los Abencerrajes,** Boabdil had the throats of 16 sons of the Abencerrajes family slit after one of them allegedly had amorous encounters with the sultana. According to legend, dust-colored stains in the basin are traces of the massacre.

Over a bridge, across the Callejón de los Cipreses and the Callejón de las Adelfas, are the vibrant blossoms, towering cypresses, and streaming waterways of **El Generalife,** vacation retreat of the sultans. The two buildings of El Generalife, the **Palacio** and the **Sala Regia,** connect across the Patio de la Acequia, embellished with a pool fed by fountains forming an archway.

When the Christians drove the first Nasrid King Alhamar from the Albaicín to this more strategic hill, he built the series of rust-colored brick towers which form the **Alcazaba** (fortress). A dark, spiraling staircase leads to the **Torre de la Vela** (watchtower), where visitors have a 360° view of Granada and the surrounding mountains. After the Reconquista drove the Moors from Spain, Fernando and Isabel restored the Alcázar. Only two generations later, Emperor Carlos V demolished part of it to make way for his Palacio, a Renaissance masterpiece by Pedro Machuca, a disciple of Michelangelo. While incongruous with the surrounding Moorish splendor, it is considered one of the most beautiful Renaissance buildings in Spain. *(☎902 44 12 21; www.alhambra-patronato.es; reservations ☎902 22 44 60; www.alhambra-tickets.es. Open daily Apr.-Sept. 8:30am-8pm; Oct.-Mar. 8:30am-6pm. Also open June-Sept. Tu-Sa 10-11:30pm; Oct.-May F-Sa 8-9:30pm. Audio tours are worth the €5 and are available in English, French, German, Italian, and Spanish. €12, under 12 and the disabled free. €13 if bought online. EU students with ID, EU seniors 65+ €9.)*

THE ALBAICÍN. A labyrinth of steep, narrow alleys, the Albaicín was the only Moorish neighborhood to escape the torches of the Reconquista. After the fall of the Alhambra, a small Muslim population remained here until their expulsion in the 17th century. Today, with North African cuisine, outdoor bazaars blasting Arabic music, teahouses, and the mosque near Pl. San Nicolás, the Albaicín attests to the persistence of Islamic culture in Andalucía. The best way to explore this maze is to proceed along Carrera del Darro off Pl. Santa Ana, climb the Cuesta del Chapiz on the left, then wander through the Muslim ramparts, cisterns, and gates. On Pl. Santa Ana, the 16th-century Real Cancillería, with its arcaded patio and stalactite ceiling, was the Christians' city hall. Farther uphill are the 11th-century Arab baths. *(Carrera del Darro, 31. ☎958 22 97 38. Call ☎958 22 56 03 to confirm hours. Free.)* The **mirador,** adjacent to Iglesia de San Nicolás, affords the city's best view of the Alhambra, especially in winter when snow adorns the Sierra Nevada behind it.

NIGHTLIFE

Granada's policy of "free *tapas* with a drink" lures students and tourists to its many pubs and bars. Great *tapas* bars can be found off the side streets near Pl. Nueva. The most boisterous nightspots belong to Calle Pedro Antonio de Alarcón, between Pl. Albert Einstein and Ancha de Gracia, while hip new bars and clubs line Calle Elvira. Gay bars are around Carrera del Darro.

Camborio, Camino del Sacromonte, 48 (☎958 22 12 15), a quick taxi ride or 20min. walk uphill from Pl. Nueva; bus #34 stops at midnight. DJ-spun pop music echoes through dance floors to the rooftop patio above. Striking view of the Alhambra. Beer €4. Mixed drinks €5. Cover €6, includes 1 drink. Open Tu-Sa midnight-7am. Cash only.

Salsero Mayor, C. la Paz, 20 (☎958 52 27 41). An ageless group of locals and tourists alike flocks here for crowded nights of salsa, bachata, and merengue. Beer €2-3. Mixed drinks €5. Open M-Th and Su 10pm-3am, F-Sa 1pm-4am. Cash only.

Granada 10, C. Cárcel Baja 3 (☎958 22 40 01). Movie theater by evening (shows Sept.-June at 8, 10pm), raging dance club by night. Flashy and opulent. No sneakers or sportswear. Open M-Th and Su 12:30-4am, F-Sa 12:30-6am. Cover €10. MC/V.

SPAIN

COSTA DEL SOL

MÁLAGA ☎952

Málaga (pop. 550,000) is the transportation hub of the coast, and while its beaches are known more for bars than for natural beauty, the city has much to offer. Towering high above the city, the medieval **Alcazaba** is Málaga's most imposing sight. At the east end of Po. del Parque, the 11th-century structure was originally used as both a military fortress and royal palace for Moorish kings. (Open June-Aug. Tu-Su 9:30am-8pm; Sept.-May Tu-Sa 8:30am-7pm. €2, students and seniors €0.60. Free Su after 2pm.) Málaga's breathtaking **cathedral,** C. Molina Lario 4, is nicknamed *La Manquita* (One-Armed Lady) because one of its two towers was never completed. (☎952 22 03 45. Open M-F 10am-6pm, Sa 10am-5pm. Mass daily 9am. Entrance €3.50, includes audio tour.) **Picasso's birthplace,** Pl. de la Merced 15, is now home to the **Casa Natal y Fundación Picasso,** which organizes concerts, exhibits, and lectures. Upstairs is a permanent collection of Picasso's drawings, photographs, and pottery. (☎952 06 02 15; www.fundacionpicasso.es. Open daily 9:30am-8pm. €1; students, seniors, and under 17 free.) The **Museo Picasso,** C. San Augustin 8, details the transition of Málaga's most famous son from child prodigy to renowned master. (☎952 44 33 77; www.museopicassomalaga.org. Open Tu-Th, Su, and holidays 10am-8pm; F-Sa 10am-9pm. €6 permanent collection, €4.50 for temporary, €8 combined; students, youth €3. Free entrance last Su of every month 3-8pm.

One of a few spots in Málaga just for backpackers, friendly **Picasso's Corner** ❷, C. San Juan de Letrán 9, off Pl. de la Merced, offers free Internet and top-notch bathrooms. (☎952 21 22 87; www.picassoscorner.com. Dorms €18-19; doubles €45. MC/V.) **ComoLoco** ❷, C. José Denis Belgradno, 17 (☎952 21 65 71) specializes in salads and pitas (€4.85-10), and is one of many trendy restaurants by C. Granada. Salads are large enough to quiet a grumbling stomach, but you'll have to wait the typical 20-70min. for a table. Open daily 1pm-1am. Cash only.

RENFE **trains** (☎902 24 02 02) leave from Explanada de la Estación for: Barcelona (13hr., 2 per day, €58); Córdoba (2hr., 9 per day, €19); Madrid (5hr., 7 per day, €71-79); Seville (3hr., 5-6 per day, €17-33). **Buses** run from Po. de los Tilos (☎952 35 00 61), one block from the RENFE station along C. Roger de Flor, to: Barcelona (13 hr., 2 per day, €75); Cádiz (5hr., 3-6 per day, €22); Córdoba (3hr., 7 per day, €12); Granada (2hr., 17-19 per day, €9.40); Madrid (7hr., 8-12 per day, €20); Marbella (1hr., 1 per hr., €5); Ronda (3hr., 4-12 per day, €10); Seville (3hr., 11-12 per day, €15). To get to the **city center** from the bus station, take bus #3, 4, or 21 (€1) or exit right onto Callejones del Perchel, walk through the Av. de la Aurora intersection, turn right on Av. de Andalucía, and cross Puente de Tetuán. Alameda Principal leads into Pl. de la Marina and the **tourist office.** (☎952 12 20 20. Open M-F 9am-7pm.) **Postal Code:** 29080.

NORTHERN SPAIN

BARCELONA ☎93

Barcelona is a city that has grown young as it has grown old. In the 17 years since it hosted the Olympics, travelers have been drawn to this European hot-spot's beaches, clubs, and first-rate restaurants. Once home to Pablo Picasso and Joan Miró, the city has a strong art scene, which continues the tradition of the whimsical and daring *Modernisme* architectural movement. Barcelona is a gateway—not only to Catalan art and culture, but also to the Mediterranean and the Pyrenees—and its vibrant aura lingers long after you leave.

INTERCITY TRANSPORTATION

Flights: Aeroport El Prat de Llobregat (BCN; ☎902 40 47 04; www.aena.es), 13km southwest of Barcelona. To get to Pl. Catalunya, take the **Aerobus** (☎934 15 60 20) in front of terminals A, B, or C (35-40min.; every 6-15min.; to Pl. Catalunya daily 6am--1am, to the airport 5:30am-12:15am; €4.05, round-trip €7.30).

Trains: Barcelona has 2 main train stations. **Estació Barcelona-Sants,** in Pl. Països Catalans (ⓂSants Estació), is the main terminal for domestic and international traffic. **Estació de França,** on Av. Marquès de l'Argentera (ⓂBarceloneta), services regional destinations, including Tarragona and Zaragoza, and a limited number of international locations. Note that trains often stop before the main stations; check the schedule. **RENFE** (reservations and info ☎902 24 02 02, international 24 34 02) to: **Bilbao** (6½-9hr., 12:30 and 11pm, €41-60); **Madrid** (3hr.; from mid-June to mid-Sept. 14-21 per day, from mid-Sept. to mid-June 4-7 per day; €44); **Sevilla** (5½-12hr., 3 per day 8am-10:05pm, €59-132); **Valencia** (3-4 hr., 14 per day, €34-41). International destinations include **Milan, ITA** (via **Figueres** and **Turin**) and **Montpellier, FRA,** with connections to Geneva, Paris, and the French Riviera. 20% discount on round-trip tickets.

Buses: Arrive at the **Barcelona Nord Estació d'Autobusos,** C. Alí-bei, 80 (☎902 26 06 06; www.barcelonanord.com). ⓂArc de Triomf or #54 bus. Info booth open 7am-9pm. Buses also depart from Estació Sants and the airport. **Sarfa** (☎902 30 20 25; www.sarfa.es). Bus stop and ticket office also at Ronda Sant Pere, 21 (☎933 02 62 23). To: **Cadaqués** (2¾hr.; M-F 2-4 per day 10:30am-7pm Sa-Su 2-4 per day 10:30am-8:45pm; €21); **Palafrugell** (2hr., 8-15 per day 8:15am-8:30pm, €16); **Tossa de Mar** via **Lloret de Mar** (1½hr., 7-13 per day 8am-8:30pm, €11). **Eurolines** (☎93 265 07 88; www.eurolines.es) goes to **Paris, FRA** via **Lyon** (15hr., M-Sa 9:30pm, €75-91); 10% discount under 26 or over 60. **ALSA/Enatcar** (☎902 42 22 42; www.alsa.es) goes to: **Alicante** (7-9hr., 8 per day, €41-46); **Bilbao** (7-8½hr., 4-7 per day, €42); **Madrid** (8hr., 18-21 per day 7am-1am, €29-41); **Sevilla** (15-20hr., 3 per day, €89); **Valencia** (4-5hr., 8 per day, €25-30); **Zaragoza** (4hr., 3-21 per day, €14-21).

Ferries: Transmediterránea (☎902 45 46 45; www.transmediterranea.es), in Terminal Drassanes, Moll Sant Bertran. **"Fast" ferry** (€51-69; round-trip €96-€103) June-Aug. to **Ibiza** (8-9hr., 1 per day Tu and Th-Su), **Mahón** (8½hr., M and W-Su 10:30pm), and **Palma de Mallorca** (8hr., 1-2 per day).

ORIENTATION

Imagine yourself perched on Columbus's head at the **Monument a Colom** (on Passeig de Colom, along the shore), viewing the city with the sea at your back. From the harbor, the city slopes upward to the mountains. From the Monument a Colom, **La Rambla,** a pedestrian thoroughfare, runs from the harbor to **Plaça de Catalunya** (M: Catalunya), the city center. *Let's Go* uses "Las Ramblas" to refer to the general area and "La Rambla" in address listings. The **Ciutat Vella** (Old City) centers around Las Ramblas and includes the neighborhoods of Barri Gòtic, La Ribera, and El Raval. The **Barri Gòtic** is to the right (with your back to the ocean) of Las Ramblas, enclosed on the other side by Vía Laietana. East of V. Laietana lies the maze-like **La Ribera,** bordered by Parc de la Ciutadella and Estació de França. Beyond La Ribera—farther east outside the Ciutat Vella—are **Poble Nou** and **Port Olímpic.** To the west of Las Ramblas is **El Raval.** Farther west rises **Montjuïc,** with sprawling gardens, museums, the 1992 Olympic grounds, and a fortress. Directly behind the Monument a Colom is the **Port Vell** (old port) development, where a wavy bridge leads across to the ultra modern shopping and entertainment complexes Moll d'Espanya and Maremàgnum. North of the Ciutat Vella is **l'Eixample,** a gridded neighborhood created during the expansion of the 1860s, which sprawls from Pl. Catalunya toward the mountains. Gran Vía de les Corts Catalanes defines its lower edge, and the **Passeig de Gràcia,** l'Eixample's main avenue, bisects the neighborhood. **Avinguda Diagonal** marks the border between l'Eixample and the **Zona Alta** (Uptown), which includes **Pedralbes, Gràcia,** and other older neighborhoods in the foothills. The peak of **Tibidabo,** the northwest border of the city, offers the best view of Barcelona.

LOCAL TRANSPORTATION

Public Transportation: ☎010. Passes *(abonos)* work for the Metro, bus, urban lines of FGC commuter trains, RENFE *cercanías,* Trams, and Nitbus. A *sencillo* ticket (1 ride) costs €1.40. A **T-10 pass** (€7.70) is valid for 10 rides; a **T-Día pass** entitles you to unlimited bus and Metro travel for 1 day (€5.80) and the **T-mes** (€48) for 1 month.

Metro: ☎93 298 7000; www.tmb.net. Vending machines and ticket windows sell passes. Hold on to your ticket until you exit or risk a €40 fine. Trains run M-Th, Su and holidays 5am-midnight, F 5am-2am, Sa non-stop service. €1.40.

Ferrocarrils de la Generalitat de Catalunya (FGC): (☎932 05 15 15; www.fgc.es). Commuter trains to local destinations with main stations at Pl. de Catalunya and Pl. d'Espanya. The commuter line costs the same as the Metro (€1.40) as far as Tibidabo. After that, rates go up by zone: Zone 2 €2.10, Zone 3 €2.90, etc. Metro passes are valid on FGC trains. Info office at the Pl. de Catalunya station open M-F 7am-9pm.

Buses: Go just about anywhere, usually 5am-10pm. Most stops have maps posted. Buses run 4-6 per hr. in central locations. €1.40.

Nitbus: (www.emt-amb.cat/links/cat/cnitbus.htm). 18 different lines run every 20-30min. 10:30pm-4:30am, depending on the line; a few run until 5:30am. All buses depart from around Pl. de Catalunya, stop in front of most club complexes, and work their way through Ciutat Vella and the Zona Alta.

Taxis: Try **RadioTaxi033** (☎93 303 3033; www.radiotaxi033.com; AmEx/MC/V)

Car Rental: Avis, C. Corcega 293-295 (☎93 237 5680; www.avis.com). Also at airport (☎93 298 3600) and Estació Barcelona-Sants, Pl. dels Països Catalans. (☎93 330 4193. Open M-F 7:30am-10:30pm, Sa 8am-7pm, Su 9am-7pm.)

PRACTICAL INFORMATION

Tourist Offices: ☎90 730 1282; www.barcelonaturisme.com. In addition to several tourist offices, Barcelona has numerous mobile information kiosks. **Aeroport del Prat de Llobregat,** terminals A and B (☎93 478 0565). Info and last-minute accommodation booking. Open daily 9am-9pm. **Estació Barcelona-Sants,** Pl. Països Catalans. M: Sants-Estació. Info and last-minute accommodations booking. Open June 24-Nov. 24 daily 8am-8pm; Nov. 25-June 23 M-F 8am-8pm, Sa-Su 8am-2pm. **Oficina de Turisme de Catalunya,** Pg. de Gràcia 107 (☎93 238 4000; www.gencat.es/probert). M: Diagonal. Open M-Sa 10am-7pm, Su 10am-2pm. **Plaça de Catalunya,** Pl. de Catalunya 17S. M: Catalunya. The biggest, best, and busiest tourist office. Free **maps,** brochures on sights and public transportation, booking service for accommodations, gift shop, currency exchange, and box office. Open daily 9am-9pm. **Plaça de Sant Jaume,** C. Ciutat 2. M: Jaume I. Open M-F 9am-8pm, Sa 10am-8pm, Su and holidays 10am-2pm.

Currency Exchange: ATMs give the best rates; the next-best rates are available at banks. General banking hours are M-F 8:30am-2pm. Las Ramblas has many exchange stations open late, but the rates are not as good and a commission will be taken.

Luggage Storage: Estació Barcelona-Sants, ⓂSants-Estació. Lockers €4.50 per day. Open daily 5:30am-11pm. **Estació Nord,** ⓂArc de Triomf. Lockers €3.50-5 per day, 90-day limit. Also at the **El Prat Airport.** €5 per day.

Library: Biblioteca Sant Pau-Santa Creu, C. Hospital, 56 (☎933 02 07 97), in El Raval 1 block up C. Hospital from Las Ramblas. ⓂLiceu. Open M-Tu 3:30-8:30pm, W-Th 10am-2pm, F 3:30-8:30pm.

Laundromat: Lavomatic, Pl. Joaquim Xirau, 1, a block off La Rambla and 1 block below C. Escudellers. Branch at C. Consolat del Mar, 43-45 (☎932 68 47 68), 1 block north of Pg. Colon and 2 blocks off Via Laietana. Wash €4.80. Dry €0.90 per 5min. Both open M-Sa 9am-9pm.

Tourist Police: La Rambla, 43 (☎932 56 24 30). ⓂLiceu. English spoken. Open 24hr.

Late-Night Pharmacy: Rotates; check any pharmacy window for the nearest on duty.

Medical Services: Medical Emergency: ☎061. **Hospital Clínic i Provincal,** C. Villarroel,170 (☎932 27 54 00). ⓂHospital Clínic. Main entrance at C. Roselló and C. Casanova.

Internet: **Easy Internet Café,** La Rambla, 31 (☎933 01 7507; www.easyinternetcafe.com). ⓂLiceu. Fairly reasonable prices and over 200 terminals in a bright, modern center. €2.10 per hr., min. €2. 1-day unlimited pass €7; 1 week €15; 1 month €30. Open 8am-2:30am. **Branch** at Ronda Universitat, 35. ⓂCatalunya. €2 per hour; 1-day pass €3; 1 week €7; 1 month €15. Open daily 8am-2:30am.

Navegaweb, La Rambla, 88-94 (☎933 17 90 26; navegabarcelona@terra.es). ⓂLiceu. Good rates for international calls ($0.20 per min. to USA). Internet €2 per hr. Open M-Th 9am-midnight, F 9am-1am, Sa 9am-2am, Su 9am-midnight.

Bcnet, C. Barra de Ferro, 3 (☎932 68 15 07; www.bornet-bcn.com), down the street from the Museu Picasso. ⓂJaume I. €1 for 15min; €3 per hr.; 10hr. ticket €19. Open M-F 10am-11pm, Sa-Su noon-11pm.

Post Office: Pl. d'Antoni López (☎902 197 197). ⓂJaume I or Barceloneta. Fax and **Lista de Correos.** Open M-F 8:30am-9:30pm, Su noon-10pm. Dozens of branches; consult www.correos.es. **Postal Code:** 08001.

ACCOMMODATIONS

While there are plenty of accommodations in Barcelona, finding an affordable room can be difficult. To crash in touristy **Barri Gòtic** or **Las Ramblas** during the busier months (June-Sept. and Dec.), make reservations weeks, even months, ahead. Consider staying outside the tourist hub of *Ciutat Vella;* there are many affordable and enjoyable hostels in **l'Eixample** and **Gràcia** that tend to have more vacancies. Travelers should not assume that rooms have A/C, phone, or TV unless specified. A handful of campgrounds lie on the outskirts of the city, accessible by intercity buses (20-45min., €1.50). The **Associació de Càmpings i C.V. de Barcelona,** Gran Via de les Corts Catalanes 608 (☎93 412 5955; www.campingsbcn.com), has more info.

LOWER BARRI GÒTIC

Backpackers flock to these hostels to be close to the buzz of Las Ramblas.

Hostal Levante, Baixada de San Miquel, 2 (☎933 17 95 65; www.hostallevante.com). ⓂLiceu. New rooms are large and tasteful, with light wood furnishings, exceptionally clean bathrooms, A/C, and fans; some have balconies. Ask for a newly renovated room. Apartments have kitchens, living rooms, and washing machines. Internet €1 per hr. Singles €35, with bath 45; doubles from €55/€65; 4-person apartments €30 per person. Credit card number required with reservation. MC/V. ❸

Pensión Mariluz, C. Palau, 4 (☎933 17 34 63; www.pensionmariluz.com), 3rd fl. ⓂLiceu or Jaume I. Gorgeous renovations turned this hostel into a warm, bright space around a classy old courtyard. Shared bathrooms are clean but a bit cramped. Offers short-term apartments nearby. A/C. Locker, sheets, and towels included. Free Wi-Fi in common area. Dorms €15-24; singles €30-41; doubles €40-60; triples €48-72; quads €65-90, with bath €94. MC/V. ❷

Hostal Fernando, C. Ferran, 31 (☎933 01 79 93; www.hfernando.com). ⓂLiceu. Clean rooms with a little more attention and care than most places in this price range. Dorms with A/C and lockers. Common kitchen with dining room and TV on 3rd fl. Private rooms have TV and bath. Towels €1.50. Internet €1 per 30min. Free Wi-Fi. Dorms €20-24; singles €45-55; doubles €65-77; triples €75-90. MC/V. ❷

Kabul Youth Hostel, Pl. Reial, 17 (☎933 18 51 90; www.kabul.es). ⓂLiceu. Legendary among backpackers—it's hosted nearly a million since its establishment in 1985. Rooms with balconies overlooking Pl. Reial available by request. Lounge and terrace. Breakfast and dinner included. Linens €2. Free Wi-Fi. Computers provided with 20min. of free use per day. Check-out 11am. Reservations available only on website with credit card. Dorms €20-30. MC/V. ❷

UPPER BARRI GÒTIC

SPAIN

Accommodations here can be costlier; those farther from Las Ramblas are generally more serene. Early reservations are essential in summer, when hostels become crowded.

Hostal Maldà, C. Pi, 5 (☎933 17 30 02). ⓂLiceu. Enter the small shopping center and follow the signs upstairs. Clean, no-frills rooms that would cost twice as much money at other places. All rooms have shared bath. Call for reservations. Singles €15; doubles €30; triples with shower €45. Cash only. ❶

Hostal-Residència Rembrandt, C. de la Portaferrissa, 23 (☎933 18 10 11; www.hostalrembrandt.com). ⓂLiceu. Range of unique rooms. Cheapest are fairly standardbut some have large baths, patios, and sitting areas. Breakfast €5. Reception 9am-11pm. Reservations require credit card or €50 deposit. Singles with shower around €30, with bath €40; doubles €50/65; triples €75/85. MC/V. ❷

Hostal Campi, C. Canuda, 4 (☎933 01 35 45; www.hostalcampi.com). Central location, warmly decorated rooms, and helpful staff. Most rooms have balconies, some have TVs. Internet €1 per hr. Singles €32; doubles €55, with bath €65; triples €75/85. Prices rise in high season. MC/V. ❸

Pensión Hostal Paris, C. del Cardenal Casañas, 4 (☎993 301 37 85). ⓂLiceu. Basic clean bedrooms but an exceptional common room with lavish gilt-framed paintings and a balcony overlooking La Rambla. Free Wi-Fi. Must pay one night with reservation. Singles €30; doubles €55, with bath 65; triples €85. MC/V. ❷

LA RIBERA AND EL RAVAL

La Ribera, while still touristed, can be calmer than the Barri Gòtic. Be careful in El Raval (near the port) and farther from Las Ramblas at night.

Gothic Point Youth Hostel, C. dels Vigatans, 5 (☎932 68 78 08; www.gothicpoint.com). ⓂJaume I. Jungle-gym rooms with A/C. Most beds come with curtains and personal lockers. Highly social, with lots of events, including a weekly DJ jam and free concerts. Rooftop terrace and colorful lounge area with TV. Breakfast included. Lockers €3. Linens €2. Free internet. Refrigerator and kitchen access. Dorms €24. €1 credit card fee per night. AmEx/MC/V. ❶

Hotel Peninsular, C. de Sant Pau, 34 (☎934 12 36 99; www.hpeninsular.com). M: Liceu. This *Modernista* building has 78 rooms with green doors, phones, and A/C around a beautiful 4-story interior courtyard festooned with hanging plants. Breakfast included.

Safety deposit boxes €2 per day with €20 deposit. Free internet and Wi-Fi. Check-out 11am. Singles €55; doubles €78; triples €95; quads €120; quints €140. MC/V. ❺

Barcelona Mar Youth Hostel, C. de Sant Pau, 80 (☎933 24 85 30; www.barcelonamar.es). M: Paral·lel. This hostel hosts Spanish cooking classes (€18), a tapas-and-flamenco-night (€22), a pub crawl that includes cover and 1 drink per bar (€15), a free walking tour, and more. Shared bathrooms with separate rooms for toilets and new shower curtains. 125 dorm-style beds and ocean-themed decor. Breakfast and lockers included. Linens €2.50, towels €2.50; both €3.50. Self-service laundry €4.50. Free internet and Wi-Fi. 6- to 16-bed dorms in summer €26, in winter €16-19; Doubles €46-58, F-Sa add €2 per person. AmEx/MC/V. ❷

Hostal de Ribagorza, C. de Trafalgar, 39 (☎933 19 19 68; www.hostalribagorza.com). ⓂUrquinaona. Ornate Modernista building with attractive rooms, homey decorations, and colorfully tiled floors. TV and A/C. Doubles €45-60; triples €60-75. MC/V. ❹

L'EIXAMPLE

Although L'Eixample may be far from the sights of Las Ramblas and the Barri Gòtic, it is home to Barcelona's most beautiful architecture. Accommodations here tend to be much nicer than those in Ciutat Vella.

Sant Jordi Hostel Aragó, C. Aragó, 268 (☎932 15 67 43; www.santjordihostels.com). ⓂPasseig de Gràcia. Walk 3 blocks up Pg. de Gràcia and make a left on C. Arago; it's on the left. Crash in this recently renovated hostel's sleek and homey common room and recuperate from a long day. They'll plan your night out for you if you so desire. Board games, DVDs, lockers, sheets, towels, TV, use of guitar all free. Laundry €5. Breakfast €3. Kitchen. Laundry €5. Internet and Wi-Fi. Parties and bar crawls organized regularly; call ahead. 4-bed dorms €14-17; 6-bed dorms €13-25. ❶

Somnio Hostel, C. Diputació 251. (☎932 72 53 08, www.somniohostels.com) ⓂPg. de Gràcia. Chic, clean, and neatly arranged rooms just blocks from Pl. de Catalunya. A/C throughout, free internet and Wi-Fi, TV in common area. Drinks available at the front desk. Breakfast €5. Single-sex dorms, complete with sheets and locker €25; singles €42; doubles €77, with bath €85. MC/V. ❷

Hostal Residència Oliva, Pg. de Gràcia, 32, 4th fl. (☎934 88 01 62; www.hostaloliva.com). ⓂPg. de Gràcia. Classy ambience—wooden bureaus, mirrors, and a light marble floor. Fragrant bouquets of flowers in the hallways are perhaps to be expected from a hostel that has been in operation since 1931. Rooms have TV, A/C, and Wi-Fi. Singles €38; doubles €66, with bath €85. Cash only. ❹

Hostal Qué Tal, C. Mallorca, 290 (☎934 59 23 66; www.quetalbarcelona.com), near C. Bruc. ⓂPg. de Gràcia or Verdaguer. Plants, both potted and painted, adorn the hallways of this *hostal.* Warm decorations make the spacious rooms feel cozy. Free internet. Singles €45; doubles €55-65, with bath €75-80. MC/V. ❺

ZONA ALTA: GRÀCIA AND OUTER BARRIS

The most visited part of Zona Alta is Gràcia, incorporated into Barcelona in 1897 despite the protests of many of its residents. Calls for Gràcian independence continue even today. Gràcia is Barcelona's "undiscovered" quarter, so last-minute arrivals may find vacancies here, even though options are scarce.

Pensión Norma, C. Gran de Gràcia, 87 (☎932 37 44 78). ⓂFontana. Meticulously kept rooms with sinks and wardrobes. The spacious shared bath is clean with speckled tile floors. Free Wi-Fi. Singles €27-32; doubles €38-47, with bath €55-60. MC/V. ❷

Hostal Lesseps, C. Gran de Gràcia, 239 (☎932 18 44 34; www.hostallesseps.com). ⓂLesseps. 16 spotless rooms, each with a high ceiling, classy velvet walls, small desk, TV, and bath. A/C €5. Cats and dogs allowed. Free internet and Wi-Fi. Singles €40; doubles €65; triples €75; quads €90. MC/V. ❹

FOOD

Port Vell and **Port Olímpic** are known for seafood. The restaurants on **Carrer Aragó** by Pg. de Gràcia have great lunchtime *menús*, and the **Passeig de Gràcia** has beautiful outdoor dining. Gràcia's **Plaça Sol** and the area around La Ribera's **Santa Maria del Mar** are the best *tapas* (or cheap, laid-back dinner) spots. For fruit, cheese, and wine, head to **La Boqueria** (Mercat de Sant Josep), off La Rambla outside M: Liceu. (Open M-Sa 8am-8pm.) Buy groceries at **Champion,** La Rambla 13. (M: Liceu. Open M-Sa 9am-10pm.)

BARRI GÒTIC

Les Quinze Nits, Pl. Reial, 6 (☎933 17 30 75; www.lesquinzenits.com). ⓂLiceu. Popular restaurant with lines halfway through the plaza every night; arrive early for excellent Catalan cuisine at unusually low prices. Sit in the classy interior or eat outside for no extra charge and keep an eye on your fellow tourists in Pl. Reial. Starters €4-7. Entrees €6-11. Wine €3. Sangria €4.70. Open daily 1-3:45pm and 8:30-11:30pm. AmEx/MC/V. ❷

L'Antic Bocoi del Gòtic, Baixada de Viladecols, 3 (☎933 10 50 67; www.bocoi.net). ⓂJaume I. Excellent salads (€7.20-9.20), *coques de recapte* (open-faced toasted sandwiches; €9), and cheese platters (€13-19) feature *jamón ibérico* and local produce. Look for the 1st-century Roman wall inside. Open M-Sa 8:30pm-midnight. Reserve in advance. AmEx/D/MC/V. ❸

Attic, La Rambla, 120 (☎933 02 48 66; www.angrup.com). ⓂLiceu. This chic restaurant promises high-class food at manageable prices. The modern, orange interior will feel like a refuge from touristy La Rambla. Mediterranean fusion cuisine, including fish (€10-14), meat (€8-15), and their specialty, ox burger (€11). Open daily 1-4:30pm and 7pm-12:30am. AmEx/MC/V. ❸

Arc Café, C. Carabassa, 19 (☎933 02 52 04; www.arccafe.com). ⓂDrassanes. This secluded, handsome cafe serves curries (€9.50-12) and salads (€4-7). Entrees €8-17. *Menú del mediodía* €9.60. Breakfast until 1pm. Thai dinner menu Th-F. Open M-Th 10am-1am, F 10am-3am, Sa 11am-3am, Su 11am1am. MC/V. ❸

Juicy Jones, C. Cardenal Casañas, 7 (☎93 302 43 30; reservations 60 620 49 06). ⓂLiceu, L3. A vegan's haven, Juicy Jones is a refreshing touch of the psychedelic, with wildly decorated walls and a long bar spilling over with fresh fruit. The creative vegan *menú* (€8.50) features Spanish and Indian inspired dishes (after 1pm). They offer a full juice bar with every conceivable mixture of fresh juices and soy milkshakes (€3-5). Open daily 12:30pm-12am. Kitchen closes at 11:30pm. Cash only. ❷

Xaloc, C. de la Palla, 13-17 (☎933 01 19 90). ⓂLiceu. Classy local favorite. A clean look complements the butcher counter where pig legs hang from the ceiling. Expect simple plates with high-quality ingredients. Tapas €3-7. *Cocas* €4-6. Open M-F 9am-midnight, Sa-Su 10am-midnight. AmEx/MC/V. ❷

The Bagel Shop, C. Canuda, 25 (☎93 302 41 61). ⓂCatalunya, L3. Walk down La Rambla and take the 1st left, and then bear right onto C. Canuda; it's on the left in Pl. Vila de Madrid. Bagels are rare in Spain, but here you'll find a diverse selection (€1, toasted €0.15 more) and a variety of spreads, from cream cheese to mango chutney. Good place to go for a tasty, inexpensive lunch with plenty of vegetarian options. Bagel sandwiches €4-6. Open M-Sa 9:30am-9:30pm, Su 11am-4pm. MC/V. ❶

OTHER NEIGHBORHOODS

La Llavor dels Origens, C. d'Enric Granados, 9 (☎934 53 11 20; www.lallavordelsorigens.com); C. de la Vidrieria, 6-8 (☎933 10 75 31); Pg. del Born, 4 (☎932 95 66 90); and C. de Ramón y Cajal, 12 (☎932 13 60 31). A hip dining room with a new-school twist. Delectable entrees include beef-stuffed onion (€6.40) and rabbit with chocolate

SPAIN

and almonds (€6.40). Soups, meat dishes, and some vegetarian dishes €4.30-7. Open daily 12:30pm-1am. AmEx/MC/V. ❷

Petra, C. dels Sombrerers, 13 (☎933 19 99 99). ⓂJaume I. Some of the best food in the area at shockingly low prices. Clever decor—stained-glass windows, menus printed on wine glasses, and light fixtures made from silverware—give the place a charming bohemian feel. Try the duck with brie and apple or the rigatoni with *foie gras* sauce and peach. Salads and pasta €5. Entrees €8. Open Tu-Th 1:30-4pm and 9-11:30pm, F-Sa 1:30-4pm and 9pm-midnight, Su 1:30-4pm. MC/V. ❷

El Pebre Blau, C. dels Banys Vells, 21 (☎933 19 13 08). ⓂJaume I. A *nouveau gourmet* restaurant serving Mediterranean and Middle Eastern fusion dishes under starry lanterns. Throw in a cheeky menu (available in English) and an attentive waitstaff for the win. Most dishes €10-18. Open daily 8pm-midnight. Reserve ahead, especially for weekend. MC/V. ❸.

Organic, C. Junta de Comerç, 11 (☎933 01 09 02; www.antoniaorganickitchen.com). This vegan-friendly eatery provides wholesome, healthy dishes—starting with the filtered water used to prepare the food. Vegan salad bar and lunch *menú* (M-F €10, Sa-Su €14) served under candlelight and exposed ceiling. Salad bar regulars include cheese-and-mushroom *croquetas* and cucumbers and yogurt. Dinner served a la carte. 2nd location in La Boqueria market also has a *menú* and *bocadillos;* takeout only. Open daily 12:30pm-midnight. MC/V. ❷

Rita Rouge, Pl. Gardunya (☎934 81 36 86; ritarouge@ritablue.com). M: Liceu. 2nd branch **Rita Blue,** Pl. Sant Augustí, 3 (☎933 42 40 86; www.ritablue.com). Savor a healthy, delicious, and high-quality lunch *menú* (€11; weekends €14) full of creative offerings and vegetarian choices on a shady, black-and-red terrace just behind La Boqueria, or come at night for a mixed drink (€6-8) on zebra-striped cushions or in the glittery bar's red and silver bucket seats. Entrees (€9.50-22) include chicken tandoori with yogurt and *basmati* rice. Salads and wok dishes €6-12. Open M-Sa noon-2am, Su 6pm-2am. ❸

Taktika Berri, C. Valencia, 169 (☎934 53 47 59). ⓂUniversitat. Walk up C. d'Aribau and make a left onto C. Valencia. Many consider this Basque restaurant the best one in Barcelona. While you can always eat *pintxos* (skewered tapas) such as *montaditos* (small sandwiches) at the bar, you won't get a table unless you call weeks in advance. Entrees like battered cheek and cod omelette are delicious, but not cheap—expect to pay €35 for a full meal, whether of tapas or entrees. Good selection of Basque wines. Open M-F 1-4pm and 8:30-11pm, Sa 1-4pm. AmEx/MC/V. ❺

SIGHTS AND MUSEUMS

The **Ruta del Modernisme** pass is the cheapest and most flexible option for those with an interest in seeing Barcelona's major sights. Passes give holders a 25-30% discount on attractions including Palau de la Música Catalana, the Museu de Zoología, and tours of Hospital de la Santa Creu i Sant Pau. Purchase passes at the Pl. Catalunya tourist office or at the Modernisme Centre at Hospital Santa Creu i Sant Pau, C. Sant Antoni Maria Claret 167. (☎933 17 76 52; www.rutadelmodernisme.com. Passes free with the purchase of a €12 guidebook, €5 per additional adult, adult accompanying someone under 18 free.)

LAS RAMBLAS

This pedestrian-only strip (roughly 1km long) is a cornucopia of street performers, fortune-tellers, human statues, pet and flower stands, and artists. The wide, tree-lined street, known in Catalan as Les Rambles, is actually six *ramblas* (promenades) that form one boulevard from the Pl. de Catalunya. According to legend, visitors who sample the water from the **Font de Canaletes** at the

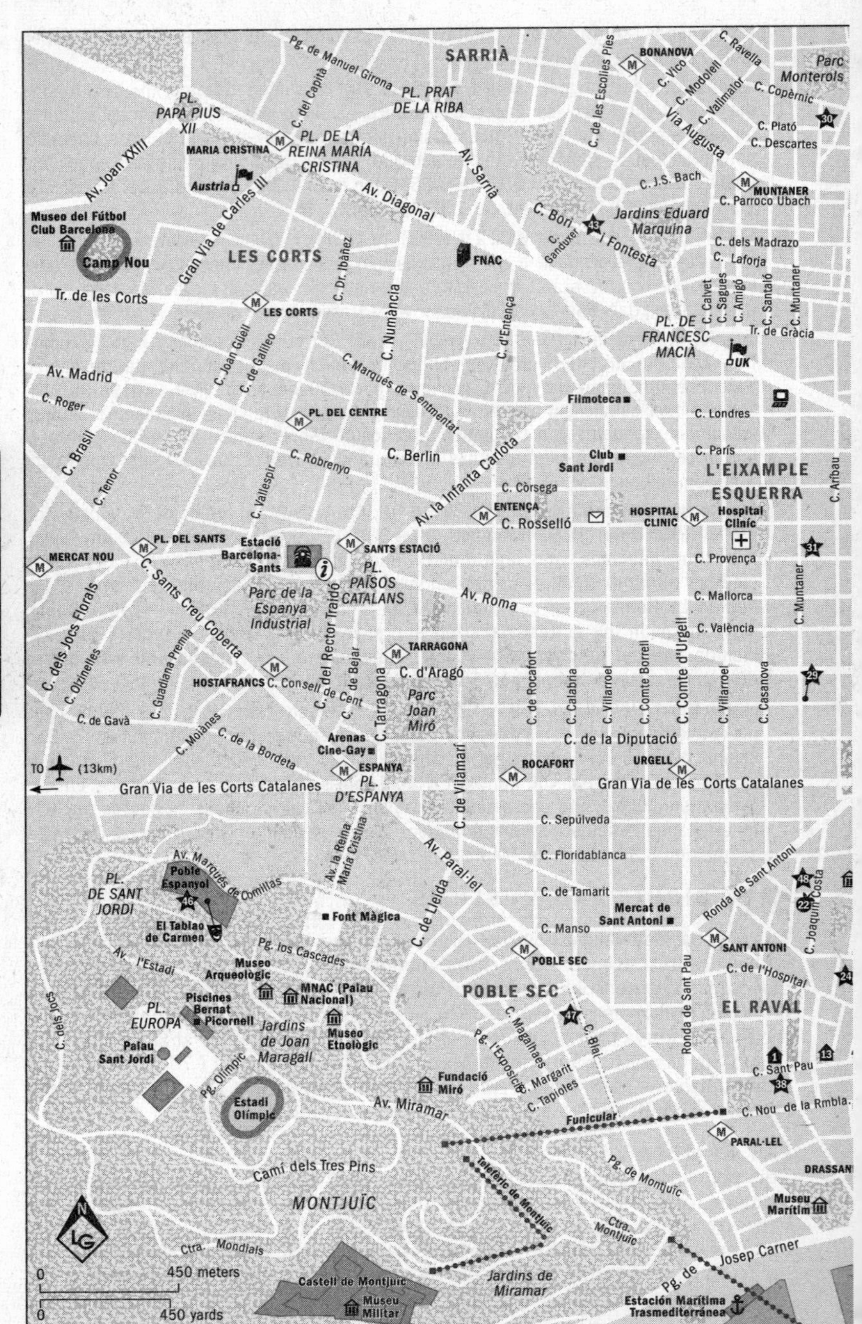
SARRIÀ
LES CORTS
L'EIXAMPLE ESQUERRA
POBLE SEC
EL RAVAL
MONTJUÏC
Pg. de Manuel Girona
PL. PRAT DE LA RIBA
PL. PAPA PIUS XII
PL. DE LA REINA MARÍA CRISTINA
MARIA CRISTINA
Austria
Av. Joan XXIII
Museo del Fútbol Club Barcelona
Camp Nou
Gran Via de Carles III
Av. Diagonal
Av. Sarrià
FNAC
BONANOVA
C. de les Escolies Pies
C. Vico
C. Modolell
C. Vallmalor
C. Ravella
Parc Monterols
C. Copèrnic
C. Plató
C. Descartes
Via Augusta
C. J.S. Bach
MUNTANER
C. Parroco Ubach
Jardins Eduard Marquina
C. Bori i Fontesta
C. Ganduxer
C. dels Madrazo
C. Laforja
C. Calvet
C. Sagues
C. Amigó
C. Santaló
C. Muntaner
Tr. de Gràcia
PL. DE FRANCESC MACIÀ
UK
Tr. de les Corts
LES CORTS
C. Dr. Ibáñez
C. Numància
C. d'Entença
C. Joan Güell
C. de Galileo
Av. Madrid
C. Roger
C. Marqués de Sentmenat
PL. DEL CENTRE
Filmoteca
C. Londres
C. París
C. Brasil
C. Tenor
C. Berlin
C. Robrenyo
Club Sant Jordi
Av. la Infanta Carlota
C. Còrsega
C. Vallespir
ENTENÇA
C. Rosselló
HOSPITAL CLINIC
Hospital Clinic
C. Aribau
PL. DEL SANTS
MERCAT NOU
Estació Barcelona-Sants
SANTS ESTACIÓ
PL. PAÏSOS CATALANS
C. Provença
C. Sants Creu Coberta
Parc de la Espanya Industrial
C. del Rector Triadó
Av. Roma
C. Mallorca
C. València
C. dels Jocs Florals
C. Olzinelles
C. Guadiana Premià
HOSTAFRANCS
C. Consell de Cent
C. de Bejar
TARRAGONA
C. d'Aragó
C. Tarragona
Parc Joan Miró
C. de Rocafort
C. Calabria
C. Villarroel
C. Comte Borrell
C. Comte d'Urgell
C. Casanova
C. de Gavà
C. Moianes
C. de la Bordeta
Arenas Cine-Gay
C. de la Diputació
TO (13km)
ESPANYA
PL. D'ESPANYA
ROCAFORT
URGELL
Gran Via de les Corts Catalanes
C. de Vilamarí
C. Sepúlveda
Av. la Reina Maria Cristina
Av. Paral·lel
C. Floridablanca
PL. DE SANT JORDI
Av. Marqués de Comillas
Poble Espanyol
El Tablao de Carmen
C. de Lleida
C. de Tamarit
Ronda de Sant Antoni
C. Joaquín Costa
Font Màgica
Mercat de Sant Antoni
C. Manso
SANT ANTONI
Pg. los Cascades
Av. l'Estadi
Museo Arqueològic
MNAC (Palau Nacional)
POBLE SEC
C. de l'Hospital
PL. EUROPA
Piscines Bernat Picornell
C. dels Jocs
Jardins de Joan Maragall
Museo Etnològic
C. Magalhaes
Pg. l'Exposició
C. Blai
Ronda de Sant Pau
Palau Sant Jordi
Pg. Olímpic
Estadi Olímpic
Fundació Miró
C. Margarit
C. Tapioles
C. Sant Pau
Av. Miramar
Funicular
C. Nou de la Rmbla.
PARAL·LEL
Camí dels Tres Pins
Telefèric de Montjuïc
Pg. de Montjuïc
DRASSAN
Museu Marítim
Ctra. Montjuïc
Ctra. Mondials
Pg. de Josep Carner
0 450 meters
0 450 yards
Castell de Montjuïc
Museu Militar
Jardins de Miramar
Estación Marítima Trasmediterránea
LG

SPAIN

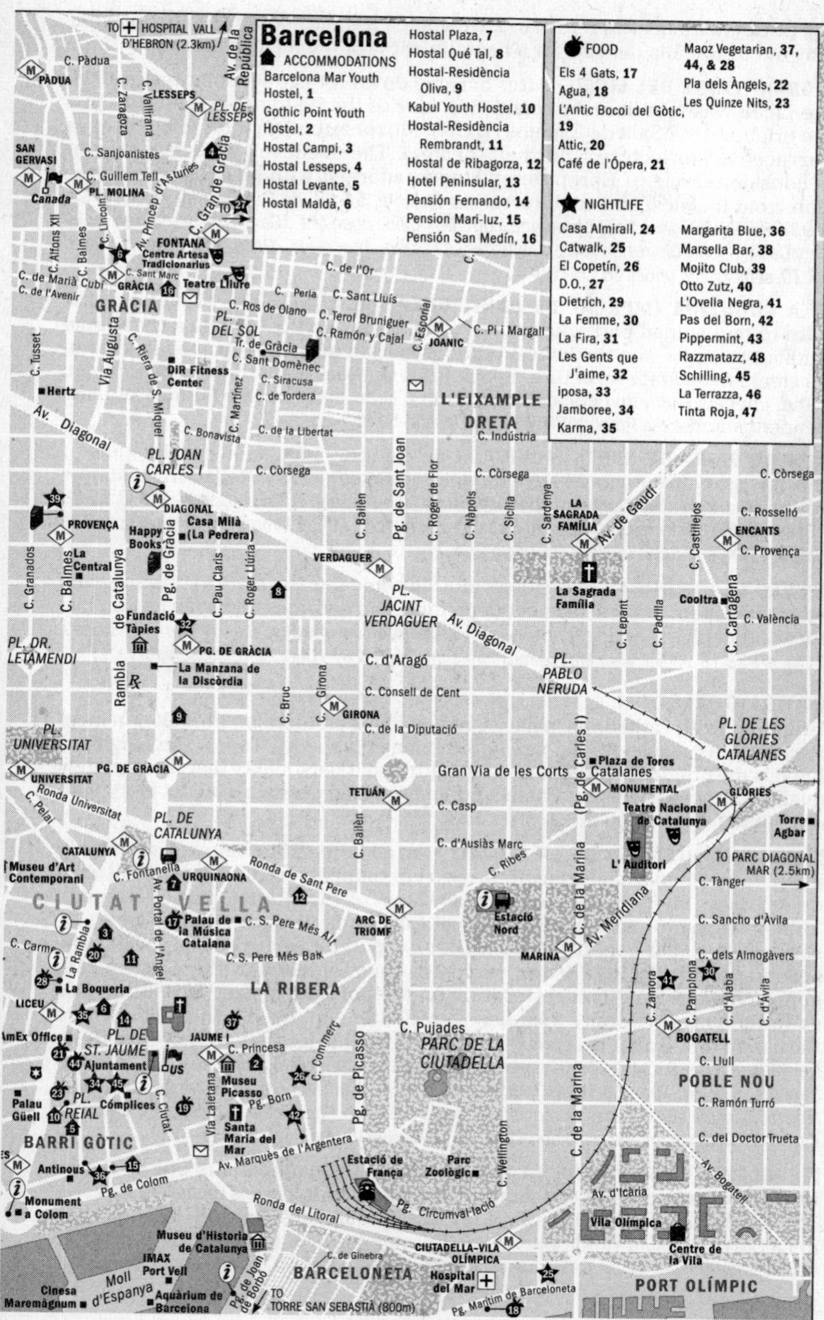
Barcelona
ACCOMMODATIONS
Barcelona Mar Youth Hostel, 1
Gothic Point Youth Hostel, 2
Hostal Campi, 3
Hostal Lesseps, 4
Hostal Levante, 5
Hostal Maldà, 6
Hostal Plaza, 7
Hostal Qué Tal, 8
Hostal-Residència Oliva, 9
Kabul Youth Hostel, 10
Hostal-Residència Rembrandt, 11
Hostal de Ribagorza, 12
Hotel Peninsular, 13
Pensión Fernando, 14
Pension Mari-luz, 15
Pensión San Medín, 16
FOOD
Els 4 Gats, 17
Agua, 18
L'Antic Bocoi del Gòtic, 19
Attic, 20
Café de l'Ópera, 21
Maoz Vegetarian, 37, 44, & 28
Pla dels Àngels, 22
Les Quinze Nits, 23
NIGHTLIFE
Casa Almirall, 24
Catwalk, 25
El Copetín, 26
D.O., 27
Dietrich, 29
La Femme, 30
La Fira, 31
Les Gents que J'aime, 32
iposa, 33
Jamboree, 34
Karma, 35
Margarita Blue, 36
Marsella Bar, 38
Mojito Club, 39
Otto Zutz, 40
L'Ovella Negra, 41
Pas del Born, 42
Pippermint, 43
Razzmatazz, 48
Schilling, 45
La Terrazza, 46
Tinta Roja, 47
TO HOSPITAL VALL D'HEBRON (2.3km)
Av. de la República
PÀDUA
LESSEPS
PL. DE LESSEPS
SAN GERVASI
Canada
PL. MOLINA
FONTANA
Centre Artesa Tradicionarius
GRÀCIA
Teatre Lliure
PL. DEL SOL
JOANIC
DIR Fitness Center
Hertz
L'EIXAMPLE DRETA
Av. Diagonal
PL. JOAN CARLES I
DIAGONAL
PROVENÇA
Casa Milà (La Pedrera)
Happy Books
La Central
VERDAGUER
PL. JACINT VERDAGUER
LA SAGRADA FAMÍLIA
La Sagrada Família
Av. de Gaudí
ENCANTS
Cooltra
Fundació Tàpies
PG. DE GRÀCIA
La Manzana de la Discòrdia
PL. DR. LETAMENDI
PL. PABLO NERUDA
GIRONA
PL. UNIVERSITAT
UNIVERSITAT
PL. DE LES GLÒRIES CATALANES
Gran Via de les Corts Catalanes
Plaza de Toros
MONUMENTAL
TETUÁN
GLÒRIES
Teatre Nacional de Catalunya
Torre Agbar
PL. DE CATALUNYA
CATALUNYA
Museu d'Art Contemporani
URQUINAONA
L' Auditori
TO PARC DIAGONAL MAR (2.5km)
CIUTAT VELLA
Palau de la Música Catalana
ARC DE TRIOMF
Estació Nord
MARINA
Av. Meridiana
La Boqueria
LA RIBERA
LICEU
PL. DE ST. JAUME
JAUME I
Ajuntament
US
AmEx Office
PARC DE LA CIUTADELLA
BOGATELL
POBLE NOU
Palau Güell
PL. REIAL
Còmplices
Museu Picasso
Santa Maria del Mar
BARRI GÒTIC
Antinous
Estació de França
Parc Zoològic
Av. Icària
Vila Olímpica
Monument a Colom
Ronda del Litoral
Museu d'Historia de Catalunya
CIUTADELLA-VILA OLÍMPICA
Centre de la Vila
IMAX Port Vell
BARCELONETA
Hospital del Mar
PORT OLÍMPIC
Cinesa Maremàgnum
Moll d'Espanya
Aquàrium de Barcelona
TO TORRE SAN SEBASTIÀ (800m)
Pg. Marítim de Barceloneta
C. Pàdua
C. Sanjoanistes
C. Guillem Tell
Av. Príncep d'Asturies
C. Gran de Gràcia
Via Augusta
C. Tusset
C. Bonavista
C. Còrsega
Pg. de Sant Joan
C. Rosselló
C. Provença
C. València
Rambla de Catalunya
Pg. de Gràcia
C. d'Aragó
C. Consell de Cent
C. de la Diputació
Ronda Universitat
C. Casp
C. d'Ausiàs Marc
Ronda de Sant Pere
C. Fontanella
Av. Portal de l'Àngel
C. de la Marina
La Rambla
Via Laietana
C. Princesa
Pg. Born
C. Pujades
Pg. de Picasso
C. Wellington
Av. Marquès de l'Argentera
Pg. de Colom
Pg. Circumval·lació
Av. Bogatell
C. Llull
C. Ramón Turró
C. del Doctor Trueta
C. Tànger
C. Sancho d'Àvila
C. dels Almogàvers

SPAIN

top of Las Ramblas will return to Barcelona. Pass the **Mirador de Colom** on your way out to Rambla del Mar for a beautiful view of the Mediterranean.

GRAN TEATRE DEL LICEU. After burning down for the second time in 1994, the Liceu was rebuilt and expanded; a tour of the building includes not just the original 1847 Sala de Espejos (Hall of Mirrors), but also the 1999 Foyer (a curvaceous bar/lecture hall/small theater). The five-level, 2292-seat theater is considered one of Europe's top stages, adorned with palatial ornamentation, gold facades, and sculptures. *(La Rambla, 51-59, by C. Sant Pau. ⓂLiceu, L3. ☎934 85 99 00; www.liceubarcelona.com. Box office open M-F 10am-1pm and 2-6pm or by ServiCaixa. Short 20min. non-guided visits daily 11:30am-1pm every 30min, €4. 1hr. tours 10am; €8.70, seniors and under 26 €6.70.)*

LA BOQUERIA (MERCAT DE SANT JOSEP). Just the place to pick up that hard-to-find animal part you've been looking for, La Boqueria is a traditional Catalan *mercat*—and the largest outdoor market in Spain—located in a giant, all-steel *Modernista* structure. Specialized vendors sell produce, fish, bread, wine, cheese, nuts, sweets and meat from a seemingly infinite number of independent stands. *(La Rambla, 89. ⓂLiceu. Open M-Sa 8am-8pm.)*

CENTRE D'ART DE SANTA MÓNICA. One can only imagine what the nuns of this former convent would have thought of the edgy art installations that now rotate through this large modern gallery. *(La Rambla, 7. ⓂDrassanes. ☎933 16 28 10; www.artsantamonica.cat. Open Tu-Sa noon-10pm. Free. Punt d'Informació Cultural open M-F 9:30am-2pm and 3:30-7:30pm, Sa 10am-2pm.)*

MUSEU DE L'ERÒTICA. Barcelona's most intrepid tourists flock to this museum, which houses an odd assortment of pictures and figurines that span human history and depict seemingly impossible **sexual acrobatics.** *(La Rambla, 96. ⓂLiceu, L1/3. ☎933 18 98 65; www.erotica-museum.com. Open daily 10am-9pm. €9, students €8.)*

SPAIN

BARRI GÒTIC

Brimming with cathedrals, palaces, and unabashed tourism, Barcelona's most ancient zone masks its old age with unflagging energy. Today, the neighborhood is the political center of the city, with a split personality that is alternately quaint and overwhelming. Catalan commercialism persists in all its glory with store-lined streets and fine restaurants.

MUSEU D'HISTÒRIA DE LA CIUTAT. Buried some 20m below a seemingly innocuous old plaza lies one of the two components to the Museu d'Història de la Ciutat: the subterranean excavations of the Roman city of Barcino. This 4000-square-meter **archaeological exhibit** displays incredibly well-preserved 1st- to 6th-century ruins. Built on top of those 4th-century walls, the second part, **Palau Reial Major,** served as the residence of the Catalan-Aragonese monarchs. When restoration on the building began, the Gothic **Saló de Tinell** (Throne Room) was discovered; it is supposedly the place where Fernando and Isabel received Columbus after his journey to America. *(Pl. del Rei. ⓂJaume I. ☎932 56 21 00; www.museuhistoria.bcn.cat. Wheelchair-accessible. Open Apr.-Sept. Tu-Sa 10am-8pm, Su 10am-3pm; Oct.-Mar. Tu-Sa 10am-2pm and 4-7pm, Su 10am-3pm. Free multilingual audio guides. Pamphlets available in English. Museum €6, students €4. Exhibition €1.80/1.10. Museum and exhibition €6.80/5.10. Under 16 free.)*

ESGLÉSIA CATEDRAL DE LA SANTA CREU. This cathedral is one of Barcelona's most recognizable monuments. The altar holds a cross designed by Frederic Marès in 1976, and the Crypt of Santa Eulàlia lies beneath. The museum in La Sala Capitular holds Bartolomé Bermejo's *Pietà*. *(ⓂJaume I, L4. In Pl. Seu, up C. Bisbe from Pl. St. Jaume. Cathedral open daily 8:30am-12:30pm, 1-5pm, and 5:15-7:30pm.*

Museum open daily 10am-12:30pm, 1-5pm, and 5:15-7pm. Elevator to the roof open M-Sa 10am-12:30pm and 1-6pm. Services Su at noon and 6:30pm. From 1-5pm €5 (includes cathedral, elevator, and museum), otherwise free. Museum €2. Elevator €2.50.)

LA RIBERA

This neighborhood has recently evolved into an artsy nucleus, with art galleries, chic eateries, and exclusive bars. La Ribera's streets are even closer together than those in the Barri Gòtic, but feels much less congested.

PALAU DE LA MÚSICA CATALANA. In 1891, the Orfeó Català Choir Society commissioned *Modernista* master Luis Domènech i Montaner to design this must-see concert venue. By day, the music hall is illuminated by tall stained-glass windows and an ornate stained-glass skylight, which gleam again after dark by electric light. Sculptures of wild horses and busts of the seven muses are on the walls flanking the stage. The **Sala de Luis Millet** has an up close view of the intricate *trencadis* pillars. *(C. del Palau de la Música, 4-6. ☎902 44 28 82; www.palaumusica.org. Ⓜ Jaume I, Urinaona. Mandatory 50min. tours in English every hr. Open daily Sept.-July 10am-3:30pm, Semana Santa and Aug. 10am-6pm. €12, students and seniors €11. Check website for scheduled performances. Concert tickets €8-175. Box office open 9am-9pm. MC/V.)*

MUSEU PICASSO. Barcelona's most visited museum traces Picasso's artistic development with the world's most comprehensive collection of work from his formative Barcelona period. Picasso donated 1700 of the museum's 3600 works. *(C. de Montcada, 15-23. Ⓜ Jaume I, L4. From the metro, head down C. de la Princesa and turn right on C. de Montcada. ☎932 56 30 00; www.museupicasso.bcn.es. Open Tu-Su 10am-8pm. Last entry 30min. before closing. Wheelchair-accessible. €9, students and seniors €6, under 16 free. Special exhibits €5.80. Free Su after 3pm. 1st Su of each month free.)*

PARC DE LA CIUTADELLA. Host of the 1888 World's Fair, the park harbors several museums, well-labeled horticulture, the Cascada fountains, a pond, and a zoo. The sprawling lawns are filled with strolling families, students smoking and playing instruments, and affectionate couples. Buildings of note include Domènech i Montaner's *Modernista* **Castell dels Tres Dracs** (now the Museu de Zoología) and Josep Amergós's **Hivernacle.** The **Parc Zoològic** is home to several threatened and endangered species, including the Iberian wolf and the Sumatran tiger. *(Ⓜ Ciutadella or Marina. Park open daily 8am-11pm)*

MUSEU DE LA XOCOLATA (CHOCOLATE MUSEUM). The museum presents gobs of information about the history, production, and ingestion of this sensuous sweet. Chocolate sculptures include La Sagrada Família and football star Ronaldo. The cafe offers tasting and baking workshops. *(Pl. Pons i Clerch, C. del Comerç, 26. Ⓜ Jaume I. ☎932 68 78 78; www.museudelaxocolata.com. Open M and W-Sa 10am-7pm, Su 10am-3pm. €4.30, students and seniors €3.70, with Barcelona Card €3, under 7 free. Alcohol and chocolate tasting €7.70; reservations required. Workshops for kids from €5.40; reservations required.)*

EL RAVAL

Located next to Las Ramblas and the Barri Gòtic, the northern part of El Raval is a favorite among Barcelona's natives rather than its tourists. The southern portion of the area is home to many Indian and Middle Eastern immigrants. This diverse and mostly working-class neighborhood has a special charm, with quirky shops and eateries, welcoming bars, and hidden historical attractions. In the late 19th and early 20th centuries, overcrowding here led to an urban nightmare of rampant crime, prostitution, and drug use. Revitalization efforts, especially since the 1992 Olympic Games, have cleaned up the neighborhood.

MUSEU D'ART CONTEMPORANI (MACBA). The MACBA has received worldwide acclaim for its focus on post-avant-garde art and contemporary works. The main attractions are the highly innovative rotating exhibits and the *Nits de MACBA*, when the museum stays open until midnight for concerts and guided tours—tickets are cheap. *(Pl. Des Àngels, 1. M: Catalunya ☎934 12 08 10; www.macba.es. Open M and W-F 11am-8pm, Sa 10am-8pm, Su 10am-3pm. Tours in Catalan and English M and Th 6pm; Catalan and Spanish W and F 6pm, Su noon and 6pm. €7.50, students €6, under 14 free; temporary exhibitions €4. From mid-May to Sept. restaurant and bar service on 1st-fl. terrace. Restaurant and bar phone ☎672 20 73 89.)*

PALAU GÜELL. Gaudí's 1886 Palau Güell, the Modernist residence built for patron Eusebi Güell, has one of Barcelona's most spectacular interiors. Güell spared no expense on this house, considered to be the first example of Gaudí's revolutionary style. At the time of writing the Palau is closed for renovations until an undisclosed date. *(C. Nou de La Rambla, 3-5. M: Liceu. ☎933 17 39 74; www.palauguell.cat. Partial entrance only. Open Tu-Sa 10am-2:30pm. Free.)*

CENTRE DE CULTURA CONTEMPORÀNIA DE BARCELONA (CCCB). The center stands out for its mixture of architectural styles, incorporating an early 20th-century theater with a sleek wing of black glass. CCCB has a bookstore, a cafe, gallery space, and screening room. It's also the main daytime venue for the **Sonar Music Festival;** check the *Guía del Ocio* for scheduled events. *(asa de Caritat. C. Montalegre, 5. M: Catalunya or Universitat. ☎933 06 41 00; www.cccb.org. Open Tu-W and F-Su 11am-8pm, Th 11am-10pm. Expositions €4.70, students €3.60, under 16 free. 2 expositions for €6. 1st W of the month, Th 8-10pm and Su 3-8pm free.)*

SPAIN

L'EIXAMPLE

The Catalan Renaissance and Barcelona's 19th-century growth pushed the city past its medieval walls and into modernity. **Ildefons Cerdà** drew up a plan for a new neighborhood where people of all social classes could live side by side; however, l'Eixample (luh-SHOMP-luh) did not thrive as a utopian community but became a playground for the bourgeoisie. Despite gentrification, L'Eixample remains an innovative neighborhood full of *Modernista* oddities.

LA SAGRADA FAMÍLIA. Antoni Gaudí's masterpiece is far from finished, which makes La Sagrada Família the world's most visited construction site. Only 8 of the 18 planned towers have been completed and the church still lacks an "interior," yet millions of people make the touristic pilgrimage to witness its work-in-progress majesty. Of the three facades, only the **Nativity Facade** was finished under Gaudí. A new team of architects led by Jordi Bonet hopes to lay the last stone by 2026 (the 100th anniversary of Gaudí's death). The affiliated museum displays plans and computer models of the fully realized structure. *(C. Mallorca, 401. ☎932 08 04 14; www.sagradafamilia.org. Ⓜ Sagrada Família. Open daily Apr.-Sept. 9am-8pm, Oct.-Mar. 9am-6pm. Last elevator to the tower 15min. before close. Guided tours in English (€3) May-Oct. at 11am, 1, 3, 5pm; Nov.-Apr. at 11am and 1pm. €11, students €9, under 10 free. Elevator €2.50. Combined ticket with Casa-Museu Gaudí €13, students €11.)*

LA MANZANA DE LA DISCÒRDIA. A short walk from Pl. de Catalunya, the odd-numbered side of Pg. de Gràcia between C. Aragó and C. Consell de Cent has been leaving passersby scratching their heads for a century. The Spanish nickname, which translates to the "block of discord," comes from the stylistic clashing of its three most extravagant buildings. Sprouting flowers, stained glass, and legendary doorway sculptures adorn **Casa Lleó i Morera,** #35, by Domènech i Montaner, on the far left corner of the block (admire from the outside; entrance is not permitted). Two buildings down, Puig i Cadafalch's geometric, Moorish-influenced facade makes **Casa Amatller,** #41, perhaps the most beautiful building on the block (guided tour with chocolate tasting M-F 4 per day 11am-6pm, Su at noon; €8). The real discord comes next door at **Casa Batlló,** #43, popularly believed to represent Catalonia's patron Sant Jordi (St. Jordi) slaying a dragon. The chimney plays the lance, the scaly roof is the dragon's back, and the bony balconies are the remains of his victims. The house was built using shapes from nature—the balconies ripple like the ocean. *(Pg. de Gràcia, 43. ☎932 16 03 06; www.casabatllo.cat. Open daily 9am-8pm. €17, students, BCN card €13. Cash only. Call for group discounts for more than 20 people. Free multilingual audio tour.)*

CASA MILÀ (LA PEDRERA). From the outside, this Gaudí creation looks like the sea—the undulating walls seem like waves and the iron balconies are reminiscent of seaweed. Chimneys resembling armored soldiers have views of every corner of Barcelona. The entrance fee entitles visitors to tour one well-equipped apartment, the roof, and the winding brick attic, now functioning as the **Espai Gaudí,** a multimedia presentation of Gaudí's life and works. The summer concert series transforms the roof into a jazz cabaret on weekend nights. *(Pg. de Gràcia, 92. ☎902 40 09 73; www.lapedreraeducacio.org. Open daily Mar.-Oct. 9am-8pm, last admission 7:30pm; Nov.-Feb. 9am-6:30pm. €9.50, students and seniors €5.50. Free audio tour. Concerts last weekend of June-July F-Sa 9pm-midnight. €12, glass of cava included.)*

FUNDACIÓ ANTONI TÀPIES. Less than 20 years old, this museum has a floor devoted to **Antoni Tàpies,** a Barcelonese sculptor and painter. But the real attractions are the rotating exhibitions on the two lower floors, which feature some of the world's best modern photography and video art as well as film screenings and lectures. In summer, DJ nights on the terrace have free drinks and after-hours gallery access. *(C. Aragó, 255. ☎934 87 03 15. ⓂPg. de Gràcia. Closed for renovation as of summer 2009. Call for more information.)*

SPAIN

MONTJUÏC

Historically, whoever controlled Montjuïc (mon-joo-EEK; "Hill of the Jews") controlled the city. Dozens of rulers have occupied and modified the **Castell de Montjuïc,** a fortress built atop an ancient Jewish cemetery. Franco made it one of his "interrogation" headquarters. Today, the area is home to a park and **Poble Espanyol,** a recreation of famous buildings and sights from all regions of Spain.

FUNDACIÓ MIRÓ. An large collection of sculptures, drawings, and paintings from Miró's career, ranging from sketches to wall-sized canvases, engages visitors with the work of this Barcelona-born artist. His best-known pieces here include *El carnival de Arlequín, La masia,* and *L'or de l'Azuz.* The gallery also displays experimental work by young artists and pieces by Alexander Calder. *(Take the funicular from M: Paral·lel or catch the Park Montjuïc bus from Pl. Espanya. ☎934 43 94 70; www.fundaciomiro-bcn.org. Library open M and Sa 10am-2pm, Tu-F 10am-2pm and 3-6pm. Fundació open July-Sept. Tu-W and F-Sa 10am-8pm, Th 10am-9:30pm, Su and holidays 10am-2:30pm; Oct.-June Tu-W and F-Sa 10am-7pm, Th 10am-9:30pm, Su and holidays 10am-2:30pm. Last entry 15min. before closing. €8, students and seniors €6, under 13 €4. Temporary exhibitions €4/3/4. Headphones €4. Concert tickets €10.)*

MUSEU NACIONAL D'ART DE CATALUNYA (PALAU NACIONAL). Designed by Enric Catà and Pedro Cendoya for the 1929 International Exposition, the magnificent Palau Nacional has housed the Museu Nacional d'Art de Catalunya (MNAC) since 1934. Its main hall is a public event space, while the wings are home to the world's finest collection of Catalan Romanesque art and a wide variety of Gothic pieces. Highlights include Miró's *Gorg Bleu* stained glass, a gallery of Romanesque cathedral apses, and works by Joaquím Mir, a modernist painter known for color-saturated landscapes. The museum recently acquired the entire holdings of the Museu d'Art Modern, formerly located in the Parc de la Ciutadella, and is now the principal art museum of Catalonia. The **Fonts Luminoses** and the central **Font Màgica** are lit up by weekend laser shows. *(From M: Espanya, walk up Av. Reina María Cristina, away from the twin brick towers, and take the escalators to the top. ☎936 22 03 76; www.mnac.es. Open Tu-Sa 10am-7pm, Su and holidays 10am-2:30pm. Wheelchair-accessible. €8.50, students and seniors €6, under 14 free. First Su of the month free. Audio tour included.)*

WATERFRONT

MUSEU D'HISTÒRIA DE CATALUNYA. The last gasp of the Old City before entering the tourist trap of Barceloneta, the Museu provides an exhaustive and patriotic introduction to Catalan history, politics, and culture. There is a particularly good section devoted to Franco. Exhibits include recreations of a 1930s Spanish bar and an 8th-century Islamic prayer tent. *(Pl. Pau Vila, 3. Near entrance to the Moll d'Espanya; left walk out toward Barceloneta. ☎932 25 47 00; www.mhcat.com. Open Tu and Th-Sa 10am-7pm, W 10am-8pm, Su 10am-2:30pm. €4; under 18 and students €3; university students, under 7, and over 65 free. Free 1st Su of the month.)*

VILA OLÍMPICA. The Vila Olímpica, beyond the east side of the zoo, was built to house 15,000 athletes and entertain millions of tourists for the 1992 Summer Olympics. It's home to several public parks, a shopping center, and offices. In nearby **Barceloneta,** beaches stretch out from the old port. *(M: Ciutadella or Vila Olímpica. Walk along the water on Ronda Litoral toward the 2 towers.)*

SPAIN

ZONA ALTA

Zona Alta (Uptown) is the section of Barcelona that lies at the top of most maps: past l'Eixample, in and around the Collserola Mountains, and away from the low-lying waterfront districts. The most visited part of Zona Alta is Gràcia, which packs a surprising number of *Modernista* buildings and parks, international cuisine, and chic shops into a relatively small area.

PARC GÜELL. This fantastical park was designed entirely by Gaudí but, in typical Gaudí fashion, was not completed until after his death. Gaudí intended Parc Güell to be a garden city, and its buildings and ceramic-mosaic stairways were designed to house the city's elite. However, only one house, now know as the **Casa-Museu Gaudí,** was built. Two staircases flank the park, leading to a towering *Modernista* pavilion originally designed as an open-air market but is now only occasionally used as a stage by street musicians. The longest park bench in the world, a multicolored serpentine wonder made of tile shards, decorates the top of the pavilion. *(Bus #24 from Pl. Catalunya stops at the upper entrance. Info center ☎93 284 62 00. Park and info center open daily 9am-dusk. Free.)*

MUSEU DEL FÚTBOL CLUB BARCELONA. A close second to the Picasso Museum as Barcelona's most-visited museum, the FCB merits all the attention it gets from football fanatics. Fans will appreciate the storied history of the team. The high point is entering the stadium and taking in the 100,000-seat **Camp Nou.** (*Next to the stadium. ☎93 496 3608. M: Collblanc. Enter through access gate 7 or 9. Open M-Sa 10am-6:15pm, Su and holidays 10am-2pm. €8.50, students and 13 or under €7. Museum and Camp Nou tour €13/10.40. Free parking.*)

ENTERTAINMENT

For tips on entertainment, nightlife, and food, pick up the *Guía del Ocio* (www.guiadelociobcn.es; €1) at any newsstand. The best shopping in the city is in the **Barri Gòtic,** but if you feel like dropping some extra cash, check out the posh **Passeig de Gràcia** in l'Eixample. Grab face paint to join fans of F.C. Barcelona (Barça) at the Camp Nou stadium for **fútbol.** (Box office C. Arístedes Maillol

12-18. ☎90 218 99 00. Tickets €30-60.) **Barceloneta** and **Poble Nou** feature specific sand for topless tanning and many places to rent sailboats and water-sports equipment. Head up to Montjuïc to take advantage of the **Olympic Facilities,** which are now open for public use, including **Piscines Bernat Picornell,** a gorgeous pool complex. (Av. de l'Estadi 30-40. ☎93 423 4041. Open M-F 6:45am-midnight, Sa 7am-9pm, Su 6am-4pm.)

MOONLIGHT MOVIES AT MONTJUIC. For a movie under the stars, head up the hill to Sala Montjuïc, an annual 5-week film series in the moat of Castell de Montjuïc. Bring a picnic and listen to live music before the show.

FESTIVALS

Check sight and museum hours during festival times, as well as during the Christmas season and *Semana Santa* (Holy Week). The **Festa de Sant Jordi** (St. George; Apr. 23, 2009) celebrates Catalunya's patron saint with a feast. Men give women roses, and women give men books. In the last two weeks of August, city folk jam at Gràcia's **Festa Mayor;** lights blaze in *plaças* and music plays all night. The three-day **Sónar** music festival comes to town in mid-June, attracting renowned DJs and electronica enthusiasts from all over the world. Other major music festivals include **Summercase** (indie and pop) and **Jazzaldia**. Check www.mondosonoro.com or pick up the *Mondo Sonoro* festival guide for more info. In July and August, the **Grec Festival** hosts dance performances, concerts, and film screenings. The **Festa Nacional de Catalunya** (Sept. 11) brings traditional costumes and dancing. **Festa de Sant Joan** takes place the night of June 23; ceaseless fireworks will prevent any attempts to sleep. The largest celebration in Barcelona is the **Festa de Mercè,** the weeks before and after September 24 when *barceloneses* revel with fireworks, *sardana* dancing, and concerts.

SPAIN

NIGHTLIFE

Barcelona's wild, varied nightlife treads the line between slick and kitschy. In many ways, the city is clubbing heaven—things don't get going until late (don't bother showing up at a club before 1am), and they continue until dawn. Yet for every full-blown dance club, there are 100 more relaxed bars, from Irish pubs to absinthe dens. Check the *Guía del Ocio* (www.guiadelocio.com) for the address of that place your hip *Barcelonese* friend just told you about.

DON'T FEAR FLYERS. Many clubs hand out flyers, particularly in La Ribera. They are far from a tourist trap—travelers can save lots of money with free admission and drink passes.

BARRI GÒTIC

Main streets like C. Ferran have *cervecerías* and *bar-restaurantes* every five steps. C. Escudellers is the location for post-bar dancing, while Pl. Reial remains packed until the early morning. Las Ramblas becomes a little questionable at night, as prostitutes emerge where families roamed in the daylight.

El Bosq de les Fades, Pg. de la Banca, 16 (☎933 17 26 49), near the Wax Museum. Ⓜ Drassanes. This spooky cafe-bar used to be the horror section of the Wax Museum and retains a fairytale look, with gnarled trees, gourd-lanterns, and a wishing well. Fills up early, so it's a good place to start the night. Beer €3. *Cava* €3. Tequila Sunrise €7.20. Open M-Th and Su 10am-1am, F-Sa 10am-2am. MC/V.

Barcelona Pipa Club, Pl. Reial, 3 (☎933 02 47 32; www.bpipaclub.com). ⓂLiceu, L3. Unmarked—look for the small plaque on the door to the left of Glaciar Bar, on your left as you enter the square from Las Ramblas, and ring the doorbell. Don't let the pseudo-secrecy deter you. A welcoming place for late-night drinks. The decor is 100% Sherlock Holmes, the music mostly jazz and fusion, and the people are a mix of local bartenders, artists, and tourists in the know. An impressive collection of pipes from around the world is housed in a side-room along with a small pool table (€1.50 a game). Live music (often jazz) F 11pm. Mixed drinks €7, beer €4. Open daily 11pm-4:30am. Cash only.

Shangó, C. d'En Groch, 2 (☎662 10 51 65). ⓂJaume I. Walk down Via Laietana and take a right on C. d'Àngel Baixeras. Continue as it turns into C. Gignàs and take a right on the small C. d'en Groch. This colorful bar blasts Latin beats and attracts young locals with its delicious mojitos (€6). Free salsa classes Tu and W at 11pm. Beer from €2.20. Happy hour 9-11pm. Open daily 9pm-3am. Cash only.

Smoll Bar, C. Comtesa de Sobradiel, 9. ⓂLiceu, L3. Between Pl. Reial and Via Laietana. As promised, this chic, neon-lit bar is quite small, and fills up quickly and reliably. Be prepared to get cozy with a young, mostly gay crowd. Beer €3.50. Mixed drinks €6-7. Open M-Th 9:30pm-2:30am, F-Sa 9:30pm-3am. Cash only.

Sincopa, C. Avinyò, 35. ⓂLiceu, L3. Coming from Las Ramblas, take a right off C. Ferran. Bright, instrument-laden walls enclose a lively young crowd. Always blasting music, mostly Latin. When the upside-down musicians on the ceiling orient themselves you know you've had too much to drink. Wine €3. Mixed drinks €7. Open daily 6pm-3am. Cash only.

LA RIBERA AND EL RAVAL

La Ribera has become a hip, artsy district, attracting young locals and tourists in the know. The streets of El Raval hold a place for every variety of bar-hopper—Irish pubbers, American backpackers, absinthe aficionados, lounge lizards, and foosball maniacs will find themselves at home. Keep in mind that the depths of El Raval see less tourism and wandering there late at night is not advised.

El Copetín, Pg. del Born, 19 (☎607 20 21 76). ⓂJaume I. Cuban rhythms invade this casual, dimly lit nightspot. Copetín fills up before some places open, making it a good place to start the night. When the bartenders break out the maracas and cowbell, be ready to get down. Mojitos €7. Open M-Th and Su 6pm-2:30am, F-Sa 6pm-3am. Cash only.

Ribborn, C. Antic de Sant Joan, 3 (☎933 10 71 48; www.ribborn.com). ⓂBarceloneta. Deep crimson light and an eclectic music selection, from jazz to funk to soul. Beer €2.50. Mixed drinks €7. Jazz piano W 9pm. Happy hour Tu-Sa 7-10pm. Open Tu-Su 7pm-3am. MC/V.

El Born, Pg. del Born, 26 (☎933 19 53 33). ⓂJaume I. Sit at the marble counter over the basins where they used to sell fish or follow the tiny spiral staircase for more casual seating. Free Wi-Fi. Beer €2. Open Tu-Su 10am-2:30am. MC/V over €10.

Pitin Bar, Pg. del Born, 34 (☎93 319 59 87; www.pitinbar.com). ⓂJaume I. A shiny interior on the 1st floor and a cozy attic upstairs fill up nightly with the young and the young-at-heart. Start off with a beer (€2.50) and if that doesn't do enough for you, contemplate a shot of absinthe (€3.50). Or just skip right to the absinthe. Open Sept.-May Tu-Su 10am-2am, June-Aug. daily 10am-2am. Cash only.

Alma, C. de Sant Antoni dels Sombrerers, 7 (☎933 19 76 07). ⓂJaume I. The tattoos and body piercings on display in this bar rival its dramatic red decor. Come during happy hour (8:30-9:30pm) to snag €4 mixed drinks and €8 pitchers of sangria. Open M-Th and Su 8:30pm-2:30am, F-Sa 8:30pm-3am. Cash only.

No Se, Pg. del Born, 29 (☎671 48 59 14). ⓂJaume I. Walk down C. Princesa, make a right onto C. Montcada, and follow it until Pg. del Born. Perhaps in keeping with its laid-back name, this bar doesn't try as hard as some of its competitors on the busy Pg. del Born. The intimate space has a few canvases thrown up on the walls and a relaxing ambience. Mixed drinks €8-10. Open daily 8pm-2:30am. MC/V.

Kama, C. del Rec, 69 (☎932 68 10 29; www.kamabar.com). ⓂBarceloneta. Walk up Pl. del Palau, make a right on Av. del Marqués de l'Argentera, and a left on C. del Rec; the bar is on the right. Kama means "desire" in Sanskrit. At this fuschia-lit restaurant, you'll find what you desire—assuming that it's Indian dishes like *kheema mutter* and*palak paneer,* mixed drinks, and a sharp, cosmopolitan ambience. Lunch *menù* €10. Entrees €15-26. Mixed drinks €8-10. Open M 8:30pm-midnight, Tu-Sa 1-4pm and 8:30pm-midnight, Su 8:30pm-midnight. MC/V.

L'EIXAMPLE

Home to some of Europe's best gay nightlife, L'Eixample is dotted with upscale bars. Get to know the **NitBus** schedule or bring money for a taxi home.

Zeltas, C. Casanova, 75 (☎934 50 84 69; www.zeltas.net). Complete with shimmering cloth hangings, feather boas, and low white couches, this exotic bar welcomes a classy clientele—usually gay—to sip a drink and enjoy the ambience. Wine €3. Beer €4.50. Mixed drinks €7. Open daily 10:30pm-3am. MC/V.

Les Gents que J'aime, C. València, 286, downstairs (☎932 15 68 79). ⓂPg. de Gràcia. You'll feel like Serge Gainsbourg at his hippest lounging in this dark, subterranean bar's velvet furniture. Background soul, funk, and jazz soothe patrons enjoying drinks like Les Gents (kiwi, lime, and pineapple juice; €7). Shotgun the chairs tucked beneath the staircase. Beer €4. Mixed drinks €6-7. Open daily 7pm-2:30am. AmEx/MC/V.

Espit Chupitos (Aribau), C. Aribau, 77 (www.espitchupitos.com). ⓂUniversitat. From Pl. de la Universitat, walk up C. Aribau. Colloquially known as "The Chupito Bar" (the bar has grown so popular that there are actually now three locations in Barcelona), this bar serves shots with flair. Servers perform when delivering so-called spectacle shots (€2): the Harry Potter shot involves lighting the bar on fire and the Monica Lewinsky shot...well, let's just say it's best ordered for an unsuspecting friend. Other locations at Carrer de la Unió 35 and Passeig de Colom 8. Open M-Th and Su 8pm-2:30am, F and Sa 8pm-3am. MC/V.

Dietrich Gay Teatro Cafe, C. Consell de Cent, 255 (☎934 51 77 07). ⓂUniversitat or Pg. de Gràcia. An unflattering caricature of a semi-nude Marlene Dietrich greets patrons at this inclusive gay bar. Beer €3.50. Mixed drinks €6. Drag shows, acrobatics, and dancing; check with the restaurant ahead of time. Open M-Th and Su 6pm-2am, F-Sa midnight-3am. MC/V.

La Chapelle, C. Mutaner, 67 (☎934 53 30 76). ⓂUniversitat. Walk up C. Mutaner. La Chapelle's decor juxtaposes antique devotional carvings with ultra-modern bubble lights. Gay-friendly. Beer €2.50. Mixed drinks €5. Open daily 4pm-2am. MC/V.

MONTJUÏC

Lower Montjuïc is home to **Poble Espanyol,** Av. Marqués de Comillas, a recreation of famous buildings and sights from all regions of Spain. At night the complex becomes a disco theme park that offers some of the craziest clubbing experiences in all of Barcelona. (☎93 508 6300; www.poble-espanyol.com. M: Espa-

SPAIN

nya.) When Poble Espanyol closes, buses take serious party animals to "los afters"—clubs open 6am-7pm, such as the popular **Merci** and **Souvenir.**

Tinta Roja, C. Creus dels Molers, 17 (☎934 43 32 43; www.tintaroja.net). Located just off Av. Paral·lel in a newly pedestrian section of Poble Sec. Red tinted lights, red velvet chairs. The dance floor gets serious, especially during tango classes W 9-10:30pm, (call for details). Specialties include tropical mixed drinks (€7) and Argentine *yerba-mate* (€4.80) Open Th 9:30pm-2:30am, F-Sa 9:30pm-3am. Cash only.

La Terrazza, Avda. Marquès de Comillas, s/n (☎932 72 49 80). On weekend summer nights, Poble Espanyol succumbs to the irrepressible revelry of La Terrazza, an outdoor dance club to one side of the village where you can sway along to techno with the masses. Get here after 2am and you may find yourself in a line of up to 100. Beer €6. Mixed drinks €9-10, although bars scattered in Poble Espanyol stay open late and serve cheaper alcohol. Cover €18, gets you into the village and club, plus 1 drink. Open June-Oct. Th midnight-5am, F-Sa midnight-6am. MC/V.

WATERFRONT

Once mostly a wasteland of old factories and warehouses, **Poble Nou** and **Port Olímpic** today are home to docked sailboats, restaurants, and a long strip of nightclubs that draws crowds long into the night. The entire waterfront area, which stretches all the way from **Maremàgnum** to **Port Vell,** may be as hedonistic and touristy as Barcelona gets. Come nightfall, Maremàgnum, the city's biggest mall, turns into a tri-level maze of clubs packed with crowds even on weeknights. There is no cover at the Maremàgnum clubs; they make their money by charging exorbitant drink prices (beer €6; mixed drinks €9-11). With so many people, catching a cab home can be difficult.

SPAIN

Absenta, C. Sant Carles, 36. ⓂBarceloneta. Walking down Pg. Joan de Borbó and take a left on C. Sant Carles. A green interior with vintage posters suits the star beverage at this absinthe bar, although most choose to sit out on the terrace during summer. Beer €2.50. Wine €2.80. Absinthe €4-7. Open M, W-Th, and Su 11am-2am, Tu 6pm-2am, F-Sa 11am-3am. Cash only.

Ke?, C. del Beluart, 54. (☎932 24 15 88) ⓂBarceloneta. Walking down Pg. Joan de Borbó, take a left on C. Sant Carles and another left at the plaza onto C. del Beluart. Decor meanders between tropical surf, the American west, and Popeye the Sailor. Hosts an equally eclectic crowd, from rowdy beachgoers to locals using the Wi-Fi on the back sofa over a beer (€2). Open daily 11:30am-2:30am. Cash only.

Opium Mar, Pg. Marítim de la Barceloneta, 34 (☎902 26 74 86; www.opiummar.com). The indoor-outdoor restaurant serves seafood until 1am, at which point the DJ starts blasting house music and the place turns into a glitzy, colorful club. When they aren't platform-dancing, bikini-clad waitresses serve drinks as chic patrons bust a move. Beer €8. Mixed drinks €10-15. Wheelchair-accessible. Cover €20 includes one drink. Restaurant open daily 1pm-1am. Club open M-Th and Su midnight-5am, F-Sa 1am-6am. AmEx/MC/V.

GRÀCIA

Gràcia is all about busy-but-intimate bars—the kind of venues where you run into friends and have to raise your voice to talk with them. If you feel a bit more adventurous, head to **Plaça de la Revolució de Septiembre 1868** or **Plaça del Sol** and take it from there; in this young, vibrant neighborhood, you really can't go wrong..

Vinil, C. Matilde, 2 (☎669 17 79 45; www.vinilus.blogspot.com). This bar's dim orange lighting, mismatched pillows, mellow background music, and screened daily movies make you never want to leave. Beer and wine €2.70. Mojitos and *caipirinhas* (the only mixed drinks served) €6. Open in summer M-Th 8pm-2am, F-Sa 8pm-3am; in winter M-Th and Su 8pm-2am, F-Sa 8pm-3am.

Cafe del Sol, Pl. del Sol, 16 (☎932 37 14 48). ⓂFontana. Walk down C. Gran de Gràcia, make a left on C. Ros de Olano and then a right on C. Cano/C.Leopoldo Alas. Locals pack the 8 tapas bars around Pl. del Sol every night and spill out into the plaza. This mainstay offers perfect tostadas (€3-5) and tapas (€1.70-5) as well as beer (€2-3), wine, and mixed drinks (€5-6). Come for lunch and take your tapas out into the plaza. Open M-Th and Su noon-2:30am, F and Sa noon-3am.

Nictalia, C. St. Domenec, 15 (☎932 37 23 23). ⓂFontana. Walk down C. Gran de Gràcia to C. St. Domenec and make a left; Nictalia is 2 blocks down on the left. Step into this intimate bar and feel the magic—it's got blue fairy lights, purple walls, and colorful chalkboards (not to mention a buzzing crowd of locals and cheap shots). Beer €2-3. Mixed drinks €5. Shots €1.80. Open M-Th 6:30pm-2am, F and Sa 6pm-3am. Cash only.

NAVARRA

PAMPLONA (IRUÑA) ☎948

El encierro, la Fiesta de San Fermín, the Running of the Bulls, utter debauchery: call it what you will, the outrageous festival of the city's patron saint is the principal cause of the international notoriety Pamplona (pop. 200,000) enjoys. Since the city's immortalization in Ernest Hemingway's *The Sun Also Rises*, hordes of travelers have flocked to Pamplona for one week each July to witness the daily *corridas* and ensuing chaos. The city's monuments, museums, and parks merit exploration as well.

TRANSPORTATION AND PRACTICAL INFORMATION. **Trains** (☎902 24 02 02) run from Estación RENFE. To travel the two kilometers take the #9 bus from Po. Sarasate to the station, (20 mins., €1, buses every 15 min., Av. de San Jorge, to Barcelona (6-8hr., 3 per day, from €36), Madrid (3hr., 4 per day, €52), and San Sebastián (1hr., 5 per day, €19). **Buses** leave from the bus station by the Ciudadela on C. Yangüas y Miranda for Barcelona (6-8hr., 4 per day, €26), Bilbao (2hr., 5-6 per day, €14), and Madrid (5hr., 6-10 per day, €28). From Pl. del Castillo, take C. San Nicolás, turn right on C. San Miguel, and walk through Pl. San Francisco to reach the **tourist office,** C. Hilarión Eslava. (☎948 42 04 20; www.turismo.navarra.es. Open during *San Fermín* daily 8am-8pm; July-Aug. M-Sa 9am-8pm, Su 10am-2pm; Sept.-June M-Sa 10am-2pm and 4-7pm, Su 10am-2pm.) **Luggage storage** is at the Escuelas de San Francisco in Pl. San Francisco during *San Fermín.* (€3.40 per day. Open 24hr. from July 4 at 8am to July 16 at 2pm.) The **biblioteca** has free Internet and Wi-Fi. (Open Sept.-June M-F 8:30am-8:45pm, Sa 8:30am-1:45pm, July-Aug. M-F 8:30am-2:45pm.) **Postal Code:** 31001.

ACCOMMODATIONS AND FOOD. Smart San Ferministas book their rooms up to a year ahead; without a reservation, it's nearly impossible to find a room. Expect to pay rates up to four times the normal price. Check the tourist office for a list of official accommodations with openings or the newspaper *Diario de Navarra* for *casas particulares* (private homes that rent rooms). Be aware, though, that some owners prefer Spanish guests. Many roomless backpackers are forced to fluff up their sweatshirts and sleep on Pl. de los Fueros, Pl. del Castillo, the lawns of the Ciudadela, along the banks of the river, or not at all. Be careful—stay in large groups, and if you can't store your backpack, sleep on top of it. During the rest of the year, finding a room in Pamplona is no problem. Budget accommodations line Calle San Gregorio and **Calle San Nicolás** off Pl. del Castillo. Deep within the *casco antiguo* (Old Town), **Pensión Eslava ❶**, C. Hilarión Eslava 13, 2nd fl., is quieter and less crowded than other *pensiones*. Older rooms have a balcony and shared bath. (☎948 22 15 58. Singles €15; doubles €20-30, during San Fermín €100. Cash only.) Small **Horno de Aralar ❸**, C. San Nicolás 12, above the restaurant, has five spotless, bright rooms with bath and TV. (☎948 22 11 16. Singles €40; doubles €50; during San Fermín all rooms €200-300. MC/V.) To get to **Camping Ezcaba ❶**, 7km from the city in Eusa, take city bus line 4-V (4 per day, 26 per day during San Fermín) from Pl. de las Merindades. (☎948 33 03 15. €4.90 per person, €5.35 per tent, €4.90 per car. San Fermín €10.59, €11.68. €10.59 per car MC/V.)

Look for hearty *menús* at the cafe-bars above **Plaza de San Francisco** and around **Paseo de Ronda.** Thoroughfares **Calle Navarrería** and **Paseo de Sarasate** are home to good *bocadillo* bars. **Café-Bar Iruña ❸**, Pl. del Castillo, the former casino made famous in Hemingway's *The Sun Also Rises*, is notable for its storied past and elegant interior. The *menú* (€13) is required if eating at a table, but the restaurant serves drinks and sandwiches at the bar. (☎948 22 20 64. Open M-Th 8am-11pm, F 8am-2am, Sa 9am-2am, Su 9am-11pm. MC/V.) Get groceries at **Vendi Supermarket**, C. Hilarión Eslava and C. Mayor. (☎948 22 15 55. Open M-F 9am-2pm and 5:30-7:30pm, Sa 9am-2pm; *San Fermín* M-Sa 9am-2pm. MC/V.)

SPAIN

SIGHTS AND NIGHTLIFE. Pamplona's rich architectural legacy is reason enough to visit during the 51 other weeks of the year. The restored 14th-century Gothic **Catedral de Santa María,** at the end of C. Navarrería is one of only four cathedrals of its kind in Europe. (☎948 22 29 90. Open Sept. 16-July 14 M-F 10am-2pm and 4-7pm, Sa 10am-2pm. July 15-Sept. 15 M-F 10am-7pm, Sa 10am-2:30 pm. €4.40.) The walls of the pentagonal **Ciudadela** enclose free art exhibits, various summer concerts, and an amazing San Fermín fireworks display. Follow Po. de Sarasate to its end and go right on C. Navas de Tolosa, then take the next left onto C. Chinchilla and follow it to its end. (☎948 22 82 37. Open M-Sa 7:30am-9:30pm, Su 9am-9:30pm. Closed for San Fermín. Free.)

Central **Plaza del Castillo**, with outdoor seating galore, is the heart of Pamplona's social scene. A young crowd parties in the *casco antiguo*, particularly along the bar-studded **Calle San Nicolás, Calle Jarauta,** and **Calle San Gregorio.** The small plaza **Travesía de Bayona,** 600m past the Ciudela (follow Av. del Ejército as it turns into Av. de Bayona, the Travesía is just before Mo. de la Oliva branches off), has bars and *discotecas*. **Blue Shadow** (☎948 27 51 09) and **Tandem** (☎948 26 92 85), Tr. de Bayona 3 and 4, have good dancing and big crowds. (Beer €3.50. Mixed drinks €6. Both open Th-Sa 10pm-4am.)

RUNNING SCARED. So, you're going to run, and nobody's going to stop you. But because nobody—except the angry, angry bulls—wants to see you get seriously injured, here are a few words of *San Fermín* wisdom:

1. Research the *encierro* before you run; the tourist office has a pamphlet that outlines the route and offers tips for the inexperienced. Running the entire 850m course is highly inadvisable; it would mean 2-8min. of evading 6 bulls moving at 24kph (15mph). Instead, pick a 50m stretch.
2. Don't stay up all night drinking and carousing. Experienced runners get lots of sleep the night before and arrive at the course around 6:30am.
3. Take a fashion tip from the locals: wear the traditional white-and-red outfit with closed-toe shoes. Ditch the baggy clothes, backpacks, and cameras.
4. Give up on getting near the bulls and concentrate on getting to the bullring in one piece. Though some whack the bulls with rolled newspapers, runners should never distract or touch the animals.
5. Never stop in doorways, alleys, or corners; you can be trapped and killed.
6. Run in a straight line; if you cut someone off, they can easily fall.
7. Be particularly wary of isolated bulls—they seek company in the crowds. In 2007, 13 runners were seriously injured by an isolated bull.
8. If you fall, stay down. Curl up into a fetal position, lock your hands behind your head, and do not get up until the clatter of hooves has passed.

SPAIN

FIESTA DE SAN FERMÍN (JULY 1-14, 2009). Visitors overcrowd the city as it delivers an eight-day frenzy of bullfights, concerts, dancing, fireworks, parades, parties, and wine in what is perhaps Europe's premier party. *Pamploneses*, clad in white with red sashes and bandanas, throw themselves into the merry-making, displaying obscene levels of both physical stamina and alcohol tolerance. *El encierro*, or "The Running of the Bulls," is the highlight of *San Fermín;* the first *encierro* takes place on July 7 at 8am and is repeated at 8am every day for the next seven days. Hundreds of bleary-eyed, hungover, hyper-adrenalized runners flee from large bulls as bystanders cheer from balconies, barricades, doorways, and windows. Both the bulls and the mob are dangerous; terrified runners react without concern for those around them. To participate in the bullring excitement without the risk of the *encierro*, onlookers should arrive at 6:45am. Tickets for the *grada* section of the ring are available at 7am in the bullring box office (July 7, 8 and 14 €5.50, July 9-13 €4.50). You can watch for free, but the free section is overcrowded, making it hard to see and breathe. To watch a **bullfight,** wait in the line that forms at the bullring around 7:30pm. As one fight ends, the next day's tickets go on sale. (Tickets from €10; check www.feriadeltoro.com for details.) Tickets are incredibly hard to get at face value, as over 90% belong to season holders. Once the running ends, insanity spills into the streets and explodes at night with singing in bars, dancing in alleyways, spontaneous parades, and a no-holds-barred party in **Plaza del Castillo.**

NOT JUST A LOAD OF BULL. Although Pamplona is generally safe, crime skyrockets during San Fermín. Beware of assaults and muggings and do not walk alone at night during the festival.

BASQUE COUNTRY (PAÍS VASCO)

BILBAO (BILBO) ☎944

The once gritty, industrial Bilbao (pop. 354,000) has risen to international cultural prominence since the creation of the shining **Guggenheim Museum.** However, this city, with its expansive parks, efficient transport, and grand architecture of all kinds has plenty to offer beyond its oddly-shaped claim to fame.

TRANSPORTATION. To reach the **airport** (**BIO;** ☎944 86 96 64), 25km from Bilbao, take the Bizkai bus (☎902 22 22 65) marked *Aeropuerto* from the Termibús terminal or Pl. Moyúa (line A-3247; 25min., 2 per hr., €1.10). RENFE **trains** (☎902 24 02 02) leave from **Estación de Abando,** Pl. Circular 2, for Barcelona (9-10hr., 2 per day, €39-51), Madrid (5-6hr., 2 per day, €40-45), and Salamanca (5hr., 2pm, €27). Trains run between Bilboa's Estación de Atxuri and San Sebastián (2hr., 17-18 per day). FEVE trains run from **Estación de Santander,** C. Bailén, 2 (☎944 25 06 15; www.feve.es) to: León (7hr., 2:30pm, €20.55) and Santander (3hr.; 8am, 1, 7:30pm; €7.25). Most **bus** companies leave from **Termibús,** C. Gurtubay 1 (☎944 39 52 05; M: San Mamés), for: Barcelona (7hr., 4 per day, €41); Madrid (4-5hr., 10-18 per day, €26); Pamplona (2hr., 4-6 per day, €13); San Sebastián (1hr., 1-2 per hr., €8.70). Within Bilbao, a **Creditrans pass** (purchased in denominations of €5, €10, or €15) allows access to Metro, BizkaiBus, Bilbobús, and EuskoTran, the new tram/train line, at a discounted rate.

ORIENTATION AND PRACTICAL INFORMATION. The **Río de Bilbao** runs through the city and separates the historic *casco viejo* from the newer parts of town. The train stations are across the river west of the *casco viejo*. The city's major thoroughfare, **Gran Vía de Don Diego López de Haro,** connects three of Bilbao's main plazas. Heading east from Pl. de Sagrado Corazón, Gran Vía continues through the central **Pl. Moyúa** and ends at **Pl. Circular.** Past Pl. Circular, cross the Río de Bilbao on Puente del Arenal to arrive in **Plaza de Arriaga,** and **Plaza Nueva.** The **tourist office** is at Pl. Ensanche 11. (☎944 79 57 60; www.bilbao.net/bilbaoturismo. Open M-F 9am-2pm and 4-7:30pm.) with branches at Teatro Arriaga and near the Guggenheim. Free **Internet** and Wi-Fi at **Biblioteca Municipal,** C. Bidebarrieta, 4 (☎944 15 09 15; open Sept. 16-May 31 M 2:30-8pm, Tu-F 8:30am-8:30pm, Sa 10am-1pm; July M-F 8:30am-7:30pm; Aug. M-F 8:30am-1:45pm; June Tu-F 8:30am-7:30pm, Sa 10am-2pm). **Postal Code:** 48008.

ACCOMMODATIONS AND FOOD. Plaza Arriaga and Calle Arenal have many budget accommodations, while upscale hotels are in the new city off Gran Vía. Rates climb during Semana Grande. **Pensión Méndez ❷,** C. Sta. María 13, 4th fl., provides cheery rooms with spacious balconies. (☎944 16 03 64. Singles €25; doubles €35; triples €50. MC/V.) **Hostal Méndez ❸,** on the first floor of the same building, is even more comfortable; rooms all have large windows, full bath, and TV. (Singles €38-40; doubles €50-55; triples €65-70. MC/V.) **Pensión Manoli ❷,** C. Libertad, 2, 4th fl. (☎944 15 56 36) is tucked away on the tiny C. Libertad just outside the Pl. Nueva by the Casco Viejo metro stop with small, tidy rooms and shared baths. Rooms have balconies overlooking the street. (Free Wi-Fi. Singles €25; doubles €30.)

Restaurants and bars in the *casco viejo* offer a wide selection of local dishes, *pintxos (tapas)*, and *bocadillos*. The new city has even more variety. **Restaurante Peruano Ají Colorado ❸,** C. Barrenkale 5, specializes in traditional Andean *ceviche* (marinated raw fish; €10), and also serves Peruvian mountain dishes.

(☎944 15 22 09. M-F lunch *menú* €12. Open M-Sa 1:30-4pm and 9-11pm, Su 1:30-4pm. MC/V.) **Restaurante Vegetariano Garibolo ❸,** C. Fernandez del Campo, 7, serves a vegetarian *menú* (€12) that lines locals up at lunchtime. (☎942 22 32 55; M-F 1-4pm, F-Sa 1-4pm and 9-11pm). **Mercado de la Ribera,** on the river-bank, is the biggest indoor market in Spain. (Open M-Th and Sa 8am-2:30pm, F 8am-2:30pm and 4:30-7:30pm.) Pick up groceries at **Carrefour Express,** Pl. Santos Juanes, past Mercado de la Ribera. (Open M-Sa 9am-9pm. AmEx/MC/V.)

SIGHTS. Frank Gehry's **Museo Guggenheim Bilbao,** Av. Abandoibarra 2, is awe-inspiring. Lauded in the international press with every superlative imaginable, it has catapulted Bilbao straight into cultural stardom. Sheathed in titanium, limestone, and fluid glass, the €95 million building is said to resemble either an iridescent fish or a blossoming flower. The dramatic, spacious interior features a towering atrium and a series of unconventional exhibition spaces. The museum hosts rotating exhibits drawn from the Guggenheim Foundation's often eccentric collection; don't be surprised if you are asked to take your shoes off, lie on the floor, or even sing throughout your visit. (☎944 35 90 80; www.guggenheim-bilbao.es. Wheelchair-accessible. Admission includes English-language audioguide, as well as guided tours Tu-Su 11am, 12:30, 4:30, 6:30pm; sign up 30min. before tour at the info desk. Open July-Aug. daily 10am-8pm; Sept.-June Tu-Su 10am-8pm. €13, students €7.50, under 12 free.) Although the **Museo de Bellas Artes,** Pl. del Museo 2, can't boast the name recognition of the Guggenheim, it wins the favor of locals. Holding artistic riches behind an unassuming facade, the museum has an impressive collection of 12th- to 20th-century art, including excellent 15th- to 17th-century Flemish paintings, canvases by Basque artists, and works by Mary Cassatt, El Greco, Gauguin, Goya, and Velázquez. Take C. Elcano to Pl. del Museo or bus #10 from Pte. del Arenal. (☎944 39 60 60, Open Tu-Sa 10am-8pm, Su 10am-2pm. €5.50, students and seniors €4, under 12 and W free.)

ENTERTAINMENT AND NIGHTLIFE. Bilbao has a thriving bar scene. In the *casco viejo*, locals spill out into the streets to sip their *txikitos* (chee-KEE-tos; small glasses of wine), especially on **Calle Barrenkale,** one of Bilbao's seven original streets. A young crowd fills **Calle Licenciado Poza** on the west side of town, especially between C. General Concha and Alameda de Recalde, where a covered alleyway connecting C. Licenciado Poza and Alameda de Urquijo teems with bars. Mellow **Alambique,** Alda. Urquijo 37, provides elegant seating and chance for conversation under chandeliers and photos of old Bilbao. (☎944 43 41 88. Beer €2-3. Open M-Th 8am-2am, F-Sa 8am-3am, Su 5pm-3am.) The **Cotton Club,** C. Gregorio de la Revilla 25 (entrance on C. Simón Bolívar around the corner from the metro stop), decorated with over 30,000 beer bottle caps and featuring over 100 whiskeys, draws a huge crowd on Friday and Saturday nights, while the rest of the week is a little more low-key. (☎944 10 49 51. Beer €3. Mixed drinks €6. Rum €6. Open M-Th 5pm-3:30am, F-Sa 5pm-6am, Su 6:30pm-3:30am.) The massive **fiesta** in honor of *Nuestra Señora de Begoña* (Our Lady of Begoña)—complete with bullfighting, concerts, fireworks, and theater—occurs during *Semana Grande* (mid-August). Pick up a *Bilbao Guide* from the tourist office for event listings.

SWITZERLAND (SCHWEIZ, SUISSE, SVIZZERA)

While the stereotype of Switzerland as a country of bankers, chocolatiers, and watchmakers still exists, an energetic youth culture is also reviving old images of a pastoral Swiss culture. The country's gorgeous lakes and formidable peaks entice outdoor enthusiasts from around the globe. Mountains dominate about two-thirds of the country: the Jura cover the northwest region, the Alps stretch across the lower half, and the eastern Rhaetian Alps border Austria. Only in Switzerland can one indulge in decadent chocolate as a cultural experience.

LIFE AND TIMES

HISTORY

AGAINST THE EMPIRE (1032-1520). Switzerland was a loose union of relatively united cantons as part of the **Holy Roman Empire** until 1032. But when **Emperor Rudolf of Hapsburg** tried to assert control over the region in the late 13th century, the Swiss rebelled. Three Alemanni communities (the Forest Cantons) signed an **Everlasting Alliance** in 1291, agreeing to defend each other from outside attack—which they did in a series of sporadic territorial struggles with the Hapsburg empire over the next 350 years. The Swiss consider the alliance to be the beginning of the **Swiss Confederation.** However, the union of culturally distinct states made for uneasy cooperation. The **Swabian War** (1499-1500) against the empire brought the alliance virtual independence from the Hapsburgs, but internal struggles over cultural and religious differences continued.

REFORMATION TO REVOLUTION (1520-1800). With no strong central government to settle religious squabbles among cantons, Switzerland was divided by the **Protestant Reformation.** Zürich's **Huldrych Zwingli** and Geneva's **John Calvin** instituted Protestant reforms, but the rural cantons remained loyal to the Catholic Church. When religious differences between the urban Protestant cantons and the rural Catholic cantons escalated into full-fledged battle in the mid-16th century, the Confederation intervened, granting Protestants freedom but prohibiting them from imposing their faith on others. The Swiss remained neutral during the **Thirty Years' War,** escaping the devastation wrought on the rest of Europe. The Peace of Westphalia, which ended the war in 1648, officially granted the neutral Confederation independence from the Hapsburg empire—which it had, at that point, been unofficially enjoying for 150 years. Swiss independwence was fairly short-lived: **Napoleon Bonaparte** invaded in 1798 and established the **Helvetic Republic.** After Napoleon's defeat at Waterloo in 1815, Swiss neutrality was officially recognized again in the **Treaty of Vienna.**

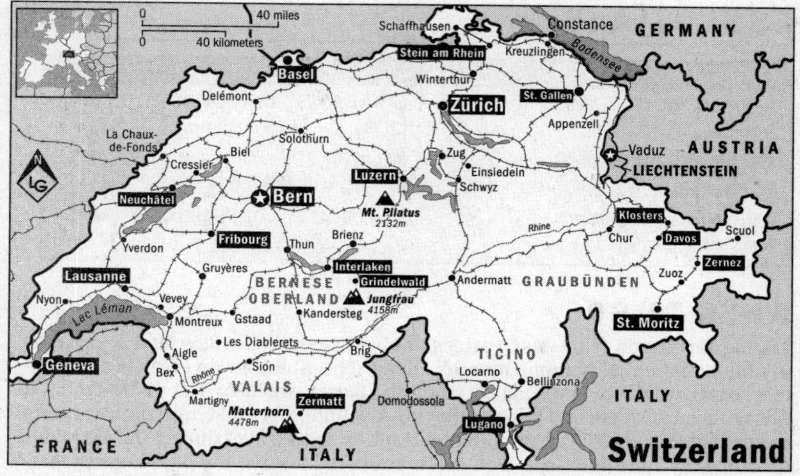

NEUTRALITY AND DIPLOMACY (1815-2002). Switzerland then turned its attention to domestic issues. Industrial growth brought prosperity, but religious differences continued to fuel tension. A short, 25-day civil war broke out in 1847. The Protestants were victorious, and the country enacted a new constitution modeled on the United States Constitution. Once it stabilized, Switzerland established a reputation for resolving international conflicts. The **Geneva Convention** of 1864 established international laws for conduct during war, and Geneva became the headquarters for the **International Red Cross** (p. 594).

The country's neutrality was tested in **World War I,** when French- and German-speaking areas of Switzerland claimed different cultural loyalties. In 1920, the Allies chose Geneva as the headquarters of the **League of Nations,** solidifying Switzerland's reputation as a center for international mediation. During **World War II**, both sides viewed Switzerland (and its banks) as neutral territory. As the rest of Europe cleared the rubble of two global wars, Switzerland nurtured its already robust economy: Zürich emerged as a center for banking and insurance, while Geneva solidified its position as the world's diplomatic headquarters. Although Switzerland joined the United Nations in 2002, it remains isolationist, declining membership in the NATO and the EU.

TODAY

Since WWII, Switzerland has remained fiercely independent, and has also become increasingly wealthy and liberal. The Swiss elected **Ruth Dreifuss** as both their first female and first Jewish president in 1998, and they maintain one of the world's most stringent ecological policies to protect their Alpine environment. Under the Swiss constitution, the Confederation incorporates the 26 cantons and its legislature, the Federal Assembly. The executive branch consists of a group of seven members, the **Bundesrat** (Federal Council). The Bundesrat chooses a president from among its ranks. The president holds office for one year, though the post is more symbolic than functional.

ESSENTIALS

FACTS AND FIGURES

OFFICIAL NAME: Swiss Confederation.
CAPITAL: Bern.
MAJOR CITIES: Basel, Geneva, Zürich.
POPULATION: 7,582l,000
LAND AREA: 41,300 sq. km.
TIME ZONE: GMT+1.
LANGUAGES: German (64%), French (20%), Italian (10%), Romansch (1%).
RELIGIONS: Roman Catholic (48%), Protestant (44%), other (8%).
CHOCOLATE CONSUMED IN 2007: 93,501 tons.

WHEN TO GO

During ski season (Nov.-Mar.) prices double in eastern Switzerland and travelers must make reservations months ahead. The situation reverses in the summer, especially July and August, when the flatter, western half of Switzerland fills with vacationers and hikers enjoying low humidity and temperatures rarely exceeding 26°C (80°F). A good budget option is to travel during the shoulder season: May-June and Sept.-Oct., when tourism lulls and the daytime temperature ranges from -2 to 7°C (46-59°F). Many mountain towns throughout Switzerland shut down completely in May and June, however, so call ahead.

DOCUMENTS AND FORMALITIES

EMBASSIES. Most foreign embassies in Switzerland are in Bern (p. 576). Swiss embassies abroad include: **Australia**, 7 Melbourne Ave., Forrest, Canberra, ACT, 2603 (☎02 6162 8400; www.eda.admin.ch/australia); **Canada**, 5 Marlborough Ave., Ottawa, ON, K1N 8E6 (☎613-235-1837; www.eda.admin.ch/canada); **Ireland,** 6 Ailesbury Rd., Ballsbridge, Dublin, 4 (☎353 12 18 63 82; www.eda.admin.ch/dublin); **New Zealand**, 22 Panama St., Wellington (☎04 472 15 93; www.eda.admin.ch/wellington); **UK,** 16-18 Montagu Pl., London, W1H 2BQ (☎020 76 16 60 00; www.eda.admin.ch/london); **US,** 2900 Cathedral Ave., NW, Washington, D.C., 20008 (☎202-745-7900; www.eda.admin.ch/washington).

VISA AND ENTRY INFORMATION. EU citizens do not need a visa. Citizens of Australia, Canada, New Zealand, and the US do not need a visa for stays of up to 90 days. For stays longer than 90 days, all visitors need visas (around US$52), available at Swiss consulates.

TOURIST SERVICES AND MONEY

EMERGENCY Ambulance: ☎144. Fire: ☎118. Police: ☎117.

TOURIST OFFICES. Branches of the **Swiss National Tourist Office,** marked by a standard blue "i" sign, are present in nearly every town in Switzerland; most agents speak English. The official tourism website for Switzerland is www.myswitzerland.com.

THE REAL DEAL. If you're planning on spending a long time in Switzerland, consider the **Museum Pass** (30CHF). Available at some tourist offices and participating venues, it lets you into most major Swiss museums.

MONEY. The Swiss unit of currency is the **Swiss franc (CHF);** plural Swiss francs. One Swiss franc is equal to 100 centimes (called *Rappen* in German Switzerland), with standard denominations of 5, 10, 20, and 50 centimes and 1, 2, and 5CHF in coins; and 10, 20, 50, 100, 200, 500, and 1000CHF in notes. Widely accepted credit cards include American Express, MasterCard, and Visa. Euros (€) are also accepted at many museums and restaurants. Switzerland is not cheap; if you stay in hostels and prepare most of your own food, expect to spend 55-80CHF per day. Generally, it's less expensive to exchange money at home than in Switzerland. ATMs offer the best exchange rates. Although restaurant bills already include a 15% service charge, an additional tip of 1-2CHF for a modest meal or 5-10CHF for a more upscale dinner is expected. Give hotel porters and doormen about 1CHF per bag and airport porters 5CHF per bag.

Switzerland has a 7.6% **value added tax (VAT),** a sales tax applied to goods and services. The prices given in *Let's Go* include VAT. In the airport upon exiting Switzerland, non-Swiss citizens can claim a refund on the tax paid for goods purchased at participating stores. In order to qualify for a refund in a store, you must spend at least 500CHF; make sure to ask for a refund form when you pay. For more info on qualifying for a VAT refund, see p. 13.

SWISS FRANC		
	AUS$1 = 0.95CHF	1CHF = AUS$1.05
	CDN$1 = 1.03CHF	1CHF = CDN$0.97
	EUR€1 = 1.61CHF	1CHF = EUR€0.62
	NZ$1 = 0.78CHF	1CHF = NZ$1.28
	UK£1 = 2.04CHF	1CHF = UK£0.49
	US$1 = 1.09CHF	1CHF = US$0.92

TRANSPORTATION

BY PLANE. Major international airports are in **Bern** (BRN; ☎031 960 21 11; www.alpar.ch), **Geneva** (GVA; ☎022 717 71 11; www.gva.ch), and **Zürich** (ZRH; ☎043 816 22 11; www.zurich-airport.com). From London, **easyJet** (☎0871 244 23 66; www.easyjet.com) has flights to Geneva and Zürich. **Aer Lingus** (Ireland ☎0818 365 000, Switzerland ☎442 86 99 33, UK ☎0870 876 5000; www.aerlingus.com) sells tickets from Dublin, IRE to Geneva. For info on flying to Switzerland from other locations, see p. 33.

BY TRAIN. Federal (**SBB, CFF**) and private railways connect most towns with frequent trains. For times and prices, check online (www.sbb.ch). **Eurail, Europass,** and **Inter Rail** are all valid on federal trains. The **Swiss Pass,** sold worldwide, offers four, eight, 15, 22, or 30 consecutive days of unlimited rail travel (www.swisstravelsystem.com). It also doubles as a **Swiss Museum Pass,** allowing free entry to 400 museums. (2nd-class 4-day pass US$222, 8-day US$315, 15-day US$384, 22-day US$446, 1-month US$496.)

BY BUS. PTT Post Buses, a barrage of government-run yellow coaches, connect rural villages and towns that trains don't service. Swiss Passes are valid on many buses; Eurail passes are not. Even with the Swiss Pass, you might have to pay 5-10CHF extra if you're riding certain buses.

BY CAR. Roads, generally in good condition, may become dangerous at higher altitudes in the winter. The speed limit is 50kph in towns and cities, 80kph on open roads, and 120kph on highways. Be sure to drive under the speed limit; radar traps are frequent. Many small towns forbid cars; some require special permits or restrict driving hours. US and British citizens 18 and older with a valid driver's license may drive in Switzerland for up to one year following their arrival; for stays longer than one year, drivers should contact the **Service des automobiles et de la navigation** (SAN; ☎022 388 30 30; www.geneve.ch/san) about acquiring a Swiss permit. Custom posts sell windshield stickers (US$33) required for driving on Swiss roads. Call ☎140 for roadside assistance.

BY BIKE. Cycling is a splendid way to see the country. The **Touring Club Suisse,** with locations throughout Switzerland (☎022 417 22 20; www.tcs.ch), is a good source for maps and route descriptions.

KEEPING IN TOUCH

PHONE CODES	**Country code:** 41. **International dialing prefix:** 00. For more information on how to place international calls, see **Inside Back Cover.**

EMAIL AND INTERNET. Most Swiss cities, as well as a number of smaller towns, have at least one Internet cafe with web access available for about 12-24CHF per hour. Hostels and restaurants frequently offer Internet access as well, but it seldom comes for free: rates can climb as high as 12CHF per hour.

TELEPHONE. Whenever possible, use a calling card for international phone calls, as long-distance rates are often exorbitant for national phone services. For info about using mobile phones abroad, see p. 21. Most pay phones in Switzerland accept only prepaid taxcards, which are available at kiosks, post offices, and train stations. Direct access numbers include: **AT&T Direct** (☎800 89 00 11); **Canada Direct** (☎800 55 83 30); **MCI WorldPhone** (☎800 89 02 22); **Sprint** (☎800 899 777); **Telecom New Zealand** (☎800 55 64 11).

MAIL. Airmail from Switzerland averages three to 15 days to North America, although times are unpredictable from smaller towns. Domestic letters take one to three days. Bright yellow logos mark Swiss national post offices, referred to as **Die Post** in German or **La Poste** in French. Letters from Switzerland cost 1.40CHF to mail to the US, 1.20CHF to mail to the UK, and 0.85CHF mailed domestically. To receive mail in Switzerland, have mail delivered **Poste Restante.** Mail will go to the main post office unless you specify a subsidiary by street address. Address mail to be held as follows: LAST NAME, First Name, *Postlagernde Briefe*, Postal Code, City, SWITZERLAND. Bring a passport to pick up your mail; there may be a small fee.

ACCOMMODATIONS AND CAMPING

SWITZERLAND	❶	❷	❸	❹	❺
ACCOMMODATIONS	under 30CHF	30-42CHF	43-65CHF	66-125CHF	over 125CHF

There are hostels (*Jugendherbergen* in German, *Auberges de Jeunesse* in French, *Ostelli* in Italian) in all cities in Switzerland as well as in most towns. **Schweizer Jugendherbergen** (SJH; www.youthhostel.ch) runs HI hostels throughout Switzerland. Non-HI members can stay in any HI hostel, where beds are usually 30-44CHF; members typically receive a 6CHF discount. The more informal **Swiss Backpackers** (SB) organization (☎062 892 2675; www.backpacker.ch) lists over 40 hostels aimed at young, foreign travelers interested in socializing.

Most **Swiss campgrounds** are not idyllic refuges but large plots glutted with RVs. Prices average 12-20CHF per tent site and 6-9CHF per extra person. **Hotels** and **pensions** tend to charge at least 65-80CHF for a single room and 80-120CHF for a double. The cheapest have *Gasthof*, *Gästehaus*, or *Hotel-Garni* in the name. **Privatzimmer** (rooms in a family home) run about 30-60CHF per person. Breakfast is included at most hotels, pensions, and *Privatzimmer*.

HIKING AND SKIING. Nearly every town has **hiking trails:** Interlaken (p. 579), Grindelwald, Luzern, and Zermatt offer particularly good hiking opportunities. Trails are marked with either red-white-red markers (only sturdy boots and hiking poles needed) or blue-white-blue markers (mountaineering equipment needed). **Skiing** in Switzerland is less expensive than in North America, provided you avoid pricey resorts. **Ski passes** run 40-70CHF per day, 100-300CHF per week; a week of lift tickets, equipment rental, lessons, lodging, and demi-pension (breakfast plus one other meal) averages 475CHF. **Summer skiing** is available in a few towns.

FOOD AND DRINK

SWITZERLAND	❶	❷	❸	❹	❺
FOOD	under 9CHF	9-23CHF	24-32CHF	33-52CHF	over 52CHF

Switzerland is not for the lactose intolerant. The Swiss are serious about dairy products, from rich and varied **cheeses** to decadent **milk chocolate**—even the major Swiss soft drink, **Rivella,** contains dairy. Swiss dishes vary from region to region. Bernese **rösti,** a plateful of hash-brown potatoes (sometimes flavored with bacon or cheese), is prevalent in the German regions; cheese or meat **fondue** is popular in the French regions. Try Valaisian **raclette,** made by melting cheese over a fire, scraping it onto a baked potato, and garnishing it with meat or vegetables. Supermarkets **Migros** and **Co-op** double as cafeterias; stop in for a cheap meal and groceries. Water from the fountains that adorn cities and large towns is usually safe; filling your bottle with it will save you money. *Kein Trinkwasser* or *Eau non potable* signs indicate unclean water. Each canton has its own local beer, which is often cheaper than soda.

BEYOND TOURISM

Although Switzerland's volunteer opportunities are limited, a number of ecotourism and rural development organizations allow you to give back to the country. Your best bet is to go through a placement service. Look for opportunities for short-term work on websites like www.emploi.ch. For more info on opportunities across Europe, see **Beyond Tourism**, see p. 45.

Bergwald Projekt/Mountain Forest Project, Hauptstr. 24, 7014 Trin (☎081 650 40 40; www.bergwaldprojekt.ch). Organizes week-long conservation projects in Austria, Germany, and Switzerland.

Workcamp Switzerland, Komturei Tobel, Postfach 7, 9555 Tobel (☎071 917 24 86; www.workcamp.ch). Offers 2-4 week sessions during which volunteers live in a group environment and work on a community service project.

SWITZERLAND

GERMAN SWITZERLAND

German Switzerland encompasses 65% of the country. While the region's intoxicating brews and industrious cities will remind visitors of Germany, the natural beauty at every turn is uniquely Swiss. Different forms of Swiss German, a dialect distinct from High German, are spoken here.

BERN ☎031

Bern (pop. 128,000) has been Switzerland's capital since 1848, but don't expect power politics or businessmen in suits—the Bernese prefer to focus on the more leisurely things in life, like strolling through the arcades of the *Altstadt* or meandering along the banks of the serpentine Aare River.

TRANSPORTATION AND PRACTICAL INFORMATION. Bern's small **airport** (**BRN;** ☎031 960 2111) is 20min. from the city. A **bus** runs from the train station 50min. before each flight (10min., 14CHF). **Trains** run from the station at Bahnhofpl. to: Geneva (2hr., 2 per hr., 45CHF); Luzern (1hr., 2 per hr., 35CHF); St. Gallen (2hr., every hr., 65CHF); Zürich (1hr., 4 per day, 46CHF); Berlin, GER (12hr., 1-2 per hr., 95CHF); Paris, FRA (6hr., 4-5 per day, 115CHF). Local Bernmobil **buses** (departing from the left of the train station) and **trams** (departing from the front of the station) run 5:45am-midnight. (☎321 86 41; www.bernmobil.ch. Single ride 3.80CHF, day pass 12CHF.) Buses depart from the back of the station and post office. **Free bikes** are available from Bern Rollt at two locations: on Hirscheng. near the train station and on Zeugausg. near Waisenhauspl. (☎079 652 2319; www.bernrollt.ch. Passport and 20CHF deposit. Open May-Oct. daily 7:30am-9:30pm.)

Most of old Bern lies to your left as you leave the train station, along the Aare River. Bern's main train station is an often-confusing tangle of essential services and extraneous shops. Take extra caution in the parks around the Parliament (Bundeshaus), especially at night. The **tourist office** is on the street level of the station. (☎031 328 1212; www.berninfo.ch. Open June-Sept. daily 9am-8:30pm; Oct.-May M-Sa 9am-6:30pm, Su 10am-5pm.) The **post office,** Schanzenpost 1, is one block to the right from the train station. (Open M-F 7:30am-9pm, Sa 8am-4pm, Su 4-9pm.) **Postal Codes:** CH-3000 to CH-3030.

Embassies in Bern include: **Canada,** Kirchenfeldstr. 88 (☎031 357 3200; www.geo.international.gc.ca/canada-europa/switzerland); **Ireland,** Kirchenfeldstr. 68 (☎031 352 1442); **UK,** Thunstr. 50 (☎031 359 7700; www.britishembassy.gov.uk/switzerland); **US,** Jubilaumsstr. 93 (☎031 357 7011; bern.usembassy.gov). The **Australian** consulate is in Geneva (p. 589). **New Zealanders** should contact their embassy in Berlin, GER (p. 253).

ACCOMMODATIONS AND FOOD. If Bern's cheaper hostels are full, check at the tourist office for a list of private rooms. **Backpackers Bern/Hotel Glocke ❷,** Rathausg. 75, in the middle of the *Altstadt*, has friendly owners and a large common room. From the train station, cross the tram lines and turn left on Spitalg., continuing onto Marktg. Turn left at Kornhauspl., then right on Rathausg. (☎031 311 3771; www.bernbackpackers.ch. Internet 1CHF per 10min. Reception 8am-noon and 3-10pm. Dorms 33CHF; singles 69CHF; doubles 82CHF, with bath 140CHF; quads 172CHF. AmEx/MC/V.) At **Jugendherberge (HI) ❷,** Weiherg. 4, near the river, guests receive free access to a public swimming pool. From the station, go down Christoffelg.; take the stairs to the left of

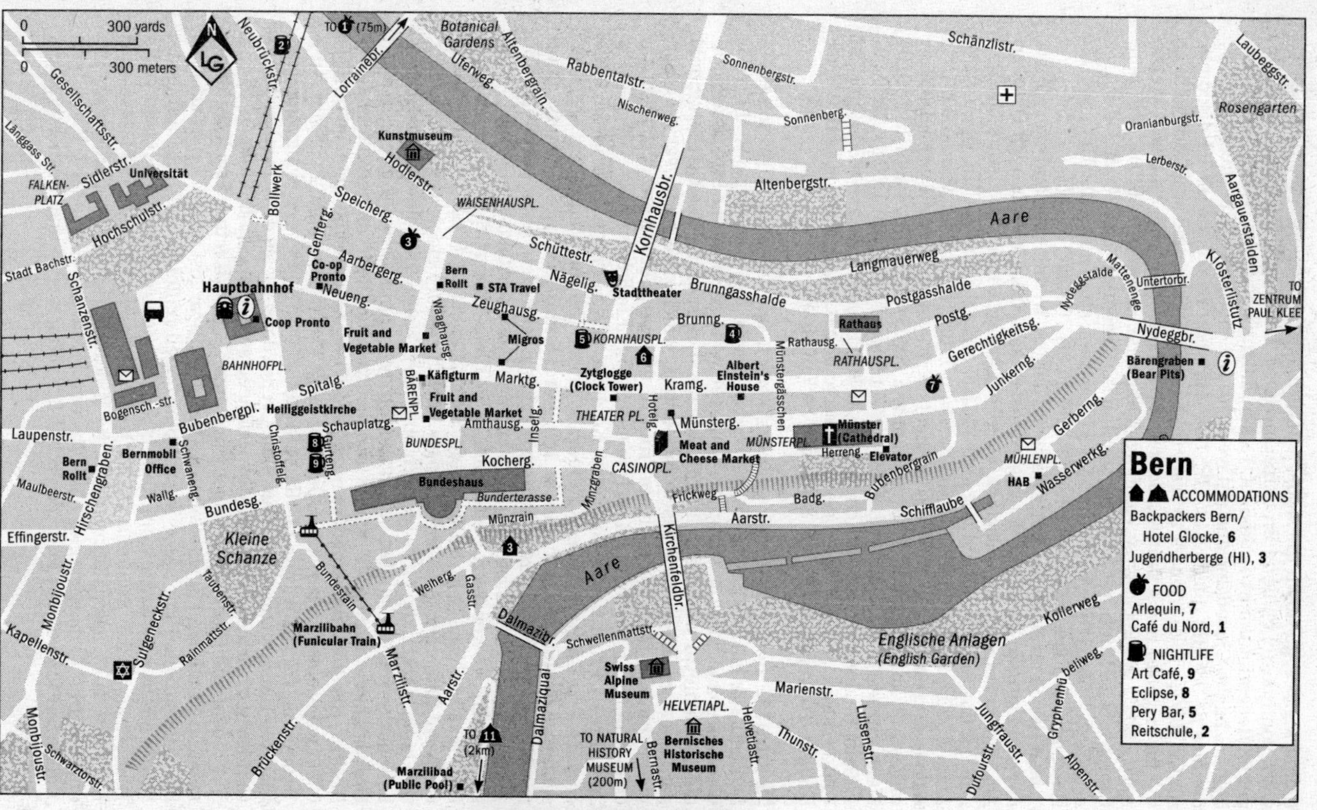
Bern
ACCOMMODATIONS
Backpackers Bern/
Hotel Glocke, 6
Jugendherberge (HI), 3
FOOD
Arlequin, 7
Café du Nord, 1
NIGHTLIFE
Art Café, 9
Eclipse, 8
Pery Bar, 5
Reitschule, 2
0 300 yards
0 300 meters
TO 1 (75m)
Botanical Gardens
Aare
Hauptbahnhof
Coop Pronto
Co-op Pronto
Universität
Kunstmuseum
Stadttheater
Rathaus
Zytglogge (Clock Tower)
Albert Einstein's House
Münster (Cathedral)
Meat and Cheese Market
Elevator
Bärengraben (Bear Pits)
Käfigturm
Fruit and Vegetable Market
Migros
STA Travel
Bern Rollt
Heiliggeistkirche
Bernmobil Office
Bundeshaus
Kleine Schanze
Marzilibahn (Funicular Train)
Marzilibad (Public Pool)
Swiss Alpine Museum
Bernisches Historische Museum
TO NATURAL HISTORY MUSEUM (200m)
TO 11 (2km)
Englische Anlagen (English Garden)
HAB
Kornhausbr.
Kirchenfeldbr.
Nydeggbr.
Dalmazibr.
Lorrainebr.
TO ZENTRUM PAUL KLEE

the park gates, go down the slope, and turn left on Weiherg. (☎031 311 6316; www.youthhostel.ch/bern. Breakfast included. Lockers 20CHF. Internet 6CHF per hr. Reception June to mid-Sept. 7am-midnight; mid-Sept. to May 7-10am and 5pm-midnight. Closed 2nd and 3rd weeks of Jan. Dorms 33CHF; singles 55CHF; doubles 84-98CHF; quads 148CHF. 1.30CHF visitor's fee; 6CHF HI discount. AmEx/MC/V.) Take tram #9 to Wabern, backtrack 50m, and walk downhill at the first right to reach **Camping Eichholz ❶**, Strandweg 49, near a beach on the Aare. (☎031 961 2602; www.campingeichholz.ch. Showers 1.50CHF per 5min. Laundry 5CHF. Internet 2.50CHF per 15min. Reception 7am-10pm. Open late Apr.-Sept. 7.50CHF per person, 15-17CHF per tent; students 14-16CHF/6.50CHF. Bungalow doubles 35CHF; triples 60CHF; quads 100CHF. MC/V.)

Markets sell produce, cheese, and meats daily at Weinhauspl. and every Tuesday and Saturday on Bundespl. and Munstergasse from May through October. A friendly couple owns **Arlequin ❷**, Gerechtigkeitsg. 51, an 80s-inspired restaurant. (☎031 311 3946. Sandwiches 6-12CHF. Meat fondue 35CHF. Open Tu-W 11am-11:30pm, Th-F 11am-1:30am, Sa 11am-11pm. AmEx/MC/V; min. 20CHF.) A diverse crowd gathers under stage lights on the terrace at **Café du Nord ❸**, Lorrainestr. 2, and enjoys an all-organic menu. (☎031 332 2328. Pasta 19-25CHF. Meat entrees 22-32CHF. Open M-W 8am-11:30pm, Th-F 8am-1:30am, Sa 9am-1:30am, Su 4pm-11:30pm. Kitchen open M-Sa 11:30am-2pm and 6:30-10pm, Su 4:30-11:30pm. MC/V.) For groceries, head to **Migros**, Marktg. 46. (Open M 9am-6:30pm, Tu 8am-6:30pm, W-F 8am-9pm, Sa 7am-4pm.)

SIGHTS. Bern's historic center *(Altstadt)*, one of the best-preserved in Switzerland, is a UNESCO World Heritage sight. Covered arcades allow for wandering and window shopping, while the wide cobblestone streets are dotted by medieval wells topped with Renaissance statues. The Swiss national parliament meets in the massive **Bundeshaus**, which rises high over the Aare; water tumbles from fountains in front of the entrance. (www.parlament.ch. One 45min. tour per hr. M-Sa 9-11am and 2-4pm. English-language tour usually 2pm. Free.) From the Bundeshaus, Kocherg. and Herreng. lead to the 15th-century Protestant **Münster** (Cathedral); above the main entrance, a golden sculpture depicts the torments of hell. For a fantastic view of the city, climb the Münster's 100m spire. (Cathedral open Easter-Oct. Tu-Sa 10am-5pm, Su 11:30am-5pm; Nov.-Easter Tu-Sa 10am-noon, Su 11:30am-2pm. Free. Audio guide 5CHF. Tower open Easter-Oct. M-Sa 10am-4:30pm, Su 11:30am-4:30pm; Nov.-Mar. M-F 2pm-3pm, Sa 2pm-5pm, Su 11:30am-1pm. 4CHF.) For some early medieval flair, check out the **Zytglogge**, a 12th-century clock tower on Kramg. that once marked the city's western boundary. Watch the golden figure use his hammer to ring the golden bell at the top every hour. Down the road is **Albert Einstein's house**, Kramg. 49, where he conceived the theory of general relativity in 1915. His small apartment is now filled with photos and letters. (☎031 312 0091; www.einstein-bern.ch. Open Apr.-Sept. daily 10am-5pm; Feb.-Mar. Tu-F 10am-5pm, Sa 10am-4pm. 6CHF, students 4.50CHF.) Several walkways lead from the Bundeshaus to the **Aare River.** On hot days, locals dive from the banks to ride the river's currents; only experienced swimmers should join.

A recent addition to Bern's many museums is the **Zentrum Paul Klee**, Monument im Fruchtland 3, which houses the world's largest collection of artwork by the renowned Paul Klee in a ripple-shaped building built into a hillside. (☎031 359 0101; www.zpk.org. Take bus #12 to Zentrum Paul Klee. Open Tu-Su 10am-5pm. 16CHF, students 14CHF.) Near Lorrainebrücke, the **Kunstmuseum**, Hodlerstr. 8-12, has paintings from the Middle Ages to the contemporary era and features a smattering of big 20th-century names: Giacometti, Kandinsky, Kirchner, Picasso, and Pollock. (☎031 328 0944; www.kunstmuseumbern.ch.

Open Tu-Su 10am-5pm. 7CHF, students 5CHF. Special exhibits up to 18CHF.) At the east side of the river, across the Nydeggbrücke, lie the **Bärengraben** (Bear Pits), where gawking crowds can observe three European brown bears—the city's namesake. (Open daily June-Sept. 9:30am-5pm; Oct.-May 10am-4pm.) The path up the hill to the left leads to the **Rosengarten** (Rose Garden), which provides visitors with a breathtaking view of Bern's *Altstadt*, especially at sunset. Anything and everything relating to Bern's long history is on display in the jam-packed **Bernisches Historische Museum,** Helvetiapl. 5. (☎031 350 7711; www.bhm.ch. Open Tu-F 10am-5pm. 13CHF, students 8CHF.)

ENTERTAINMENT AND NIGHTLIFE. Check out *Bewegungsmelder*, available at the tourist office, for events. July's **Gurten Festival** (www.gurtenfestival.ch) draws young and energetic crowds and has attracted such luminaries as Bob Dylan and Elvis Costello, while jazz-lovers arrive in early May for the **International Jazz Festival** (www.jazzfestivalbern.ch). Bern's traditional folk festival is the **Onion Market,** which brings 50 tons of onions to the city (late Nov. 2009). The orange grove at **Stadtgärtnerei Elfenau** (tram #19, dir.: Elfenau, to Luternauweg) has free Sunday concerts in the summer. From mid-July to mid-August, **OrangeCinema** (☎0800 07 80 78; www.orangecinema.ch) screens recent films outdoors; tickets are available from the tourist office in the train station.

Find new DJs at **Art Café,** Gurteng. 6, a cafe and club with huge windows overlooking the street. (☎031 318 2070. Open M-W 7am- 1:30am, Th-F 7am-3:30am, Sa 8am-3:30am, Su 10am-3:30am. Cash only.) The Art Café crowd wanders next door to dance to funky beats at **Eclipse,** which has the same owners. (☎031 882 0888; www.eclipse-bar.ch. Open M-W 7am-1:30am, Th-F 7am-3am, Sa 9am-3am.) Many locals gather at **Gut Gelaunt,** Shauptplatzgasse 22, just around the corner, to relax outside and enjoy the special 12-14CHF alcoholic gelato sundaes. (☎031 312 8989; www.gutgelaunt.ch. Beer 4-6CHF. Wine 6-8CHF. Open daily noon-midnight.) The candlelit **Pery Bar,** Schmiedenpl. 3, provides a romantic setting for early-evening drinks. (☎031 311 5908. Beer 5.50CHF. Wine 7CHF. DJs W-Sa. Open M-W 5pm-1:30am, Th 5pm-2:30am, F 5pm-3:30am, Sa 4pm-3:30am. AmEx/MC/V.) To escape the fashionable folk that gather in the *Altstadt* at night, head to the **Reitschule,** Neubrückestr. 8, a graffiti-covered center for Bern's counterculture. (Open daily 8pm-late.)

JUNGFRAU REGION

The most famous region of the Bernese Oberland, Jungfrau draws tourists with its hiking trails, glacier lakes, and snow-capped peaks. From Interlaken, the valley splits at the foot of the Jungfrau Mountain. The eastern valley contains Grindelwald, with easy access to two glaciers, while the western valley harbors many smaller towns. The two valleys are divided by an easily hikeable ridge.

INTERLAKEN ☎033

Interlaken (pop. 5,700) lies between the Thunersee and the Brienzersee at the foot of the largest mountains in Switzerland. Countless hiking trails, raging rivers, and peaceful lakes have turned the town into one of Switzerland's prime tourist attractions and its top adventure-sport destination.

TRANSPORTATION AND PRACTICAL INFORMATION. Westbahnhof (☎033 826 4750) and Ostbahnhof (☎033 828 7319) have **trains** to: Basel (2-3hr.,

1-2 per hr., 55CHF); Bern (1hr., 1-2 per hr., 26CHF); Geneva (3hr., 1-2 per hr., 65CHF); Zürich (2hr., every 2hr., 63CHF). Ostbahnhof also sends trains to Grindelwald (1-2 per hr., 10.20CHF) and Luzern (2hr., 1-2 per hr., 55CHF).

The **tourist office**, Höheweg 37, in Hotel Metropole, gives out **maps** and books accommodations for free. (☎033 826 5300; www.interlaken.ch. Open May-Oct. M-F 8am-7pm, Sa 8am-5pm, Su 10am-noon and 5pm-7pm; Nov.-Apr. M-F 8am-noon and 1:30-6pm, Sa 9am-noon.) Both train stations rent **bikes.** (33CHF per day. Open M-F 6am-8pm, Sa-Su 8am-8pm.) For weather info, call ☎033 828 7931. The **post office** is at Marktg. 1. (Open M-F 8am-noon and 1:45-6pm, Sa 8:30am-11am.) **Postal Code:** CH-3800.

ACCOMMODATIONS AND FOOD. Interlaken is a backpacking hot spot, especially in summer months, so hostels tend to fill up quickly; reserve more than a month ahead. Diagonally across the Höhenmatte from the tourist office, the friendly, low-key **Backpackers Villa Sonnenhof ❷,** Alpenstr. 16, includes admission to a nearby spa for the duration of your stay, minigolf, and free use of local buses. (☎033 826 7171; www.villa.ch. Breakfast included. Laundry 10CHF. Internet 1CHF per 8min. Free Wi-Fi. Reception 7:30-11am and 4-10pm. Dorms 35-37CHF; doubles 98CHF; triples 135CHF; quads 156CHF. AmEx/MC/V.) In contrast, **Balmer's Herberge ❶,** Hauptstr. 23, Switzerland's oldest private hostel, is a place to party. Services include mountain bike rental (35CHF per day), nightly movies, and an extremely popular bar. This hostel also features its own ticket desk for adventure companies, which provides both convenient booking and comparatively cheap package deals. (☎033 822 1961; www.balmers.ch. Breakfast included. Laundry 4CHF. Free Wi-Fi. 24hr. reception. Dorms 27-30CHF; doubles 74-80CHF; triples 99-105CHF; quads 132-146CHF. AmEx/MC/V.) **Funny Farm ❶,** just off Hauptstr., attracts partiers with bonfires, a climbing wall, a swimming pool, and Saturday night beach volleyball. (☎033 828 1281; www.funny-farm.ch. Laundry 10CHF. Internet 5CHF per 25min. or 10CHF for your entire stay. Reception 24hr. Dorms 20-28CHF, with bath 30-39CHF. MC/V.) To camp at **Sackgut ❶,** Brienzstr. 24, turn right from the Ostbanhof, cross the bridge, go right, then turn right again. (☎033 822 4434; www.campingtcs.ch. Open Apr.-Oct. Reception 9-11:30am and 4-6pm. 8CHF per person, 15CHF per tent site. Cash only.)

SWITZERLAND

My Little Thai ❷, Hauptstr. 19 (right next to Balmer's Herberge), fills with hungry backpackers in the evening. (☎033 821 1017; www.mylittlethai.ch. Pad thai 16-22CHF. Vegetarian options available. Open daily 11:30am-10pm. AmEx/MC/V.) **El Azteca ❷,** Jungfraustr. 30, serves cactus salad (16CHF), fajitas (28-38CHF), and other Mexican fare. (☎033 822 7131. Open daily 7:30am-2pm and 6:30pm-11:30pm. AmEx/MC/V.) There are **Migros** and **Coop** supermarkets by both train stations. (Open M-Th 8am-6:30pm, F 8am-9pm, Sa 7:30am-5pm.)

OUTDOOR ACTIVITIES. With the incredible surrounding Alpine scenery, it's no wonder that many of Interlaken's tourists seem compelled to try otherwise unthinkable adventure sports. **Alpin Raft,** Hauptstr. 7 (☎033 823 4100; www.alpinraft.ch), the most established company in Interlaken, has qualified, entertaining guides and offers a wide range of activities, including paragliding (150CHF), river rafting (99-110CHF), skydiving (380-430CHF), and hang-gliding (185CHF). They also offer two different types of **bungee jumping.** At the 85m **Glacier Bungee Jump** (125CHF), thrill-seekers leap off a ledge above the Lutschine River. At the **Alpin Rush Jump** (165CHF), jumpers attached to one of the longest bungee cords in the world leap out of a gondola 134m above a lake, surrounded by the green peaks of the Simmental Valley and herds of grazing cattle. One of the most popular adventure activities at Alpin Raft is **canyoning**

(110-175CHF), which involves rappeling down a series of gorge faces, jumping off cliffs into pools of churning water, and swinging—Tarzan-style—from ropes and zip cords through the canyon. All prices include transportation to and from any hostel in Interlaken and usually a beer upon completion. **Skywings Adventures** has witty professionals and a wide range of activities from paragliding (150-220CHF) to river rafting (99CHF); their booth is across the street from the tourist office (☎079 266 8228; www.skywings.ch). **Outdoor Interlaken,** Hauptstr. 15 (☎826 7719; www.outdoor-interlaken.ch), offers many of the same activities as Alpin Raft at similar prices, as well as rock-climbing lessons (½-day 89CHF) and whitewater **kayaking** tours (½-day 155CHF). At **Skydive Xdream,** you can skydive with one of the best in the world; the owner, Stefan Heuser, was on the Swiss skydiving team for 12 years and won three world championship medals. (☎079 759 3483; www.justjump.ch. 380CHF per tandem plane jump; 430CHF per tandem helicopter jump. Open year-round. Pick-ups 9am and 1pm, Sa-Su also 4pm. Call for winter availability.) Swiss Alpine Guide offers **ice climbing,** running full-day trips to a nearby glacier and providing all the equipment needed to scale vertical glacier walls and rappel into icy crevasses. (☎033 822 6000; www.swissalpineguides.ch. Trips May-Nov. daily, weather permitting. 160CHF.)

Interlaken's most-traversed trail climbs **Harder Kulm** (1310m). From the Ostbahnhof, head toward town, take the first road bridge right across the river, and follow the yellow signs that give way to white-red-white rock markings. From the top, signs lead back down to the Westbahnhof. The hike should be about 2hr. up and 1hr. down. In summer, the Harderbahn **funicular** runs from the trailhead to the top. (Open daily May to Oct. 15CHF, round-trip 25CHF. 25% Eurail and 50% SwissPass discount.) For a flatter trail, turn left from the train station and left again before the bridge; follow the canal over to the nature reserve on the shore of the **Thunersee.** The 3hr. trail winds along the Lombach River, through pastures at the base of Harder Kulm, and back toward town.

ADVENTURE WITH CAUTION. Interlaken's adventure sports industry is thrilling, but accidents do happen. On July 27, 1999, 21 tourists were killed by a sudden flash flood while canyoning. Be aware that you participate in all adventure sports at your own risk.

CENTRAL SWITZERLAND

ZÜRICH ☎044

Battalions of executives charge daily through Zürich, Switzerland's largest city (pop. 370,000) and the world's fourth-largest stock exchange—bringing with them enough money to keep upper-crust boutiques thriving. But only footsteps away from the flashy Bahnhofstr. shopping district is the old town and city's student quarter, home to cobblestoned pieces of history and an energetic counter-culture that has inspired generations of Swiss philosophers and artists.

TRANSPORTATION

Flights: Zürich-Kloten Airport (**ZRH;** ☎044 816 2211; www.zurich-airport.com) is a major hub for Swiss International Airlines (☎084 885 2000; www.swiss.com). Daily connections to: **Frankfurt, GER; London, BRI; Paris, FRA.** Trains connect the airport to the Hauptbahnhof in the city center. 3-6 per hr., 6CHF; Eurail and SwissPass valid.

Trains: Run to: **Basel** (1hr., 2-3 per hr., 31CHF); **Bern** (1hr., 3-4 per hr., 46CHF); **Geneva** (3hr., 1-2 per hr., 88CHF); **Luzern** (1hr., 1-2 per hr., 23CHF); **St. Gallen** (30min.; 2-3 per hr.; 28CHF); **Milan, ITA** (4hr., every 2hr., 72-87CHF); **Munich, GER** (5hr., 4-5 per day, 90CHF); **Paris, FRA** (5hr., 4 per day, 112-140CHF, under 26 86CHF).

Public Transportation: Trams criss-cross the city, originating at the *Hauptbahnhof.* Tickets valid for 1hr. cost 4CHF (press the blue button on automatic ticket machines); tickets (valid for 30min.) cost 2.40CHF (yellow button). If you plan to ride several times, buy a 24hr. **Tageskarte** (7.60CHF; green button), valid on trams, buses, and ferries. **Night buses** (5CHF ticket valid all night) run from the city center to outlying areas (F-Su).

Car Rental: The tourist office offers a 20% discount and free upgrade deal with **Europcar** (☎044 804 4646; www.europcar.ch). Prices from 155CHF per day with unlimited mileage. 20+. Branches at the airport (☎043 255 5656), Josefstr. 53 (☎044 271 5656), and Lindenstr. 33 (☎044 383 1747). Rent in the city; 40% tax is added at the airport.

Bike Rental: Bike loans from **Züri Rollt** (☎043 288 3400; www.zuerirollt.ch) are free for 6hr. during business hours; otherwise 5CHF per day, 20CHF per night. Pick up a bike from **Globus City,** the green hut on the edge of the garden between Bahnhofstr. and Löwenstr.; **Opernhaus**, by the opera house past Bellevuepl.; **Velogate,** across from Hauptbahnhof's tracks next to the Landesmuseum castle. Bikes must be returned to original rental station. Passport and 20CHF deposit. Open May-Oct. 7:30am-11:30pm.

ORIENTATION AND PRACTICAL INFORMATION

Zürich is in north-central Switzerland, close to the German border and on some of the lowest land in the country. The **Limmat River** splits the city down the middle on its way to the **Zürichsee** (Lake Zürich). The **Hauptbahnhof** (train station) lies on the western bank and marks the beginning of **Bahnhofstraße,** the city's main shopping street. Two-thirds of the way down Bahnhofstr. lies **Paradeplatz,** the banking center of Zürich, which marks the beginning of the last stretch of the shopping street (reserved for those with trust funds). The eastern bank of the river is dominated by the university district, which stretches above the narrow **Niederdorfstraße** and pulses with bars, clubs, and restaurants.

Tourist Office: In the **Hauptbahnhof** (☎044 215 4000; www.zuerich.com). An electronic hotel reservation board is at the front of the station. Also sells the **ZürichCARD,** which is good for unlimited public transportation, free museum admission, and discounts on sights and tours (1-day 17CHF, 3-day 34CHF). Open May-Oct. M-Sa 8am-8:30pm, Su 8:30am-6:30pm; Nov.-Apr. M-Sa 8:30am-7pm, Su 9am-6:30pm.

Currency Exchange: On the main floor of the train station. Cash advances for MC/V with photo ID; min. 200CHF, max. 1000CHF. Open daily 6:30am-9:30pm. **Crédit Suisse,** at Paradepl. 5CHF commission. Open M-F 8:15am-5pm.

Luggage Storage: Middle level of *Hauptbahnhof.* 5-8CHF. Open daily 4:15am-1:30am.

Bookstore: The Orell Füssli Bookshop, Bahnhofstr. 70, has an extensive selection of English books. (☎044 211 0444. Open M-F 9am-8pm, Sa 9am-6pm. AmEx/MC/V.)

GLBT Resources: Homosexuelle Arbeitsgruppe Zürich (HAZ), on the 3rd fl. of Sihlquai 67 (☎044 271 2250; www.haz.ch), has a library and meetings. Open W 2-6pm.

24hr. Pharmacy: Bellevue Apotheke, Theaterstr. 14, on Bellevuepl. (☎044 266 6222).

Internet: Quanta Virtual Fun Space (☎044 260 7266), at the corner of Mühleg. and Niederdorfstr. 3CHF per 15min., 5CHF per 30min. Open daily 9am-midnight.

Post Office: Sihlpost, Kasernestr. 95-97, behind the station. Open M-F 6:30am-10:30pm, Sa 6:30am-8pm, Su 10am-10:30pm. **Postal Code:** CH-8021.

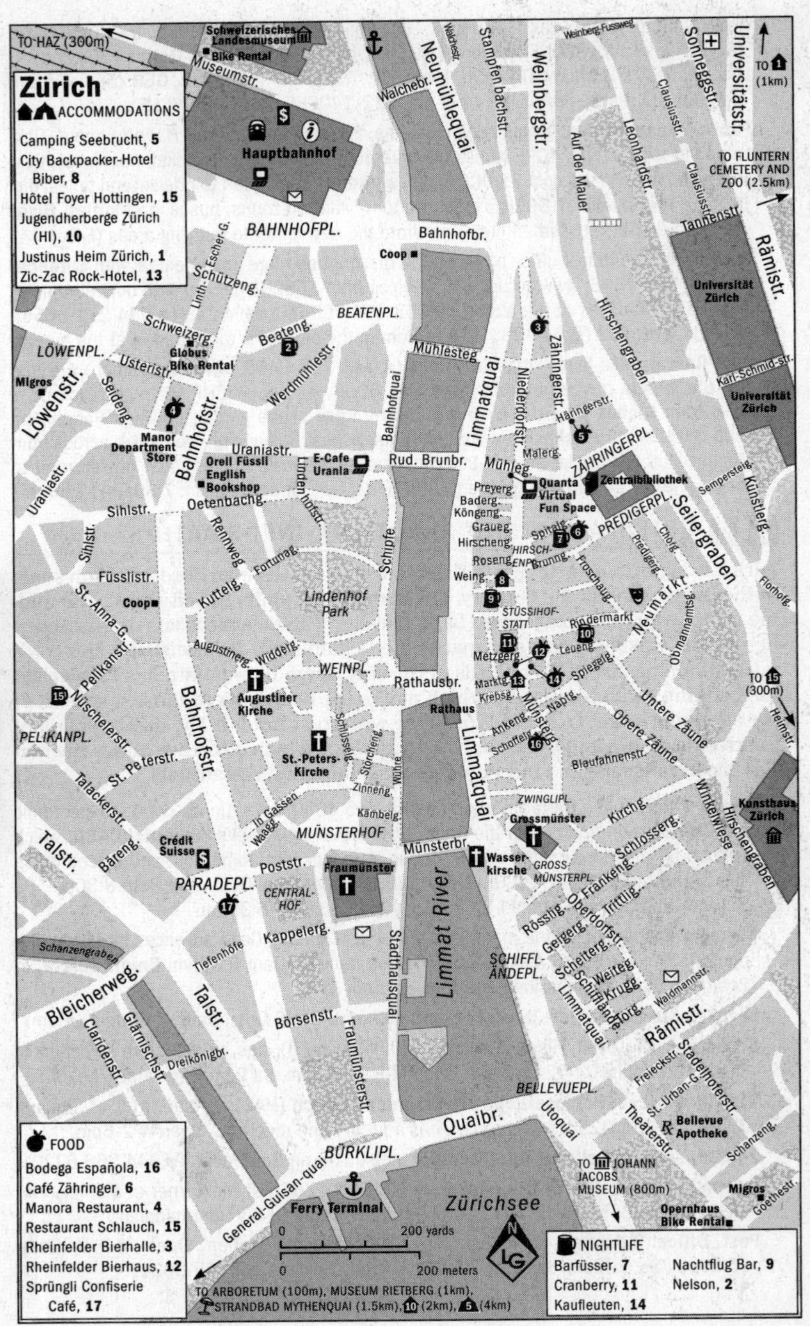

SWITZERLAND

ACCOMMODATIONS AND CAMPING

Zürich's few budget accommodations are easily accessible by foot or public transportation. Reserve ahead, especially in summer.

Justinus Heim Zürich, Freudenbergstr. 146 (☎044 361 3806; justinuszh@bluewin.ch). Take tram #9 or 10 (dir.: Bahnhof Oerlikon) to Seilbahn Rigiblick, then take the funicular to the top (open daily 5:20am-12:40am). This hillside hostel, which hosts students during the term period, is removed from the downtown bustle but easily accessible. Beautiful view of the city. Breakfast included. Reception 8am-noon and 5-9pm. Singles 50CHF, with shower 65CHF; doubles 90-110CHF. Rates rise July-Aug. V. ❸

The City Backpacker-Hotel Biber, Niederdorfstr. 5 (☎044 251 9015; www.city-backpacker.ch). From the Hauptbanhof, cross the bridge and Limmatquai, turn right onto Niederdorfst., and walk for 5min. The beds are somewhat uncomfortable and the street noise constant—but with Niederdorfstr. nightlife right outside, you may not need your bunk bed. Reception 8-11am and 3-10pm. Check-out 10am. Dorms 34CHF; singles 71CHF; doubles 98CHF; triples 135CHF; quads 176CHF. MC/V. ❷

Hôtel Foyer Hottingen, Hottingenstr. 31 (☎044 256 1919; www.foyer-hottingen.ch). Take tram #3 (dir.: Kluspl.) to Hottingerpl. Families and student backpackers fill this house a block from the Kunsthaus. Breakfast included. Reception 7am-11pm. Partitioned dorms (40CHF) provide privacy. Singles 85-95CHF, with bath 120-135CHF; doubles 120/160-170CHF; triples 145/190CHF; quads 180CHF. MC/V. ❷

Jugendherberge Zürich (HI), Mutschellenstr. 114 (☎044 399 7800; www.youthhostel.ch/zuerich). From the station, take tram #7 (dir.: Wollishofen) to Morgental, then backtrack 20m and head down Mutschellenstr. 24hr. snack bar with beer on tap. Breakfast included. Internet 1CHF per 4min. Reception 24hr. Dorms 44CHF; singles with shower 105CHF; doubles with shower 123CHF; triples 141CHF, with shower 156CHF; quads 178CHF; quints 194CHF. Rates rise July-Aug. HI discount 6CHF. MC/V. ❸

Zic-Zac Rock-Hotel, Marktg. 17 (☎044 261 2181; www.ziczac.ch). Hotel is 1min. down the road past City Backpacker. Each room is named after a band and decorated with funky paintings. Rooms have TV, phone, and sink. Internet 1CHF per 4min. Free Wi-Fi. Reception 24hr. Singles 83CHF, with shower 94CHF; doubles 133/147CHF; triples 173/180CHF; quads with shower 280CHF. AmEx/MC/V. ❹

THE LOCAL STORY

A SAINTLY BREED

In AD 1050, the Archdeacon Bernard de Menthon founded a hospice in a Jungfrau region mountain pass, bringing with him a breed of large, furry dogs of Gallic origin. In addition to providing shelter for passing merchants, Bernard and the monks working under him would venture into blizzards in search of stranded travelers. Though it is uncertain whether the dogs accompanied the monks on their rescue missions—early accounts relate that dogs were used to run an exercise wheel that turned a cooking spit—by the time of Bernard's canonization, dogs bearing his name had become famous, and regularly patrolled the pass.

Gifted with a fine sense of smell, a thick coat, an amiable manner, and a neck made to tie a barrel of brandy to, the St. Bernards made a name for themselves by saving over 2000 lives throughout centuries. In the 1810s, a dog named Barry saved 40 lost travelers. Today, few St. Bernards still work as rescue dogs—smaller, lighter breeds less liable to sink in the snow have taken their place. The St. Bernard is now a popular household pet, as well as the star of popular films like *Cujo* and the *Beethoven* moviesm, but it will always have dignity as the Alpine fixture it once was.

Camping Seebrucht, Seestr. 559 (☎044 482 1612; www.camping-zurich.ch). Take tram #11 to Bürklipl., then bus #161 or 165 to Stadtgrenze. Showers 2CHF. Reception 8am-noon and 3-9pm. Check-out 11:30am. 8CHF per person, 12CHF per tent. MC/V. ❶

FOOD

Zürich's has over 1300 restaurants, offering a bite of everything. The cheapest meals are available at *Würstli* (sausage) stands for 5CHF. The **farmer's markets** at Bürklipl. (Tu and F 6-11am) and Rosenhof (Th 10am-8pm, Sa 10am-5pm) sell produce and flowers. Head to **Niederdorfstraße** for a variety of snack bars and cheaper restaurants interspersed among fancier establishments.

Café Zähringer, Zähringerpl. 11 (☎044 252 0500; www.cafe-zaehringer.ch). Enjoy mainly vegetarian and vegan fare in this colorful, student-friendly cafe. Try their *Kefirwasser,* a purple, fizzy drink made from dates and mushrooms fed with sugar (4CHF). Salads 7-13CHF. Pastas 4-14CHF. Stir-fry 18.50-26.50CHF. Breakfast specials 8.50-23CHF. Open M 6pm-midnight, Tu-Su 8am-midnight. Cash only. ❷

Restaurant Schlauch, Münstergasse 20 (☎044 251 2304). Enjoy the billiard tables at this affordable downtown eatery. Soups 5-8.50CHF. Salads 7-14CHF. Entrees 8-20CHF. Open Tu-Sa 11:30am-2pm and 6-9pm. AmEx/MC/V. ❷

Bodega Española, Münstergasse 15 (☎044 251 2310). Has been serving Catalán delights since 1874. Egg-and-potato tortilla dishes 16-18CHF. Tapas 4.80CHF. Open daily 10am-midnight. Kitchen open noon-2pm and 6-10pm. AmEx/MC/V. ❷

Sprüngli Confiserie Café, Paradepl. (☎044 224 4711). This Zürich landmark was founded by one of the original Lindt chocolate makers. Pick up a handful of the bite-size *Luxemburgerli* (8.40CHF per 100g) or eat a full meal (19-28CHF). Open M-F 7am-8pm, Sa 8am-7pm, Su 10am-6pm. **Branches** at Stadelhoferpl. near the lake (open M-F 7am-6:30pm, Sa 8am-4pm) and in the Hauptbanhof (open M-F 6:45am-9pm, Sa 6:45am-8pm, Su 8:45am-5pm). AmEx/MC/V. ❷

Rheinfelder Bierhalle, Niederdorfst. 76 (☎044 251 5464). This restaurant/bar near the Hauptbanhof attracts patrons looking for hearty meals and plentiful liquor. Soups 4-6CHF. *Würste* 5-15CHF. Entrees 9-20CHF. Open daily 9am-midnight. MC/V. ❷

Manora Restaurant, Banhofst. 75. Mingle with bankers at this fast-paced self-serve restaurant on the 5th fl. of the Manor department store. Sandwiches 3-6CHF. Salads 4-11CHF. Entrees 6-15CHF. Open M-F 9am-8pm, Sa 9am-5pm. AmEx/MC/V. ❶

Rheinfelder Bierhaus, Marktg. 19. Night crowds fill the outdoor seating at this bright, very Swiss downtown restaurant (not to be confused with Rheinfelder Bierhalle down the street). Entrees 12-21CHF. Vegetarian dishes 12-16CHF. Open daily 8:30am-midnight. Kitchen open 11am-11pm. AmEx/MC/V. ❷

SIGHTS

Bahnhofstraße leads into the city from the train station. The street is filled with shoppers during the day but falls quiet after 6pm and on weekends. At the Zürichsee end of Bahnhofstr., **Bürkliplatz** is a good place to begin walking along the lake shore. The *platz* itself hosts a Saturday **flea market** *(May-Oct. 6am-3pm).* On the other side of the Limmat River, the pedestrian zone continues on Niederdorfstr. and Münsterg., where shops run from ritzy to erotic and crowds keep busy until after midnight. Off Niederdorfstr., **Spiegelgasse** was once home to Goethe and Lenin. **Fraumünster, Grossmünster,** and **St. Peters Kirche** grace the Limmat River. For a view of Zürich from the water, as well as a chance to see some of the towns on the banks of the Zürichsee, **boat tours,** costing a fraction of those in other Swiss cities, leave from the ferry terminal at Bürklipl. The shortest tour, A Kleine Rundfahrten, lasts 1hr. *(May-Sept. daily 11am-6:30pm. 7.80CHF.)*

FRAUMÜNSTER. Marc Chagall's stained glass windows depicting Biblical scenes add vibrancy to this otherwise austere 13th-century Gothic cathedral. A mural on the courtyard's archway depicts Felix and Regula (the decapitated patron saints of Zürich) with their heads in their hands. *(Off Paradepl. Open May-Nov. M-Sa 10am-6pm, Su 11:30am-6pm; Dec.-Apr. M-Sa 10am-4pm, Su 11:30am-4pm. Free.)*

GROSSMÜNSTER. Ulrich Zwingli kickstarted the Swiss German Reformation at Grossmünster in the 16th century. Today, the cathedral is Zürich's main landmark. Its defining twin towers are best viewed on the bridge near the Fraumünster. *(Towers open daily Mar.-Oct. 9:15am-5pm; Nov.-Feb. 10:15am-4:30pm. 2CHF.)*

ZOO ZÜRICH. Far from downtown's bustle, this hillside zoo holds around 2000 animals of 250 different species, along with a few million children. Explore tropical rainforests and their inhabitants at the enormous Masoala biosphere. *(Take tram #6 (dir.: Zoo) to the last stop, then walk up Zürichbergst. to your left. ☎ 044 254 2505; www.zoo.ch. Zoo open daily Mar.-Oct. 9am-6pm; Nov.-Mar. 9am-5pm. Biosphere open Mar.-Oct. 10am-6pm; Nov-Mar. 9am-5pm. 22CHF, ages 16-25 16CHF. AmEx/MC/V.)*

BEACHES. When the weather heats up, a visit to the beaches along the Zürichsee offers respite. The city has numerous free swimming spots, which are labeled on a map distributed by the tourist office. The convenient and popular **Arboretum** is about 100m down from the Quaibrücke. *(Tram #5 to Rentenanstalt and head to the water.)* Across the lake, **Zürichhorn** draws crowds with its peaceful gardens and a famous statue by Jean Tinguely. *(Tram #2 or 4 to Frolichst., then walk towards the lake.)* **Strandbad Mythenquai,** along the western shore, offers diving towers and a water trampoline. *(Tram #7 to Brunaustr. and walk 2min. in the same direction until you see a set of stairs. Look for signs. ☎ 044 201 0000. Check out www.sportamt.ch for info on water quality. Open daily May to early Sept. 9am-8pm. 6CHF, ages 16-20 4.50CHF.)*

GARDENS AND PARKS. For views of the city and river, climb up to **Lindenhof,** once a checkpoint for Roman settlement; walk uphill on Strehlg., Rennweg, or Glockeng. The lush **Rieter-Park,** overlooking the city, creates a romantic backdrop for the **Museum Rietberg.** *(Tram #7 to Museum Rietberg. Turn right onto Sternenstr. and follow the signs uphill to the museum. Free.)* The **Stadtgärtnerel's** aviary attracts botanists and ornithologists alike—17 species of tropical birds swoop overhead. *(Sackzelg. 25-27. Tram #3 to Hubertus; head down Gutstr. ☎ 044 492 1423; www.stadtgaertnerei.ch. Open daily 9-11:30am and 1:30-4:30pm. Free.)*

MUSEUMS

MUSEUM RIETBERG. Rietberg presents an outstanding collection of Asian, African, and other non-European art, housed in three structures spread around the Rieter-Park. The basement of the new **Emerald Building** houses masterpieces from Asia and Africa; highlights include Chinese boddhisatvas and Japanese Noh masks. **Villa Wesendonck** (where Wagner wrote *Tristan and Isolde*) holds works from South Asia, Central America, and Oceania, while **Park-Villa Rieter** includes a small collection of Near Eastern art. *(Gablerstr. 15. Tram #7 to Museum Rietberg. ☎ 044 206 3131; www.rietberg.ch. Buy tickets in the Emerald building. All buildings open Apr.-Sept. Tu and F-Su 10am-5pm, W-Th 10am-8pm. 16CHF, students 12CHF. MC/V.)*

KUNSTHAUS ZÜRICH. The Kunsthaus, Europe's largest privately funded museum, houses a vast collection ranging from religious works by the Old Masters to 21st-century American Pop Art. Compositions by Chagall, Dalí, Gauguin, van Gogh, Munch, Picasso, Rembrandt, Renoir, and Rubens stretch from wall to wall in a patchwork of rich color while a Modern sculpture made of car tops adorns the entrance. *(Heimpl. 1. Take tram #3, 5, 8, or 9 to Kunsthaus. ☎ 044 253*

8484; www.kunsthaus.ch. English-language audio tour and brochure. Open T and Sa-Su 10am-6pm, W-F 10am-8pm. 18CHF, students 12CHF. AmEx/MC/V.)

SCHWEIZERISCHES LANDESMUSEUM. In the cement imitation-castle next to the Hauptbahnhof, this museum of Swiss history and culture displays centuries-old artifacts. Highlights include 16th-century astrological tools, Ulrich Zwingli's weapons from the 1531 Battle of Kappel, and a tiny jeweled clock with a golden skeleton indicating the hour. *(Museumstr. 2. ☎044 218 6511; www.musee-suisse.com. Open Tu-Su 10am-5pm, Th 10am-7pm. 10CHF, students 8CHF.)*

JOHANN JACOBS MUSEUM. Exhibits on the cultural history of coffee are best viewed while sipping a free cup. *(Seefldquai 17. Take tram #2, 4, 5, 8, 9, 11, or 15 to Bellevue, then walk along the lake and turn onto Seefeldquai. ☎044 388 6151; www.johann-jacobs-museum.ch. Open F 2-7pm, Sa 2-5pm, Su 10am-5pm. 5CHF, students 3CHF.)*

ENTERTAINMENT AND NIGHTLIFE

Most English-language movies in Zürich are screened with French and German subtitles (marked "E/D/F"). Films generally cost 15CHF and up, but less on Mondays. From mid-July to mid-August, the **OrangeCinema,** an open-air cinema at Zürichhorn (tram #2 or 4 to Fröhlichstr.), attracts huge crowds to its lakefront screenings. In mid-August, the **Street Parade** brings together ravers from all over for the world's biggest techno party.

THAT EXPLAINS THE TASSELS. Beware the deceptive and common title of "night club"—it's really just a euphemism for "strip club."

For information on after-dark happenings, check **ZüriTipp** (www.zueritipp.ch) or pick up a free copy of *ZürichGuide* or *ZürichEvents* from the tourist office. On **Niederdorfstraße,** the epicenter of Zürich's *Altstadt* nightlife, bars are packed to the brim almost every night. **Kreis 5,** once the industrial area of Zürich, has recently developed into party central, with ubiquitous clubs, bars, and lounges taking over former factories. Kreis 5 lies northwest of the *Hauptbahnhof*, with Hardstr. as its axis. To get there, take tram #4 (dir.: Werdholzi) or #13 (dir.: Albisgütli) to Escher-Wyss-Pl. and follow the crowds. Closer to the Old Town, **Langstraße,** reached by walking away from the river on the city's western side, is the reputed red-light district, with many bars and clubs (some sleazier than others). Beer in Zürich is pricey (from 6CHF), but an array of cheap bars have established themselves on Niederdorfstr. near Mühleg.

Kaufleuten, Pelikanstr. 18 (☎044 225 3322; www.kaufleuten.ch). For a memorable evening, visit this former theater transformed into trendy club. Still decked out in red velvet, it attracts the who's who of Zürich by throwing nightly themed parties. Madonna and Prince have both paid visits. Check website for events. Cover 10-30CHF. Hours vary, but generally open M-Th and Su 11pm-2am, F-Sa 11pm-4am. MC/V.

Nelson, Beateng. 11 (☎044 212 6016). Locals, backpackers, and businessmen chug beer (9CHF per pint) at this large Irish pub. 20+. Open M-W 11:30am-2am, Th 11:30am-3am, F 11:30am-4:30am, Sa 3pm-4:30am, Su 3pm-2am. MC/V.

Barfüsser, Spitalg. 14 (☎044 251 4064), off Zähringerpl. Freely flowing mixed drinks (14-17CHF) and wine (6-9CHF) accompany delicious sushi at this gay bar. Open M-Th noon-1am, F-Sa noon-2am, Su 5pm-1am. AmEx/MC/V.

Nachtflug Bar, Café, and Lounge, Stüssihofstatt 4 (☎044 261 9966; www.n8flug.ch). Sleek bar with outdoor seating. Wine from 6CHF. Beer from 4.90CHF. Open M-Th 9am-midnight, F-Sa 9am-1:30am, Su 11am-midnight. Outdoor bar open M-W 9am-midnight, Th-F 9am-10pm, Sa-Su 11am-10pm. AmEx/MC/V.

Cranberry, Metzgerg. 3 (☎044 261 2772; www.cranberry.ch). Attracts a sociable clientele with funky lights, peppy music, and a wide selection of mixed drinks (6-19CHF). Happy hour 5-7pm; drinks are double-sized. Open M-W and Su 5pm-12:30am, Th 5pm-1am, F-Sa 5pm-2am. AmEx/MC/V.

FRENCH SWITZERLAND

The picturesque scenery and refined cities of French Switzerland have attracted herds of tourists for centuries, and there's no denying that the area's charm often comes at a steep price. But the best experiences in French Switzerland are free: strolling down tree-lined avenues, soaking up endearing *vieilles villes* (Old Towns), and taking in the mountain vistas from across Lac Léman (Lake Geneva) and Lac Neuchâtel.

GENEVA (GENÈVE) ☎022

Geneva (pop. 186,000) began with a tomb, blossomed into a religious center, became the "Protestant Rome," and ultimately emerged as a center for world diplomacy. Today, thanks to the presence of dozens of multinational organizations, including the United Nations and the Red Cross, the city is easily the most worldly in Switzerland. But Geneva's heritage lingers; you can sense it in the street names paying homage to Genevese patriots of old and the ubiquitous presence of the cherished cuckoo clock.

TRANSPORTATION

Flights: Cointrin Airport (**GVA;** ☎022 717 7111, flight info ☎022 717 7105) is a hub for **Swiss International Airlines** (☎0848 85 20 00) and also serves **Air France** (☎827 8787) and **British Airways** (☎0848 80 10 10). Several direct flights per day to **Amsterdam, NTH; London, BRI; New York, USA; Paris, FRA;** and **Rome, ITA.** Bus #10 runs to the Gare Cornavin (15min., 6-12 per hr., 3CHF), but the train trip is shorter (6min., 6 per hr., 3CHF).

Trains: Trains run 4:30am-1am. **Gare Cornavin,** pl. Cornavin, is the main station. To: **Basel** (2hr., every 2 hr., 69CHF); **Bern** (2hr., 2 per hr., 46CHF); **Lausanne** (40min., 3-4 per hr., 20.60CHF); **Zürich** (3hr., 1-2 per hr., 80CHF); **Nyon** (20 min., 8.20CHF); **St. Gallen** (4hr., 1-2 per hr., 95CHF). Ticket counter open M-F 5:15am-9:30pm, Sa-Su 5:30am-9:30pm. **Gare des Eaux-Vives** (☎022 736 1620), on av. de la Gare des Eaux-Vives (tram #12 to Amandoliers SNCF), connects to France's regional rail through **Annecy, FRA** (1hr., 6 per day, 15CHF) or **Chamonix, FRA** (2hr., 4 per day, 25CHF).

Public Transportation: Geneva has an efficient **bus and tram** network (☎022 308 3311; www.tpg.ch). Single tickets, which can be purchased in the train station, are valid for 1hr. within the "orange" city zone (which includes the airport) are 3CHF; rides of 3 stops or less 2CHF. **Day passes** (10CHF) and a **9hr. pass** (7CHF) are available for the canton of Geneva; day passes for the whole region 18CHF. MC/V. Stamp multi-use tickets before boarding at machines in the station. Buses run 5am-12:30am; **Noctambus** (F-Sa 12:30-3:45am, 3CHF) offers night service. Tram use is free with the **Geneva visitor card,** usually distributed by hotels and hostels—make sure to ask for one.

Taxis: Taxi-Phone (☎022 331 4133). 6.80CHF plus 3CHF per km. 30CHF from airport.

Bike Rental: Geneva has well-marked bike paths and special traffic signals. Behind the station, **Genève Roule,** pl. Montbrillant 17 (☎022 740 1343), has **free bikes.** (Passport and 20CHF deposit. First 4 hours free, 1CHF per hour thereafter. Fines are 60CHF for lost free bike. Mountain bikes 17CHF per day. Touring bikes 28CHF per day. May-Oct. only.) Other locations at Bains des Pâquis, Plain de Plainpalis, Place de l'Octroi, and pl.

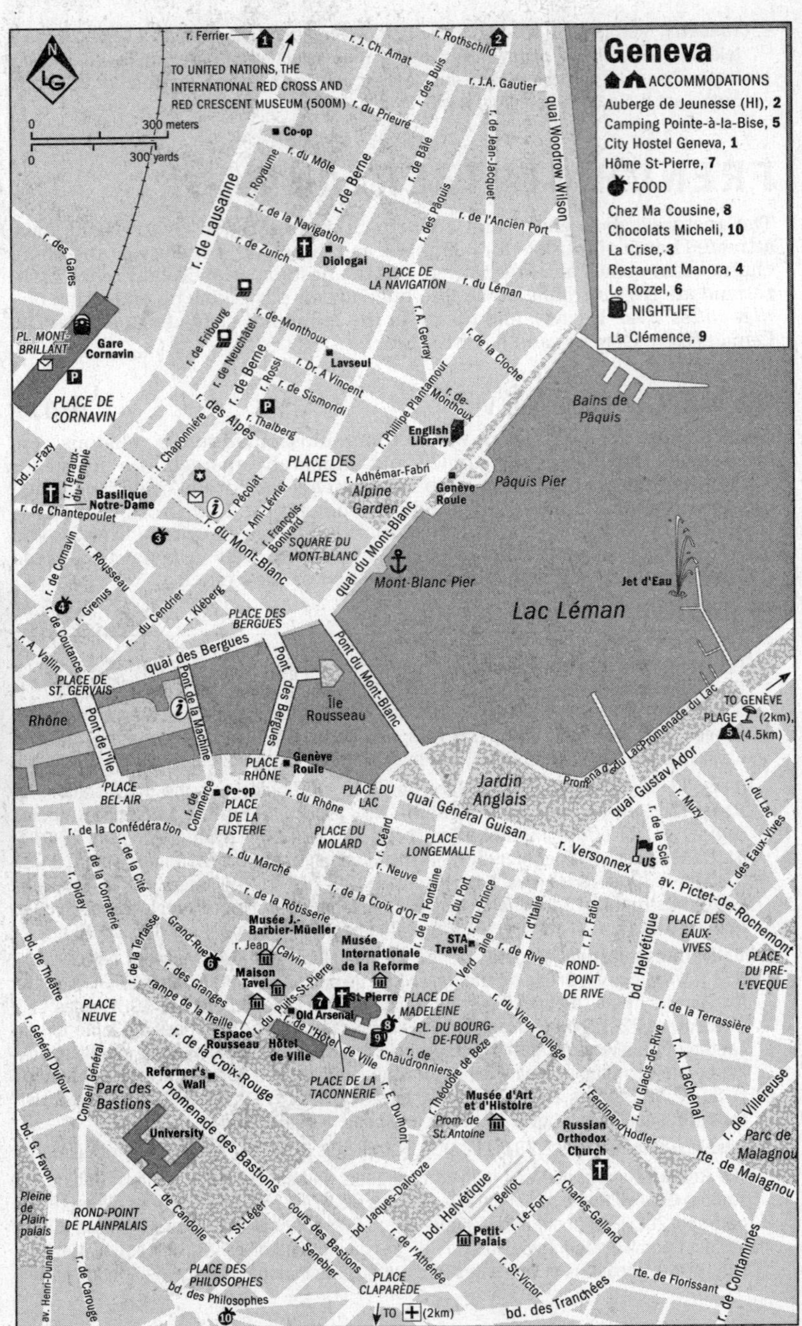
Geneva
ACCOMMODATIONS
Auberge de Jeunesse (HI), 2
Camping Pointe-à-la-Bise, 5
City Hostel Geneva, 1
Hôme St-Pierre, 7
FOOD
Chez Ma Cousine, 8
Chocolats Micheli, 10
La Crise, 3
Restaurant Manora, 4
Le Rozzel, 6
NIGHTLIFE
La Clémence, 9
TO UNITED NATIONS, THE INTERNATIONAL RED CROSS AND RED CRESCENT MUSEUM (500M)
300 meters
300 yards
Gare Cornavin
PLACE DE CORNAVIN
PL. MONT-BRILLANT
PLACE DES ALPES
PLACE DE LA NAVIGATION
Basilique Notre-Dame
English Library
Alpine Garden
Genève Roule
Pâquis Pier
Bains de Pâquis
SQUARE DU MONT-BLANC
Mont-Blanc Pier
Jet d'Eau
Lac Léman
Rhône
Île Rousseau
Jardin Anglais
TO GENÈVE PLAGE (2km), (4.5km)
Musée J.-Barbier-Müeller
Musée Internationale de la Reforme
Maison Tavel
St-Pierre
Old Arsenal
Espace Rousseau
Hôtel de Ville
Reformer's Wall
Parc des Bastions
University
Musée d'Art et d'Histoire
Russian Orthodox Church
Petit-Palais
Parc de Malagnou
PLACE NEUVE
PLACE DE MADELEINE
PL. DU BOURG-DE-FOUR
PLACE DE LA TACONNERIE
ROND-POINT DE PLAINPALAIS
ROND-POINT DE RIVE
PLACE DES PHILOSOPHES
PLACE CLAPARÈDE
TO (2km)
STA Travel
Co-op
Diologai
Lavseul
US

du Rhône. Arrive before 9am, as bikes go quickly. Free **bike maps** available. Open daily May-Oct. 8am-9pm; Nov.-Apr. 8am-6pm. Cash only.

Hitchhiking: *Let's Go* does not recommend hitchhiking. Those headed to Germany or northern Switzerland take bus #4 to Jardin Botanique, where they try to catch a ride. Those headed to France take bus #4 to Palettes, then line D to St. Julien.

ORIENTATION AND PRACTICAL INFORMATION

The twisting streets and quiet squares of the historic *vieille ville* (Old Town), centered on **Cathédrale de St-Pierre,** make up the heart of Geneva. Across the **Rhône River** to the north, five-star hotels give way to lakeside promenades, **International Hill,** and rolling parks. Across the **Arve River** to the south lies the village of **Carouge,** home to bars and clubs (take tram #12 or 13 to pl. du Marché).

Tourist Office: r. du Mont-Blanc 18 (☎022 909 7000; www.geneva-tourism.ch), in the Central Post Office Building. From Cornavin, walk 5min. toward the Pont du Mont-Blanc. Staff books hotel rooms for 5CHF, gives out free city **maps,** and leads English-language walking tours (daily 10am; 15CHF). Open M 10am-6pm, Tu-Su 9am-6pm.

Consulates: Australia, chemin des Fins 2 (☎022 799 9100). **Canada,** Laurenzerberg 2 (☎531 38 3000). **New Zealand,** chemin des Fins 2 (☎022 929 0350). **UK,** r. de Vermont 37 (☎022 918 2400). **US,** r. Versonnex 7 (☎022 840 5160).

Currency Exchange: ATMs have the best rates. The currency exchange inside the **Gare Cornavin** has good rates with no commission on traveler's checks, makes cash advances on credit cards (min. 200CHF), and arranges **Western Union** transfers. Open M-Sa 7am-8pm, Su 8am-5:50pm.

GLBT Resources: Dialogai, r. de la Navigation 11-13, entrance Rue d. Levant 5 (☎022 906 4040). From Gare Cornavin, turn left, walk 5min. down r. de Lausanne, and turn right onto r. de la Navigation. Has brochures and maps on **GBLT nightlife;** doubles as a cafe and nighttime hot spot. Mostly male crowd, but women welcome. Open M 9am-10pm, Tu-Th 9am-6pm, F 9am-5pm.

Laundromat: Laundrenet, r. de la servette 83. (☎022 734 8383; www.laundrenet.com) From the Gare Cornavin walk along r. de Lyon and turn right onto r. de la Servette. New, state of the art facilities. Wash 6-9CHF, dry 1CHF per 10min. Internet 6CHF per hr., students 5.50 CHF. Open July-Aug M and W noon-9pm, T 10am-9pm, Th-Sa 10am-8pm, Su noon-8pm; Sept.-June M-Tu noon-9pm, W-Su noon-8pm. **Lavseul,** r. de Monthoux 29 (☎022 735 9051). Wash 5CHF, dry 1CHF per 9min. Open daily 7am-midnight.

Police: R. de Berne 6 (☎117). Open M-F 9am-noon and 3-6:30pm, Sa 9am-noon.

Hospital: Geneva University Hospital, r. Micheli-du-Crest 24 (☎022 372 3311; www.hug-ge.ch). Bus #1 or 5 or tram #7, or Bus #35 from Place du Augustines. Door #2 is for emergency care; door #3 is for consultations. For info on walk-in clinics, contact the **Association des Médecins** (☎022 320 8420). 24 hr. medical centers at **Permanence De Chantelpoulet,** Rue de Chantepoulet 1-3 (☎022 731 2120); and **Permanence De La Tour,** Avenue J.D. Maillard 3 (☎022 719 6111).

Internet: Charly's Multimedia Check Point, r. de Fribourg 7 (☎022 901 1313; www.charlys.com). 4CHF per hr. Free Wi-Fi. Open M-Sa 9am-midnight, Su 1-11pm.

Post Office: Poste Centrale, r. du Mont-Blanc 18, 1 block from Gare Cornavin. Open M-F 7:30am-6pm, Sa 9am-4pm. **Postal Code:** CH-1200.

ACCOMMODATIONS AND CAMPING

The indispensable *Info Jeunes* lists about 30 budget options, and the tourist office publishes *Budget Hotels,* which stretches the definition of budget to 120CHF per person. Cheap beds are relatively scarce, so reserve ahead.

Hôme St-Pierre, Cour St-Pierre 4 (☎022 310 3707; info@homestpierre.ch). Take bus #5 to pl. Neuve, then walk up Rampe de la Treille, turn left onto R. Puits-St.-Pierre, then right on R. du Solil Levant. The hostel will be on your left. This 150-year-old "home" has comfortable beds and a great location beside the cathedral. It acts primarily as a dorm for women, so backpackers (especially men) may be cramped. Church bells ring at all hours of the night. Breakfast M-Sa 7CHF. Wi-Fi available. Reception M-Sa 9am-noon and 4-8pm, Su 9am-noon. Dorms 27CHF; singles 40CHF; doubles 60CHF. MC/V. ❶

City Hostel Geneva, r. Ferrier 2 (☎022 901 1500; www.cityhostel.ch). From the train station, head down r. de Lausanne. Take the 1st left on r. du Prieuré, which becomes r. Ferrier. Spotless, cozy rooms. Kitchens on each floor. Linens 3.50CHF. Internet 5CHF per hr. Reception 7:30am-noon and 1pm-midnight. 3-4 bed single-sex dorms 28.50CHF; singles 59-64CHF; doubles 72-86CHF. Reserve ahead in summer. MC/V. ❷

Auberge de Jeunesse (HI), r. Rothschild 30 (☎022 732 6260; www.youthhostel.ch/geneva). Standard rooms, some of which have lakeviews. Chess lovers can duke it out on the life-size chess board outside. Breakfast included. Laundry 8CHF. Internet 4CHF per hr. Max. 6-night stay. Reception 6:30-10am and 2pm-midnight. Dorms 35CHF; doubles 85CHF, with shower 95CHF; quads 135CHF. 6CHF HI discount. AmEx/MC/V. ❷

Camping Pointe-à-la-Bise, chemin de la Bise (☎022 752 1296). Take bus #8 or tram #16 to Rive, then bus E north to Bise. Reception July-Aug. 8am-noon and 2-9pm; Apr.-June and Sept. 8am-noon and 4-8pm. Open Apr.-Sept. Reserve ahead. 7CHF per person, 12 CHF per tent; 4-person bungalows 98CHF. AmEx/MC/V. ❶

FOOD

Geneva has it all, from sushi to paella, but you may need a banker's salary to foot the bill. Pick up basics at *boulangeries*, *pâtisseries*, or supermarkets, which often have attached cafeterias. Try the **Coop** on the corner of r. du Commerce and r. du Rhône, in the Centre Rhône Fusterie, or the **Migros** in the basement of the Places des Cygnes shopping center on r. de Lausanne, down the street from the station. A variety of relatively cheap ethnic eateries center in the **Les Pâquis** area, bordered by r. de Lausanne and Gare Cornavin on one side and the quais Mont-Blanc and Wilson on the other. Around **place du Cirque** and **plaine de Plainpalais** are student-oriented tea rooms. To the south, the neighborhood of **Carouge** is known for its cozy pizzerias and funky brasseries.

Chez Ma Cousine, pl. du Bourg-de-Four 6 (☎022 310 9696; www.chezmacousine.ch), down the stairs behind the cathedral. This cheery cafe has perfected *poulet* with its half-chicken with salad and french fries special (14.90CHF) and a variety of chicken salads (14-15CHF). Open M-Sa 11am-11:30pm, Su 11am-10:30pm. AmEx/MC/V. ❷

Restaurant Manora, r. de Cornavin 4 (☎022 909 490), on the top floor of the Manor department store, near the train station. Offers a wide selection of entrees, fresh fruits and vegetables, and free water (a rarity in Switzerland). Entrees 5-12CHF. Open M-W 9am-7pm, Th 9am-9pm, F 9am-7:30pm, Sa 8:30am-6pm. AmEx/MC/V. ❶

Le Rozzel, Grand-Rue 18 (☎022 312 4272). Take bus #5 to pl. Neuve, then walk up the hill on r. Jean-Calvin to Grand-Rue. Pleasant outdoor seating on a winding street. Sweet and savory crepes 8-19CHF. Open M-Sa 10am-7pm, Su 10am-noon. MC/V. ❷

La Crise, r. de Chantepoulet 13 (☎022 738 0264). Walk up Chantepoulet, the street that branches off from the central Mont-blanc St., past the tourist office, and the restaurant will be on the left side. Every morning, the vegetables for the soup of the day (3.50CHF) are prepared in front of customers at this tiny but popular snack bar. *Plat du jour* 15CHF; smaller portion CHF. Open M-F 6am-3pm and 6-8pm, Sa 6am-3pm. Lunch served after noon. Cash only. ❷

Chocolats Micheli, r. Micheli-du-Crest 1 (☎022 329 9006). Take tram #13 to Plainpalais and walk up bd. des Philosophes until it intersects with r. Micheli-du-Crest. Con-

SWITZERLAND

fectionary masterpieces (1-3CHF) abound in this Victorian cafe. Purists should try the "100% chocolate." Coffee 3.40CHF. Store open M-F 8am-6:45pm, Sa 8am-5pm. Cafe open M-F 8am-6pm, Sa 8am-3:30pm. MC/V. ❶

SIGHTS

The city's most interesting historical sights are located within walking distance from the *vieille ville* (Old Town). The tourist office has 2hr. English-language walking tours. (Mid-June to Sept. M, W, F-Sa 10am, Tu and Th at 6:30pm; Oct. to mid-June Sa 10am. 15CHF, students 10CHF.)

VIEILLE VILLE. From 1536 to 1564, Calvin preached at the **Cathédrale de St-Pierre,** which looms over the *vieille ville* from its hilltop location. Climb the north tower for an unparalleled view of the city, and the south tower for some interesting information about the bells. *(Cathedral open June-Sept. M-F 9:30-6:30, Sa 9:30am-5pm, Su 10am-6:30pm. Concert Sa 6pm; service Su 10am. Tower open June-Sept. M-F 9am-6pm, Sa 9am-4:30pm. Cathedral free, tower 4CHF.)* Ruins, including a Roman sanctuary and an AD 4th-century basilica, rest in an **archaeological site** below the cathedral; you can even see the tomb around which the city was built. *(Open June-Sept. Tu-Su 10am-5pm; Oct.-May Tu-F 2-5pm, Sa-Su 1:30-5:30pm. Last entry 4:30. 8CHF, students 4CHF.)* For a dense presentation of Reformation 101, visit the **Musée International de la Réforme,** 4 r. du Cloitre, housed on the site of the city's official acceptance of Protestantism in 1536. *(☎022 310 2431; www.musee-reforme.ch. Open Tu-Su 10am-5pm. 10CHF, students 7CHF.)* At the western end of the *vieille ville* sits the 12th-century **Maison Tavel,** r. de Puits Saint Pierre 6. The oldest privately owned home in Geneva contains a wonderful scale model of the city as well a wide selection of trinkets from everyday life throughout the years. *(☎022 418 3700; www.ville-ge.ch/mah. Open Tu-Su 10am-5pm. Free.)* Across the street is the **Hôtel de Ville** (Town Hall), where world leaders met on August 22, 1864 for the first Geneva Convention. The **Grand-Rue,** beginning at the Hôtel de Ville, is lined with medieval workshops and 18th-century mansions. Plaques commemorate famous residents like **Jean-Jacques Rousseau,** who was born at #40. Visit the **Espace Rousseau** there for a short but informative audiovisual presentation of his life and work. *(☎022 310 1028; www.espace-rousseau.ch. Open Tu-Su 11am-5:30pm. 5CHF, students 3CHF.)* Below the cathedral, along r. de la Croix-Rouge, the **Parc des Bastions** stretches from pl. Neuve to pl. des Philosophes and includes **Le Mur des Réformateurs** (The Reformers' Wall), a sprawling collection of bas-relief figures depicting Protestant Reformers. The hulking **Musée d'Art et d'Histoire,** R. Charles-Galland 2, offers everything from prehistoric relics to contemporary art. *(☎022 418 2610; mah.ville-ge.ch. Open Tu-Su 10am-5pm. Free.)*

WATERFRONT. As you descend from the cathedral to the lake, medieval lanes give way to wide streets and chic boutiques. Down Gustave Ardor, the **Jet d'Eau,** Europe's highest fountain and Geneva's city symbol, spews a seven-ton plume of water 134m into the air. The **floral clock** in the **Jardin Anglais** pays homage to Geneva's watch industry. Possibly the city's most overrated attraction, it was once its most hazardous—the clock had to be cut back because tourists intent on taking the perfect photograph repeatedly backed into oncoming traffic. For a day on the waterfront, head up the south shore of the lake to Genève Plage, where there is a water slide and an enormous pool. *(☎022 736 2482; www.geneve-plage.ch. Open mid-May to mid-Sept. daily 10am-8pm. 7CHF, students 4.50CHF.)*

INTERNATIONAL HILL. North of the train station, the International Red Cross building contains the impressive **International Red Cross and Red Crescent Museum,** av. de la Paix 17. *(Bus #8, F, V or Z to Appia ☎022 748 9511; www.micr.org. Open M and W-Su 10am-5pm. 10CHF, students 5CHF. English-language audio tour 3CHF.)* Across the street, the European headquarters of the **United Nations,** av. de la Paix 14, is in the same building that once held the League of Nations. The constant traffic of international diplomats is entertainment in itself. *(☎022 917 4896; www.unog.ch. Mandatory 1hr. tour. English tours every hour. Open July-Aug. daily 10am-5pm; Apr.-June and Sept.-Oct. daily 10am-noon and 2-4pm; Nov.-Mar. M-F 10am-noon and 2-4pm. 10CHF, students 8CHF.)*

ENTERTAINMENT AND NIGHTLIFE

Genève Agenda, available at the tourist office, features event listings from major festivals to movies. In late June, the **Fête de la Musique** fills the city with nearly 500 free concerts of all styles. Parc de la Grange has free **jazz concerts.** Geneva hosts the biggest celebration of **American Independence Day** outside the US (July 4), and the **Fêtes de Genève** in early August fill the city with international music and fireworks. **L'Escalade** (Dec. 2009) commemorates the successful blockade of invading Savoyard troops.

Nightlife in Geneva is divided by neighborhood. **Place Bourg-de-Four,** below the cathedral in the *vieille ville,* attracts students to its charming terraces. **Place du Molard** has loud, somewhat upscale bars and clubs. For something more frenetic, head to **Les Pâquis,** near Gare Cornavin and pl. de la Navigation. As the city's red-light district, it has a wide array of rowdy, low-lit bars and some nightclubs. This neighborhood is also home to many of the city's gay bars. Carouge, across the Arve River, is a locus of student-friendly nightlife. In the *vieille ville,* generations of students have had their share of drinks at the intimate **La Clémence,** pl. du Bourg-de-Four 20. You can count on it to be open even when the rest of the city has shut down. Try the local **Calvinus beer** (7.40CHF) to do your part for Protestantism. (Sandwiches 3.30-6.40CHF. Open M-Th 7am-12:30am, F-Sa 7am-1:30am. MC/V.)

APPENDIX

CLIMATE

AVG. TEMP. (LOW/ HIGH), PRECIP.	JANUARY			APRIL			JULY			OCTOBER		
	°C	°F	mm	°C	°F	mm	°C	°F	mm	°C	°F	mm
Amsterdam	1/5	33/41	69	4/12	40/54	53	12/20	54/68	76	7/13	45/56	74
Athens	6/13	43/55	46	11/20	52/68	28	22/32	72/90	5	14/23	58/73	48
Berlin	-3/2	26/35	43	4/13	39/55	43	13/23	55/73	53	6/13	42/55	36
Copenhagen	-2/2	28/36	53	2/10	36/49	43	13/20	55/69	74	7/12	44/54	58
Dublin	3/8	37/46	69	4/12	40/53	51	12/19	53/66	51	8/14	46/57	71
London	2/7	35/45	51	5/13	41/56	46	13/22	55/71	33	8/14	46/58	71
Madrid	0/11	32/51	46	6/17	42/63	46	16/32	61/90	10	8/20	47/68	46
Paris	1/6	34/43	7	6/14	42/57	33	14/24	58/75	8	8/15	46/59	17
Rome	2/12	35/53	84	7/19	44/66	69	17/31	62/88	23	10/22	50/72	107
Vienna	-3/2	27/36	38	5/14	41/57	51	15/25	59/77	64	6/14	43/57	41

MEASUREMENTS

Like the rest of the rational world, Western Europe uses the metric system. The basic unit of length is the meter (m), which is divided into 100 centimeters (cm) or 1000 millimeters (mm). One thousand meters make up one kilometer (km). Fluids are measured in liters (L), each divided into 1000 milliliters (mL). A liter of pure water weighs one kilogram (kg), the unit of mass that is divided into 1000 grams (g). One metric ton is 1000kg.

MEASUREMENT CONVERSIONS	
1 inch (in.) = 25.4mm	1 millimeter (mm) = 0.039 in.
1 foot (ft.) = 0.305m	1 meter (m) = 3.28 ft.
1 yard (yd.) = 0.914m	1 meter (m) = 1.094 yd.
1 mile (mi.) = 1.609km	1 kilometer (km) = 0.621 mi.
1 ounce (oz.) = 28.35g	1 gram (g) = 0.035 oz.
1 pound (lb.) = 0.454kg	1 kilogram (kg) = 2.205 lb.
1 fluid ounce (fl. oz.) = 29.57mL	1 milliliter (mL) = 0.034 fl. oz.
1 gallon (gal.) = 3.785L	1 liter (L) = 0.264 gal.

Britain uses the metric system, although its longtime conversion to the metric system is still in progress—road signs indicate distance in miles. Gallons in the US and those in Britain are not identical: one US gallon equals 0.83 Imperial gallons. Pub aficionados will note that an Imperial pint (20 oz.) is larger than its US counterpart (16 oz.).

LANGUAGE PHRASEBOOK

DANISH

In Danish, stress is usually placed on the first syllable of the word. Unfortunately, there is no firm rules for pronouncing the alphabet. Danish is a North Germanic language, and thus resembles Swedish, Norwegian, and Icelandic.

ENGLISH	DANISH	PRONOUNCED	ENGLISH	DANISH	PRONOUNCED
Yes/No	Ja/ne	yah/ney	**Ticket**	Billet	bih-LEHD
Please	Vær så venlig	vair soh VEN-lee	**Train/Bus**	Tog/Bus	too/boos
Thank you	Tak	tahk	**Airport**	Lufthavn	LOFD-haown
Hello	Hallo	HAH-lo	**Departure**	Afgang	OW-gahng
Goodbye	Farvel	fah-VEL	**Market**	Marked	MAH-gehth
Sorry/Excuse me	undskyld	OHN-scoolt	**City center**	Centrum	SEHN-trum
Help!	Hjælp!	yailp	**Hotel/Hostel**	Hotel/Vandrerhjem	ho-TEL/VAN-druh-yem
Police	Politiet	poh-lee-TEE-ehth	**Pharmacy**	Apotek	ah-poh-TEYG
Embassy	Ambassade	ahm-bah-SAH-theh	**Toilet**	Toilet	toe-ah-LEHD

ENGLISH	DANISH	PRONUNCIATION
Where is...?	Hvor er...?	voa air
How do I get to...?	Hvordan kommer jeg til...?	vo-DAN KOM-ah yey tee
How much does this cost?	Hvad koster det?	vah KOS-ter day
I'd like a...	Jeg vil geme have en...	yay vee GEHR-neh hah en
Do you speak English?	Taler du engelsk?	TAY-luh doo ENG-elsk

DANISH CARDINAL NUMBERS										
0	**1**	**2**	**3**	**4**	**5**	**6**	**7**	**8**	**9**	**10**
nul	en	to	tre	fire	fem	seks	syv	otte	ni	ti

DUTCH

Most Dutch consonants, with a few exceptions, share their sounds with English, sometimes rendering Dutch into a phonetic version of English with a foreign accent. Vowels are a different story. The combinations "e," "ee," "i," and "ij" are occasionally pronounced "er" as in "mother."

ENGLISH	DUTCH	PRONOUNCED	ENGLISH	DUTCH	PRONOUNCED
Yes/No	Ja/Nee	yah/nay	**Ticket**	Kaartje	KAHR-chuh
Please/You're welcome	Alstublieft	Als-too-BLEEFT	**Train/Bus**	Trein/Bus	train/boos
Thank you	Dank u wel	DAHNK oo vell	**Station**	Station	stah-SHON
Hello	Dag/Hallo	Dakh/Hallo	**Taxi**	Taxi	TAHK-see
Goodbye	Tot ziens	Tot zeens	**Grocery**	Kruidenier	kraow-duh-NEER
Excuse me	Neem me niet kwalijk	neym muh neet KWAH-lek	**Tourist office**	VVV	fay-fay-fay
Help!	Help!	helup	**City center**	Centrum	SEHN-trum
Police	Politie	po-LEET-see	**Shop**	winkel	VIN-kerl
Embassy	Ambassade	ahm-bah-SAH-duh	**Toilet**	Toilet	twah-LEYT
Pharmacy	Apotheek	ah-po-TEYK	**Wooden shoes**	Klompen	KLOM-pem

ENGLISH	DUTCH	PRONUNCIATION
Where is...?	Waar is...?	VAHR ihss
I'm lost.	Ik ben verdwaald.	Ik ben fer-VAHLDT

How much does this cost?	Wat kost het?	wat KOST et
Do you have...?	Heeft u...?	HEYFT oo
Do you speak English?	Sprekt u Engels?	SPREYKT oo ENG-els

DUTCH CARDINAL NUMBERS										
0	**1**	**2**	**3**	**4**	**5**	**6**	**7**	**8**	**9**	**10**
nul	een	twee	drie	vier	vijf	zes	zeven	acht	negen	tien

FRENCH

Le is the masculine singular definite article (the), *la* the feminine; both are abbreviated to *l'* before a vowel, while *les* is the plural definite article for both genders. *Un* is the masculine singular indefinite article (a or an), *une* the feminine, while *des* is the plural indefinite article for both genders ("some").

ENGLISH	FRENCH	PRONOUNCED	ENGLISH	FRENCH	PRONOUNCED
Hello	Bonjour	bohn-zhoor	**Exchange**	L'échange	lay-shanzh
Please	S'il vous plaît	see voo pley	**Grocery**	L'épicerie	lay-pees-ree
Thank you	Merci	mehr-see	**Market**	Le marché	leuh marzh-chay
Excuse me	Excusez-moi	ex-ku-zey mwah	**Police**	La police	la poh-lees
Yes/No	Oui/Non	wee/nohn	**Embassy**	L'ambassade	lahm-ba-sahd
Goodbye	Au revoir	oh ruh-vwahr	**Passport**	Le passeport	leuh pass-por
Help!	Au secours!	oh seh-coor	**Post Office**	La poste	la pohst
I'm lost.	Je suis perdu.	zhe swee pehr-doo	**One-way**	Le billet simple	leuh bee-ay samp
Train/Bus	Le train/Le bus	leuh tran/leuh boos	**Round-trip**	Le billet aller-retour	leuh bee-ay a-lay-re-toor
Station	La gare	la gahr	**Ticket**	Le billet	leuh bee-ay
Airport	L'aéroport	la-ehr-o-por	**Single room**	Une chambre simple	oon shahm-br samp
Hotel	L'hôtel	lo-tel	**Double room**	Une chambre pour deux	oon shahm-br poor duh
Hostel	L'auberge	lo-berzhe	**With shower**	Avec une douche	ah-vec une doosh
Bathroom	La salle de bain	la sal de bahn	**Taxi**	Le taxi	leuh tax-ee
Open/Closed	Ouvert/Fermé	oo-ver/fer-may	**Ferry**	Le bac	leuh bak
Doctor	Le médecin	leuh mehd-sen	**Tourist office**	Le bureau de tourisme	leuh byur-oh de toor-eesm
Hospital	L'hôpital	loh-pee-tal	**Town hall**	L'hôtel de ville	lo-tel de veel
Pharmacy	La pharmacie	la far-ma-see	**Vegetarian**	Végétarien	vay-jay-ta-ree-ehn
Left/Right	À gauche/À droite	a gohsh/a dwat	**Kosher/Halal**	Kascher/Halal	ka-shey/ha-lal
Straight	Tout droit	too dwa	**Newsstand**	Le tabac	leuh ta-bac
Turn	Tournez	toor-neh	**Cigarette**	La cigarette	la see-ga-ret

ENGLISH	FRENCH	PRONUNCIATION
Do you speak English?	Parlez-vous anglais?	par-leh voo ahn-gleh
Where is...?	Où se trouve...?	oo seh-trhoov
When is the next...?	À quelle heure part le prochain..?	ah kel ur par leuh pro-chan
How much does this cost?	Ça fait combien?	sah f com-bee-en?
Do you have rooms available?	Avez-vous des chambres disponibles?	av-eh voo deh shahm-br dees-pon-eeb-bl?
I would like...	Je voudrais...	zhe voo-dreh
I don't speak French.	Je ne parle pas Français.	zhe neuh parl pah frawn-seh
I'm allergic to...	Je suis allergique à...	zhe swee al-ehr-zheek a
I love you.	Je t'aime.	zhe tem

FRENCH CARDINAL NUMBERS										
0	**1**	**2**	**3**	**4**	**5**	**6**	**7**	**8**	**9**	**10**
zéro	un	deux	trois	quatre	cinq	six	sept	huit	neuf	dix

GERMAN

In German, every letter in the word is pronounced. Consonants are pronounced exactly as they are in English, with the following exceptions: "j" is pronounced as "y"; "qu" is pronounced "kv"; a single "s" is pronounced "z"; "v" is pronounced "f"; "w" is pronounced "v"; and "z" is pronounced "ts." "Sch" is "sh," "st" is "sht," and "sp" is "shp." The "ch" sound, as in "ich" ("I") and "nicht" ("not"), is tricky; you can substitute a "sh." The letter ß (ess-tset) represents a double "s"; pronounce it "ss."

ENGLISH	GERMAN	PRONOUNCED	ENGLISH	GERMAN	PRONOUNCED
Yes/No	Ja/Nein	yah/nein	**Train/Bus**	Zug/Bus	tsoog/boos
Please	Bitte	BIH-tuh	**Station**	Bahnhof	BAHN-hohf
Thank you	Danke	DAHNG-kuh	**Airport**	Flughafen	FLOOG-hah-fen
Hello	Hallo	HAH-lo	**Taxi**	Taxi	TAHK-see
Goodbye	Auf Wiedersehen	owf VEE-der-zehn	**Ticket**	Fahrkarte	FAR-kar-tuh
Excuse me	Entschuldigung	ent-SHOOL-dih-gung	**Departure**	Abfahrt	AHB-fart
Help!	Hilfe!	HIL-fuh	**One-way**	Einfache	AYHN-fah-kuh
I'm lost.	Ich habe mich verlaufen.	eesh HAH-buh meesh fer-LAU-fun	**Round-trip**	Hin und zurück	hin oond tsuh-RYOOK
Police	Polizei	poh-lee-TSAI	**Reservation**	Reservierung	reh-zer-VEER-ung
Embassy	Botschaft	BOAT-shahft	**Ferry**	Fährschiff	FAYHR-shiff
Passport	Reisepass	RYE-zeh-pahss	**Bank**	Bank	bahnk
Doctor/Hospital	Arzt/Krankenhaus	ahrtst/KRANK-en-house	**Exchange**	Wechseln	VEHK-zeln
Pharmacy	Apotheke	AH-po-TAY-kuh	**Grocery**	Lebensmittelgeschäft	LAY-bens-miht-tel-guh-SHEFT
Hotel/Hostel	Hotel/Jugendherberge	ho-TEL/YOO-gend-air-BAIR-guh	**Tourist office**	Touristbüro	TU-reest-byur-oh
Single room	Einzellzimmer	EIN-tsel-tsihm-meh	**Post Office**	Postamt	POST-ahmt
Double room	Doppelzimmer	DOP-pel-tsihm-meh	**Old Town/City Center**	Altstadt	AHLT-shtat
Dorm	Schlafsaal	SHLAF-zahl	**Vegetarian**	Vegetarier	Feh-geh-TAYR-ee-er
With shower	Mit dusche	mitt DOO-shuh	**Vegan**	Veganer	FEH-gan-er
Bathroom	Badezimmer	BAH-deh-tsihm-meh	**Kosher/Halal**	Koscher/Halaal	KOH-shehr/hah-LAAL
Open/Closed	Geöffnet/Geschlossen	geh-UHF-net/geh-SHLOS-sen	**Nuts/Milk**	Nüsse/Milch	NYOO-seh/mihlsh
Left/Right	Links/Rechts	lihnks/rekhts	**Bridge**	Brücke	BRUKE-eh
Straight	Geradeaus	geh-RAH-de-OWS	**Castle**	Schloß	shloss
(To) Turn	Drehen	DREH-ehn	**Square**	Platz	plahtz

ENGLISH	GERMAN	PRONUNCIATION
Where is...?	Wo ist...?	vo ihst
How do I get to...?	Wie komme ich nach...?	vee KOM-muh eesh NAHKH
How much does that cost?	Wieviel kostet das?	VEE-feel KOS-tet das
Do you have...?	Haben Sie...?	HOB-en zee
I would like...	Ich möchte...	eesh MERSH-teh
I'm allergic to...	Ich bin zu...allergisch.	eesh bihn tsoo...ah-LEHR-gish

Do you speak English?	Sprechen sie Englisch?	SHPREK-en zee EHNG-lish
I do not speak German.	Ich spreche kein Deutsch.	eesh-SHPREK-eh kyne DOYCH
I'm waiting for my boyfriend/ husband.	Ich warte auf meinen Freund/ Mann.	eesh VAHR-tuh owf MYN-en froynd/ mahn

GERMAN CARDINAL NUMBERS										
0	**1**	**2**	**3**	**4**	**5**	**6**	**7**	**8**	**9**	**10**
null	eins	zwei	drei	vier	fünf	sechs	sieben	acht	neun	zehn

GREEK

The Greek alphabet has 24 letters. Greek words often havean accent mark called a *tonos* (τόνος). The *tonos* appears over the vowels of multi-syllabic words and tells you where the stress lies. The stress can change the meaning of the word so the *tonos* is essential for understanding and communication. The semicolon (;) is the Greek question mark (?).

ALPHABET

SYMBOL	NAME	PRONOUNCED	SYMBOL	NAME	PRONOUNCED
Α α	alpha	*a* as in f**a**ther	Ν ν	nu	*n* as in **n**et
Β β	beta	*v* as in **v**elvet	Ξ ξ	xi	*x* as in mi**x**
Γ γ	gamma	*y* or *g* as in **y**o**g**a	Ο ο	omicron	*o* as in r**o**w
Δ δ	delta	*th* as in **th**ere	Π π	pi	*p* as in **p**eace
Ε ε	epsilon	*e* as in j**e**t	Ρ ρ	rho	*r* as in **r**oll
Ζ ζ	zeta	*z* as in **z**ebra	Σ σ/ς	sigma	*s* as in **s**ense
Η η	eta	*ee* as in qu**ee**n	Τ τ	tau	*t* as in **t**ent
Θ θ	theta	*th* as in **th**ree	Υ υ	upsilon	*ee* as in gr**ee**n
Ι ι	iota	*ee* as in tr**ee**	Φ φ	phi	*f* as in **f**og
Κ κ	kappa	*k* as in **k**ite	Χ χ	chi	*h* as in **h**orse
Λ λ	lambda	*l* as in **l**and	Ψ ψ	psi	*ps* as in oo**ps**
Μ μ	mu	*m* as in **m**oose	Ω ω	omega	*o* as in Let's G**o**

LANGUAGE

ENGLISH	GREEK	PRONOUNCED	ENGLISH	GREEK	PRONOUNCED
Yes/No	Ναι/Οχι	neh/OH-hee	**Train/Bus**	Τραίνο/ Λεωφορείο	TREH-no/leh-o-fo-REE-o
Please	Παρακαλώ	pah-rah-kah-LO	**Ferry**	Πλοίο	PLEE-o
Thank you	Ευχαριστώ	ef-hah-ree-STO	**Station**	Σταθμός	stath-MOS
Hello/ Goodbye	Γειά σας	YAH-sas	**Airport**	Αεροδρόμιο	ah-e-ro-DHRO-mee-o
Sorry/ Excuse me	Συγνόμη	sig-NO-mee	**Taxi**	Ταξί	tah-XEE
Help!	Βοήθειά!	vo-EE-thee-ah	**Hotel/Hostel**	Ξενοδοχείο	kse-no-dho-HEE-o
I'm lost.	Εχω χαθεί.	EH-o ha-THEE	**Rooms to let**	Δωμάτια	do-MA-tee-ah
Police	Αστυνομία	as-tee-no-MEE-a	**Bathroom**	Τουαλέττα	tou-ah-LET-ta
Embassy	Πρεσβεία	prez-VEE-ah	**Open/Closed**	Ανοικτό/ Κλειστό	ah-nee-KTO/ klee-STO
Passport	Διαβατήριο	dhee-ah-vah-TEE-ree-o	**Left/Right**	Αριστερά/Δεξία	aris-te-RA/ de-XIA
Doctor	Γιατρός	yah-TROSE	**Bank**	Τράπεζα	TRAH-peh-zah

Pharmacy	Φαρμακείο	fahr-mah-KEE-o	Exchange	Ανταλλάσσω	an-da-LAS-so
Post Office	Ταχυδρομείο	ta-hi-dhro-MEE-o	Market	Αγορά	ah-go-RAH

ENGLISH	GREEK	PRONUNCIATION
Where is...?	Που είναι...?	poo-EE-neh
How much does this cost?	Πόσο κάνει?	PO-so KAH-nee
Do you have (a vacant room)?	Μηπώς έχετε (ελέυθερα δωμάτια)?	mee-POSE EK-he-teh (e-LEF-the-ra dho-MA-tee-a)
I would like...	Θα ήθελα...	thah EE-the-lah
Do you speak English?	Μιλατε αγγλικά?	mee-LAH-teh ahn-glee-KAH
I don't speak Greek.	Δεν μιλαώ ελληνικά.	dthen mee-LOW el-lee-nee-KAH

GREEK CARDINAL NUMBERS										
0	1	2	3	4	5	6	7	8	9	10
miden	ena	dio	tria	tessera	pente	eksi	epta	okto	ennea	deka
ουδέν	ενα	δυο	τρια	τεσσερα	πρια	εξι	επτα	οκτω	εννεα	δεκα

ITALIAN

In many Italian words, stress falls on the next-to-last syllable. When stress falls on the last syllable, accents indicate where stress falls: *città* (cheet-TAH) or *perchè* (pair-KAY). Stress can fall on the first syllable, but this occurs less often.

ENGLISH	ITALIAN	PRONOUNCED	ENGLISH	ITALIAN	PRONOUNCED
Yes/No	Sì/No	see/no	Departure	La partenza	lah par-TEN-zuh
Please	Per favore/Per piacere	pehr fah-VOH-reh/pehr pyah-CHEH-reh	One-way	Solo andata	SO-lo ahn-DAH-tah
Thank you	Grazie	GRAHT-see-yeh	Round-trip	Andata e ritorno	ahn-DAH-tah eh ree-TOHR-noh
Hello (informal/formal)	Ciao/Buongiorno	chow/bwohn-JOHR-noh	Reservation	La prenotazione	lah pray-no-taht-see-YOH-neh
Goodbye	Arrivederci/Arrivederla	ah-ree-veh-DAIR-chee/ah-ree-veh-DAIR-lah	Ticket	Il biglietto	eel beel-YEHT-toh
Sorry/Excuse me	Mi dispiace/Scusi	mee dees-PYAH-cheh/SKOO-zee	Train/Bus	Il treno/l'autobus	eel TRAY-no/aow-toh-BOOS
Help!	Aiuto!	ah-YOO-toh	Station	La stazione	lah staht-see-YOH-neh
Police	La Polizia	lah po-LEET-ZEE-ah	Airport	L'aeroporto	LAYR-o-PORT-o
Embassy	L'Ambasciata	lahm-bah-SHAH-tah	Taxi	Il tassi	eel tahs-SEE
Passport	Il passaporto	eel pahs-sah-POHR-toh	Ferry	Il traghetto	eel tra-GHEHT-toh
Hotel/Hostel	L'albergo/L'ostello	lal-BEHR-go/los-TEHL-loh	Bank	La banca	lah bahn-KAH
Single room	Una camera singola	OO-nah CAH-meh-rah SEEN-goh-lah	Exchange	Il cambio	eel CAHM-bee-oh
Double room	Una camera doppia	OO-nah CAH-meh-rah DOH-pee-yah	Grocery	Gli alimentari	lee ah-lee-mehn-TA-ree
With shower	Con doccia	kohn DOH-cha	Pharmacy	La farmacia	lah far-mah-SEE-ah

Bathroom	Un gabinetto/Un Bagno	oon gah-bee-NEHT-toh/oon BAHN-yoh	**Tourist office**	L'Azienda Promozione Turistica	lah-tzee-EHN-da-pro-mo-tzee-O-nay tur-EES-tee-kah
Open/Closed	Aperto/Chiuso	ah-PAIR-toh/KYOO-zoh	**Doctor**	Il medico	eel MEH-dee-koh
Left/Right	Sinistra/destra	see-NEE-strah/DEH-strah	**Vegetarian**	Vegetariano	veh-jeh-tar-ee-AN-oh
Straight	Sempre diritto	SEHM-pray-DREET-toh	**Kosher/Halal**	Kasher/Halal	KA-sher/HA-lal
Turn	Gira a	JEE-rah ah	**Nuts/Milk**	La noce/Il latte	lah NO-cheh/eel LA-teh

ENGLISH	ITALIAN	PRONUNCIATION
Where is...?	Dov'è...?	doh-VEH
How do I get to...?	Come si arriva a...?	KOH-meh see ahr-REE-vah ah
How much does that cost?	Quanto costa?	KWAN-toh CO-stah
Do you have...?	Hai...?	hi
Do you speak English?	Parla inglese?	PAHR-lah een-GLEH-zeh
I'd like...	Vorrei...	VOH-ray
I'm allergic to...	Ho delle allergie...	oh DEHL-leh ahl-lair-JEE-eh

ITALIAN CARDINAL NUMBERS										
0	**1**	**2**	**3**	**4**	**5**	**6**	**7**	**8**	**9**	**10**
zero	uno	due	tre	quattro	cinque	sei	sette	otto	nove	dieci

PORTUGUESE

Vowels with a *til* (ã, õ, etc.) or before "m" or "n" are pronounced with a nasal twang. At the end of a word, "o" is pronounced "oo" as in "room," and "e" is sometimes silent. "S" is pronounced "sh" or "zh" when it occurs before another consonant. "Ch" and "x" are pronounced "sh"; "j" and "g" (before e or i) are pronounced "zh." The combinations "nh" and "lh" are pronounced "ny" and "ly" respectively.

ENGLISH	PORTUGUESE	PRONOUNCED	ENGLISH	PORTUGUESE	PRONOUNCED
Hello	Olá/Oi	oh-LAH/oy	**Hotel**	Pousada	poh-ZAH-dah
Please	Por favor	pohr fah-VOHR	**Bathroom**	Banheiro	bahn-YEH-roo
Thank you (m/f)	Obrigado/Obrigada	oh-bree-GAH-doo/dah	**Open/Closed**	Aberto/Fechado	ah-BEHR-toh/feh-CHAH-do
Sorry/Excuse me	Desculpe	dish-KOOLP-eh	**Doctor**	Médico	MEH-dee-koo
Yes/No	Sim/Não	seem/now	**Pharmacy**	Farmácia	far-MAH-see-ah
Goodbye	Adeus	ah-DEH-oosh	**Left/Right**	Esquerda/Direita	esh-KER-dah/dee-REH-tah
Help!	Socorro!	soh-KOO-roh	**Bank**	Banco	BAHN-koh
I'm lost.	Estou perdido.	ish-TOW per-DEE-doo	**Exchange**	Câmbio	CAHM-bee-yoo
Ticket	Bilhete	beel-YEHT	**Market**	Mercado	mer-KAH-doo
Train/Bus	Comboio/Autocarro	kom-BOY-yoo/OW-to-KAH-roo	**Police**	Polícia	po-LEE-see-ah
Station	Estação	eh-stah-SAO	**Embassy**	Embaixada	ehm-bai-SHAH-dah
Airport	Aeroporto	aye-ro-POR-too	**Post Office**	Correio	coh-REH-yoh

ENGLISH	PORTUGUESE	PRONUNCIATION
Do you speak English?	Fala inglês?	FAH-lah een-GLEYSH
Where is...?	Onde é...?	OHN-deh eh
How much does this cost?	Quanto custa?	KWAHN-too KOOSH-tah
Do you have rooms available?	Tem quartos disponíveis?	teng KWAHR-toosh dish-po-NEE-veysh

I want/would like...	En quero/gostaria de...	eh-oo KER-oh/gost-ar-EE-ah day
I don't speak Portuguese.	Não falo Português	now FAH-loo por-too-GEZH
I cannot eat...	Não posso comer...	now POH-soo coh-MEHR
Another round, please.	Mais uma rodada, por favor.	maish OO-mah roh-DAH-dah pohr fah-VOHR

PORTUGUESE CARDINAL NUMBERS										
0	**1**	**2**	**3**	**4**	**5**	**6**	**7**	**8**	**9**	**10**
zero	um	dois	três	quatro	cinco	seis	sete	oito	nove	dez

SPANISH

Spanish words receive stress on the syllable marked with an accent. Each vowel has only one pronunciation: *a* ("ah" in "father"); *e* ("eh" in "pet"); *i* ("ee" in "eat"); *o* ("oh" in "oat"); *u* ("oo" in "boot"); *y*, by itself, is pronounced the same as the Spanish i ("ee"). Most consonants are the same as in English. Important exceptions are: *j* ("h" in "hello"); *ll* ("y" in "yes"); *ñ* ("ny" in "canyon"); and *r* at the beginning of a word or *rr* anywhere in a word (trilled). *H* is always silent. *G* before *e* or *i* is pronounced like the "h" in "hen;" elsewhere it is pronounced like the "g" in "gate." *X* has a bewildering variety of pronunciations; it can sound like the English "h," "s," "sh," or "x."

ENGLISH	SPANISH	PRONOUNCED	ENGLISH	SPANISH	PRONOUNCED
Hello	Hola	O-lah	**Hotel/Hostel**	Hotel/Hostal	oh-TEL/ohs-TAHL
Please	Por favor	pohr fah-VOHR	**Bathroom**	Baño	BAHN-yoh
Thank you	Gracias	GRAH-see-ahs	**Open/Closed**	Abierto(a)/ Cerrado(a)	ah-bee-EHR-toh/sehr-RAH-doh
Sorry/Excuse me	Perdón	pehr-DOHN	**Doctor**	Médico	MEH-dee-koh
Yes/No	Sí/No	see/no	**Pharmacy**	Farmacia	far-MAH-see-ah
Goodbye	Adiós	ah-DYOYS	**Left/Right**	Izquierda/ Derecha	ihz-kee-EHR-da/ deh-REH-chah
Help!	¡Ayuda!	ay-YOOH-dah	**Bank**	Banco	BAHN-koh
I'm lost.	Estoy perdido (a).	ess-TOY pehr-DEE-doh (dah)	**Exchange**	Cambio	CAHM-bee-oh
Ticket	Boleto	boh-LEH-toh	**Grocery**	Supermercado	soo-pehr-mer-KAH-doh
Train/Bus	Tren/Autobús	trehn/ow-toh-BOOS	**Police**	Policía	poh-lee-SEE-ah
Station	Estación	es-tah-SYOHN	**Embassy**	Embajada	em-bah-HA-dah
Airport	Aeropuerto	ay-roh-PWER-toh	**Post Office**	Oficina de correos	oh-fee-SEE-nah deh coh-REH-ohs

ENGLISH	SPANISH	PRONUNCIATION
Do you speak English?	¿Habla inglés?	AH-blah een-GLEHS?
Where is...?	¿Dónde está?	DOHN-deh eh-STA?
How much does this cost?	¿Cuánto cuesta?	KWAN-toh KWEHS-tah?
Do you have rooms available?	¿Tiene habitaciones libres?	tee-YEH-neh ah-bee-tah-see-YOH-nehs LEE-brehs?
I want/would like...	Quiero/Me gustaría...	kee-YEH-roh/meh goo-tah-REE-ah
I don't speak Spanish.	No hablo español.	no AH-bloh ehs-pahn-YOHL
I cannot eat...	No puedo comer...	no PEWH-doh coh-MEHR...

SPANISH CARDINAL NUMBERS										
0	**1**	**2**	**3**	**4**	**5**	**6**	**7**	**8**	**9**	**10**
cero	uno	dos	tres	cuatro	cinco	seis	siete	ocho	nueve	diez

INDEX

R

S

T

U

V

W

Z

MAP INDEX

SUGGESTED ITINERARIES:

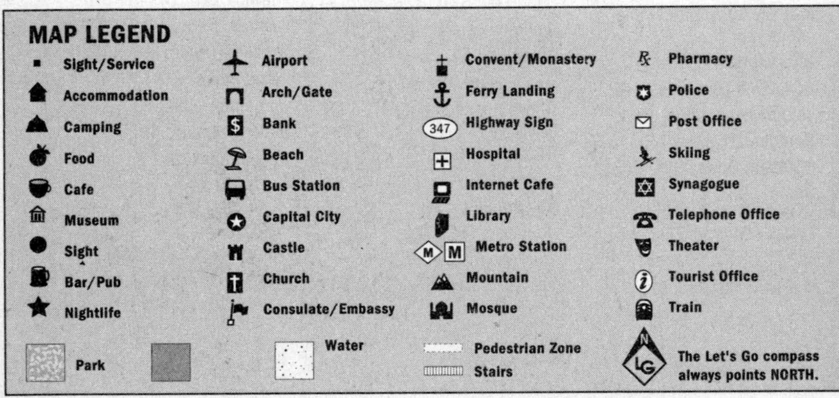

ABOUT LET'S GO

THE STUDENT TRAVEL GUIDE

Let's Go publishes the world's favorite student travel guides, written entirely by Harvard students. Armed with pens, notebooks, and a few changes of clothes stuffed into their backpacks, our student researchers go across continents, through time zones, and above expectations to seek out invaluable travel experiences for our readers. Because we are a completely student-run company, we have a unique perspective on how students travel, where they want to go, and what they're looking to do when they get there. If your dream is to grab a machete and forge through the jungles of Costa Rica, we can take you there. If you'd rather bask in the Riviera sun at a beachside cafe, we'll set you a table. In short, we write for readers who know that there's more to travel than tour buses. To keep up, visit our website, www.letsgo.com, where you can sign up to blog, post photos from your trips, and connect with the Let's Go community.

TRAVELING BEYOND TOURISM

We're on a mission to provide our readers with sharp, fresh coverage packed with socially responsible opportunities to go beyond tourism. Each guide's Beyond Tourism chapter shares ideas about responsible travel, study abroad, and how to give back to the places you visit while on the road. To help you gain a deeper connection with the places you travel, our fearless researchers scour the globe to give you the heads-up on both world-renowned and off-the-beaten-track opportunities. We've also opened our pages to respected writers and scholars to hear their takes on the countries and regions we cover, and asked travelers who have worked, studied, or volunteered abroad to contribute first-person accounts of their experiences.

FIFTY YEARS OF WISDOM

Let's Go has been on the road for 50 years and counting. We've grown a lot since publishing our first 20-page pamphlet to Europe in 1960, but five decades and 54 titles later our witty, candid guides are still researched and written entirely by students on shoestring budgets who know that train strikes, stolen luggage, food poisoning, and marriage proposals are all part of a day's work. This year, for our 50th anniversary, we're publishing 26 titles—including 6 brand new guides—brimming with editorial honesty, a commitment to students, and our irreverent style. Here's to the next 50!

THE LET'S GO COMMUNITY

More than just a travel guide company, Let's Go is a community that reaches from our headquarters in Cambridge, MA all across the globe. Our small staff of dedicated student editors, writers, and tech nerds comes together because of our shared passion for travel and our desire to help other travelers get the most out of their experience. We love it when our readers become part of the Let's Go community as well—when you travel, drop us a postcard (67 Mt. Auburn St., Cambridge, MA 02138, USA), send us an e-mail (feedback@letsgo.com), or sign up on our website (www.letsgo.com) to tell us about your adventures and discoveries.

For more information, updated travel coverage, and news from our researcher team, visit us online at www.letsgo.com.

HELPING LET'S GO. If you want to share your discoveries, suggestions, or corrections, please drop us a line. We appreciate every piece of correspondence, whether a postcard, a 10-page email, or a coconut. Visit Let's Go at **http://www.letsgo.com,** or send email to:

feedback@letsgo.com, subject: "Let's Go Western Europe"

Address mail to:

Let's Go Western Europe, 67 Mount Auburn St., Cambridge, MA 02138 , USA

In addition to the invaluable travel advice our readers share with us, many are kind enough to offer their services as researchers or editors. Unfortunately, our charter enables us to employ only currently enrolled Harvard students.

Distributed by Publishers Group West.
Printed in Canada by Friesens Corp.

ISBN-13: 978-1-59880-314-3
ISBN-10: 1-59880-314-X
Tenth edition
10 9 8 7 6 5 4 3 2 1

Let's Go Western Europe is written by Let's Go Publications, 67 Mount Auburn St., Cambridge, MA 02138, USA.